The Inequality Reader

SECOND EDITION

The Inequality Reader

Contemporary and Foundational Readings in
Race, Class, and Gender

Edited by
David B. Grusky
Szonja Szelényi

**WESTVIEW
PRESS**
A Member of the Perseus Books Group

Westview Press was founded in 1975 in Boulder, Colorado, by notable publisher and intellectual Fred Praeger. Westview Press continues to publish scholarly titles and high-quality undergraduate- and graduate-level textbooks in core social science disciplines. With books developed, written, and edited with the needs of serious nonfiction readers, professors, and students in mind, Westview Press honors its long history of publishing books that matter.

Published by Westview Press,
A Member of the Perseus Books Group

Every effort has been made to secure required permissions of all text, images, maps, and other art included in this volume.

Westview Press books are available at special discounts for bulk purchases in the United States by corporations, institutions, and other organizations. For more information, please contact the Special Markets Department at the Perseus Books Group, 2300 Chestnut Street, Suite 200, Philadelphia, PA 19103, or call (800) 810-4145, ext. 5000, or e-mail special.markets@perseusbooks.com.

Library of Congress Cataloging-in-Publication Data
    The inequality reader : contemporary and foundational readings in race, class, and gender / edited by David B. Grusky, Szonja Szelényi.—2nd ed.
        p.   cm.
    Includes bibliographical references and index.
    ISBN 978-0-8133-4484-3 (pbk. : alk. paper)
    1. Equality. 2. Social stratification.   3. Social classes.   4. Race.   5. Sex role.   I. Grusky, David B.   II. Szelényi, Szonja, 1960–
HM821.I54 2011
305.01—dc22

                                                                                    2010044319

E-book ISBN 978-0-8133-4517-8

10 9 8 7 6 5 4

To Robert M. Hauser
in the year of his retirement

Contents

Part IV
Inequality at the Extremes

Part V
Racial and Ethnic Inequality

Part VI
Gender Inequality

Part VII
Generating Inequality

Part VIII
The Consequences of Inequality

Part IX
Globalization and Inequality

Part X
What Is To Be Done?

Preface and Acknowledgments

Why publish yet another anthology of research on poverty and inequality? Although it wouldn't serve us well to draw too much attention to our many high quality competitors, it surely can't come as a surprise that the market is increasingly well-stocked. If we've gone boldly forth nonetheless, it's mainly because recent developments in the field demand a new type of anthology that's quite unlike existing ones. These new developments, which we list below, are part of the ongoing transformation of sociology as it refashions a place for itself within an increasingly competitive social science landscape.

A renaissance of policy: It wasn't so long ago that sociologists and other social scientists were roundly blamed for losing the War on Poverty, for designing poorly-conceived programs rife with unintended consequences, for naively believing that they could intervene in a complex social ecology and achieve anything even remotely resembling what was intended. It's no wonder given this interpretation of history that social scientists with policy interests have sometimes been just a bit gun shy. But all that's changed as a spate of programs have been carefully evaluated (e.g., Harlem Children's Zone, Perry Preschool) and shown to be quite promising. Quite suddenly, policy optimism is back in fashion, and it's become increasingly difficult to follow what's happening in the field without studying at least some of the policy behind it. We have accordingly included in this edition a new section on social policy and its successes and failings.

Rise of a multidisciplinary inequality field: For better or worse, there's no longer a consensual, interdisciplinary division of labor that has economists studying the total output of goods and sociologists studying how goods and resources are unequally distributed. Although such a simple division of labor never obtained even in the past, clearly economists have turned to the study of poverty and inequality, once the special province of sociologists, with unprecedented vigor. As a result, sociology is no longer a dominant force in the field, and "head-in-the-sand anthologies" that continue to pretend otherwise by relying exclusively on contributions by sociologists clearly do not prepare our students well. We have sought to incorporate into our reader some of the most important contributions by economists and other social scientists, contributions that have in many cases already entered into sociological discourse and have accordingly become, in effect, part of sociology.

Public intellectuals and inequality: As poverty and inequality increasingly become mainstream concerns, public intellectuals have become yet another new group of practicing sociologists, with their work often proving influential and ignored at one's peril. This research has taken not only the usual small-scale form characteristic of qualitative research in sociology but also a more heavily funded "big journalism" form in which cadres of investigators investigate a well-defined sociological question as part of a long-term research project. If one wants a searing expose or a provocative hypothesis, it often pays to turn to journalists and public intellectuals.

The new post-survey world: Over the last decade, the standard survey instrument has come to be appreciated as but one useful approach to studying poverty and inequality, while other approaches, especially quasi-experimental ones, have clearly gained in prominence. We have incorporated the most influential quasi-experimental studies and also drawn more heavily than in prior anthologies on ethnographic and mixed-method studies. In many cases, these qualitative studies have also attracted much attention and become widely celebrated, and not just among a narrow academic audience.

The editing rules adopted throughout this anthology are in most cases conventional. For example, brackets are used to mark off a passage that has been inserted for the purpose of clarifying meaning, whereas ellipses are used whenever a passage appearing in the original contribution has been excised altogether. The ellipses have been omitted when the excised text was a footnote, a minor reference to a table or passage (e.g., "see table 1"), or simply quite short in length. When necessary, tables and footnotes are renumbered without so indicating in the text, and all articles that were cited in excised passages are likewise omitted, without indication, from the list of references appearing at the end of each chapter.

We were obliged for reasons of space to omit all footnotes (or endnotes) that were not strictly necessary. In the lead footnotes for each article, we have detailed any of the potentially controversial editing decisions, including resequencing paragraphs and smoothing out transitional prose between adjacent sections. We have also inserted references to the source article whenever it seemed appropriate to remind the reader that more detail is available in that source. The spelling, grammatical, and stylistic conventions of the original contributions have otherwise been preserved. In this respect, the reader should be forewarned that some of the terms appearing in the original contributions would now be regarded as inappropriate (e.g., Negro), whereas others have passed out of common usage and will possibly be unfamiliar. While a strong argument could clearly be made for eliminating all language that is no longer acceptable, this type of sanitizing would not only exceed usual editorial license but would also generate a final text that contained inconsistent, and possibly confusing, temporal cues.

The selections reproduced here have been pre-tested in graduate and under-graduate inequality classes at Stanford University. We are indebted to the many students in these classes who shared their reactions to the selections and thereby shaped the final product more than they may realize. The anonymous reviewers of the proposal for this book also provided unusually constructive criticisms. We are further indebted to Alice Chou and Annie Lenth for assisting in every phase of the book's production, including tracking down possible selections, coordinating the proofing, and uncannily finding all too many errors. Finally, we thank our Westview Press Editor, Evan Carver, for pressing us to get it done rather than revise and tinker well beyond the point of diminishing returns.

David B. Grusky
Stanford, California

PART I

Introduction

The Stories About Inequality
That We Love to Tell

DAVID B. GRUSKY

There is a growing consensus among academics, policy makers, and even politicians that poverty and inequality should no longer be treated as soft social issues that can safely be subordinated to more fundamental interests in maximizing total economic output. The most important sources of this newfound concern with poverty and inequality are (1) the spectacular increase in economic inequality and other forms of disadvantage in many late-industrial countries (the *takeoff account*); (2) the striking persistence of many noneconomic forms of inequality despite decades of quite aggressive egalitarian reform (the *persistence account*); (3) an emerging concern that poverty and inequality may have negative macrolevel effects on terrorism, total economic production, and ethnic unrest (the *macrolevel externalities account*); (4) a growing awareness of the negative individual-level effects of poverty on health, political participation, and a host of other life conditions (the *microlevel externalities account*); (5) the rise of a global village in which regional disparities in the standard of living have become more

widely visible and hence increasingly difficult to ignore (the *visibility account*); (6) the ongoing tendency to expose and delegitimate new types of inequalities (based on sexual orientation, disability, or citizenship) that, not so long ago, were taken for granted, rarely discussed, and barely seen (the *new inequalities account*); (7) a confluence of recent events (e.g., Hurricane Katrina, the Great Recession, and high pay for poorly performing CEOs) that have brought poverty and inequality into especially sharp relief (the *idiographic account*); and (8) a growing commitment to a conception of human entitlements that include, at minimum, the right to seek or secure employment and thereby be spared extreme deprivation (the *social inclusion account*).

The foregoing list is remarkable in two ways. First, only three of the eight reasons for this newfound interest are about the brute empirics of inequality (i.e., its growth or intransigence), while all others are about changes in how we have come to view, study, and evaluate those empirics. When scholars now argue, for example, that in-

---

David B. Grusky, "The Stories About Inequality That We Love to Tell." Original article prepared for this book.

equality has multifarious effects (i.e., an *externalities account*), they presumably don't mean to suggest that such effects suddenly multiplied in the contemporary period. Rather, we are to understand that inequality was always rife with externalities, however inadequately we may have appreciated them in the past. Although changes in empirics hardly exhaust, then, the sources of our growing concern with inequality, this is not to gainsay the equally important point that such changes, especially the takeoff in income inequality and the Great Recession, are likely very important in explaining why inequality has come to be understood as a fundamental social problem of our time.

The above list is no less remarkable for the relatively minor role that normative concerns play. To be sure, there appears to be a growing sentiment that, at minimum, contemporary social systems should guarantee an opportunity for all citizens to participate in economic life and hence avoid the most extreme forms of social and economic exclusion (i.e., the *social inclusion account*). It would nonetheless be a mistake to understand the rising interest in poverty and inequality as principally fueled by some sudden realization that social inclusion is a fundamental social good. Indeed, far from treating inequality as a moral problem in itself, the contemporary tendency is to emphasize its profound consequences and threats for the world community as a whole (i.e., the *macrolevel externalities account*). The rhetoric of sustainability, although more frequently featured in discussions of environmental problems, is increasingly taken as relevant to discussions of inequality as well. In adopting this rhetoric, the claim is that extreme inequality is counterproductive not just because it reduces total economic output but also because other very legitimate objectives, such as reducing mortality rates, might also be compromised. By this logic, social policy must simultaneously be oriented toward increasing economic output *and* restraining the rise of debilitating and counterproductive forms of inequality, a rather more complicated maximization problem than conventionally taken on in economics (see Ch. 3, Fischer et al.; and Ch. 4, Krueger).

The Role of Benign Narratives in Past Scholarship

The foregoing orientation toward poverty and inequality should be understood as a sea change relative to the sensibilities that prevailed after World War II and even into the 1960s and 1970s. To be sure, the standard-issue sociologist of the past also embraced the view that inequality was an important social problem, but overlaid on this sensibility was an appreciation of various logics of history that operated in the main to reduce inequality, if only gradually and fitfully. The problem of inequality was understood, then, as a tractable moral problem, an unfortunate side circumstance of capitalism (and even socialism) that would become yet more manageable with the transition into the increasingly affluent forms of advanced industrialism. This orientation toward inequality, which we characterize as "benign," is expressed in the standard postwar narratives about three types of outcomes: (1) the distribution of income, power, and other valued resources; (2) the distribution of opportunities for securing income, power, and other valued resources; and (3) the formation of social classes and other institutionalized groups (e.g., racial groups and gender groups). We review each of these three types of benign narratives below.

The Long-Term Trend in Inequality

The dominant inequality narrative of the postwar period featured the emergence of egalitarian ideologies and the consequent delegitimation of the extreme forms of inequality found in agrarian systems (e.g., Bell 1973; Kerr et al. 1964; and Parsons 1970). The Enlightenment was understood as fostering a critical rhetoric of equality that unleashed one of the most profound revolutions in human history. The resulting decline in inequality can be seen, for example, in (1) the European revolutions of the eighteenth and nineteenth centuries against the privileges of rank (honorific equality); (2) the gradual elimination of inequalities in the rights to vote, own property, and speak and assemble (civil equality); (3) the abolition of slavery and the establishment of the radically egalitarian principle of self-ownership (equality of human assets); and (4) the equalization of economic assets via the rise of socialism, welfare capitalism, and their many institutions (economic equality).[1]

As is well known, the latter commitment to equalizing economic assets was rather weaker than the commitment to other forms of equalization, with the result that economic inequalities remained extreme in all market economies. There was nonetheless a decline in economic inequality throughout the postwar period in the United States. According to the classic Kuznets curve (1955), the initial stages of capitalist development bring about an increase in income inequality as capital is increasingly concentrated among a small number of investors, whereas more advanced forms of capitalism entail a growth in the size of the middle class and a consequent reversal of the upward trend. The causal dynamics behind the resulting inverted-U pattern remain unclear (see Acemoglu and Robinson 2002), but most sociologists attribute the late-industrial decline in inequality to the increasingly crucial role that the skilled working class played in production, the associated growth in working-class productivity, and the leverage that this growth in skills and productivity conferred on skilled workers.

The careful reader might inquire as to the mechanisms by which cultural egalitarianism of this sort diffuses and takes hold. The conventional view in this regard is that a series of crucial historical events after the Enlightenment (e.g., the defeat of Nazism) served to define equality as one of our core cultural commitments. Absent some revolutionary event that changes this cultural trajectory, the course of human history then becomes the working out of this commitment, a task that involves shedding subsidiary values that sometimes come into conflict with our deeper commitment to egalitarianism. The core mechanism that drives this cultural diffusion may therefore be understood as the gradual reconciling of competing values to a new value, that of equality, that has been elevated by one or more historical events to a position of prominence.

The Long-Term Trend in Inequality of Opportunity

The second narrative of interest rests on a sharp distinction between the distribution of social rewards (e.g., income) and the distribution of opportunities for securing these rewards. In liberal welfare regimes, extreme inequalities in rewards may be tolerated, but only insofar as opportunities for attaining these rewards are understood to be equally distributed. It is inequalities of opportunity that are regarded, then, as especially illegitimate in the context of liberal welfare regimes.

The dominant narratives of the postwar period have these inequalities of opportunity gradually weakening. The narratives of this period may be understood as benign because they describe the withering away of precisely those types of inequalities (i.e., inequalities of opportunity) that are regarded as problematic or illegitimate. The trademark of the benign narrative is this simple correspondence between what we want and what we think will likely happen. We describe below four benign subnarratives that characterize some of the processes by which inequalities of opportunity come to be weakened.

The most famous such subnarrative pertains to the discrimination-reducing effects of competitive market economies. In his original formulation of the "taste for discrimination" model, Becker (1957) argued that discrimination would be eroded by competitive market forces because it requires employers to pay a premium to hire members of the preferred class of labor, such as males, whites, or any other ascriptively defined category. This taste is discriminatory because it rests on exogenous preferences for a certain category of labor that cannot be understood as arising from some larger concern for maximizing profitability or market share. When managers make hiring decisions in accord with such tastes, their firms will not be competitive with nondiscriminating firms because they must pay extra to secure labor from the preferred class (without any compensating increase in productivity). In standard renditions of this account, it is presumed that discriminating firms will gradually be selected out by the market, although it is also possible that some discrimi-

nating firms will change their hiring practices to remain competitive.

This economic subnarrative works in tandem with a second organizational one that emphasizes the diffusion of modern personnel practices in the form of universalistic hiring practices (e.g., open hiring and credentialism) and bureaucratized pay scales and promotion procedures (see Ch. 7, Weber; Ch. 44, Charles and Grusky; and Reskin and McBrier 2000). The essence of such bureaucratic personnel practices is a formal commitment to universalism (i.e., treating all workers equally) and to meritocratic hiring and promotion (i.e., hiring and promoting on the basis of credentials). In its ideal-typical form, the spread of bureaucracy becomes an organizational process with its own dynamic, a process of diffusion that rests not on actual efficiencies, as with the economic subnarrative, but simply on the *presumption* that bureaucratic practices are efficient and that modern firms must therefore adopt them. This subnarrative, like the economic one, implies that firms will gradually come to embrace organizational procedures that reduce inequalities of opportunity.

The third subnarrative of interest is the political one. Whereas the economic and organizational subnarratives treat change in inequality as an unintended by-product of macrolevel forces (i.e., competition and bureaucratization), the political subnarrative is about instrumental action explicitly oriented toward effecting a decline in inequality. In theory, such political action could be oriented toward reducing inequalities of either opportunity or outcome, but historically a main emphasis within liberal welfare regimes has been legislation aimed at reducing inequality of opportunity (e.g., antidiscrimination legislation, early education programs, and educational loans). The distinctive assumption of the political sub-narrative is that straightforward social engineering is an important source of change and that the unintended or unanticipated consequences of such engineering are too often overemphasized.

The final subnarrative, a simple cultural one, rests on the argument that Western ideals of justice and equality continue to be endogenously worked out through a logic that diffuses independently of the economic efficiency of such ideals. The cultural subnarrative can be straightforwardly distinguished from the economic one because the growing taste for equality is presumed to be an exogenous shift rather than some accommodation to the rising economic cost of exercising discriminatory tastes. Likewise, the cultural subnarrative is distinct from the organizational subnarrative by virtue of focusing on the spread of tastes for equality and equality-enhancing practices, not the spread of organizational forms (e.g., bureaucratization) that are deemed efficient, normatively desirable, or both. Finally, the cultural and political subnarratives are closely related because political commitments to equal opportunity, antidiscrimination legislation, and school reform may be partly or even largely motivated by these newfound tastes for equal opportunity. At the same time, the cultural commitment to equal opportunity is not expressed exclusively in such political terms but is additionally expressed in the attitudes, behaviors, and personnel practices of employers. Most obviously, employers may gradually shed their preferences for certain categories of labor and instead develop tastes for equality in hiring, firing, and promotion, tastes that might at the limit be exercised in the labor market even with some loss in profits or efficiency.

The spread of such tastes for equal opportunity may again be viewed as part of our Enlightenment legacy, albeit a particular liberal variant of that legacy that emphasizes equalizing opportunities, not outcomes. This commitment is expressed not only at the individual level (e.g., changes in attitudes) but also at the collective level through various types of political reform (e.g., antidiscrimination legislation) as well as the diffusion of bureaucratic personnel policies (e.g., open hiring).

The Long-Term Trend in Class Formation

The final benign narrative of interest describes the gradual transition from lumpy class-based labor markets to more purely gradational ones (see Ch. 8, Chan and Goldthorpe; and Ch. 54, Jonsson et al.). Within this narrative, the early-industrial economy is represented as deeply balkanized into partly independent labor markets defined by detailed occupations (e.g., economist, carpenter), big social classes (e.g., manager, farmer), or yet more aggregated factors of production (e.g., worker, capitalist). For our purposes, what is principally of interest is our collective fascination with arguments describing how these classes, however they may be defined (see Wright 2005), tend to gradually dissipate and leave us with gradational labor markets that increasingly approximate the seamless neoclassical ideal. The first step in this transition, as described most famously by Dahrendorf (1959), is the gradual institutionalization of class conflict, a regularization of labor-capital relations achieved through the establishment of unions, collective bargaining agreements, and other laws defining how labor and capital should negotiate (see also Parsons 1970). The second step in this transition involves the dismantling of unions and other institutionalized residues of classes as the liberal welfare ideals of deregulation and flexibility are increasingly pursued.

This line of argumentation is somewhat differently expressed in more recent postmodernist narratives. Although the postmodern literature is itself notoriously fragmented, most variants have proceeded from the assumption that class identities, ideologies, and organization are attenuating and that "new theories, perhaps more cultural than structural, [are] in order" (Davis 1982, 585). The core claim is that politics, lifestyles, and consumption practices are no longer class determined and have increasingly become a "function of individual taste, choice, and commitment" (Crook, Pakulski, and Waters 1992, 222; see also Pakulski 2005).

In more ambitious variants of postmodernism, the focus shifts away from simply claiming that attitudes and practices are less class determined, and the older class-analytic objective of understanding macrolevel stratificational change is resuscitated. This ambition underlies, for example, all forms of postmodernism that seek to represent new social movements (e.g., environmentalism) as the vanguard force behind future stratificatory change. As argued by Eyerman (1992) and others (e.g., Touraine 1981), the labor movement can be seen as a fading enterprise rooted in the old conflicts of the workplace and industrial capitalism, whereas new social movements provide a more appealing call for collective action by virtue of their emphasis on issues of lifestyle, personal identity, and normative change. With this formulation, the proletariat is stripped of its privileged status as a universal class, and new social movements emerge as an alternative

and far more benign force "shaping the future of modern societies" (Haferkamp and Smelser 1992, 17).

New Approaches to Studying Inequality

The foregoing narratives, all of which were fixtures of the postwar intellectual landscape, describe the emergence of a world in which inequalities are less profound, opportunities are more equally distributed, and class conflicts and interclass differences become attenuated. These narratives are benign in the sense that they push us toward equilibriums that most commentators, even neo-Marxian ones, might well regard as appealing. The benign narrative is accordingly built on the happy correspondence between what should be and what will be.

If there is any theme to contemporary analyses of inequality, it is that the benign narrative has fallen largely out of fashion. We have nonetheless laid out these narratives in some detail because they still motivate some contemporary research (e.g., Ch. 51, Breen et al.), often provide an important backdrop to current theorizing, and are sometimes used as foils by contemporary scholars seeking to motivate their own analyses. The benign narrative is in this sense lurking in the background of contemporary discussions of inequality. We turn now to a closer discussion of how contemporary analyses of inequality have developed partly in reaction to the benign narratives of the postwar period.

Multidimensionalism and New Inequalities

As a natural starting point for this discussion, we note that contemporary inequality scholarship is increasingly concerned with new

Table 1.1 Types of Assets and Examples of Advantaged and Disadvantaged Groups

Assets		Examples	
Asset group	Examples of types	Advantaged	Disadvantaged
1. Economic	Wealth	Billionaire	Bankrupt worker
	Income	Professional	Laborer
	Ownership	Capitalist	Worker (i.e., employed)
2. Power	Political power	Prime minister	Disenfranchised person
	Workplace authority	Manager	Subordinate worker
	Household authority	Head of household	Child
3. Cultural	Knowledge	Intelligentsia	Uneducated
	Digital culture	Silicon Valley resident	Residents of other places
	"Good" manners	Aristocracy	Commoner
4. Social	Social clubs	Country club member	Nonmember
	Workplace associations	Union member	Nonmember
	Informal networks	Washington A-list	Social unknown
5. Honorific	Occupational	Judge	Garbage collector
	Religious	Saint	Excommunicate
	Merit-based	Nobel Prize winner	Nonwinner
6. Civil	Right to work	Citizen	Illegal immigrant
	Due process	Citizen	Suspected terrorist
	Franchise	Citizen	Felon
7. Human	On-the-job	Experienced worker	Inexperienced worker
	General schooling	College graduate	High school dropout
	Vocational training	Law school graduate	Unskilled worker
8. Physical	Mortality	Person with long life	A premature death
(i.e., health)	Physical disease	Healthy person	Person with AIDS, asthma
	Mental health	Healthy person	Depressed, alienated

forms of inequality, forms that either were ignored in the past or have been spawned by new technologies or institutions. This growing emphasis on new inequalities is consistent with the now fashionable view that inequality is multidimensional and that conventional studies of economic, socioeconomic, or cultural inequality hardly exhaust its many forms (e.g., Sen 2006).

If a multidimensional approach is taken, one might usefully distinguish between the eight forms of inequality listed in Table 1.1, each such form pertaining to a type of good that is intrinsically valuable (as well as possibly an investment). The multidimensional space formed by these variables may be labeled the "inequality space." We can characterize the social location of an individual within this inequality space by specifying her or his constellation of scores on each of the eight classes of variables in this table.

This framework allows scholars to examine how individuals are distributed among the less conventionally studied dimensions of the inequality space. Are new assets as unequally distributed as old ones? Is inequality becoming more of an "all or nothing" affair in which upper-class workers are advantaged on all dimensions of interest and lower-class workers are disadvantaged on all dimensions of interest? Are new assets sometimes distributed in ways that compensate for shortfalls in older ones? In the present volume, multidimensionalist questions of this kind are posed for such "new" outcomes as health (Ch. 65, Scott; Ch. 66, Mullahy, Robert, and Wolfe), computer literacy (Ch. 69, Hargittai), imprisonment or capital punishment (Ch. 22, Western), and networks and social capital (Ch. 61, Granovetter; Ch. 62, Lin; Ch. 63, Burt; Ch. 64, Fernandez and Fernandez-Mateo). These new types of inequality may be understood in some cases as truly new divides generated by new technologies (e.g., the digital divide) or new social institutions (e.g., modern mass prisons). More typically, the "new" outcomes are just increasingly popular topics of study among academics, not truly new forms (e.g., health inequalities).

The Intransigence of Poverty and Inequality

The foregoing line of research typically takes the form of an exposé of the extent to which seemingly basic human entitlements, such as living outside of prison, freely participating in digital culture, or living a long and healthy life, are unequally distributed in ways that sometimes amplify well-known differentials of income or education. The continuing attraction of such exposés (at least among academics) may be attributed to our collective discomfort with an economic system that generates rather more inequality than is palatable under contemporary cultural standards. Although the equalizing reforms of social democracy have historically been a main solution to this tension, the declining legitimacy of such reform (especially in Europe and the United States) leaves the tension an increasingly unresolved one.

Whereas the old narratives focused, then, on the forces making for decline in inequality, a more pessimistic assessment of the trajectory of late industrialism has now taken hold, and much scholarship accordingly focuses on documenting that inequality has persisted at higher levels than had been anticipated. This sensibility underlies, for example, contemporary research showing that residential segregation in the United States is so extreme as to constitute a modern form of apartheid (Ch. 19, Massey and Denton); that racial discrimination in labor markets likewise remains extreme (Ch. 28, Bertrand and Mullainathan); that the occupational structure is hypersegregated by gender (Ch. 44, Charles and Grusky); that income inequality has increased markedly in many countries over the past thirty-five years (Ch. 9, Saez; Ch. 10, Grusky and Weeden); that poverty rates in the United States remain strikingly high (Ch. 17, Smeeding); that African Americans are routinely harassed, slighted, and insulted in public places (Ch. 30, Feagin; Ch. 35, Bobo); that working-class and middle-class children tend to be raised in profoundly different ways (Ch. 68, Lareau); and that massive class disparities in access to health services persist (Ch. 65, Scott; Ch. 66, Mullahy, Robert, and Wolfe).

The cynic might ask whether this new muckraking tradition is really all that necessary. Is there truly a large public that doesn't already appreciate the persistence of many of these inequalities? We live, after all, in a market society in which virtually everything is commodified, meaning that almost all goods and services are allocated on the basis of our ability to pay for them. Because we are so deeply and (seemingly) irrevocably marketized, the real intellectual challenge would be to find a good, service, or outcome that is somehow untouched by class, one that is perfectly and equally distributed to all.

We suspect that our contributors would react to such (hypothetical) criticism by emphasizing that only some inequalities may be understood as the inevitable outcome of our collective decision to allocate resources on the basis of a market. It is at least possible to imagine markets that do not entail racial or gender discrimination and encompass institutions that have a substantial inequality-moderating effect. It is likewise possible to imagine that class differences in politics, culture, and child-rearing practices would have by now abated. The benign narratives of the postwar period in fact laid out precisely such imaginings. If it is now clear that these imagined futures have not been realized, surely we need to document that conclusion with all the rigor that can possibly be mustered. To be sure, many of us well know that the world is a massively unequal one, but even so the force of the known can be readily lost when we live with profound inequality on a day-to-day basis. This commitment to remind us of what comes to be taken for granted is the cornerstone, we suspect, of the renewed interest in the inequality-documenting function.

The Rise of New and Less Benign Narratives

The rise of this muckraking exposé of inequality has been coupled, moreover, with increasing interest in developing narratives that explain why inequality has persisted or grown more extreme. These narratives are typically less grand than the quite encompassing narratives of the postwar period; that is, rather specialized narratives have recently developed around many of the various unit trends of interest (e.g., the expansion of income inequality), and rather little attention has been paid to developing some grand metanarrative that links these specialized narratives. The signature, then, of the contemporary narrative is this highly delimited focus, a commitment to developing a rigorously empirical foundation, and a special interest in identifying those more insidious social forces that undermine the benign narratives of the past.

By way of example, consider the historic rise in income inequality, a development that has spawned one of the most sustained efforts at narrative building of our time (see Ch. 10, Grusky and Weeden). As noted above, the classic Kuznets curve aligns nicely with the facts of inequality up to the early 1970s, but then a dramatic, unprecedented upswing in inequality in the post-1970 period made it clear that inequality history had not ended. We have since witnessed one of the most massive research efforts in the history of social science as scholars sought to identify the smoking gun that accounted for this dramatic increase in inequality.

Initially, the dominant hypothesis was that deindustrialization (i.e., the relocation of manufacturing jobs to offshore labor markets) brought about a decline in demand for less-educated manufacturing workers, a decline that generated increases in inequality by hollowing out the middle class and sending manufacturing workers into unemployment or the ranks of poorly paid service work. Although this line of argumentation still has its advocates, it cannot easily be reconciled with evidence suggesting that the computerization of the workplace is an important force behind the heightened demand for highly educated workers. Because of this result (and other supporting evidence), the deindustrialization story has now been largely supplanted by the converse hypothesis that "skill-biased technological change" has increased the demand for high-skill workers beyond the increase in supply, thus inducing a short-term disequilibrium and a corresponding increased payoff for high-skill labor. At the same time, most scholars acknowledge that this story is at best an incomplete one and that other accounts, especially more narrowly political ones, must additionally be entertained (e.g., Card and DiNardo 2002). Most notably, some of the rise in income inequality in the United States was clearly attributable to the declining minimum wage (in real dollars), a decline that in turn has to be understood as the outcome of political processes that increasingly favor proinequality forces. The same conclusion applies yet more obviously to the recent round of tax cuts in the United States.

The future of income inequality depends on which of these underlying mechanisms is principally at work. The silver lining of the deindustrialization story is that within-country increases in inequality should be offset by between-country declines (as poor countries profit from new manufacturing jobs), whereas the silver lining of skill-biased technological change is that the heightened demand for high-skill workers is presumably a onetime short-term disequilibrium that will, by virtue of the higher payoff to high-skill jobs, trigger a compensating growth

in the supply of high-skill workers. There is, unfortunately, no shortage of competing stories that imply more disturbing futures, even futures consistent with a classical Marxian account in which low-skill workers are emiserated within some countries by virtue of a globalization-induced race to the bottom.

We have focused on the rise of income inequality and the various narratives it has generated only because this literature is especially well known and central to the field. The larger point that we seek to make is that, no matter the subfield, there appears to be much interest in developing narratives that explain why long-standing declines in inequality have slowed down, stalled altogether, or even reversed themselves. We are referring, for example, to (1) narratives of globalization that describe how the liberalization of financial and capital markets has harmed poor countries (Ch. 70, Stiglitz); (2) narratives of deindustrialization that describe the loss of inner-city jobs and the associated rise of an urban underclass (Ch. 18, Wilson); (3) narratives of segmented assimilation that describe the relatively bleak prospects for at least some new immigrant groups (Ch. 26, Portes and Zhou); (4) narratives of "opting out" that have highly trained women eschewing stressful careers in favor of recommitting to their children, spouses, and domestic responsibilities (Ch. 38, Belkin; cf. Ch. 39, Stone); and (5) narratives of essentialist segregation that describe how sex-typed occupational ghettos continue to be built around presumed differences in male and female aptitudes (Ch. 44, Charles and Grusky). Although counternarratives of the more optimistic sort are also being developed (e.g., Alba and Nee 2003; Ch. 71, Firebaugh; and Ch. 51,

Breen et al.), they seem not to be as frequently generated or as readily embraced, and the proponents of such narratives find themselves beleaguered, outnumbered, and on the defensive.

Conclusion

We have fashioned our review and introduction around the revolutionary changes over the past half century in the types of narratives that sociologists and other social scientists have applied to make sense of trends in inequality. The narratives of the postwar period took on a strikingly benign form in which the dominant logics of history were understood as operating in the main to reduce inequality. These benign narratives, which now mainly seem naive and quaint, have been supplanted by a host of new narratives that give far greater weight to the forces making for inequality.

Has the pendulum swung too far? It is child's play to posit any number of nonempirical sources of our fascination, some might say obsession, with the pessimistic narrative. The following are perhaps the most obvious of such accounts:

1. *The newsworthiness account.* If the postwar period of the 1950s and 1960s was indeed one in which many types of inequality declined (e.g., income inequality), then perhaps a special incentive has since emerged to ferret out results that are newsworthy by virtue of revealing a counteracting persistence or even growth in inequality. It is surely difficult to market analyses and forge careers on the basis of business-as-usual evidence. We might ask, for example, whether the digital divide emerged as a newsworthy topic partly because it catered to this simple muckraking sensibility. If instead access to computing had been found to be equal, wouldn't we have quickly discarded the topic and set off to find some other more unequal outcome? This type of selection on the dependent variable (i.e., inequality) will create a research literature that exaggerates how unequal the world is.

2. *The moral credentials account.* It is well to bear in mind that the contemporary academic, far from taking a vow of poverty, is now firmly ensconced in the middle class, often the upper middle class. When relatively privileged scholars study poverty and disadvantage, they often feel a special obligation to demonstrate a strong commitment to amelioration and to display political sentiments that are liberal, progressive, or even radical. In some cases, this pressure may motivate them to downplay any evidence of decline in inequality or disadvantage, presumably out of concern that undue emphasis on the progress achieved so far will make it appear that the remaining disadvantage is regarded as acceptable or unproblematic.

3. *The "obsession with small differences" account.* The continuing diffusion of egalitarian values renders any departures from equality, no matter how small, as problematic and newsworthy. By this logic, even increasingly small intergroup differences will attract much attention, especially because ever more powerful models and statistical methods now make it possible to tease them out (see Nisbet 1959, 12).

If these nonempirical interpretations shouldn't be dismissed out of hand, neither should they be taken too seriously. It is relevant in this regard that many of the pessimistic narratives involve indisputably dramatic changes in outcomes (e.g., income) that were frequently studied well before any reversal in the trend line was detected. Although some of the pessimistic narratives featured in this volume are still in incipient form and are not yet well researched, it will of course be difficult to continue to maintain these narratives should strong disconfirming evidence turn up. The implication, then, is that our exaggerated taste for pessimism might conceivably lead us to cycle through a great many pessimistic stories (and fail to develop enough benign ones), but at least in the long run the usual rules of evidence will have us excise egregiously flawed narratives, no matter how benign or pessimistic they may be.

NOTE

1. This is not to suggest that *all* postwar sociologists and social scientists emphasized forces making for a decline in inequality. However, even when a benign narrative was not adopted, there was usually some effort to engage with it and to explain or defend the decision not to take it up. This defensiveness was especially apparent in neo-Marxian analyses of the postwar era. Although such analyses were based on deeply pessimistic subnarratives about the trajectory of capitalism, these subnarratives were typically attached to larger and more benign narratives about the postcapitalist trajectory (see Ch. 5, Marx; and Ch. 6, Wright).

REFERENCES

Acemoglu, Daron, and James A. Robinson. 2002. "The Political Economy of the Kuznets Curve." *Review of Development Economics* 6: 183–203.

Alba, Richard, and Victor Nee. 2003. *Remaking the American Mainstream: Assimilation and Contemporary Immigration.* Cambridge: Harvard University Press.

Becker, Gary S. 1957. *The Economics of Discrimination.* Chicago: University of Chicago Press.

Bell, Daniel. 1973. *The Coming of Post-Industrial Society.* New York: Basic Books.

Card, D., and J. E. DiNardo. 2002. "Skill-Biased Technological Change and Rising Wage Inequality: Some Problems and Puzzles." *Journal of Labor Economics* 20: 733–783.

Charles, Maria, and David B. Grusky. 2004. *Occupational Ghettos: The Worldwide Segregation of Women and Men.* Stanford: Stanford University Press.

Crook, Stephen, Jan Pakulski, and Malcolm Waters. 1992. *Postmodernization.* London: Sage.

Dahrendorf, Ralf. 1959. *Class and Class Conflict in Industrial Society.* Stanford: Stanford University Press.

Davis, James. 1982. "Achievement Variables and Class Cultures: Family, Schooling, Job, and Forty-nine Dependent Variables in the Cumulative GSS." *American Sociological Review* 47: 569–586.

Eyerman, Ron. 1992. "Modernity and Social Movements." In *Social Change and Modernity*, edited by Hans Haferkamp and Neil J. Smelser. Berkeley and Los Angeles: University of California Press.

Haferkamp, Hans, and Neil J. Smelser. 1992. Introduction to *Social Change and Modernity*, edited by Hans Haferkamp and Neil J. Smelser. Berkeley and Los Angeles: University of California Press.

Kerr, Clark, John T. Dunlop, Frederick H. Harbison, and Charles A. Myers. 1964. *Industrialism and Industrial Man.* New York: Oxford University Press.

Kuznets, Simon. 1955. "Economic Growth and Income Inequality (Presidential Address)." *American Economic Review* 45: 1–28.

Nisbet, Robert A. 1959. "The Decline and Fall of Social Class." *Pacific Sociological Review* 2: 11–17.

Pakulski, J. 2005. "Foundations of a Post-Class Analysis." In *Approaches to Class Analysis,* edited by E. Wright. Cambridge: Cambridge University Press.

Parsons, Talcott. 1970. "Equality and Inequality in Modern Society; or, Social Stratification Revisited." In *Social Stratification: Research and Theory for the 1970s*, edited by Edward O. Laumann. Indianapolis: Bobbs-Merrill.

Reskin, Barbara F., and Debra Branch McBrier. 2000. "Why Not Ascription? Organizations' Employment of Male and Female Man-

agers." *American Sociological Review* 65: 210–233.

Sen, A. 2006. "Conceptualizing and Measuring Poverty." In *Inequality and Poverty*, edited by D. Grusky and R. Kanbur. Stanford: Stanford University Press.

Touraine, Alain. 1981. *The Voice and the Eye: An Analysis of Social Movements*. Cambridge: Cambridge University Press.

Wright, Erik O. 2005. *Approaches to Class Analysis*. Cambridge: Cambridge University Press.

PART II

Does Inequality
Serve a Purpose?

2

Some Principles of Stratification

KINGSLEY DAVIS AND
WILBERT E. MOORE

In a previous paper some concepts for handling the phenomena of social inequality were presented.[1] In the present paper a further step in stratification theory is undertaken—an attempt to show the relationship between stratification and the rest of the social order.[2] Starting from the proposition that no society is "classless," or unstratified, an effort is made to explain, in functional terms, the universal necessity which calls forth stratification in any social system.

Throughout, it will be necessary to keep in mind one thing—namely, that the discussion relates to the system of positions, not to the individuals occupying those positions. It is one thing to ask why different positions carry different degrees of prestige, and quite another to ask how certain individuals get into those positions. Although, as the argument will try to show, both questions are related, it is essential to keep them separate in our thinking.

Most of the literature on stratification has tried to answer the second question (particularly with regard to the ease or difficulty of mobility between strata) without tackling the first. The first question, however, is logically prior and, in the case of any particular individual or group, factually prior.

The Functional Necessity of Stratification

Curiously the main functional necessity explaining the universal presence of stratification is precisely the requirement faced by any society of placing and motivating individuals in the social structure. As a functioning mechanism a society must somehow distribute its members in social positions and induce them to perform the duties of these positions. It must thus concern itself with motivation at two different levels: to instill in the proper individuals the desire to fill certain positions, and, once in these positions, the desire to perform the duties attached to them. Even though the social order may be relatively static in form, there is a continuous process of metabolism as new individuals are born into it, shift with age, and die off. Their absorption into the positional system must somehow be arranged and motivated. This is true whether the system is competitive or non-competitive. A

Kingsley Davis and Wilbert E. Moore, "Some Principles of Stratification," *American Sociological Review* 10 (April 1945), pp. 242–249.

competitive system gives greater importance to the motivation to achieve positions, whereas a non-competitive system gives perhaps greater importance to the motivation to perform the duties of the positions; but in any system both types of motivation are required.

If the duties associated with the various positions were all equally pleasant to the human organism, all equally important to societal survival, and all equally in need of the same ability or talent, it would make no difference who got into which positions, and the problem of social placement would be greatly reduced. But actually it does make a great deal of difference who gets into which positions, not only because some positions are inherently more agreeable than others, but also because some require special talents or training and some are functionally more important than others. Also, it is essential that the duties of the positions be performed with the diligence that their importance requires. Inevitably, then, a society must have, first, some kind of rewards that it can use as inducements, and, second, some way of distributing these rewards differentially according to positions. The rewards and their distribution become a part of the social order, and thus give rise to stratification.

One may ask what kind of rewards a society has at its disposal in distributing its personnel and securing essential services. It has, first of all, the things that contribute to sustenance and comfort. It has, second, the things that contribute to humor and diversion. And it has, finally, the things that contribute to self-respect and ego expansion. The last, because of the peculiarly social character of the self, is largely a function of the opinion of others, but it nonetheless ranks in importance with the first two. In any social system all three kinds of rewards must be dispensed differentially according to positions.

In a sense the rewards are "built into" the position. They consist in the "rights" associated with the position, plus what may be called its accompaniments or perquisites. Often the rights, and sometimes the accompaniments, are functionally related to the duties of the position. (Rights as viewed by the incumbent are usually duties as viewed by other members of the community.) However, there may be a host of subsidiary rights and perquisites that are not essential to the function of the position and have only an indirect and symbolic connection with its duties, but which still may be of considerable importance in inducing people to seek the positions and fulfill the essential duties.

If the rights and perquisites of different positions in a society must be unequal, then the society must be stratified, because that is precisely what stratification means. Social inequality is thus an unconsciously evolved device by which societies insure that the most important positions are conscientiously filled by the most qualified persons. Hence every society, no matter how simple or complex, must differentiate persons in terms of both prestige and esteem, and must therefore possess a certain amount of institutionalized inequality.

It does not follow that the amount or type of inequality need be the same in all societies. This is largely a function of factors that will be discussed presently.

The Two Determinants of Positional Rank

Granting the general function that inequality subserves, one can specify the two factors that determine the relative rank of different positions. In general those positions convey the best reward, and hence have the highest rank, which (a) have the greatest importance for the society and (b) require the greatest training or talent. The first factor concerns function and is a matter of relative significance; the second concerns means and is a matter of scarcity.

Differential Functional Importance. Actually a society does not need to reward positions in proportion to their functional importance. It merely needs to give sufficient reward to them to insure that they will be filled competently. In other words, it must see that less essential positions do not compete successfully with more essential ones. If a position is easily filled, it need not be heavily rewarded, even though important. On the other hand, if it is important but hard to fill, the reward must be high enough to get it filled anyway. Functional importance is therefore a necessary but not a sufficient cause of high rank being assigned to a position.[3]

Differential Scarcity of Personnel. Practically all positions, no matter how acquired, require some form of skill or capacity for performance. This is implicit in the very notion of position, which implies that the incumbent must, by virtue of his incumbency, accomplish certain things.

There are, ultimately, only two ways in which a person's qualifications come about: through inherent capacity or through training. Obviously, in concrete activities both are always necessary, but from a practical standpoint the scarcity may lie primarily in one or the other, as well as in both. Some positions require innate talents of such high degree that the persons who fill them are bound to be rare. In many cases, however, talent is fairly abundant in the population but the training process is so long, costly, and elaborate that relatively few can qualify. Modern medicine, for example, is within the mental capacity of most individuals, but a medical education is so burdensome and expensive that virtually none would undertake it if the position of the M.D. did not carry a reward commensurate with the sacrifice.

If the talents required for a position are abundant and the training easy, the method of acquiring the position may have little to do with its duties. There may be, in fact, a virtually accidental relationship. But if the skills required are scarce by reason of the rarity of talent or the costliness of training, the position, if functionally important, must have an attractive power that will draw the necessary skills in competition with other positions. This means, in effect, that the position must be high in the social scale—must command great prestige, high salary, ample leisure, and the like.

How Variations Are to Be Understood. In so far as there is a difference between one system of stratification and another, it is attributable to whatever factors affect the two determinants of differential reward— namely, functional importance and scarcity of personnel. Positions important in one society may not be important in another, because the conditions faced by the societies, or their degree of internal development, may be different. The same conditions, in turn, may affect the question of scarcity; for in some societies the stage of development, or the external situation, may wholly obviate the necessity of certain kinds of skill or talent. Any particular system of stratification, then, can be understood as a product of the special conditions affecting the two afore-mentioned grounds of differential reward.

NOTES

1. Kingsley Davis, "A Conceptual Analysis of Stratification," *American Sociological Review.* 7:309–321, June, 1942.

2. The writers regret (and beg indulgence) that the present essay, a condensation of a longer study, covers so much in such short space that adequate evidence and qualification cannot be given and that as a result what is actually very tentative is presented in an unfortunately dogmatic manner.

3. Unfortunately, functional importance is difficult to establish. To use the position's prestige to establish it, as is often unconsciously done, constitutes circular reasoning from our point of view. There are, however, two independent clues: (a) the degree to which a position is functionally unique, there being no other positions that can perform the same function satisfactorily; and (b) the degree to which other positions are dependent on the one in question. Both clues are best exemplified in organized systems of positions built around one major function. Thus, in most complex societies the religious, political, economic, and educational functions are handled by distinct structures not easily interchangeable. In addition, each structure possesses many different positions, some clearly dependent on, if not subordinate to, others. In sum, when an institutional nucleus becomes differentiated around one main function, and at the same time organizes a large portion of the population into its relationships, the *key* positions in it are of the highest functional importance. The absence of such specialization does not prove functional unimportance, for the whole society may be relatively unspecialized; but it is safe to assume that the more important functions receive the first and clearest structural differentiation.

3

Inequality by Design

CLAUDE S. FISCHER, MICHAEL HOUT, MARTÍN SÁNCHEZ JANKOWSKI, SAMUEL R. LUCAS, ANN SWIDLER, AND KIM VOSS

Why do some Americans have a lot more than others? Perhaps, inequality follows inevitably from human nature. Some people are born with more talent than others; the first succeed while the others fail in life's competition. Many people accept this explanation, but it will not suffice. Inequality is not fated by nature, nor even by the "invisible hand" of the market; it is a social construction, a result of our historical acts. *Americans have created the extent and type of inequality we have, and Americans maintain it.*

To answer the question of what explains inequality in America, we must divide it in two. First, who gets ahead and who falls behind in the competition for success? Second, what determines how much people get for being ahead or behind? To see more clearly that the two questions are different, think of a ladder that represents the ranking of affluence in a society. Question one asks why this person rather than that person ended up on a higher or lower rung. Question two asks why some societies have tall and narrowing ladders—ladders that have huge distances between top and bottom

rungs and that taper off at the top so that there is room for only a few people—while other societies have short and broad ladders—ladders with little distance between top and bottom and with lots of room for many people all the way to the top.

The answer to the question of who ends up where is that people's social environments largely influence what rung of the ladder they end up on.[1] The advantages and disadvantages that people inherit from their parents, the resources that their friends can share with them, the quantity and quality of their schooling, and even the historical era into which they are born boost some up and hold others down. The children of professors, our own children, have substantial head starts over children of, say, factory workers. Young men who graduated from high school in the booming 1950s had greater opportunities than the ones who graduated during the Depression. Context matters tremendously.

The answer to the question of why societies vary in their structure of rewards is more political. In significant measure, societies choose the height and breadth of their "ladders." By loosening markets or regulating them, by providing services to all citizens or rationing them according to income, by subsidizing some groups more than others, societies, through their politics, build their ladders. To be sure, historical and external constraints deny full freedom of action, but a substantial freedom of action remains. In a democracy, this means that the inequality Americans have is, in significant measure, the historical result of policy choices Americans—or, at least, Americans' representatives—have made. In the United States, the result is a society that is distinctively *un*equal. Our ladder is, by the standards of affluent democracies and even by the standards of recent American history, unusually extended and narrow—and becoming more so.

To see how policies shape the structure of rewards (i.e., the equality of outcomes), consider these examples: Laws provide the ground rules for the marketplace—rules covering incorporation, patents, wages, working conditions, unionization, security transactions, taxes, and so on. Some laws widen differences in income and earnings among people in the market; others narrow differences. Also, many government programs affect inequality more directly through, for example, tax deductions, food stamps, social security, Medicare, and corporate subsidies.

To see how policies also affect which particular individuals get to the top and which fall to the bottom of our ladder (i.e., the equality of opportunity), consider these examples: The amount of schooling young Americans receive heavily determines the jobs they get and the income they make. In turn, educational policies—what sorts of schools are provided, the way school resources are distributed (usually according to the community in which children live), teaching methods such as tracking, and so on—strongly affect how much schooling children receive. Similarly, local employment opportunities constrain how well people can do economically. Whether and where governments promote jobs or fail to do so will, in turn, influence who is poised for well-paid employment and who is not.

Claiming that intentional policies have significantly constructed the inequalities we have and that other policies could change those inequalities may seem a novel idea in the current ideological climate. So many voices tell us that inequality is the result of individuals' "natural" talents in a "natural" market. Nature defeats any sentimental efforts by society to reduce inequality, they say; such efforts should therefore be dropped as futile and wasteful. Appeals to nature are common and comforting. As Kenneth Bock wrote in his study of social philosophy, "We have been quick to seek explanations of our problems and failures in what we *are* instead of what we *do*. We seem wedded to the belief that our situation is a consequence of our nature rather than of our historical acts."[2] In this case, appeals to nature are shortsighted.

Arguments from nature are useless for answering the question of what determines the structure of rewards because that question concerns differences in equality *among societies*. Theories of natural inequality cannot tell us why countries with such similar genetic stocks (and economic markets) as the United States, Canada, England, and Sweden can vary so much in the degree of economic inequality their citizens experience. The answer lies in deliberate policies.

Appeals to nature also cannot satisfactorily answer even the first question: Why do some *individuals* get ahead and some fall behind? Certainly, genetic endowment helps. Being tall, slender, good-looking, healthy, male, and white helps in the race for success, and these traits are totally or partly determined genetically. But these traits matter to the degree that society makes them matter—determining how much, for example, good looks or white skin are rewarded. More important yet than these traits are the social milieux in which people grow up and live.

Realizing that intentional policies account for much of our expanding inequality is not only more accurate than theories of natural inequality; it is also more optimistic. We are today more unequal than we have been in seventy years. We are more unequal than any other affluent Western nation. Intentional policies could change those conditions, could reduce and reverse our rush to a polarized society, could bring us closer to the average inequality in the West, could expand both equality of opportunity and equality of result.

Still, the "natural inequality" viewpoint is a popular one. Unequal outcomes, the best-selling *Bell Curve* argues, are the returns from a fair process that sorts people out according to how intelligent they are.[3] But *The Bell Curve*'s explanation of inequality is inadequate. The authors err in assuming that human talents can be reduced to a single, fixed, and essentially innate skill they label intelligence. They err in asserting that this trait largely determines how people end up in life. And they err in imagining that individual competition explains the structure of inequality in society. . . .

Disparities in income and wealth, [other] analysts argue, encourage hard work and saving. The rich, in particular, can invest their capital in production and thus create jobs for all.[4] This was the argument of "supply-side" economics in the 1980s, that rewarding the wealthy—for example, by reducing income taxes on returns from their investments—would stimulate growth to the benefit of all. The 1980s did not work out that way, but the theory is still influential. We *could* force more equal outcomes, these analysts say, but doing so would reduce living standards for all Americans.

Must we have so much inequality for overall growth? The latest economic research concludes *not;* it even suggests that inequality may *retard* economic growth. In a detailed statistical analysis, economists Torsten Persson and Guido Tabellini reported finding that, historically, societies that had more inequality of earnings tended to have lower, not higher, subsequent economic growth. Replications by other scholars substantiated the finding: More unequal nations grew less quickly than did more equal societies.[5] . . .

This recent research has not demonstrated precisely how greater equality helps economic growth,[6] but we can consider a few possibilities. Increasing resources for those of lower income might, by raising health, educational attainment, and hope, increase people's abilities to be productive and entrepreneurial. Reducing the income of those at the top might reduce unproductive and speculative spending. Take, as a concrete example, the way American corporations are run compared with German and Japanese ones. The American companies are run by largely autonomous managers whose main responsibility is to return short-term profits and high stock prices to shareholders and—because they are often paid in stock options—to themselves as well. Japanese and German managers are more like top employees whose goals largely focus on keeping the company a thriving enterprise. The latter is more conducive to reinvesting profits and thus to long-term growth.[7] Whatever the mechanisms may be, inequality appears to undermine growth. Americans certainly need not feel that they must accept the high levels of inequality we currently endure in order to have a robust economy.

A related concern for Americans is whether "leveling" stifles the drive to get ahead. Americans prefer to encourage Horatio Alger striving and to provide opportunities for everyone. Lincoln once said "that some would be rich shows that others may become rich."[8] Many, if not most, Americans believe that inequality is needed to encourage people to work hard.[9] But, if so, *how much* inequality is needed?

For decades, sociologists have been comparing the patterns of social mobility across societies, asking: In which countries are people most likely to overcome the disadvantages of birth and move up the ladder? In particular, does more or less equality encourage such an "open" society? The answer is that Western societies vary little in the degree to which children's economic successes are constrained by their parents' class positions. America, the most unequal Western society, has somewhat more fluid intergenerational mobility than do other nations, but so does Sweden, the most equal Western society.[10] There is no case for encouraging inequality in this evidence, either.

In sum, the assumption that considerable inequality is needed for, or even encourages, economic growth appears to be false. We do not need to make a morally wrenching choice between more affluence and more equality; we can have both. But even if such a choice were necessary, both sides of the debate, the "altruists" who favor intervention for equalizing and the supposed "realists" who resist it, agree that inequality can be shaped by policy decisions: Wittingly or unwittingly, we choose our level of inequality.

NOTES

1. We know that in statistical models of individual status attainment much, if not most, of the variance is unaccounted for. Of the explained variance, however, the bulk is due to social environment broadly construed. Also, we believe that much of the residual, unexplained variance is attributable to unmeasured social rather than personal factors.

2. Kenneth Bock, *Human Nature Mythology* (Urbana 1994), p. 9.

3. Richard J. Herrnstein and Charles Murray, *The Bell Curve: Intelligence and Class Structure in American Life* (New York 1994).

4. See, for example, Rich Thomas, "Rising Tide Lifts the Yachts: The Gap Between Rich and Poor Has Widened, but There Are Some Comforting Twists," *Newsweek,* May 1, 1995. See also George Will, "What's Behind Income Disparity," *San Francisco Chronicle,* April 24, 1995.

5. Torsten Persson and Guido Tabellini, "Is Inequality Harmful for Growth?," *American Economic Review* 84, 1994; Roberto Chang, "Income Inequality and Economic Growth: Evidence and Recent Theories," *Economic Review* 79, 1994; George R. G. Clarke, "More Evidence on Income Distribution and Growth," *Journal of Development Economics* 47, 1995. See also Peter H. Lindert, "The Rise of Social Spending," *Explorations in Economic History* 31, 1994.

6. Persson and Tabellini's explanation ("Is Inequality Harmful?") for their results is that in societies with greater earnings inequality, there is less political pressure for government redistribution; such redistribution impairs growth. However, their evidence for the explanation is thin, and Clarke's results ("More Evidence") are inconsistent with that argument. Chang ("Income Inequality") suggests that with more equality, lower-income families could make longer-term investment decisions. In any event, the statistical

results suggest that government intervention on behalf of equality in the market, rather than after the market, would be beneficial.

7. See, for example, Michael Porter, *Capital Choices: Changing the Way America Invests in Industry* (Washington 1992).

8. Quoted by Alan Trachtenberg, *The Incorporation of America: Culture and Society in the Gilded Age* (New York 1982), p. 75.

9. See, for example, Lee Rainwater, *What Money Buys: Inequality and the Social Meanings of Income* (New York 1974); James R. Kluegel and E. R. Smith, "Beliefs About Stratification," *Annual Review of Sociology* 7, 1981.

10. Harry B. G. Ganzeboom, Donald J. Treiman, and Wout C. Ultee, "Comparative Intergenerational Stratification Research," *Annual Review of Sociology* 17, 1991.

4

Inequality,
Too Much of a Good Thing

ALAN B. KRUEGER

As the title of this essay suggests, I believe inequality has both positive and negative effects. On the positive side, differential rewards provide incentives for individuals to work hard, invest, and innovate. On the negative side, differences in rewards that are unrelated to productivity—those that result from racial discrimination, for example—are corrosive to civil society and cause resources to be misallocated. Even if discrimination did not exist, however, income inequality is problematic in a democratic society if those who are privileged use their economic muscle to curry favor in the political arena and thereby secure monopoly rents or other advantages. Moreover, for several reasons discussed in the next section, poverty and income inequality create negative externalities.[1] Consequently, it can be in the interest of the wealthy as well as the poor to raise the incomes of the poor, especially by using education and training as a means for redistribution.

The term *inequality* is often used rather loosely and can be a lightning rod. Some have argued that only extreme poverty is a concern. Others have argued that the gap in income or wealth between the well off and the poor is a concern. Yet others have argued that the rapid growth in income disparity between the richest of the rich and everyone else is an issue. I will argue that, for various reasons elaborated below, all of these forms of inequality are of concern to contemporary American society, and that America has reached a point at which, on the margin, efficiently redistributing income from rich to poor is in the nation's interest.

A theme of my contribution to this debate is that societies must strike a *balance* between the beneficial incentive effects of inequality and the harmful welfare-decreasing effects of inequality. The optimal balance will differ across societies and time, but too much inequality can be harmful in any society, just as too much equality can suppress innovation and drive. . . .

Why Care about Rising Inequality?

Philosophers have argued about income inequality and social justice for centuries. I will

---

sidestep most of that debate. What follows is a thumbnail sketch of reasons why I think it is in our interest for U.S. public policy to try to restore a more balanced distribution of income in the country. Because such a conclusion fundamentally rests on one's values as well as an empirical view of the world, I will touch lightly on these reasons. Suffice it to say that I hope there are enough arguments here to persuade the reader that it is worth considering using education and training as part of an overall strategy to reduce income inequality in America.

Philosophy

As Atkinson (1983) observes, "different principles of justice lead to quite different views about inequality" (p. 5). Principles of justice provide guidelines for society's welfare function, and with a welfare function for a particular society, economists could judge the distribution of inequality in that society against the optimal level. The rub, of course, is that the welfare function in a society is *not* observable and depends on philosophical arguments that are not testable. In addition, one has the Arrow impossibility theorem[2] with which to contend. Consequently, appealing to philosophical arguments can never be universally dispositive.

Principles of social justice can be divided into those that focus on fair exchange starting from a just distribution of endowments, and those that focus on the equality of outcomes. Rawls invites readers to arrive at a theory of justice by selecting the principles they would desire if they were choosing such principles in an original position behind a veil of ignorance, unaware of their standing in society or initial endowment of talents. He argues that in this case the social justice that would be desired would involve two principles: one protecting liberties and

the other providing for an egalitarian distribution of opportunities and material goods. This leads him to a maximin welfare function in which the well-being of the worst off in society should be as high as possible. Interestingly, Adam Smith arrived at a somewhat similar conclusion nearly two hundred years earlier, positing that "[n]o society can surely be flourishing and happy, of which the far greater part of the members are poor and miserable. It is but equity, besides, that they who feed, clothe and lodge the whole body of the people, should have such a share of the produce of their own labour as to be themselves tolerably well fed, clothed and lodged" (Smith 1776, 110–111).

Nozick (1974) questions whether a theory of justice can be based on the distribution of outcomes. Using the analogy of fans who are willing to pay a fee to watch Wilt Chamberlain play basketball—an updated analogy might substitute Shaquille O'Neal—Nozick argues that "no end-state principle or distributional patterned principle of justice can be continuously realized without continuous interference with people's lives" (p. 163). Who could complain about Wilt Chamberlain's exorbitant salary if it results from rational choices? Nozick also raises the issue of the adverse incentive effects Rawls's theory of justice would have on the acquisition of talent.

Religion

I would argue that religious beliefs provide as strong (or weak) a justification for views toward society's implicit welfare function as do philosophical reflections behind a veil of ignorance. Indeed, I would go further and say that religious tenets reflect the demand for equality among the public. If people did not adhere to the basic tenets of their religion, they would not practice or would eventually change faiths. Thus, long-standing religious views toward inequality provide something of a revealed-preference argument.[3] And with regard to wealth inequality, the world's major religions are united in favoring redistribution of wealth toward the poor. Robert Nelson (1991), for example, observes that "Roman Catholicism has traditionally instilled a strong concern for the poor; in the Middle Ages the church itself provided much of the care for the indigent. The welfare state today similarly accomplishes substantial internal redistribution with the approval of many of the wealthier contributing members of the community" (p. 326). The Jewish *Siddur* advises followers to "Be just to the poor and the orphan; Deal righteously with the afflicted and the destitute" and comments, "Happy are they who are thoughtful of the needy; In time of trouble may the Lord Keep them from harm." And the Koran criticizes the egoism of the rich inhabitants of Mecca and urges believers in Islam to support poor people, orphans, and captives. Islam requires five major obligations of its followers, including *zakat,* an obligatory contribution to the needy (which today is implemented in the form of a tax).

Enlightened Self-Interest

Another line of argument for achieving and maintaining a minimum level of equality rests on self-interest. If wide disparities in income or education create negative externalities for a majority of people, then it clearly is in the self-interest of members of society to reduce those disparities. Individuals acting on their individual preferences (e.g., paying to see Shaquille O'Neal play basketball) will not internalize these externalities. What might such exter-

nalities be? An incomplete list would involve the following.

- More educated voters make the democratic process work better. First, people with more education are more likely to be informed and more likely to participate in democracy. Second, more-informed citizens are likely (though not guaranteed) to make better decisions. For the latter reason, even a devout defender of free markets like Milton Friedman (1982) can be found supporting a minimum compulsory level of education.
- Available evidence suggests a link between crime and inequality (e.g., Ehrlich 1973; Freeman 1983, 1995; and Imrohoroglu, Merlo, and Rupert 2001). Other things being equal, the incentive for those with limited market opportunities to commit property crimes rises as inequality increases. From the criminal's perspective, the potential gain from crime is higher if inequality is higher, and the opportunity cost is lower. Society can devote more resources to crime prevention and incarceration, or to reducing inequality.
- Society is not willing to allow citizens to be totally destitute, to fall below some minimum level of basic consumption when it comes to food or health care (see, e.g., Pauly 1971). By providing those likely to have low incomes with skills, therefore, and thereby raising their future earnings, society can reduce the cost of providing transfer payments later on. . . .
- Nelson and Phelps (1966) and Romer (1990) model the level of education in a society as generating positive externalities for economic growth, although

empirical support for this model is mixed (see Krueger and Lindahl 2001).

Low Wages, Imperfect Monitoring, and Public Safety

In an advanced economy, people are connected via markets in a myriad of ways. Employee performance can be monitored only imperfectly. If an employee performs poorly because he or she feels poorly compensated, others may suffer as a result of his or her poor performance. The tragic events of September 11th, for example, highlighted the importance of paying baggage screeners better wages.

Market Failure

More generally, market failures could lead the distribution of income in a society to be suboptimal. Credit constraints, for example, might prevent children from poor families from investing adequately in education. Monopsony power on the part of employers might enable firms to pay workers less than the value of their marginal products.[4] Statistical discrimination might lead to lower-than-optimal investment in education for discriminated-against groups (e.g., Lundberg and Startz 1983).

Efficient Policy Changes

Another type of externality could arise in the political arena in a society if income inequality in that society is viewed as excessive. Treaties to reduce international trade barriers offer an example. A policy that reduces trade barriers undoubtedly will increase national income in the society that enacts it. However, there will be winners and losers from such a policy. If some segments of society feel that they have not benefited from developments in the economy, then they are unlikely to support efforts to reduce trade barriers. I am not talking here just about the losers from the trade barrier reduction policy specifically, who are usually few in number and concentrated in a handful of industries. Instead, views toward free trade seem to be class related. For example, Blendon et al. (1997) find that 72 percent of those with less than a college education say one reason the U.S. economy is not doing better is that "companies are sending jobs overseas," whereas only 53 percent of college graduates agree with the same statement, and just 6 percent of American Economic Association members. Less-educated people are also less likely than those with more education to respond in the survey that trade agreements are good for the economy. I suspect that one reason Presidents (George W.) Bush and Clinton had difficulty securing fast-track authority for the passage of trade agreement is that large segments of the public perceived that they would lose from free trade, an inference that they drew because they had seen their real incomes stagnate or decline over the previous twenty years while trade expanded. Although I suspect trade has had little to do with rising wage inequality in the United States, it is understandable why so many people would draw such an inference.

Unless the public perceives that it will benefit from more efficient policies, there is little reason to suspect it will support such policies, and with 94 percent of income growth accruing to the top 1 percent of the U.S. population since 1973, it is understandable why the American public might be a little skeptical that it gained from past changes such as expanded trade.

Money Buys Influence

Economists at least since Adam Smith have fretted that wealthy merchants and manufacturers would be led by self-interest to seek government regulation and privilege to protect their monopoly position, thereby preventing the invisible hand from working its magic. Money buys access and influence in politics. It also buys influence through think tanks. A negative consequence of the skewed distribution of income in the United States is that some individuals have much more political influence than others.

Benabou (2000) develops a formal model in which the progressivity of educational funding and taxation is endogenous. He shows that the political influence of the wealthy interacts with income inequality to block efficient progressive policies or impose inefficient regressive ones. When income inequality is high, he finds, the wealthy are more likely to block *efficiency-enhancing* programs that would improve educational opportunities for the less well off.

Growth and Income Inequality

Persson and Tabellini (1994) develop a model of economic growth in which income inequality negatively influences growth through the political process. In their model, income inequality leads to policies that do not protect property rights and therefore do not allow full private appropriation of the returns from investment. A growing body of cross-country and cross-state studies have estimated the relationship between initial income inequality and subsequent GDP growth.[5] Although attributing causality is difficult in these studies, the correlation between income inequality and growth is negative, conditional on variables like initial GDP per capita and average education. Two-stage least-squares estimates that use variables such as initial literacy and infant mortality as instruments for income

inequality also show an inverse relationship between GDP growth and such inequality.

Health and Income Inequality

One common argument I will *not* make concerns health and income inequality. Wilkinson (1996), for example, argues that average health is negatively affected by the societal level of income inequality. The evidence in support of this view, however, is far from compelling (see, e.g., Smith 1999 and Deaton 2001), although Eibner and Evans (2002) provide evidence that relative deprivation affects health, and a large body of evidence finds that a person's own income level is related to his or her health.

Winner-Take-All Inefficiency in Superstar Markets

Frank and Cook (1996) argue that technological changes have facilitated a shift to superstar markets in many top-paying professions. The reward received by the one who finishes first is much greater than the reward received by the also-rans. They lament that this shift is inefficient and inequitable, causing too many students to pursue careers in law, finance, and consulting at the expense of more socially beneficial fields such as engineering, manufacturing, civil service, and teaching. The winner-take-all society engendered by this shift may create the same type of misallocation of talent that Murphy, Shleifer, and Vishny (1991) attribute to rent seeking. To some extent, income inequality probably leads to legions of tax lawyers and lobbyists who look for ways to help wealthy clients avoid taxation. Frank and Cook believe that superstar markets have led to inefficient investment and wasteful competition. Although I think we are at little risk of becoming a nation of Tonya Hardings, there may be something to the argument that superstar salaries provide perverse incentives and unnecessary competition in some sectors and divert some workers from pursuing more socially rewarding careers.

Public Preference

Last but not least, I would surmise that a majority of the public demands a certain amount of equality and is particularly supportive of using education and training to achieve more equality of outcomes. A survey of 1,001 adults by Lake, Snell, Perry & Associates in July 2000 posed the following request to respondents: "I am going to read some different ways the government can help poor Americans find and keep good jobs. For each, please tell me if you strongly support, somewhat support, somewhat oppose, or strongly oppose this idea." Fully 90 percent supported "helping to pay for education and job training for people leaving welfare." Similarly, a Gallup poll sponsored by General Motors in May 1998 asked the following free-form question: "Just your opinion, in what ways do you think the government should help the poor?" By far, the top two responses were providing better/more affordable education (38 percent) and providing job training/skills training (29 percent). The next-highest response was providing more jobs/job opportunities, at 16 percent. Only 5 percent of those surveyed cited lowering taxes as a way the government might assist poor people.

Even when given an explicit choice of lower taxes, the public prefers education and training. A CBS News poll in September 1999, for example, asked 1,376 respondents, "Which comes closer to your view? Government should provide tools to help families better their lives, such as education and job training programs. The best thing

that government can do for families is to cut taxes and allow individual families to decide for themselves how to allocate their money." Fifty-five percent of respondents said the first statement more closely reflected their views, whereas only 42 percent replied that the second statement came closer to what they believed.

Wrapping Up

In supporting minimum schooling, Milton Friedman (1982) argued that "[a] stable and democratic society is impossible without a minimum degree of literacy and knowledge on the part of most citizens and without widespread acceptance of some common set of values" (p. 86). I would argue that inequality could grow so extreme that it eventually jeopardizes any type of "widespread acceptance" of a democratic capitalist society that might be established. This leads me to agree with Victor Fuchs (1979): "For me the key word is *balance,* both in the goals that we set and in the institutions that we nourish in order to pursue these goals. I value freedom *and* justice *and* efficiency, and economics tells me that I may have to give up a little of one goal to insure the partial achievement of others" (p. 180).

Targeted Education and Training: Part of the Solution

In a perfect world, children from all families would invest in educational resources up to the point that their marginal return equaled their discount rate, and all families would have equal access to credit and discount investments at the same prevailing rate. The evidence suggests, however, that education decisions are not made in a perfect world. Children from poor families *behave* as if they have higher discount rates.

The most plausible explanations for this phenomenon are that poor families are credit constrained (i.e., cannot borrow at the same rate as everyone else), or that they discount future benefits of human capital investments at a higher than market rate because they are impatient, have a greater disutility of schooling, or fail to appreciate the benefits of education. Of these possible explanations, credit constraints have received the most attention in the literature, because students cannot easily use the return on their future human capital as collateral to borrow for human capital investments. This may be a reason for discount rates to vary. Poor families face different borrowing costs than rich ones.

The following five observations are consistent with the view that low-income families face credit constraints when it comes to education. First, Ellwood and Kane (2000) find that when the return to college education increased in the 1980s, four-year college enrollment increased for children from all quartiles of the income distribution except the bottom one. Second, Behrman and Taubman (1990) find that the timing of parental income matters for children's educational attainment. Using data from the Panel Study of Income Dynamics (PSID), they find that father's income earned when children are teenagers has a stronger effect on children's educational attainment than income earned later on. Third, Shea (2000) looks at the effect on children's human capital of differences in parental income emanating from noncompetitive factors, such as employment in a high-paying union job or industry. Wage differences for reasons such as these arguably are independent of parents' ability. Shea finds that family income matters for children's human capital investment in a

sample of low-income families, but not for the broader population. He concludes that this finding is consistent with the idea that the accumulation of observable skills by poverty sample fathers may have been suboptimal due to liquidity constraints. Fourth, Björklund and Jantti (1997) find stronger family income effects on children's outcomes in the United States than in Sweden, which provides much more generous educational subsidies than the United States. Fifth, the reaction of college enrollment to changes in tuition, especially at the two-year-college level, is substantially larger than the reaction of college enrollment to equivalent, present-value changes in the payoff to education (see Kane 1999).

Although it is possible to construct complicated explanations of the above findings that are consistent with all families' having equal access to credit—and I suspect part of the association between education and parental income reflects intergenerational transmission of ability and motivation for schooling, as Cameron and Heckman (2001) argue—Occam's razor and common sense suggest that families have different access to credit. For example, some families borrow for college costs by accumulating debt on their credit cards at exorbitant rates, whereas others tap into their family finances or take out home equity loans that are given tax-preferred treatment.

One does not have to resort to theoretical assumptions or indirect tests of credit constraints, however, to support the view that redistribution of wealth via targeted education and training is desirable. *It is clear that returns to education and training are at least as big at the bottom of the income distribution as at the top.* I have presented evidence elsewhere (Krueger 2003) that the *social return* from investment in education and training for poor children, from infancy through early adulthood, is at least as great as the social return from investments in education and training in the general public.

A theme that emerges from my survey of the evidence (see Krueger 2003) is that the real rate of return from investment in various education and training programs for the disadvantaged is 6 to 11 percent. This range applies to a diverse set of programs, ranging from preschool to Job Corps to conventional K–12 public schools. To put this figure in perspective, note that the historical real rate of return on the stock market has been calculated at 6.3 percent (Burtless 1999). So investment in human capital for the disadvantaged seems to yield at least as great a return as investment in the equity market. Also, because there is not currently universal access to most of the educational and training programs, and many willing participants are thus turned away, I would argue that the returns estimated from various evaluations reviewed below would approximately apply if the programs were greatly expanded to accommodate more participants. . . .

I would emphasize that I do not envision investment in human capital development as the sole component of a program to address the adverse consequences of income inequality. It is part of the solution, not the whole solution. In principle, the optimal government policy regarding income inequality would employ multiple instruments, up to the point at which the social benefit per additional dollar of cost of each instrument is equal across the instruments.

NOTES

1. In referring to "negative externalities," Krueger is claiming that decisions resulting in poverty and inequality are made without taking into account the full costs of those decisions, just as decisions by firms to pollute are often made without those firms having to bear the full costs of such decisions (e.g., the social costs of the resulting asthma).—EDS.

2. The Arrow impossibility theorem refers in this context to the impossibility of devising a "fair" procedure for translating individual preferences about how much inequality should be allowed into a collective decision about how much inequality should be allowed.—EDS.

3. The simple point that Krueger is making here is that consumers of religion are, by virtue of their decision to consume, revealing a taste for the egalitarian doctrines of most major religions.—EDS.

4. When workers face a single employer to whom they can sell their labor, that employer has "monopsony power" that makes it possible to offer wages that are lower than would be predicted in competitive markets.—EDS.

5. The GDP (Gross Domestic Product) is the total value of the final goods and products produced in a year within a country.—EDS.

REFERENCES

Atkinson, Anthony. 1983. *The Economics of Inequality,* 2d ed. Oxford: Oxford University Press.

Behrman, Jere, and Paul Taubman. 1990. "The Intergenerational Correlation between Children's Adult Earnings and Their Parents' Income: Results from the Michigan Panel Survey of Income Dynamics." *Review of Income and Wealth* 36, no. 2: 115–127.

Benabou, Roland. 2000. "Unequal Societies: Income Distribution and the Social Contract." *American Economic Review* 90, no. 1 (March): 96–129.

Björklund, Anders, and Markus Jantti. 1997. "Intergenerational Income Mobility in Sweden Compared to the United States." *American Economic Review* 87, no. 5 (December): 1009–1018.

Blendon, Robert, John Benson, Mollyann Brodie, Richard Morin, Drew Altman, Daniel Gitterman, Mario Brossard, and Matt James. 1997. "Bridging the Gap between the Public's and Economists' Views of the Economy." *Jour-*

nal of Economic Perspectives 11, no. 3 (Summer): 105–118.

Burtless, Gary. 1999. "Risk and Returns of Stock Market Investments Held in Individual Retirement Accounts." Testimony before the House Budget Committee Task Force on Social Security Reform, May 11.

Cameron, Stephen, and James Heckman. 2001. "The Dynamics of Educational Attainment for Black, Hispanic, and White Males." *Journal of Political Economy* 109, no. 3 (June): 455–499.

Deaton, Angus. 2001. "Health, Inequality, and Economic Development." Research Program in Development Studies working paper, Princeton University.

Ehrlich, Isaac. 1973. "Participation in Illegitimate Activities: A Theoretical and Empirical Investigation." *Journal of Political Economy* 81, no. 3 (May): 521–565.

Eibner, Christine, and William Evans. 2002. "Relative Deprivation, Poor Health Habits and Mortality." University of Maryland, College Park, mimeo.

Ellwood, David, and Thomas Kane. 2000. "Who Is Getting a College Education? Family Background and the Growing Gaps in Enrollment." In *Securing the Future: Investing in Children from Birth to College*, Sheldon Danziger and Jane Waldfogel, eds. New York: Russell Sage.

Frank, Robert H., and Philip J. Cook. 1996. *The Winner Take All Society*. New York: Free Press.

Freeman, Richard. 1983. "Crime and the Labor Market." In *Crime and Public Policy*, James Wilson, ed. San Francisco: Institute for Contemporary Studies.

Freeman, Richard. 1995. "The Labor Market." In *Crime*, James Wilson and Joan Petersilia, eds. San Francisco: Institute for Contemporary Studies.

Friedman, Milton. 1982. *Capitalism and Freedom*. Chicago: University of Chicago Press.

Fuchs, Victor. 1979. "Economics, Health, and Post-Industrial Society." *Health and Society* 57, no. 2 (Spring): 153–182.

Imrohoroglu, Ayse, Antonio Merlo, and Peter Rupert. 2001. "What Accounts for the Decline in Crime?" Penn Institute for Economic Research working paper no. 01–012.

Kane, Thomas. 1999. *The Price of Admission: Rethinking How Americans Pay for College*. Washington, D.C.: Brookings Institution Press.

Krueger, Alan. 2003. "Economic Considerations and Class Size." *Economic Journal*, forthcoming.

Krueger, Alan, and Mikael Lindahl. 2001. "Education and Growth: Why and for Whom?" *Journal of Economic Literature* 39, no. 4 (December): 1101–1136.

Lundberg, Shelly, and Richard Startz. 1983. "Private Discrimination and Social Intervention in Competitive Labor Markets." *American Economic Review* 73, no. 3 (June): 340–347.

Murphy, Kevin M., Andrei Shleifer, and Robert Vishny. 1991. "The Allocation of Talent: Implications for Growth." *Quarterly Journal of Economics* 106, no. 2 (May): 503–530.

Nelson, Richard, and Edmund Phelps. 1966. "Investment in Humans, Technological Diffusion, and Economic Growth." *American Economic Review* 56, no. 2 (March): 69–75.

Nelson, Robert. 1991. *Reaching for Heaven on Earth*. Savage, Md.: Rowman & Littlefield.

Nozick, Robert. 1974. *Anarchy, State, and Utopia*. New York: Basic.

Pauly, Mark V. 1971. *Medical Care at Public Expense: A Study in Applied Welfare Economics*. New York: Praeger.

Persson, Torsten, and Guido Tabellini. 1994. "Is Inequality Harmful for Growth?" *American Economic Review* 84, no. 3 (June): 600–621.

Rawls, John. 1971. *A Theory of Justice*. Cambridge: Belknap Press of Harvard University Press.

Romer, Paul. 1990. "Endogenous Technological Change." *Journal of Political Economy* 98, no. 5 (October): 71–102.

Shea, John. 2000. "Does Parents' Money Matter?" *Journal of Public Economics* 77, no. 2 (August): 155–184.

Smith, Adam. [1776]. *The Wealth of Nations*. New York: Random House.

Smith, James P. 1999. "Healthy Bodies and Thick Wallets: The Dual Relation between Health and Economic Status." *Journal of Economic Perspectives* 13, no. 2 (Spring): 145–166.

Wilkinson, Richard. 1996. *Unhealthy Societies: The Afflictions of Inequality*. London: Routledge.

PART III

The Structure of Social Inequality

5

Classes in Capitalism and Pre-Capitalism

KARL MARX

The history of all hitherto existing society[1] is the history of class struggles.

Freeman and slave, patrician and plebeian, lord and serf, guild-master[2] and journeyman, in a word, oppressor and oppressed, stood in constant opposition to one another, carried on an uninterrupted, now hidden, now open fight, a fight that each time ended, either in a revolutionary re-constitution of society at large, or in the common ruin of the contending classes.

In the earlier epochs of history, we find almost everywhere a complicated arrangement of society into various orders, a manifold gradation of social rank. In ancient Rome we have patricians, knights, plebeians, slaves; in the Middle Ages, feudal lords, vassals, guild-masters, journeymen, apprentices, serfs; in almost all of these classes, again, subordinate gradations.

The modern bourgeois society that has sprouted from the ruins of feudal society has not done away with class antagonisms. It has but established new classes, new conditions of oppression, new forms of struggle in place of the old ones.

Our epoch, the epoch of the bourgeoisie, possesses, however, this distinctive feature: it has simplified the class antagonisms. Society as a whole is more and more splitting up into two great hostile camps, into two great classes directly facing each other: Bourgeoisie and Proletariat.

From the serfs of the Middle Ages sprang the chartered burghers of the earliest towns. From these burgesses the first elements of the bourgeoisie were developed.

The discovery of America, the rounding of the Cape, opened up fresh ground for the rising bourgeoisie. The East-Indian and Chinese markets, the colonisation of America, trade with the colonies, the increase in the means of exchange and in commodities generally, gave to commerce, to navigation, to industry, an impulse never before known, and thereby, to the revolutionary element in the tottering feudal society, a rapid development.

Karl Marx, "The Communist Manifesto," in *Selected Works*, vol. 1 (Moscow: Progress Publishers, 1964), pp. 108–119. Reprinted by permission of Progress Publishers. *The Poverty of Philosophy* (New York: International Publishers, 1963), pp. 172–175. Reprinted by permission of International Publishers. "The Eighteenth Brumaire of Louis Bonaparte," in *Selected Works*, vol. 1 (Moscow: Progress Publishers, 1963), pp. 478–479. Reprinted by permission of Progress Publishers. *Capital*, vol. 3 (Moscow: Progress Publishers, 1967), pp. 885–886. Reprinted by permission of Progress Publishers.

The feudal system of industry, under which industrial production was monopolised by closed guilds, now no longer sufficed for the growing wants of the new markets. The manufacturing system took its place. The guild-masters were pushed on one side by the manufacturing middle class; division of labour between the different corporate guilds vanished in the face of division of labour in each single workshop.

Meantime the markets kept ever growing, the demand ever rising. Even manufacture no longer sufficed. Thereupon, steam and machinery revolutionised industrial production. The place of manufacture was taken by the giant, Modern Industry, the place of the industrial middle class, by industrial millionaires, the leaders of whole industrial armies, the modern bourgeois.

Modern industry has established the world-market, for which the discovery of America paved the way. This market has given an immense development to commerce, to navigation, to communication by land. This development has, in its turn, reacted on the extension of industry; and in proportion as industry, commerce, navigation, railways extended, in the same proportion the bourgeoisie developed, increased its capital, and pushed into the background every class handed down from the Middle Ages.

We see, therefore, how the modern bourgeoisie is itself the product of a long course of development, of a series of revolutions in the modes of production and of exchange.

Each step in the development of the bourgeoisie was accompanied by a corresponding political advance of that class. An oppressed class under the sway of the feudal nobility, an armed and self-governing association in the mediaeval commune;[3] here independent urban republic (as in Italy and Germany), there taxable "third estate" of the monarchy (as in France), afterwards, in the period of manufacture proper, serving either the semi-feudal or the absolute monarchy as a counterpoise against the nobility, and, in fact, cornerstone of the great monarchies in general, the bourgeoisie has at last, since the establishment of Modern Industry and of the world-market, conquered for itself, in the modern representative State, exclusive political sway. The executive of the modern State is but a committee for managing the common affairs of the whole bourgeoisie.

The bourgeoisie, historically, has played a most revolutionary part. The bourgeoisie, wherever it has got the upper hand, has put an end to all feudal, patriarchal, idyllic relations. It has pitilessly torn asunder the motley feudal ties that bound man to his "natural superiors," and has left remaining no other nexus between man and man than naked self-interest, than callous "cash payment." It has drowned the most heavenly ecstasies of religious fervour, of chivalrous enthusiasm, of philistine sentimentalism, in the icy water of egotistical calculation. It has resolved personal worth into exchange value, and in place of the numberless indefeasible chartered freedoms, has set up that single, unconscionable freedom—Free Trade. In one word, for exploitation, veiled by religious and political illusions, it has substituted naked, shameless, direct, brutal exploitation.

The bourgeoisie has stripped of its halo every occupation hitherto honoured and looked up to with reverent awe. It has converted the physician, the lawyer, the priest, the poet, the man of science, into its paid wage-labourers.

The bourgeoisie has torn away from the family its sentimental veil, and has reduced the family relation to a mere money relation.

The bourgeoisie has disclosed how it came to pass that the brutal display of vigour in the Middle Ages, which Reactionists so much admire, found its fitting complement in the most slothful indolence. It has been the first to show what man's activity can bring about. It has accomplished wonders far surpassing Egyptian pyramids, Roman aqueducts, and Gothic cathedrals; it has conducted expeditions that put in the shade all former Exoduses of nations and crusades.

The bourgeoisie cannot exist without constantly revolutionising the instruments of production, and thereby the relations of production, and with them the whole relations of society. Conservation of the old modes of production in unaltered form, was, on the contrary, the first condition of existence for all earlier industrial classes. Constant revolutionising of production, uninterrupted disturbance of all social conditions, everlasting uncertainty and agitation distinguish the bourgeois epoch from all earlier ones. All fixed, fast-frozen relations, with their train of ancient and venerable prejudices and opinions, are swept away, all new-formed ones become antiquated before they can ossify. All that is solid melts into air, all that is holy is profaned, and man is at last compelled to face with sober senses, his real conditions of life, and his relations with his kind.

The need of a constantly expanding market for its products chases the bourgeoisie over the whole surface of the globe. It must nestle everywhere, settle everywhere, establish connexions everywhere.

The bourgeoisie has through its exploitation of the world-market given a cosmopolitan character to production and consumption in every country. To the great chagrin of Reactionists, it has drawn from under the feet of industry the national ground on which it stood. All old-established national industries have been destroyed or are daily being destroyed. They are dislodged by new industries, whose introduction becomes a life and death question for all civilised nations, by industries that no longer work up indigenous raw material, but raw material drawn from the remotest zones; industries whose products are consumed, not only at home, but in every quarter of the globe. In place of the old wants, satisfied by the productions of the country, we find new wants, requiring for their satisfaction the products of distant lands and climes. In place of the old local and national seclusion and self-sufficiency, we have intercourse in every direction, universal inter-dependence of nations. And as in material, so also in intellectual production. The intellectual creations of individual nations become common property. National one-sidedness and narrow-mindedness become more and more impossible, and from the numerous national and local literatures, there arises a world literature.

The bourgeoisie, by the rapid improvement of all instruments of production, by the immensely facilitated means of communication, draws all, even the most barbarian, nations into civilisation. The cheap prices of its commodities are the heavy artillery with which it batters down all Chinese walls, with which it forces the barbarians' intensely obstinate hatred of foreigners to capitulate. It compels all nations, on pain of extinction, to adopt the bourgeois mode of production; it compels them to introduce what it calls civilisation into their midst, *i.e.,* to become bourgeois themselves. In one word, it creates a world after its own image.

The bourgeoisie has subjected the country to the rule of the towns. It has created enormous cities, has greatly increased the urban population as compared with the rural, and has thus rescued a considerable part of the population from the idiocy of rural life. Just as it has made the country dependent on the towns, so it has made barbarian and semi-barbarian countries dependent on the civilised ones, nations of peasants on nations of bourgeois, the East on the West.

The bourgeoisie keeps more and more doing away with the scattered state of the population, of the means of production, and of property. It has agglomerated population, centralised means of production, and has concentrated property in a few hands. The necessary consequence of this was political centralisation. Independent, or but loosely connected provinces, with separate interests, laws, governments and systems of taxation, became lumped together into one nation, with one government, one code of laws, one national class-interest, one frontier and one customs-tariff.

The bourgeoisie, during its rule of scarce one hundred years, has created more massive and more colossal productive forces than have all preceding generations together. Subjection of Nature's forces to man, machinery, application of chemistry to industry and agriculture, steam-navigation, railways, electric telegraphs, clearing of whole continents for cultivation, canalisation of rivers, whole populations conjured out of the ground—what earlier century had even a presentiment that such productive forces slumbered in the lap of social labour?

We see then: the means of production and of exchange, on whose foundation the bourgeoisie built itself up, were generated in feudal society. At a certain stage in the development of these means of production and of exchange, the conditions under which feudal society produced and exchanged, the feudal organisation of agriculture and manufacturing industry, in one word, the feudal relations of property became no longer compatible with the already developed productive forces; they became so many fetters. They had to be burst asunder; they were burst asunder.

Into their place stepped free competition, accompanied by a social and political constitution adapted to it, and by the economical and political sway of the bourgeois class.

A similar movement is going on before our own eyes. Modern bourgeois society with its relations of production, of exchange and of property, a society that has conjured up such gigantic means of production and of exchange, is like the sorcerer, who is no longer able to control the powers of the nether world whom he has called up by his spells. For many a decade past the history of industry and commerce is but the history of the revolt of modern productive forces against modern conditions of production, against the property relations that are the conditions for the existence of the bourgeoisie and of its rule. It is enough to mention the commercial crises that by their periodical return put on its trial, each time more threateningly, the existence of the entire bourgeois society. In these crises a great part not only of the existing products, but also of the previously created productive forces, are periodically destroyed. In these crises there breaks out an epidemic that, in all earlier epochs, would have seemed an absurdity—the epidemic of over-production. Society suddenly finds itself put back into a state of momentary barbarism; it appears as if a famine, a universal war of devastation had cut off the supply of every means of subsistence; industry and commerce seem to be destroyed; and why? Because there is too much civilisation, too much means of subsistence, too much industry, too much commerce. The productive forces at the disposal of society no longer tend to further the development of the conditions of bourgeois property; on the contrary, they have become too powerful for these conditions, by which they are fettered, and so soon as they overcome these fetters, they bring disorder into the whole of bourgeois society, endanger the existence of bourgeois property. The conditions of bourgeois society are too narrow to comprise the wealth created by them. And how does the bourgeoisie get over these crises? On the one hand by enforced destruction of a mass of productive forces; on the other, by the conquest of new markets, and by the more thorough exploitation of the old ones. That is to say, by paving the way for more extensive and more destructive crises, and by diminishing the means whereby crises are prevented.

The weapons with which the bourgeoisie felled feudalism to the ground are now turned against the bourgeoisie itself.

But not only has the bourgeoisie forged the weapons that bring death to itself; it has also called into existence the men who are to wield those weapons—the modern working class—the proletarians.

In proportion as the bourgeoisie, *i.e.,* capital, is developed, in the same proportion is the proletariat, the modern working class, developed—a class of labourers, who live only so long as they find work, and who find work only so long as their labour increases capital. These labourers, who must sell themselves piecemeal, are a commodity, like every other article of commerce, and are consequently exposed to all the vicissitudes of competition, to all the fluctuations of the market.

Owing to the extensive use of machinery and to division of labour, the work of the proletarians has lost all individual character, and, consequently, all charm for the workman. He becomes an appendage of the machine, and it is only the most simple, most monotonous, and most easily acquired knack, that is required of him. Hence, the cost of production of a workman is restricted, almost entirely, to the means of subsistence that he requires for his maintenance, and for the propagation of his race. But the price of a commodity, and therefore also of labour, is equal to its cost of production. In proportion, therefore, as the repulsiveness of the work increases, the wage decreases. Nay more, in proportion as the use of machinery and division of labour increases, in the same proportion the burden of toil also increases, whether by prolongation of the working hours, by increase of the work exacted in a given time or by increased speed of the machinery, etc.

Modern industry has converted the little workshop of the patriarchal master into the great factory of the industrial capitalist. Masses of labourers, crowded into the factory, are organised like soldiers. As privates of the industrial army they are placed under the command of a perfect hierarchy of officers and sergeants. Not only are they slaves of the bourgeois class, and of the bourgeois State; they are daily and hourly enslaved by the machine, by the overlooker, and, above all, by the individual bourgeois manufacturer himself. The more openly this despotism proclaims gain to be its end and aim, the more petty, the more hateful and the more embittering it is.

The less the skill and exertion of strength implied in manual labour, in other words, the more modern industry becomes developed, the more is the labour of men superseded by that of women. Differences of age and sex have no longer any distinctive social validity for the working class. All are instruments of labour, more or less expensive to use, according to their age and sex.

No sooner is the exploitation of the labourer by the manufacturer, so far, at an end, and he receives his wages in cash, than he is set upon by the other portions of the bourgeoisie, the landlord, the shopkeeper, the pawnbroker, etc.

The lower strata of the middle class—the small tradespeople, shopkeepers, and retired tradesmen generally, the handicraftsmen and peasants—all these sink gradually into the proletariat, partly because their diminutive capital does not suffice for the scale on which Modern Industry is carried on, and is swamped in the competition with the large capitalists, partly because their specialised skill is rendered worthless by new methods of production. Thus the proletariat is recruited from all classes of the population.

The proletariat goes through various stages of development. With its birth begins its struggle with the bourgeoisie. At first the contest is carried on by individual labourers, then by the workpeople of a factory, then by the operatives of one trade, in one locality, against the individual bourgeois who directly exploits them. They direct their attacks not against the bourgeois conditions of production, but against the instruments of production themselves: they destroy imported wares that compete with their labour, they smash to pieces machinery, they set factories ablaze, they seek to restore by force the vanished status of the workman of the Middle Ages.

At this stage the labourers still form an incoherent mass scattered over the whole country, and broken up by their mutual competition. If anywhere they unite to form more compact bodies, this is not yet the consequence of their own active union, but of the union of the bourgeoisie, which class, in order to attain its own political ends, is compelled to set the whole proletariat in motion, and is moreover yet, for a time, able to do so. At this stage, therefore, the proletarians do not fight their enemies, but the enemies of their enemies, the remnants of absolute monarchy, the landowners, the nonindustrial bourgeois, the petty bourgeoisie. Thus the whole historical movement is concentrated in the hands of the bourgeoisie; every victory so obtained is a victory for the bourgeoisie.

But with the development of industry the proletariat not only increases in number; it becomes concentrated in greater masses, its strength grows, and it feels that strength more. The various interests and conditions of life within the ranks of the proletariat are more and more equalised, in proportion as machinery obliterates all distinctions of labour, and nearly everywhere reduces wages to the same low level. The growing competition among the bourgeois, and the resulting commercial crises, make the wages of the workers ever more fluctuating. The unceasing improvement of machinery, ever more rapidly developing, makes their livelihood more and more precarious; the collisions between individual workmen and individual bourgeois take more and more the character of collisions between two classes. Thereupon the workers begin to form combinations (Trades' Unions) against the bourgeois; they club together in order to keep up the rate of wages; they found permanent associations in order to make provision beforehand for these occasional revolts. Here and there the contest breaks out into riots.

Now and then the workers are victorious, but only for a time. The real fruit of their battles lies, not in the immediate result, but in the ever-expanding union of the workers. This union is helped on by the improved means of communication that are created by modern industry and that place the workers of different localities in contact with one another. It was just this contact that was needed to centralise the numerous local struggles, all of the same character, into one national struggle between classes. But every class struggle is a political struggle. And that union, to attain which the burghers of the Middle Ages, with their miserable highways, required centuries, the modern proletarians, thanks to railways, achieve in a few years.

This organisation of the proletarians into a class, and consequently into a political party, is continually being upset again by the competition between the workers themselves. But it ever rises up again, stronger, firmer, mightier. It compels legislative recognition of particular interests of the workers, by taking advantage of the divisions among the bourgeoisie itself. Thus the ten-hours' bill in England was carried.

Altogether collisions between the classes of the old society further, in many ways, the course of development of the proletariat. The bourgeoisie finds itself involved in a constant battle. At first with the aristocracy; later on, with those portions of the bourgeoisie itself, whose interests have become antagonistic to the progress of industry; at all times, with the bourgeoisie of foreign countries. In all these battles it sees itself compelled to appeal to the proletariat, to ask for its help, and thus, to drag it into the political arena. The bourgeoisie itself, therefore, supplies the proletariat with its own elements of political and general education, in other words, it furnishes the proletariat with weapons for fighting the bourgeoisie.

Further, as we have already seen, entire sections of the ruling classes are, by the advance of industry, precipitated into the proletariat, or are at least threatened in their conditions of existence. These also supply the proletariat with fresh elements of enlightenment and progress.

Finally, in times when the class struggle nears the decisive hour, the process of dissolution going on within the ruling class, in fact within the whole range of old society, assumes such a violent, glaring character, that a small section of the ruling class cuts itself adrift, and joins the revolutionary class, the class that holds the future in its hands. Just as, therefore, at an earlier period, a section of the nobility went over to the bourgeoisie, so now a portion of the bourgeoisie goes over to the proletariat, and in particular, a portion of the bourgeois ideologists, who have raised themselves to the level of comprehending theoretically the historical movement as a whole.

Of all the classes that stand face to face with the bourgeoisie today, the proletariat alone is a really revolutionary class. The other classes decay and finally disappear in the face of Modern Industry; the proletariat is its special and essential product.

The lower middle class, the small manufacturer, the shopkeeper, the artisan, the peasant, all these fight against the bourgeoisie, to save from extinction their existence as fractions of the middle class. They are therefore not revolutionary, but conservative. Nay more, they are reactionary, for they try to roll back the wheel of history. If by chance they are revolutionary, they are so only in view of their impending transfer into the proletariat, they thus defend not their present, but their future interests, they desert their own standpoint to place themselves at that of the proletariat.

The "dangerous class," the social scum, that passively rotting mass thrown off by the lowest layers of old society, may, here and there, be swept into the movement by a proletarian revolution, its conditions of life, however, prepare it far more for the part of a bribed tool of reactionary intrigue.

In the conditions of the proletariat, those of old society at large are already virtually swamped. The proletarian is without property; his relation to his wife and children has no longer anything in common with the bourgeois family-relations; modern, industrial labour, modern subjection to capital, the same in England as in France, in America as in Germany, has stripped him of every trace of national character. Law, morality, religion, are to him so many bourgeois prejudices, behind which lurk in ambush just as many bourgeois interests.

All the preceding classes that got the upper hand, sought to fortify their already acquired status by subjecting society at large to their conditions of appropriation. The proletarians cannot become masters of the productive forces of society, except by abolishing their own previous mode of appropriation, and thereby also every other previous mode of appropriation. They have nothing of their own to secure and to fortify; their mission is to destroy all previous securities for, and insurances of, individual property.

All previous historical movements were movements of minorities, or in the interests of minorities. The proletarian movement is the self-conscious, independent movement of the immense majority, in the interests of the immense majority. The proletariat, the lowest stratum of our present society, cannot stir, cannot raise itself up, without the whole superincumbent strata of official society being sprung into the air.

Though not in substance, yet in form, the struggle of the proletariat with the bourgeoisie is at first a national struggle. The proletariat of each country must, of course, first of all settle matters with its own bourgeoisie.

In depicting the most general phases of the development of the proletariat, we traced the more or less veiled civil war, raging within existing society, up to the point where that war breaks out into open revolution, and where the violent overthrow of the bourgeoisie lays the foundation for the sway of the proletariat.

Hitherto, every form of society has been based, as we have already seen, on the antagonism of oppressing and oppressed classes. But in order to oppress a class, certain conditions must be assured to it under which it can, at least, continue its slavish existence. The serf, in the period of serfdom, raised himself to membership in the commune, just as the petty bourgeois, under the yoke of feudal absolutism, managed to develop into a bourgeois. The modern labourer, on the contrary, instead of rising with the progress of industry, sinks deeper and deeper below the conditions of existence of his own class. He becomes a pauper, and pauperism develops more rapidly than population and wealth. And here it becomes evident, that the bourgeoisie is unfit any longer to be the ruling class in society, and to impose its conditions of existence upon society as an overriding law. It is unfit to rule because it is incompetent to assure an existence to its slave within his slavery, because it cannot help letting him sink into such a state, that it has to feed him, instead of being fed by him. Society can no longer live under this bourgeoisie, in other words, its existence is no longer compatible with society.

The essential condition for the existence, and for the sway of the bourgeois class, is the formation and augmentation of capital; the condition for capital is wage-labour. Wage-labour rests exclusively on competition between the labourers. The advance of industry, whose involuntary promoter is the bourgeoisie, replaces the isolation of the labourers, due to competition, by their revolutionary combination, due to association. The development of Modern Industry, therefore, cuts from under its feet the very foundation on which the bourgeoisie produces and appropriates products. What the bourgeoisie, therefore, produces, above all, is its own grave-diggers. Its fall and the victory of the proletariat are equally inevitable.

NOTES

1. That is, all *written* history. In 1847, the pre-history of society, the social organisation existing previous to recorded history, was all but unknown. [*Note by Engels to the English edition of 1888.*]

2. Guild-master, that is, a full member of a guild, a master within, not a head of a guild. [*Note by Engels to the English edition of 1888.*]

3. "Commune" was the name taken, in France, by the nascent towns even before they had conquered from their feudal lords and masters local self-government and political rights as the "Third Estate." Generally speaking, for the economical development of the bourgeoisie, England is here taken as the typical country; for its political development, France. [*Note by Engels to the English edition of 1888.*]

This was the name given their urban communities by the townsmen of Italy and France, after they had purchased or wrested their initial rights of self-government from their feudal lords. [*Note by Engels to the German edition of 1890.*]

The Communist Manifesto, pp. 108–119

The first attempts of workers to *associate* among themselves always take place in the form of combinations.

Large-scale industry concentrates in one place a crowd of people unknown to one another. Competition divides their interests. But the maintenance of wages, this common interest which they have against their boss, unites them in a common thought of resistance—*combination*. Thus combination always has a double aim, that of stopping competition among the workers, so that they can carry on general competition with the capitalist. If the first aim of resistance was merely the maintenance of wages, combinations, at first isolated, constitute themselves into groups as the capitalists in their turn unite for the purpose of repression, and in face of always united capital, the maintenance of the association becomes more necessary to them than that of wages. This is so true that English economists are amazed to see the workers sacrifice a good part of their wages in favour of associations, which, in the eyes of these economists, are established solely in favour of wages. In this struggle—a veritable civil war—all the elements necessary for a coming battle unite and develop. Once it has reached this point, association takes on a political character.

Economic conditions had first transformed the mass of the people of the country into workers. The combination of capital has created for this mass a common situation, common interests. This mass is thus already a class as against capital, but not yet for itself. In the struggle, of which we have noted only a few phases, this mass becomes united, and constitutes itself as a class for itself. The interests it defends become class interests. But the struggle of class against class is a political struggle.

In the bourgeoisie we have two phases to distinguish: that in which it constituted itself as a class under the regime of feudalism and absolute monarchy, and that in which, already constituted as a class, it overthrew feudalism and monarchy to make society into a bourgeois society. The first of these phases was the longer and necessitated the greater efforts. This too began by partial combinations against the feudal lords.

Much research has been carried out to trace the different historical phases that the bourgeoisie has passed through, from the commune up to its constitution as a class.

But when it is a question of making a precise study of strikes, combinations and other forms in which the proletarians carry out before our eyes their organization as a class, some are seized with real fear and others display a *transcendental* disdain.

An oppressed class is the vital condition for every society founded on the antagonism of classes. The emancipation of the oppressed class thus implies necessarily the creation of a new society. For the oppressed class to be able to emancipate itself it is necessary that the productive powers already acquired and the existing social relations should no longer be capable of existing side by side. Of all the instruments of production, the greatest productive power is the revolutionary class itself. The organization of revolutionary elements as a class supposes the existence of all the productive forces which could be engendered in the bosom of the old society.

Does this mean that after the fall of the old society there will be a new class domination culminating in a new political power? No.

The condition for the emancipation of the working class is the abolition of every class, just as the condition for the liberation of the third estate, of the bourgeois order, was the abolition of all estates[1] and all orders.

The working class, in the course of its development, will substitute for the old civil society an association which will exclude classes and their antagonism, and there will be no more political power properly so-called, since political power is precisely the official expression of antagonism in civil society.

Meanwhile the antagonism between the proletariat and the bourgeoisie is a struggle of class against class, a struggle which carried to its highest expression is a total revolution. Indeed, is it at all surprising that a society founded on the opposition of classes should culminate in brutal *contradiction,* the shock of body against body, as its final *dénouement?*

Do not say that social movement excludes political movement. There is never a political movement which is not at the same time social.

It is only in an order of things in which there are no more classes and class antagonisms that *social evolutions* will cease to be *political revolutions.* Till then, on the eve of every general reshuffling of society, the last word of social science will always be:

"Le combat ou la mort; la lutte sanguinaire ou le néant. C'est ainsi que la question est invinciblement posée." [2]

NOTES

1. Estates here in the historical sense of the estates of feudalism, estates with definite and

limited privileges. The revolution of the bourgeoisie abolished the estates and their privileges. Bourgeois society knows only *classes*. It was, therefore, absolutely in contradiction with history to describe the proletariat as the "fourth estate." [*Note by F. Engels to the German edition,* 1885.]

2. "Combat or death; bloody struggle or extinction. It is thus that the question is inexorably put." George Sand, *Jean Ziska*.

The Poverty of Philosophy, pp. 172–175

The small-holding peasants form a vast mass, the members of which live in similar conditions but without entering into manifold relations with one another. Their mode of production isolates them from one another instead of bringing them into mutual intercourse. The isolation is increased by France's bad means of communication and by the poverty of the peasants. Their field of production, the small holding, admits of no division of labour in its cultivation, no application of science and, therefore, no diversity of development, no variety of talent, no wealth of social relationships. Each individual peasant family is almost self-sufficient; it itself directly produces the major part of its consumption and thus acquires its means of life more through exchange with nature than in intercourse with society. A small holding, a peasant and his family; alongside them another small holding, another peasant and another family. A few score of these make up a village, and a few score of villages make up a Department. In this way, the great mass of the French nation is formed by simple addition of homologous magnitudes, much as potatoes in a sack form a sack of potatoes. In so far as millions of families live under economic conditions of existence that separate their mode of life, their interests and their culture from those of the other classes, and put them in hostile opposition to the latter, they form a class. In so far as there is merely a local interconnection among these small-holding peasants, and the identity of their interests begets no community, no national bond and no political organisation among them, they do not form a class. They are consequently incapable of enforcing their class interests in their own name, whether through a parliament or through a convention. They cannot represent themselves, they must be represented. Their representative must at the same time appear as their master, as an authority over them, as an unlimited governmental power that protects them against the other classes and sends them rain and sunshine from above. The political influence of the small-holding peasants, therefore, finds its final expression in the executive power subordinating society to itself.

The Eighteenth Brumaire of Louis Bonaparte, pp. 478–479

The owners merely of labour-power, owners of capital, and landowners, whose respective sources of income are wages, profit and ground-rent, in other words, wage-labourers, capitalists and landowners, constitute then three big classes of modern society based upon the capitalist mode of production.

In England, modern society is indisputably most highly and classically developed in economic structure. Nevertheless, even here the stratification of classes does not appear in its pure form. Middle and intermediate strata even here obliterate lines of demarcation everywhere (although incomparably less in rural districts than in the cities). However, this is immaterial for our analysis. We have seen that the continual tendency and law of development of the capitalist mode of production is more and more to divorce the means of production from labour, and more and more to concentrate the scattered means of production into large groups, thereby transforming labour into wage-labour and the means of production into capital. And to this tendency, on the other hand, corresponds the independent separation of landed property from capital and labour, or the transformation of all landed property into the form of landed property corresponding to the capitalist mode of production.

The first question to be answered is this: What constitutes a class?—and the reply to this follows naturally from the reply to another question, namely: What makes wage-labourers, capitalists and landlords constitute the three great social classes?

At first glance—the identity of revenues and sources of revenue. There are three great social groups whose members, the individuals forming them, live on wages, profit and ground-rent respectively, on the realisation of their labour-power, their capital, and their landed property.

However, from this standpoint, physicians and officials, e.g., would also constitute two classes, for they belong to two distinct social groups, the members of each of these groups receiving their revenue from one and the same source. The same would also be true of the infinite fragmentation of interest and rank into which the division of social labour splits labourers as well as capitalists and landlords—the latter, e.g., into owners of vineyards, farm owners, owners of forests, mine owners and owners of fisheries.

[Here the manuscript breaks off.]

Capital, Vol. III, pp. 885–886

6

Class Counts

ERIK OLIN WRIGHT

A story from the *Li'l Abner* comic strips from the late 1940s will help to set the stage for the discussion of the concept of class structure. Here is the situation of the episode: Li'l Abner, a resident of the hill-billy community of Dogpatch, discovers a strange and wonderful creature, the "shmoo," and brings a herd of them back to Dogpatch. The shmoo's sole desire in life is to please humans by transforming itself into the material things human beings need. They do not provide humans with luxuries, but only with the basic necessities of life. If you are hungry, they can become ham and eggs, but not caviar. What's more, they multiply rapidly so you never run out of them. They are thus of little value to the wealthy, but of great value to the poor. . . .

In the episode from *Li'l Abner* reproduced here, a manager working for a rich capitalist, P.U., does a study to identify the poorest place in America in order to hire the cheapest labor for a new factory. The place turns out to be Dogpatch. P.U. and the manager come to Dogpatch to recruit employees for the new factory. The story unfolds in a sequence of comic strips from 1948 (Al Capp 1992: 134–136).

The presence of shmoos is a serious threat to class relations. Workers are more difficult to recruit for toilsome labor and no longer have to accept "guff" and indignities from their bosses. . . .

The saga of the shmoo helps to clarify the sense in which the interests of workers and capitalists are deeply antagonistic, one of the core ideas of Marxist class analysis. How do shmoos affect the material interests of people in these two classes? This depends upon the level of generosity of the shmoo. If the shmoo provides less than bare physical sub-sistence, it probably has a positive effect on the material interests of both workers and capitalists. For workers it makes their lives a little bit less precarious; for capitalists, such sub-subsistence shmoos could be considered a subsidy to the wage bill. All other things being equal, capitalists can pay lower wages if part of the subsistence of workers is provided outside of the market. At the other extreme, if shmoos provide for superabundance, grati-fying every material desire of humans from basic necessities to the most expensive luxu-ries, then they would also positively serve the material interests of capitalists. Between these two extremes, however, the impact of the

shmoo on the material interests of the two classes diverges. The welfare of workers is continuously improved as the generosity of shmoos increases, whereas for capitalists, after a point, their material interests are adversely affected. Once shmoos provide workers with a respectable standard of living, workers no longer have to work in order to live at an acceptable standard. As P.U.'s manager states in panic, "Do you realize what the shmoo means? Nobody'll have to work hard any more!!" This does not mean, of course, that no workers would be willing to work for an employer. Work fills many needs for people besides simply providing earnings, and in any case, so long as the shmoo does not provide superabundance, many people will have consumption desires beyond the shmoo level of provision. Nevertheless, workers would be in a much more powerful bargaining position with modestly generous shmoos at home, and it will be more difficult, in P.U.'s words, to get them to "do the long, dreary, backbreaking labor at our canning factories.". . .

What the story of the shmoo illustrates is that the deprivations of the propertyless in a capitalist system are not simply an unfortunate by-product of the capitalist pursuit of profit; they are a necessary condition for that pursuit. This is what it means to claim that capitalist profits depend upon "exploitation." Exploiting classes have an interest in preventing the exploited from acquiring the means of subsistence even if, as in the case of the shmoo story, that acquisition does not take the form of a redistribution of wealth or income from capitalists to workers.

The Concept of Exploitation

The story of the shmoo revolves around the linkage between class divisions, class interests and exploitation. There are two main classes in the story—capitalists who own the means of production and workers who do not. By virtue of the productive assets which they own (capital and labor power) they each face a set of constraints on how they can best pursue their material interests. The presence of shmoos fundamen-

tally transforms these constraints and is a threat to the material interests of capitalists. Why? Because it undermines their capacity to exploit the labor power of workers. "Exploitation" is thus the key concept for understanding the nature of the *interests* generated by the class relations.

Exploitation is a loaded theoretical term, since it suggests a moral condemnation of particular relations and practices, not simply an analytical description. To describe a social relationship as exploitative is to condemn it as both harmful and unjust to the exploited. Yet, while this moral dimension of exploitation is important, the core of the concept revolves around a particular type of *antagonistic interdependence of material interests* of actors within economic relations, rather than the injustice of those relations as such. As I will use the term, class exploitation is defined by three principal criteria:

A. *The material welfare of one group of people causally depends on the material deprivations of another.*
B. *The causal relation in (A) involves the asymmetrical exclusion of the exploited from access to certain productive resources.* Typically this exclusion is backed by force in the form of property rights, but in special cases it may not be.
C. *The causal mechanism which translates exclusion (B) into differential welfare (A) involves the appropriation of the fruits of labor of the exploited by those who control the relevant productive resources.*

This is a fairly complex set of conditions. Condition (A) establishes the antagonism of material interests. Condition (B) establishes that the antagonism is rooted in the way people are situated within the social organization of production. The expression "asymmetrical" in this criterion is meant to exclude "fair competition" from the domain of possible exploitations. Condition (C) establishes the specific mechanism by which the interdependent, antagonistic material interests are generated. The welfare of the exploiter depends upon the *effort* of the exploited, not merely the deprivations of the exploited.

If only the first two of these conditions are met we have what can be called "nonexploitative economic oppression," but not "exploitation." In nonexploitative economic oppression there is no transfer of the fruits of labor from the oppressed to the oppressor; the welfare of the oppressor depends simply on the exclusion of the oppressed from access to certain resources, but not on their effort. In both instances, the inequalities in question are rooted in ownership and control over productive resources.

The crucial difference between exploitation and nonexploitative oppression is that in an exploitative relation, the exploiter *needs* the exploited since the exploiter depends upon the effort of the exploited. In the case of nonexploitative oppression, the oppressors would be happy if the oppressed simply disappeared. Life would have been much easier for the European settlers in North America if the continent had been uninhabited by people. Genocide is thus always a potential strategy for nonexploitative oppressors. It is not an option in a situation of economic exploitation because exploiters require the labor of the exploited for their material well-being. It is no accident that culturally we have the abhorrent saying, "the only good Indian is a dead Indian," but not the saying "the only good worker is a dead worker" or "the only good slave is a dead slave." It makes sense to say "the only good worker is an obedient and conscientious worker," but not "the only good worker is a dead worker." The contrast between North America and South Africa in the treatment of indigenous peoples reflects this difference poignantly: in North America, where the indigenous people were oppressed (by virtue of being coercively displaced from the land) but not exploited, genocide was the basic policy of social control in the face of resistance; in South Africa, where the European settler population heavily depended upon African labor for its own prosperity, this was not an option.

Exploitation, therefore, does not merely define a set of *statuses* of social actors, but a pattern of on-going *interactions* structured by a set of social relations, relations which mutually bind the exploiter and the exploited together. This dependency of the exploiter on the exploited gives the exploited a certain form of power, since human beings always retain at least some minimal control over their own expenditure of effort. Social control of labor which relies exclusively on repression is costly and, except under special circumstances, often fails to generate optimal levels of diligence and effort on the part of the exploited. As a result, there is generally systematic pressure on exploiters to moderate their domination and in one way or another to try to elicit some degree of consent from the exploited, at least in the sense of gaining some level of minimal cooperation from them. Paradoxically perhaps, exploitation is thus a constraining force on the practices of the exploiter. This constraint constitutes a basis of power for the exploited. . . .

Class and Exploitation

In capitalist society, the central form of exploitation is based on property rights in the means of production. These property rights generate three basic classes: *capitalists* (exploiters), who own the means of production and hire workers; *workers* (exploited), who do not own the means of production and sell their labor power to capitalists; and *petty bourgeois* (neither exploiter nor exploited), who own and use the means of production without hiring others. The Marxist account of how the capital-labor relation generates exploitation is a familiar one: propertyless workers, in order to acquire their means of livelihood, must sell their labor power to people who own the means of production. In this exchange relation, they agree to work for a specified length of time in exchange for a wage which they use to buy their means of subsistence. Because of the power relation between capitalists and workers, capitalists are able to force workers to produce more than is needed to provide them with this subsistence. As a result, workers produce a surplus which is owned by the capitalist and takes the form of profits. Profits, the amount of the social product that is left over after the costs of producing and reproducing all of the inputs (both labor power inputs and physical inputs) have been deducted, constitute an appropriation of the fruits of labor of workers.

Describing this relation as exploitative is a claim about the basis for the inherent conflict between workers and capitalists in the employment relation. It points to the crucial fact that the conflict between capitalists and workers is not simply over the *level of wages,* but over the *amount of work effort* performed for those wages. Capitalists always want workers to expend more effort than workers willingly want to do. . . .

For some theoretical and empirical purposes, this simple image of the class structure may be sufficient. For example, if the main purpose of an analysis is to explore the basic differences between the class structures of feudalism and capitalism, then an analysis which revolved entirely around the relationship between capitalists and workers might be adequate. However, for many of the things we want to study with class analysis, we need a more nuanced set of categories. In particular, we need concepts which allow for two kinds of analyses: first, the analysis of the variation across time and place in the class structures of concrete capitalist societies, and second, the analysis of the ways individual lives are affected by their location within the class structure. The first of these is needed if we are to explore macro-variations in a fine-grained way; the second is needed if we are to use class effectively in micro-analysis.

Both of these tasks involve elaborating a concept of class structure in capitalist societies that moves beyond the core polarization between capitalists and workers. More specifically, this involves solving two general problems in class structural analysis: first, the problem of locating the "middle class" within the class structure, and second, locating people not in the paid labor force in the class structure.

The Problem of the "Middle Class" Among Employees

If we limit the analysis of class structure in capitalism to the ownership of, and exclusion from, the means of production, we end up with a class structure in which there are only three locations—the capitalist class, the working class and the petty bourgeoisie (those who own means of production but do not hire workers)— and in which around 85–90% of the population in most developed capitalist countries falls into a single class. While this may in some sense reflect a profound truth about capitalism—that the large majority of the population are separated from the means of production and must sell their labor power on the labor market in order to survive—it does not provide us with an adequate conceptual framework for explaining many of the things we want class to help explain. In particular, if we want class structure to help explain class consciousness, class formation and class conflict, then we need some way of understanding the class-relevant divisions within the employee population.

In ordinary language terms, this is the problem of the "middle class"—people who do not own their own means of production, who sell their labor power on a labor market, and yet do not seem part of the "working class." The question, then, is on what basis can we differentiate class locations among people who share a common location of nonownership within capitalist property relations? In my analyses, I divide the class of employees along two dimensions: first, their relationship to authority within production, and second, their possession of skills or expertise.

Authority

There are two rationales for treating authority as a dimension of class relations among employees. The first concerns the role of *domination* within capitalist property relations. In order to insure the performance of adequate effort on the part of workers, capitalist production always involves an apparatus of domination involving surveillance, positive and negative sanctions and varying forms of hierarchy. Capitalists do not simply *own* the means of production and *hire* workers; they also *dominate* workers within production.

In these terms, managers and supervisors can be viewed as exercising delegated capitalist class powers in so far as they engage in the practices of domination within production. In this sense they can be considered *simultaneously* in the capitalist class *and* the working class: they are like capitalists in that they dominate workers; they are like workers in that they are controlled by capitalists and exploited within production. They thus occupy what I have called *contradictory locations within class relations*. The term "contradictory" is used in this expression rather than simply "dual" since the class interests embedded in managerial jobs combine the inherently antagonistic interests of capital and labor. The higher one moves in the authority hierarchy, the greater will be the weight of capitalist interests within this class location. Thus upper managers, and especially Chief Executive Officers in large corporations will be very closely tied to the capitalist class, while the class character of lower level supervisor jobs will be much closer to that of the working class.

The second rationale for treating the authority dimension as a criterion for differentiating class locations among employees centers on the relationship between their earnings and the appropriation of surplus. The strategic position of managers within the organization of production enables them to make significant claims on a portion of the social surplus (defined in the counterfactual manner discussed above) in the form of relatively high earnings. In effect this means that the wages and salaries of managerial labor power are above the costs of producing and reproducing their labor power (including whatever skills they might have). . . .

Skills and Expertise

The second axis of class differentiation among employees centers on the possession of skills or expertise. Like managers, employees who possess high levels of skills/expertise are potentially in a privileged appropriation location within exploitation relations. There are two primary mechanisms through which this can happen. First, skills and expertise are frequently scarce in labor markets, not simply because they are in short supply, but also because there are systematic obstacles in the way of increasing the supply of those skills to meet the requirements of employing organizations. One important form of these obstacles is credentials, but rare talents could also constitute the basis for sustained restrictions on the supply of a particular form of labor power. The result of such restrictions on supply is that owners of the scarce skills are able to receive a wage above the costs of producing and reproducing their labor power.

Second, the control over knowledge and skills frequently renders also the labor effort of skilled workers difficult to monitor and control. The effective control over knowledge by such employees means that employers must rely to some extent on loyalty enhancing mechanisms in order to achieve desired levels of cooperation and effort from employees with high levels of skills and expertise, just as they have to do in the case of managers. Employees with high levels of expertise, therefore, are able to appropriate surplus both because of their strategic location within the organization of production (as controllers of knowledge), and because of their strategic location in the organization of labor markets (as controllers of a scarce form of labor power).. . .

A Map of Middle-Class Class Locations

Adding position within authority hierarchies and possession of scarce skills and expertise to the fundamental dimension of capitalist property relations generates the map of class locations presented in Figure 6.1. It is important to stress that this is a map of class *locations*. The cells in the typology are not "classes" as such; they are lo-

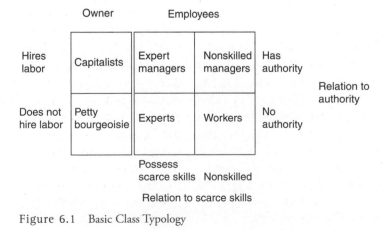

Figure 6.1   Basic Class Typology

cations within class relations. Some of these are contradictory locations within class relations, others are privileged appropriation locations within exploitation relations and still others are polarized locations within capitalist property relations. By convention the polarized locations—"capitalists" and "workers" in capitalism—are often called "classes," but the more precise terminology would be to describe these as the fundamental locations within the capitalist class structure. The typology is thus not a proposal for a six-class model of the class structure of capitalism, but rather a model of a class structure which differentiates six locations within class relations.

REFERENCES

Capp, Al. 1992. *Li'L Abner,* vol 14: 1948. Princeton, WI: Kitchen Sink Press.

7

Class, Status, Party

MAX WEBER

Economically Determined Power and the Social Order

Law exists when there is a probability that an order will be upheld by a specific staff of men who will use physical or psychical compulsion with the intention of obtaining conformity with the order, or of inflicting sanctions for infringement of it.[1] The structure of every legal order directly influences the distribution of power, economic or otherwise, within its respective community. This is true of all legal orders and not only that of the state. In general, we understand by 'power' the chance of a man or of a number of men to realize their own will in a communal action even against the resistance of others who are participating in the action.

'Economically conditioned' power is not, of course, identical with 'power' as such. On the contrary, the emergence of economic power may be the consequence of power existing on other grounds. Man does not strive for power only in order to enrich himself economically. Power, including economic power, may be valued 'for its own sake.' Very frequently the striving for power is also conditioned by the social 'honor' it entails. Not all power, however, entails social honor: The typical American Boss, as well as the typical big speculator, deliberately relinquishes social honor. Quite generally, 'mere economic' power, and especially 'naked' money power, is by no means a recognized basis of social honor. Nor is power the only basis of social honor. Indeed, social honor, or prestige, may even be the basis of political or economic power, and very frequently has been. Power, as well as honor, may be guaranteed by the legal order, but, at least normally, it is not their primary source. The legal order is rather an additional factor that enhances the chance to hold power or honor; but it cannot always secure them.

The way in which social honor is distributed in a community between typical groups participating in this distribution we may call the 'social order.' The social order and the economic order are, of course, similarly related to the 'legal order.' However, the social and the economic order are not identical. The economic order is for us

Max Weber, "Class, Status, Party," in *From Max Weber: Essays in Sociology*, edited by H. H. Gerth & C. Wright Mills, and translated by H. H. Gerth & C. Wright Mills, pp. 180–195. Translation copyright © 1946, 1958 by H. H. Gerth and C. Wright Mills.

merely the way in which economic goods and services are distributed and used. The social order is of course conditioned by the economic order to a high degree, and in its turn reacts upon it.

Now: 'classes,' 'status groups,' and 'parties' are phenomena of the distribution of power within a community.

Determination of Class-Situation by Market-Situation

In our terminology, 'classes' are not communities; they merely represent possible, and frequent, bases for communal action. We may speak of a 'class' when (1) a number of people have in common a specific causal component of their life chances, in so far as (2) this component is represented exclusively by economic interests in the possession of goods and opportunities for income, and (3) is represented under the conditions of the commodity or labor markets. [These points refer to 'class situation,' which we may express more briefly as the typical chance for a supply of goods, external living conditions, and personal life experiences, in so far as this chance is determined by the amount and kind of power, or lack of such, to dispose of goods or skills for the sake of income in a given economic order. The term 'class' refers to any group of people that is found in the same class situation.]

It is the most elemental economic fact that the way in which the disposition over material property is distributed among a plurality of people, meeting competitively in the market for the purpose of exchange, in itself creates specific life chances. According to the law of marginal utility this mode of distribution excludes the non-owners from competing for highly valued

goods; it favors the owners and, in fact, gives to them a monopoly to acquire such goods. Other things being equal, this mode of distribution monopolizes the opportunities for profitable deals for all those who, provided with goods, do not necessarily have to exchange them. It increases, at least generally, their power in price wars with those who, being propertyless, have nothing to offer but their services in native form or goods in a form constituted through their own labor, and who above all are compelled to get rid of these products in order barely to subsist. This mode of distribution gives to the propertied a monopoly on the possibility of transferring property from the sphere of use as a 'fortune,' to the sphere of 'capital goods'; that is, it gives them the entrepreneurial function and all chances to share directly or indirectly in returns on capital. All this holds true within the area in which pure market conditions prevail. 'Property' and 'lack of property' are, therefore, the basic categories of all class situations. It does not matter whether these two categories become effective in price wars or in competitive struggles.

Within these categories, however, class situations are further differentiated: on the one hand, according to the kind of property that is usable for returns; and, on the other hand, according to the kind of services that can be offered in the market. Ownership of domestic buildings; productive establishments; warehouses; stores; agriculturally usable land, large and small holdings—quantitative differences with possibly qualitative consequences—ownership of mines; cattle; men (slaves); disposition over mobile instruments of production, or capital goods of all sorts, especially money or objects that can be exchanged for money easily and at any time;

disposition over products of one's own labor or of others' labor differing according to their various distances from consumability; disposition over transferable monopolies of any kind—all these distinctions differentiate the class situations of the propertied just as does the 'meaning' which they can and do give to the utilization of property, especially to property which has money equivalence. Accordingly, the propertied, for instance, may belong to the class of rentiers or to the class of entrepreneurs.

Those who have no property but who offer services are differentiated just as much according to their kinds of services as according to the way in which they make use of these services, in a continuous or discontinuous relation to a recipient. But always this is the generic connotation of the concept of class: that the kind of chance in the *market* is the decisive moment which presents a common condition for the individual's fate. 'Class situation' is, in this sense, ultimately 'market situation.' The effect of naked possession *per se,* which among cattle breeders gives the nonowning slave or serf into the power of the cattle owner, is only a forerunner of real 'class' formation. However, in the cattle loan and in the naked severity of the law of debts in such communities, for the first time mere 'possession' as such emerges as decisive for the fate of the individual. This is very much in contrast to the agricultural communities based on labor. The creditor-debtor relation becomes the basis of 'class situations' only in those cities where a 'credit market,' however primitive, with rates of interest increasing according to the extent of dearth and a factual monopolization of credits, is developed by a plutocracy. Therewith 'class struggles' begin.

Those men whose fate is not determined by the chance of using goods or services for themselves on the market, e.g. slaves, are not, however, a 'class' in the technical sense of the term. They are, rather, a 'status group.'

Communal Action Flowing from Class Interest

According to our terminology, the factor that creates 'class' is unambiguously economic interest, and indeed, only those interests involved in the existence of the 'market.' Nevertheless, the concept of 'class-interest' is an ambiguous one: even as an empirical concept it is ambiguous as soon as one understands by it something other than the factual direction of interests following with a certain probability from the class situation for a certain 'average' of those people subjected to the class situation. The class situation and other circumstances remaining the same, the direction in which the individual worker, for instance, is likely to pursue his interests may vary widely, according to whether he is constitutionally qualified for the task at hand to a high, to an average, or to a low degree. In the same way, the direction of interests may vary according to whether or not a *communal* action of a larger or smaller portion of those commonly affected by the 'class situation,' or even an association among them, e.g. a 'trade union,' has grown out of the class situation from which the individual may or may not expect promising results. [Communal action refers to that action which is oriented to the feeling of the actors that they belong together. Societal action, on the other hand, is oriented to a rationally motivated adjustment of interests.] The rise of societal or even of communal action from a common class situation is by no means a universal phenomenon.

The class situation may be restricted in its effects to the generation of essentially *similar* reactions, that is to say, within our terminology, of 'mass actions.' However, it may not have even this result. Furthermore, often merely an amorphous communal action emerges. For example, the 'murmuring' of the workers known in ancient oriental ethics: the moral disapproval of the work-master's conduct, which in its practical significance was probably equivalent to an increasingly typical phenomenon of precisely the latest industrial development, namely, the 'slow down' (the deliberate limiting of work effort) of laborers by virtue of tacit agreement. The degree in which 'communal action' and possibly 'societal action,' emerges from the 'mass actions' of the members of a class is linked to general cultural conditions, especially to those of an intellectual sort. It is also linked to the extent of the contrasts that have already evolved, and is especially linked to the *transparency* of the connections between the causes and the consequences of the 'class situation.' For however different life chances may be, this fact in itself, according to all experience, by no means gives birth to 'class action' (communal action by the members of a class). The fact of being conditioned and the results of the class situation must be distinctly recognizable. For only then the contrast of life chances can be felt not as an absolutely given fact to be accepted, but as a resultant from either (1) the given distribution of property, or (2) the structure of the concrete economic order. It is only then that people may react against the class structure not only through acts of an intermittent and irrational protest, but in the form of rational association. There have been 'class situations' of the first category (1), of a specifically naked and transparent sort, in the urban centers of Antiquity and during the Middle Ages; especially then, when great fortunes were accumulated by factually monopolized trading in industrial products of these localities or in foodstuffs. Furthermore, under certain circumstances, in the rural economy of the most diverse periods, when agriculture was increasingly exploited in a profit-making manner. The most important historical example of the second category (2) is the class situation of the modern 'proletariat.'

Types of 'Class Struggle'

Thus every class may be the carrier of any one of the possibly innumerable forms of 'class action,' but this is not necessarily so: In any case, a class does not in itself constitute a community. To treat 'class' conceptually as having the same value as 'community' leads to distortion. That men in the same class situation regularly react in mass actions to such tangible situations as economic ones in the direction of those interests that are most adequate to their average number is an important and after all simple fact for the understanding of historical events. Above all, this fact must not lead to that kind of pseudo-scientific operation with the concepts of 'class' and 'class interests' so frequently found these days, and which has found its most classic expression in the statement of a talented author, that the individual may be in error concerning his interests but that the 'class' is 'infallible' about its interests. Yet, if classes as such are not communities, nevertheless class situations emerge only on the basis of communalization. The communal action that brings forth class situations, however, is not basically action between members of the identical class; it is an action between members of different classes. Communal actions that directly determine the class situation of the worker and the entrepreneur are: the labor market, the commodities market, and the capitalistic enterprise. But, in its turn, the existence of a capitalistic enterprise presupposes that a very specific communal action exists and that it is specifically structured to protect the possession of goods *per se,* and especially the power of individuals to dispose, in principle freely, over the means of production. The existence of a capitalistic enterprise is preconditioned by a specific kind of 'legal order.' Each kind of class situation, and above all when it rests upon the power of property *per se,* will become most clearly efficacious when all other determinants of reciprocal relations are, as far as possible, eliminated in their significance. It is in this way that the utilization of the power of property in the market obtains its most sovereign importance.

Now 'status groups' hinder the strict carrying through of the sheer market principle. In the present context they are of interest to us only from this one point of view. Before we briefly consider them, note that not much of a general nature can be said about the more specific kinds of antagonism between 'classes' (in our meaning of the term). The great shift, which has been going on continuously in the past, and up to our times, may be summarized, although at the cost of some precision: the struggle in which class situations are effective has progressively shifted from consumption credit toward, first, competitive struggles in the commodity market and, then, toward price wars on the labor market. The 'class struggles' of antiquity—to the extent that they were genuine class struggles and not struggles between status groups—were initially carried on by indebted peasants, and perhaps also by artisans threatened by debt bondage and struggling against urban creditors. For debt bondage is the normal result

of the differentiation of wealth in commercial cities, especially in seaport cities. A similar situation has existed among cattle breeders. Debt relationships as such produced class action up to the time of Cataline. Along with this, and with an increase in provision of grain for the city by transporting it from the outside, the struggle over the means of sustenance emerged. It centered in the first place around the provision of bread and the determination of the price of bread. It lasted throughout antiquity and the entire Middle Ages. The propertyless as such flocked together against those who actually and supposedly were interested in the dearth of bread. This fight spread until it involved all those commodities essential to the way of life and to handicraft production. There were only incipient discussions of wage disputes in antiquity and in the Middle Ages. But they have been slowly increasing up into modern times. In the earlier periods they were completely secondary to slave rebellions as well as to fights in the commodity market.

The propertyless of antiquity and of the Middle Ages protested against monopolies, pre-emption, forestalling, and the withholding of goods from the market in order to raise prices. Today the central issue is the determination of the price of labor.

This transition is represented by the fight for access to the market and for the determination of the price of products. Such fights went on between merchants and workers in the putting-out system of domestic handicraft during the transition to modern times. Since it is quite a general phenomenon we must mention here that the class antagonisms that are conditioned through the market situation are usually most bitter between those who actually and directly participate as opponents in price wars. It is not the rentier, the share-holder, and the banker who suffer the ill will of the worker, but almost exclusively the manufacturer and the business executives who are the direct opponents of workers in price wars. This is so in spite of the fact that it is precisely the cash boxes of the rentier, the share-holder, and the banker into which the more or less 'unearned' gains flow, rather than into the pockets of the manufacturers or of the business executives. This simple state of affairs has very frequently been decisive for the role the class situation has played in the formation of political parties. For example, it has made possible the varieties of patriarchal socialism and the frequent attempts—formerly, at least—of threatened status groups to form alliances with the proletariat against the 'bourgeoisie.'

Status Honor

In contrast to classes, *status groups* are normally communities. They are, however, often of an amorphous kind. In contrast to the purely economically determined 'class situation' we wish to designate as 'status situation' every typical component of the life fate of men that is determined by a specific, positive or negative, social estimation of *honor*. This honor may be connected with any quality shared by a plurality, and, of course, it can be knit to a class situation: class distinctions are linked in the most varied ways with status distinctions. Property as such is not always recognized as a status qualification, but in the long run it is, and with extraordinary regularity. In the subsistence economy of the organized neighborhood, very often the richest man is simply the chieftain. However, this often means only an honorific preference. For example, in the so-called pure modern 'democracy,' that is, one devoid of any expressly ordered

status privileges for individuals, it may be that only the families coming under approximately the same tax class dance with one another. This example is reported of certain smaller Swiss cities. But status honor need not necessarily be linked with a 'class situation.' On the contrary, it normally stands in sharp opposition to the pretensions of sheer property.

Both propertied and propertyless people can belong to the same status group, and frequently they do with very tangible consequences. This 'equality' of social esteem may, however, in the long run become quite precarious. The 'equality' of status among the American 'gentlemen,' for instance, is expressed by the fact that outside the subordination determined by the different functions of 'business,' it would be considered strictly repugnant—wherever the old tradition still prevails—if even the richest 'chief,' while playing billiards or cards in his club in the evening, would not treat his 'clerk' as in every sense fully his equal in birthright. It would be repugnant if the American 'chief' would bestow upon his 'clerk' the condescending 'benevolence' marking a distinction of 'position,' which the German chief can never dissever from his attitude. This is one of the most important reasons why in America the German 'clubby-ness' has never been able to attain the attraction that the American clubs have.

Guarantees of Status Stratification

In content, status honor is normally expressed by the fact that above all else a specific *style of life* can be expected from all those who wish to belong to the circle. Linked with this expectation are restrictions on 'social' intercourse (that is, intercourse which is not subservient to economic or any other of business 'functional' purposes). These restrictions may confine normal marriages to within the status circle and may lead to complete endogamous closure. As soon as there is not a mere individual and socially irrelevant imitation of another style of life, but an agreed-upon communal action of this closing character, the 'status' development is under way.

In its characteristic form, stratification by 'status groups' on the basis of conventional styles of life evolves at the present time in the United States out of the traditional democracy. For example, only the resident of a certain street ('the street') is considered as belonging to 'society,' is qualified for social intercourse, and is visited and invited. Above all, this differentiation evolves in such a way as to make for strict submission to the fashion that is dominant at a given time in society. This submission to fashion also exists among men in America to a degree unknown in Germany. Such submission is considered to be an indication of the fact that a given man *pretends* to qualify as a gentleman. This submission decides, at least *prima facie,* that he will be treated as such. And this recognition becomes just as important for his employment chances in 'swank' establishments, and above all, for social intercourse and marriage with 'esteemed' families, as the qualification for dueling among Germans in the Kaiser's day. As for the rest: certain families resident for a long time, and, of course, correspondingly wealthy, e.g. 'F. F. V., i.e. First Families of Virginia,' or the actual or alleged descendants of the 'Indian Princess' Pocahontas, of the Pilgrim fathers, or of the Knickerbockers, the members of almost inaccessible sects and all sorts of circles setting themselves apart by means of any other characteristics

and badges . . . all these elements usurp 'status' honor. The development of status is essentially a question of stratification resting upon usurpation. Such usurpation is the normal origin of almost all status honor. But the road from this purely conventional situation to legal privilege, positive or negative, is easily traveled as soon as a certain stratification of the social order has in fact been 'lived in' and has achieved stability by virtue of a stable distribution of economic power.

'Ethnic' Segregation and 'Caste'

Where the consequences have been realized to their full extent, the status group evolves into a closed 'caste.' Status distinctions are then guaranteed not merely by conventions and laws, but also by *rituals.* This occurs in such a way that every physical contact with a member of any caste that is considered to be 'lower' by the members of a 'higher' caste is considered as making for a ritualistic impurity and to be a stigma which must be expiated by a religious act. Individual castes develop quite distinct cults and gods.

In general, however, the status structure reaches such extreme consequences only where there are underlying differences which are held to be 'ethnic.' The 'caste' is, indeed, the normal form in which ethnic communities usually live side by side in a 'societalized' manner. These ethnic communities believe in blood relationship and exclude exogamous marriage and social intercourse. Such a caste situation is part of the phenomenon of 'pariah' peoples and is found all over the world. These people form communities, acquire specific occupational traditions of handicrafts or of other arts, and cultivate a belief in their ethnic community. They live in a 'diaspora' strictly segregated from all personal intercourse, except that of an unavoidable sort, and their situation is legally precarious. Yet, by virtue of their economic indispensability, they are tolerated, indeed, frequently privileged, and they live in interspersed political communities. The Jews are the most impressive historical example.

A 'status' segregation grown into a 'caste' differs in its structure from a mere 'ethnic' segregation: the caste structure transforms the horizontal and unconnected coexistences of ethnically segregated groups into a vertical social system of super- and subordination. Correctly formulated: a comprehensive societalization integrates the ethnically divided communities into specific political and communal action. In their consequences they differ precisely in this way: ethnic coexistences condition a mutual repulsion and disdain but allow each ethnic community to consider its own honor as the highest one; the caste structure brings about a social subordination and an acknowledgment of 'more honor' in favor of the privileged caste and status groups. This is due to the fact that in the caste structure ethnic distinctions as such have become 'functional' distinctions within the political societalization (warriors, priests, artisans that are politically important for war and for building, and so on). But even pariah people who are most despised are usually apt to continue cultivating in some manner that which is equally peculiar to ethnic and to status communities: the belief in their own specific 'honor.' This is the case with the Jews.

Only with the negatively privileged status groups does the 'sense of dignity' take a specific deviation. A sense of dignity is the precipitation in individuals of social honor and of conventional demands which a positively privileged status group raises for the deportment of its members. The sense of dignity that characterizes positively privileged status groups is naturally related to their 'being' which does not transcend itself, that is, it is to their 'beauty and excellence.' Their kingdom is 'of this world.' They live for the present and by exploiting their great past. The sense of dignity of the negatively privileged strata naturally refers to a future lying beyond the present, whether it is of this life or of another. In other words, it must be nurtured by the belief in a providential 'mission' and by a belief in a specific honor before God. The 'chosen people's' dignity is nurtured by a belief either that in the beyond 'the last will be the first,' or that in this life a Messiah will appear to bring forth into the light of the world which has cast them out the hidden honor of the pariah people. This simple state of affairs, and not the 'resentment' which is so strongly emphasized in Nietzsche's much admired construction in the *Genealogy of Morals,* is the source of the religiosity cultivated by pariah status groups. In passing, we may note that resentment may be accurately applied only to a limited extent; for one of Nietzsche's main examples, Buddhism, it is not at all applicable.

Incidentally, the development of status groups from ethnic segregations is by no means the normal phenomenon. On the contrary, since objective 'racial differences' are by no means basic to every subjective sentiment of an ethnic community, the ultimately racial foundation of status structure is rightly and absolutely a question of the concrete individual case. Very frequently a status group is instrumental in the production of a thoroughbred anthropological type. Certainly a status group is to a high degree effective in producing extreme types, for they select personally qualified individuals (e.g. the Knighthood selects those who are fit for warfare, physically and psychically). But selection is far from being the only, or the predominant, way in which status groups are formed: political membership or class situation has at all times been at least as frequently decisive. And today the class situation is by far the predominant factor, for of course the possibility of a style of life expected for members of a status group is usually conditioned economically.

Status Privileges

For all practical purposes, stratification by status goes hand in hand with a monopolization of ideal and material goods or opportunities, in a manner we have come to know as typical. Besides the specific status honor, which always rests upon distance and exclusiveness, we find all sorts of material monopolies. Such honorific preferences may consist of the privilege of wearing special costumes, of eating special dishes taboo to others, of carrying arms—which is most obvious in its consequences—the right to pursue certain non-professional dilettante artistic practices, e.g. to play certain musical instruments. Of course, material monopolies provide the most effective motives for the exclusiveness of a status group; although, in themselves, they are rarely sufficient, almost always they come into play to some extent. Within a status circle there is the question of intermarriage: the interest of the families in the monopolization of potential bridegrooms is at least of equal importance and is parallel to the interest in the monopolization of daughters. The daughters of the circle must be provided for. With an increased inclosure of the status group, the conventional preferential opportunities for special employment grow into a legal monopoly of special offices for the members. Certain goods become objects

for monopolization by status groups. In the typical fashion these include 'entailed estates' and frequently also the possessions of serfs or bondsmen and, finally, special trades. This monopolization occurs positively when the status group is exclusively entitled to own and to manage them; and negatively when, in order to maintain its specific way of life, the status group must *not* own and manage them.

The decisive role of a 'style of life' in status 'honor' means that status groups are the specific bearers of all 'conventions.' In whatever way it may be manifest, all 'stylization' of life either originates in status groups or is at least conserved by them. Even if the principles of status conventions differ greatly, they reveal certain typical traits, especially among those strata which are most privileged. Quite generally, among privileged status groups there is a status disqualification that operates against the performance of common physical labor. This disqualification is now 'setting in' in America against the old tradition of esteem for labor. Very frequently every rational economic pursuit, and especially 'entrepreneurial activity,' is looked upon as a disqualification of status. Artistic and literary activity is also considered as degrading work as soon as it is exploited for income, or at least when it is connected with hard physical exertion. An example is the sculptor working like a mason in his dusty smock as over against the painter in his salon-like 'studio' and those forms of musical practice that are acceptable to the status group.

Economic Conditions and Effects of Status Stratification

The frequent disqualification of the gainfully employed as such is a direct result of the principle of status stratification peculiar to the social order, and of course, of this principle's opposition to a distribution of power which is regulated exclusively through the market. These two factors operate along with various individual ones, which will be touched upon below.

We have seen above that the market and its processes 'knows no personal distinctions': 'functional' interests dominate it. It knows nothing of 'honor.' The status order means precisely the reverse, viz.: stratification in terms of 'honor' and of styles of life peculiar to status groups as such. If mere economic acquisition and naked economic power still bearing the stigma of its extra-status origin could bestow upon anyone who has won it the same honor as those who are interested in status by virtue of style of life claim for themselves, the status order would be threatened at its very root. This is the more so as, given equality of status honor, property *per se* represents an addition even if it is not overtly acknowledged to be such. Yet if such economic acquisition and power gave the agent any honor at all, his wealth would result in his attaining more honor than those who successfully claim honor by virtue of style of life. Therefore all groups having interests in the status order react with special sharpness precisely against the pretensions of purely economic acquisition. In most cases they react the more vigorously the more they feel themselves threatened. Calderon's respectful treatment of the peasant, for instance, as opposed to Shakespeare's simultaneous and ostensible disdain of the *canaille* illustrates the different way in which a firmly structured status order reacts as compared with a status order that has become economically precarious. This is an example of a state of affairs that recurs everywhere. Precisely be-

cause of the rigorous reactions against the claims of property *per se,* the 'parvenu' is never accepted, personally and without reservation, by the privileged status groups, no matter how completely his style of life has been adjusted to theirs. They will only accept his descendants who have been educated in the conventions of their status group and who have never besmirched its honor by their own economic labor.

As to the general *effect* of the status order, only one consequence can be stated, but it is a very important one: the hindrance of the free development of the market occurs first for those goods which status groups directly withheld from free exchange by monopolization. This monopolization may be effected either legally or conventionally. For example, in many Hellenic cities during the epoch of status groups, and also originally in Rome, the inherited estate (as is shown by the old formula for indication against spendthrifts) was monopolized just as were the estates of knights, peasants, priests, and especially the clientele of the craft and merchant guilds. The market is restricted, and the power of naked property *per se,* which gives its stamp to 'class formation,' is pushed into the background. The results of this process can be most varied. Of course, they do not necessarily weaken the contrasts in the economic situation. Frequently they strengthen these contrasts, and in any case, where stratification by status permeates a community as strongly as was the case in all political communities of antiquity and of the Middle Ages, one can never speak of a genuinely free market competition as we understand it today. There are wider effects than this direct exclusion of special goods from the market. From the contrariety between the status order and the purely economic order mentioned above, it follows that in most instances the notion of honor peculiar to status absolutely abhors that which is essential to the market: higgling. Honor abhors higgling among peers and occasionally it taboos higgling for the members of a status group in general. Therefore, everywhere some status groups, and usually the most influential, consider almost any kind of overt participation in economic acquisition as absolutely stigmatizing.

With some over-simplification, one might thus say that 'classes' are stratified according to their relations to the production and acquisition of goods; whereas 'status groups' are stratified according to the principles of their *consumption* of goods as represented by special 'styles of life.'

An 'occupational group' is also a status group. For normally, it successfully claims social honor only by virtue of the special style of life which may be determined by it. The differences between classes and status groups frequently overlap. It is precisely those status communities most strictly segregated in terms of honor (viz. the Indian castes) who today show, although within very rigid limits, a relatively high degree of indifference to pecuniary income. However, the Brahmins seek such income in many different ways.

As to the general economic conditions making for the predominance of stratification by 'status,' only very little can be said. When the bases of the acquisition and distribution of goods are relatively stable, stratification by status is favored. Every technological repercussion and economic transformation threatens stratification by status and pushes the class situation into the foreground. Epochs and countries in which the naked class situation is of predominant significance are regularly the periods of technical and economic transformations. And every slowing down of the shifting of economic stratifications leads, in due course, to the growth of status structures and makes for a resuscitation of the important role of social honor.

Parties

Whereas the genuine place of 'classes' is within the economic order, the place of 'status groups' is within the social order, that is, within the sphere of the distribution of 'honor.' From within these spheres, classes and status groups influence one another and they influence the legal order and are in turn influenced by it. But 'parties' live in a house of 'power.'

Their action is oriented toward the acquisition of social 'power,' that is to say, toward influencing a communal action no matter what its content may be. In principle, parties may exist in a social 'club' as well as in a 'state.' As over against the actions of classes and status groups, for which this is not necessarily the case, the communal actions of 'parties' always mean a societalization. For party actions are always directed toward a goal which is striven for in planned manner. This goal may be a 'cause' (the party may aim at realizing a program for ideal or material purposes), or the goal may be 'personal' (sinecures, power, and from these, honor for the leader and the followers of the party). Usually the party action aims at all these simultaneously. Parties are, therefore, only possible within communities that are societalized, that is, which have some rational order and a staff of persons available who are ready to enforce it. For parties aim precisely at influencing this staff, and if possible, to recruit it from party followers.

In any individual case, parties may represent interests determined through 'class situation' or 'status situation,' and they may recruit their following respectively from one or the other. But they need be neither purely 'class' nor purely 'status' parties. In most cases they are partly class parties and partly status parties, but sometimes they are neither. They may represent ephemeral or enduring structures. Their means of attaining power may be quite varied, ranging from naked violence of any sort to canvassing for votes with coarse or subtle means: money, social influence, the force of speech, suggestion, clumsy hoax, and so on to the rougher or more artful tactics of obstruction in parliamentary bodies.

The sociological structure of parties differs in a basic way according to the kind of communal action which they struggle to influence. Parties also differ according to whether or not the community is stratified by status or by classes. Above all else, they vary according to the structure of domination within the community. For their leaders normally deal with the conquest of a community. They are, in the general concept which is maintained here, not only products of specially modern forms of domination. We shall also designate as parties the ancient and medieval 'parties,' despite the fact that their structure differs basically from the structure of modern parties. By virtue of these structural differences of domination it is impossible to say anything about the structure of parties without discussing the structural forms of social domination *per se*. Parties, which are always structures struggling for domination, are very frequently organized in a very strict 'authoritarian' fashion. . . .

Concerning 'classes,' 'status groups,' and 'parties,' it must be said in general that they necessarily presuppose a comprehensive societalization, and especially a political framework of communal action, within which they operate. This does not mean that parties would be confined by the frontiers of any individual political community. On the contrary, at all times it has been the order of the day that the societalization (even when it aims at the use of military force in common) reaches beyond the frontiers of politics. This has been the case in the solidarity of interests among the Oligarchs and among the democrats in Hellas, among the Guelfs and among Ghibellines in the Middle Ages, and within the Calvinist party during the period of religious struggles. It has been the case up to the solidarity of the landlords (international congress of agrarian landlords), and has continued among princes (holy alliance, Karlsbad decrees), socialist workers, conservatives (the longing of Prussian conservatives for Russian intervention in 1850). But their aim is not necessarily the establishment of new international political, i.e. *territorial,* dominion. In the main they aim to influence the existing dominion.[2]

NOTES

1. *Wirtschaft und Gesellschaft,* part III, chap. 4, pp. 631–40. The first sentence in paragraph one and the several definitions in this chapter which are in brackets do not appear in the original text. They have been taken from other contexts of *Wirtschaft und Gesellschaft.*

2. The posthumously published text breaks off here. We omit an incomplete sketch of types of 'warrior estates.'

8

Is There a Status Order in Contemporary British Society?

Evidence from the Occupational Structure of Friendship

TAK WING CHAN AND JOHN H. GOLDTHORPE

Introduction

The main question we consider in this paper is that of whether present-day British society has a recognisable status order. We treat this question, however, in the context of a larger problem concerning the stratification of modern societies in general: namely, that of whether it is still empirically defensible and conceptually valuable to distinguish, on broadly Weberian lines (Weber, 1922/1968: 302–307, 926–939), between a status order and a class structure.

By a status order we understand a set of hierarchical relations that express perceived and typically accepted social superiority, equality or inferiority of a quite generalised kind, attaching not to qualities of particular individuals but rather to social positions that they hold or to certain of their ascribed attributes (e.g. 'birth' or ethnicity). A class structure, in contrast, we would see as being grounded specifically, and quite objectively, in the social relations of economic life—i.e. in the social relations of labour markets and production units. While typically generating differential, and often extreme, advantage and disadvantage, a class structure does not necessarily take on the consistently hierarchical form that is inherent to a status order (cf. Dahrendorf, 1959: 74–77; Giddens, 1973: 106).

At least up to the middle decades of the last century, it was in fact commonplace for sociologists to distinguish between status and class much on the lines indicated above (e.g. see Mills, 1951; Marshall, 1953/1963; Lockwood, 1958). Subsequently, though, this approach has been far less often followed, as a result, it would seem, of a number of only rather loosely connected developments.

On the one hand, doubts have arisen over whether in the more advanced soci-

Tak Wing Chan and John H. Goldthorpe, "Is There a Status Order in Contemporary British Society?" *European Sociological Review* 20, no. 5 (2004), pp. 383–391, 393–397.

eties of the present day well-defined status orders still exist. Historians, drawing in part on earlier sociological work, have produced evidence of a long-term decline in deference. Individuals treated by others as social inferiors would appear to have become less ready to accept such derogation or at all events to acknowledge it through words or actions—such as the use of honorifics, curtseying, cap-touching etc. The overt expression of social superiority has also, perhaps, become less acceptable (cf. Runciman, 1997: 153–158 esp). At the same time, 'local status systems' that in an earlier period were often documented in fascinating detail in community studies (e.g. Warner and Lunt, 1941; Warner et al., 1949; Plowman et al., 1962) have been seen as increasingly threatened by the mobility and anonymity of modern 'mass' society (Goldthorpe, 1978).

On the other hand, though, sociologists would seem to have become attracted to 'one-dimensional' understandings of social stratification, which discount or override the status/class distinction as much out of methodological or theoretical predilections as of any responsiveness to actual social change. Thus, in North America the popularity of the concept of 'socioeconomic status' has clearly reflected the advantages, as demonstrated by Duncan and others, of being able to treat stratification through a single continuous measure, such as the Duncan SEI (Duncan, 1961), in work using correlation and OLS regression techniques (e.g. Duncan and Hodge, 1963; Blau and Duncan, 1967). In Europe, in contrast, a more important influence has probably been the theoretical efforts of Bourdieu (1984) to 're-think', and indeed overcome, Weber's 'opposition' of status

and class: that is, by treating status as the symbolic aspect of class structure, which is itself seen as not reducible to 'economic' relations alone. For Bourdieu and his followers attention thus focuses on the lifestyle or underlying habitus that is specific and distinctive to different classes (or 'class fractions') rather than, as in Weber's case, on 'the most varied ways' in which class and status, and thus lifestyle, may be contingently related to each other.

However, while the developments in question cannot be lightly disregarded, they do not, in our view, amount in themselves to a demonstration that, in the study of contemporary societies, the distinction between status and class as qualitatively different forms of stratification is now either empirically outmoded or conceptually redundant. In particular, the two following issues remain to be determined:

(i) Can status orders still be identified in modern societies, even if of a less overt, less sharply demarcated and less localised kind than previously existed, and as a form of stratification that can be empirically as well as conceptually differentiated from class structure?

(ii) In so far as this is so, what is the relative importance of these two forms of stratification as determinants of individuals' experience and action in different areas of their social lives—or, in other words, of the pattern of their life-chances and life-choices?

In the present chapter, our primary concern is with the first of these questions which we take up in the case of present-day British society. We aim to show that the question can in fact be answered positively, i.e. a status order can be identified and one that, we suggest, maps onto the class structure in an intelligible, though far from straightforward, way. In subsequent papers, we will then address the second question on the basis of an ongoing research programme.

Methodological Approach

In our attempt to trace a status order in present-day Britain we follow the approach pioneered in the USA by Laumann (1966, 1973; Laumann and Guttman 1966) in seeking to move beyond 'small town' studies of social stratification such as those of Warner and his associates previously cited. Laumann accepted that differential association could be taken as a key indicator of status. He recognised, however, that in the urban 'mass' society of the later twentieth century individuals' associational networks were not restricted by the boundaries of local communities but could extend over a wide geographical area. Thus, in studying differential association, ethnographic work, reliant on participant observation, would need to give way to survey-based research of a more spatially extensive kind.

More specifically, Laumann proceeded by collecting information from samples of urban populations on respondents' own occupations and on the occupations of other individuals within respondents' more immediate social networks. For different occupational groupings of respondents, the occupational distributions of reported associates could then be established and, in turn, the extent to which these distributions differed from one grouping to another. Finally, by using the (at the time) novel technique of multidimensional scaling, the dimensionality of these differences could be investigated, and the further ques-

tions addressed of whether a dimension emerged that could be plausibly interpreted as one of status and, if so, of what ordering occupational groupings took along this dimension. In his earlier work, it should be added, Laumann sought information on a relatively wide range of respondents' associates, including kin, neighbours and friends; but in later work he made what for us is a significant change in concentrating on friends alone.

Laumann's approach depends on two basic assumptions, both of which we believe are defensible. The first is that in modern societies occupation is one of the most salient characteristics to which status attaches. That this is indeed the case would, at all events, appear to be a matter of some consensus among sociologists of otherwise often divergent views (e.g. Blau and Duncan, 1967; Parkin, 1971; Coxon and Jones, 1978; Stewart et al., 1980; Bourdieu, 1984; Grusky and Sørensen, 1998).

The second assumption is that recurrent association is a good indicator of a state of social equality between individuals and is, moreover, a better indicator of such equality, the 'freer' the choice of associates and the closer or more intimate the association—which would appear to be the reason for Laumann's eventual decision to work with data on friends only. Again, this assumption would seem a plausible one, and, for Britain at least, there is evidence to show that differential association is in fact more marked in the case of friends who are regarded as 'close' than in the case of those who are simply frequent leisure time companions (Goldthorpe, 1987: ch.7). While association with the latter may result primarily from shared interests and activities (cultural, sporting, hobby, political etc.), relations with the former are more likely to be based on 'pure' sociability, thus making social inequality within the relationship especially unlikely—which, from our point of view, is the crucial consideration.

In this regard, it is relevant to refer the work of Prandy and his associates, who have also sought to apply Laumann's approach to the British case. In their initial work in constructing a stratification scale, the 'Cambridge Scale', (Stewart et al., 1973, 1980), this group also rely on occupationally linked data on friendship, but define friendship in a deliberately loose way so as to allow even relatively transient associations to be included. However, for the purposes of a revision and updating of the scale (Prandy and Lambert, 2003), they then abandon analysis of data of this kind in favor of data on the (current) occupations of married couples, mainly because they can then draw on samples of census data and gain the advantage of working with large numbers of cases.

Whether the revised 'CAMSIS' scale that is based on such marriage data is essentially the same as the original Cambridge scale based on friendship data, as Prandy and Lambert claim, is, in our view, debatable; and they indeed concede that '[c]ertainly, the strength of the relationship between marriage partners is less, statistically speaking, than it is between friends' (Prandy and Lambert, 2003: 401). But what must be recognised here is that a fundamental theoretical difference exists between our position and that of Prandy and his associates. In an early statement, they assert that 'the Weberian distinction of classes . . . from status groups . . . is neither useful nor necessary' (Stewart et al., 1980: 28). More recently, Bottero and Prandy (2003: 180) maintain that 'social interaction distance is taken as a stratification order in its own right' and that 'research has tended to elim-

inate the distinction between class and status, or the economic and the cultural, which was once seen as central analytically to conventional stratification theory'. The implication then is that their scale reflects 'stratification arrangements' in some quite general and undifferentiated sense. In contrast, we would believe that the Weberian distinction between class and status is conceptually clear and potentially highly important; that it cannot be rejected by fiat; and that whether or not a status order is still identifiable in contemporary British, or any other, society must be treated as an empirical question.

Data and Analytical Techniques

The data we use come from wave 10 (year 2000) of the British Household Panel Study (BHPS). We restrict our analysis to respondents aged 20–64 but, unlike Laumann and most others who have subsequently taken his approach, we include women, categorised on the basis of their own occupations. The idea of a status order from which we begin could be described as 'gender neutral'. That is to say, one would expect there to be a common status order for men and women together rather than two separate, gender-specific orders. By including women, we can then of course investigate how far this expectation holds good.

In wave 10 of the BHPS, respondents were asked to think of three people they considered to be their closest friends. Information about these friends, such as their age, sex, employment status, and their relationship to respondents was recorded. For the first-mentioned friend, respondents were also asked to report his or her occupational title. Data on the current (or last) occupation of these 'first' close friends, together

Table 8.1 Occupational Categories Used in the Analysis and Their Constituent Minor Occupational Groups

Code	Descriptive title	OPCS MOGs	%
GMA	General managers and administrators	10, 13, 15	2.5
PDM	Plant, depot and site managers	11, 14, 16	2.7
SM	Specialist managers	12	2.7
MPS	Managers and proprietors in services	17	4.4
OMO	Managers and officials, not elsewhere classified	19	2.0
SET	Scientists, engineers and technologists	20, 21	1.9
HP	Higher professionals	22, 24, 25, 26, 27, 29	3.3
TPE	Teachers and other professionals in education	23	4.5
API	Associate professionals in industry	30, 31, 32, 33, 39	3.9
APH	Associate professionals in health and welfare	34, 37	4.8
APB	Associate professionals in business	35, 36, 38	2.6
AOA	Administrative officers and assistants	40	2.1
NCC	Numerical clerks and cashiers	41	3.7
FRC	Filing and record clerks	42	1.9
OCW	Other clerical workers	43	3.5
SDC	Store and dispatch clerks	44, 49	2.1
SEC	Secretaries and receptionists	45, 46	3.3
SMC	Skilled and related manual workers in construction and maintenance	50, 52	3.5
SMM	Skilled and related manual workers in metal trade	51, 53, 54	3.5
SMO	Skilled and related manual workers not elsewhere classified	55, 56, 57, 58, 59	3.9
PSP	Protective service personnel	60, 61	1.9
CW	Catering workers	62	2.3
PSW	Personal service workers	63, 66, 67, 69	2.2
HW	Health workers	64	2.6
CCW	Childcare workers	65	2.6
BSR	Buyers and sales representatives	70, 71	1.6
SW	Sales workers	72, 73, 79	6.3
PMO	Plant and machine operatives	80, 81, 82, 83, 84, 85, 86, 89	6.2
TO	Transport operatives	87, 88	3.3
GL	General labourers	90, 91, 92, 93, 99	2.2
RWS	Routine workers in services	94, 95	6.1

with similar data on the current (or last) occupation of respondents, form the basis of our empirical analyses.

These data were coded to the three-digit unit groups of the UK standard occupational classification (OPCS, UK, 1990) and could thence be allocated to the 77 two-digit minor occupational groups (MOGs). Although the BHPS affords us a relatively large sample size ($n = 9160$), the MOGs were still a more detailed classification than

we could sensibly employ. A 77×77 contingency table would, on average, have had less than two observations per cell. Some collapsing of the MOGs was therefore necessary. Operationally, we combined MOGs according to their functions, while taking into account their relative size and the work milieu of their constituent occupations at the same time. In the end, we worked with the 31 categories of Table 8.1. As can be seen from the last column of the table, each of these categories accounts for between 1.6 and 6.3 per cent of our respondents.

Our basic data arrays are therefore 31 × 31 contingency tables, for men and women separately and together, in which respondent's occupational group is related to the occupational group of respondent's 'first' close friend. We subject these contingency tables to multidimensional scaling (MD-SCAL), the technique used by Laumann and most of those following him.

Our MDSCAL exercise proceeds as follows. We first generate 'outflow' rates from our contingency tables, i.e. the percentage distributions of friends across our occupational categories for each category of respondent. We then compute the index of dissimilarity for each pair of rows of outflow rates. This gives us a measure of the between-category dissimilarity, δ. We then use the half-matrix of δs as input to the simplest form of MDSCAL analysis.

That is, we seek to represent our 31 occupational categories as points in a Euclidean space, such that the distance between category A and category B in this space, d_{AB}, best approximates the observed dissimilarity between the two categories δ_{AB}. Formally, this idea can be represented as follows:

$$d_{AB} = \alpha + \beta\,\delta_{AB},$$

$$d_{AB} = \left[\sum_{m=1}^{M} (x_{Am} - x_{Bm})^2 \right]^{1/2},$$

where x_{Am} and x_{Bm} are the coordinates of points A and B in the mth dimension, and α and β are parameters.

Results

In Figure 8.1 we report stress-values from our MDSCAL analyses. It can be seen that,

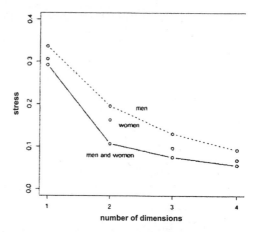

Figure 8.1 Stress Values of Multidimensional Scaling Applied to 2000 BHPS Best Friend Data, Using Data for All, and for Male and Female Respondents Separately

if men and women are taken together in the analysis, the three-dimensional solution achieves a stress-value of 0.075, indicating a rather good fit. However, if men and women are analyzed separately, the fit is generally worse, requiring, in the case of men, a four-dimensional solution to obtain a stress value that falls below 0.10. Since it is difficult to visualise a space of four, or more, dimensions, we would incline here not to go beyond the three-dimensional solution.

So what, then, are the main features of our favoured MDSCAL solution? The panels of Figure 8.2 show the positions of our 31 occupational categories as projected onto the three planes involved—with men and women included in the analysis together.

The first dimension, shown horizontally in the first and second panels of Figure 8.2 is, at least prima facie, that which captures status. Thus, at the left extreme of the dimension are located six categories comprising manual occupations, while moving in from the right extreme come the categories of Higher professionals, Associate professionals in

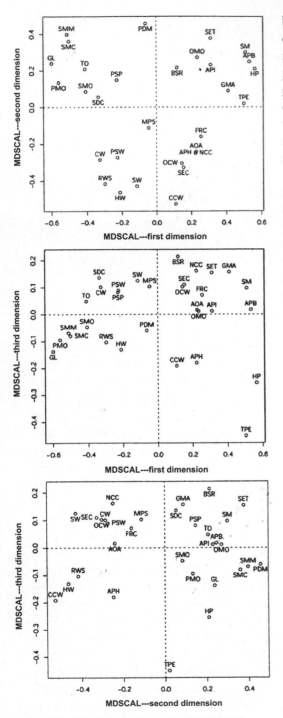

business, Specialist managers, Teachers and other professionals in education, General managers and administrators, Associate professionals in industry, and Scientists, engineers and technologists. In between, the categories can be seen as ordered according to what might be described as a manual/non-manual continuum that we discuss further below.

In this respect, our findings are in fact much in line with those of Laumann and others. That is to say, these earlier investigators have also found a first dimension in their MDSCAL analyses that is likewise interpretable as reflecting status. However, it has been a recurrent finding in previous work that while more than one dimension is required in order to obtain a well-fitting MDSCAL solution, the further dimensions introduced have not been open to interpretation, or only in a rather speculative way (e.g. see Laumann, 1966: 102–104, 1973: 79–80; Pappi, 1973; Stewart *et al.*, 1980: 41–44; Prandy, 1998).

In fact, it turns out that this second dimension can be interpreted rather convincingly—and in a way that follows directly from our inclusion of women in the analysis. It can be taken as a dimension that expresses the degree to which our 31 occupational categories are characterised by sex segregation. Thus, looking at the first panel of Figure 8.2, where the dimension is shown vertically, one finds at the top occupational categories in which men predominate—Plant, depot and site managers, Skilled and related manual workers in metal trades, Skilled and related manual workers in construction and maintenance, and Scientists, engineers and technologists; while at the bottom come categories in which women predominate—Childcare workers, Health workers, Sales workers,

Figure 8.2 The Three Dimensional MDSCAL Solution Projected onto Three Basic Planes

Routine workers in services, and Secretaries and receptionists. We can check this interpretation of our second dimension by relating the scores of our categories on it to their sex composition (i.e. percentage female) within our sample. We obtain a correlation of r = -0.92.

If, then, we do capture here the effects on the occupational structure of friendship of differences in work environments according to the degree to which they constitute male or female 'worlds'—the effects of, say, the engineering shop, building site or maintenance department as against those of the care home, supermarket floor or word-processing room—an important implication follows. Because our second dimension in this way represents the gendering of opportunities for friendship formation, our first dimension, being thus 'purified' of this influence, should, if it does indeed reflect actual friendship choice as influenced by status, apply to men and women alike. For, as we earlier observed, the conception of a status order with which we operate entails gender-neutrality. We can easily check whether or not this expectation is met by turning to our MDSCAL analyses for men and women separately.

The relevant results are shown in Figure 8.3 in which category scores on the first, putatively status, dimension for men and women are plotted against each other. As can be seen, there is a quite high correlation (r = 0.75). Moreover, the two obvious 'outlier' categories, which are identified, have one feature in common that suggest that their significance should not be over-estimated: they fall towards the extremes of the second dimension (see Figure 8.2), i.e. they are markedly sex-segregated. Only 2.3 per cent of the Secretaries and receptionists are men, and only 3.1 per cent of the Skilled and re-

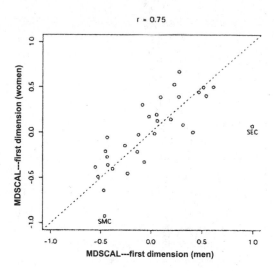

Figure 8.3 First Dimension MDSCAL Scores Estimated Separately for Men and for Women Plotted Against Each Other

lated manual workers in construction and maintenance are women. We would then believe that these discrepant scores are likely to come about mainly by chance, because respondents of the 'minority' sex are too few in number to allow reliable results. From this point of view, the outlier categories are, at least to some extent, artefacts of inescapable limitations of our study in terms of sample size; and in turn, we would regard Figure 8.3 as giving quite strong support to the idea that the first dimension of our three-dimensional MDSCAL solution does reflect a status order that is, as it should be, common to men and women.

Finally here we should comment briefly on the third dimension of our MDSCAL solution. It should be recognised that the dimensions of MDSCAL solutions do not have to be interpreted in terms of some single factor: they may simply 'mop up' a number of different effects. With this point in mind, it may be noted that on the third dimension—as a detailed examination of the plots of Figure 8.2 will confirm—several categories come into close proximity whose members will tend to occupy similar occupational situses (Morris and Murphy, 1959): for example, Plant, depot and site managers, our three categories of Skilled and related manual workers and Plant and machine operatives; or Managers and proprietors in services and Sales workers, Catering workers and Personal service workers; or again, Associate professionals in health and welfare and Health workers and Childcare workers. In so far, then, as the third dimension, like the second, even if in a less straightforwardly interpretable way, does capture features of the occupational structure of friendship that derive primarily from the different opportunities for friendship that are offered by particular work environments, rather than from actual friendship choices expressing status considerations, we are further encouraged to believe that in our first dimension it is status per se that is primarily reflected.

The Status Dimension in More Detail

We now turn to a more detailed examination of what we would take to be the status dimension of our MDSCAL analyses, although, as will be seen, with a continuing concern for the validity of this interpretation. This concern is important since the ordering of categories along any MDSCAL dimension is in itself indicative only of their relative closeness or separation according to some metric. Thus, it could be suggested that our first dimension reflects no more than homophily—the tendency for people to make friends with others like themselves. To sustain the stronger claim that it captures a hierarchical ordering by status, further evidence is called for, external to that of the MDSCAL analysis.

To begin with, we show in Table 8.2 the rank-ordering of our 31 categories on the putative status dimension and, to make our discussion somewhat more concrete, we also identify 'representative' occupations: that is, occupations that account for relatively large numbers of individuals within each category and at the same time give some idea of its range. There are two features of the rank-ordering to which we would draw attention.

The first, on which we have in fact already commented, is that the categories can be seen as ordered overall according to the degree of 'manuality' of the work involved in their constituent occupations. More specifically, occupations in categories 1–7 in the ranking are essentially non-manual in character, and categories 8–18, only slightly less so. Or, somewhat more specifically, one might say that these occupations require working predominantly with symbols and/or people rather than directly with inanimate material entities. Categories 19–25 are then ones that cover occupations, falling mostly within the services sector, that tend to some significant degree to have both non-manual and manual components—the former usually involving some kind of 'people processing'. And, finally, categories 26–31 comprise occupations that require the performance of predominantly manual tasks, in effect working with things rather than with either symbols or people.

The second feature of the ranking that we would pick out relates specifically to its non-manual range—i.e. categories 1–18. It can be seen that within this range there is a tendency for managerial categories to rank lower than do professional categories. It is true that the two highest ranking categories, Higher professionals and Associate professionals in business, are followed in

Table 8.2　The 31 Occupational Categories Ranked by Status Score and Representative Occupations Within Each Category

	Code	Representative Occupations
1	HP	Chartered accountants, clergy, medical practitioners, solicitors
2	APB	Journalists, investment analysts, insurance brokers, designers
3	SM	Company treasurers, financial managers, computer systems managers, personnel managers
4	TPE	College lecturers, education officers and inspectors, school teachers
5	GMA	Bank and building society managers, general managers in industry, national and local government officers
6	API	Computer analysts and programmers, quantity surveyors, vocational and industrial trainers
7	SET	Civil and structural engineers, clinical biochemists, industrial chemists, planning engineers, software engineers
8	FRC	Conveyancing clerks, computer clerks, library assistants
9	OMO	Security managers, cleaning managers
10	AOA	Clerical officers in national and local government
11	NCC	Accounts assistants, bank clerks
12	APH	Community workers, nurses, occupational therapists, youth workers
13	SEC	Personal assistants, receptionists, secretaries, word processor operators
14	OCW	General assistants, commercial and clerical assistants
15	BSR	Buyers and purchasing officers, technical sales representatives, wholesale representatives
16	CCW	Educational assistants, nursery nurses
17	MPS	Catering managers, hoteliers, publicans, shopkeepers and managers
18	PDM	Clerks of works, farm managers, maintenance managers, transport managers, works managers
19	SW	Cash desk and check-out operators, sales and shop assistants, window dressers
20	HW	Ambulance staff, dental nurses, nursing auxiliaries
21	PSW	Caretakers and housekeepers, hairdressers and beauticians, travel attendants, undertakers
22	PSP	Fire service and police officers, security guards
23	RWS	Car park attendants, cleaners, counter-hands, couriers and messengers, hotel porters, postal workers
24	CW	Bar staff, chefs, cooks, waiters and waitresses
25	SDC	Despatch and production control clerks, storekeepers
26	SMO	Gardeners and groundsmen, printers, textile workers, woodworkers
27	TO	Bus and coach drivers, lorry and van drivers, taxi drivers
28	SMC	Bricklayers, electricians, painters and decorators, plasterers, roofers, telephone repairmen
29	SMM	Fitters, setters, setter-operators, sheet metal workers, turners, welders
30	PMO	Assemblers, canners, fillers and packers, food processors, moulders and extruders, routine inspectors and testers
31	GL	Agricultural workers, factory labourers, goods porters, refuse collectors

third place by a managerial category, Specialist managers. But individuals falling in this latter category are more likely than other managers to have professional qualifications and to be operating to some extent in a professional role. Following Teachers and other professionals in other professionals in education, General managers and administrators then rank fifth, but other managers and officials rank only ninth, below in fact the highest ranking clerical category, and the two remaining managerial categories, Managers and proprietors in services and Plant, depot and site managers are found together at the very end of the non-manual range.

These two features of the ranking we would regard as having particular significance in that they lend support to the idea that it does indeed express status rather than homophily alone. This is so because both can be taken as providing rather clear 'echoes' of the relatively explicit and well-defined status order that prevailed in British society from, say, the later nineteenth through to the mid-twentieth century. Sociologists and historians would appear largely to concur (for useful reviews see Runciman, 1997: 153–163, 212–229; McKibbin, 2000: chs I–IV) that the non-manual/manual distinction marked a major boundary within this order, and one that was strongly upheld even in fact as the distinction became less consequential in terms of economic conditions; and, further, that professional employment was generally regarded as being socially superior to managerial employment, and especially to managerial employment in industry or 'trade'.

At the same time, though, it should also be recognised that, today, the non-manual/manual distinction is in itself less clear-cut than it was previously, chiefly as a result of the growth of the services sector of the economy. Many occupations that have concurrently expanded are ones to which the distinction does not all that easily apply. As we have observed, categories 19–25 are largely made up of occupations in services that involve both non-manual and manual work, and official statistics would indicate (cf. Table 8.1 and also Jackson, 2002) that these occupations now account for as much as a quarter of the total employed population. Even if, then—as we would

believe to be the case—the degree of 'manuality' of work remains an important influence on social status, it would seem likely that the resulting lines of division will now be rather more blurred than they were half a century ago.

Finally, change in this regard may be in part related to one further feature of the ranking of Table 8.2 that calls for some comment: that is, the relatively low positions of the skilled manual worker categories. To some degree, this result may be artefactual in that the official occupational groupings from which these categories are constructed are not, despite their labels, drawn up according to skill in any very strict way (hence the 'skilled and related . . . ' formulation). However, we would doubt if this is a factor of major importance, and would emphasise, rather, the real changes that have occurred over recent decades in the nature and occupational distribution of skills, in consequence of developments in economic structure, technology and organisation (cf. Gallie *et al.*, 1998: ch. 2), and that indeed underlie the difficulties that arise in using earlier nomenclature. It is usually supposed (e.g. Roberts, 1971: ch. 1) that, under the 'old' status order, skilled, 'time-served' craftsmen formed an 'aristocracy of labour' and ranked clearly above semi-and unskilled manual workers and also above the typical service works of the day—domestics, shop hands etc. But the fact that we do not reproduce this pattern has to be understood, we would suggest, in relation to the declining demand for, or dilution of, many traditional craft skills at the same time as new kinds of skill with different sectoral and occupational linkages have emerged—including technical skills as, say, in connection with computerisation, but also communication and 'social' skills more generally.

Table 8.3 The Goldthrope Class Schema (Nine-Class Version)

Class	Description
I	Professional, administrative and managerial employees, higher grade; large employers
II	Professional, administrative and managerial employees, lower grade; technicians, higher grade
IIIa	Routine non-manual employees, higher grade
IIIb	Routine non-manual employees, lower grade
IVac	Small employers (other than professionals) including farmers
IVb	Self-employed workers (other than professionals)
V	Technicians, lower grade; supervisors of manual workers
VI	Skilled manual workers
VII	Non-skilled (i.e., semi- and unskilled) manual workers

In sum, while the present-day status order that is suggested by our empirical analyses can claim to show continuities with that of an earlier period that, we believe, can scarcely be dismissed as coincidental, this order would at the same time appear to be in several respects less sharply demarcated than previously, as well as being less openly recognised and acknowledged.

Status and Class

Having now presented evidence to suggest that through the analysis of the occupational structure of friendship a status order in contemporary British society can still be identified, at least in its broad lines, we come finally to the issue that is salient in the Weberian perspective that we have adopted: that of the relationship between status and class. As we have already indicated, we take the view that the distinction between class and status is, conceptually, a well-defined and coherent one and that its applicability and value in the context of present-day British society, as in any other, has to be a matter for investigation, not assertion. In this regard, therefore, a question of immediate interest that we seek here to address is that of how the status order we hope to have identified in present-day Britain maps onto the class structure.

The Goldthorpe class schema, which treats class positions as being defined by social relations in economic life or, more specifically, by employment relations (Goldthorpe, 1997, 2000: ch. 10) has been shown to possess an acceptable level of criterion validity and also of construct validity in being strongly predictive of individuals' economic security, stability and prospects (Evans and Mills, 1998; Goldthorpe and McKnight, 2004). The nine-class version of this schema is displayed in Table 8.3. Figure 8.4 then gives a first indication of how status is distributed within and between classes. It is evident that there is a status gradient across classes, as might be expected. In terms of the median or interquartile range of the status of their members, the non-manual classes (I, II and IIIa) rank clearly above the manual classes (V, VI and VII); and, within the non-manual classes, the median status of members of Class I is above that of members of Class II who in turn rank above the members of Class IIIa.

However, it also appears from Figure 8.4 that the spread of status within classes is often quite considerable and that there is a good deal of overlap in status between classes, both in the case of the non-manual and manual classes considered separately and across the non-manual/manual divide.

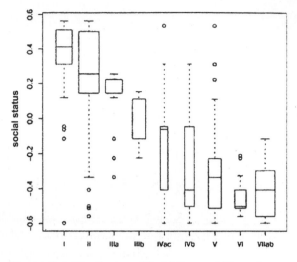

Figure 8.4 Distribution of Social Status within and Between Classes
Note: The boxes are drawn with width proportional to the square-root of n of the classes. Because of the small n of classes IVc and VIIb, they are collapsed with classes IVa and VIIa respectively.

These features of Figure 8.4, we should recognise, may well be in some degree arte-factual—most obviously as the result simply of any measurement error in regard to both status and class. Further, as we have acknowledged, the categories on which our status ordering is based are by no means as refined as we would ideally wish. Thus, when these categories are related to classes, the category members represented in one class may in fact have higher or lower status than those represented in another. In other words, classes may pick up variation in status within categories in a systematic way. But, even with all reasonable allowance being made for these possibilities, the lack of congruence between status and class has still to be regarded as far from negligible, and likewise the differences in the degree of such congruence from one region of Figure 8.4 to another.

To provide further information on the interrelation between status and class, and

especially on status stratification within classes, we show in Figure 8.5 the composition of each class in terms of our occupational categories as ordered by status.

To begin with the salariat, it could be said that in Class I status stratification is quite limited: 77 per cent of those in this class are in fact covered by the seven highest categories in the status order. Moreover, so far as the remainder are concerned, the point made above concerning artefactual effects could well apply. For example, we know that the Plant, depot and site managers who are the main discrepant—i.e. relatively low status—category within Class I will be employed in large establishments and individuals in this subset of the category may then have higher status than their counterparts employed in small establishments and allocated to Class II. When we turn to Class II itself, however, stratification by status is far more extensive and would seem less likely to be of an artefactual kind. From Figure 8.5 three broad status levels can in fact be identified. First comes a grouping of professionals and specialist managers, secondly, one of administrative officials and associate professionals in health, and thirdly, one in which managers in industry and services predominate, i.e. those occupational groupings that, as we have seen tend to have low status relative to both their income and educational qualifications.

With the classes of routine non-manual employees, Classes IIIa and IIIb, we again find only rather limited status stratification. In IIIa, two status levels might perhaps be distinguished—the higher comprising routine non-manual employees working in predominantly administrative contexts, and the lower, such employees working in sales

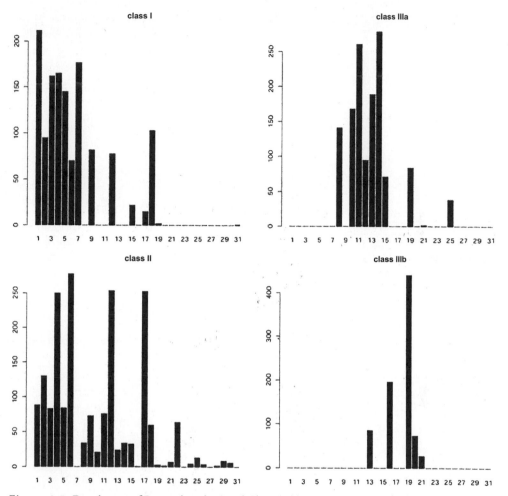

Figure 8.5 Distribution of Respondents by Social Class, and by Occupational Group within Social Class (*continues*)

Note: The occupational groups are numbered according to their status ranking.

and services. But in IIIb two thirds of those in the class fall within just three occupational categories that are in fact neighbours in our status order.

Turning next to the two classes of 'independents', IVac and IVb, status stratification is in these cases quite marked, as might be expected given the occupational range that is covered. In both cases alike, Figure 8.5 points to two main groupings, the higher comprising those running largely

service or small industrial enterprises and the lower involved in enterprises entailing various kinds of mainly artisanal, that is, manual work.

Finally, with the 'blue-collar' classes, V, VI and VII, the finding of variable degrees of status stratification persists. Such stratification is least apparent in Class VI, that of skilled manual workers, with 85 per cent of those in the class being accounted for by five neighbouring categories in the status

82

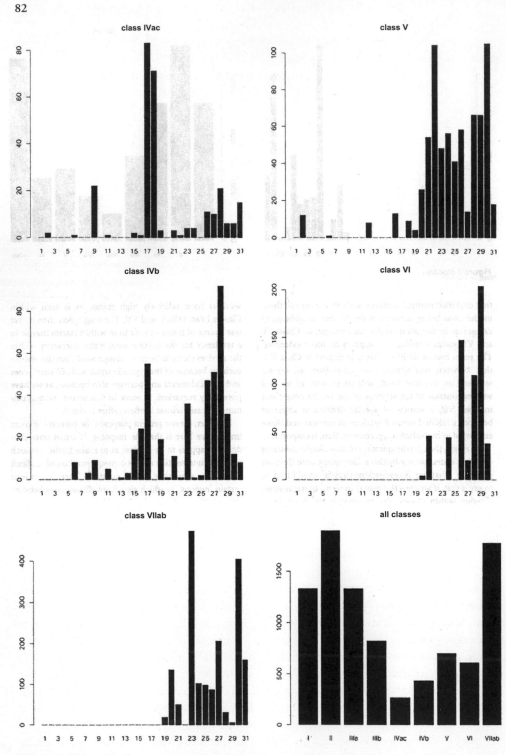

Figure 8.5 (*continued*)

order. In contrast, in Classes V and VII status stratification appears far more extensive. The main line of division that is indicated in Class V is that between technicians and supervisors of service workers, on the one hand, and supervisors of manual workers outside of the services sector, on the other; and in Class VII, a somewhat similar division is apparent between unskilled manual workers in services and those employed in manufacturing, construction, transport etc.

To revert, then, to the question of how closely the status order of contemporary British society maps onto the class structure, what our investigations thus far would lead us to say is that, if we view the matter in terms of status stratification within classes, the mapping is much closer in some cases than it is in others. More specifically, status homogeneity appears relatively high in Class I, the higher division of the salariat, in Classes IIIa and IIIb, those of routine non-manual employees, and in Class VI, that of skilled manual workers. But in the remaining classes status stratification would appear far from negligible.

Why such a pattern should exist calls for further inquiry, although one pointer to emerge from the foregoing, relating to the services sector, may be noted. In this sector, and especially in sales and personal services, 'white-collar', that is, managerial and other non-manual, workers would appear to have relatively low status, as is seen within Class II (and also perhaps Class IIIa), while independents, and blue-collar supervisory and manual workers have relatively high status, as is seen within Classes IVac, IVb, V and VII. The suggestion then is that one source of status stratification within classes may lie in a tendency for the occupational status hierarchy within the services sector to be more compressed than elsewhere—perhaps

because of the typically small scale of enterprises and establishments and perhaps also because, as we have previously remarked, in work in this sector the manual/non-manual division is often rather blurred.

However, for our present purposes, the outcome of main importance here is that the mapping of status onto class does not appear to be so close as to make further research into their interrelation and its consequences unduly difficult and, at the same time, rather pointless. There are at least certain 'regions' in which significant disjunctions between class position and status level would appear to occur.

Conclusions

In this paper we have been concerned, as a first step in a larger research programme, with investigating how far in contemporary British society it is still possible to identify a status order, despite an evident decline in deference and in the readiness of individuals to openly assert their social superiority over others. Using the approach pioneered by Laumann, and focusing on the occupational structure of close friendship—within which social equality can be supposed—we have presented empirical analyses to show that there is one dimension of this structure that can be plausibly interpreted as reflecting a hierarchy of status and one that is, as it should be, essentially 'gender-neutral'. We attach particular significance to the fact that this hierarchy displays clear continuities with that depicted for the later nineteenth and earlier twentieth centuries in historical and earlier sociological research, although there are also indications that the present-day hierarchy is less sharply demarcated. This would appear to be largely the result of the growth of occupations, especially within the services sector of the economy, to which the manual/non-manual distinction does not easily apply.

Also, as regards status and class, we have argued that it is important to treat these as two distinct concepts and then to consider as an empirical question in what way, in any particular society at any particular time, the status order and the class structure relate to each other. So far as present-day Britain is concerned—and assuming of course that a status order does indeed exist broadly on the lines we have claimed—we find that while some classes show a rather high degree of status homogeneity, in others the extent of status stratification is quite extensive. And in this connection also we have raised the possibility that the growth of the services sector may play a significant role.

Following our programme, we are presently addressing the second question that we initially posed: that of the relative importance of status and class as determinants of individuals' experience and action in different domains of their social lives. Thus, we are examining the relationship between the positions individuals hold within the status order, as we would envisage it, and their cultural tastes and preferences and, in particular, in areas where 'high' and 'low' tastes and preferences are widely recognised as marking out distinctive lifestyles. To the extent that in this regard we can show that the effects of status clearly outweigh those of class—and our preliminary results indicate that they in fact do—then the validity of the status order that we have proposed will be further confirmed. And moreover, to the extent that we can in other domains—as, for example, those of experience in economic life and in turn the perception of economic and polit-

ical interests—show that the reverse is the case—i.e. that class is a more potent force than status—then the value of a Weberian perspective will be underlined and the way opened up to an understanding of the form of stratification of modern societies more consistent with the complexity that, we would believe, it does indeed display.

REFERENCES

Blau, P. M. and Duncan, O. D. (1967) *The American Occupational Structure*. New York, NY: John Wiley and Sons.

Bottero, W. and Prandy, K. (2003). Social interaction distance and stratification. *British Journal of Sociology*, 54, 177–197.

Bourdieu, P. (1984). *Distinction: A Social Critique of the Judgement of Taste*. London, UK: Routledge & Kegan Paul.

Coxon, A. and Jones, C. (1978). *The Images of Occupational Prestige*. London, UK: Macmillan.

Dahrendorf, R. (1959). *Class and Class Conflict in Industrial Societies*. London, UK: Routledge & Kegan Paul.

Duncan, O. D. (1961). A socioeconomic index for all occupations. In Reiss, A. (Ed.), *Occupations and Social Status*. New York, NY: Free Press.

Duncan, O. D. and Hodge, R. W. (1963). Education and occupational mobility. *American Journal of Sociology*, 68, 629–644.

Evans, G. and Mills, C. (1998). Identifying class structure: A latent class analysis of the criterion-related and construct validity of the Goldthorpe class schema. *European Sociological Review*, 14, 87–106.

Gallie, D., White, M., Cheng, Y. and Tomlinson, M. (Eds.) (1998). *Restructuring the Employment Relationship*. Oxford, UK: Clarendon Press.

Giddens, A. (1973). *The Class Structure of the Advanced Societies*. London, UK: Hutchinson.

Goldthorpe, J. H. (1978). The current inflation: towards a sociological account. In Hirsch, F. and Goldthorpe, J. H. (Eds), *The Political Economy of Inflation*. London, UK: Martin Robertson, 186–214.

Goldthorpe, J. H. (1987). *Social Mobility and Class Structure in Modern Britain*, second edn. Oxford, UK: Clarendon Press.

Goldthorpe, J. H. (1997). The 'Goldthorpe' class schema. In Rose, D. and O'Reilly, K. (Eds), *Constructing Classes*. London, UK: Office of National Statistics.

Goldthorpe, J. H. (2000). *On Sociology: Numbers, Narratives, and the Integration of Research and Theory*. Oxford, UK: Oxford University Press.

Goldthorpe, J. H. and McKnight, A. (2004). *The economic basis of social class*. CASEpaper 80, London School of Economics.

Grusky, D. B. and Sørensen, J. B. (1998). Can class analysis be salvaged? *American Journal of Sociology*, 103, 1187–1234.

Jackson, M. (2002). *Explaining Class Mobility: Meritocracy, Education and Employers*. DPhil thesis, University of Oxford, UK.

Laumann, E. O. (1966). *Prestige and Association in an Urban Community*. Indianapolis, IN: Bobbs-Merrill.

Laumann, E. O. (1973). *Bonds of Pluralism*. New York, NY: Wiley.

Laumann, E. O. and Guttman, L. (1966). The relative associational contiguity of occupations in an urban setting. *American Sociological Review*, 31, 169–178.

Lockwood, D. (1958). *The Blackcoated Worker: A Study in Class Consciousness*. London, UK: Allen & Unwin.

Marshall, T. (1953/1963). *Sociology At the Crossroads and Other Essays*. London, UK: Heinemann.

McKibbin, R. (2000). *Classes and Cultures: England 1918–1951*. Oxford, UK: Oxford University Press.

Mills, C. W. (1951). *White Collar: The American Middle Classes*. New York, NY: Oxford University Press.

Morris, R. and Murphy, R. (1959). The situs dimension in occupational structure. *American Sociological Review*, 24, 231–239.

Pappi, F. (1973). Sozialstruktur und soziale Schichtung in einer Kleinstadt mit heterogener Bevölkerung. In Friedrichs, J., Mayer, K. and Schluchter, W. (Eds). *Soziologische Theorie und Empirie*. Opladen: Westdeutschen Verlag.

Parkin, F. (1971). *Class Inequality and Political Order*. London, UK: MacGibbon and Kee.

Plowman, D., Minchinton, W. and Stacey, M. (1962). Local social status in England and Wales. *Sociological Review*, 10, 161–202.

Prandy, K. (1998). Deconstructing classes, *Work, Employment and Society*, 12, 743–753.

Prandy, K. and Lambert, P. S. (2003). Marriage, social distance and the social space: An alternative derivation and validation of the Cambridge scale. *Sociology*, 37, 397–411.

Roberts, R. (1971). *The Classic Slum*. Harmondsworth, UK: Penguin.

Runciman, W. G. (1997). *Applied Social Theory, Vol. 3 of A Treatise On Social Theory*. Cambridge, UK: Cambridge University Press.

Stewart, A., Prandy, K. and Blackburn, R. M. (1973). Measuring the class structure. *Nature*, 245 (5426), 415–417.

Stewart, A., Prandy, K. and Blackburn, R. M. (1980). *Social Structure and Occupations*. London, UK: Macmillan.

Warner, W. and Lunt, P. (1941). *The Social Life of a Modern Community*. New Haven, CT: Yale University Press.

Warner, W., Meeker, M. and Eells, K. (1949). *Social Class in America*. Chicago, IL: Science Research Associates.

Weber, M. (1922/1968). *Economy and Society*. Berkeley and Los Angeles, CA: University of California Press.

9

Striking It Richer

The Evolution of Top Incomes in the United States

EMMANUEL SAEZ

The recent dramatic rise in income inequality in the United States is well documented. But we know less about which groups are winners and which are losers, or how this may have changed over time. Is most of the income growth being captured by an extremely small income elite? Or is a broader upper middle class profiting? And are capitalists or salaried managers and professionals the main winners? I explore these questions with a uniquely long-term historical view that allows me to place current developments in deeper context than is typically the case.

Efforts at analyzing long-term trends are often hampered by a lack of good data. In the United States, and most other countries, household income surveys virtually did not exist prior to 1960. The only data source consistently available on a long-run basis is tax data. The U.S. government has published detailed statistics on income reported for tax purposes since 1913, when the modern federal income tax started. These statistics report the number of taxpayers and their total income and tax liability for a large number of income brackets. Combining these data with population census data and aggregate income sources, one can estimate the share of total personal income accruing to various upper-income groups, such as the top 10 percent or top 1 percent.

We define income as the sum of all income components reported on tax returns (wages and salaries, pensions received, profits from businesses, capital income such as dividends, interest, or rents, and realized capital gains) before individual income taxes. We exclude government transfers such as Social Security retirement benefits or unemployment compensation benefits from our income definition. Therefore, our income measure is defined as market income before individual income taxes.

Evidence on U.S. Top Income Shares

Figure 9.1 presents the income share of the top decile from 1917 to 2005 in the United States. In 2005, the top decile includes all families with market income above $99,200. The overall pattern of the top decile share over the century is U-shaped. The share of the top decile is around 45

Emmanuel Saez, "Striking It Richer," *Pathways* (Winter 2008), pp. 5, 7.

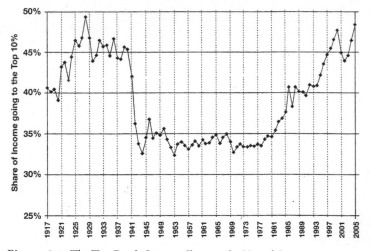

Figure 9.1 The Top Decile Income Share in the United States, 1917–2005

percent from the mid-1920s to 1940. It declines substantially to just above 32.5 percent in four years during World War II and stays fairly stable around 33 percent until the 1970s. Such an abrupt decline, concentrated exactly during the war years, cannot easily be reconciled with slow technological changes and suggests instead that the shock of the war played a key and lasting role in shaping income concentration in the United States. After decades of stability in the postwar period, the top decile share has increased dramatically over the last twenty-five years and has now regained its pre-war level. Indeed, the top decile share in 2005 is equal to 48.3 percent, a level higher than any other year since 1917, except 1928, which was the peak of the stock market bubble in the "roaring" 1920s.

Figure 9.2 decomposes the top decile into the top percentile (families with income above $350,500 in 2005), the next 4 percent (families with income between $140,100 and $350,500 in 2005), and the bottom half of the top decile (families with income between $99,200 and $140,100 in 2005). Interestingly, most of the fluctuations of the top decile are due to fluctuations within the top percentile. The drop in the next two groups during World War II is far less dramatic, and they recover from the WWII shock relatively quickly. Finally, their shares do not increase much during the recent decades. In contrast, the top percentile has gone through enormous fluctuations along the course of the twentieth century, from about 18 percent before WWI, to a peak above 20 percent in the late 1920s, to only about 9 percent during the 1960s–1970s, and back to almost 22 percent by 2005. Those at the very top of the income distribution therefore play a central role in the evolution of U.S. inequality over the course of the twentieth century.

The implications of these fluctuations at the very top can also be seen when we examine trends in *real* income growth per family between the top 1 percent and the bottom 99 percent in recent years. From

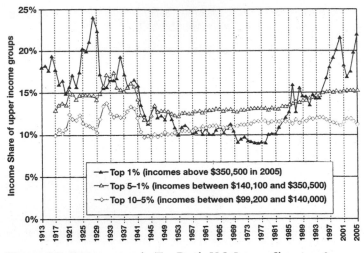

Figure 9.2 Decomposing the Top Decile U.S. Income Share into 3
Groups, 1913–2005

1994 to 2005, for example, average real incomes per family grew at a 1.9 percent annual rate (implying a growth of 23 percent over the eleven-year period). However, if one excludes the top 1 percent, average real income growth is halved to about 1 percent per year (implying a growth of 12 percent over the eleven-year period). Top 1 percent incomes grew at a much faster rate of 6 percent per year (implying a 90 percent growth over the eleven-year period). This implies that top 1 percent incomes captured about half of the overall economic growth over the period 1994–2005.

The 1994–2005 period encompasses, however, a dramatic shift in how the bottom 99 percent of the income distribution fared. I next distinguish between the 1994–2000 expansion of the Clinton administration and the 2002–2005 expansion of the Bush administration. During both expansions, the incomes of the top 1 percent grew extremely quickly, as seen in Figure 9.2, at an annual rate of over 10 percent. However, while the bottom 99 percent of incomes

grew at a solid pace of 2.7 percent per year from 1994–2000, these incomes grew less than 1 percent per year from 2002–2005. Therefore, in the economic expansion of 2002–2005, the top 1 percent captured almost three-quarters of income growth. Those results may help explain the disconnect between the economic experiences of the public and the solid macroeconomic growth posted by the U.S. economy since 2002. Those results may also help explain why the dramatic growth in top incomes during the Clinton administration did not generate much public outcry while there has been an extraordinary level of attention to top incomes in the press and in the public debate over the last two years. Moreover, top income tax rates went up in 1993 during the Clinton administration (and hence a larger share of the gains made by top incomes was redistributed) while top income tax rates went down in 2001 during the Bush administration.

The top percentile share declined during WWI, recovered during the 1920s boom, and declined again during the Great Depression and WWII. This very specific timing, together with the fact that very high incomes account for a disproportionate share of the total decline in inequality, strongly suggests that the shocks incurred by capital owners during 1914 to 1945 (depression and wars) played a key role. Indeed, from 1913 and up to the 1970s, very top incomes were mostly composed of capital income (mostly dividend income) and to a smaller extent business income, the wage income share being very modest. Therefore, the large decline of top incomes observed during the 1914–1960 period is predominantly a capital income phenomenon.

Interestingly, the income composition pattern at the very top has changed considerably over the century. The share of wage and salary income has increased sharply from the 1920s to the present, and especially since the 1970s. Therefore, a significant fraction of the surge in top incomes since the 1970s is due to an explosion of top wages and salaries. Indeed, estimates based purely on wages and salaries show that the share of total wages and salaries earned by the top 1 percent wage income earners has jumped from 5.1 percent in 1970 to 12.0 percent in 2006.

Evidence based on the wealth distribution is consistent with those facts. Estimates of wealth concentration, measured by the share of total wealth accruing to top 1 percent wealth holders, constructed by Wojciech Kopczuk and myself from estate tax returns for the 1916–2000 period in the United States, show a precipitous decline in the first part of the century with only fairly modest increases in recent decades. The evidence suggests that top incomes earners today are not "rentiers" deriving their incomes from past wealth but rather are "working rich," highly paid employees or new entrepreneurs who have not yet accumulated fortunes comparable to those accumulated during the Gilded Age. Such a pattern might not last for very long. The possible repeal of the federal tax on large estates in coming years would certainly accelerate the path toward the reconstitution of the great wealth concentration that existed in the U.S. economy before the Great Depression.

The labor market has been creating much more inequality over the last thirty years, with the very top earners capturing a large fraction of macroeconomic productivity gains. A number of factors may help explain this increase in inequality, not only underlying technological changes but also the retreat of institutions developed during the New Deal and World War II—such as progressive tax policies, powerful unions, corporate provision of health and retirement benefits, and changing social norms regarding pay inequality. We need to decide as a society whether this increase in income inequality is efficient and acceptable and, if not, what mix of institutional reforms should be developed to counter it.

10

Is Market Failure Behind
the Takeoff in Inequality?

DAVID B. GRUSKY AND
KIM A. WEEDEN

The growth in wage inequality within many late-industrial countries is one of the most spectacular and consequential developments of our time, spectacular because the turnaround was so sudden and undermined the conventional view that economic development would bring about widely diffused affluence, consequential because it is affecting the lives of so many people and in such profound ways. During the early stages of this takeoff in inequality, the dramatic changes in remuneration were happening under the radar, with the public not just unconcerned by the changes but also largely unaware of them (McCall and Kenworthy 2008). But that's no longer the case. We are now in the midst of a historic moment in which public debates about the legitimacy of extreme poverty and inequality have taken on a new prominence and urgency.

We don't harbor any illusions that a major change in poverty or inequality policy could easily be achieved. In any late-industrial country, one will find a well-developed and deeply institutionalized apparatus for ad-dressing poverty and inequality, and any changes in that apparatus will at this point likely be glacial. It is nonetheless important to continue revisiting and redefining the rationale behind such an apparatus and thereby ensure that any further changes and elaborations are consistent with that rationale. We will attempt in this chapter to lay out what we think is a promising rationale and how existing policies might then be elaborated to better serve it.

This type of exercise is only infrequently attempted. In many countries, perhaps especially the United States, there's a rather strong strand of pragmatism underlying poverty and inequality policy. If an antipoverty program can be shown to work at low cost, then that's enough for us and we will embrace it. This pragmatist movement to identify what works and what doesn't elevates to center stage the very simple empirical question of whether a given program has its intended effects. It's surely important to know whether a program works. But the typical evaluation exercises, almost by definition and certainly by convention,

---

David B. Grusky and Kim A. Weeden, "Is Market Failure Behind the Takeoff in Inequality?" New contribution written for this edition.

don't ask whether the program under study resonates well with our larger ideals.

The United States would be well served by an ideology, a constitution of sorts, that underlies its reform apparatus, just as it has an ideology underlying its efforts to fashion a more productive economy. The latter type of economic reform is an ongoing process: There's endless discussion about trade alliances, tax reform, corporate regulation, and so forth. These debates are occasionally guided by explicit evidence of whether the proposed reforms will work, but it's also conventional to refer back to first principles by asking whether the proposed reform will allow the invisible hand to better operate and thus be competition enhancing. The United States is understood as a market economy precisely because of this a priori commitment. For a variety of reasons, debates about poverty and inequality reform are rather less tethered to any a priori commitments, and they become quite technical and pragmatic as a result. In the absence of principles, policy interventions tend to grow and accumulate into a sprawling array, one without any obviously unifying rhyme or reason. Although clearly it's crucial to know whether programs work as intended, our argument in this chapter is that there are also returns to building policy around principle.

What might that principle be? We did not by chance choose to contrast ideology-rich economic policy and ideology-poor inequality policy. The contrast is especially instructive, we argue, because poverty and inequality policy is best founded on the same market principles that now inform our economic policy. We make this argument in particular for countries, such as the United States, Germany, and the United Kingdom, in which market principles are deeply written into the cultural DNA and hence have a special and abiding resonance. For other countries (e.g., Nordic countries), such principles are a less fundamental cultural commitment, and the rationale for building them into poverty and inequality policy is less compelling.

The reader may at this point be perplexed. How, it might be asked, could one possibly build anti-inequality interventions around market principles? Aren't profound poverty and inequality the main consequences of adopting market principles? Wouldn't labor-market institutions that adhere rigorously to market principles generate yet more poverty and inequality? These are important questions, and the rest of our chapter will be devoted principally to answering them. We will suggest that market principles, if the United States were truly to commit to them, might yield far less poverty and inequality than we now have.

We well realize that this is a radical view. The conventional wisdom is that poverty and inequality are straightforward consequences of market processes, that those with a promarket commitment must reconcile themselves to much market-generated inequality, and that insofar as less inequality is preferred, the only recourse is to take on such market-generated inequality with after-market redistribution. This conventional wisdom is so widely diffused and taken for granted that many people presume that progressive taxation and other redistributive after-market interventions are the *only* way to address poverty and inequality. The presumption, in other words, is that the market generates inequality and that after-market interventions are therefore the only way to undo inequality. We will argue that in fact nothing could be further from the truth.

We take the obverse position that *market failure* is a main source of poverty and inequality. Put simply: There would be less inequality in the United States if labor markets were more competitive, if our commitment to competition went beyond lip-service appeals, and if this commitment could be implemented even when the rich and powerful might be harmed by it. If, in other words, market failure is the cause of poverty and inequality, then the correct prescription is market repair. We argue that market economies can take on poverty and inequality by making their labor-market institutions more competitive and reducing the amount of illicit, noncompetitive inequality generated within the market. This approach reduces the pressure to take on poverty and inequality via redistributive approaches that are typically viewed as ideologically suspect.

But so much for preliminaries. The principal type of market failure that generates inequality is, we contend, the growing extraction of rent at the top of the class structure, where "rent" refers in this context to wages or returns in excess of what a fully competitive market would pay. The most common examples of rent include the minimum wage, the so-called union wage, excessive returns to schooling (occasioned by restrictions on access to schooling), and the wage premiums that accrue to certification, licensing, and related forms of occupational closure. Among countries with increasing inequality (e.g., the United States), rents that formerly accrued to workers in the lower half of the income distribution have been reduced by the decline of unionization, the decline in the real value of the minimum wage, and by other institutional reforms that reduce the bargaining power of labor. This rent destruction at the bottom of the income distribution is well known and doesn't require further study. The standard literature on rent destruction has, however, shown a perplexing tendency to assume that rents are being destroyed at the top of the class structure as much as at the bottom. The evidence of the past thirty years suggests, to the contrary, that rent destruction and rent creation are deeply asymmetric, with fundamental forces at work creating new potential for rent at the top of the class structure just as rent is being eliminated at the bottom. It's precisely such asymmetry that has generated much inequality of late.

This new capacity for rent creation at the top of the class structure takes the form of rent that accrues to (1) occupations that create artificial scarcity by controlling who is qualified to enter the occupation (i.e., occupation rent), (2) capitalists who, by virtue of operating in increasingly concentrated and union-free industries, can use their new-found leverage to more effectively squeeze labor (i.e., capital rent), (3) educated workers who benefit from a reduced supply of competitors by virtue of substandard precollege schooling and rationed college slots (i.e., education rent), and (4) CEOs who secure sweetheart deals because the members of governing boards have no incentive to tie CEO pay to performance.

Although much has been written about these sources of rent at the top of the class structure, they haven't been incorporated into testable models of inequality or used to understand trends and cross-national differences in inequality. We think it's high time to build a comprehensive theory of the rent-based takeoff that may then be tested against more conventional theories that stress technological rather than sociopolitical sources of the takeoff. In the present chapter, we will focus on just two of the four types of rent, as doing so will serve to illustrate the type of analysis that could be developed more generally. We begin by arguing that rising returns to schooling, well appreciated as a main cause of rising inequality, are attributable to market failure in the form of barriers to free and open competition for higher education. We then argue that excessive executive compensation is likewise rooted in noncompetitive practices and that a market wage might be inequality reducing. Because of space limitations, we can't render the arguments in any comprehensive way, and instead we refer the reader elsewhere for a related and more sustained treatment (Weeden and Grusky 2010). The two examples laid out here should be taken as mere illustrations of the larger claim that market failure is a principal cause of inequality. We can use these two examples to show that, insofar as market failure is indeed a driving force behind the rise of inequality, one can reduce inequality not just by shifts from postmarket redistribution but also by market repair.

Education and Market Failure

The takeoff in inequality is typically understood as the consequence of technological changes (e.g., increasing computerization) that increase the demand for educated labor. Because this demand can't be immediately met, the payoff to educated labor increases as employers compete with one another and bid up its price, and the earnings gap between educated and uneducated labor accordingly widens. This account, which treats such skill-biased technological change (i.e., SBTC) as the smoking gun behind the takeoff in inequality, remains exceedingly popular. Although anti-SBTC carping is growing more common, a com-

prehensive alternative to SBTC hasn't yet been developed.

The SBTC story thus stresses that rising returns to education arise from the increase in demand for skilled labor. We might reasonably ask why workers don't simply go ahead and pursue a college education when they well know that there's a high payoff to college. Are there real structural impediments that prevent workers from realizing their hopes and aspirations for a credential? Or are there instead cognitive impediments that prevent them from formulating such aspirations in the first place? The cognitive impediments story, stated baldly, is that workers are either stupid or lazy: That is, they either don't understand that college yields a high payoff or understand that it yields a high payoff but even so just can't be bothered to pursue a college degree. We will suggest here that the cognitive-impediments story is less plausible than an account that recognizes that workers may simply not be in a position to secure a degree even though they appreciate its benefits.

The main structural impediments at stake here are supply-side and demand-side barriers that prevent sufficient numbers of workers (relative to demand) from securing a college education. The *supply* of potential college students is artificially lowered because children born into poor families and neighborhoods don't have the training (in primary and secondary schools) that qualifies them for entry into college (Goldin and Katz 2008). The *demand* for college students is kept artificially low because, in at least some countries, elite private and public schools engage in explicit rationing of their available slots. It's not as if Stanford University, for example, is meeting the rising interest in its degrees by selling some profit-maximizing number of them. If top universities did meet the demand in this way, the excessive returns to a high-prestige education would disappear, as indeed happened in the 1970s in the United States. We haven't, however, witnessed an analogous takeoff in higher education in recent decades. Instead, elite private universities have evidently decided to ration their slots, while public universities have been prevented from expanding because of declining state subsidies (and other forces).

This failure of educational institutions to expand in the face of rising demand stands in direct contrast to the expected response in competitive markets. When demand for hybrid cars, for example, increased dramatically in the United States, car manufacturers responded by ramping up production to a profit-maximizing level. They didn't typically respond by setting up hybrid-car admissions committees, by rigorously interviewing and testing prospective buyers, or by asking them to submit detailed résumés and statements about how the hybrid-owning experience will change their lives. Why did education and automobile manufacturers respond so differently to increased demand? The answer is simple: The market for cars more closely approximates a competitive market, whereas the market for education is anything but. We have become so accustomed to the contemporary practice of rationing higher education that we no longer appreciate what a profound form of market failure it is.

These bottlenecks on the supply and demand sides mean that those lucky enough to have a college education are artificially protected from competition and reap excessive pay as a result. If all children, even those born into poor families, had fair and open access to higher education, these excessive returns would disappear under the force of competition. It's in this very important sense that market failure is generating inequality. The prescription is likewise clear: If market failure is the cause of inequality, the proper response is market repair. We can straightforwardly repair the market by addressing the supply-side and demand-side bottlenecks that now prevent workers from acquiring college degrees.

Who would win and who would lose under such market repair? We have already noted that the losers would be those who are now artificially protected from competition and are therefore reaping excessive returns. The winners are those who are currently locked out of higher education, but would gain access once markets were repaired. But these are not the only winners. The other main winners would be the businesses that currently pay inflated prices for high-skill employees, but will no longer have to do so once higher education is opened up fully to competition. It's surely not in the interest of businesses to pay excessive returns to rationed secondary education, nor is it in the wider interest of any country to settle for the lower GDP that such restrictions on competition imply. The upshot is that market repair yields many winners.

It's high time, then, to move beyond the usual lip-service appeals to educational reform and appreciate that the current system makes a mockery of our ostensible commitment to markets. To be sure, the rise of for-profit educational institutions is often championed (and perhaps more often decried) as some nascent implementation of market principles, but such for-profits remain a small fraction of the higher-education sector, enrolling fewer than 4 percent of students in two-year programs and fewer than 2 percent of students in four-year programs (Bailey, Badway, and Gumport 2001). Moreover, it's altogether unclear whether there is a payoff to a for-profit credential, let alone whether that payoff equals the payoff to a traditional credential. If the payoff is indeed as small as some research suggests, then even a substantial increase in the number of for-profit credentials won't necessarily reduce inequality by much (Chung 2009; Grubb 1993).

Executive Pay and Market Failure

If one next considers CEO and executive pay, one again can't be all that impressed by our commitment to market principles. The main and well-known problem is that board members, sitting at the behest of the CEO, make decisions about that CEO's pay (Bebchuk and Fried 2004). This setup lends itself to board members favoring ample compensation packages because their own interests are best served by attending to the CEO's interests. It should come as no surprise, for example, that CEO pay is higher when many of the outside directors have been appointed under the CEO.[1] It becomes difficult with such pay-setting practices to represent the resulting pay in market terms. It's rather like asking a professor's students to decide on the professor's pay in advance of receiving their grades. When the fox is guarding the henhouse, one has to believe the fox's interests are better served than those of the hens.

The board's particularism is, however, nicely camouflaged by the practice of hiring outside consultants to examine the pay of peer firms and to make a recommendation accordingly, with that recommendation then typically represented as the pay level set by a competitive market (DiPrete, Eirich, and Pittinsky 2010). It's indeed the case that one can't expect CEOs to accept compensation below the prevailing compensation and

that an individual firm may therefore have no reasonable alternative but to compensate at the prevailing level. It shouldn't, however, be concluded that this package reflects the marginal product of the CEO. Rather, it's nothing more or less than the prevailing package, and the prevailing package simply reflects the prevailing practice of allowing CEOs to appoint board members who are then beholden to them. The resulting "market pay" is simply the pay that's generated when nonmarket forces are allowed to affect the board's compensation decisions.

The foregoing story about CEO pay is not universally accepted. Indeed, a large contingent of scholars view executive-pay arrangements as the product of arm's-length contracting between boards and executives, with the resulting compensation package indeed reflecting the marginal product of CEOs (Murphy and Zabojnik 2007; Gabaix and Landier 2008). If existing corporate practices deliver compensation that simply equals the value of the decisions the executive is making, then there's no market failure. The debate between scholars who hold this view (i.e., the optimal contracting view) and those who reject it (i.e., the managerial power view) is long, acrimonious, and far from resolved.

Although we are skeptical that existing governance practices can successfully deliver market pay, it goes well beyond our charge to review the relevant literature here and attempt to make that case. We instead make the fallback point that one should at least avoid compensation practices that create the strong *appearance* of impropriety. It's possible that economists working within the optimal contracting view are entirely right that, at the end of the day, contemporary compensation levels are efficient and only appear improper. But here's the rub: Even if this were true, the legitimacy of compensation practices is still everywhere doubted and called into question, and much corporate energy must accordingly be devoted to concealing, justifying, or explaining packages that the public and stockholders treat with much understandable suspicion. Because these packages are so public, the mere appearance of impropriety can lead to widespread cynicism about how fair our system is, with resulting costs in the form of increased disaffection and reduced initiative. If the optimal contracting view is on the mark, then CEOs will continue to be paid at the same high level even after the appearance of impropriety is removed. The best way to test this view thus involves doing away with the smoking gun practices that suggest wholesale corruption.

The upshot is that even those who hold to the optimal contracting view should have an interest in setting up compensation practices that eliminate the appearance of corruption. It's useful in this regard to contrast two rather different approaches to reining in compensation. The institutionalist approach, which we have been advocating here, requires that we reform pay-setting institutions that make boards beholden to CEOs, thereby eliminating at least the appearance of impropriety. This institutionalist approach differs from a reformist approach that instead takes the existing corporate pay-setting institutions as given and layers various pay-governing controls on top of them. These secondary controls may take the form, for example, of (1) internalized moral restraints on the amount of pay that executives should accept or be offered, (2) government regulations capping total compensation, (3) corporate pay scales constituting voluntary caps on compensation, or (4) government taxation of excessive compensation.

The foregoing reformist approaches operate, it would seem, from the premise that two wrongs make a right. That is, instead of repairing institutions that are susceptible to nonmarket influence, they instead take deeply flawed institutions and layer on top of them additional nonmarket correctives (e.g., pay caps). The evident premise is either that two layers of nonmarket practices will, in conjunction, magically hit upon the true market wage or that the main objective shouldn't be to capture that elusive competitive market wage but instead just limit compensation any way possible.

We think such cynicism underestimates the public and, in particular, its commitment to competitive markets. As we see it, the informed public wants nothing more or less than competitive market wages, and high levels of compensation are quite unproblematic in market-focused societies (e.g., the United States) when they're justifiable in market terms. There's much empirical evidence suggesting, for example, that the U.S. population is prepared to accept quite extreme inequality insofar as it's fairly generated under competitive market rules (Hochschild 1995). It's accordingly wrong to interpret the current public outrage about CEO pay as some mass protest against high compensation. Rather, it's a mass protest against corruption, against sweetheart deals, against foxes guarding the henhouse. If we're right on this point, the institutionalist approach is clearly preferred, and we should accordingly turn to developing corporate practices that will plausibly yield market pay.

Conclusion

We've argued here that there is much market failure in late-industrial societies, that such failure generates high inequality, and that market repair is our best bet for reducing inequality in a way that resonates well with our core commitments. The conventional wisdom, by contrast, is that competitive markets are inequality-generating machines and that perhaps the worst-possible principle around which to build a commitment to equality is the market principle. This conventional formula confuses markets as they are with markets as they should be. In their current form, markets are indeed inequality-generating machines, but that's partly because they encompass various forms of closure, corruption, and supply bottlenecks that are inconsistent with a purely competitive market. If such market failure could be taken on, and we think it can, we might end up with strikingly less inequality. We have focused here on two especially important examples of this argument but suspect that it applies more widely.

We don't want to press our argument too far by suggesting that inequality should exclusively be addressed via market repair. To the contrary, after-market redistribution clearly is an important tool for inequality reduction, and our objective here has simply been to remind that it's not the *only* tool. The obvious problem with focusing exclusively on after-market intervention is that in some countries it's ideologically suspect and doesn't garner enough support to reduce inequality appreciably or permanently. The market principle is, by contrast, one of the core commitments of most late-industrial countries and hence a promising base upon which to build anti-inequality initiatives that deliver over the long run.

NOTE

1. For a review of relevant evidence, see Bebchuk and Wiesbach 2009.

REFERENCES

Bailey, Thomas, Norena Badway, and Patricia Gumport. 2001. *For-Profit Higher Education and Community Colleges.* Stanford, CA: National Center for Postsecondary Improvement.

Bebchuk, Lucian A., and J. Fried. 2004. *Pay Without Performance.* Cambridge: Harvard University Press.

Bebchuk, Lucian A., and Michael S. Wiesbach. 2009. "The State of Corporate Governance Research." Dice Center Working Paper 2009-21. Ohio State University, Columbus.

Chung, Anna S. 2009. "Effects of For-Profit College Training on Earnings." MPRA Paper 18972. University Library of Munich, Germany.

DiPrete, Thomas A., Greg Eirich, and Matthew Pittinsky. 2010. "Compensation Benchmarking, Leapfrogs, and the Surge in Executive Pay." *American Journal of Sociology* 115, no. 6: 1671–1712.

Gabaix, X., and A. Landier. 2008. "Why Has CEO Pay Increased So Much?" *Quarterly Journal of Economics* 123: 49–100.

Goldin, Claudia, and Lawrence Katz. 2008. *The Race Between Education and Technology.* Cambridge: Harvard University Press.

Grubb, W. N. 1993. "The Long-Run Effects of Proprietary Schools on Wages and Earnings: Implications for Federal Policy." *Educational Evaluation and Policy Analysis* 15: 17–33.

Hochschild, Jennifer. 1995. *Facing Up to the American Dream: Race, Class, and the Soul of the Nation.* Princeton: Princeton University Press.

McCall, Leslie, and Lane Kenworthy. 2008. "Inequality, Public Opinion, and Redistribution." *Socio-Economic Review* 8: 35–68.

Murphy, K. J., and J. Zabojnik. 2007. "Managerial Capital and the Market for CEOs." Working Paper. Queen's University, Kingston, Ontario.

Weeden, Kim A., and David B. Grusky. 2010. "Can Inequality Be Reduced by Repairing Markets?" Working Paper. Department of Sociology, Cornell University, Ithaca, NY.

PART IV

Inequality at the Extremes

11

The Power Elite

C. WRIGHT MILLS

The powers of ordinary men are circumscribed by the everyday worlds in which they live, yet even in these rounds of job, family, and neighborhood they often seem driven by forces they can neither understand nor govern. 'Great changes' are beyond their control, but affect their conduct and outlook none the less. The very framework of modern society confines them to projects not their own, but from every side, such changes now press upon the men and women of the mass society, who accordingly feel that they are without purpose in an epoch in which they are without power.

But not all men are in this sense ordinary. As the means of information and of power are centralized, some men come to occupy positions in American society from which they can look down upon, so to speak, and by their decisions mightily affect, the everyday worlds of ordinary men and women. They are not made by their jobs; they set up and break down jobs for thousands of others; they are not confined by simple family responsibilities; they can escape. They may live in many hotels and houses, but they are bound by no one community. They need

not merely 'meet the demands of the day and hour'; in some part, they create these demands, and cause others to meet them. Whether or not they profess their power, their technical and political experience of it far transcends that of the underlying population. What Jacob Burckhardt said of 'great men,' most Americans might well say of their elite: 'They are all that we are not.'[1]

The power elite is composed of men whose positions enable them to transcend the ordinary environments of ordinary men and women; they are in positions to make decisions having major consequences. Whether they do or do not make such decisions is less important than the fact that they do occupy such pivotal positions: their failure to act, their failure to make decisions, is itself an act that is often of greater consequence than the decisions they do make. For they are in command of the major hierarchies and organizations of modern society. They rule the big corporations. They run the machinery of the state and claim its prerogatives. They direct the military establishment. They occupy the strategic command posts of the social structure, in which are now centered the effective means of the power and the wealth and the celebrity which they enjoy.

The power elite are not solitary rulers. Advisers and consultants, spokesmen and opinion-makers are often the captains of their higher thought and decision. Immediately below the elite are the professional politicians of the middle levels of power, in the Congress and in the pressure groups, as well as among the new and old upper classes of town and city and region. Mingling with them in curious ways are those professional celebrities who live by being continually displayed but are never, so long as they remain celebrities, displayed enough. If such celebrities are not at the head of any dominating hierarchy, they do often have the power to distract the attention of the public or afford sensations to the masses, or, more directly, to gain the ear of those who do occupy positions of direct power. More or less unattached, as critics of morality and technicians of power, as spokesmen of God and creators of mass sensibility, such celebrities and consultants are part of the immediate scene in which the drama of the elite is enacted. But that drama itself is centered in the command posts of the major institutional hierarchies.

1

The truth about the nature and the power of the elite is not some secret which men of affairs know but will not tell. Such men hold quite various theories about their own roles in the sequence of event and decision. Often they are uncertain about their roles, and even more often they allow their fears and their hopes to affect their assessment of their own power. No matter how great their actual power, they tend to be less acutely aware of it than of the resistances of others to its use. Moreover, most American men of affairs have learned well the rhetoric of public relations, in some cases even to the point of using it when they are alone, and thus coming to believe it. The personal awareness of the actors is only one of the several sources one must examine in order to understand the higher circles. Yet many who believe that there is no elite, or at any rate none of any consequence, rest their argument upon what men of affairs believe about themselves, or at least assert in public.

There is, however, another view: those who feel, even if vaguely, that a compact and powerful elite of great importance does now prevail in America often base that feeling upon the historical trend of our time. They have felt, for example, the domination of the military event, and from this they infer that generals and admirals, as well as other men of decision influenced by them, must be enormously powerful. They hear that the Congress has again abdicated to a handful of men decisions clearly related to the issue of war or peace. They know that the bomb was dropped over Japan in the name of the United States of America, although they were at no time consulted about the matter. They feel that they live in a time of big decisions; they know that they are not making any. Accordingly, as they consider the present as history, they infer that at its center, making decisions or failing to make them, there must be an elite of power.

On the one hand, those who share this feeling about big historical events assume that there is an elite and that its power is great. On the other hand, those who listen carefully to the reports of men apparently involved in the great decisions often do not believe that there is an elite whose powers are of decisive consequence.

Both views must be taken into account, but neither is adequate. The way to understand the power of the American elite lies neither solely in recognizing the historic scale of events nor in accepting the personal awareness reported by men of apparent decision. Behind such men and behind the events of history, linking the two, are the major institutions of modern society. These hierarchies of state and corporation and army constitute the means of power; as such they are now of a consequence not before equaled in human history—and at their summits, there are now those command posts of modern society which offer us the sociological key to an understanding of the role of the higher circles in America.

Within American society, major national power now resides in the economic, the political, and the military domains. Other institutions seem off to the side of modern history, and, on occasion, duly subordinated to these. No family is as directly powerful in national affairs as any major corporation; no church is as directly powerful in the external biographies of young men in America today as the military establishment; no college is as powerful in the shaping of momentous events as the National Security Council. Religious, educational, and family institutions are not autonomous centers of national power; on the contrary, these decentralized areas are increasingly shaped by the big three, in which developments of decisive and immediate consequence now occur. . . .

Within each of the big three, the typical institutional unit has become enlarged, has become administrative, and, in the power of its decisions, has become centralized. Behind these developments there is a fabulous technology, for as institutions, they have incorporated this technology and guide it, even as it shapes and paces their developments.

The economy—once a great scatter of small productive units in autonomous balance—has become dominated by two or three hundred giant corporations, administratively and politically interrelated, which together hold the keys to economic decisions.

The political order, once a decentralized set of several dozen states with a weak spinal cord, has become a centralized, executive establishment which has taken up into itself many powers previously scattered, and now enters into each and every cranny of the social structure.

The military order, once a slim establishment in a context of distrust fed by state militia, has become the largest and most expensive feature of government, and, although well versed in smiling public relations, now has all the grim and clumsy efficiency of a sprawling bureaucratic domain.

In each of these institutional areas, the means of power at the disposal of decisionmakers have increased enormously; their central executive powers have been enhanced; within each of them modern administrative routines have been elaborated and tightened up.

As each of these domains becomes enlarged and centralized, the consequences of its activities become greater, and its traffic with the others increases. The decisions of a handful of corporations bear upon military and political as well as upon economic developments around the world. The decisions of the military establishment rest upon and grievously affect political life as well as the very level of economic activity. The decisions made within the political domain determine economic activities and military programs. There is no longer, on the one hand, an economy, and, on the other hand, a political order containing a military establishment unimportant to politics and to money-making. There is a political economy linked, in a thousand ways, with military institutions and decisions. On each side of the world-split running through central Europe and around the Asiatic rimlands, there is an ever-increasing interlocking of economic, military, and political structures.[2] If there is government intervention in the corporate economy, so is there corporate intervention in the governmental process. In the structural sense, this triangle of power is the source of the interlocking directorate that is most important for the historical structure of the present.

The fact of the interlocking is clearly revealed at each of the points of crisis of modern capitalist society—slump, war, and boom. In each, men of decision are led to an awareness of the interdependence of the major institutional orders. In the nineteenth century, when the scale of all institutions was smaller, their liberal integration was achieved in the automatic economy, by an autonomous play of market forces, and in the automatic political domain, by the bargain and the vote. It was then assumed that out of the imbalance and friction that followed the limited decisions then possible a new equilibrium would in due course emerge. That can no longer be assumed, and it is not assumed by the men at the top of each of the three dominant hierarchies.

For given the scope of their consequences, decisions—and indecisions—in any one of these ramify into the others, and hence top decisions tend either to become co-ordinated or to lead to a commanding indecision. It has not always been like this.

When numerous small entrepreneurs made up the economy, for example, many of them could fail and the consequences still remain local; political and military authorities did not intervene. But now, given political expectations and military commitments, can they afford to allow key units of the private corporate economy to break down in slump? Increasingly, they do intervene in economic affairs, and as they do so, the controlling decisions in each order are inspected by agents of the other two, and economic, military, and political structures are interlocked.

At the pinnacle of each of the three enlarged and centralized domains, there have arisen those higher circles which make up the economic, the political, and the military elites. At the top of the economy, among the corporate rich, there are the chief executives; at the top of the political order, the members of the political directorate; at the top of the military establishment, the elite of soldier-statesmen clustered in and around the Joint Chiefs of Staff and the upper echelon. As each of these domains has coincided with the others, as decisions tend to become total in their consequence, the leading men in each of the three domains of power—the warlords, the corporation chieftains, the political directorate—tend to come together, to form the power elite of America.

2

The higher circles in and around these command posts are often thought of in terms of what their members possess: they have a greater share than other people of the things and experiences that are most highly valued. From this point of view, the elite are simply those who have the most of what there is to have, which is generally held to include money, power, and prestige—as well as all the ways of life to which these lead.[3] But the elite are not simply those who have the most, for they could not 'have the most' were it not for their positions in the great institutions. For such institutions are the necessary bases of power, of wealth, and of prestige, and at the same time, the chief means of exercising power, of acquiring and retaining wealth, and of cashing in the higher claims for prestige.

By the powerful we mean, of course, those who are able to realize their will, even if others resist it. No one, accordingly, can be truly powerful unless he has access to the command of major institutions, for it is over these institutional means of power that the truly powerful are, in the first instance, powerful. Higher politicians and key officials of government command such institutional power; so do admirals and generals, and so do the major owners and executives of the larger corporations. Not all power, it is true, is anchored in and exercised by means of such institutions, but only within and through them can power be more or less continuous and important. . . .

If we took the one hundred most powerful men in America, the one hundred wealthiest, and the one hundred most celebrated away from the institutional positions they now occupy, away from their resources of men and women and money, away from the media of mass communication that are now focused upon them—then they would be powerless and poor and uncelebrated. For power is not of a man. Wealth does not center in the person of the wealthy. Celebrity is not inherent in any personality. To be celebrated, to be wealthy, to have power requires access to major institutions, for the institutional positions men occupy determine in large part their chances to have and to hold these valued experiences.

3

The people of the higher circles may also be conceived as members of a top social stratum, as a set of groups whose members know one another, see one another socially and at business, and so, in making decisions, take one another into account. The elite, according to this conception, feel themselves to be, and are felt by others to be, the inner circle of 'the upper social classes.'[4] They form a more or less compact social and psychological entity; they have become self-conscious members of a social class. People are either accepted into this class or they are not, and there is a qualitative split, rather than merely a numerical scale, separating them from those who are not elite. They are more or less aware of themselves as a social class and they behave toward one another differently from the way they do toward members of other classes. They accept one another, understand one another, marry one another, tend to work and to think if not together at least alike.

Now, we do not want by our definition to prejudge whether the elite of the command posts are conscious members of such a socially recognized class, or whether considerable proportions of the elite derive from such a clear and distinct class. These are matters to be investigated. Yet in order to be able to recognize what we intend to investigate, we must note something that all biographies and memoirs of the wealthy and the powerful and the eminent make clear: no matter what else they may be, the people of these higher circles are involved in a set of overlapping 'crowds' and intricately connected 'cliques.' There is a kind of mutual attraction among those who 'sit on the same terrace'—although this often becomes clear to them, as well as to others, only at the point at which they feel the need to draw the line; only when, in their common defense, they come to understand what they have in common, and so close their ranks against outsiders.

The idea of such ruling stratum implies that most of its members have similar social origins, that throughout their lives they maintain a network of informal connections, and that to some degree there is an interchangeability of position between the various hierarchies of money and power and celebrity. We must, of course, note at once that if such an elite stratum does exist, its social visibility and its form, for very solid historical reasons, are quite different from those of the noble cousinhoods that once ruled various European nations.

That American society has never passed through a feudal epoch is of decisive importance to the nature of the American elite, as well as to American society as a historic whole. For it means that no nobility or aristocracy, established before the capitalist era, has stood in tense opposition to the higher bourgeoisie. It means that this bourgeoisie has monopolized not only wealth but prestige and power as well. It means that no set of noble families has commanded the top positions and monopolized the values that are generally held in high esteem; and certainly that no set has done so explicitly by inherited right. It means that no high church dignitaries or court nobilities, no entrenched landlords with honorific accouterments, no monopolists of high army posts have opposed the enriched bourgeoisie and in the name of

birth and prerogative successfully resisted its self-making.

But this does *not* mean that there are no upper strata in the United States. That they emerged from a 'middle class' that had no recognized aristocratic superiors does not mean they remained middle class when enormous increases in wealth made their own superiority possible. Their origins and their newness may have made the upper strata less visible in America than elsewhere. But in America today there are in fact tiers and ranges of wealth and power of which people in the middle and lower ranks know very little and may not even dream. There are families who, in their well-being, are quite insulated from the economic jolts and lurches felt by the merely prosperous and those farther down the scale. There are also men of power who in quite small groups make decisions of enormous consequence for the underlying population.

The American elite entered modern history as a virtually unopposed bourgeoisie. No national bourgeoisie, before or since, has had such opportunities and advantages. Having no military neighbors, they easily occupied an isolated continent stocked with natural resources and immensely inviting to a willing labor force. A framework of power and an ideology for its justification were already at hand. Against mercantilist restriction, they inherited the principle of *laissez-faire;* against Southern planters, they imposed the principle of industrialism. The Revolutionary War put an end to colonial pretensions to nobility, as loyalists fled the country and many estates were broken up. The Jacksonian upheaval with its status revolution put an end to pretensions to monopoly of descent by the old New England families. The Civil War broke the power, and so in due course the prestige, of the antebellum South's claimants for the higher esteem. The tempo of the whole capitalist development made it impossible for an inherited nobility to develop and endure in America.

No fixed ruling class, anchored in agrarian life and coming to flower in military glory, could contain in America the historic thrust of commerce and industry, or subordinate to itself the capitalist elite—as capitalists were subordinated, for example, in Germany and Japan. Nor could such a ruling class anywhere in the world contain that of the United States when industrialized violence came to decide history. Witness the fate of Germany and Japan in the two world wars of the twentieth century; and indeed the fate of Britain herself and her model ruling class, as New York became the inevitable economic, and Washington the inevitable political capital of the western capitalist world.

4

The elite who occupy the command posts may be seen as the possessors of power and wealth and celebrity; they may be seen as members of the upper stratum of a capitalistic society. They may also be defined in terms of psychological and moral criteria, as certain kinds of selected individuals. So defined, the elite, quite simply, are people of superior character and energy.

The humanist, for example, may conceive of the 'elite' not as a social level or category, but as a scatter of those individuals who attempt to transcend themselves, and accordingly, are more noble, more efficient, made out of better stuff. It does not matter whether they are poor or rich, whether they hold high position or low, whether they are

acclaimed or despised; they are elite because of the kind of individuals they are. The rest of the population is mass, which, according to this conception, sluggishly relaxes into uncomfortable mediocrity.[5]

This is the sort of socially unlocated conception which some American writers with conservative yearnings have recently sought to develop. But most moral and psychological conceptions of the elite are much less sophisticated, concerning themselves not with individuals but with the stratum as a whole. Such ideas, in fact, always arise in a society in which some people possess more than do others of what there is to possess. People with advantages are loath to believe that they just happen to be people with advantages.

They come readily to define themselves as inherently worthy of what they possess; they come to believe themselves 'naturally' elite; and, in fact, to imagine their possessions and their privileges as natural extensions of their own elite selves. In this sense, the idea of the elite as composed of men and women having a finer moral character is an ideology of the elite as a privileged ruling stratum, and this is true whether the ideology is elite-made or made up for it by others.

In eras of equalitarian rhetoric, the more intelligent or the more articulate among the lower and middle classes, as well as guilty members of the upper, may come to entertain ideas of a counter-elite. In western society, as a matter of fact, there is a long tradition and varied images of the poor, the exploited, and the oppressed as the truly virtuous, the wise, and the blessed. Stemming from Christian tradition, this moral idea of a counter-elite composed of essentially higher types condemned to a lowly station, may be and has been used by the underlying population to justify harsh criticism of ruling elites and to celebrate utopian images of a new elite to come.

The moral conception of the elite, however, is not always merely an ideology of the overprivileged or a counter-ideology of the underprivileged. It is often a fact: having controlled experiences and select privileges, many individuals of the upper stratum do come in due course to approximate the types of character they claim to embody. Even when we give up—as we must—the idea that the elite man or woman is born with an elite character, we need not dismiss the idea that their experiences and trainings develop in them characters of a specific type. . . .

5

These several notions of the elite, when appropriately understood, are intricately bound up with one another, and we shall use them all in this examination of American success. We shall study each of several higher circles as offering candidates for the elite, and we shall do so in terms of the major institutions making up the total society of America; within and between each of these institutions, we shall trace the interrelations of wealth and power and prestige. But our main concern is with the power of those who now occupy the command posts, and with the role which they are enacting in the history of our epoch.

Such an elite may be conceived as omnipotent, and its powers thought of as a great hidden design. Thus, in vulgar Marxism, events and trends are explained by reference to 'the will of the bourgeoisie'; in Nazism, by reference to 'the conspiracy of the Jews'; by the petty right in America today, by reference to 'the hidden force' of Communist spies. According to such notions of the omnipotent elite as historical cause, the elite is never an entirely visible agency. It is, in fact, a secular substitute for the will of God, being realized in a sort of providential design, except that usually non-elite men are thought capable of opposing it and eventually overcoming it.

The opposite view—of the elite as impotent—is now quite popular among liberal-minded observers. Far from being omnipotent, the elites are thought to be so scattered as to lack any coherence as a historical force. Their invisibility is not the invisibility of secrecy but the invisibility of the multitude. Those who occupy the formal places of authority are so check-mated—by other elites exerting pressure, or by the public as an electorate, or by constitutional codes—that, although there may be upper classes, there is no ruling class; although there may be men of power, there is no power elite; although there may be a system of stratification, it has no effective top. In the extreme, this view of the elite, as weakened by compromise and disunited to the point of nullity, is a substitute for impersonal collective fate; for, in this view, the decisions of the visible men of the higher circles do not count in history.

Internationally, the image of the omnipotent elite tends to prevail. All good events and pleasing happenings are quickly imputed by the opinion-makers to the leaders of their own nation; all bad events and unpleasant experiences are imputed to the enemy abroad. In both cases, the omnipotence of evil rulers or of virtuous leaders is assumed. Within the nation, the use of such rhetoric is rather more complicated: when men speak of the power of their own party or circle, they and their leaders are, of course, impotent; only 'the people' are omnipotent. But, when they speak of the power of their opponent's party or circle, they impute to them omnipotence; 'the people' are now powerlessly taken in.

More generally, American men of power tend, by convention, to deny that they are powerful. No American runs for office in order to rule or even govern, but only to serve; he does not become a bureaucrat or even an official, but a public servant. And nowadays, as I have already pointed out, such postures have become standard features of the public-relations programs of all men of power. So firm a part of the style of power-wielding have they become that conservative writers readily misinterpret them as indicating a trend toward an 'amorphous power situation.'

But the 'power situation' of America today is less amorphous than is the perspective of those who see it as a romantic confusion. It is less a flat, momentary 'situation' than a graded, durable structure. And if those who occupy its top grades are not omnipotent, neither are they impotent. It is the form and the height of the gradation of power that we must examine if we would understand the degree of power held and exercised by the elite.

If the power to decide such national issues as are decided were shared in an absolutely equal way, there would be no power elite; in fact, there would be no *gradation* of power, but only a radical homogeneity. At the opposite extreme as well, if the power to decide issues were absolutely monopolized by one small group, there would be no gradation of power; there would simply be this small group in command, and below it, the undifferentiated, dominated masses. American society today represents neither the one nor the other of these extremes, but a conception of them is

none the less useful: it makes us realize more clearly the question of the structure of power in the United States and the position of the power elite within it.

Within each of the most powerful institutional orders of modern society there is a gradation of power. The owner of a roadside fruit stand does not have as much power in any area of social or economic or political decision as the head of a multi-million-dollar fruit corporation; no lieutenant on the line is as powerful as the Chief of Staff in the Pentagon; no deputy sheriff carries as much authority as the President of the United States. Accordingly, the problem of defining the power elite concerns the level at which we wish to draw the line. By lowering the line, we could define the elite out of existence; by raising it, we could make the elite a very small circle indeed. In a preliminary and minimum way, we draw the line crudely, in charcoal as it were: By the power elite, we refer to those political, economic, and military circles which as an intricate set of overlapping cliques share decisions having at least national consequences. In so far as national events are decided, the power elite are those who decide them. . . .

6

It is not my thesis that for all epochs of human history and in all nations, a creative minority, a ruling class, an omnipotent elite, shape all historical events. Such statements, upon careful examination, usually turn out to be mere tautologies,[6] and even when they are not, they are so entirely general as to be useless in the attempt to understand the history of the present. The minimum definition of the power elite as those who decide whatever is decided of major consequence, does not imply that the members of this elite are always and necessarily the history-makers; neither does it imply that they never are. We must not confuse the conception of the elite, which we wish to define, with one theory about their role: that they are the history-makers of our time. To define the elite, for example, as 'those who rule America' is less to define a conception than to state one hypothesis about the role and power of that elite. No matter how we might define the elite, the extent of its members' power is subject to historical variation. If, in a dogmatic way, we try to include that variation in our generic definition, we foolishly limit the use of a needed conception. If we insist that the elite be defined as a strictly coordinated class that continually and absolutely rules, we are closing off from our view much to which the term more modestly defined might open to our observation. In short, our definition of the power elite cannot properly contain dogma concerning the degree and kind of power that ruling groups everywhere have. Much less should it permit us to smuggle into our discussion a theory of history.

During most of human history, historical change has not been visible to the people who were involved in it, or even to those enacting it. Ancient Egypt and Mesopotamia, for example, endured for some four hundred generations with but slight changes in their basic structure. That is six and a half times as long as the entire Christian era, which has only prevailed some sixty generations; it is about eighty times as long as the five generations of the United States' existence. But now the tempo of change is so rapid, and the means of observation so accessible, that the interplay of event and decision seems often to be quite historically

visible, if we will only look carefully and from an adequate vantage point.

When knowledgeable journalists tell us that 'events, not men, shape the big decisions,' they are echoing the theory of history as Fortune, Chance, Fate, or the work of The Unseen Hand. For 'events' is merely a modern word for these older ideas, all of which separate men from history-making, because all of them lead us to believe that history goes on behind men's backs. History is drift with no mastery; within it there is action but no deed; history is mere happening and the event intended by no one.[7]

The course of events in our time depends more on a series of human decisions than on any inevitable fate. The sociological meaning of 'fate' is simply this: that, when the decisions are innumerable and each one is of small consequence, all of them add up in a way no man intended—to history as fate. But not all epochs are equally fateful. As the circle of those who decide is narrowed, as the means of decision are centralized and the consequences of decisions become enormous, then the course of great events often rests upon the decisions of determinable circles. This does not necessarily mean that the same circle of men follow through from one event to another in such a way that all of history is merely their plot. The power of the elite does not necessarily mean that history is not also shaped by a series of small decisions, none of which are thought out. It does not mean that a hundred small arrangements and compromises and adaptations may not be built into the going policy and the living event. The idea of the power elite implies nothing about the process of decision-making as such: it is an attempt to delimit the social areas within which that process, whatever its character, goes on. It is a conception of who is involved in the process.

The degree of foresight and control of those who are involved in decisions that count may also vary. The idea of the power elite does not mean that the estimations and calculated risks upon which decisions are made are not often wrong and that the consequences are sometimes, indeed often, not those intended. Often those who make decisions are trapped by their own inadequacies and blinded by their own errors.

Yet in our time the pivotal moment does arise, and at that moment, small circles do decide or fail to decide. In either case, they are an elite of power. The dropping of the A-bombs over Japan was such a moment; the decision on Korea was such a moment; the confusion about Quemoy and Matsu, as well as before Dienbienphu were such moments; the sequence of maneuvers which involved the United States in World War II was such a 'moment.' Is it not true that much of the history of our times is composed of such moments? And is not that what is meant when it is said that we live in a time of big decisions, of decisively centralized power?

Most of us do not try to make sense of our age by believing in a Greek-like, eternal recurrence, nor by a Christian belief in a salvation to come, nor by any steady march of human progress. Even though we do not reflect upon such matters, the chances are we believe with Burckhardt that we live in a mere succession of events; that sheer continuity is the only principle of history. History is merely one thing after another; history is meaningless in that it is not the realization of any determinate plot. It is true, of course, that our sense of continuity, our feeling for the history of our time, is affected by crisis. But we seldom look beyond the immediate crisis or the crisis felt to be just ahead. We believe neither in fate nor

providence; and we assume, without talking about it, that 'we'—as a nation—can decisively shape the future but that 'we' as individuals somehow cannot do so.

Any meaning history has, 'we' shall have to give to it by our actions. Yet the fact is that although we are all of us within history we do not all possess equal powers to make history. To pretend that we do is sociological nonsense and political irresponsibility. It is nonsense because any group or any individual is limited, first of all, by the technical and institutional means of power at its command; we do not all have equal access to the means of power that now exist, nor equal influence over their use. To pretend that 'we' are all history-makers is politically irresponsible because it obfuscates any attempt to locate responsibility for the consequential decisions of men who do have access to the means of power.

From even the most superficial examination of the history of the western society we learn that the power of decision-makers is first of all limited by the level of technique, by the *means* of power and violence and organization that prevail in a given society. In this connection we also learn that there is a fairly straight line running upward through the history of the West; that the means of oppression and exploitation, of violence and destruction, as well as the means of production and reconstruction, have been progressively enlarged and increasingly centralized.

As the institutional means of power and the means of communications that tie them together have become steadily more efficient, those now in command of them have come into command of instruments of rule quite unsurpassed in the history of mankind. And we are not yet at the climax of their development. We can no longer lean upon or take soft comfort from the historical ups and downs of ruling groups of previous epochs. In that sense, Hegel is correct: we learn from history that we cannot learn from it.

NOTES

1. Jacob Burckhardt, *Force and Freedom* (New York: Pantheon Books, 1943), pp. 303 ff.

2. Cf. Hans Gerth and C. Wright Mills, *Character and Social Structure* (New York: Harcourt, Brace, 1953), pp. 457 ff.

3. The statistical idea of choosing some value and calling those who have the most of it an elite derives, in modern times, from the Italian economist, Pareto, who puts the central point in this way: 'Let us assume that in every branch of human activity each individual is given an index which stands as a sign of his capacity, very much the way grades are given in the various subjects in examinations in school. The highest type of lawyer, for instance, will be given 10. The man who does not get a client will be given 1—reserving zero for the man who is an out-and-out idiot. To the man who has made his millions—honestly or dishonestly as the case may be—we will give 10. To the man who has earned his thousands we will give 6; to such as just manage to keep out of the poor-house, 1, keeping zero for those who get in. . . . So let us make a class of people who have the highest indices in their branch of activity, and to that class give the name of *elite*.' Vilfredo Pareto, *The Mind and Society* (New York: Harcourt, Brace, 1935), par. 2027 and 2031. Those who follow this approach end up not with one elite, but with a number corresponding to the number of values they select. Like many rather abstract ways of reasoning, this one is useful because it forces us to think in a clear-cut way. For a skillful use of this approach, see the work of Harold D. Lasswell, in particular, *Politics: Who Gets What, When, How* (New York: McGraw-Hill, 1936); and for a more systematic use, H. D. Lasswell and Abraham Kaplan, *Power and Society* (New Haven: Yale University Press, 1950).

4. The conception of the elite as members of a top social stratum, is, of course, in line with the prevailing common-sense view of stratification. Technically, it is closer to 'status group' than to 'class,' and has been very well stated by Joseph A. Schumpeter, 'Social Classes in an Ethically Homogeneous Environment,' *Imperialism and Social Classes* (New York: Augustus M. Kelley, Inc., 1951), pp. 133 ff., especially pp. 137–47. Cf. also his *Capitalism, Socialism and Democracy,* 3rd ed. (New York: Harper, 1950), Part II. For the distinction between class and status groups, see *From Max Weber: Essays in Sociology* trans. and ed. by Gerth and Mills (New York: Oxford University Press, 1946). For an analysis of Pareto's conception of the elite compared with Marx's conception of classes, as well as data on France, see Raymond Aron, 'Social Structure and Ruling Class,' *British Journal of Sociology,* vol. I, nos. 1 and 2 (1950).

5. The most popular essay in recent years which defines the elite and the mass in terms of a morally evaluated character-type is probably José Ortega y Gasset's, *The Revolt of the Masses,* 1932 (New York: New American Library, Mentor Edition, 1950), esp. pp. 91 ff.

6. As in the case, quite notably, of Gaetano Mosca, *The Ruling Class* (New York: McGraw-Hill, 1939). For a sharp analysis of Mosca, see Fritz Morstein Marx, 'The Bureaucratic State,' *Review of Politics,* vol. I, 1939, pp. 457 ff. Cf. also Mills, 'On Intellectual Craftsmanship,' April 1952, mimeographed, Columbia College, February 1955.

7. Cf. Karl Löwith, *Meaning in History* (Chicago: University of Chicago Press, 1949), pp. 125 ff. for concise and penetrating statements of several leading philosophies of history.

12

Who Rules America?

Power and Politics

G. WILLIAM DOMHOFF

Do corporations have far too much power in the United States? Does the federal government ignore the interests of everyday people? The great majority of Americans— 70 to 75 percent in some surveys—answer "yes" to both questions.[1] This chapter explains why their answers are accurate even though there is freedom of speech, the possibility of full political participation, and increasing equality of opportunity due to the civil rights and women's movements. In other words, it attempts to resolve a seeming paradox that has bedeviled social scientists and political activists for a long time: How is it possible to have such extreme corporate domination in a democratic country?

This paradox is made all the more striking because corporations do not have as much power in most other democratic countries. The wealth and income differences between people at the top and the bottom are not as great, and the safety net for those who are poor, ill, or elderly is stronger. Why does the richest nation in the world also have the most poverty compared to any other democratic country?

Using a wide range of systematic empirical findings, this chapter shows how the owners and top-level managers in large companies work together to maintain themselves as the core of the dominant power group. Their corporations, banks, and agribusinesses form a *corporate community* that shapes the federal government on the policy issues of interest to it, issues that have a major impact on the income, job security, and well-being of most other Americans. At the same time, there is competition within the corporate community for profit opportunities, which can lead to highly visible policy conflicts among rival corporate leaders that are sometimes fought out in Congress. Yet the corporate community is cohesive on the policy issues that affect its general welfare, which is often at stake when political challenges are made by organized workers, liberals, or strong environmentalists. The chapter therefore deals with another seeming paradox: How can a highly competitive group of corporate leaders cooperate enough to work their common will in the political and policy arenas? . . .

G. William Domhoff, *Who Rules America? Power and Politics*, Fourth Edition, pp. xi–xii, 45–51, 57, 67–68, 216–218. Copyright © 2002 by McGraw-Hill Companies.

Partly because the owners and high-level managers within the corporate community share great wealth and common economic interests, but also due to political opposition to their interests, they band together to develop their own social institutions—gated neighborhoods, private schools, exclusive social clubs, debutante balls, and secluded summer resorts. These social institutions create social cohesion and a sense of group belonging, a "we" feeling, and thereby mold wealthy people into a *social upper class*. In addition, the owners and managers supplement their small numbers by financing and directing a wide variety of nonprofit organizations—e.g., tax-free foundations, think tanks, and policy-discussion groups—to aid them in shaping public policy. The highest-ranking employees in these non-profit organizations become part of a general leadership group for the corporate community and the upper class. . . .

The Corporate Community and the Upper Class

Why does it matter whether or not the corporate community and the upper class are intertwined? If the corporate community and the upper class are essentially one and the same in terms of people and objectives, then it is more likely that they have the wealth, social cohesion, and awareness of their common interests to organize themselves well enough to dominate government. If they are separate, the wealth and status of the upper class might form a rival power base and make the power structure more open.

The nationwide social upper class has its own exclusive social institutions and is based in the ownership of great wealth. The social cohesion that develops among members of

the upper class . . . is based in the two types of relationships found in a membership network: common membership in specific social institutions and friendships based on social interactions within those institutions. Research on small groups in laboratory settings suggests that social cohesion is greatest when (1) the social groups are seen to be exclusive and of high status; and (2) when the interactions take place in relaxed and informal settings.[2] Many of the social institutions of the upper class fit these specifications very well. From the viewpoint of social psychology, the people who make up the upper class can be seen as members of numerous small groups that meet at private schools, social clubs, retreats, and resorts. . . .

Prepping for Power

From infancy through young adulthood, members of the upper class receive a distinctive education. This education begins early in life in preschools that sometimes are attached to a neighborhood church of high social status. Schooling continues during the elementary years at a local private school called a day school. The adolescent years may see the student remain at day school, but there is a strong chance that at least one or two years will be spent away from home at a boarding school in a quiet rural setting. Higher education is obtained at one of a small number of prestigious private universities. Although some upper-class children may attend public high school if they live in a secluded suburban setting, or go to a state university if there is one of great esteem and tradition in their home state, the system of formal schooling is so insulated that many upper-class students never see the inside of a public school in all their years of education. This separate educational system is important evidence for the distinctiveness of the mentality and lifestyle that exists within the upper class, because schools play a large role in transmitting the class structure to their students.

The linchpins in the upper-class educational system are the dozens of boarding schools developed in the last half of the nineteenth and the early part of the twentieth centuries, coincident with the rise of a nationwide upper class whose members desired to insulate themselves from an inner city that was becoming populated by lower-class immigrants. They become surrogate families that play a major role in creating an upper-class subculture on a national scale in America.[3] The role of boarding schools in providing connections to other upper-class social institutions is also important. . . .

Virtually all graduates of private secondary schools go on to college, and most do so at prestigious universities. Graduates of the New England boarding schools, for example, historically found themselves at three or four large Ivy League universities: Harvard, Yale, Princeton, and Columbia. However, that situation changed somewhat after World War II as the universities grew and provided more scholarships. An analysis of admission patterns for graduates of 14 prestigious boarding schools between 1953 and 1967 demonstrated this shift by showing that the percentage of their graduates attending Harvard, Yale, or Princeton gradually declined over those years from 52 to 25 percent. Information on the same 14 schools for the years 1969 to 1979 showed that the figure had bottomed out at 13 percent in 1973, 1975, and 1979, with some schools showing very little change from the late 1960s and others dropping even more dramatically.[4] Now many upper-class students attend a select handful of smaller private colleges, most of which are in the East, but a few in the South and West as well.

Graduates of private schools outside of New England most frequently attend a prominent state university in their area, but a significant minority go to eastern Ivy League and top private universities in other parts of the country. For example, the Cate School, a boarding school near Santa Barbara, California, is modeled after its New England counterparts and draws most of its students from California and other western states. In the four years between 1993 and 1996, 35 percent of the 245 graduates went to one of fifteen prestigious Ivy League schools, with Middlebury (12), Harvard (10), and Brown (7) topping the list. The other leading destinations for Cate graduates were the University of California (27), Stanford (9), University of Colorado (9), Georgetown (8), Duke (7), Vanderbilt (6), and University of Chicago (5). Or, to take another example, St. John's in Houston is a lavishly endowed day school built in the Gothic architecture typical of many universities. From 1992 through 1996, 22 percent of its 585 graduates went to the fifteen Ivy League schools used in the Cate analysis, with Princeton (27), the University of Pennsylvania (15), Cornell (13), Harvard (12), and Yale (12) the most frequent destinations. As might be expected, 105 graduates went to the University of Texas (18 percent), but Rice (49), Vanderbilt (33), and Stanford (15) were high on the list. Few graduates of either Cate or St. John's went to less prestigious state schools.[5]

Most private school graduates pursue careers in business, finance, or corporate law, which is the first evidence for the intertwining of the upper class and the corporate community. Their business-oriented preoccupations are demonstrated in the greatest detail in a study of all those who graduated from Hotchkiss between 1940 and 1950. Using the school's alumni files, the researcher followed the careers of 228 graduates from their date of graduation until 1970.[6] Fifty-six percent of the sample are either bankers or business executives, with 80 of the 91 businessmen serving as president, vice-president, or partner in their firms. Another 10 percent of the sample are lawyers, mostly as partners in large firms closely affiliated with the corporate community.

The involvement of private school graduates on boards of directors is demonstrated in a study of all alumni over the age of 45 from one of the most prestigious eastern boarding schools, St. Paul's. Using *Poor's Register of Corporations, Directors and Executives,* and *Who's Who in America,* one finds that 303 of these several thousand men are serving as officers or directors in corporations in general, and that 102 are directors of 97 corporations in the *Fortune* 800. Their involvement is especially great in the financial sector. Most striking of all, 21 graduates of St. Paul's are either officers or directors at J. P. Morgan Bank, which for a time was one of the five largest banks in the country until it merged with Chase Manhattan Bank in late 2000. This finding suggests that the alumni of particular schools may tend to cluster at specific banks or corporations.

Social Clubs

Private social clubs are a major point of orientation in the lives of upper-class adults. These clubs also have a role in differentiating members of the upper class from other members of society. The clubs of the upper class are many and varied, ranging from family-oriented country clubs and downtown men's and women's clubs to highly specialized clubs for yachtsmen, sportsmen, gardening enthusiasts, and fox hunters. Downtown men's clubs originally were places for having lunch and dinner, and occasionally for attending an evening performance or a weekend party. As upper-class families deserted the city for large suburban estates, a new kind of club, the country club, gradually took over some of these functions. The downtown club became almost entirely a luncheon club, a site to hold meetings, or a place to relax on a free afternoon. The country club, by contrast, became a haven for all members of the family. It offered social and sporting activities ranging from dances, parties, and banquets to golf, swimming, and tennis. Special group dinners were often arranged for all members on Thursday night, the traditional maid's night off across the United States.

Initiation fees, annual dues, and expenses vary from a few thousand dollars in downtown clubs to tens of thousands of dollars in some country clubs, but money is not the primary barrier in gaining membership to a club. Each club has a very rigorous screening process before accepting new members. Most require nomination by one or more active members, letters of recommendation from three to six members, and interviews with at least some members of the membership committee. Negative votes by two or three members of what is typically a 10- to 20-person committee often are enough to deny admission to the candidate. The carefulness with which new members are selected extends to a guarding of club membership lists, which are usually available only to club members. Research on clubs therefore has to be based on out-of-date membership lists that have been given to historical libraries by members or their surviving spouses.

Men and women of the upper class often belong to clubs in several cities, creating a nationwide pattern of overlapping memberships. These overlaps provide evidence for social cohesion within the upper class. An indication of the nature and extent of this overlapping is revealed in a study of membership lists for 20 clubs in several major cities across the country, including the Links in New York, the Duquesne in Pittsburgh, the Chicago in Chicago, the Pacific Union in San Francisco, and the California in Los Angeles. There is sufficient overlap among 18 of the 20 clubs to form three regional groupings and a fourth group that provides a bridge between the two largest regional groups. The several dozen men who are in three or more of the clubs, most of them very wealthy people who also sit on several corporate boards, are especially important in creating the overall pattern.[7]

The overlap of this club network with corporate boards of directors provides important evidence for the intertwining of the upper class and corporate community. In one study, the club memberships of the chairpersons and outside directors of the 20 largest industrial corporations were counted. The overlaps with upper-class clubs in general are ubiquitous, but the concentration of directors in a few clubs is especially notable. At least one director from 12 of the 20 corporations is a member of the Links Club, which is the New York meeting grounds of the national corporate establishment. Seven of General Electric's directors are members, as are four from Chrysler, four from Westinghouse, and three from IBM. In addition to the Links, several other clubs have directors from four or more corporations. Another study, using membership lists from 11 prestigious clubs in different parts of the country, confirms and extends these findings. A majority of the top 25 corporations in every major sector of the economy have directors in at least one of these clubs, and several have many more. For example, all of the 25 largest industrials have one or more directors in these 11 clubs. The Links in New York, with 79 connections to 21 industrial corporations, has the most.[8] . . .

Continuity and Upward Mobility

Americans always have believed that anyone can rise from rags to riches if they try hard enough, but in fact a rise from the bottom to the top is very rare and often a matter of luck—being at the right place at the right time. In the late nineteenth century, a wealthy upper-class Bostonian with a Harvard education, Horatio Alger, became a best-selling author by writing short fictional books on young boys who had gone from penniless adversity to great wealth. In real life, the commentators of his day pointed to three or four actual examples. Subsequent research showed that most of the business leaders of that era did not fit the Horatio Alger myth. As one historian put it, Horatio Algers appeared more frequently in magazines and textbooks than they did in reality.[9]

Since 1982, the Horatio Alger story line has been taken up by *Forbes*, a business magazine that publishes an annual list of the allegedly 400 richest Americans. "Forget old money," says the article that introduces the 1996 list. "Forget silver spoons. Great fortunes are being created almost monthly in the U.S. today by young entrepreneurs who hadn't a dime when we created this list 14 years ago."[10] But the Horatio Alger story is no less rare today than it was in the 1890s. A study of all those on the *Forbes* lists for 1995 and 1996 showed that at least 56 percent of them came from millionaire families and that another 14 percent came from the top 10 percent of the income ladder.[11]. . .

Class Awareness:
A Capitalist Mentality

The institutions that establish the owners and high-level executives of corporations as a national upper class transcend the presence or absence of any given person or family. Families can rise and fall in the class structure, but the institutions of the upper class persist. Not everyone in this nationwide upper class knows everyone else, but everybody knows somebody who knows someone in other areas of the country, thanks to a common school experience, a summer at the same resort, membership in the same social club, or membership on the same board of directors. The upper class at any given historical moment consists of a complex network of overlapping social circles knit together by the members they have in common and by the numerous signs of equal social status that emerge from a similar lifestyle. Viewed from the standpoint of social psychology, the upper class is made up of innumerable face-to-face small groups that are constantly changing in their composition as people move from one social setting to another.

Involvement in these institutions usually instills a class awareness that includes feelings of superiority, pride, and justified privilege. Deep down, most members of the upper class think they are better than other people, and therefore fully deserving of their station in life. This class awareness is based in corporate ownership, but it is reinforced by the shared social identities and interpersonal ties created through participation in the social institutions of the upper class.

The fact that the upper class is based in the ownership and control of profit-producing investments in stocks, bonds, and real estate shows that it is a capitalist class as well as a social class. Its members are not concerned simply with the interests of one corporation or business sector, but with such matters as the investment climate, the rate of profit, and the overall political climate. That is, they have a capitalist mentality.

NOTES

1. Aaron Bernstein, "Too Much Corporate Power?," *BusinessWeek*, 11 September 2000, 145–149.

2. Michael Hogg, *The Social Psychology of Group Cohesiveness* (New York: New York University Press, 1992).

3. Peter W. Cookson and Caroline Hodges Persell, *Preparing for Power: America's Elite Boarding Schools* (New York: Basic Books, 1985).

4. Michael Gordon, "Changing Patterns of Upper-Class Prep School College Placements," *Pacific Sociological Review* 12, no. 1 (1969): 23–26.

5. These figures were obtained from the admissions offices at Cate and St. John's in 1997.

6. Christopher Armstrong, "Privilege and Productivity: The Cases of Two Private Schools and Their Graduates," Ph.D. Dissertation, University of Pennsylvania, 1974.

7. G. William Domhoff, "Social Clubs, Policy-Planning Groups, and Corporations: A Network Study of Ruling-Class Cohesiveness," *Insurgent Sociologist* 5, no. 3 (1975): 173–184.

8. G. William Domhoff, "Social Clubs, Policy-Planning Groups, and Corporations: A Network Study of Ruling-Class Cohesiveness," *Insurgent Sociologist* 5, no. 3 (1975): 173–184; G. William Domhoff, *Who Rules America?*, 1st ed. (Englewood Cliffs, N.J.: Prentice-Hall, 1967).

9. William Miller, "American Historians and the Business Elite," *Journal of Economic History* 9 (1949): 184–208.

10. Ann Marsh, "The Forbes Four Hundred," *Forbes*, 14 October 1996, 100.

11. Chuck Collins, *Born on Third Base: The Sources of Wealth of the 1996 Forbes 400* (Boston: United for a Fair Economy, 1997).

13

The Future of Intellectuals and the Rise of the New Class

ALVIN W. GOULDNER

In all countries that have in the twentieth century become part of the emerging world socioeconomic order, a New Class composed of intellectuals and technical intelligentsia—not the same—enters into contention with the groups already in control of the society's economy, whether these are businessmen or party leaders. A new contest of classes and a new class system is slowly arising in the third world of developing nations, in the second world of the USSR and its client states, and in the first world of late capitalism of North America, Western Europe, and Japan.

The early historical evolution of the New Class in Western Europe, its emergence into the public sphere as a structurally differentiated and (relatively) autonomous social stratum, may be defined in terms of certain critical episodes. What follows is only a synoptic inventory of some episodes decisive in the formation of the New Class.

1. A process of secularization in which most intelligentsia are no longer trained by, living within, and subject to close supervision by a churchly organization, and thus separated from the everyday life of society.[1]

Secularization is important because it desacralizes authority-claims and facilitates challenges to definitions of social reality made by traditional authorities linked to the church. Secularization is important also because it is an infrastructure on which there develops the modern grammar of rationality, or culture of critical discourse, with its characteristic stress on self-groundedness—in Martin Heidegger's sense of the "mathematical project."[2]

2. A second episode in the emergence of the New Class is the rise of diverse vernacular languages, the corresponding decline of Latin as the language of intellectuals, and especially of their scholarly production. Latin becomes a ritual, rather than a technical language. This development further dissolves the membrane between everyday life and the intellectuals—whether clerical or secular.

3. There is a breakdown of the feudal and old regime system of personalized *patronage* relations between the old hegemonic elite and individual members of the New Class as cultural producers; and

Alvin W. Gouldner, *The Future of Intellectuals and the Rise of the New Class* (New York: Continuum Publishing Service, 1979), pp. 1–8, 18–20, 28–29, 83–85, 102–104, 106, 110, 112–113. Reprinted by permission of Continuum International Publishing Group.

4. A corresponding growth of an anonymous *market* for the products and services of the New Class, thus allowing them to make an independent living apart from close supervision and *personalized controls by patrons.* Along with secularization, this means that the residence and work of intellectuals are both now less closely supervised by others.

They may now more readily take personal initiatives in the public, political sphere, while also having a "private" life.

5. The character and development of the emerging New Class also depended importantly on the multi-national structure of European polities. That Europe was not a single empire with a central authority able to impose a single set of norms throughout its territory, but a system of competing and autonomous states with diverse cultures and religions, meant that dissenting intellectuals, scientists, and divines could and did protect their own intellectual innovations by migrating from their home country when conditions there grew insupportable and sojourning in foreign lands. Even the enforced travel of exiled intellectuals also enabled them to enter into a European-wide communication network. In an article (as yet unpublished), Robert Wuthnow has suggested that their often extensive travel led many intellectuals to share a cosmopolitan identity transcending national limits and enhancing their autonomy from local elites.

6. A sixth episode in the formation of the New Class is the waning of the extended, patriarchical family system and its replacement by the smaller, nuclear family. As middle class women become educated and emancipated, they may increasingly challenge paternal authority and side with their children in resisting it. With declining paternal authority and growing maternal influence, the autonomy strivings of children are now more difficult to repress; hostility and rebellion against paternal authority can become more overt. There is, correspondingly, increasing difficulty experienced by paternal authority in imposing and reproducing its social values and political ideologies in their children.

7. Following the French Revolution, there is in many parts of Europe, especially France and Germany, a profound reformation and extension of *public, non*-church controlled, (relatively more) *multi-class* education, at the lower levels as well as at the college, polytechnical, and university levels. On the one hand, higher education in the public school becomes the institutional basis for the *mass* production of the New Class of intelligentsia and intellectuals. On the other hand, the expansion of primary and secondary public school teachers greatly increases the jobs available to the New Class.

As teachers, intellectuals come to be defined, and to define themselves, as responsible for and "representative" of society as a *whole,*[3] rather than as having allegiance to the class interests of their students or their parents. As teachers, they are not defined as having an *obligation* to reproduce parental values in their children. Public teachers supersede private tutors.

8. The new structurally differentiated educational system is increasingly insulated from the family system, becoming an important source of values among students divergent from those of their families. The socialization of the young by their families is now mediated by a *semi*-autonomous group of teachers.

9. While growing public education limits family influence on education, it also

increases the influence of the state on education. The public educational system thus becomes a major *cosmopolitanizing* influence on its students, with a corresponding distancing from *localistic* interests and values.

10. Again, the new school system becomes a major setting for the intensive linguistic conversion of students from casual to reflexive speech, or (in Basil Bernstein's terms) from "restricted" linguistic codes to "elaborated" linguistic codes,[4] to a culture of discourse in which claims and assertions may *not* be justified by reference to the speaker's social status. This has the profound consequence of making all *authority-referring* claims potentially problematic.

11. This new culture of discourse often diverges from assumptions fundamental to everyday life, tending to put them into question even when they are linked to the upper classes. These school-inculcated modes of speech are, also, (relatively) situation-free language variants. Their situation-freeness is further heightened by the "communications revolution" in general, and by the development of printing technology, in particular. With the spread of printed materials, definitions of social reality available to intellectuals may now derive increasingly from *distant* persons, from groups geographically, culturally, and historically distant and even from dead persons, and may therefore diverge greatly from any local environment in which they are received. Definitions of social reality made by local elites may now be invidiously contrasted (by intellectuals) with definitions made in other places and times.

12. With the spread of public schools, literacy spreads; humanistic intellectuals lose their exclusiveness and privileged market position, and now experience a status disparity between their "high" culture, as they see it, and their lower deference, repute, income and social power. The social position of humanistic intellectuals, *particularly in a technocratic and industrial society,* becomes more marginal and alienated than that of the technical intelligentsia. The New Class becomes internally differentiated.

13. Finally, a major episode in the emergence of the modern intelligentsia is the changing form of the revolutionary *organization.* Revolution itself becomes a technology to be pursued with "instrumental rationality." The revolutionary organization evolves from a ritualistic, oath-bound secret society into the modern "vanguard" party. When the *Communist Manifesto* remarks that Communists have nothing to hide,[5] it is exactly a proposed emergence into *public* life which is implied. The *Communist Manifesto* was written by Marx and Engels for the "League of Communists," which was born of the "League of the Just" which, in turn, was descended from the "League of Outlaws." This latter group of German emigrants in Paris had a pyramidal structure, made a sharp distinction between upper and lower members, blindfolded members during initiation ceremonies, used recognition signs and passwords, and bound members by an oath.[6] The vanguard organization, however, de-ritualizes participation and entails elements of both the "secret society" and of the public political party. In the vanguard organization, public refers to the public availability of the *doctrine* rather than the availability of the organization or its membership to public scrutiny. Here, to be "public" entails the organization's rejection of "secret doctrines" known only to an elite in the organization—as, for instance, Bakunin's doctrine of an elite dictatorship of anarchists.[7] The

modern vanguard structure is first clearly encoded in Lenin's *What Is to Be Done?* Here it is plainly held that the proletariat cannot develop a *socialist* consciousness by itself, but must secure this from a scientific theory developed by the intelligentsia.[8] The "vanguard" party expresses the *modernizing* and elite ambitions of the New Class as well as an effort to overcome its political limitations. Lenin's call for the development of "professional" revolutionaries, as the core of the vanguard, is a rhetoric carrying the tacit promise of a *career*-like life which invites young members of the New Class to "normalize" the revolutionary existence. . . .

There are several distinguishable conceptions of the New Class:

1. *New Class as Benign Technocrats:* Here the New Class is viewed as a new historical elite already entrenched in institutional influence which it uses in benign ways for society; it is more or less inevitable and trustworthy: e.g., Galbraith,[9] Bell,[10] Berle and Means.[11]

(*Sed contra:* This obscures the manner in which the New Class egoistically pursues its own special vested interests. Moreover, the power of the New Class today is scarcely entrenched. This view also ignores the limits on the rationality of the New Class.)

2. *New Class as Master Class:* Here the New Class is seen as another moment in a long-continuing circulation of historical elites, as a socialist intelligentsia that brings little new to the world and continues to exploit the rest of society as the old class had, but now uses education rather than money to exploit others: Bakunin,[12] Machajski.[13]

(*Sed contra:* The New Class is more historically unique and discontinuous than this sees; while protecting its own special interests, it is not bound by the same *limits* as the old class and, at least transiently, contributes to collective needs.)

3. *New Class as Old Class Ally:* The New Class is here seen as a benign group of dedicated "professionals" who will uplift the old (moneyed) class from a venal group to a collectivity-oriented elite and who, fusing with it, will forge a new, genteel elite continuous with but better than the past: Talcott Parsons.[14]

(*Sed contra:* Neither group is an especially morally bound agent; the old class is constrained to protect its profits, the New Class is cashing in on its education. Immersed in the present, this view misses the fact that each is ready to exploit the other, if need be, and shows little understanding of the profound (if different) limits imposed on the rationality and morality of each of these groups, and of the important tensions between them.)

4. *New Class as Servants of Power:* Here the New Class is viewed as subservient to the old (moneyed) class which is held to retain power much as it always did, and is simply using the New Class to maintain its domination of society: Noam Chomsky[15] and Maurice Zeitlin.[16]

(*Sed contra:* This ignores the revolutionary history of the twentieth century in which radicalized elements of the New Class played a major leadership role in the key revolutions of our time. It greatly overemphasizes the common interests binding the New and old class, systematically missing the tensions between them; it ignores the fact that elimination of the old class is an historical option open to the New Class. This static conception underestimates the growth in the numbers and influence of the New Class. The view is also unexpectedly Marcusean in overstressing the prospects of old class continuity; it really sees the old class as having no effective opponents, either in the New Class or in the old adversary class, the proletariat. It thus ends as seeing even less social change in prospect than the Parsonian view [#3 above].)

5. *New Class as Flawed Universal Class* (*my own view*): The New Class is elitist and self-seeking and uses its special knowledge to advance its own interests and power, and to control its own work situation. Yet the New Class may also be the best card that history has presently given us to play. The power of the New Class is growing. It is substantially more powerful and independent than Chomsky suggests, while still much less powerful than is suggested by Galbraith who seems to conflate present reality with future possibility. The power of this morally ambiguous New Class is on the ascendent and it holds a mortgage on at least *one* historical future.

In my own left Hegelian sociology, the New Class bearers of knowledge are seen as an embryonic new "universal class"—as the prefigured embodiment of such future as the working class still has. It is that part of the working class which will survive cybernation. At the same time, a left Hegelian sociology also insists that the New Class is profoundly flawed as a universal class. Moreover, the New Class is not some unified subject or a seamless whole; it, too, has its own internal contradictions. It is a class internally divided with tensions between (technical) intelligentsia and (humanistic) intellectuals. No celebration, mine is a critique of the New Class which does not view its growing power as inevitable, which sees it as morally ambivalent, embodying the collective interest but partially and tran-

siently, while simultaneously cultivating its own guild advantage. . . .

The New Class as a Cultural Bourgeoisie

1. The New Class and the old class are at first undifferentiated; the New Class commonly originates in classes with property advantages, that is, in the old class, or is sponsored by them. The New Class of intellectuals and intelligentsia are the relatively more *educated* counterpart—often the brothers, sisters, or children—of the old moneyed class. Thus the New Class contest sometimes has the character of a *civil war within the upper classes.* It is the differentiation of the old class into contentious factions. To understand the New Class contest it is vital to understand how the *privileged* and advantaged, not simply the suffering, come to be alienated from the very system that privileges them.

2. The "non-negotiable" objectives of the old moneyed class are to reproduce their capital, at a minimum, but, preferably, to make it accumulate and to appropriate profit: M-C-M´, as Marx said. This is done within a structure in which all of them must compete with one another. This unrelenting competition exerts pressure to rationalize their productive and administrative efforts and unceasingly to heighten efficiency. (Marx called it, "revolutionizing" production.) But this rationalization is dependent increasingly on the efforts of the New Class intelligentsia and its expert skills. It is inherent in its structural situation, then, that the old class must bring the New Class into existence.

3. Much of the New Class is at first trained under the direct control of the old

class's firms or enterprises. Soon, however, the old class is separated from the reproduction of the New Class by the emergence and development of a public system of education whose costs are "socialized."[17]

4. The more that the New Class's reproduction derives from specialized systems of public education, the more the New Class develops an ideology that stresses its *autonomy*, its separation from and presumable independence of "business" or political interests. This autonomy is said to be grounded in the specialized knowledge or cultural capital transmitted by the educational system, along with an emphasis on the obligation of educated persons to attend to the welfare of the collectivity. In other words, the *ideology* of "professionalism" emerges.

5. Professionalism is one of the public *ideologies* of the New Class, and is the genteel subversion of the old class by the new. Professionalism is a phase in the historical development of the "collective consciousness" of the New Class. While not overtly a critique of the old class, professionalism is a tacit claim by the New Class to *technical and moral superiority* over the old class, implying that the latter lack technical credentials and are guided by motives of commercial venality. Professionalism silently installs the New Class as the paradigm of virtuous and legitimate authority, performing with technical skill and with dedicated concern for the society-at-large. Professionalism makes a focal claim for the legitimacy of the New Class which tacitly deauthorizes the old class.

On the one side, this is a bid for prestige *within* the established society; on the other, it tacitly presents the New Class as an *alternative* to the old. In asserting its own claims to authority, professionalism in effect *devalues the authority of the old class.*

6. The special privileges and powers of the New Class are grounded in their *individual* control of special cultures, languages, techniques, and of the skills resulting from these. The New Class is a cultural bourgeoisie who appropriates privately the advantages of a historically and collectively produced cultural capital. Let us be clear, then: the New Class is not just *like* the old class; its special culture is not just *like* capital. No metaphor is intended. The special culture of the New Class *is* a stock of capital that generates a stream of income (some of) which it appropriates privately.

7. The fundamental objectives of the New Class are: to increase its own share of the national product; to produce and reproduce the special social conditions enabling them to appropriate privately larger shares of the incomes produced by the special cultures they possess; to control their work and their work settings; and to increase their political power partly in order to achieve the foregoing. The struggle of the New Class is, therefore, to *institutionalize a wage system,* i.e., a social system with a distinct principle of distributive justice: "from each according to his ability, to each according to his work," which is also the norm of "socialism." Correspondingly, the New Class may oppose other social systems and their different systems of privilege, for example, systems that allocate privileges and incomes on the basis of controlling stocks of money (i.e., old capital). The New Class, then, is prepared to be egalitarian so far as the privileges of the *old* class are concerned. That is, under certain conditions it is prepared to remove or restrict the special incomes of the old class: profits, rents, interest. The New Class is anti-egalitarian, however, in that it seeks

special guild advantages—political powers and incomes—on the basis of its possession of cultural capital. . . .

The New Class as a Speech Community

1. The culture of critical discourse (CCD)[18] is an historically evolved set of rules, a grammar of discourse, which (1) is concerned to *justify* its assertions, but (2) whose *mode* of justification does not proceed by invoking authorities, and (3) prefers to elicit the *voluntary* consent of those addressed solely on the basis of arguments adduced. CCD is centered on a specific speech act: justification. It is a culture of discourse in which there is nothing that speakers will on principle permanently refuse to discuss or make problematic; indeed, they are even willing to talk about the value of talk itself and its possible inferiority to silence or to practice. This grammar is the deep structure of the common ideology shared by the New Class. *The shared ideology of the intellectuals and intelligentsia is thus an ideology about discourse.* Apart from and underlying the various technical languages (or sociolects) spoken by specialized professions, intellectuals and intelligentsia are commonly committed to a culture of critical discourse (CCD). CCD is the latent but mobilizable infrastructure of modern "technical" languages.

2. The culture of critical discourse is characterized by speech that is *relatively* more *situation-free*, more context or field "independent." This speech culture thus values expressly legislated meanings and devalues tacit, context-limited meanings. Its ideal is: "one word, one meaning," for everyone and forever.

The New Class's special speech variant also stresses the importance of particular modes of *justification*, using especially explicit and articulate rules, rather than diffuse precedents or tacit features of the speech context. The culture of critical speech requires that the validity of claims be justified without reference to the speaker's *societal position or authority.* Here, good speech is speech that can make its own principles *explicit* and is oriented to conforming with them, rather than stressing context-sensitivity and context-variability. Good speech here thus has *theoreticity.*[19]

Being pattern-and-principle-oriented, CCD implies that that which is said may *not* be correct, and may be *wrong.* It recognizes that "What Is" may be mistaken or inadequate and is therefore open to alternatives. CCD is also relatively more *reflexive,* self-monitoring, capable of more metacommunication, that is, of talk about talk; it is able to make its own speech problematic, and to edit it with respect to its lexical and grammatical features, as well as making problematic the validity of its assertions. CCD thus requires considerable "expressive discipline," not to speak of "instinctual renunciation."

3. Most importantly, the culture of critical speech forbids reliance upon the speaker's person, authority, or status in society to justify his claims. As a result, CCD de-authorizes all speech grounded in traditional societal authority, while it authorizes itself, the elaborated speech variant of the culture of critical discourse, as the standard of *all* "serious" speech. From now on, persons and their social positions must not be visible in their speech. Speech becomes impersonal. Speakers hide behind their speech. Speech seems to be dis-embodied, de-contextualized and self-grounded. (This is especially so for the speech of intellectuals and somewhat less

so for technical intelligentsia who may not invoke CCD except when their paradigms break down.) The New Class becomes the guild masters of an invisible pedagogy.

4. The culture of critical discourse is the common ideology shared by the New Class, although technical intelligentsia sometimes keep it in latency. The skills and the social conditions required to reproduce it are among the common *interests* of the New Class. Correspondingly, it is in the common interest of the New Class to prevent or oppose all censorship of its speech variety and to install it as the standard of good speech. *The New Class thus has both a common ideology in CCD and common interests in its cultural capital. . . .*

The Flawed Universal Class

1. The New Class is the most progressive force in modern society and is a center of whatever human emancipation is possible in the foreseeable future. It has no motives to curtail the forces of production and no wish to develop them solely in terms of their profitability. The New Class possesses the scientific knowledge and technical skills on which the future of modern forces of production depend. At the same time, members of the New Class also manifest increasing sensitivity to the ecological "side effects" or distant diseconomies of continuing technical development. The New Class, further, is a center of opposition to almost all forms of censorship, thus embodying a universal societal interest in a kind of rationality broader than that invested in technology. Although the New Class is at the center of nationalist movements throughout the world, after that phase is secured, the New Class is also the most internationalist and most universalist of all social

strata; it is the most cosmopolitan of all elites. Its control over ordinary "foreign" languages, as well as of technical sociolects, enable it to communicate with other nationalities and it is often a member of a technical guild of international scope.

2. For all that, however, the New Class is hardly the end of domination. While its ultimate significance is the end of the old moneyed class's domination, the New Class is also the nucleus of a *new* hierarchy and the elite of a new form of cultural capital.

The historical limits of the New Class are inherent in both the nature of its own characteristic rationality, and in its ambitions as a cultural bourgeoisie. Its culture of critical discourse fosters a purely "theoretical" attitude toward the world. Speakers are held competent to the degree that they know and can *say* the rules, rather than just happening to follow them. The culture of critical discourse thus values the very theoreticity that the "common sense" long suspected was characteristic of intellectuals.

Intellectuals have long believed that those who know the rule, who know the theory by which they act, are superior because they lead an "examined" life. They thus exalt theory over practice, and are concerned less with the success of a practice than that the practice should have submitted itself to a reasonable rule. Since intellectuals and intelligentsia are concerned with doing things in the right way and for the right reason—in other words, since they value doctrinal conformity for its own sake—they (we) have a native tendency toward ritualism and *sectarianism*.

3. The culture of the New Class exacts still other costs: since its discourse emphasizes the importance of carefully edited speech, this has the vices of its virtues: in its *virtuous* aspect, self-editing implies a commendable

circumspection, carefulness, self-discipline and "seriousness." In its negative modality, however, self-editing also disposes toward an unhealthy self-consciousness, toward stilted convoluted speech, an inhibition of play, imagination and passion, and continual pressure for expressive discipline. The new rationality thus becomes the source of a new alienation.

Calling for watchfulness and self-discipline, CCD is productive of intellectual reflexivity *and* the loss of warmth and spontaneity. Moreover, that very reflexivity stresses the importance of adjusting action to some pattern of propriety. There is, therefore, a structured inflexibility when facing changing situations; there is a certain disregard of the differences in situations, and an insistence on hewing to the required rule.

This inflexibility and insensitivity to the force of differing contexts, this inclination to impose one set of rules on different cases also goes by the ancient name of "dogmatism." Set in the context of human relationships, the vulnerability of the New Class to dogmatism along with its very *task*-centeredness, imply a certain insensitivity to *persons,* to their feelings and reactions, and open the way to the disruption of human solidarity. Political brutality, then, finds a grounding in the culture of critical discourse; the new rationality may paradoxically allow a new darkness at noon.

4. The paradox of the New Class is that it is both emancipatory *and* elitist. It subverts all establishments, social limits, and privileges, including its own. The New Class bears a culture of critical and careful discourse which is an historically emancipatory rationality. The new discourse (CCD) is the grounding for a critique of established forms of domination and provides an escape from tradition, but it also bears the seeds of a new domination. Its discourse is a lumbering machinery of argumentation that can wither imagination, discourage play, and curb expressivity. The culture of discourse of the New Class seeks to *control* everything, its topic and itself, believing that such domination is the only road to truth. The New Class begins by monopolizing truth and by making itself its guardian. It thereby makes even the claims of the old class dependent on it. The New Class sets itself above others, holding that its speech is better than theirs; that the examined life (*their* examination) is better than the unexamined life which, it says, is sleep and no better than death. Even as it subverts old inequities, the New Class silently inaugurates a new hierarchy of the knowing, the knowledgeable, the reflexive and insightful. Those who talk well, it is held, excel those who talk poorly or not at all. It is now no longer enough simply to be good. Now, one has to explain it. The New Class is the universal class in embryo, but badly flawed.

NOTES

1. It is not my intention to suggest that modern intellectuals are merely the secular counterpart of clericals. Indeed, my own stress (as distinct, say, from Edward Shils who does appear to view intellectuals as priests *manqués*) is on the discontinuity of the two.

2. For full development of this, see chapter 2, especially p. 42, of my *Dialectic of Ideology and Technology* (New York, 1976).

3. Doubtless some will insist this is a "false consciousness." But this misses the point. My concern here is with their own definitions of their social role, precisely because these influence the manner in which they perform their roles. As W. I. Thomas and Florian Znaniecki long ago (and correctly) insisted, a thing defined as real is real in its consequences. Moreover, the state who employs most of these teachers is itself interested in having

teachers consolidate the tie between students and it itself, rather than with the students' parents.

4. See Basil Bernstein, *Class, Codes and Control,* vol. 1, *Theoretical Studies Towards a Sociology of Language* (London, 1971), vol. 2, *Applied Studies Towards a Sociology of Language* (London, 1973), vol. 3, *Towards a Theory of Educational Transmission* (London, 1975). Bernstein's theory is used here in a critical appropriation facilitated by the work of Dell Hymes and William Labov. My own critique of Bernstein emerges, at least tacitly, in the discussion of [the "Flawed Universal Class"] in the text. It is developed explicitly in my *Dialectic of Ideology and Technology,* pp. 58–66. While Labov has sharply criticized Bernstein, he himself also stresses the general importance of self-monitored speech and of speech *reflexivity* in general (i.e., not only of careful pronunciation) thus converging with Bernstein's focus on reflexivity as characterizing the elaborated linguistic variant and distinguishing it from the restricted variant. See William Labov, *Sociolinguistic Patterns* (Philadelphia, 1972), p. 208.

5. For example: "The Communists disdain to conceal their views and aims. They openly declare . . ." (*Communist Manifesto* [Chicago, 1888], authorized English edition edited by Engels, p. 58).

6. See E. Hobsbawm, *Primitive Rebels* (Manchester, 1959), p. 167 ff.

7. A secret doctrine is one which, because it is reserved only for the organization elite, can be made known only after persons join organizations and reach a certain membership position in it. A secret doctrine thus is never one which can have been a *motive* for joining the organization in the first instance.

8. Lenin's *What Is to Be Done?* was originally published in 1902.

9. *The New Industrial State* (Boston, 1967).

10. *The Coming of Post-Industrial Society* (New York, 1973).

11. *The Modern Corporation and Private Property* (New York, 1932).

12. "It stands to reason that the one who knows more will dominate the one who knows less," M. Bakouinine, *Oeuvres,* Vol. 5 (Paris, 1911), p. 106.

13. See V. F. Calverton, *The Making of Society* (New York, 1937).

14. Talcott Parsons, *The Social System* (Glencoe, 1951), chapter 10; *Essays in Sociological Theory* (Glencoe, 1954), chapter 18; "The Professions," *International Encyclopedia of Social Sciences* (New York, 1968).

15. While Chomsky's position is exhibited in various of his writings, I shall rely here on his most recent statement in his Huizinga lecture, "Intellectuals and the State," delivered at Leiden, 9 October 1977. Citations will be from the manuscript copy. Cf. N. Chomsky, *American Power and the New Mandarins* (New York, 1969).

16. Maurice Zeitlin, "Corporate Ownership and Control: The Large Corporations and the Capitalist Class," *American Journal of Sociology* (March 1974), pp. 1073–1119.

17. Cf. James O'Connor, *Corporations and the State* (New York, 1974), pp. 126–28 for the argument that government financing of R & D and advanced education constitute a socialization of part of the costs of production whose net surplus is privately appropriated.

18. This section is indebted to Basil Bernstein and is based on a critical appropriation of his "elaborated and restricted linguistic codes," which have gone through various re-workings. That controversial classic was published in J. J. Gumperz and D. Hymes, *Directions in Sociolinguistics* (New York, 1972). A recent re-working is to be found in Bernstein's "Social Class, Language, and Socialization," in T. A. Sebeok, ed., *Current Trends in Linguistics* (The Hague, 1974). For full bibliographic and other details see note 4 above.

19. Cf. Peter McHugh, "A Common-Sense Perception of Deviance," in H. P. Dreitzel, ed., *Recent Sociology, Number 2* (London, 1970), pp. 165 ff. For good speech as "serious" speech see David Silverman, "Speaking Seriously," *Theory and Society* (Spring, 1974).

14

Bobos in Paradise

The New Upper Class and How They Got There

DAVID BROOKS

The Rise of the Educated Class

I'm not sure I'd like to be one of the people featured on the *New York Times* wedding page, but I know I'd like to be the father of one of them. Imagine how happy Stanley J. Kogan must have been, for example, when his daughter Jamie was admitted to Yale. Then imagine his pride when Jamie made Phi Beta Kappa and graduated summa cum laude. Stanley himself is no slouch in the brains department: he's a pediatric urologist in Croton-on-Hudson, with teaching positions at the Cornell Medical Center and the New York Medical College. Still, he must have enjoyed a gloat or two when his daughter put on that cap and gown.

And things only got better. Jamie breezed through Stanford Law School. And then she met a man—Thomas Arena—who appeared to be exactly the sort of son-in-law that pediatric urologists dream about. He did his undergraduate work at Princeton, where he, too, made Phi Beta Kappa and graduated summa cum laude. And he, too, went to law school, at Yale. After school they both went

to work as assistant U.S. attorneys for the mighty Southern District of New York.

These two awesome résumés collided at a wedding ceremony in Manhattan, and given all the school chums who must have attended, the combined tuition bills in that room must have been staggering. The rest of us got to read about it on the *New York Times* weddings page. The page is a weekly obsession for hundreds of thousands of *Times* readers and aspiring Balzacs. Unabashedly elitist, secretive, and totally honest, the "mergers and acquisitions page" (as some of its devotees call it) has always provided an accurate look at at least a chunk of the American ruling class. And over the years it has reflected the changing ingredients of elite status.

When America had a pedigreed elite, the page emphasized noble birth and breeding. But in America today it's genius and geniality that enable you to join the elect. And when you look at the *Times* weddings page, you can almost feel the force of the mingling SAT scores. It's Dartmouth marries Berkeley, MBA weds Ph.D., Fulbright hitches with Rhodes, Lazard Frères joins with CBS, and summa cum laude embraces summa cum laude (you rarely see a summa settling for a magna—the tension in such a marriage would be too great). The *Times* emphasizes four things about a person— college degrees, graduate degrees, career path, and parents' profession—for these are the markers of upscale Americans today. . . .

The Fifties

The *Times* weddings page didn't always pulse with the accomplishments of the Résumé Gods. In the late 1950s, the page projected a calm and more stately ethos. The wedding accounts of that era didn't emphasize jobs or advanced degrees. The profession of the groom was only sometimes mentioned, while the profession of the bride was almost never listed (and on the rare occasions when the bride's profession was noted, it was in the past tense, as if the marriage would obviously end her career). Instead, the *Times* listed pedigree and connections. Ancestors were frequently mentioned. The ushers were listed, as were the bridesmaids. Prep schools were invariably mentioned, along with colleges. The *Times* was also careful to list the groom's clubs— the Union League, the Cosmopolitan Club. It also ran down the bride's debutante history, where she came out, and whatever women's clubs she might be a member of, such as the Junior League. In short, the page was a galaxy of restricted organizations. . . .

The section from the late fifties evokes an entire milieu that was then so powerful and is now so dated: the network of men's clubs, country clubs, white-shoe law firms, oak-paneled Wall Street firms, and WASP patriarchs. Everybody has his or her own mental images of the old Protestant Estab-lishment: lockjaw accents, the Social Register, fraternity jocks passing through Ivy League schools, constant rounds of martinis and highballs, bankers' hours, starched old men like Averell Harriman, Dean Acheson, and John J. McCloy, the local bigwigs that appear in John Cheever and John O'Hara stories. . . .

It really was possible to talk about an aristocratic ruling class in the fifties and early sixties, a national elite populated by men who had gone to northeastern prep schools like Groton, Andover, Exeter, and St. Paul's and then ascended through old-line firms on Wall Street into the boardrooms of the Fortune 500 corporations and into the halls of Washington power. The WASPs didn't have total control of the country or anything like it, but they did have the hypnotic magic of prestige. As Richard Rovere wrote in a famous 1962 essay entitled "The American Establishment," "It has very nearly unchallenged power in deciding what is and what is not respectable opinion in this country.". . .

This was the last great age of socially acceptable boozing. It was still an era when fox hunting and polo didn't seem antiquarian. But the two characteristics of that world that strike us forcefully today are its unabashed elitism and its segregation. Though this elite was nowhere near as restrictive as earlier elites—World War II had exerted its leveling influence—the 1950s establishment was still based on casual anti-Semitism, racism, sexism, and a thousand other silent barriers that blocked entry for those without the correct pedigree. Wealthy Jewish and Protestant boys who had been playing together from childhood were forced to endure "The Great Division" at age 17, when Jewish and Gentile society parted into two entirely separate orbits, with separate debutante seasons, dance schools, and social secretaries. A Protestant business executive may have spent his professional hours working intimately with his Jewish colleague, but he never would have dreamed of putting him up for membership in his club. When Senator Barry Goldwater attempted to play golf at the restricted Chevy Chase Club, he was told the club was restricted. "I'm only half Jewish, so can't I play nine holes?" he is said to have replied.

The WASP elite was also genially anti-intellectual. Its members often spoke of "eggheads" and "highbrows" with polite disdain. Instead, their status, as F. Scott Fitzgerald had pointed out a few decades before, derived from "animal magnetism and money." By contrast with today's ruling class, they had relatively uncomplicated attitudes about their wealth. They knew it was vulgar to be gaudy, they tended toward thriftiness, but they seem not to have seen their own money as an affront to American principles of equality. On the contrary, most took their elite status for granted, assuming that such position was simply part of the natural and beneficent order of the universe. There was always going to be an aristocracy, and so for the people who happened to be born into it, the task was to accept the duties that came along with its privileges. . . .

The Hinge Years

Then came the change. By 1960 the average verbal SAT score for incoming freshmen at Harvard was 678, and the math score was 695—these are stratospheric scores. The average Harvard freshman in 1952 would have placed in the bottom 10 percent of the Harvard freshman class of 1960. Moreover, the 1960 class was drawn from a much wider socioeconomic pool. Smart kids from Queens or Iowa or California, who wouldn't have thought of applying to Harvard a decade earlier, were applying and getting accepted. Harvard had transformed itself from a school catering mostly to the northeastern social elite to a high-powered school reaching more of the brightest kids around the country. And this transformation was replicated in almost all elite schools. . . .

History, as Pareto once remarked, is the graveyard of aristocracies, and by the late fifties and early sixties the WASP Establishment had no faith in the code—and the social restrictions—that had sustained it. Maybe its members just lost the will to fight for their privileges. As the writer David Frum theorizes, it had been half a century since the last great age of fortune making. The great families were into at least their third genteel generation. Perhaps by then there wasn't much vigor left. Or perhaps it was the Holocaust that altered the landscape by discrediting the sort of racial restrictions that the Protestant Establishment was built on.

In any case, in 1964 Digby Baltzell astutely perceived the crucial trends. "What seems to be happening," he wrote in *The Protestant Establishment*, "is that a scholarly hierarchy of campus communities governed by the values of admissions committees is gradually supplanting the class hierarchies of local communities which are still governed by the values of parents. . . . Just as the hierarchy of the Church was the main avenue of advancement for the talented and ambitious youth from the lower orders during the medieval period, and just as the business enterprise was responsible for the nineteenth century rags-to-riches dream (when we were predominantly an Anglo-Saxon country), so the campus community has now become the principal guardian of our traditional opportunitarian ideals."

The campus gates were thus thrown open on the basis of brains rather than blood, and within a few short years the university landscape was transformed. Harvard, as we've seen, was changed from a school for the well-connected to a school for brainy strivers. The remaining top schools eliminated their Jewish quotas and eventually dropped their restrictions on women. Furthermore, the sheer numbers of educated Americans exploded. The portion of Americans going to college had been rising steadily throughout the 20th century, but between 1955 and 1974 the growth rate was off the charts. Many of the new students were women. Between 1950 and 1960 the number of female students increased by 47 percent. It then jumped by an additional 168 percent between 1960 and 1970. Over the following decades the student population kept growing and growing. In 1960 there were about 2,000 institutions of higher learning. By 1980 there were 3,200. In 1960 there were 235,000 professors in the United States. By 1980 there were 685,000. . . .

The Sixties

The educated-class rebellion we call "the sixties" was about many things, some of them important and related to the Civil Rights movement and Vietnam, some of them entirely silly, and others, like the sexual revolution, overblown (actual sexual behavior was affected far more by the world wars than by the Woodstock era). But at its core the cultural radicalism of the sixties was a challenge to conventional notions of success. It was not only a political effort to

dislodge the establishment from the seats of power. It was a cultural effort by the rising members of the privileged classes to destroy whatever prestige still attached to the WASP lifestyle and the WASP moral code, and to replace the old order with a new social code that would celebrate spiritual and intellectual ideals. The sixties radicals rejected the prevailing definition of accomplishment, the desire to keep up with the Joneses, the prevailing idea of social respectability, the idea that a successful life could be measured by income, manners, and possessions. . . .

And Then Comes Money

The hardest of the hard-core sixties radicals believed the only honest way out was to reject the notion of success altogether: drop out of the rat race, retreat to small communities where real human relationships would flourish. But that sort of utopianism was never going to be very popular, especially among college grads. Members of the educated class prize human relationships and social equality, but as for so many generations of Americans before them, achievement was really at the core of the sixties grads' value system. They were meritocrats, after all, and so tended to define themselves by their accomplishments. Most of them were never going to drop out or sit around in communes smelling flowers, raising pigs, and contemplating poetry. Moreover, as time went by, they discovered that the riches of the universe were lying at their feet.

At first, when the great hump of baby boom college graduates entered the workforce, having a college degree brought few financial rewards or dramatic life changes. As late as 1976, the labor economist Richard

Freeman could write a book called *The Overeducated American,* arguing that higher education didn't seem to be paying off in the marketplace. But the information age kicked in, and the rewards for education grew and grew. In 1980, according to labor market specialist Kevin Murphy of the University of Chicago, college graduates earned roughly 35 percent more than high school graduates. But by the mid-1990s, college graduates were earning 70 percent more than high school graduates, and those with graduate degrees were earning 90 percent more. The wage value of a college degree had doubled in 15 years.

The rewards for intellectual capital have increased while the rewards for physical capital have not. That means that even liberal arts majors can wake up one day and find themselves suddenly members of the top-income brackets. A full professor at Yale who renounced the capitalist rat race finds himself making, as of 1999, $113,100, while a professor at Rutgers pulls in $103,700 and superstar professors, who become the object of academic bidding wars, now can rake in more than $300,000 a year. Congressional and presidential staffers top out at $125,000 (before quintupling that when they enter the private sector), and the journalists at national publications can now count on six-figure salaries when they hit middle age, not including lecture fees. Philosophy and math majors head for Wall Street and can make tens of millions of dollars from their quantitative models. America has always had a lot of lawyers, and now the median income for that burgeoning group is $72,500, while income for the big-city legal grinds can reach seven figures. And super-students still flood into medicine— three-quarters of private practitioners net more than $100,000. Meanwhile, in Silicon Valley there are more millionaires than people. . . .

The Anxieties of Abundance

Those who want to win educated-class approval must confront the anxieties of abundance: how to show—not least to themselves—that even while climbing toward the top of the ladder they have not become all the things they still profess to hold in contempt. How to navigate the shoals between their affluence and their self-respect. How to reconcile their success with their spirituality, their elite status with their egalitarian ideals. Socially enlightened members of the educated elite tend to be disturbed by the widening gap between rich and poor and are therefore made somewhat uncomfortable by the fact that their own family income now tops $80,000. Some of them dream of social justice yet went to a college where the tuition costs could feed an entire village in Rwanda for a year. Some once had "Question Authority" bumper stickers on their cars but now find themselves heading start-up software companies with 200 people reporting to them. The sociologists they read in college taught that consumerism is a disease, and yet now they find themselves shopping for $3,000 refrigerators. They took to heart the lessons of *Death of a Salesman,* yet now find themselves directing a sales force. They laughed at the plastics scene in *The Graduate* but now they work for a company that manufactures . . . plastic. Suddenly they find themselves moving into a suburban house with a pool and uncomfortable about admitting it to their bohemian friends still living downtown. . . .

The Reconcilers

The grand achievement of the educated elites in the 1990s was to create a way of living that lets you be an affluent success and at the same time a free-spirit rebel. Founding design firms, they find a way to be an artist and still qualify for stock options. Building gourmet companies like Ben & Jerry's or Nantucket Nectars, they've found a way to be dippy hippies and multinational corporate fat cats. Using William S. Burroughs in ads for Nike sneakers and incorporating Rolling Stones anthems into their marketing campaigns, they've reconciled the antiestablishment style with the corporate imperative. Listening to management gurus who tell them to thrive on chaos and unleash their creative potential, they've reconciled the spirit of the imagination with service to the bottom line. Turning university towns like Princeton and Palo Alto into entrepreneurial centers, they have reconciled the highbrow with the high tax bracket. Dressing like Bill Gates in worn chinos on his way to a stockholders' meeting, they've reconciled undergraduate fashion with upper-crust occupations. Going on eco-adventure vacations, they've reconciled aristocratic thrill-seeking with social concern. Shopping at Benetton or the Body Shop, they've brought together consciousness-raising and cost control.

When you are amidst the educated upscalers, you can never be sure if you're living in a world of hippies or stockbrokers. In reality you have entered the hybrid world in which everybody is a little of both.

Marx told us that classes inevitably conflict, but sometimes they just blur. The values of the bourgeois mainstream culture and the values of the 1960s counterculture have merged. That culture war has ended, at least within the educated class. In its place that class has created a third culture, which is a reconciliation between the previous two. The educated elites didn't set out to create this reconciliation. It is the product of millions of individual efforts to have things both ways. But it is now the dominant tone of our age. In the resolution between the culture and the counterculture, it is impossible to tell who co-opted whom, because in reality the bohemians and the bourgeois co-opted each other. They emerge from this process as bourgeois bohemians, or Bobos.

The New Establishment

Today the *New York Times* weddings section is huge once again. In the early 1970s the young rebels didn't want to appear there, but now that their own kids are in college and getting married, they are proud to see their offspring in the Sunday paper. For a fee the *Times* will send you a reproduction of your listing, suitable for framing.

And the young people, the second-generation Bobos, are willing to see their nuptials recorded. Look at the newlyweds on any given Sunday morning, beaming out at you from the pages of the *Times*. Their smiles seem so genuine. They all look so nice and approachable, not dignified or fearsome, the way some of the brides on the 1950s pages did. Things are different but somehow similar. . . .

Today's establishment is structured differently. It is not a small conspiracy of well-bred men with interlocking family and school ties who have enormous influence on the levers of power. Instead, this establishment is a large, amorphous group of meritocrats who share a consciousness and who unself-consciously reshape institutions to accord with their values. They are not confined to a few East Coast institutions. In 1962, Richard Rovere could write, "Nor has the Establishment ever made much headway in such fields as advertising, television or motion pictures." Today's establishment is everywhere. It exercises its power subtly, over ideas and concepts, and therefore pervasively. There are no sure-fire demographic markers to tell who is a member of this establishment. Members tend to have gone to competitive colleges, but not all have. They tend to live in upscale neighborhoods, such as Los Altos, California, and Bloomfield, Michigan, and Lincoln Park, Illinois, but not all do. What unites them is their shared commitment to the Bobo reconciliation. People gain entry into the establishment by performing a series of delicate cultural tasks: they are prosperous without seeming greedy; they have pleased their elders without seeming conformist; they have risen toward the top without too obviously looking down on those below; they have achieved success without committing certain socially sanctioned affronts to the ideal of social equality; they have constructed a prosperous lifestyle while avoiding the old clichés of conspicuous consumption (it's OK to hew to the new clichés).

Obviously, none of this is to suggest that all members of the new Bobo establishment think alike, any more than it's true to say that all members of any establishment think alike. Some of the bourgeois bohemians are more on the bourgeois side; they are stockbrokers who happen to like artists' lofts. Some are on the bohemian side; they are art professors who dabble in the market. Nonetheless, if you look at some quintessential figures of the new establishment—such as Henry Louis Gates, Charlie Rose, Steven Jobs, Doris Kearns Goodwin, David

Geffen, Tina Brown, Maureen Dowd, Jerry Seinfeld, Stephen Jay Gould, Lou Reed, Tim Russert, Steve Case, Ken Burns, Al Gore, Bill Bradley, John McCain, George W. Bush—you can begin to sense a common ethos that mingles 1960s rebellion with 1980s achievement. You can feel the Bobo ethos, too, in the old institutions that have been taken over by the new establishment, such as the *New Yorker,* Yale University, the American Academy of Arts and Letters (which now includes people like Toni Morrison, Jules Feiffer, and Kurt Vonnegut among its members), or the *New York Times* (which now runs editorials entitled "In Praise of the Counterculture"). You can sense the ethos with special force in the new establishment institutions that would have been alien to the old elite: NPR, DreamWorks, Microsoft, AOL, Starbucks, Yahoo, Barnes & Noble, Amazon, and Borders.

And over the past few years, this new educated establishment has begun to assume the necessary role of an establishment. That is to say, it has begun to create a set of social codes that give coherent structure to national life. Today, America once again has a dominant class that defines the parameters of respectable opinion and taste—a class that determines conventional wisdom, that promulgates a code of good manners, that establishes a pecking order to give shape to society, that excludes those who violate its codes, that transmits its moral and etiquette codes down to its children, that imposes social discipline on the rest of society so as to improve the "quality of life," to use the contemporary phrase. . . .

Class Rank

This has got to be one of the most anxious social elites ever. We Bobos are not anxious because there is an angry mob outside the gates threatening to send us to the guillotine. There isn't. The educated elite is anxious because its members are torn between their drive to succeed and their fear of turning into sellouts. Furthermore, we are anxious because we do not award ourselves status sinecures. Previous establishments erected social institutions that would give their members security. In the first part of the 20th century, once your family made it into the upper echelons of society, it was relatively easy to stay there. You were invited on the basis of your connections to the right affairs. You were admitted, nearly automatically, to the right schools and considered appropriate for the right spouses. The pertinent question in those circles was not what do you do, but who are you. Once you were established as a Biddle or an Auchincloss or a Venderlip, your way was clear. But members of today's educated class can never be secure about their own future. A career crash could be just around the corner. In the educated class even social life is a series of aptitude tests; we all must perpetually perform in accordance with the shifting norms of propriety, ever advancing signals of cultivation. Reputations can be destroyed by a disgraceful sentence, a lewd act, a run of bad press, or a terrible speech at the financial summit at Davos.

And more important, members of the educated class can never be secure about their children's future. The kids have some domestic and educational advantages—all those tutors and developmental toys—but they still have to work through school and ace the SATs just to achieve the same social rank as their parents. Compared to past elites, little is guaranteed.

The irony is that all this status insecurity only makes the educated class stronger. Its members and their children must constantly be alert, working and achieving. Moreover, the educated class is in no danger of becoming a self-contained caste. Anybody with the right degree, job, and cultural competencies can join. Marx warned that "the more a ruling class is able to assimilate the most prominent men [or women] of the dominated classes, the more stable and dangerous its rule." And in truth it is hard to see how the rule of the meritocrats could ever come to an end. The WASP Establishment fell pretty easily in the 1960s. It surrendered almost without a shot. But the meritocratic Bobo class is rich with the spirit of self-criticism. It is flexible and amorphous enough to co-opt that which it does not already command. The Bobo meritocracy will not be easily toppled, even if some group of people were to rise up and conclude that it should be.

15

Nickel-and-Dimed

On (not) Getting by in America

BARBARA EHRENREICH

At the beginning of June 1998 I leave behind everything that normally soothes the ego and sustains the body—home, career, companion, reputation, ATM card—for a plunge into the low-wage workforce. There, I become another, occupationally much diminished "Barbara Ehrenreich"—depicted on job-application forms as a divorced homemaker whose sole work experience consists of housekeeping in a few private homes. I am terrified, at the beginning, of being unmasked for what I am: a middle-class journalist setting out to explore the world that welfare mothers are entering, at the rate of approximately 50,000 a month, as welfare reform kicks in. Happily, though, my fears turn out to be entirely unwarranted: during a month of poverty and toil, my name goes unnoticed and for the most part unuttered. In this parallel universe where my father never got out of the mines and I never got through college, I am "baby," "honey," "blondie," and, most commonly, "girl."

My first task is to find a place to live. I figure that if I can earn $7 an hour—which, from the want ads, seems doable—I can afford to spend $500 on rent, or maybe, with severe economies, $600. In the Key West

area, where I live, this pretty much confines me to flophouses and trailer homes—like the one, a pleasing fifteen-minute drive from town, that has no air-conditioning, no screens, no fans, no television, and, by way of diversion, only the challenge of evading the landlord's Doberman pinscher. The big problem with this place, though, is the rent, which at $675 a month is well beyond my reach. . . .

So I decide to make the common trade-off between affordability and convenience, and go for a $500-a-month efficiency thirty miles up a two-lane highway from the employment opportunities of Key West, meaning forty-five minutes if there's no road construction and I don't get caught behind some sun-dazed Canadian tourists. . . .

I am not doing this for the anthropology. My aim is nothing so mistily subjective as to "experience poverty" or find out how it "really feels" to be a long-term low-wage worker. I've had enough unchosen encounters with poverty and the world of low-wage work to know it's not a place you want to visit for touristic purposes; it just smells too much like fear. And with all my real-life assets—bank account, IRA, health

Barbara Ehrenreich, "Nickel-and-Dimed," *Harper's Magazine*, January 1999, pp. 37–52.

insurance, multiroom home—waiting indulgently in the background, I am, of course, thoroughly insulated from the terrors that afflict the genuinely poor.

No, this is a purely objective, scientific sort of mission. The humanitarian rationale for welfare reform—as opposed to the more punitive and stingy impulses that may actually have motivated it—is that work will lift poor women out of poverty while simultaneously inflating their self-esteem and hence their future value in the labor market. Thus, whatever the hassles involved in finding child care, transportation, etc., the transition from welfare to work will end happily, in greater prosperity for all. Now there are many problems with this comforting prediction, such as the fact that the economy will inevitably undergo a downturn, eliminating many jobs. Even without a downturn, the influx of a million former welfare recipients into the low-wage labor market could depress wages by as much as 11.9 percent, according to the Economic Policy Institute (EPI) in Washington, D.C.

But is it really possible to make a living on the kinds of jobs currently available to unskilled people? Mathematically, the answer is no, as can be shown by taking $6 to $7 an hour, perhaps subtracting a dollar or two an hour for child care, multiplying by 160 hours a month, and comparing the result to the prevailing rents. According to the National Coalition for the Homeless, for example, in 1998 it took, on average nationwide, an hourly wage of $8.89 to afford a one-bedroom apartment, and the Preamble Center for Public Policy estimates that the odds against a typical welfare recipient's landing a job at such a "living wage" are about 97 to 1. If these numbers are right,

low-wage work is not a solution to poverty and possibly not even to homelessness. . . .

On the morning of my first full day of job searching, I take a red pen to the want ads, which are auspiciously numerous. Everyone in Key West's booming "hospitality industry" seems to be looking for someone like me—trainable, flexible, and with suitably humble expectations as to pay. I know I possess certain traits that might be advantageous—I'm white and, I like to think, well-spoken and poised—but I decide on two rules: One, I cannot use any skills derived from my education or usual work—not that there are a lot of want ads for satirical essayists anyway. Two, I have to take the best-paid job that is offered me and of course do my best to hold it; no Marxist rants or sneaking off to read novels in the ladies' room. . . .

Most of the big hotels run ads almost continually, just to build a supply of applicants to replace the current workers as they drift away or are fired, so finding a job is just a matter of being at the right place at the right time and flexible enough to take whatever is being offered that day. This finally happens to me at one of the big discount hotel chains, where I go for housekeeping and am sent, instead, to try out as a waitress at the attached "family restaurant," a dismal spot with a counter and about thirty tables that looks out on a parking garage and features such tempting fare as "Pollish [sic] sausage and BBQ sauce" on 95-degree days. Phillip, the dapper young West Indian who introduces himself as the manager, interviews me with about as much enthusiasm as if he were a clerk processing me for Medicare, the principal questions being what shifts can I work and when can I start. I mutter something about being woefully out of practice as a waitress, but he's already on to the uniform: I'm to show up tomorrow wearing black slacks and black shoes; he'll provide the rust-colored polo shirt with Hearthside embroidered on it, though I might want to wear my own shirt to get to work, ha ha. At the word "tomorrow," something between fear and indignation rises in my chest. I want to say, "Thank you for your time, sir, but this is just an experiment, you know, not my actual life."

So begins my career at the Hearthside, I shall call it, one small profit center within a global discount hotel chain, where for two weeks I work from 2:00 till 10:00 P.M. for $2.43 an hour plus tips. In some futile bid for gentility, the management has barred employees from using the front door, so my first day I enter through the kitchen, where a red-faced man with shoulder-length blond hair is throwing frozen steaks against the wall and yelling, "Fuck this shit!" "That's just Jack," explains Gail, the wiry middle-aged waitress who is assigned to train me. "He's on the rag again"—a condition occasioned, in this instance, by the fact that the cook on the morning shift had forgotten to thaw out the steaks. For the next eight hours, I run after the agile Gail, absorbing bits of instruction along with fragments of personal tragedy. All food must be trayed, and the reason she's so tired today is that she woke up in a cold sweat thinking of her boyfriend, who killed himself recently in an upstate prison. No refills on lemonade. And the reason he was in prison is that a few DUIs caught up with him, that's all, could have happened to anyone. Carry the creamers to the table in a monkey bowl, never in your hand. And after he was gone she spent several months living in her truck, peeing in a plastic pee bottle and reading by candlelight at night, but you can't live in a truck in the summer, since you need to have the windows down, which means anything can get in, from mosquitoes on up.

At least Gail puts to rest any fears I had of appearing overqualified. From the first day on, I find that of all the things I have left behind, such as home and identity, what I miss the most is competence. Not that I have ever felt utterly competent in the writing business, in which one day's success augurs nothing at all for the next. But in my writing life, I at least have some notion of procedure: do the research, make the outline, rough out a draft, etc. As a server, though, I am beset by requests like bees: more iced tea here, ketchup over there, a to-go box for table fourteen, and where are the high chairs, anyway? Of the twenty-seven tables, up to six are usually mine at any time, though on slow afternoons or if Gail is off, I sometimes have the whole place to myself. There is the touch-screen computer-ordering system to master, which is, I suppose, meant to minimize server-cook contact, but in practice requires constant verbal fine-tuning: "That's gravy on the mashed, okay? None on the meatloaf," and so forth—while the cook scowls as if I were inventing these refinements just to torment him. Plus, something I had forgotten in the years since I was eighteen: about a third of a server's job is "side work" that's invisible to customers—sweeping, scrubbing, slicing, refilling, and restocking. If it isn't all done, every little bit of it, you're going to face the 6:00 P.M. dinner rush defenseless and probably go down in flames. I screw up dozens of times at the beginning, sustained in my shame entirely by Gail's support—"It's okay, baby, everyone does that sometime"—because, to my total surprise and despite the scientific detachment I am doing my best to maintain, I care. . . .

Sometimes I play with the fantasy that I am a princess who, in penance for some tiny transgression, has undertaken to feed each of her subjects by hand. But the non-princesses working with me are just as indulgent, even when this means flouting management rules—concerning, for example, the number of croutons that can go on a salad (six). "Put on all you want," Gail whispers, "as long as Stu isn't looking." She dips into her own tip money to buy biscuits and gravy for an out-of-work mechanic who's used up all his money on dental surgery, inspiring me to pick up the tab for his milk and pie. . . .

Ten days into it, this is beginning to look like a livable lifestyle. I like Gail, who is "looking at fifty" but moves so fast she can alight in one place and then another without apparently being anywhere between them. I clown around with Lionel, the teenage Haitian busboy, and catch a few fragments of conversation with Joan, the svelte fortyish hostess and militant feminist who is the only one of us who dares to tell Jack to shut the fuck up. I even warm up to Jack when, on a slow night and to make up for a particularly unwarranted attack on my abilities, or so I imagine, he tells me about his glory days as a young man at "coronary school"—or do you say "culinary"?—in Brooklyn, where he dated a knock-out Puerto Rican chick and learned everything there is to know about food. I finish up at 10:00 or 10:30, depending on how much side work I've been able to get done during the shift, and cruise home to the tapes I snatched up at random when I left my real home—Marianne Faithfull, Tracy Chapman, Enigma, King Sunny Ade, the Violent Femmes—just drained enough for the music to set my cranium resonating but hardly dead. Midnight snack is Wheat Thins and Monterey Jack, accompanied by cheap white wine on ice and whatever AMC has to offer. To bed by 1:30 or 2:00, up at 9:00 or 10:00, read for an hour while my uniform whirls around in the landlord's washing machine, and then it's another eight hours spent following Mao's central instruction, as laid out in the Little Red Book, which was: Serve the people.

I could drift along like this, in some dreamy proletarian idyll, except for two things. One is management. If I have kept this subject on the margins thus far it is because I still flinch to think that I spent all those weeks under the surveillance of men (and later women) whose job it was to monitor my behavior for signs of sloth, theft, drug abuse, or worse. Not that managers and especially "assistant managers" in low-wage settings like this are exactly the class enemy. In the restaurant business, they are mostly former cooks or servers, still capable of pinch-hitting in the kitchen or on the floor, just as in hotels they are likely to be former clerks, and paid a salary of only about $400 a week. But everyone knows they have crossed over to the other side, which is, crudely put, corporate as opposed to human. Cooks want to prepare tasty meals; servers want to serve them graciously; but managers are there for only one reason—to make sure that money is made for some theoretical entity that exists far away in Chicago or New York, if a corporation can be said to have a physical existence at all. . . .

Managers can sit—for hours at a time if they want—but it's their job to see that no one else ever does, even when there's nothing to do, and this is why, for servers, slow times can be as exhausting as rushes. You start dragging out each little chore, because if the manager on duty catches you in an idle moment, he will give you something far nastier to do. So I wipe, I clean, I consolidate ketchup bottles and recheck the cheesecake supply, even tour the tables to make sure the customer evaluation forms are all standing perkily in their places—wondering all the time how many calories I burn in these strictly theatrical exercises. When, on a particularly dead afternoon, Stu finds me glancing at a *USA Today* a customer has left behind, he assigns me to vacuum the entire floor with the broken vacuum cleaner that has a handle only two feet long, and the only way to do that without incurring orthopedic damage is to proceed from spot to spot on your knees. . . .

The other problem, in addition to the less-than-nurturing management style, is that this job shows no sign of being financially viable. You might imagine, from a comfortable distance, that people who live, year in and year out, on $6 to $10 an hour have discovered some survival stratagems unknown to the middle class. But no. It's not hard to get my co-workers to talk about their living situations, because housing, in almost every case, is the principal source of disruption in their lives, the first thing they fill you in on when they arrive for their shifts. After a week, I have compiled the following survey:

- Gail is sharing a room in a well-known downtown flophouse for which she and a roommate pay about $250 a week. Her roommate, a male friend, has begun hitting on her, driving her nuts, but the rent would be impossible alone.
- Claude, the Haitian cook, is desperate to get out of the two-room apartment he shares with his girlfriend and two other, unrelated, people. As far as I can

determine, the other Haitian men (most of whom only speak Creole) live in similarly crowded situations.
- Annette, a twenty-year-old server who is six months pregnant and has been abandoned by her boyfriend, lives with her mother, a postal clerk.
- Marianne and her boyfriend are paying $170 a week for a one-person trailer.
- Jack, who is, at $10 an hour, the wealthiest of us, lives in the trailer he owns, paying only the $400-a-month lot fee.
- The other white cook, Andy, lives on his dry-docked boat, which, as far as I can tell from his loving descriptions, can't be more than twenty feet long. He offers to take me out on it, once it's repaired, but the offer comes with inquiries as to my marital status, so I do not follow up on it.
- Tina and her husband are paying $60 a night for a double room in a Days Inn. This is because they have no car and the Days Inn is within walking distance of the Hearthside. When Marianne, one of the breakfast servers, is tossed out of her trailer for subletting (which is against the trailer-park rules), she leaves her boyfriend and moves in with Tina and her husband.
- Joan, who had fooled me with her numerous and tasteful outfits (hostesses wear their own clothes), lives in a van she parks behind a shopping center at night and showers in Tina's motel room. The clothes are from thrift shops.

It strikes me, in my middle-class solipsism, that there is gross improvidence in some of these arrangements. When Gail and I are wrapping silverware in napkins—the only task for which we are permitted to sit—she tells me she is thinking of escaping from her roommate by moving into the Days Inn herself. I am astounded: How can she even think of paying between $40 and $60 a day? But if I was afraid of sounding like a social worker, I come out just sounding like a fool. She squints at me in disbelief, "And where am I supposed to get a month's rent and a month's deposit for an apartment?" I'd been feeling pretty smug about my $500 efficiency, but of course it was made possible only by the $1,300 I had allotted myself for start-up costs when I began my low-wage life: $1,000 for the first month's rent and deposit, $100 for initial groceries and cash in my pocket, $200 stuffed away for emergencies. In poverty, as in certain propositions in physics, starting conditions are everything.

There are no secret economies that nourish the poor; on the contrary, there are a host of special costs. If you can't put up the two months' rent you need to secure an apartment, you end up paying through the nose for a room by the week. If you have only a room, with a hot plate at best, you can't save by cooking up huge lentil stews that can be frozen for the week ahead. You eat fast food, or the hot dogs and Styrofoam cups of soup that can be microwaved in a convenience store. If you have no money for health insurance—and the Hearthside's niggardly plan kicks in only after three months—you go without routine care or prescription drugs and end up paying the price. Gail, for example, was fine until she ran out of money for estrogen pills. She is supposed to be on the company plan by now, but they claim to have lost her application form and need to begin the paperwork all over again. So she spends $9 per migraine pill to control the headaches she wouldn't have, she insists, if her estrogen supplements were covered. Similarly, Marianne's boyfriend lost his job as a roofer because he missed so much time after getting a cut on his foot for which he couldn't afford the prescribed antibiotic.

My own situation, when I sit down to assess it after two weeks of work, would not be much better if this were my actual life. The seductive thing about waitressing is that you don't have to wait for payday to feel a few bills in your pocket, and my tips usually cover meals and gas, plus something left over to stuff into the kitchen drawer I use as a bank. But as the tourist business slows in the summer heat, I sometimes leave work with only $20 in tips (the gross is higher, but servers share about 15 percent of their tips with the busboys and bartenders). With wages included, this amounts to about the minimum wage of $5.15 an hour. Although the sum in the drawer is piling up, at the present rate of accumulation it will be more than a hundred dollars short of my rent when the end of the month comes around. Nor can I see any expenses to cut. True, I haven't gone the lentil-stew route yet, but that's because I don't have a large cooking pot, pot holders, or a ladle to stir with (which cost about $30 at Kmart, less at thrift stores), not to mention onions, carrots, and the indispensable bay leaf. I do make my lunch almost every day—usually some slow-burning, high-protein combo like frozen chicken patties with melted cheese on top and canned pinto beans on the side. Dinner is at the Hearthside, which offers its employees a choice of BLT, fish sandwich, or hamburger for only $2. The burger lasts longest, especially if it's heaped with gut-puckering jalapeños, but by midnight my stomach is growling again.

So unless I want to start using my car as a residence, I have to find a second, or alternative, job. I call all the hotels where I filled out housekeeping applications weeks ago—the Hyatt, Holiday Inn, Econo Lodge, HoJo's, Best Western, plus a half dozen or so locally run guesthouses. Nothing. Then I start making the rounds again, wasting whole mornings waiting for some assistant manager to show up, even dipping into places so creepy that the front-desk clerk greets you from behind bulletproof glass and sells pints of liquor over the counter. But either someone has exposed my real-life housekeeping habits—which are, shall we say, mellow—or I am at the wrong end of some infallible ethnic equation: most, but by no means all, of the working housekeepers I see on my job searches are African Americans, Spanish-speaking, or immigrants from the Central European post-Communist world, whereas servers are almost invariably white and monolingually English-speaking. When I finally get a positive response, I have been identified once again as server material. Jerry's, which is part of a well-known national family restaurant chain and physically attached here to another budget hotel chain, is ready to use me at once. The prospect is both exciting and terrifying, because, with about the same number of tables and counter seats, Jerry's attracts three or four times the volume of customers as the gloomy old Hearthside. . . .

I start out with the beautiful, heroic idea of handling the two jobs at once, and for two days I almost do it: the breakfast/lunch shift at Jerry's, which goes till 2:00, arriving at the Hearthside at 2:10, and attempting to hold out until 10:00. In the ten minutes between jobs, I pick up a spicy chicken sandwich at the Wendy's drive-through window, gobble it down in the car, and change from khaki slacks to black, from Hawaiian to rust polo. There is a problem, though. When during the 3:00 to 4:00 P.M. dead time I finally sit down to wrap silver, my flesh seems to bond to the seat. I try to refuel with a purloined cup of soup, as I've seen Gail and Joan do dozens of times, but a manager catches me and hisses "No eating!" though there's not a customer around to be offended by the sight of food making contact with a server's lips. So I tell Gail I'm going to quit, and she hugs me and says she might just follow me to Jerry's herself.

But the chances of this are minuscule. She has left the flophouse and her annoying roommate and is back to living in her beat-up old truck. But guess what? she reports to me excitedly later that evening: Phillip has given her permission to park overnight in the hotel parking lot, as long as she keeps out of sight, and the parking lot should be totally safe, since it's patrolled by a hotel security guard! With the Hearthside offering benefits like that, how could anyone think of leaving? . . .

Management at Jerry's is generally calmer and more "professional" than at the Hearthside, with two exceptions. One is Joy, a plump, blowsy woman in her early thirties, who once kindly devoted several minutes to instructing me in the correct one-handed method of carrying trays but whose moods change disconcertingly from shift to shift and even within one. Then there's B. J., a.k.a. B. J.-the-bitch, whose contribution is to stand by the kitchen counter and yell, "Nita, your order's up, move it!" or, "Barbara, didn't you see you've got another table out there? Come on, girl!" Among other things, she is hated for having replaced the whipped-cream squirt cans with big plastic whipped-cream-filled baggies that have to be squeezed with both hands—because, reportedly, she saw or thought she saw employees trying to inhale the propellant gas from the squirt cans, in the hope that it might be nitrous oxide. On my third night, she pulls me aside abruptly and brings her face so close that it looks as if she's planning to butt me with her forehead. But instead of saying, "You're fired," she says, "You're doing fine." The only trouble is I'm spending time chatting with customers: "That's how they're getting you." Furthermore I am letting them "run me," which means harassment by sequential demands: you bring the ketchup and they decide they want extra Thousand Island; you bring that and they announce they now need a side of fries; and so on into distraction. Finally she tells me not to take her wrong. She tries to say things in a nice way, but you get into a mode, you know, because everything has to move so fast. . . .

I make friends, over time, with the other "girls" who work my shift: Nita, the tattooed twenty-something who taunts us by going around saying brightly, "Have we started making money yet?" Ellen, whose teenage son cooks on the graveyard shift and who once managed a restaurant in Massachusetts but won't try out for management here because she prefers being a "common worker" and not "ordering people around." Easy-going fiftyish Lucy, with the raucous laugh, who limps toward the end of the shift because of something that has gone wrong with her leg, the exact nature of which cannot be determined without health insurance. We talk about the usual girl things—men, children, and the sinister allure of Jerry's chocolate peanut-butter cream pie—though no one, I notice,

ever brings up anything potentially expensive, like shopping or movies. As at the Hearthside, the only recreation ever referred to is partying, which requires little more than some beer, a joint, and a few close friends. Still, no one here is homeless, or cops to it anyway, thanks usually to a working husband or boyfriend. All in all, we form a reliable mutual-support group: If one of us is feeling sick or overwhelmed, another one will "bev" a table or even carry trays for her. If one of us is off sneaking a cigarette or a pee, the others will do their best to conceal her absence from the enforcers of corporate rationality. . . .

I make the decision to move closer to Key West. First, because of the drive. Second and third, also because of the drive: gas is eating up $4 to $5 a day, and although Jerry's is as high-volume as you can get, the tips average only 10 percent, and not just for a newbie like me. Between the base pay of $2.15 an hour and the obligation to share tips with the busboys and dishwashers, we're averaging only about $7.50 an hour. Then there is the $30 I had to spend on the regulation tan slacks worn by Jerry's servers—a setback it could take weeks to absorb. (I had combed the town's two downscale department stores hoping for something cheaper but decided in the end that these marked-down Dockers, originally $49, were more likely to survive a daily washing.) Of my fellow servers, everyone who lacks a working husband or boyfriend seems to have a second job: Nita does something at a computer eight hours a day; another welds. Without the forty-five-minute commute, I can picture myself working two jobs and having the time to shower between them.

So I take the $500 deposit I have coming from my landlord, the $400 I have earned toward the next month's rent, plus the $200 reserved for emergencies, and use the $1,100 to pay the rent and deposit on trailer number 46 in the Overseas Trailer Park, a mile from the cluster of budget hotels that constitute Key West's version of an industrial park. Number 46 is about eight feet in width and shaped like a barbell inside, with a narrow region—because of the sink and the stove—separating the bedroom from what might optimistically be called the "living" area, with its two-person table and half-sized couch. The bathroom is so small my knees rub against the shower stall when I sit on the toilet, and you can't just leap out of the bed, you have to climb down to the foot of it in order to find a patch of floor space to stand on. Outside, I am within a few yards of a liquor store, a bar that advertises "free beer tomorrow," a convenience store, and a Burger King—but no supermarket or, alas, laundromat. By reputation, the Overseas park is a nest of crime and crack, and I am hoping at least for some vibrant, multicultural street life. But desolation rules night and day, except for a thin stream of pedestrian traffic heading for their jobs at the Sheraton or 7-Eleven. There are not exactly people here but what amounts to canned labor, being preserved from the heat between shifts. . . .

When my month-long plunge into poverty is almost over, I finally land my dream job—housekeeping. I do this by walking into the personnel office of the only place I figure I might have some credibility, the hotel attached to Jerry's, and confiding urgently that I have to have a second job if I am to pay my rent and, no, it couldn't be front-desk clerk. "All right," the personnel lady fairly spits, "So it's housekeeping," and she marches me back to meet Maria, the housekeeping manager, a tiny, frenetic Hispanic woman who greets me as "babe" and hands me a pamphlet emphasizing the need for a positive attitude. The hours are nine in the morning till whenever, the pay is $6.10 an hour, and there's one week of vacation a year. I don't have to ask about health insurance once I meet Carlotta, the middle-aged African-American woman who will be training me. Carla, as she tells me to call her, is missing all of her top front teeth.

On that first day of housekeeping and last day of my entire project—although I don't yet know it's the last—Carla is in a foul mood. We have been given nineteen rooms to clean, most of them "checkouts," as opposed to "stay-overs," that require the whole enchilada of bed-stripping, vacuuming, and bathroom-scrubbing. When one of the rooms that had been listed as a stay-over turns out to be a checkout, Carla calls Maria to complain, but of course to no avail. "So make up the motherfucker," Carla orders me, and I do the beds while she sloshes around the bathroom. For four hours without a break I strip and remake beds, taking about four and a half minutes per queen-sized bed, which I could get down to three if there were any reason to. We try to avoid vacuuming by picking up the larger specks by hand, but often there is nothing to do but drag the monstrous vacuum cleaner—it weighs about thirty pounds—off our cart and try to wrestle it around the floor. Sometimes Carla hands me the squirt bottle of "BAM" (an acronym for something that begins, ominously, with "butyric"; the rest has been worn off the label) and lets me do the bathrooms. No service ethic challenges me here to new heights of performance. I just concentrate on removing the pubic hairs from the bathtubs, or at least the dark ones that I can see. . . .

When I request permission to leave at about 3:30, another housekeeper warns me that no one has so far succeeded in combining housekeeping at the hotel with serving at Jerry's: "Some kid did it once for five days, and you're no kid." With that helpful information in mind, I rush back to number 46, down four Advils, shower, stooping to fit into the stall, and attempt to compose myself for the oncoming shift. So much for what Marx termed the "reproduction of labor power," meaning the things a worker has to do just so she'll be ready to work again. . . .

Then it comes, the perfect storm. Four of my tables fill up at once. Four tables is nothing for me now, but only so long as they are obligingly staggered. As I bev table 27, tables 25, 28, and 24 are watching enviously. As I bev 25, 24 glowers because their bevs haven't even been ordered. Twenty-eight is four yuppyish types, meaning everything on the side and agonizing instructions as to the chicken Caesars. Twenty-five is a middle-aged black couple, who complain, with some justice, that the iced tea isn't fresh and the tabletop is sticky. But table 24 is the meteorological event of the century: ten British tourists who seem to have made the decision to absorb the American experience entirely by mouth. Here everyone has at least two drinks—iced tea and milk shake, Michelob and water (with lemon slice, please)—and a huge promiscuous orgy of breakfast specials, mozz sticks, chicken strips, quesadillas, burgers with cheese and without, sides of hash browns with cheddar, with onions, with gravy, seasoned fries, plain fries, banana splits. Poor Jesus (the cook)! Poor me! Because when I arrive with their first tray of food—after three prior trips just to refill bevs—Princess Di refuses to eat her chicken strips with her pancake-and-

sausage special, since, as she now reveals, the strips were meant to be an appetizer. Maybe the others would have accepted their meals, but Di, who is deep into her third Michelob, insists that everything else go back while they work on their "starters." Meanwhile, the yuppies are waving me down for more decaf and the black couple looks ready to summon the NAACP.

Much of what happened next is lost in the fog of war. Jesus starts going under. The little printer on the counter in front of him is spewing out orders faster than he can rip them off, much less produce the meals. Even the invincible Ellen is ashen from stress. I bring table 24 their reheated main courses, which they immediately reject as either too cold or fossilized by the microwave. When I return to the kitchen with their trays (three trays in three trips), Joy confronts me with arms akimbo: "What is this?" She means the food—the plates of rejected pancakes, hash browns in assorted flavors, toasts, burgers, sausages, eggs. "Uh, scrambled with cheddar," I try, "and that's. . . " "NO," she screams in my face. "Is it a traditional, a super-scramble, an eye-opener?" I pretend to study my check for a clue, but entropy has been up to its tricks, not only on the plates but in my head, and I have to admit that the original order is beyond reconstruction. "You don't know an eye-opener from a traditional?" she demands in outrage. All I know, in fact, is that my legs have lost interest in the current venture and have announced their intention to fold. I am saved by a yuppie (mercifully not one of mine) who chooses this moment to charge into the kitchen to bellow that his food is twenty-five minutes late. Joy screams at him to get the hell out of her kitchen, please, and then turns on Jesus in a fury, hurling an empty tray across the room for emphasis.

I leave. I don't walk out, I just leave. I don't finish my side work or pick up my credit-card tips, if any, at the cash register or, of course, ask Joy's permission to go. And the surprising thing is that you *can* walk out without permission, that the door opens, that the thick tropical night air parts to let me pass, that my car is still parked where I left it. There is no vindication in this exit, no fuck-you surge of relief, just an overwhelming, dank sense of failure pressing down on me and the entire parking lot. I had gone into this venture in the spirit of science, to test a mathematical proposition, but somewhere along the line, in the tunnel vision imposed by long shifts and relentless concentration, it became a test of myself, and clearly I have failed. . . .

When I moved out of the trailer park, I gave the key to number 46 to Gail and arranged for my deposit to be transferred to her. She told me that Joan is still living in her van and that Stu had been fired from the Hearthside. . . .

In one month, I had earned approximately $1,040 and spent $517 on food, gas, toiletries, laundry, phone, and utilities. If I had remained in my $500 efficiency, I would have been able to pay the rent and have $22 left over (which is $78 less than the cash I had in my pocket at the start of the month). During this time I bought no clothing except for the required slacks and no prescription drugs or medical care (I did finally buy some vitamin B to compensate for the lack of vegetables in my diet). Perhaps I could have saved a little on food if I had gotten to a supermarket more often, instead of convenience stores, but it should be noted that I lost almost four pounds in four weeks, on a diet weighted heavily toward burgers and fries.

How former welfare recipients and single mothers will (and do) survive in the low-wage workforce, I cannot imagine. Maybe they will figure out how to condense their lives—including child-raising, laundry, romance, and meals—into the couple of hours between full-time jobs. Maybe they will take up residence in their vehicles, if they have one. All I know is that I couldn't hold two jobs and I couldn't make enough money to live on with one. And I had advantages unthinkable to many of the long-term poor—health, stamina, a working car, and no children to care for and support. . . .

The thinking behind welfare reform was that even the humblest jobs are morally uplifting and psychologically buoying. In reality they are likely to be fraught with insult and stress. But I did discover one redeeming feature of the most abject low-wage work— the camaraderie of people who are, in almost all cases, far too smart and funny and caring for the work they do and the wages they're paid. The hope, of course, is that someday these people will come to know what they're worth, and take appropriate action.

16

The Missing Class

Portraits of the Near Poor in America

KATHERINE S. NEWMAN AND
VICTOR TAN CHEN

Valerie Rushing starts her shift at midnight. A train pulls into the station, and she hops on it, mop in hand. The thirty-three-year-old mother of one is an employee for the Long Island Rail Road, the busiest commuter railroad in North America, which every morning carries an army of groggy suburbanites to their Manhattan offices, and every night shuttles them back home. When their day ends, hers begins. Most nights she'll mop twenty cars. Tonight it's twice that because she's working a double shift—midnight to 8 A.M., and 8 A.M. to 4 P.M.

Toilet duty, of course, is the worst. Long Islanders are a more slovenly sort than the city's notorious subway riders, Valerie grouses. "You figure that they would have some consideration for the next person that is going to use the bathroom, but they don't. They'll throw their whatevers there in the garbage, in the toilet. . . . And they are the most alcoholic people that I know." Every night, an eclectic assortment of paper-sheathed beer cans and bottles awaits her.

But don't feel sorry for Valerie Rushing. With a union card in her pocket, she makes $13.68 an hour (in 1999 dollars), plus full benefits. Her earlier life at the minimum wage—as a child-care worker, shoe-store employee, and fast-food cashier—is a distant memory.

Two years with the Long Island Rail Road have broadened Valerie's outlook. Before, she hardly ventured into the other boroughs; now she feels comfortable traversing the city and doesn't think twice about heading out to Manhattan to shop. Yes, it's janitorial work, but Valerie doesn't complain. "If it's sweeping, it's sweeping," she says. The point is, it pays the bills.

And Valerie has a lot of bills. She has sole responsibility for her daughter and has custody of her niece's six-year-old son because his own grandmother, Valerie's crack-addled sister, can't be bothered. Valerie sets aside part of every paycheck for the children's clothes, toys, and excursions. She puts aside another part to pay for her $700-a-month Brooklyn apartment, and she stashes away what she can toward that suburban house she hopes to buy someday soon.

Valerie is not poor, but she is not middle class. Instead, she occupies an obscure place between rungs of the nation's social ladder— somewhere between working hard and succeeding, between dreaming big and living in the shadow of her ambitions. People like Valerie don't make the headlines. They aren't invited to focus groups. Blue-ribbon commissions on poverty do not include them. They are a forgotten labor force—too prosperous to be the "working poor," too insecure to be "middle income."

They are America's Missing Class.

They are people like Tomás Linares. A year shy of fifty, he is still clocking in seven days a week at two jobs in centers for people with developmental disabilities, where Tomás spends his days patiently demonstrating to his charges how to brush their teeth, reprimanding them for stealing and scratching, and occasionally wrestling an unruly resident to the floor. For his efforts, he makes a little less than $20,000 a year.

Tomás is not poor, but a look at his rundown Brooklyn apartment might suggest otherwise. He lives in an urban borderland sandwiched between two extremes: the concentrated poverty of rampant drug dealing, sporadic gang violence, and shuttered factories that Tomás has known since his youth and the collateral prosperity that middle-class newcomers and mounting real estate prices bring to Brooklyn these days. Divorced and lacking a college education, Tomás has few prospects for rising much higher in life and no illusion that he'll ever leave his seedy corner.

Gloria Hall is part of the Missing Class as well, but perhaps for not much longer. An employee of the city's health department, she stopped working after falling seriously ill. She has insurance, but her policy won't cover the specialized treatment recom-mended for her rare form of cancer. So Gloria is a frequent visitor to the local teaching hospital, a drab health-care assembly line where patients like her are nonchalantly wheeled from room to room, waiting interminably for their release. For Gloria, living in near poverty means walking a tightrope over this frayed net, unsure of what each new step in her treatment will bring.

It also means worrying about what her deteriorating health will mean for her two adolescent sons, who suffer from the affliction of a deadbeat dad. What will happen to them if she dies? Who will care for them when she's not there? She knows that the odds are stacked against children like hers, those who are unlucky enough to be born black and male and statistically at risk—as crime victims and perpetrators, developmentally disabled and dropouts. Her two boys are unluckier still: they live in a household that is not poor but near poor. "I know some parents that are in worse situations than I am, financially," Gloria says. "And they get everything. Every year their kids go away to summer camp.

"You either got to be on the bottom, or you've got to be on the top."

Thirty-seven million Americans live below the poverty line. We know a lot about them because journalists, politicians, think tanks, and social scientists track their lives in great detail. Every time the poverty rate goes up or down, political parties take credit or blame for this important bellwether.

Yet there is a much larger population of Americans that virtually no one pays attention to: the near poor. Fifty-four million Americans—including 21 percent of the nation's children—live in this nether region above the poverty line but well below a secure station. This "Missing Class" is composed of households earning roughly between $20,000 and $40,000 for a family of four.[1]

The hard-won wages of Missing Class families place them beyond the reach of most policies that speak to the conditions of life among the poor. Yet they are decidedly *not* middle-class Americans. In decades past we might have called them working class, but even that label fails to satisfy, now that many Missing Class workers toil in traditionally white-collar domains like health clinics and schools, even as their incomes, households, and neighborhoods lack the solidity of an earlier generation's blue-collar, union-sheltered way of life. Missing Class families earn less money, have few savings to cushion themselves, and send their kids to schools that are underfunded and crowded. The near poor live in inner-ring suburbs and city centers where many of the social problems that plague the truly poor constrain their lives as well. Crime, drugs, and delinquency are less of a problem in near-poor neighborhoods than they are in blighted ghettos, but they are down the block, within earshot, and close enough to threaten their kids.

Sending Missing Class teens to college, the single most important fault line in determining their long-range prospects, is difficult for the near poor. Many are unaware of the financial aid that might await their children. Parents who have never navigated the shoals of college admission are poorly prepared to offer advice, and the schools that might take over this stewardship are overwhelmed with the task of getting kids to graduate in the first place. Near-poor kids are the ones who work many hours while still in high school, who hardly ever see their guidance counselor, and who struggle to complete homework assignments that no one nearby can help them with.

Yet, because their earnings place them above the poverty line, the Missing Class is rarely on the national radar screen. We just don't think about them. This needs to change. The fate of Missing Class families is a test for this country of what it can offer to those citizens—immigrants and native-born alike—who have pulled themselves off the floor that poverty represents. If they can move up, they clear the way for those coming behind them. If they can at least stay where they are, their example will matter to others. But if their children fail to advance— if they fall back into the hole that the parents labored so hard to escape from—we will have defaulted on the promise of this wealthy nation. We will have seen a temporary respite in a single generation from the problems of poverty, only to see it emerge again in the children of the Missing Class. The danger is real—and growing with every new crack in our increasingly open and vulnerable economy.

Ironically, some of their problems stem from what most would agree is an entirely positive aspect of Missing Class life. Near-poor parents are firmly attached to the world of work. While many arrived in the Missing Class as graduates from the ranks of the welfare dependent, they are now lodged in jobs as transit workers, day-care providers, hospital attendants, teachers' aides, and clerical assistants. They pay their taxes and struggle to keep afloat on wages that are better than the minimum—if not by a huge margin. Yet even as these men and women dutifully turn the wheels of the national economy, their devotion to work takes a toll on their family life, especially on their children, who spend long hours in substandard day care or raise themselves in their teen years.

Of necessity, Missing Class families live fairly close to the margins. They have a hard time saving to buffer themselves from downturns in the economy because a large portion of their income disappears into the pockets of landlords and cash registers of grocery stores every month. As long as the adults—and many of the teens—stay on the job, they can manage. But the slightest push can send them hurtling down the income ladder again. In fact, even in the prosperous years of 1996–2002, about 16 percent of the nation's near-poor families lost a tenth or more of their income. It is important to recognize that the majority actually went in the other direction: they gained income in excess of 30 percent. These upwardly mobile families are headed out of the Missing Class for something much better. Nonetheless, the group that slides is not insignificant, and its ranks have probably grown, now that the economy has cooled.

Missing Class Americans live in safer communities than the truly poor. Indeed, many look out upon their neighborhoods in amazement because they are barely recognizable from the destitute and crime-ridden days of yore. As gentrification has taken root in overheated real estate markets, once-affordable enclaves are now almost beyond the reach of the Missing Class. The arrival of affluent new neighbors brings with it more attention from city officials and the police, more investment in the aesthetics of the community, and something closer to a rainbow of complexions on the streets. For the African Americans, Dominicans, and Puerto Ricans who used to "own" these neighborhoods, this is mainly a blessing. Still, some wonder whether they still belong—whether they are still welcome on their own turf.

The children of the Missing Class won't enjoy anything approaching the inheri-tance—in property, cash, or other assets—that their middle-class counterparts will surely reap. These wealth differences are crucial: savings are the safety net that catches you when you falter, but Missing Class families have no such bulwark. As a result, they experience an odd fusion of optimism and insecurity: the former from their upward mobility, the latter from the nagging concern that it could all disappear if just one thing goes wrong. One uninsured child sick enough to pull a parent off the job; one marriage spiraling into divorce; one layoff that shuts off the money spigot.

What's more, Missing Class families live in neighborhoods that are chronically underserved by financial institutions and scrupulously avoided by grocery chains and other major retail outlets. Denied even the most basic infrastructure for savings or loans at reasonable rates and forced to pay a premium on virtually everything they buy, these harried workers turn to check-cashing stores that exact a cut before handing over their wages. They purchase their food, household goods, and furniture at corner bodegas and other small shops with high margins.

At the same time that the pull of rising wages and the push of welfare reform have drawn millions of low-income parents deeper into the labor market, new policies governing the lives of their children have emerged that clash with the demands of the adult work world. The No Child Left Behind Act has thrust the burly arm of the state into third-grade classrooms, where kids used to the demands of finger paints and Autoharps are now sweating high-stakes tests every year. Eight-year-olds wake up with stomachaches because they are afraid of being held back in school if they cannot pass these exams. Missing Class kids do not fret needlessly; the failure rates on statewide tests are high in their neighborhoods.

School district officials have their own problems to contend with. If their charges do not show significant improvement every year, they find their schools on watch lists, threatened with the loss of funds. How do they exact these improvements? Not by themselves. School systems see parents as an auxiliary teaching force. Notes come home every day explaining to parents that they must take their children to the library, read to them, and drill them on their arithmetic. For those who have the time and the skills to tutor their kids, this is not an onerous task. For the immigrant factory worker who leaves home at 7 A.M., commutes ninety minutes each way to a bottle-packing plant, and works a back-breaking eight-hour shift on an assembly line, the additional burden of helping her son with his reading every day is simply too much. All this "neglect" adds up in the end and yields dismal outcomes on high-stakes tests. For teenagers, it also means a license to misbehave. When Mom and Dad are working every hour they can find, no one is around to make sure that Johnny is doing his homework, and now that he's fourteen, there is no longer an after-school program to occupy him. Johnny may live in a safer, higher-income community than his poorer cousins, but chances are his neighborhood abuts rougher enclaves. This sets up temptations and risks that snare many a Missing Class teen.

The kinds of jobs that sustain the near poor may not come with health insurance or retirement benefits attached. For the more fortunate whose employers do bestow these perks, the versions they enjoy are likely to be of lower quality than the middle-class kind. Medical insurance often comes with very high deductibles, amounting to something closer to catastrophic coverage. It's a big step beyond no insurance at all, but it often exposes the Missing Class to medicine of middling quality, not to mention a host of bureaucratic complications not unlike what the uninsured face, including delayed care and expensive emergency-room treatment. And yet Missing Class families, more so than their wealthier counterparts, *need* first-rate health care. They live in apartments laden with lead paint and plagued by roaches. Asthma is epidemic in low-income neighborhoods in part because the housing there is in shambles and situated near highways belching out exhaust fumes. When it comes to health, the near poor and the real poor can be hard to tell apart.

Every family has its own way of making decisions about finances and responsibilities, but among the fragile households of the Missing Class the negotiations are especially contentious and complex. Figuring out who does what and for whom is no easy matter where "recombinant families"—made up of stepparents and children by different fathers—are concerned. What is a stepfather's financial responsibility for his wife's child from an earlier relationship? Is he supposed to buy him new Nikes? Or is that the responsibility of the boy's "real" father? What is a mother to do if her new man doesn't feel like paying for a school uniform? Should she take some of the money that he gives her for the phone bill to cover the cost? And how, exactly, should a mother feel when her tight household budget has to stretch even further because her husband has obligations to the children he had with his first wife?

Millions of divorced Americans cope with these sticky questions, albeit with difficulty. But many Missing Class families have only enough to get by, even when two parents are working. The stress of their dicey finances never bodes well for their marriages. Secrecy is rife. Husbands don't tell their wives what they make; they just dole out money for approved purposes. Working wives keep their earnings to themselves as well. Single mothers lean on boyfriends for help and may make their continued affection contingent on some form of support. Men who live alone make regular cash donations to their girlfriends. Thrusting monetary considerations into relationships of intimacy can lead to mutual wariness, even distrust. It is one of the many ways that life in the Missing Class is so delicately held together, even if it is clearly more comfortable than living below the poverty line.

With all these complexities and uncertainties, one might imagine that being near poor is a bleak existence. Not so. Missing Class families know far too many people who are genuinely mired in hardship to think that they deserve pity. In general, they see a good deal of promise in their lives. Comparisons with others who are in distress are always at hand because the near poor live cheek by jowl with the real poor. Chances are good that the less well-off members of their own extended family are among the truly disadvantaged. The Missing Class sees itself as a success story from this vantage point—albeit one hanging on by its fingernails.

NOTE

1. This is 100–200 percent of the official poverty line in 2006.

17

Poorer by Comparison
Poverty, Work, and Public Policy in Comparative Perspective

TIMOTHY M. SMEEDING

The United States is a famously parochial and "exceptional" country, but nowhere is it more parochial and exceptional than in its treatment of domestic antipoverty policy. By examining cross-nationally comparable measures of income and poverty, we can shed some of that parochialism and come to appreciate how our poverty compares to that of other nations, why we've embarked on the path we have, and where we might go in the future. Comparing recent trends in poverty rates across several nations can also help us understand the relative effectiveness of American social policy and, even more importantly, how it might be made more effective.

While every nation has its own idiosyncratic institutions and policies, reflecting its values, culture, institutions, and history, wide differences in success and failure in fighting poverty are evident from the comparisons that follow. All nations value low poverty, high levels of economic self-reliance, and equality of opportunity for young people, but they differ dramatically in the extent to which they realize these goals. In examining these differences, the United States does not always look very supportive of low-income families. Moreover, we could do much better at reaching these goals if we made it a national priority to help those who try to escape poverty through their own work efforts.

What Is Poverty?

While most rich nations share a concern over low incomes, poverty measurement began as an Anglo American social indicator. In fact, "official" measures of poverty exist in only the United States and the United Kingdom. In Northern Europe and Scandinavia, the debate centers instead on the level of income at which minimum benefits for social programs should be set and what level of income constitutes exclusion from everyday society, not on measuring poverty. Because Northern European and Scandinavian nations recognize that their social programs already ensure a low

Timothy Smeeding, "Poorer by Comparison: Poverty, Work, and Public Policy in Comparative Perspective," *Pathways* (Winter 2008), pp. 3–5.

poverty rate under any reasonable set of measurement standards, there is no need to calculate poverty rates.

For purposes of international comparisons, poverty is almost always a relative concept. A majority of cross-national studies define the poverty threshold as one-half of the average family's income. The official United States poverty line was 28 percent of this level in 2000, though it was 50 percent of this level in 1963 when it was first employed. I define poverty rates in the analyses that follow using this standard relative concept. The measurement utilized here is based on disposable cash income (DPI), which includes all types of money income, minus direct income and payroll taxes and including all cash transfers, such as food stamps and cash housing allowances, and refundable tax credits such as the Earned Income Tax Credit (EITC).

What Do We Find?

Across twenty-one countries with fully comparable data, the overall poverty rate for all persons using the 50 percent poverty threshold varies from 5 percent in Finland to 20 percent in Mexico. The poverty rate is 17 percent in the United States, the second highest of all nations and the highest of all rich nations. The average rate of poverty is 10 percent across the twenty-one countries we observe here (Figure 17.1). Higher overall poverty rates are found, as one might expect, in Mexico, but also in Anglo-Saxon nations (United States, Australia, Canada, Ireland, and the United Kingdom), and southern European nations (Greece, Spain, Italy) with a relatively high level of overall inequality. But even so, Australian, Canadian, and British poverty remain below U.S. levels.

The lowest poverty rates are more common in smaller, well-developed, and high-spending welfare states (Sweden, Finland), where they are about 5 or 6 percent. Moderate rates are found in major European countries, where social policies provide more generous support to single mothers and working women (through paid family leave, for example), and where social assistance benefits are high.

On average, the percentage of children under age 18 who are poor is a slightly larger problem than is overall poverty in these nations, but the cross-national patterns are very similar (Figure 17.2). After Mexico, the U.S. child poverty rate is at 22 percent compared with the 12 percent average over these twenty-one nations. European child poverty rates are lower and Anglo Saxon rates higher among these nations, but the U.S. child poverty rate is more than 4 percentage points higher than in any other rich nation.

Many in America believe that the story of child poverty is one of poor immigrants, given the idea that immigrants are more likely than native citizens both to have low incomes and many children. But two nations with substantially higher fractions of children born to foreigners, Canada and Australia, both have substantially lower child poverty rates than the United States.

Why Are Persons Poor?

But what explains these differences? The short answer is that they result from two main causes: the amount of support we give to the poor (especially the working poor) and the level of wages paid in the United States compared to other nations. Redistributive social expenditures vary greatly across nations. Social expenditures (health,

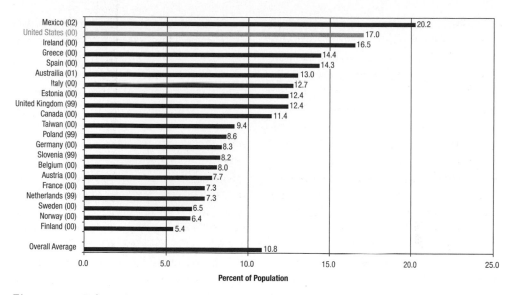
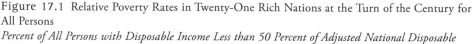

Figure 17.1 Relative Poverty Rates in Twenty-One Rich Nations at the Turn of the Century for All Persons
Percent of All Persons with Disposable Income Less than 50 Percent of Adjusted National Disposable Median Income

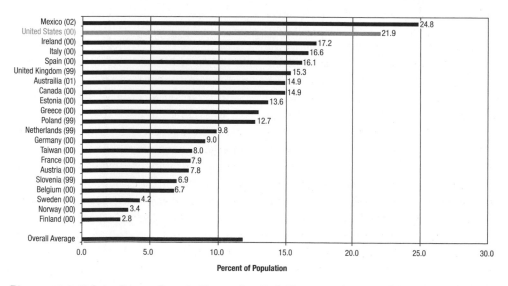

Figure 17.2 Relative Poverty Rates in Twenty-One Rich Nations at the Turn of the Century for Children
Percent of Children with Disposable Income Less than 50 Percent of Adjusted National Disposable Median Income

education, cash, and near cash support) as a fraction of total government spending in Organisation for Economic Co-Operation and development (OECD) nations ranges from 67 percent in Australia to 90 percent in Denmark and Sweden. That is, 67 to 90 percent of all government spending is made up of redistributive cash or in-kind (health, education) benefits. Therefore, social expenditure constitutes most of what most governments actually do. The United States is significantly below all these others in levels of cash spending on the nonelderly and families with children. We spend about 3 percent of national income on benefits for these groups, a level closer to Mexico (which is at 2 percent) than to any of the richer OECD nations (which are all spending at least 6 percent of national income on family benefits).

The United States also has the highest proportion of workers in poorly paid jobs, and the highest number of annual hours worked by poor families with children. Thus despite the larger work effort in the United States, our poverty rates are higher for two reasons: because our jobs pay low wages and because, even with high levels of low-wage work, U.S. antipoverty policy does less to compensate low-wage workers and lift them out of poverty than do other nations.

Of course, antipoverty and social insurance programs are in most respects unique to each country. There is no one kind of program or set of programs that are conspicuously successful in all countries that use them. Social benefits (such as child allowances or fundable tax credits) and targeted social assistance transfer programs for low-income populations are mixed in different ways in different countries. So, too, are minimum wages, worker preparation

and training programs, work-related benefits (such as child care and family leave), and other social benefits.

The United States differs from most nations that achieve lower poverty rates because of its emphasis on work and self-reliance for working-age adults, regardless of the wages workers must accept or the family situations of those workers. For over a decade, U.S. unemployment has been well below average, and until recently American job growth has been much faster than the average. A strong economy coupled with a few specific antipoverty devices (like the expanded support for low income workers through the EITC) has produced most of the poverty reduction of recent years. Despite these factors, the United States does not spend enough to make up for lower levels of pay, and we therefore end up with a relatively higher poverty rate than is found in other nations.

When There Is a Will

As Emmanuel Saez shows in this book, the real incomes of Americans across the income spectrum did rise in the late 1990s, but they fell again after 2000. Most of the gains in recent years have been captured by Americans much further up the income scale, producing a conspicuously wide gap between the incomes of the nation's rich and poor children, elders, and adults. In recent years, the U.K. and especially the U.S. economies have performed better than many other economies where income disparities are smaller. Employment growth has been relatively faster, joblessness lower, and economic growth higher than in most other rich countries where public policy and social convention have kept income disparities low. But if we compare child poverty in the United States with the United Kingdom, using the exact same poverty standards, we see a large difference in recent trends.

Child poverty in both nations began to fall without the help of policy from the mid- to the late 1990s, owning mainly to the strong wage growth and tight labor markets in both countries. Then, after 2000, the patterns of child poverty trends diverged, falling by about half in the United Kingdom as U.S. child poverty actually rose by several percentage points.

Why so? In 1997, Prime Minister Blair announced his nation would rid itself of high child poverty, and in 1999 he instituted a wide and deep set of policies to reduce child poverty. These included high-quality child care and extensive work supports, programs that combine welfare and work (not forcing low-income mothers to give up benefits and survive on work alone), and a working family tax credit (similar to the U.S. EITC program) to increase the return to going to work. As we entered the twenty-first century, when both economies turned sour, the United Kingdom continued to have policy-driven reductions in child poverty while the U.S. poverty decline stopped and even reversed. The poverty rate for U.K. children fell to 11 percent by 2004–2005, while the official U.S. child poverty rate was 18 percent in 2005, according to U.S. Census estimates.

The reason for the big improvement in the United Kingdom is that they had a leader who set a national goal of improving living standards and eradicating child poverty in Britain over the next decade, one who then matched that political rhetoric with large measures of real and continuing fiscal effort to reduce poverty, improve living standards, and support

work. In Britain, former Prime Minister Blair spent an *extra* .9 percent of national incomes since 1999 for low-income families with children. Nine-tenths of a percent of U.S. national income is about $120 billion. This is substantially more than we now spend on the EITC, food stamps, child care support, and other targeted programs combined. The result of this spending in Britain is that child poverty rates in 2000 were 45 percent below their 1999 level, while children's real living standards and the employment levels of their mothers also rose. Meanwhile, children in the United States enjoyed no such gains.

Where to Go From Here?

As long as the United States relies almost exclusively on the job market and low wages to generate incomes for working-age families, economic changes that reduce the earnings of less-skilled workers will inevitably have a big negative effect on poverty among children and prime-age adults. Welfare reform has pushed many low-income women into the labor market and they have stayed there as welfare rolls continue to fall. Even with the $25.4 billion spent on Temporary Assistance for Needy Families today, less than $10 billion is in the form of cash assistance. The rest is now in the form of child care, transportation assistance, training, and other services, which do increase work, but do not address low pay. While the switch from cash to services has undoubtedly helped account for higher earnings among low-income parents, it has not helped move many of them from poverty. In fact, serious gaps with work assistance policies still exist, especially in the child care arena, family leave policy, and health insurance provision.

Labor markets alone cannot reduce poverty because not all of the poor can be expected to "earn" their way out of poverty. Single parents with young children, disabled workers, and the unskilled all face significant challenges earning an adequate income, no matter how much they work. The relationship between antipoverty spending and poverty rates is of course complicated, but the evidence discussed above is very suggestive. U.S. poverty rates, especially among children, are high when compared with those in other industrialized countries. Yet U.S. economic performance has also been good compared with that in most other rich countries. As the British have demonstrated, carefully crafted public policy can certainly reduce poverty if the policy effort is made.

Of course, the high direct and indirect costs of our child poverty are now widely recognized in public debate. The wisdom of expanding programs targeted at children and poor families depends on one's values and subjective views about the economic, political, and moral trade-offs of poverty alleviation. It is hard to argue that the United States cannot afford to do more to help the poor, particularly those that also help themselves via their work efforts. But it has not done so thus far. If the nation is to be successful in reducing poverty, it will need to do a better job of combining work and benefits targeted to low-wage workers in low-income families. There is already hard evidence that such programs produce better outcomes for kids.

If the political history of the United States is any guide, a 5 percent overall relative poverty rate is not a plausible goal. But a gradual reduction in the overall poverty rate from 17 percent overall and 21 percent for children to a level under, say, 12 percent is certainly feasible. This rate would represent a considerable achievement by U.S. standards, but it is worth remembering that this "target" poverty rate is higher than the average poverty levels in the twenty-one nations examined here and would still leave us just below the poverty levels of our Irish, Australian, British, and Canadian counterparts.

18

Jobless Poverty

A New Form of Social Dislocation in the Inner-City Ghetto

WILLIAM JULIUS WILSON

In September 1996 my book, *When Work Disappears: The World of the New Urban Poor,* was published. It describes a new type of poverty in our nation's metropolises: poor, segregated neighborhoods in which a majority of adults are either unemployed or have dropped out of the labor force altogether. What is the effect of these "jobless ghettos" on individuals, families, and neighborhoods? What accounts for their existence? I suggest several factors and conclude with policy recommendations: a mix of public-and-private sector projects is more effective than relying on a strategy of employer subsidies.

The Research Studies

When Work Disappears was based mainly on three research studies conducted in Chicago between 1986 and 1993. The first of these three studies included a variety of data: a random survey of nearly 2,500 poor and nonpoor African American, Latino, and white residents in Chicago's poor neighborhoods; a more focused survey of 175 participants who were reinterviewed and answered open-ended questions; a survey of 179 employers selected to reflect distribution of employment across industry and firm size in the Chicago metropolitan areas; and comprehensive ethnographic research, including participant-observation research and life-history interviews by ten research assistants in a representative sample of inner-city neighborhoods.

The first of the two remaining projects also included extensive data: a survey of a representative sample of 546 black mothers and up to two of their adolescent children (aged eleven to sixteen—or 887 adolescents) in working-class, middle-class, and high-poverty neighborhoods; a survey of a representative sample of 500 respondents from two high-joblessness neighborhoods on the South Side of Chicago; and six focus-group discussions involving the residents and former residents of these neighborhoods.

Jobless Ghettos

The jobless poverty of today stands in sharp contrast to previous periods. In 1950, a substantial portion of the urban black population was poor but they were working. Urban poverty was quite extensive but people held jobs. However, as we entered the 1990s most adults in many inner-city ghetto neighborhoods were not working. For example, in 1950 a significant majority of adults held jobs in a typical week in the three neighborhoods that represent the historic core of the Black Belt in Chicago—Douglas, Grand Boulevard, and Washington Park. But by 1990, only four in ten in Douglas worked in a typical week, one in three in Washington Park, and one in four in Grand Boulevard.[1] In 1950, 69 percent of all males aged fourteen and older who lived in these three neighborhoods worked in a typical week, and in 1960, 64 percent of this group were so employed. However, by 1990 only 37 percent of all males aged sixteen and over held jobs in a typical week in these three neighborhoods.

The disappearance of work has had negative effects not only on individuals and families, but on the social life of neighborhoods as well. Inner-city joblessness is a severe problem that is often overlooked or obscured when the focus is mainly on poverty and its consequences. Despite increases in the concentration of poverty since 1970, inner cities have always featured high levels of poverty. But the levels of inner-city joblessness reached during the first half of the 1990s were unprecedented.

Joblessness versus
Informal Work Activity

I should note that when I speak of "joblessness" I am not solely referring to official unemployment. The unemployment rate represents only the percentage of workers in the *official* labor force—that is, those who are *actively* looking for work. It does not include those who are outside of or have dropped out of the labor market, including the nearly six million males aged twenty-five to sixty who appeared in the census statistics but were not recorded in the labor market statistics in 1990 (Thurow 1990).

These uncounted males in the labor market are disproportionately represented in the inner-city ghettos. Accordingly, in *When Work Disappears,* I use a more appropriate measure of joblessness, a measure that takes into account both official unemployment and non–labor-force participation. That measure is the employment-to-population ratio, which corresponds to the percentage of adults aged sixteen and older who are working. Using the employment-to-population ratio we find, for example, that in 1990 only one in three adults aged sixteen and older held a job in the ghetto poverty areas of Chicago, areas representing roughly 425,000 men, women, and children. And in the ghetto tracts of the nation's one hundred largest cities, for every ten adults who did not hold a job in a typical week in 1990 there were only six employed persons (Kasarda 1993).

The consequences of high neighborhood joblessness are more devastating than those of high neighborhood poverty. A neighborhood in which people are poor but employed is much different than a neighborhood in which people are poor and jobless. *When Work Disappears* shows that many of today's problems in the inner-city ghetto neighborhoods—crime, family dissolution, welfare, low levels of social organization, and so on—are fundamentally a consequence of the disappearance of work.

It should be clear that when I speak of the disappearance of work, I am referring to the declining involvement in or lack of attachment to the formal labor market. It could be argued that, in the general sense of the term, "joblessness" does not necessarily mean "nonwork." In other words, to be officially unemployed or officially outside the labor market does not mean that one is totally removed from all forms of work activity. Many people who are officially jobless are nonetheless involved in informal kinds of work activity, ranging from unpaid housework to work that draws income from the informal or illegal economies.

Housework is work, baby-sitting is work, even drug dealing is work. However, what contrasts work in the formal economy with work activity in the informal and illegal economies is that work in the formal economy is characterized by, indeed calls for, greater regularity and consistency in schedules and hours. Work schedules and hours are formalized. The demands for discipline are greater. It is true that some work activities outside the formal economy also call for discipline and regular schedules. Several studies reveal that the social organization of the drug industry is driven by discipline and a work ethic, however perverse.[2] However, as a general rule, work in the informal and illegal economies is far less governed by norms or expectations that place a premium on discipline and regularity. For all these reasons, when I speak of the disappearance of work, I mean work in the formal economy, work that provides a framework for daily behavior because of the discipline, regularity, and stability that it imposes.

Effect of Joblessness on Routine and Discipline

In the absence of regular employment, a person lacks not only a place in which to work and the receipt of regular income but also a coherent organization of the present—that is, a system of concrete expectations and goals. Regular employment provides the anchor for the spatial and temporal aspects of daily life. It determines where you are going to be and when you are going to be there. In the absence of regular employment, life, including family life, becomes less coherent. Persistent unemployment and irregular employment hinder rational planning in daily life, a necessary condition of adaptation to an industrial economy (Bourdieu 1965).

Thus, a youngster who grows up in a family with a steady breadwinner and in a neighborhood in which most of the adults are employed will tend to develop some of the disciplined habits associated with stable or steady employment—habits that are reflected in the behavior of his or her parents and of other neighborhood adults. These might include attachment to a routine, a recognition of the hierarchy found in most work situations, a sense of personal efficacy attained through the routine management of financial affairs, endorsement of a system of personal and material rewards associated with dependability and responsibility, and so on. Accordingly, when this youngster enters the labor market, he or she has a distinct advantage over the youngsters who grow up in households without a steady breadwinner and in neighborhoods that are not organized around work—in other words, a milieu in which one is more exposed to the less disciplined habits associated with casual or infrequent work.

With the sharp recent rise of solo-parent families, black children who live in inner-city households are less likely to be socialized in a work environment for two main reasons. Their mothers, saddled with child-care responsibilities, can prevent a slide deeper into poverty by accepting welfare. Their fathers, removed from family responsibilities and obligations, are more likely to become idle as a response to restricted employment opportunities, which further weakens their influence in the household and attenuates their contact with the family. In short, the social and cultural responses to joblessness are reflected in the organization of family life and patterns of family formation; there they have implications for labor-force attachment as well.

Given the current policy debates that assign blame to the personal shortcomings of the jobless, we need to understand their behavior as responses and adaptations to chronic subordination, including behaviors that have evolved into cultural patterns. The social actions of the jobless—including their behavior, habits, skills, styles, orientations, attitudes—ought not to be analyzed as if they are unrelated to the broader structure of their opportunities and constraints that have evolved over time. This is not to argue that individuals and groups lack the freedom to make their own choices, engage in certain conduct, and develop certain styles and orientations; but I maintain that their decisions and actions occur within a context of constraints and opportunities that are drastically different from those in middle-class society.

Explanations of the Growth of Jobless Ghettos

What accounts for the growing proportion of jobless adults in inner-city communities? An easy explanation would be racial segregation. However, a race-specific argument is not sufficient to explain recent changes in such neighborhoods. After all, these historical Black Belt neighborhoods were *just as segregated by skin color in 1950* as they are today, yet the level of employment was much higher then. One has to account for the ways in which racial segregation interacts with other changes in society to produce the recent escalating rates of joblessness. Several factors stand out: the decreasing demand for low-skilled labor, the suburbanization of jobs, the social deterioration of ghetto neighborhoods, and negative employer attitudes. I discuss each of these factors next.

Decreasing Demand for Low-Skilled Labor

The disappearance of work in many inner-city neighborhoods is in part related to the nationwide decline in the fortunes of low-skilled workers. The sharp decline in the relative demand for unskilled labor has had a more adverse effect on blacks than on whites because a substantially larger proportion of African Americans are unskilled. Although the number of skilled blacks (including managers, professionals, and technicians) has increased sharply in the last several years, the proportion of those who are unskilled remains large, because the black population, burdened by cumulative experiences of racial restrictions, was overwhelmingly unskilled just several decades ago (Schwartzman 1997).[3]

The factors involved in the decreased relative demand for unskilled labor include changes in skill-based technology, the rapid growth in college enrollment that increased the supply and reduced the relative cost of skilled labor, and the growing internationalization of economic activity, including trade liberalization policies, which reduced the price of imports and raised the output of export industries (Schwartzman 1997). The increased output of export industries aids skilled workers, simply because they are heavily represented in export industries. But increasing imports, especially those from developing countries that compete with labor-intensive industries (for example, apparel, textile, toy, footwear, and some manufacturing industries), hurts unskilled labor (Schwartzman 1997).

Accordingly, inner-city blacks are experiencing a more extreme form of the economic marginality that has affected most unskilled workers in America since 1980. Unfortunately, there is a tendency among policy makers, black leaders, and scholars alike to separate the economic problems of the ghetto from the national and international trends affecting American families and neighborhoods. If the economic problems of the ghetto are defined solely in racial terms they can be isolated and viewed as only requiring race-based solutions as proposed by those on the left, or as only requiring narrow political solutions with subtle racial connotations (such as welfare reform), as strongly proposed by those on the right.

Overemphasis on Racial Factors

Race continues to be a factor that aggravates inner-city black employment problems as we shall soon see. But the tendency to overemphasize the racial factors obscures other more fundamental forces that have sharply increased inner-city black joblessness. As the late black economist Vivian Henderson put it several years ago, "[I]t is as if racism having put blacks in their economic place steps aside to watch changes in the economy destroy that place" (Henderson 1975, 54). To repeat, the concentrated joblessness of the inner-city poor represents the most dramatic form of the growing economic dislocations among the unskilled stemming in large measure from changes in the organization of the economy, including the global economy.

Suburbanization of Jobs

But inner-city workers face an additional problem: the growing suburbanization of jobs. Most ghetto residents cannot afford an automobile and therefore have to rely on public transit systems that make the connection between inner-city neighborhoods and suburban job locations difficult and time consuming.

Although studies based on data collected before 1970 showed no consistent or convincing effects on black employment as a consequence of this spatial mismatch, the employment of inner-city blacks relative to suburban blacks has clearly deteriorated since then. Recent research (conducted mainly by urban labor economists) strongly shows that the decentralization of employment is continuing and that employment in manufacturing, most of which is already suburbanized, has decreased in central cities, particularly in the Northeast and Midwest (Holzer 1996).

Blacks living in central cities have less access to employment (as measured by the ratio of jobs to people and the average travel time to and from work) than do central-city whites. Moreover, unlike most other groups of workers across the urban-suburban divide, less-educated central-city blacks receive lower wages than suburban blacks who have similar levels of education. And the decline in earnings of central-city blacks is related to the decentralization of employment—that is, the movement of jobs from the cities to the suburbs—in metropolitan areas (Holzer 1996).

Social Deterioration of Ghetto Neighborhoods

Changes in the class, racial, and demographic composition of inner-city neighborhoods have also contributed to the high percentage of jobless adults in these neighborhoods. Because of the steady out-migration of more advantaged families, the proportion of nonpoor families and prime-age working adults has decreased sharply in the typical inner-city ghetto since 1970 (Wilson 1987). In the face of increasing and prolonged joblessness, the declining proportion of nonpoor families and the overall depopulation has made it increasingly difficult to sustain basic neighborhood institutions or to achieve adequate levels of social organization. The declining presence of working- and middle-class blacks has also deprived ghetto neighborhoods of key structural and cultural resources. Structural resources include residents with income high enough to sustain neighborhood services, and cultural resources include conventional role models for neighborhood children.

On the basis of our research in Chicago, it appears that what many high jobless neighborhoods have in common is a relatively high degree of social integration (high levels of local neighboring while being relatively isolated from contacts in the broader mainstream society) and low levels of informal social control (feelings that they have little control over their immediate environment, including the environment's negative influences on their children). In such areas, not only are children at risk because of the lack of informal social controls, they are also disadvantaged because the social interaction among neighbors tends to be confined to those whose skills, styles, orientations, and habits are not as conducive to promoting positive social outcomes (academic success, pro-social behavior, employment in the formal labor market, etc.) as those in more stable neighborhoods. Although the close

interaction among neighbors in such areas may be useful in devising strategies, disseminating information, and developing styles of behavior that are helpful in a ghetto milieu (teaching children to avoid eye-to-eye contact with strangers and to develop a tough demeanor in the public sphere for self-protection), they may be less effective in promoting the welfare of children in society at large.

Despite being socially integrated, the residents in Chicago's ghetto neighborhoods shared a feeling that they had little informal social control over the children in their environment. A primary reason is the absence of a strong organizational capacity or an institutional resource base that would provide an extra layer of social organization in their neighborhoods. It is easier for parents to control the behavior of the children in their neighborhoods when a strong institutional resource base exists and when the links between community institutions such as churches, schools, political organizations, businesses, and civic clubs are strong or secure. The higher the density and stability of formal organizations, the less illicit activities such as drug trafficking, crime, prostitution, and the formation of gangs can take root in the neighborhood.

Few Community Institutions

A weak institutional resource base is what distinguishes high jobless inner-city neighborhoods from stable middle-class and working-class areas. As one resident of a high jobless neighborhood on the South Side of Chicago put it, "Our children, you know, seems to be more at risk than any other children there is, because there's no library for them to go to. There's not a center they can go to, there's no field house that they can go into. There's nothing.

There's nothing at all." Parents in high jobless neighborhoods have a much more difficult task controlling the behavior of their adolescents and preventing them from getting involved in activities detrimental to pro-social development. Given the lack of organizational capacity and a weak institutional base, some parents choose to protect their children by isolating them from activities in the neighborhood, including avoiding contact and interaction with neighborhood families. Wherever possible, and often with great difficulty when one considers the problems of transportation and limited financial resources, they attempt to establish contacts and cultivate relations with individuals, families, and institutions, such as church groups, schools, and community recreation programs, outside their neighborhood. A note of caution is necessary, though. It is just as indefensible to treat inner-city residents as super heroes who overcome racist oppression as it is to view them as helpless victims. We should, however, appreciate the range of choices, including choices representing cultural influences that are available to inner-city residents who live under constraints that most people in the larger society do not experience.

Effect of Joblessness on Marriage and Family

It is within the context of labor-force attachment that the public policy discussion on welfare reform and family values should be couched. The research that we have conducted in Chicago suggests that as employment prospects recede, the foundation for stable relationships becomes weaker over time. More permanent relationships such as marriage give way to temporary liaisons that result in broken unions, out-of-wedlock pregnancies, and, to a lesser extent, separation and divorce. The changing norms concerning marriage in the larger society reinforce the movement toward temporary liaisons in the inner city, and therefore economic considerations in marital decisions take on even greater weight. Many inner-city residents have negative outlooks toward marriage, outlooks that are developed in and influenced by an environment featuring persistent joblessness.

The disrupting effect of joblessness on marriage and family causes poor inner-city blacks to be even more disconnected from the job market and discouraged about their role in the labor force. The economic marginality of the ghetto poor is cruelly reinforced, therefore, by conditions in the neighborhoods in which they live.

Negative Employer Attitudes

In the eyes of employers in metropolitan Chicago, the social conditions in the ghetto render inner-city blacks less desirable as workers, and therefore many are reluctant to hire them. One of the three studies that provided the empirical foundation for *When Work Disappears* included a representative sample of employers in the greater Chicago area who provided entry-level jobs. An overwhelming majority of these employers, both white and black, expressed negative views about inner-city ghetto workers, and many stated that they were reluctant to hire them. For example, a president of an inner-city manufacturing firm expressed a concern about employing residents from certain inner-city neighborhoods:

> If somebody gave me their address, uh, Cabrini Green I might unavoidably have some concerns.
> *Interviewer:* What would your concerns be?

That the poor guy probably would be frequently unable to get to work and . . . I probably would watch him more carefully even if it wasn't fair, than I would with somebody else. I know what I should do though is recognize that here's a guy that is trying to get out of his situation and probably will work harder than somebody else who's already out of there and he might be the best one around here. But I, I think I would have to struggle accepting that premise at the beginning. (Wilson 1996, field notes)

In addition to qualms about the neighborhood milieu of inner-city residents, the employers frequently mentioned concerns about applicants' language skills and educational training. An employer from a computer software firm in Chicago expressed the view "that in many businesses the ability to meet the public is paramount and you do not talk street talk to the buying public. Almost all your black welfare people talk street talk. And who's going to sit them down and change their speech patterns?" (Wilson 1996, field notes) A Chicago real estate broker made a similar point:

A lot of times I will interview applicants who are black, who are sort of lower class. . . . They'll come to me and I cannot hire them because their language skills are so poor. Their speaking voice for one thing is poor . . . they have no verbal facility with the language . . . and these . . . you know, they just don't know how to speak and they'll say "salesmens" instead of "salesmen" and that's a problem. . . . They don't know punctuation, they don't know how to use correct grammar, and they cannot spell. And I can't hire them. And I feel bad about

that and I think they're being very disadvantaged by the Chicago Public School system. (Wilson 1996, field notes)

Another respondent defended his method of screening out most job applicants on the telephone on the basis of their use of "grammar and English":

I have every right to say that that's a requirement for this job. I don't care if you're pink, black, green, yellow or orange, I demand someone who speaks well. You want to tell me that I'm a bigot, fine, call me a bigot. I know blacks, you don't even know they're black. (Wilson 1996, field notes)

Finally, an inner-city banker claimed that many blacks in the ghetto "simply cannot read. When you're talking our type of business, that disqualifies them immediately, we don't have a job here that doesn't require that somebody have minimum reading and writing skills" (Wilson 1996, field notes).

How should we interpret the negative attitudes and actions of employers? To what extent do they represent an aversion to blacks *per se* and to what degree do they reflect judgments based on the job-related skills and training of inner-city blacks in a changing labor market? I should point out that the statements made by the African American employers concerning the qualifications of inner-city black workers did not differ significantly from those of the white employers. Whereas 74 percent of all the white employers who responded to the open-ended questions expressed negative views of the job-related traits of inner-city blacks, 80 percent of the black employers did so as well.

This raises a question about the meaning and significance of race in certain situations—in other words, how race intersects with other factors. A key hypothesis in this connection is that given the recent shifts in the economy, employers are looking for workers with a broad range of abilities: "hard" skills (literacy, numerical ability, basic mechanical ability, and other testable attributes) and "soft" skills (personalities suitable to the work environment, good grooming, group-oriented work behaviors, etc.). While hard skills are the product of education and training—benefits that are apparently in short supply in inner-city schools—soft skills are strongly tied to culture, and are therefore shaped by the harsh environment of the inner-city ghetto. For example, our research revealed that many parents in the inner-city ghetto neighborhoods of Chicago wanted their children not to make eye-to-eye contact with strangers and to develop a tough demeanor when interacting with people on the streets. While such behaviors are helpful for survival in the ghetto, they hinder successful interaction in mainstream society.

Statistical Discrimination

If employers are indeed reacting to the difference in skills between white and black applicants, it becomes increasingly difficult to discuss the motives of employers: are they rejecting inner-city black applicants out of overt racial discrimination or on the basis of qualifications?

Nonetheless, many of the selective recruitment practices do represent what economists call "statistical discrimination": employers make assumptions about the inner-city black workers *in general* and reach decisions based on those assumptions before they have had a chance to review systematically the qualifications of an individual applicant. The net effect is that many black inner-city applicants are never given the chance to prove their qualifications on an individual level because they are systematically screened out by the selective recruitment process.

Statistical discrimination, although representing elements of class bias against poor workers in the inner city, is clearly a matter of race both directly and indirectly. Directly, the selective recruitment patterns effectively screen out far more black workers from the inner city than Hispanic or white workers from the same types of backgrounds. But indirectly, race is also a factor, even in those decisions to deny employment to inner-city black workers on the basis of objective and thorough evaluations of their qualifications. The hard and soft skills among inner-city blacks that do not match the current needs of the labor market are products of racially segregated communities, communities that have historically featured widespread social constraints and restricted opportunities.

Thus the job prospects of inner-city workers have diminished not only because of the decreasing relative demand for low-skilled labor in the United States economy, the suburbanization of jobs, and the social deterioration of ghetto neighborhoods, but also because of negative employer attitudes. This combination of factors presents a real challenge to policy makers. Indeed, considering the narrow range of social policy options in the "balance-the-budget" political climate, how can we immediately alleviate the inner-city jobs problem—a problem which will undoubtedly grow when the new welfare reform bill takes full effect and creates a situation that will be even more harmful to inner-city children and adolescents?

Public Policy Dilemmas

What are the implications of these studies on public policy? A key issue is public-sector employment. If firms in the private sector cannot hire or refuse to hire low-skilled adults who are willing to take minimum-wage jobs, then policy makers should consider a policy of public-sector employment-of-last-resort. Indeed, until current changes in the labor market are reversed or until the skills of the next generation of workers can be upgraded before they enter the labor market, many workers, especially those who are not in the official labor force, will not be able to find jobs unless the government becomes an employer-of-last-resort (Danziger and Gottschalk 1995). This argument applies especially to low-skilled inner-city black workers. It is bad enough that they face the problem of shifts in labor-market demand shared by all low-skilled workers; it is even worse that they confront negative employer perceptions about their work-related skills and attitudes.

For all these reasons, the passage of the 1996 welfare reform bill, which did not include a program of job creation, could have very negative social consequences in the inner city. Unless something is done to enhance the employment opportunities of inner-city welfare recipients who reach the time limit for the receipt of welfare, they will flood a pool already filled with low-skilled, jobless workers. . . .

West Virginia, a state that has been plagued with a severe shortage of work opportunities, has provided community service jobs to recipients of welfare for several years. In Wisconsin, Governor Thompson's welfare reform plan envisions community service jobs for many parents in the more depressed areas of the state, and the New Hope program in Milwaukee provides community service jobs for those unable to find employment in the private sector (Center on Budget and Policy Priorities 1996). It is especially important that this mixed strategy include a plan to make *adequate* monies available to localities or communities with high jobless and welfare dependency rates.

Obviously, as more people become employed and gain work experience, they will have a better chance of finding jobs in the private sector when jobs become available. The attitudes of employers toward inner-city workers could change, in part because they would be dealing with job applicants who have steady work experience and who could furnish references from their previous supervisors. Children are more likely to be socialized in a work-oriented environment and to develop the job readiness skills that are seen as important even for entry-level jobs.

Thus, given the recent welfare reform legislation, *adequate* strategies to enhance the employment opportunities of inner-city residents should be contemplated, strategies that would be adequately financed and designed to address the employment problems of low-skilled workers not only in periods of tight labor markets, but, even more important, in periods when the labor market is slack.

NOTES

1. The figures on adult employment are based on calculations from data provided by the 1990 U.S. Bureau of the Census (1993) and the *Local Community Fact Book for Chicago—1950* (1953) and the *Local Community Fact Book for Chicago—1960* (1963). The adult employment rates represent the number of employed individuals (aged fourteen and older in 1950 and sixteen

and older in 1990) among the total number of adults in a given area. Those who are not employed include both the individuals who are members of the labor force but are not working and those who have dropped out or are not part of the labor force.

2. See, for example, Bourgois (1995) and Venkatesh (1996).

3. The economist David Schwartzman defines "unskilled workers to include operators, fabricators, and laborers, and those in service occupations, including private household workers, those working in protective service occupations, food service, and cleaning and building service." On the basis of this definition he estimates that 80 percent of all black workers and 38 percent of all white workers were unskilled in 1950. By 1990, 46 percent of black workers and 27 percent of white workers were employed in unskilled occupations (Schwartzman 1997).

BIBLIOGRAPHY

Bourdieu, Pierre. 1965. *Travail et Travailleurs en Algerie.* Paris: Editions Mouton.

Bourgois, Philippe. 1995. *In Search of Respect: Selling Crack in El Barrio.* New York: Cambridge University Press.

Center on Budget and Policy Priorities. 1996. *The Administration's $3 Billion Jobs Proposal.* Washington, DC: Center on Budget and Policy Priorities.

Danziger, Sheldon H., and Peter Gottschalk. 1995. *America Unequal.* Cambridge, MA: Harvard University Press.

Henderson, Vivian. 1975. "Race, Economics, and Public Policy." *Crisis* 83 (Fall):50–55.

Holzer, Harry J. 1996. *What Employers Want: Job Prospects for Less-Educated Workers.* New York: Russell Sage.

Kasarda, John D. 1993. "Inner-City Concentrated Poverty and Neighborhood Distress: 1970–1990." *Housing Policy Debate* 4(3): 253–302.

Local Community Fact Book for Chicago—1950. 1953. Chicago: Community Inventory, University of Chicago.

Local Community Fact Book for Chicago—1960. 1963. Chicago: Community Inventory, University of Chicago.

Schwartzman, David. 1997. *Black Unemployment: Part of Unskilled Unemployment.* Westport, CT: Greenwood.

Thurow, Lester. 1990. "The Crusade That's Killing Prosperity." *American Prospect* March/April:54–59.

U.S. Bureau of the Census. 1993. *Census of Population: Detailed Characteristics of the Population.* Washington, DC: U.S. Government Printing Office.

Venkatesh, Sudhir. 1996. "Private Lives, Public Housing: An Ethnography of the Robert Taylor Homes." Ph.D. dissertation, University of Chicago.

Wilson, William Julius. 1987. *The Truly Disadvantaged: The Inner City, the Underclass, and Public Policy.* Chicago: University of Chicago Press.

———. 1996. *When Work Disappears: The World of the New Urban Poor.* New York: Alfred A. Knopf.

19

American Apartheid

Segregation and the Making of the Underclass

DOUGLAS S. MASSEY AND
NANCY A. DENTON

It is quite simple. As soon as there is a group area then all your uncertainties are removed and that is, after all, the primary purpose of this Bill [requiring racial segregation in housing].

—Minister of the Interior, Union of South Africa
legislative debate on the Group Areas Act of 1950

During the 1970s and 1980s a word disappeared from the American vocabulary.[1] It was not in the speeches of politicians decrying the multiple ills besetting American cities. It was not spoken by government officials responsible for administering the nation's social programs. It was not mentioned by journalists reporting on the rising tide of homelessness, drugs, and violence in urban America. It was not discussed by foundation executives and think-tank experts proposing new programs for unemployed parents and unwed mothers. It was not articulated by civil rights leaders speaking out against the persistence of racial inequality; and it was nowhere to be found in the thousands of pages written by social scientists on the urban underclass. The word was segregation.

Most Americans vaguely realize that urban America is still a residentially segregated society, but few appreciate the depth of black segregation or the degree to which it is maintained by ongoing institutional arrangements and contemporary individual actions. They view segregation as an unfortunate holdover from a racist past, one that is fading progressively over time. If racial residential segregation persists, they reason, it is only because civil rights laws passed during the 1960s have not had enough time to work or because many blacks still prefer to live in black neighborhoods. The residential segregation of blacks is viewed charitably as a "natural" out-

Douglas S. Massey and Nancy A. Denton, *American Apartheid: Segregation and the Making of the Underclass* (Cambridge, Mass.: Harvard University Press, 1993), pp. 1–9, 12–16, 239–241. Copyright © 1993 by the President and Fellows of Harvard University Press. Reprinted by permission of the publisher.

come of impersonal social and economic forces, the same forces that produced Italian and Polish neighborhoods in the past and that yield Mexican and Korean areas today.

But black segregation is not comparable to the limited and transient segregation experienced by other racial and ethnic groups, now or in the past. No group in the history of the United States has ever experienced the sustained high level of residential segregation that has been imposed on blacks in large American cities for the past fifty years. This extreme racial isolation did not just happen; it was manufactured by whites through a series of self-conscious actions and purposeful institutional arrangements that continue today. Not only is the depth of black segregation unprecedented and utterly unique compared with that of other groups, but it shows little sign of change with the passage of time or improvements in socioeconomic status.

If policymakers, scholars, and the public have been reluctant to acknowledge segregation's persistence, they have likewise been blind to its consequences for American blacks. Residential segregation is not a neutral fact; it systematically undermines the social and economic well-being of blacks in the United States. Because of racial segregation, a significant share of black America is condemned to experience a social environment where poverty and joblessness are the norm, where a majority of children are born out of wedlock, where most families are on welfare, where educational failure prevails, and where social and physical deterioration abound. Through prolonged exposure to such an environment, black chances for social and economic success are drastically reduced.

Deleterious neighborhood conditions are built into the structure of the black community. They occur because segregation concen-

trates poverty to build a set of mutually reinforcing and self-feeding spirals of decline into black neighborhoods. When economic dislocations deprive a segregated group of employment and increase its rate of poverty, socioeconomic deprivation inevitably becomes more concentrated in neighborhoods where that group lives. The damaging social consequences that follow from increased poverty are spatially concentrated as well, creating uniquely disadvantaged environments that become progressively isolated—geographically, socially, and economically—from the rest of society.

The effect of segregation on black well-being is structural, not individual. Residential segregation lies beyond the ability of any individual to change; it constrains black life chances irrespective of personal traits, individual motivations, or private achievements. For the past twenty years this fundamental fact has been swept under the rug by policymakers, scholars, and theorists of the urban underclass. Segregation is the missing link in prior attempts to understand the plight of the urban poor. As long as blacks continue to be segregated in American cities, the United States cannot be called a race-blind society.

The Forgotten Factor

The present myopia regarding segregation is all the more startling because it once figured prominently in theories of racial inequality. Indeed, the ghetto was once seen as central to black subjugation in the United States. In 1944 Gunnar Myrdal wrote in *An American Dilemma* that residential segregation "is basic in a mechanical sense. It exerts its influence in an indirect and impersonal way: because Negro people do not live near white people, they cannot . . . associate with each other in the many activities founded on common neighborhood. Residential segregation . . . becomes reflected in uni-racial schools, hospitals, and other institutions" and creates "an artificial city . . . that permits any prejudice on the part of public officials to be freely vented on Negroes without hurting whites."[2]

Kenneth B. Clark, who worked with Gunnar Myrdal as a student and later applied his research skills in the landmark *Brown v. Topeka* school integration case, placed residential segregation at the heart of the U.S. system of racial oppression. In *Dark Ghetto,* written in 1965, he argued that "the dark ghetto's invisible walls have been erected by the white society, by those who have power, both to confine those who have *no* power and to perpetuate their powerlessness. The dark ghettos are social, political, educational, and—above all—economic colonies. Their inhabitants are subject peoples, victims of the greed, cruelty, insensitivity, guilt, and fear of their masters."[3]

Public recognition of segregation's role in perpetuating racial inequality was galvanized in the late 1960s by the riots that erupted in the nation's ghettos. In their aftermath, President Lyndon B. Johnson appointed a commission chaired by Governor Otto Kerner of Illinois to identify the causes of the violence and to propose policies to prevent its recurrence. The Kerner Commission released its report in March 1968 with the shocking admonition that the United States was "moving toward two societies, one black, one white—separate and unequal."[4] Prominent among the causes that the commission identified for this growing racial inequality was residential segregation.

In stark, blunt language, the Kerner Commission informed white Americans that "discrimination and segregation have long permeated much of American life; they now threaten the future of every American."[5] "Segregation and poverty have created in the racial ghetto a destructive environment totally unknown to most white Americans. What white Americans have never fully understood—but what the Negro can never forget—is that white society is deeply implicated in the ghetto. White institutions created it, white institutions maintain it, and white society condones it."[6]

The report argued that to continue present policies was "to make permanent the division of our country into two societies; one, largely Negro and poor, located in the central cities; the other, predominantly white and affluent, located in the suburbs."[7] Commission members rejected a strategy of ghetto enrichment coupled with abandonment of efforts to integrate, an approach they saw "as another way of choosing a permanently divided country."[8] Rather, they insisted that the only reasonable choice for America was "a policy which combines ghetto enrichment with programs designed to encourage integration of substantial numbers of Negroes into the society outside the ghetto."[9]

America chose differently. Following the passage of the Fair Housing Act in 1968, the problem of housing discrimination was declared solved, and residential segregation dropped off the national agenda. Civil rights leaders stopped pressing for the enforcement of open housing, political leaders increasingly debated employment and educational policies rather than housing integration, and academicians focused their theoretical scrutiny on everything from culture to family structure, to institutional racism, to federal welfare systems. Few people spoke of racial segregation as a problem or acknowledged its persisting consequences. By the end of the 1970s residential segregation became the forgotten factor in American race relations.[10]

While public discourse on race and poverty became more acrimonious and more focused on divisive issues such as school busing, racial quotas, welfare, and affirmative action, conditions in the nation's ghettos steadily deteriorated.[11] By the end of the 1970s, the image of poor minority families mired in an endless cycle of unemployment, unwed childbearing, illiteracy, and dependency had coalesced into a compelling and powerful concept: the urban underclass.[12] In the view of many middle-class whites, inner cities had come to house a large population of poorly educated single mothers and jobless men—mostly black and Puerto Rican—who were unlikely to exit poverty and become self-sufficient. In the ensuing national debate on the causes for this persistent poverty, four theoretical explanations gradually emerged: culture, racism, economics, and welfare.

Cultural explanations for the underclass can be traced to the work of Oscar Lewis, who identified a "culture of poverty" that he felt promoted patterns of behavior inconsistent with socioeconomic advancement.[13] According to Lewis, this culture originated in endemic unemployment and chronic social immobility, and provided an ideology that allowed poor people to cope with feelings of hopelessness and despair that arose because their chances for socioeconomic success were remote. In individuals, this culture was typified by a lack of impulse control, a strong present-time orientation, and little ability to defer gratifica-

tion. Among families, it yielded an absence of childhood, an early initiation into sex, a prevalence of free marital unions, and a high incidence of abandonment of mothers and children.

Although Lewis explicitly connected the emergence of these cultural patterns to structural conditions in society, he argued that once the culture of poverty was established, it became an independent cause of persistent poverty. This idea was further elaborated in 1965 by the Harvard sociologist and then Assistant Secretary of Labor Daniel Patrick Moynihan, who in a confidential report to the President focused on the relationship between male unemployment, family instability, and the intergenerational transmission of poverty, a process he labeled a "tangle of pathology."[14] He warned that because of the structural absence of employment in the ghetto, the black family was disintegrating in a way that threatened the fabric of community life.

When these ideas were transmitted through the press, both popular and scholarly, the connection between culture and economic structure was somehow lost, and the argument was popularly perceived to be that "people were poor because they had a defective culture." This position was later explicitly adopted by the conservative theorist Edward Banfield, who argued that lower-class culture—with its limited time horizon, impulsive need for gratification, and psychological self-doubt—was primarily responsible for persistent urban poverty.[15] He believed that these cultural traits were largely imported, arising primarily because cities attracted lower-class migrants.

The culture-of-poverty argument was strongly criticized by liberal theorists as a self-serving ideology that "blamed the victim."[16] In the ensuing wave of reaction, black families were viewed not as weak but, on the contrary, as resilient and well-adapted survivors in an oppressive and racially prejudiced society.[17] Black disadvantages were attributed not to a defective culture but to the persistence of institutional racism in the United States. According to theorists of the underclass such as Douglas Glasgow and Alphonso Pinkney, the black urban underclass came about because deeply imbedded racist practices within American institutions—particularly schools and the economy—effectively kept blacks poor and dependent.[18]

As the debate on culture versus racism ground to a halt during the late 1970s, conservative theorists increasingly captured public attention by focusing on a third possible cause of poverty: government welfare policy. According to Charles Murray, the creation of the underclass was rooted in the liberal welfare state.[19] Federal antipoverty programs altered the incentives governing the behavior of poor men and women, reducing the desirability of marriage, increasing the benefits of unwed childbearing, lowering the attractiveness of menial labor, and ultimately resulted in greater poverty.

A slightly different attack on the welfare state was launched by Lawrence Mead, who argued that it was not the generosity but the permissiveness of the U.S. welfare system that was at fault.[20] Jobless men and unwed mothers should be required to display "good citizenship" before being supported by the state. By not requiring anything of the poor, Mead argued, the welfare state undermined their independence and competence, thereby perpetuating their poverty.

This conservative reasoning was subsequently attacked by liberal social scientists, led principally by the sociologist William

Julius Wilson, who had long been arguing for the increasing importance of class over race in understanding the social and economic problems facing blacks.[21] In his 1987 book *The Truly Disadvantaged*, Wilson argued that persistent urban poverty stemmed primarily from the structural transformation of the inner-city economy.[22] The decline of manufacturing, the suburbanization of employment, and the rise of a low-wage service sector dramatically reduced the number of city jobs that paid wages sufficient to support a family, which led to high rates of joblessness among minorities and a shrinking pool of "marriageable" men (those financially able to support a family). Marriage thus became less attractive to poor women, unwed childbearing increased, and female-headed families proliferated. Blacks suffered disproportionately from these trends because, owing to past discrimination, they were concentrated in locations and occupations particularly affected by economic restructuring.

Wilson argued that these economic changes were accompanied by an increase in the spatial concentration of poverty within black neighborhoods. This new geography of poverty, he felt, was enabled by the civil rights revolution of the 1960s, which provided middle-class blacks with new opportunities outside the ghetto.[23] The out-migration of middle-class families from ghetto areas left behind a destitute community lacking the institutions, resources, and values necessary for success in post-industrial society. The urban underclass thus arose from a complex interplay of civil rights policy, economic restructuring, and a historical legacy of discrimination.

Theoretical concepts such as the culture of poverty, institutional racism, welfare disincentives, and structural economic change have all been widely debated. None of these explanations, however, considers residential segregation to be an important contributing cause of urban poverty and the underclass. In their principal works, Murray and Mead do not mention segregation at all;[24] and Wilson refers to racial segregation only as a historical legacy from the past, not as an outcome that is institutionally supported and actively created today.[25] Although Lewis mentions segregation sporadically in his writings, it is not assigned a central role in the set of structural factors responsible for the culture of poverty, and Banfield ignores it entirely. Glasgow, Pinkney, and other theorists of institutional racism mention the ghetto frequently, but generally call not for residential desegregation but for race-specific policies to combat the effects of discrimination in the schools and labor markets. In general, then, contemporary theorists of urban poverty do not see high levels of black-white segregation as particularly relevant to understanding the underclass or alleviating urban poverty.[26]

The purpose of this chapter is to redirect the focus of public debate back to issues of race and racial segregation, and to suggest that they should be fundamental to thinking about the status of black Americans and the origins of the urban underclass. Our quarrel is less with any of the prevailing theories of urban poverty than with their systematic failure to consider the important role that segregation has played in mediating, exacerbating, and ultimately amplifying the harmful social and economic processes they treat.

We join earlier scholars in rejecting the view that poor urban blacks have an autonomous "culture of poverty" that explains their failure to achieve socioeconomic success in American society. We argue instead that residential segregation has been instrumental in creating a structural niche within which a deleterious set of attitudes and behaviors—a culture of segregation—has arisen and flourished. Segregation created the structural conditions for the emergence of an oppositional culture that devalues work, schooling, and marriage and that stresses attitudes and behaviors that are antithetical and often hostile to success in the larger economy. Although poor black neighborhoods still contain many people who lead conventional, productive lives, their example has been overshadowed in recent years by a growing concentration of poor, welfare-dependent families that is an inevitable result of residential segregation.

We readily agree with Glasgow, Pinkney, and others that racial discrimination is widespread and may even be institutionalized within large sectors of American society, including the labor market, the educational system, and the welfare bureaucracy. We argue, however, that this view of black subjugation is incomplete without understanding the special role that residential segregation plays in enabling all other forms of racial oppression. Residential segregation is the institutional apparatus that supports other racially discriminatory processes and binds them together into a coherent and uniquely effective system of racial subordination. Until the black ghetto is dismantled as a basic institution of American urban life, progress ameliorating racial inequality in other arenas will be slow, fitful, and incomplete.

We also agree with William Wilson's basic argument that the structural transformation of the urban economy undermined economic supports for the black community during the 1970s and 1980s.[27] We argue, however, that in the absence of segregation, these structural changes would not have produced the disastrous social and economic outcomes observed in inner cities during these decades. Although rates of black poverty were driven up by the economic dislocations Wilson identifies, it was segregation that confined the increased deprivation to a small number of densely settled, tightly packed, and geographically isolated areas.

Wilson also argues that concentrated poverty arose because the civil rights revolution allowed middle-class blacks to move out of the ghetto. Although we remain open to the possibility that class-selective migration did occur,[28] we argue that concentrated poverty would have happened during the 1970s with or without black middle-class migration. Our principal objection to Wilson's focus on middle-class out-migration is not that it did not occur, but that it is misdirected: focusing on the flight of the black middle class deflects attention from the real issue, which is the limitation of black residential options through segregation.

Middle-class households—whether they are black, Mexican, Italian, Jewish, or Polish—always try to escape the poor. But only blacks must attempt their escape within a highly segregated, racially segmented housing market. Because of segregation, middle-class blacks are less able to escape than other groups, and as a result are exposed to more poverty. At the same time, because of segregation no one will move into a poor black neighborhood except other poor blacks. Thus both middle-class blacks and poor blacks lose compared with the poor and middle class of other groups: poor blacks live under unrivaled concentrations of poverty and affluent blacks live in neighborhoods that are far less advanta-

geous than those experienced by the middle class of other groups.

Finally, we concede Murray's general point that federal welfare policies are linked to the rise of the urban underclass, but we disagree with his specific hypothesis that generous welfare payments, by themselves, discouraged employment, encouraged unwed childbearing, undermined the strength of the family, and thereby caused persistent poverty.[29] We argue instead that welfare payments were only harmful to the socioeconomic well-being of groups that were residentially segregated. As poverty rates rose among blacks in response to the economic dislocations of the 1970s and 1980s, so did the use of welfare programs. Because of racial segregation, however, the higher levels of welfare receipt were confined to a small number of isolated, all-black neighborhoods. By promoting the spatial concentration of welfare use, therefore, segregation created a residential environment within which welfare dependency was the norm, leading to the intergenerational transmission and broader perpetuation of urban poverty.

Coming to Terms with American Apartheid

Our fundamental argument is that racial segregation—and its characteristic institutional form, the black ghetto—are the key structural factors responsible for the perpetuation of black poverty in the United States. Residential segregation is the principal organizational feature of American society that is responsible for the creation of the urban underclass. . . . It can be shown that any increase in the poverty rate of a residentially segregated group leads to an immediate and automatic increase in the geographic concentration of poverty. When the rate of minority poverty is increased under conditions of high segregation, all of the increase is absorbed by a small number of neighborhoods. When the same increase in poverty occurs in an integrated group, the added poverty is spread evenly throughout the urban area, and the neighborhood environment that group members face does not change much.

During the 1970s and 1980s, therefore, when urban economic restructuring and inflation drove up rates of black and Hispanic poverty in many urban areas, underclass communities were created only where increased minority poverty coincided with a high degree of segregation—principally in older metropolitan areas of the northeast and the midwest. Among Hispanics, only Puerto Ricans developed underclass communities, because only they were highly segregated; and this high degree of segregation is directly attributable to the fact that a large proportion of Puerto Ricans are of African origin.

The interaction of intense segregation and high poverty leaves black neighborhoods extremely vulnerable to fluctuations in the urban economy, because any dislocation that causes an upward shift in black poverty rates will also produce a rapid change in the concentration of poverty and, hence, a dramatic shift in the social and economic composition of black neighborhoods. The concentration of poverty, for example, is associated with the wholesale withdrawal of commercial institutions and the deterioration or elimination of goods and services distributed through the market.

Neighborhoods, of course, are dynamic and constantly changing, and given the high rates of residential turnover characteristic of contemporary American cities, their well-being depends to a great extent on the characteristics and actions of their residents. Decisions taken by one actor affect the subsequent decisions of others in the neighborhood. In this way isolated actions affect the well-being of the community and alter the stability of the neighborhood.

Because of this feedback between individual and collective behavior, neighborhood stability is characterized by a series of thresholds, beyond which various self-perpetuating processes of decay take hold. Above these thresholds, each actor who makes a decision that undermines neighborhood well-being makes it increasingly likely that other actors will do the same. Each property owner who decides not to invest in upkeep and maintenance, for example, lowers the incentive for others to maintain their properties. Likewise, each new crime promotes psychological and physical withdrawal from public life, which reduces vigilance within the neighborhood and undermines the capacity for collective organization, making additional criminal activity more likely.

Segregation increases the susceptibility of neighborhoods to these spirals of decline. During periods of economic dislocation, a rising concentration of black poverty is associated with the simultaneous concentration of other negative social and economic conditions. Given the high levels of racial segregation characteristic of American urban areas, increases in black poverty such as those observed during the 1970s can only lead to a concentration of housing abandonment, crime, and social disorder, pushing poor black neighborhoods beyond the threshold of stability.

By building physical decay, crime, and social disorder into the residential structure of black communities, segregation creates a harsh and extremely disadvantaged environment to which ghetto blacks must adapt. In concentrating poverty, moreover, segregation also concentrates conditions such as drug use, joblessness, welfare dependency, teenage childbearing, and unwed parenthood, producing a social context where these conditions are not only common but the norm. By adapting to this social environment, ghetto dwellers evolve a set of behaviors, attitudes, and expectations that are sharply at variance with those common in the rest of American society.

As a direct result of the high degree of racial and class isolation created by segregation, for example, Black English has become progressively more distant from Standard American English, and its speakers are at a clear disadvantage in U.S. schools and labor markets. Moreover, the isolation and intense poverty of the ghetto provides a supportive structural niche for the emergence of an "oppositional culture" that inverts the values of middle-class society. Anthropologists have found that young people in the ghetto experience strong peer pressure not to succeed in school, which severely limits their prospects for social mobility in the larger society. Quantitative research shows that growing up in a ghetto neighborhood increases the likelihood of dropping out of high school, reduces the probability of attending college, lowers the likelihood of employment, reduces income earned as an adult, and increases the risk of teenage childbearing and unwed pregnancy.

Segregation also has profound political consequences for blacks, because it so isolates them geographically that they are the only ones who benefit from public expenditures in their neighborhoods. The relative integration of most ethnic groups means that jobs or services allocated to them will

generally benefit several other groups at the same time. Integration thus creates a basis for political coalitions and pluralist politics, and most ethnic groups that seek public resources are able to find coalition partners because other groups can anticipate sharing the benefits. That blacks are the only ones to benefit from resources allocated to the ghetto—and are the only ones harmed when resources are removed—makes it difficult for them to find partners for political coalitions. Although segregation paradoxically makes it easier for blacks to elect representatives, it limits their political influence and marginalizes them within the American polity. Segregation prevents blacks from participating in pluralist politics based on mutual self-interest.

Because of the close connection between social and spatial mobility, segregation also perpetuates poverty. One of the primary means by which individuals improve their life chances—and those of their children—is by moving to neighborhoods with higher home values, safer streets, higher-quality schools, and better services. As groups move up the socioeconomic ladder, they typically move up the residential hierarchy as well, and in doing so they not only improve their standard of living but also enhance their chances for future success. Barriers to spatial mobility are barriers to social mobility, and by confining blacks to a small set of relatively disadvantaged neighborhoods, segregation constitutes a very powerful impediment to black socioeconomic progress.

Despite the obvious deleterious consequences of black spatial isolation, policymakers have not paid much attention to segregation as a contributing cause of urban poverty and have not taken effective steps to dismantle the ghetto. Indeed, for most of the past two decades public policies tolerated and even supported the perpetuation of segregation in American urban areas. Although many political initiatives were launched to combat discrimination and prejudice in the housing and banking industries, each legislative or judicial act was fought tenaciously by a powerful array of people who believed in or benefited from the status quo.

Although a comprehensive open housing bill finally passed Congress under unusual circumstances in 1968, it was stripped of its enforcement provisions as its price of enactment, yielding a Fair Housing Act that was structurally flawed and all but doomed to fail. As documentation of the law's defects accumulated in multiple congressional hearings, government reports, and scholarly studies, little was done to repair the situation until 1988, when a series of scandals and political errors by the Reagan administration finally enabled a significant strengthening of federal antidiscrimination law.

Yet even more must be done to prevent the permanent bifurcation of the United States into black and white societies that are separate and unequal. As of 1990, levels of racial segregation were still extraordinarily high in the nation's large urban areas, particularly those of the north. Segregation has remained high because fair housing enforcement relies too heavily on the private efforts of individual victims of discrimination. Whereas the processes that perpetuate segregation are entrenched and institutionalized, fair housing enforcement is individual, sporadic, and confined to a small number of isolated cases.

As long as the Fair Housing Act is enforced individually rather than systemically, it is unlikely to be effective in overcoming the structural arrangements that support

segregation and sustain the ghetto. Until the government throws its considerable institutional weight behind efforts to dismantle the ghetto, racial segregation will persist. . . .

Ultimately, however, dismantling the ghetto and ending the long reign of racial segregation will require more than specific bureaucratic reforms; it requires a moral commitment that white America has historically lacked. The segregation of American blacks was no historical accident; it was brought about by actions and practices that had the passive acceptance, if not the active support, of most whites in the United States. Although America's apartheid may not be rooted in the legal strictures of its South African relative, it is no less effective in perpetuating racial inequality, and whites are no less culpable for the socioeconomic deprivation that results.

As in South Africa, residential segregation in the United States provides a firm basis for a broader system of racial injustice. The geographic isolation of Africans within a narrowly circumscribed portion of the urban environment—whether African townships or American ghettos—forces blacks to live under extraordinarily harsh conditions and to endure a social world where poverty is endemic, infrastructure is inadequate, education is lacking, families are fragmented, and crime and violence are rampant.[30] Moreover, segregation confines these unpleasant by-products of racial oppression to an isolated portion of the urban geography far removed from the experience of most whites. Resting on a foundation of segregation, apartheid not only denies blacks their rights as citizens but forces them to bear the social costs of their own victimization.

Although Americans have been quick to criticize the apartheid system of South

Africa, they have been reluctant to acknowledge the consequences of their own institutionalized system of racial separation. The topic of segregation has virtually disappeared from public policy debates; it has vanished from the list of issues on the civil rights agenda; and it has been ignored by social scientists spinning endless theories of the underclass. Residential segregation has become the forgotten factor of American race relations, a minor footnote in the ongoing debate on the urban underclass. Until policymakers, social scientists, and private citizens recognize the crucial role of America's own apartheid in perpetuating urban poverty and racial injustice, the United States will remain a deeply divided and very troubled society.[31]

NOTES

1. Epigraph from Edgar H. Brookes, *Apartheid: A Documentary Study of Modern South Africa* (London: Routledge and Kegan Paul, 1968), p. 142.

2. Gunnar Myrdal, *An American Dilemma*, vol. 1 (New York: Harper and Brothers, 1944), p. 618; see also Walter A. Jackson, *Gunnar Myrdal and America's Conscience* (Chapel Hill: University of North Carolina Press, 1990), pp. 88–271.

3. Kenneth B. Clark, *Dark Ghetto: Dilemmas of Social Power* (New York: Harper and Row, 1965), p. 11.

4. U.S. National Advisory Commission on Civil Disorders, *The Kerner Report* (New York: Pantheon Books, 1988), p. 1.

5. Ibid.

6. Ibid., p. 2.

7. Ibid., p. 22.

8. Ibid.

9. Ibid.

10. A few scholars attempted to keep the Kerner Commission's call for desegregation alive, but their voices have largely been unheeded in the ongoing debate. Thomas Pettigrew has continued to assert the central importance of residential segregation, calling it the "linchpin" of American race relations; see "Racial Change and Social Policy," *Annals of the American Academy of Political and Social Science* 441 (1979):114–31. Gary Orfield has repeatedly pointed out segregation's deleterious effects on black prospects for education, employment, and socioeconomic mobility; see "Separate Societies: Have the Kerner Warnings Come True?" in Fred R. Harris and Roger W. Wilkins, eds., *Quiet Riots: Race and Poverty in the United States* (New York: Pantheon Books, 1988), pp. 100–122; and "Ghettoization and Its Alternatives," in Paul E. Peterson, ed., *The New Urban Reality* (Washington, D.C.: Brookings Institution, 1985), pp. 161–96.

11. See Thomas B. Edsall and Mary D. Edsall, *Chain Reaction: The Impact of Race, Rights, and Taxes on American Politics* (New York: Norton, 1991).

12. For an informative history of the evolution of the concept of the underclass, see Michael B. Katz, *The Undeserving Poor: From the War on Poverty to the War on Welfare* (New York: Pantheon, 1989), pp. 185–235.

13. Oscar Lewis, *La Vida: A Puerto Rican Family in the Culture of Poverty—San Juan and New York* (New York: Random House, 1965); "The Culture of Poverty," *Scientific American* 215 (1966): 19–25; "The Culture of Poverty," in Daniel P. Moynihan, ed., *On Understanding Poverty: Perspectives from the Social Sciences* (New York: Basic Books, 1968), pp. 187–220.

14. The complete text of this report is reprinted in Lee Rainwater and William L. Yancey, *The Moynihan Report and the Politics of Controversy* (Cambridge: MIT Press, 1967), pp. 39–125.

15. Edward C. Banfield, *The Unheavenly City* (Boston: Little, Brown, 1970).

16. William Ryan, *Blaming the Victim* (New York: Random House, 1971).

17. Carol Stack, *All Our Kin: Strategies of Survival in a Black Community* (New York: Harper and Row, 1974).

18. Douglas C. Glasgow, *The Black Underclass: Poverty, Unemployment, and Entrapment of Ghetto Youth* (New York: Vintage, 1981), p. 11; Alphonso Pinkney, *The Myth of Black Progress*

(Cambridge: Cambridge University Press, 1984), pp. 78–80.

19. Charles Murray, *Losing Ground: American Social Policy, 1950–1980* (New York: Basic Books, 1984).

20. Lawrence M. Mead, *Beyond Entitlement: The Social Obligations of Citizenship* (New York: Free Press, 1986).

21. William Julius Wilson, *The Declining Significance of Race: Blacks and Changing American Institutions* (Chicago: University of Chicago Press, 1978).

22. William Julius Wilson, *The Truly Disadvantaged: The Inner City, the Underclass, and Public Policy* (Chicago: University of Chicago Press, 1987), pp. 1–108.

23. Ibid., pp. 49–62.

24. The subject indices of *Losing Ground* and *Beyond Entitlement* contain no references at all to residential segregation.

25. The subject index of *The Truly Disadvantaged* contains two references to pre1960s Jim Crow segregation.

26. Again with the exception of Thomas Pettigrew and Gary Orfield.

27. We have published several studies documenting how the decline of manufacturing, the suburbanization of jobs, and the rise of low-wage service employment eliminated high-paying jobs for manual workers, drove up rates of black male unemployment, and reduced the attractiveness of marriage to black women, thereby contributing to a proliferation of female-headed families and persistent poverty. See Mitchell L. Eggers and Douglas S. Massey, "The Structural Determinants of Urban Poverty," *Social Science Research* 20 (1991): 217–55; Mitchell L. Eggers and Douglas S. Massey, "A Longitudinal Analysis of Urban Poverty: Blacks in U.S. Metropolitan Areas between 1970 and 1980," *Social Science Research* 21 (1992): 175–203.

28. The evidence on the extent of middle-class out-migration from ghetto areas is inconclusive. Because racial segregation does not decline with rising socioeconomic status, out-movement from poor black neighborhoods certainly has not been to white areas. When Kathryn P. Nelson measured rates of black out-migration from local "zones" within forty metropolitan areas, however, she found higher rates of out-movement for middle- and upper-class blacks compared with poor blacks; but her "zones" contained more than 100,000 inhabitants, making them considerably larger than neighborhoods (see "Racial Segregation, Mobility, and Poverty Concentration," paper presented at the annual meetings of the Population Association of America, Washington, D.C., March 19–23, 1991). In contrast, Edward Gramlich and Deborah Laren found that poor and middle-class blacks displayed about the same likelihood of out-migration from poor census tracts (see "Geographic Mobility and Persistent Poverty," Department of Economics, University of Michigan, Ann Arbor, 1990).

29. See Eggers and Massey, "A Longitudinal Analysis of Urban Poverty."

30. See International Defense and Aid Fund for Southern Africa, *Apartheid: The Facts* (London: United Nations Centre against Apartheid, 1983), pp. 15–26.

31. We are not the first to notice the striking parallel between the institutionalized system of racial segregation in U.S. cities and the organized, state-sponsored system of racial repression in South Africa. See John H. Denton, *Apartheid American Style* (Berkeley, Calif.: Diablo Press, 1967); James A. Kushner, "Apartheid in America: An Historical and Legal Analysis of Contemporary Racial Residential Segregation in the United States," *Howard Law Journal* 22 (1979):547–60.

20

Neighborhoods, Poverty, and Children's Well-Being

ANNE R. PEBLEY AND NARAYAN SASTRY

Research on neighborhood effects suggests that neighborhood characteristics such as poverty, crime, and residential turnover influence several interrelated aspects of the neighborhood environment that, in turn, affect families and children. These mechanisms can be summarized in four categories: child and family-related institutions; social organization and interaction; normative environment; and labor and marriage markets. We will briefly describe each of these.

Child and family-related institutions include schools, child care providers, public libraries, recreational programs and activities (such as music lessons, youth organizations, sports activities, arts and theater activities, and mentoring programs), parks, religious institutions, and social service providers. These institutions play a vital role in the general process of socialization, but many also impart important skills and provide specific services. While the availability and quality of these institutions may be affected directly by public policy (for example, by school improvement programs in poorer neighborhoods), they are also likely to be determined by neighborhood socioeconomic characteristics (Jencks and Mayer 1990; Aber et al. 1997). For example, child care centers and after-school programs may be more readily available, hire better staff, and provide better service in more affluent or well-educated neighborhoods, because residents demand it and can afford to pay for it. As described later, more socially organized neighborhoods may also be able to demand better institutions through collective action and the political process, even if income and educational levels are low. Poorer neighborhoods may be worse off than others not only because they have weaker institutions but also because the greater needs of families are likely to overtax the existing institutions (Aber et al. 1997).

Neighborhood *social organization and interaction* has recently received considerable attention in research on neighborhood effects. Social disorganization theory suggests that some neighborhood characteristics (such as poverty, ethnic heterogeneity,

Anne R. Pebley and Narayan Sastry, "Neighborhoods, Poverty, and Children's Well-Being," *Social Inequality*, edited by Kathryn M. Neckerman, pp. 120–123, 129–135, 138–145. Copyright © 2004 by the Russell Sage Foundation.

high residential turnover rates, low home-ownership rates, and concentration of recent immigrants) make it harder for residents to establish social ties and agree on the values needed to exercise social control and work together on common goals. As a result, socially disorganized neighborhoods are more difficult, dangerous, and stressful places to live. Parents and children in these neighborhoods are both more likely to participate in deviant behavior (delinquency, crime, violence, substance abuse) and to suffer the consequences of this behavior in others (Shaw and McKay 1969; Sampson, Morenoff, and Gannon-Rowley 2002). Sampson and his colleagues (Sampson, Morenoff, and Earls 1999; Sampson, Morenoff, and Gannon-Rowley 2002) argue that neighborhood collective efficacy—that is, shared expectations and the involvement of neighborhood residents in active support and social control of children—is key to a positive neighborhood environment for children. In neighborhoods with higher collective efficacy, residents are more likely to monitor and, when necessary, correct children's behavior. They are also more likely to work together on neighborhood problems and to build and maintain strong local institutions.

Two other theoretical perspectives—William Julius Wilson's (1987, 1996) collective socialization model and James Coleman's (1988) social capital theory—suggest related ways in which neighborhood social interaction may be important for children. Collective socialization models posit that neighborhood adults play an important role by monitoring children's behavior (as Sampson and his colleagues emphasize) and by providing role models. For example, Wilson argues that the selec-tive out-migration of middle-class professionals from African American inner-city neighborhoods has resulted in fewer positive role models for the children in those neighborhoods. Social capital models suggest that the key elements are the dense and overlapping social ties among adults and children. In neighborhoods with more social capital, children know that they will be held accountable for their actions and that they can rely on neighborhood adults for support. However, as Wilson (1996) and Sampson, Morenoff, and Earls (1999) note, high levels of social capital can facilitate the enforcement of *both* negative and positive norms and behavior. Wilson (1996, 62) points out, for example, that in neighborhoods "characterized by high levels of individual and family involvement in aberrant behavior," a high degree of social integration among adults can in fact help to create and reinforce problem behavior among children.

Connections with the world outside the neighborhood may also be important. Especially in disadvantaged neighborhoods, extralocal social ties can provide access to information about, or assistance with, opportunities, services, or normative feedback from those who move in other social circles (Coleman 1988; Stack 1974; Edin 1991; Tigges, Browne, and Green 1998). Melvin Oliver's (1988) study of social networks in urban African American communities in Los Angeles shows that extralocal social ties vary considerably among neighborhoods. He concludes that in poor neighborhoods the lack of outside social ties may be a significant disadvantage. In recent decades urban sociologists have argued that despatialized social networks have displaced the role of neighborhoods in urban life; neighborhoods are increasingly *un*important, they argue, in individuals' lives (South 2001; Fischer 1984; Wellman 1999). However, Barry Wellman (1999, 27), a proponent of this view, admits that "communities have not totally lost their domestic roots. . . . Local relationships are necessary for domestic safety, controlling actual land use, and quickly getting goods and services." He shows, for example, that much of Toronto residents' telephone contact is with neighbors rather than with extralocal ties (Wellman 1996). As Sampson and his colleagues (2002) point out, social ties among neighbors do not need to be strong or close in order to be effective. In fact, social disorganization theory suggests that neighborhood environments depend on weak and limited ties among neighbors who share a minimum level of trust, agreement on basic standards, and willingness to live by and enforce those standards. Nonetheless, the relative importance for children's development of urban neighborhood environments versus social networks is an empirical question for which we do not yet have complete answers.

The economic models suggest that *labor and marriage markets* are key elements in neighborhood effects on families and children (Duncan and Hoffman 1990; Haveman and Wolfe 1994). Local labor markets, marriage markets, and, in some neighborhoods, the illicit economy provide constraints and opportunities for neighborhood residents. Market conditions affect adults and adolescents most directly. However, by affecting their *parents'* probabilities of employment and marriage, local markets may have indirect effects on younger children. For example, in neighborhoods with poor labor markets, higher rates of parental un-

employment may affect children by increasing stress on parents, depressing household income, and creating a more stressful home environment.

Neighborhood characteristics, such as high levels of marriage, are thought to affect children's well-being both directly, by providing a positive normative environment, strong institutions, effective monitoring and social control, and a supportive climate for children, and indirectly, through effects on parents and the home environment. As noted earlier, neighborhood labor market and marriage market conditions can affect parents' income, family structure, and the home environment. Neighborhoods may also directly affect parenting behavior and family dynamics (Aneshensel and Sucoff 1996; Klebanov et al. 1997; Coulton 1996; Korbin and Coulton 1997). For example, parents in extremely disadvantaged neighborhoods are more likely to exhibit more punitive, authoritarian, and coercive parenting styles and to use corporal punishment (McLoyd 1990; Sampson and Laub 1994) as well as to withdraw emotionally from their children (Klebanov, Brooks-Gunn, and Duncan 1994). These responses are likely to have detrimental consequences for children's emotional, cognitive, and social development, and those consequences may later be reinforced by other negative aspects of neighborhood life.

Several theorists emphasize the key role of the *normative environment* itself in linking neighborhood compositional characteristics (such as poverty or high turnover rates) and child outcomes. Neighborhood norms may be a consequence of the characteristics of the people who live in the neighborhood—their income level, ethnic background, education, or immigrant experience. Those norms may also be affected by the social organization and interaction and by marriage and labor markets, as described earlier. The central idea in this literature is that the greater the concentration of like-minded people, the stronger the normative climate and the greater the exposure of neighborhood residents to these norms. For example, black children in poor inner-city neighborhoods may be more likely to be exposed to social problems, because the extreme concentration of poverty in inner-city African American neighborhoods since 1970 has created negative normative environments in which behavior considered negative by the middle class is reinforced and valued (Massey, Gross, and Eggers 1991; Massey and Denton 1993; Wilson, 1987, 1996; Fordham and Ogbu 1986). However, this process is not necessarily limited to concentrated-poverty neighborhoods or to negative outcomes—for example, some observers have argued that concentrated immigrant communities in Los Angeles can provide supportive climates for social mobility (Waldinger 1996). The "epidemic" hypothesis (Crane 1991; Case and Katz 1991) is a specific version of theories about normative environments. Jonathan Crane (1991) argues that concentrated-poverty neighborhoods dramatically increase adolescents' exposure to problem behavior and negative norms through contacts with peers. Epidemics of social problems can occur once neighborhoods reach a critically high level of negative social behaviors. . . .

Neighborhood Selection

A serious problem in studying neighborhood effects on children's well-being is the potential endogeneity of neighborhood (and school) characteristics. Endogenous characteristics are independent variables that may be correlated with unobserved factors not included in the model. In the case of neighborhood selection, the problem is that parents can choose the neighborhood in which they live but they can also affect children's development in many other ways. Thus, parents' attitudes about child development may affect both the type of neighborhood their children grow up in and other factors that affect their children's development, such as parenting and the home environment. Parents who move to help their children escape the influences of gang activity, drug use, teenage pregnancy, or crime, or who choose a neighborhood for the quality of its schools, may also be better parents in other ways. Other neighborhood attributes that may influence both parents' choice of where to live and children's behavior and development include the strength of neighborhood ties and characteristics of other families and children in the neighborhood. To the extent that neighborhood of residence is a choice, all neighborhood characteristics should be treated as endogenous. It is important, however, to understand the source of the endogeneity in order to identify appropriate analytic strategies.

Neighborhood attributes may be endogenous because place of residence is a choice variable and is determined in part by factors that also influence children's behavior and development. Thus, a common set of parent and family characteristics determines both children's behavior and development *and* neighborhood choice. Some of these characteristics, such as household income and parents' education, are measurable and can be controlled in models of children's behavior and development. However, some are unobserved and hence are picked up in the random component of statistical models, where correlation with included regressors—neighborhood characteristics—leads to biased and inconsistent estimates of all model parameters. As Greg Duncan and his colleagues explain (see, for example, Duncan, Connell, and Klebanov 1997), the problem of neighborhood selection is thus really one of omitted variables. Specific unobserved (omitted) parent and family factors are the parents' cognitive ability and family motivation and aspirations, which may influence the degree to which a family values its children's behavior and development (as well as its choice of place of residence). . . .

Neighborhood-Effects Analyses

The extensive neighborhood-effects literature published since 1990 has generally sought to answer one or more of the following three questions:

1. Are children who grow up in poor neighborhoods worse off than other children?
2. Are disparities in children's welfare by neighborhood poverty level due to differences in their families' characteristics, or do neighborhood conditions themselves play a role?
3. What mechanisms link concentrated-poverty neighborhoods to poorer outcomes for children?

Studies addressing these questions have generally been of two types. The largest group is non-experimental or observational studies, generally based on sample survey data. More recently, several experimental studies have assessed the consequences for poor families of moving into nonpoor neighborhoods. Both types of studies have usually sought to investigate the first two questions—whether children's outcomes differ by neighborhood characteristics and whether this variation persists if family attributes are held constant. A smaller number of studies have attempted to answer the third question by exploring the mechanisms that may link the characteristics of concentrated-poverty neighborhoods to poorer outcomes for children.

Recent reviews by psychologists, economists, and sociologists have thoroughly cataloged and critiqued this literature (Leventhal and Brooks-Gunn 2000; Ginter, Haveman, and Wolfe 2000; Duncan and Raudenbush 1999, 2001; Sampson, Morenoff, and Gannon-Rowley 2002). In this section, we draw on these critiques and our own reading of the literature to summarize the results of non-experimental research on neighborhood effects. We then consider more recent experimental studies.

Observational Studies

Observational studies are typically based on individual and household data from sample surveys linked with census data on the local areas (usually census tracts) in which children and families live. These studies have employed a wide range of study designs, survey datasets, theoretical approaches, neighborhood, family, and outcome measures, and statistical methods. Here we summarize the results of this very diverse group of studies.

First, basic descriptive analyses have shown that many dimensions of children's well-being (including teen sexual behavior, substance abuse, mental health, cognitive and achievement scores, high school completion, youth violence, delinquency, and child abuse) vary significantly by neighborhood income levels and, less often, by other neighborhood characteristics such as residential stability, high school completion rate, female headship, social disorder, and social cohesion. Children and teens living in poorer neighborhoods generally have worse outcomes.

Second, a substantial part of the variation in children's outcomes by neighborhood income level is accounted for by differences in family income and other family characteristics. In other words, when family characteristics such as income, family structure, and parents' educational attainment are held constant, the relationship between children's outcomes and neighborhood income levels is substantially reduced. Moreover, Ginter and her colleagues (2000) show that the more complete the set of family characteristics that is held constant, the greater the decline in the size and significance of coefficients on neighborhood variables. They conclude that the results of many neighborhood-effects studies are likely due, at least in part, to omitted variables at the family level. Nonetheless, these researchers and others find that some neighborhood characteristics retain significant effects even after extensive controls for family and individual characteristics are introduced.

Third, the size of neighborhood effects on children's outcomes is generally modest and considerably smaller than the effects of family and individual characteristics. For example, in studies reviewed by Leventhal and Brooks-Gunn (2000), neighborhood characteristics accounted for 5 to 10 percent of the variance in children's outcomes. Duncan and Raudenbush (2001, 132) argue, however, that "the degree of neighborhood-based 'action' may still be large

enough to be consistent with cost-effective, neighborhood-based interventions."

Fourth, results from these studies, not surprisingly, suggest that the effects of neighborhood conditions (net of family SES) vary by type of child outcome investigated (behavior problems, school readiness, teen sex, delinquency) and by the child's age, ethnicity, and gender. For example, Brooks-Gunn, Duncan, and their colleagues examined an extensive set of child development indicators across a broader age range (Brooks-Gunn, Duncan, and Aber 1997). Duncan and Raudenbush (1999) summarize the results as follows: (1) neighborhood effects appear in the preschool years but are most consistent for school-age children; (2) neighborhood effects appear to be stronger for cognitive and achievement outcomes than for behavior and mental health measures; and (3) white children appear to be more affected by neighborhood conditions than African American children. Sampson and his colleagues (2002) argue that the evidence of neighborhood effects on crime rates is stronger than the evidence for other types of outcomes.

Fifth, several studies suggest that the presence of affluent neighbors has a greater impact on children's outcomes than neighborhood poverty (Brooks-Gunn, Duncan, and Aber 1997; Duncan and Raudenbush 1999; Sampson, Morenoff, and Earls 1999). However, Ginther and her colleagues (2000) dispute this conclusion. Their reanalysis of the PSID data includes variables indicating the percentage of households with high and low income as well as the income of the child's family relative to that of other families in the neighborhood. Their results suggest that "the income of the family relative to that of its neighbors—rather than the extent to which the neighborhood is populated by high (low) income families—may be the more relevant consideration" (628). This is an important topic for future neighborhood-effects research.

Sixth, reliable methods for assessing neighborhood social and physical environments are not well developed and tested. Those studies that have examined intervening processes have investigated a broad range of potential mechanisms. For example, Sampson and his colleagues (Sampson et al. 1997; Sampson and Raudenbush 1999; Morenoff, Sampson, and Raudenbush 2001) show that informal social control, collective efficacy, and social ties are significantly related to outcomes such as delinquency, crime, and homicide. Scott South and Eric Baumer's (2000; Baumer and South 2001) results suggest that peer attitudes and behaviors account for a substantial proportion of neighborhood effects on adolescents, particularly teen parenthood and sexual activity. Dawn Upchurch and her colleagues (1999) and Carol Aneshensel and Clea Sucoff (1996) show that perceived "ambient hazards" (for example, neighborhood disorder, disorganization, and threats) are an important mediating factor between neighborhood disadvantage and teen sexual behavior and mental health.

Finally, a few studies have tackled endogenous residential choice using non-experimental data and statistical models. William Evans, Wallace Oates, and Robert Schwab (1992), Anne Case and Lawrence Katz (1991), and Eric Foster and Sara McLanahan (1996) used instrumental variables to eliminate the correlation between unobserved parent attributes and neighborhood variables. However, finding credible and viable instruments is a very difficult task. Instead, Daniel Aaronson (1997, 1998) and Robert Plotnick and Saul Hoffman (1996) have used sibling fixed effects in analyses of educational attainment, adult economic status, and teen pregnancy in the PSID. While Aaronson found significant neighborhood effects once unobserved family characteristics were controlled, Plotnick and Hoffman did not. Aaronson (1998) suggests that the difference in results lies in the types of sibling pairs included and the measurement of neighborhood variables. Gary Solon, Marianne Page, and Greg Duncan (2000) take another approach: they compare correlations for sibling pairs with correlations among neighbors within sampling clusters in the PSID. Their results suggest that the size of neighborhood effects is small and considerably smaller than family effects.

Experimental Studies

More recently, several experimental or quasi-experimental studies have attempted to tackle the issue of endogenous neighborhood selection. The initial effort was the Gautreaux Program, in which low-income African American families from Chicago housing projects were given Section 8 housing vouchers that could be used only in predominantly white or multi-ethnic neighborhoods (typically in suburban areas). The control group was Section 8 voucher recipients who used their vouchers in the city of Chicago. James Rosenbaum (1991, 1995) shows that children who move to the suburbs rather than cities are less likely to drop out of school and more likely to attend college, have a job, and receive higher pay. However, the study has several methodological limitations, including self-selection into the study and substantial sample attrition.

The Moving To Opportunity (MTO) experiment was a more carefully designed outgrowth of the Gautreaux Program developed by the U.S. Department of Housing and Urban Development (HUD) and implemented by local public housing authorities and non-profits between 1994 and 1999 in Baltimore, Boston, Chicago, Los Angeles, and New York (Brennan 2002). Participants were volunteers from very low-income families with children in public housing or Section 8 project-based housing in inner-city, high-poverty neighborhoods. Each participant family was assigned randomly to one of three groups: the *experimental group,* which received vouchers that could be used only in low-poverty areas plus counseling and assistance locating housing; the *comparison group,* which received geographically unrestricted vouchers and standard housing authority briefings and assistance; and the *control group,* which continued to receive project-based assistance. The study sought to answer two questions: What impact does mobility counseling have on families' residential choices and housing and neighborhood conditions? And what are the effects of neighborhood conditions on the well-being of MTO families?

The follow-up design and analyses of MTO in each city have been conducted by separate groups of researchers using different data collection and analytic strategies. This approach has the disadvantage that it is harder to make comparisons across cities (and hence generalizations beyond each city). But it also has the advantage that the multiple research strategies used provide a richer picture of the experimental process and outcomes. The one commonality among all five sites is that HUD conducted a self-administered baseline survey of all families who volunteered to participate. Researchers in most study sites conducted follow-up telephone surveys two to three years after families were assigned to treatment groups. The Boston and Los Angeles projects also conducted qualitative studies with a sample of participants. In contrast, analyses of Boston participants have relied on baseline passive and active tracking of respondents and administrative data on arrests and school performance. Furthermore, the project in each city focused on a somewhat different set of children's outcomes.

As in almost all social experiments, the MTO project encountered significant problems in implementation of the experimental treatment (Matulef 1999). Large proportions of families who were offered vouchers did not move during the period when the vouchers were valid, and analyses comparing movers to nonmovers in the experimental and comparison groups show that movers are significantly different from nonmovers. As a result, most (but not all) MTO analyses adopt analytic strategies that account for this selection. For example, Jens Ludwig and his colleagues (Ludwig, Duncan, and Pinkston 2000; Ludwig, Ladd, and Duncan 2001) in Baltimore and Lawrence Katz and his colleagues (Katz, Kling, and Liebman 2001) in Boston produce both intent-to-treat (ITT) and treatment-on-treated (TOT) estimates. ITT analyses compare outcomes for families assigned to the two treatment groups whether or not they actually moved with outcomes for the control group. Thus, ITT results are "lower bounds" on the effects of the treatment because the two treatment groups include substantial proportions of families who never moved. These researchers also estimate an "effects of TOT" parameter, which is a measure of the effect of moving on those who actually moved during the program. The TOT analysis uses instrumental variables methods to estimate the difference between families in the treatment groups who moved with those in the control group who would have moved if offered the opportunity. In the New York study, Leventhal and Brooks-Gunn (2003) use a conceptually similar approach by comparing treatment group movers with both treatment group nonmovers and those who were assigned to the control group. . . .

In general, most studies show some improvements in children's outcomes in the treatment groups compared with the controls. In particular, the Boston and Baltimore studies show significant differences in behavior problems, including juvenile arrests and respondent-reported behavior problems. This result is particularly striking since both studies report that children in the experimental group were more likely than those in the other groups to be arrested prior to their move. Experimental group children in New York, especially boys, experienced fewer depressive and anxiety-related behaviors.

Baltimore children in the treatment groups also had better test scores. Compared with the control group, children in the experimental group had better test scores overall, while those in the comparison group had better reading scores. There is some evidence in the Baltimore results that experimental-group children were more likely to be suspended from and drop out of school. Ludwig, Ladd, and Duncan (2001) suggest that middle-income schools are less likely to tolerate behavior that is acceptable in schools in poor neighborhoods. Health outcomes were better for children in the experimental group in Boston. The Boston and Chicago studies also report significant declines in fears about safety and increases in feelings of safety, a point of view echoed in the Los Angeles and New York studies.

An important concern of the New York and Los Angeles studies was the impact of moving into middle-class neighborhoods on poor children's social adjustment, social capital, and friendship patterns. If children move to better neighborhoods but feel left out or are socially isolated, they may not be better off in the long run. In general, the results to date are reassuring. Children in all three groups were as likely to have a friend in the neighborhood. In some cases, children were less likely to participate in extracurricular activities in the experimental group. Maria Hanratty, Sara McLanahan, and Becky Pettit (1998) speculate that experimental group families may face more stringent financial situations because of higher rents and large security deposits compared with other groups.

In summary, the early results of the MTO experiments provide important new evidence that neighborhood social and physical conditions affect family life and at least some aspects of children's well-being. The results of these experimental studies are limited by implementation problems and unexpected events as well as by difficulties in generalizing to the rest of the population. Nonetheless, the results of experiments combined with those from observational studies will play an important role over the next several years in helping us understand the role of residential patterns in children's well-being.

Discussion

Despite the serious methodological problems that are only beginning to be addressed adequately, a review of previous experimental and observational studies suggests that growing up in a poor neighborhood negatively affects children's outcomes over and above the effects of family socioeconomic status. However, the effects may be complex and difficult to observe. For example, the MTO results suggest that a major effect of moving to a better neighborhood is feeling safer and less anxious and depressed. Although we might expect a greater sense of safety and lower anxiety and depression to have very important long-run effects on children's emotional development and outlook on life, the effects may be less immediately apparent on school performance, skills acquisition, and behaviors, outcomes that are more typically measured in surveys and administrative data.

Research to date also suggests that family effects on children's outcomes are significantly larger than neighborhood effects. However, it is important to keep in mind that the measurement of neighborhood characteristics is at a much more rudimentary stage of development than measurement of family processes in large-scale surveys. Because of their pervasive role in most children's lives, it makes sense that families would have a greater influence on children's well-being than neighborhoods or other social environments. However, public policy generally has considerably less ability to influence parents' behavior and attributes directly than to affect neighborhood quality. Hence, even modest neighborhood effects may be of considerable interest to policymakers.

Moreover, it is important to consider residential segregation and neighborhood and family effects on children's well-being in a larger context. The finding that neighborhood effects are more modest in size than family effects can be misleading to the extent that neighborhood conditions, and residential segregation more generally, have an important influence on families' socioeconomic status and family dynamics. Residential segregation has been implicated by many scholars as a key mechanism for the intergenerational transmission of inequality (Massey and Denton 1993; Wilson 1987, 1996; Jargowsky 1997). The argument is that restriction to concentrated-poverty neighborhoods compounds the difficulty that poor, minority families face in escaping poverty because in poor neighborhoods housing values remain low, the chances of criminal victimization remain higher, high-paying jobs are less available, exposure to disease and substance abuse is greater, and individuals are more socially isolated. Thus, residential segregation and residence in concentrated-poverty neighborhoods may be an important determinant of the family socioeconomic status and a major indirect influence on children's outcomes.

If residence in a poor and dangerous neighborhood affects parents' attitudes, mental health, and parenting practices (Furstenberg et al. 1999; Kling, Liebman, and Katz 2001; Brooks-Gunn, Duncan, and Aber 1997), it is even more difficult to disentangle "family" effects from "neighborhood" effects. Nonetheless, several recent experimental and observational studies promise to provide clearer answers than past research on the direct and indirect pathways through which residential segregation affects children growing up in poor neighborhoods.

REFERENCES

Aaronson, Daniel. 1997. "Sibling Estimates of Neighborhood Effects." In *Neighborhood Poverty: Policy Implications in Studying Neighborhoods,* vol. 2, edited by Jeanne Brooks-Gunn, Greg J. Duncan, and J. Lawrence Aber. New York: Russell Sage Foundation.

———. 1998. "Using Sibling Data to Estimate the Impact of Neighborhoods on Children's Educational Outcomes." *Journal of Human Resources* 33(4): 915–46.

Aber, J. Lawrence, Martha A. Gephart, Jeanne Brooks-Gunn, and James P. Connell. 1997. "Development in Context: Implications for Studying Neighborhood Effects." In *Neighborhood Poverty: Context and Consequences for Children,* vol. 1, edited by Jeanne Brooks-Gunn, Greg J. Duncan, and J. Lawrence Aber. New York: Russell Sage Foundation.

Aneshensel, Carol S., and Clea A. Sucoff. 1996. "The Neighborhood Context of Adolescent Mental Health." *Journal of Health and Social Behavior* 37: 293–310.

Baumer, Eric P., and Scott J. South. 2001. "Community Effects on Youth Sexual Activity." *Journal of Marriage and the Family* 63: 540–54.

Brennan, Brian. 2002. "Background on MTO." *Moving To Opportunity Research.* Created August 30, 2000; last modified August 22, 2002. Available at: www.princeton.edu/~kling/mto/background.htm.

Bronfenbrenner, Urie. 1986. "Ecology of the Family as Context for Human Development." *Developmental Psychology* 22(6): 723–42.

Brooks-Gunn, Jeanne, Greg J. Duncan, and J. Lawrence Aber, eds. 1997. *Neighborhood Poverty.* New York: Russell Sage Foundation.

Brooks-Gunn, Jeanne, Greg J. Duncan, Pamela K. Klebanov, and Naomi Sealand. 1993. "Do Neighborhoods Influence Child and Adolescent Development?" *American Journal of Sociology* 99(2): 353–95.

Case, Anne C., and Lawrence F. Katz. 1991. "The Company You Keep: The Effects of Family and Neighborhood on Disadvantaged Youth." Working paper. Cambridge, Mass.: National Bureau of Economic Research.

Coleman, James S. 1988. "Social Capital in the Creation of Human Capital." *American Sociological Review* 94 (supp.): S95–120.

Coulton, Claudia J. 1996. "Effects of Neighborhoods on Families and Children: Implications for Services." In *Children and Their Families in Big Cities: Strategies for Service Reform,* edited by A. J. Kahn and S. B. Kamerman. New York: Columbia University.

Crane, Jonathan. 1991. "The Epidemic Theory of Ghettos and Neighborhood Effects on Dropping Out and Teenage Childbearing." *American Sociological Review* 96(5): 1226–59.

Duncan, Greg J., James P. Connell, and Pamela K. Klebanov. 1997. "Conceptual and Methodological Issues in Estimating Causal Effects of Neighborhoods and Family Conditions on Individual Development." In *Neighborhood Poverty: Context and Consequences for Children,* vol. 1, edited by Jeanne Brooks-Gunn, Greg J. Duncan, and J. Lawrence Aber. New York: Russell Sage Foundation.

Duncan, Greg J., and Saul D. Hoffman. 1990. "Welfare Benefits, Economic Opportunities, and Out-of-Wedlock Births Among Black Teenage Girls." *Demography* 27(4): 519–35.

Duncan, Greg J., and Stephen W. Raudenbush. 1999. "Assessing the Effects of Context in Studies of Child and Youth Development." *Educational Psychologist* 34(1): 29–41.

———. 2001. "Neighborhoods and Adolescent Development: How Can We Determine the Links?" In *Does It Take a Village? Community Effects on Children, Adolescents, and Families,* edited by Alan Booth and Ann C. Crouter. Mahwah, N.J.: Lawrence Erlbaum Associates.

Edin, Kathryn. 1991. "Surviving the Welfare System: How AFDC Recipients Make Ends Meet in Chicago." *Social Problems* 38(4): 462–74.

Evans, William N., Wallace E. Oates, and Robert M. Schwab. 1992. "Measuring Peer Group Effects: A Study of Teenage Behavior." *Journal of Political Economy* 100(3): 966–91.

Fischer, Claude S. 1984. *The Urban Experience.* New York: Harcourt, Brace, Jovanovich.

Fordham, Signithia, and John U. Ogbu. 1986. "Black Students' School Success: Coping with the Burden of 'Acting White.'" *The Urban Review* 18: 176–206.

Foster, Eric M., and Sara McLanahan. 1996. "An Illustration of the Use of Instrumental Variables: Do Neighborhood Conditions Affect a Young Person's Chance of Finishing High School?" Unpublished paper. Princeton University.

Furstenberg, Frank F., Jr., Thomas D. Cook, Jacquelynne Eccles, Glen H. Elder Jr., and Arnold J. Sameroff. 1999. *Managing to Make It: Urban Families and Adolescent Success.* Chicago: University of Chicago Press.

Ginther, Donna, Robert Haveman, and Barbara Wolfe. 2000. "Neighborhood Attributes as Determinants of Children's Outcomes: How Robust Are the Relationships?" *Journal of Human Resources* 35(4): 603–42.

Hanratty, Maria, Sara McLanahan, and Becky Pettit. 1998. "The Impact of the Los Angeles Moving To Opportunity Program on Residential Mobility, Neighborhood Characteristics, and Early Child and Parent Outcomes." Working paper 98–18. Princeton, N.J.: Princeton University, Center for Research on Child Wellbeing.

Haveman, Robert, and Barbara Wolfe. 1994. *Succeeding Generations: On the Effects of Investments in Children.* New York: Russell Sage Foundation.

Jargwosky, Paul A. 1997. *Poverty and Place: Ghettos, Barrios, and the American City.* New York: Russell Sage Foundation.

Jencks, Christopher, and Susan E. Mayer. 1990. "The Social Consequences of Growing up in a Poor Neighborhood." In *Inner-City Poverty in the United States,* edited by Laurence E. Lynn Jr. and Michael G. H. McGeary. Washington, D.C.: National Academy Press.

Katz, Lawrence F., Jeffrey R. Kling, and Jeffrey B. Liebman. 2001. "Moving To Opportunity in Boston: Early Results of a Randomized Mobility Experiment." *Quarterly Journal of Economics* (May): 607–54.

Klebanov, Pamela K., Jeanne Brooks-Gunn, P. Lindsay Chase-Lansdale, and R. A. Gordon. 1997. "Are Neighborhood Effects on Young Children Mediated by Features of the Home Environment?" In *Neighborhood Poverty,* vol. 1, edited by Jeanne Brooks-Gunn, Greg J. Duncan, and J. Lawrence Aber. New York: Russell Sage Foundation.

Klebanov, Pamela K., Jeanne Brooks-Gunn, and Greg J. Duncan. 1994. "Does Neighborhood and Family Poverty Affect Mother's Parenting, Mental Health and Social Support?" *Journal of Marriage and the Family* 56: 441–55.

Kling, Jeffrey R., Jeffrey B. Liebman, and Lawrence F. Katz. 2001. "Bullets Don't Got No Name: Consequences of Fear in the Ghetto." Working paper 225. Chicago: Northwestern University and the University of Chicago, Joint Center for Poverty Research.

Korbin, Jill E., and Claudia J. Coulton. 1997. "Understanding the Neighborhood Context for Children and Families: Combining Epidemiological and Ethnographic Approaches." In *Neighborhood Poverty,* vol. 2, edited by Jeanne Brooks-Gunn, Greg J. Duncan, and J. Lawrence Aber. New York: Russell Sage Foundation.

Leventhal, Tama, and Jeanne Brooks-Gunn. 2000. "The Neighborhoods They Live In: The Effects of Neighborhood Residence on Child and Adolescent Outcomes." *Psychological Bulletin* 126(2): 309–37.

———. 2003. "The Early Impacts of Moving To Opportunity on Children and Youth in New York City." In *Choosing a Better Life: Evaluating the Moving To Opportunity Social Experiment,* edited by John Goering and Judith Feins. Washington, D.C.: Urban Institute Press.

Ludwig, Jens, Greg J. Duncan, and Joshua C. Pinkston. 2000. "Evidence from a Randomized Housing-Mobility Experiment." Unpublished paper. Georgetown University, Washington, D.C.

Ludwig, Jens, Helen F. Ladd, and Greg J. Duncan. 2001. "Urban Poverty and Educational Outcomes." *Brookings-Wharton Papers on Urban Affairs* 2001: 147–201.

Massey, Douglas S., and Nancy A. Denton. 1993. *American Apartheid: Segregation and the Making of the Underclass.* Cambridge, Mass.: Harvard University Press.

Massey, Douglas S., and Mitchell L. Eggers. 1990. "The Ecology of Inequality: Minorities and the Concentration of Poverty, 1970 to 1980." *American Journal of Sociology* 95(5): 1153–88.

Massey, Douglas S., Andrew B. Gross, and M. L. Eggers. 1991. "Segregation, the Concentration of Poverty, and the Life Chances of Individuals." *Social Science Research* 20(4): 397–420.

Massey, Douglas S., Andrew B. Gross, and K. Shibuya. 1994. "Migration, Segregation, and the Concentration of Poverty." *American Sociological Review* 59: 425–45.

Matulef, Mark. 1999. "Moving To Opportunity (MTO) Demonstration for Fair Housing Program, Los Angeles Demonstration Site Interim Outcomes of Housing Search and Counseling Strategies: Early Lessons for Experimental Design and Implementation." Available at: www.wws.princeton.edu/~kling/mto/quick.htm.

McLoyd, Vonnie C. 1990. "The Impact of Economic Hardship on Black Families and Children: Psychological Distress, Parenting, and Socioemotional Development." *Child Development* 61: 311–46.

Morenoff, Jeffrey D., Robert J. Sampson, and Stephen W. Raudenbush. 2001. "Neighborhood Inequality, Collective Efficacy, and the Spatial Dynamics of Urban Violence." *Criminology* 39(3): 517–59.

Oliver, Melvin L. 1988. "The Urban Black Community as Network: Toward a Social Network Perspective." *Sociological Quarterly* 29(4): 623–45.

Rosenbaum, James E. 1991. "Black Pioneers: Do Their Moves to the Suburbs Increase Economic Opportunity for Mothers and Children?" *Housing Policy Debate* 2(4): 1179–1213.

———. 1995. "Changing the Geography of Opportunity by Expanding Residential Choice: Lessons from the Gautreaux Program." *Housing Policy Debate* 6(1): 231–70.

Sampson, Robert J., and John H. Laub. 1994. "Urban Poverty and the Family Context of Delinquency: A New Look at Structure and Process in a Classic Study." *Child Development* 65: 523–40.

Sampson, Robert J., Jeffrey D. Morenoff, and Felton Earls. 1999. "Beyond Social Capital: Spatial Dynamics of Collective Efficacy for Children." *American Sociological Review* 64(5): 633–60.

Sampson, Robert J., Jeffrey D. Morenoff, and Thomas Gannon-Rowley. 2002. "Assessing 'Neighborhood Effects': Social Processes and New Directions in Research." *Annual Review of Sociology* 28: 443–78.

Sampson, Robert J., and Stephen W. Raudenbush. 1999. "Systematic Social Observation of Public Spaces: A New Look at Disorder in Urban Neighborhoods." *American Journal of Sociology* 105(3): 603–51.

Sampson, Robert J., Stephen W. Raudenbush, and Felton Earls. 1997. "Neighborhoods and Violent Crime: A Multilevel Study of Collective Efficacy." *Science* 277 (August 15): 918–24.

Shaw, Clifford R., and McKay, Henry D. 1969. *Juvenile Delinquency and Urban Areas.* Chicago: The University of Chicago Press.

Solon, Gary, Marianne E. Page, and Greg J. Duncan. 2000. "Correlations Between Neighboring Children in Their Subsequent Educational Attainment." *Review of Economics and Statistics* 82(3): 383–92.

South, Scott J. 2001. "Issues in the Analysis of Neighborhoods, Families and Children." In *Does It Take A Village? Community Effects on Children, Adolescents, and Families,* edited by Alan Booth and Ann C. Crouter. Mahwah, N.J.: Lawrence Erlbaum Associates, Inc.

South, Scott J., and Eric P. Baumer. 2000. "Deciphering Community and Race Effects on Adolescent Premarital Childbearing." *Social Forces* 78: 1379–1407.

Stack, Carol. 1974. *All Our Kin: Survival Strategies.* New York: Harper Torchback.

Tigges, Leann M., Irene Browne, and Gary P. Green. 1998. "Social Isolation of the Urban Poor: Race, Class and Neighborhood Effects on Social Resources." *Sociological Quarterly* 39(1): 53–77.

Upchurch, Dawn M., Carol S. Aneshensel, Clea A. Sucoff, and Lene Levy-Storms. 1999. "Neighborhood and Family Contexts of Adolescent Sexual Activity." *Journal of Marriage and the Family* 61: 920–33.

Waldinger, Roger. 1996. "Ethnicity and Opportunity in the Plural City." In *Ethnic Los Angeles,* edited by Roger Waldinger and Mehdi Bozorgmehr. New York: Russell Sage Foundation.

Wellman, Barry. 1996. "Are Personal Communities Local? A Dumptarian Reconsideration." *Social Networks* 17(2): 423–36.

———. 1999. "Preface." In *Networks in the Global Village,* edited by Barry Wellman. Boulder, Colo.: Westview Press.

Wilson, William Julius. 1987. *The Truly Disadvantaged.* Chicago: University of Chicago Press.

———. 1996. *When Work Disappears: The World of the New Urban Poor.* New York: Alfred A. Knopf.

21

Flat Broke with Children
Women in the Age of Welfare Reform

SHARON HAYS

Money and Morality

A nation's laws reflect a nation's values. The 1996 federal law reforming welfare offered not just a statement of values to the thousands of local welfare offices across the nation, it also backed this up with something much more tangible. Welfare reform came with money. Lots of it. Every client and caseworker in the welfare office experienced this. New social workers and employment counselors were hired. New signs were posted. New workshops were set up. In Arbordale and Sunbelt City, the two welfare offices I studied, every caseworker found a new computer on her desk. (Arbordale and Sunbelt City are pseudonyms for the two towns where I studied the effects of welfare reform. I gave them these fictitious names to protect all the clients and caseworkers who shared with me their experiences of reform.) In small-town Arbordale, the whole office got a facelift: new carpets, new paint, a new conference room, new office chairs, and plush new office dividers. The reception area, completely remodeled with plants and posters and a children's play area, came

to resemble the waiting room of an elite pediatrician's office more than the entrance to a state bureaucracy. Sunbelt City acquired new carpets, a new paint job, and new furniture as well. And all the public areas in that welfare office were newly decorated with images of nature's magnificence—glistening raindrops, majestic mountains, crashing waves, setting sun—captioned with inspirational phrases like "perseverance," "seizing opportunities," "determination," "success."

As I walked the halls of the Sunbelt City welfare office back in 1998, situated in one of the poorest and most dangerous neighborhoods of a western boom town, those scenes of nature's magnificence struck me as clearly out of place. But the inspirational messages they carried nonetheless seemed an apt symbolic representation of the new legislative strategy to train poor families in "mainstream" American values. Welfare reform, Congress had decreed, would "end the dependence of needy parents on government benefits by promoting job preparation, work, and marriage."[1] Welfare mothers, those Sunbelt signs im-

Sharon Hays, *Flat Broke with Children*, pp. 3–5, 10, 139, 141–147, 215, 217–220, 226–228, 230, 241, 254, 259–260, 263, 265–267, 270–274, 276–278. Copyright © 2003 by Oxford University Press.

plied, simply needed a *push*—to get them out to work, to keep them from having children they couldn't afford to raise, to get them married and safely embedded in family life. Seizing opportunities.

States were awash in federal funds. And the economy was booming in those early years of reform. Everyone was feeling it. There was change in the air. A sense of possibilities—with just a tinge of foreboding.

The Personal Responsibility and Work Opportunity Reconciliation Act of 1996, the law that ended 61 years of poor families' entitlement to federal welfare benefits—the law that asserted and enforced a newly reformulated vision of the appropriate values of work and family life—provided all that additional funding as a way of demonstrating the depth of the nation's commitment to change in the welfare system. It provided state welfare programs with federal grants in amounts matching the peak years of national welfare caseloads (1992 to 1995)—even though those caseloads had everywhere since declined. This meant an average budget increase of 10 percent, before counting the tremendous amount of additional federal funding coming in for new childcare and welfare-to-work programs. Even though there was lots more money, most states did not pass it on to poor mothers in the form of larger welfare checks. In fact, only two states raised their benefit amounts, while two others lowered theirs at the inception of reform.

Most of the welfare caseworkers I met were optimistic about the new law, at least in the first year of its enactment. "Welfare reform is the best thing that ever happened," was a phrase I heard frequently. A number of caseworkers, echoing popular sentiment, told me that "welfare had be-come a trap" and the clients had become "dependent." Some focused on the tax money that would be saved. Others pointed out that lots of caseworkers are mothers too, and economic necessity forces them to come to work every day and leave their children in day care, so it seemed only fair that welfare mothers should be required to do the same. . . .

The purpose of this chapter is to explore the cultural norms, beliefs, and values embedded in welfare reform. While millions of dollars have been spent to track the outcomes of this legislation, and while scholars, politicians, and pundits have fiercely debated the effects of every policy contained within it, I want to focus attention on the broad *cultural* significance of this reform effort. What does the Personal Responsibility Act tell us about the values of our society? How have its moral prescriptions been translated into concrete practices? What message does it send to the poor and to the nation? In particular, I was interested from the start in determining just what welfare reform is saying about work and family life in American society today. . . .

Invisibility and Inclusion

Invisibility was a problem experienced by the majority of the welfare mothers I encountered. Most emphasized, in one way or another, that they were not "born to welfare" (as one put it), and almost all felt fairly certain that—time limits or no time limits—they would find some way to survive. These mothers did not, in other words, tell me their stories primarily to convince listeners that they were worthy of continued welfare receipt. Many did, on the other hand, share their tales because they wanted people to understand how they came to participate in one of the most universally despised social programs in U.S. history. They had heard more than once the stereotypes labeling them as lazy, dependent, ignorant, promiscuous, and manipulative cheats. They told their stories, therefore, with the hope that they would be recognized not simply as a composite of clichés, but as whole persons. . . .

Sheila's Downward Spiral

The spiral for Sheila began just after she finished high school. Sheila is white and was 29 years old at the time I met her in the old and notoriously dangerous housing project where she lived, not far from the Sunbelt City welfare office. From a working-class background, she was raised in a small town "with small town values." She was engaged to be married to her high school sweetheart. The summer after they graduated he was killed in an auto accident.

> I wish that then and there I had just said, "Okay, forward," instead of sitting and mourning and moping and weeping and thinking about what could have and should have and would have been. I should have just gone on ahead to college like I had intended. And I didn't do it. But you know what they say, hindsight is 20–20.

She moved to Sunbelt City with her parents and took a part-time job. Less than a year later her father left her mother.

> It was in February. He left a note on the kitchen table. It said, "I'm leaving you for good." And he left the keys to the car that was not paid for. He left one month owing in rent. My mom at the time was not working, and I was still mourning my boyfriend.

Shortly after that me and my mom found jobs at a dry cleaners. We opened it in the morning, and we worked for 15 hours a day. We'd come home, go to sleep, get up, and go right back there. Six days a week. And we were doing good. We had paid up the back rent, and the car was being paid for.

And then my mother got blood clots. She almost lost her leg. And the doctor said she shouldn't work any more. This meant we lost $1,500 a month in income and we were trying to make it on my little $1,200. With the medical bills and the car payments, I got a month behind on rent, and they evicted us.

We were homeless. In all the hoopla and everything, I lost my job. It just kind of dominoed. We were actually homeless, living with friends and things like that. And I mean we went hungry—we ate the throwaways from McDonald's.

A lot of people don't realize how close they live to being homeless. I mean, you're just one or two paychecks away from the street. And once you hit bottom, you're gonna hit and you're gonna hit hard. But you have to remember that once you hit bottom you're as low as you can go. There's only one way to go, and that's up.

Unfortunately for Sheila, the downward spiral had not yet reached its lowest point. It was while she and her mother were homeless that she met the man who was to become the father of her daughter. He was, at that moment, her savior, but only a temporary one:

> I met Sam, and I thought he was a very nice gentleman. Sam was living with a friend, and they took the two of us in. I found another job. We were hopeful; even

though my mom still couldn't work, we were beginning to get back on our feet.

Sam had told me he was divorced. I was still young; I was 21 at the time. And, like I said, I come from a small community. Well, after we'd been together for almost a year, I got a phone call one morning—and it was his wife! So I used the money I had to put him on a bus back to his wife in Florida. And that's the last I heard of him.

A month later I found out I was pregnant. Sam still doesn't know he's got a daughter. The child support people haven't found him yet.

Putting Sam on that bus meant that pregnant Sheila and her disabled mom were homeless again. And then Sheila was raped:

For a while I wasn't sure if Sam was the father. There was the small issue of the fact that three weeks almost to the day after he left I was raped. That's a part of living on the street; that's a danger for women who live on the street.

And that's how I came to find out I was pregnant—I went to the clinic to check a few weeks after the rape. So there were two possible identities to the father. I had a hard time knowing what to do. But as soon as she was born I saw what she looked like and I knew who she was; I knew who she belonged to. She looks too much like her dad.

Sheila was just 22 years old when she gave birth to her daughter. If things had gone as she had originally planned, she would have been starting her last year of college at that time.

Sheila first went to the welfare office in the last months of her pregnancy, hoping to get medical coverage for the birth.

I was a high-risk pregnancy all the way through my pregnancy. I went down to the welfare office and applied for medical assistance. My mother and I were still homeless. I worked a part-time job until things [with the pregnancy] got too bad. My mother had gotten a job [against her doctor's advice] and we managed, with my first welfare check, to finally get our very own small studio apartment. Just two weeks later my daughter was born.

Sheila's daughter (who was busy with her homework during most of my visit), was seven years old when I met her.

From the time she gave birth to the time of our interview, Sheila had a string of jobs. She went back to work when her daughter was just three months old. That job she described as a "really good one," where she worked her way up to a management position in a fast-food restaurant. The rest of the jobs were temporary or low-paying jobs, mainly entry-level fast foods and unskilled clerical work. She left every one. She quit the good one after more than two years, and she's still sorry about it, even though she remembers well all the time she spent agonizing over that decision. She left because the hours and the bus rides were so long that she was spending over 12 hours a day away from home, and she never had a chance to see her daughter. "My daughter was nearly three years old and she was calling my mother 'mom' and calling me 'Sheila.' It was just too hard. I just wanted to get to know her, to do her ABCs and her 1–2–3s. I wanted to be there."

She went back on welfare and spent almost a year getting to know her daughter before again seeking work. She spoke nostalgically of that time with her three-year-old, but she also emphasized that leaving that job was her "third big mistake," alongside mourning rather than continuing on to college, and getting involved with a married man.

Sheila left subsequent jobs because she hurt her back, loading boxes ("the doctors say I'm not allowed to lift over 15 pounds now"), because the pay was too poor, because the jobs were only temporary (through a "temp" agency), and most recently, because her mother was diagnosed as terminally ill and needed to be cared for. Her mother suffered respiratory failure first, then a massive heart attack and, by the time I met her, Sheila was afraid to leave her alone most of the time. "That's my greatest fear, that I'll go to work, and I'll be at work, and something will happen to my mom. I don't know what to do."

Sheila's combined time on welfare, including the time when her child was born, between jobs, and since her mother's illness, added up to about three and a half years, including the last year and a half since welfare reform. She'd been using the resources offered by the welfare office to train herself on computers and in accounting skills. She told me about the contacts she'd made with state agencies that might hire her, and she was feeling somewhat optimistic, though still quite worried about her mom. Her primary goal was to find an employer flexible enough to allow her to care for both her daughter and her mother.

The sheer number of tragedies in Sheila's young life—her fiancé's death, her father leaving, her homelessness, her affair with a married man, her rape, her high-risk pregnancy, and now her mother's terminal illness—testify to the unique circumstances that led her to go on welfare. But every mother I talked to had a story of hardship to tell. And every mother I met had experienced some version of the domino effect: one problem leading to another and compounding it, until too many dominoes fall and the situation becomes impossible to manage. In this, Sheila's story represents the most prominent pattern in the road to welfare.

A second, partially hidden, pattern that Sheila shares with many welfare mothers who have children out of wedlock involves the issue of birth control. Most observers of Sheila's life would agree that she has had some very tough luck. Yet many would also want to know why she allowed herself to get pregnant. After all, it is clear from this vantage point that the last thing Sheila needed was a child to support. She answered, "I did use birth control, but it must not have worked. I don't know what happened."

The truth is, it could very well be that Sheila simply did not use birth control faithfully enough, or that the methods she and her partner used were not sufficiently foolproof. The crucial point here, however, is that a substantial number of sexually active young men and women do not use birth control faithfully enough. This fact does not appear to vary significantly by one's race or economic status. About 50 percent of female teens are sexually active. About 70 percent of those say they used birth control the last time they had sex. But this percentage is based on self-reporting— in which case Sheila, for instance, would be included as a "yes." And equally important, having used birth control recently is not the same thing as using it consistently. There tends to be a good deal of variation in answers to the questions "used at most recent sex," and "used at first sex," for example, which confirms that "recently" is not the same as "always."[2] Putting all this together, it becomes clear that a large number of sexually active young people do not use foolproof birth control every time they have sex. Sheila, in this sense, is a member of the majority.

The central factor separating poor and working-class youth from the middle and upper classes on this score is that financially privileged young women who find themselves pregnant before they are ready are more likely to get an abortion.[3] I asked Sheila if she had thought about having an abortion.

Oh no, no. Well, I can't say it didn't cross my mind. But I'm a person who believes if you're gonna play, you're gonna pay. And it's not her fault. I'm the kind of person who thinks that, as soon as they have that heartbeat, which is like ten days after conception, then that's a live human being. I just couldn't do it. I love my daughter.

No matter what we might think of the consequences of this choice in the context of Sheila's life, the vast majority of Americans agree that she has a right to make this decision. And few would argue that her problem, in this instance, is a problem of bad values.

There is a third important pattern that Sheila shares with the majority of welfare mothers—the pushes toward work and the pulls toward home. The stress associated with those pushes and pulls is something welfare mothers have in common with parents of all classes and backgrounds. Sheila's desire to stay at home with her daughter is no different from all the other working moms who long to have more time to spend with their young children. Her longing for a job flexible enough to allow her to care for her child is shared by most working parents today. Her sense of regret over taking off those career-building years in order to be with her daughter mimics all the stay-at-home mothers who worry that they will never be able to recoup their lost time in the labor market.[4] And the fact that Sheila feels committed to staying at home with her terminally ill mother puts her in the same position as the millions of (mainly) women who care for their aging parents—many of whom suffer serious economic hardship because of it.[5] What makes Sheila's case distinct is solely that these realities landed her in the welfare office.

No matter what the edicts of welfare reform might mean to Sheila in the coming years, and no matter what we might think of the paths she chose at the multiple crossroads of her early adulthood, the difficulties she has faced speak to much larger social problems. To the extent that the Personal Responsibility Act is our collective cultural response, it is clear that this law has done little to address the underlying causes of the strains Sheila has experienced and the choices she was forced to make. . . .

The "Success" of Welfare Reform

Most welfare mothers share the core values of most Americans. They share a concern with contemporary problems in work and family life and a commitment to finding solutions—including the overhaul of the welfare system. The trouble is, welfare reform was founded on the assumption that welfare mothers do not share American values and are, in fact, personally responsible for *undermining* our nation's moral principles. The policies and procedures instituted by welfare reform have thus been aimed at "fixing" these women. . . .

Shared Values, Symbolic Boundaries, and the Politics of Exclusion

In responding to welfare reform, the welfare mothers I met often offered a perfect mirror of the complex mix of higher values, genuine concerns, exclusionary judgments, and cultural distortions that informed the Personal Responsibility Act. One mother, Denise, captured nearly all these elements in her response, offering the full range of the more prominent patterns I encountered and mimicking the words of welfare mothers you have heard throughout the book. A black woman with two daughters, at the time I met her Denise was recently employed at Mailboxes-R-Us for $6.50 an hour and was making ends meet with the help of welfare reform's (time-limited) income supplement, transportation vouchers, and childcare subsidy. This is what she had to say when I asked her for her overall assessment of reform:

> When I was younger, years ago, anybody could get on welfare. And I think that's what's good about welfare reform. People have to show some sort of initiative. Before, the welfare office didn't pressure you to find a job, but now they do. And I think that's a good system. They've really helped me out a lot.
>
> Plus, I think people are sick of having to pay their tax money. They say, "Look, I am out here working, and I don't make that much money, and I have kids of my own. I'm tired of having to take care of your babies." People are getting upset and it's rightly so. I think it's rightly so.
>
> And lots of people abuse the system. You see it every day. A lot of people that you run into and a lot of people that live in your neighborhood—I mean a lot of peo-

ple do hair and get paid in cash. And I hear about these people who had children just to get a welfare check, just because they didn't want to go out and work. I've seen women that's on welfare, they're looking good and their children look poorly. I see that happening.

> Some of them are lazy and don't want to work. I think that some just want to stay home with their kids. But then they should have thought about that before they had the children.

At this point in her argument, Denise had hit upon nearly all the concerns of hardworking Americans who conscientiously pay their taxes, raise their children, and struggle to make it all work. She had also hit upon nearly all the well-worn stereotypes of poor mothers—implicitly labeling them as welfare cheats, lazy couch potatoes, promiscuous breeders, and lousy parents. But Denise wasn't finished.

> I think some people on welfare are being greedy—taking away from people that are homeless, people that really need the help. I mean there are truly people out there living at the Salvation Army. I hear tell that there are people who can't get in those shelters because they're so full. And I think that's the sad part about it. Those women that don't really need welfare shouldn't be taking money away from the homeless.
>
> But there are gonna be problems. Like, there are women that want to go out there and get a job, but who's gonna watch their kids? And there are people who will still need that little extra help to pay the bills. So that's a glitch in the system. And some of these women are already pregnant, and they're already poor, and they really do need the help. I think that we have to

weigh things and maybe investigate a bit more. There are a lot of people that are disabled and need welfare; there are women who have been abused. Some of those people that are in a lot of trouble, you know, their kids are gonna be the ones you see on TV, shooting up the schools and everything.[6]

I know a lot of people say that this welfare reform is a good thing—and it is really gonna help a lot of people. But in the end things are probably gonna get worse. There's gonna be more crime 'cause people can't get on welfare and they're not gonna have any money and they're gonna go out and rob people, and kill people. And it happens, it happens. So that's a problem with the system.

This same sort of ambivalence is evident in Americans' response to welfare reform. Although most are positive about reform, the majority of Americans also say that they are "very" concerned about poverty. Most additionally believe that the national standards for poverty are set too low, stating that a family of four with an income of less than $20,000 is, in fact, "poor," even if the federal government does not label them as such. More significantly, a majority of Americans are in favor of further aid to the poor—including the expansion of job opportunities, tax credits, medical coverage, subsidies for childcare and housing, and the provision of better schools. Still, Americans worry about the government's ability to appropriately and effectively provide that aid, and many don't want to have to pay higher taxes to subsidize the poor.

Denise is also much like most Americans in that the central moral categories she uses to frame her response are work and family values, independence and commitment to others, self-sufficiency and concern for the common good. Women should take the "initiative," they should work, they should not rely on the help of others, they should support their own children, they should think twice before they give birth to children they cannot afford to raise. At the same time, people should not be "greedy," they should care for those who are more vulnerable than themselves, and they should consider the impact of their actions on the nation as a whole. All this makes perfect sense, and all this resonates perfectly with our nation's values. The trouble is that managing these commitments is hard enough if you have a spouse, a house in the suburbs, two cars in the garage, good health insurance, reliable childcare, a willingness to make compromises, a great deal of determination, empathy, and energy, and a household income of $60,000. The more items on this list that you lack, the tougher it becomes to live up to this demanding system of values. Denise, like most Americans, implicitly understands these "glitches." Yet her reasoning becomes a bit cloudy at this point—in large measure, I would argue, because of the loophole provided by the final significant element in her response to welfare reform.

It is hard to miss that Denise's support for the Personal Responsibility Act is predicated on the construction of a moral distinction between herself and all those "other" bad welfare mothers who fail to live up to social standards. Denise is making use of what Michèle Lamont has called "symbolic boundaries" to develop an implicit hierarchy of social worth. Like most people who use this strategy, she is not simply engaging in a mean-spirited attack on others or a self-interested attempt to highlight her own virtues. These symbolic boundaries also allow her to positively affirm shared values and specify the proper way to live one's life.[7]

Yet, given that many observers consider Denise herself a member of the deviant group she describes, the fact that she and other welfare mothers persist in this technique is curious. It testifies not just to the power and ubiquity of boundary making as a social strategy, it also speaks to the power and ubiquity of the demonization of poor single mothers. When welfare mothers distinguish themselves from those other "bad" women, they are calling on widely disseminated negative images of welfare mothers. These images seem to match all those strangers, those loud neighbors, those people who appear to spend their lives hanging out on street corners. The lives of the women they actually know, on the other hand, seem much more complex, their actions more understandable, their futures more redeemable.

The demonization of welfare mothers and the dichotomy between "us" and "them" can thus provide a dividing line that allows Denise and other Americans to say, if some welfare mothers can't make it, it's not because the problems they encounter in trying to manage work and family and still keep their heads above water are that bad or that widespread; it's because they didn't try hard enough or weren't good enough. Symbolic boundaries thus become *exclusionary* boundaries—simultaneously offering a means to affirm shared values and a means to think of "outsiders" in terms of individual blame. The obvious problem, in Denise's case, is that her own logic might ultimately leave her as one of the "accused." In broader terms, this exclusionary process means that all those Americans who are suffering from childcare woes, second shifts, inadequate health insurance, precarious jobs, unmanageable debt, and unstable communities are left to feel that their problems are *personal* problems for which no public solutions can be found. . . .

Winners and Losers

The extent to which the facts about the declining welfare rolls are read as a success ultimately depends on one's primary goals. If the goal of reform was solely to trim the rolls, then it has surely succeeded. If the goal was to place more single mothers in jobs regardless of wages, that goal has been met. If we sought to ensure that more welfare mothers would face a double shift of paid work and childcare, placing them on an "equal" footing with their middle-class counterparts, then some celebrations are in order. If the aim was to ensure that poor men are prosecuted for failure to pay child support, then welfare reform has been relatively effective. If the goal was to make low-income single mothers more likely to seek out the help of men, no matter what the costs, there is some (inconclusive) evidence that this strategy may be working.[8] If the goal was to decrease poverty overall, there is no indication that anything but the cycle of the economy has had an impact. Beyond this, the answers are more complicated.

Thinking about losers, one can start with the families who have left welfare. One-half are sometimes without enough money to buy food. One-third have to cut the size of meals. Almost half find themselves unable to pay their rent or utility bills. Many more families are turning to locally funded services, food banks, churches, and other charities for aid. Many of those charities are already overburdened. In some locales, homeless shelters and housing assistance programs are closing their doors to new customers, food banks are running out of food, and other charities are being forced to tighten their eligibility requirements.[9]

Among the former welfare families who are now living with little or no measurable income, will those charities be enough? At ground level, Nancy, the supervisor in Arbordale's welfare office, told me more than once that she was deeply concerned about these families, particularly the children. Melissa, the supervisor in Sunbelt City, on the other hand, repeatedly responded to my questions regarding the fate of former welfare recipients with the simple statement, "They have other resources." Melissa was referring not only to all those (overloaded) charities, but also to all the boyfriends and family members who could help in paying the bills, and to all those unreported or underreported side jobs (doing hair, cleaning houses, caring for other people's children, selling sex or drugs).[10] Between these two welfare supervisors, both of whom have spent many years working with poor mothers, who is right? And what about Denise, who both agreed with Melissa that many welfare mothers didn't *really* need the help, and who predicted that welfare reform would result in frightening hardship, including a rise in crime?

Consider the "other resources" available to the women I have introduced in this chapter. In the case of Sheila, the Sunbelt mother who was caring for her seven-year-old daughter and her terminally ill mother, the three of them might be able to survive somehow on her mom's disability check (about $550 per month) with the help of food stamps and local charities. If worse came to worst, she might be able to find some work on the graveyard shift so that she wouldn't have to leave her mom and daughter alone during the day (but she would be faced with leaving them alone at night in that very dangerous housing project).

Most welfare mothers *do* have other resources. Yet many of those resources are only temporary, and many are, at best, inadequate. Most will likely add greater instability and uncertainty to the lives of these families. And nearly all these resources have their own price tags—practical, emotional, moral, and social. . . .

The real winners in the story of welfare reform are all the restaurant, hotel, retail, and food service chains, and all the corporations, manufacturers, and small business owners across America who employ low-wage workers. These owners (and their stockholders) benefit not just from the availability of millions of poor women desperate to find work and willing to accept the lowest wages and the worst working conditions, they benefit not just from the additional availability of all those now more-desperate poor men, they also benefit because all this desperation creates more profitable labor market conditions overall. Welfare reform helps to convince all low-wage workers that they can be easily displaced by former welfare recipients and therefore makes them less likely to complain, change jobs, join unions, or demand higher wages. The logic of reform also means that low-wage employers can rest assured, for the moment at least, that no one will be calling into question the fact that their policies are less than family friendly and their workers are unable to support their children on the wages they take home.[11]

On a superficial level, the "end of welfare" appears to hold in place the symbolic messages that work is better than welfare and marriage is better than single parenthood. But by no stretch of the imagination could one argue that welfare reform brings with it anything resembling the triumph of "family values." And the practical reality of most low-wage employment no more offers

"independence" and self-sufficiency to former welfare recipients than it does to all the
middle-class teenagers who spend their
summers working in fast-food restaurants
and retail chains.

NOTES

1. U.S. Congress (1996, PL104–193, Title I, Section 401).

2. Terry and Manlove (1999); see also Luker (1996) and Waller (1999).

3. Luker (1996), Waller (1999), and Ventura et al. (2000).

4. See, for instance, Hays (1996), Hochschild (1989, 1997).

5. See Arno et al. (1999) and Harvard School of Public Health (2000) on the number of women caring for disabled or aged family members.

6. Denise is referring to then-prominent news stories on the Columbine school shooting and the other school shootings that followed.

7. On symbolic boundaries, see Lamont (1992, 2000).

8. See Sorenson and Zibman (2000); Cherlin and Fomby (2002).

9. See Loprest (1999), Boushev and Gunderson (2001), Sherman et al. (1998), National Campaign for Jobs and Income Support (2001A, 2001B). A study of major U.S. cities found that from 2000 to 2001, requests for food had increased by 23 percent and requests for emergency housing were up by 13 percent (U.S. Conference of Mayors 2001).

10. See Edin and Lein (1997).

11. See, for instance, Newman (1988, 1999), Piven (1999), Blau (1999), Edin and Lein (1997), Ehrenreich (2001).

REFERENCES

Arno, Peter, Carol Levine, and Margaret Memmott. 1999. "The Economic Value of Informal Caregiving." *Health Affairs* 18: 182–188.

Boushev, Heather and Bethney Gunderson. 2001. *When Work Just Isn't Enough: Measuring Hardships Faced by Families after Moving from Welfare to Work*. Washington, DC: Economic Policy Institute.

Cherlin, Andrew J. and Paula Fomby. 2002. *A Closer Look at Changes in Children's Living Arrangements*. Welfare, Children, and Families: A Three-City Study, Working Paper 02–01. Baltimore, MD: Johns Hopkins University.

Edin, Kathryn and Laura Lein. 1997. *Making Ends Meet: How Single Mothers Survive Welfare and Low-Wage Work*. New York: Russell Sage Foundation.

Ehrenreich, Barbara. 2001. *Nickel and Dimed: On (Not) Getting By in America*. New York: Metropolitan Books.

Harvard School of Public Health. 2000. *Caregiving by Women: A Disproportionately Large Load.*" Project on Global Working Families. Cambridge, MA: President and Fellows of Harvard College.

Hays, Sharon. 1996. *The Cultural Contradictions of Motherhood*. New Haven, CT: Yale University Press.

Hochschild, Arlie Russell with Anne Machung. 1989. *The Second Shift: Working Parents and the Revolution at Home*. New York: Viking.

Hochschild, Arlie Russell. 1997. *The Time Bind: When Work Becomes Home and Home Becomes Work*. New York: Metropolitan Books.

Lamont, Michèle. 1992. *Money, Morals, and Manners*. Chicago: University of Chicago Press.

Lamont, Michèle. 2000. *The Dignity of Working Men: Morality and the Boundaries of Race, Class, and Immigration*. New York: Russell Sage Foundation.

Loprest, Pamela. 1999. *Families Who Left Welfare: Who Are They and How Are They Doing?* Washington, DC: Urban Institute.

Luker, Kristin. 1996. *Dubious Conceptions: The Politics of Teenage Pregnancy*. Cambridge, MA: Harvard University Press.

National Campaign for Jobs and Income Support. 2001A. *A Recession Like No Other: New Analysis Finds Safety Net in Tatters as Economic Slump Deepens*. Washington, DC: National Campaign for Jobs and Income Support.

National Campaign for Jobs and Income Support. 2001B. *Leaving Welfare, Left Behind:*

Employment Status, Income, and Well-Being of Former TANF Recipients. Washington, DC: National Campaign for Jobs and Income Support.

Newman, Katherine S. 1988. *Falling from Grace.* New York: Free Press.

Newman, Katherine S. 1999. *No Shame in My Game: The Working Poor in the Inner City.* New York: Vintage Books.

Piven, Frances Fox. 1999. "Welfare and Work," pp. 83–99 in *Whose Welfare?* edited by Gwendolyn Mink. Ithaca, NY: Cornell University Press.

Sherman, Arloc, Cheryl Amey, Barbara Duffield, Nancy Ebb, and Deborah Weinstein. 1998. *Welfare to What? Early Findings on Family Hardship and Well-Being.* National Coalition for the Homeless. Washington, DC: Children's Defense Fund.

Sorensen, Elaine and Chava Zibman. 2000. *Child Support Offers Some Protection Against Poverty.* Assessing the New Federalism, Series B, No. B–10. Washington, DC: Urban Institute.

Terry, Elizabeth and Jennifer Manlove. 1999. *Trends in Sexual Activity and Contraceptive Use Among Teens.* Washington, DC: Child Trends.

U.S. Conference of Mayors. 2001. *A Status Report on Hunger and Homelessness in America's Cities:* A 27-City Survey. Washington, DC: Conference of Mayors.

U.S. Congress. 1996. *Personal Responsibility and Work Opportunity Reconciliation Act of 1996.* Public Law 104–193, H.R. 3734.

Ventura, Stephanie and Christine A. Bachrach. 2000. *Nonmarital Childbearing in the United States, 1940–99.* U.S. Department of Health and Human Services, National Vital Statistics Reports 48 (16). Washington, DC: U.S. Government Printing Office.

Waller, Maureen R. 1999. "Meanings and Motives in New Family Stories: The Separation of Reproduction and Marriage Among Low-Income Black and White Parents," pp. 182–218 in *The Cultural Territories of Race: Black and White Boundaries,* edited by Michèle Lamont. Chicago: University of Chicago Press.

22

Incarceration, Unemployment, and Inequality

BRUCE WESTERN

In the later 1990s, two remarkable conditions influenced the employment opportunities of young, unskilled men in the United States. First, the unemployment rate fell to its lowest level in 30 years—around 4.5 percent by the summer of 1998. Second, the incarceration rate rose to its highest level in U.S. history. In 1998 1.78 million men were detained in American prisons and jails.

In removing so many from the labor force, U.S. incarceration policy has had significant but largely overlooked effects on unemployment. In the short run, it has lowered conventional measures of unemployment by concealing joblessness among a large group of able-bodied, working-age men. In the long run, it may raise unemployment rates by curtailing the job prospects of exconvicts and will certainly deepen economic inequality, because its effects are increasingly detrimental to young, black, unskilled men, whose incarceration rates are the highest of all and whose market power is weak. In this chapter I explore both short- and long-run effects.

The Penal System as a Labor Market Institution

In industrial relations and welfare state development, the United States stands apart from other major western nations. Its employment system is far more market-driven: rates of unionization and unemployment insurance coverage are lower than in most other countries in the Organisation for Economic Co-operation and Development (OECD), and social welfare spending accounts for only about 15 percent of gross domestic product (GDP), compared to about a quarter of GDP in the large European countries.

In recent years, the highly regulated European labor market has been burdened with persistent unemployment and apparently stagnant rates of economic growth, whereas the unregulated U.S. labor market has seen unemployment steadily falling in a booming economy. These trends have been used to buttress the argument that unregulated labor markets yield stronger economic performance than highly regulated markets.

Bruce Western, "Incarceration, Unemployment, and Inequality," *Focus* 21 (Spring 2001), pp. 32–36.

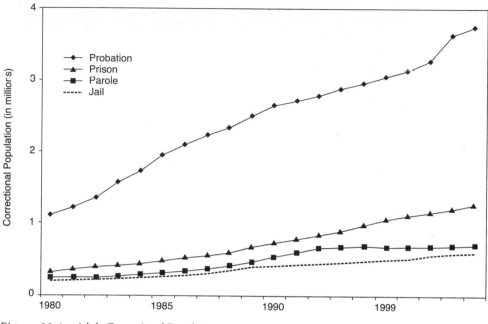

Figure 22.1   Adult Correctional Populations, 1980–99.

Source: Bureau of Justice Statistics http://www.ojp.usdoj.gov/bjs/glance/corr2.txt.

But the argument is too narrowly framed. Labor markets are embedded in a wide array of social arrangements that extend beyond the welfare state or industrial relations. The weakness of social protection mechanisms does not alone explain the superior U.S. employment record. In the United States, criminal justice policy constitutes a significant state intervention, providing a sizeable, nonmarket reallocation of labor that has significant effects on employment trends.

The magnitude of this intervention is reflected in incarceration and budget figures. Rates of incarceration began to increase in the early 1970s, but the most rapid growth took place in the 1980s and 1990s (see Figure 22.1). Between 1980 and 1999, the number of people in prisons and jails in the United States grew from half a million to almost two million. . . .

Incarceration is spread unevenly across the adult population. Men make up more than 90 percent of all inmates. In the mid-1990s, about two-thirds of those inmates were under 35, and about half had not completed high school. The dramatic expansion of the prison population most seriously affected young African Americans. In 1930, blacks accounted for 22 percent of all those in prison. In 1992, over half the prison population was black. By 1995, one out of three black male youths was under some form of state supervision and nearly 7 percent of all black males were incarcerated.

The U.S. incarceration rate—the number incarcerated on a single day per 100,000 of the adult population—is very much greater than incarceration rates in other industrialized democracies. In 1992–93, for instance, the overall U.S. rate was 5–10 times greater

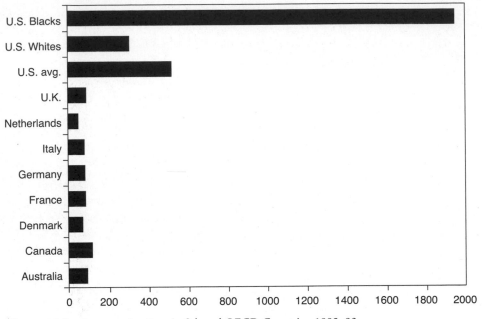

Figure 22.2   Incarceration Rate in Selected OECD Countries, 1992–93.

Source: B. Western and K. Beckett, "How Unregulated Is the U.S. Labor Market? The Penal System as a Labor Market Institution," *American Journal of Sociology* 104, no. 4 (1999): 130–60, Table 2.

than the rate for other OECD countries; among American blacks, the incarceration rate was 20 times greater (Figure 22.2). These high rates correspond to large absolute numbers. The entire Western European prison population is measured in hundreds of thousands, the prison and jail population in the United States in millions. This disparity does not reflect higher crime rates in the United States. The evidence, indeed, suggests that U.S. crime rates are only slightly above the average among industrialized countries. Thus U.S. incarceration rates appear to result from more aggressive prosecutorial practices, tougher sentencing standards, and intensified criminalization of drug-related activity.

The Short-Run Effect of Incarceration

The performance of national labor markets is commonly summarized by the unem-

ployment rate—the percentage of unemployed individuals among the civilian labor force. This definition excludes from its calculations those in the military and those in prison and jail, as well as the "discouraged," those no longer looking for work and therefore out of the labor force. A broader concept tries to tap the idleness or economic dependence of a group by extending the definition of "unemployed" to include those incarcerated.

In the short run, incarceration keeps those with a high risk of unemployment out of the labor market. National surveys of prisons and jails from the early 1990s indicate that, on average, more than a third of male inmates were unemployed at the time they were sent to prison. If, for example, we count among the unemployed those inmates who were not working when incarcerated, the adjusted unemployment rate for 1995 was 6.2 percent, versus the conventional rate of 5.6 percent.

If we pursue the calculation further, including all inmates among the unemployed, the adjusted U.S. unemployment rate for 1995 rises to 7.5 percent, an increase of 1.9 percentage points over the conventional rate.[1] According to this adjusted measure, U.S. rates of labor inactivity never fell below 7 percent throughout the 1980s. In the economically buoyant period of the mid-1990s, the rate of inactivity was about 8 percent, higher than any conventional unemployment rate since the recession of the early 1980s.

In Europe, the short-run effect of incarceration is tiny, because incarceration rates are so low. In all European countries, unemployed males outnumber imprisoned males by very large ratios—between 20:1 and 50:1 (in the United States the ratio is 3:1). Including prison inmates in the jobless count, therefore, changes the unemployment rate for most European countries by only a few tenths of a percentage point, a striking contrast with the large U.S. difference.

By the conventional measure, the United States enjoyed consistently lower unemployment than Europe after the mid-1980s. But adjusted figures that count the incarcerated population as unemployed suggest that the U.S. labor market performed worse, not better, than Europe for most of the period between 1976 and 1994.

The Long-Run Effect of Incarceration

The long-run effects of incarceration highlight the employment experiences of convicts after they are released. Ex-convicts must reintegrate themselves into mainstream society, surmounting the psychological, social, and financial consequences of imprisonment. In this process, the ability to find stable, legal employment is crucial, yet job prospects for ex-convicts are poorer than the prospects of applicants with no criminal record. Incarceration erodes the value of vocational skills, and the increasingly violent and overcrowded state of prisons and jails produces attitudes and practices that may enhance survival in the prison but are not compatible with success in the conventional job market. Job prospects may be even worse in the current context, because resources for educational and vocational training in prisons have declined. Such experiences are better observed through survey data than through aggregate labor market statistics; I drew upon the National Longitudinal Survey of Youth (NLSY), which surveys a national sample of Americans aged 14 to 21 in 1979, to follow workers as they moved from prison to the labor market. I examined employment as a function of youth incarceration, jail time, and work experience, controlling also for personal and regional characteristics such as the extent of juvenile contact with the criminal justice system and the local unemployment rate. I included employment status both before and after incarceration, because the same characteristics that place men at risk of unemployment or low wages also raise their chances of criminal conviction.

The regression analysis indicates that youth who spent time in prison worked less four years later than youth who had no prison time. Incarceration, on average, reduced employment by about 5 percentage points, or three weeks a year. The effect is particularly large for black youth, whose employment was reduced by about 9 percentage points (5 weeks) by juvenile jail time. The effect of jail time on adult employment was greater than the effect of dropping out of high school or living in a high-unemployment area. Moreover, these effects did not decay over time. Even after 15 years, men incarcerated as juveniles worked between 5 and 10 percentage points less than their counterparts who never went to prison. The effects of adult incarceration, although large in the short run (5–10 weeks a year), were less persistent, and largely disappeared within four to five years of release.

With nearly two million men now in prison, these effects are not small. The penal system, when viewed as a labor market institution, appears to significantly undermine the productivity and employment chances of the male workforce.

The Penal System and Racial Inequality in Employment

A large and growing proportion of young black men has had experience with the penal system; can we estimate the likely effect on their future prospects and on black-white economic inequality?

The short-run effects of incarceration are very much worse for black than for white men. As the prison and jail population grew throughout the 1980s, the labor market effects of incarceration for black men becomes much larger if all those incarcerated are counted among the unemployed. In 1990–94, the adjusted unemployment rate is only one percentage point higher for white men, but it is seven percentage points higher for black men. During the 1990s almost one in five African American men, on average, was without a job.

Standard labor force data report a persistent gap in joblessness between black and white men that dates at least from the late 1960s.[2] Employment-population ratios calculated from these data show that employment inequality grew most sharply for young high school dropouts.[3] By including the incarcerated in calculating these ratios, we gain a more accurate picture, because marginalized groups at the fringes of the labor market have especially high incarceration rates.

If we include men in prison or jail, employment among black high school dropouts aged 20–35 declines from 46 to 29.3 percent in 1996. Furthermore, the adjusted employment ratios for black high school dropouts show steady decline over time, whereas conventional ratios show black employment as stable or even rising slightly.

The long-run effects are also serious. The incarceration of youth disrupts transitions from school to a career and hinders the acquisition of work experience. Ex-prisoners find it difficult to access jobs in the primary sector that offer opportunities for training, pay schedules that rise strongly with experience and age, and other characteristics of stable employment.[4] Instead, many ex-inmates find themselves stuck in low-wage job trajectories, confined to casual or illegitimate employment in the secondary labor market.

These kinds of disruptions materially affect earnings. In general, black ex-convicts earn about 10 percent less per hour than comparable men who were never incarcerated, after adjusting for such factors as work experience, schooling, youth delinquency, and drug use. They also have generally flat earnings profiles. My estimates suggest that, by 1998, the disproportionate incarceration of black men and the low-wage job trajectory of ex-inmates, taken together, had raised black-white earnings inequality by about 15 percent. . . .

By the end of the twentieth century, the prison experience was routinely shaping the working lives of young, less-educated, minority men. Because their incarceration rates are so high, labor market and earnings statistics as conventionally measured may significantly understate the extent of racial inequality in employment. The evidence suggests that the U.S. prison system may be exercising a systematic influence on large-scale patterns of economic inequality.

NOTES

1. The unemployed are usually defined as those without paid employment who are actively seeking work in the month before the survey.

2. F. Wilson, M. Tienda, and L. Wu, "Race and Unemployment: Labor Market Experiences of Black and White Men, 1968–1988," *Work and Occupations* 22, no. 3 (1995): 245–70.

3. J. Bound and R. Freeman, "What Went Wrong? The Erosion of Relative Earnings and Employment among Young Black Men in the 1980s," *Quarterly Journal of Economics* 107 (1992): 201–32.

4. M. Duneier, *Sidewalk* (New York: Farrar, Strauss, and Giroux, 1999), R. Sampson and J. Laub, *Crime in the Making: Pathways and Turning Points Through Life* (Cambridge, MA: Harvard University Press, 1993), J. Waldfogel, "The Effect of Criminal Conviction on Income and the Trust 'Reposed in the Workmen'," *Journal of Human Resources* 29 (1994): 62–81, and "Does Conviction Have a Persistent Effect on Income and Employment?" *International Review of Law and Economics* 14 (1994): 103–19.

23

Escaping Poverty

Can Housing Vouchers Help?

STEFANIE DELUCA AND
JAMES E. ROSENBAUM

It makes sense that helping poor minority families leave dangerous neighborhoods would bring about immediate improvements in their lives. Urban sociologists have long described the horrors of public housing, drug-related violence, and the high levels of racial isolation and segregation common in many American cities. Dozens of studies have also shown that growing up in poor neighborhoods predicts a range of diminished social and economic outcomes for families and children.

Essentially, the logic is that if poor and minority families had access to the same schools, communities, and labor markets as middle-class families, they could start the path to middle-class success. Unfortunately, it's not so easy for these families to obtain access to such opportunity-rich communities. When black families move, they usually move between poor neighborhoods, not out of them. This is due in part to housing discrimination and lending practices that channel black families into undesirable neighborhoods. We must consider whether a voucher mobility strategy is enough on its own to alleviate the problems of the urban poor, or whether it's one essential part of a larger set of interventions. Will helping poor families escape the ghetto break the cycle of poverty?

In some ways this thought experiment has already been tested—poor families have relocated to different neighborhoods through a number of unique housing voucher programs. The first major residential mobility program, the Gautreaux program, came as a result of a 1976 Supreme Court ruling in a housing desegregation lawsuit filed on behalf of public housing residents against the Chicago Housing Authority (CHA) and the U.S. Department of Housing and Urban Development (HUD). Between 1976 and 1998, the court remedy provided vouchers for over 7,000 families in the Chicago metro area to move to nonsegregated communities. About half moved to mostly white, middle- and upper-income suburbs, and half moved to nonpublic housing city neighborhoods. However, unlike the Section 8 program, families did not choose the new housing units—they were offered specific apartments in new neighborhoods by housing counselors (who were working with land-

Stefanie DeLuca and James E. Rosenbaum, "Escaping Poverty: Can Housing Vouchers Help?" *Pathways* (Winter 2008), pp. 29–32.

lords) on a first-come, first-served basis, similar to a random draw lottery. Suburbs with a population that was more than 30 percent black were excluded by the consent decree.

Early results from the Gautreaux program showed that low-income black children moving to middle-class white suburbs had better educational and employment outcomes than their counterparts relocating to other city areas—they were more likely to complete high school, attend college, and attend four-year colleges. Suburban youth who didn't attend college were more likely to get jobs with better pay and benefits. Mothers who moved to the suburbs also benefited from higher levels of employment postmove. This early research was powerful, showing how neighborhoods could be policy levers. These findings suggest that the life chances of low-income families depend not just on *who* they are but *where* they live. In recent work, we have examined the long-term outcomes for the Gautreaux families to see if the earlier results held up years later. We found that the program was very successful in helping former public housing families relocate to safer, more integrated neighborhoods and stay there. These families came from very poor neighborhoods originally, with census-tract poverty rates averaging 40 to 60 percent, or three to five times the national poverty rate. After their move, families moving to suburbs were living in neighborhoods that were 5 percent poor. As of the late 1990s, fifteen to twenty years later, mothers continued to live in neighborhoods with lower poverty rates.

The Gautreaux program also achieved striking success in moving low-income black families into more racially integrated neighborhoods. For example, 83 percent of their neighbors in their origin communities were black. The program placed its families moving to suburbs in communities that reduced this percentage to less than 10 percent black. While the later moves of Gautreaux suburb families were to neighborhoods that contained considerably more blacks (33 percent on average), these levels were less than half of what they had been in the origin neighborhoods, and more than half of the families were still in mostly white neighborhoods. Families who moved to the most integrated neighborhoods were also more likely to live in similar areas fifteen years later. The children of Gautreaux families who had relocated to less segregated neighborhoods were also more likely to reside in such neighborhoods when they became adults.

Early research on Gautreaux had also shown large relationships between placement neighborhoods and gains in adult employment. For example, 26 percent of families moving to neighborhoods with the highest proportions of educated residents received welfare in 1989 (about six years after relocation for most families) compared to 39 percent of families who moved to neighborhoods with the lowest proportion of educated individuals. But did these improvements also last? The short answer is yes. Using state and federal data on employment and welfare receipt up to twenty years later, we found that women placed in more affluent, less-segregated neighborhoods spent less time on welfare and more time employed than women placed in areas with mostly black residents, more crime, and higher unemployment rates. Over fifteen years later, women placed in areas with higher economic resources and less segregation earned between $2,400 and $2,900 more per year than women placed in any other kind of neighborhood.

While the results from the Gautreaux program had a profound effect on social scientists and policy makers, it wasn't a perfect experiment. All families moved somewhere, so there was no way to compare them to similar kinds of families who did not relocate to better neighborhoods. As a result, the Moving to Opportunity (MTO) program was designed as a rigorous social experiment, in part to test the promise of the Gautreaux program. Beginning in 1994, MTO allowed public housing residents in five cities (New York, Boston, Baltimore, Chicago, and Los Angeles) to apply for a chance to receive a housing voucher. Families were assigned at random to one of three groups. An experimental group received a Section 8 voucher that would allow them to rent an apartment in the private market, but they could only use this voucher in census tracts with 1990 poverty rates of less than 10 percent (unlike Gautreaux, there were no racial restrictions on the destination neighborhoods). This group also received housing counseling to assist them in relocating. Another group received a Section 8 voucher with no geographical restrictions. Finally, the control group received no new housing assistance but could continue to live in public housing or apply for other housing assistance.

Like Gautreaux, families with MTO vouchers relocated to neighborhoods with much lower poverty rates than their public housing neighborhoods. These new neighborhoods were 11 percent poor on average, compared to their original communities, which were usually 40 percent poor or more. At the time of the four- to seven-year follow-up study, MTO families who had moved with low-poverty vouchers were still in neighborhoods that were significantly less poor than the control group but more disadvantaged than their first MTO community. MTO set no race-based limits on placement neighborhoods, and MTO families moving in conjunction with the program both began and ended up in neighborhoods with high minority concentrations.

When families first signed up for MTO, over three-quarters reported that the most important reason for wanting to move was to get away from inner-city gangs, drugs, and violence. Four to seven years later, movers reported higher levels of neighborhood and housing quality than those families who did not move with the program. Fewer experimental movers were victimized and they felt safer at night—in part because they reported greater success getting police to respond to calls in their neighborhood and they saw less drug-related loitering outside. These improvements in safety may have also led to the significant reduction in psychological distress observed among experimental mothers who relocated.

Teenage girls who moved with MTO also benefited from the relief of escaping high-poverty neighborhoods. Not only did they report significantly lower levels of depression and anxiety, they were also less likely to use drugs, drink, and smoke. Unfortunately, the young men who relocated to low-poverty areas were actually *more* likely to engage in risky behavior and more likely to be arrested for property crimes. Interviews suggest that girls and boys socialize in different ways—boys were more likely to hang out with their friends on the corner or on a neighborhood basketball court, and girls were more likely to visit friends inside their homes or to go downtown to a mall. Boys may have been at higher risk of delinquency because these routines do fit in as well in low-poverty neighborhoods, which may explain why they did not benefit as much as girls from peers in their new neighborhoods.

In terms of what many policy makers were hoping for—increases in economic self-suffi-ciency for parents and better schooling out-comes for children—the MTO results were not as encouraging. MTO mothers were no more likely to be employed, earned no more, and received welfare no less often than moth-ers assigned to the control group. However, it should be stressed that MTO occurred in an unusual historical era, a period in which welfare reform and a very strong labor mar-ket combined to generate an amazing 100 percent gain in employment in the control group. That the MTO movers failed to demonstrate better employment outcomes may not generalize to different times. In terms of educational outcomes, early MTO research had shown that moving to less poor neighborhoods helped children attend better schools and increased test scores and school engagement (especially in Baltimore). How-ever, four to seven years after program moves, virtually no educational benefits were found for these youth. This may be partially because almost 70 percent of the MTO chil-dren were attending schools in the same district they attended when they signed up for the program. Some children did attend higher-performing schools in the suburbs as a result of their move—but average differ-ences were small. For example, while 88 percent of Gautreaux suburban movers at-tended schools with above-average achieve-ment on national exams, less than 10 percent of MTO experimental group children at-tended such schools. While it seems surpris-ing that more movers didn't send their children to better schools, few families had experience with better educational environ-

ments, and families lacked the information that middle-class parents use to make choices about their children's education.

Overall, the Gautreaux and MTO pro-grams both succeeded admirably in enabling families to achieve their stated goal of escap-ing violent, gang-ridden neighborhoods and finding better quality housing; these escapes were permanent for many families in the case of Gautreaux. The significance of the improved safety and mental health should not be ignored. In fact, the reductions in MTO mothers' psychological distress are comparable to what is achieved through current antidepressant drug treatments. However, in terms of long-term gains in eco-nomic self-sufficiency, residential location and children's academic achievement, find-ings from the two programs are mixed. How do we reconcile these differences?

Despite some similarities, the Gautreaux program differed from MTO in important ways. First, MTO's criterion for a place-ment neighborhood was based on the poverty rate, while Gautreaux moved fami-lies to mostly white suburban neighbor-hoods (which were more affluent than MTO destinations). As a result, MTO fam-ilies did not move as far away from their original neighborhoods as Gautreaux's fam-ilies did.

Second, the way participants secured housing units differed between the two pro-grams, which may have led to differences in long-term neighborhood residence. In Gautreaux, real estate staff worked with landlords to locate units for participants and helped identify housing that participants could not find on their own; this may have facilitated permanent relocations through overcoming landlord discrimination. In con-trast, although they received housing coun-seling, MTO experimental families found units on their own. While only 10 percent of Gautreaux suburban families moved less than ten miles, 84 percent of the MTO treatment group did so. Such short-distance moves may have reduced changes in employment opportunities and school quality, and may have reduced the possibility of changes in social outcomes through new networks or by permitting interaction with prior neighbors and family. Therefore, the mix of housing counselor assistance and placement in high-resource communities seemed to yield the greatest long-term benefits for families, and indicates the policy significance of both components for mobility programs.

A third important difference is methodological. In Gautreaux, we can only compare families that moved to a variety of *different* neighborhoods. Therefore, Gautreaux can inform us about what happens when families move from uniformly poor and highly segregated neighborhoods into communities not chosen by the families themselves, neighborhoods that show wide variations in degree of racial integration, poverty, and safety. MTO, on the other hand, tracks the fortunes of a randomly assigned control group of families who expressed interest in the program but, owing to the luck of the draw, were not offered access to it. Thus, MTO compares the effects of both being offered a low-poverty voucher and moving to lower-poverty neighborhoods with not being offered assistance at all. This design is better for inferring causal effects of reductions in neighborhood poverty, but might tell us less about the effects of moving to neighborhoods that vary by race and class and (it turns out) include more affluent neighbors and high-achieving schools.

In the future, we will have the opportunity to better understand the implications of mobility programs. Researchers are planning

a ten-year follow up to the MTO evaluation, to see whether some of the early improvements experienced by families have more substantial long-term benefits. In Baltimore, families are currently moving as part of the ongoing Thompson program— a desegregation remedy very similar to the one ordered in Gautreaux. Stefanie DeLuca is following over 1,000 families who have moved to low-poverty, nonsegregated neighborhoods around the Baltimore metropolitan area. Housing counselors are working with families to prepare them for moves and are also organizing monthly bus trips to outlying counties so that families can explore new neighborhoods and meet landlords. Unlike other mobility programs, Thompson involves multipartner efforts to help directly connect these families to resources in their new communities. For example, one local foundation provides cars with low financing to families moving to the suburbs and another foundation has been supporting ways to connect families to better health care, employment training, and high-quality schools after their move.

How do these current results from Gautreaux and MTO inform antipoverty policy? First, the initial gains in neighborhood quality that many of the Gautreaux families achieved with vouchers and housing assistance persisted for at least one to two decades. This is extremely encouraging and suggests that it is possible for low-income black families to make permanent escapes from neighborhoods with concentrated racial segregation, crime, and poverty. In the absence of such a program, it is rare to see poor families maintaining long-term residence in nonpoor, nonsegregated communities.

Second, housing mobility vouchers *by themselves* do not guarantee moves to better neighborhoods or large gains in economic and social success for families and children. Therefore, housing mobility may be a necessary but insufficient lever for improving the lives of poor families. For parents to acquire better jobs and transition off welfare, we may need to couple housing mobility with additional services and supports. Recent research showed that many experimental work support programs run in the 1990s boosted work, family income, and children's achievement. Some of these programs supplied poor parents with earnings supplements and child care assistance that helped them balance employment and family needs. To help promote children's educational and behavioral achievement, mobility counselors should be trained to inform parents about the benefits of schooling opportunities in their new communities, since low-income parents are not always aware of these choices. When transfers do occur, counselors can make sure that receiving schools have information about the child, so that little instruction time is lost. Last, postmove assistance to help tenants and landlords work out problems might ensure that families remain in opportunity-rich communities, and might encourage landlords to participate in the program.

This nation has a strong commitment to improving education and employment outcomes of its citizens; providing opportunities to live in safe communities where families can prosper should also be part of that commitment. Evidence from housing voucher programs suggests that well-designed residential mobility programs can be important instruments for helping families improve the quality of their lives.

PART V

Racial and Ethnic Inequality

24

Racial Formation in the United States

From the 1960s to the 1990s

MICHAEL OMI AND
HOWARD WINANT

In 1982–83, Susie Guillory Phipps unsuccessfully sued the Louisiana Bureau of Vital Records to change her racial classification from black to white. The descendant of an 18th-century white planter and a black slave, Phipps was designated "black" in her birth certificate in accordance with a 1970 state law which declared anyone with at least 1/32nd "Negro blood" to be black.

The Phipps case raised intriguing questions about the concept of race, its meaning in contemporary society, and its use (and abuse) in public policy. Assistant Attorney General Ron Davis defended the law by pointing out that some type of racial classification was necessary to comply with federal record-keeping requirements and to facilitate programs for the prevention of genetic diseases. Phipps's attorney, Brian Begue, argued that the assignment of racial categories on birth certificates was unconstitutional and that the 1/32nd designation was inaccurate. He called on a retired Tulane University professor who cited research indicating that most Louisiana whites have at least 1/20th "Negro" ancestry.

In the end, Phipps lost. The court upheld the state's right to classify and quantify racial identity.[1]

Phipps's problematic racial identity, and her effort to resolve it through state action, is in many ways a parable of America's unsolved racial dilemma. It illustrates the difficulties of defining race and assigning individuals or groups to racial categories. It shows how the racial legacies of the past— slavery and bigotry—continue to shape the present. It reveals both the deep involvement of the state in the organization and interpretation of race, and the inadequacy of state institutions to carry out these functions. It demonstrates how deeply Americans both as individuals and as a civilization are shaped, and indeed haunted, by race.

Having lived her whole life thinking that she was white, Phipps suddenly discovers that by legal definition she is not. In U.S. society, such an event is indeed catastrophic. But if she is not white, of what race is she? The *state* claims that she is black, based on its rules of classification, and another state agency, the court, upholds this judgment.

But despite these classificatory standards which have imposed an either-or logic on racial identity, Phipps will not in fact "change color." Unlike what would have happened during slavery times if one's claim to whiteness was successfully challenged, we can assume that despite the outcome of her legal challenge, Phipps will remain in most of the social relationships she had occupied before the trial. Her socialization, her familial and friendship networks, her cultural orientation, will not change. She will simply have to wrestle with her newly acquired "hybridized" condition. She will have to confront the "Other" within.

The designation of racial categories and the determination of racial identity is no simple task. For centuries, this question has precipitated intense debates and conflicts, particularly in the U.S.—disputes over natural and legal rights, over the distribution of resources, and indeed, over who shall live and who shall die.

A crucial dimension of the Phipps case is that it illustrates the inadequacy of claims that race is a mere matter of variations in human physiognomy, that it is simply a matter of skin color. But if race cannot be understood in this manner, how *can* it be understood? We cannot fully hope to address this topic—no less than the meaning of race, its role in society, and the forces which shape it—in one chapter, nor indeed in one book. Our goal in this chapter, however, is far from modest: we wish to offer at least the outlines of a theory of race and racism.

What Is Race?

There is a continuous temptation to think of race as an *essence,* as something fixed, concrete, and objective. And there is also an op-

posite temptation: to imagine race as a mere *illusion,* a purely ideological construct which some ideal non-racist social order would eliminate. It is necessary to challenge both these positions, to disrupt and reframe the rigid and bipolar manner in which they are posed and debated, and to transcend the presumably irreconcilable relationship between them.

The effort must be made to understand race as an unstable and "decentered" complex of social meanings constantly being transformed by political struggle. With this in mind, let us propose a definition: *race is a concept which signifies and symbolizes social conflicts and interests by referring to different types of human bodies.* Although the concept of race invokes biologically based human characteristics (so-called "phenotypes"), selection of these particular human features for purposes of racial signification is always and necessarily a social and historical process. In contrast to the other major distinction of this type, that of gender, there is no biological basis for distinguishing among human groups along the lines of race. Indeed, the categories employed to differentiate among human groups along racial lines reveal themselves, upon serious examination, to be at best imprecise, and at worst completely arbitrary.

If the concept of race is so nebulous, can we not dispense with it? Can we not "do without" race, at least in the "enlightened" present? This question has been posed often, and with greater frequency in recent years. An affirmative answer would of course present obvious practical difficulties: it is rather difficult to jettison widely held beliefs, beliefs which moreover are central to everyone's identity and understanding of the social world. So the attempt to banish the concept as an archaism is at best counterintuitive. But a deeper difficulty, we believe, is inherent in the very formulation of this schema, in its way of posing race as a *problem,* a misconception left over from the past, and suitable now only for the dustbin of history.

A more effective starting point is the recognition that despite its uncertainties and contradictions, the concept of race continues to play a fundamental role in structuring and representing the social world. The task for theory is to explain this situation. It is to avoid both the utopian framework which sees race as an illusion we can somehow "get beyond," and also the essentialist formulation which sees race as something objective and fixed, a biological datum. Thus we should think of race as an element of social structure rather than as an irregularity within it; we should see race as a dimension of human representation rather than an illusion. These perspectives inform the theoretical approach we call racial formation.

Racial Formation

We define *racial formation* as the sociohistorical process by which racial categories are created, inhabited, transformed, and destroyed. Our attempt to elaborate a theory of racial formation will proceed in two steps. First, we argue that racial formation is a process of historically situated *projects* in which human bodies and social structures are represented and organized. Next we link racial formation to the evolution of hegemony, the way in which society is organized and ruled. Such an approach, we believe, can facilitate understanding of a whole range of contemporary controversies and dilemmas involving race, including the nature of racism, the relationship of race to other forms of differences, inequalities, and

oppression such as sexism and nationalism, and the dilemmas of racial identity today.

From a racial formation perspective, race is a matter of both social structure and cultural representation. Too often, the attempt is made to understand race simply or primarily in terms of only one of these two analytical dimensions.[2] For example, efforts to explain racial inequality as a purely social structural phenomenon are unable to account for the origins, patterning, and transformation of racial difference.

Conversely, many examinations of racial difference—understood as a matter of cultural attributes *à la* ethnicity theory, or as a society-wide signification system, *à la* some poststructuralist accounts—cannot comprehend such structural phenomena as racial stratification in the labor market or patterns of residential segregation.

An alternative approach is to think of racial formation processes as occurring through a linkage between structure and representation. Racial *projects* do the ideological "work" of making these links. *A racial project is simultaneously an interpretation, representation, or explanation of racial dynamics, and an effort to reorganize and redistribute resources along particular racial lines.* Racial projects connect what race *means* in a particular discursive practice and the ways in which both social structures and everyday experiences are racially *organized,* based upon that meaning. Let us consider this proposition, first in terms of large-scale or macro-level social processes, and then in terms of other dimensions of the racial formation process.

Racial Formation as a Macro-Level Social Process

To *interpret the meaning of race is to frame it social structurally.* Consider for example, this statement by Charles Murray on welfare reform:

My proposal for dealing with the racial issue in social welfare is to repeal every bit of legislation and reverse every court decision that in any way requires, recommends, or awards differential treatment according to race, and thereby put us back onto the track that we left in 1965. We may argue about the appropriate limits of government intervention in trying to enforce the ideal, but at least it should be possible to identify the ideal: Race is not a morally admissible reason for treating one person differently from another. Period.[3]

Here there is a partial but significant analysis of the meaning of race: it is not a morally valid basis upon which to treat people "differently from one another." We may notice someone's race, but we cannot act upon that awareness. We must act in a "color-blind" fashion. This analysis of the meaning of race is immediately linked to a specific conception of the role of race in the social structure: it can play no part in government action, save in "the enforcement of the ideal." No state policy can legitimately require, recommend, or award different status according to race. This example can be classified as a particular type of racial project in the present-day U.S.—a "neoconservative" one.

Conversely, *to recognize the racial dimension in social structure is to interpret the meaning of race.* Consider the following statement by the late Supreme Court Justice Thurgood Marshall on minority "set-aside" programs:

A profound difference separates governmental actions that themselves are racist, and governmental actions that seek to remedy the effects of prior racism or to prevent neutral government activity from perpetuating the effects of such racism.[4]

Here the focus is on the racial dimensions of *social structure*—in this case of state activity and policy. The argument is that state actions in the past and present have treated people in very different ways according to their race, and thus the government cannot retreat from its policy responsibilities in this area. It cannot suddenly declare itself "color-blind" without in fact perpetuating the same type of differential, racist treatment. Thus, race continues to signify difference and structure inequality. Here, racialized social structure is immediately linked to an interpretation of the meaning of race. This example too can be classified as a particular type of racial project in the present-day U.S.—a "liberal" one. . . .

These two examples of contemporary racial projects are drawn from mainstream political debate; they may be characterized as center-right and center-left expressions of contemporary racial politics. We can, however, expand the discussion of racial formation processes far beyond these familiar examples. In fact, we can identify racial projects in several other analytical dimensions: first, the political spectrum can be broadened to include radical projects, on both the left and right, as well as along other political axes. Second, analysis of racial projects can take place not only at the macro-level of racial policy-making, state activity, and collective action, but also at the micro-level of everyday experience. . . .

The Political Spectrum of Racial Formation

We have encountered examples of a neoconservative racial project, in which the significance of race is denied, leading to a "color-blind" racial politics and "hands off" policy orientation; and of a "liberal" racial project, in which the significance of race is affirmed, leading to an egalitarian and "activist" state policy. But these by no means exhaust the political possibilities. Other racial projects can be readily identified on the contemporary U.S. scene. For example, "far right" projects, which uphold biologistic and racist views of difference, explicitly argue for white supremacist policies. "New right" projects overtly claim to hold "color-blind" views, but covertly manipulate racial fears in order to achieve political gains. On the left, "radical democratic" projects invoke notions of racial "difference" in combination with egalitarian politics and policy.

Further variations can also be noted. For example, "nationalist" projects, both conservative and radical, stress the incompatibility of racially defined group identity with the legacy of white supremacy, and therefore advocate a social structural solution of separation, either complete or partial. Nationalist currents represent a profound legacy of the centuries of racial absolutism that initially defined the meaning of race in the U.S. Nationalist concerns continue to influence racial debate in the form of Afrocentrism and other expressions of identity politics.

Taking the range of politically organized racial projects as a whole, we can "map" the current pattern of racial formation at the level of the public sphere, the "macro-level" in which public debate and mobilization takes place. But important as this is, the terrain on which racial formation occurs is broader yet.

Racial Formation as Everyday Experience

At the micro-social level, racial projects also link signification and structure, not so much as efforts to shape policy or define large-scale meaning, but as the applications of "common sense." To see racial projects operating at the level of everyday life, we have only to examine the many ways in which, often unconsciously, we "notice" race.

One of the first things we notice about people when we meet them (along with their sex) is their race. We utilize race to provide clues about *who* a person is. This fact is made painfully obvious when we encounter someone whom we cannot conveniently racially categorize—someone who is, for example, racially "mixed" or of an ethnic/racial group we are not familiar with. Such an encounter becomes a source of discomfort and momentarily a crisis of racial meaning.

Our ability to interpret racial meanings depends on preconceived notions of a racialized social structure. Comments such as, "Funny, you don't look black," betray an underlying image of what black should be. We expect people to act out their apparent racial identities; indeed we become disoriented when they do not. The black banker harassed by police while walking in casual clothes through his own well-off neighborhood, the Latino or white kid rapping in perfect Afro patois, the unending *faux pas* committed by whites who assume that the non-whites they encounter are servants or tradespeople, the belief that non-white colleagues are less qualified persons hired to fulfill affirmative action guidelines, indeed the whole gamut of racial stereotypes—that "white men can't jump," that Asians can't dance, etc., etc.—all testify to the way a racialized social structure shapes racial experience and conditions meaning. Analysis of such stereotypes reveals the always present, already active link between our view of the social structure—its demography, its laws, its customs, its threats—and our conception of what race means.

Conversely, our ongoing interpretation of our experience in racial terms shapes our relations to the institutions and organizations through which we are imbedded in social structure. Thus we expect differences in skin color, or other racially coded characteristics, to explain social differences. Temperament, sexuality, intelligence, athletic ability, aesthetic preferences, and so on are presumed to be fixed and discernible from the palpable mark of race. Such diverse questions as our confidence and trust in others (for example, clerks or salespeople, media figures, neighbors), our sexual preferences and romantic images, our tastes in music, films, dance, or sports, and our very ways of talking, walking, eating, and dreaming become racially coded simply because we live in a society where racial awareness is so pervasive. Thus in ways too comprehensive even to monitor consciously, and despite periodic calls—neoconservative and otherwise—for us to ignore race and adopt "color-blind" racial attitudes, skin color "differences" continue to rationalize distinct treatment of racially identified individuals and groups.

To summarize the argument: the theory of racial formation suggests that society is suffused with racial projects, large and small, to which all are subjected. This racial "subjection" is quintessentially ideological. Everybody learns some combination, some version, of the rules of racial classification, and of her own racial identity, often without obvious teaching or conscious inculcation. Thus are we inserted in a comprehensively racialized social structure. Race becomes "common sense"—a way of comprehend-

ing, explaining, and acting in the world. A vast web of racial projects mediates between the discursive or representational means in which race is identified and signified on the one hand, and the institutional and organizational forms in which it is routinized and standardized on the other. These projects are the heart of the racial formation process.

Under such circumstances, it is not possible to represent race discursively without simultaneously locating it, explicitly or implicitly, in a social structural (and historical) context. Nor is it possible to organize, maintain, or transform social structures without simultaneously engaging, once more either explicitly or implicitly, in racial signification. Racial formation, therefore, is a kind of synthesis, an outcome, of the interaction of racial projects on a society-wide level. These projects are, of course, vastly different in scope and effect. They include large-scale public action, state activities, and interpretations of racial conditions in artistic, journalistic, or academic fora, as well as the seemingly infinite number of racial judgments and practices we carry out at the level of individual experience. . . .

NOTES

1. *San Francisco Chronicle,* 14 September 1982, 19 May 1983.

2. Michael Omi and Howard Winant, "On the Theoretical Status of the Concept of Race" in Warren Crichlow and Cameron McCarthy, eds., *Race, Identity, and Representation in Education* (New York: Routledge, 1993).

3. Charles Murray, *Losing Ground: American Social Policy, 1950–1980* (New York: Basic Books, 1984), p. 223.

4. Justice Thurgood Marshall, dissenting in *City of Richmond v. J. A. Croson Co.,* 488 U.S. 469 (1989).

25

Racial Identities in 2000

The Response to the Multiple-Race Response Option

REYNOLDS FARLEY

The greatest change in the measurement of race in the history of the United States occurred in the census of 2000. For more than two centuries, the federal statistical system had classified each respondent into a single race. That is no longer the case. According to the new rules, anyone may now identify with as many races as he or she desires. . . .

The efforts to change the one-race-only classification system came from individuals who believed that many Americans shared multiple racial origins, but information about the size or growth of this population was seldom presented. Indeed, no reliable data existed before the Census Bureau pretested queries for the census of 2000. Although a small number of studies attempted to estimate changes over time in the frequency of interracial marriages (Kalmijn 1993, 1998), few data sets lend themselves to the measurement of rare events; until 1967, some states prohibited marriages across racial lines, and so there are few data on the mixed-race offspring of interracial unions. However, public-use files from census data may be used to ascertain the percentage of married couples in which the husband and wife reported different races. As a result, studies of interracial marriage have become numerous (Fu 2001; Gilbertston, Fitzpatrick, and Yang 1996; Heer 1974; Hwang, Saenz, and Aguirre 1995; Model and Fisher 2001; Qian 1997; Rosenfield 2001; Sandefur and McKinnell 1986; Schoen and Thomas 1989). Presumably, as the proportion of interracial marriages increases, so too will the percentage of children who think of themselves as multiple by race.

Table 25.1 reports data about interracial marriage compiled from the 1990 census and the March 2000 Current Population Survey. Spouses were classified into one of five mutually exclusive and exhaustive categories: Hispanic, non-Hispanic white, non-Hispanic black or African American, non-Hispanic Asian or Pacific Islander, and non-Hispanic American Indian. For these tabulations, Hispanic origin is treated as if it were equivalent to a race.

According to the table, the percentage of married couples in which the races of the

Reynolds Farley, "Racial Identities in 2000: The Response to the Multiple-Race Response Option," in *The New Race Question: How the Census Counts Multiracial Individuals*, edited by Joel Perlmann and Mary C. Waters, pp. 33, 38–40, 44–49, 57–60. Copyright © 2002 by the Russell Sage Foundation.

Table 25.1 Estimates of Racial Intermarriage, 1990 and 2000, by Race and Sex (Thousands)

Racial Group	Men		Women	
	1990	*2000*	*1990*	*2000*
White				
Number	43,710	43,809	43,546	43,590
Percentage married out	2.7	3.4	2.2	2.9
Black				
Number	3,566	4,089	3,383	3,872
Percentage married out	6.3	8.4	2.4	3.3
Hispanic				
Number	3,489	5,181	3,562	5,318
Percentage married out	18.7	15.0	19.9	17.2
Asian				
Number	1,299	1,922	1,543	2,201
Percentage married out	11.3	9.9	24.1	21.3
American Indian				
Number	300	351	330	371
Percentage married out	57.8	52.3	61.5	53.9
Total				
Number	52,364	55,352	52,364	55,352
Percentage married out	4.5	5.4	4.5	5.4

Source: U.S. Bureau of the Census, Public Use Microdata Files from the 5 Percent Sample of the Census of 1990 and from the March 2000 Current Population Survey.
Note: These data tabulate the race of spouses for persons married and living with a spouse. Five mutually exclusive races were used: Hispanic, non-Hispanic white, non-Hispanic black, non-Hispanic Asian (including Pacific Islanders), and non-Hispanic American Indian.

spouses differ rose from 4.5 percent at the start of the 1990s to 5.4 percent at the end—an increase from 2.4 million interracial couples to about 3.0 million. This finding is consistent with previous studies that reported a secular trend toward increasing interracial marriage, especially among blacks and whites (Farley 1999, figures 5.7 and 5.8). Presumably, a growing but still small minority of children have parents of different races.

The primary reason for change through the 1990s was that white and black men and women increasingly married persons from races other than their own. The percentage of black men with nonblack wives rose from 6.3 to 8.4 percent, while that of white men with nonwhite wives went from 2.7 to 3.4 percent. Interestingly, the percentage of Hispanic and Asian spouses marrying outside their race decreased. Migration from abroad has produced rapid growth for these groups. Immigrant enclaves are getting much larger, and this presumably promotes greater racial homogamy for Hispanics and Asians who marry, especially among immigrants. . . .

The Official Governmental Decision About Measuring Race

Because the new 1997 OMB (Office of Management and Budget) guidelines for measuring race will have consequences for decades to come, it is important to summarize them carefully. They include the following:

- When self-identification is used to identify race in the federal statistical system, respondents should be given the opportunity to identify with more than one race, but the term "multiracial" is not to be used. Rather, the names of specific races are to be presented as choices for the respondent.
- When self-identification is the method of data collection, separate questions should be asked to determine race and Hispanic ethnicity.
- The Hispanic-ethnicity question should precede the race question (an important change from the 1990 census procedure).
- "Arab" and "Cape Verdean" should not be used as races. (Spokespersons for these groups had advocated the addition of these terms as races.)
- The term "American Indian" should not be replaced by "Native American," but the term "Hawaiian" should be replaced by "Native Hawaiian."
- The term "Alaskan Native" should replace "Aleut" or "Eskimo."
- Asian races should be distinguished from Pacific Islander races. A broad racial category called "Native Hawaiian or Other Pacific Islander" (NHOPI or NHPI) should be used.
- The five major racial categories to be used are white, black or African American, American Indian, Asian, and Native Hawaiian or other Pacific Islander.

The radical shift away from the assumption that each person had only one racial identity did not occur because powerful civil rights organization or professional associations advocated a change nor because federal enforcement agencies demanded improved data to carry out the responsibilities mandated by Congress and the courts. Rather, a small number of persistent advocates who were greatly upset by the status quo effectively challenged the traditional system. They found a sympathetic hearing in Congress and in the Clinton administration: elected and appointed officials did not want to be in the untenable position of insisting that a person had only one racial identity when he or she wished to identify with two or more races. The idea that every individual can be classified as a member of a single race may gradually disappear in the United States, just as the idea that people were either Anglos or Saxons disappeared in England.

How the OMB Guidelines Were Put into Operation for the 2000 Enumeration

After data were gathered in 2000, the Census Bureau developed coding rules to process the results. These rules increased the number of major races by adding a sixth option, "some other race." Persons who identified with a single race—those who either checked only one box or checked no box but wrote a term directly denoting race, such as white, black, or African American, in the "some other race" space or anywhere near the race question on the census questionnaire—were classified into one major race.

Other respondents presented challenges, and the Census Bureau devised new procedures for their classification. A person who marked two Asian races, such as Chinese and Vietnamese, or two Pacific Islander races, such as Guamanian and Samoan, was classified as identifying with a single major race—Asian or NHOPI, respectively.

Although not consistent with OMB recommendations, the Census 2000 enumeration form included a "some other race" box where a respondent could write a word or phrase. The size of the multiple race population depended greatly upon the coding procedures the Census Bureau developed for coding entries written in the "some other race" box.

If a person wrote any term indicating a Hispanic origin, he or she was automatically considered to be "other" by race. For example, a person who wrote Castilian, Cuban, or Argentinean was classified into the "other" race category. If the respondent had already checked a box for his or her race and then wrote a Hispanic term, he or she was multiple by race. Thus persons who marked white or black for their race and then went on to write Dominican or Puerto Rican in the "some other race" box were classified as multiracial. This explains why two of the most frequently reported combinations were white and "some other race" and black and "some other race."

If a person wrote a term in the "some other race" box indicating an origin other than Hispanic, the Census Bureau may or may not have classified that individual into the "other" race category. The agency considered the word or phrase written on the 2000 Census form and then examined data for persons who wrote that same word or phrase for their ancestry in the enumeration of 1990. If 70 percent or more of the persons reporting that ancestry in 1990 identified with a specific race, that race was assigned to the 2000 respondent. If less than 70 percent of those reporting that ancestry in 1990 had identified with a race,

then the person was considered "other" by race in 2000. Several examples illustrate this procedure. Those who wrote French or Irish in the "some other race" box on the Census 2000 form were classified as white since more than 70 percent of those reporting French or Irish as their ancestry in 1990 had marked white for their race. Those who wrote South African in the "some other race" box in Census 2000 were considered to be "other" by race since, in the 1990 census, those writing South African for their ancestry reported a variety of races: white, black, and Asian Indian. These coding rules mean that if a person marked white in 2000 and then went on to write "Spanish" in the "some other race" box, he or she was multiracial just as was a person who checked black and then wrote "Dominican" in the "some other race" box. However, a person who checked white on the Census 2000 and then wrote "French" or "Italian" in the "some other race" box was not multiple by race.

Identifying with Multiple Races: How Many Used This Option?

There were no instructions on the census form telling a respondent what to do to be tabulated as multiracial. Thus, the reported size of the multiracial population largely results from Census Bureau coding rules.

As table 25.2 indicates, 6.8 million of the 281.4 million Americans counted in 2000 marked two or more boxes or wrote a Hispanic-origin term for their second race, such that they were classified as identifying with two or more of the six major races used in the census. Approximately one American in forty identified with two races, whereas about one in one thousand marked boxes to identify with three or more races.

Table 25.2 Population by Number of Races Reported, 2000 Census

Number of Races Reported	Number	Percentage of Total Population
One only	274,595,678	97.4
Two	6,368,075	2.3
Three	410,285	0.1
Four	38,408	<0.1
Five	8,637	<0.1
Six	823	<0.1
Total	281,421,906	100.0

Source: U.S. Bureau of the Census 2001, table 1.

Fewer than one thousand persons checked sufficient numbers of boxes to identify with all six major races.

Table 25.3 lists the racial combinations reported by at least one hundred thousand in 2000; the pie chart in figure 25.1 illustrates the distribution of the multirace population. The most popular combination—reported by one-third of those who identified with two or more races—was white and "some other race." Typically, these were people who marked both the box for white and the box for "some other race" and then wrote in a term denoting Hispanic origin. White and American Indian was the next most popular combination, followed by white and Asian. The most commonly reported second race for those who marked the box for black was also "some other race," just as it was for whites. Subsequent data from the census will allow us to confirm the hypothesis that many of the individuals who identified themselves as black and "some other race" were Caribbeans or Central Ameri-

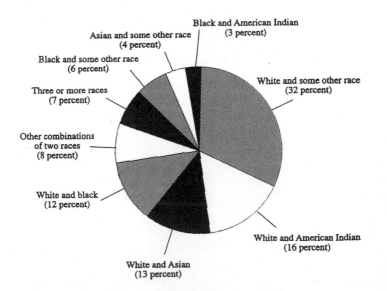

Figure 25.1 Distribution of the Multiple-Race Population, 2000
Source: U.S. Bureau of the Census 2001.

Table 25.3 Frequency of Report of Multiple-Race Ancestry, 2000 Census

Racial Combination	Number Reported	Share of the Total Multiple-Race Population (Percentage)
Most Frequently Reported		
White and some other race	2,206,251	32.3
White and American Indian	1,082,683	15.9
White and Asian	868,395	12.7
White and black	784,764	11.5
Black and some other race	417,249	6.1
Asian and some other race	249,108	3.6
Black and American Indian	182,494	2.7
Asian and NHOPI	138,802	2.0
White and NHOPI	112,964	1.7
White, black, and American Indian	112,207	1.6
Black and Asian	106,782	1.6
All other combinations	564,529	8.3
Least Frequently Reported		
White–Black–Indian–NHOPI—some other race	68	<0.1
Black–Indian–NHOPI—some other race	111	<0.1
Indian–Asian–NHOPI—some other race	207	<0.1
Black–Indian–Asian–NHOPI—some other race	216	<0.1
White–Indian–NHOPI—some other race	309	<0.1
White–black–NHOPI—some other race	325	<0.1
Black–Indian–Asian—some other race	334	<0.1
White–black–Asian–NHOPI—some other race	379	<0.1
Indian–NHOPI—some other race	586	<0.1
White–Indian–Asian–NHOPI—some other race	639	<0.1
Total	6,826,228	100.0

Source: U.S. Bureau of the Census 2001.

Note: NHOPI refers to the major racial group of Native Hawaiians and other Pacific Islanders. Ninety-seven percent of those who marked "Some other race" as their only race went on to identify with a Spanish-Hispanic-Latino origin on the separate Hispanic-origin inquiry. Fifty-eight percent of those who marked "Some other race" in combination with one or more other major races went on to identify with a Spanish-Hispanic-Latino origin.

cans who identified with their African origin and then wrote a Spanish term, such as Dominican. The only three-race combination marked by one hundred thousand or more respondents was white, black, and American Indian—reflecting, undoubtedly, the high rates at which American Indians have married outside their own race since the arrival of the first Europeans.

The Census of 2000 provides counts for 6 major race designations (including "some other") and for all possible combi-

nations of multiple reporting. There are 57 such possible combinations of 2 to 6 races—implying that this enumeration gives us counts for 63 distinct races or combinations of races down to the lowest level of census geography, the city block. When these 63 races are tabulated according to reported Hispanic ethnicity, data are available for 126 different groups.

Table 25.3 also lists the ten least frequently reported races. Some people identified with every one of the combinations,

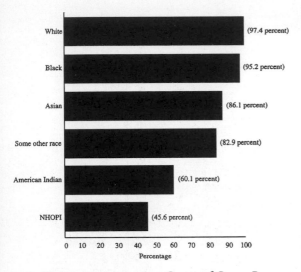

Figure 25.2 Minimum Counts of Census Race Groups—Races as Percentage of Maximum Counts, 2000
Source: U.S. Bureau of the Census 2001.

but fewer than ten thousand persons identified with 35 of the 57 possible multiple race groups, and fewer than one thousand persons checked boxes to identify with 14 of the combinations. As this table shows, the combination white–black–American Indian–NHOPI–some other race was chosen least frequently, with a national count of just sixty-eight persons. Most of the 57 multiple-race combinations were reported so infrequently that the groups will not be subject to scholarly analysis.

Maximum and Minimum Counts of the Race in 2000

The 2000 census data generate thirty-two different estimates of the size of each of the major races; that is, it provides a count of those who identified with each race only, five different counts for the two-race combination involving each race, ten different counts for both three-race and four-race combinations, five different counts for five-race combinations, and, finally, the count that includes persons who claimed all six major races. No longer is there an unambiguous answer to the question, how many whites, or how many American Indians, did the census count.

Figure 25.2 presents a comparison of the minimum and maximum counts of each of the six major race categories. There are substantial differences between these counts. Among those who marked a box to report they were white by race, for example, few went on to identify with a second race, and so the minimum count of whites is close to the maximum count. Among Native Hawaiians and other Pacific Islanders, however, there were many more who identified with a second or third race than who identified as NHOPI only.

Whites and African Americans differed from the other major races in that those who identified as white or black were relatively unlikely to identify with a second race—thus the minimum and maximum counts are fairly similar. Although 5.2 million Americans marked both white and a second race, 97.4 percent of those who marked white claimed white as their only race. Among those who marked black, 95.2 percent marked only black–African American–Negro.

The "some other race" group presented in figure 25.2 is largely—but not entirely—made up of Latinos; 90.4 percent of those who checked the "some other race" box went on to claim a Spanish-Hispanic-Latino identity on the distinct Hispanic-ethnicity question. Of those who checked only the "some other race" box, 97 percent marked themselves as Hispanic in origin.

American Indians and the NHOPI races were distinguished by the frequency with which they were reported in combination with other races. The estimates of the American Indian population are spread across a broad range in the census of 2000: from 2.5 million who identified uniquely with this race to a maximum of 4.1 million, if those who marked Indian along with a second or third race are included in the count. . . .

Conclusion

Putting this new conceptualization of race into practice on the self-administered census form presented a formidable challenge to the Census Bureau. Their decision was to classify all persons into one or more of six race categories: white, black, American Indian, Asian, Native Hawaiian and other Pacific Islander, and "some other race."

Current regulations of the Office of Management and Budget strongly recommend that the Hispanic-origin question be asked, in addition to the mandatory race question. This may confuse respondents and certainly adds a burden for users of data: approximately 40 percent of those who identified with a Hispanic origin in both the 1990 and 2000 censuses did not mark a box for any one of the major races. Instead, they wrote a term denoting a Hispanic origin for their race and were thereby classified by the Census Bureau as "some other race."

In the census of 2000, approximately 2.4 percent of the total population—one person in forty—identified with two or more races. This number is misleading, however, because it includes those who wrote in a term denoting Hispanic origin for their second race. If those who wrote in a Hispanic-origin term are excluded, approximately 1.6 percent of the population identified with

two or more of the five major races—that is, about one person in sixty-five.

Multiple-race reporting was more common among the young, reflecting the demographic consequences of increasing interracial marriage. Among those under the age of eighteen, 4.4 percent identified with two or more races; among those eighteen years and older, that figure fell to 1.9 percent. If those who were counted as multiple in race because they wrote in a Hispanic-origin term for their second race are excluded, then the multiple-race population accounted for 3.2 percent of the population under the age of eighteen and 1.4 percent for their elders. Stated differently, about one American child in thirty-one was reported to be multiracial, compared with one in seventy-one for the population eighteen and older.

The reporting of multiple races displays strong geographic patterns. It is most common in Hawaii, Alaska, and California. Given the large black and white populations, the history of miscegenation, and a significant literature describing generations of mulattoes, one might expect multiple-race reporting to be high in the southern states. Instead, such reporting was lowest in the Deep South. . . .

The social movement that led to the change in racial identification has not been active in the years since census data were collected. It has faded. Because of apparent increases in marriages across racial lines, however, there will inevitably be a growing population of children whose parents differ by race. At this point, we do not know whether the current OMB racial classification system will be readily used by these individuals or whether many of them may identify with the race of one parent in some circumstances and that of the other parent in other circumstances. The traditional system of categorizing persons according to membership in a unique race is no longer accurate nor acceptable, but it is far from certain that the approach used in Census 2000 is practical, ideal, or useful (Skerry 2000).

We have yet to determine whether the concept "multiracial" will enter popular discourse. I believe that it will not, and that into the foreseeable future, most people will continue to assume that every American has a "basic" or "essential" race.

The multiple-race option is a dramatic change in the federal statistical system, but there is a telling demographic analogy. From 1870 through 1970 the census asked the birthplaces of respondents' parents. After the restrictive immigration laws of the early twentieth century went into effect, the second-generation population declined, and in 1980, an open-ended question about ancestry supplanted the query on parents' birthplaces. Respondents were encouraged to write in a term or terms to identify their ethnicity, ancestry, or national origin. The Census Bureau coded the first two terms unless the individual had entered a religious identity. At first glance, one might assume that analysts would exploit these new ancestry data to describe patterns of ethnic intermarriage, the nation's ethnic heterogeneity, and the way ancestry or national origin was linked to achievement. Few scholars, however, have analyzed ancestry and multiple-ancestry information from the last three censuses, and as far as I know, these data have not been used by governmental agencies.

REFERENCES

Farley, Reynolds. 1999. "Racial Issues: Recent Trends in Residential Patterns and Intermar-

riage." In *Diversity and Its Discontents: Cultural Conflict and Common Ground in Contemporary American Society,* edited by Neil J. Smelser and Jeffrey C. Alexander. Princeton, N.J.: Princeton University Press.

Fu, Vincent Kang. 2001. "Racial Intermarriage Pairings." *Demography* 38(2): 147–59.

Gilberston, Greta, Joseph Fitzpatrick, and Lijun Yang. 1996. "Hispanic Intermarriage in New York City: New Evidence from 1991." *International Migration Review* 30(summer): 445–59.

Heer, David. 1974. "The Prevalence of Black-White Intermarriage in the United States: 1960 and 1970." *Journal of Marriage and the Family* 36(2): 246–58.

Hwang, Sean-Smong, Rogelio Saenz, and Benigno Aguirre. 1995. "The SES Selectivity of Interracially Married Asians." *International Migration Review* 29(summer): 469–91.

Kalmijn, Matthijs. 1993. "Trends in Black-White Intermarriage." *Social Forces* 72(1): 19–146.

———. 1998. "Intermarriage and Homogamy: Causes, Patterns, and Trends." *Annual Review of Sociology* 24: 395–421.

Model, Suzanne, and Gene Fisher. 2001. "Black-White Unions: West Indians and African Americans Compared." *Demography* 38(2): 177–85.

Qian, Zhenchao. 1997. "Breaking the Racial Barriers: Variations in Interracial Marriage Between 1980 and 1990." *Demography* 34(3): 263–76.

Rosenfield, Michael J. 2001. "The Salience of Pan-National Hispanic and Asian Identities in U.S. Marriage Markets." *Demography* 38(2): 161–75.

Sandefur, Gary, and Trudy McKinnell. 1986. "American Indian Intermarriage." *Social Science Research* 15(4): 347–71.

Schoen, Robert, and B. Thomas. 1989. "Intergroup Marriage in Hawaii: 1969–1971 and 1979–1981." *Sociological Perspectives* 32: 365–82.

Skerry, Peter. 2000. *Counting on the Census? Race, Group Identity, and the Evasion of Politics.* Washington, D.C.: Brookings Institution.

26

The New Second Generation
Segmented Assimilation and Its Variants

ALEJANDRO PORTES
AND MIN ZHOU

My name is Herb
and I'm not poor;
I'm the Herbie that you're looking for,
like Pepsi,
a new generation
of Haitian determination—
I'm the Herbie that you're looking for.

A beat tapped with bare hands, a few dance steps, and the Haitian kid was rapping. His song, titled "Straight Out of Haiti," was being performed at Edison High, a school that sits astride Little Haiti and Liberty City, the largest black area of Miami. The lyrics captured well the distinct outlook of his immigrant community. The panorama of Little Haiti contrasts sharply with the bleak inner city. In Miami's Little Haiti, the storefronts leap out at the passersby. Bright blues, reds, and oranges vibrate to Haitian merengue blaring from sidewalk speakers.[1] Yet, behind the gay Caribbean exteriors, a struggle goes on that will define the future of this community. As we will see later on, it involves the second generation—children like Herbie—subject to conflicting pressure from parents and peers and to pervasive outside discrimination.

Growing up in an immigrant family has always been difficult, as individuals are torn by conflicting social and cultural demands while they face the challenge of entry into an unfamiliar and frequently hostile world. And yet the difficulties are not always the same. The process of growing up American oscillates between smooth

Alejandro Portes and Min Zhou, "The New Second Generation: Segmented Assimilation and Its Variants," *The Annals of the American Academy of Political and Social Science* 530 (November 1993), pp. 75–77, 81–92, 96.

acceptance and traumatic confrontation depending on the characteristics that immigrants and their children bring along and the social context that receives them. In this article, we explore some of these factors and their bearing on the process of social adaptation of the immigrant second generation. We propose a conceptual framework for understanding this process and illustrate it with selected ethnographic material and survey data from a recent survey of children of immigrants.

Research on the new immigration—that which arose after the passage of the 1965 Immigration Act—has been focused almost exclusively on the first generation, that is, on adult men and women coming to the United States in search of work or to escape political persecution. Little noticed until recently is the fact that the foreign-born inflow has been rapidly evolving from single adult individuals to entire family groups, including infant children and those born to immigrants in the United States. By 1980, 10 percent of dependent children in households counted by the census were second-generation immigrants.[2] In the late 1980s, another study put the number of students in kindergarten through twelfth grade in American schools who spoke a language other than English at home at 3 to 5 million.[3]

The great deal of research and theorizing on post–1965 immigration offers only tentative guidance on the prospects and paths of adaptation of the second generation because the outlook of this group can be very different from that of their immigrant parents. For example, it is generally accepted among immigration theorists that entry-level menial jobs are performed without hesitation by newly arrived immigrants but are commonly shunned by their U.S.-reared offspring. This disjuncture gives rise to a race between the social and economic progress of first-generation immigrants and the material conditions and career prospects that their American children grow to expect.[4]

Nor does the existing literature on second-generation adaptation, based as it is on the experience of descendants of pre-World War I immigrants, offer much guidance for the understanding of contemporary events. The last sociological study of children of immigrants was Irving Child's *Italian or American? The Second Generation in Conflict,* published fifty years ago.[5] Conditions at the time were quite different from those confronting settled immigrant groups today. Two such differences deserve special mention. First, descendants of European immigrants who confronted the dilemmas of conflicting cultures were uniformly white. Even if of a somewhat darker hue than the natives, their skin color reduced a major barrier to entry into the American mainstream. For this reason, the process of assimilation depended largely on individual decisions to leave the immigrant culture behind and embrace American ways. Such an advantage obviously does not exist for the black, Asian, and mestizo children of today's immigrants.

Second, the structure of economic opportunities has also changed. Fifty years ago, the United States was the premier industrial power in the world, and its diversified industrial labor requirements offered to the second generation the opportunity to move up gradually through better-paid occupations while remaining part of the working class. Such opportunities have increasingly disappeared in recent years following a rapid process of national deindustrialization and global industrial restructuring. This process has left entrants to the American labor force confronting a widening gap between the minimally paid menial jobs that immigrants commonly accept and the high-tech and professional occupations requiring college degrees that native elites occupy.[6] The gradual disappearance of intermediate opportunities also bears directly on the race between first-generation economic progress and second-generation expectations, noted previously. . . .

Assimilation as a Problem

The Haitian immigrant community of Miami is composed of some 75,000 legal and clandestine immigrants, many of whom sold everything they owned in order to buy passage to America. First-generation Haitians are strongly oriented toward preserving a strong national identity, which they associate both with community solidarity and with social networks promoting individual success.[7] In trying to instill national pride and an achievement orientation in their children, they clash, however, with the youngsters' everyday experiences in school. Little Haiti is adjacent to Liberty City, the main black inner-city area of Miami, and Haitian adolescents attend predominantly inner-city schools. Native-born youths stereotype Haitians as too docile and too subservient to whites and they make fun of French and Creole and of the Haitians' accent. As a result, second-generation Haitian children find themselves torn between conflicting ideas and values: to remain Haitian they would have to face social ostracism and continuing attacks in school; to become American— black American in this case—they would have to forgo their parents' dreams of making it in America on the basis of ethnic solidarity and preservation of traditional values.[8]

An adversarial stance toward the white mainstream is common among inner-city minority youths who, while attacking the newcomers' ways, instill in them a con sciousness of American-style discrimination. A common message is the devaluation of education as a vehicle for advancement of all black youths, a message that directly contradicts the immigrant parents' expectations. Academically outstanding Haitian American students, "Herbie" among them, have consciously attempted to retain their ethnic identity by cloaking it in black American cultural forms, such as rap music. Many others, however, have followed the path of least effort and become thoroughly assimilated. Assimilation in this instance is not into mainstream culture but into the values and norms of the inner city. In the process, the resources of solidarity and mutual support within the immigrant community are dissipated.

An emerging paradox in the study of today's second generation is the peculiar forms that assimilation has adopted for its members. As the Haitian example illustrates, adopting the outlooks and cultural ways of the native-born does not represent, as in the past, the first step toward social and economic mobility but may lead to the exact opposite. At the other end, immigrant youths who remain firmly ensconced in their respective ethnic communities may, by virtue of this fact, have a better chance for educational and economic mobility through use of the material and social capital that their communities make available.[9]

This situation stands the cultural blueprint for advancement of immigrant groups in American society on its head. As presented in innumerable academic and journalistic writings, the expectation is that the foreign-born and their offspring will first

acculturate and then seek entry and acceptance among the native-born as a prerequisite
for their social and economic advancement.
Otherwise, they remain confined to the
ranks of the ethnic lower and lower-middle
classes.[10] This portrayal of the requirements
for mobility, so deeply embedded in the national consciousness, stands contradicted
today by a growing number of empirical
experiences.

A closer look at these experiences indicates, however, that the expected consequences of assimilation have not entirely
reversed signs, but that the process has become segmented. In other words, the question is into what sector of American society
a particular immigrant group assimilates.
Instead of a relatively uniform mainstream
whose mores and prejudices dictate a common path of integration, we observe today
several distinct forms of adaptation. One
of them replicates the time-honored portrayal of growing acculturation and parallel
integration into the white middle-class; a
second leads straight in the opposite direction to permanent poverty and assimilation into the underclass; still a third
associates rapid economic advancement
with deliberate preservation of the immigrant community's values and tight solidarity. This pattern of segmented assimilation
immediately raises the question of what
makes some immigrant groups become
susceptible to the downward route and
what resources allow others to avoid this
course. In the ultimate analysis, the same
general process helps explain both outcomes. We advance next our hypotheses as
to how this process takes place and how
the contrasting outcomes of assimilation
can be explained. This explanation is then
illustrated with recent empirical material
in the final section.

Vulnerability and Resources

Along with individual and family variables,
the context that immigrants find upon arrival in their new country plays a decisive
role in the course that their offspring's lives
will follow. This context includes such broad
variables as political relations between sending and receiving countries and the state of
the economy in the latter and such specific
ones as the size and structure of preexisting
coethnic communities. The concept of
modes of incorporation provides a useful
theoretical tool to understand this diversity.
As developed in prior publications, modes of
incorporation consist of the complex formed
by the policies of the host government; the
values and prejudices of the receiving society; and the characteristics of the coethnic
community. These factors can be arranged in
a tree of contextual situations, illustrated by
Figure 26.1. This figure provides a first ap-
proximation to our problem.[11]

To explain second-generation outcomes
and their segmented character, however, we
need to go into greater detail into the meaning of these various modes of incorporation
from the standpoint of immigrant youths.
There are three features of the social contexts encountered by today's newcomers
that create vulnerability to downward assimilation. The first is color, the second is
location, and the third is the absence of mobility ladders. As noted previously, the majority of contemporary immigrants are
nonwhite. Although this feature may appear
at first glance as an individual characteristic,
in reality it is a trait belonging to the host
society. Prejudice is not intrinsic to a particular skin color or racial type, and, indeed,
many immigrants never experienced it in
their native lands. It is by virtue of moving
into a new social environment, marked by

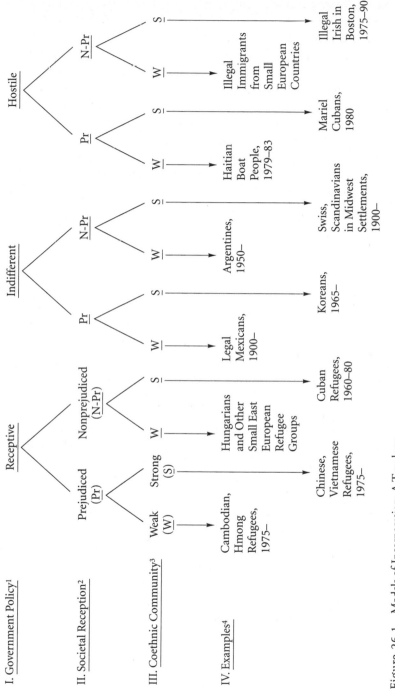

Figure 26.1 Models of Incorporation: A Typology

Source: Adapted from Alejandro Portes and Rubén G. Rumbaut, *Immigrant America: A Portrait* (Berkeley: University of California Press, 1990), p. 91. Copyright © 1990 by the Regents of the University of California.

1. Receptive policy is defined as legal entry with resettlement assistance, indifferent as legal entry without resettlement assistance, hostile as active opposition to a group's entry or permanence in the country; 2. Prejudiced reception is defined as that accorded to nonphenotypically white groups; nonprejudiced is that accorded to European and European-origin whites; 3. Weak coethnic communities are either small in numbers or composed primarily of manual workers; strong communities feature sizable numerical concentrations and a diversified occupational structure including entrepreneurs and professionals; 4. Examples include immigrant groups arriving from the start of the century to the present. Dates of migration are approximate. Groups reflect broadly but not perfectly the characteristics of each ideal type.

different values and prejudices, that physical features become redefined as a handicap.

The concentration of immigrant households in cities and particularly in central cities, as documented previously, gives rise to a second source of vulnerability because it puts new arrivals in close contact with concentrations of native-born minorities. This leads to the identification of the condition of both groups—immigrants and the native poor—as the same in the eyes of the majority. More important, it exposes second-generation children to the adversarial subculture developed by marginalized native youths to cope with their own difficult situation.[12] This process of socialization may take place even when first-generation parents are moving ahead economically and, hence, their children have no objective reasons for embracing a counter-cultural message. If successful, the process can effectively block parental plans for intergenerational mobility.

The third contextual source of vulnerability has to do with changes in the host economy that have led to the evaporation of occupational ladders for intergenerational mobility. As noted previously, new immigrants may form the backbone of what remains of labor-intensive manufacturing in the cities as well as in their growing personal services sector, but these are niches that seldom offer channels for upward mobility. The new hourglass economy, created by economic restructuring, means that children of immigrants must cross a narrow bottleneck to occupations requiring advanced training if their careers are to keep pace with their U.S.-acquired aspirations. This race against a narrowing middle demands that immigrant parents accumulate sufficient resources to allow their children to effect the passage and to simultaneously prove to them the viability of aspirations for upward mobility. Otherwise, assimilation may not be into mainstream values and expectations but into the adversarial stance of impoverished groups confined to the bottom of the new economic hourglass.

The picture is painted in such stark terms here for the sake of clarity, although in reality things have not yet become so polarized. Middle-level occupations requiring relatively modest educational achievements have not completely vanished. By 1980, skilled blue-collar jobs—classified by the U.S. census as "precision production, craft, and repair occupations"—had declined by 1.1 percent relative to a decade earlier but still represented 13 percent of the experienced civilian labor force, or 13.6 million workers. Mostly clerical administrative support occupations added another 16.9 percent, or 17.5 million jobs. In 1980, occupations requiring a college degree had increased by 6 percent in comparison with 1970, but they still employed less than a fifth—18.2 percent—of the American labor force.[13] Even in the largest cities, occupations requiring only a high school diploma were common by the late 1980s. In New York City, for example, persons with 12 years or less of schooling held just over one half of the jobs in 1987. Clerical, service, and skilled blue-collar jobs not requiring a college degree represented 46 percent.[14] Despite these figures, there is little doubt that the trend toward occupational segmentation has increasingly reduced opportunities for incremental upward mobility through well-paid blue-collar positions. The trend forces immigrants today to bridge in only one generation the gap between entry-level jobs and professional positions that earlier groups took two or three generations to travel.

Different modes of incorporation also make available, however, three types of resources to confront the challenges of contemporary assimilation. First, certain groups, notably political refugees, are eligible for a variety of government programs including educational loans for their children. The Cuban Loan Program, implemented by the Kennedy administration in connection with its plan to resettle Cuban refugees away from South Florida, gave many impoverished first- and second-generation Cuban youths a chance to attend college. The high proportion of professionals and executives among Cuban American workers today, a figure on a par with that for native white workers, can be traced, at least in part, to the success of that program.[15] Passage of the 1980 Refugee Act gave to subsequent groups of refugees, in particular Southeast Asians and Eastern Europeans, access to a similarly generous benefits package.[16]

Second, certain foreign groups have been exempted from the traditional prejudice endured by most immigrants, thereby facilitating a smoother process of adaptation. Some political refugees, such as the early waves of exiles from Castro's Cuba, Hungarians and Czechs escaping the invasions of their respective countries, and Soviet Jews escaping religious persecution, provide examples. In other cases, it is the cultural and phenotypical affinity of newcomers to ample segments of the host population that ensures a welcome reception. The Irish coming to Boston during the 1980s are a case in point. Although many were illegal aliens, they came into an environment where generations of Irish Americans had established a secure foothold. Public sympathy effectively neutralized governmental hostility in this case, culminating in a change of the immigration law directly benefiting the newcomers.[17]

Third, and most important, are the resources made available through networks in the coethnic community. Immigrants who join well-established and diversified ethnic groups have access from the start to a range of moral and material resources well beyond those available through official assistance programs. Educational help for second-generation youths may include not only access to college grants and loans but also the existence of a private school system geared to the immigrant community's values. Attendance at these private ethnic schools insulates children from contact with native minority youths, while reinforcing the authority of parental views and plans.

In addition, the economic diversification of several immigrant communities creates niches of opportunity that members of the second generation can occupy, often without a need for an advanced education. Small-business apprenticeships, access to skilled building trades, and well-paid jobs in local government bureaucracies are some of the ethnic niches documented in the recent literature.[18] In 1987, average sales per firm of the smaller Chinese, East Indian, Korean, and Cuban enterprises exceeded $100,000 per year and they jointly employed over 200,000 workers. These figures omit medium-sized and large ethnic firms, whose sales and work forces are much larger.[19] Fieldwork in these communities indicates that up to half of recently arrived immigrants are employed by coethnic firms and that self-employment offers a prime avenue for mobility to second-generation youths.[20] Such community-mediated opportunities provide a solution to the race between material resources and second-generation aspirations not available through competition in the open labor market. Through creation of a capitalism of their own, some immigrant groups have thus been able to circumvent outside discrimination and the threat of vanishing mobility ladders.

In contrast to these favorable conditions are those foreign minorities who either lack a community already in place or whose coethnics are too poor to render assistance. The condition of Haitians in South Florida, cited earlier, provides an illustration of one of the most handicapped modes of incorporation encountered by contemporary immigrants, combining official hostility and widespread social prejudice with the absence of a strong receiving community.[21] From the standpoint of second-generation outcomes, the existence of a large but downtrodden coethnic community may be even less desirable than no community at all. This is because newly arrived youths enter into ready contact with the reactive subculture developed by earlier generations. Its influence is all the more powerful because it comes from individuals of the same national origin, "people like us" who can more effectively define the proper stance and attitudes of the newcomers. To the extent that they do so, the first-generation model of upward mobility through school achievement and attainment of professional occupations will be blocked.

Three Examples

Mexicans and Mexican Americans

Field High School (the name is fictitious) is located in a small coastal community of central California whose economy has long been tied to agricultural production and immigrant farm labor. About 57 percent of the student population is of Mexican descent. An intensive ethnographic study of the class of 1985 at Field High began with school records that showed that the majority of U.S.-born Spanish-surname students who had entered the school in 1981 had dropped out by their senior year. However,

only 35 percent of the Spanish-surname students who had been originally classified by the school as limited English proficient (LEP) had dropped out. The figure was even lower than the corresponding one for native white students, 40 percent. LEP status is commonly assigned to recently arrived Mexican immigrants.[22]

Intensive ethnographic fieldwork at the school identified several distinct categories in which the Mexican-origin population could be classified. Recent Mexican immigrants were at one extreme. They dressed differently and unstylishly. They claimed an identity as Mexican and considered Mexico their permanent home. The most academically successful of this group were those most proficient in Spanish, reflecting their prior levels of education in Mexico. Almost all were described by teachers and staff as courteous, serious about their schoolwork, respectful, and eager to please as well as naive and unsophisticated. They were commonly classified as LEP.

The next category comprised Mexican-oriented students. They spoke Spanish at home and were generally classified as fluent English proficient (FEP). They had strong bicultural ties with both Mexico and the United States, reflecting the fact that most were born in Mexico but had lived in the United States for more than five years. They were proud of their Mexican heritage but saw themselves as different from the first group, the *recién llegados* (recently arrived), as well as from the native-born Chicanos and Cholos, who were derided as people who had lost their Mexican roots. Students from this group were active in soccer and the Sociedad Bilingue and in celebrations of May 5th, the anniversary of the Mexican defeat of French occupying forces. Virtually all of the Mexican-descent students who graduated in the top 10 percent of their class in 1981 were identified as members of this group.

Chicanos were by far the largest Mexican-descent group at Field High. They were mostly U.S.-born second- and third-generation students whose primary loyalty was to their in-group, seen as locked in conflict with white society. Chicanos referred derisively to successful Mexican students as "schoolboys" and "schoolgirls" or as "wannabes." According to M. G. Matute-Bianchi,

To be a Chicano meant in practice to hang out by the science wing . . . *not* eating lunch in the quad where all the "gringos" and "schoolboys" hang out . . . cutting classes by faking a call slip so you can be with your friends at the 7–11 . . . sitting in the back of classes and not participating . . . *not* carrying your books to class . . . *not* taking the difficult classes . . . doing the minimum to get by.[23]

Chicanos merge imperceptibly into the last category, the Cholos, who were commonly seen as "low riders" and gang members. They were also native-born Mexican Americans, easily identifiable by their deliberate manner of dress, walk, speech, and other cultural symbols. Chicanos and Cholos were generally regarded by teachers as "irresponsible," "disrespectful," "mistrusting," "sullen," "apathetic," and "less motivated," and their poor school performance was attributed to these traits.[24] According to Matute-Bianchi, Chicanos and Cholos were faced with what they saw as a forced-choice dilemma between doing well in school or being a Chicano. To act white was regarded as disloyalty to one's group.

The situation of these last two groups exemplifies losing the race between first-generation achievements and later generations' expectations. Seeing their parents and grandparents confined to humble menial jobs and increasingly aware of discrimination against them by the white mainstream, U.S.-born children of earlier Mexican immigrants readily join a reactive subculture as a means of protecting their sense of self-worth. Participation in this subculture then leads to serious barriers to their chances of upward mobility because school achievement is defined as antithetical to ethnic solidarity. Like Haitian students at Edison High, newly arrived Mexican students are at risk of being socialized into the same reactive stance, with the aggravating factor that it is other Mexicans, not native-born strangers, who convey the message. The principal protection of *mexicanos* against this type of assimilation lies in their strong identification with home-country language and values, which brings them closer to their parents' cultural stance.

Punjabi Sikhs in California

Valleyside (a fictitious name) is a northern California community where the primary economic activity is orchard farming. Farm laborers in this area come often from India; they are mainly rural Sikhs from the Punjab. By the early 1980s, second-generation Punjabi students already accounted for 11 percent of the student body at Valleyside High. Their parents were no longer only farm laborers, since about a third had become orchard owners themselves and another third worked in factories in the nearby San Francisco area. An ethnographic study of Valleyside High School in 1980–82 revealed a very difficult process of assimilation for Punjabi Sikh students. According to its author, M. A. Gibson, Valleyside is "redneck country," and white residents are extremely hostile to immigrants who look different and speak a different language: "Punjabi teenagers are told they stink . . . told to go back to India . . . physically abused by majority students who spit at them, refuse to sit by them in class or in buses, throw food at them or worse."[25]

Despite these attacks and some evidence of discrimination by school staff, Punjabi students performed better academically than majority Anglo students. About 90 percent of the immigrant youths completed high school, compared to 70–75 percent of native whites. Punjabi boys surpassed the average grade point average, were more likely to take advanced science and math classes, and expressed aspirations for careers in science and engineering. Girls, on the other hand, tended to enroll in business classes, but they paid less attention to immediate career plans, reflecting parental wishes that they should marry first. This gender difference is indicative of the continuing strong influence exercised by the immigrant community over its second generation. According to Gibson, Punjabi parents pressured their children against too much contact with white peers who may "dishonor" the immigrants' families, and defined "becoming Americanized" as forgetting one's roots and adopting the most disparaged traits of the majority, such as leaving home at age 18, making decisions without parental consent, dating, and dancing. At the same time, parents urged children to abide by school rules, ignore racist remarks and avoid fights, and learn useful skills, including full proficiency in English.[26]

The overall success of this strategy of selective assimilation to American society is remarkable because Punjabi immigrants were generally poor on their arrival in the United States and confronted widespread discrimination from whites without the benefit of either governmental assistance or a well-established coethnic community. In terms of our typology of vulnerability and resources, the Punjabi Sikh second generation was very much at risk except for two crucial factors. First, immigrant parents did not settle in the inner city or in close proximity to any native-born minority whose offspring could provide an alternative model of adaptation to white-majority discrimination. In particular, the absence of a downtrodden Indian American community composed of children of previous immigrants allowed first-generation parents to influence decisively the outlook of their offspring, including their ways of fighting white prejudice. There was no equivalent of a Cholo-like reactive subculture to offer an alternative blueprint of the stance that "people like us" should take.

Second, Punjabi immigrants managed to make considerable economic progress, as attested by the number who had become farm owners, while maintaining a tightly knit ethnic community. The material and social capital created by this first-generation community compensated for the absence of an older coethnic group and had decisive effects on second-generation outlooks. Punjabi teenagers were shown that their parents' ways paid off economically, and this fact, plus their community's cohesiveness, endowed them with a source of pride to counteract outside discrimination. Through this strategy of selective assimilation, Punjabi Sikhs appeared to be winning the race against the inevitable acculturation of their children to American-style aspirations.

Caribbean Youths in South Florida

Miami is arguably the American city that has been most thoroughly transformed by post–1960 immigration. The Cuban Revolution had much to do with this transformation, as it sent the entire Cuban upper class out of the country, followed by thousands of refugees of more modest backgrounds. Over time, Cubans created a highly diversified and prosperous ethnic community that provided resources for the adaptation process of its second generation. Reflecting this situation are average Cuban family incomes that, by 1989, approximated those of the native-born population; the existence in 1987 of more than 30,000 Cuban-owned small businesses that formed the core of the Miami ethnic enclave; and the parallel rise of a private school system oriented toward the values and political outlook of this community.[27] In terms of the typology of vulnerability and resources, well-sheltered Cuban American teenagers lack any extensive exposure to outside discrimination, they have little contact with youths from disadvantaged minorities, and the development of an enclave creates economic opportunities beyond the narrowing industrial and tourist sectors on which most other immigrant groups in the area depend. Across town, Haitian American teenagers face exactly the opposite set of conditions, as has been shown.

Among the other immigrant groups that form Miami's ethnic mosaic, two deserve mention because they represent intermediate situations between those of the Cubans and Haitians. One comprises Nicaraguans escaping the Sandinista regime during the 1980s. They were not as welcomed in the United States as were the Cuban exiles, nor were they able to develop a large and diversified community. Yet they shared with Cubans their language and culture, as well as a militant anti-Communist discourse. This common political outlook led the Cuban American community to extend its resources

in support of their Nicaraguan brethren, smoothing their process of adaptation.[28] For second-generation Nicaraguans, this means that the preexisting ethnic community that provides a model for their own assimilation is not a downtrodden group but rather one that has managed to establish a firm and positive presence in the city's economy and politics.

The second group comprises West Indians coming from Jamaica, Trinidad, and other English-speaking Caribbean republics. They generally arrive in Miami as legal immigrants, and many bring along professional and business credentials as well as the advantage of fluency in English. These individual advantages are discounted, however, by a context of reception in which these mostly black immigrants are put in the same category as native-born blacks and discriminated against accordingly. The recency of West Indian migration and its small size have prevented the development of a diversified ethnic community in South Florida. Hence new arrivals experience the full force of white discrimination without the protection of a large coethnic group and with constant exposure to the situation and attitudes of the inner-city population. Despite considerable individual resources, these disadvantages put the West Indian second generation at risk of bypassing white or even native black middle-class models to assimilate into the culture of the underclass. . . .

Conclusion

Fifty years ago, the dilemma of Italian American youngsters studied by Irving Child consisted of assimilating into the American mainstream, sacrificing in the process their parents' cultural heritage in contrast to taking refuge in the ethnic community from the challenges of the outside world. In the contemporary context of segmented assimilation, the options have become less clear. Children of nonwhite immigrants may not even have the opportunity of gaining access to middle-class white society, no matter how acculturated they become. Joining those native circles to which they do have access may prove a ticket to permanent subordination and disadvantage. Remaining securely ensconced in their coethnic community, under these circumstances, may be not a symptom of escapism but the best strategy for capitalizing on otherwise unavailable material and moral resources. As the experiences of Punjabi Sikh and Cuban American students suggest, a strategy of paced, selective assimilation may prove the best course for immigrant minorities. But the extent to which this strategy is possible also depends on the history of each group and its specific profile of vulnerabilities and resources. The present analysis represents a preliminary step toward understanding these realities.

NOTES

1. Alejandro Portes and Alex Stepick, *City on the Edge: The Transformation of Miami* (Berkeley: University of California Press, 1993), chap. 8.

2. Defined as native-born children with at least one foreign-born parent or children born abroad who came to the United States before age 12.

3. Joan N. First and John W. Carrera, *New Voices: Immigrant Students in U.S. Public Schools* (Boston: National Coalition of Advocates for Students, 1988).

4. Michael Piore, *Birds of Passage* (New York: Cambridge University Press, 1979); Herbert Gans, "Second-Generation Decline: Scenarios for the Economic and Ethnic Futures of the Post–1965 American Immigrants," *Ethnic and Racial Studies* 15:173–92 (Apr. 1992).

5. Irving L. Child, *Italian or American? The Second Generation in Conflict* (New Haven, CT: Yale University Press, 1943).

6. See, for example, Saskia Sassen, "Changing Composition and Labor Market Location of Hispanic Immigrants in New York City, 1960–1980," in *Hispanics in the U.S. Economy*, ed. George J. Borjas and Marta Tienda (New York: Academic Press, 1985), pp. 299–322.

7. See Alex Stepick, "Haitian Refugees in the U.S." (Report no. 52, Minority Rights Group, London, 1982); Alex Stepick and Alejandro Portes, "Flight into Despair: A Profile of Recent Haitian Refugees in South Florida," *International Migration Review*, 20:329–50 (Summer 1986).

8. This account is based on fieldwork in Miami conducted in preparation for a survey of immigrant youths in public schools.

9. On the issue of social capital, see James S. Coleman, "Social Capital in the Creation of Human Capital," *American Journal of Sociology*, supplement, 94:S95–121 (1988); Alejandro Portes and Min Zhou, "Gaining the Upper Hand: Economic Mobility among Immigrant and Domestic Minorities," *Ethnic and Racial Studies*, 15:491–522 (Oct. 1992). On ethnic entrepreneurship, see Ivan H. Light, *Ethnic Enterprise in America: Business and Welfare among Chinese, Japanese, and Blacks* (Berkeley: University of California Press, 1972); Kenneth Wilson and W. Allen Martin, "Ethnic Enclaves: A Comparison of the Cuban and Black Economies in Miami," *American Journal of Sociology*, 88:135–60 (1982).

10. See W. Lloyd Warner and Leo Srole, *The Social Systems of American Ethnic Groups* (New Haven, CT: Yale University Press, 1945); Thomas Sowell, *Ethnic America: A History* (New York: Basic Books, 1981).

11. See Alejandro Portes and Rubén G. Rumbaut, *Immigrant America: A Portrait* (Berkeley: University of California Press, 1990), chap. 3.

12. See Mercer L. Sullivan, *"Getting Paid": Youth, Crime, and Work in the Inner City* (Ithaca, NY: Cornell University Press, 1989), chaps. 1, 5.

13. U.S. Department of Commerce, Bureau of the Census, *Census of Population and Housing, 1980: Public Use Microdata Samples A (MRDF)*

(Washington, DC: Department of Commerce, 1983).

14. Thomas Bailey and Roger Waldinger, "Primary, Secondary, and Enclave Labor Markets: A Training System Approach," *American Sociological Review,* 56:432–45 (1991).

15. Professionals and executives represented 25.9 percent of Cuban-origin males aged 16 years and over in 1989; the figure for the total adult male population was 26 percent. See Jesus M. García and Patricia A. Montgomery, *The Hispanic Population of the United States: March 1990,* Current Population Reports, ser. P-20, no. 449 (Washington, DC: Department of Commerce, 1991).

16. Portes and Rumbaut, *Immigrant America,* pp. 23–25; Robert L. Bach et al., "The Economic Adjustment of Southeast Asian Refugees in the United States," in *World Refugee Survey, 1983* (Geneva: United Nations High Commission for Refugees, 1984), pp. 51–55.

17. The 1990 Immigration Act contains tailor-made provisions to facilitate the legalization of Irish immigrants. Those taking advantage of the provisions are popularly dubbed "Kennedy Irish" in honor of the Massachusetts Senator who coauthored the act. On the 1990 act, see Michael Fix and Jeffrey S. Passel, "The Door Remains Open: Recent Immigration to the United States and a Preliminary Analysis of the Immigration Act of 1990" (Working paper, Urban Institute and RAND Corporation, 1991). On the Irish in Boston, see Karen Tumulty, "When Irish Eyes Are Hiding. . . ," *Los Angeles Times,* 29 Jan. 1989.

18. Bailey and Waldinger, "Primary, Secondary, and Enclave Labor Markets"; Min Zhou, *New York's Chinatown: The Socioeconomic Potential of an Urban Enclave* (Philadelphia: Temple University Press, 1992); Wilson and Martin, "Ethnic Enclaves"; Suzanne Model, "The Ethnic Economy: Cubans and Chinese Reconsidered" (Manuscript, University of Massachusetts at Amherst, 1990).

19. U.S. Department of Commerce, Bureau of the Census, *Survey of Minority-Owned Business Enterprises, 1987,* MB–2 and MB–3 (Washington, DC: Department of Commerce, 1991).

20. Alejandro Portes and Alex Stepick, "Unwelcome Immigrants: The Labor Market Experiences of 1980 (Mariel) Cuban and Haitian Refugees in South Florida," *American Sociological Review,* 50:493–514 (Aug. 1985); Zhou, *New York's Chinatown;* Luis E. Guarnizo, "One Country in Two: Dominican-Owned Firms in New York and the Dominican Republic" (Ph.D. diss. Johns Hopkins University, 1992); Bailey and Waldinger, "Primary, Secondary, and Enclave Labor Markets."

21. Stepick, "Haitian Refugees in the U.S."; Jake C. Miller, *The Plight of Haitian Refugees* (New York: Praeger, 1984).

22. M. G. Matute-Bianchi, "Ethnic Identities and Patterns of School Success and Failure among Mexican-Descent and Japanese-American Students in a California High School," *American Journal of Education,* 95:233–55 (Nov. 1986). This study is summarized in Rubén G. Rumbaut, "Immigrant Students in California Public Schools: A Summary of Current Knowledge" (Report no. 11, Center for Research on Effective Schooling for Disadvantaged Children, Johns Hopkins University, Aug. 1990).

23. Matute-Bianchi, "Ethnic Identities and Patterns," p. 253.

24. Rumbaut, "Immigrant Students," p. 25.

25. M. A. Gibson, *Accommodation without Assimilation: Sikh Immigrants in an American High School* (Ithaca, NY: Cornell University Press, 1989), p. 268.

26. Gibson, *Accommodation without Assimilation.* The study is summarized in Rumbaut, "Immigrant Students," pp. 22–23.

27. García and Montgomery, Hispanic Population; U.S. Department of Commerce, Bureau of the Census, *Survey of Minority-Owned Business Enterprises,* MB–2.

28. Portes and Stepick, *City on the Edge,* chap. 7.

27

Black Identities

West Indian Immigrant Dreams and American Realities

MARY C. WATERS

A key proposition of the new models of immigrant incorporation studies how the social capital immigrants bring with them, and the racial and ethnic definitions of nonwhite immigrants as minorities, combine to create a situation where becoming American in terms of culture and identity and achieving economic success are decoupled. Some immigrants and their children do better economically by maintaining a strong ethnic identity and culture and by resisting American cultural and identity influences. In fact, many authors now suggest that remaining immigrant-or ethnic-identified eases economic and social incorporation into the United States. These new assumptions turn models of identity change on their head—now those who resist becoming American do well and those who lose their immigrant ethnic distinctiveness become downwardly mobile. West Indians, it turns out, fit this model very well because when West Indians lose their distinctiveness as immigrants or ethnics they become not just Americans, but black Americans.

Given the ongoing prejudice and discrimination in American society, this represents downward mobility for the immigrants and their children. . . .

The main argument of this chapter is that black immigrants from the Caribbean come to the United States with a particular identity/culture/worldview that reflects their unique history and experiences. This culture and identity are different from the immigrant identity and culture of previous waves of European immigrants because of the unique history of the origin countries and because of the changed contexts of reception the immigrants face in the United States. This culture and identity are also different from the culture and identity of African Americans.

At first, two main aspects of the culture of West Indians help them to be successful in America. First, because they are immigrants they have a different attitude toward employment, work, and American society than native-born Americans. Employers value this highly. Their background characteristics, including human capital and social network ties, ease their entry into the U.S. labor force. Middle-class immigrants come with qualifications and training that are needed in the U.S. economy (nurses, for example). Because English is their native language, they are able to transfer their foreign qualifications (teaching credentials, nursing degrees) into American credentials. In addition, working-class immigrants have extensive networks of contacts that facilitate their entry into low-level jobs.

Second, the immigrants' unique understanding and expectations of race relations allow them to interact with American racial structures in a successful way. Specifically, their low anticipation of sour race relations allows them to have better interpersonal interactions with white Americans than many native African Americans. Because they come from a society with a majority of blacks and with many blacks in high positions, the immigrants have high ambitions and expectations. Yet their experience with blocked economic mobility due to race and their strong racial identities lead them to challenge blocked mobility in a very militant fashion when they encounter it. This combination of high ambitions, friendly relations with whites on an interpersonal level, and strong militance in encountering any perceived discrimination leads to some better outcomes in the labor market for West Indians than for black Americans.

Ultimately, however, the structural realities of American race relations begin to swamp the culture of the West Indians. Persistent and obvious racial discrimination undermines the openness toward whites the immigrants have when they first arrive. Low wages and poor working conditions are no longer attractive to the children of the immigrants,

who use American, not Caribbean, yardsticks to measure how good a job is. Racial discrimination in housing channels the immigrants into neighborhoods with inadequate city services and high crime rates. Inadequate public schools undermine their hopes for their children's future. Over time the distinct elements of West Indian culture the immigrants are most proud of—a willingness to work hard, a lack of attention to racialism, a high value on education, and strong interests in saving for the future—are undermined by the realities of life in the United States.

These changes are particularly concentrated among the working-class and poor immigrants. Middle-class immigrants are able to pass along aspects of their culture and worldview to their children, but the majority of the working-class immigrants are not. Race as a master status in the United States soon overwhelms the identities of the immigrants and their children, and they are seen as black Americans. Many of the children of the immigrants develop "oppositional identities" to deal with that status. These identities stress that doing well in school is "acting white." The cultural behaviors associated with these oppositional identities further erode the life chances of the children of the West Indian immigrants.

While many white conservatives blame the culture of African Americans for their failures in the economy, the experiences of the West Indians show that even "good culture" is no match for racial discrimination. Over the course of one generation the structural realities of American race relations and the American economy undermine the cultures of the West Indian immigrants and create responses among the immigrants, and especially their children, that resemble the cultural responses of

African Americans to long histories of exclusion and discrimination. . . .

The key factor brought to fresh light by the West Indian immigrants' experiences is the role of continuing racial inequality—the institutional failures in our inner cities to provide jobs, education, and public safety—in sustaining a cultural response of disinvestment in the face of discrimination rather than increased striving. A lifetime of interpersonal attacks based on race can lead to bitterness and anger on the part of an individual. A community of people coping with economic marginality and a lack of any avenues of institutional support for individual mobility leads to a culture of opposition. That culture might serve individuals well for those times when it protects them from the sting of racism and discrimination, but ultimately as a long-term political response to discrimination and exclusion it serves to prevent people from taking advantage of the new opportunities that do arise. Those opportunities are reserved by whites in power for immigrants who make them feel less uncomfortable about relations between the races and especially about taking orders from white supervisors or customers.

One of the African-American teachers [interviewed in this study] eloquently describes how even one act of cruelty or disdain by a white person can have long-standing effects on a young black person and on the whole cycle of black-white race relations:

I have had this happen to me so let me relate this incident. I have been going or coming from a building and held the door for some old white person and had them walk right past me, as if I am supposed to hold the door for them. Not one word, a thank-you, or an acknowledgment of your presence was made. A seventeen-year-old, when he has something like that happen to him, the next time he is going to slam that door in the old lady's face, because I had that tendency myself. I had the hostility build up in me. The next time it happens I won't do that because I am older, but when I was seventeen it might not have made any difference to me that this was a different old lady. I would have flashed back to that previous incident and said I am not holding that door for you. Now that old lady who may have been a perfectly fine individual, who got this door slammed in her face by this young black person, her attitude is "boy, all those people are really vicious people." Her not understanding how it all came to pass. That on a large scale is what is happening in our country today. That's why our young people are very aggressive and very, very hostile when they are put in a situation of black-white confrontation. They say to themselves, "I am not going to let you treat me the way you treated my grandparents, or the way I have read or seen in books or movies that they were treated." I would rather for you to hate me than to disrespect me, is the attitude I think is coming out from our black youth today. (Black American male teacher, age 41)

The policy implications of this study lie in the ways in which the economic and cultural disinvestment in American cities erodes the social capital of immigrant families. The families need recognition of their inherent strengths and the supports necessary to maintain their ambitions. The erosion of the optimism and ambition of the first generation that I saw in their children could be stopped if job opportunities were more plentiful, inner-city schools were nurturing and safe environments that provided good educations, and neighborhoods were safer. Decent jobs, effective schools, and safe streets are not immigrant- or race-based policies. They are universal policies that would benefit all urban residents. Indeed, the strengths these immigrant families have may be in part due to their immigrant status, but the problems they face are much more likely to be due to their class status and their urban residence. Policies that benefit immigrants would equally benefit Americans.

But, in addition, the experience of these immigrants tells us that we must recognize the continuing significance of interpersonal racism in creating psychological tensions and cultural adaptations in the black community. The cycle of attack and disrespect from whites, anger and withdrawal from blacks, and disengagement and blaming behaviors by whites must be broken by changing whites' behaviors. This involves policies that specifically address racial discrimination. The immigrants' tales of blatant housing and job discrimination directly point to needed vigilance in protecting all blacks in the United States from unequal treatment in the private sector. The more difficult problem is dealing with the everyday subtle forms of prejudice and discrimination that also plague foreign-born and American-born blacks. We cannot pass laws forbidding white women from clutching their handbags when black teenagers walk past them. We cannot require old white women to thank young black men who show them courteous behavior. Those kinds of behaviors can only change when whites no longer automatically fear blacks and when whites begin to perceive the humanity and diversity of the black people they encounter.

28

Are Emily and Greg More Employable Than Lakisha and Jamal?

A Field Experiment on Labor Market Discrimination

MARIANNE BERTRAND AND
SENDHIL MULLAINATHAN

Every measure of economic success reveals significant racial inequality in the U.S. labor market. Compared to Whites, African-Americans are twice as likely to be unemployed and earn nearly 25 percent less when they are employed (Council of Economic Advisers, 1998). This inequality has sparked a debate as to whether employers treat members of different races differentially. When faced with observably similar African-American and White applicants, do they favor the White one? Some argue yes, citing either employer prejudice or employer perception that race signals lower productivity. Others argue that differential treatment by race is a relic of the past, eliminated by some combination of employer enlightenment, affirmative action programs and the profit-maximization motive. In fact, many in this latter camp even feel that stringent enforcement of affirmative action programs has produced an environment of reverse discrimination. They would argue that faced with identical candidates, employ-

ers might favor the African-American one. Data limitations make it difficult to empirically test these views. Since researchers possess far less data than employers do, White and African-American workers that appear similar to researchers may look very different to employers. So any racial difference in labor market outcomes could just as easily be attributed to differences that are observable to employers but unobservable to researchers.

To circumvent this difficulty, we conduct a field experiment that builds on the correspondence testing methodology that has been primarily used in the past to study minority outcomes in the United Kingdom. We send resumes in response to help-wanted ads in Chicago and Boston newspapers and measure callback for interview for each sent resume. We experimentally manipulate perception of race via the name of the fictitious job applicant. We randomly assign very White-sounding names (such as Emily Walsh or Greg Baker) to half the resumes and very

Marianne Bertrand and Sendhil Mullainathan, "Are Emily and Greg More Employable Than Lakisha and Jamal? A Field Experiment on Labor Market Discrimination," *The American Economic Review* (September 2004), pp. 991–992, 1006–1007, 1009–1013.

African-American-sounding names (such as Lakisha Washington or Jamal Jones) to the other half. Because we are also interested in how credentials affect the racial gap in callback, we experimentally vary the quality of the resumes used in response to a given ad. Higher-quality applicants have on average a little more labor market experience and fewer holes in their employment history; they are also more likely to have an e-mail address, have completed some certification degree, possess foreign language skills, or have been awarded some honors. In practice, we typically send four resumes in response to each ad: two higher-quality and two lower-quality ones. We randomly assign to one of the higher- and one of the lower-quality resumes an African-American-sounding name. In total, we respond to over 1,300 employment ads in the sales, administrative support, clerical, and customer services job categories and send nearly 5,000 resumes. The ads we respond to cover a large spectrum of job quality, from cashier work at retail establishments and clerical work in a mail room, to office and sales management positions.

We find large racial differences in callback rates. Applicants with White names need to send about 10 resumes to get one callback whereas applicants with African-American names need to send about 15 resumes. This 50-percent gap in callback is statistically significant. A White name yields as many more callbacks as an additional eight years of experience on a resume. Since applicants' names are randomly assigned, this gap can only be attributed to the name manipulation.

Race also affects the reward to having a better resume. Whites with higher-quality resumes receive nearly 30-percent more callbacks than Whites with lower-quality re-sumes. On the other hand, having a higher-quality resume has a smaller effect for African-Americans. In other words, the gap between Whites and African-Americans widens with resume quality. While one may have expected improved credentials to alleviate employers' fear that African-American applicants are deficient in some unobservable skills, this is not the case in our data.

The experiment also reveals several other aspects of the differential treatment by race. First, since we randomly assign applicants' postal addresses to the resumes, we can study the effect of neighborhood of residence on the likelihood of callback. We find that living in a wealthier (or more educated or Whiter) neighborhood increases callback rates. But, interestingly, African-Americans are not helped more than Whites by living in a "better" neighborhood. Second, the racial gap we measure in different industries does not appear correlated to Census-based measures of the racial gap in wages. The same is true for the racial gap we measure in different occupations. In fact, we find that the racial gaps in callback are statistically indistinguishable across all the occupation and industry categories covered in the experiment. Federal contractors, who are thought to be more severely constrained by affirmative action laws, do not treat the African-American resumes more preferentially; neither do larger employers or employers who explicitly state that they are "Equal Opportunity Employers." In Chicago, we find a slightly smaller racial gap when employers are located in more African-American neighborhoods.[1] . . .

Interpretation

Three main sets of questions arise when interpreting the results above. First, does a higher callback rate for White applicants imply that employers are discriminating against African-Americans? Second, does our design only isolate the effect of race or is the name manipulation conveying some other factors than race? Third, how do our results relate to different models of racial discrimination?

Interpreting Callback Rates

Our results indicate that for two identical individuals engaging in an identical job search, the one with an African-American name would receive fewer interviews. Does differential treatment within our experiment imply that employers are discriminating against African-Americans (whether it is rational, prejudice-based, or other form of discrimination)? In other words, could the lower callback rate we record for African-American resumes *within our experiment* be consistent with a racially neutral review of the *entire pool* of resumes the surveyed employers receive?

In a racially neutral review process, employers would rank order resumes based on their quality and call back all applicants that are above a certain threshold. Because names are randomized, the White and African-American resumes we send should rank similarly on average. So, irrespective of the skill and racial composition of the applicant pool, a race-blind selection rule would generate equal treatment of Whites and African-Americans. So our results must imply that employers use race as a factor when reviewing resumes, which matches the legal definition of discrimination.

But even rules where employers are not trying to interview as few African-American applicants as possible may generate observed differential treatment in our experiment. One such hiring rule would be

employers trying to interview a target level of African-American candidates. For example, perhaps the average firm in our experiment aims to produce an interview pool that matches the population base rate. This rule could produce the observed differential treatment if the average firm receives a higher proportion of African-American resumes than the population base rate because African-Americans disproportionately apply to the jobs and industries in our sample.

Some of our other findings may be consistent with such a rule. For example, the fact that "Equal Opportunity Employers" or federal contractors do not appear to discriminate any less may reflect the fact that such employers receive more applications from African-Americans. On the other hand, other key findings run counter to this rule. As we discuss above, we find no systematic difference in the racial gap in callback across occupational or industry categories, despite the large variation in the fraction of African-Americans looking for work in those categories. African-Americans are underrepresented in managerial occupations, for example. If employers matched base rates in the population, the few African-Americans who apply to these jobs should receive a higher callback rate than Whites. Yet, we find that the racial gap in managerial occupations is the same as in all the other job categories. This rule also runs counter to our findings on returns to skill. Suppose firms are struggling to find White applicants but are overwhelmed with African-American ones. Then they should be less sensitive to the quality of White applicants (as they are trying to fill in their hiring quota for Whites) and much more sensitive to the quality of Black applicants (when they have so many to pick from). Thus, it is unlikely that the differential treatment we observe is generated by hiring rules such as these.

Potential Confounds

While the names we have used in this experiment strongly signal racial origin, they may also signal some other personal trait. More specifically, one might be concerned that employers are inferring social background from the personal name. When employers read a name like "Tyrone" or "Latoya," they may assume that the person comes from a disadvantaged background. In the extreme form of this social background interpretation, employers do not care at all about race but are discriminating only against the social background conveyed by the names we have chosen.

While plausible, we feel that some of our earlier results are hard to reconcile with this interpretation. For example, we found that while employers value "better" addresses, African-Americans are not helped more than Whites by living in Whiter or more educated neighborhoods. If the African-American names we have chosen mainly signal negative social background, one might have expected the estimated name gap to be lower for better addresses. Also, if the names mainly signal social background, one might have expected the name gap to be higher for jobs that rely more on soft skills or require more interpersonal interactions. We found no such evidence.

There is one final potential confound to our results. Perhaps what appears as a bias against African-Americans is actually the result of *reverse discrimination*. If qualified African-Americans are thought to be in high demand, then employers with average quality jobs might feel that an equally talented African-American would never accept an offer from them and thereby never call her or him in for an interview. Such an argument might also explain why African-Americans do not receive as strong a return as Whites to better resumes, since higher qualification only strengthens this argument. But this interpretation would suggest that among the better jobs, we ought to see evidence of reverse discrimination, or at least a smaller racial gap. However, we do not find any such evidence. The racial gap does not vary across jobs with different skill requirements, nor does it vary across occupation categories. Even among the better jobs in our sample, we find that employers significantly favor applicants with White names.

Relation to Existing Theories

What do these results imply for existing models of discrimination? Economic theories of discrimination can be classified into two main categories: taste-based and statistical discrimination models. Both sets of models can obviously "explain" our average racial gap in callbacks. But can these models explain our other findings? More specifically, we discuss the relevance of these models with a focus on two of the facts that have been uncovered in this paper: (i) the lower returns to credentials for African-Americans; (ii) the relative uniformity of the race gap across occupations, job requirements and, to a lesser extent, employer characteristics and industries.

Taste-based models (Gary S. Becker, 1961) differ in whose prejudiced "tastes" they emphasize: customers, coworkers, or employers. Customer and co-worker discrimination models seem at odds with the lack of significant variation of the racial gap by occupation and industry categories, as the amount of customer contact and the fraction of White employees vary quite a lot across these categories. We do not find a larger racial gap among jobs that explicitly require "communication skills" and jobs for which we expect either customer or coworker contacts to be higher (retail sales for example).

Because we do not know what drives employer tastes, employer discrimination models could be consistent with the lack of occupation and industry variation. Employer discrimination also matches the finding that employers located in more African-American neighborhoods appear to discriminate somewhat less. However, employer discrimination models would struggle to explain why African-Americans get relatively lower returns to their credentials. Indeed, the cost of indulging the discrimination taste should increase as the minority applicants' credentials increase.

Statistical discrimination models are the prominent alternative to the taste-based models in the economics literature. In one class of statistical discrimination models, employers use (observable) race to proxy for *unobservable* skills (e.g., Edmund S. Phelps, 1972; Kenneth J. Arrow, 1973). This class of models struggle to explain the credentials effect as well. Indeed, the added credentials should lead to a larger update for African-Americans and hence greater returns to skills for that group.

A second class of statistical discrimination models "emphasize the precision of the information that employers have about individual productivity" (Altonji and Blank, 1999). Specifically, in these models, employers believe that the same observable signal is more precise for Whites than for African-Americans (Dennis J. Aigner and Glenn G. Cain, 1977; Shelly J. Lundberg and Richard Startz, 1983; Bradford Cornell and Ivo Welch, 1996). Under such models,

African-Americans receive lower returns to observable skills because employers place less weight on these skills. However, how reasonable is this interpretation for our experiment? First, it is important to note that we are using the same set of resume characteristics for both racial groups. So the lower precision of information for African-Americans cannot be that, for example, an employer does not know what a high school degree from a very African-American neighborhood means (as in Aigner and Cain, 1977). Second, many of the credentials on the resumes are in fact externally and easily verifiable, such as a certification for a specific software.

An alternative version of these models would rely on bias in the observable signal rather than differential variance or noise of these signals by race. Perhaps the skills of African-Americans are discounted because affirmative action makes it easier for African-Americans to get these skills. While this is plausible for credentials such as an employee-of-the-month honor, it is unclear why this would apply to more verifiable and harder skills. It is equally unclear why work experience would be less rewarded since our study suggests that getting a job is more, not less, difficult for African-Americans.

The uniformity of the racial gap across occupations is also troubling for a statistical discrimination interpretation. Numerous factors that should affect the level of statistical discrimination, such as the importance of unobservable skills, the observability of qualifications, the precision of observable skills and the ease of performance measurement, may vary quite a lot across occupations.

This discussion suggests that perhaps other models may do a better job at explaining our findings. One simple alternative model is lexicographic search by employers. Employers receive so many resumes that they may use quick heuristics in reading these resumes. One such heuristic could be to simply read no further when they see an African-American name. Thus they may never see the skills of African-American candidates and this could explain why these skills are not rewarded. This might also to some extent explain the uniformity of the race gap since the screening process (i.e., looking through a large set of resumes) may be quite similar across the variety of jobs we study.

Conclusion

This paper suggests that African-Americans face differential treatment when searching for jobs and this may still be a factor in why they do poorly in the labor market. Job applicants with African-American names get far fewer callbacks for each resume they send out. Equally importantly, applicants with African-American names find it hard to overcome this hurdle in callbacks by improving their observable skills or credentials.

Taken at face value, our results on differential returns to skill have possibly important policy implications. They suggest that training programs alone may not be enough to alleviate the racial gap in labor market outcomes. For training to work, some general-equilibrium force outside the context of our experiment would have to be at play. In fact, if African-Americans recognize how employers reward their skills, they may rationally be less willing than Whites to even participate in these programs.

NOTE

1. For further details on this experiment, see Bertrand and Mullainathan (2004).

REFERENCES

Aigner, Dennis J. and Cain, Glenn G. "Statistical Theories of Discrimination in Labor Markets." *Industrial and Labor Relations Review,* January 1977, *30*(1), pp. 175–87.

Altonji, Joseph G. and Blank, Rebecca M. "Race and Gender in the Labor Market," in Orley Ashenfelter and David Card, eds., *Handbook of labor economics,* Vol. 30. Amsterdam: North-Holland, 1999, pp. 3143–259.

Arrow, Kenneth, J. "The Theory of Discrimination," in Orley Ashenfelter and Albert Rees, eds., *Discrimination in labor markets.* Princeton, NJ: Princeton University Press, 1973, pp. 3–33.

Becker, Gary S. *The economics of discrimination,* 2nd Ed. Chicago: University of Chicago Press, 1961.

Bertrand, Marianne and Sendhil Mullainathan. "Are Emily and Greg More Employable Than Lakisha and Jamal? A Field Experiment on Labor Market Discrimination." *American Economic Review* 94 (September 2004): 991–1013.

Cornell, Bradford and Welch, Ivo. "Culture, Information, and Screening Discrimination." *Journal of Political Economy,* June 1996, *104*(3), pp. 542–71.

Council of Economic Advisers. *Changing America: Indicators of social and economic well-being by race and Hispanic origin.* September 1998, http://w3.access.gpo.gov/eop/ca/pdfs/ca.pdf.

Lundberg, Shelly J. and Starz, Richard. "Private Discrimination and Social Intervention in Competitive Labor Market." *American Economic Review,* June 1983, *73*(3), pp. 340–47.

Phelps, Edmund S. "The Statistical Theory of Racism and Sexism." *American Economic Review,* September 1972, *62*(4), pp. 659–61.

29

Marked

Race, Crime, and Finding Work in an Era of Mass Incarceration

DEVAH PAGER

While stratification researchers typically focus on schools, labor markets, and the family as primary institutions affecting inequality, a new institution has emerged as central to the sorting and stratifying of young disadvantaged men: the criminal justice system. With over two million individuals currently incarcerated, and well over half a million prisoners released each year, the large and growing numbers of men being processed through the criminal justice system raises important questions about the consequences of this massive institutional intervention. Further, large racial disparities in incarceration lead us to question the degree to which mass incarceration has particular implications for stratification along racial lines.

This [chapter] focuses on the consequences of incarceration for the employment outcomes of black and white men. I adopt an experimental audit approach to formally test the degree to which race and criminal background affect subsequent employment opportunities. By using matched pairs of individuals to apply for real entry-level jobs, it becomes possible to directly measure the extent to which contact with the criminal justice system—in the absence of other disqualifying characteristics—serves as a barrier to employment among equally qualified applicants. Further, by varying the race of the tester pairs, it becomes possible to assess the ways in which the effects of race and criminal record interact to produce new forms of labor market inequalities.

Mass Incarceration and the Credentialing of Stigma

Over the past three decades, the number of prison inmates has increased by more than 700 percent, leaving the United States the country with the highest incarceration rate in the world (Bureau of Justice Statistics, 2006; Mauer, 1999). During this time, incarceration changed from a punishment reserved primarily for the most heinous offenders to one extended to a much greater range of crimes and a much larger segment of the population. Recent trends in crime policy have led to the imposition

This is a commissioned chapter that draws heavily on material in a previous publication (Devah Pager, "The Mark of a Criminal Record," *American Journal of Sociology* 108 [2003], pp. 937–975).

of harsher sentences for a wider range of offenses, thus casting an ever widening net of penal intervention.

For each individual processed through the criminal justice system, police records, court documents, and corrections databases detail dates of arrest, charges, conviction, and terms of incarceration. Most states make these records publicly available, often through on-line repositories, accessible to employers, landlords, creditors, and other interested parties. With increasing numbers of occupations, public services, and other social goods becoming off-limits to ex-offenders, these records can be used as the official basis for eligibility determination or exclusion. The state, in this way, serves as a credentialing institution, providing official and public certification of those among us who have been convicted of wrongdoing. The "credential" of a criminal record, like educational or professional credentials, constitutes a formal and enduring classification of social status, which can be used to regulate access and opportunity across numerous social, economic, and political domains. As increasing numbers of young men are marked by their contact with the criminal justice system, it becomes a critical priority to understand the costs and consequences of this now prevalent form of negative credential (Pager, 2007b).

Racial Stereotypes in an Era of Mass Incarceration

The expansion of the correctional population has been particularly consequential for blacks. Blacks today represent over 40 percent of current prison inmates relative to just 12 percent of the U.S. population. Over the course of a lifetime, nearly one in three young black men—and well over half of young black high school dropouts—will spend some time in prison. According to these estimates, young black men are more likely to go to prison than to attend college, serve in the military, or, in the case of high school dropouts, to be in the labor market (Bureau of Justice Statistics, 1997; Pettit and Western, 2004). Prison is no longer a rare or extreme event among our nation's most marginalized groups. Rather it has now become a normal and anticipated marker in the transition to adulthood.

There is reason to believe that the implications of these trends extend well beyond the prison walls, with assumptions of criminality among blacks generalizing beyond those directly engaged in crime. Blacks in this country have long been regarded with suspicion and fear; but unlike progressive trends in other racial attitudes, associations between race and crime have changed little in recent years. Survey respondents consistently rate blacks as more prone to violence than any other American racial or ethnic group, with the stereotype of aggressiveness and violence most frequently endorsed in ratings of African Americans (Sniderman and Piazza, 1993; Smith, 1990). The stereotype of blacks as criminals is deeply embedded in the collective consciousness of white Americans, irrespective of the perceiver's level of prejudice or personal beliefs (Devine and Elliot, 1995; Eberhardt et al., 2004; Graham and Lowery, 2004).

While it would be impossible to trace the source of contemporary racial stereotypes to any one factor, the disproportionate growth of criminal justice intervention in the lives of young black men—and corresponding media coverage of this phenomenon, which presents an even more skewed representation—has likely played an important role. Experimental research shows that exposure to news coverage of a violent incident committed by a black perpetrator not only increases punitive attitudes about crime but further increases negative attitudes about blacks generally (Gilliam and Iyengar, 2000). The more exposure we have to images of blacks in custody or behind bars, the stronger our expectations become regarding the race of assailants or the criminal tendencies of black strangers (Cole, 1995).

The consequences of mass incarceration then may in fact extend far beyond the costs to the individual bodies behind bars, and to the families that are disrupted or the communities whose residents cycle in and out. The criminal justice system may itself legitimate and reinforce deeply embedded racial stereotypes, contributing to the persistent chasm in this society between black and white.

Assessing the Impact of Race and Criminal Background

In considering the labor market impacts of race and criminal background, questions of causality loom large. For example, while employment disparities between blacks and whites have been well established, the causes of these disparities remain widely contested. Where racial discrimination may represent one explanation, a growing number of researchers have pointed instead to individual-level factors such as skill deficits and other human capital characteristics as a key source of racial wage differentials (Neal and Johnson, 1996; Farkas and Vicknair, 1996). Likewise, assessing the impact of incarceration is not altogether straightforward. On the one hand, it's not hard to imagine that a prison record would carry a weighty stigma, with members of the general public (employers included) reluctant to associate or work with former inmates. On the other hand, criminal offenders aren't typically the image of the model employee. It's certainly possible that the poor employment outcomes of ex-offenders stem rather from characteristics of the offenders themselves, as opposed to any consequence of their criminal conviction. Poor work habits, substance abuse problems, or deficient interpersonal skills may be sufficient to explain the employment disadvantages of ex-offenders, and yet these characteristics are difficult to capture using standard data sources.

Given the difficulties inherent to evaluating the impact of race and imprisonment through conventional measures, I set out to investigate this issue by constructing an experiment. I wanted to bracket the range of personal characteristics associated with African Americans and ex-offenders in order to home in on the causal impact of race and a criminal record. The experimental audit methodology allowed me to do just that. Using this approach, I pose the questions: Given two equally qualified job applicants, how much does a criminal record affect the chances of being selected by an employer? To what extent does race condition employers' responses? In answering these questions, we can begin to understand the ways in which race and criminal background shape and constrain important economic opportunities.

The Audit Methodology

The basic design of an employment audit involves sending matched pairs of individuals (called testers) to apply for real job openings in order to see whether employers respond differently to applicants on the basis of selected characteristics. The current study included four male testers, two blacks and two whites, matched into two teams—the two black testers formed one team, and the two white testers formed a second team.[1] The testers were college students from Milwaukee who were matched on the basis of age, race, physical appearance, and general style of self-presentation. The testers were assigned fictitious resumes that reflected equivalent levels of education and work experience.[2] In addition, within each team, one auditor was randomly assigned a "criminal record" for the first week; the pair then rotated which member presented himself as the ex-offender for each successive week of employment searches, such that each tester served in the criminal record condition for an equal number of cases.[3] By varying which member of the pair presented himself as having a criminal record, unobserved differences within the pairs of applicants were effectively controlled.

Before initiating the fieldwork, testers participated in a common training program to become familiar with the details of their assumed profile and to ensure uniform behavior in job interviews. The training period lasted for one week, during which testers participated in mock interviews with one another and practice interviews with cooperating employers. The testers were trained to respond to common interview questions in standardized ways, and were well-rehearsed for a wide range of scenarios that emerge in hiring situations. Frequent communication between myself and the testers throughout each day of fieldwork allowed for regular supervision and troubleshooting in the event of unexpected occurrences.

A random sample of entry-level positions (those jobs requiring no previous experience and no education beyond high school) was drawn each week from the Sunday classified advertisement section of the *Milwaukee Journal Sentinel*. The most common job titles included waitstaff, laborers and warehouse, production/operators, customer service, sales, delivery drivers, and cashiers; a handful of clerical and managerial positions were also included. I excluded from the sample those occupations with legal restrictions on ex-offenders, such as jobs in the health care industry, work with children and the elderly, jobs requiring the handling of firearms (e.g., security guards), and jobs in the public sector. Of course, any true estimate of the collateral consequences of incarceration would also need to take account of the wide range of employment fully off-limits to individuals with prior felony convictions.

Each of the audit pairs was randomly assigned fifteen job openings each week. The white pair and the black pair were assigned separate sets of jobs, with the same-race testers applying to the same jobs. One member of the pair applied first, with the second applying one day later (randomly varying whether the ex-offender was first or second). A total of 350 employers were audited during the course of this study: 150 by the white pair and 200 by the black pair. Additional tests were performed by the black pair because black testers received fewer callbacks on average, and there were thus fewer data points with which to draw comparisons. A larger sample size enables the calculation of more precise estimates of the effects under investigation (for a more in-depth discussion of the study design, see Pager, 2003).

This study focused only on the first stage of the employment process, as this is the stage most likely to be affected by the barriers of race and criminal record. Testers visited

employers, filled out applications, and proceeded as far as they could during the
course of one visit. If testers were asked to
interview on the spot, they did so, but they
did not return to the employer for a second
visit. The primary dependent variable then
is the proportion of applications that
elicited callbacks from employers. Individual voice mail boxes were set up for each
tester to record employer responses.

An advantage of the call-back as our key
outcome variable—as opposed to a job
offer—is that it does not require employers
to narrow their selection down to a single
applicant. At the job offer stage, if presented
with an ex-offender and an equally qualified
nonoffender, even employers with little concern over hiring ex-offenders would likely select the applicant with no criminal record,
an arguably safer choice. Equating the two
applicants could in fact magnify the impact
of the criminal record, as it becomes the only
remaining basis for selection between the
two (Heckman, 1998). The call-back, by
contrast, does not present such complications. Typically employers interview multiple candidates for entry-level positions
before selecting a hire. In fact, in a subsequent survey, employers in this study reported interviewing an average of eight
applicants for the last entry-level position
filled. At the call-back stage, then, employers
need not yet choose between the ex-offender
and nonoffender. If the applicants appear
well-qualified, and if the employer does not
view the criminal record as an automatic dis-
qualifier, s/he can interview them both.[4]

Hiring Outcomes by Race and Criminal Background

Results are based on the proportion of applications submitted by each tester which

elicited callbacks from employers. Three
main findings should be noted from the
audit results, presented in Figure 29.1.
First, there is a large and significant effect
of a criminal record for all job seekers.
Among whites, for example, 34 percent of
those without criminal records received
callbacks relative to only 17 percent of
those with criminal records. A criminal
record is thus associated with a 50 percent
reduction in the likelihood of a callback
among whites. Often testers reported seeing employers' levels of responsiveness
change dramatically once they had glanced
down at the criminal record question on
the application form. Many employers
seem to use the information as a screening
mechanism, weeding out applicants at the
initial stage of review.

Second, there is some indication that the
magnitude of the criminal record effect
may be even larger for blacks. While the interaction between race and criminal record
is not statistically significant, the substantive difference is worth noting. The ratio of
callbacks for nonoffenders relative to offenders for whites was two to one (34 percent vs. 17 percent), while this same ratio
for blacks is close to three to one (14 percent vs. 5 percent).[5] The estimated effect of
a criminal record is thus 40 percent larger
for blacks than for whites. The combination of minority status and criminal background appears to intensify employers'
negative reactions, leaving few employment
prospects for black ex-offenders (200 applications resulted in only 10 callbacks).

Finally, looking at the callback rates for
black and white tester pairs side by side, the
fundamental importance of race becomes
vividly clear. Among those without criminal
records, black applicants were less than half
as likely to receive callbacks compared to

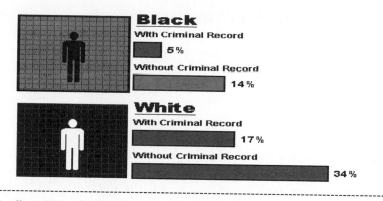

The effects of race and criminal record are large and statistically significant (p<.01). The interaction between the two is not significant in the full sample.

Figure 29.1 The Effects of Race and Criminal Background on Employment

equally qualified whites (14 percent vs. 34 percent). This implies that young black men needed to work more than twice as hard (apply to twice as many jobs) to secure the same opportunities as whites with identical qualifications. Even more striking, the powerful effects of race rival even the strong stigma conveyed by a criminal record. In this study, a white applicant *with a criminal record* was just as likely, if not more, to receive a callback as a black applicant with no criminal history (17 percent vs. 14 percent). Despite the fact that the white applicant revealed evidence of a felony drug conviction, and despite the fact that he reported having only recently returned from a year and a half in prison, employers seemed to view this applicant as no more risky than a young black man with no history of criminal involvement. Racial disparities have been documented in many contexts, but here, comparing the two effects side by side, we are confronted with a troubling reality: Being black in America today is just about the same as having a felony conviction in terms of one's chances of finding a job.[6]

The results of this research suggest that both race and criminal background represent extremely powerful barriers to job entry. The matched design allows us to separate speculation about applicant qualifications (supply-side influences) from the preferences or biases of employers (demand-side influences). While this study remains silent on the many supply-side factors that may also contribute to the employment difficulties of blacks and ex-offenders, it speaks loud and clear about the significance of employer demand in shaping the opportunities available to job seekers on the basis of their race or criminal background. Before applicants have an opportunity to demonstrate their capabilities in person, a large proportion are weeded out on the basis of a single categorical distinction.

Discussion

There is serious disagreement among academics, policy makers, and practitioners over the extent to which contact with the criminal justice system—in itself—leads to harmful consequences for employment. The present study takes a strong stand in this debate by offering direct evidence of the causal relationship between a criminal record and employment outcomes. Using matched pairs and an experimentally assigned criminal record, this estimate is unaffected by the problems of selection which plague observational data. While certainly there are additional ways in which incarceration may affect economic outcomes, this study provides convincing evidence that mere contact with the criminal justice system, in the absence of any transformative or selective effects, severely limits subsequent employment opportunities. And while the audit study investigates employment barriers to ex-offenders from a micro-perspective, the implications are far-reaching. The finding that ex-offenders are one-half to one-third as likely to be considered by employers suggests that a criminal record indeed presents a major barrier to employment. With over two million people currently behind bars and over 12 million people with prior felony convictions, the consequences for labor market inequalities are potentially profound.

Second, the persistent effect of race on employment opportunities is painfully clear in these results. Blacks are less than half as likely to receive consideration by employers relative to their white counterparts, and black nonoffenders fall behind even whites with prior felony convictions. While this research cannot identify the precise source of employers' reluctance to hire blacks, it is important to consider the influence of high incarceration rates among blacks as one possible source of racial bias. Indeed, the available evidence points to the pervasiveness of images associating blacks with crime, and the power of these images to strengthen negative feelings about blacks as a group. It may be the case, then, that increasing rates of incarceration among blacks, and the disproportionate coverage of criminal justice contact among blacks in the media, heighten negative reactions toward African Americans generally, irrespective of their personal involvement in crime.

No longer a peripheral institution, the criminal justice system has become a dominant presence in the lives of young disadvantaged men, playing a key role in the sorting and stratifying of labor market opportunities. The "criminal credential" now represents a common marker among young disadvantaged men, allowing for the easy identification and exclusion of those with a prior arrest or conviction. Further, because blacks are so strongly associated with the population under correctional supervision, it becomes common to assume that any given young black man is likely to have—or to be on his way to acquiring—a criminal record.

At this point in history, it is impossible to tell whether the massive presence of incarceration in today's stratification system represents a unique anomaly of the late twentieth century or part of a larger movement toward a system of stratification based on the official certification of individual character and competence. Whether this process will continue to form the basis of emerging social cleavages remains to be seen.

NOTES

1. The two teams were sent to different employers in order to minimize suspicion that might otherwise arise from two similar applicants with similar criminal backgrounds applying within a short time interval. In the present design, the criminal record effect is estimated as a within-team effect while race is measured as a between-team effect. While the latter is less efficient, the comparison should be unbiased. Black and white testers used *identical* resumes (something that would not have been possible had they visited the same employers) and were selected and trained to

present comparable profiles to employers. Likewise, employers were randomly assigned across tester pairs, minimizing heterogeneity in employer characteristics by team.

2. Testers presented themselves as high school graduates with steady work experience in entry level jobs.

3. The criminal record in all cases was a drug felony, possession with intent to distribute (cocaine), and 18 months of prison time. Testers presented the information to employers by checking the box "yes" in answer to the standard application question, "Have you ever been convicted of a crime?" As additional cues, testers also reported work experience in the correctional facility and listed their parole officer as a reference (see Pager, 2003 for a more in-depth discussion of these issues).

4. A more in-depth discussion of methodological concerns, including limits to generalizability, representativeness of testers, sample restrictions, and experimenter effects is presented in Pager (2007b), appendix 4A.

5. While not significant in the full sample, this interaction becomes significant when analyzed specifically for suburban employers or among employers with whom the testers had extended personal contact (see Pager, 2007b, chap. 7).

6. These results do not appear specific to Milwaukee. Other audit studies have revealed effects of similar magnitude (see Pager, 2007a for a summary); and a replication of the present study in New York City comes to similar conclusions (Pager and Western, 2005).

REFERENCES

Bureau of Justice Statistics. 2002. "Recidivism of Prisoners Released in 1994," edited by Patrick Langan and David Levin. Washington, DC: U.S. Department of Justice.

——— 2006. "Prison and Jail Inmates at Midyear 2005." Washington, DC: U.S. Department of Justice.

Bureau of Justice Statistics Special Report 1997. March. *Lifetime Likelihood of Going to State or Federal Prison*, by Thomas P. Bonczar and Allen J. Beck. Washington, DC: U.S. Department of Justice.

Cole, David. 1995. "The paradox of race and crime: A comment on Randall Kennedy's 'politics of distinction.'" *Georgetown Law Journal* 83:2547–2571.

Devine, P. G., and A. J. Elliot. 1995. "Are Racial Stereotypes Really Fading? The Princeton Trilogy Revisited." *Personality and Social Psychology Bulletin* 21(11): 1139–1150.

Eberhardt, Jennifer L., Phillip Atiba Goff, Valerie J. Purdie, and Paul G. Davies. 2004. "Seeing black: Race, crime, and visual processing." *Journal of Personality & Social Psychology* 87:876–893.

Farkas, George, and Kevin Vicknair. 1996. "Appropriate tests of racial wage discrimination require controls for cognitive skill: comment on Cancio, Evans, and Maume." *American Sociological Review* 61:557–560.

Freeman, Richard B. 1987. "The Relation of Criminal Activity to Black Youth Employment." *Review of Black Political Economy* 16(1–2): 99–107.

Gilliam, Franklin D., and Shanto Iyengar. 2000. "Prime suspects: The influence of local television news on the viewing public." *American Journal of Political Science* 44:560–573.

Graham, Sandra, and Brian S. Lowery. 2004. "Priming unconscious racial stereotypes about adolescent offenders." *Law and Human Behavior* 28:483–504.

Heckman, James J. 1998. "Detecting discrimination." *The Journal of Economic Perspectives* 12:101–116.

Heckman, James, and Peter Seligman. 1993. "The Urban Institute Audit Studies: Their Methods and Findings." In Michael Fix and Raymond J. Struyk (eds.), *Clear and Convincing Evidence: Measurement of Discrimination in America*. Washington, DC: Urban Institute Press.

Mauer, Marc. 1999. *Race to Incarcerate*. New York: New Press.

Neal, Derek, and William Johnson. 1996. "The Role of Premarket Factors in Black-White Wage Differences." *Journal of Political Economy,* 104(5): 869–895.

Pager, Devah. 2003. "The Mark of a Criminal Record." *American Journal of Sociology* 108(5): 937–975.

————. 2007a. "The Use of Field Experiments for Studies of Employment Discrimination: Contributions, Critiques, and Directions for the Future." *Annals of the American Academy of Political and Social Science* 609: 104–133.

————. 2007b. *Marked: Race, Crime, and Finding Work in an Era of Mass Incarceration.* Chicago: University of Chicago Press.

Pager, Devah, and Bruce Western. 2005. "Discrimination in Low Wage Labor Markets: Evidence from New York City." Paper presented at Population Association of America. Philadelphia, PA.

Pettit, Becky, and Bruce Western. 2004. "Mass Imprisonment and the Life Course: Race and Class Inequality in U.S. Incarceration." *American Sociological Review* 69: 151–169.

Sampson, Robert J., and John H. Laub. 1993. *Crime in the Making: Pathways and Turning Points Through Life.* Cambridge, MA: Harvard University Press.

Schwartz, Richard, and Jerome Skolnick. 1962. "Two Studies of Legal Stigma." *Social Problems,* Fall: 133–142.

Smith, Tom W. 1991. "Ethnic Images. General Social Survey Technical Report, 19." Chicago: National Opinion Research Center, University of Chicago.

Sniderman, Paul M., and Thomas Piazza. 1993. *The Scar of Race.* Cambridge, MA: Harvard University Press.

Travis, Jeremy, Amy Solomon, and Michelle Waul. 2001. *From Prison to Home: The Dimensions and Consequences of Prisoner Reentry.* Washington, DC: Urban Institute Press.

Uggen, Christopher. 2000. "Work as a Turning Point in the Life Course of Criminals: A Duration Model of Age, Employment, and Recidivism." *American Sociological Review* 65(4): 529–546.

Uggen, Christopher, Jeff Manza, and Melissa Thompson. 2006. "Citizenship and Reintegration: The Socioeconomic, Familial, and Civic Lives of Criminal Offenders." *The Annals of the American Academy of Social and Political Science* 605:281–310.

Western, Bruce. 2002. "The Impact of Incarceration on Wage Mobility and Inequality." *American Sociological Review* 67(4): 526–546.

Western, Bruce, and Katherine Beckett. 1999. "How Unregulated Is the U.S. Labor Market? The Penal System as a Labor Market Institution." *American Journal of Sociology* 104(4): 1030–60.

Wilson, William Julius. 1996. *When Work Disappears: The World of the New Urban Poor.* New York: Vintage Books.

30

The Continuing Significance of Race
Antiblack Discrimination in Public Places

JOE R. FEAGIN

Racial discrimination as a continuing and major problem for middle-class blacks has been downplayed as analysts have turned to the various problems of the "underclass." For example, Wilson (1978, pp. 110–1) has argued that the growth of the black middle class since the 1960s is the result of improving economic conditions and of government civil rights laws, which virtually eliminated overt discrimination in the workplace and public accommodations. According to Wilson, the major problem of the 1964 Civil Rights Act is its failure to meet the problems of the black underclass (Wilson 1987, pp. 146–7).

Here I treat these assertions as problematic. Do middle-class black Americans still face hostile treatment in public accommodations and other public places? If so, what form does this discrimination take? Who are the perpetrators of this discrimination? What is the impact of the discrimination on its middle-class victims? How do middle-class blacks cope with such discrimination?

Discrimination can be defined in social-contextual terms as "actions or practices carried out by members of dominant racial or ethnic groups that have a differential and negative impact on members of subordinate racial and ethnic groups" (Feagin and Eckberg 1980, pp. 1–2). This differential treatment ranges from the blatant to the subtle (Feagin and Feagin 1986). Here I focus primarily on blatant discrimination by white Americans targeting middle-class blacks. . . .

To examine discrimination, I draw primarily on 37 in-depth interviews from a larger study of 135 middle-class black Americans in Boston, Buffalo, Baltimore, Washington, D.C., Detroit, Houston, Dallas, Austin, San Antonio, Marshall, Las Vegas, and Los Angeles. The interviewing was done in 1988–1990; black interviewers were used. . . .

Responses to Discrimination: Public Accommodations

Two Fundamental Strategies: Verbal Confrontation and Withdrawal

In the following account, a black news director at a major television station shows the interwoven character of discriminatory

---

Joe R. Feagin, "The Continuing Significance of Race: Antiblack Discrimination in Public Places," *American Sociological Review* 56 (February 1991), pp. 101–103, 105–106, 108–112, 114–116.

action and black response. The discrimination took the form of poor restaurant service, and the responses included both suggested withdrawal and verbal counterattack.

He [her boyfriend] was waiting to be seated. . . . He said, "You go to the bathroom and I'll get the table. . . ." He was standing there when I came back; he continued to stand there. The restaurant was almost empty. There were waiters, waitresses, and no one seated. And when I got back to him, he was ready to leave, and said, "Let's go." I said, "What happened to our table?" He wasn't seated. So I said, "No, we're not leaving, please." And he said, "No, I'm leaving." So we went outside, and we talked about it. And what I said to him was, you have to be aware of the possibilities that this is not the first time that this has happened at this restaurant or at other restaurants, but this is the first time it has happened to a black news director here or someone who could make an issue of it, or someone who is prepared to make an issue of it.

So we went back inside after I talked him into it and, to make a long story short, I had the manager come. I made most of the people who were there (while conducting myself professionally the whole time) aware that I was incensed at being treated this way. . . . I said, "Why do you think we weren't seated?" And the manager said, "Well, I don't really know." And I said, "Guess." He said, "Well I don't know, because you're black?" I said, "Bingo. Now isn't it funny that you didn't guess that I didn't have any money," (and I opened up my purse) and I said, "because I certainly have money. And isn't it odd that you didn't guess that it's because I couldn't pay for it because I've got two American

Express cards and a Master Card right here. I think it's just funny that you would have assumed that it's because I'm black.". . . And then I took out my card and gave it to him and said, "If this happens again, or if I hear of this happening again, I will bring the full wrath of an entire news department down on this restaurant." And he just kind of looked at me. "Not [just] because I am personally offended. I am. But because you have no right to do what you did, and as a people we have lived a long time with having our rights abridged. . . ." There were probably three or four sets of diners in the restaurant and maybe five waiters/waitresses. They watched him standing there waiting to be seated. His reaction to it was that he wanted to leave. I understood why he would have reacted that way, because he felt that he was in no condition to be civil. He was ready to take the place apart and . . . sometimes it's appropriate to behave that way. We hadn't gone the first step before going on to the next step. He didn't feel that he could comfortably and calmly take the first step, and I did. So I just asked him to please get back in the restaurant with me, and then you don't have to say a word, and let me handle it from there. It took some convincing, but I had to appeal to his sense of this is not just you, this is not just for you. We are finally in a position as black people where there are some of us who can genuinely get their attention. And if they don't want to do this because it's right for them to do it, then they'd better do it because they're afraid to do otherwise. If it's fear, then fine, instill the fear.

This example provides insight into the character of modern discrimination. The discrimination was not the "No Negroes" exclusion of the recent past, but rejection in the form of poor service by restaurant personnel. The black response indicates the change in black-white interaction since the 1950s and 1960s, for discrimination is handled with vigorous confrontation rather than deference. It is possible that the white personnel defined the couple as "poor blacks" because of their jeans, although the jeans were fashionable and white patrons wear jeans. In comments not quoted here the news director rejects such an explanation. She forcefully articulates a theory of rights—a response that signals the critical impact of civil rights laws on the thinking of middle-class blacks. The news director articulates the American dream: she has worked hard, earned the money and credit cards, developed the appropriate middle-class behavior, and thus has under the law a *right* to be served. There is defensiveness in her actions too, for she feels a need to legitimate her status by showing her purse and credit cards. One important factor that enabled her to take such assertive action was her power to bring a TV news team to the restaurant. This power marks a change from a few decades ago when very few black Americans had the social or economic resources to fight back successfully.

This example underscores the complexity of the interaction in such situations, with two levels of negotiation evident. The negotiation between the respondent and her boyfriend on withdrawal vs. confrontation highlights the process of negotiating responses to discrimination and the difficulty in crafting such responses. Not only is there a process of dickering with whites within the discriminatory scene but also a negotiation between the blacks involved. . . .

The confrontation response is generally so costly in terms of time and energy that acquiescence or withdrawal are common options. An example of the exit response was provided by a utility company executive in an east coast city:

I can remember one time my husband had picked up our son . . . from camp; and he'd stopped at a little store in the neighborhood near the camp. It was hot, and he was going to buy him a snowball. And the proprietor of the store—this was a very old, white neighborhood, and it was just a little sundry store. But the proprietor said he had the little window where people could come up and order things. Well, my husband and son had gone into the store. And he told them, "Well, I can't give it to you here, but if you go outside to the window, I'll give it to you." And there were other [white] people in the store who'd been served [inside]. So, they just left and didn't buy anything.

Here the act seems a throwback to the South of the 1950s, where blacks were required to use the back or side of a store. This differential treatment in an older white neighborhood is also suggestive of the territorial character of racial relations in many cities. The black response to degradation here was not to confront the white person or to acquiesce abjectly, but rather to reject the poor service and leave. . . .

Careful Situation Assessments

We have seen in the previous incidents some tendency for blacks to assess discriminatory incidents before they act. . . .

The complex process of evaluation and response is described by a college dean, who commented generally on hotel and restaurant discrimination encountered as he travels across the United States:

> When you're in a restaurant and . . . you notice that blacks get seated near the kitchen. You notice that if it's a hotel, your room is near the elevator, or your room is always way down in a corner somewhere. You find that you are getting the undesirable rooms. And you come there early in the day and you don't see very many cars on the lot and they'll tell you that this is all we've got. Or you get the room that's got a bad television set. You know that you're being discriminated against. And of course you have to act accordingly. You have to tell them, "Okay, the room is fine, [but] this television set has got to go. Bring me another television set." So in my personal experience, I simply cannot sit and let them get away with it [discrimination] and not let them know that I know that that's what they are doing. . . .
>
> When I face discrimination, first I take a long look at myself and try to determine whether or not I am seeing what I think I'm seeing in 1989, and if it's something that I have an option [about]. In other words, if I'm at a store making a purchase, I'll simply walk away from it. If it's at a restaurant where I'm not getting good service, I first of all let the people know that I'm not getting good service, then I [may] walk away from it. But the thing that I have to do is to let people know that I know that I'm being singled out for a separate treatment. And then I might react in any number of ways— depending on where I am and how badly I want whatever it is that I'm there for.

This commentary adds another dimension to our understanding of public discrimination, its cumulative aspect. Blacks confront not just isolated incidents—such as a bad room in a luxury hotel once every few years—but a lifelong series of such incidents. Here again the omnipresence of careful assessments is underscored. The dean's interview highlights a major difficulty in being black—one must be constantly prepared to assess accurately and then decide on the appropriate response. This long-look approach may indicate that some middle-class blacks are so sensitive to white charges of hypersensitivity and paranoia that they err in the opposite direction and fail to see discrimination when it occurs. In addition, as one black graduate student at a leading white university in the Southeast put it: "I think that sometimes timely and appropriate responses to racially motivated acts and comments are lost due to the processing of the input." The "long look" can result in missed opportunities to respond to discrimination. . . .

Responses to Discrimination: The Street

Reacting to White Strangers

As we move away from public accommodations settings to the usually less protected street sites, racial hostility can become more fleeting and severer, and thus black responses are often restricted. The most serious form of street discrimination is violence. Often the reasonable black response to street discrimination is withdrawal, resigned acceptance, or a quick verbal retort. The difficulty of responding to violence is seen in this report by a man working for a media surveying firm in a southern industrial city:

> I was parked in front of this guy's house. . . . This guy puts his hands on the

window and says, "Get out of the car, nigger.". . . So, I got out, and I thought, "Oh, this is what's going to happen here." And I'm talking fast. And they're, "What are you doing here?" And I'm, "This is who I am. I work with these people. This is the man we want to put in the survey." And I pointed to the house. And the guy said, "Well you have an out-of-state license tag, right?" "Yea." And he said, "If something happened to you, your people at home wouldn't know for a long time, would they?". . . I said, "Look, I deal with a company that deals with television. [If] something happens to me, it's going to be a national thing. . . . So, they grab me by the lapel of my coat, and put me in front of my car. They put the blade on my zipper. And now I'm thinking about this guy that's in the truck [behind me], because now I'm thinking that I'm going to have to run somewhere. Where am I going to run? Go to the police? [laughs] So, after a while they bash up my headlight. And I drove [away].

Stigmatized and physically attacked solely because of his color, this man faced verbal hostility and threats of death with courage. Cautiously drawing on his middle-class resources, he told the attackers his death would bring television crews to the town. This resource utilization is similar to that of the news director in the restaurant incident. Beyond this verbal threat his response had to be one of caution. For most whites threatened on the street, the police are a sought-after source of protection, but for black men this is often not the case.

At the other end of the street continuum is nonverbal harassment such as the "hate stare.". . . A middle-class student with dark skin reported that on her way to university classes she had stopped at a bakery in a white residential area where very few blacks live or shop. A white couple in front of the store stared intently and hatefully at her as she crossed the sidewalk and entered and left the bakery. She reported that she had experienced this hate stare many times. The incident angered her for some days thereafter, in part because she had been unable to respond more actively to it. . . .

It seems likely that for middle-class blacks the street is the site of recurring encounters with various types of white malevolence. A vivid example of the cumulative character and impact of this discrimination was given by another black student at a white university, who recounted his experiences walking home at night from a campus job to his apartment in a predominantly white residential area:

So, even if you wanted to, it's difficult just to live a life where you don't come into conflict with others. Because every day you walk the streets, it's not even like once a week, once a month. It's every day you walk the streets. Every day that you live as a black person you're reminded how you're perceived in society. You walk the streets at night; white people cross the streets. I've seen white couples and individuals dart in front of cars to not be on the same side of the street. Just the other day, I was walking down the street, and this white female with a child, I saw her pass a young white male about 20 yards ahead. When she saw me, she quickly dragged the child and herself across the busy street. What is so funny is that this area has had an unknown white rapist in the area for about four years. [When I pass] white men tighten their grip on their women. I've seen people turn around and seem like they're going to take blows from me. The police constantly make circles around me as I walk home, you know, for blocks. I'll walk, and they'll turn a block. And they'll come around me just to make sure, to find out where I'm going. So, every day you realize [you're black]. Even though you're not doing anything wrong; you're just existing. You're just a person. But you're a black person perceived in an unblack world. (This quote includes a clarification sentence from a follow-up interview.)

Unable to "see" his middle-class symbols of college dress and books, white couples (as well as individuals) have crossed the street in front of cars to avoid walking near this modest-build black student, in a predominantly white neighborhood. Couples moving into defensive postures are doubtless reacting to the stigma of "black maleness." The student perceives such avoidance as racist, however, not because he is paranoid, but because he has previously encountered numerous examples of whites taking such defensive measures. . . .

Conclusion

I have examined the sites of discrimination, the types of discriminatory acts, and the responses of the victims and have found the color stigma still to be very important in the public lives of affluent black Americans. The sites of racial discrimination range from relatively protected home sites, to less protected workplace and educational sites, to the even less protected public places. The 1964 Civil Rights Act guarantees that black Americans are "entitled to the full and equal enjoyment of the goods, services, facilities, privileges, advantages, and accommodations" in public accommodations. Yet the interviews indicate that deprivation of

full enjoyment of public facilities is not a relic of the past; deprivation and discrimination in public accommodations persist. Middle-class black Americans remain vulnerable targets in public places. . . .

Particular instances of discrimination may seem minor to outside white observers when considered in isolation. But when blatant acts of avoidance, verbal harassment, and physical attack combine with subtle and covert slights, and these accumulate over months, years, and lifetimes, the impact on a black person is far more than the sum of the individual instances. . . .

The cumulative impact of racial discrimination accounts for the special way that blacks have of looking at and evaluating interracial incidents. One respondent, a clerical employee at an adoption agency, described the "second eye" she uses:

I think that it causes you to have to look at things from two different perspectives. You have to decide whether things that are done or slights that are made are made because you are black or they are made because the person is just rude, or unconcerned and uncaring. So it's kind of a situation where you're always kind of looking to see with a second eye or a second antenna just what's going on.

The language of "second eye" suggests that blacks look at white-black interaction through a lens colored by personal and group experience with cross-institutional and cross-generational discrimination.

Blacks must be constantly aware of the repertoire of possible responses to chronic and burdensome discrimination. One older respondent spoke of having to put on her "shield" just before she leaves the house each morning. When quizzed, she said that for more than six decades, as she leaves her home, she has tried to be prepared for insults and discrimination in public places, even if nothing happens that day. This extraordinary burden of discrimination was eloquently described by the female professor who resented having to worry about life-threatening incidents that her "very close white friends . . . simply don't have to worry about." Another respondent was articulate on this point:

. . . if you can think of the mind as having one hundred ergs of energy, and the average man uses fifty percent of his energy dealing with the everyday problems of the world—just general kinds of things—then he has fifty percent more to do creative kinds of things that he wants to do. Now that's a white person. Now a black person also has one hundred ergs; he uses fifty percent the same way a white man does, dealing with what the white man has [to deal with], so he has fifty percent left. But he uses twenty-five percent fighting being black, [with] all the problems being black and what it means. Which means he really only has twenty-five percent to do what the white man has fifty percent to do, and he's expected to do just as much as the white

man with that twenty-five percent. . . . So, that's kind of what happens. You just don't have as much energy left to do as much as you know you really could if you were free, [if] your mind were free.

The individual cost of coping with racial discrimination is great, and, as he says, you cannot accomplish as much as you could if you retained the energy wasted on discrimination. This is perhaps the most tragic cost of persisting discrimination in the United States. In spite of decades of civil rights legislation, black Americans have yet to attain the full promise of the American dream.

REFERENCES

Feagin, Joe R. and Douglas Eckberg. 1980. "Prejudice and Discrimination." *Annual Review of Sociology* 6:1–20.

Feagin, Joe R. and Clairece Booher Feagin. 1986. *Discrimination American Style* (rev. ed). Melbourne, FL: Krieger Publishing Co.

Wilson, William J. 1978. *The Declining Significance of Race*. Chicago: University of Chicago Press.

———. 1987. *The Truly Disadvantaged: The Inner City, the Underclass, and Public Policy*. Chicago: University of Chicago Press.

Stereotype Threat and African-American Student Achievement

CLAUDE STEELE

Over the past four decades African-American college students have been more in the spotlight than any other American students. This is because they aren't just college students; they are a cutting edge in America's effort to integrate itself in the nearly forty years since the passage of the Civil Rights Act. These students have borne much of the burden for our national experiment in racial integration. And to a significant degree the success of the experiment will be determined by their success.

Nonetheless, throughout the 1990s the national college dropout rate for African Americans has been 20 to 25 percent higher than that for whites. Among those who finish college, the grade point average of Black students is two-thirds of a grade below that of whites. . . .

Virtually all aspects of underperformance—lower standardized test scores, lower college grades, lower graduation rates—persist among students from the African-American middle class. This situation forces on us an uncomfortable recognition: that beyond class, something racial is depressing the academic performance of these students.

Some time ago two of my colleagues, Joshua Aronson and Steven Spencer, and I tried to see the world from the standpoint of African-American students, concerning ourselves less with features of theirs that might explain their troubles than with features of the world they see. A story I was told recently depicts some of these. The storyteller was worried about his friend, a normally energetic Black student who had broken up with his longtime girlfriend and had since learned that she, a Hispanic, was now dating a white student. This hit him hard. Not long after hearing about his girlfriend, he sat through an hour's discussion of *The Bell Curve* in his psychology class, during which the possible genetic inferiority of his race was openly considered. Then he overheard students at lunch arguing that affirmative action allowed in too many underqualified Blacks. By his own account, this young man had experienced very little of what he thought of as racial discrim-

Claude Steele, "Stereotype Threat and African-American Student Achievement," *Young, Gifted, and Black: Promoting High Achievement Among African-American Students,* Theresa Perry, Claude Steele, and Asa Hilliard III, pp. 109-116, 120-123, 172-174, 176-177. Copyright © 2003 by Theresa Perry, Claude Steele, and Asa Hilliard III. Reprinted by permission of Beacon Press, Boston.

ination on campus. Still, these were features of his world. Could they have a bearing on his academic life?

My colleagues and I have called such features "stereotype threat"—the threat of being viewed through the lens of a negative stereotype, or the fear of doing something that would inadvertently confirm that stereotype. Everyone experiences stereotype threat. We are all members of some group about which negative stereotypes exist, from white males and Methodists to women and the elderly. And in a situation where one of those stereotypes applies—a man talking to women about pay equity, for example, or an aging faculty member trying to remember a number sequence in the middle of a lecture—we know that we may be judged by it.

Like the young man in the story, we can feel mistrustful and apprehensive in such situations. For him, as for African-American students generally, negative stereotypes apply in many situations, even personal ones. Why was that old roommate unfriendly to him? Did that young white woman who has been so nice to him in class not return his phone call because she's afraid he'll ask her for a date? Is it because of his race or something else about him? He cannot know the answers, but neither can his rational self fully dismiss the questions. Together they raise a deeper question: Will his race be a boundary to his experience, to his emotions, to his relationships?. . .

Measuring Stereotype Threat

Can stereotype threat be shown to affect academic performance? And if so, who would be most affected—stronger or weaker students? Which has a greater influence on academic success among Black college students—the degree of threat or the level of preparation with which they enter college?

As we confronted these questions in the course of our research, we came in for some surprises. We began with what we took to be the hardest question: Could something as abstract as stereotype threat really affect something as irrepressible as intelligence? Ours is an individualistic culture; forward movement is seen to come from within. Against this cultural faith one needs evidence to argue that something as "sociological" as stereotype threat can repress something as "individualistic" as intelligence.

To acquire such evidence, Joshua Aronson and I (following a procedure developed with Steven Spencer) designed an experiment to test whether the stereotype threat that Black students might experience when taking a difficult standardized test could depress their performance on the test to a statistically reliable degree. We brought white and Black Stanford students into the laboratory and gave them, one at a time, a very difficult thirty-minute section of a Graduate Record Exam subject test in English literature. Most of these students were sophomores, which meant that the test—designed for graduating seniors—was particularly hard for them—precisely the feature, we reasoned, that would make this simple testing situation different for our Black participants than for our white participants, despite the fact that all the participants were of equal ability levels measured by all available criteria. (The difficulty of the test guaranteed that both Black and white students would find the test frustrating. And it is in these situations that members of ability-stereotyped groups are most likely to experience the extra burden of stereotype threat. First, the experience of frustration with the test gives credibility to the limitation alleged in the stereotype. For this reason, frustration can be especially stinging and disruptive for test-takers to whom the stereotype is relevant. Second, it is on a demanding test that one can least afford to be bothered by the thoughts that likely accompany stereotype threat.)

A significant part of the negative stereotype about African Americans concerns intellectual ability. Thus, in the stereotype threat conditions of the experiments in this series, we merely mentioned to participants that the test was a measure of verbal ability. This was enough, we felt, to make the negative stereotype about African Americans' abilities relevant to their performance on the test, and thus to put them at risk of confirming, or being seen to confirm, the negative stereotype about their abilities. If the pressure imposed by the relevance of a negative stereotype about one's group is enough to impair an important intellectual performance, then Black participants should perform worse than whites in the "diagnostic" condition of this experiment but not in the "nondiagnostic" condition. As figure 31.1 depicts, this is precisely what happened: Blacks performed a full standard deviation lower than whites under the stereotype threat of the test being "diagnostic" of their intellectual ability, even though we had statistically matched the two groups in ability level. Something other than ability was involved; we believed it was stereotype threat.

But maybe the Black students performed less well than the white students because they were less motivated, or because their skills were somehow less applicable to the advanced material of this test. We needed some way to determine if it was indeed

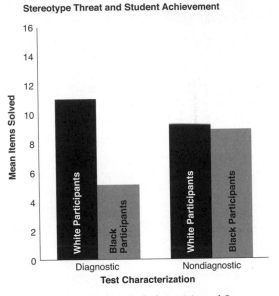

Stereotype Threat and Student Achievement

Figure 31.1   White and Black Participants' Score (Controlled for SAT) on a Difficult English Test as a Function of Characterization of the Test

stereotype threat that depressed the Black students' scores. We reasoned that if stereotype threat had impaired their performance on the test, then reducing this threat would allow their performance to improve. We presented the same test as a laboratory task that was used to study how certain problems are generally solved. We stressed that the task did not measure a person's level of intellectual ability. A simple instruction, yes, but it profoundly changed the meaning of the situation. In one stroke "spotlight anxiety," as the psychologist William Cross once called it, was turned off—and the Black students' performance on the test rose to match that of equally qualified whites (see figure 31.1). In the nonstereotype threat conditions, we presented the same test as an instrument for studying problem solving that was "nondiagnostic" of individual differences in ability—thus making the racial stereotype irrelevant to their performance.

Aronson and I decided that what we needed next was direct evidence of the subjective state we call stereotype threat. To seek this, we looked into whether simply sitting down to take a difficult test of ability was enough to make Black students mindful of their race and stereotypes about it. This may seem unlikely. White students I have taught over the years have sometimes said that they have hardly any sense of even having a race. But Blacks have many experiences with the majority "other group" that make their race salient to them.

We again brought Black and white students in to take a difficult verbal test. But just before the test began, we gave them a long list of words, each of which had two letters missing. They were told to complete the words on this list as fast as they could. We knew from a preliminary survey that twelve of the eighty words we had selected could be completed in such a way as to relate to the stereotype about Blacks' intellectual ability. The fragment "—ce," for example, could become "race." If simply taking a difficult test of ability was enough to make Black students mindful of stereotypes about their race, these students should complete more fragments with stereotype-related words. That is just what happened. When Black students were told that the test would measure ability, they completed the fragments with significantly more stereotype-related words than when they were told that it was not a measure of ability. Whites made few stereotype-related completions in either case. . . .

How Stereotype Threat Affects People Differently

Is everyone equally threatened and disrupted by a stereotype? One might expect, for example, that it would affect the weakest stu-

dents most. But in all our research the most achievement-oriented students, who were also the most skilled, motivated, and confident, were the most impaired by stereotype threat. This fact had been under our noses all along—in our data and even in our theory. A person has to care about a domain in order to be disturbed by the prospect of being stereotyped in it. That is the whole idea of disidentification—protecting against stereotype threat by ceasing to care about the domain in which the stereotype applies. Our earlier experiments had selected Black students who identified with verbal skills and women who identified with math. But when we tested participants who identified less with these domains, what had been under our noses hit us in the face. None of them showed any effect of stereotype threat whatsoever.

These weakly identified students did not perform well on the test: once they discovered its difficulty, they stopped trying very hard and got a low score. But their performance did not differ depending on whether they felt they were at risk of being judged stereotypically.

This finding, I believe, tells us two important things. The first is that the poorer college performance of Black students may have another source in addition to the one—lack of good preparation and, perhaps, of identification with school achievement—that is commonly understood. This additional source—the threat of being negatively stereotyped in the environment—has not been well understood. The distinction has important policy implications: different kinds of students may require different pedagogies of improvement.

The second thing is poignant: what exposes students to the pressure of stereotype threat is not weaker academic identity and skills but stronger academic identity and skills. They may have long seen themselves as good students—better than most. But led into the domain by their strengths, they pay an extra tax on their investment—vigilant worry that their future will be compromised by society's perception and treatment of their group.

This tax has a long tradition in the Black community. The Jackie Robinson story is a central narrative of Black life, literature, and journalism. *Ebony Magazine* has run a page for fifty years featuring people who have broken down one or another racial barrier. Surely the academic vanguard among Black college students today knows this tradition— and knows, therefore, that the thing to do, as my father told me, is to buckle down, pay whatever tax is required, and disprove the damn stereotype.

That, however, seems to be precisely what these students are trying to do. In some of our experiments we administered the test of ability by computer, so that we could see how long participants spent looking at different parts of the test questions. Black students taking the test under stereotype threat seemed to be trying too hard rather than not hard enough. They reread the questions, reread the multiple choices, rechecked their answers, more than when they were not under stereotype threat. The threat made them inefficient on a test that, like most standardized tests, is set up so that thinking long often means thinking wrong, especially on difficult items like the ones we used. . . .

In the old song about the "steel-drivin' man," John Henry races the new steam-driven drill to see who can dig a hole faster. When the race is over, John Henry has prevailed by digging the deeper hole—only to drop dead. The social psychologist Sherman James uses the term "John Henryism" to describe a psychological syndrome that he

found to be associated with hypertension in several samples of North Carolina Blacks: holding too rigidly to the faith that discrimination and disadvantage can be overcome with hard work and persistence. Certainly this is the right attitude. But taken to extremes, it can backfire. A deterioration of performance under stereotype threat by the skilled, confident Black students in our experiments may be rooted in John Henryism.

This last point can be disheartening. Our research, however, offers an interesting suggestion about what can be done to overcome stereotype threat and its detrimental effects. The success of Black students may depend less on expectations and motivation—things that are thought to drive academic performance—than on trust that stereotypes about their group will not have a limiting effect in their school world.

Putting this idea to the test, Joseph Brown and I asked, How can the usual detrimental effect of stereotype threat on the standardized-test performance of these students be reduced? By strengthening students' expectations and confidence, or by strengthening their trust that they are not at risk of being judged on the basis of stereotypes? In the ensuing experiment we strengthened or weakened participants' confidence in their verbal skills, by arranging for them to have either an impressive success or an impressive failure on a test of verbal skills, just before they took the same difficult verbal test we had used in our earlier research. When the second test was presented as a test of ability, the boosting or weakening of confidence in their verbal skills had no effect on performance: Black participants performed less well than equally skilled white participants. What does this say about the commonsense idea that black students' academic problems are rooted in lack of self-confidence?

What did raise the level of black students' performance to that of equally qualified whites was reducing stereotype threat—in this case by explicitly presenting the test as racially fair. When this was done, Blacks performed at the same high level as whites even if their self-confidence had been weakened by a prior failure.

These results suggest something that I think has not been made clear elsewhere: when strong Black students sit down to take a difficult standardized test, the extra apprehension they feel in comparison with whites is less about their own ability than it is about having to perform on a test and in a situation that may be primed to treat them stereotypically. We discovered the extent of this apprehension when we tried to develop procedures that would make our Black participants see the test as "race-fair." It wasn't easy. African-Americans have endured so much bad press about test scores for so long that, in our experience, they are instinctively wary about the tests' fairness. We were able to convince them that our test was race-fair only when we implied that the research generating the test had been done by Blacks. When they felt trust, they performed well regardless of whether we had weakened their self-confidence beforehand. And when they didn't feel trust, no amount of bolstering of self-confidence helped.

REFERENCES

Aronson, J. 1997. *The Effects of Conceptions of Ability on Task Valuation.* Unpublished manuscript, New York University.

_____. 1999. *The Effects of Conceiving Ability as Fixed or Improvable on Responses to Stereotype Threat.* Unpublished manuscript, New York University.

Brown, J. L., and C. M. Steele. 2001. *Performance Expectations Are Not a Necessary Mediator of Stereotype Threat in African American Verbal Test Performance.* Unpublished manuscript, Stanford University.

Cross, W. E., Jr. 1991. *Shades of Black: Diversity in African-American Identity.* Philadelphia: Temple University Press.

Spencer, S. J., E. Iserman, P. G. Davies, and D. M. Quinn. 2001. *Suppression of Doubts, Anxiety, and Stereotypes as a Mediator of the Effect of Stereotype Threat on Women's Math Performance.* Unpublished manuscript, University of Waterloo.

Spencer, S. J., C. M. Steele, and D. M. Quinn. 1999. "Stereotype Threat and Women's Math Performance." *Journal of Experimental Social Psychology* 35: 4–28.

Steele, C. M. 1975. "Name-Calling and Compliance." *Journal of Personality and Social Psychology* 31: 361–69.

_____. 1992. "Race and the Schooling of Black Americans." *Atlantic Monthly* 269: 68–78.

_____. 1997. "A Threat in the Air: How Stereotypes Shape Intellectual Identity and Performance." *American Psychologist* 52: 613–29.

_____. 1999. "Thin Ice: Stereotype Threat and Black College Students." *Atlantic Monthly* 248: 44–54.

Steele, C. M., and J. Aronson. 1995. "Stereotype Threat and the Intellectual Test Performance of African Americans." *Journal of Personality and Social Psychology* 69: 797–811.

Steele, C. M., S. J. Spencer, and J. Aronson. 2002. "Contending with Group Image: The Psychology of Stereotype and Social Identity Threat." In *Advances in Experimental Social Psychology,* vol. 34, ed. M. Zanna. Academic Press.

Steele, C. M., S. J. Spencer, P. G. Davies, K. Harber, and R. E. Nisbett. 2001. *African American College Achievement: A "Wise" Intervention.* Unpublished manuscript, Stanford University.

Steele, S. 1990. *The Content of Our Character: A New Vision of Race in America.* New York: St. Martin's.

32

The Declining Significance of Race
Blacks and Changing American Institutions

WILLIAM JULIUS WILSON

Race relations in America have undergone fundamental changes in recent years, so much so that now the life chances of individual blacks have more to do with their economic class position than with their day-to-day encounters with whites. In earlier years the systematic efforts of whites to suppress blacks were obvious to even the most insensitive observer. Blacks were denied access to valued and scarce resources through various ingenious schemes of racial exploitation, discrimination, and segregation, schemes that were reinforced by elaborate ideologies of racism. But the situation has changed. However determinative such practices were for the previous efforts of the black population to achieve racial equality, and however significant they were in the creation of poverty-stricken ghettoes and a vast underclass of black proletarians—that massive population at the very bottom of the social class ladder plagued by poor education and low-paying, unstable jobs—they do not provide a meaningful explanation of the life chances of black Americans today. The traditional patterns of interaction between blacks and whites, particularly in the labor market, have been fundamentally altered.

In the antebellum period, and in the latter half of the nineteenth century through the first half of the twentieth century, the continuous and explicit efforts of whites to construct racial barriers profoundly affected the lives of black Americans. Racial oppression was deliberate, overt, and is easily documented, ranging from slavery to segregation, from the endeavors of the white economic elite to exploit black labor to the actions of the white masses to eliminate or neutralize black competition, particularly economic competition.[1] As the nation has entered the latter half of the twentieth century, however, many of the traditional barriers have crumbled under the weight of the political, social, and economic changes of the civil rights era. A new set of obstacles has emerged from basic structural shifts in the economy. These obstacles are therefore impersonal but may prove to be even more formidable for certain segments of the black population. Specifically, whereas the previous barriers were usually designed to control

---

and restrict the entire black population, the new barriers create hardships essentially for the black underclass; whereas the old barriers were based explicitly on racial motivations derived from intergroup contact, the new barriers have racial significance only in their consequences, not in their origins. In short, whereas the old barriers bore the pervasive features of racial oppression, the new barriers indicate an important and emerging form of class subordination.

It would be shortsighted to view the traditional forms of racial segregation and discrimination as having essentially disappeared in contemporary America; the presence of blacks is still firmly resisted in various institutions and social arrangements, for example, residential areas and private social clubs. However, in the economic sphere, class has become more important than race in determining black access to privilege and power. It is clearly evident in this connection that many talented and educated blacks are now entering positions of prestige and influence at a rate comparable to or, in some situations, exceeding that of whites with equivalent qualifications. It is equally clear that the black underclass is in a hopeless state of economic stagnation, falling further and further behind the rest of society. . . .

Three Stages of American Race Relations

My basic thesis is that American society has experienced three major stages of black-white contact and that each stage embodies a different form of racial stratification structured by the particular arrangement of both the economy and the polity. Stage one coincides with antebellum slavery and the early post-bellum era and may be designated the period

of *plantation economy and racial-caste oppression.* Stage two begins in the last quarter of the nineteenth century and ends at roughly the New Deal era and may be identified as the period of *industrial expansion, class conflict, and racial oppression.* Finally, stage three is associated with the modern, industrial, post–World War II era, which really began to crystallize during the 1960s and 1970s, and may be characterized as the period of *progressive transition from racial inequalities to class inequalities.* For the sake of brevity I shall identify the different periods respectively as the preindustrial, industrial, and modern industrial stages of American race relations.

Although this abbreviated designation of the periods of American race relations seems to relate racial change to fundamental economic changes rather directly, it bears repeating that the different stages of race relations are structured by the unique arrangements and interactions of the economy and the polity. Although I stress the economic basis of structured racial inequality in the preindustrial and industrial periods of race relations, I also attempt to show how the polity more or less interacted with the economy either to reinforce patterns of racial stratification or to mediate various forms of racial conflict. Moreover, for the modern industrial period, I try to show how race relations have been shaped as much by important economic changes as by important political changes. Indeed, it would not be possible to understand fully the subtle and manifest changes in race relations in the modern industrial period without recognizing the dual and often reciprocal influence of structural changes in the economy and political changes in the state. Thus, my central argument is that different systems of production and/or different arrangements of the polity have imposed different constraints on the way in which racial groups have interacted in the United States, constraints that have structured the relations between racial groups and that have produced dissimilar contexts not only for the manifestation of racial antagonisms but also for racial group access to rewards and privileges.

In contrast to the modern industrial period in which fundamental economic and political changes have made economic class affiliation more important than race in determining Negro prospects for occupational advancement, the preindustrial and industrial periods of black-white relations have one central feature in common, namely, overt efforts of whites to solidify economic racial domination (ranging from the manipulation of black labor to the neutralization or elimination of black economic competition) through various forms of juridical, political, and social discrimination. Since racial problems during these two periods were principally related to group struggles over economic resources, they readily lend themselves to the economic class theories of racial antagonisms that associate racial antipathy with class conflict. A brief consideration of these theories, followed by a discussion of their basic weaknesses, will help to raise a number of theoretical issues that will be useful for analyzing the dynamics of racial conflict in the preindustrial and industrial stages of American race relations. However, in a later section of this chapter I shall attempt to explain why these theories are not very relevant to the modern industrial stage of American race relations.

Economic Class Theories

Students of race relations have paid considerable attention to the economic basis of racial antagonism in recent years, particularly to the theme that racial problems in historical situations are related to the more general problems of economic class conflict. A common assumption of this theme is that racial conflict is merely a special manifestation of class conflict. Accordingly, ideologies of racism, racial prejudices, institutionalized discrimination, segregation, and other factors that reinforce or embody racial stratification are seen as simply part of a superstructure determined and shaped by the particular arrangement of the class structure.[2] However, given this basic assumption, which continues to be the most representative and widely used economic class argument,[3] proponents have advanced two major and somewhat divergent explanations of how class conflicts actually shape and determine racial relations—the orthodox Marxist theory of capitalist exploitation,[4] and the *split labor-market theory* of working-class antagonisms.[5]

The orthodox Marxist theory, which is the most popular variant of the Marxists' explanations of race,[6] postulates that because the ultimate goal of the capitalist class is to maximize profits, efforts will be made to suppress workers' demands for increased wages and to weaken their bargaining power by promoting divisions within their ranks. The divisions occur along racial lines to the extent that the capitalist class is able to isolate the lower-priced black labor force by not only supporting job, housing, and educational discrimination against blacks, but also by developing or encouraging racial prejudices and ideologies of racial subjugation such as racism. The net effect of such a policy is to insure a marginal working class of blacks and to establish a relatively more privileged position for the established white labor force. Since discrimination guarantees a situation where the average wage rate of the black labor force is less than the average wage rate of the established white labor force, the probability of labor solidarity against the capitalist class is diminished.

At the same time, orthodox Marxists argue, the members of the capitalist class benefit not only because they have created a reserved army of labor that is not united against them and the appropriation of surplus from the black labor force is greater than the exploitation rate of the white labor force,[7] but also because they can counteract ambitious claims of the white labor force for higher wages either by threatening to increase the average wage rate of black workers or by replacing segments of the white labor force with segments of the black labor force in special situations such as strikes. The weaker the national labor force, the more likely it is that it will be replaced by lower-paid black labor especially during organized strikes demanding wage increases and improved working conditions. In short, orthodox Marxists argue that racial antagonism is designed to be a "mask for privilege" that effectively conceals the efforts of the ruling class to exploit subordinate minority groups and divide the working class.

In interesting contrast to the orthodox Marxist approach, the split labor-market theory posits the view that rather than attempting to protect a segment of the laboring class, business "supports a liberal or *laissez faire* ideology that would permit all workers to compete freely in an open market. Such open competition would displace higher paid labor. Only under duress does business yield to a labor aristocracy [i.e., a privileged position for white workers]."[8]

The central hypothesis of the split labor-market theory is that racial antagonism first develops in a labor market split along racial lines. The term "antagonism" includes all aspects of intergroup conflict, from beliefs and ideologies (e.g., racism), to overt behavior (e.g., discrimination), to institutions (e.g., segregationist laws). A split labor market occurs when the price of labor for the same work differs for at least two groups, or would differ if they performed the same work. The price of labor "refers to labor's total cost to the employer, including not only wages, but the cost of recruitment, transportation, room and board, education, health care (if the employer must bear these), and the cost of labor unrest."[9]

There are three distinct classes in a split labor market: (1) business or employers; (2) higher-paid labor; and (3) cheaper labor. Conflict develops between these three classes because of different interests. The main goal of business or employers is to maintain as cheap a labor force as possible in order to compete effectively with other businesses and to maximize economic returns. Employers will often import laborers from other areas if local labor costs are too high or if there is a labor shortage. Whenever a labor shortage exists, higher-paid labor is in a good bargaining position. Accordingly, if business is able to attract cheaper labor to the market place, the interests of higher-paid labor are threatened. They may lose some of the privileges they enjoy, they may lose their bargaining power, and they may even lose their jobs. Moreover, the presence of cheaper labor in a particular job market may not only represent actual competition but potential competition as well. An "insignificant trickle" could be seen as the beginning of a major immigration. If the labor market is split along ethnic lines, for example, if higher-paid labor is white and lower-paid labor is black, class antagonisms are transformed into racial antagonisms. Thus, "while much rhetoric of ethnic antagonism concentrates on ethnicity and race, it really in large measure (though probably not entirely) expresses this class conflict."[10]

In some cases members of the lower-paid laboring class, either from within the territorial boundaries of a given country or from another country, are drawn into or motivated to enter a labor market because they feel they can improve their standard of living. As Edna Bonacich points out, "the poorer the economy of the recruits, the less the inducement needed for them to enter the new labor market."[11] In other cases, individuals are forced into a new labor-market situation, such as the involuntary migration of blacks into a condition of slavery in the United States. In this connection, the greater the employer's control over lower-priced labor, the more threatening is lower-paid labor to higher-paid labor.

However, if more expensive labor is strong enough, that is, if it possesses the power resources to preserve its economic interests, it can prevent being replaced or undercut by cheaper labor. On the one hand it can exclude lower-paid labor from a given territory. "Exclusion movements clearly serve the interests of higher paid labor. Its standards are protected, while the capitalist class is deprived of cheaper labor."[12] On the other hand, if it is not possible for higher-paid labor to rely on exclusion (cheaper labor may be indigenous to the territory or may have been imported early in business-labor relations when higher-paid labor could not prevent the move) then it will institutionalize a system of ethnic stratification which could (1) monopolize skilled positions, thereby ensuring the effectiveness of strike action; (2) prevent cheaper labor from developing the skills necessary to compete with higher-paid labor (for example, by imposing barriers to equal access to education); and (3) deny cheaper labor the political resources that

would enable them to undercut higher-paid labor through, say, governmental regulations. "In other words, the solution to the devastating potential of weak, cheap labor is, paradoxically, to weaken them further, until it is no longer in business' immediate interest to use them as replacement."[13] Thus, whereas orthodox Marxist arguments associate the development and institutionalization of racial stratification with the motivations and activities of the capitalist class, the split labor-market theory traces racial stratification directly to the powerful, higher-paid working class.

Implicit in both of these economic class theories is a power-conflict thesis associating the regulation of labor or wages with properties (ownership of land or capital, monopolization of skilled positions) that determine the scope and degree of a group's ability to influence behavior in the labor market. Furthermore, both theories clearly demonstrate the need to focus on the different ways and situations in which various segments of the dominant racial group perceive and respond to the subordinate racial group. However, as I examine the historical stages of race relations in the United States, I find that the patterns of black/white interaction do not consistently and sometimes do not conveniently conform to the propositions outlined in these explanations of racial antagonism. In some cases, the orthodox Marxian explanation seems more appropriate; in other instances, the split labor-market theory seems more appropriate; and in still others, neither theory can, in isolation, adequately explain black-white conflict.

If we restrict our attention for the moment to the struggle over economic resources, then the general pattern that seems to have characterized race relations in the United States during the preindustrial and industrial stages was that the economic elite segments of the white population have been principally responsible for those forms of racial inequality that entail the exploitation of labor (as in slavery), whereas whites in the lower strata have been largely responsible for those forms of imposed racial stratification that are designed to eliminate economic competition (as in job segregation). Moreover, in some situations, the capitalist class and white workers form an alliance to keep blacks suppressed. Accordingly, restrictive arguments to the effect that racial stratification was the work of the capitalist class or was due to the "victory" of higher-paid white labor obscure the dynamics of complex and variable patterns of black-white interaction.

However, if we ignore the more categorical assertions that attribute responsibility for racial stratification to a particular class and focus seriously on the analyses of interracial contact in the labor market, then I will be able to demonstrate that, depending on the historical situation, each of the economic class theories provides arguments that help to illuminate race relations during the preindustrial and industrial periods of black-white contact. By the same token, I hope to explain why these theories have little application to the third, and present, stage of modern industrial race relations. My basic argument is that the meaningful application of the arguments in each theory for any given historical period depends considerably on knowledge of the constraints imposed by the particular systems of production and by the particular laws and policies of the state during that period, constraints that shape the structural relations between racial and class groups and which thereby produce different patterns of intergroup interaction. . . .

The Influence of the System of Production

The term "system of production" not only refers to the technological basis of economic processes or, in Karl Marx's terms, the "forces of production," but it also implies the "social relations of production," that is, "the interaction (for example, through employment and property arrangement) into which men enter at a given level of the development of the forces of production."[14] As I previously indicated, different systems of production impose constraints on racial group interaction. In the remainder of this section I should like to provide a firmer analytical basis for this distinction as it applies specifically to the three stages of American race relations, incorporating in my discussion relevant theoretical points raised in the foregoing sections of this chapter.

It has repeatedly been the case that a non-manufacturing or plantation economy with a simple division of labor and a small aristocracy that dominates the economic and political life of a society has characteristically generated a paternalistic rather than a competitive form of race relations, and the antebellum South was no exception.[15] Paternalistic racial patterns reveal close symbiotic relationships marked by dominance and subservience, great social distance and little physical distance, and clearly symbolized rituals of racial etiquette. The southern white aristocracy created a split labor market along racial lines by enslaving blacks to perform tasks at a cheaper cost than free laborers of the dominant group. This preindustrial form of race relations was not based on the actions of dominant-group laborers, who, as we shall see, were relatively powerless to effect significant change in race relations during this period, but on the structure of the relations established by the aristocracy. Let me briefly amplify this point.

In the southern plantation economy, public power was overwhelmingly concentrated in the hands of the white aristocracy. This power was not only reflected in the control of economic resources and in the development of a juridical system that expressed the class interests of the aristocracy, but also in the way the aristocracy was able to impose its viewpoint on the larger society.[16] This is not to suggest that these aspects of public power have not been disproportionately controlled by the economic elite in modern industrialized Western societies; rather it indicates that the hegemony of the southern ruling elite was much greater in degree, not in kind, than in these societies. The southern elite's hegemony was embodied in an economy that required little horizontal or vertical mobility. Further, because of the absence of those gradations of labor power associated with complex divisions of labor, white workers in the antebellum and early postbellum South had little opportunity to challenge the control of the aristocracy. Because white laborers lacked power resources in the southern plantation economy, their influence on the form and quality of racial stratification was minimal throughout the antebellum and early postbellum periods. Racial stratification therefore primarily reflected the relationships established between blacks and the white aristocracy, relationships which were not characterized by competition for scarce resources but by the exploitation of black labor.[17] Social distance tended to be clearly symbolized by rituals of racial etiquette: gestures and behavior reflecting dominance and subservience. Consequently, any effort to impose a system of public segregation was superfluous. Furthermore, since the social gap between the aristocracy and black slaves was wide and stable, ideologies of racism played less of a role in the subordination of blacks than they subsequently did in the more competitive systems of race relations following the Civil War. In short, the relationship represented intergroup paternalism because it allowed for "close symbiosis and even intimacy, without any threat to status inequalities."[18] This was in sharp contrast to the more competitive forms of race relations that accompanied the development of industrial capitalism in the late nineteenth century and first few decades of the twentieth century (the industrial period of American race relations), wherein the complex division of labor and opportunities for greater mobility not only produced interaction, competition, and labor-market conflict between blacks and the white working class, but also provided the latter with superior resources (relative to those they possessed under the plantation economy) to exert greater influence on the form and content of racial stratification.

The importance of the system of production in understanding race relations is seen in a comparison of Brazil and the southern United States during the post-slavery periods. In the United States, the southern economy experienced a fairly rapid rate of expansion during the late nineteenth century, thereby creating various middle level skilled and unskilled positions that working-class whites attempted to monopolize for themselves. The efforts of white workers to eliminate black competition in the South generated an elaborate system of Jim Crow segregation that was reinforced by an ideology of biological racism. The white working class was aided not only by its numerical size, but also by its increasing accumulation of political resources that accompanied changes in its relation to the means of production.

As white workers gradually translated their increasing labor power into political power, blacks experienced greater restrictions in their efforts to achieve a satisfactory economic, political, and social life. In Brazil, on the other hand, the large Negro and mulatto population was not thrust into competition with the much smaller white population over access to higher-status positions because, as Marvin Harris notes, "there was little opportunity for any member of the lower class to move upward in the social hierarchy."[19] No economic class group or racial group had much to gain by instituting a rigid system of racial segregation or cultivating an ideology of racial inferiority. Racial distinctions were insignificant to the landed aristocracy, who constituted a numerically small upper class in what was basically a sharply differentiated two-class society originally shaped during slavery. The mulattoes, Negroes, and poor whites were all in the same impoverished lower-ranking position. "The general economic stagnation which has been characteristic of lowland Latin America since the abolition of slavery," observes Marvin Harris, "tends to reinforce the pattern of pacific relationships among the various racial groups in the lower ranking levels of the social hierarchy. Not only were the poor whites out-numbered by the mulattoes and Negroes, but there was little of a significant material nature to struggle over in view of the generally static condition of the economy."[20] Accordingly, in Brazil, segregation, discrimination, and racist ideologies failed to crystallize in the first several decades following the end of slavery. More recently, however, industrialization has pushed Brazil toward a competitive type of race relations, particularly the southern region (for example, São Paulo) which has experienced rapid industrialization and has blacks in economic competition with many lower-status white immigrants.[21]

Whereas the racial antagonism in the United States during the period of industrial race relations (such as the Jim Crow segregation movement in the South and the race riots in northern cities) tended to be either directly or indirectly related to labor-market conflicts, racial antagonism in the period of modern industrial relations tends to originate outside the economic order and to have little connection with labor-market strife. Basic changes in the system of production have produced a segmented labor structure in which blacks are either isolated in the relatively non-unionized, low-paying, basically undesirable jobs of the noncorporate sector, or occupy the higher-paying corporate and government industry positions in which job competition is either controlled by powerful unions or is restricted to the highly trained and educated, regardless of race. If there is a basis for labor-market conflict in the modern industrial period, it is most probably related to the affirmative action programs originating from the civil rights legislation of the 1960s. However, since affirmative action programs are designed to improve job opportunities for the talented and educated, their major impact has been in the higher-paying jobs of the expanding government sector and the corporate sector. The sharp increase of the more privileged blacks in these industries has been facilitated by the combination of affirmative action and rapid industry growth. Indeed despite the effectiveness of affirmative action programs the very expansion of these sectors of the economy has kept racial friction over higher-paying corporate and government jobs to a minimum.

Unlike the occupational success achieved by the more talented and educated blacks, those in the black underclass find themselves locked in the low-paying and dead-end jobs of the noncorporate industries, jobs which are not in high demand and which therefore do not generate racial competition or strife among the national black and white labor force. Many of these jobs go unfilled, and employers often have to turn to cheap labor from Mexico and Puerto Rico. As Nathan Glazer has pointed out, "Expectations have changed, and fewer blacks and whites today will accept a life at menial labor with no hope for advancement, as their fathers and older brothers did and as European immigrants did."[22]

Thus in the modern industrial era neither the corporate nor government sectors nor the noncorporate low-wage sector provide the basis for the kind of interracial competition and conflict that has traditionally plagued the labor market in the United States. This, then, is the basis for my earlier contention that the economic class theories which associate labor-market conflicts with racial antagonism have little application to the present period of modern industrial race relations.

The Polity and American Race Relations

If the patterned ways in which racial groups have interacted historically have been shaped in major measure by different systems of production, they have also been undeniably influenced by the changing policies and laws of the state. For analytical purposes, it would be a mistake to treat the influences of the polity and the economy as if they were separate and unrelated. The legal and political systems in the antebellum South were effectively used as instruments of the slaveholding elite to strengthen and legitimate the institution of slavery. But as industrialization altered the economic class structure in the postbellum South, the organizing power and political consciousness of the white lower class increased and its members were able to gain enough control of the political and juridical systems to legalize a new system of racial domination (Jim Crow segregation) that clearly reflected their class interests.

In effect, throughout the preindustrial period of race relations and the greater portion of the industrial period the role of the polity was to legitimate, reinforce, and regulate patterns of racial inequality. However, it would be unwarranted to assume that the relationship between the economic and political aspects of race necessarily implies that the latter is simply a derivative phenomenon based on the more fundamental processes of the former. The increasing intervention, since the mid-twentieth century, of state and federal government agencies in resolving or mediating racial conflicts has convincingly demonstrated the political system's autonomy in handling contemporary racial problems. Instead of merely formalizing existing racial alignments as in previous periods, the political system has, since the initial state and municipal legislation of the 1940s, increasingly created changes leading to the erosion of traditional racial alignments; in other words, instead of reinforcing racial barriers created during the preindustrial and industrial periods, the political system in recent years has tended to promote racial equality.

Thus, in the previous periods the polity was quite clearly an instrument of the white population in suppressing blacks. The government's racial practices varied, as I indicated above, depending on which segment of the white population was able to assert its class interests. However, in the past two decades the interests of the black population have been significantly reflected in the racial policies of the government, and this change is one of the clearest indications that the racial balance of power has been significantly altered. Since the early 1940s the black population has steadily gained political resources and, with the help of sympathetic white allies, has shown an increasing tendency to utilize these resources in promoting or protecting its group interests.

By the mid-twentieth century the black vote had proved to be a major vehicle for political pressure. The black vote not only influenced the outcome of national elections but many congressional, state, and municipal elections as well. Fear of the Negro vote produced enactment of public accommodation and fair employment practices laws in northern and western municipalities and states prior to the passage of federal civil rights legislation in 1964. This political resurgence for black Americans increased their sense of power, raised their expectations, and provided the foundation for the proliferation of demands which shaped the black revolt during the 1960s. But there were other factors that helped to buttress Negro demands and contributed to the developing sense of power and rising expectations, namely, a growing, politically active black middle class following World War II and the emergence of the newly independent African states.

The growth of the black middle class was concurrent with the growth of the black urban population. It was in the urban areas, with their expanding occupational opportunities, that a small but significant number of blacks were able to upgrade their occupations, increase their income, and improve their standard of living. The middle-class segment of an oppressed minority is most likely to participate in a drive for social justice that is disciplined and sustained. In the early phases of the civil rights movement, the black middle class channeled its energies through organizations such as the National Association for the Advancement of Colored People, which emphasized developing political resources and successful litigation through the courts. These developments were paralleled by the attack against traditional racial alignments in other parts of the world. The emerging newly independent African states led the assault. In America, the so-called "leader of the free world," the manifestation of racial tension and violence has been a constant source of embarrassment to national government officials. This sensitivity to world opinion made the national government more vulnerable to pressures of black protest at the very time when blacks had the greatest propensity to protest.

The development of black political resources that made the government more sensitive to Negro demands, the motivation and morale of the growing black middle class that resulted in the political drive for racial equality, and the emergence of the newly independent African states that increased the federal government's vulnerability to civil rights pressures all combined to create a new sense of power among black Americans and to raise their expectations as they prepared to enter the explosive decade of the 1960s. The national government was also aware of this developing sense of power and responded to the pressures of black protest in the 1960s with an unprecedented series of legislative enactments to protect black civil rights.

The problem for blacks today, in terms of government practices, is no longer one of legalized racial inequality. Rather the problem for blacks, especially the black underclass, is that the government is not organized to deal with the new barriers imposed by structural changes in the economy. With the passage of equal employment legislation and the authorization of affirmative action programs the government has helped clear the path for more privileged blacks, who have the requisite education and training, to enter the mainstream of American occupations. However, such government programs do not confront the impersonal economic barriers confronting members of the black underclass, who have been effectively screened out of the corporate and government industries. And the very attempts of the government to eliminate traditional racial barriers through such programs as affirmative action have had the unintentional effect of contributing to the growing economic class divisions within the black community.

Class Stratification and Changing Black Experiences

The problems of black Americans have always been compounded because of their low position in both the economic order (the average economic class position of blacks as a group) and the social order (the social prestige or honor accorded individual blacks because of their ascribed racial status). It is of course true that the low economic position of blacks has helped to shape the categorical social definitions attached to blacks as a racial group, but it is also true that the more blacks become segmented in terms of economic class position, the more their concerns about the social significance of race will vary.

In the preindustrial period of American race relations there was of course very little variation in the economic class position of blacks. The system of racial-caste oppression relegated virtually all blacks to the bottom of the economic class hierarchy. Moreover, the social definitions of racial differences were heavily influenced by the ideology of racism and the doctrine of paternalism, both of which clearly assigned a subordinate status for blacks vis-à-vis whites. Occasionally, a few individual free blacks would emerge and accumulate some wealth or property, but they were the overwhelming exception. Thus the uniformly low economic class position of blacks reinforced and, in the eyes of most whites, substantiated the social definitions that asserted Negroes were culturally and biogenetically inferior to whites. The uniformly low economic class position of blacks also removed the basis for any meaningful distinction between race issues and class issues within the black community.

The development of a black middle class accompanied the change from a preindustrial to an industrial system of production. Still, despite the fact that some blacks were able to upgrade their occupation and increase their education and income, there were severe limits on the areas in which blacks could in fact advance. Throughout most of the industrial period of race relations, the growth of the black middle class occurred because of the expansion of institutions created to serve the needs of a growing urbanized black population. The black doctor, lawyer, teacher, minister, businessman, mortician, excluded from the white community, was able to create a niche in the segregated black community. Although the income levels and life-styles of the black professionals were noticeably and sometimes conspicuously different from those of the black masses, the two groups had one basic thing in common, a racial status contemptuously regarded by most whites in society. If E. Franklin Frazier's analysis of the black bourgeoisie is correct, the black professionals throughout the industrial period of American race relations tended to react to their low position in the social order by an ostentatious display of material possessions and a conspicuous effort to disassociate themselves from the black masses.[23]

Still, as long as the members of the black middle class were stigmatized by their racial status; as long as they were denied the social recognition accorded their white counterparts; more concretely, as long as they remained restricted in where they could live, work, socialize, and be educated, race would continue to be a far more salient and important issue in shaping their sense of group position than their economic class position. Indeed, it was the black middle class that provided the leadership and generated the momentum for the civil rights movement during the mid-twentieth century. The influence and interests of this class were clearly reflected in the way the race issues were defined and articulated. Thus, the concept of "freedom" quite clearly implied, in the early stages of the movement, the right to swim in certain swimming pools, to eat in certain restaurants, to attend certain movie theaters, and to have the same voting privileges as whites. These basic concerns were reflected in the 1964 Civil Rights Bill which helped to create the illusion that, when the needs of the black middle class were met, so were the needs of the entire black community.

However, although the civil rights movement initially failed to address the basic needs of the members of the black lower class, it did increase their awareness of racial oppression, heighten their expectations about improving race relations, and increase their impatience with existing racial arrangements. These feelings were dramatically manifested in a series of violent ghetto outbursts that rocked the nation throughout the late 1960s. These outbreaks constituted the most massive and sustained expression of lower-class black dissatisfaction in the nation's history. They also forced the political system to recognize the problems of human survival and de facto segregation in the nation's ghettoes—problems pertaining to unemployment and underemployment, inferior ghetto schools, and deteriorated housing.

However, in the period of modern industrial race relations, it would be difficult indeed to comprehend the plight of inner-city blacks by exclusively focusing on racial discrimination. For in a very real sense, the current problems of lower-class blacks are substantially related to fundamental structural changes in the economy. A history of discrimination and oppression created a huge black underclass, and the technological and economic revolutions have combined to insure it a permanent status.

As the black middle class rides on the wave of political and social changes, benefiting from the growth of employment opportunities in the growing corporate and government sectors of the economy, the black underclass falls behind the larger society in every conceivable respect. The economic and political systems in the United States have demonstrated remarkable flexibility in allowing talented blacks to fill positions of prestige and influence at the same time that these systems have shown persistent rigidity in handling the problems of lower-class blacks. As a result, for the first time in American history class issues can meaningfully compete with race issues in the way blacks develop or maintain a sense of group position.[24]

Conclusion

The foregoing sections of this chapter present an outline and a general analytical basis for the arguments that will be systematically explored [elsewhere].[25] I have tried to show that race relations in American society have been historically characterized by three major stages and that each stage is represented by a unique form of racial interaction which is shaped by the particular arrangement of the economy and the polity. My central argument is that different systems of production and/or different policies of the state have imposed different constraints on the way in which racial groups interact—constraints that have structured the relations between racial groups and produced dissimilar contexts not only for the manifestation of racial antagonisms but also for racial-group access to rewards and privileges. I emphasized in this connection that in the preindustrial and industrial periods of American race relations the systems of production primarily shaped the patterns of racial stratification and the role of the polity was to legitimate, reinforce, or regulate these patterns. In the modern industrial period, however, both the system of production and the polity assume major importance in creating new patterns of race relations and in altering the context of racial strife. Whereas the preindustrial and industrial stages were principally related to group struggles over economic resources as different segments of the white population overtly sought to create and solidify economic racial domination (ranging from the exploitation of black labor in the preindustrial period to the elimination of black competition for jobs in the industrial period) through various forms of political, juridical, and social discrimination; in the modern industrial period fundamental economic and political changes have made economic class posi-

tion more important than race in determining black chances for occupational mobility. Finally, I have outlined the importance of racial norms or belief systems, especially as they relate to the general problem of race and class conflict in the preindustrial and industrial periods.

My argument that race relations in America have moved from economic racial oppression to a form of class subordination for the less-privileged blacks is not meant to suggest that racial conflicts have disappeared or have even been substantially reduced. On the contrary, the basis of such conflicts have shifted from the economic sector to the sociopolitical order and therefore do not play as great a role in determining the life chances of individual black Americans as in the previous periods of overt economic racial oppression.

NOTES

1. See William J. Wilson, *Power, Racism and Privilege: Race Relations in Theoretical and Sociohistorical Perspectives* (New York: The Free Press, 1973).

2. In Marxist terminology, the "superstructure" refers to the arrangements of beliefs, norms, ideologies, and noneconomic institutions.

3. However, not all theorists who emphasize the importance of economic class in explanations of race relations simply relegate problems of race to the superstructure. The Marxist scholars Michael Burawoy and Eugene Genovese recognize the reciprocal influence between the economic class structure and aspects of the superstructure (belief systems, political systems, etc.), a position which I also share and which is developed more fully in subsequent sections of this chapter. See Eugene D. Genovese, *Roll, Jordan, Roll: The World the Slaves Made* (New York: Pantheon, 1974); idem, *In Red and Black: Marxian Explorations in Southern and Afro-American History* (New York: Vintage Press, 1971); and Michael Burawoy, "Race, Class, and

Colonialism," *Social and Economic Studies* 23 (1974): 521–50.

4. Oliver C. Cox, *Caste, Class and Race: A Study in Social Dynamics* (Garden City, New York: Doubleday, 1948); Paul A. Baran and Paul M. Sweezy, *Monopoly Capital: An Essay on the American Economic and Social Order* (Harmondsworth: Penguin, 1966); Michael Reich, "The Economics of Racism," in *Problems in Political Economy,* ed. David M. Gordon (Lexington, Mass.: Heath, 1971); and M. Nikolinakos, "Notes on an Economic Theory of Racism," *Race: A Journal of Race and Group Relations* 14 (1973): 365–81.

5. Edna Bonacich, "A Theory of Ethnic Antagonism: The Split Labor Market," *American Sociological Review* 37 (October 1972): 547–59; idem, "Abolition, the Extension of Slavery and the Position of Free Blacks: A Study of Split Labor Markets in the United States," *American Journal of Sociology* 81 (1975): 601–28.

6. For examples of alternative and less orthodox Marxist explanations of race, see Eugene D. Genovese, *The Political Economy of Slavery: Studies in the Economy and Society of the Slave South* (New York: Pantheon, 1966); idem, *The World the Slaveholders Made: Two Essays in Interpretation* (New York: Pantheon, 1969); idem, *In Red and Black;* idem, *Roll, Jordan, Roll;* and Burawoy, "Race, Class, and Colonialism."

7. "Exploitation," in Marxian terminology, refers to the difference between the wages workers receive and the value of the goods they produce. The size of this difference, therefore, determines the degree of exploitation.

8. Bonacich, "A Theory of Ethnic Antagonism," p. 557.

9. Ibid., p. 549.

10. Ibid., p. 553.

11. Ibid., p. 549.

12. Ibid., p. 555.

13. Ibid., p. 556.

14. Neil J. Smelser, *Karl Marx on Society and Social Change* (Chicago: University of Chicago Press, 1974), p. xiv. According to Smelser, Marx used the notions "forces of production" and "social relations of production" as constituting the "mode of production." However, in Marx's writings the mode of production is often discussed as equivalent only to the "forces of production." To avoid confusion, I have chosen the term "system of production" which denotes the interrelation of the forces of production and the mode of production.

15. Pierre L. van den Berghe, *Race and Racism: A Comparative Perspective* (New York: John Wiley and Sons, 1967), p. 26.

16. See, for example, Genovese, *Roll, Jordan, Roll.*

17. An exception to this pattern occurred in the cities of the antebellum South, where nonslaveholding whites played a major role in the development of urban segregation. However, since an overwhelming majority of the population resided in rural areas, race relations in the antebellum southern cities were hardly representative of the region.

18. van den Berghe, *Race and Racism,* p. 27.

19. Marvin Harris, *Patterns of Race in the Americas* (New York: Walker, 1964), p. 96.

20. Ibid., p. 96.

21. van den Berghe, *Race and Racism,* p. 28.

22. Nathan Glazer, "Blacks and Ethnic Groups: The Difference, and the Political Difference It Makes," in *Key Issues in the Afro-American Experience,* ed. Nathan I. Huggins, Martin Kilson, and Daniel M. Fox (New York: Harcourt Brace Jovanovich, 1971), 2: 209.

23. E. Franklin Frazier, *Black Bourgeoisie* (New York: The Free Press, 1957). See also Nathan Hare, *Black Anglo-Saxons* (New York: Collier, 1965).

24. The theoretical implications of this development for ethnic groups in general are discussed by Milton Gordon under the concept "ethclass." See Milton M. Gordon, *Assimilation in American Life* (New York: Oxford University Press, 1964).

25. See William Julius Wilson, *The Declining Significance of Race: Blacks and Changing American Institutions* (Chicago and London: University of Chicago Press, 1978).

33

Black Wealth/White Wealth

A New Perspective on Racial Inequality

MELVIN L. OLIVER AND
THOMAS M. SHAPIRO

Each year two highly publicized news reports capture the attention and imagination of Americans. One lists the year's highest income earners. Predictably, they include glamorous and highly publicized entertainment, sport, and business personalities. For the past decade that list has included many African Americans: musical artists such as Michael Jackson, entertainers such as Bill Cosby and Oprah Winfrey, and sports figures such as Michael Jordan and Magic Johnson. During the recent past as many as half of the "top ten" in this highly exclusive rank have been African Americans.

Another highly publicized list, by contrast, documents the nation's wealthiest Americans. The famous *Forbes* magazine profile of the nation's wealthiest 400 focuses not on income, but on wealth.[1] This list includes those people whose assets—or command over monetary resources—place them at the top of the American economic hierarchy. Even though this group is often ten times larger than the top earners list, it contains few if any African Americans. An examination of these two lists creates two very different perceptions of the well-being of America's black community on the eve of the twenty-first century. The large number of blacks on the top income list generates an optimistic view of how black Americans have progressed economically in American society. The near absence of blacks in the *Forbes* listing, by contrast, presents a much more pessimistic outlook on blacks' economic progress.

This chapter develops a perspective on racial inequality that is based on the analysis of private wealth. Just as a change in focus from income to wealth in the discussion above provides a different perspective on racial inequality, our analysis reveals deep patterns of racial imbalance not visible when viewed only through the lens of income. This analysis provides a new perspective on racial inequality by exploring how material assets are created, expanded, and preserved.

The basis of our analysis is the analytical distinction between wealth and other traditional measures of economic status, of how people are "making it" in America (for example, income, occupation, and education). Wealth is a particularly important indicator of individual and family access to life chances. Income refers to a flow of money over time, like a rate per hour, week, or year; wealth is a stock of assets owned at a particular time. Wealth is what people own, while income is what people receive for work, retirement, or social welfare. Wealth signifies the command over financial resources that a family has accumulated over its lifetime along with those resources that have been inherited across generations. Such resources, when combined with income, can create the opportunity to secure the "good life" in whatever form is needed—education, business, training, justice, health, comfort, and so on. Wealth is a special form of money not used to purchase milk and shoes and other life necessities. More often it is used to create opportunities, secure a desired stature and standard of living, or pass class status along to one's children. In this sense the command over resources that wealth entails is more encompassing than is income or education, and closer in meaning and theoretical significance to our traditional notions of economic well-being and access to life chances.

More important, wealth taps not only contemporary resources but material assets that have historic origins. Private wealth thus captures inequality that is the product of the past, often passed down from generation to generation. Given this attribute, in attempting to understand the economic status of blacks, a focus on wealth helps us avoid the either-or view of a march toward progress or a trail of despair. Conceptualizing racial inequality through wealth revolutionizes our conception of its nature and magnitude, and of whether it is declining or increasing. While most recent analyses have concluded that contemporary class-based factors are most important in understanding the sources of continuing racial inequality, our focus on wealth sheds light on both the historical and the contemporary impacts not only of class but of race. . . .

The argument for class, most eloquently and influentially stated by William Julius Wilson in his 1978 book *The Declining Significance of Race,* suggests that the racial barriers of the past are less important than present-day social class attributes in determining the economic life chances of black Americans. Education, in particular, is the key attribute in whether blacks will achieve economic success relative to white Americans. Discrimination and racism, while still actively practiced in many spheres, have marginally less effect on black Americans' economic attainment than whether or not blacks have the skills and education necessary to fit in a changing economy. In this view, race assumes importance only as the lingering product of an oppressive past. As Wilson observes, this time in his *The Truly Disadvantaged,* racism and its most harmful injuries occurred in the past, and they are today experienced mainly by those on the bottom of the economic ladder, as "the accumulation of disadvantages . . . passed from generation to generation."[2]

We believe that a focus on wealth reveals a crucial dimension of the seeming paradox of continued racial inequality in American society. Looking at wealth helps solve the riddle of seeming black progress alongside economic deterioration. Black wealth has grown, for example, at the same time that it has fallen further behind that of whites. Wealth reveals an array of insights into black and white inequality that challenge our conception of racial and social justice in America.

The empirical heart of our analysis resides in an examination of differentials in black and white wealth holdings. This focus paints a vastly different empirical picture of social inequality than commonly emerges from analyses based on traditional inequality indicators. The burden of our claim is to demonstrate not simply the taken-for-granted assumption that wealth reveals "more" inequality—income multiplied x times is not the correct equation. More importantly we show that wealth uncovers a qualitatively different pattern of inequality on crucial fronts. Thus the goal of this work is to provide an analysis of racial differences in wealth holding that reveals dynamics of racial inequality otherwise concealed by income, occupational attainment, or education. It is our argument that wealth reveals a particular network of social relations and a set of social circumstances that convey a unique constellation of meanings pertinent to race in America. This perspective significantly adds to our understanding of public policy issues related to racial inequality; at the same time it aids us in developing better policies for the future. In stating our case, we do not discount the important information that the traditional indicators provide, but we argue that by adding to the latter an analysis of wealth a more thorough, comprehensive and powerful explanation of social inequality can be elaborated. . . .

Economists argue that racial differences in wealth are a consequence of disparate class and human capital credentials (age, education, experience, skills), propensities to save, and consumption patterns. A sociology of wealth seeks to properly situate the social context in which wealth generation occurs. Thus the sociology of wealth accounts for racial differences in wealth holding by demonstrating the unique and diverse social circumstances that blacks and whites face. One result is that blacks and whites also face different structures of investment opportunity, which have been affected historically and contemporaneously by both race and class. We develop three concepts to provide a sociologically grounded approach to understanding racial differentials in wealth accumulation. These concepts highlight the ways in which this opportunity structure has disadvantaged blacks and helped contribute to massive wealth inequalities between the races.

Our first concept, "racialization of state policy," refers to how state policy has impaired the ability of many black Americans to accumulate wealth—and discouraged them from doing so—from the beginning of slavery throughout American history. From the first codified decision to enslave African Americans to the local ordinances that barred blacks from certain occupations to the welfare state policies of today that discourage wealth accumulation, the state has erected major barriers to black economic self-sufficiency. In particular, state policy has structured the context within which it has been possible to acquire land, build community, and generate wealth. Historically, policies and actions of the United States government have promoted homesteading, land acquisition, home ownership, retirement, pensions, education, and asset accumulation for some sectors of the population and not for others. Poor people—blacks in particular—generally have been excluded from participation in these state-sponsored opportunities. In this way, the distinctive relationship between whites and blacks has been woven into the fabric of state actions. The modern welfare state has racialized citizenship, social organization, and economic status while consigning blacks to a relentlessly impoverished and subordinate position within it.

Our second focus, on the "economic detour," helps us understand the relatively low level of entrepreneurship among and the small scale of the businesses owned by black Americans. While blacks have historically sought out opportunities for self-employment, they have traditionally faced an environment, especially from the post-bellum period to the middle of the twentieth century, in which they were restricted by law from participation in business in the open market. Explicit state and local policies restricted the rights of blacks as free economic agents. These policies had a devastating impact on the ability of blacks to build and maintain successful enterprises. While blacks were limited to a restricted African American market to which others (for example, whites and other ethnics) also had easy access, they were unable to tap the more lucrative and expansive mainstream white markets. Blacks thus had fewer opportunities to develop successful businesses. When businesses were developed that competed in size and scope with white businesses, intimidation and ultimately, in some cases, violence were used to curtail their expansion or get rid of them altogether. The lack of important assets and indigenous community development has thus played a crucial role in limiting the wealth-accumulating ability of African Americans.

The third concept we develop is synthetic in nature. The notion embodied in the "sedimentation of racial inequality" is that in central ways the cumulative effects of the past have seemingly cemented blacks to the bottom of society's economic hierarchy. A history of low wages, poor schooling, and segregation affected not one or two generations of blacks but practically all

African Americans well into the middle of the twentieth century. Our argument is that the best indicator of the sedimentation of racial inequality is wealth. Wealth is one indicator of material disparity that captures the historical legacy of low wages, personal and organizational discrimination, and institutionalized racism. The low levels of wealth accumulation evidenced by current generations of black Americans best represent the economic status of blacks in the American social structure.

To argue that blacks form the sediment of the American stratificational order is to recognize the extent to which they began at the bottom of the hierarchy during slavery, and the cumulative and reinforcing effects of Jim Crow and de facto segregation through the mid-twentieth century. Generation after generation of blacks remained anchored to the lowest economic status in American society. The effect of this inherited poverty and economic scarcity for the accumulation of wealth has been to "sediment" inequality into the social structure. The sedimentation of inequality occurred because the investment opportunity that blacks faced worked against their quest for material self-sufficiency. In contrast, whites in general, but well-off whites in particular, were able to amass assets and use their secure financial status to pass their wealth from generation to generation. What is often not acknowledged is that the same social system that fosters the accumulation of private wealth for many whites denies it to blacks, thus forging an intimate connection between white wealth accumulation and black poverty. Just as blacks have had "cumulative disadvantages," many whites have had "cumulative advantages." Since wealth builds over a lifetime and is then passed along to kin, it is, from our perspective, an essential indicator of black economic well-being. By focusing on wealth we discover how a black's socioeconomic status results from a socially layered accumulation of disadvantages passed on from generation to generation. In this sense we uncover a racial wealth tax.

Our empirical analysis enables us to raise and answer several key questions about wealth: How has wealth been distributed in American society over the twentieth century? What changes in the distribution of wealth occurred during the 1980s? And finally, what are the implications of these changes for black-white inequality?

During the eighties the rich got much richer, and the poor and middle classes fell further behind. Why? The Reagan tax cuts provided greater discretionary income for middle- and upper-class taxpayers. One asset whose value grew dramatically during the eighties was real estate, an asset that is central to the wealth portfolio of the average American. Home ownership makes up the largest part of wealth held by the middle class, whereas the upper class more commonly hold a greater degree of their wealth in financial assets. Owning a house is the hallmark of the American Dream, but it is becoming harder and harder for average Americans to afford their own home and fewer are able to do so.

In part because of the dramatic rise in home values, the wealthiest generation of elderly people in America's history is in the process of passing along its wealth. Between 1987 and 2011 the baby boom generation stands to inherit approximately $7 trillion. Of course, all will not benefit equally, if at all. One-third of the worth of all estates will be divided by the richest 1 percent, each legatee receiving an average inheritance of $6 million. Much of this wealth will be in the form of property, which, as the philosopher Robert Nozick is quoted as saying in a 1990 *New York Times* piece, "sticks out as a special kind of unearned benefit that produces unequal opportunities."[3] Kevin, a seventy-five-year-old retired homeowner interviewed for this study, captures the dilemma of unearned inheritance:

> You heard that saying about the guy with a rich father? The kid goes through life thinking that he hit a triple. But really he was born on third base. He didn't hit no triple at all, but he'll go around telling everyone he banged the fucking ball and it was a triple. He was born there!

Inherited wealth is a very special kind of money imbued with the shadows of race. Racial difference in inheritance is a key feature of our story. For the most part, blacks will not partake in divvying up the baby boom bounty. America's racist legacy is shutting them out. The grandparents and parents of blacks under the age of forty toiled under segregation, where education and access to decent jobs and wages were severely restricted. Racialized state policy and the economic detour constrained their ability to enter the post–World War II housing market. Segregation created an extreme situation in which earlier generations were unable to build up much, if any, wealth. The average black family headed by a person over the age of sixty-five has no net financial assets to pass down to its children. Until the late 1960s there were few older African Americans with the ability to save much at all, much less invest. And no savings and no inheritance meant no wealth.

The most consistent and strongest common theme to emerge in interviews conducted with white and black families was that family assets expand choices, horizons, and opportunities for children while lack of assets limit opportunities. Because parents want to give their children whatever advantages they can, we wondered about the ability of the average American household to expend assets on their children. We found that the lack of private assets intrudes on the dreams that many Americans have for their children. Extreme resource deficiency characterizes several groups. It may surprise some to learn that 62 percent of households headed by single parents are without savings or other financial assets, or that two of every five households without a high school degree lack a financial nest egg. Nearly one-third of all households—and 61 percent of all black households—are without financial resources. These statistics lead to our focus on the most resource-deficient households in our study—African Americans.

We argue that, materially, whites and blacks constitute two nations. One of the analytic centerpieces of this work tells a tale of two middle classes, one white and one black. Most significant, the claim made by blacks to middle-class status depends on income and not assets. In contrast, a wealth pillar supports the white middle class in its drive for middle-class opportunities and a middle-class standard of living. Middle-class blacks, for example, earn seventy cents for every dollar earned by middle-class whites but they possess only fifteen cents for every dollar of wealth held by middle-class whites. For the most part, the economic foundation of the black middle class lacks one of the pillars that provide stability and security to middle-class whites—assets. The black middle class position is precarious and fragile with insubstantial wealth resources. This analysis means it is entirely premature to celebrate the rise of the black

middle class. The glass is both half empty and half full, because the wealth data reveal the paradoxical situation in which blacks' wealth has grown while at the same time falling further behind that of whites.

The social distribution of wealth discloses a fresh and formidable dimension of racial inequality. Blacks' achievement at any given level not only requires that greater effort be expended on fewer opportunities but also bestows substantially diminished rewards. Examining blacks and whites who share similar socioeconomic characteristics brings to light persistent and vast wealth discrepancies. Take education as one prime example: the most equality we found was among the college educated, but even here at the pinnacle of achievement whites control four times as much wealth as blacks with the same degrees. This predicament manifests a disturbing break in the link between achievement and results that is essential for democracy and social equality.

The central question of this study is, Why do the wealth portfolios of blacks and whites vary so drastically? The answer is not simply that blacks have inferior remunerable human capital endowments—substandard education, jobs, and skills, for example—or do not display the characteristics most associated with higher income and wealth. We are able to demonstrate that even when blacks and whites display similar characteristics—for example, are on a par educationally and occupationally—a potent difference of $43,143 in home equity and financial assets still remains. Likewise, giving the average black household the same attributes as the average white household leaves a $25,794 racial gap in financial assets alone.

The extent of discrimination in institutions and social policy provides a persuasive index of bias that undergirds the drastic differences between blacks and whites. We show that skewed access to mortgage and housing markets and the racial valuing of neighborhoods on the basis of segregated markets result in enormous racial wealth disparity. Banks turn down qualified blacks much more often for home loans than they do similarly qualified whites. Blacks who do qualify, moreover, pay higher interest rates on home mortgages than whites. Residential segregation persists into the 1990s, and we found that the great rise in housing values is color-coded.[4] Why should the mean value of the average white home appreciate at a dramatically higher rate than the average black home? Home ownership is without question the single most important means of accumulating assets. The lower values of black homes adversely affect the ability of blacks to utilize their residences as collateral for obtaining personal, business, or educational loans. We estimate that institutional biases in the residential arena have cost the current generation of blacks about $82 billion. Passing inequality along from one generation to the next casts another racially stratified shadow on the making of American inequality. Institutional discrimination in housing and lending markets extends into the future the effects of historical discrimination within other institutions.

Placing these findings in the larger context of public policy discussions about racial and social justice adds new dimensions to these discussions. A focus on wealth changes our thinking about racial inequality. The more one learns about wealth differences, the more mistaken current policies appear. To take these findings seriously, as we do, means not shirking the responsibility of seeking alternative policy

ideas with which to address issues of inequality. We might even need to think about social justice in new ways. In some key respects our analysis of disparities in wealth between blacks and whites forms an agenda for the future, the key principle of which is to link opportunity structures to policies promoting asset formation that begin to close the racial wealth gap.

Closing the racial gap means that we have to target policies at two levels. First, we need policies that directly address the situation of African Americans. Such policies are necessary to speak to the historically generated disadvantages and the current racially based policies that have limited the ability of blacks, as a group, to accumulate wealth resources.

Second, we need policies that directly promote asset opportunities for those on the bottom of the social structure, both black and white, who are locked out of the wealth accumulation process. More generally, our analysis clearly suggests the need for massive redistributional policies in order to reforge the links between achievement, reward, social equality, and democracy. These policies must take aim at the gross inequality generated by those at the very top of the wealth distribution. Policies of this type are the most difficult ones on which to gain consensus but the most important in creating a more just society.

This chapter's underlying goal is to establish a way to view racial inequality that will serve as a guide in securing racial equality in the twenty-first century. Racial equality is not an absolute or idealized state of affairs, because it cannot be perfectly attained. Yet the fact that it can never be perfectly attained in the real world is a wholly insufficient excuse for dismissing it as utopian or impossible. What is important are the bearings by which a nation chooses to orient its character. We can choose to let racial inequality fester and risk heightened conflict and violence. Americans can also make a different choice, a commitment to equality and to closing the gap as much as possible.

NOTES

1. Harold Senecker, 1993, "The *Forbes* 400: The Richest People in America," *Forbes,* 18 October, pp. 110–113.

2. William J. Wilson, 1987, *The Truly Disadvantaged,* Chicago: University of Chicago Press.

3. Nick Ravo, 1990, "A Windfall Nears in Inheritances from the Richest Generation," *New York Times,* 22 July E4.

4. Reynolds Farley and William H. Frey, 1994, "Changes in the Segregation of Whites from Blacks During the 1980s: Small Steps Toward a More Integrated Society," *American Sociological Review* 59: 23–45. Douglas S. Massey and Nancy A. Denton, 1993, *American Apartheid: Segregation and the Making of the Underclass,* Cambridge: Harvard University Press.

34

The Possibility of
a New Racial Hierarchy in the
Twenty-First-Century United States

HERBERT J. GANS

Over the last decade, a number of social scientists writing on race and ethnicity have suggested that the country may be moving toward a new racial structure (Alba 1990; Sanjek 1994; Gitlin 1995). If current trends persist, today's multiracial hierarchy could be replaced by what I think of as a dual or bimodal one consisting of "nonblack" and "black" population categories, with a third, "residual," category for the groups that do not, or do not yet, fit into the basic dualism.[1]

More important, this hierarchy may be based not just on color or other visible bodily features, but also on a distinction between undeserving and deserving, or stigmatized and respectable, races.[2] The hierarchy is new only insofar as the old white-nonwhite dichotomy may be replaced by a nonblack-black one, but it is hardly new for blacks, who are likely to remain at the bottom once again. I fear this hierarchy could develop even if more blacks achieve educa-

tional mobility, obtain professional and managerial jobs, and gain access to middle-class incomes, wealth, and other "perks." Still, the hierarchy could also end, particularly if the black distribution of income and wealth resembles that of the then dominant races, and if interracial marriage eliminates many of the visible bodily features by which Americans now define race. . . .

The Dual Racial Hierarchy

Before what is now described, somewhat incorrectly, as the post–1965 immigration, the United States was structured as a predominantly Caucasian, or white, society, with a limited number of numerically and otherwise inferior races, who were typically called Negroes, Orientals, and American Indians—or blacks, yellows, and reds to go with the pinkish-skinned people called whites. There was also a smattering of groups involving a huge

---

number of people who were still described by their national or geographic origins rather than language, including Filipinos, Mexicans and Puerto Ricans, Cubans, etc.[3]

After 1965, when many other Central and Latin American countries began to send migrants, the Spanish-speaking groups were all recategorized by language and called Hispanics. Newcomers from Southeast Asia were classified by continental origin and called Asians, which meant that the later Indian, Pakistani, and Sri Lankan newcomers had to be distinguished regionally, and called South Asians.

At the end of the twentieth century, the country continues to be dominated by whites. Nevertheless, both the immigrants who started to arrive after the end of World War II and the political, cultural, and racial changes that took place in the wake of their arrival have further invalidated many old racial divisions and labels. They have also set into motion what may turn out to be significant transformations in at least part of the basic racial hierarchy.

These transformations are still in an early phase but one of the first has been the elevation of a significant, and mostly affluent, part of the Asian and Asian-American population into a "model minority" that also bids to eradicate many of the boundaries between it and whites. Upward socioeconomic mobility and increasing intermarriage with whites may even end up in eliminating the boundary that now constructs them as a separate race. Thus, one possible future trend may lead to all but poor Asians and Asian-Americans being perceived and even treated so much like whites that currently visible bodily differences will no longer be judged negatively or even noticed, except when and where

Asians or Asian-Americans threaten white interests (e.g., Newman 1993). The same treatment as quasi whites may spread to other successfully mobile and intermarrying immigrants and their descendants, for example Filipinos and white Hispanics.[4]

What these minorities have in common now with Asians, and might have in common even more in the future, is that they are all nonblack, although not as many are currently as affluent as Asians. Nonetheless, by the middle of the twenty-first century, as whites could perhaps become, or will worry about becoming, a numerical minority in the country, they might cast about for political and cultural allies.[5] Their search for allies, which may not even be conscious or deliberate, could hasten the emergence of a new, non-black racial category, whatever it is named, in which skin color, or in the case of "Hispanics," racially constructed ethnic differences, will be ignored, even if whites would probably remain the dominant subcategory.

The lower part of the emerging dual hierarchy will likely consist of people classified as blacks, including African-Americans, as well as Caribbean and other blacks, dark-skinned or black Hispanics, Native Americans, and anyone else who is dark skinned enough and/or possessed of visible bodily features and behavior patterns, actual or imagined, that remind nonblacks of blacks. Many of these people will also be poor, and if whites and other nonblacks continue to blame America's troubles on a low-status scapegoat, the new black category will be characterized as an undeserving race.

In effect, class will presumably play nearly as much of a role in the boundary changes as race, but with some important exceptions. For example, if a significant number of very poor whites remain as the twenty-first-century equivalent of today's "white trash," they will probably be viewed as less undeserving than equally poor blacks simply because they are whites.[6]

Furthermore, the limits of class are indicated, at least for today, by the continued stigmatization of affluent and otherwise high-status blacks, who suffer some of the same indignities as poor blacks (Feagin and Sykes 1994).[7] So, of course, do moderate- and middle-income members of the working class, who constitute the majority of blacks in America even if whites do not know it. The high visibility of "black" or Negroid physical features renders class position invisible to whites, so that even affluent blacks are suspected of criminal or pathological behavior that is actually found only among a minority of very poor blacks.

Despite continuing white hatreds and fears of blacks that continue almost 150 years after the Civil War, racial classification systems involving others have been more flexible. When the first Irish immigrants came to New York, they were so poor that they were perceived by Anglo-Saxon whites as the black Irish and often treated like blacks. Even so, it did not take the Irish long to separate themselves from blacks, and more important, to be so separated by the city's Anglo-Saxons. A generation later, the Irish were whites (Roediger 1991; Ignatiev 1995).

Perhaps their new whiteness was reinforced by the arrival of the next set of newcomers: people from Eastern and Southern Europe who were often described as members of "swarthy races." Even though the word *race* was used the way we today use *ethnicity,* the newcomers were clearly not white in the Anglo-Saxon sense, and Southern Italians were sometimes called "guineas" because of their dark skin. Nonetheless, over

time, they too became white, thanks in part to their acculturation, their integration into the mainstream economy, and after World War II, their entry into the middle class. Perhaps the disappearance of their swarthiness was also reinforced by the arrival in the cities of a new wave of Southern blacks during and after World War II.

A less typical racial transformation occurred about that time in Mississippi, where whites began to treat the Chinese merchants who provided stores for poor blacks as near whites. As Loewen (1988) tells the story, increased affluence and acculturation were again relevant factors. Although whites neither socialized nor intermarried with the Chinese, they accorded them greater social deference and political respect than when they had first arrived. They turned the Chinese into what I previously called a residual category, and in the process created an early version of the nonblack-black duality that may appear in the United States in the next century.

As the Mississippi example suggests, changes in racial classification schemes need not require racial or class equality, for as long as scarce resources or positions remain, justifications for discrimination also remain and physical features that are invisible in some social settings can still become visible in others. Glass ceilings supply the best example, because they seem to change more slowly than some other hierarchical boundaries. Even ceilings for Jews, non-Irish Catholics, and others long classified as whites are still lower than those for WASPs in the upper reaches of the class and prestige structures.

I should note that the racial hierarchy I have sketched here, together with the qualifications that follow, are described both from the perspective of the (overtly) detached social scientist, and also from the perspective of the populations that end up as dominant in the structure. A longer paper would analyze how very differently the people who are fitted into the lower or residual parts of the hierarchy see it.[8]

Qualifications to the Dual Hierarchy

Even if the country would someday replace its current set of racial classifications, the result would not be a simple dual structure, and this model needs to be qualified in at least three ways.

Residuals

The first qualification is the near certainty of a residual or middle category that includes groups placed in a waiting position by the dominant population until it becomes clear whether they will be allowed to become non-black, face the seemingly permanent inferiority that goes with being black, or become long-term residuals.

If such a structure were to develop in the near future, those likely to be placed in a residual category would include the less affluent members of today's Asian, Hispanic and Filipino, Central and South American Indian, and mixed Indian-Latino populations. The future of the dark-skinned members of the South Asian newcomers is harder to predict. Indeed, their treatment will become an important test of how whites deal with the race-class nexus when the people involved are very dark skinned but are not Negroid—and when their class position is so high that in 1990 it outranked that of all other immigrants (Rumbaut 1997, table 1.4).[9]

Who is classified as residual will, like all other categorizations, be shaped by both

class and race. To borrow Milton Gordon's (1964) useful but too rarely used notion of "ethclass," what may be developing are "race-classes," with lower-class members of otherwise racially acceptable groups and higher-class members of racially inferior ones being placed in the residual category.

It is also possible for two or more residual categories to emerge, one for nonwhite and Hispanic populations of lower- and working-class position, and another for nonwhites and Hispanics of higher-class position, with the latter more likely to be eligible eventually to join whites in the nonblack portion of a dual hierarchy. Yet other variations are conceivable, however, for white America has not yet given any clues about how it will treat middle-class Latinos of various skin colors and other bodily features. Perhaps today's ad hoc solution, to treat nonblack Hispanics as a quasi-racial ethnic group that is neither white nor black, may survive for another generation or more, particularly if enough Hispanics remain poor or are falsely accused of rejecting linguistic Americanization.

Being placed in a residual classification means more than location in a middle analytic category; it is also a socially enforced, even if covert, category, and it will be accompanied by all the social, political, and emotional uncertainties that go with being placed in a holding pattern and all the pains these create (Marris 1996). True, residuals may not know they are waiting, but then the second-generation white ethnic "marginal men" identified by Stonequist (1937) did not know they were waiting for eventual acculturation and assimilation.

Multiracials

A second qualification to the dual model is created by the emergence of biracials or multiracials that result from the rising in-termarriage rates among Asian, Hispanic, and black and white immigrants as well as black and white native-born Americans.[10] Interracial marriages increased from 1 per-cent of all marriages in 1960 to 3 percent in 1990 (Harrison and Bennett 1995, 165).[11] They are expected to increase much faster in the future, particularly Asian-white ones, since even now, about a third of all Asian marriages, and more than half of all Japan-ese ones, are intermarriages.[12] If Hispanic-white marriages were also counted, they would exceed all the rest in current number and expected growth, but these are usually treated as ethnic rather than racial inter-marriages.

Another set of recruits for a residual po-sition includes the light-skinned blacks, once called mulattos, who today dominate the African-American upper class, some of whom may be sufficiently elite and light-skinned to be viewed as nonblack. Even now, the most prominent among the light-skinned black-white biracials, including business and civic leaders, celebrities and entertainers, are already treated as honorary whites, although many refuse this option and take special pride in their blackness and become "race leaders."[13]

Meanwhile, "multiracial" is in the process of slowly becoming a public racial category, and someday it could become an official one codified by the U.S. Census.[14] At this writing, however, many people of mixed race are not ready to define themselves pub-licly as such, and those who can choose which racial origin to use are sometimes flexible on instrumental grounds, or may choose different racial origins on different occasions.[15] How people of various racial mixtures construct themselves in the longer run is impossible to tell, since issues of their identification and treatment by others, their own identity, and the social, occupational, financial, and political benefits and costs in-volved cannot be predicted either.

As far as the country's long-term future racial structure is concerned, however, what matters most is how whites will eventually view and treat multiracial people. This will be affected by the variations in class and vis-ible physical features among multiracial people—for example, how closely they re-semble whites or other deserving races. An-other question is the future of the traditional identification of race with "blood," which counts all nonwhites in halves, quarters, or even eighths, depending on how many and which ancestors intermarried with whom.[16] If the late twentieth-century belief in the power of genes continues, blood might sim-ply be replaced by genes someday.

Mixed race is a particularly complex cate-gory, for several reasons. In any racial inter-marriage with more than one offspring, each sibling is likely to look somewhat dif-ferent racially from the others, ranging from darker to lighter or more and less nonwhite. Thus, one black-white sibling could be viewed as black and another as nonblack—even before they decide how they view themselves. What happens in subsequent generations is virtually unimaginable, since even if mixed-race individuals marry others of the same mixture, their children will not resemble their grandparents and some may barely resemble their parents. Eventually, a rising number will be treated as, and will think of themselves as, white or nonblack, but this is possible only when people of multiracial origin can no longer bear chil-dren who resemble a black ancestor.

Empirical evidence about the effects of racial intermarriage from countries where it has taken place for a long time is unfortunately not very relevant. The closest case, the Caribbean islands, are for the most part, tiny. They are also former plantation societies, with a small number of white and light-skinned elites, and a large number of nonwhites—and a differential conception of white and nonwhite from island to island.[17] Caribbean nonwhites appear to intermarry fairly freely but skin color does count and the darkest-skinned peoples are invariably lowest in socioeconomic class and status (Mintz 1989; Rodriguez 1989).

The only large country, Brazil, also began as a plantation society, and it differs from the United States particularly in that the Brazilian state eschewed racial legislation. As a result, Brazil never passed Jim Crow laws, but as of this writing (January 1998) it has not passed civil rights legislation either. Racial stratification, as well as discrimination and segregation, has persisted nonetheless, but it has been maintained through the class system. Drastic class inequalities, including a high rate of illiteracy among the poor, have enabled whites to virtually monopolize the higher class and status positions.

The absence of state involvement has given Brazil an undeserved reputation as a society that encourages intermarriage but ignores racial differences, a reputation the state has publicized as "racial democracy." The reality is not very different from that of the United States, however, for while there has been more intermarriage, it appears to have taken place mainly among blacks and black-white biracials, who together make up about half the country's population. Moreover, biracials gain little socioeconomic advantage from their lighter skins, even as the darkest-skinned blacks are kept at the bottom, forced into slums and prisons as in the United States.[18]

In effect, the Brazilian experience would suggest an empirical precedent for my hypothesis that blacks will remain a separate, and discriminated-against, population in the United States of the future. Indeed, in just about every society in which blacks first arrived as slaves, they are still at the bottom, and the political, socioeconomic, and cultural mechanisms to keep them there remain in place. Although blacks obtain higher incomes and prestige than Asians or white Hispanics in a number of American communities, the descendants of nonblack immigrants are, with some notable exceptions, still able to overtake most blacks in the long run.

Since parts of the United States were also a plantation society in which the slaves were black, the leftovers of the racial stratification pattern will likely continue here as well. Thus, children of black-white intermarriages who turn out to be dark skinned are classified as blacks, even if the United States is on the whole kinder to light-skinned biracials than Brazil.

The future of Asian-white biracials remains more unpredictable, in part because no empirical data exist that can be used to shore up guesses about them. The same observation applies to the endless number of other multiracial combinations that will be created when the children of multiracial parents intermarry with yet other multiracials. There will be few limits to new variations in bodily features, though which will be visible or noticed, and which of the latter will be stigmatized or celebrated as exotic cannot be guessed now.[19] Most likely, however, the larger the number of multiracials and of multiracial variations, the more difficult it will be for nonblacks to define and enforce racial boundaries, or to figure out which of the many darker-skinned varieties of multiracials had black ancestors. In that case, an eventual end to racial discrimination is possible.

If future racial self-identification patterns will also resemble today's ethnic ones, the racial equivalent of today's voluntary white ethnicity and its associated lack of ethnic loyalty may mean that many future triracial, quadriracial, and other multiracial people may eventually know little, and care even less, about the various racial mixtures they have inherited. It is even conceivable that this change will extend to black multiracials, and should race become voluntary for them as well, the possibility of an end to racial discrimination will be increased. Unfortunately, at the moment such extrapolations are far closer to utopian thinking than to sociological speculation.

Regional Variations

A third qualification to the dual model is that the portrait I have drawn is national, but given the regional variations in old racial groups and new immigrant populations, it fits no single U.S. region. Moreover, some parts of the country are now still so devoid of new immigrants, with the exception of the handful who come to establish "ethnic" restaurants, that the present racial hierarchies, categories, and attitudes, many of them based on stereotypes imported from elsewhere, could survive unchanged for quite a while in such areas. Furthermore, some areas that have experienced heavy immigration from Asia and Latin America are currently seeing an outmigration of whites, especially lower-income ones (Frey 1996). Thus, even current patterns in the racial makeup of U.S. regions could change fairly quickly.

In addition, regional differences remain in the demography of the lowest strata. The racial hierarchy of the Deep South will probably continue to bear many direct marks of slavery, although the de facto black experience elsewhere in the country has so far not been totally different. Moreover, in some regions, Latin American and other poor non-black immigrants have already been able to jump over the poor black population economically and socially, partly because whites, including institutions such as banks, are less hostile—or less necessary—to them than they are to blacks.

In the Southwest, Mexicans and other Hispanics remain at the socioeconomic bottom, although in California, they may be joined by the Hmong, Laotians, and other very poor Asians. And Native Americans still occupy the lowest socioeconomic stratum in the handful of mostly rural parts of the country where they now live, although tribes with gambling casinos may be able to effect some changes in that pattern.

Even though some of the new immigrants can by now be found just about everywhere in America, the Los Angeles and New York City areas not only remain the major immigrant arrival centers but also contain the most diverse populations. As a result, a number of the issues discussed in this paper will be played out there, even as they are barely noticeable in the many smaller American cities that may have attracted only a handful of the newcomers. Since these two cities are also the country's prime creators of popular culture, however, their distinctive racial and ethnic characteristics will probably be diffused in subtle ways through the country as a whole. . . .

Conclusion

Since no one can even guess much less model the many causal factors that will influence the future, the observations above are not intended to be read as a prediction but as an exercise in speculative analysis. The weakness of such an analysis is its empirical reliance on the extrapolation of too many current trends and the assumed persistence of too many current phenomena. The analysis becomes a justifiable exercise, however, because it aims only to speculate about what future "scenarios" are possible, and what variables might shape these.

Obviously, the observations about such a hierarchy are not meant to suggest that it is desirable. Indeed, I wrote the paper with the hope that if such a future threatens to become real, it can be prevented.

NOTES

I am grateful for comments on earlier drafts of this paper from Margaret Chin, Jennifer Lee, an anonymous reviewer—and from my fellow authors in the volume *The Cultural Territories of Race: Black and White Boundaries,* edited by Michèle Lamont (Chicago and New York: University of Chicago Press and Russell Sage Foundation, 1999).

1. These categories are constructions, but they also contain populations experiencing all the pleasures and pains of being located in a hierarchy. And although I am often discussing constructions, I will forgo the practice of putting all racial, national, and related names and labels between quotes, except for unusual racial stereotypes.

2. The two races may not be called that openly, but ambiguous pejoratives have long been part of the American vocabulary, for example *underclass* now, and *pauper* a century earlier (Gans 1995). Since races are social constructions, their names will depend in large part on who does the naming—and whose names become dominant in the public vocabulary.

3. Puerto Ricans are still often described as immigrants, even though they have been American citizens for a long time and their move from the island to the mainland is a form of interstate mo-

bility. Racial, class, and linguistic considerations have undoubtedly influenced this labeling.

The same dominant-race thinking led Irving Kristol and other neoconservatives to argue in the 1960s that blacks were similar enough to the white European immigrants to be able to adopt and act on immigrant values. They also assumed that blacks would then assimilate like immigrants, ignoring such facts as that blacks had originally come as slaves, not immigrants; had been here several centuries; and had not yet been allowed by whites to assimilate. Thirty years later, many whites ignore the same facts to propose the newest immigrants as role models for blacks.

4. Much less is said about black Hispanics, including Puerto Ricans, who suffer virtually all of the discriminatory and other injustices imposed on African-Americans.

5. Some highly placed whites are already worrying, for example in a *Time* cover story by William Henry III (1990), but then similar whites worried a century earlier what the then arriving Catholic and Jewish newcomers would do to *their* country. The current worries are as meaningless as the old ones, since they are based on extrapolations of current patterns of immigration, not to mention current constructions of (nonwhite) race and (Hispanic) ethnicity.

6. Hacker (1996) notes, for example, that the term "white trash" is no longer in common use. Indeed, for reasons worth studying, the more popular term of the moment is "trailer trash," which nonetheless seems to be applied solely to poor whites.

7. In this respect, the United States differs from many other countries in the Western hemisphere, where blacks who have managed to become affluent are treated, within limits, as whites.

8. Not only might they perceive it more angrily than I am here doing, but they might be angrier about it than about the present hierarchy, simply because it is new but no great improvement. One result could be their constructions of new racial identities for themselves that depart drastically from the ones future nonblacks consider reasonable.

9. Being far fewer than Asians in number, South Asians are nationally not very visible now.

Moreover, for religious and other reasons, South Asian immigrants have so far often been able to discourage their children from intermarrying.

10. My observations on multiracial constructions and people have benefited from many conversations with Valli Rajah.

11. Between 1970 and 1994, the number of people in interracial marriages grew from 676,000 to more than three million (Fletcher 1997). In 1990, biracial children made up 4 percent of all children, increasing from half a million in 1970 to about two million that year. The largest number were Asian-white children, followed by Native American-white and African American-white ones (Harrison and Bennett 1995).

12. Some observers currently estimate that 70 percent of all Japanese and Japanese-Americans are intermarried, mostly with whites. Since they came to the United States as families long before 1965, this estimate may supply a clue about what will happen to second-, third-, and later-generation descendants of other Asian-American populations.

13. Presumably class position will affect how other descendants of old Southern mulatto and creole populations (Dominguez 1986) will be classified.

14. In the political debates over the racial categories to be used in the Year 2000 Census, vocal multiracials preferred to be counted as and with various people of color. African-Americans and other officially recognized racial groups also indicated their opposition to a multiracial category, being reluctant to reduce the power of their numbers or the federal benefits that now go to racial minorities (e.g., Holmes 1996).

15. Kohne (1996) reports that light-skinned biracial Columbia University students who identify as whites also apply for scholarships as blacks. But then, four decades earlier, I met Italian-Americans in Boston's West End who took Irish names in order to obtain jobs in Irish-dominated city hall.

16. The practice of quantifying racial bloods has a long history in Europe and the United States, thanks to both eugenics and slavery. Perhaps it will disappear when enough people have to start counting three or more races. However, peo-ple also still use blood fractions when they marry across religions, so that the notion of racial, ethnic, or religious "blood" is by no means obsolete.

17. They are also different, for "one and the same person may be considered white in the Dominican Republic or Puerto Rico . . . 'colored' in Jamaica, Martinique, or Curacao . . . [and] a 'Negro' in Georgia" (Hoetink 1967, xii).

18. This account is based mainly on the data summarized in Fiola 1990 and Skidmore 1992, the classic analysis of the Brazilian racial system in Skidmore 1993, Adamo's 1983 case study of race and class in Rio de Janeiro, and the sociopolitical analyses by Marx (1995, 1996). I am indebted to Anthony Marx for guiding me into the literature on Brazil, although there is still precious little social research, especially with current data, in English.

19. No one has so far paid much attention to who is constructed as exotic and why, except the multiracial people, mostly women, to whom it is applied. Some of them benefit because they are sought by industries that hire workers with exotic facial features; but women without these occupational interests resent such labeling because it turns them into sexual objects.

Industries that employ workers with exotic features, facial and otherwise, such as the fashion and entertainment industries, play an interesting, and probably unduly influential, role in the country's public racial construction.

REFERENCES

Adamo, Samuel C. 1983. "The Broken Promise: Race, Health and Justice in Rio de Janeiro, 1890–1940." Ph.D. diss., University of New Mexico.

Alba, Richard D. 1990. *Ethnic Identity.* New Haven: Yale University Press.

Dominguez, Virginia R. 1986. *White by Definition.* New Brunswick: Rutgers University Press.

Feagin, Joe R., and Michael P. Sykes. 1994. *Living with Racism.* Boston: Beacon.

Fiola, Jan. 1990. "Race Relations in Brazil: A Reassessment of the 'Racial Democracy' Thesis." Occasional Papers Series no. 34. University of

Massachusetts Latin American Studies Program, Amherst.

Fletcher, Michael A. 1997. "More Than a Black-White Issue." *Washington Post National Weekly Edition,* May 26, 34.

Frey, William H. 1996. "Immigration, Domestic Migration and Demographic Balkanization in America." *Population and Development Review* 22:741–63.

Gans, Herbert J. 1995. *The War Against the Poor.* New York: Basic.

Gitlin, Todd. 1995. *The Twilight of Common Dreams.* New York: Metropolitan.

Gordon, Milton M. 1964. *Assimilation in American Life.* New York: Oxford University Press.

Hacker, Andrew. 1996. Foreword to *The Coming Race War?* by Richard Delgado. New York: New York University Press.

Harrison, Roderick J., and Claudette Bennett. 1995. "Racial and Ethnic Diversity." In *State of the Union: America in the 1990s,* vol. 2, *Social Trends,* edited by Reynolds Farley. New York: Russell Sage Foundation.

Henry, William, III. 1990. "Beyond the Melting Pot." *Time,* April 9, 29–32.

Hoetink, Harry. 1967. *The Two Variants in Caribbean Race Relations.* London: Oxford University Press.

Holmes, Steven. 1996. "Census Tests New Category to Identify Racial Groups." *New York Times,* December 4, A25.

Ignatiev, Noel. 1995. *How the Irish Became White.* New York: Routledge.

Kohne, Natasha G. 1996. "The Experience of Mixed-Race Women: Challenging Racial Boundaries." Unpublished senior thesis, Department of Sociology, Columbia University, New York.

Loewen, James W. 1988. *The Mississippi Chinese.* 2d ed. Prospect Heights, Ill.: Waveland.

Marris, Peter. 1996. *The Politics of Uncertainty.* New York: Routledge.

Marx, Anthony W. 1995. "Contested Citizenship: The Dynamics of Racial Identity and Social Movements." *International Review of History* 40, supplement 3: 159–83.

———. 1996. "Race-Making and the Nation-State." *World Politics,* January, 180–208.

Mintz, Sidney W. 1989. *Caribbean Transformations.* New York: Columbia University Press.

Newman, Katherine. 1993. *Declining Fortunes.* New York: Basic.

Rodriguez, Clara E. 1989. *Puerto Ricans: Born in the U.S.A.* Boston: Unwin Hyman.

Roediger, David R. 1991. *Wages of Whiteness.* London: Verso.

Rumbaut, Ruben G. 1997. "Ties that Bind: Immigration and Immigrant Families in the United States." In *Immigration and the Family,* edited by Alan Booth, Ann C. Crouter, and Nancy Landale. Mahwah, N.J.: Erlbaum.

Sanjek, Roger. 1994. "Intermarriage and the Future of the Races in the United States." In *Race,* edited by Steven Gregory and Roger Sanjek. New Brunswick: Rutgers University Press.

Skidmore, Thomas L. 1992. "Fact and Myth: Discovering a Racial Problem in Brazil." Working paper 173. Helen Kellogg Institute for International Studies, University of Notre Dame.

———. 1993. *Black into White.* Durham: Duke University Press.

Stonequist, Everett V. 1937. *The Marginal Man.* New York: Scribner's.

35

What Do You Call a
Black Man with a Ph.D.?

LAWRENCE BOBO

Ain't nothing post-racial about the United States of America.

I say this because my best friend, a well-known, middle-aged, affluent, black man, *was arrested on his own front porch* after showing his identification to a white police officer who was responding to a burglary call. Though the officer quickly determined that my friend was the rightful resident of the house and knew by then that there was no burglary in progress, he decided to place my friend in handcuffs, put him in the back of a police cruiser and have him fingerprinted and fully "processed," at our local police station.

This did not happen at night. It happened in the middle of the day. It did not happen to a previously unknown urban black male. It happened to internationally known, 58-year-old Henry Louis "Skip" Gates Jr. I am writing about this event because it is an outrage, because I want others to know that it is an outrage, and because, even now, I have not fully processed the meaning of it.

Here's what I understand to have happened: The officer in my friend's case was really motivated by a simmering cauldron of anger that my friend had not immediately complied with his initial command to step out of the house. In hindsight, that was the right thing to do since I think my friend could have been physically injured by this police officer (if not worse) had he, in fact, stepped out of his home before showing his ID. Black Americans recall all too well that Amadou Diallo reached for his identification in a public space when confronted by police and, 42 gun shots later, became the textbook case of deadly race-infected police bias.

Skip is one of the most readily recognized black men in America and the most broadly influential black scholar of this generation. And yes, in the liberal, politically correct cocoon of "the people's Republic of Cambridge," a famous, wealthy and important black man was arrested on his front porch. The ultimate charge? "Disorderly conduct." Whatever that means.

Even before the charges were dropped Tuesday, I knew in my bones that this officer was wrong. I knew in my bones that this situation was about the level of deference from a black male that a white cop expects. I say this even though I did not see

Lawrence Bobo, "What Do You Call a Black Man with a Ph.D.?" *The Root*, July 21, 2009, www.theroot.com.

the events themselves unfold. What I do know with certainty is that the officer, even by his own written report, understood that he was dealing with a lawful resident of the house when he made the arrest. That same report makes it clear that at the time of the arrest, the officer was no longer concerned about the report of a "burglary in progress" involving "two black males." No, by this point we're talking about something else entirely.

Maybe this "situation" had something to do with Harvard University and social class. It is possible that one element of what happened here involved a policeman with working-class roots who faced an opportunity to "level the playing field" with a famous and successful Harvard professor. But even if class mattered, it did so mostly because of how, in this situation, it was bound up with race.

Imagine the scenario. An influential man, in his own home, is ordered to step outside by a policeman. Naturally and without disrespect he asks "Why?" or perhaps "Who are you?" The officer says words to the effect, "I'm responding to a burglary report. Step outside now!"

To which, our confident man, in his own home, says, "No. This is my house. I live here. I work for the university, and the university manages this property." The response prompts the officer to demand identification. "Fine," our resident says, and he pulls out two forms of identification from his wallet.

The officer now knows with high certainty that he is dealing with the legitimate resident of the home. Does he ask, "Is everything alright, sir? We had a report of a burglary." No, he does not. Does he say, "I'm sorry, sir, if I frightened you before.

We had a report of a burglary, and all they said was 'two black men at this address.' You can understand my concern when I first got to the house?"

No, he didn't do that either. He also could have disengaged by walking away. But no, he didn't do that either.

This officer continued to insist that my friend step outside. By now, it is clear to my friend that the officer has, well, "an attitude problem." So, as I suspect would happen with any influential, successful person, in their own home, who has provided authoritative identification to a policeman would do in this situation: My friend says, "I want your name and badge number." The cop says nothing sensible in response but continues to wait at the door.

The request for the officer's name and badge number is pressed again. No response. Social scientists have plenty of hard data showing that African Americans, across the social-class spectrum, are deeply distrustful of the police. The best research suggests that this perception has substantial roots in direct personal encounters with police that individuals felt were discriminatory or motivated by racism. But this perception of bias also rests on a shared collective knowledge of a history of discriminatory treatment of blacks by police and of social policies with built-in forms of racial bias (i.e., stiffer sentences for use of crack versus powder cocaine).

In the age of Obama, however, with all the talk of post-racial comity, you might have thought what happened to Skip Gates was an impossibility. Even the deepest race cynic—picture comedian Dave Chappelle as "Conspiracy Brother" from the movie *Undercover Brother*—couldn't predict such an event. But, I will say that when I moved into the same affluent area as Gates, I wondered whether someone might mistakenly report me, a black man, for breaking into my own house in a largely white neighborhood and what I would have to do to prove that the house actually belonged to me if the police showed up at the door.

I remember joking with my wife that maybe I should keep a copy of the mortgage papers and deed in the front foyer, just in case. I do now. And it is no longer a joke.

There is no way to completely erase and undo what has been done. And there is, indeed, a larger lesson here about the problem of racial bias and misuse of discretion by police that still, all too often, works against blacks, especially poor blacks. If Skip Gates can be arrested on his front porch and end up in handcuffs in a police cruiser then, sadly, there, but for the grace of God, goes every other black man in America. That is one sad statement, and it should also be enough to end all this post-racial hogwash.

Maybe events will prove my cynicism and anger unwarranted. Perhaps the officer involved will be fully held to account for his actions. Perhaps Gates will hear the apology he so richly deserves to hear. Perhaps a review of training, policy and practice by police in my fair city and many others will take place and move us closer to a day of bias-free policing. If you're inclined to believe all that will happen, then I've got a shiny, new, post-racial narrative I'd be happy to sell.

PART VI

Gender Inequality

36

The Social Construction of Gender

JUDITH LORBER

Talking about gender for most people is the equivalent of fish talking about water. Gender is so much the routine ground of everyday activities that questioning its taken-for-granted assumptions and presuppositions is like thinking about whether the sun will come up. Gender is so pervasive that in our society we assume it is bred into our genes. Most people find it hard to believe that gender is constantly created and re-created out of human interaction, out of social life, and is the texture and order of that social life. Yet gender, like culture, is a human production that depends on everyone constantly "doing gender" (West and Zimmerman 1987).

And everyone "does gender" without thinking about it. Today, on the subway, I saw a well-dressed man with a year-old child in a stroller. Yesterday, on a bus, I saw a man with a tiny baby in a carrier on his chest. Seeing men taking care of small children in public is increasingly common—at least in New York City. But both men were quite obviously stared at—and smiled at, approvingly. Everyone was doing gender—the men who were changing the role of fathers and the other passengers, who were applauding them silently. But there was more gendering going on that probably fewer people noticed. The baby was wearing a white crocheted cap and white clothes. You couldn't tell if it was a boy or a girl. The child in the stroller was wearing a dark blue T-shirt and dark print pants. As they started to leave the train, the father put a Yankee baseball cap on the child's head. Ah, a boy, I thought. Then I noticed the gleam of tiny earrings in the child's ears, and as they got off, I saw the little flowered sneakers and lace-trimmed socks. Not a boy after all. Gender done.

Gender is such a familiar part of daily life that it usually takes a deliberate disruption of our expectations of how women and men are supposed to act to pay attention to how it is produced. Gender signs and signals are so ubiquitous that we usually fail to note them—unless they are missing or ambiguous. Then we are uncomfortable until we have successfully placed the other person in a gender status; otherwise, we feel socially dislocated. In our society, in addition to man and woman, the status can be *transvestite* (a person who dresses in opposite-gender clothes) and *transsexual* (a person who has had sex-change surgery). Transvestites and transsexuals carefully construct their gender status by dressing, speaking, walking, gesturing in the ways prescribed for women or men—whichever they want to be taken for—and so does any "normal" person.

For the individual, gender construction starts with assignment to a sex category on the basis of what the genitalia look like at birth. Then babies are dressed or adorned in a way that displays the category because parents don't want to be constantly asked whether their baby is a girl or a boy. A sex category becomes a gender status through naming, dress, and the use of other gender markers. Once a child's gender is evident, others treat those in one gender differently from those in the other, and the children respond to the different treatment by feeling different and behaving differently. As soon as they can talk, they start to refer to themselves as members of their gender. Sex doesn't come into play again until puberty, but by that time, sexual feelings and desires and practices have been shaped by gendered norms and expectations. Adolescent boys and girls approach and avoid each other in an elaborately scripted and gendered mating dance. Parenting is gendered, with different expectations for mothers and for fathers, and people of different genders work at different kinds of jobs. The work adults do as mothers and fathers and as low-level workers and high-level bosses, shapes women's and men's life experiences, and these experiences produce different feelings, consciousness, relationships, skills—ways of being that we call feminine or masculine. All of these processes constitute the social construction of gender.

Gendered roles change—today fathers are taking care of little children, girls and boys are wearing unisex clothing and getting the same education, women and men are working at the same jobs. Although many traditional social groups are quite strict about maintaining gender differences, in other social groups they seem to be blurring. Then why the one-year-old's earrings? Why is it still so important to mark a child as a girl or a boy, to make sure she is not taken for a boy or he for a girl? What would happen if they were? They would, quite literally, have changed places in their social world.

To explain why gendering is done from birth, constantly and by everyone, we have to look not only at the way individuals experience gender but at gender as a social institution. As a social institution, gender is one of the major ways that human beings organize their lives. Human society depends on a predictable division of labor, a designated allocation of scarce goods, assigned responsibility for children and others who cannot care for themselves, common values and their systematic transmission to new members, legitimate leadership, music, art, stories, games, and other symbolic productions. One way of choosing people for the different tasks of society is on the basis of their talents, motivations, and competence—their demonstrated achievements. The other way is on the basis of gender, race, ethnicity—ascribed membership in a category of people. Although societies vary in the extent to which they use one or the other of these ways of allocating people to work and to carry out other responsibilities, every society uses gender and age grades. Every society classifies people as "girl and boy children," "girls and boys ready to be married," and "fully adult women and men," constructs similarities among them and differences between them, and assigns them to different roles and responsibilities. Personality characteristics, feelings, motivations, and ambitions flow from these different life experiences so that the members of these different groups become different kinds of people. The process of gendering and its outcome are legitimated by religion, law, science, and the society's entire set of values. . . .

Western society's values legitimate gendering by claiming that it all comes from physiology—female and male procreative differences. But gender and sex are not equivalent, and gender as a social construction does not flow automatically from genitalia and reproductive organs, the main physiological differences of females and males. In the construction of ascribed social statuses, physiological differences such as sex, stage of development, color of skin, and size are crude markers. They are not the source of the social statuses of gender, age grade, and race. Social statuses are carefully constructed through prescribed processes of teaching, learning, emulation, and enforcement. Whatever genes, hormones, and biological evolution contribute to human social institutions is materially as well as qualitatively transformed by social practices. . . .

For Individuals, Gender Means Sameness

Although the possible combinations of genitalia, body shapes, clothing, mannerisms, sexuality, and roles could produce infinite varieties in human beings, the social institution of gender depends on the production and maintenance of a limited number of gender statuses and of making the mem-

bers of these statuses similar to each other. Individuals are born sexed but not gendered, and they have to be taught to be masculine or feminine. As Simone de Beauvoir said: "One is not born, but rather becomes, a woman. . . ; it is civilization as a whole that produces this creature . . . which is described as feminine." (1952, 267).

Children learn to walk, talk, and gesture the way their social group says girls and boys should. Ray Birdwhistell, in his analysis of body motion as human communication, calls these learned gender displays *tertiary* sex characteristics and argues that they are needed to distinguish genders because humans are a weakly dimorphic species—their only sex markers are genitalia (1970, 39–46). Clothing, paradoxically, often hides the sex but displays the gender.

In early childhood, humans develop gendered personality structures and sexual orientations through their interactions with parents of the same and opposite gender. As adolescents, they conduct their sexual behavior according to gendered scripts. Schools, parents, peers, and the mass media guide young people into gendered work and family roles. As adults, they take on a gendered social status in their society's stratification system. Gender is thus both ascribed and achieved (West and Zimmerman 1987). . . .

For human beings there is no essential femaleness or maleness, femininity or masculinity, womanhood or manhood, but once gender is ascribed, the social order constructs and holds individuals to strongly gendered norms and expectations. Individuals may vary on many of the components of gender and may shift genders temporarily or permanently, but they must fit into the limited number of gender statuses their society recognizes. In the process, they re-create their society's version of women and men: "If we do gender appropriately, we simultaneously sustain, reproduce, and render legitimate the institutional arrangements. . . . If we fail to do gender appropriately, we as individuals—not the institutional arrangements—may be called to account (for our character, motives, and predispositions)" (West and Zimmerman 1987, 146).

The gendered practices of everyday life reproduce a society's view of how women and men should act (Bourdieu [1980] 1990). Gendered social arrangements are justified by religion and cultural productions and backed by law, but the most powerful means of sustaining the moral hegemony of the dominant gender ideology is that the process is made invisible; any possible alternatives are virtually unthinkable (Foucault 1972; Gramsci 1971).

For Society, Gender Means Difference

The pervasiveness of gender as a way of structuring social life demands that gender statuses be clearly differentiated. Varied talents, sexual preferences, identities, personalities, interests, and ways of interacting fragment the individual's bodily and social experiences. Nonetheless, these are organized in Western cultures into two and only two socially and legally recognized gender statuses, "man" and "woman."[1] In the social construction of gender, it does not matter what men and women actually do; it does not even matter if they do exactly the same thing. The social institution of gender insists only that what they do is *perceived* as different.

If men and women are doing the same tasks, they are usually spatially segregated to maintain gender separation, and often the tasks are given different job titles as well, such as executive secretary and administrative assistant (Reskin 1988). If the differences between women and men begin to blur, society's "sameness taboo" goes into action (G. Rubin 1975, 178). At a rock and roll dance at West Point in 1976, the year women were admitted to the prestigious military academy for the first time, the school's administrators "were reportedly perturbed by the sight of mirror-image couples dancing in short hair and dress gray trousers," and a rule was established that women cadets could dance at these events only if they wore skirts (Barkalow and Raab 1990, 53). Women recruits in the U.S. Marine Corps are required to wear makeup—at a minimum, lipstick and eye shadow—and they have to take classes in makeup, hair care, poise, and etiquette. This feminization is part of a deliberate policy of making them clearly distinguishable from men Marines. Christine Williams quotes a twenty-five-year-old woman drill instructor as saying: "A lot of the recruits who come here don't wear makeup; they're tomboyish or athletic. A lot of them have the preconceived idea that going into the military means they can still be a tomboy. They don't realize that you are a *Woman* Marine" (1989, 76–77).

If gender differences were genetic, physiological, or hormonal, gender bending and gender ambiguity would occur only in hermaphrodites, who are born with chromosomes and genitalia that are not clearly female or male. Since gender differences are socially constructed, all men and all women can enact the behavior of the other, because they know the other's social script: "'Man' and 'woman' are at once empty and overflowing categories. Empty because they have no ultimate, transcendental meaning.

Overflowing because even when they appear to be fixed, they still contain within them alternative, denied, or suppressed definitions." (J. W. Scott 1988, 49). . . .

Gender as Process, Stratification, and Structure

As a social institution, gender is a process of creating distinguishable social statuses for the assignment of rights and responsibilities. As part of a stratification system that ranks these statuses unequally, gender is a major building block in the social structures built on these unequal statuses.

As a *process,* gender creates the social differences that define "woman" and "man." In social interaction throughout their lives, individuals learn what is expected, see what is expected, act and react in expected ways, and thus simultaneously construct and maintain the gender order: "The very injunction to be a given gender takes place through discursive routes: to be a good mother, to be a heterosexually desirable object, to be a fit worker, in sum, to signify a multiplicity of guarantees in response to a variety of different demands all at once" (J. Butler 1990, 145). Members of a social group neither make up gender as they go along nor exactly replicate in rote fashion what was done before. In almost every encounter, human beings produce gender, behaving in the ways they learned were appropriate for their gender status, or resisting or rebelling against these norms. Resistance and rebellion have altered gender norms, but so far they have rarely eroded the statuses.

Gendered patterns of interaction acquire additional layers of gendered sexuality, parenting, and work behaviors in childhood, adolescence, and adulthood. Gendered norms and expectations are enforced through informal sanctions of gender-inappropriate behavior by peers and by formal punishment or threat of punishment by those in authority should behavior deviate too far from socially imposed standards for women and men.

Everyday gendered interactions build gender into the family, the work process, and other organizations and institutions, which in turn reinforce gender expectations for individuals.[2] Because gender is a process, there is room not only for modification and variation by individuals and small groups but also for institutionalized change (J. W. Scott 1988, 7).

As part of a *stratification* system, gender ranks men above women of the same race and class. Women and men could be different but equal. In practice, the process of creating difference depends to a great extent on differential evaluation. As Nancy Jay (1981) says: "That which is defined, separated out, isolated from all else is A and pure. Not-A is necessarily impure, a random catchall, to which nothing is external except A and the principle of order that separates it from Not-A" (45). From the individual's point of view, whichever gender is A, the other is Not-A; gender boundaries tell the individual who is like him or her, and all the rest are unlike. From society's point of view, however, one gender is usually the touchstone, the normal, the dominant, and the other is different, deviant, and subordinate. In Western society, "man" is A, "wo-man" is Not-A. (Consider what a society would be like where woman was A and man Not-A.)

The further dichotomization by race and class constructs the gradations of a heterogeneous society's stratification scheme. Thus, in the United States, white is A,

African American is Not-A; middle class is A, working class is Not-A, and "African-American women occupy a position whereby the inferior half of a series of these dichotomies converge" (P. H. Collins 1990, 70). The dominant categories are the hegemonic ideals, taken so for granted as the way things should be that white is not ordinarily thought of as a race, middle class as a class, or men as a gender. The characteristics of these categories define the Other as that which lacks the valuable qualities the dominants exhibit.

In a gender-stratified society, what men do is usually valued more highly than what women do because men do it, even when their activities are very similar or the same. In different regions of southern India, for example, harvesting rice is men's work, shared work, or women's work: "Wherever a task is done by women it is considered easy, and where it is done by [men] it is considered difficult" (Mencher 1988, 104). A gathering and hunting society's survival usually depends on the nuts, grubs, and small animals brought in by the women's foraging trips, but when the men's hunt is successful, it is the occasion for a celebration. Conversely, because they are the superior group, white men do not have to do the "dirty work," such as housework; the most inferior group does it, usually poor women of color (Palmer 1989). . . .

Societies vary in the extent of the inequality in social status of their women and men members, but where there is inequality, the status "woman" (and its attendant behavior and role allocations) is usually held in lesser esteem than the status "man." Since gender is also intertwined with a society's other constructed statuses of differential evaluation—race, religion, occupation, class, country of origin, and so on—men

and women members of the favored groups command more power, more prestige, and more property than the members of the disfavored groups. Within many social groups, however, men are advantaged over women. The more economic resources, such as education and job opportunities, are available to a group, the more they tend to be monopolized by men. In poorer groups that have few resources (such as working-class African Americans in the United States), women and men are more nearly equal, and the women may even outstrip the men in education and occupational status (Almquist 1987).

As a *structure,* gender divides work in the home and in economic production, legitimates those in authority, and organizes sexuality and emotional life (Connell 1987, 91–142). As primary parents, women significantly influence children's psychological development and emotional attachments, in the process reproducing gender. Emergent sexuality is shaped by heterosexual, homosexual, bisexual, and sadomasochistic patterns that are gendered—different for girls and boys, and for women and men—so that sexual statuses reflect gender statuses.

When gender is a major component of structured inequality, the devalued genders have less power, prestige, and economic rewards than the valued genders. In countries that discourage gender discrimination, many major roles are still gendered; women still do most of the domestic labor and child rearing, even while doing full-time paid work; women and men are segregated on the job and each does work considered "appropriate"; women's work is usually paid less than men's work. Men dominate the positions of authority and leadership in government, the military, and the law; cultural productions, religions, and sports reflect men's interests.

In societies that create the greatest gender difference, such as Saudi Arabia, women are kept out of sight behind walls or veils, have no civil rights, and often create a cultural and emotional world of their own (Bernard 1981). But even in societies with less rigid gender boundaries, women and men spend much of their time with people of their own gender because of the way work and family are organized. This spatial separation of women and men reinforces gendered differentness, identity, and ways of thinking and behaving (Coser 1986).

Gender inequality—the devaluation of "women" and the social domination of "men"—has social functions and a social history. It is not the result of sex, procreation, physiology, anatomy, hormones, or genetic predispositions. It is produced and maintained by identifiable social processes and built into the general social structure and individual identities deliberately and purposefully. The social order as we know it in Western societies is organized around racial ethnic, class, and gender inequality. I contend, therefore, that the continuing purpose of gender as a modern social institution is to construct women as a group to be the subordinates of men as a group. The life of everyone placed in the status "woman" is "night to his day—that has forever been the fantasy. Black to his white. Shut out of his system's space, she is the repressed that ensures the system's functioning" (Cixous and Clément [1975] 1986, 67).

NOTES

1. Other societies recognize more than two categories, but usually no more than three or four (Jacobs and Roberts 1989).

2. On the "logic of practice," or how the experience of gender is embedded in the norms of everyday interaction and the structure of formal organizations, see Acker 1990; Bourdieu [1980] 1990; Connell 1987; Smith 1987.

BIBLIOGRAPHY

Acker, Joan. 1990. "Hierarchies, Jobs, and Bodies: A Theory of Gendered Organizations." *Gender and Society* 4: 139–58.

Almquist, Elizabeth M. 1987. "Labor Market Gendered Inequality in Minority Groups." *Gender and Society* 1:400–14.

Barkalow, Carol, with Andrea Raab. 1990. *In the Men's House.* New York, NY: Poseidon Press.

Bernard, Jessie. 1981. *The Female World.* New York, NY: Free Press.

Birdwhistell, Ray L. 1970. *Kinesics and Context: Essays on Body Motion Communication.* Philadelphia: University of Pennsylvania Press.

Bourdieu, Pierre. [1980] 1990. *The Logic of Practice.* Stanford, California: Stanford University Press.

Butler, Judith. 1990. *Gender Trouble: Feminism and the Subversion of Identity.* New York and London: Routledge.

Cixous, Hélène and Catherine Clément. [1975] 1986. *The Newly Born Woman,* translated by Betsy Wing. Minneapolis: University of Minnesota Press.

Collins, Patricia Hill. 1990. *Black Feminist Thought: Knowledge, Consciousness, and the Politics of Empowerment.* Boston: Unwin Hyman.

Connell, R. W. 1987. *Gender and Power: Society, the Person, and Sexual Politics.* Stanford, California: Stanford University Press.

Coser, Rose Laub. 1986. "Cognitive Structure and the Use of Social Space." *Sociological Forum* 1:1–26.

De Beauvoir, Simone. 1953. *The Second Sex,* translated by H. M. Parshley. New York, NY: Knopf.

Foucault, Michel. 1972. *The Archeology of Knowledge and the Discourse on Language,* translated by A. M. Sheridan Smith. New York, NY: Pantheon.

Gramsci, Antonio. 1971. *Selections from the Prison Notebooks,* translated and edited by

Quintin Hoare and Geoffrey Nowell Smith. New York, NY: International Publishers.

Jacobs, Sue-Ellen and Christine Roberts. 1989. "Sex, Sexuality, Gender, and Gender Variance." In *Gender Anthropology,* edited by Sandra Morgen. Washington, DC: American Anthropological Association.

Jay, Nancy. 1981. "Gender and Dichotomy." *Feminist Studies* 7: 38–56.

Mencher, Joan. 1988. "Women's Work and Poverty: Women's Contribution to Household Maintenance in South India. In *A Home Divided: Women and Income in the Third World,* edited by Daisy Dwyer and Judith Bruce. Stanford, CA: Stanford University Press.

Palmer, Phyllis. 1989. *Domesticity and Dirt: Housewives and Domestic Servants in the United States, 1920–1945.* Philadelphia: Temple University Press.

Reskin, Barbara F. 1988. "Bringing the Men Back In: Sex Differentiation and the Devaluation of Women's Work." *Gender and Society* 2:58–81.

Rubin, Gayle. 1975. "The Traffic in Women: Notes on the Political Economy of Sex." In *Toward an Anthropology of Women,* edited by Rayna R. Reiter. New York, NY: Monthly Review Press.

Scott, Joan Wallach. 1988. *Gender and the Politics of History.* New York, NY: Columbia University Press.

Smith, Dorothy. 1987. *The Everyday World as Problematic: A Feminist Sociology.* Toronto: University of Toronto Press.

West, Candace and Don Zimmerman. 1987. "Doing Gender." *Gender and Society* 1:125–51.

Williams, Christine L. 1989. *Gender Differences at Work: Women and Men in Nontraditional Occupations.* Berkeley, CA: University of California Press.

37

The Time Bind

When Work Becomes Home and Home Becomes Work

ARLIE RUSSELL HOCHSCHILD

The Waving Window

It is 6:45 A.M. on a fine June day in the midwestern town of Spotted Deer. At a childcare center in the basement of the Baptist church, Diane Caselli, a childcare worker in blue jeans and loose shirt, methodically turns over small upended chairs that rest on a Lilliputian breakfast table. She sets out small bowls, spoons, napkins, and a pitcher of milk around a commanding box of Cheerios. The room is cheerful, clean, half-asleep. Diane moves slowly past neatly shelved puzzles and toys, a hat rack hung with floppy, donated dress-up hats and droopy pocketbooks, a tub filled with bits of colored paper. Paintings of swerving trains and tipsy houses are taped to the wall.

At seven, a tall, awkward-looking man peers hesitantly into the room, then ventures a few steps forward looking for Diane. His son Timmy tromps in behind him. Diane walks over, takes Timmy's hand, and leads him to the breakfast table, where she seats him and helps him pour cereal and

milk into his bowl. Timmy's dad, meanwhile, hurries toward the door.

One wall of the room has four large windows that overlook a sidewalk. In front of the second window is a set of small wooden steps children climb to wave good-bye to their departing parents. It's called "the waving window." Timmy dashes from the breakfast table, climbs up the wooden steps, and waits.

His dad, an engineer, briskly strides past the first window toward his red Volvo parked down the street. He stops for a moment in front of the waving window, tilts his head, eyebrows lifted clownishly, then walks on without a backward glance. Timmy returns to his cereal, sighs, and declares excitedly, "My Dad sawed me wave!". . .

At 7:40 A.M., four-year-old Cassie sidles in, her hair half-combed, a blanket in one hand, a fudge bar in the other. "I'm late," her mother explains to Diane. "Cassie wanted the fudge bar so bad, I gave it to her," she adds apologetically—though Diane has said nothing. Gwen Bell is a sturdy young woman, with short-cropped dark hair. Lightly made up and minimally adorned with gold stud earrings, she is neatly dressed in khaki slacks and jacket. Some Amerco mothers don business suits as soldiers don armor while a few wear floral dresses suggesting festivity and leisure. But Cassie's mother is dressed in a neutral way, as if she were just getting the job of self-presentation done.

"Pleeese, can't you take me with you?" Cassie pleads.

"You know I can't take you to work," Gwen replies in a tone that suggests she's heard this request before. Cassie's shoulders droop in defeat. She's given it a try, but now she's resigned to her mother's imminent departure, and she's agreed, it seems, not to make too much fuss about it. Aware of her mother's unease about her long day at childcare, however, she's struck a hard bargain. Every so often she gets a morning fudge bar. This is their deal, and Cassie keeps her mother to it. As Gwen Bell later explained to me, she continually feels that she owes Cassie more time than she actually gives her. She has a time-debt to her daughter. If many busy parents settle such debts on evenings or weekends when their children eagerly "collect" promised time, Cassie insists on a morning down payment, a fudge bar that makes her mother uneasy but saves her the trouble and embarrassment of a tantrum. Like other parents at the center, Gwen sometimes finds herself indulging her child with treats or softened rules in exchange for missed time together. Diane speaks quietly to Cassie, trying to persuade her to stop sulking and join the others.

The center works on "child time." Its rhythms are child-paced, flexible, mainly slow. Teachers patiently oversee the laborious task of tying a shoelace, a prolonged sit on the potty, the scrambled telling of a tall tale. In this and other ways it is an excellent childcare center, one of a dozen islands of child time I was to discover in my three summers of field research at Amerco, a Fortune 500 company headquartered in Spotted Deer.[1] Scattered throughout the town, such islands—a playground, a pediatrician's waiting room, the back of a family van—stand out against the faster paced, more bureaucratically segmented blocks of adult work time. . . .

At the Spotted Deer Childcare Center, the group of young breakfasters gradually expands, early arrivals watching the entertainment provided by yet more newcomers. Sally enters sucking her thumb. Billy's mother carries him in even though he's already five. Jonathan's mother forgets to wave, and soon after, Jonathan kicks the breakfast table from below, causing milk to spill and children to yell. Marie ushers him away to dictate a note to his mother explaining that it hurts his feelings when she doesn't wave.

Cassie still stands at the front door holding her fudge bar like a flag, the emblem of a truce in a battle over time. Every now and then, she licks one of its drippy sides while Diane, uncertain about what to do, looks on disapprovingly. The cereal eaters watch from their table, fascinated and envious. Gwen Bell turns to leave, waving goodbye to Cassie, car keys in hand. By our prior arrangement, I am her shadow for this day, and I follow her out the door and into the world of Amerco.

Arriving at her office, as always, exactly at 7:50 A.M., Gwen finds on her desk a cup of coffee in her personal mug, milk no sugar (exactly as she likes it), prepared by a coworker who has managed to get in ahead of her. The remaining half of a birthday cake has been left on a table in the hall outside her office by a dieting coworker who wants someone else to eat it before she does. Gwen prepares materials for her first meeting (having e-mailed messages to the other participants from home the previous night), which will inaugurate her official 8 A.M. to 5:45 P.M. workday. As she does so, she nibbles at a sliver of the cake while she proofreads a memo that must be Xeroxed and handed out at a second meeting scheduled for 9 A.M.

As the assistant to the head of the Public Relations Office, Gwen has to handle Amerco's responses to any press reports that may appear about the company. This time the impending media attention is positive, and her first meeting has been called to discuss how to make the most of it. As the members of the publicity team straggle into her office and exchange friendly greetings, she sighs. She's ready.

Gwen loves her job at Amerco, and she is very good at it. Whatever the daily pressures, she also feels remarkably at home there. Her boss, a man who she says reminds her of the best aspects of her father, helps her deal with work problems and strongly supports her desire to rise in the company. In many ways, her "Amerco dad" has been better to her than her own father, who, when she was small, abruptly walked out on her mother and her. She feels lucky to have such a caring boss, and working for him has reinforced her desire to give her all to work—insofar as she can. She and her husband need her salary, she tells me, since his job, though more lucrative than hers, is less steady.

Gradually, over the last three years Gwen's workday has grown longer. She used to work a straight eight-hour day.

Now it is regularly eight and a half to nine hours, not counting the work that often spills over into life at home. Gwen is not happy about this. She feels Cassie's ten-hour day at Spotted Deer is too long, but at the same time she is not putting energy into curbing her expanding workday. What she does do is complain about it, joke about it, compare stories with friends at work. Hers are not the boastful "war stories" of the older men at Amerco who proudly proclaim their ten-hour workdays and biweekly company travel schedules. Rather, Gwen's stories are more like situation comedies: stories about forgetting to shop and coming home to a refrigerator containing little more than wilted lettuce and a jar of olives, stories told in a spirit of hopeless amusement. Gwen is reasonably well informed about Amerco's flextime and reduced-hours policies, which are available to white-collar employees like her. But she has not talked with her boss about cutting back her hours, nor have her joking coworkers, and her boss hasn't raised the possibility himself. There is just so much to get done at the office.

At 5:45 P.M. on the dot, Gwen arrives back at Spotted Deer. Cassie is waiting eagerly by the door, her coat over her arm, a crumpled picture she has drawn in her hand. Gwen gives Cassie a long, affectionate hug. By the time Gwen and Cassie roll into the driveway of their two-story white frame house, surrounded by a border of unruly shrubs, it is 6:25 P.M. John Bell is already there, having shopped, taken the messages off the phone machine, set the table, and heated the oven. This is one of two days a week he leaves home and returns earlier than his wife. He has eaten an ample lunch, knowing that they usually have a late, light dinner, but this evening he's hungrier than he means to be. He plays with Cassie while Gwen makes dinner.

To protect the dinner "hour"—8:00 to 8:30—Gwen checks that the phone machine is on, and we hear a series of abbreviated rings several times during dinner. John says grace, and we all hold hands. It is time, it seems, to let go and relax. Right after dinner, though, it's Cassie's bath time. Cassie both loves and protests her nightly bath. Gwen has come to expect Cassie to dawdle as she undresses or searches for a favorite bath toy, trying to make a minivacation of it. Gwen lets Cassie linger, scans through her phone messages, and sets them aside.

At 9 P.M., the bath over, Gwen and Cassie have "quality time" or "QT," as John affectionately calls it. This they see as their small castle of time protected from the demands of the outside world. Half an hour later, at 9:30 P.M., Gwen tucks Cassie into bed.

Later, as Gwen and John show me around their home, John points out in passing an expensive electric saw and drill set he bought two years earlier with the thought of building a tree house for Cassie, a bigger hutch for her rabbit Max, and a guest room for visiting friends. "I have the tools," John confides. "I just don't have the time to use them." Once, those tools must have represented the promise of future projects. Now they seemed to be there in place of the projects. Along with the tools, perhaps John has tried to purchase the illusion of leisure they seemed to imply. Later, as I interviewed other working parents at Amerco, I discovered similar items banished to attics and garages. Timmy's father had bought a boat he hadn't sailed all year. Jarod and Tylor's parents had a camper truck they had hardly driven. Others had cameras, skis, guitars, encyclopedia sets,

even the equipment to harvest maple syrup, all bought with wages that took time to earn.

John's tools seemed to hold out the promise of another self, a self he would be "if only I had time." His tools had become for him what Cassie's fudge bar was for her—a magical substitute for time, a talisman.

There were, in a sense, two Bell households: the rushed family they actually were and the relaxed family they imagined they could be if only they had time. Gwen and Bill complained that they were in a time bind: they wanted more time for life at home than they had. It wasn't that they wanted more small segments of "quality time" added into their over-busy days. They wanted a quality life, and Gwen, at least, worked for a family-friendly company whose policies seemed to hold out hope for just that. So what was preventing them from getting it?

Time in the Balance

We've gotten ourselves into a time bind. Feeling that we are always late, having no free time, trying to adapt as best we can to the confines of our time prisons—these are all symptoms of what has become a national way of life. There are several reasons for this. Over the past two decades, global competition and inflation have lowered the buying power of the male wage. In response, many women have gone to work in order to maintain the family income. But the legacy of patriarchy has given cultural shape to this economic story. As women have joined men at work, they have absorbed the views of an older, male-oriented work world—its views of "an honest day's work"—at a much faster rate than men have absorbed their share of domestic work and culture. One reason women have changed more than men is that the world of "male" work seems more honorable and valuable than the "female" world of home and children.

There is another factor too—we are increasingly anxious about our "culture of care." Where do we turn when we are down and out? This is a question we ask, understandably, even when we are up and in. With recent welfare "reform," the government is cutting off aid to women and the poor. With the growth of the benefit-less contingency labor force, many corporations are doing the same thing to middle-class men. Meanwhile, modern families have grown more ambiguous: It's a little less clear than it once was who's supposed to take care of whom, how much and for how long. So we've grown more anxious. Given our tradition of individualism, many of us feel alone in this anxiety, and insofar as work is our rock, we cling to it.

In this context, the idea of cutting back the workday is an idea that seems to have died, gone to heaven and become an angel of an idea. We dream about it, but it's something we'd never really expect to do. No matter how a movement for work-family balance is structured, in the long run, no such balance will ever take hold if the social conditions that would make it possible—men who are willing to share parenting and housework, supportive communities, and policy-makers and elected officials who are prepared to demand family-friendly reforms—remain out of reach. . . .

As my study of Amerco has shown, however, even when the jobs of working parents are secure, pay a sufficient wage and provide family-friendly programs, many working parents are still reluctant to spend more time at home. American fathers spend less time at home than mothers do, expand their work hours when children are small and, if Amerco is any indication, are reluctant to take paternity leaves. We know from previous research that many men have found a haven at work. This isn't news. The news is that growing numbers of working women are leery of spending more time at home as well. They feel guilty and stressed out by long hours at work, but they feel ambivalent about cutting back on those hours.

Women fear losing their place at work; having such a place has become a source of security, pride and a powerful sense of being valued. As a survey conducted by Bright Horizons (a Boston-based company that runs on-site daycare centers in twenty-three states) indicates, women are just as likely to feel appreciated as men at the workplace; as likely as men to feel underappreciated at home; and even more likely than men to have friends at work. To cut back on work hours means risking loosening ties to a world that, tension-filled as it is, offers insurance against even greater tension and uncertainty at home. For a substantial number of time-bound working parents, the stripped-down home and the community-denuded neighborhood are simply losing out to the pull of the workplace.

Many women are thus joining men in a flight from the "inner city" of home to the "suburbs" of the workplace. In doing so, they have absorbed the views of an older, male-oriented work world about what a "real career" and "full commitment to the job" really mean. Women now make up nearly half the labor force. The vast majority of them need and want to be there. There is definitely no going back. But women have entered the workplace on "male" terms. It would be less problematic for women to adopt a male model of work—to finally enjoy privileges formerly reserved for men—if the male model of work were one of balance. But it is not.

All this is unsettling news, in part because the children of working parents are being left to adjust to or resist the time bind—and all of its attendant consequences—more or less on their own. It is unsettling because while children remain precious to their parents, the "market value" of the world in which they are growing up has declined drastically. One need not compare their childhoods with a perfect childhood in a mythical past to conclude that our society needs to face up to a serious problem.

NOTE

1. To protect the privacy of the people in this chapter, I have given the company a fictional name and declined to specify what its workers produce or where they live. I've also altered the names, occupations, and defining details of the personal lives of individuals. I have, however, tried to document as accurately as possible their experiences of life at home and at work and to capture the essence of the culture that infuses both worlds.

38

The Opt-Out Revolution

LISA BELKIN

The scene in this cozy Atlanta living room would—at first glance—warm an early feminist's heart. Gathered by the fireplace one recent evening, sipping wine and nibbling cheese, are the members of a book club, each of them a beneficiary of all that feminists of 30-odd years ago held dear.

The eight women in the room have each earned a degree from Princeton, which was a citadel of everything male until the first co-educated class entered in 1969. And after Princeton, the women of this book club went on to do other things that women once were not expected to do. They received law degrees from Harvard and Columbia. They chose husbands who could keep up with them, not simply support them. They waited to have children because work was too exciting. They put on power suits and marched off to take on the world.

Yes, if an early feminist could peer into this scene, she would feel triumphant about the future. Until, of course, any one of these polished and purposeful women opened her mouth.

"I don't want to be on the fast track leading to a partnership at a prestigious law firm," says Katherine Brokaw, who left that track in order to stay home with her three children. "Some people define that as success. I don't."

"I don't want to be famous; I don't want to conquer the world; I don't want that kind of life," says Sarah McArthur Amsbary, who was a theater artist and teacher and earned her master's degree in English, then stepped out of the work force when her daughter was born. "Maternity provides an escape hatch that paternity does not. Having a baby provides a graceful and convenient exit."

Wander into any Starbucks in any Starbucks kind of neighborhood in the hours after the commuters are gone. See all those mothers drinking coffee and watching over toddlers at play? If you look past the Lycra gym clothes and the Internet-access cell phones, the scene could be the '50s, but for the fact that the coffee is more expensive and the mothers have M.B.A.s. . . .

Arguably, the barriers of 40 years ago are down. Fifty percent of the undergraduate class of 2003 at Yale was female; this year's graduating class at Berkeley Law School was 63 percent women; Harvard was 46

Lisa Belkin, "The Opt-Out Revolution," *The New York Times Magazine* (October 26, 2003, Section 6), pp. 42, 44–46, 85–86.

percent; Columbia was 51. Nearly 47 percent of medical students are women, as are 50 percent of undergraduate business majors (though, interestingly, about 30 percent of M.B.A. candidates). They are recruited by top firms in all fields. They start strong out of the gate.

And then, suddenly, they stop. Despite all those women graduating from law school, they comprise only 16 percent of partners in law firms. Although men and women enter corporate training programs in equal numbers, just 16 percent of corporate officers are women, and only eight companies in the Fortune 500 have female C.E.O.s. Of 435 members of the House of Representatives, 62 are women; there are 14 women in the 100-member Senate.

Measured against the way things once were, this is certainly progress. But measured against the way things were expected to be, this is a revolution stalled. During the '90s, the talk was about the glass ceiling, about women who were turned away at the threshold of power simply because they were women. The talk of this new decade is less about the obstacles faced by women than it is about the obstacles faced by mothers. As Joan C. Williams, director of the Program on WorkLife Law at American University, wrote in the *Harvard Women's Law Journal* last spring, "Many women never get near" that glass ceiling, because "they are stopped long before by the maternal wall."

Look, for example, at the Stanford class of '81. Fifty-seven percent of mothers in that class spent at least a year at home caring for their infant children in the first decade after graduation. One out of four have stayed home three or more years. Look at Harvard Business School. A survey of women from the classes of 1981, 1985 and 1991 found that only 38 percent were working full time. Look at professional women in surveys across the board. Between one-quarter and one-third are out of the work force, depending on the study and the profession. Look at the United States Census, which shows that the number of children being cared for by stay-at-home moms has increased nearly 13 percent in less than a decade. At the same time, the percentage of new mothers who go back to work fell from 59 percent in 1998 to 55 percent in 2000.

Look, too, at the mothers who have not left completely but have scaled down or redefined their roles in the crucial career-building years (25 to 44). Two-thirds of those mothers work fewer than 40 hours a week—in other words, part time. Only 5 percent work 50 or more hours weekly. Women leave the workplace to strike out on their own at equally telling rates; the number of businesses owned or co-owned by women jumped 11 percent since 1997, nearly twice the rate of businesses in general.

Look at how all these numbers compare with those of men. Of white men with M.B.A.'s, 95 percent are working full time, but for white women with M.B.A.'s, that number drops to 67 percent. (Interestingly, the numbers for African-American women are closer to those for white men than to those for white women.)

And look at the women of this Atlanta book club. A roomful of Princeton women each trained as well as any man. Of the 10 members, half are not working at all; one is in business with her husband; one works part time; two freelance; and the only one with a full-time job has no children.

Social scientists—most of them women—have made a specialty in recent years of studying why all this is so. Joan Williams ("Unbending Gender"), Sylvia Ann Hewlett ("Creating a Life"), Arlie Russell Hochschild (who coined the phrase "the second shift") and Felice N. Schwartz (who made popular the phrase "the mommy track"), to name just a few, have done important work about how the workplace has failed women.

But to talk to the women of the book club—or to the women of a San Francisco mothers' group with whom I also spent time, or the dozens of other women I interviewed, or the countless women I have come to know during the four years I have reported on the intersection of life and work—is to sense that something more is happening here. It's not just that the workplace has failed women. It is also that women are rejecting the workplace. . . .

As these women look up at the "top," they are increasingly deciding that they don't want to do what it takes to get there. Women today have the equal right to make the same bargain that men have made for centuries—to take time from their family in pursuit of success. Instead, women are redefining success. And in doing so, they are redefining work.

Time was when a woman's definition of success was said to be her apple-pie recipe. Or her husband's promotion. Or her well-turned-out children. Next, being successful required becoming a man. Remember those awful padded-shoulder suits and floppy ties? Success was about the male definition of money and power.

There is nothing wrong with money or power. But they come at a high price. And lately when women talk about success they use words like satisfaction, balance and sanity.

That's why a recent survey by the research firm Catalyst found that 26 percent of women at the cusp of the most senior levels of management don't want the promotion. And it's why *Fortune* magazine found that of the 108 women who have appeared on its list of the top 50 most powerful women over the years, at least 20 have chosen to leave their high-powered jobs, most voluntarily, for lives that are less intense and more fulfilling.

It's why President Bush's adviser Karen Hughes left the White House, saying her family was homesick and wanted to go back to Austin. It's why Brenda C. Barnes, who was the president and C.E.O. of Pepsi-Cola North America, left that job to move back to Illinois with her family. And it's why Wendy Chamberlin, who was ambassador to Pakistan, resigned, because security concerns meant she never saw her two young daughters.

Why don't women run the world?

Maybe it's because they don't want to.

Attitudes cluster in place and time. This is particularly true of a college campus, where one-quarter of the student population turns over every year. Undergraduates tend to think that the school they find is the one that always was, with no knowledge of the worldview of those even a few short years before. Looked at that way, the women of the Atlanta book club are a panoramic snapshot of change.

Sally Sears, the oldest of the group, entered Princeton in the fall of 1971. Women had been fully admitted two years earlier, and the school was still very much a boys club. Sears had gone to a small public school in Alabama and entered college "very conscious of being a representative of women and a representative of the South." As she describes it the air was electric with feminism. "Margaret Mead came to talk one night, and I was stunned by how penetrating her questions were about what it was like to be the first women," she says. "I thought, my God, she's thinking of us as Samoans."

Upon graduation in 1975, Sears felt both entitled and obligated to make good. "The clear message was, 'You've been given the key to a kingdom that used to be denied to people like you,'" she says. "It never occurred to me that my choices would be proscribed. I could have anything I wanted."

What she wanted, at first, was to be "a confirmed single person, childless, a world traveler." She spent a couple of years running *The Childersburg Star*, a small Alabama newspaper owned by her family, and then, in 1978, she took a job on the air at a television station in Birmingham. That led to a job in Memphis, followed by a year-long trip around the world, then another TV job in Dallas. By 1984 she was on the air in Atlanta, where she became a local celebrity and where she met Richard Belcher, a fellow reporter and now a local anchor. They were married in 1988, when Sears was 35.

Three years later, their son, Will, was born. Soldiers of feminism take only the shortest of maternity leaves, and as soon as Sears recovered from her C-section she was back at work. The O.J. Simpson trial was the first real test of what she calls "work plus love plus a child," because both she and her husband were sent out to California for the duration. "I got my mom and dad to bring Will out, and we all camped out at the New Otani Hotel for a few weeks," she says. "I was determined not to blink.". . .

Sears took nine years to quit. And she did so with great regret. "I would have hung in there, except the days kept getting longer and longer," she explains. "My five-day 50-hour week was becoming a 60-hour

week." As news reports could be transmitted farther and farther from the "mother ship," she found herself an hour or two from home when the nightly news was done. "Will was growing up, and I was driving home from a fire," she says. "I knew there would always be wrecks and fires, but there wouldn't always be his childhood."

First she tried to reduce her schedule. "The station would not give me a part-time contract," she says. "They said it was all or nothing." So in August 2000, she walked away from her six-figure income and became a homeroom mom at her son's school.

"It was wrenching for me to leave Channel 2," she says. "I miss being the lioness in the newsroom—to walk through and have the interns say, 'There she goes.' It kills me that I'm not contributing to my 401(k) anymore. I do feel somehow that I let the cause down.". . .

Sarah McArthur Amsbary of the Atlanta group leads a much-examined life. Back in college, she says, she gave no thought to melding life and work, but now, "I think about it almost constantly."

And what she has concluded, after all this thinking, is that the exodus of professional women from the workplace isn't really about motherhood at all. It is really about work. "There's a misconception that it's mostly a pull toward motherhood and her precious baby that drives a woman to quit her job, or apparently, her entire career," she says. "Not that the precious baby doesn't magnetize many of us. Mine certainly did. As often as not, though, a woman would have loved to maintain some version of a career, but that job wasn't cutting it anymore. Among women I know, quitting is driven as much from the job-dissatisfaction side as from the pull-to-motherhood side."

She compares all this to a romance gone sour. "Timing one's quitting to coincide with a baby is like timing a breakup to coincide with graduation," she says. "It's just a whole lot easier than breaking up in the middle of senior year."

That is the gift biology gives women, she says. It provides pauses, in the form of pregnancy and childbirth, that men do not have. And as the workplace becomes more stressful and all-consuming, the exit door is more attractive. "Women get to look around every few years and say, 'Is this still what I want to be doing?'" she says. "Maybe they have higher standards for job satisfaction because there is always the option of being their child's primary caregiver. When a man gets that dissatisfied with his job, he has to stick it out."

This, I would argue, is why the workplace needs women. Not just because they are 50 percent of the talent pool, but for the very fact that they are more willing to leave than men. That, in turn, makes employers work harder to keep them. It is why the accounting firm Deloitte & Touche has more than doubled the number of employees on flexible work schedules over the past decade and more than quintupled the number of female partners and directors (to 567, from 97) in the same period. It is why

I.B.M. employees can request up to 156 weeks of job-protected family time off. It is why Hamot Medical Center in Erie, Pa., hired a husband and wife to fill one neonatology job, with a shared salary and shared health insurance, then let them decide who stays home and who comes to the hospital on any given day. It is why, everywhere you look, workers are doing their work in untraditional ways.

Women started this conversation about life and work—a conversation that is slowly coming to include men. Sanity, balance and a new definition of success, it seems, just might be contagious. And instead of women being forced to act like men, men are being freed to act like women. Because women are willing to leave, men are more willing to leave, too—the number of married men who are full-time caregivers to their children has increased 18 percent. Because women are willing to leave, 46 percent of the employees taking parental leave at Ernst & Young last year were men.

Looked at that way, this is not the failure of a revolution, but the start of a new one. It is about a door opened but a crack by women that could usher in a new environment for us all.

Why don't women run the world?

"In a way," Amsbary says, "we really do."

39

Getting to Equal

Progress, Pitfalls, and Policy Solutions on the Road to Gender Parity in the Workplace

PAMELA STONE

Kate Hadley aspired to do it all—pursue a successful career and raise a family. With a BA and MBA from Ivy League schools, Kate was a poster girl for the feminist movement, having easily cracked the boys' club of the corporate suite. She was committed to her job, experienced (with more than 10 years as an international marketing executive), and—when I interviewed her—at home full time with her kids. Part of the so-called "opt-out revolution" popularized by the media, Kate epitomizes high-achieving women who are said to be throwing over careers for family, their decision to be home a choice and part of a larger social movement, not simply a retro echo. Stay-at-home moms like Kate might not be the first group of women you'd think to study if you wanted to learn more about inequality in the workplace, but in fact their experiences are central to understanding recent trends. These women offer a unique lens for viewing the processes underlying women's progress—and lack thereof—in achieving gender parity in employment.

Trends in the Gender Revolution

Since the 1970s, women have made great and, by historical standards, rapid gains in the workplace. They have closed the college education gap, and their graduation rate now eclipses men's. While their labor force participation rate is still lower than men's (60 percent versus 75 percent in 2008 for those aged 16 and over), it has risen rapidly over a period that saw men's begin to dip. Importantly, over this same period, women (particularly white and middle-class women) began eschewing the pattern of dropping out of the labor force after becoming mothers, instead working continuously throughout the years of peak family formation (as less-privileged women have always done). Fully two-thirds of mothers of preschoolers are in the labor force today. And fulfilling the basis for those old "You've come a long way, baby" ads, many women have entered formerly male-dominated, high-prestige, lucrative, and powerful professions once all but closed to them.

Pamela Stone, "Getting to Equal: Progress, Pitfalls, and Policy Solutions on the Road to Gender Parity in the Workplace," *Pathways* (Spring 2009), pp. 3–7.

With respect to advancing in the workplace, women have been doing everything right for close to four decades now: getting educated, working more and more continuously, and moving out of dead-end, low-paying "pink-collar" jobs. That's the good news. The bad news is that despite women's best and sustained efforts, progress toward gender equality is uneven and appears to be stalling.

Let's start by looking at one of the bright spots: the mobility of women out of low-paying historically "female" jobs such as child care providers and secretaries. One such measure of this movement is the index of dissimilarity, which expresses the extent of sex segregation in terms of the proportion of workers who would have to change jobs in order to create a fully integrated workplace. A fully integrated workplace is defined as one in which women's representation in any occupation would be equal to their representation in the labor force as a whole. In 1970, this index stood at 0.57; today, it is around 0.47. Progress, yes, but there's a long way to go when you consider that about half of all workers would still have to switch jobs for the workplace to be completely integrated.

Another sobering observation is that most of the gains in this index resulted from dramatic declines in segregation in the distant 1970s. Recent decades have shown virtually no change. Nor has women's progress in integrating jobs occurred across the board. Rather, integration has been experienced almost entirely by middle-class, college-educated, predominately white women who were able to respond quickly to opportunities afforded by the late 20th-century shift to a postindustrial economy and the attendant growth of professional and managerial jobs. Less well-educated women did not enjoy similar opportunities and remain mired in low-wage jobs. Finally, even in professional fields where women are well- and long-represented, they are often concentrated in less prestigious and less lucrative niches, and do not appear to be making it to the very top. Law, one of the first fields to open up to women, is a notable case in point. Women received about half of all law degrees conferred in 2001, when they made up 30 percent of the profession. At the same time, however, they accounted for only 15 percent of federal judges, 15 percent of law firm partners (only 5 percent of managing partners), 10 percent of law school deans, and 10 percent of general counsels.

The most widely used bottom-line indicator of gender inequality is the wage gap, computed as the ratio of women's to men's median earnings. Since the 1970s, when women earned roughly 59 cents to every dollar earned by a man, the gap has narrowed considerably, and now stands at 78 cents to every dollar. This progress is largely a function of women's entry into higher-paying fields, but also of declines in men's earnings. Trends in the gender wage gap show rapid and sizeable improvement, starting in the 1980s (see Figure 39.1). This improvement, however, was followed by a subsequent slowdown.

For today's twentysomethings, the wage gap narrows to near parity, as would be expected for these beneficiaries of the gender revolution. By the time they reach their thirties, however, women have become parents. And despite the fact that these women have become more experienced workers, the wage gap widens, approaching overall levels. The wage gap is also wider for women of color (African American women earn 63 cents and Latinas 53 cents to every

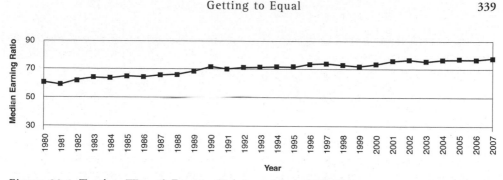

Figure 39.1 Trends in Women's Earnings (Relative to Men): 1980–2007
Source: Institute for Women's Policy Research, *Fact Sheet on the Gender Wage Gap: 2007*, August 2008, based on compilation of data from Current Population Survey.

dollar earned by a white man). Even in the professional and managerial ranks, where formal credentials are critical (and merito-cratic principles govern recruitment, pro-motion, and pay), sizeable gender gaps remain. In 2000, these gaps were 65 cents to the dollar for financial managers, 72 cents for physicians, 73 cents for lawyers, and 81 cents for editors and reporters, to name but a few fields in which women have made considerable inroads.

What explains the overall gender wage gap? Between 1983 and 2000, according to a 2003 report by the U.S. Government Accountability Office, just over half of the gap is due to "legitimate" or "valid" sources, including differences in human capital (such as education and training), hours worked, industrial and occupational posi-tions, and unionization levels. The re-maining 45 percent is unexplained, which most analysts attribute to differences in tastes or preferences and/or outright dis-crimination, although some suggest that it is attributable to very fine-grained oc-cupational segregation.

Not only are major sources of the gap unknown, so too are prospects for future progress. Leading experts on gender in-equality, such as sociologist Reeve Vanne-

man and his colleagues, have raised the worrying question: "Are we seeing the end of the gender revolution?" Others, such as psychologist Virginia Valian, ask impa-tiently "Why so slow?" The decade-long slowdown in integrating jobs and closing the wage gap—at a virtual standstill in the new millennium—is a red flag to scholars, activists, and policymakers alike that some-thing is seriously amiss on the road to gen-der equality.

Opting Out? Or Pushed Out?

This is where women like Kate Hadley come in. I talked with Kate as part of a larger study I conducted of women who had transitioned from lives that combined professional careers with family—a con-temporary, feminist model—to lives in which careers were left behind and taking care of children and family became their major focus—typically understood as a neo-traditional, counter-feminist lifestyle. Kate and women like her in their 30s and 40s were responsible for much of the im-provement registered in the aggregate indi-cators described above. If these women are retreating from professional success, or "opting out" as media pundits claim, this

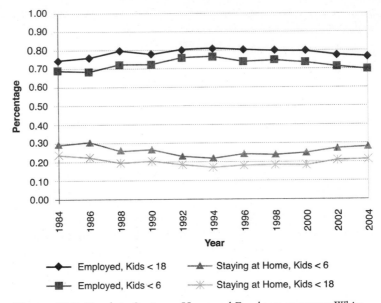

Figure 39.2 Trends in Staying at Home and Employment among White, Non-Hispanic College-Educated Mothers

Source: Tabulation of March Current Population Survey microdata, 1984–2004, by Cordelia Reimers, Department of Economics, Hunter College and Graduate Center, CUNY

might explain some of the slowdown in women's progress, or even portend a greater stall. I wanted to learn two things: (1) What was happening to this cohort of fast-track women? Were they turning away from combining careers with motherhood and, if so, how widespread was this phenomenon? (2) Among women who have "opted out," what led them to do so? In particular, what role did those hard-to-measure, unexplained "choices," tastes, and preferences (said to be evolving to reflect traditional gender roles) play? Likewise, what role did discrimination play?

In answer to the first question, Figure 39.2 shows trends in full-time family caregiving and employment among the demographic said to be heading home (white, married, college-educated mothers). The overall trend in caregiving is downward,

but not straightforward: In 1981, 25.2 percent of women stayed home, which declined to an all-time low in 1993 of 16.5 percent, rising again in 2005 to 21.3 percent. The uptick in staying home in the mid-1990s was attributable primarily to unemployment levels, rising husbands' earnings, and deferred childbearing. Furthermore, among mothers, college-educated women exhibit the highest rates of labor force participation, and more recent cohorts of professional women are combining careers with motherhood in greater proportions than ever before: 77 percent in 2004. Overall, these trends show little sign of women reverting to 1950s stereotypes. Whether looking at staying at home or employment, however, we see a plateau or slowdown after an initial burst of rapid change. And, as with trends in job desegregation and the wage gap, this leveling off is not fully understood, though the parallels strongly suggest that the trends are interrelated.

To understand more about the decision-making underlying these trends, I interviewed dozens of at-home moms across the country who had worked in a variety of high-status professional and managerial jobs (more than half of whom had advanced degrees). What I found is that working moms are not "opting out" of the workplace because of family. They're being shut out. Their decisions did not reflect a change in favor of domesticity nor even a newfound appreciation of mothering (that came after they quit). Women spoke much more about work than about family in discussing why and how they'd come to quit. Nor did outright old-fashioned sex discrimination play a role (these women were surprisingly resilient, recounting overtly sexist experiences with tough matter-of-factness, almost gusto).

Instead, the combination of rising hours, travel, and 24/7 accountability demanded in today's workplaces, coupled with insufficient and inadequate part-time and flexible options, put these working moms in a classic time bind. As I talked with them, I heard the same thing over and over: that their jobs were "all-or-nothing," forcing these high-achieving women into decisions to reluctantly interrupt, and sometimes terminate, their once-flourishing careers. Married to men with comparable credentials and work histories—until they became parents—women found themselves "home alone" and primarily responsible for child care, their husbands' inability to help out a function of their own high-demand jobs.

One of the paradoxes of my findings is that these at-home moms, seemingly the most traditional of women, were actually highly work-committed. Despite being married to equally successful men who could support them at home, most women, after becoming mothers, stuck it out, trying to make work work. Some were denied flexibility outright, but more quit because their efforts to fashion flexible careers— efforts that should have been applauded— were instead penalized. Indicative of the mommy-tracking and stigma these innovators experienced, one woman invoked *Scarlet Letter*–like imagery as she explained to me "When you job share, you have 'MOMMY' stamped in huge letters on your head." Once women shifted away from a full-time-plus schedule, their formerly high-flying careers nose-dived, undermining their attachment to their careers in a classic scenario of negative reinforcement.

My results highlight the way in which time demands and professional occupations' inflexibility create a de facto "motherhood bar." This bar operates in tandem with the secondary influence of intensive parenting to cause women to quit their careers. Ostensibly meritocratic and unbiased time demands, coupled with ideal worker standards of commitment, appear to be replacing essentialist stereotypes in preventing women's full integration in professional fields. More women than ever are professionals and managers (over a third of all employed women), and the hours of these jobs have ratcheted up, such that the United States now enjoys the dubious distinction of having the world's longest workweek. That's not to say that essentialist stereotypes have disappeared. Indeed, they are at the heart of the double bind of work-family conflict. But stereotypes now operate in less overt ways, under the cover of time norms and related job imperatives. And because women facing untenable work conditions voluntarily "quit," unequal outcomes become their "choice" rather than a reflection of employers' (often discriminatory) practices.

Most women, of course, cannot quit, and instead persevere in the face of inflexible schedules, mommy tracking, and low pay. Less-educated and less-advantaged women accommodate their caregiving needs by cycling in and out of the labor force through a series of low-wage jobs, often fired when they take time off or show up late because they have to attend to family needs. These different strategies to accommodate family responsibilities share the same result: considerable costs not just to women in the form of lost earnings, but also to firms and the economy in the form of underused skills and talent. The motherhood penalty has now been well-documented. Incidentally, men—perceived as primary breadwinners—enjoy a "fatherhood premium" that further exacerbates the gender gap. The deep-seated and entrenched nature of motherhood bias means that it is more difficult to discern, more taken for granted as the norm, than is outright old-style sexism. Witness the easy acceptance of the notion that women like the ones I studied, who've spent a lifetime devoted to the pursuit of professional success, happily throw it all over in a (baby's) heartbeat.

Remembering the Ladies: Policies for Gender Equality

The motherhood penalty reminds us that workplace inequality is deeply rooted in the division of labor at home. The gendered nature of care, coupled with the absence of public supports in the United States for caregiving, redound to women's detriment and remain a lingering basis of labor market inequality. Women must trade time in paid employment for time devoted to unpaid caregiving, a trade-off that looms ever larger as we face a widely acknowledged care crisis occasioned by an aging society, changes in family and household structure, and gaps in the social safety net. An effective policy response requires that we confront both sides of the work-family equation to neutralize the penalty to caregiving and break the link between gender and care. To accomplish this, we must provide supports for more gender-equitable caring *and* earning. In devising policy initiatives, we do not need to start from scratch, but can instead look to Europe's experience to draw both positive and negative lessons. While work-family policies and supports are more widespread and well-established there, somewhat surprisingly these countries exhibit less gender equality than the United States. This outcome alerts us to steer clear of policies that unintentionally cement women's secondary labor market position as part-time workers in highly segregated female ghettoes. Such policies include the long unpaid leave in Germany that reinforces a traditional division of labor and women's lesser labor force attachment. A better approach would be to err in favor of more egalitarian approaches like those in Sweden and Norway, which provide generous wage-replacement policies and family leave provisions to promote men's caregiving.

Current economic circumstances, coupled with a new administration led by President Barack Obama, create a moment of crisis and opportunity. Congress and the Obama administration are off to a good start, putting more teeth into existing equal pay laws with the swift passage and signing into law of the Lilly Ledbetter Fair Pay Act. As the Ledbetter case demonstrated, garden variety sexism is alive and well. Ledbetter, an experienced plant manager for the Goodyear Tire & Rubber Company, filed suit when she learned that she was earning less than her male counterparts, a case that made its way to the Supreme Court. The court did not deny that Ledbetter had suffered pay discrimination, but ruled that she had failed to file her claim in time. The Ledbetter bill closes that loophole, effectively extending the deadline under which plaintiffs can bring suit under existing equal pay laws. Several pending fair pay bills go even further, requiring proactive oversight and enforcement of anti-discrimination laws. The new stimulus package also contains provisions to strengthen and re-energize the Equal Employment Opportunity Commission (EEOC). Together, these laws send a powerful signal that puts employers on notice and empowers women workers who are experiencing sex discrimination. Under the Bush administration, the EEOC was already paying increased attention to family caregiving discrimination (FCD). Currently the fastest-growing area of employment discrimination litigation, FCD attacks the motherhood penalty directly, and these cases must be vigorously pursued.

The recently passed stimulus package, insofar as it contains numerous tax and spending policies related to employment and earnings, can also be used to advance gender equity and parity—a true win-win—and must be evaluated and implemented with this goal in mind. A guiding principle should be to maintain and hasten the progress women have made, largely at the top, while increasing opportunities for those at the bottom who have not enjoyed the same gains and suffer the triple penalty of gender, race, and class. Thus, we need a two-pronged approach to move closer to gender equality, one that raises the ceiling and lifts the floor.

Women's jobs appear to be a little more recession-proof than men's in the current downturn, but women's groups have called on the new administration to "remember the ladies" to create more public-sector jobs in fields such as education, health care, and social services. While the stimulus package does so, it appears to be weighted somewhat more heavily toward creating male-dominated infrastructure jobs. The enormous scale of new job creation offers a rare chance to challenge existing stereotypes about what constitutes "women's" and "men's" work. By coupling job creation with new training and recruitment efforts, the employment-stimulus package can bring more women into high-paying "male" jobs, while at the same time encouraging men to enter lower-paying, but seemingly reliable "female" jobs, thereby reducing unemployment *and* shrinking the wage gap.

The kind of job creation entailed in the stimulus package would especially benefit women at the true middle and bottom of the income spectrum. The problem for women at the very bottom is that work doesn't pay enough to offset its associated costs, especially child care. In addition to creating more employment opportunities, we need to make work worth it for these women, and the enhanced earned income tax credits in the stimulus package are a good beginning. Nearly one-third of women in the labor force work in low-wage jobs compared with one-fifth of male workers. To really move women out of poverty and to economic self-sufficiency and parity with men, we need more aggressive policies that address low pay directly, such as raising the minimum wage or implementing more comprehensive policies like living wage and pay equity reforms. All of these, but especially pay equity, which expands the reach of equal pay laws to level earnings for comparable jobs with similar requirements and responsibilities, will go far to increase women's earnings and narrow the gender gap by addressing the sizeable pay disparities associated with job segregation.

Policies that facilitate mothers' labor force attachment by nullifying the trade-off between unpaid care work and employment are also needed. In this regard, extension of the Family and Medical Leave Act to provide *paid* family leave with fewer restrictions in coverage is the obvious answer, and already a reality in a number of states, notably California and New Jersey. Providing child care, either directly or in the form of subsidies, as well as universal early childhood education, will make it possible for women to hold on to jobs and accrue valuable experience while simultaneously affording their children well-documented educational benefits. Finally, universal health insurance, insofar as it promotes health and wellness, reduces the need for women to take costly absences and interruptions from work to care for sick children and other family members.

Last, we need to find ways to undermine the long-hour work culture that effectively bars women's progress in elite jobs and robs all parents, fathers and mothers, of time with their families. One way to reduce hours is to extend overtime provisions to the professional and managerial jobs that

are now exempt from them, requiring employers to pay workers for those 40-hour-plus workweeks. A good place to start would be to overturn Bush-era policies that broadened exempt coverage. Absent this, we need to look to the private sector to come up with meaningful, non-stigmatized, and gender-neutral ways of working flexibly, including better-paying and more equitable part-time jobs with prorated benefits (health care reform will advance this goal by making part-time positions less costly to employers). Many American companies already have innovative and successful work-life and work-family policies and practices in place that can serve as a model. While some argue that curtailed hours and family-friendly flexibility are no longer feasible in an era of economic insecurity, news reports make clear that both are being used in innovative ways to avoid layoffs in the current deep recession. Similar strategies of shortening the workweek and encouraging flexibility have a long track record in dealing with unemployment in Europe. As an added attraction, research demonstrates that flexibility and family-friendly innovations enhance employee morale, productivity, and retention.

Current policies and work arrangements shortchange women's employment and earnings, but they also shortchange men's participation in parenting and family life. We'll know we have achieved true gender parity when men and women participate equally and fully in market-based work and the unpaid work of the family, when women are not only just as likely as men to be CEOs, but men are just as likely as women to stay at home.

40

The Time Divide

Work, Family, and Gender Inequality

JERRY A. JACOBS AND
KATHLEEN GERSON

As families diversify and workers face new challenges, people feel increasingly torn between their public and private worlds. Whether they are working more or less, workers confront new pressures and dilemmas as they attempt to cope with the conflicts that inevitably arise between family and work. These conflicts are real and growing. Yet it remains unclear whether they stem from workers' preferences to spend more time at work or, alternatively, from a growing gap between what workers prefer and what they feel they must do.

Some have argued that the emergence of time binds reflects a widespread cultural shift in which workers increasingly look to work as an escape from the complexities of contemporary family life. From this perspective, workers' preferences are at the heart of changes at work and at home. Arlie Hochschild's study of Amerco, a fictionally named American company, shows in illuminating and powerful detail how some workers cope with complexities at home by spending more time at work (Hochschild

1997). The average employee at Amerco, however, works nearly one day per week more than the average American worker. This makes Amerco a great place to study the coping strategies of overworked parents, but it is not an ideal vantage point from which to generalize about overall trends in labor force behavior and cultural changes in America. Nearly all the vignettes presented by Hochschild describe workers who put in fifty or more hours per week, from the sixty-hour-per-week executive to the "over-time hound" assembly-line worker. This is an important and growing segment of the labor force, but it does not represent the average worker.

To reach broad conclusions about general cultural, structural, and individual change, we need a broader look at workers in a range of work settings. How are workers' experiences embedded in larger social and economic forces, and how do workers' options and perceptions vary with their circumstances? . . .

Changes in family structure have transformed the lives of workers in several ways. As men have faced stagnant wages and women have become increasingly committed to work outside the home, most households now rely on women's earnings. These economic transformations have fueled women's need and desire for secure, well-paying jobs and left dual-earner and single-parent households to cope without an unpaid worker at home. Women are thus likely to prefer good jobs with reasonable hours, and fathers who share breadwinning responsibilities with an employed partner also need flexible hours and some measure of control at work.

These profound changes in the private lives of women and men are thus generating changes in worker preferences that may not fit with the supply of jobs. While people face new needs for balance and flexibility in their working lives, employers have good reasons to offer jobs with either long or short workweeks. This forces workers to choose between time and income—a difficult decision that clashes with the exigencies of the new family economy.

Ideal versus Actual Working Hours

If changes in the shape and character of the labor force are clashing with economic forces that influence the structure of jobs, workers are indeed likely to feel caught in the conflict. This clash between job demands and private needs can take several forms. Many may feel compelled to work more than they would wish, while others are likely to wish to work more than they are able. As workers' circumstances vary, so do the kinds of time binds workers experience. Yet so many now face family time squeezes that those who desire to put in less time at work are likely to outnumber those who wish to work more.

The 1997 Changing Workforce survey (Bond, Galinsky, and Swanberg 1998) pro-

vides a wide array of information about workers' actual and preferred commitments to work, family, and personal pursuits, which makes it possible to examine the contours and causes of actual and ideal working time. This survey is distinctive in terms of the range of questions asked regarding workers' values and preferences and in its focus on the links, tensions, and conflicts between work and family. People were asked how many hours per week they usually worked at their principal job and also at any additional jobs they held. They were also asked: "Ideally, how many hours, in total, would you like to work each week?" Thus, because people were asked about their ideal as well as their actual working hours, we can examine whether their overall level of work reflects their desires. We can also ascertain whether variation in preferences across groups of workers corresponds to variations in actual work levels.

Comparing people's actual and ideal hours also makes it possible to measure the difference between a worker's usual time on all jobs and his or her ideal working time. Table 40.1, which compares ideal hours to total hours worked for employed women and men, demonstrates that most American workers experience a significant gap between how much they work and how much they would like to work. One fifth said that their actual and ideal hours correspond precisely; but fully three in five felt that their usual workweek was longer than their ideal hours, and an additional one in five preferred to work more than they currently do. (The unemployed should be added to this group of underworked Americans, but the Changing Workforce survey only includes the currently employed.)

The vast majority of those who preferred fewer working hours wished to work at

Table 40.1   Comparison of Total Hours Worked and Ideal Hours, by Gender

	Men	*Women*
Total hours usually worked (all jobs)	47.3	41.4
Ideal hours	37.5	32.1
Difference (actual – ideal)	9.8	9.3
Percent wanting to work less	60.2	60.1
Percent ideal equals actual	20.5	21.4
Percent wanting to work more	19.3	18.5
Percent wanting to work at least 5 hours less	58.4	58.6
Percent wanting to work at least 10 hours less	47.4	48.8
Percent wanting to work at least 20 hours less	28.3	27.9

Source: National Study of the Changing Workforce, 1997.

Note: All percentages are of total male and female samples, respectively. Thus, 60.2% of men reported wanting to work less; 58.4% of the total wanted to work at least 5 hours less. In other words, the great majority (58.4% over 60.2%) of those men who reported wanting to work less reported at least a 5-hour gap between their actual and ideal working hours.

least 5 hours less per week. Nearly half (over 47 percent of both men and women) wished to work 10 hours less per week, and over one quarter wanted to work at least 20 hours less.

While women work an average of about 6 fewer hours per week than men, the difference between their actual and ideal hours is quite similar. Women and men wished to work less by approximately the same amount. Men preferred to work 9.8 fewer hours, compared to 9.3 fewer hours for women (a difference that is not statistically significant). If both groups were able to realize their wishes, the gender gap in hours worked—which, at about 6 hours per week, is not large—would probably not change significantly.

Whether or not contemporary Americans are actually working more than earlier generations, the majority seem to *feel* overworked—at least compared to their ideals. Excessively long workweeks certainly do not emerge as ideal or an aspiration. But neither are short workweeks desirable to those who wish to work more. . . .

Occupational Position

Professional, managerial, and technical workers are most likely to feel overworked (Table 40.2). Women in these positions would prefer to work 13 hours less than they do, while women in other occupations want to work about 7 fewer hours. Male professionals want to work just under 12 hours less, while their counterparts in other occupational categories wish to work about 9 hours less. And while professionals and managers tend to put in longer workweeks than others, their *ideal* work schedules are not longer. Men who are professionals and managers wish to work about the same amount of time as other male workers. Women professionals and managers prefer to work about 2 hours less per week but actually work 4 hours more than women in other occupations.

Occupational position is a key factor in shaping the needs and desires of both men and women. Despite the persistent view that female professionals are less committed to work than their male counterparts,

Table 40.2   Total Hours Worked and Ideal Hours, by Occupation, Marital Status, and Gender

	Men			Women		
	Total Hours	Ideal Hours	Difference	Total Hours	Ideal Hours	Difference
Occupation						
Managerial, professional, and technical	48.9	37.3	11.6	43.9	30.9	13.0
Other	46.4	37.7	8.7	39.6	33.0	6.6
Marital Status						
Married (or living with partner)	48.2	37.8	10.4	40.9	30.8	10.1
Not currently married	45.7	37.1	8.6	42.0	33.8	8.2
Married, employed spouse	48.1	38.2	9.9	41.4	30.4	11.0
Married, nonemployed spouse	48.3	37.3	11.0	38.5	32.8	5.7
Children						
With children under six	49.3	38.9	10.4	39.4	30.0	9.4
Without children under six	46.8	37.3	9.5	41.8	32.5	9.3

Source: National Study of the Changing Workforce, 1997.

workers of both sexes appear to be looking for a reasonable balance between paid work and other pursuits. Those who put in long hours, regardless of gender, would like to cut back, while those who face shortened workweeks would like to work more. The most highly educated and well remunerated professionals and managers face the greatest demands to put in many hours at work. Rather than insulating one from overwork, well-paid jobs that offer advancement may actually increase the pressures to work more as well as the penalties for working less.

It could be argued that since those with the highest levels of education and income are working as much as, if not more than, other employees, these choices simply reflect a reasonable preference to enhance financial and career opportunities through hard work. Yet affluent workers, no less than other workers, face economic and other workplace constraints. Our analysis supports the widespread conviction and case histories presented elsewhere that exceptionally long workweeks are routinely required for career advancement, but not necessarily

desired by those who experience them (see, for example, Epstein et al. 1999)....

Marriage, Children, and Gender

The life course has grown increasingly fluid and unpredictable, and age may simply be too crude a measure to reveal the dynamics between personal circumstances and work constraints. Regardless of the age at which people choose to marry or have children, family commitments are almost certain to increase the need for domestic time. Marriage and parenthood should thus influence the gap between ideal and actual working time.

Gender also shapes the pressures and dilemmas of private life; marriage and especially parenthood are likely to affect women and men in different ways. Although men's participation in domestic work has increased in recent decades, women continue to bear a greater share of the load, especially when children arrive. And amid the growing strength of mothers' work commitments, fathers continue to face pressures to provide primary economic support for their families (see, for example, Gerson 1993). This means that, while both men and women are likely to feel torn between family and work, they are also likely to feel this conflict in different degrees and to respond in different ways.

Despite the growing convergence between women's and men's work commitments, they continue to face different pressures as parents. And though women and men express roughly equal desires to work fewer hours, a more complicated relationship emerges between gender and family situation in Table 40.2. First, married and single workers of both sexes differ in their ideal working hours. Married women work almost 1 hour less per week than women who are not married, but they would like to work 3 hours less. The gap between actual and ideal working time is thus 2 hours greater for married than for single women. Ideally, married women would prefer to work 10 hours less per week, while single women would prefer to work 8 hours less per week.

In contrast, married men work more than single men, by about 2.5 hours per week. Married and single men wish, however, to work about the same amount of time.[1] Married men thus experience a larger gap between actual and ideal hours (10 hours per week) than do single men (8 hours per week). For both women and men, married life adds to the feeling of being squeezed for time, but they have somewhat different reasons for feeling this way. Married men feel torn because they are spending more time on the job than single men. Married women are prone to cut back slightly in their working time, but would like to cut back more.

Within marriage, differences emerge among women living in different family situations, although they are not as large as might be expected. Women with employed husbands work about 3 hours per week less than those few whose husbands do not work, but this small difference is not statistically significant. Women in dual-earner marriages want to work 30 hours per week instead of the 41 hours they actually work, creating a sizable gap of 11 hours per week. For those with husbands who are not employed, the gap is 6 hours (and, again, the difference between the two is not statistically significant).

Women with preschool children show a similar pattern. These women work 39 hours per week on average, but would prefer to work 30 hours per week, for a gap of 9 hours per week. For women without children under six, there is also a 9 hour per week differential, which is statistically indistinguishable from the gap for those with preschool children. Having preschool children and employed husbands thus shapes women's desired and actual working time, but does not create a dramatic change in the gap between the two.

Marriage and parenthood also influence men's actual and ideal working time but, as in the case of women, in only modest ways. Surprisingly, men whose wives are employed do not differ from those with nonemployed partners in either actual or ideal working time. Having preschool children does increase the total number of hours worked per week for men, but it also increases their desired working time. The fathers of young children are thus likely to conclude that their family's financial needs require them to put in more time at work. And since actual working time increases by more than desired time, a higher proportion of these men want to work less.

To some extent, the modest gap in women's actual and ideal working time reflects the fact that they have already made strategic adjustments to avoid work-family conflict. After all, their average working hours are lower than men's at the outset. The larger pattern nevertheless suggests that family circumstances are as important as gender and that both mothers *and* fathers with young children want more time away from work than do other groups. Marriage clearly creates a context that pulls both women and men toward personal commitments outside of work. Yet we find little support for the oft-stated argument that married women with young children are the primary group wishing to work less. In fact, about half of married men and women across a range of family situations express such a desire. While some have argued that the arrival of children increases the number of hours that both mothers and fathers spend at the workplace, we find that women with small children cut back on their time at paid work, but to a smaller extent than in previous generations. The larger message in these findings is that all parents, whether they are mothers or fathers, need job arrangements that enable them to strike a balance between the economic and caretaking work that parenthood entails. . . .

Divided Options, Shared Aspirations

Although much of the debate concerning overwork in America has focused on the time women and men are spending at the workplace, we have looked closely in this chapter at how contemporary workers *feel* about their time at work. The concept of overwork depends as much on ideals as on actual working time, and we have found a notable gap between what workers do and what they would prefer. Most workers experience a significant time divide between their circumstances and their aspirations.

Yet this does not mean that all, or even most, workers feel overworked. Workers disagree considerably about whether they would like to work more or less. This disagreement makes it clear that the perception of overwork is not a general problem, but is nevertheless an important one to those whose jobs require that they put in very long workweeks and those whose family responsibilities are at their height. Far from using work to avoid family time, these workers would prefer more balance in their lives, with more time for private and family pursuits.

The problems of overworked Americans should also not blind us to the difficulties faced by those workers who cannot find sufficient employment to meet their own or their families' needs. As we have seen, many of those with relatively short workweeks would actually prefer to work more. Essentially, the gap between ideals and realities, rather than overwork *per se,* is the core problem for contemporary workers. Among women and men alike, most aspire to a balance that neither the overworked nor the underworked can achieve.

NOTE

1. The difference between single and married men in their ideal working hours is not statistically significant.

REFERENCES

Bond, James T., Ellen Galinsky, and Jennifer E. Swanberg. 1998. *The 1997 National Study of the Changing Workforce.* New York, NY: Families and Work Institute.

Epstein, Cynthia Fuchs, Carroll Seron, Bonnie Oglensky, and Robert Sauté. 1999. *The Part-Time Paradox: Time Norms, Professional Lives, Family, and Gender.* New York: Routledge.

Hochschild, Arlie. 1997. *The Time Bind: When Work Becomes Home and Home Becomes Work.* New York, NY: Metropolitan Books.

41

Orchestrating Impartiality

The Impact of "Blind" Auditions on Female Musicians

CLAUDIA GOLDIN AND CECILIA ROUSE

Sex-biased hiring has been alleged for many occupations but is extremely difficult to prove. The empirical literature on discrimination, deriving from the seminal contributions of Gary Becker (1971) and Kenneth Arrow (1973), has focused mainly on disparities in earnings between groups (e.g., males and females), given differences in observable productivity-altering characteristics. With the exception of various audit studies (e.g., Genevieve Kenney and Douglas A. Wissoker, 1994; David Neumark et al., 1996 and others), few researchers have been able to address directly the issue of bias in hiring practices. A change in the way symphony orchestras recruit musicians provides an unusual way to test for sex-biased hiring.

Until recently, the great symphony orchestras in the United States consisted of members who were largely handpicked by the music director. Although virtually all had auditioned for the position, most of the contenders would have been the (male) students of a select group of teachers. In an attempt to overcome this seeming bias in the hiring of musicians, most major U.S. orchestras changed their audition policies in the 1970s and 1980s, making them more open and routinized. Openings became widely advertised in the union papers, and many positions attracted more than 100 applicants where fewer than 20 would have been considered before. Audition committees were restructured to consist of members of the orchestra, not just the conductor and section principal. The audition procedure became democratized at a time when many other institutions in America did as well.

But democratization did not guarantee impartiality, because favorites could still be identified by sight and through resumes. Another set of procedures was adopted to ensure, or at least give the impression of, impartiality. These procedures involve hiding the identity of the player from the jury. Although they take several forms, we use the terms "blind" and "screen" to describe the group. The question we pose is whether

Claudia Goldin and Cecilia Rouse, "Orchestrating Impartiality: The Impact of 'Blind' Auditions on Female Musicians," *American Economic Review* 90 (2000), pp. 715–726, 734–738, 740–741.

the hiring process became more impartial through the use of blind auditions. Because we are able to identify sex, but no other characteristics, for a large sample, we focus on the impact of the screen on the employment of women.

Screens were not adopted by all orchestras at once. Among the major orchestras, one still does not have any blind round to their audition procedure (Cleveland) and one adopted the screen in 1952 for the preliminary round (Boston Symphony Orchestra), decades before the others. Most other orchestras shifted to blind preliminaries from the early 1970s to the late 1980s. The variation in screen adoption at various rounds in the audition process allows us to assess its use as a treatment.

The change in audition procedures with the adoption of the screen allows us to test whether bias exists in its absence. In both our study and studies using audits, the issue is whether sex (or race or ethnicity), apart from objective criteria (e.g., the sound of a musical performance, the content of a resume), is considered in the hiring process. Why sex might make a difference is another matter. . . .

Sex Composition of Orchestras

Symphony orchestras consist of about 100 musicians and, although the number has varied between 90 and 105, it is rarely lower or higher. The positions, moreover, are nearly identical between orchestras and over time. As opposed to firms, symphony orchestras do not vary much in size and have virtually identical numbers and types of jobs. Thus we can easily look at the proportion of women in an orchestra without being concerned about changes in the composition of occupations and

the number of workers. An increase in the number of women from, say, 1 to 10 cannot arise because the number of harpists (a female-dominated instrument) has greatly expanded. It must be because the proportion female within many groups has increased.

Among the five highest-ranked orchestras in the nation (known as the "Big Five")—the Boston Symphony Orchestra (BSO), the Chicago Symphony Orchestra, the Cleveland Symphony Orchestra, the New York Philharmonic (NYPhil), and the Philadelphia Orchestra—none contained more than 12 percent women until about 1980.[1] As can be seen in Figure 41.1A, each of the five lines (giving the proportion female) greatly increases after some point. For the NYPhil, the line steeply ascends in the early 1970s. For the BSO, the turning point appears to be a bit earlier. The percentage female in the NYPhil is currently 35 percent, the highest among all 11 orchestras in our sample after being the lowest (generally at zero) for decades. Thus the increase of women in the nation's finest orchestras has been extraordinary. The increase is even more remarkable because, as we discuss below, turnover in these orchestras is exceedingly low. The proportion of new players who were women must have been, and indeed was, exceedingly high.

Similar trends can be discerned for four other orchestras—the Los Angeles Symphony Orchestra (LA), the San Francisco Philharmonic (SF), the Detroit Symphony Orchestra, and the Pittsburgh Symphony Orchestra (PSO)—given in Figure 41.1B.[2] The upward trend in the proportion female is also obvious in Figure 41.1B, although initial levels are higher than in Figure 41.1A. There is somewhat more choppiness to the graph, particularly during the 1940s.

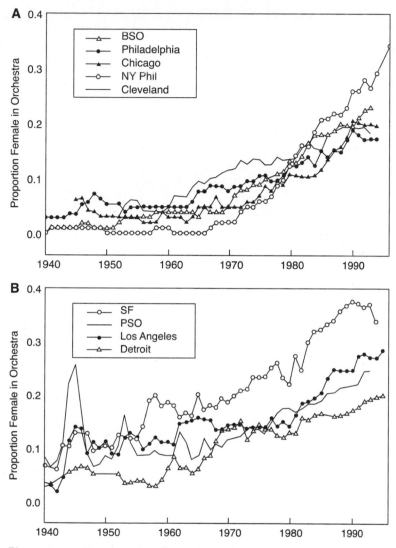

Figure 41.1   Proportion Female in Nine Orchestras, 1940 to 1990s. A: The "Big Five"; B: Four Others

Source: Roster sample. See text.

Although we have tried to eliminate all substitute, temporary, and guest musicians, especially during World War II and the Korean War, this was not always possible.

The only way to increase the proportion women is to hire more female musicians and turnover during most periods was low.

The number of new hires is graphed in Figure 41.2 for five orchestras. Because "new hires" is a volatile construct, we use a centered five-year moving average. In most years after the late 1950s, the top-ranked orchestras in the group (Chicago and NYPhil) hired about four musicians a year,

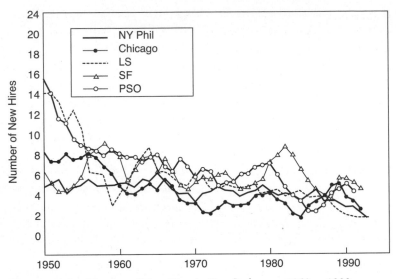

Figure 41.2   Number of New Hires in Five Orchestras, 1950 to 1990s
Source: Roster Sample. See text.

whereas the other three hired about six. Prior to 1960 the numbers are extremely high for LA and the PSO, because, it has been claimed, their music directors exercised their power to terminate, at will, the employment of musicians. Also of interest is that the number of new hires trends down, even excluding years prior to 1960. The important points to take from Figure 41.2 are that the number of new hires was small after 1960 and that it declined over time.

The proportion female among the new hires must have been sizable to increase the proportion female in the orchestras. Figure 41.3 shows the trend in the share of women among new hires for four of the "Big Five" (Figure 41.3A) and four other orchestras (Figure 41.3B).[3] In both groups the female share of new hires rose over time, at a somewhat steeper rate for the more prestigious orchestras. Since the early 1980s the share female among new hires has been about 35 percent for the BSO and Chicago, and

about 50 percent for the NYPhil, whereas before 1970 less than 10 percent of new hires were women.

Even though the fraction of new hires who are female rises at somewhat different times across the orchestras, there is a discernible increase for the group as a whole from the late 1970s to early 1980s, a time when the labor force participation of women increased generally and when their participation in various professions greatly expanded. The question, therefore, is whether the screen mattered in a direct manner or whether the increase was the result of a host of other factors, including the appearance of impartiality or an increased pool of female contestants coming out of music schools. Because the majority of new hires are in their late twenties and early thirties, the question is whether the most selective music schools were producing considerably more female students in the early 1970s. We currently have information by instrument for only the Juilliard School

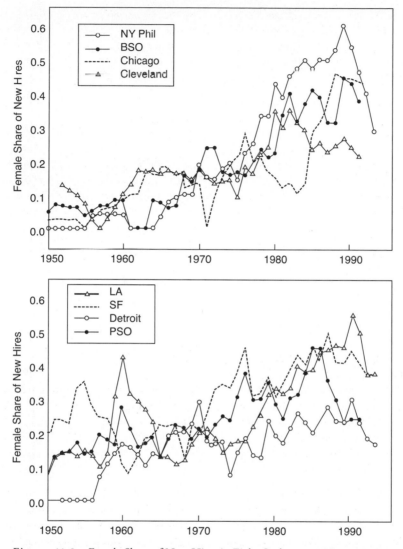

Figure 41.3   Female Share of New Hires in Eight Orchestras, 1950 to 1990s.
A: Four of the "Big Five"; B: Four Others

Source: Roster sample. See text.

Note: A five-year centered moving average is used. New hires are musicians who were not
with the orchestra the previous year, who remain for at least one additional year and who
were not substitute musicians in the current year.

of Music. With the exception of the brass section, the data, given in Figure 41.4, do not reveal any sharp breaks in the fraction of all graduates who are female. Thus, it is not immediately obvious that an expansion in the supply of qualified female musicians explains the marked increase in female symphony orchestra members; it could, therefore, be because of changes in the hiring procedures of orchestras.

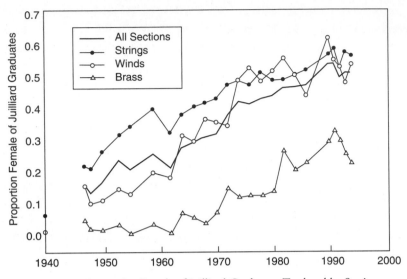

Figure 41.4   Proportion Female of Juilliard Graduates, Total and by Section:
1947 to 1995.
Source: Juilliard Music School files

But why would changes in audition pro-cedures alter the sex mix of those hired? Many of the most renowned conductors have, at one time or another, asserted that female musicians are not the equal of male musicians. Claims abound in the world of music that "women have smaller techniques than men," "are more temperamental and more likely to demand special attention or treatment," and that "the more women [in an orchestra], the poorer the sound."[4] Zubin Mehta, conductor of the Los Ange-les Symphony from 1964 to 1978 and of the New York Philharmonic from 1978 to 1990, is credited with saying, "I just don't think women should be in an orchestra."[5] Many European orchestras had, and some continue to have, stated policies not to hire women. The Vienna Philharmonic has only recently admitted its first female member (a harpist). Female musicians, it can be con-vincingly argued, have historically faced considerable discrimination. Thus a blind

hiring procedure, such as a screen that con-ceals the identity of the musician audition-ing, could eliminate the possibility of discrimination and increase the number of women in orchestras.

Orchestral Auditions

To understand the impact of the democra-tization of the audition procedure and the screen, we must first explain how orchestra auditions are now conducted. After deter-mining that an audition must be held to fill an opening, the orchestra advertises that it will hold an audition. Each audition at-tracts musicians from across the country and, often, from around the world. Musi-cians interested in auditioning are required to submit a resume and often a tape of compulsory music (recorded according to specific guidelines) to be judged by mem-bers of the orchestra. In some orchestras this prescreening is dispositive; in others the musician has the right to audition live in the preliminary round, even if the audition committee rejects the candidate on the basis of the tape. All candidates are given, in advance, most of the music they are expected to perform at the live audition.

Live auditions today generally consist of three rounds: preliminary, semifinal, and final. But there is considerable variation. Although all orchestras now have a preliminary round, some have two final rounds and in many there was no semifinal round until the 1980s. The preliminary is generally considered a screening round to eliminate unqualified candidates. As a result, the committee is free to advance as many, or as few, as they wish. Candidates advanced from the semifinal round are generally considered "acceptable for hire" by the audition committee (which does not include the music director, a.k.a. conductor, until the finals). Again, this means that the committee can advance as many as it wishes. The final round generally results in a hire, but sometimes does not.

In blind auditions (or audition rounds) a screen is used to hide the identity of the player from the committee. The screens we have seen are either large pieces of heavy (but sound-porous) cloth, sometimes suspended from the ceiling of the symphony hall, or look like large room dividers. Some orchestras also roll out a carpet leading to center stage to muffle footsteps that could betray the sex of the candidate. Each candidate for a blind audition is given a number, and the jury rates the candidate's performance next to the number on a sheet of paper. Only the personnel manager knows the mapping from number to name and from name to other personal information. The names of the candidates are not revealed to the juries until after the last blind round.

Almost all preliminary rounds are now blind. The semifinal round, added as the number of applicants grew, may be blind. Finals are rarely blind and almost always involve the attendance and input of the music director. Although the music director still wields considerable power, the self-governance that swept orchestras in the 1970s has served to contain the conductor's authoritarianism. The music director can ignore the audition committee's advice, but does so at greater peril. Once an applicant is chosen to be a member of an orchestra, lifetime tenure is awarded after a brief probationary period. The basis for termination is limited and rarely used. The positions we are analyzing are choice jobs in the musical world. In 1995 the *minimum starting* base salary for musicians at the BSO was $1,400 per week (for a 52-week year), not including recording contracts, soloist fees, overtime and extra service payments, bonuses, and per diem payments for tours and Tanglewood. . . .

The audition procedures of the 11 orchestras in the roster sample are summarized in Table 41.1.[6] Although audition procedures are now part of union contracts, that was not the case in the more distant past and the procedures were not apparently recorded in any surviving documents. We gathered information on these procedures from various sources, including union contracts, interviews with personnel managers, archival documents on auditions, and a mail survey we conducted of orchestral musicians concerning the procedures employed during the audition that won them their current position.

An obvious question to ask is whether the adoption of the screen is endogenous. Of particular concern is that more meritocratic orchestras adopted blind auditions

Table 41.1   Orchestra Audition Procedure Summary Table

Orchestra	Preliminaries	Semifinals	Finals
A	Blind since 1973	Blind (varies) since 1973	Not Blind
B	Blind since at least 1967	Use of screen varies	Blind 1967–1969; since winter 1994
C	Blind since at least 1979 (definitely after 1972)	Not blind: 1991–present Blind: 1984–1987	Not blind
D	Blind since 1986	Blind since 1986; varies until 1993	1st part blind since 1993; 2nd part not blind
E	Use of screen varies until 1981	Use of screen varies	Not blind
F	Blind since at least 1972	Blind since at least 1972	Blind since at least 1972
G	Blind since 1986	Use of screen varies	Not blind
H	Blind since 1970	Not blind	Not blind
I	Blind since 1979	Blind since 1979	Blind since fall 1983
J	Blind since 1952	Blind since 1952	Not blind
K	Not blind	Not blind	Not blind

Notes: The eleven orchestras (A through K) are those in the roster sample described in the text. A subset of eight form the audition sample (also described in the text). All orchestras in the sample are major big-city U.S. symphony orchestras and include the "Big Five."

Sources: Orchestra union contracts (from orchestra personnel managers and libraries), personal conversations with orchestra personnel managers, and our mail survey of current orchestra members who were hired during the probable period of screen adoption.

earlier, producing the spurious result that the screen increased the likelihood that women were hired.[7] We estimate a probit model of screen adoption by year, conditional on an orchestra's not previously having adopted the screen (an orchestra exits the exercise once it adopts the screen). Two time-varying covariates are included to assess commonly held notions about screen adoption: the proportion female (lagged) in the orchestra, and a measure of tenure (lagged) of then-current orchestra members. Tenure is included because personnel managers maintain the screen was advocated more by younger players.

As the proportion female in an orchestra increases, so does the likelihood of screen adoption in the preliminary round, as can be seen in columns (1) and (2) in Table 41.2, although the effects are very small and far from statistically significant. We estimate a similar effect when we assess the role of female presence on the adoption of blind finals [see column (3)]. The impact of current tenure, measured by the proportion with less than six years with the orchestra, is—contrary to general belief—negative and the results do not change controlling for whether the orchestra is one of the "Big Five." In all, it appears that orchestra sex composition had little influence on screen adoption, although the stability of the personnel may have increased its likelihood.

Table 41.2   Estimated Probit Models for the Use of a Screen

	Preliminaries blind		Finals blind
	(1)	(2)	(3)
(Proportion female)$_{t-1}$	2.744	3.120	0.490
	(3.265)	(3.271)	(1.163)
	[0.006]	[0.004]	[0.011]
(Proportion of orchestra personnel with <6 years tenure)$_{t-1}$	−26.46	−28.13	−9.467
	(7.314)	(8.459)	(2.787)
	[−0.058]	[−0.039]	[−0.207]
"Big Five" orchestra		0.367	
		(0.452)	
		[0.001]	
pseudo R^2	0.178	0.193	0.050
Number of observations	294	294	434

Notes: The dependent variable is 1 if the orchestra adopts a screen, 0 otherwise. Huber standard errors (with orchestra random effects) are in parentheses. All specifications include a constant. Changes in probabilities are in brackets. "Proportion female" refers to the entire orchestra. "Tenure" refers to years of employment in the current orchestra. "Big Five" includes Boston, Chicago, Cleveland, New York Philharmonic, and Philadelphia. The data begin in 1947 and an orchestra exits the exercise once it adopts the screen. The unit of observation is an orchestra-year.

Source: Eleven-orchestra roster sample. See text.

The Role of Blind Auditions on the Audition and Hiring Process

A. Data and Methods

Audition Records.   We use the actual audition records of eight major symphony orchestras obtained from orchestra personnel managers and the orchestra archives. The records are highly confidential and occasionally contain remarks (including those of the conductor) about musicians currently with the orchestra. To preserve the full confidentiality of the records, we have not revealed the names of the orchestras in our sample.

Although availability differs, taken together we obtained information on auditions dating from the late 1950s through 1995. Typically, the records are lists of the names of individuals who attended the auditions, with notation near the names of those advanced to the next round. For the preliminary round, this would indicate advancement to either the semifinal or final round. Another list would contain the names of the semifinalists or finalists with an indication of who won the audition. From these records, we recorded the instrument and position (e.g., section, principal, substitute) for which the audition was held. We also know whether the individual had an "automatic" placement in a semifinal or final round. Automatic placement occurs when a musician is already known to be above some quality cutoff and is invited to compete in a semifinal or final round. We also recorded whether the individual was advanced to the next round of the current audition.

We rely on the first name of the musicians to determine sex. For most names establishing sex was straightforward. Sexing the Japanese and Korean names was equally straightforward, at least for our Japanese and Korean consultants. For more difficult cases, we checked the names in three baby books (Connie Lockhard Ellefson, 1990; Alfred J. Kolatch, 1990; Bruce Lansky, 1995). If the name was listed as male- or female-only, we considered the sex known. The gender-neutral names (e.g., Chris, Leslie, and Pat) and some Chinese names (for which sex is indeterminate in the absence of Chinese characters) remained ambiguous. Using these procedures, we were able to determine the sex of 96 percent of our audition sample.

In constructing our analysis sample, we exclude incomplete auditions, those in which there were no women (or only women) competing, rounds from which no one was advanced, and the second final round, if one exists, for which the candidates played with the orchestra. In addition, we generally consider each round of the audition separately. These sample restrictions exclude 294 rounds (199 contained no women) and 1,539 individuals. Our final analysis sample has 7,065 individuals and 588 audition rounds (from 309 separate auditions) resulting in 14,121 person-rounds and an average of 2.0 rounds per musician. . . .

Roster Data.   Our second source of information comes from the final results of the audition process, the orchestra personnel rosters. We collected these data from the personnel page of concert programs, one each year for eleven major symphony orchestras. These records are in the public domain and thus we have used the orchestra names in the graphs containing those data alone. As opposed to the auditionees, we were able to confirm the sex of the players with the orchestra personnel managers and archivists. We considered a musician to be

new to the orchestra in question if he or she had not previously been a regular member of that orchestra (i.e., we did not count returning members as new). We excluded, when possible, temporary and substitute musicians, as well as harpists and pianists. Our final sample for 1970 to 1996 has 1,128 new orchestra members. . . .

B. The Effect of the Screen on the Hiring of Women

Using the Audition Sample.   We turn now to the effect of the screen on the actual hire and estimate the likelihood an individual is hired out of the initial audition pool.[8] Whereas the use of the screen for each audition round was, more or less, an unambiguous concept, that for the entire process is not and we must define a blind audition. The definition we have chosen is that a blind audition contains all rounds that use the screen. In using this definition, we compare auditions that are completely blind with those that do not use the screen at all or use it for the early rounds only. We divide the sample into auditions that have a semifinal round and those that do not, because the earlier analysis suggested they might differ (Goldin and Rouse 2000).

The impact of completely blind auditions on the likelihood of a woman's being hired is given in Table 41.3, for which all results include individual fixed effects.[9] The impact of the screen is positive and large in magnitude, but only when there is no semifinal round. Women are about 5 percentage points more likely to be hired than are men in a completely blind audition, although the effect is not statistically significant. The effect is nil, however, when there is a semifinal round. The impact for all rounds [columns (5) and (6)] is about 1 percentage point, although the standard errors are

Table 41.3   Linear Probability Estimates of the Effect of Blind Auditions on the Likelihood of Being Hired with Individual Fixed Effects

	Without semifinals		With semifinals		All	
	(1)	(2)	(3)	(4)	(5)	(6)
Completely blind audition	−0.024 (0.028)	0.047 (0.041)	0.001 (0.009)	0.006 (0.011)	0.001 (0.008)	0.005 (0.009)
Completely blind audition × female	0.051 (0.046)	0.036 (0.048)	0.001 (0.016)	−0.004 (0.016)	0.011 (0.013)	0.006 (0.013)
Year effects?	No	Yes	No	Yes	No	Yes
Other covariates?	No	Yes	No	Yes	No	Yes
R^2	0.855	0.868	0.692	0.707	0.678	0.691
Number of observations	4,108	4,108	5,883	5,883	9,991	9,991

Notes: The unit of observation is a person-round. The dependent variable is 1 if the individual is advanced (or hired) from the final round and 0 if not. Standard errors are in parentheses. All specifications include individual fixed effects, whether the sex is missing, and an interaction for sex being missing and a completely blind audition. "Other covariates" are the size of the audition, the proportion female at the audition, the number of individuals advanced (hired), whether a "Big Five" orchestra, the number of previous auditions, and whether the individual had an automatic semifinal or final.

Source: Eight-orchestra audition sample. See text.

large and thus the effect is not statistically significant. Given that the probability of winning an audition is less than 3 percent, we would need more data than we currently have to estimate a statistically significant effect, and even a 1-percentage-point increase is large, as we later demonstrate.

Using the Roster Data.   The roster data afford us another way to evaluate the effect of the screen on the sex composition of orchestras. Using the rosters we know the sex of new hires each year for 11 orchestras, and we also have information (see Table 41.1) on the year the screen was adopted by each orchestra. We treat the orchestra position as the unit of observation and ask whether the screen affects the sex of the individual who fills the position. We model the likelihood that a female is hired in a

particular year as a function of whether the orchestra's audition procedure involved a screen, again relying on the variation over time within a particular orchestra. Thus, in all specifications, we include orchestra fixed effects and an orchestra-specific time trend.

The roster data extend further back in time than do the audition data and could conceivably begin with the orchestra's founding, although there is no obvious reason to include many years when none used the screen. We report, in Table 41.4, the effects of the screen on the hiring of women from 1970 to 1996 using a probit model. The screen is first defined to include any blind auditions [column (1)]. In column (2) we estimate separate effects for orchestras using blind preliminary (and semifinal) rounds but not blind finals and those with completely blind auditions.

Table 41.4   Probit Estimates of the Effect of Blind Auditions on the Sex of New Members: 1970 to 1996

	Any blind auditions	Only blind preliminaries and/or semifinals vs. completely blind auditions
	(1)	(2)
Any blind auditions	0.238 (0.183) [0.075]	
Only blind preliminaries and/or semifinals		0.232 (0.184) [0.074]
Completely blind auditions		0.361 (0.438) [0.127]
Section:		
Woodwinds	−0.187 (0.114) [−0.058]	−0.188 (0.114) [−0.058]
Brass	−1.239 (0.157) [−0.284]	−1.237 (0.157) [−0.284]
Percussion	−1.162 (0.305) [−0.235]	−1.164 (0.305) [−0.235]
p-value of test: only blind preliminaries and/or semifinals = completely blind		0.756
pseudo R²	0.106	0.106
Number of observations	1,128	1,128

Notes: The dependent variable is 1 if the individual is female and 0 if male. Standard errors are in parentheses. All specifications include orchestra fixed effects and orchestra-specific time trends. Changes in probabilities are in brackets; see text for an explanation of how they are calculated. New members are those who enter the orchestra for the first time. Returning members are not considered new. The omitted section is strings.

Source: Eleven-orchestra roster sample. See text.

To interpret the probit coefficient, we first predict a base probability, under the assumption that each orchestra does not use a screen. We then predict a new probability assuming the orchestra uses a screen. The mean difference in the probabilities is given in brackets.

The coefficient on blind in column (1) is positive, although not significant at any usual level of confidence. The estimates in column (2) are positive and equally large in magnitude to those in column (1). Further,

these estimates show that the existence of any blind round makes a difference and that a completely blind process has a somewhat larger effect (albeit with a large standard error). According to the point estimates in column (1) of Table 41.4, blind auditions increase the likelihood a female will be hired by 7.5 percentage points. The magnitude of the effect must be judged relative to the overall average and, for the period under consideration, it was about 30 percent. Thus blind auditions increased the likelihood a female would be hired by 25 percent. . . .[10]

Conclusion

The question is whether hard evidence can support an impact of discrimination on hiring. Our analysis of the audition and roster data indicates that it can, although we mention various caveats before we summarize the reasons. Even though our sample size is large, we identify the coefficients of interest from a much smaller sample. Some of our coefficients of interest, therefore, do not pass standard tests of statistical significance and there is, in addition, one persistent result that goes in the opposite direction. The weight of the evidence, however, is what we find most persuasive and what we have emphasized. . . .

As in research in economics and other fields on double-blind refereeing (see, e.g., Blank, 1991), the impact of a blind procedure is toward impartiality and the costs to the journal (here to the orchestra) are relatively small. We conclude that the adoption of the screen and blind auditions served to help female musicians in their quest for orchestral positions.

NOTES

1. The data referred to, and used in Figures 41.1 to 41.3, are from orchestral rosters, described in more detail below.

2. Our roster sample also includes the Metropolitan Opera Orchestra and the St. Louis Symphony.

3. A centered five-year moving average is also used for this variable.

4. Seltzer (1989), p. 215.

5. Seltzer (1989), p. 215.

6. We identify the orchestras by letter, rather than by name, to preserve confidentiality of the audition sample.

7. Note, however, it is unlikely that the orchestras that sought to hire more women chose to adopt the screen earlier since the best way to increase the number of women in the orchestra is to have not-blind auditions (so that one could be sure to hire more women).

8. The original article (Goldin and Rouse 2000) includes much additional analysis examining the effect of the screen on the likelihood of being advanced through each stage of the audition process.—EDS

9. There are four auditions in which the committee could not choose between two players and therefore asked each to play with the orchestra. We consider both to be winners. The results are not sensitive to this classification. For this analysis we exclude auditions with no women, all women, or no winner; these exclusions do not change the results.

10. In Table 41.3 we are identified off of individuals who competed in auditions that were completely blind *and* those that were not completely blind (that is, *any* one round could not be blind). The unit of observation is the person-round and there are 92 fulfilling this criterion for auditions without a semifinal [columns (1) and (2)]; on average these persons competed in 3.6 auditions in this sample. There are 625 person-rounds fulfilling this criterion that included a semifinal [columns (3) and (4)] and on average these persons competed in 3.5 auditions in this sample. Finally, there are 911 person-rounds fulfilling this criterion across all auditions [columns (5) and (6)] and on average these persons competed in 3.5 auditions in this sample. The sample off of which we are identified is larger for all auditions than for the sum of the other two because some individuals auditioned both with and without a semifinal round.

REFERENCES

Arrow, Kenneth. "The Theory of Discrimination," in Orley Ashenfelter and Albert Rees, eds., *Discrimination in labor markets*. Princeton, NJ: Princeton University Press, 1973, pp. 3–33.

Becker, Gary. *The economics of discrimination*, 2nd Ed. Chicago: University of Chicago Press, 1971 [orig. pub. 1957].

Blank, Rebecca. "The Effects of Double-Blind versus Single-Blind Refereeing: Experimental Evidence from the *American Economic Review*." *American Economic Review,* December 1991, *81*(5), pp. 1041–67.

Ellefson, Connie Lockhard. *The melting pot book of baby names,* 2nd Ed. Cincinnati, OH: Better Way Books, 1990.

Goldin, Claudia and Cecilia Rouse. 2000. "Orchestrating Impartiality: The Impact of 'Blind' Auditions on Female Musicians." *American Economic Review* 90 (September): 715–741.

Kenney, Genevieve and Wissoker, Douglas A. "An Analysis of the Correlates of Discrimination Facing Young Hispanic Job-Seekers." *American Economic Review,* June 1994, *84*(3), pp. 674–83.

Kolatch, Alfred J. *The Jonathan David dictionary of first names.* New York: Perigee Books, 1990.

Lansky, Bruce. *35,000+ baby names.* New York: Meadowbrook Press, 1995.

Neumark, David (with Bank, Roy and Van Nort, Kyle D.). "Sex Discrimination in Restaurant Hiring: An Audit Study." *Quarterly Journal of Economics,* August 1996, *111*(3), pp. 915–41.

Seltzer, George. *Music matters: The performer and the American Federation of Musicians.* Metuchen, NJ: Scarecrow Press, 1989.

42

Getting a Job

Is There a Motherhood Penalty?

SHELLEY J. CORRELL,
STEPHEN BENARD, AND
IN PAIK

Mothers experience disadvantages in the workplace in addition to those commonly associated with gender. Recent studies show employed mothers in the United States suffer a 5 percent per-child wage penalty on average after controlling for the usual human capital and occupational factors that affect wages (Budig and England 2001; Anderson, Binder, and Krause 2003). The pay gap between mothers and nonmothers under age 35 is larger than the pay gap between men and women (Crittenden 2001), and employed mothers now account for most of the "gender gap" in wages (Glass 2004).

The disadvantages are not limited to pay. Describing a consultant as a mother leads evaluators to rate her as less competent than when she is described as not having children (Cuddy, Fiske, and Glick 2004), and visibly pregnant managers are judged as less committed to their jobs, less dependable, less authoritative, but warmer, more emotional, and more irrational than otherwise equal women managers (Halpert, Wilson, and Hickman 1993; Corse 1990). While the pattern is clear, the underlying mechanism remains opaque. Why would being a parent lead to disadvantages in the workplace for women? And why might similar disadvantages not occur for men?

This paper presents a laboratory experiment and an audit study. The laboratory experiment evaluates the hypothesis that the "motherhood penalty" occurs because cultural understandings of motherhood lead evaluators to, perhaps unconsciously, expect mothers to be less competent and less committed to their jobs (Blair-Loy 2003; Ridgeway and Correll 2004). As a result, we argue, employers will discriminate against mothers when making hiring, promotion, and salary decisions. We do not expect fathers to experience similar workplace disadvantages since being a good father is not seen in our culture as incompatible with being a good worker (Townsend 2002). By having participants

This is a commissioned chapter that draws heavily on material in a previous publication (Shelley J. Correll, Stephen Benard, and In Paik, "Getting a Job: Is There a Motherhood Penalty?" *American Journal of Sociology* 112 [March 2007], pp. 1297–1338).

rate job applicants, we expect that applicants presented as women with children will be viewed as less competent and less committed to work, will need to present evidence that they are more qualified for the job, will be rated as less promotable, and will be offered lower starting salaries compared with otherwise similar applicants presented as women without children. While the laboratory experiment isolates and examines the mechanism of discrimination, the audit study provides external validity by evaluating whether actual employers discriminate against mothers.

Wage Penalty for Motherhood

Explanations for the motherhood wage penalty generally can be classified as worker explanations, which seek to identify differences in the traits, skills, and behaviors between mothers and nonmothers, and discrimination explanations, which rely on the differential preference for or treatment of mothers and nonmothers. Empirical evaluations of these explanations have largely focused on the former.

Budig and England (2001) find that interruptions from work, working part-time, and decreased seniority/experience collectively explain no more than about one-third of the motherhood penalty. In addition, "mother-friendly" job characteristics (i.e., differences in the type of jobs chosen) explain very little of the penalty. Similarly, Anderson, Binder, and Krause (2003) find that human capital and occupational and household resource variables (e.g., number of adults in household) collectively account for 24 percent of the total penalty for one child and 44 percent for women with two or more children. As Budig and England (2001) conclude, the remaining wage gap

likely arises either because mothers are somehow less productive at work than nonmothers or because employers discriminate against mothers (or some combination of the two processes).

Productivity and Discrimination

To distinguish between discrimination and productivity explanations, ideally one would compare the outcomes of employed mothers and nonmothers who have equal levels of workplace productivity. If differences in pay or promotion rates were found between equally productive mothers and nonmothers, this would suggest that discrimination factors were at work. However, the datasets analyzed in the previous studies lack direct measures of worker productivity. One likely reason for this is that it is inherently problematic to specify what makes someone a productive employee. This difficulty leads to another: unexplained gaps in wages between employed mothers and nonmothers can always be attributed to unmeasured productivity differences between the two groups.

To address these problems, we experimentally held constant the workplace performances and other relevant characteristics of a pair of fictitious job applicants and varied only their parental status. By holding constant workplace-relevant characteristics, differences between the ratings of mothers and nonmothers cannot be attributed to productivity or skill differences. While this design cannot rule out the possibility that productivity differences account for part of the wage penalty found in previous studies, the laboratory study will isolate a potential status-based discrimination mechanism by evaluating whether being a parent disadvantages mothers in the workplace even when no productivity differences exist between them and women without children.

Performance Expectations and Evaluations of Workplace Competence

Status Characteristics Theory

The laboratory study evaluates the theoretical claim that motherhood is a "status characteristic" that, when salient, results in biased evaluations of competence and commitment, a stricter standard for evaluating the workplace performances of mothers, and a bias against mothers in hiring, promotion, and salary decisions. A status characteristic is a categorical distinction among people, such as race or occupational status, that has attached to it widely held cultural beliefs associating greater status worthiness and competence with one category of the distinction over others (Berger et al. 1977).

Theory and empirical research suggest that ability standards are stricter for those with lower performance expectations (Foschi 1989). The logic behind this prediction is that good performances are inconsistent with expectations for lower status actors; therefore when they perform well, their performances are critically scrutinized and judged by a stricter standard compared with higher status actors. Thus, performances of low status actors—even when "objectively" equal to that of their high status counterparts—are less likely to be judged as demonstrating task ability or competence (for a comparison of status discrimination and economic theories of statistical discrimination, see Correll and Benard 2006).

Motherhood as a Status Characteristic

To understand how motherhood might function as a devalued status characteristic in workplace settings, it is helpful to broaden the conventional usage of "performance expectations." While researchers typically focus on the anticipated relative *competence* of group members, cultural beliefs about the relative *effort* that social groups exert in task situations can also be the basis for forming differentiated performance expectations. While it is logically difficult to understand why taking on the motherhood role should affect a person's underlying competence, there is considerable evidence that contemporary cultural beliefs assume that employed mothers are less committed to work than nonmothers and, consequently, put less *effort* into it (Ridgeway and Correll 2004). Motherhood affects perceptions of commitment because contradictory schemas govern conceptions of "family devotion" and "work devotion" (Blair-Loy 2003: 5). A cultural norm that mothers should always be on call for their children coexists in tension with another widely held normative belief in our society that the "ideal worker" be unencumbered by competing demands and "always there" for his or her employer (Acker 1990; Hays 1996; Williams 2001; Blair-Loy 2003). The tension between these two roles occurs at the level of normative cultural assumptions, and not necessarily at the level of mothers' own commitment to work. Indeed, Bielby and Bielby (1984) found no differences in the workplace commitment of mothers and nonmothers. Instead it is the *perceived* tension between these two roles that leads us to suggest that motherhood is a devalued status in workplace settings.

Therefore, we predict that mothers will be rated as less competent, less committed, less suitable for hire and promotion, and deserving of lower starting salaries compared with otherwise equal women who are not mothers. In addition, we expect mothers will be judged by a harsher standard. Since being a good father is not seen as culturally incompatible with being an ideal worker (Townsend 2002), we do not expect that fathers will experience lower workplace evaluations.

The Laboratory Experiment

Paid undergraduate volunteers (84 men and 108 women) rated a pair of equally qualified, same-gender (either male or female), same-race (either African American or white) fictitious job applicants, presented as real, who differed on parental status. Since there were very few significant effects of participant gender or applicant race, we do not discuss these results here.

The Use of Undergraduates

The laboratory setting ensures sufficient control over factors that would interfere with tests of our hypotheses, such as other people in the room to prime other status characteristics, telephones, or other distractions, and it allows us to collect detailed measures to fully test our argument. By necessity we rely on a sample of undergraduates. The theory presented here implies that to the extent that employers share the belief that mothers are less committed to or competent in workplace settings, they too will subtly discriminate against mothers. Qualitative and quantitative research provides some evidence that employers share this belief (Blair-Loy 2003; Crittenden 2001; Kennelly 1999; Cleveland and Berman 1987; Cleveland 1991; Olian and Schwab 1988). The audit study, described below, will provide more direct evidence regarding the extent to which employers discriminate against mothers.

Procedure

Participants read a description of a company that was purportedly hiring for a mid-level marketing position and examined application materials for two equally qualified applicants who differed on parental status. To increase their task orientation, participants were told that their input would impact actual hiring decisions. They then inspected each applicant's file, containing three items: a short memo, a "fact sheet," and a resume. The memos contained notes purportedly from a company human resources staff member who conducted a screening interview with the applicant. The "fact sheet" summarized relevant information about the potential employee (e.g., college GPA) not presented on the resume. The fact sheets and the resumes established that the candidates were equally productive in their past jobs and had equivalent skills and backgrounds. Prior to the actual experiment, pretesting of the two versions of the materials confirmed that the resumes were perceived to be of equivalent quality.

Experimental Manipulations

The race and gender of applicants were manipulated by altering first names on the applicant files (Bertrand and Mullainathan 2003). Parental status was manipulated on the resume and on the human resources memo. The resume described one applicant as an officer in an elementary school Parent-Teacher Association, and the accompanying memo included the following phrase: "Mother/Father to Tom and Emily. Married to John/Karen." The nonparent was presented as married, but with no mention of children.

Dependent Measures

There are eight dependent measures: two that measure competence and commitment, two that measure the ability standard participants used to judge the applicants, and four that serve as our key evaluation measures. The competence measure is a weighted average of participants' ratings of the applicants on seven-point scales ranging from "not at all" to "extremely" capable, efficient, skilled, intelligent, independent, self-confident, aggressive, and organized (alpha=.85). The commitment measure comes from a single-item question that asked participants how committed they thought the applicant would be relative to other employees in similar positions at the company.

There are two ability standard items. Participants were asked: (1) what percentile the applicant would need to score on an exam diagnostic of management ability, and (2) "how many days could this applicant be late or leave early per month before you would no longer recommend him/her for management track?" We predict that mothers will be required to score in a *higher* percentile than nonmothers before being considered hirable and will be allowed *fewer* days of being late or leaving early.

There are four evaluation measures. Participants were asked: (1) to recommend a *salary* for each applicant, (2) to estimate the likelihood that an applicant would be subsequently *promoted* if hired, (3) to judge whether the applicant, if hired, should be recommended for a *management-training* course designed for those with strong advancement potential, and (4) to decide if they would recommend each applicant for *hire*. We predict that mothers will be of-fered lower starting salaries, will be rated as less promotable, will be less likely to be recommended for management, and will be less likely to be recommended for hire than nonmothers.

Laboratory Experiment Results

As predicted, mothers were judged significantly less competent and committed than women without children (see Table 42.1, left side) and were held to harsher performance and punctuality standards. They were allowed significantly fewer times of being late to work and needed a significantly higher score on the management exam than nonmothers before being considered hirable. Similarly, the evaluation measures show significant and substantial penalties for motherhood. The recommended starting salary for mothers was $11,000 (7.4 percent) less than that offered nonmothers, a significant difference. Mothers were also rated significantly less promotable and were less likely to be recommended for management. Finally, while participants recommended 84 percent of female nonmothers for hire, they recommended a significantly lower 47 percent of mothers.

Fathers were not disadvantaged, and in fact were advantaged on some of these measures. Relative to nonfathers, fathers were rated significantly more committed to their jobs, allowed to be late to work significantly more times, and offered significantly higher salaries.

Multivariate Analysis

We now turn to multivariate models to evaluate the motherhood penalty hypothesis by estimating the effects of gender of applicant, parental status, and the interaction

Table 42.1 Means or Proportions of Status, Standards and Evaluation Variables by Gender and Parental Status of Applicant (Standard Deviations in Parentheses)

	Female Applicants Mothers	Female Applicants Non-mothers	Male Applicants Fathers	Male Applicants Non-fathers
Competence	5.19 (0.73)**	5.75 (0.58)	5.51 (0.68)	5.44 (0.66)
Commitment	67.0 (19.1)**	79.2 (15.2)	78.5** (16.3)	74.2 (18.6)
Days allowed late	3.16 (1.98)**	3.73 (2.01)	3.69** (2.55)	3.16 (1.85)
Percent score required on exam	72.4 (27.5)**	67.9 (27.7)	67.3 (32.7)	67.1 (33.0)
Salary recommended	$137,000**	$148,000	$150,000**	$144,000
	(21,000)	(25,000)	(23,000)	(20,700)
Proportion recommend for management	.691++	.862	.936+	.851
Likelihood of promotion	2.74 (0.65)**	3.42 (0.54)	3.30* (0.62)	3.11 (0.70)
Proportion recommend for hire	.468++	.840	.734+	.617

* $p<.1$, test for difference in means between parent and non-parents
** $p<.05$, test for difference in means between parent and non-parents
+ $z<.1$, test for difference in proportion between parents and non-parents
++ $z<.05$, test for difference in proportion between parents and non-parents
Notes: 94 participants rated female applicants and 94 rated male applicants. For this table, the data for male and female subjects are pooled, as are the data by race of applicant.

of gender of applicant with parental status on each of the eight dependent variables. We refer to the interaction term (gender of applicant x parental status) as the "motherhood penalty interaction." Applicant race and participant gender are included in all models, and standard errors are clustered by participant ID to take into account the nonindependence of observations that results from asking participants to rate applicants in pairs. Linear regression models are used for the continuous dependent variables. Logistic regression models are estimated for the binary evaluation variables (recommend for management and recommend for hire). Ordered logistic regression, with the proportional odds specification, is used for the ordered categorical evaluation variable, likelihood of promotion. Parental status, gender of applicant, gender of participant, and race of applicant are dummy variables, with parents, females, and African Americans coded as 1.

The estimated regression coefficients are presented in Tables 42.2–4. For all eight dependent variables, the motherhood penalty interaction is significant and in the predicted direction. This result shows strong support for the main prediction that parental status negatively impacts ratings for female, but not male, applicants.

Confirming our prediction, mothers were viewed as less competent than nonmothers. The significant, negative motherhood

Table 42.2 Estimated Regression Coefficients for the Effects of Gender, Parental Status and Race on Applicant's Perceived Competence and Commitment (Robust Standard Errors in Parentheses Clustered by Participant ID)

Independent Variables	Competence	Commitment
Parent	0.089	5.15 ***
	(0.088)	(1.73)
Female applicant	0.376 ***	5.68 **
	(0.104)	(2.51)
African American	-0.038	-2.01
	(0.090)	(2.27)
Female participant	0.060	-2.61
	(0.094)	(2.26)
Motherhood interaction^	-0.750 ***	-17.3 ***
	(0.132)	(2.32)
Intercept	5.42 ***	75.8 ***
	(0.100)	(2.55)

^ Parent * Female applicant
* p<.1
** p<.05
*** p<.001
Note: N=188 participants

penalty interaction indicates that being a parent lowers the competence ratings for women, but not men (see left column, Table 42.2). Participants also perceived mothers as less committed than other applicants: the motherhood penalty interaction is significant and negative in the model predicting commitment ratings (see right column, Table 42.2). The positive and significant main effect for parental status implies that fathers are actually rated as more committed than nonfathers.

Consistent with the status-based discrimination argument, mothers were held to a stricter performance standard (see Table 42.3). The motherhood interaction is significant and positive in the model predicting the required test score, while the main effects of gender of applicant and parental status are insignificant, showing that participants require mothers (but not

fathers) to score higher on a test of management ability than other applicants before considering them for a job. Mothers are also held to a higher standard of punctuality, being allowed fewer days of being late.

In Table 42.4, the motherhood penalty interaction is significant and negative across all four models, indicating that mothers, relative to other applicants, are believed to deserve lower salaries and to be less suitable for hiring, promoting, and training for management. In the model predicting likelihood of promotion, the main effect of parental status is marginally significant and positive, while the motherhood penalty interaction is significant and negative, indicating that the negative effect of parental status on perceptions of promotability accrues only to women.

Consistent with previous literature on the motherhood wage penalty, mothers are offered lower starting salaries than other

Table 42.3 Estimated Regression Coefficients for the Effects of Gender, Parental Status and Race on Ability Standard Variables (Robust Standard Errors in Parentheses, Clustered by Participant ID)

Independent Variables	Days allowed late	Test score required (%)
Parent	0.515 ***	1.03
	(0.137)	(0.968)
Female applicant	0.572 **	1.25
	(0.294)	(4.52)
African American	-0.361	-4.06
	(0.294)	(4.38)
Female participant	0.234	-9.44 **
	(0.289)	(4.30)
Motherhood interaction^	-1.10 ***	3.56 ***
	(0.213)	(1.21)
Intercept	3.22 ***	73.7 ***
	(0.322)	(4.27)

^ Parent * Female applicant
* p<.1
** p<.05
*** p<.001
Note: N=188 participants

Table 42.4 Estimated Regression Coefficients for the Effects of Gender, Parental Status and Race on Evaluation Variables (Robust Standard Errors in Parentheses, Clustered by Participant ID)

Independent Variables	Promotion likelihood (ordered logistic estimates)	Mgmt training? (binary logistic estimates)	Hire? (binary logistic estimates)	Recommended salary in thousands of dollars (linear estimates)
Parent	1.03 *	0.605 *	0.570	4.47 ***
	(0.545)	(0.321)	(0.366)	(1.84)
Female applicant	0.256	1.009 ***	1.21 ***	2.56
	(0.425)	(0.319)	(0.365)	(3.18)
African American	0.309	-0.211	-0.163	-6.80 **
	(0.299)	(0.218)	(0.197)	(2.94)
Female participant	0.496 *	0.526 **	0.606 ***	0.691
	(0.298)	(0.226)	(0.199)	(2.82)
Motherhood interaction^	-2.14 ***	-2.72 ***	-2.38 ***	-15.9 ***
	(0.651)	(0.426)	(0.548)	(2.42)
Intercept	^^	4.56 ***	0.210	148
		(0.601)	(0.266)	(2.55)

^ Parent * Female applicant
^^ Since ordered logistic regression produces multiple intercepts, we do not present them here.
* p<.1
** p<.05
*** p<.001
Note: N=188 participants

Table 42.5 Estimated Regression Coefficients for the Mediation of Competence and Commitment on the Impact of Parental Status on Workplace Evaluations (Robust Standard Errors in Parentheses, Clustered by Participant ID)

Independent Variables	Promotion likelihood (ordered logistic estimates)	Mgmt training? (binary logistic estimates)	Hire? (binary logistic estimates)	Recommended salary in thousands of dollars (linear estimates)
Competence	0.628 **	1.263 ***	1.21 ***	7.00 ***
	(0.295)	(0.281)	(0.258)	(1.99)
Commitment	0.237 ***	0.206 **	0.308 ***	1.08
	(0.095)	(0.099)	(0.081)	(0.762)
Parent	0.901 *	0.508	0.433	3.23 *
	(0.558)	(0.340)	(0.426)	(1.78)
Female applicant	-0.140	0.661 **	0.755 *	-0.817
	(0.426)	(0.332)	(0.410)	(3.31)
African American	0.374	-0.154	-0.092	-6.30 ***
	(0.319)	(0.237)	(0.244)	(2.86)
Female participant	0.557 *	0.606 ***	0.755 ***	0.512
	(0.316)	(0.236)	(0.254)	(2.81)
Motherhood interaction^	-1.34 **	-1.89 ***	-1.39 **	-8.52 ***
	(0.646)	(0.437)	(0.606)	(2.66)
Intercept	^^	3.64 ***	-2.09 ***	140
		(0.947)	(0.702)	(6.37)
Percent reduction of motherhood penalty	37.4 %	30.5 %	41.6 %	46.4 %

^ Parent * Female applicant
^^ Since ordered logistic regression produces multiple intercepts, we do not present them here.
* p<.1
** p<.05
*** p<.001
Note: N=188 participants

types of applicants, as indicated by the significant, negative coefficient for the motherhood interaction term. Childless men were recommended an average salary of approximately $148,000. Fathers were offered a significantly higher salary of approximately $152,000. Women without children were offered approximately $151,000, whereas mothers were recommended a significantly lower salary of about $139,000, or about 7.9 percent less than otherwise equal childless women.

While the motherhood penalty interaction is significant and its sign is in the predicted direction for each model, to complete our argument, we need to give evidence that motherhood disadvantages job applicants *because* it is a status characteristic. If the theory is correct, then evaluations of competence and commitment should mediate the motherhood penalty.

When the competence and commitment ratings were added as independent variables to the models (see Table 42.5), the negative

Table 42.6 Proportions of Applicants Receiving Callbacks by Gender and Parental Status

	Callbacks / Total Jobs	Proportion Called Back
Mothers	10 / 320	.0313
Childless women	21 / 320	.0656++
Fathers	16 / 318	.0503
Childless men	9 / 318	.0283

++ z<.05, test for difference in proportions between parents and non-parents
Notes: Mothers and childless women applied to the same 320 jobs; fathers and childless men applied to the same 318 jobs.

effect of motherhood status on workplace evaluations was significantly reduced, by a magnitude of 31–46 percent. Thus, mothers are rated as less hirable, less suitable for promotion and management training, and deserving of lower salaries in part because they are believed to be less competent and less committed to paid work. Having established support for the causal mechanism with the laboratory data, we turn to the audit study to assess whether actual employers discriminate against mothers.

The Audit Study

The audit methodology combines experimental design with real-life settings. As in laboratory experiments, audit studies isolate a characteristic (e.g., race or gender) and test for discriminatory behavior. Distinct from most laboratory studies, audit study participants are the people who make important decisions about actual applicants, such as employers conducting new employee searches. While laboratory experiments permit closer investigation of social and cognitive processes, audit studies provide greater generalizability of results.

Resumes and cover letters from a pair of fictitious, equally qualified, same-gender applicants were sent to employers advertising for marketing and business job openings in a large, northeastern city newspaper over an 18-month period of time. The same-sex pair contained one parent and one nonparent. Job openings were randomly assigned to either the male or female condition. We manipulated parental status on the resume and on the cover letter. We did not manipulate race in this study.

We monitor whether gender and parental status impact the odds that an employer will call back an applicant. Based on the 5–8 percent callback rate found in an audit study of race in hiring (Bertrand and Mullainathan 2003), and to ensure that we had sufficient statistical power to evaluate the effect of parental status, we submitted 1,276 resumes and cover letters to 638 employers.

Results

The results suggest that real employers do discriminate against mothers (see Table 42.6). Childless women received 2.1 times as many callbacks as equally qualified mothers. This finding is similar to the laboratory experiment (see Table 42.1) in which childless women were recommended for hire 1.8 times more frequently than mothers. In the laboratory study, fathers were recommended for hire at a slightly *higher* rate, although the difference was only marginally significant; in the audit study, fa-

Table 42.7 Estimated Binary Logistic Regression Coefficients for the Effects of Parental Status and Gender on the Odds of Receiving a Callback (Robust Standard Errors in Parentheses, Clustered by Job)

Independent Variables	Callback?
Parent	0.598
	(.433)
Female applicant	0.887**
	(.407)
Motherhood interaction^	-1.38**
	(.590)
Intercept	-3.54***
	(.338)

^ Parent * Female applicant
* p<.1
** p<.05
*** p<.001
Notes: Mothers and childless women applied to the same 320 jobs; fathers and childless men applied to the same 318 jobs, for a total of 1276 applications to 638 jobs.

thers were called back at a higher rate, although the difference was not significant.

We now consider a multivariate model for the effects of parental status, applicant gender, and the interaction of parental status and applicant gender on the odds that an applicant receives a callback from an employer. Table 42.7 shows the motherhood penalty interaction is significant and negative, while the main effect for parental status is insignificant, and the main effect for the female applicant variable is significant and positive. The significant negative motherhood penalty interaction term indicates that being a parent lowers the odds that a woman, but not a man, will receive a callback from employers. In sum, the audit data show that, compared with their equally qualified childless counterparts, mothers are disadvantaged when actual employers make hiring decisions.

Strengths and Limitations

While the audit study evaluates whether actual employers discriminate against mothers in the hiring process, it does not give us insight into the mechanism underlying discrimination, because it was not possible to collect employers' rankings of commitment, competence, performance standards, and other relevant variables. These limits mean that while the audit study establishes that actual employers discriminate against mothers, it cannot establish why.

By considering the results of these two companion studies simultaneously, however, we find support for the status-based discrimination mechanism using the laboratory data and see real world implications of the argument with data generated from the audit study. Further, these results are consistent with qualitative work showing that employers discriminate against mothers (Blair-Loy 2003; Crittenden 2001; Kennelly 1999) and with survey research that consistently finds a wage penalty for motherhood (Budig and England 2001; Anderson, Binder, and Krause 2003). Thus, across a wide range of methodological approaches—each of which has its unique strengths and weaknesses—we find evidence that mothers experience disadvantages in workplace settings and that discrimination plays a role in producing these disadvantages.

Summary and Conclusions

This project makes two main contributions. First, it isolates and experimentally evaluates a status-based discrimination mechanism that explains some of the disadvantages mothers experience in the paid labor market. Second, it shows that real employers discriminate against mothers.

The results of this study have implications for understanding some of the enduring patterns of gender inequality in paid work. Studies have documented the motherhood penalty in at least 15 countries (Harkness and Waldfogel 1999; Misra, Budig, and Moller 2005) and shown its stability over time (Avellar and Smock 2003). This study offers a partial explanation for the mechanism behind a widespread, durable phenomenon with implications for a broad segment of the population.

More generally, a gender gap in wages has persisted despite the vast movement of women into paid labor in the United States since the early 1970s, and employed mothers account for most of this gap (Glass 2004). This study suggests that cultural beliefs about the tension between the motherhood and "ideal worker" roles may play a part in reproducing this pattern of inequality. A second enduring pattern of gender inequality is the so-called "glass ceiling," a metaphor for the barriers that restrict women's movement up the career ladder to the highest positions in organizations and firms. To the extent that employers view mothers as less committed to their jobs and less "promotable," the glass ceiling women face could be, in part, a motherhood ceiling.

Writing for the National Center for Policy Analysis, Denise Venable (2002) reports that among people ages 27 to 33 who have never had children, women's earnings approach 98 percent of men's. She concludes, "When women behave in the workplace as men do, the wage gap between them is small." Claims of unequal pay, she continues, "almost always involve comparing apples and oranges." However, since most employed men and employed women have children at some point in their lives, the most illustrative "within fruit" comparison is not the comparison of childless men to childless women, but the comparison of men with children to women with children. As the two studies reported here show, when women "behave as men do," by giving evidence of being a parent, they are discriminated against, while their male counterparts are often advantaged. Far from being an "apples to oranges" comparison, the male and female applicants who were evaluated in these studies were exactly equal by experimental design. That parental status disadvantaged only female applicants is strong evidence of discrimination.

REFERENCES

Acker, Joan. 1990. "Hierarchies, jobs, and bodies: a theory of gendered organizations." *Gender & Society* 4: 139–158.

Anderson, Deborah J., Melissa Binder, and Kate Krause. 2003. "The motherhood wage penalty revisited: Experience, heterogeneity, work effort and work-schedule flexibility." *Industrial and Labor Relations Review* 56: 273–294.

Avellar, Sarah, and Pamela Smock. 2003. "Has the price of motherhood declined over time? A cross-cohort comparison of the motherhood wage penalty." *Journal of Marriage and the Family* 65: 597–607.

Berger, Joseph, Hamit Fisek, Robert Norman, and Morris Zelditch, Jr. 1977. *Status Characteristics and Social Interaction.* New York: Elsevier.

Bertrand, Marianne, and Sendhil Mullainathan. 2003. "Are Emily and Greg more employable than Lakisha and Jamal? A field experiment on labor market discrimination." *National Bureau of Economic Research Working Paper Series,* Working Paper no. 9873. Retrieved September 2003. (http://www.nber.org/papers/w9873).

Bielby, Denise D., and William T. Bielby. 1984. "Work commitment, sex-role attitudes, and women's employment." *American Sociological Review* 49: 234–247.

Blair-Loy, Mary. 2003. *Competing Devotions: Career and Family Among Women Executives.* Cambridge, MA: Harvard University Press.

Budig, Michelle, and Paula England. 2001. "The wage penalty for motherhood." *American Sociological Review* 66: 204–225.

Cleveland, Jeanette N. 1991. "Using hypothetical and actual applicants in assessing person-organization fit: A methodological note." *Journal of Applied Social Psychology* 21: 1004–1011.

Cleveland, Jeanette N., and Andrew H. Berman. 1987. "Age perceptions of jobs: Agreement between samples of students and managers." *Psychological Reports* 61: 565–566.

Correll, Shelley J., and Stephen Benard. 2006. "Biased estimators? Comparing status and statistical theories of gender discrimination." Pp. 89–116 in *Social Psychology of the Workplace (Advances in Group Process Volume 23)*, edited by Shane R. Thye and Edward J. Lawler. New York: Elsevier.

Corse, Sara J. 1990. "Pregnant managers and their subordinates: The effects of gender expectations on hierarchical relationships." *Journal of Applied Behavioral Science* 26: 25–48.

Crittenden, Ann. 2001. *The Price of Motherhood: Why the Most Important Job in the World Is Still the Least Valued.* New York: Metropolitan Books.

Cuddy, Amy J. C., Susan T. Fiske, and Peter Glick. 2004. "When professionals become mothers, warmth doesn't cut the ice." *Journal of Social Issues* 60: 701–718.

Foschi, Martha. 1989. "Status characteristics, standards and attributions." Pp. 58–72 in *Sociological Theories in Progress: New Formulations*, edited by Joseph Berger, Morris Zelditch, Jr., and Bo Anderson. Boston: Houghton Mifflin.

Glass, Jennifer. 2004. "Blessing or curse? Work-family policies and mother's wage growth over time." *Work and Occupations* 31: 367–394.

Halpert, Jane A., Midge L. Wilson, and Julia Hickman. 1993. "Pregnancy as a source of bias in performance appraisals." *Journal of Organizational Behavior* 14: 649–663.

Harkness, Susan, and Jane Waldfogel. 1999. "The family gap in pay: Evidence from seven industrialised countries." CASE paper 29: Centre for Analysis of Social Exclusion.

Hays, Sharon. 1996. *The Cultural Contradictions of Motherhood.* New Haven, CT: Yale University Press.

Kennelly, Ivy. 1999. "That single mother element: How white employers typify black women." *Gender & Society* 13: 168–192.

Misra, Joya, Michelle Budig, and Stephanie Moller. 2005. "Employment, wages, and poverty: Reconciliation policies and gender equity." Paper presented at the Annual Meeting of the American Sociological Association, Philadelphia, PA.

Olian, Judy D., and Donald P. Schwab. 1988. "The impact of applicant gender compared to qualifications on hiring recommendations: A meta-analysis of experimental studies." *Organizational Behavior and Human Decision Processes* 41: 180–195.

Ridgeway, Cecilia, and Shelley J. Correll. 2004. "Motherhood as a status characteristic." *Journal of Social Issues* 60: 683–700.

Townsend, Nicholas W. 2002. *The Package Deal: Marriage, Work and Fatherhood in Men's Lives.* Philadelphia, PA: Temple University Press.

Venable, Denise. 2002. "The wage gap myth." National Center for Policy Analysis, April 12, 2002, Brief Analysis no. 392. Retrieved December 12, 2004. (http://www.ncpa.org/pub/ba/ba392/).

Waldfogel, Jane. 1997. "The effect of children on women's wages." *American Sociological Review* 62: 209–217.

Williams, Joan. 2001. *Unbending Gender: Why Work and Family Conflict and What to Do About It.* Oxford: Oxford University Press.

43

Rethinking Employment Discrimination and Its Remedies

BARBARA F. RESKIN

The paradigmatic definition of discrimination is the differential treatment of persons because of status characteristics that are functionally irrelevant to the outcome in question (Merton 1972; see also Allport 1954, 51). Implicit in this definition is the proposition that individuals discriminate because of their negative feelings (antipathy, distaste, fear) toward or negative beliefs (social stereotypes) about members of a status group (Allport 1954, 14; Becker 1957). Media accounts of whites' hostility toward blacks prior to and during the civil rights movement lent face validity to an antipathy-based theory of discrimination. Although the success of the civil rights movement depended partly on its ability to expose the antagonism that many whites harbored toward blacks, it simultaneously reinforced the theory that discrimination resulted from the deliberate efforts of individual whites to harm blacks because of their hostility to them.

In emphasizing differential treatment *based on* or *because of* an irrelevant charac-teristic, social scientists construed discrimination as *intentional* behavior. So too did the major antidiscrimination law, Title VII of the 1964 Civil Rights Act. Although the statute did not explicitly define discrimination, it conceptualized it as an intended and consciously motivated act (Stryker 2001, 18). Thus, the law operationalized illegal employment discrimination as intentional.

Economists have theorized that employers may also intentionally discriminate against individuals on the rational rather than emotional ground that they belong to a race or sex thought to be less productive or more costly to employ, or that they will otherwise adversely affect business because of customers' or coworkers' prejudices (Phelps 1972; Bergmann and Darity 1981). Economists term this intentional, non-animus-based discrimination "statistical discrimination." The Equal Employment Opportunity Commission (EEOC) and the Supreme Court (*Los Angeles Department of Water and Power v. Manhart* 1978; 435 U.S. 702)—the federal agencies charged with enforcing and inter-

Barbara F. Reskin, "Rethinking Employment Discrimination and Its Remedies," in *The New Economic Sociology: Developments in an Emerging Field*, edited by Mauro F. Guillén, Randall Collins, Paula England, and Marshall Meyer, pp. 218–230, 232–233, 237, 239–244. Copyright © 2002 by the Russell Sage Foundation. Reprinted with permission.

preting Title VII—have interpreted the law as prohibiting intentional, non-animus-based discrimination, including statistical (stereotype-based) discrimination. The law prohibits employers from *deliberately* using race and sex in personnel decisions, regardless of their motive (except to redress egregious discrimination of the past; see Reskin 1998). Thus, the major U.S. antidiscrimination law bans individuals—whether acting on their own behalf or as agents of their employer—from intentionally discriminating regardless of whether their motives derive from negative sentiments toward a group or from concerns about the economic ramifications of employing members of that group.

There is ample evidence that individuals continue to engage in intentional acts that conform to the paradigmatic definition of discrimination (Kirschenman and Neckerman 1991; Kasinitz and Rosenberg 1996; Browne and Kennelly 1999; U.S. Equal Employment Opportunity Commission 2001a–g). However, both the paradigmatic theory of intentional disparate treatment and the theory of statistical discrimination ignore another important source of employment discrimination: automatic, nonconscious cognitive processes.[1] In this chapter, I review research that implies that employment decisions are routinely biased as a result of normal cognitive processes. If nonconscious cognitive processes—unless checked by employment structures—regularly contribute to discrimination, our theoretical approach to discrimination needs to be modified.

In the years since the animus theory of discrimination gained paradigmatic status, social cognition researchers have established that automatic cognitive processes give rise to cognitive errors whose results are likely to be discriminatory. Largely outside individ-

ual control, these processes are marked by a cognitive efficiency that makes them generally adaptive. Because of their automaticity, neither intention nor antipathy is a necessary condition for discriminatory outcomes. The role of automatic cognitive processes in discrimination means that we also cannot continue to view discrimination as anomalous acts by a few biased individuals within an otherwise fair system of employment opportunities (Black 1989). Instead, we must recognize that discriminatory outcomes—many of them involving micro acts of discrimination—are pervasive, permitting members of favored groups to accumulate advantages while members of disfavored groups accumulate disadvantages.

Social Cognitive Processes and Employment Discrimination

Categorization

The core cognitive process that links gender and race to workplace outcomes is categorization. We automatically categorize the people we encounter into ingroups and outgroups, into "we" and "they" (Rothbart and Lewis 1994; Brewer and Brown 1998). In 1908 Georg Simmel wrote that we necessarily think of others in terms of general categories (1971 [1908], 10–12). Almost half a century later Gordon Allport (1954, 19) echoed this insight, asserting that "the human mind must think with the aid of categories." Recent research supports these claims: we understand the social world in terms of categorical distinctions and readily categorize others into ingroups and outgroups, on the basis of both highly visible as well as arbitrary and trivial characteristics (Brewer 1997, 200; Brewer and Brown 1998, 566; Fiske 1998, 364, 375).

A critical concomitant of categorization is the generalization of similarity and difference. Having categorized others on trait A, we infer both that ingroup members resemble us and that outgroup members differ from us on traits B, C, D, and so on. As a result, we systematically underestimate within-group differences and exaggerate between-group differences on a variety of characteristics (Brown 1995, 78). Categorization also affects how and how quickly we encode and recall information about others, thereby (unbeknownst to us) distorting our perceptions and shaping our preferences (Perdue et al. 1990).

It is important to note that we automatically prefer ingroup members to outgroup members. We are more comfortable with them, feel more obligated and loyal to them, impute to them positive attributes, trust them, remember their positive traits while forgetting their negative ones, are predisposed to cooperate with them, and favor them when distributing rewards (Perdue et al. 1990; Baron and Pfeffer 1994; Rothbart and Lewis 1994, 369; Brown 1995; Brewer 1997, 201; Brewer and Brown 1998, 567; Fiske 1998, 361).

Although we tend to distrust and depersonalize outgroup members and see them as competitors (Brewer 1997, 201), laboratory research indicates that we apparently do not automatically see them in negative ways (Perdue et al. 1990, 482) or discriminate against them when allocating negative outcomes (Brewer and Brown 1998, 559). Together, this body of research suggests that automatic categorization gives rise to discrimination primarily through pervasive ingroup favoritism rather than pervasive outgroup antipathy.

Automatic categorization is not inevitably group-serving. We categorize others into ingroups and outgroups largely independently of our conscious feelings toward the groups or our desire to protect our own status (Fiske 1998, 364). Nonetheless, ingroup preferences reinforce dominant groups' privileges. For example, group status affects whether people infer "illusory correlations" between positive traits and group membership. Members of high-status ingroups show more ingroup favoritism than do members of low-status ingroups (Brewer and Brown 1998, 570). Also, ingroup attachment is especially strong among people who think that group membership affects their opportunities or risks, both among competing groups and among ingroups in a numerical minority (Weber 1994).

Group membership is often based on ascribed characteristics. Ingroup favoritism cannot operate unless we can readily distinguish who is "us" and who is "them" (Brewer 1997, 205). Given its cultural salience and socially exaggerated visibility, we habitually use sex in assigning others to ingroups or outgroups (Brewer and Brown 1998). Because sex and race are strongly correlated with control over workplace opportunities, with white men monopolizing these roles, ingroup preference favors whites, men, and especially white men. Thus, ingroup favoritism produces status-group discrimination.

In sum, concomitant to our automatic sorting of people into categories are automatic biases in our feelings toward others based on whether we see them as "us" or "them." The effects of such biases are discriminatory, although they are neither intended nor even known to us as we perpetrate them (Fiske 1998, 362). In addition, they apparently operate more through our automatic inclination to favor others like ourselves than to deprive or punish those who differ (Brewer and Brown 1998; DiTomaso 2000).

Stereotyping

Categorization leads to a second automatic cognitive process with potentially discriminatory effects: stereotyping. Stereotyping is an inferential process in which we attribute traits that we habitually associate with a group to individuals who belong to that group. Although *conscious* stereotypes can culminate in intentional statistical discrimination (see, for example, Wilson 1996, ch. 5; Moss and Tilly 1996, 264), here I address the *unintentional* discriminatory effects of *nonconscious* stereotypes. Almost invariably, noticing that a "target" belongs to a stereotyped group automatically brings to mind characteristics that are stereotypically linked to that group, even when we consciously reject those stereotypes as false (Bodenhausen, Macrae, and Garst 1998, 316). In fact, we automatically pursue, prefer, and remember "evidence" that supports our stereotypes (including untrue "evidence") and ignore, discount, and forget facts that challenge them. Stereotypes have been described as "hypotheses in search of evidence" (Brown 1995) because we are predisposed toward behavioral interpretations that conform to our stereotypes, blind to stereotype-inconsistent interpretations, and cognitively better able to find stereotype-consistent than -inconsistent evidence (Fiske 1998, 367). This selectivity means that our nonconscious stereotypes include a confirmatory bias (Brown 1995).

Given our cognitive capacity to override evidence with stereotypes, it stands to reason that we invoke stereotypes when we lack complete information about others. For example, given the stereotype of blacks as lazy (Bobo 2001), an employer who is choosing between a black applicant and a white applicant and

has limited information about the black is likely to assume automatically that the black applicant is lazy. Stereotypes also distort our recollections of others. We more readily remember stereotypical than nonstereotypical descriptions—an attractive flight attendant, for example, is more memorable than an unattractive flight attendant (Brown 1995, 96). As discussed later, stereotypes also bias the attributions we automatically construct for others' behavior; these attribution errors in turn distort our assessments of others and our expectations of their future behavior.

Automatic stereotypes often prevail even when we are consciously motivated not to stereotype. For instance, experimental subjects asked to judge the heights of women and men from photographs routinely underestimated women's height relative to same-height men, although they had been instructed to judge each photograph as an individual and they knew that accurate judgments could yield a substantial payoff (Brown 1995, 92). Subjects in another study who were instructed to suppress their stereotypes were able to do so, but in a subsequent task they expressed stronger stereotypes than members of a control group who had not been told to avoid stereotyping (Bodenhausen et al. 1998, 326).

Automatic stereotyping is tenacious because it is cognitively efficient (Fiske 1998, 366; Fiske, Lin, and Neuberg 1999, 237, 244). We can process information that supports our stereotypes more quickly than inconsistent information. Time pressure, information overload, mental busyness, and pressure to make a decision—conditions that characterize the work lives of many decisionmakers—increase our likelihood of stereotyping and exacerbate the effects of stereotypes on judgment and memory, presumably because these situations require cognitive efficiency (Bodenhausen et al. 1998: 319; Fiske 1998, 389; Goodwin, Operario, and Fiske 1998, 694). For example, subjects in a sentence-completion task could refrain from making sexist statements when they had ample time; given time limits, however, their statements were more sexist than those of members of a control group (Bodenhausen et al. 1998, 326).

Any attribute that is stereotypically linked to a status characteristic can activate (or "prime") group stereotypes (Heilman 1995; Fiske 1998, 366). For example, research subjects who were subliminally exposed to the words "black" and "white" were more likely to link negative traits to blacks and positive traits to whites than those who were not subliminally exposed (Dovidio et al. 1997), and men who were primed with stereotypic statements about women were more likely to ask a female job applicant sexist questions than were nonprimed men, and they took longer to recognize nonsexist words (Fiske et al. 1999). These findings imply that an idle remark can activate sex or race stereotypes that in turn affect how decision-makers assess job or promotion candidates or other workers (Heilman 1995). Importantly, by priming race or sex stereotypes, diversity training may actually foster distorted impressions and differential treatment based on sex or race.

Status affects the propensity to automatic stereotyping. Subordinates are less likely to stereotype members of dominant groups than the reverse, presumably because they need to make accurate assessments of the people who control their work environment and rewards (Fiske et al. 1999, 241). In addition, dominant-group members appear to have greater confidence in their stereotyped assessments than do members of subordinate groups, probably both be-cause their dominant-group status gives them confidence *and* because being wrong is less likely to have negative consequences.

In sum, social cognition research suggests that unconscious sex and race stereotyping can lead to discrimination by distorting our impressions of individuals based on group membership. This occurs, unless checked, when group-based stereotypes automatically are applied to individuals, replace missing information about individuals, distort what we recall of others' behavior, bias our attributions of others' success and failures, and influence our predictions of others' future behavior.

Attribution Error

How we expect others to perform affects the meaning we assign to their behavior. When people's performance conforms to our expectations, we attribute it to their stable, internal traits (for example, ability); when it contradicts our expectations, we attribute it to transient, external causes (for example, task difficulty or luck). Both ingroup versus outgroup membership and sex and race stereotypes influence our expectations about others' performance. We expect members of socially preferred groups to succeed and members of devalued groups to fail. Thus, we tend to chalk up successes by ingroup members and white men and failures by outgroup members, minorities, and white women to their stable predispositions, while we attribute failures by ingroup members and white men and successes by outgroup members, minorities, and white women to external (and hence, unstable) factors (Crocker, Major, and Steele 1998, 539). For example, we credit a man's talents for his success in a customarily male job, while we attribute a woman's success to situational factors, such as help from others. Importantly, we do not see successes or failures that we have attributed to external causes as predicting future success (Swim and Sanna 1996; Brewer and Brown 1998, 560).

Moreover, our brains tend to encode behavior that conforms to our expectations in terms of abstract traits (intelligence, honesty, laziness) and encode unexpected behavior in concrete terms (his car would not start; she took the class twice). Thus, we attribute an ingroup member losing his temper to provocation and the same behavior by an outgroup member to personality. Attributions in abstract terms are more likely than ones in concrete terms to affect our global evaluation of others as well as our predictions of their future performance, and they are more resistant to challenge by counterevidence. As a result, these cognitive propensities give ingroup members and persons from socially valued groups the benefit of the doubt, while preventing new data on outgroup members and persons in socially subordinate status groups from dispelling negative attributions.

Once again, while these propensities are universal, perceptions by members of majority groups are more prone to attribution error than those by minority-group members (Brown 1995, 101–2).

Micro-Macro Links

Automatic categorization, ingroup preference, and stereotyping are cognitively efficient for individuals. Their efficiency frees up cognitive resources for other purposes, making these propensities cognitively adaptive to individuals, especially those who are juggling multiple demands (Brown 1995, 95). Given what seems to be the near-impossibility of suppressing these cognitive propensities, the resulting biases are pervasive and predictable. Because they link employment outcomes to functionally irrelevant group membership, they are also discriminatory.

In addition, although many of the daily discriminatory events stemming from cognitive biases such as excluding someone from a project or denying them credit for a success may seem trivial (and certainly not legally actionable), over time members of preferred groups accumulate advantages and members of disparaged groups accumulate disadvantages. Eventually group differences emerge that appear to justify unequal career outcomes (Krieger 1995). Thus, unless employers implement structures to check the biasing effects of these microlevel processes, their long-term consequences create or exacerbate macrolevel disparities across race and sex groups in their economic and social fates.

In view of the automaticity of these cognitive processes, the proximate cause of employment discrimination becomes whether employers' personnel practices prevent or permit these cognitive propensities from linking workers' status characteristics to their employment outcomes (Bielby 2000; Reskin 2000). In the next section, I discuss employment structures and practices that can reduce their discriminatory impact.

Organizational Practices, Cognitive Biases, and Discriminatory Outcomes

Work organizations cannot stamp out our propensities to categorize others automatically or to treat ingroup members more favorably than outgroup members. As we have seen, attempts to repress stereotyping can backfire. But employment structures can curb the *biasing effects* of these cognitive processes, thus inhibiting the discrimination that would otherwise result (Fiske 1998,

375). The impact of audition practices on women's share of positions in major symphony orchestras illustrates my point. With the adoption in the 1970s and 1980s of blind auditions that physically screened the musician from the auditors, women's odds of being selected rose sharply (Goldin and Rouse 2000). Screens that concealed the sex of the candidates circumvented intentional discrimination and obviated the discriminatory consequences of nonconscious sex stereotyping and ingroup favoritism. Social cognition and organizational research points to employment practices or structures that can arrest—or activate—the biasing effects of cognitive processes. Based on that scholarship, this section proposes organizational practices that mitigate the biasing effects of automatic cognitive processes.

Organizational Practices and Categorization

The automaticity of ingroup preference probably plays an important role in producing disparate employment outcomes for different race or sex groups. One way to minimize its discriminatory effects is to dissociate ingroup membership from ascribed statuses. As Marilynn Brewer (1997, 205) observes, a precursor of ingroup favoritism is the identification of who is "us" and who is "them." Employers can take advantage of this fact by discouraging ingroups based on race or sex through *decategorization* and *recategorization*.

Decategorization conveys individuating information about workers to decisionmakers (which in turn reduces stereotyping). Recategorization recognizes that people have many characteristics that compete to serve as the basis of categorization. According to Galen Bodenhausen and her colleagues (1998, 316), "the stereotypes associated with the category that 'wins' the competition" are activated, while we suppress the "losing" stereotype. Consider, for example, an experiment in which exposure to a photograph of a Chinese woman activated subjects' stereotypes about women, while inhibiting their stereotypes about Asians, but exposure to a picture of the same woman eating noodles with chopsticks triggered stereotypes about Asians, while suppressing stereotypes about women (Bodenhausen et al. 1998, 317). In general, recategorization exploits people's readiness to categorize others on the most trivial criteria by encouraging the categorization of workers on characteristics that are independent of their sex and race (Brewer and Brown 1998, 583). Employers can encourage recategorization based on work-related functions, for example. Function-based categories such as teams, projects, and divisions are cognitively available and exploitable by employers through work-group culture and structured competition. Firms can also emphasize recategorization to a "superordinate category" such as an officer of the law or a UPS employee (Brewer 1997, 202). . . .

Organizational Practices and Stereotyping

Although the propensity to automatic stereotyping is universal, whether we stereotype others varies, and whether our stereotypes give rise to biased cognitions depends on several factors, such as the type and quality of information that is available to decisionmakers about "targets"; whether the decisionmaking process highlights status-group membership and hence primes stereotyping; decisionmakers' awareness of potential biases and their motivation to perceive others accurately; and whether decisionmakers have the cognitive resources to consciously minimize stereotype-based distortions (Bodenhausen et al. 1998, 330).

Making available accurate individuating information about persons from negatively stereotyped groups can prevent stereotyping. (But feeling informed in the absence of objective information may promote stereotyping; see Fiske 1998, 387.) When we lack information that we need to make employment decisions, our descriptive stereotypes automatically provide it. Because stereotypes about socially devalued groups tend to be negative and those about socially favored groups to be positive, the effect is usually discriminatory. In addition, because multiple bases for categorizing a person compete for activation, providing relevant information (Is the applicant a college graduate? An experienced manager?) about members of stereotyped groups can prevent their being stereotyped by sex, race, and other ascribed characteristics (Bodenhausen et al. 1998, 316). Thus, employment practices that increase the amount of unambiguous, relevant information available to decisionmakers may suppress stereotyping (Heilman 1995, 12). By compiling and disseminating to decisionmakers standardized information for all candidates on all the criteria relevant to a personnel decision, organizations can reduce stereotyping. . . .

Decisionmakers' Discretion

Discretion is an important perquisite for managers. It not only permits autonomy but allows decisionmakers to control the amount of effort they must expend. Although organizational members tend to assume that managers' decisions are rational (Baron 1984, 56), discretion invites unconscious and conscious biases to influence their decisions, thus spawning discriminatory treatment. Employment decisions that are based on unstructured observations are especially vulnerable to cognitive biases (Fiske et al. 1991). The key to preventing such automatic biases from giving rise to unintended micro acts of discrimination lies in curbing decisionmakers' discretion by requiring specific procedures for distributing opportunities. . . .

Conclusion

In keeping with the paradigmatic conception of discrimination as conscious invidious treatment motivated by antipathy, Congress outlawed intentional discrimination in Title VII of the 1964 Civil Rights Act. Although the enforcement of Title VII has reduced employment discrimination (Burstein 1989; Burstein and Edwards 1994), decades after the enactment of Title VII the careers of thousands of Americans continue to be stunted by employment discrimination (Blumrosen et al. 1998; Reskin 2001). Discrimination persists partly because antidiscrimination remedies misconstrue discrimination as based in antipathy toward a group. Despite the applicability of the paradigmatic construction of discrimination in many instances, that construction ignores an even more important reason individuals' sex and race are routinely and illegitimately linked to employment rewards: automatic nonconscious cognitive processes that distort our perceptions and treatment of others.

Categorization, ingroup preference, stereotyping, attribution error—all part of the normal information processing that occurs largely outside our conscious control—bias our perceptions, evaluations, and treatment of people because of their sex, color, accent, and other discernible characteristics that signal membership in more or less valued groups. They engender biases because we automatically categorize others into ingroups and outgroups—often based on these same characteristics. Moreover, we prefer ingroup members to outgroup members, evaluate them more favorably, treat as factual impressions that are based on stereotypes, and make erroneous inferences about the successes or failures of ingroup and outgroup members.

These cognitive biases occur during interpersonal relations, and interpersonal relations are an intrinsic part of most jobs. Thus, ordinary, everyday cross-sex and cross-race interactions elicit automatic ingroup favoritism, stereotyping, and attribution biases. These cognitive distortions lead on a daily basis to micro acts of discrimination: omitting a qualified but female inside candidate from the short list for a top position because no one thinks of her; not recognizing the contribution that a Japanese woman makes to a project; assuming that women do not want challenging assignments; not inviting a black man to a meeting of his specialty group; being confused about which black worker made a suggestion; giving a white male a tip on a job opening (Cose 1993; Fiske 1998, 371–72; Catalyst 1999; Barrett 1999; DiTomaso 2000; Reskin and McBrier 2000, 224; Sturm 2001, 113, 136).

At the individual level, these "countless small acts by a changing cast of characters . . . *incrementally* and consistently limit the employment prospects of one group of workers compared with those of another" (Nelson and Bridges 1999, 241–43, emphasis added; see also Feagin 2000, 139; Sturm 2001, 113). As a result, workers who regularly benefit from ingroup preference accumulate advantages, and members of disparaged groups who suffer the negative discriminatory effects of cognitive biases accumulate disadvantages. Over time, career disparities between sex- and race-based groups also accumulate. In the aggregate, the unchecked consequences of automatic cognitive biases help to preserve job segregation, promotion differences, and earnings disparities by race and sex. That they result from nonconscious cognitive processes rather than conscious antipathy does not mitigate their impact or reduce the need for more effective policy remedies. The results are the same.

NOTE

1. According to Shiffrin and Schneider (1977), automatic cognitive processes are those that are not effortful, intentional, or consciously controlled.

REFERENCES

Allport, Gordon W. 1954. *The Nature of Prejudice.* Reading, Mass.: Addison-Wesley.

Baron, James N. 1984. "Organizational Perspectives on Stratification." *Annual Review of Sociology* 10: 37–69.

Baron, James N., and Jeffrey Pfeffer. 1994. "The Social Psychology of Organizations and Inequality." *Social Psychology Quarterly* 57: 190–209.

Barrett, Paul M. 1999. *The Good Black: A True Story of Race in America.* New York: Dutton.

Becker, Gary. 1957. *The Economics of Discrimination.* Chicago: University of Chicago Press.

Bergmann, Barbara R., and William Darity Jr. 1981. "Social Relations, Productivity, and Employer Discrimination." *Monthly Labor Review* 104(April): 47–49.

Bielby, William T. 2000. "Minimizing Workplace Gender and Racial Bias." *Contemporary Sociology* 29(1): 120–29.

Black, Donald. 1989. *Sociological Justice.* New York: Oxford University Press.

Blumrosen, Alfred W., Mark Bendick, J. J. Miller, and Ruth G. Blumrosen. 1998. "Employment Discrimination Against Women in Washington State, 1997." Employment Discrimination Project Report 3. Newark, N.J.: Rutgers University School of Law.

Bobo, Lawrence D. 2001. "Racial Attitudes and Relations at the Close of the Twentieth Century." In *America Becoming: Racial Trends and Their Consequences,* vol. 1, edited by Neil J. Smelser, William J. Wilson, and Faith N. Mitchell. Washington: National Academy Press.

Bodenhausen, Galen V., C. Neil Macrae, and Jennifer Garst. 1998. "Stereotypes in Thought and Deed: Social Cognitive Origins of Intergroup Discrimination." In *Intergroup Cognition and Intergroup Behaviors*, edited by Constantine Sedikides, John Schopler, and Chester A. Insko. Mahwah, N.J.: Erlbaum.

Brewer, Marilynn B. 1997. "The Social Psychology of Intergroup Relations: Can Research Inform Practice?" *Journal of Social Issues* 53(1): 197–211.

Brewer, Marilynn B., and Rupert J. Brown. 1998. "Intergroup Relations." In *Handbook of Social Psychology*, edited by Daniel T. Gilbert, Susan T. Fiske, and Gardner Lindzey. New York: McGraw-Hill.

Brown, Rupert. 1995. *Prejudice*. Oxford: Blackwell.

Browne, Irene, and Ivy Kennelly. 1999. "Stereotypes and Realities: Images of Black Women in the Labor Market." In *Latinas and African American Women at Work*, edited by Irene Browne. New York: Russell Sage Foundation.

Burstein, Paul. 1989. "Attacking Sex Discrimination in the Labor Market: A Study in Law and Politics." *Social Forces* 67: 641–65.

Burstein, Paul, and Mark E. Edwards. 1994. "The Impact of Employment Discrimination Litigation on Racial Disparity in Earnings: Evidence and Unresolved Issues." *Law and Society Review* 28: 79–111.

Catalyst. 1999. "Women of Color Report a 'Concrete Ceiling' Barring Their Advancement in Corporate America." *Catalyst Press Room,* July 13. Available at: www.catalystwomen.org/press/mediakit/release071399woc.html (May 20, 2001).

Cose, Ellis. 1993. *Rage of the Privileged Class.* New York: HarperCollins.

Crocker, Jennifer, Brenda Major, and Claude Steele. 1998. "Social Stigma." In *Handbook of Social Psychology*, edited by Daniel T. Gilbert, Susan T. Fiske, and Gardner Lindzey. New York: McGraw-Hill.

DiTomaso, Nancy. 2000. "Why Antidiscrimination Policies Are Not Enough: The Legacies and Consequences of Affirmative Inclusion—for Whites." Rutgers University, Newark. Unpublished manuscript.

Dovidio, John F., Kerry Kawakami, Craig Johnson, Brenda Johnson, and Adaiah Howard. 1997. "On the Nature of Prejudice: Automatic and Controlled Processes." *Journal of Experimental Social Psychology* 33: 510–40.

Feagin, Joe R. 2000. *Racist America: Roots, Current Realities, and Future Reparations.* New York: Routledge.

Fiske, Susan T. 1998. "Stereotyping, Prejudice, and Discrimination." In *Handbook of Social Psychology*, edited by Daniel T. Gilbert, Susan T. Fiske, and Gardner Lindzey. New York: McGraw-Hill.

Fiske, Susan T., Donald N. Bersoff, Eugene Borgida, Kay Deaux, and Madeline E. Heilman. 1991. "Social Science Research on Trial: Use of Sex Stereotyping Research in *Price Waterhouse v. Hopkins.*" *American Psychologist* 46: 1049–60.

Fiske, Susan T., Monica Lin, and Steven L. Neuberg. 1999. "The Continuum Model: Ten Years Later." In *Dual Process Theories in Social Psychology*, edited by Shelly Chaiken and Yaacov Trope. New York: Guilford Press.

Goldin, Claudia, and Cecilia Rouse. 2000. "Orchestrating Impartiality: The Impact of 'Blind' Auditions on Female Musicians." *American Economic Review* 90: 715–41.

Goodwin, Stephanie A., Don Operario, and Susan T. Fiske. 1998. "Situational Power and Interpersonal Dominance Facilitate Bias and Inequality." *Journal of Social Issues* 54: 677–98.

Heilman, Madeline E. 1995. "Sex Stereotypes and Their Effects in the Workplace: What We Know and What We Don't Know." *Journal of Social Issues* 10: 3–26.

Kasinitz, Philip S., and Jan Rosenberg. 1996. "Missing the Connection: Social Isolation and Employment on the Brooklyn Waterfront." *Social Problems* 43: 180–96.

Kirschenman, Joleen, and Kathryn M. Neckerman. 1991. "'We'd Love to Hire Them But . . .': The Meaning of Race for Employers." In *The Urban Underclass*, edited by Christopher Jencks and Paul Peterson. Washington, D.C.: Brookings Institution.

Krieger, Laura H. 1995. "The Contents of Our Categories: A Cognitive Bias Approach to

Discrimination and Equal Employment Opportunity." *Stanford Law Review* 47: 1161–1248.

Merton, Robert K. 1972. "Insiders and Outsiders." *American Journal of Sociology* 78: 9–47.

Moss, Philip, and Chris Tilly. 1996. "Soft Skills and Race: An Investigation of Black Men's Employment Problems." *Work and Occupations* 23: 252–76.

Nelson, Robert L., and William S. Bridges. 1999. *Legalizing Gender Inequality.* New York: Oxford University Press.

Perdue, Charles, John F. Dovidio, Michael B. Gutman, and Richard B. Tyler. 1990. "Us and Them: Social Categorization and the Process of Intergroup Bias." *Journal of Personality and Social Psychology* 59: 475–86.

Phelps, Edmund S. 1972. "The Statistical Theory of Racism and Sexism." *American Economic Review* 62: 659–61.

Reskin, Barbara F. 1998. *The Realities of Affirmative Action.* Washington, D.C.: American Sociological Association.

———. 2000. "The Proximate Causes of Discrimination: Research Agenda for the Twenty-First Century." *Contemporary Sociology* 29: 319–29.

———. 2001. "Employment Discrimination and Its Remedies." In *Sourcebook on Labor Market Research: Evolving Structures and Processes,* edited by Ivar Berg and Arne Kalleberg. New York: Plenum.

Reskin, Barbara F., and Debra B. McBrier. 2000. "Why Not Ascription?: Organizations' Employment of Male and Female Managers." *American Sociological Review* 65: 210–33.

Rothbart, Myron, and Susan Lewis. 1994. "Cognitive Processes and Intergroup Relations: A Historical Perspective." In *Social Cognition: Impact on Social Psychology,* edited by Patricia G. Devine and David L. Hamilton. San Diego: Academic Press.

Simmel, Georg. 1971 [1908]. *On Individuality and Social Forms: Selected Writings.* Edited and with an introduction by Donald N. Levine. Chicago: University of Chicago Press.

Stryker, Robin. 2001. "Disparate Impact and the Quota Debates: Law, Labor Market Sociology, and Equal Employment Policies." *Sociological Quarterly* 42(1): 13–46.

Sturm, Susan. 2001. "Second Generation Employment Discrimination: A Structural Approach." *Columbia Law Review* 101(3): 101–207.

Swim, Janet K., and Lawrence J. Sanna. 1996. "He's Skilled, She's Lucky: A Meta-analysis of Observers' Attributions for Women's and Men's Successes and Failures." *Personality and Social Psychology Bulletin* 22: 507–19.

U.S. Equal Employment Opportunity Commission. 2001a. "EEOC and Private Plaintiffs Settle Harassment Suit for $485,000 Against Chicken Processing Plant." *EEOC Press Releases* (April 10). Available at: www.eeoc.gov/press/4-10-01.html (June 20, 2001).

———. 2001b. "EEOC Responds to Final Report of Mitsubishi Consent Decree Monitors." *EEOC Press Releases* (May 23). Available at: www.eeoc.gov/press/5-23-01.html (June 20, 2001).

———. 2001c. "EEOC Seeks to Join Nationwide Sex Discrimination Suit Against Rent-A-Center." *EEOC Press Releases* (March 12). Available at: www.eeoc.gov/press/3-1201.html (June 20, 2001).

———. 2001d. "EEOC Settles Bias Suit for $2.6 Million Against TWA." *EEOC Press Releases* (May 24). Available at: www.eeoc.gov/press/5-24-01.html (June 20, 2001).

———. 2001e. "EEOC Settles Racial Harassment Suit Against Georgia-Pacific Corporation." *EEOC Press Releases* (April 3). Available at: www.eeoc.gov/press/4-3-01.html (June 20, 2001).

———. 2001f. "EEOC Sues Two Indiana Employers for Race Harassment." *EEOC Press Releases* (May 22). Available at: www.eeoc.gov/press/5-22-01.html (June 20, 2001).

———. 2001g. "Joe's Stone Crab Liable for Intentional Discrimination Court Rules in Sex Bias Suit Brought by EEOC." *EEOC Press Releases* (March 28). Available at: www.eeoc.gov/press/3-28-01.html (June 20, 2001).

Weber, Joseph G. 1994. "The Nature of Ethnocentric Attribution Bias: Ingroup Protection or Enhancement?" *Journal of Experimental Social Psychology* 20: 177–94.

Wilson, William J. 1996. *When Work Disappears.* Chicago: University of Chicago Press.

44

Egalitarianism and Gender Inequality

MARIA CHARLES AND
DAVID B. GRUSKY

The rise of egalitarian values and associated egalitarian institutional reforms is a distinctive feature of modernity and postmodernity. This development, which dates at least to the Enlightenment, intensified throughout the twentieth century as formal legal rights were extended to previously excluded groups (e.g., women), wide-reaching institutional reforms were implemented to equalize life chances (e.g., bureaucratic personnel policies), and anti-egalitarian doctrines (e.g., racism) were challenged. These processes of equalization, dramatic though they are, obviously do not exhaust the story of modernity and postmodernity. As is well known, this story is replete with counterpoints at which the forces for egalitarianism have been resisted, sometimes violently (as with recurrences of eugenics and fascism) and sometimes in quieter but still profound ways (as in the persistence of residential segregation).

This chapter is about one of those quieter anti-egalitarian forces currently playing out in the domain of gender stratification. At first blush, the forces for equalization may appear to be straightforwardly triumphing in this domain, as evidenced by (a) the rapid diffusion of egalitarian views on gender roles, (b) the withering away of the long-standing gender gap in college attendance and graduation, and (c) the steady increase in rates of female labor force participation (see Figure 44.1). These developments, although spectacular and unprecedented, have nonetheless been coupled with equally spectacular forms of resistance to equalization, especially within the workplace. Most notably, women and men continue to work in very different occupations, with women crowding into a relatively small number of historically female occupations (e.g., teacher, secretary, nurse). If one sought, for example, to undo all sex segregation by reallocating women to less segregated occupations, a full 52 percent of the employed women in the United States would have to be shifted out of their current occupational categories (Jacobs 2003). This extreme sex segregation is typical of what prevails throughout the advanced industrial world. Because sex segregation is so

This is a commissioned chapter that draws heavily on material in a previous publication (Maria Charles and David B. Grusky, *Occupational Ghettos: The Worldwide Segregation of Women and Men.* Copyright © 2004 by the Board of Trustees of the Leland Stanford Junior University).

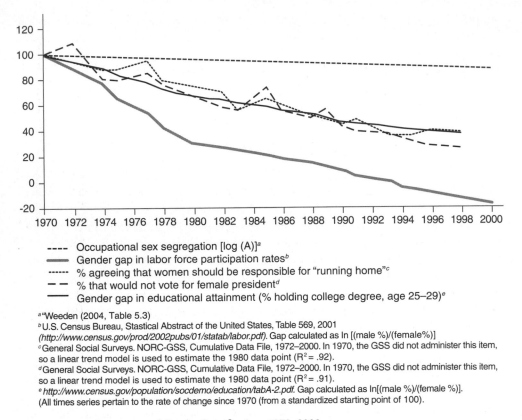

---- Occupational sex segregation [log (A)][a]
▬▬ Gender gap in labor force participation rates[b]
······ % agreeing that women should be responsible for "running home"[c]
– – % that would not vote for female president[d]
—— Gender gap in educational attainment (% holding college degree, age 25–29)[e]

[a]"Weeden (2004, Table 5.3)
[b]U.S. Census Bureau, Stastical Abstract of the United States, Table 569, 2001
(http://www.census.gov/prod/2002pubs/01/statab/labor.pdf). Gap calculated as ln [(male %)/(female%)]
[c]General Social Surveys. NORC-GSS, Cumulative Data File, 1972–2000. In 1970, the GSS did not administer this item,
so a linear trend model is used to estimate the 1980 data point ($R^2 = .92$).
[d]General Social Surveys. NORC-GSS, Cumulative Data File, 1972–2000. In 1970, the GSS did not administer this item,
so a linear trend model is used to estimate the 1980 data point ($R^2 = .91$).
[e] *http://www.census.gov/population/socdemo/education/tabA-2.pdf.* Gap calculated as ln[(male %)/(female %)].
(All times series pertain to the rate of change since 1970 (from a standardized starting point of 100).

Figure 44.1   Parameters of Gender Stratification, 1970–2000

extreme, and because it colors the life chances and life experiences of so many women and men, we characterize the contemporary occupational structure as "hypersegregated" (see Massey and Denton 1993 for a related usage).

Why is the occupational structure so resistant to egalitarian forces? It could be argued that fundamental institutional change is inevitably prolonged and that full integration will ultimately be achieved through ongoing reform efforts (Jackson 1998). Although we cannot rule out the possibility of full integration in the distant future, we would stress that this outcome is by no means inevitable under prevailing policies, practices, and commitments. That is, rather than viewing sex segregation as a residual that is destined to wither away under contemporary egalitarian pressures, it is best regarded as an organic feature of modern economies that is ideologically consistent with egalitarianism, at least as the latter is understood and practiced today. In this sense, there is a deep structure to sex segregation that makes it a viable long-term feature of modern economies, even as pressures for equalization mount in other domains of the social stratification system.

The foregoing interpretation is consistent with the relatively slow pace of integrative change, the failure of conventional egalitarian policy to reduce occupational segregation, and the long-term persistence of pockets of especially extreme segregation ("occupational ghettos"). We briefly review each of these pieces of supporting evidence in the following paragraphs.

Slow Pace of Change

The clearest evidence of resistance to egalitarian pressures emerges in comparing the rate of desegregative change with corresponding rates of change elsewhere in the gender stratification system. As indicated in Figure 44.1, the moderate declines in occupational sex segregation over the past thirty years stand in stark contrast to the more precipitous changes in (a) attitudes toward gender roles, (b) rates of female labor force participation, and (c) the gender gap in educational investments. These differences in the pacing of change suggest that the segregation regime has been shielded from the equalizing forces that have played out more dramatically in other domains.

The Failure of Egalitarianism

It is also instructive to ask whether countries that have committed most explicitly to family-friendly policies, antidiscrimination legislation, and other forms of egalitarianism have made substantial headway in reducing sex segregation. If they have, such progress suggests that conventional egalitarian commitments, at least when carried out to their logical extremes, can serve to more quickly root out residual segregative processes. The available evidence is largely disappointing on this front. For example, Sweden is well known for its egalitarian and family-friendly policies, yet it remains deeply sex segregated to the present day. Conversely, countries that are commonly viewed as bastions of conservative gender

practice, such as Japan and Italy, are *not* any more segregated than less conservative countries.

Unevenness of Change

There is, to be sure, clear and substantial evidence of desegregation in many sectors of the occupational structure, yet any careful observer of this process has to be struck by its unevenness and by the persistence, in particular, of many female occupational ghettos (e.g., secretary, nursery school teacher). Moreover, when male-dominated occupations embark on what appears to be integrative trajectories, the influx of women often continues well past the point of gender parity and ultimately creates a new female-dominated ghetto (e.g., Reskin and Roos 1990). These results suggest that sex segregation, far from being a holdover, is actively advanced by dynamics that are part and parcel of modern industrialism.

We therefore present the following puzzle: Why has sex segregation proven resistant to egalitarian pressures even as other forms of gender inequality have given way? Although we return to this puzzle repeatedly, it is important to recognize that it is but one part of a larger complex of perplexing findings that scholars of segregation have recently reported. The following two puzzles might, in particular, be cited: (a) the common view that male power and privilege allows men to dominate the best occupations fails to accord with the typical pattern of contemporary sex segregation; and (b) the highest levels of segregation are often found in socially and culturally progressive countries (such as Sweden) rather than in their more traditional counterparts (such as Japan). Taken together, these findings seem to suggest a topsy-turvy world in which males do not straightforwardly dominate the best jobs, family-friendly policies have a perverse segregating effect, and contemporary gender regimes continue to have a highly segregated "1950s feel" even in the twenty-first century.

We argue here that these empirical puzzles have emerged in the literature because stratification scholars tend to treat sex segregation in unidimensional terms and accordingly fail to appreciate that a complex amalgam of processes underlies gender inequality and renders some forms of segregation more entrenched than others. Although the tendency to represent segregation unidimensionally is widespread, it emerges especially clearly in classical theorizing about long-term trends in inequality. For example, structural-functional theorists typically treat all forms of "ascription," including sex segregation, as a generic residue destined to wither away either because discriminatory practices are inefficient or because bureaucratic forms of social organization have diffused widely and served to undermine discriminatory practices (e.g., Parsons 1970). In similar fashion, neoinstitutionalists assume that egalitarian practices and organizational forms will gradually diffuse and generate across-the-board reductions in segregation, although the main impetus for such diffusion is not so much the intrinsic efficiency of universalistic practices as the characteristically modern commitment to cultural *stories* about their efficiency (e.g., Meyer 2001). Finally, some early feminist scholars (e.g., Huber 1988) conceptualized occupational sex segregation as one of the main outcomes of "patriarchal" forms of social organization, again implying that the fate of sex segregation is simply a function of the larger fate of patriarchal social relations

that "create solidarity and interdependence among men and enable them to dominate women" (Hartmann 1981, p. 14). This approach typically treats both patriarchy and inequality in monolithic terms and thus draws scholars into weaving stories about the extent of segregation rather than its many dimensions and their different responsiveness to egalitarian forces.

These various theories share the prejudice that the explanandum of interest (segregation) may be represented in unidimensional terms, but they differ in their claims about the extent or pacing of change in this explanandum. If segregation is seen as persistent or ubiquitous, then reference is made to the strength and durability of patriarchal norms, institutions, or values (Chafetz 1988; Hartmann 1981; Ridgeway 1997; Williams 2000). If segregation is seen as relatively weak or declining in strength, this is attributed to (a) the gradual displacement of traditional gender roles and ideologies with universalistic values, (b) the diffusion of bureaucratic forms of organization, or (c) the discrimination-eroding discipline of the competitive market (Goode 1963; Ramirez 1987). These discrepant interpretations are typically evaluated by applying scalar measures of segregation that likewise presume unidimensionality (such as the index of dissimilarity). There is accordingly a close correspondence between classical unidimensional theorizing and the methodologies that have until now been adopted to describe and compare sex segregation.

We argue, then, that various puzzles have emerged in the literature because conventional theories and methods blind us to the multidimensional structure of segregation. By advancing a two-dimensional conceptualization of sex segregation and a matching methodological approach, we seek to solve

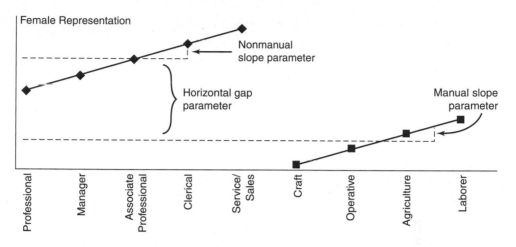

Note: In our models, the major occupational categories are coded in terms of a socioeconomic scale, thus allowing the intercategory distances to vary freely. For the purpose of simplifying the presentation, we have assumed here that intercategory distances are the same.

Figure 44.2   Anatomy of a Hypothetical Sex-Segregation Regime

the puzzles and build an alternative understanding of the development of segregation regimes.

A New Multidimensional Model

It is useful to begin by asking whether the underlying structure of sex segregation is consistent with unidimensional accounts of segregation. In many such accounts, it is simply presumed that the best occupations will be dominated by men, either because women have disproportionate domestic responsibilities that reduce their incentive to invest in demanding careers (e.g., Becker 1991), or because employers practice discrimination through "glass ceiling" personnel policies and other forms of male-biased queuing in the labor market (e.g., Reskin and Roos 1990).

This conventional account falls short because it fails to appreciate the distinction between vertical and horizontal forms of segregation and, in particular, the interac-

tion between these two forms (see Blackburn, Jarman, and Brooks 2000; Semyonov and Jones 1999). The model in Figure 44.2, which underlies all our analysis, builds explicitly on this distinction: the "nonmanual slope parameter" governs the extent to which men dominate the most desirable classes in the nonmanual sector; the "manual slope parameter" governs the extent to which men dominate the most desirable classes in the manual sector; and the "horizontal gap parameter" governs the extent to which men are disproportionately allocated into the manual sector rather than the nonmanual one.

The horizontal axis of this figure arrays the nine major occupational categories defined by the International Labour Office (ILO) on an approximate socioeconomic scale ranging from high (professional) to low (agricultural). Following convention, the first five categories in this list may be characterized as nonmanual, and the second four may be characterized as manual.

The vertical axis of this figure, labeled "female representation," indicates the extent to which women or men are overrepresented in each of these nine categories. In the interior of the figure, the slopes of the two lines reveal the strength of vertical segregation, with a steep positive slope indicating that men are much advantaged in the competition for desirable occupations, a moderate positive slope indicating that men are only weakly advantaged in this competition, and a negative slope (which is logically possible but empirically unlikely) indicating that women are advantaged. The extent of horizontal segregation (the "horizontal gap parameter") is given by the vertical distance between the manual and nonmanual lines.[1] The foregoing three-parameter specification, which serves to summarize the aggregate structure of segregation, allows us to resolve long-standing empirical puzzles in the field that arose because most scholars have defaulted to a unidimensional view.

The two vertical slope parameters in Figure 44.2 are partly consistent with a unidimensional queuing formulation (whereby men secure better occupations than women), but our specification may be understood as a revision of this formulation because queuing theory does not allow for a "horizontal gap" expressing the tendency of women to be disproportionately allocated to the nonmanual sector (even though nonmanual occupations are, on average, more desirable than manual ones). Moreover, we allow the vertical principle to be stronger in some regions of the labor market (i.e., the manual sector) than in others, and we also allow the vertical principle to be stronger at the aggregate level than at the level of detailed occupations (which are not represented in Figure 44.2). Although queuing theory thus motivates some aspects of our parame-

terization, it cannot provide a complete account of segregation (see Reskin and Roos 1990; Strober 1984).

The deficiencies of queuing theory and other unidimensional formulations arise in large part because the cultural underpinnings of segregation are fundamentally two-dimensional. Under the parameterization of Figure 44.2, it is assumed that (a) the cultural tenet of male primacy undergirds vertical segregation, and (b) the complementary cultural tenet of gender essentialism undergirds horizontal segregation. The tenet of male primacy represents men as more status-worthy than women and better suited for positions of authority and domination, and the tenet of gender essentialism represents women as more competent than men in personal service, nurturance, and social interaction. In the modern context, these two cultural tenets tend to coexist with one another, thus giving segregation systems a hybrid character. We review these two tenets below.

Essentialism

Why do women crowd into the nonmanual sector and men crowd into the manual sector? In addressing this question, one has to be struck by the strong correspondence between (a) the traits that are regarded as distinctively male or female (gender essentialism) and (b) the task requirements of manual and nonmanual labor. Although prevailing characterizations of male and female traits are complex and multifaceted, a core feature of such characterizations is that women are presumed to excel in personal service, nurturance, and interpersonal interaction, and men are presumed to excel in interaction with things (rather than people) and in strenuous or physical labor. These stereotypes about natural male and female characteristics are disseminated and perpetuated through popular culture and media, through social interaction in which significant others (parents, peers, teachers) implicitly or explicitly support such interpretations, and through micro-level cognitive processes in which individuals pursue and remember evidence consistent with their preexisting stereotypes and ignore, discount, or forget evidence that undermines those stereotypes (Fiske 1998; Reskin 2000). The main claim we wish to advance is that horizontal segregation is maintained and reproduced in large part because nonmanual occupations embody characteristics (such as service orientation) regarded as prototypically female, while manual occupations embody characteristics (such as strenuousness and physicality) regarded as prototypically male (see, e.g., Crompton 2001; Lorber 1993; Milkman and Townsley 1994; Tilly 1998). This linkage is converted into durable horizontal segregation because (a) employers internalize these essentialist presumptions and allocate occupations to men and women in accord with them (i.e., essentialist discrimination), and (b) workers internalize the same essentialist presumptions and aspire to occupations that satisfy them (i.e., essentialist preferences). It follows that horizontal segregation has both demand-side and supply-side sources.

Male Primacy

Why are men disproportionately allocated to the best-paid and most desirable occupations in both the nonmanual and manual sectors? In accounting for such vertical segregation, we again understand the main forces at work as being cultural in form, but now the relevant cultural principle is the long-standing belief that men are more status-worthy than women and accordingly better suited for positions of high pay or authority. Despite the rise of universalistic ideals, there persist deeply rooted and widely shared cultural beliefs that men are better suited than women for all forms of labor outside the family, and that men are, in particular, better suited than women for labor involving the exercise of authority and power (Deaux and Kite 1987; Ridgeway 1997). We argue, then, that vertical segregation is maintained and reproduced in part because it is consistent with the cultural value of male primacy. The main proximate mechanisms by which beliefs in male primacy are translated into vertical segregation are (a) the recognition among men that, because they are regarded as primary breadwinners, they should make substantial investments in human capital (i.e., supply-side sources), and (b) the recognition among employers that, because men are regarded as primary breadwinners, their commitment to the labor force will be greater and hence there is a greater payoff to investing in them rather than in women (who may exhibit intermittency). Moreover, employers reward men with better jobs not just because they assume that men have a greater commitment to the labor force, but also because they regard men as intrinsically more competent. Because such assumptions about intrinsic competency are internalized by everyone, male workers will also come to believe that they are more competent at high-status tasks than females and hence more likely to succeed in those tasks, thereby motivating them to make the requisite investments in human capital. The premise of male primacy, like that of gender essentialism, is therefore expressed in supply-side as well as demand-side processes.

The Dynamics of Gender Segregation

This two-dimensional understanding of segregation casts light on the processes by which the spread of egalitarian commitments will affect the structure of gender inequality. Within the cultural domain, the diffusion of egalitarianism is an extremely important development, one that will likely continue apace unless some unforeseen catastrophic event has a recalibrating effect. Although the future of egalitarianism appears bright, one should consider the limits of the particular version of egalitarianism that has taken hold and that continues to diffuse. Among the many competing egalitarian visions, it is clear that "liberal egalitarian" strands remain dominant, implying that our collective commitment to gender equality mainly takes the form of developing procedural guarantees of equal opportunity. This commitment to liberal egalitarianism is quite compatible with the essentialist presumption that men and women have fundamentally different tastes, skills, and abilities (see Charles and Grusky 2004). That is, the liberal egalitarian vision of women and men as autonomous agents entitled to equal rights, opportunities, and treatment allows for the persistence of fundamentally gendered outlooks and identities. For a liberal egalitarian, it is enough to defend the right of women to fairly compete for any occupation to which they aspire, without in any way questioning how those aspirations were formed or why they may differ from the aspirations of men. It follows that liberal egalitarians embrace an "equal but different" conceptualization of gender and social justice.

Insofar as this version of egalitarianism continues to diffuse, the push toward complete equality may be slowed. This suppressive effect occurs through proximate mechanisms on both the supply and demand sides. On the supply side, we cannot expect liberal egalitarians to pay much attention to individual aspirations and self-assessments, meaning that the persistence of gender differences in these outlooks and identities will not be scrutinized or challenged to the extent that they would be under more radical egalitarian commitments. On the demand side, the liberal egalitarian commitment delegitimates all forms of pure discrimination, but it does not as directly challenge statistical discrimination that rests on essentialist presumptions. In a world in which women have disproportionately "invested" in nurturance and service, essentialist presumptions about gender differences in capabilities have ample room to flourish, and employers may well reason that gender provides a good signal of capabilities in nurturing and service. The main argument we would make, then, is that liberal variants of egalitarianism serve principally to undermine the presumption of male primacy rather than gender essentialism; and, consequently, horizontal forms of segregation may prove to be quite resistant to egalitarianism.

Is the Argument Supported?

This argument can be addressed with the international data archive described in Table 44.1. We apply a cross-nationally harmonized classification of sixty-four detailed occupational categories to census segregation data from ten industrial market economies. The data are organized in the form of a three-dimensional, 1,280-cell matrix with sixty-four occupations, two sexes, and ten countries. For most of our

Table 44.1   Data and Sample Characteristics

Country	Census Year	Sample Size
Belgium	1991	3,418,512
France	1990	900,255
West Germany	1993	128,912
Italy	1991	21,071,282
Portugal	1991	4,037,130
Sweden	1990	4,059,813
Switzerland	1990	3,076,445
United Kingdom	1991	2,405,091
United States	1990	1,152,885
Japan	1990	12,220,974

analyses, we examine segregation principally in terms of nine major classes, each of which is an aggregation of a subset of the sixty-four detailed occupations in the full array. We report results based on "self-weighted" data in which the actual sample size in each country is preserved. Because large-sample countries (such as Italy and Japan) have much leverage on our estimates, we have reestimated many of our models after standardizing sample sizes to an arbitrary constant ($N = 10,000$), but such standardized results have proved to be much the same as self-weighted results and therefore will not be reported here.

We have measured horizontal inequality at the aggregate level by distinguishing the five nonmanual categories (managerial, professional, associate professional, clerical, service/sales) from the four manual categories (agriculture, craft, operative, laborer). We measure vertical inequality with the internationally standardized socioeconomic index (SEI) published by Ganzeboom and Treiman (1996). This index, which is constructed as a weighted average of the educational attainment and income of occupational incumbents, is highly correlated with an international occupational prestige index. We apply two variants of this scale in our analy-

ses: (a) the aggregate variant (V1) assigns average SEI values to each of the nine major categories, and (b) the detailed variant (V2) assigns SEI values to each of the sixty-four detailed occupations. The aggregate variant of this scale is used to examine the extent to which aggregate segregation is vertically organized, whereas the detailed variant is used to examine the extent to which detailed segregation is vertically organized.

The key question that arises is whether the between-category component may be explained in vertical terms. In its purest form, a queuing model implies that men are disproportionately allocated to the most desirable major occupations, thus suggesting the following specification:

$$m_{ijk} = \alpha_k \beta_{ik} \gamma_{jk} e^{\varepsilon(Z_i V1_j)},$$

where i, j, and k index gender, occupation, and country respectively, α_k is the grand mean in the kth country, β_{ik} is the country-specific marginal effect for the ith gender, γ_{jk} is the country-specific marginal effect for the jth occupation, ε refers to the effect of socioeconomic status on female representation (at the aggregate level), Z_i is an indicator variable for gender (i.e., $Z_1 = 0$ and $Z_2 = 1$), and $V1_j$ refers to the aggregate version of our socioeconomic scale. We have identified this model by imposing standard constraints on the parameters.

The test statistic for this model, L^2 = 16,081,116 with 629 df, implies that only 2.5 percent of the total association at the aggregate level can be explained in vertical terms. Moreover, our estimate of ε under this model is .008, meaning that female representation increases by a factor of 1.008 for each unit increase in socioeconomic status. This estimate, which indicates that women are (slightly) overrepresented in high-status occupations, is of course inconsistent with simple queuing perspectives (see Blackburn, Brooks, and Jarman 2001; Charles and Grusky 1995; Roos 1985). Although such a result is counterintuitive, it is consistent with the long-standing argument that socioeconomic scores overstate the desirability of routine nonmanual occupations and hence create the (misleading) appearance of female advantage (e.g., Acker 1980; England 1979). We have no quarrels with this long-standing account, but it may not be complete. The queuing model fails, as we see it, not only because socioeconomic scales are flawed or because the vertical dynamic is weak but also because this dynamic is obscured in the absence of controls for horizontal segregation. The structure of segregation is in this sense fundamentally multidimensional.

We can test this argument by examining whether the vertical coefficient reverses sign and strengthens in the context of a multidimensional model. When vertical and horizontal effects are simultaneously fit, the following model is generated:

$$m_{ijk} = \alpha_k \beta_{ik} \gamma_{jk} e^{\varepsilon(Z_i V1_j) + \omega(Z_i H_j)},$$

where H_j is the horizontal term (i.e., $H_j = 1$ if j is a manual occupation and $H_j = 0$ otherwise), ω is the effect of horizontal status

on female representation, and the remaining terms are defined as before. The explained association under this specification increases dramatically from 2.5 to 80.4 percent, and the vertical coefficient further assumes the expected negative sign and becomes quite strong (-.050). The horizontal coefficient is likewise very strong: The estimate of ω, -1.96, implies that female representation is 7.10 times greater in a nonmanual occupation than a corresponding manual occupation of the same socioeconomic status. This effect, which is equivalent to that associated with a downward shift in status of nearly forty points, is surely strong enough to suggest that scholars of gender stratification should move beyond their long-standing focus on vertical inequality and begin attending to horizontal forms of stratification.

We might also allow the strength of the vertical effect to differ across sectors. This model may be represented as follows:

$$m_{ijk} = \alpha_k \beta_{ik} \gamma_{jk} e^{\psi(Z_i N_j V1_j) + \varepsilon(Z_i M_j V1_j) + \omega(Z_i H_j)},$$

where N_j is an indicator variable for nonmanual occupations (i.e., $N_j = 1$ if j is a nonmanual occupation and $N_j = 0$ otherwise), M_j is an indicator variable for manual occupations (i.e., $M_j = H_j$), and ψ and ε express the strength of vertical segregation within the nonmanual and manual sectors respectively.[2] With this specification, the explained association increases modestly (from 80.4 to 85.3 percent), and the vertical effect is revealed to be slightly weaker in the nonmanual sector (-.040) than in the manual sector (-.047). The modern segregation regime thus takes on the three-parameter form represented in Figure 44.2: The horizontal gap parameter captures the dramatic overrepresentation of women in the nonmanual sector, and the two slope parameters capture the tendency for men to dominate the best occupations within the manual and nonmanual sectors.

It follows that our three-parameter specification effectively exhausts the structure of segregation at the aggregate level. Is disaggregate segregation equally amenable to a parsimonious account? Although we shall not attempt any elaborate modeling here, we can at least test the simple claim that segregation across detailed categories assumes a simple vertical form. This hypothesis can be tested with the following model:

$$m_{ijk} = \alpha_k \beta_{ik} \gamma_{jk} e^{\varepsilon(Z_i V2_j) + \rho_c(Z_i)},$$

where ρ refers to the scale values for major occupational categories (indexed by c), and $V2_j$ refers to the detailed variant of our socioeconomic scale. This model explains a mere 3.3 percent of the total disaggregate association; and the vertical coefficient, estimated at -.034, is only 68 percent as strong as the corresponding vertical coefficient (-.050) at the aggregate level (under the model of equation 2). We can conclude that the forces of patriarchy do not operate all that efficiently in allocating men to the most desirable occupations within each major category. It is possible, of course, that the vertical coefficient is suppressed because various types of essentialist effects (such as a nurturing effect or service effect) have been improperly omitted from our model. It is surely worth exploring this possibility in future research. Without explicit evidence of such bias, our provisional conclusion is nonetheless that disaggregate segregation does not have a clear vertical character to it, again calling conventional queuing models into question.

We next ask whether our three-parameter specification suffices to describe the structure of aggregate segregation in *all* advanced in-

dustrial countries. We have estimated single-country models analogous to the foregoing pooled models and reported the relevant parameters and fit statistics in Table 44.2. The main conclusions that emerge are: (a) a simple unidimensional model explains only a small minority of the aggregate association in each country (see panel A); (b) the vertical segregation coefficient from this unidimensional model assumes the same positive (and counterintuitive) sign in each country; (c) our alternative multidimensional specification explains more than 70 percent of the aggregate association in each country (see panel D); (d) the vertical segregation coefficients from this model become strong and negative in each country; (e) the horizontal segregation effect is likewise strong in most countries (except Italy and Portugal) and may therefore be regarded as an important, if neglected, source of contemporary hypersegregation; and (f) the nonmanual slope coefficient is weaker than the corresponding manual coefficient in all but two countries (the United States and Japan).

We can now turn to the question of why countries with a comparatively deep commitment to egalitarianism, such as France, West Germany, Sweden, the United Kingdom, and the United States, have remained quite sex segregated. As shown in Panel C of Table 44.2, the average value of the horizontal segregation parameter for these five "egalitarian" countries is −3.20, whereas the corresponding average for the five less egalitarian countries in our sample is −2.07. There is accordingly no evidence that egalitarianism reduces the horizontal variant of segregation. To the contrary, it would appear to increase such segregation, an effect that may arise because egalitarianism has drawn women into the labor force at precisely the time when the nonmanual sector

Table 44.2 Single-Country Models of Vertical and Horizontal Sex Segregation

Model	Aggregate Segregation Explained (%)	Segregation Coefficient Vertical	Horizontal
A. Vertical Effect			
Belgium	3.66	0.01	
France	2.40	0.01	
West Germany	1.54	0.01	
Italy	12.78	0.01	
Portugal	0.52	0.00	
Sweden	1.02	0.01	
Switzerland	0.68	0.01	
United Kingdom	0.71	0.01	
United States	9.15	0.02	
Japan	0.61	0.00	
B. Horizontal Effect			
Belgium	43.48		−1.10
France	40.41		−1.40
West Germany	42.34		−1.32
Italy	59.55		−0.83
Portugal	18.36		−0.49
Sweden	41.64		−1.53
Switzerland	42.01		−1.49
United Kingdom	39.34		−1.39
United States	55.44		−1.54
Japan	20.82		−0.65
C. Vertical and Horizontal Effect (Additive)			
Belgium	75.08	−.053	−2.37
France	79.64	−.086	−3.45
West Germany	84.82	−.077	−3.14
Italy	75.73	−.027	−1.38
Portugal	39.02	−.034	−1.19
Sweden	79.95	−0.80	−3.40
Switzerland	82.43	−.080	−3.23
United Kingdom	83.03	−0.84	−3.34
United States	75.02	−.049	−2.69
Japan	77.63	−.075	−2.16

D. Vertical and Horizontal Effect (Ineractive)

Model	Aggregate Segregation Explained (%)	Vertical Nonmanual	Vertical Manual	Horizontal
Belgium	85.84	−.039	−.085	−2.89
France	87.99	−.066	−.110	−4.09
West Germany	92.11	−0.62	−.090	−3.61
Italy	83.84	−.017	−.046	−1.56
Portugal	71.93	−.004	−.089	−1.42
Sweden	87.84	−.065	−.114	−4.13
Switzerland	88.37	−.068	−.101	−3.86
United Kingdom	87.42	−.071	−.077	−3.80
United States	75.64	−.045	−.027	−2.86
Japan	77.94	−.078	−.013	−2.11

Table 44.3   Frequencies for Gender Egalitarianism Variable

Country	Value
Belgium	51.52
France	58.95
West Germany	58.46
Italy	47.66
Portugal	54.27
Sweden	87.93
Switzerland	54.70
United Kingdom	58.62
United States	71.06
Japan	25.71

is expanding (see Charles and Grusky 2004 for details).

This counterintuitive result can be formalized by developing an explicit measure of gender egalitarianism and then asking how it varies with horizontal segregation. We may define "gender egalitarianism" as a commitment to gender-based equality of opportunity and operationalize it as the percentage of respondents in each country disagreeing with the statement that "men have greater rights to jobs during periods of high unemployment." This survey item, which comes out of the 1990 World Values Survey (WVS), signals whether respondents accept the assumption of male economic dominance or reject it in favor of the norms of universalism and equal opportunity (see Table 44.3 for country-level values). If we then regress the coefficients for horizontal segregation (Panel C) on our measure of egalitarianism, we secure a coefficient of –.026. This coefficient implies that a 40 point increase in egalitarianism, a difference roughly equal to that between Italy and Sweden, raises horizontal segregation by a factor of 2.83. The "Swedish puzzle" is solved, therefore, by recognizing that the logic of egalitarian policy is not inconsistent with the persistence and even the growth of horizontal forms of segregation.

We of course appreciate that many other macro-level variables may well affect the extent of vertical and horizontal segregation. For example, we have argued elsewhere that service-sector expansion and economic rationalization are important structural forces affecting modern segregation, forces that can again perversely work to increase rather than reduce horizontal segregation (Charles and Grusky 2004). Although the effects of service-sector expansion and rationalization rest on complicated mechanisms that cannot be reviewed here, they are consistent with our larger argument that sex segregation cannot necessarily be expected to straightforwardly decline.

Conclusion

The preceding discussion suggests that the future of gender inequality rests on a struggle between egalitarian and essentialist forces that is not quite as one-sided as modernization theorists have sometimes claimed (see, e.g., Jackson 1998; Parsons 1970). If gender segregation is especially durable, it is partly because it has a deep essentialist undergirding. The "first revolution" in gender inequality, which has generated important reductions in segregation over the past thirty years, has been driven in large part by declines in vertical inequality (see Weeden 2004). Will there be a "second revolution" that leads to an analogous decline in horizontal segregation? In answering this question, conventional functionalist and neoinstitutionalist accounts fall short because they fail to recognize that horizontal segregation proceeds from an essentialist ideology that can persist—even thrive—in the context of liberal egalitarian norms of equal opportunity.

In the contemporary context, men and women are presumed to have rather different tastes and aptitudes, and liberal egalitarianism works merely to ensure that such differences, however they might be generated, can then be pursued or expressed in a fair (gender-neutral) contest. The assumption that men and women have fundamentally different tastes and capacities is reinforced in various social settings, not just in families (with their gender-specific socialization practices) and work organizations (with their discriminatory hiring practices) but in other institutional contexts as well. By way of (trivial) example, consider the practice among American fast-food restaurants of providing gender-specific toys to children, a practice of interest only because it is widely diffused and evidently unobjectionable to all but a small minority of "gender progressives." If these same restaurants distributed toys on the basis of racial or class standing, the practice would be deemed absurd at best and racist or classist at worst. This example suggests that, at least in the United States, it is less legitimate to interpret racial or class-based inequalities in essentialist terms than to interpret gender segregation and inequality in these terms.

In the long run, it is of course possible that a yet deeper form of egalitarianism will emerge and delegitimate (a) the tendency of males and females to develop different tastes, aspirations, and market capacities, and (b) the tendency of employers to make judgments about productivity through essentialist lenses. There are indeed many signs that just such a form of egalitarianism is developing. Most notably, conventional sociological understandings of the roles of socialization, social exchange, and power differentials in generating preferences have diffused widely in contemporary industrial

societies, suggesting that preferences and choices formerly regarded as sacrosanct are increasingly treated as outcomes of unequal and unfair social processes. This deeper form of egalitarianism is reflected in attempts by some parents to minimize gender bias in the socialization of their children, at least in the early years of childrearing before the unremitting influence of societywide essentialism typically undermines their efforts. It is surely plausible that this deeper form of egalitarianism will ultimately take hold (see Ramirez 1987, p. 270).

For our part, we would merely stress that prevailing forms of egalitarianism do not fully delegitimate essentialist processes and that a true "second revolution," one that establishes this new and broader definition of equality, will therefore be needed to eliminate essentialist segregation. There should be no illusions about how formidable the remaining barriers are. Far from being some "inevitable destiny" (Jackson 1998, p. 271), the second revolution will face many obstacles, not the least of which is an entrenched tradition of classical liberalism that celebrates individual choice and thus supports and sustains those forms of inequality that can be represented as consistent with it.

NOTES

1. If the two vertical segregation lines are parallel, the distance between them is of course constant. However, insofar as the slopes of these lines are allowed to differ, the size of the horizontal parameter will depend on the implicit zero point of the vertical scale.

2. Under this specification, the two vertical parameters no longer generate parallel lines, meaning that the estimated size of the horizontal parameter depends on the implied zero point of the socioeconomic scale. We have fixed the zero point of this scale at 37 (which is the midpoint between the score for the lowest nonmanual cate-

gory [40] and the highest manual category [34]). The two vertical segregation lines are furthest from one another at this point (assuming that the nonmanual slope is weaker than the manual one).

REFERENCES

Acker, Joan R. 1980. "Women and Stratification: A Review of Recent Literature." *Contemporary Sociology* 9: 25–39.

Becker, Gary S. 1991. *A Treatise on the Family.* Cambridge, MA: Harvard University Press.

Blackburn, Robert M., Jennifer Jarman, and Bradley Brooks. 2000. "The Puzzle of Gender Segregation and Inequality: A Cross-National Analysis." *European Sociological Review* 16: 119–135.

_____. 2001. "Occupational Stratification: The Vertical Dimension of Occupational Segregation." *Work, Employment, and Society* 15: 5111–5138.

Chafetz, Janet Saltzman. 1988. "The Gender Division of Labor and the Reproduction of Female Disadvantage: Toward an Integrated Theory." *Journal of Family Issues* 9: 108–131.

Charles, Maria, and David B. Grusky. 1995. "Models for Describing the Underlying Structure of Sex Segregation." *American Journal of Sociology* 100: 931–971.

_____. 2004. *Occupational Ghettos: The Worldwide Segregation of Women and Men.* Stanford, CA: Stanford University Press.

Crompton, Rosemary. 2001. "The Gendered Restructuring of the Middle Classes." In Janeen Baxter and Mark Western, eds., *Reconfigurations of Class and Gender*, pp. 29–54. Stanford, CA: Stanford University Press.

Deaux, Kay, and Mary Kite. 1987. "Thinking about Gender." In B. Hess and M. Ferree, eds., *Analyzing Gender: A Handbook of Social Science Research*, pp. 92–117. Newbury Park, CA: Sage.

England, Paula. 1979. "Women and Occupational Prestige: A Case of Vacuous Sex Equality." *Signs* 5: 252–265.

Fiske, Susan T. 1998. "Stereotyping, Prejudice, and Discrimination." In D. T. Gilbert, S.T. Fiske, and G. Lindzey, eds., *Handbook of Social Psychology*, pp. 357–411. New York: McGraw-Hill.

Ganzeboom, Harry B. G., and Donald J. Treiman. 1996. "Internationally Comparable Measures of Occupational Status for the 1988 International Standard Classification of Occupations." *Social Science Research* 25: 201–239.

Goode, William J. 1963. *World Revolution and Family Patterns.* New York: Free Press.

Hartmann, Heidi I. 1981. "The Unhappy Marriage of Marxism and Feminism: Towards a More Progressive Union." In Lydia Sargent, ed., *Women and Revolution: A Discussion of the Unhappy Marriage of Marxism and Feminism*, pp. 1–41. Boston: South End Press.

Huber, Joan. 1988. "A Theory of Family, Economy, and Gender." *Journal of Family Issues* 9: 9–26.

Jackson, Robert Max. 1998. *Destined for Equality: The Inevitable Rise of Women's Status.* Cambridge, MA: Harvard University Press.

Jacobs, Jerry. 2003. "Detours on the Road to Equality: Women, Work, and Higher Education." *Contexts* 2: 32–41.

Lorber, Judith. 1993. *Paradoxes of Gender.* New Haven, CT: Yale University Press.

Massey, Douglas S., and Nancy A. Denton. 1993. *American Apartheid: Segregation and the Making of the Underclass.* Cambridge, MA: Harvard University Press.

Meyer, John W. 2001. "The Evolution of Modern Stratification Systems." In David B. Grusky, ed., *Social Stratification: Class, Race, and Gender in Sociological Perspective*, 2d ed., pp. 881–90. Boulder, CO: Westview Press.

Milkman, Ruth, and Eleanor Townsley. 1994. "Gender and the Economy." In Neil J. Smelser and Richard Swedberg, eds., *The Handbook of Economic Sociology*, pp. 600–619. Princeton, NJ: Princeton University Press.

Parsons, Talcott. 1970. "Equality and Inequality in Modern Society, or Social Stratification Revisited." In Edward O. Laumann, ed., *Social Stratification: Research and Theory for the 1970s*, pp. 14–72. Indianapolis: Bobbs-Merrill.

Ramirez, Francisco O. 1987. "Global Changes, World Myths, and the Demise of Cultural Gender: Implications for the United States." In Terry Boswell and Albert Bergesen, eds., *America's Changing Role in the World System*, pp. 257–73. New York: Praeger.

Reskin, Barbara F. 2000. "The Proximate Causes of Employment Discrimination." *Contemporary Sociology* 29: 319–328.

Reskin, Barbara F., and Patricia A. Roos. 1990. *Job Queues, Gender Queues: Explaining Women's Inroads into Male Occupations*. Philadelphia: Temple University Press.

Ridgeway, Cecilia L. 1997. "Interaction and the Conservation of Gender Inequality: Considering Employment." *American Sociological Review* 62: 218–235.

Roos, Patricia A. 1985. *Gender and Work: A Comparative Analysis of Industrial Societies*. New York: State University of New York Press.

Semyonov, Moshe, and Frank L. Jones. 1999. "Dimensions of Gender Occupational Differentiation in Segregation and Inequality: A Cross-National Analysis." *Social Indicators Research* 46: 225–247.

Strober, Myra H. 1984. "Toward a General Theory of Occupational Sex Segregation: The Case of Public School Teaching." In Barbara F. Reskin, ed., *Sex Segregation in the Workplace*. Washington, DC: National Academy Press.

Tilly, Charles. 1998. *Durable Inequality*. Berkeley: University of California Press.

Weeden, Kim A. 2004. "Profiles of Change: Sex Segregation in the United States." In Maria Charles and David B. Grusky, *Occupational Ghettos: The Worldwide Segregation of Women and Men*. Stanford, CA: Stanford University Press.

Williams, Joan. 2000. *Unbending Gender: Why Family and Work Conflict and What to Do About It*. New York: Oxford University Press.

45

Detours on the Road to Equality
Women, Work, and Higher Education

JERRY A. JACOBS

News stories about the first woman entering a field—astronaut, firefighter, professional basketball player, Ivy League university president—have largely faded, although Carly Fiorina's selection as head of Hewlett Packard was widely extolled in both the business and popular press. It is commonly assumed that the barriers that once blocked women's entry into new fields have been dismantled. But there has been less change than meets the eye. The slow but steady movement of women into formerly male-dominated occupations has tapered off, if not completely stopped, during the 1990s. Women have made greater strides, however, in their pursuit of higher education. Indeed, the second development may be the result of the roadblocks they are facing in finding employment in traditionally male fields.

Layers of Segregation

Despite highly visible exceptions, such as local television news anchor teams, most occupations remain skewed toward either men or women. For every news anchor-woman, there are literally thousands of women who work in traditional female settings such as at a receptionist's desk, in an elementary school classroom, or at the take-out window of a fast-food restaurant. Whether she is a white single mother in Florida or a black empty-nester in Michigan, a woman more often works next to other women than to men. Women remain crowded in certain jobs such as secretaries or administrative assistants (99 percent female), child care workers (98 percent) or registered nurses (93 percent). Among the remaining male bastions are construction trades, such as carpenters, plumbers and electricians (3 percent female), mechanics and repairers (5 percent) and engineers (10 percent). This concentration of women and men in different jobs, occupations and industries is what sociologists mean when they refer to the gender segregation of work.

Among the highest-status professions, law, medicine and management have experienced a large influx of women. Nearly half of managers, law students and medical students are women. But within these fields, gender disparities are unmistakable. Few female

Jerry A. Jacobs, "Detours on the Road to Equality: Women, Work, and Higher Education," *Contexts* 2, no. 1 (Winter 2003), pp. 32–41.

managers have reached the highest echelons of large corporations, and women middle-managers are less likely than their male counterparts to have authority over staffs and budgets. Female lawyers are more likely to be found in family law or working for the government than practicing in the more lucrative specializations at major firms. And female physicians are more likely to specialize in pediatrics or family practice than surgery or anesthesiology. Indeed, the closer you look within nominally integrated occupations, the more segregation you find. Men and women are segregated by occupation, by firms within occupation, and by jobs and specializations within firms. There are "men's jobs" and "women's jobs" at all levels of education, skills, and experience, and at each level, the women's jobs tend to be paid less. Moreover, female-dominated fields pay less even when working time, qualifications and experience are taken into account.

One way to appreciate the income disparity is to compare the pay for male- and female-dominated occupations that have similar job qualifications. Women are 50 percent of bus drivers but only 3 percent of railroad conductors. Women are 71 percent of accountants and auditors but only 29 percent of securities and financial services sales representatives. Women are 88 percent of dressmakers but only 22 percent of upholsterers. In each of these cases, the male occupation pays more than the female one. These heavily-skewed numbers suggest that, despite good intentions, many jobs are not truly open to everyone.

Explaining Job Segregation

Why do women and men end up in different occupations? A popular view is that gender distinctions at work are as natural as boys and girls playing separately on the school playground. But sociologists tend to view gender roles as social conventions rather than natural phenomena.

People are taught to distinguish men's work from women's work, just as they are taught right from wrong. Gender stereotypes in the workplace are readily apparent, even to young children, and are often self-perpetuating. Children in elementary school report without hesitation that nurses are usually women, and firefighters, engineers and presidents are usually men. Young girls may no longer be encouraged to stay home, but now many are encouraged to work in 'suitable' jobs that emphasize helping others. Ideals pressed on boys include abstract reasoning, competitive prowess in sports and business, tinkering with things and financial success.

But persistent sex segregation at work is not the simple product of young men and women's choices. American youngsters' occupational aspirations are notoriously fickle. Occupational goals change often during the teenage years. More than half of college students change majors at least once. Even workers in their 20s and 30s continue to change occupations. For example, women engaged in emotionally demanding jobs, such as assisting children with learning disabilities, suffer from burnout, while other women working in male-dominated fields find that such jobs are not always worth the isolation and long hours. That this turnover has failed to reduce sex segregation suggests that continued pressure to pursue sex-typed work lasts well into adulthood.

For example, working in a masculine field can raise questions about a woman's femininity. Christine Williams found that female

Marines feel they need to show how tough they are on the job but also how feminine they can be off the job. Men who work as nurses face some of the same issues, and respond by emphasizing the heroic aspects of nursing. Beyond the pressure of gender expectations, a web of social factors tends to press women into traditionally female occupations and hold them there in adulthood. Women have fewer acquaintances with knowledge about openings in male-dominated settings. They often lack the co-worker support necessary to succeed. They face job tasks and hours that assume a male bread-winner with a supportive stay-at-home wife. And their family and friends are often dubious about or hostile to a new or unconventional occupation. Some of the remaining barriers to women's economic advancement are rooted in the structure of work. For example, excessive hours in a number of demanding fields limit the opportunities of those with parental and other caregiving obligations, especially mothers. Over the last 30 years, the work week has lengthened and the pace of work has intensified for many in the labor force, accentuating the strain on women.

Historical experiences also instruct us about just how flexible these gender distinctions can be. When seats in medical school classrooms became vacant during World War II, young women rushed to fill them. Other women were recruited to fill manufacturing jobs, with the media stressing how the required skills were similar to women's domestic talents. In the 1960s young women switched rapidly from education into medicine, business, and other fields as professional schools in these fields opened their doors. These examples suggest that the gender stereotypes with which

women grow up do not prevent them from seizing new opportunities as they become available.

And the things men and women say they want from their jobs are more similar than different. For example, Alison Konrad has shown that men and women overlap a great deal in the specific features of jobs they rank as important. In other words, gender segregation cannot be reduced to what men and women look for in jobs.

Hitting a Wall?

The early 1980s was a period of great energy and optimism both for research and policy on occupational gender segregation. An entirely new dimension of social inequality appeared to be open for exploration—not an everyday event. Comparable worth—the idea of equalizing pay not only for the same work, but also for work of comparable value—seemed a realistic and even imminent possibility. Women were making notable strides, entering new occupations and receiving graduate training in professions such as law, medicine and business. And women's entry into male fields even helped the women who remained in female fields. Fields such as nursing and teaching now face severe shortages, which stimulate higher wages for these undervalued professions.

At that time I was confident that these trends would continue, while some other analysts feared that the rate of change was so slow that it would take many decades to rectify the gender disparities at work. As it turns out, even the skeptics were too optimistic. Progress toward greater gender integration of occupations largely ground to a halt during the 1990s. The most widely used measure of segregation is the "index of dissimilarity," which measures the proportion of women who would have to change fields in order to be represented across types of occupations in the same proportions as men are. (Zero represents complete integration; 100 complete segregation.) This index fell from 67 in 1970 to 60 in 1980 to 56 in 1990, and then to 52 by 2000. But the modest change that occurred during the 1990s was almost all due to shifts in the size of occupations, rather than greater integration within occupations. (The more integrated occupational groups—professionals, technical workers, managers and sales occupations—grew, while the more segregated occupational groups—clerical workers and craft workers—declined.) More mixing within occupations did not happen in the 1990s.

Stagnation is evident in several related areas as well. The gender gap in median weekly earnings has been stuck at the same level since 1993—76 percent in 2001—and segregation by gender across medical specialties actually inched upward during the 1990s.

Why has the gender integration of occupations slowed to a crawl? A longer view suggests that this stability is typical and it is the unusual changes of the 1970s and 1980s that need to be explained. For most of the century gender differentiation remained roughly constant, despite economic booms and depressions, revolutions in marriage, fertility, and divorce, and the incremental but inexorable entry of women into the labor force.

Social change often occurs in brief intervals followed by periods of renewed stagnation. The feminist movement of the late 1960s and 1970s challenged many traditional assumptions, but its force waned by the late 1980s. The idea that a woman could do anything a man could do had tremendous force, but gradually was contested by the notion that women have special values and strengths which should be better appreciated. And inevitably a backlash against ostensibly special treatment challenged affirmative action and other measures designed to broaden opportunities for women and minorities.

Gender integration occurred largely through women entering formerly male-dominated settings. Few men showed interest in breaking into the pink-collar frontier. The stigma of doing "women's work," coupled with low pay, makes many jobs performed by women unattractive to men. The puzzle, of course, is why women have not left traditional female fields in even greater numbers for the better pay, benefits, promotion opportunities, and even job flexibility found in many men's occupations. Since women continue to join the labor market in ever greater numbers and take shorter and shorter breaks from work for childbearing, one would expect that they would continue to seek out avenues toward economic self-sufficiency. Such commitments to work should keep the pressure on to open male-dominated fields. Yet, while some pressure continues, many women have sought economic independence by the alternative and time-honored route of enrolling in higher education.

Degrees of Difference

Women first surpassed men in obtaining bachelor's degrees in 1982, and the gap continues to widen. In 1998, the most current data available, 56 percent of bachelor's degrees went to women. Before long, college graduates will probably be roughly 60:40 women to men, or a 1.5 to 1 ratio of young women to young men. Women are even more disproportionately concentrated among associate degree recipients, and are at parity with men in garnering master's and professional degrees.

Women's domination of undergraduate education represents a remarkable turn of events. Just 40 years ago, men were earning two-thirds of college degrees, and just 20 years ago, men and women were at parity. While many expected and welcomed women's catching up to men in educational attainment, I am not aware of anyone—economist, sociologist or educator—who predicted that women would surpass men by so much so quickly. What happened?

The surge in women's education is probably linked to gender segregation at work in several ways. First, women realize that the low wages that they face in unskilled women's jobs do not offer a living wage. In 1998, women with a high school degree working full-time, year-round brought home a median income of $22,800 a year; high school dropouts earned $16,700. Male high school graduates made $31,200 a year on average ($24,000 for high school dropouts). Young men consequently have less of a pressing need to pursue higher education. If skilled crafts and other relatively high-wage jobs open to male high school graduates were equally open to women, it is possible that fewer women would pursue higher education.

Second, by seeking specific vocational credentials, women gain some protection against hiring discrimination. If a pharmacy position requires a master's degree, women with such a diploma can expect that they will be given serious consideration. Many women returning to higher education do so to pursue particular vocational degree programs, to become nurse's aides, to get a teacher's certificate and to update office skills. The laundry list of rationalizations for turning away women is less readily available in professional settings, especially when there is a tight market for highly specialized skills. Accordingly, sex segregation has declined more sharply for college graduates than for those with fewer educational credentials.

Finally, the educational credentials women garner are themselves segregated, which limits the financial returns they can expect. In a national survey of the college class of 1999, I found that women college seniors expected to earn 30 percent less than their male classmates when they reached age 30, and the field of the degree they were pursuing explained the largest slice of this gap.

Women are pursuing a broader set of college programs than in the past, but here too change has slowed. About 30 percent of women would have to change fields to match their male counterparts, a difference that has been roughly constant since the mid-1980s. Biology, business and math are among the fields that have reached a rough gender balance. Engineering and the physical sciences (astronomy, chemistry and physics) remain male-dominated fields while psychology, education, nursing, and the romance languages are leading feminine fields of study. Girls are increasingly taking math and science in high school and testing better in those subjects, but this convergence in courses and scores has not translated into a convergence in college majors.

Looking Toward 2020

While forecasting trends is treacherous, it seems safe to predict that the gender segregation of jobs in the year 2020 will resemble current patterns. The major engines of gender integration have all lost steam. There are two ways in which women enter male fields: by starting their careers there or by switching later in life. The numbers taking either route have shrunk in recent years and are no longer enough to make up for the women who drop out of male-dominated careers.

As a result, it seems unrealistic to expect total gender integration. Basic changes in the way work is structured are needed, but we are in a period of political retrenchment, with bold new proposals unlikely to gain serious attention. Further reductions in occupational segregation will take another wave of political, cultural, social and economic reforms like those initiated during the 1960s. Specific policy measures would include: vigorous enforcement of anti-discrimination laws; training programs that target highly gender-typed fields; and a broad reconsideration of the value of women's work, especially caregiving work. Restructuring of working time to make all jobs parent-friendly is needed so that responsible parents (mostly women) are not trapped in so-called 'mommy track' positions or part-time jobs with no job security or employment benefits. Specifically policies that reduce the length of the work week—especially for professionals and managers—could reduce work-family conflict, increase the time working parents can spend with their children and advance gender equality at work. Reducing artificial gender barriers at work can improve economic efficiency while promoting gender equity. Recruiting more women into fields such as computer science and engineering could help to provide much needed talent in these areas, while recruiting more men to be elementary school teachers would help solve the looming national shortages we face in this area. There are many simple and effective measures that can be taken to broaden opportunities for women at work. We simply need the political will. Of course, the gender gap in voting—women were 11 percentage points more likely to vote for Gore than Bush in 2000—could return gender equality to the center of public policy discussions and put the labor force back on a course of incremental progress toward gender equality.

Most observers view the large and growing number of women in colleges and universities as yet another indication of how far women have come. But this welcome development may also have a darker side, as it reflects in part the continued obstacles women face in obtaining high-paying jobs that require no diploma. In other words, until we see more women wearing mechanic's overalls, we can expect to see more and more women marching in caps and gowns at graduation.

REFERENCES

Boulis, Ann, Jerry A. Jacobs, and Jon Veloski. "Gender Segregation by Specialty During Medical School." *Academic Medicine.* 76 (October 2001): S65–7. A study of gender and fields of specialization among medical students.

Cotter, David A., JoAnn M. DeFiore, Joan M. Hermsen, Breda M. Kowalewski, and Reeve Vanneman. "All Women Benefit: The Macro-Level Effect of Occupational Integration on Gender Earnings Inequality." *American Socio-*

logical Review 62 (October 1997): 714–734. An analysis of the impact of gender segregation on women's wages.

Jacobs, Jerry A. "Gender Inequality and Higher Education." *Annual Review of Sociology* 22 (1996): 153–85. Reviews women's uneven progress in higher education.

Konrad, Alison M., J. Edgar Ritchie, Pamela Lieb, and Elizabeth Corrigall. "Sex Differences and Similarities in Job Attribute Preferences: A Meta-Analysis." *Psychological Bulletin* 126 (July 2000): 593–641. Analyzes data on what women and men want from their jobs.

Neumark, David. "Sex Discrimination in Restaurant Hiring: An Audit Study." *The Quarterly Journal of Economics* 111 (August 1996): 915–941. A case study of hiring discrimination in restaurants.

Rab, Sara. "Sex Discrimination in Restaurant Hiring Practices." Master's Thesis, Department of Sociology, University of Pennsylvania, 2001. A study of gender and elite restaurants in New York City and Philadelphia.

Padavic, Irene, and Barbara Reskin. *Women and Men at Work.* Second Edition. Thousand Oaks, CA: Pine Forge Press, 2002. Broad overview of gender inequality at work.

Williams, Christine L. *Gender Differences at Work: Women and Men in Nontraditional Occupations.* Berkeley, CA: University of California Press, 1989. Case studies of female Marines and male nurses.

46

The Within-Job Gender Wage Gap

TROND PETERSEN AND
LAURIE A. MORGAN

There are three types of discrimination that can produce wage differences between men and women. (1) Women are differentially allocated to occupations and establishments that pay lower wages. This may involve discrimination partly through differential access to occupations and establishments—that is, the matching process at the point of hire—and partly through subsequent promotions. We call this process *allocative discrimination.* (2) Occupations held primarily by women are paid lower wages than those held primarily by men, although skill requirements and other wage relevant factors are the same. This process, which we call *valuative discrimination,* is addressed by comparable worth initiatives. (3) Women receive lower wages than men within a given occupation and establishment. We call this process *within-job wage discrimination.* Allocative and valuative discrimination involve the segregation of men and women into different occupations, establishments, or both, and may occur without within-job wage discrimina-

tion. Thus, although it may be the case that where men and women share the same jobs they receive the same pay, they simply do not share the same jobs all that often. One conjecture currently accepted by many researchers is that wage differences are less an issue of within-job wage discrimination and more a matter of allocative and valuative processes. That is, the segregation of women into lower paying occupations, establishments, or both, and lower pay in occupations held primarily by women are more important than pay differences within the same job in explaining the gender wage gap. Treiman and Hartmann (1981, 92–93) write, "Although the committee recognizes that instances of unequal pay for the same work have not been entirely eliminated, we believe that they are probably not now the major source of differences in earnings."

This conjecture is drawn primarily from a large literature that focuses on pay differences across and within occupations. One pattern of findings is that the wage gap between

---

This is a commissioned chapter that draws heavily on material in a previous publication (Trond Petersen and Laurie A. Morgan, "Separate and Unequal: Occupation-Establishment Sex Segregation and the Gender Wage Gap," *American Journal of Sociology* 101 [September 1995], pp. 329–361. Copyright © 1995 by the University of Chicago Press).

men and women becomes smaller as occupational controls become finer, suggesting that a large proportion of the wage gap is explained by occupational distribution (Treiman and Hartmann 1981; Reskin and Roos 1990). For example, Treiman and Hartmann (1981, 33–39) explained 10 to 20 percent of the raw gap using 222 occupational categories and 35 to 40 percent using 479 categories. These studies usually draw on data from the Census or national probability samples that allow no analysis of practices in specific establishments. Additional evidence suggests that, within occupations, the distribution of women across firms or establishments also accounts for some portion of the wage gap. For example, Blau (1977) found that in 11 clerical occupations, differences in men's and women's wages were larger between than within establishments.

Yet the prevailing conjecture remains a conjecture. It has not been shown that men and women receive equal pay within given occupations in given establishments. What has been shown is that sex segregation is extensive and pervasive (Bielby and Baron 1984; Petersen and Morgan 1995), but not the extent to which sex segregation accounts for the wage gap or that, when sex segregation is absent, the sexes receive more or less equal treatment. To confirm such a claim, one needs data on wages of men and women in the same detailed occupational group or position within the same establishment. Such data are not widely available except for isolated establishments.

This article reports a large-scale empirical investigation of wage differences between men and women within the same detailed occupational position within the same establishment. We use establishment-level data from a wide variety of industries. In each establishment, individual-level wage data for a large array of detailed occupational groups were collected, providing more accurate wage as well as occupational data than probably any other surveys available, except in some case studies of single establishments (e.g., Hartmann 1987). We focus first on production and clerical employees in 16 U.S. industries in the 1974 to 1983 period, primarily 1974 to 1978, analyzing data on 787,577 employees, 705 industry-specific occupations, 6,057 establishments, and 71,214 occupation-establishment pairs. Second, we focus on seven professional and three administrative occupations across a broad range of industries in 1981, analyzing data on about 740,000 employees distributed across 2,162 establishments and 16,433 occupation-establishment pairs.

We make no attempt to settle the important conceptual issues that go along with the empirical patterns we address, namely the sources of observed patterns, neither from the demand side—that is, discriminatory behavior by employers—or the supply side—that is, behaviors by employees and prospective employees (see England 1992, chap. 2). Nevertheless, our results have implications for the kinds of theoretical issues that are most in need of being addressed and for the type of data that need to be collected and analyzed.

Data

We use two large-scale data sets. The first data set comes from 16 Industry Wage Surveys (IWS) conducted by the U.S. Bureau of Labor Statistics (BLS) in the period 1974 to 1983 (see, e.g., U.S. Department of Labor 1976), corresponding to industry codes at three and more digits as defined in the *Standard Industrial Classification Manual* (see U.S. Executive Office of the President 1987). Eleven industries were surveyed in 1974 to 1978, whereas 5 were surveyed in 1980 to 1983. The populations for the surveys and the sampling from the populations are described in several U.S. Department of Labor publications (see Petersen and Morgan 1995, table 1). Of the 16, 11 are manufacturing industries, and 5 are service industries.

In each industry, the BLS drew a sample of several hundred establishments, often covering a large proportion of the establishments in the industry. For each establishment, information was obtained from establishment records both on establishment characteristics and on a large number of the production and/or clerical workers in the establishment. Within each industry, only a selection of occupations were surveyed—on average 42 occupations per industry. The occupations were selected by the BLS in order to provide a wide representation of production or clerical occupations in an industry. The individual-level data provide information on each individual in the relevant occupation and establishment. Excluded from the data collection were professional and managerial employees. Because these occupations may have exhibited wider variations in wages, even at the occupation-establishment level, there may have been less occupation-establishment level variation in wages here than in samples including professionals and managers.

For each employee surveyed, information was obtained on sex, occupation (an industry-specific code), method of wage payment (incentive- or time-rated), and hourly earnings. No information was collected on race, age, experience, or educa-

tion. The occupational classification is unusually detailed, corresponding in many cases to nine digits in the *Dictionary of Occupational Titles* (see U.S. Department of Labor 1977). In other cases, the titles are specific to the BLS data, based on industry-specific codes, but are usually as detailed as the nine-digit titles in the *Dictionary of Occupational Titles*.

Wage data are straight-time hourly wages in 13 industries and full-time weekly earnings in the other three, excluding premium pay for overtime and work on weekends, holidays, and late shifts. Thus, we do not conflate pay earned on regular hours with pay earned on overtime and irregular hours, making the wage data less prone to bias than virtually any other study used for assessing wage discrimination. Men work more overtime hours than women, due either to preference for or better access to overtime hours, and overtime hours are usually paid at a higher rate. Non-production bonuses, such as year-end bonuses, are also excluded, whereas incentive pay is included.

The second data set we use is the National Survey of Professional, Administrative, Technical, and Clerical (PATC) employees in 1981, also conducted by the BLS (U.S. Department of Labor 1981). The sampling and data collection design for this survey is similar to that in the IWS data. We use the data on weekly pay for full-time employees in seven professional and three administrative occupations.

Methods

We report all statistics separately for each of the 16 industries in the IWS data.[1] The raw (average) wages, either hourly or full-time weekly earnings, for women and men in an industry are given by $\overline{w}_f$ and $\overline{w}_m$, and the raw proportional wage between women and men is $w_{r,r} = \overline{w}_f / \overline{w}_m$. The average wages for women and men in occupation o are $\overline{w}_{o,f}$ and $\overline{w}_{o,m}$, and the proportional wage is $w_{o,r} = \overline{w}_{o,f} / \overline{w}_{o,m}$. The average wages for women and men in establishment e are $\overline{w}_{e,f}$ and $\overline{w}_{e,m}$, and the proportional wage is $w_{e,r} = \overline{w}_{e,f} / \overline{w}_{e,m}$. The average wages for women and men in occupation-establishment pair oe are $\overline{w}_{oe,f}$ and $\overline{w}_{oe,m}$, and the proportional wage is $w_{oe,r} = \overline{w}_{oe,f} / \overline{w}_{oe,m}$. These computations can only be done for units that are integrated by sex. We multiply each proportional wage by 100 in order to get the average female wage as percent of average male wage at the relevant level. This percentage is referred to as the relative wage in what follows.

We make three computations with relative wages. Each computation answers the following question: suppose sex segregation—by occupation, establishment, or occupation-establishment—were abolished, what then would the remaining relative wage be? These computations are defined in the appendix.

At the occupation level, we report the average of the relative wage across all sex-integrated occupations. We do the same at the establishment level. At the occupation-establishment level, we likewise report the average of the relative wage ($w_{oe,r} \times 100$) across all sex-integrated occupation-establishment units (oe). The female wage gap at each of these levels is then given as 100 minus the average of the relative wage at each level. This equals the percent by which women are paid less than men.

The remaining wage gap at the occupation-establishment level can reasonably be interpreted as an estimate of the upper bound on the amount of within-job wage discrimination, the gap one would observe in the absence of occupation-establishment sex segregation. It is an upper bound because the remaining gap at that level could have been caused by other factors, such as differences in experience and human capital between men and women in a given category. The difference between the raw wage gap and the wage gap at the occupation-establishment level can thus be interpreted as being attributable to occupation-establishment sex segregation. This part of course need not be caused by discrimination alone.

Results

Table 46.1 gives first in column 2 the raw relative wage and then in columns 3 to 5 the relative wages controlling for occupation, for establishment, and for occupation-establishment, computed from equations (1) to (4) in the appendix. Column 1 shows the percentage female in each industry. Column 2 shows that the average of the industry-specific raw relative wages between men and women was 81 percent. Thus the average of the industry-specific female wage gaps was 19 percent, where the wage gap is the percentage by which women earned less than men, computed as 100 minus the relative wage.

Column 3 shows that the female wage gap is reduced to an average, across the 16 industries, of 8 percent when we control for occupation, using equation (2). Column 4 shows that the female wage gap is reduced, across the 16 industries, to an average of 15 percent when we control for establishment, using equation (3). Column 5 shows that the female wage gap is reduced to about 0 to 4 percent when we control for the occupation-establishment pair, using equation (4). The average of the industry-specific female wage

Table 46.1   Women's Wages Relative to Men's With and Without Occupation, Establishment, and Occupation-Establishment Controls

		Women's Wages as a Percentage of Men's				Percent of Raw Wage Gap Explained by:		
	%F	Raw	Occ	Est	Occ-Est	Occ	Est	Occ-Est
Industry	1	2	3	4	5	6	7	8
Men's and Boys' Shirts	92.5	84.0	92.7	83.1	98.0	54.5	–5.4	87.5
Hospitals	84.8	105.3	95.8	103.7	101.0	178.7	30.7	81.3
Banking*	82.8	64.7	97.3	65.5	98.1	92.4	2.3	94.6
Life Insurance*	75.9	61.5	98.0	61.4	98.9	94.8	–0.3	97.1
Wool Textiles	55.4	87.3	93.8	91.7	98.6	51.3	34.8	89.0
Cotton Man-Made Fiber Textiles	54.6	89.2	96.5	90.5	99.7	67.5	11.8	97.2
Miscellaneous Plastics Products	51.9	77.5	87.4	80.6	97.8	44.1	14.0	90.2
Hotels and Motels	51.5	87.0	91.9	89.1	99.7	37.9	16.4	97.7
Computer and Data Processing*	44.5	67.5	98.4	81.4	98.9	95.1	42.8	96.6
Wood Household Furniture	35.9	85.4	91.3	90.4	95.7	40.3	34.2	70.5
Textile Dyeing and Finishing	19.8	82.7	92.2	90.2	99.0	55.0	43.4	94.2
Machinery	15.5	74.3	88.8	89.0	99.6	56.4	57.2	98.4
Nonferrous Foundries	9.4	81.3	84.1	84.4	97.5	15.1	16.7	86.7
Paints and Varnishes	5.6	85.1	92.6	91.8	96.6	50.2	44.8	77.1
Industrial Chemicals	2.5	83.2	93.2	90.1	97.1	59.6	41.2	82.8
Fabricated Structural Steel	0.6	80.7	86.0	81.5	96.9	27.4	4.1	83.9
Average Across Industries**	42.7	81.0	92.5	85.3	98.3	63.8	24.3	89.1

Note: Column 1, %F, gives the percent female in the industry. Column 2 gives the raw relative wage, from equation (1) in the Appendix. Columns 3–5 give the average of the within occupation, within establishment and within occupation-establishment relative wages, computed from equations (2)–(4). Columns 6–8 give the percent of the raw wage gap, defined as 100 minus the number in column 2, that can be attributed to occupation, establishment, and occupation-establishment segregation, computed from equations (5)–(7).

*This is based on weekly wages for full-time employees.

**Each column gives the unweighted average across industries of the percentages in the respective column.

gaps is 1.7 percent, after controlling for the occupation-establishment pair.

These results are striking. Controlling for occupation or establishment alone reduces the wage gap somewhat, but not drastically. However, controlling for the occupation-establishment pair reduces the wage gap to a point of virtually no difference between men and women. The remaining female wage gap is on average 1.7 percent across the 16 industries, even without controlling for any individual-level characteristics such as education, age, seniority, and race. Occupation-establishment segregation accounts better for wage differences between men and women than any other set of variables studied in the literature on wage differences.[2]

Columns 6 to 8 give a decomposition of the raw wage gap, calculated as 100 minus the relative wage from column 2, into the percentage that is due to occupation, to establishment, and to occupation-establishment segregation, when each dimension is considered alone. These results are based on equations (5) to (7) in the appendix. Column 6 shows that occupational sex segregation alone accounts for about 64 percent of the wage gap, somewhat more than other studies have shown (e.g., Treiman and Hartmann 1981; Reskin and Roos 1990). Column 7 shows that establishment sex segregation alone accounts for about 24 percent of the wage gap. This is a new result. To date, occupational segregation has been the primary focus of gender wage gap studies. Column 8 shows that occupation-establishment sex segregation alone accounts for a large percentage of the wage gap, ranging from a low of 70.5 percent to a high of 98.4 percent. In 14 of 16 industries, more than 80 percent of the wage gap is explained by occupation-establishment segregation, and among seven of those more than 90 percent is explained, whereas in two industries only 70 percent and 77 percent of the gap is explained.

Again, we have the striking result that the interaction of occupation and establishment segregation not only explains dramatically more of the wage gap than either establishment or occupational segregation alone, it also explains most of the wage differences between men and women. Had men and women been equally distrib-

uted on occupation-establishment pairs, on the average 89 percent of the wage gap would have disappeared, assuming that other forms of discrimination would not have emerged.

One point requires discussion here. The female wage gap for the workers in our sample is about 20 percent. This is substantially less than the about 40 percent gap for all full-time workers during the period of the surveys (e.g., Goldin 1990, 61). There are several reasons for this discrepancy. One is that prior studies look at median or average annual earnings for full-time employees. It is probable that men on the average work more hours per year than women and that they also work more overtime hours. Therefore, differences between men and women are likely overstated. Another reason for this difference is that the occupations covered here comprise a relatively narrow range of the overall spectrum. In particular, professional and managerial occupations are excluded from the sample. The excluded occupations are expected to be on average higher paid than those included and to be occupied primarily by men. As a result, we have, when computing the raw wage gap of 19 percent, some degree of de facto control for occupation.

The latter results were based on data mostly for blue-collar, clerical, and some technical employees. It might be suspected that the wage gap among professional, administrative, and managerial employees is greater. However, when we turn our attention to analysis of wage differences among these employees using PATC data, the results are similar to those in the IWS data. The wage gap in the PATC data is just 3.1 percent among men and women in the same position (occupation and rank) and the same establishment.

Conclusion and Discussion

The findings of this article are simple to summarize. First, wage differences within given occupation-establishment pairs were relatively small: on average 1.7 percent among blue-collar and clerical as well as some technical employees, and on average 3.1 percent in seven professional and three administrative occupations, ranging from 1 percent in the lower to 5 percent in the higher ranks in an occupation. Thus, occupation-establishment segregation, not within-job wage discrimination was the driving force for observed wage differences.[3] Second, establishment segregation, was important for wage differences between men and women, although not as important as occupational segregation, a result we could compute only for the blue-collar, clerical, and some technical employees in the IWS data.

The first finding is important. It shows that occupation-establishment segregation accounted for more of the gender wage gap than any other variable or set of variables currently used in studying the gender wage gap. Occupational segregation alone tends to account for about 40 percent of the wage gap, and human capital and other variables also account for about 40 percent (e.g., Treiman and Hartmann 1981, chap. 2). But no set of variables, either individual or structural, accounts for as much as 89 percent, as occupation-establishment segregation did here in the case of blue-collar, clerical, and some technical employees in the IWS data.

This first finding establishes the conjecture already made in the literature, but not yet documented: wage differences are to a larger extent generated by occupation-establishment segregation than by within-job wage discrimination. Along with the first, the second finding shows the need to study establishment as well as occupational segregation.

The implications of the findings are straightforward. In terms of policy, allocative and valuative processes should be given the most attention, and within-job wage discrimination, which is covered by the Equal Pay Act of 1963 and which has been the implicit or explicit focus of much discussion and research, should receive less. Future research on differential wage attainment between men and women should be refocused as follows. The emphasis should be less on within-job wage discrimination and more on three prior processes: (1) the entry of employees into occupations and establishments, that is, the differential access of men and women to positions during the initial hiring or matching process, an allocative mechanism that is not easy to research; (2) career advancement within establishments, that is, the differential rates of promotion for men and women, also an allocative mechanism, but one which is more easily studied (Spilerman 1986); and (3) how jobs occupied primarily by women tend to be paid less than those occupied by men—the comparable worth issue, or what we refer to as valuative discrimination, also a line of research well under way (see England 1992).

Two issues arise in the identification of allocative processes as responsible for the gender wage gap. The first is whether segregation patterns are due primarily to discrimination or to differences in productive capacities. The meaning of our results for theory and policy depends on which mechanism operated here. This cannot be settled with our data and is obviously a task for future research. It requires information about productive capacities and would require an analysis of the matching between these and particular jobs.

The second issue concerns the role of supply-side sources of differential attainment between men and women. Of particular interest are the constraints put on women's career attainment from family obligations and household choices. Although these constraints may result most proximally from a traditional household division of labor, not directly from discriminatory behaviors by employers, household decisions are made in light of labor market opportunities, so the two are interdependent. The role of supply-side behaviors and their interrelationship with employer behaviors in generating the observed occupation-establishment segregation is in need of research.

Appendix

The *raw* relative wage between women and men is given as

$$w_{(r,r)} = \frac{\overline{w}_f}{\overline{w}_m} \times 100. \qquad (1)$$

The relative wage controlling for occupation obtains as

$$w_{(o,r)} = \frac{1}{N_{o(I)}} \ [\Sigma_{o=1}^{N_{o(I)}} (w_{o,r})] \times 100. \qquad (2)$$

Here, $N_{o(I)}$ is the number of occupations in which both men and women are present.

The establishment-level relative wage obtains as

$$w_{(e,r)} = \frac{1}{N_{e(I)}} \ [\Sigma_{e=1}^{N_{e(I)}} (w_{e,r})] \times 100. \qquad (3)$$

Here, $N_{e(I)}$ is the number of establishments where both men and women are present.

The occupation-establishment-level relative wage obtains as

$$w_{(oe,r)} = \frac{1}{N_{oe(I)}} \ [\Sigma_{oe=1}^{N_{oe(I)}} (w_{oe,r})] \times 100. \qquad (4)$$

Here, $N_{oe(I)}$ is the number of occupation-establishment pairs in which both men and women are present.

The raw wage gap obtains as 100 minus the number in (1). The percentage of the raw wage gap due to occupational segregation alone is given by

$$\%w_{(o,r)} = \frac{w_{(o,r)} - w_{(r,r)}}{100 - w_{(r,r)}} \times 100. \qquad (5)$$

The percentage of the raw wage gap due to establishment segregation alone is given by

$$\%w_{(e,r)} = \frac{w_{(e,r)} - w_{(r,r)}}{100 - w_{(r,r)}} \times 100. \qquad (6)$$

The percentage of the raw wage gap due to occupation-establishment segregation alone is given by

$$\%w_{(oe,r)} = \frac{w_{(oe,r)} - w_{(r,r)}}{100 - w_{(r,r)}} \times 100. \qquad (7)$$

NOTES

The article is a version of Petersen and Morgan (1995) that was excerpted and partially rewritten for this volume by Petersen and Morgan with the help of David Grusky.

1. Unfortunately, we cannot compare wages across industries, because the industry data come from different years and hence reflect inflation as well as general wage increases.

2. Although Groshen (1991) and Tomaskovic-Devey (1993) report similar results on wage differences, neither author reported the wage gap at the occupation-establishment level.

3. Similar results are shown in Petersen et al. (1997) for Norway in 1984 and 1990.

REFERENCES

Bielby, William T., and James N. Baron. 1984. "A Woman's Place Is with Other Women: Sex Segregation Within Organizations." Pages 27–55 in *Sex Segregation in the Workplace: Trends, Explanations, Remedies,* edited by Barbara F. Reskin. Washington, D.C.: National Academy Press.

Blau, Francine D. 1977. *Equal Pay in the Office.* Lexington, MA: Lexington Books.

England, Paula. 1992. *Comparable Worth: Theories and Evidence.* Hawthorne, NY: Aldine de Gruyter.

Goldin, Claudia. 1990. *Understanding the Gender Gap: An Economic History of American Women.* New York: Oxford University Press.

Groshen, Erica L. 1991. "The Structure of the Female/Male Wage Differential: Is It Who You Are, What You Do, or Where You Work?" *Journal of Human Resources* 26(3):457–72.

Hartmann, Heidi I. 1987. "Internal Labor Markets and Gender: A Case Study of Promotion." Pages 59–92 in *Gender in the Workplace,* edited by Clair Brown and Joseph Pechman. Washington, D.C.: Brookings Institution.

Petersen, Trond, and Laurie A. Morgan. 1995. "Separate and Unequal: Occupation-Establishment Sex Segregation and the Gender Wage Gap." *American Journal of Sociology* 101(2): 329–61.

Petersen, Trond, Vemund Snartland, Lars-Erik Becken, and Karen Modesta Olsen. 1997. "Within-Job Wage Discrimination and the Gender Wage Gap, The Case of Norway." *European Sociological Review* 13(2):199–215.

Reskin, Barbara F., and Patricia Roos (Eds.). 1990. *Job Queues, Gender Queues: Explaining Women's Inroads into Male Occupations.* Philadelphia: Temple University Press.

Spilerman, Seymour. 1986. "Organizational Rules and the Features of Work Careers." *Research in Social Stratification and Mobility* 5:41–102.

Tomaskovic-Devey, Donald. 1993. *Gender and Race Inequality at Work: The Sources and Consequences of Job Segregation.* Ithaca, NY: ILR Press.

Treiman, Donald J., and Heidi I. Hartmann (Eds.). 1981. *Women, Work, and Wages: Equal Pay for Jobs of Equal Value.* Washington, D.C.: National Academy Press.

U.S. Department of Labor. 1976. *Industry Wage Survey: Miscellaneous Plastics, September 1974.* Bureau of Labor Statistics, Bulletin 1914. Washington, D.C.: U.S. Government Printing Office.

———. 1977. *Dictionary of Occupational Titles.* 4th ed. Bureau of Employment Security. Washington, D.C.: U.S. Government Printing Office.

———. 1981. *National Survey of Professional, Administrative, Technical, and Clerical Pay, March 1981.* Bureau of Labor Statistics, Bulletin 2108. Washington, D.C.: U.S. Government Printing Office.

U.S. Executive Office of the President. 1987. *Standard Industrial Classification Manual.* 1987. Office of Management and Budget. Washington, D.C.: U.S. Government Printing Office.

47

Devaluation and the Pay of Comparable Male and Female Occupations

PAULA ENGLAND

The terms *comparable worth* and *pay equity* refer to a form of sex discrimination that went virtually unrecognized until the 1980s. Evidence abounds that jobs filled mostly by women have pay levels lower than they would be if the jobs were filled mostly by men. This is seen as sex discrimination by advocates of the principle of comparable worth, which posits that jobs that are equally demanding and onerous and of equal value to society should be paid equally. The theory positing that employers assign lower wages to some jobs because they are filled largely with women has come to be called the devaluation perspective. Petersen and Saporta (2004) have referred to this type of discrimination as "valuative discrimination."

At first glance, the issue of comparable worth sounds like the more familiar issue of "equal pay for equal work," which refers to men and women in the same job with the same seniority, performing the same work equally well, but being paid differently. Petersen and Saporta (2004) have called this

"within job discrimination," and it has been illegal in the United States since the 1963 Equal Pay Act and Title VII of the 1964 Civil Rights Act. However, comparable worth is distinct because it refers to comparisons between the pay in different jobs that entail at least some distinct tasks. Comparable worth advocates compare jobs that are largely male with those that are largely female (which I will sometimes, for brevity, refer to as "male" and "female" jobs) and, in some cases, claim that the difference between the pay of the two jobs results from gender bias in wage setting rather than from other job characteristics. Needless to say, this approach creates a thorny issue in distinguishing when two distinct jobs are comparable in the sense that we would expect them to pay the same in the absence of sex discrimination.

The wage discrimination at issue in a comparable worth scenario is also distinct from discrimination in hiring, initial job placement, and promotion, all of which Petersen and Saporta (2004) refer to as "allocative discrimination." Such discrimination is a

---

This is a commissioned chapter that draws heavily on material in previous publications (Paula England, *Comparable Worth: Theories and Evidence.* Copyright © 1992 by Aldine Press; Paula England, Joan M. Hermsen, and David A. Cotter, "The Devaluation of Women's Work: A Comment on Tam," *American Journal of Sociology* 105 [2000], pp. 1741–1751).

violation of Title VII of the Civil Rights Act of 1964. Hiring discrimination against women seeking to enter traditionally male jobs is one (although not the only) reason for occupational sex segregation. There are supply-side processes at work as well, such as those that lead women and men to major in different fields in college. Without segregation of jobs, female jobs could not be given a discriminatory pay level. But engaging in discrimination on the basis of sex in setting the pay levels assigned to male and female jobs is analytically distinct from engaging in hiring discrimination on the basis of sex. Moreover, valuative discrimination may exist whether or not the segregation came from allocative discrimination or from supply-side forces.

Some examples may help the reader to visualize the sorts of comparisons at issue in comparable worth. In 1975, nurses in Denver, Colorado, sued the city claiming that their jobs paid less than male jobs such as tree trimmer and sign painter. It would be hard to argue that the latter two jobs require as much skill or are as demanding as nursing. Women workers for the city of San Jose, California, discovered that secretaries were generally earning less than workers in male jobs that required no more than an eighth grade education, including, for example, men who washed cars for the city. Eventually, women in San Jose succeeded in getting the city to do a job evaluation study. The results showed, to choose some examples, that nurses earned $9,120 less annually than fire truck mechanics and that legal secretaries made $7,288 less annually than equipment mechanics. In 1985, the California School Employees Association complained that school librarians and teaching assistants (female jobs) were paid less than custodians and groundskeepers (male jobs). In recent years, the city of Philadelphia, Pennsylvania,

was paying practical nurses (mostly women) less than gardeners (mostly men). These are not atypical examples. In addition, one is hard-pressed to come up with a single example of a male job paying less than a female job that reasonable people would find comparable in skill, effort, and difficulty of working conditions. Nor are these differences in pay a result of men averaging more years of seniority than women, since in the above comparisons (from England 1992: 2), a constant level of experience was assumed.

U.S. courts have ruled that, under most conditions, this type of valuative discrimination and lack of comparable worth is not a violation of U.S. law (Nelson and Bridges 1999; England 1992: Chapter 5). Studies on data from a single employer like those reviewed here are not seen as evidence of illegal discrimination in wage setting. At present there is no legal remedy for this kind of discrimination unless there is a "smoking-gun" statement by employers that the reason they paid one job less than another was simply because it was filled with women. Statistical evidence of consistently biased pay levels is not enough. However, occasionally, some of the job evaluation studies have led private and city or state government entities to revise their pay scales to equalize salaries in jobs deemed comparable.

Economists propose two explanations for the lower pay of occupations with a high percent of female workers. The first is the theory of compensating differentials, which posits that the full pay of a job consists of both pecuniary (wage) and nonpecuniary compensation (the utility experienced from doing the work itself). Jobs with more comfortable, less hazardous working conditions can be filled with workers easily at lower wages, ceteris paribus. If women care more about nonpecuniary rewards (such as avoiding physical danger or having mother-friendly work conditions such as flexible hours or on-site child care centers) than men, and men focus more on maximizing earnings, then women will trade off earnings for amenities by choosing safer, more mother-friendly jobs. Most tests have failed to find that greater nonpecuniary amenities explain much of the lower pay of women's jobs (England 1992; Glass 1990; Glass and Camarigg 1992; Jacobs and Steinberg 1990; Kilbourne et al. 1994). The idea that women might choose lower-paying jobs for other compensations seems on first glance consistent with the finding that mothers earn less than nonmothers, even after controlling for part-time work status, experience, and seniority (Budig and England 2001; Lundberg and Rose 2000; Waldfogel 1997). But neither Glass (1990) nor Glass and Camarigg (1992) found women's jobs to have more mother-friendly characteristics than men's jobs. Similarly, Budig and England (2001) could not find any job characteristics (except part-time status) that reduced the motherhood wage penalty. Nonmothers were about as concentrated in female jobs as mothers. Thus, oddly enough, in the United States, segregation by sex does not seem to stem from women choosing or being consigned to more mother-friendly jobs. The "motherhood penalty" explains only some of the sex gap in pay, and this portion is largely unrelated to the effect of occupational sex segregation on the sex gap in pay. Thus, although the general theory of compensating differentials may have some merit, it cannot explain most of the lower pay of female jobs.

A second explanation offered by economists for the lower pay in female jobs is crowding. Bergmann (1986) argues that women's jobs pay less because they are crowded. According to this view, women seeking to enter male occupations face sex discrimination in hiring (the allocative discrimination discussed above), leading to a supply of applicants for traditionally female jobs larger than it would be in the absence of hiring discrimination as women denied entrance to male jobs crowd the female jobs. The excess supply lowers wages in female jobs. Although this is plausible, it is very difficult to test directly.

Sociologists have proposed the devaluation thesis, which posits that gender bias leads to valuing (and thus paying) female jobs less than comparably skilled male jobs (England et al. 2000; Steinberg 2001). According to these sociologists, it doesn't matter if segregation arises from allocative discrimination (in hiring and job placement) or not; employers engage in valuative discrimination once the segregation has occurred. Of course, the same evidence offered for this view would also be consistent with crowding. However, sociologists believe it is unlikely that hiring is the only place where bias occurs; it occurs in wage-setting between jobs as well.

Evidence that the sex composition of an occupation or job affects its wage level supports the devaluation theory. Such effects of sex composition, after statistically controlling for the other factors already discussed, have led some researchers to conclude that employers set lower wages (relative to job demands) when jobs are filled largely by women. One type of study takes the U.S. Census Bureau's detailed occupational categories as units of analysis. The measures include the percent female of those in the occupation, average or median male wage, median female wage, average education of incumbents, and a myriad of measures of skill demands from the *Dictionary of Occupational Titles*. These studies examine the effect of occupational percent female on average male and female wages (separately for men and women) after adding all the educational, skill, and working condition demands as control variables whose effects are adjusted out statistically. These studies find that both men and women earn less when in a more female occupation (England 1992; England et al. 2001). That is, in a regression predicting median wage, percent female of the occupation is significant and negative. (See Filer 1989 for a contrary finding.)

Other studies use individuals as units of analysis, and find that individuals in more female occupations earn less, after similar statistical controls to those described above (England et al. 2000; see Tam 1997, 2000 for a contrary view). Other studies take person/years as units of analysis, and percent female in occupations as contextual variables. The studies with person/years as units employ person-fixed effects to remove omitted variable bias; that is, they use persons as their own control and generally show that the same person earns more when moving to a more male-dominated occupation or earns less when moving to a more female-dominated occupation (Kilbourne et al. 1994; MacPherson and Hirsch 1995).

Other studies use jobs from a single employer as cases and show that female jobs pay less than male jobs when a job evaluation (of skill demands and working conditions) finds these jobs comparable (reviewed in England 1992).

All of these studies suggest that jobs pay either men or women less if they are filled mostly by women. The low pay of the largely female jobs cannot be entirely explained by how much skill the job requires or how onerous the working conditions are, because measures of these factors are controlled in the regression analyses that find a significant negative effect of the percent female in the occupation or job. These studies convince many sociologists that employers' evaluation of jobs is gendered—and that devaluation infects the wage levels of female jobs. Sociologists posit that this devaluation is perpetuated through cultural, institutional, and market mechanisms. Although the evidence of devaluation is quite strong, there is little direct evidence of the mechanisms through which it occurs.

I close with a somewhat speculative description of the process by which the devaluation of female jobs has probably occurred. At certain points in the life of organizations, particularly when they are first formed, or undergo significant restructuring, the relative wages of various jobs are somewhat up for grabs, although not unaffected by market forces. At these points, gender bias infects the decisions managers or consultants make about the wage levels for various jobs. In part, this results from a cognitive distortion in underestimating the relative contribution to profits or other organization goals of the work done in female jobs. In part, this bias on the part of organizational decision makers results from generalizing to women's jobs the relatively low status accorded women as persons by our culture. Later, bureaucratic inertia takes over, setting the wage consequences of these cultural biases in stone; the relative wage levels of jobs within an organization often remain quite constant for decades. Relative wage scales get institutionalized. If any attempt is made to change relative wage levels in a way favorable to female occupations, individual or collective action by male workers may increase the wages in male-dominated jobs over those of female-dominated jobs again. Market processes then reproduce all these effects. That is, if most employers have at some point inscribed these biases into their wage structures, this affects the "going wage" in predominantly female and male occupations that other new organizations must pay to hire workers of typical quality into the occupation. These market forces dictate that even an organization not beset by these cognitive and cultural biases will be forced to pay a higher wage to recruit in male occupations than comparable female occupations. Although they could choose to pay more than they need to in female occupations—more than the market or average wage—few profit-minded employers will do so. In these ways, gender bias is perpetuated over time. Absent significant collective action or new legislation that requires comparable worth in pay scales, the devaluing social and inertial forces described above may keep the pay penalty for working in female jobs in force indefinitely.

REFERENCES CITED

Bergmann, Barbara. 1986. *The Economic Emergence of Women*. New York: Basic Books.

Budig, Michelle J., and Paula England. 2001. "The Wage Penalty for Motherhood." *American Sociological Review* 66: 204–225.

England, Paula. 1992. *Comparable Worth: Theories and Evidence*. New York: Aldine.

England, Paula, Jennifer Thompson, and Carolyn Aman. 2001. "The Sex Gap in Pay and Comparable Worth: An Update." Pp. 551–556 in Ivar Berg and Arne Kalleberg, eds., *Sourcebook on Labor Markets: Evolving Structures and Processes*. New York: Plenum.

England, Paula, Joan M. Hermsen, and David A. Cotter. 2000. "The Devaluation of Women's Work: A Comment on Tam." *American Journal of Sociology* 105: 1741–1751.

Filer, Randall K. 1989. "Occupational Segregation, Compensating Differentials and Comparable Worth." Pp. 153–170 in Michael, Robert T., Heidi I. Hartmann, and Brigid O. Farrell, eds., *Pay Equity: Empirical Inquiries*. Washington, DC: National Academy Press.

Glass, Jennifer. 1990. "The Impact of Occupational Segregation on Working Conditions." *Social Forces* 68: 779–796.

Glass, Jennifer, and Valerie Camarigg. 1992. "Gender, Parenthood, and Job-Family Compatibility." *American Journal of Sociology* 98: 131–151.

Jacobs, Jerry, and Ronnie Steinberg. 1990. "Compensating Differentials and the Male-Female Wage Gap: Evidence from the New York State Comparable Worth Study." *Social Forces* 69: 439–468.

Kilbourne, Barbara S., Paula England, George Farkas, Kurt Beron, and Dorothea Weir. 1994. "Returns to Skill, Compensating Differentials, and Gender Bias: Effects of Occupational Characteristics on the Wages of White Women and Men." *American Journal of Sociology* 100: 689–719.

Lundberg, Shelley, and Elaina Rose. 2000. "Parenthood and the Earnings of Married Men and Women." *Labour Economics* 7:689–710.

MacPherson, D. A., and B. T. Hirsch. 1995. "Wages and Gender Composition: Why Do Women's Jobs Pay Less?" *Journal of Labor Economics* 13: 426–471.

Nelson, Robert, and William Bridges. 1999. *Legalizing Gender Inequality*. New York: Cambridge University Press.

Petersen, Trond, and Ishak Saporta. 2004. "The Opportunity Structure for Discrimination." *American Journal of Sociology* 109: 852–901.

Steinberg, Ronnie. J. 2001. "Comparable Worth in Gender Studies." Pp. 2293–2397 in N. J. Smelser and P. B. Baltes, eds., *International Encyclopedia of the Social and Behavioral Sciences*, vol. 4. London: Elsevier.

Tam, Tony. 1997. "Sex Segregation and Occupational Gender Inequality in the United States: Devaluation or Specialized Training?" *American Journal of Sociology* 102: 1652–1692.

Tam, Tony. 2000. "Occupational Wage Inequality and Devaluation: A Cautionary Tale of Measurement Error." *American Journal of Sociology* 105: 1752–1760.

Waldfogel, Jane. 1997. "The Effect of Children on Women's Wages." *American Sociological Review* 62: 209–217.

48

The Gender Pay Gap
Have Women Gone as Far as They Can?

FRANCINE D. BLAU AND
LAWRENCE M. KAHN

After half a century of stability in the earnings of women relative to men, there has been a substantial increase in women's relative earnings since the late 1970s. One of the things that make this development especially dramatic and significant is that the recent changes contrast markedly with the relative stability of earlier years.

These post–1980 earnings changes are also interesting because, when you compare women to their male counterparts, gains have been prevalent across a wide spectrum. So, for example, at first much of the female gains were centered on younger women, but now, while the gains may be a bit larger for younger women, women of all ages have narrowed the pay gap with men. The same broad progress is visible when we look at the trends in the gender pay gap by education. Less-educated women have narrowed the pay gap with less-educated men and highly educated women have narrowed the pay gap with highly educated men.

The earnings gains of women are particularly remarkable because they have occurred during a period when overall wage inequality was rising. That is, the difference in pay between workers with high wages and workers with low wages has widened considerably over the past 25 years or so. And yet, women, a low paid group, have nonetheless been able to narrow the pay gap with a relatively higher paid group, men.

The foregoing supports our initial observation that there has been important, significant progress for women. On the other hand, however, there is still a gender pay gap. Women continue to earn considerably less than men on average. It is also true that convergence slowed noticeably in the 1990s after women had especially gained relative to men in the 1980s. Although there were some larger gains for women in the early 2000s, the long-run significance of this recent experience is unclear. With the evidence suggesting that convergence has slowed in recent years, the possibility arises that the narrowing of the gender pay gap will not continue into the future. Moreover, there is evidence that although discrimination against women in the labor market has declined, some discrimination does still continue to exist.

Francine D. Blau and Lawrence M. Kahn, "The Gender Pay Gap: Have Women Gone as Far as They Can?" *Academy of Management Perspectives* 21 (2007), pp. 7–23.

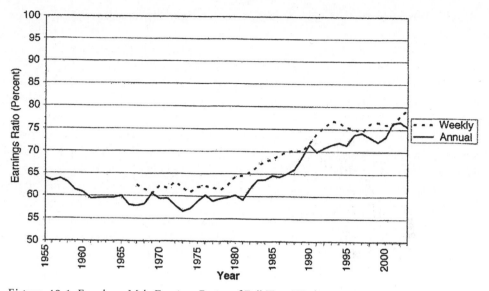

Figure 48.1 Female-to-Male Earnings Ratios of Full-Time Workers, 1955–2003

Trends in the Gender Pay Gap

In this section we look in more detail at the trends in the relative wages of women. Figure 48.1 presents data drawn from published government statistics on female-to-male earnings ratios of full-time workers. We focus on full-time workers to adjust for gender differences in hours worked. This is important because women are more likely than men to work part-time. Ideally we would like a measure of wages or an hourly rate of pay. Unfortunately, we do not have a similar long data series for hourly wages. Thus, we focus here on the earnings of full-time workers.

The figure gives the gender earnings ratio for two data series available from published government statistics. Again, both pertain to the relative earnings of female and male full-time workers. The first, the annual earnings series, is based on annual earnings data on workers who are employed year round as well as full time. The second, the weekly earnings series, is based on the earnings of full-time workers over the survey week, regardless of how many weeks per year the individual works. The annual earnings series has been available for the longest time period, 1955 to 2003; the weekly earnings series has been available for a somewhat shorter period, 1967 to 2003.

While the exact figure for the gender earnings ratio differs a bit for the two series, they both tell the same story in terms of the trends. Until the late 1970s or early 1980s there was a remarkable constancy in the ratio, at around 60%. There were some year-to-year fluctuations, but the ratio hovered around the 60% level. Indeed, if there was any discernible trend, it was a decrease in the ratio between 1955 and 1960. Then, over the 1980s, we see a period of strong, sustained increase in the ratio. This rising trend prevailed through perhaps 1990 or 1993, depending on the series. However, during the 1990s, the pace of convergence in both the annual and the weekly earnings series slowed and both series behaved more erratically. The pace of change picked up again in the early 2000s.[1] However, as noted above, the long-run significance of this recent experience is unclear. It may signal a resumption of a strong, long-run trend towards convergence in male–female earnings or may prove to be of only short duration.[2]

Abstracting from the differential trends over the various subperiods and focusing on the period since the late 1970s as a whole, the gains have been quite remarkable, especially viewed in terms of the long constancy in the gender ratio that preceded this time. So, for example, based on the weekly earnings series, the gender ratio rose from 61.3% in 1978 to 79.4% in 2003. Again, much of this increase was accomplished in a relatively short period of time, with the ratio reaching 76.8% by 1993. Of course, the 77–79% figure remains below earnings parity. Thus, clearly all sources of the pay differential between men and women have not been eradicated.

How do we explain these earnings gains for women? To address this question as well as to understand why women continue to earn less than men, we need to first consider the basic factors that explain the gender pay gap to begin with.

Economists' Explanations for the Gender Pay Gap

The Role of Qualifications and Discrimination

Economists point to a number of factors that could be important in explaining the lower earnings of women compared to men, but traditionally have focused on two primary factors. Following Juhn, Murphy, and Pierce (1991), we call these "gender-specific" factors in that they relate specifically to differences between women and men, either in their qualifications or how they are treated. With regard to qualifications, the human capital model has been especially important in pointing out the potential role played by education and experience.

The gender gap in educational attainment was never particularly large in the United States. The biggest difference historically was that, although women were more likely to graduate from high school than men, they were less likely to go on to college and graduate education. Moreover, men tended to concentrate in career-oriented fields of study such as engineering, law, medicine and business that led to relatively high earnings. These educational differences have decreased quite a bit in recent years, especially at the college level where women are actually now over half of college students; women have also greatly increased their representation in traditionally-male professional fields. Thus gender differences in education levels have never explained a large portion of the overall gender pay gap; most recently, in some samples gender differences in years of schooling favor women.

The qualification that has proven to be quite important is work experience because traditionally women moved in and out of the labor market based on family considerations. Before World War II, most women left the labor market permanently when they got married and had children. In the immediate post-war period, a pattern arose whereby older married women returned to the labor market after their children were in school or grown. An even bigger change has occurred in the past 20 to 30 years as increasing numbers of women, including married women, started staying in the labor force fairly continuously even when they had small children at home. Today, even the majority of women with children a year or less in age are participating in the labor force. Nonetheless, on average, women have less work experience than men and that difference in qualifications is quantitatively important in explaining the gender pay gap.

Jacob Mincer and Solomon Polachek (1974) have done especially important work in highlighting the role of labor market experience in explaining the gender pay gap. Given the traditional division of labor by gender in the family, women tend to accumulate less labor market experience than men. Further, because women anticipate shorter and more discontinuous work lives, they have lower incentives to invest in market-oriented formal education and on-the-job training. Their resulting smaller human capital investments lower their earnings relative to those of men. An additional way in which the traditional division of labor may disadvantage women is that the longer hours women spend on housework may also decrease the effort they put into their market jobs compared to men, controlling for hours worked, and hence also reduce their productivity and wages (Becker, 1985).

To the extent that women choose occupations for which on-the-job training is less important, gender differences in occupations are also expected. Women may especially avoid jobs requiring large investments in skills that are unique to a particular enterprise, because the returns to such investments are reaped only as long as one remains with that employer. At the same time, employers may be reluctant to hire women for such jobs because the firm bears

some of the costs of such firm-specific training, and fears not getting a full return on that investment.

However, even controlling for experience and whatever other qualifications can readily be measured, there tends to be a pay difference between men and women that is not explained and is potentially due to discrimination. Gary Becker (1971; 1st ed., 1957) has been especially instrumental in developing analyses of labor market discrimination. Although he was looking at differences between blacks and whites, the idea of prejudice and its negative consequences are readily transferable to women versus men. Becker conceptualized discriminatory preferences as the desire to maintain social distance from the discriminated group. It may at first seem odd to hypothesize that men would not like to associate with women on the job when they generally live together with women in families. However, the issue here may be more one of socially appropriate roles than of the desire to maintain social distance, as Becker postulated was the case with race.

Standard models in economics suggest discrimination can arise in a variety of ways. In Becker's model, discrimination is due to the discriminatory tastes of employers, coworkers, or customers. Alternatively, in models of "statistical discrimination," differences in the treatment of men and women arise from average differences between the two groups in the expected value of productivity (or in the reliability with which productivity may be predicted), which may lead employers to discriminate on the basis of that average (see for example, Aigner & Cain, 1977). Finally, discriminatory exclusion of women from "male" jobs can result in an excess supply of labor in "female" occupations, depressing wages there for otherwise equally productive workers, as in Bergmann's (1974) "overcrowding" model.

The typical approach to analyzing the sources of the gender pay gap is to estimate wage regressions specifying the relationship between wages and productivity-related characteristics for men and women. The gender pay gap may then be statistically decomposed into two components: one due to gender differences in measured characteristics, and the other "unexplained" and potentially due to discrimination. Such empirical studies provide evidence consistent with both human capital differences and labor market discrimination in explaining the gender pay gap.

However, any approach that relies on a statistical residual will be open to question as to whether all the necessary explanatory variables were included in the regression. For example, even if measured human capital characteristics can explain only a portion of the wage gap between men and women, it is possible that unmeasured group differences in qualifications may explain part of the residual. If men are more highly endowed with respect to these omitted variables then we would overestimate discrimination. Alternatively, if some of the factors controlled for in such regressions—like occupation and tenure with the employer—themselves reflect the impact of discrimination, then discrimination will be underestimated. Moreover, if women face barriers to entry into certain occupations, they may have higher unmeasured productivity than men in the same jobs. This factor would also suggest an underestimate of discrimination if we controlled for occupation.[3]

Using the residual from a regression to estimate the effects of discrimination will also run into trouble if feedback effects are important. Even small initial discrimina-

Table 48.1 Contribution to the Wage Differential Between Men and Women of Differences in Measured Characteristics, 1998

Characteristics	Percent Explained
Educational attainment	-6.7
Labor force experience	10.5
Race	2.4
Occupational category	27.4
Industry category	21.9
Union status	3.5
Unexplained	41.1
Total	100.0
Wage differential (%)	20.3

Source: Calculated from data presented in Blau and Kahn (2006).

tory differences in wages may cumulate to large ones as men and women make decisions about human capital investments and time allocation in the market and the home on the basis of these wage differentials.

Results of statistical studies of the gender pay gap may nonetheless be instructive. Representative findings from analyses of this type may be illustrated by results from a recent paper of ours (Blau & Kahn, 2006). Using data from the Panel Study of Income Dynamics (PSID), which contains information on actual labor market experience for a large, nationally representative sample, we found a wage differential between male and female full-time workers in 1998 of 20%. The restriction to full-time workers is designed to focus on male and female workers who are as similar as possible.[4]

The impact of gender differences in characteristics on the male-female wage differential is shown in Table 48.1. The variables considered include indicators of "human capital," that is, those relating to education and experience, as well as measures of occupation, industry and union status. (Race is also included as a control variable, but its effect is small since the proportion of each race group in the full-time sample is about the same for men and women.)

As would be expected, women's lesser amount of labor market experience is found to be a significant determinant of the gender wage differential, explaining 11% of the gender gap in wages. This reflects a 3.5 year difference in full-time experience between men and women, which, though smaller than in previous years, is still a substantial factor explaining the wage gap. Interestingly, women in this sub-sample are found to have higher educational attainment than men, which (as indicated by the negative sign in the table) works to *lower* the gender wage gap by 7%. Putting this somewhat differently, gender differences in educational attainment do not help to explain the gender wage gap, but rather work slightly in the opposite direction. While in the population as a whole, men's educational attainment is still somewhat higher than women's, when we focus on a sub-sample of the population which is not only employed, but employed full time, women have a slight edge.

Finally, gender differences in occupation and industry are substantial and help to explain a considerable portion of the gender wage gap. Men are more likely to be in blue-collar jobs and to work in mining, construction, or durable manufacturing; they are also more likely to be in unionized employment. Women are more likely to be in clerical or professional jobs and to work in the service industry. Taken together, these variables explain 53% of the gender wage gap—27% for occupation, 22% for industry, and an additional 4% for union status.[5]

Although these findings suggest that gender differences in work-related characteristics are important, they also indicate that qualifications are only part of the story. The proportion of the wage differential that is *not* explained by these types of productivity-related characteristics includes the impact of labor market discrimination, although as mentioned above, the residual may also include the effects of gender differences in unmeasured productivity levels or non-wage aspects of jobs. In this case, 41% of the gender gap cannot be explained even when gender differences in education, experience, industries, occupations, and union status are taken into account. We can consider the results of this study somewhat differently by focusing on the gender wage ratio. The actual ("unadjusted") gender wage ratio is 80%; that is, women's wages are, on average, 80% of men's wages. If women had the same human capital characteristics (that is, education and experience), racial composition, industry and occupational distribution, and union coverage as men, the "adjusted" ratio would rise to 91% of men's wages. Thus, while measured characteristics are important, women still earn less than similar men even when all measured characteristics are taken into account. And, as we suggested above, including controls for occupation, industry, and union status may be questionable to the extent that they may be influenced by discrimination.

Nonetheless, the residual gap, however measured, may well reflect factors apart from discrimination. One that has received particular attention recently is the impact of children on women's wages, since evidence of a negative effect of children on wages has been obtained, even in analyses which control for labor market experience (Waldfogel, 1998). The reason may be that, in the past, having a child often meant that a woman withdrew from the labor force for a substantial period, breaking her tie to her employer and forgoing the returns to any firm-specific training she might have acquired, as well as any rewards for having made an especially good job match. Given the sharp increase in the labor force participation of women with young children that has occurred since the 1960s, this factor may have been of growing importance in influencing the aggregate gender gap. However, the greater availability of parental leave, legally mandated in the United States since 1993, may well mitigate the effect of this factor on more recent cohorts. Indeed, Waldfogel finds that the negative effect of children on wages is substantially reduced for mothers who have maternity leave coverage.

Some studies of discrimination have taken different approaches to the question, thus avoiding some of the problems of traditional analyses. First, two studies have applied traditional econometric techniques to especially homogeneous groups and employed extensive controls for qualifications, thus minimizing the effect of gender differences in unmeasured productivity characteristics. Wood, Corcoran, and Courant (1993) studied graduates of the University of Michigan Law School classes of 1972–1975, 15 years after graduation. The gap in pay between women and men was relatively small at the outset of their careers, but 15 years later, women graduates earned only 60% as much as men. Some of this difference reflected choices that workers had made, including the propensity of women lawyers to work shorter hours. But, even controlling for current hours worked, as well as an extensive list of worker qualifications and other covariates, including family status, race, location, grades while in law school, and detailed work history data, such as years practiced law, months of part-time work, and type and size of employer, a male advantage of 13% remained. In a similar vein, Weinberger (1998) examined wage differences among recent college graduates in 1985. Her controls included narrowly defined college major, college grade point average, and specific educational institution attended. She found an unexplained pay gap of 10 to 15% between men and women.

A second set of studies used an experimental approach. Neumark (1996) analyzed the results of a hiring "audit" in which male and female pseudojob seekers were given similar résumés and sent to apply for jobs waiting on tables at the same set of Philadelphia restaurants. In high-priced restaurants, a female applicant's probability of getting an interview was 40 percentage points lower than a male's and her probability of getting an offer was 50 percentage points lower. A second study examined the impact of the adoption of "blind" auditions by symphony orchestras in which a screen is used to conceal the identity of the candidate (Goldin & Rouse, 2000). The screen substantially increased the probability that a woman would advance out of preliminary rounds and be the winner in the final round. The switch to blind auditions was found to explain 25% of the increase in the percentage female in the top five symphony orchestras in the United States, from less than 5% of all musicians in 1970 to 25% in 1996.

Third, several recent studies have examined predictions of Becker's (1971) discrimination model. Becker and others have pointed out that competitive forces should reduce or eliminate discrimination in the long run because the least discriminatory firms, which hire more lower-priced female labor, would have lower costs of production and should drive the more discriminatory firms out of business. For this reason,

Becker suggested that discrimination would be more severe in firms or sectors that are shielded to some extent from competitive pressures. Consistent with this reasoning, Hellerstein, Neumark, and Troske (2002) found that, among plants with high levels of product market power, those employing relatively more women were more profitable. In a similar vein, Black and Strahan (2001) report that, with the deregulation of the banking industry beginning in the mid–1970s, the gender pay gap in banking declined as men's wages fell by considerably more than women's (12% vs. 3%). This suggests that during the period of regulation, banks shared the rents fostered by regulation primarily with men. It was thus men who lost the most in the shift to deregulation. And, Black and Brainerd (2004) find that increasing vulnerability to international trade reduced apparent gender wage discrimination in concentrated industries, again as predicted by Becker's (1971) model.

Finally, additional evidence on discrimination comes from court cases. A number of employment practices which explicitly discriminated against women used to be quite prevalent; including marriage bars restricting the employment of married women (Goldin, 1990), and the intentional segregation of men and women into separate job categories with associated separate and lower pay scales for women (e.g., Bowe v. Colgate-Palmolive Co., 416 F.2d 711 [7th Cir. 1969]; IUE v. Westinghouse Electric Co., 631 F.2d 1094 [3rd Cir. 1980]). While many such overt practices have receded, recent court cases suggest that employment practices still exist which produce discriminatory outcomes for women.

For example, in 1994, Lucky Stores, a major grocery chain, agreed to a settlement of $107 million after Judge Marilyn Hall Patel found that "sex discrimination was the standard operating procedure at Lucky with respect to placement, promotion, movement to full-time positions, and the allocation of additional hours" (Stender v. Lucky Stores, Inc. 803 F. Supp. 259; [N.D. Cal. 1992]; King 1997). And, in 2000, the U.S. Information Agency agreed to pay $508 million to settle a case in which the Voice of America rejected women who applied for high-paying positions in the communications field. A lawyer representing the plaintiffs said that the women were told things like, "These jobs are only for men," or "We're looking for a male voice" (FEDHR, 2000). A final example is the 1990 case against Price Waterhouse, a major accounting firm, in which the only woman considered for a partnership was denied, even though, of the 88 candidates for partner, she had brought in the most business. Her colleagues criticized her for being "overbearing, 'macho' and abrasive and said she would have a better chance of making partner if she would wear makeup and jewelry, and walk, talk and dress 'more femininely.'" The Court found that Price Waterhouse maintained a partnership evaluation system that "permitted negative sexually stereotyped comments to influence partnership selection" (BNA, 1990; Lewin, 1990).

Oftentimes, economists serve as expert witnesses in court cases alleging discrimination. Their analyses, when publicly available, provide a window into discriminatory practices that still exist to some extent in the labor market, although there is of course likely to be disagreement between experts employed by each side in the type of evidence that is relevant or in the interpretation of the evidence. For example, the Lucky Stores case cited above generated an interesting exchange summarized in Taylor (2001).[6]

Labor economist John Pencavel testified for the plaintiffs, the women who brought the suit. He found that women at Lucky earned between 76 percent and 82 percent as much as Lucky's male workers earned. Pencavel found that women were regularly placed in jobs that paid less than jobs given male coworkers, although there was no significant difference between the education and experience of the workers. There was little difference in the wages of the male and female workers within each type of job; but some jobs paid more than others and women happened to be assigned to the lower-paying jobs.

Joan Haworth, another labor economist, was an expert witness for the defendant, Lucky Stores. She reported survey evidence showing that Lucky's assignment of women and men to different jobs reflected differences in the work preferences of men and women. Thus, Lucky justified its job assignments by arguing that there was a gender difference in attitudes toward work. Lucky argued that its employment policies were based on observed differences in the career aspirations of male and female employees. For example, one manager at Lucky testified that women were more interested in cash register work and men were more interested in floor work.

As we noted above, Judge Marilyn Hall Patel decided the case in favor of the plaintiffs. With respect to the evidence cited above, she wrote: "The court finds the defendant's explanation that the statistical disparities between men and women at Lucky are caused by differences in the work interests of men and women to be unpersua-

sive." An interesting aspect of this case is that both sides agreed that male and female employees received equal pay for equal work and that the pay differential was associated with pay differences across occupations. They differed, however, over the source of the occupational differences: the choices of women vs. discrimination. This disagreement mirrors the alternative explanations economists offer in general for wage and occupational difference between men and women: differences in qualifications based on the choices men and women make versus discrimination which limits the opportunities and pay of women compared to men.

Some additional evidence supporting discrimination as a source of the type of occupational differences cited above is provided by a recent study of eight years of data from an unidentified regional grocery chain on gender differences in job titles and wage rates (Ransom & Oaxaca, 2005). As in the case of the Pencavel analysis summarized above, Ransom and Oaxaca find a pattern of gender differences in initial job assignment and upward mobility within the firm that "generally penalized women, even when the analysis account[ed] for individuals' characteristics" (p. 219). While one might again dispute the reason for these differences, the authors found that job segregation of women and men was dramatically lower in the period after the company lost a discrimination suit (1984) and reached a settlement (1986) in which it initiated affirmative action policies. This implies that it was possible to find women interested in higher-level jobs, leading one to doubt that such segregation was entirely voluntary.

These cases emphasize the role of occupational segregation by sex within firms in producing pay differences between men and women. Pencavel explicitly notes that there was little difference in pay between men and women in the same job. It is worth noting that economists and sociologists who have examined this issue across a wider range of firms have tended to come to a similar conclusion: pay differences between men and women in the same narrowly-defined occupational categories within the same firm tend to be small (Blau, 1977; Groshen, 1991; Petersen & Morgan, 1995; and Bayard, Hellerstein, Neumark, & Troske, 1999). However, even when men and women are in the same occupation, they tend to be segregated by firm, and such establishment segregation contributes substantially to the gender pay gap.

The Role of Wage Structure

In earlier work, building on a framework suggested by Chinhui Juhn, Kevin Murphy, and Brooks Pierce (1991), we point out that there is another factor that needs to be considered when analyzing gender differences in pay, and that is what we call wage structure (Blau & Kahn, 1996 and 1997). We define wage structure as being the market returns to skills and the rewards for employment in particular sectors of the economy. Market returns to skills denote the premiums the market determines for being a more experienced worker or a more highly educated worker, etc. Rewards for employment in particular sectors of the economy refer to the fact that, for example, unionized workers tend to earn more than comparable nonunionized workers or workers in some industries—durable goods, manufacturing for example—may earn more than similarly-qualified workers in other industries, say services. In addition, considerable research suggests that predominantly female occupa-

tions pay less, even controlling for measured personal characteristics of workers and a variety of characteristics of occupations, although the interpretation of such results remains in some dispute.[7]

We distinguish wage structure from gender-specific factors because the idea is that these are the returns to skills or the rewards for working in a particular industry or occupation regardless of whether you are male or female. Why should wage structure affect the gender pay gap? To see how, let's think a bit more about the two factors we discussed earlier—gender differences in qualifications and labor market discrimination. Suppose women do have less experience, on average, than men do. Then, the higher the return to experience the larger the gender pay gap will be. Or, suppose that jobs staffed primarily by women do pay less than jobs staffed primarily by men. Then, the higher the premium for being in a male occupation the larger the gender pay gap will be.

This is interesting because these market returns have in fact varied over time. In the last 25 years or so, the market returns to skills, like those acquired with work experience, have increased. So this is a factor that, taken alone, would have worked to increase the gender pay gap. The rewards to being in male occupations and industries have increased as well, and that factor, taken alone, would have increased the pay gap as well. So, one question that we have raised in our research is: How have women been able to successfully swim against the tide of rising returns to skills and rising rewards to being in particular industries and occupations? That is, how have they managed to narrow the pay differential with men in the face of the adverse trends in wage structure that have worked against them?

Before looking at the results of our research addressing these questions, let's consider the issue of why the returns to skills have been increasing. There is a fairly broad consensus among economists (though not complete unanimity) that within countries like the United States, one of the main reasons that the returns to skills have been rising is that the demand by employers for skilled workers has been rising relative to the demand for unskilled workers. Why has this occurred? There are at least two reasons. The one that that we would put the most weight on is technological change. The information and telecommunications revolution has worked to put more of a premium on skill, at least thus far. There are other scenarios possible, but thus far it has increased the demand for skilled workers compared to less skilled workers. The other reason—we would put less weight on it although it has also played a role—is international trade. Today, less skilled workers in the United States are to some extent competing against less skilled workers from around the world; many of them are available at much lower wages. Factors in addition to demand shifts that appear to have also played a role are—a decline in the union movement since unions tend to push for more egalitarian pay structures, the falling real value the minimum wage (adjusted for inflation, the minimum wage is actually lower today than it was in the 1970s), an influx of unskilled immigrants, and a decrease in the rate of growth of college-educated workers.

While rising returns to skills may be hypothesized to widen the gender pay gap, all else equal, it is possible that the demand shifts discussed above may have favored women relative to men in certain ways, and thus contributed to a decrease in the unexplained gender pay gap (Blau & Kahn, 1997; Welch, 2000). Technological change is believed to have caused within-industry demand shifts that favored white collar workers in general (Berman, Bound, & Griliches, 1994). Given the traditional male predominance in blue-collar jobs, this shift might be expected to benefit women relative to men. Similarly, to the extent that the spread of computer technology is an important source of recent technological change, the observation that women are more likely than men to use computers at work suggests that women as a group may have benefited from shifts in demand associated with computerization (Autor, Katz, & Krueger, 1998; Weinberg, 2000). Diffusion of computers likely also benefits women because computers restructure work in ways that de-emphasize physical strength (Weinberg, 2000).

Explaining the Trends: The 1980s

Returning to the trends in the gender pay gap—how do we explain them? To answer this question, we summarize results from Blau and Kahn (1997 and 2006). Using data from the PSID (we reported on some of our results above), we analyzed women's wage gains over the 1980s (1979–1989), which, as we saw in Figure 48.1, was a period of exceptionally rapid closing of the gender wage gap. We found that higher rewards to skills did indeed retard wage convergence during this period but this was more than offset by improvements in gender-specific factors.

Of particular importance was the decline in the experience difference between men and women: the gender gap in full-time experience fell from 7.5 to 4.6 years over this period. Shifts in major occupations played a significant role too, as the employment of women as professionals and managers rose relative to men's, while their relative employment in clerical and service jobs fell. Women's wages also increased relative to men's because of deunionization (the decline of unions). Deunionization had a larger negative impact on male than female workers because men, who have traditionally been more likely than women to be unionized, experienced a larger decrease in unionization than women. Another factor that worked to increase the gender pay ratio substantially was a decrease in the "unexplained" portion of the gender differential—that is, a decline in the pay difference between men and women with the same measured characteristics (i.e., experience, education, occupation, industry, and union status).

Taken together, changes in qualifications and in the unexplained gap worked to increase the gender wage ratio substantially. Working in the opposite direction, however, were changes in wage structure (or returns to characteristics) that favored men over women during this period. Of particular importance were a rise in the return to experience (since women have less of it) and increases in returns to employment in industries where men are more highly represented. These shifts in labor market returns by themselves would have reduced the gender ratio substantially. Thus, in order for the wage gap to decline, the factors favorably affecting women's wages had to be large enough to more than offset the impact of unfavorable shifts in returns. This was indeed the case, so that the gender pay gap did decline over the 1980s.

Can we say anything about the reasons for the decline in the unexplained gender wage gap that occurred over the 1980s? Such a shift may reflect a decline in labor market discrimination against women, but also an upgrading of women's *unmeasured*

labor market skills, a shift in labor market demand favoring women over men, or changes in the composition of the labor force due to the pattern of labor force entries or exits. Indeed all of these factors may well have played a role, and all appear credible during this period.

First, since women improved their relative level of measured skills, as shown by the narrowing of the gap in full-time job experience and in occupational differences between men and women, it is plausible that they also enhanced their relative level of unmeasured skills. For example, women's increasing labor force attachment may have encouraged them to acquire more on-the-job training or encouraged their employers to offer them more training. Evidence also indicates that gender differences in college major, which have been strongly related to the gender wage gap among college graduates (Brown & Corcoran, 1997), decreased over the 1970s and 1980s (Blau, Ferber, & Winkler, 2002); the marketability of women's education has probably improved. The male-female difference in SAT math scores has also been declining, falling from 46 points in 1977 to 35 points in 1996 (Blau, Ferber, & Winkler, 2002), which could be another sign of improved quality of women's education.

Second, the argument that discrimination against women declined in the 1980s may seem less credible than that their unmeasured human capital characteristics improved, since the federal government scaled back its antidiscrimination enforcement effort during the 1980s (Leonard, 1989). However, as women increased their commitment to the labor force and improved their job skills, the rationale for statistical discrimination against them diminished; thus it is plausible that this type of discrimination decreased. Further, in the presence of feed-back effects, employers' revised views can generate additional increases in women's wages by raising women's returns to invest-ments in job qualifications and skills. To the extent that such qualifications are not fully controlled for in the statistical analysis used to explain the change in the gender wage gap, this may also help to account for the decline in the "unexplained" gap. Another possible reason for a decline in discrimina-tion against women is that changes in social attitudes have made such discriminatory tastes increasingly less acceptable.

Third, the underlying labor market de-mand shifts that widened wage inequality over the 1980s may have favored women relative to men in certain ways, and thus may have also contributed to a decrease in the unexplained gender gap. Overall, manufacturing employment declined. In addition, there is some evidence that technological change produced within-in-dustry demand shifts that favored white-collar relative to blue-collar workers in general. As noted above, given the tradi-tional male predominance in blue-collar jobs, this shift might be expected to bene-fit women relative to men, as would in-creased computer use.

Finally, another factor contributing to the considerable narrowing of the "unex-plained" gender wage gap in the 1980s appears to be favorable shifts in the com-position of the female labor force. Specifi-cally, we found that, controlling for the measured characteristics mentioned earlier, the women who entered the labor force over this period tended to be those with rel-atively high (unmeasured) skills. This im-proved the quality of the female labor force and thus contributed to the narrowing of the gender wage gap. . . .

Explaining the Trends: The 1990s

Why did convergence in female and male wages slow over the 1990s? Again, drawing on our previous work (Blau & Kahn, 2006) we may suggest some tentative answers. We found that human capital trends cannot ac-count for the slowdown: women improved their relative human capital by about the same amount in both the 1980s and the 1990s. In the 1980s this upgrading con-sisted of rising relative experience while in the 1990s it consisted to a lesser extent of rising relative experience and to a greater extent of increasing educational attainment of women relative to men. Nor did changes in wage structure in the 1990s have a more adverse effect on women than changes in the previous decade—in fact the impact of changing wage structure was actually more negative for women in the 1980s. Slowing convergence in men's and women's occupa-tions and degree of unionization in the 1990s was found to account for some of the slowdown, but only a small portion.

We found that the major reason for the slowdown in wage convergence in the 1990s was the considerably smaller narrow-ing of the "unexplained" gender pay gap in the 1990s compared to the 1980s. Our rea-soning above suggests that this could be due to slower improvement in women's un-measured qualifications relative to men's in the 1990s than in the 1980s; a smaller de-cline in discrimination against women in the 1990s than in the 1980s; or less favor-able demand shifts for women in the 1990s than in the 1980s. Each of these factors ap-pears to have played a role in explaining the observed trends. In addition, controlling for measured characteristics, female labor force entrants were less skilled during the 1990s, perhaps as a result of the entry of

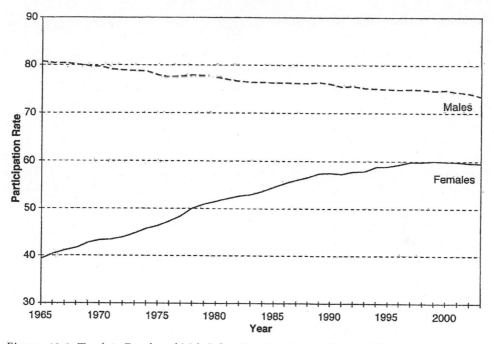

Figure 48.2 Trends in Female and Male Labor Force Participation Rates, 1965–2003

many relatively low-skilled, female single-family heads. Indeed, differences between the two decades in such shifts in labor force composition were found to explain as much as 25% of the apparent slowdown in convergence in the unexplained gender pay gap in the 1990s.

As we noted above, women narrowed the experience gap at a slower pace in the 90s than they did in the 80s. Figure 48.2 shows the trends in male and female labor force participation that underlie this development. The most striking trend shown in the figure is that the *difference* in the participation rates of men and women has narrowed considerably since the starting year, 1965. This is due to a slow steady decrease in male labor force participation combined with a much sharper and dramatic increase in female labor force participation. The decrease in male participation does not appear

to be due very much to changes in gender roles. Rather it primarily reflects the fact that men are retiring at earlier ages and are staying in school longer. Another factor has been the weakening job market for less skilled men (Juhn, 1992).

While the data in the figure begin in the mid–1960s, the large increases in female participation in fact date back to the 1940s. Interestingly, the trend towards rising female labor force participation was strong and consistent until about 1990. After that the line becomes noticeably flatter. Women's participation increased a bit through 1997, with no further increases thereafter.

How do these participation trends relate to the average experience levels of women workers? Unfortunately, it is not possible to figure this out just by looking at participation rates. This is because the labor force participation rate of women can increase for either of two reasons or a combination of both. On the one hand, participation may rise because a lot of new groups of women come into the labor market. This tends to lower the average experience of women workers because there are a lot of new entrants. On the other hand, participation can increase because women stay in the labor force more consistently over a period of time, rather than moving in and out. This works to raise average experience levels of women workers.

Research has shown that during the 1970s the average experience of women did not increase because those two factors counter balanced each other. There were a lot of new entrants and a lot of women staying in more continuously, thus average experience remained about the same (Goldin, 1990). In the 1980s, though, the increase in the labor force participation of women was due to more of them remaining in the labor force more consistently. And, as we have seen, the average experience of women workers rose accordingly. This suggests that the flattening of the trend in female labor force participation shown in the chart caused the gender gap in experience to decline more slowly in the 1990s than in the 1980s.

Before leaving the subject of the participation trends, it is interesting to consider their larger significance. Viewed more broadly, what the trends show is an enormous change in gender roles and a movement away from the traditional family of breadwinner husband and homemaker wife to a family where both husband and wife work outside the home, although not necessarily giving equal weight to each of their careers. Ralph Smith (1979) called this process a "subtle revolution." The

trends suggest that this subtle revolution, having accomplished a great deal, may be slowing down now. Is it stopping? Not necessarily. But we have reached a situation where, looking at women in the prime working ages (that is, 25 to 55), over three quarters of them are in the labor force. This means that female labor force participation rates in the United States are very high, although still below the male rates of around 90% in this age group. So it may not be surprising that, of necessity, future participation trends will be less dramatic than past trends.

Prospects for the Future

Although we readily acknowledge that predicting the future is a tricky business, we cautiously offer some thoughts on the prospects for the future. What will happen to the gender pay gap in the coming years? Recent developments make the answer to this question particularly uncertain. As we have seen, after a period of consistent and sustained narrowing of the gender pay gap over the 1980s, convergence became more fitful in the 1990s. Perhaps what we saw in the 1990s was a mere pause; perhaps we were consolidating the really massive changes that had occurred over the preceding 10 to 20 years—not just in the gender pay gap but also in women's labor force participation and in the occupations in which they work; perhaps the next 20 years will show similar renewed gains on all these fronts. That could very well be. Or we may have reached a point that we are going to stay at for quite a while, a big change from the past but not so much change in the future. It is even possible that under certain circumstances the gender pay gap could begin to widen, returning to levels of an earlier period. While we cannot choose among these options with certainty, it may be instructive to consider each of the factors that we have identified as influencing the gender pay gap and consider the possible future course of each and its likely impact on the pay gap.

One of the factors influencing the trends in the gender pay gap is overall trends in wage inequality. Rising wage inequality, to the extent that it results from increasing returns to skills like work experience that women have less of than men, on average, is expected to widen the gender pay gap, all else equal. In this respect, it has been noted that wage inequality increased less during the 1990s than during the 1980s (Katz & Autor, 1999). If this tapering off in the trend towards rising inequality should continue into the future, the negative effect of this factor on the pace of convergence in the gender pay gap will be small.

On the other hand, to the extent that rising wage inequality was due to demand shifts that favored women relative to men, it may be hypothesized that such shifts, and the relative advantage they may have given women relative to men, have also tapered off and are likely to be dampened in the future as well. This is suggested by the fact that the shedding of blue collar, manufacturing jobs was particularly pronounced in the 1980s. A closely related development, deunionization, which also disadvantaged men to a greater extent than women, is likely to occur at a slower pace in the future as unionization rates in the private sector have reached single digits, giving little scope for substantial future declines, and public sector unionization remains relatively stable. While demand shifts favoring women may have slowed, so too has the growth in the supply of women to the labor market. If this slower growth in supply continues into the future, it may mean that demand- and supply-side shifts offset each other and thus, taken together, do not have much effect on convergence in the gender pay gap.

Although overall female labor force participation increased modestly in the 1990s, welfare reforms and other government policies spurred an increase in employment among single mothers (see, for example, Meyer & Rosenbaum, 2001). The growth in participation among single heads, who tend on average to be less well educated than other women, could also have slowed wage convergence by shifting the composition of the female labor force toward low-wage women. We did indeed find some evidence consistent with this in our earlier work (Blau & Kahn, 2006), though this factor does not appear to be the main reason for the slowing convergence in the gender wage gap in the 1990s. Thus it seems unlikely that a further entry of single mothers into the labor force in the future will have a large impact on the *aggregate* gender pay gap.

Moving toward the more traditional factors of women's relative qualifications and the possibility of labor market discrimination against them, there is little reason to expect large changes here either. The flattening of the growth in women's labor force participation rates, if it continues, suggests that large increases in women's work experience and labor force commitment are unlikely, although this statement must be qualified somewhat since, as we have explained, trends in the average experience of women cannot be inferred directly from changes in participation rates. Similarly, now that women comprise the majority of college students, further large gains in the relative educational attainment of women appear unlikely, though there is room for continued reductions in the gender differences in college major and at the graduate level in professional schools and Ph.D. programs in many fields.

Turning to labor market discrimination, now that the most open and egregious forms of sex discrimination have been greatly reduced or eliminated and discrimination increasingly becomes more subtle and possibly even unconscious, future large declines in discrimination in the labor market may become more difficult to attain. In addition, the decreases in statistical discrimination that we hypothesized as occurring in response to women's increasing labor force attachment can be expected to slow as increases in women's attachment also slow. However, there seems room for some further decrease in statistical discrimination as the profound changes in gender roles that have already occurred continue to percolate through the labor market and the larger society and as additional changes continue to occur, albeit at a slower pace than in the past. And it is likely that even subtle barriers do change as women increasingly enter new areas and achieve success at higher levels. Putting this somewhat differently, while the glass ceiling may not have broken completely, it is showing a lot of cracks and is likely to show more and more cracks as time goes on.

Taking all these factors into account, our best guess is that we are going to have further changes in the direction of convergence, but most probably at a slower pace. Our own view is that one development that is extremely unlikely is that we will see a reversal of the gains in relative wages and labor force participation women have experienced over the past 25 to 30 years. We do not expect a substantial widening of the male/female pay gap or labor force participation gap to occur. On the other hand, while precisely how much narrowing we will see in the future is an open question, the gender pay gap seems unlikely to vanish in the near term.

For one thing, women continue to confront discrimination in the labor market, and, although its extent seems to be decreasing, it seems unlikely to be completely eliminated soon. In addition, at least some of the remaining pay gap is surely tied to the gender division of labor in the home, both directly through its effect on women's labor force attachment and indirectly through its impact on the strength of statistical discrimination against women. Women still retain primary responsibility for housework and child care in most American families. However, this pattern has been changing as families respond to rising labor market opportunities for women that increase the opportunity cost of such arrangements. Further, policies that facilitate the integration of work and family responsibilities, both voluntary and government-mandated, have become increasingly prevalent in recent years. Employers are likely to continue to expand such policies as they respond to the shifting composition of the work force and a desire to retain employees in whom they have made substantial investments. In the longer run, the increasing availability of such policies will make it easier for women to combine work and family, and also for men to take on a greater share of household tasks.

Finally, while our principal concern has been with the pay of women relative to men, trends in inequality among women show a deterioration in the relative economic status of less educated women that is strikingly parallel to similar trends in the labor market for men (see Table 48.2).

Table 48.2 Mean Earnings of Education Groups Relative to High School Graduates, 1974 and 2003 (%)

	1974		2003	
Education	Men	Women	Men	Women
High school:				
1–3 years	88.9	85.3	75.9	76.6
4 years	100.0	100.0	100.0	100.0
College:				
1–3 years	113.6	112.6	122.8	119.5
4 or more years	155.0	147.2	211.3	190.4

Data refer to year-round, full-time workers 18 years of age and older. In 2003, median income for 1–3 years of college is computed as a weighted average of the medians for "some college, no degree" and "associate degree."
Source: 2003: PINC04 Tables of the U.S. Census Bureau Current Population Survey, 2004 Annual Social and Economic Supplement, from http://ferrets.census.gov/macro/032004/perinc/new04_000.htm; 1974: U.S. Census Bureau Historical Income Tables—People, Table P–35, from www.census.gov/hhes/income/histinc/p35.html.

These developments for less educated women serve to underscore the widening gap between more and less skilled Americans of both sexes, as well as to emphasize its broad dimensions.

NOTES

1. Between 1980 and 1990, the average annual increase in the ratio was 1.14 percentage points for annual earnings and .74 percentage points for weekly earnings, while, between 1990 and 2000, it was only .16 percentage points for annual earnings and .42 percentage points for weekly earnings. Relative earnings growth in the early 2000s was more robust: between 2000 and 2003, the average annual increase in the ratio was .75 percentage points for annual earnings and 1.14 percentage points for weekly earnings.

2. One short-term factor could be the recession of 2001 and the relatively high unemployment rates that lingered in its aftermath. The demand for male workers tends to be more cyclically sensitive than that for female workers due to their greater concentration in blue-collar jobs and durable manufacturing industries.

3. If, as is likely, one is unable to completely control for nonwage job characteristics such as fringe benefits, safety, or job security, then the residual may again not give an accurate estimate of the extent of discrimination against women. We cannot say a priori what the effect of such omissions is. On the one hand, to the extent that men are likely to work in less safe or less secure jobs than women, such analyses may overestimate discrimination. On the other hand, to the extent that men have higher fringe benefit levels, an analysis of wage residuals will understate discrimination. To some degree, these nonwage characteristics can be accounted for by controlling for industry and occupation, although as mentioned, these controls may also reflect exclusionary hiring practices.

4. In addition to gender differences in qualifications and the extent of discrimination, the gender earnings differential may also be affected by the self-selection of women and men into full-time employment and, more generally, into the labor force. In other words, those choosing to participate—or to work full-time—may differ from those outside the labor force or part-time workers in terms of both their measured and unmeasured characteristics. One possibility, for example, is that labor force participants are a positively selected group of those who have received higher wage offers. Similarly, full-time workers may be more highly qualified and more committed to market work. We in fact find that, at a point in time, the gender pay gap is smaller if only full-time workers are considered than if

part-timers and nonparticipants are included; we examine the impact of changes in female and male selection into the labor force for trends in the gender pay gap (see below). Other research that has examined the earnings differential for white and black women has found that, if self-selection is not accounted for, the race differential is underestimated; see Neal (2004).

5. The study controls for 19 occupations and 25 industries.

6. This quotation is from the Textbook Site for *Principles of Microeconomics*, 3rd ed., *Additional Topics*, "Using Economics to Explain Gender Pay Gaps," at http://college.hmco.com/economics/taylor/econ/3e/micro/students/add_topics/ch02_genderpay.html, accessed June 28, 2002. The summary is based on materials presented in West's Federal Supplement (1993).

7. See, for example, Sorensen (1990), Kilbourne, England, Farkas, Beron, and Weir (1994), and Macpherson and Hirsch (1995).

REFERENCES

Aigner, D., & Cain, G. (1977). Statistical theories of discrimination in labor markets. *Industrial and Labor Relations Review*, 30, 175–187.

Autor, D.H., Katz, L.F., & Krueger, A.B. (1998). Computing inequality: Have computers changed the labor market? *Quarterly Journal of Economics*, 113, 1169–1214.

Bayard, K., Hellerstein, J., Neumark, D., & Troske, K. (1999). New evidence on sex segregation and sex difference in wages from matched employee-employer data. NBER Working Paper No. 7003, March.

Becker, G.S. (1957). *The economics of discrimination*, 2nd ed. Chicago: University of Chicago Press, 1971; 1st ed.

———. (1985). Human capital, effort, and the sexual division of labor. *Journal of Labor Economics*, 3, S33–S58.

Bergmann, B. (1974). Occupational segregation, wages, and profits when employers discriminate by race or sex. *Eastern Economic Journal*, 1, 1–2, 103–110.

Berman, E., Bound, J., & Griliches, Z. (1994). Changes in the demand of skilled labor within U.S. manufacturing industries: Evidence from the annual survey of manufacturing. *Quarterly Journal of Economics*, 109, 367–397.

Black, S.E., & Brainerd, E. (2004). The impact of globalization on gender discrimination. *Industrial & Labor Relations Review*, 57, 540–559.

Black, S.E., & Strahan, P.E. (2001). The division of spoils: Rent-sharing and discrimination in a regulated industry. *American Economic Review*, 91, 814–831.

Blau, F.D. (1977). *Equal pay in the office*. Lexington, MA: Lexington Books.

———. (1998). Trends in the well-being of American women, 1970–1995. *Journal of Economic Literature*, 36, 112–165.

Blau, F.D., Ferber, M.A., & Winkler, A.E. (2006). *The economics of women, men, and work*, 5th ed. Upper Saddle River, NJ: Prentice-Hall.

Blau, F.D., & Kahn, L.M. (1996). Wage structure and gender earnings differentials: An international comparison. *Economica*, 63, S29–S62.

———. (1997). Swimming upstream: Trends in the gender wage differential in the 1980s. *Journal of Labor Economics*, 15, 1–42.

———. (2006). The US gender pay gap in the 1990s: Slowing convergence. *Industrial & Labor Relations Review*, 60, 45–66.

Brown, C., & Corcoran, M. (1997). Sex-based differences in school content and the male/female wage gap. *Journal of Labor Economics*, 15, 431–65.

Bureau of National Affairs (BNA). (1990). *Daily Labor Report*, no. 235, December 6, pp. A11–A13 and F1–F10.

Federal Human Resources Week (FEDHR). (2000, April 5). Government to pay $508 million for sex discrimination at U.S. Information Agency. Vol. 6, p. 47.

Goldin, C. (1990). *Understanding the gender gap*. New York: Oxford University Press.

Goldin, C., & Rouse, C. (2000). Orchestrating impartiality: The impact of 'blind' auditions on female musicians. *American Economic Review*, 90, 715–741.

Groshen, E.L. (1991). The structure of the female/male wage differential: Is it who you are, what you do, or where you work? *Journal of Human Resources*, 26, 457–472.

Hellerstein, J.K., Neumark, D., & Troske, K. (2002). Market forces and sex discrimination. *Journal of Human Resources*, 37, 353–380.

Juhn, C. (1992). Decline of male labor market participation: The role of declining market opportunities. *Quarterly Journal of Economics*, 107, 79–121.

Juhn, C., Murphy, K.M., & Pierce, B. (1991). Accounting for the slowdown in black-white wage convergence. In M. Kosters (Ed.), *Workers and their wages* (pp. 107–143). Washington, D.C.: AEI Press.

Katz, L.F., & Autor, D.H. (1999). Changes in the wage structure and earnings inequality. In C.O. Ashenfelter & D. Card (Eds.), *Handbook of labor economics* (vol. 3A, pp. 1463–1555). Amsterdam: Elsevier.

Kilbourne, B.S., England, P., Farkas, G., Beron, K. & Weir, D. (1994). Returns to skill, compensating differentials, and gender bias: Effects of occupational characteristics on the wages of white women and men. *American Journal of Sociology*, 100, 689–719.

King, R. (1997, April 27). Women taking action against many companies. *The Times-Picayune.*

Lewin, T. (1990, May 16). Partnership awarded to woman in sex bias case. *The New York Times*, pp. A1, A12.

Leonard, J. (1989). Women and affirmative action. *Journal of Economic Perspectives*, 3, 61–75.

MacPherson, D.A., & Hirsch, B.T. (1995). Wages and gender composition: Why do women's jobs pay less? *Journal of Labor Economics*, 13, 426–471.

Meyer, B.D., & Rosenbaum, D.T. (2001). Welfare, the earned income tax credit, and the labor supply of single mothers. *Quarterly Journal of Economics*, 116, 1063–1114.

Mincer, J., & Polachek, S. (1974). Family investments in human capital: Earnings of women. *Journal of Political Economy*, 82, S76–S108.

Neal, D. (2004). The measured black-white wage gap among women is too small. *Journal of Political Economy*, 112, S1–S28.

Neumark, D.M. (1996). Sex discrimination in restaurant hiring: An audit study. *Quarterly Journal of Economics*, 111, 915–941.

Petersen, T., & Morgan, L.A. (1995). Separate and unequal: Occupation-establishment sex segregation and the gender wage gap. *American Journal of Sociology*, 10, 329–361.

Ransom, M., & Oaxaca, R.L. (2005). Intrafirm mobility and sex differences in pay. *Industrial and Labor Relations Review*, 58, 219–237.

Smith, R.E. (1979). The movement of women into the labor force. In R.E. Smith (Ed.), *The subtle revolution: Women at work* (pp. 1–29). Washington, DC: Urban Institute.

Sorensen, E. (1990). The crowding hypothesis and comparable worth issue. *Journal of Human Resources*, 25, 55–89.

Taylor, J.B. (2001). *Principles of economics*, 3rd ed. Boston, MA: Houghton Mifflin.

Waldfogel, J. (1998). The family gap for young women in the United States and Britain: Can maternity leave make a difference? *Journal of Labor Economics*, 16, 505–545.

Welch, F. (2000). Growth in women's relative wages and in inequality among men: One phenomenon or two? *American Economic Review*, 90, 444–449.

West's Federal Supplement (1993). Vol. 803, pp. 259–337. St. Paul, MN: West Publishing Company.

Weinberg, B. (2000). Computer use and the demand for female workers. *Industrial and Labor Relations Review*, 53, 290–308.

Weinberger, C.J. (1998). Race and gender wage gaps in the market for recent college graduates. *Industrial Relations*, 37, 67–84.

Wood, R.G., Corcoran, M.E., & Courant, P. (1993). Pay differences among the highly paid: The male-female earnings gap in lawyers' salaries. *Journal of Labor Economics*, 11, 417–441.

49

The Nanny Chain

ARLIE RUSSELL HOCHSCHILD

Vicky Diaz, a 34-year-old mother of five, was a college-educated schoolteacher and travel agent in the Philippines before migrating to the United States to work as a housekeeper for a wealthy Beverly Hills family and as a nanny for their two-year-old son. Her children, Vicky explained to Rhacel Parrenas,

> were saddened by my departure. Even until now my children are trying to convince me to go home. The children were not angry when I left because they were still very young when I left them. My husband could not get angry either because he knew that was the only way I could seriously help him raise our children, so that our children could be sent to school. I send them money every month.

In her book *Servants of Globalization,* Parrenas, an affiliate of the Center for Working Families at the University of California, Berkeley, tells an important and disquieting story of what she calls the "globalization of mothering." The Beverly Hills family pays "Vicky" (which is the pseudonym Parrenas gave her) $400 a week, and Vicky, in turn, pays her own family's live-in domestic worker back in the Philippines $40 a week. Living like this is not easy on Vicky and her family. "Even though it's paid well, you are sinking in the amount of your work. Even while you are ironing the clothes, they can still call you to the kitchen to wash the plates. It . . . [is] also very depressing. The only thing you can do is give all your love to [the two-year-old American child]. In my absence from my children, the most I could do with my situation is give all my love to that child."

Vicky is part of what we could call a *global care chain*: a series of personal links between people across the globe based on the paid or unpaid work of caring. A typical global care chain might work something like this: An older daughter from a poor family in a third world country cares for her siblings (the first link in the chain) while her mother works as a nanny caring for the children of a nanny migrating to a first world country (the second link), who, in turn, cares for the child of a family in a rich country (the final link). Each kind of chain expresses an invisible human *ecology of care,* one care worker depending on another and

Arlie Russell Hochschild, "The Nanny Chain," *The American Prospect* 11 (January 3, 2000), pp. 1–4.

so on. A global care chain might start in a poor country and end in a rich one, or it might link rural and urban areas within the same poor country. More complex versions start in one poor country and extend to another slightly less poor country and then link to a rich country.

Global care chains may be proliferating. According to 1994 estimates by the International Organization for Migration, 120 million people migrated—legally or illegally—from one country to another. That's 2 percent of the world's population. How many migrants leave loved ones behind to care for other people's children or elderly parents, we don't know. But we do know that more than half of legal migrants to the United States are women, mostly between ages 25 and 34. And migration experts tell us that the proportion of women among migrants is likely to rise. All of this suggests that the trend toward global care chains will continue. . . .

If it is true that attention, solicitude, and love itself can be "displaced" from one child (let's say Vicky Diaz's son Alfredo, back in the Philippines) onto another child (let's say Tommy, the son of her employers in Beverly Hills), then the important observation to make here is that this displacement is often upward in wealth and power. This, in turn, raises the question of the equitable distribution of care. It makes us wonder, is there—in the realm of love—an analogue to what Marx calls "surplus value," something skimmed off from the poor for the benefit of the rich?

Seen as a thing in itself, Vicky's love for the Beverly Hills toddler is unique, individual, private. But might there not be elements in this love that are borrowed, so to speak, from somewhere and someone else?

Is time spent with the first world child in some sense "taken" from a child further down the care chain? Is the Beverly Hills child getting "surplus" love, the way immigrant farm workers give us surplus labor? Are first world countries such as the United States importing maternal love as they have imported copper, zinc, gold, and other ores from third world countries in the past?

This is a startling idea and an unwelcome one, both for Vicky Diaz, who needs the money from a first world job, and for her well-meaning employers, who want someone to give loving care to their child. Each link in the chain feels she is doing the right thing for good reasons—and who is to say she is not?

But there are clearly hidden costs here, costs that tend to get passed down along the chain. One nanny reported such a cost when she described (to Rhacel Parrenas) a return visit to the Philippines: "When I saw my children, I thought, 'Oh children do grow up even without their mother.' I left my youngest when she was only five years old. She was already nine when I saw her again but she still wanted for me to carry her [weeps]. That hurt me because it showed me that my children missed out on a lot."

Sometimes the toll it takes on the domestic worker is overwhelming and suggests that the nanny has not displaced her love onto an employer's child but rather has continued to long intensely for her own child. As one woman told Parrenas, "The first two years I felt like I was going crazy. . . . I would catch myself gazing at nothing, thinking about my child. Every moment, every second of the day, I felt like I was thinking about my baby. My youngest, you have to understand, I left when he was only two months old. . . . You know, whenever I receive a letter from my children, I cannot sleep. I cry. It's good that my job is more demanding at night."

Despite the anguish these separations clearly cause, Filipina women continue to leave for jobs abroad. Since the early 1990s, 55 percent of migrants out of the Philippines have been women; next to electronic manufacturing, their remittances make up the major source of foreign currency in the Philippines. The rate of female emigration has continued to increase and includes college-educated teachers, businesswomen, and secretaries. . . .

The End of the Chain

Just as global capitalism helps create a third world supply of mothering, it creates a first world demand for it. The past half-century has witnessed a huge rise in the number of women in paid work—from 15 percent of mothers of children aged 6 and under in 1950 to 65 percent today. Indeed, American women now make up 45 percent of the American labor force. Three-quarters of mothers of children 18 and under now work, as do 65 percent of mothers of children 6 and under. In addition, a recent report by the International Labor Organization reveals that the average number of hours of work per week has been rising in this country.

Earlier generations of American working women would rely on grandmothers and other female kin to help look after their children; now the grandmothers and aunts are themselves busy doing paid work outside the home. Statistics show that over the past 30 years a decreasing number of families have relied on relatives to care for their children—and hence are compelled to look for nonfamily care. At the first world end of care chains, working parents are grateful to find a good nanny or child care provider, and they are generally able to pay far more than the nanny could earn in her native country. This is not just a child care problem. Many American families are now relying on immigrant or out-of-home care for their *elderly* relatives. As a Los Angeles elder-care worker, an immigrant, told Parrenas, "Domestics here are able to make a living from the elderly that families abandon." But this often means that nannies cannot take care of their own ailing parents and therefore produce an elder-care version of a child care chain—caring for first world elderly persons while a paid worker cares for their aged mother back in the Philippines.

My own research for two books, *The Second Shift* and *The Time Bind,* sheds some light on the first world end of the chain. Many women have joined the law, academia, medicine, business—but such professions are still organized for men who are free of family responsibilities. The successful career, at least for those who are broadly middle class or above, is still largely built on some key traditional components: doing professional work, competing with fellow professionals, getting credit for work, building a reputation while you're young, hoarding scarce time, and minimizing family obligations by finding someone else to deal with domestic chores. In the past, the professional was a man and the "someone else to deal with [chores]" was a wife. The wife oversaw the family, which—in pre-industrial times, anyway—was supposed to absorb the human vicissitudes of birth, sickness, and death that the workplace discarded. Today, men take on much more of the child care and housework at home, but they still base their identity on demanding careers in the context of which children are beloved impediments; hence, men resist sharing care equally at home. So when parents don't have enough "caring time" between them, they feel forced to look for that care further down the global chain.

The ultimate beneficiaries of these various care changes might actually be large multinational companies, usually based in the United States. In my research on a Fortune 500 manufacturing company I call Amerco, I discovered a disproportionate number of women employed in the human side of the company: public relations, marketing, human resources. In all sectors of the company, women often helped others sort out problems—both personal and professional—at work. It was often the welcoming voice and "soft touch" of women workers that made Amerco seem like a family to other workers. In other words, it appears that these working mothers displace some of their emotional labor from their children to their employer, which holds itself out to the worker as a "family." So, the care in the chain may begin with that which a rural third world mother gives (as a nanny) the urban child she cares for, and it may end with the care a working mother gives her employees as the vice president of publicity at your company.

PART VII

Generating Inequality

50

No Degree, and No Way Back to the Middle

TIMOTHY EGAN

Over the course of his adult life, Jeff Martinelli has married three women and buried one of them, a cancer victim. He had a son and has watched him raise a child of his own. Through it all, one thing was constant: a factory job that was his ticket to the middle class.

It was not until that job disappeared, and he tried to find something—anything—to keep him close to the security of his former life that Martinelli came to an abrupt realization about the fate of a workingman with no college degree in twenty-first-century America.

He has skills developed operating heavy machinery, laboring over a stew of molten bauxite at Kaiser Aluminum, once one of the best jobs in Spokane, Washington, a city of 200,000. His health is fine. He has no shortage of ambition. But the world has changed for people like him.

"For a guy like me, with no college, it's become pretty bleak out there," said Martinelli, who is fifty years old and deals with life's curves with a resigned shrug.

His son Caleb already knows what it is like out there. Since high school, Caleb has had six jobs, none very promising. Now twenty-eight, he may never reach the middle class, he said. But for his father and others of a generation that could count on a comfortable life without a degree, the fall out of the middle class has come as a shock. They had been frozen in another age, a time when Kaiser factory workers could buy new cars, take decent vacations, and enjoy full health care benefits.

They have seen factory gates close and not reopen. They have taken retraining classes for jobs that pay half their old wages. And as they hustle around for work, they have been constantly reminded of the one thing that stands out on their résumés: the education that ended with a high school diploma.

It is not just that the American economy has shed six million manufacturing jobs over the last three decades; it is that the market value of those put out of work, people like Jeff Martinelli, has declined considerably over their lifetimes, opening a gap that has left millions of blue-collar workers at the margins of the middle class.

And the changes go beyond the factory floor. Mark McClellan worked his way up from the Kaiser furnaces to management. He did it by taking extra shifts and learning everything he could about the aluminum business.

Still, in 2001, when Kaiser closed, McClellan discovered that the job market did not value his factory skills nearly as much as it did four years of college. He had the experience, built over a lifetime, but no degree. And for that, he said, he was marked.

He still lives in a grand house in one of the nicest parts of town, and he drives a big white Jeep. But they are a facade.

"I may look middle class," said McClellan, who is forty-five, with a square, honest face and a barrel chest. "But I'm not. My boat is sinking fast."

By the time these two Kaiser men were forced out of work, a man in his fifties with a college degree could expect to earn 81 percent more than a man of the same age with just a high school diploma. When they started work, the gap was only 52 percent. Other studies show different numbers, but the same trend—a big disparity that opened over their lifetimes.

Martinelli refuses to feel sorry for himself. He has a job in pest control now, killing ants and spiders at people's homes, making barely half the money he made at the Kaiser smelter, where a worker with his experience would make about $60,000 a year in wages and benefits.

"At least I have a job," he said. "Some of the guys I worked with have still not found anything. A couple of guys lost their houses."

Martinelli and other former factory workers say that, over time, they have come to fear that the fall out of the middle class could be permanent. Their new lives—the frustrating job interviews, the bills that arrive with red warning letters on the outside—

are consequences of a decision made at age eighteen.

The management veteran McClellan was a doctor's son, just out of high school, when he decided he did not need to go much farther than the big factory at the edge of town. He thought about going to college. But when he got on at Kaiser, he felt he had arrived.

His father, a general practitioner, now dead, gave him his blessing, even encouraged him in the choice, McClellan said.

At the time, the decision to skip college was not that unusual, even for a child of the middle class. Despite McClellan's lack of skills or education beyond the twelfth grade, there was good reason to believe that the aluminum factory could get him into middle-class security quicker than a bachelor's degree could, he said.

By twenty-two, he was a group foreman. By twenty-eight, a supervisor. By thirty-two, he was in management. Before his fortieth birthday, McClellan hit his earnings peak, making $100,000 with bonuses.

Friends of his, people with college degrees, were not earning close to that, he said.

"I had a house with a swimming pool, new cars," he said. "My wife never had to work. I was right in the middle of middle-class America and I knew it and I loved it."

If anything, the union man, Martinelli, appreciated the middle-class life even more, because of the distance he had traveled to get there. He remembers his stomach growling at night as a child, the humiliation of welfare, hauling groceries home through the snow on a little cart because the family had no car.

"I was ashamed," he said.

He was a C student without much of a future, just out of high school, when he got his break: the job on the Kaiser factory floor. Inside, it was long shifts around hot furnaces. Outside, he was a prince of Spokane.

College students worked inside the factory in the summer, and some never went back to school.

"You knew people leaving here for college would sometimes get better jobs, but you had a good job, so it was fine," said Mike Lacy, a close friend of Martinelli and a coworker at Kaiser.

The job lasted just short of thirty years. Kaiser, debt-ridden after a series of failed management initiatives and a long strike, closed the plant in 2001 and sold the factory carcass for salvage.

McClellan has yet to find work, living off his dwindling savings and investments from his years at Kaiser, though he continues with plans to open his own car wash. He pays $900 a month for a basic health insurance policy—vital to keep his wife,

Vicky, who has a rare brain disease, alive. He pays an additional $500 a month for her medications. He is both husband and nurse.

"Am I scared just a little bit?" he said. "Yeah, I am."

He has vowed that his son David will never do the kind of second-guessing that he does. Even at sixteen, David knows what he wants to do: go to college and study medicine. He said his father, whom he has seen struggle to balance the tasks of home nurse with trying to pay the bills, had grown heroic in his eyes.

He said he would not make the same choice his father did twenty-seven years earlier. "There's nothing like the Kaiser plant around here anymore," he said.

McClellan agrees. He is firm in one conclusion, having risen from the factory floor only to be knocked down: "There is no working up anymore."

51

Nonpersistent Inequality in Educational Attainment

Evidence from Eight European Countries

RICHARD BREEN,
RUUD LUIJKX,
WALTER MÜLLER, AND
REINHARD POLLAK

In their seminal study on the development of inequality in educational attainment in the 20th century, Shavit and Blossfeld (1993) summarize the results under the guiding title *Persistent Inequality*. In spite of dramatic educational expansion during the 20th century, of the 13 countries studied in their project, all but two, Sweden and the Netherlands, "exhibit stability of socio-economic inequalities of educational opportunities. Thus, whereas the proportions of all social classes attending all educational levels have increased, the relative advantage associated with privileged origins persists in all but two of the thirteen societies" (p. 22). This conclusion is based on a metaanalysis of individual country studies, all of which adopt two different approaches to assess socioeconomic inequalities of educational opportunities: one is to use ordinary least squares to regress years of education achieved

by sons and daughters on parents' education and occupational prestige; the other is to regress, using binary logistic regression, a set of successive educational transitions on the same social background variables (the "Mare model"; Mare 1980, 1981). Change or persistence in inequalities of educational opportunities is diagnosed depending on whether or not significant variation over birth cohorts is found in the regression coefficients linking social background to years of education attained and the educational transitions considered. While the two analyses address different empirical phenomena—of which Shavit and Blossfeld are well aware—the results of both suggest essentially the same conclusion, which the authors then summarize as "stability of socio-economic inequalities of educational opportunities." In the scientific community, in particular in sociology and in the education sciences,

Richard Breen, Ruud Luijkx, Walter Müller, and Reinhard Pollak, "Nonpersistent Inequality in Educational Attainment," *American Journal of Sociology* 114, no. 5 (2009), pp. 1475–1521.

the results have been viewed as evidence of a persistently high degree of class inequality of educational attainment that can change only under rather exceptional conditions.

Shavit and Blossfeld's result echoed earlier findings from some single-country studies, but subsequently several analyses have contested this finding. They have shown that equalization also took place in Germany (Müller and Haun 1994; Henz and Maas 1995; Jonsson, Mills, and Müller 1996), France (Vallet 2004), Italy (Shavit and Westerbeek 1998), and the United States (Kuo and Hauser 1995). Rijken's (1999) comparative analysis comes to the same conclusion. In other studies, Breen and Whelan (1993) and Whelan and Layte (2002) confirm persistent inequality for Ireland, whereas for Soviet Russia, Gerber and Hout (1995) find mixed results (declining inequality in secondary education and increasing inequality in transitions to university). For the postsocialist period in various countries of Eastern Europe, the origin-education association is regularly found to be very high and is likely higher than in the socialist period (Gerber [2000] for Russia; Iannelli [2003] for Hungary, Romania, and Slovakia).

The aim of this article is to reassess the empirical evidence concerning the conclusion of *Persistent Inequality* using more recent data and larger samples from a selection of European countries. In contrast to Shavit and Blossfeld, we base our conclusions on analyses using ordered logit models of educational attainment rather than on educational transition models. The reason is that we are interested in inequalities related to social origin in completed education, which constitutes the major starting condition for unequal opportunities in the life course. Another reason for not using educational transition models is that we lack data on individuals' complete educational histories. Indeed, there are no cross-nationally comparable large data sets that contain complete education histories and also cover long historical periods.

Reasons to Suppose That Educational Inequality Was Not Persistent

Differences between students from different social classes in how they fare in the educational system can, in simple terms, be seen to derive from differences in how they perform in the educational system (which Boudon [1974] called "primary effects") and differences in the educational choices they make, even given the same level of performance ("secondary effects"). In both areas, developments in the course of the 20th century would lead us to expect declining class differences.

As far as primary effects are concerned, children raised in families in the more advantaged classes encounter better conditions in their home environments that help them to do better in school. They get more intellectual stimulation that strengthens their cognitive abilities, and their parents are more highly motivated and supportive of schoolwork than parents of working-class children. Different performance at school may also derive from different nutrition and health in different classes, whereas genetic differences between individuals from different class backgrounds may play a role as well as class differences in sibship sizes (see Erikson and Jonsson 1996a). Yet, as Erikson and Jonsson (1996b, p. 81) suggest, the general improvement in conditions of living should have made working-class children less disadvantaged in terms of health and nutrition. With economic development and welfare-state protection, the minimum standards of living have improved and average family size has declined. Such changes should have been more relevant for families in the less advantaged classes, such as the working classes and the small-farmer class, who have been able to move out of absolute economic misery. Some decline in primary class effects should thus have occurred over the long term and particularly during the substantial improvement of general living conditions in the decades of economic growth and welfare-state expansion following World War II. This should have been reinforced by changes within educational institutions, such as the growth in public provision of early child care and preschool education; the development of full-day rather than part-time schooling; increased school support to counteract performance gaps of pupils; and differences in the timing, extent, and manner of tracking, all of which may reduce class differences in school performance.

As far as secondary effects are concerned, one factor that should have brought about a major reduction is the declining costs of education. Direct costs, especially in secondary education, have become smaller; school fees have been largely abolished; the number of schools has increased, even in rural areas, so schools can be reached more easily; and traveling conditions have improved. In many countries, educational support programs for less wealthy families have been set up, albeit of rather different kinds and levels of generosity. Real average family income has increased, and that should make it easier to bear the costs of education. While at least in the first half of the last century working-class children were

urged to contribute to the family income as early as possible, such pressures have declined. In most countries, economic growth and the reduction in family size have led to an increase in disposable incomes beyond what is required for basic needs. In practically all countries the length of compulsory schooling has expanded, thus reducing the number of additional school years beyond compulsory education needed to reach full secondary education. Countries certainly differ in the specifics of institutional reforms, and these probably have different implications; but the lengthening of compulsory education should everywhere have contributed to a decline in the additional costs of postcompulsory education.

Countries also differ in their welfare-state and social security arrangements and in their ability to prevent unemployment among students' parents. In countries such as Sweden, in which serious income equalization policies have been pursued successfully, the equalization of conditions is believed to have had an additional impact on reducing the class differential in the ability to bear the costs of education. The recurrence of high levels of unemployment in many countries since the 1980s, especially for the unskilled working class, and the increase in income inequality observed in some countries in recent years (Alderson and Nielsen 2002) are probably the most important changes that may have counteracted a long-term trend toward lowering the impact of costs in producing class inequalities in educational participation, but these developments are mostly too recent to be evident in our data. In sum, both primary and secondary effects changed in ways such that declining disparities between classes in educational attainment can be expected; in particular, it is the children of working-class and farm families who should have most markedly improved their relative position.

Data

Our data come from nine European countries—Germany, France, Italy, Ireland, Britain, Sweden, Poland, Hungary, and the Netherlands—and they were originally assembled for a comparative analysis of social mobility in Europe (Breen 2004). That project sought to bring together all the high-quality data sets collected between 1970 and 2000 in 11 European countries that could be used for the analysis of social mobility. The data used here are identical to those employed in that project except that the German data have been augmented by six surveys. These six surveys contain the first three German Life History Surveys for West Germany (fielded between 1981 and 1989) as well as the 2000 sample for West Germany from the German Socio-economic Panel and the ALLBUS Surveys for 2000 and 2002. The Hungarian data are excluded from the final analysis, as will be described later. The data sets that we use are listed in table 51.1. In total we use 120 surveys collected between 1970 and 2002, but each country provides rather different numbers of surveys (up to a maximum of 35 from the Netherlands). In Sweden, for example, there is a survey for every year from 1976 to 1999, whereas the analysis for Italy are based on only two surveys and those for Ireland and Poland on only three surveys each.

We use data on men ages 30–69 (30–59 in Great Britain, except for the years 1979–88, when the age range is 30–49). We adopt 30 as the lower age limit to ensure that everyone in the samples will have

attained his highest level of education, and we take 69 as an upper limit in order to minimize any effects of differential mortality. We confine our analysis to men because the inclusion of both sexes, and comparisons between them, would have made a long article excessively so. We intend to analyze educational inequality among women, and compare it with the results reported here, in a further paper.

Variables

We use four variables in our analysis. *Cohort* (C) defines five birth cohorts: 1908–24, 1925–34, 1935–44, 1945–54, and 1955–64. Thus we have information on cohorts born throughout the first two-thirds of the 20th century. *Survey period* (S) defines the five-year interval in which the data were collected: 1970–74, 1975–79, 1980–84, 1985–89, 1990–94, 1995–99, and 2000–2004.

Highest level of educational attainment (E) is measured using the CASMIN educational schema (Comparative Analysis of Social Mobility in Industrial Nations; see table 51.A1 below; Braun and Müller 1997). We have amalgamated categories 1a, 1b, and 1c and also 2a and 2b, giving us five educational categories:

1abc.—Compulsory education with or without elementary vocational education
2ab.—Secondary intermediate education, vocational or general
2c.—Full secondary education
3a.—Lower tertiary education
3b.—Higher tertiary education

We have only four educational categories in the Hungarian data, where 2ab is missing,

Table 51.1 Sources of Data

Country	No. of Tables	Sources of Data	Years for Which Data Are Included
Germany	30	Zumabus	1976–77, 1979 (2), 1980, 1982
		ALLBUS	1980, 1982, 1984, 1986, 1988, 1990–92, 1994, 1996, 1998, 2000, 2002
		Politik in der BRD	1978, 1980
		Wohlfahrtssurvey	1978
		German Life History Study	1981–83 (I), 1985–88 (II), 1988–89 (III)
		German Socio-economic Panel	1986, 1999, 2000
France	4	Formation-qualification professionnelle INSEE surveys	1970, 1977, 1985, 1993
Italy	2	National Survey on Social Mobility	1985
		Italian Household Longitudinal Survey	1997
Ireland	3	Survey of the Determinants of Occupational Status and Mobility	1973
		Survey of Income Distribution and Poverty	1987
		Living in Ireland Survey	1994
Great Britain	15	General Household Survey	1973, 1975–76, 1979–84, 1987–92
Sweden	24	Annual Surveys of Living Conditions (ULF)	1976–99
Poland	3	Zagórski (1976)	1972
		Slomczynski et al. (1989)	1988
		Social Stratification in Eastern Europe after 1989	1994
Hungary	4	Social Mobility and Life History Survey	1973, 1983, 1992
		Way of Life and Time Use Survey (Hungarian Central Statistical Office)	2000
Netherlands	35	Parliamentiary Election Study	1970, 1971, 1977, 1981, 1982, 1986, 1994, 1998
		Political Action Survey I	1974, 1979
		Justice of Income Survey	1976
		CBS Life Situation Survey	1977, 1986
		National Labour Market Survey	1982
		National Prestige and Mobility Survey	1982
		Strategic Labour Market Survey	1985, 1988, 1990, 1992, 1994, 1996, 1998
		Cultural Changes (ISSP)	1987
		Justice of Income Survey	1987
		Primary and Social Relationships	1987
		Social and Cultural Trends	1990
		Justice of Income Survey (ISJP)	1991
		Family Survey I, 1992–93	1992
		Households in the Netherlands pilot	1994
		Households in the Netherlands	1995
		Social Inequality in the Netherlands	1996
		National Crime Study	1996
		Social and Economic Attitudes	1998
		Netherlands Family Survey II	1998
		Use of Information Technology	1999

Table 51.A1 CASMIN Educational Categories

Category	Definition
1a	Inadequately completed elementary education
1b	Completed (compulsory) elementary education
1c	(Compulsory) elementary education and basic vocational qualification
2a	Secondary: intermediate vocational qualification or intermediate general qualification and vocational training
2b	Secondary: intermediate general qualification
2c_gen	Full general maturity qualification
2c_voc	Full vocational maturity certificate or general maturity certificate and vocational qualification
3a	Lower-tertiary education
3b	Higher-tertiary education

Table 51.A2   EGP Class Categories

Category	Definition
I	Higher-grade professionals, administrators, and officials; managers in large industrial establishments; large proprietors
II	Lower-grade professionals, administrators, and officials; higher-grade technicians; managers in small industrial establishments; supervisors of nonmanual employees
IIIa	Routine nonmanual employees, higher grade (administration and commerce)
IVa	Small proprietors, artisans, etc. with employees
IVb	Small proprietors, artisans, etc. without employees
IVc	Farmers and smallholders; other self-employed workers in primary production
V	Lower-grade technicians; supervisors of manual workers
VI	Skilled manual workers
VIIa	Semi- and unskilled manual workers (not in agriculture, etc.)
VIIb	Agricultural and other workers in primary production
IIIb	Routine nonmanual employees, lower grade (sales and services)

and in the Italian and the Irish data, where no distinction has been made between 3a and 3b. The CASMIN educational schema seeks to capture distinctions not only in the level of education but also in the type, and one consequence of this is that the five levels we identify cannot be considered to be sequentially ordered in any simply way. For example, in some countries lower tertiary education can be accessed directly from secondary intermediate education, whereas in most countries, higher tertiary is not usually entered after lower tertiary.

Class origins (*O*) are categorized using the Erikson-Goldthorpe-Portocarero (EGP) class schema (see app. Table 51.A2; also Erikson and Goldthorpe 1992, chap. 2). We identify seven classes:

I.—Upper service
II.—Lower service
IIIa.—Higher-grade routine nonmanual
IVab.—Self-employed and small employers
IVc.—Farmers
V + VI.—Skilled manual workers, technicians, and supervisors

Table 51.2 Sample Sizes for Cohorts by Country

| | Cohort | | | | | |
Country	1908–24	1925–34	1935–44	1945–54	1955–64	Total
Germany	2,323	3,110	4,852	4,007	2,832	17,124
France	11,283	14,169	13,126	10,517	2,610	51,705
Italy		742	1,182	1,286	827	4,037
Ireland	744	1,176	1,509	1,289	863	5,581
Great Britain	6,473	9,112	24,481	20,971	5,437	66,474
Sweden	8,032	8,209	10,875	10,145	4,093	41,354
Poland	7,729	9,248	8,851	1,002	784	27,614
Hungary	5,698	6,829	7,175	5,643	2,583	27,928
Netherlands	2,385	3,507	4,736	5,612	3,511	19,751
Total	44,667	56,102	76,787	60,472	23,540	261,568

VIIab + IIIb.—Semi- and unskilled manual, agricultural, and lower-grade routine nonmanual workers

In Britain and Poland the data allow us to identify only six class origins. In both countries we cannot distinguish classes I and II, whereas in Britain, members of Iva are included in I + II (see Goldthorpe and Mills 2004). Furthermore, in Poland, we cannot split the class III, so here IIIb is included with IIIa rather than with VIIab. In Ireland also we combine I and II because of very small numbers in class I in some cohorts.

The resulting four-way table of class origins (O) by educational attainment (E) by cohort (C) by survey period (S) is of maximum dimensions $7 \times 5 \times 5 \times 7 = 1,225$, though this number includes many structural zeros in those combinations of cohort and survey that are not observed. Furthermore, we omitted all those observations of cohort by survey in which the table of origins by education would have been extremely sparse. All the cells in such a table were treated as structural zeros.

Table 51.2 shows the resulting sample sizes for all the countries by cohort. These vary quite considerably, and this will obviously affect our ability to detect statistically significant trends. The sample sizes for Italy and Ireland are particularly small, and one consequence of this is that we have very few observations of the oldest cohort in Italy, so we omit it from our analyses.

Changes in Educational Attainment and Class Origins

Perhaps the single most striking thing that differentiates the older from the younger cohorts in our data is the massive increase in educational attainment that has occurred. Figure 51.1 shows the proportions in each cohort in each country that have attained at least upper-secondary (2c) education, and figure 51.2 shows the proportions having attained tertiary (3a and 3b) education.[1] The upward trends in both are obvious and are similar across countries.

It is not only the educational distributions that have shifted, however. During the course of the 20th century the class structures of European nations underwent major change, with a move away from farming and unskilled occupations and toward skilled jobs and white-collar jobs.

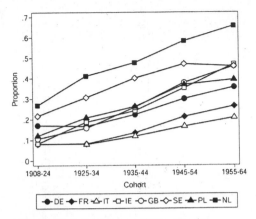

Figure 51.1 Proportion of Men Reaching at Least Upper-Secondary Education, by Country and Cohort

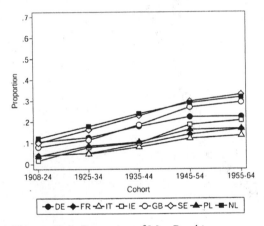

Figure 51.2 Proportion of Men Reaching Tertiary Education, by Country and Cohort

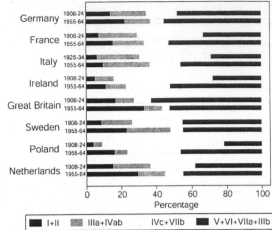

Figure 51.3 Proportions of men in various class origins for first and last cohort by country (marginal distributions). In Great Britain, class IVa is included in classes I + II; in Poland, class IIIb is included in classes IIIa + IVab.

Analyses

We focus on modeling the joint distribution of class origins and highest level of education using the ordered logit model. Letting Y be the random variable measuring educational attainment, we can write the probability that Y is less than a particular level of education, j, given background variables X, as $\gamma_j(x)$. There exists a family of statistical models that sets $g[\gamma_j(x)] = tj - \beta'x$ (McCullagh 1980), where g is a link function (such as the logit, the inverse normal, or the complementary log-log) that maps the (0, 1) interval into $(-\infty, \infty)$. The logit link, which yields the ordered logit model, sets $g[\gamma_j(x)] = \ln[\gamma_j(x)]/[1 - \gamma_j(x)]$ and for any two observations with covariate values x and x' we get

$$g[\gamma(x)] - g[\gamma(x')] = \ln\frac{\gamma(x)}{1 - \gamma(x)} - \ln\frac{\gamma(x')}{1 - \gamma(x')}$$

$$= \beta(x' - x),$$

Some aspects of this are shown in figure 51.3, which reports the share of the service class (I and II), intermediate class (IIIa and IVab), the farm classes (IVc and VIIb), and working class (V + VI, VIIa + IIIb) in the origins of the oldest and youngest cohorts in each country. The decline of the farm class and growth of the service class are evident everywhere, and the working class has grown or remained stable everywhere except Britain.

Table 51.3 Model Fits for Ordered Logit Models, by Country, Survey, and Cohort: Chi-Squared Summary Measure of Change of *OE* Effects Across Cohorts for *SCOE* Data Table (Controlling for *SOE*) and *COE* Data Table

	Data from *SCOE* Table, Controlling for *SOE*			Data from *COF* Table (Collapsed over *S*)		
Country	Change *COE* (1)	No *OE* Change (2)	ΔG^2 (3)	Change *COE* (4)	No *OE* Change (5)	ΔG^2 (6)
Germany	557.0 (468)	642.0 (492)	84.9 (24)	134.4 (90)	234.6 (114)	100.2 (24)
France	515.0 (312)	629.3 (336)	114.3 (24)	283.5 (90)	459.5 (114)	176 (24)
Italy	90.1* (96)	111.0* (114)	20.8* (18)	43.7* (48)	67* (66)	23.3* (18)
Ireland	189.2 (130)	221.1 (150)	31.8 (20)	101.8 (50)	155.3 (70)	53.4 (20)
Great Britain	709.9 (275)	780.0 (295)	70.1 (20)	502.7 (75)	604.4 (95)	101.7 (20)
Sweden	624.1 (450)	723.4 (474)	99.3 (24)	286.2 (90)	413.2 (114)	126.9 (24)
Poland	191.5 (115)	318.8 (135)	127.3 (20)	192.5 (50)	351.3 (70)	158.8 (20)
Netherlands	613.5 (516)	694.3 (540)	80.8 (24)	154.1 (90)	266.5 (114)	112.4 (24)

Note: —Numbers in parentheses are degrees of freedom.
* Not significant at *P*<.05.

and so the log odds ratio of exceeding, or failing to exceed, any particular threshold is independent of the thresholds themselves and depends only on the betas.

The ordered logit model has two attractive properties: it is more parsimonious than the multinomial logit or the Mare model, and, provided that the ordered logit is the correct model for the data, the estimates of the β parameters are unaffected by collapsing adjacent categories of *Y*. This invariance means that if the educational system makes finer distinctions than have been captured in the variable *Y*, the β's are unaffected by our having measured education less precisely. It also implies that, when making comparisons, provided that the same stochastic ordering of categories is used in all samples, we do not require the categories to be defined in exactly the same way. This facilitates both temporal and cross-national comparisons. This property is not shared by the educational transition model or by multinomial logit models, whose estimates are tied to particular categorizations of educational attainment. But the advantages of the ordered logit come at a price: the model assumes that class inequalities are identical at each level of education. This is sometimes called the parallel slopes or proportional odds assumption and is frequently found not to hold. We address this problem in our analyses.

In table 51.3 we report the goodness of fit of the ordered logit models in which we control for survey (cols. 1–3) and in which

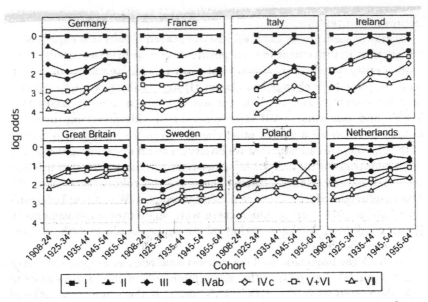

Figure 51.4 Ordered logit models for educational attainment in eight countries for men. Class origin effects over cohorts, controlled for survey effects. Class I is classes I + II in Ireland and Poland and classes I + II + IVa in Britain; educational levels 3a and 3b are merged in Italy and Ireland.

we do not (cols. 4–6). In all models the thresholds, t_j, are allowed to vary over cohort: in the models in columns 1 and 4, class origin effects are allowed to vary over cohorts, whereas in columns 2 and 5 they are held constant. The final column in each case shows the deviance comparing the model of change against the model of constancy in class effects. This shows significant change everywhere except Italy (although the Irish data barely reach significance when we control for survey period). The deviance associated with this change is lesser when we control for survey effects compared with when we do not, so our conclusions about change are unaffected, though the magnitude of that change is a little smaller.

One can also see, however, that, with the .05 level of significance, the ordered logit model fails to fit the data in almost all

countries, suggesting that the parallel slopes assumption does not hold. Elsewhere, we discuss the departures from proportionality in our data and we find that they are not consequential, so for the most part we base our findings on the results of the models whose goodness of fit is reported in column 1 of table 51.3 and whose parameter estimates are shown in figure 51.4 (see Breen et al. 2009).

In figure 51.4 each line refers to a class origin and shows how the coefficients for that class evolve over cohorts, with class I always acting as the reference category (classes I + II in Ireland and Poland and I + II + IVa in Britain) and having a coefficient of zero. The overall impression is of a decline in class inequalities everywhere (even in Italy, where the change is not statistically significant), but figure 51.4 also allows us to see how the relative positions of the various classes have shifted. In Germany there was a general narrowing of class differentials in educational attainment following the 1925–35 birth cohort and continuing until the 1945–54 cohort. Little change is evident between the latter and the youngest cohort. In France equalization started later, with the 1935–44 cohort, and continued longer, persisting into the 1955–64 cohort. It was slightly more differentiated by class origins than in Germany because men from class III showed no change in their position relative to men from class I, whereas men of farm origins (class IVc) experienced a particularly marked improvement in their relative position. In Sweden all classes have improved their position relative to class I, as in Germany, and the decline in inequality largely took place throughout the whole observation period. The Dutch case too shows a general tendency toward a narrowing of class differentials; this occurs over all cohorts, for the most part, and classes IVab, IVc, V + VI, and VII have made the greatest gains. In contrast with these four countries, the British picture is more complicated. Although all classes except III are less differentiated from class I in the youngest cohort than they were in the oldest, almost all the improvement for classes IVb and V + VI occurred between the 1908–24 and 1925–34 cohorts, whereas for class VII there has been a more prolonged improvement and for class IVc an improvement from the 1935–44 cohort onward. In Poland there has been a steady improvement in the relative positions of classes IVc, V + VI, and VII until the middle cohort, at which point the position of IVc worsens, followed by a worsening of the positions of IVab and VII in the youngest cohort. In Italy we find a modest decrease in class inequalities until the 1945–54 cohort, after which class in-

equalities tended to reassert themselves. Class VII is an exception because its position continues to improve, albeit slightly. Finally, in the Irish case, over the five cohorts the distance between class I and all other classes was reduced, and the positions of the petty bourgeoisie (IVab) and farmers (IVc) have improved noticeably.

Overall it seems to be the most disadvantaged classes that experienced the greatest improvement in their position over the first two-thirds of the 20th century. Whereas the position of class II, relative to that of class I, tends to show little change and classes III and IVab show improvements in some countries and in some cohorts but not in others, classes IVc, V + VI, and, particularly, VII show general and widespread improvement in their position vis-à-vis the other classes. As to the more precise timing of the change, we can note that we observe a trend of declining inequality in all countries for the cohorts born between 1935 and 1954, in particular for the least advantaged classes. These are the cohorts that made the crucial educational transitions in the first three post–World War II decades up to about 1975, during which there were significant improvements in living conditions during a period of strong economic growth in most European countries.

Conclusions

Even given that the weight of evidence now supports the thesis of a declining association between class origins and educational attainment, it may be argued that to interpret this trend as demonstrating an increase in equality is mistaken because education is a positional good. In this case, the value of an educational qualification diminishes in proportion to the number of people who acquire it. But for this argument to have any force it is not enough to show that, over time, the value of some qualification declines; rather, it must be demonstrated that differences between the returns to educational levels diminish. The issue is not whether the returns to a tertiary qualification are less in one cohort than in an older one, but whether, for example, the gap in returns between a tertiary and an upper-secondary qualification has narrowed. As far as we know, there is no such evidence, and indeed, there are good grounds for supposing that, as the number of graduates increases, young people with only an upper-secondary qualification will be forced to take less attractive jobs than their counterparts in older cohorts.

A potentially more telling objection to the argument that declining association implies declining class inequality is that there may be distinctions within the broad CASMIN educational categories that are consequential for life chances. For example, it is commonly the case that differences exist between classes in their choice of particular subjects of study or field of education (Lucas 2001; Van de Werfhorst 2001; Kim and Kim 2003). If these differences have become stronger as inequalities in level of education have declined, then a focus solely on educational level will overestimate the extent to which inequalities have declined. Nevertheless, it is difficult to believe that inequalities stemming from differences in field of study within a given level of education will be as important for variations in life chances as differences between the levels of education attained.

The data that we have used are uniquely suited to the purpose of describing long-term trends in educational inequality and comparing these trends across countries.

But this breadth of coverage in time and space comes at a cost: we lack many items of information that would be needed if we were to explain the trends. As a consequence, our article has been primarily empirical, descriptive, and methodological. But it is clear that our findings present a challenge to theory because much recent theorizing on educational differentials, such as Breen and Goldthorpe's (1997) relative risk aversion theory and Raftery and Hout's (1993) maximally maintained inequality hypothesis, has taken as its starting point the need to explain the supposed regularity exemplified by *Persistent Inequality*. Our results show that the focus needs to shift not only from the explanation of stability to the explanation of change, but from accounts based on the assumption of widespread commonality to those that encompass the differences between countries in the magnitude of class inequalities in educational attainment and in the timing of their decline.

NOTE

1. At this point we omit Hungary from our comparison.

REFERENCES

Alderson, Arthur S., and François Nielsen. 2002. "Globalization and the Great U-turn: Income Inequality Trends in 16 OECD Countries." *American Journal of Sociology* 107:1244–99.

Braun, Michael, and Walter Müller. 1997. "Measurement of Education in Comparative Research." *Comparative Social Research* 16:163–201.

Breen, Richard, ed. 2004. *Social Mobility in Europe*. Oxford: Oxford University Press.

———. 2007. "Statistical Models of Educational Careers." Manuscript. Yale University, CIQLE.

Breen, Richard, and John H. Goldthorpe. 1997. "Explaining Educational Differentials: Towards a Formal Rational Action Theory." *Rationality and Society* 9:275–305.

Breen, Richard, Ruud Luijkx, Walter Müller, and Reinhard Pollak. 2009. "Nonpersistent Inequality in Educational Attainment: Evidence from Eight European Countries." *American Journal of Sociology* 114: 1475–1521.

Breen, Richard, and Christopher T. Whelan. 1993. "From Ascription to Achievement? Origins, Education and Entry to the Labour Force in the Republic of Ireland during the Twentieth Century." *Acta Sociologica* 36:3–18.

Erikson, Robert, and John H. Goldthorpe. 1992. *The Constant Flux: A Study of Class Mobility in Industrial Societies*. Oxford: Clarendon.

Erikson, Robert, and Jan O. Jonsson, eds. 1996a. "Explaining Class Inequality in Education: The Swedish Test Case." Pp. 1–64 in *Can Education Be Equalized? The Swedish Case in Comparative Perspective*, edited by Robert Erikson and Jan O. Jonsson. Boulder, Colo.: Westview.

———. 1996b. "The Swedish Context: Educational Reform and Long-Term Change in Educational Inequality." Pp. 65–93 in *Can Education Be Equalized? The Swedish Case in Comparative Perspective*, edited by Robert Erikson and Jan O. Jonsson. Boulder, Colo.: Westview.

Gerber, Theodore P. 2000. "Educational Stratification in Russia during the Soviet Period." *American Journal of Sociology* 101:611–60.

Goldthorpe, John H., and Colin Mills. 2004. "Trends in Intergenerational Class Mobility in Britain in the Late Twentieth Century." Pp. 195–224 in *Social Mobility in Europe*, edited by Richard Breen. Oxford: Oxford University Press.

Henz, Ursula, and Ineke Maas. 1995. "Chancengleichheit durch die Bildungs-expansion." *Kölner Zeitschrift für Soziologie und Sozialpsychologie* 47:605–33.

Iannelli, Cristina. 2003. "Parental Education and Young People's Educational and Labour Market Outcomes: A Comparison across Europe." Pp. 27–53 in *School-to-Work Transitions in Europe: Analyses of the EU LFS 2000 Ad Hoc Module*, edited by Irena Kogan and Walter Müller. Mannheim: Mannheimer Zentrum für Europäische Sozialforschung.

Jonsson, Jan O., Colin Mills, and Walter Müller. 1996. "Half a Century of Increasing Educational Openness? Social Class, Gender and Educational Attainment in Sweden, Germany and Britain." Pp. 183–206 in *Can Education Be Equalized? The Swedish Case in Comparative Perspective*, edited by Robert Erikson and Jan O. Jonsson. Boulder, Colo.: Westview.

Kim, Anna, and Ki-Wan Kim. 2003. "Returns to Tertiary Education in Germany and the UK: Effects of Fields of Study and Gender." Working paper no. 62. Mannheimer Zentrum für Europäische Sozialforschung, Mannheim.

Kuo, Hsiang-Hui Daphne, and Robert M. Hauser. 1995. "Trends in Family Effects on the Education of Black and White Brothers." *Sociology of Education* 68:136–60.

Lucas, Samuel R. 2001. "Effectively Maintained Inequality: Education Transitions, Track Mobility, and Social Background Effects." *American Journal of Sociology* 106:1642–90.

Mare, Robert D. 1980. "Social Background and School Continuation Decisions." *Journal of the American Statistical Association* 75:295–305.

———. 1981. "Change and Stability in Educational Stratification." *American Sociological Review* 46:72–87.

McCullagh, Peter. 1980. "Regression Models for Ordinal Data." *Journal of the Royal Statistical Society*, ser. B, 42:109–42.

Müller, Walter, and Dietmar Haun. 1994. "Bildungsungleichheit im sozialen Wandel." *Kölner Zeitschrift für Soziologie und Sozialpsychologie* 46:1–42.

Müller, Walter, and Wolfgang Karle. 1993. "Social Selection in Educational Systems in Europe." *European Sociological Review* 9:1–23.

Raftery, Adrian E., and Michael Hout. 1993. "Maximally Maintained Inequality: Educational Stratification in Ireland." *Sociology of Education* 65:41–62.

Rijken, Susanne. 1999. *Educational Expansion and Status Attainment: A Cross-National and*

Over-Time Comparison. Amsterdam: Thela Thesis (ICS Dissertation).

Shavit, Yossi, and Hans-Peter Blossfeld, eds. 1993. *Persistent Inequality: Changing Educational Attainment in Thirteen Countries.* Boulder, Colo.: Westview.

Shavit, Yossi, and Karin Westerbeek. 1998. "Educational Stratification in Italy: Reforms, Expansion, and Equality of Opportunity." *European Sociological Review* 14:33–47.

Slomczynski, Kazimierz M., Ireneusz Bialecki, Henryk Domanski, et al. 1989. *Struktura spoleczna: Schemat teoretyczny i warsztat badawczy.* Warsaw: Polish Academy of Sciences.

Vallet, Louis-André. 2004. "The Dynamics of Inequality of Educational Opportunity in France: Change in the Association between Social Background and Education in Thirteen Five-Year Birth Cohorts (1908–1972)." Paper prepared for the meeting of the ISA Research Committee on Social Stratification and Mobility, Neuchâtel, May 6–8.

Van de Werfhorst, Herman. 2001. *Field of Study and Social Inequality: Four Types of Educational Resources in the Process of Stratification in the Netherlands.* Nijmegen: ICS Dissertation.

Whelan, Christopher T., and Richard Layte. 2002. "Late Industrialisation and the Increased Merit Selection Hypothesis: Ireland as a Test Case." *European Sociological Review* 18:35–50.

Zagórski, Krzysztof. 1976. *Zmiany struktury i ruchliwość społeczno-zawadowa w Polsce.* Warsaw: GUS.

52

A Refined Model of
Occupational Mobility

DAVID L. FEATHERMAN AND
ROBERT M. HAUSER

In this chapter we describe and apply a log-linear model of the mobility table. . . . The model permits us to locate groups or clusters of cells in the classification that share similar chances of mobility or immobility, freed of the confounding influences of the relative numbers of men in each origin or destination category and of changes in those relative numbers between origin and destination distributions.

By modeling the mobility table in this way we obtain new insights into the process of mobility, changes in that process, and the interactions of the mobility process with changes in the occupational structure within one mobility classification or between two or more mobility classifications. For example, we take a fresh look at the differing tendencies toward immobility in the several occupational strata, at the existence of "class" boundaries limiting certain types of mobility, at differences in upward and downward exchanges between occupational strata, and at differences among strata in the dispersion of recruit-

ment and supply. In these purposes our analysis parallels Blau and Duncan's treatment of manpower flows (1967: Chap. 2; also, see Blau, 1965).

Several sociologists have recently drawn attention to relationships between occupational mobility and class formation, for example, Giddens (1973), Parkin (1971), and Westergaard and Resler (1975). Goldthorpe and Llewellyn (1977) have critically reviewed these and related works in light of British mobility data collected in 1972. It would be easy to identify our present analytic interests with those of the class theorists, but we think such an inference unwarranted.

Although we are attempting a description of the mobility regime that is free of the distributions of occupational origins and destinations, we believe with Goldthorpe and Llewellyn that the class theorists are attempting to interpret what [might be] termed the gross flows of manpower. For the American case we have already described those flows [see Featherman and Hauser (1978: Chapter 3)], and our interest now centers on the net or underlying patterns of association in the mobility table.

We have approached the mobility table without strong theoretical presuppositions about affinities among occupational strata. Like Blau and Duncan, we have worked inductively, but our more refined analytic tools have led to substantively different conclusions than theirs about the major features of the mobility process in the United States.

Some readers may find the following discussion excessively technical, but we have tried to minimize the presentation of methodological detail. We have tried to avoid describing the methods by which empirical specifications of the mobility table may be explored, although we believe these are interesting in their own right. We have focused on the rationale and interpretation of our model, including comparisons with other ways of looking at the mobility table that seem likely to elucidate the properties of the model.

Mobility Models

The record of sociological mobility studies is paralleled by a history of statistical analysis in which occupational mobility has often served as stimulus, object, or illustration of statistical ideas (for example, see Pearson, 1904; Chessa, 1911; Rogoff, 1953; Glass, 1954; Goodman, 1961, 1968, 1969a, 1972c; Tyree, 1973; White, 1963, 1970a; Singer and Spilerman, 1976). Indeed, it is consistent with the historical pattern that sociologists were introduced to the method of path analysis primarily by way of its successful application in studies of occupational mobility (Duncan and Hodge, 1963; Blau and Duncan, 1967). Devices for the statistical analysis of mobility data range from simple descriptive measures to complex analytic

schemes. We make no systematic effort to review these measures and models, for there are several recent and comprehensive reviews (Boudon, 1973; Pullum, 1975; Bibby, 1975). We focus almost exclusively on multiplicative (loglinear) representations of the occupational mobility table. In so doing we do not intend to suggest that other methods and approaches are inferior, but to exploit features of the loglinear model that seem interesting and fruitful. . . .

In a series of papers, Goodman (1963, 1965, 1968, 1969a, 1969b, 1972c) developed and exposited methods for the analysis of contingency tables (including mobility tables) in which the significant interactions were localized in specified cells or sets of cells in the table (also, see Pullum, 1975). For example, in the case of highly aggregated (3 × 3 or 5 × 5) mobility tables Goodman showed that most of the interaction pertained to cells on or near the main diagonal (when the occupation categories of origin and destination were listed in order of increasing status). White (1963, 1970b) has made essentially the same suggestion, but some aspects of his models and methods are less appealing. Goodman (1965, 1969a) proposed that the analyst ignore or "blank out" those cells where interaction was greatest (where frequencies were thought to be especially dense or especially sparse) and attempt to fit a modified model of statistical independence, termed "quasi-independence," to the remaining frequencies in the table. In the case where only diagonal cells were blanked out in a mobility table, Goodman called the model one of "quasi-perfect mobility," after the term "perfect mobility," which had earlier been applied to the model of statistical independence in a mobility table. For an early application of this model to a large (17 × 17) table see Blau and Duncan (1967: 64–67). Goodman (1965, 1968, 1969a) noted that quasi-independence might hold over all cells in a table whose entries were not ignored, or it might hold within, but not between certain subsets of cells whose entries were not ignored. . . .

Models of quasi-independence have provided important insights into the structure of mobility tables. Aside from Goodman's expository papers, they have been applied in cross-national, interurban, and cross-temporal analyses (Iutaka et al., 1975; Featherman et al., 1975; Pullum, 1975; Hauser et al., 1975; Ramsøy, 1977; Goldthorpe et al., 1978). Goodman (1969a) also has shown how related ideas may be supplied to test any specific hypothesis about the pattern of association in a mobility table.

At the same time the application of quasi-independence models in mobility analysis has been less than satisfying in some ways. Even where large numbers of cells are blocked, quasi-independence models do not fit large tables very well (Pullum, 1975; Hauser et al., 1975). That is, when mobility data are not highly aggregated, it appears that association is not limited to the small number of cells on or near the main diagonal. The larger the number of entries blocked (or fitted exactly) before a good fit is obtained, the less substantively appealing is the model of quasi-independence. Moreover, by treating departures from quasi-independence in the blocked or ignored cells as parameters or indices of mobility and departures in the unblocked cells as error, the quasi-independence model attaches too much theoretical importance to occupational inheritance (Hope, 1976). Of course, occupational inheritance is always defined by reference to a given classification of occupations, and the problem is exacerbated by the fact that the model of quasi-independence fits best when the mo-

bility table is based on broad occupation groups. The model is of greatest validity in the measurement of immobility in classifications where the concept of occupational inheritance becomes vague.

The focus on fit on or near the main diagonal follows a traditional sociological interest in occupational inheritance, but it also draws our attention away from other aspects of association in the table. For example, one might hypothesize that certain types of mobility are as prevalent as other types of mobility or immobility. More generally, one might wish to construct a parametric model of mobility and immobility for the full table that would recognize the somewhat arbitrary character of occupational inheritance and the possible gradations of association throughout the table.

Goodman's (1972c) general multiplicative model of mobility tables and other cross-classifications substantially advanced the sophistication and precision of mobility analysis. For example, Goodman proposed and applied to the classic British and Danish mobility data a number of alternative specifications, all but two of which—the simple independence model and that of quasi-perfect mobility—assumed ordinality in the occupational categories. The models incorporated combinations of parameters for upward and downward mobility, for the number of boundaries crossed, and for barriers to crossing particular categoric boundaries. Many of these models—as well as problems in comparing their goodness of fit—are reviewed by Bishop et al. (1975: Chaps. 5, 8, 9), and some of the same models are discussed by Haberman (1974: Chap. 6). Applying Goodman's (1972c) general model we take a slightly different approach in developing models of the mobility table. Elsewhere, Hauser (1978) has applied this approach in an analysis of the classic British mobility table, and Baron (1977) has used it in a reanalysis of Rogoff's (1953) Indianapolis data.

A Refined Multiplicative Model of the Mobility Table[1]

Let x_{ij} be the observed frequency in the ijth cell of the classification of men by their own occupations ($j = 1, \ldots, J$) and their own occupations or fathers' occupations at an earlier time ($i = 1, \ldots, I$). In the context of mobility analysis the same categories will appear in rows and columns, and the table will be square with $I = J$. For $k = 1, \ldots, K$, let H_k be a mutually exclusive and exhaustive partition of the pairs (i, j) in which

$$E[x_{ij}] = m_{ij} = \alpha \beta_i \gamma_j \delta_{ij}, \qquad (1)$$

where $\delta_{ij} = \delta_k$ for $(i, j) \in H_k$, subject to the normalization $\Pi_i \beta_i = \Pi_j \gamma_j = \Pi_i \Pi_j \delta_{ij} = 1$. The normalization of parameters is a matter of convenience, and we choose the value of one so that it will hold. Note that, unlike the usual set-up, the interaction effects are not constrained within rows or columns although the marginal frequencies are fixed. The model says the expected frequencies are a product of an overall effect (α), a row effect (β_i), a column effect (γ_j), and an interaction effect (δ_{ij}). The row and column parameters represent conditions of occupational supply and demand; they reflect demographic replacement processes and past and present technologies and economic conditions. The cells (i, j) are assigned to K mutually exclusive and exhaustive levels, and each of those levels shares a common interaction parameter δ_k. Thus, aside from total, row, and column effects, each expected frequency is determined by only one

parameter, which reflects the level of mobility or immobility in that cell relative to that in other cells in the table.

The interaction parameters of the model correspond directly to our notions of variations in the density of observations (White, 1963:26). Unlike several models fitted by Goodman (1972c), this model does not assume ordinal measurement of occupations. Of course, the assumption of ordinality may help us interpret results, or our findings may be used to explore the metric properties of our occupational classification. For the model to be informative, the distribution of levels across the cells of the table must form a meaningful pattern, and one in which the parameters are identified (Mason et al., 1973; Haberman, 1974: 217). Furthermore, the number of levels (K) should be substantially less than the number of cells in the table. These latter properties are partly matters of substantive and statistical interpretation and judgment, rather than characteristics of the model or of the data. We have found it difficult to interpret models where the number of levels is much greater than the number of categories recognized in the occupational classification. . . .

Mobility to First Jobs: An Illustration

Table 52.1 gives frequencies in a classification of son's first, full-time civilian occupation by father's (or other family head's) occupation at the son's sixteenth birthday among American men who were ages 20–64 in 1973 and were not currently enrolled in school.[2] Table 52.2 gives the design matrix of a model for the data of Table 52.1. Each numerical entry in the body of the table gives the level of H_k to which the corresponding entry in the frequency table

Table 52.1   Frequencies in a Classification of Mobility from Father's (or Other Family Head's) Occupation to Son's First Full-Time Civilian Occupation: U.S. Men Aged 20–64 in March 1973

| | Son's occupation | | | | | |
| | Upper nonmanual | Lower nonmanual | Upper manual | Lower manual | Farm | Total |
Father's occupation						
Upper nonmanual	1414	521	302	643	40	2920
Lower nonmanual	724	524	254	703	48	2253
Upper manual	798	648	856	1676	108	4086
Lower manual	756	914	771	3325	237	6003
Farm	409	357	441	1611	1832	4650
Total	4101	2964	2624	7958	2265	19,912

Note: Frequencies are based on observations weighted to estimate population counts and compensate for departures of the sampling design from simple random sampling (see Featherman and Hauser [1978: Appendix B]). Broad occupation groups are upper nonmanual: professional and kindred workers, managers and officials, and non-retail sales workers; lower nonmanual: proprietors, clerical and kindred workers, and retail sales workers; upper manual: craftsmen, foremen and kindred workers; lower manual: service workers, operatives and kindred workers, and laborers, except farm; farm: farmers and farm managers, farm laborers and foremen.

was assigned. Formally, the entries are merely labels, but, for convenience in interpretation, the numerical values are inverse to the estimated density of mobility or immobility in the cells to which they refer.

On this understanding the design says that, aside from conditions of supply and demand, immobility is highest in farm occupations (Level 1) and next highest in the upper nonmanual category (Level 2). If we take the occupation groups as ranked from high to low in the order listed, we may say that there are zones of high and almost uniform density bordering the peaks at either end of the status distribution. There is one zone of high density that includes upward or downward movements between the two nonmanual groups and immobility in the lower nonmanual group. Mobility from lower to upper nonmanual occupations (Level 3) is more likely than the opposite movement, and the latter is as likely as stability in the lower nonmanual category (Level 4). Moreover, the densities of immobility in the lower nonmanual category and of downward mobility

to it are identical to those in the second zone of relatively high density, which occurs at the lower end of the occupational hierarchy. The second zone includes movements from the farm to the lower manual group and back as well as immobility in the lower manual group. Last, there is a broad zone of relatively low density (Level 5) that includes

Table 52.2   Asymmetric 5-Level Model of Mobility from Father's Occupation to First Full-Time Civilian Occupation

| | Son's occupation | | | | |
Father's occupation	(1)	(2)	(3)	(4)	(5)
1. Upper nonmanual	2	4	5	5	5
2. Lower nonmanual	3	4	5	5	5
3. Upper manual	5	5	5	5	5
4. Lower manual	5	5	5	4	4
5. Farm	5	5	5	4	1

Note: Broad occupation groups are upper nonmanual: professional and kindred workers, managers and officials, and non-retail sales workers; lower nonmanual: proprietors, clerical and kindred workers, and retail sales workers; upper manual: craftsmen, foremen and kindred workers; lower manual: service workers, operatives and kindred workers, and laborers, except farm; farm: farmers and farm managers, farm laborers and foremen.

immobility in the upper manual category, upward and downward mobility within the manual stratum, mobility between upper manual and farm groups, and all movements between nonmanual and either manual or farm groups. The design says that an upper manual worker's son is equally likely to be immobile or to move to the bottom or top of the occupational distribution; obversely, it says that an upper manual worker is equally likely to have been recruited from any location in the occupational hierarchy, including his own. Also, it is worth noting that four of the five density levels recognized in the model occur along the main diagonal, and two of these (Levels 4 and 5) are assigned both to diagonal and off-diagonal cells.

With a single exception the design is symmetric. That is, the upward and downward flows between occupations are assigned to the same density levels, except mobility from lower to upper nonmanual strata (Level 3) exceeds that from upper to lower nonmanual strata (Level 4). This asymmetry in the design is striking because it suggests the power of upper white-collar families to block at least one type of status loss and because it is the *only* asymmetry in the design. For example, Blau and Duncan (1967: 58–67) suggest that there are semipermeable class boundaries separating white-collar, blue-collar, and farm occupations, which permit upward mobility but inhibit downward mobility. The only asymmetry in the present design occurs *within* one of the broad classes delineated by Blau and Duncan.

Overall, the design resembles a river valley in which two broad plains are joined by a narrow strip of land between two great peaks. The contours of the peaks differ in that the one forming one side of the valley is both taller and more nearly symmetric than that forming the other side. This representation appears in Figure 52.1.

In some respects, this design matrix parallels Levine's (1967: Chap. 4) description of the surface of the British mobility table as a saddle (also see Levine, 1972). However, our interpretation is more extreme, since the density reaches an absolute minimum in the center of the table, not merely a minimum among the diagonal cells. In this way our model for the American 5 × 5 table is closer to Goodman's (1969a: 38, 1969b: 846) conclusion that a British 5 × 5 table shows "status disinheritance" in the middle category. We show elsewhere (Featherman and Hauser, 1978) that Levine's interpretation of the British data is based on a confounding of marginal effects and interactions which parallels that entailed in the use of mobility ratios, even though Levine did not use mobility ratios.

The model of Table 52.2 provides less than a complete description of the mobility data in Table 52.1. Under the model of statistical independence we obtain a likelihood-ratio statistic, $G^2 = 6167.7$, which is asymptotically distributed as χ^2 with 16 df. With the model of Table 52.2 as null hypothesis we obtain $G^2 = 66.5$ with 12 df, since we lose 4 df in creating the five categories of H. Clearly the model does not fit, if we take the probability associated with the test statistic as our only guide. On the other hand the model does account for 98.9% of the association in the data, that is, of the value of G^2 under independence. Given the extraordinarily large sample size we might expect small departures from frequencies predicted by the model to be statistically significant. . . .

The measures of fit we have examined have told us nothing about the several parameters of the model. That is, we have not shown that our suggested interpretation of

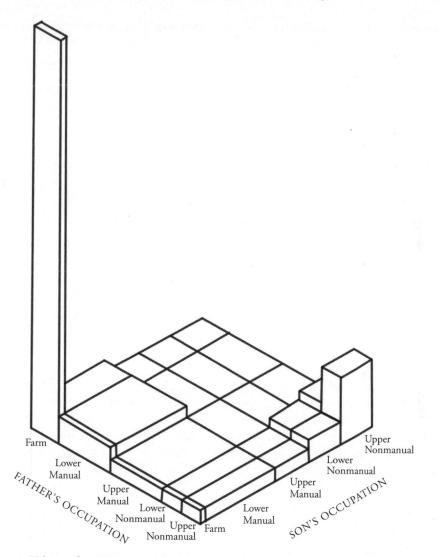

Figure 52.1 Volume of mobility from father's occupation to first full-time civilian occupation: U.S. men aged 20–64 in March 1973. The base is a unit square, and the total volume under the surface is one. Length and breadth can be read as probabilities, and height is proportionate to probability. The vertical scale has been compressed by a factor of 10.

the design matrix (Table 52.2) is substantively appealing, or even that the design correctly sorts the cells of the mobility table into zones of high and low density. Certainly, we want to look at the way in which the model fits and interprets the data as well as at deviations from fitted values.

The upper panel of Table 52.3 shows the row, column, and level parameters estimated under the model of Table 52.2 for mobility in the 1973 data from father's (or head's) occupation at son's sixteenth birthday to son's first full-time civilian occupation. The parameters are expressed in additive form, that is,

Table 52.3   Parameters and Residuals (in Additive Form) from Main, Row, and Column Effects in the Model of Table 52.2: Mobility from Father's (or Other Family Head's) Occupation to Son's First Full-Time Civilian Occupation, U.S. Men Aged 20–64 in March 1973

A. Additive parameters

	Category of row, column, or level				
Design factor	(1)	(2)	(3)	(4)	(5)
Rows (father's occupation)	−.466	−.451	.495	.570	−.148
Columns (son's occupation)	.209	.190	.240	1.020	−1.660
Levels (density)	3.044	1.234	.549	.243	−.356
	Grand mean = 6.277				

B. Level parameter plus residual (log R_{ij}^*)

	Son's occupation				
Father's occupation	(1)	(2)	(3)	(4)	(5)
1. Upper nonmanual	1.23	.25	−.34	−.36	−.45
2. Lower nonmanual	.55	.25	−.53	−.29	−.29
3. Upper manual	−.30	−.49	−.26	−.37	−.43
4. Lower manual	−.43	−.22	−.44	.24	.28
5. Farm	−.32	−.44	−.28	.24	3.04

Note: See text for explanation.

they are effects on logs of frequencies under the model of Eq. (1). The row and column parameters clearly show an intergenerational shift out of farming and into white-collar or lower blue-collar occupations. Of course these parameters reflect a number of factors, including temporal shifts in the distribution of the labor force across occupations, differential fertility, and life cycle differences in occupational positions. The level parameters show very large differences in mobility and immobility across the several cells of the classification, and these differences closely follow our interpretation of the design matrix. Differences between level parameters may readily be interpreted as differences in logs of frequencies, net of row and column effects. For example, the estimates say that immobility in farm occupations is 3.40 = 3.044 − (−.356) greater (in the metric of logged frequencies) than the estimated mobility or immobility in cells assigned to Level

5 in the design matrix. In multiplicative terms, immobility in farm occupations is $e^{3.40}$ = 29.96 times greater than mobility or immobility at Level 5. It would be incorrect to attach too much importance to the signs of the level parameters as reported in Table 52.3, for they simply reflect our normalization rule that level parameters sum to zero (in the log-frequency metric) across the cells of the table. For example, while the parameters for Levels 4 and 5 each reflect relatively low densities, it is not clear that either parameter indicates "status disinheritance" in the diagonal cells to which it pertains (compare Goodman, 1969a, 1969b).

In any event the parameters do show a sharp density gradient across the levels of the design. The smallest difference, between Levels 3 and 4, indicates a relative density $e^{.549−.243} = e^{.306}$ = 1.36 times as great at Level 3 as at Level 4. The heterogeneity of Level 5 is indicated by the fact that the difference in density between Levels 3 and 4 is about as large as the range of residuals within Level 5. Immobility in farm occupations and in upper nonmanual occupations is quite distinct from densities at other levels, but also immobility in the farm occupations is $e^{3.044-1.234} = e^{1.810} = 6.11$ times as great as in the upper nonmanual occupations.

We can write the sample counterpart of Eq. (1) as

$$\hat{m}_{ij} = \hat{\alpha}\hat{\beta}_i\hat{\gamma}_j\hat{\delta}_{ij}. \tag{2}$$

Recalling that

$$e_{ij} = x_{ij} / \hat{m}_{ij}, \tag{3}$$

we substitute Eq. (2) into (3) and rearrange terms to obtain

$$x_{ij} = \hat{\alpha}_i\hat{\gamma}_j\hat{\delta}_{ij}e_{ij}. \tag{4}$$

We divide both sides of Eq. (4) by the first three terms on the right-hand side to obtain

$$R_{ij}^* = \frac{x_{ij}}{\hat{\alpha}\hat{\beta}_i\hat{\gamma}_j} = \hat{\delta}_{ij}e_{ij}. \tag{5}$$

We shall call R_{ij}^* the new mobility ratio, or, simply, the mobility ratio. In the case of diagonal cells R_{ij}^* is equivalent to the new immobility ratio proposed by Goodman (1969a,b, 1972c; also, see Pullum, 1975: 7–8), but we suggest the ratio be computed for all cells of the table as an aid both to substantive interpretation and to the evaluation of model design.

The lower panel of Table 52.3 gives logs of the new mobility ratios for the model of Table 52.2 fitted to the classification of mobility to first jobs. While the entries in this panel depend on our specification of the model, that specification need not rigidly

govern our interpretation of the relative densities. Obviously, the pattern of relative densities does conform substantially to our earlier description of the design. The fit is good enough so there is no overlap in densities across levels recognized in the design, and all of the negative entries are neatly segregated in Level 5 of the design. If immobility among skilled workers—in cell (3, 3)—is high relative to mobility in other cells at Level 5, it is still clear that the immobility in that category is substantially less than the immobility in any other occupation group. . . .

Mobility Chances: A New Perspective

As an alternative to the Blau-Duncan interpretation, we think our multiplicative models yield a cogent and parsimonious description of occupational mobility among American men. Unlike its precursor, our description does not reflect the shape of occupational distributions of origin or destination, but only the underlying patterns of immobility and exchange between occupational strata. It may be useful here to review the major features of this description that appear in mobility between generations and within the occupational career. In doing so, of course, we do some injustice to details reported in the preceding analysis.

First, there is great immobility at the top and at the bottom of the occupational hierarchy, here represented by upper nonmanual and by farm occupations, respectively. This immobility is far more extreme than has heretofore been supposed by most students of the mobility process; it may even be consistent with the beliefs of the more extreme critics of rigidity in the American class structure.

Second, surrounding the extremes of the occupational hierarchy at both top and bottom are transitional zones, within which there are relatively homogeneous chances of immobility and of exchange with adjacent extreme strata.

Third, taken as aggregates the extreme and transitional zones of the occupational hierarchy are relatively closed both to upward and to downward movements. That is, there are sharp breaks between the density of observations within the extreme and transitional zones and the density of mobility beyond those zones. In this sense (but not in others) we may say that the data suggest the existence of barriers to movement across class boundaries.

Fourth, once the boundaries of the transitional zones have been crossed, no social distance gradient seems to underlie variations in long-distance mobility chances. These are surprisingly uniform, and observed variations in them show no consistent pattern.

Fifth, if immobility is very great at the extremes of the occupational hierarchy, it is almost nonexistent in the middle of the hierarchy. Contrary to widespread belief, men of upper blue-collar origin are about as likely to end up anywhere higher or lower in the occupational hierarchy as in their stratum of origin. Obversely, upper blue-collar workers are about as likely to have originated anywhere higher or lower in the occupational hierarchy as in their stratum of destination. Those who would find their beliefs about "class" rigidity confirmed by our estimates of immobility at the extremes of the occupational hierarchy must reconcile these with our finding that between generations immobility in upper manual occupations is no more prevalent than most types of extreme, long-distance mobility. There is no evidence of "class" boundaries

limiting the chances of movement to or from the skilled manual occupations.

Sixth, there is a rough equality in the propensities to move in one direction or the other between occupational strata. There are several exceptions to this symmetric mobility pattern, some of which may be quite important, but none suggests a dominant tendency toward upward relative to downward mobility across or within class boundaries.

Last, from a methodological perspective, our description of the mobility regime is extremely simple. In broad outline it might be fitted to a 5 × 5 table with the expenditure of as few as 2 df. None of our analyses of American mobility tables required the expenditure of more than 6 of the 16 df left unused by the model of simple statistical independence.

We reemphasize that the present description of relative mobility chances does not conflict in any way with our earlier description (Featherman and Hauser 1978: Chapter 3) of occupational inflow and outflow patterns. Rather, relative mobility chances are components of inflows and outflows, but the latter are also affected by distributions of occupational origins and destinations. Major features of the inflow and outflow tables, like the pervasiveness of upward mobility between generations and within the occupational career, are absent from the present account because they are functions of changing distributions of occupational origins and destinations.

NOTES

1. We assume the familiarity of the reader with loglinear models for frequency data. Fienberg (1970a, 1977) and Goodman (1972a,b) give useful introductions, as does the comprehensive treatise by Bishop et al. (1975). We rely heavily on methods for the analysis of incomplete tables,

which have been developed by Goodman (1963, 1965, 1968, 1969a,b, 1971, 1972c), Bishop and Fienberg (1969), Fienberg (1970b, 1972), and Mantel (1970); again, Bishop et al. (1975, especially pp. 206–211, 225–228, 282 309, 320–324) is valuable. Our model is a special case of Goodman's (1972c) general model.

2. The reported frequencies are based on a complex sampling design and have been weighted to estimate population counts while compensating for certain types of survey nonresponse. The estimated population counts have been scaled down to reflect underlying sample frequencies, and an additional downward adjustment was made to compensate for departures of the sampling design from simple random sampling (see Featherman and Hauser [1978: Appendix B]). The frequency estimates in Table 52.1 have been rounded to the nearest integer, but our computations have been based on unrounded figures. We treat the adjusted frequencies as if they had been obtained under simple random sampling.

REFERENCES

Baron, James N. 1977. "The structure of intergenerational occupational mobility: Another look at the Indianapolis mobility data." Unpublished masters thesis, University of Wisconsin–Madison.

Bibby, John. 1975. "Methods of measuring mobility." *Quality and Quantity* 9 (March): 107–136.

Bishop, Yvonne M. M., and Stephen E. Fienberg. 1969. "Incomplete two-dimensional contingency tables." *Biometrics* 25:119–128.

Bishop, Yvonne M. M., Stephen E. Fienberg, and Paul W. Holland. 1975. *Discrete Multivariate Analysis: Theory and Practice*. Cambridge: M.I.T. Press.

Blau, Peter M. 1965. "The flow of occupational supply and recruitment." *American Sociological Review* 30 (August):475–490.

Blau, Peter M., and Otis Dudley Duncan. 1967. *The American Occupational Structure*. New York: Wiley.

Boudon, Raymond. 1973. *Mathematical Structure of Social Mobility*. San Francisco: Jossey-Bass.

Chessa, Frederico. 1911. *La Trasmissione Erediteria delle Professioni*. Torino: Fratelli Bocca.

Duncan, Otis Dudley, and Robert W. Hodge. 1963. "Education and occupational mobility." *American Journal of Sociology* 68 (May): 629–644.

Featherman, David L., and Robert M. Hauser. 1978. *Opportunity and Change*. New York: Academic Press.

Featherman, David L., F. Lancaster Jones, and Robert M. Hauser. 1975. "Assumptions of social mobility research in the United States: The case of occupational status." *Social Science Research* 4:329–360.

Fienberg, Stephen E. 1970a. "The analysis of multidimensional contingency tables." *Ecology* 51:419–433.

———. 1970b. "Quasi-independence and maximum likelihood estimation in incomplete contingency tables." *Journal of the American Statistical Association* 65:1610–1616.

———. 1972. "The analysis of incomplete multiway contingency tables." *Biometrics* 23 (March):177–202.

———. 1977. *The Analysis of Cross-Classified Categorical Data*. Cambridge: M.I.T. Press.

Giddens, Anthony. 1973. *The Class Structure of the Advanced Societies*. New York: Harper and Row.

Glass, D. B. 1954. *Social Mobility in Britain*. London: Routledge and Kegan Paul.

Goldthorpe, John W., and Catriona Llewellyn. 1977. "Class mobility in modern Britain: Three theses examined." *Sociology* 11 (May): 257–287.

Goldthorpe, John W., Clive Payne, and Catriona Llewellyn. 1978. "Trends in class mobility." *Sociology* 12 (September):441–468.

Goodman, Leo A. 1961. "Statistical methods for the mover-stayer model." *Journal of the American Statistical Association* 56 (December):841–868.

———. 1963. "Statistical methods for the preliminary analysis of transaction flows." *Econometrica* 31 (January):197–208.

———. 1965. "On the statistical analysis of mobility tables." *American Journal of Sociology* 70 (March):564–585.

———. 1968. "The analysis of cross-classified data: Independence, quasi-independence, and interaction in contingency tables with or without missing entries." *Journal of the American Statistical Association* 63 (December):1091–1131.

———. 1969a. "How to ransack social mobility tables and other kinds of cross-classification tables." *American Journal of Sociology* 75 (July):1–39.

———. 1969b. "On the measurement of social mobility: An index of status persistence." *American Sociological Review* 34 (December):831–850.

———. 1971. "A simple simultaneous test procedure for quasi-independence in contingency tables." *Applied Statistics* 20:165–177.

———. 1972a. "A general model for the analysis of surveys." *American Journal of Sociology* 77 (May):1035–1086.

———. 1972b. "A modified multiple regression approach to the analysis of dichotomous variables." *American Sociological Review* 37 (February):28–46.

———. 1972c. "Some multiplicative models for the analysis of cross-classified data." Pp. 649–696 in *Proceedings of the Sixth Berkeley Symposium on Mathematical Statistics and Probability*. Berkeley: University of California Press.

Haberman, Shelby J. 1974. *The Analysis of Frequency Data*. Chicago: University of Chicago Press.

Hauser, Robert M. 1978. "A structural model of the mobility table." *Social Forces* 56 (March):919–953.

Hauser, Robert M., Peter J. Dickinson, Harry P. Travis, and John M. Koffel. 1975. "Temporal change in occupational mobility: Evidence for men in the United States." *American Sociological Review* 40 (June):279–297.

Hope, Keith. 1976. Review of Thomas W. Pullum's *Measuring Occupational Inheritance*. *American Journal of Sociology* 82 (November):726–730.

Iutaka, S., B. F. Bloomer, R. E. Burke, and O. Wolowyna. 1975. "Testing the quasi-perfect mobility model for intergenerational data: International comparison." *Economic and Social Review* 6:215–236.

Levine, Joel Harvey. 1967. Measurement in the study of intergenerational status mobility. Unpublished doctoral dissertation. Department of Social Relations. Harvard University.

———. 1972. "A two-parameter model of interaction in father-son status mobility." *Behavioral Science* 17 (September):455–465.

Mantel, Nathan. 1970. "Incomplete contingency tables." *Biometrics* 26:291–304.

Mason, Karen Oppenheim, William M. Mason, Halliman H. Winsborough, and Kenneth W. Poole. 1973. "Some methodological issues in cohort analysis of archival data." *American Sociological Review* 38 (April):242–258.

Parkin, Frank. 1971. *Class Inequality and Political Order: Social Stratification in Capitalist and Communist Societies*. New York: Praeger.

Pearson, Karl. 1904. "On the theory of contingency and its relation to association and normal correlation." Reprinted, 1948, in Karl Pearson's *Early Papers*. Cambridge: Cambridge University Press.

Pullum, Thomas. 1975. *Measuring Occupational Inheritance*. New York: Elsevier.

Ramsøy, Natalie. 1977. *Social Mobilitet i Norge (Social Mobility in Norway)*. Oslo: Tiden Forlag.

Rogoff, Natalie. 1953. *Recent Trends in Occupational Mobility*. Glencoe, Illinois: Free Press.

Singer, Burton, and Seymour Spilerman. 1976. "The representation of social processes by Markov models." *American Journal of Sociology* 82 (July):1–54.

Tyree, Andrea. 1973. "Mobility ratios and association in mobility tables." *Population Studies* 27 (July):577–588.

Westergaard, John, and Henrietta Resler. 1975. *Class in a Capitalist Society: A Study of Contemporary Britain*. New York: Basic Books.

White, Harrison C. 1963. "Cause and effect in social mobility tables." *Behavioral Science* 8:14–27.

———. 1970a. *Chains of Opportunity: System Models of Occupational Mobility in Organizations*. Cambridge: Harvard University Press.

———. 1970b. "Stayers and movers." *American Journal of Sociology* 76 (September):307–324.

53

Social Mobility in Europe

RICHARD BREEN

I discuss here the findings of a project that looks at social mobility in 11 European countries over a period of almost 30 years (see Breen 2004 for details). I want to summarize some of the main results and discuss how they relate to previous research in this area; and I also want to make some comments about the consequences of this research and of these findings for the study of social mobility. But I will begin by briefly explaining what the project is all about.

class); III (routine non-manual class); IVab (petty bourgeoisie with and without employees); IVc (farmers); V + VI (skilled manual workers, technicians and supervisors of manual workers); VIIa (unskilled manual workers not in agriculture) and VIIb (farm workers). One consequence of choosing this categorization is that it allows our results to be compared with those of *The Constant Flux* (Erikson and Goldthorpe 1993), where the same categories were used.

Data

The data used in the project comprise 117 mobility surveys covering the period 1970 to 2000. The sources of the data are shown in Table 53.1. The number of tables per country ranges from two in Israel and Italy to 35 in the Netherlands.

In general the age range of the respondents in our mobility tables is 25 to 64, and we coded social class according to the seven-class 'CASMIN' scheme (see Table 53.2). This identifies classes I + II (the service

Methodological Issues

As Table 53.1 showed, the 11 countries contribute rather different numbers of mobility tables to our cross-national analyses. Sweden, for example, has a table for every year from 1976 to 1999, whereas Poland and Ireland have only three tables each, covering the years between the early 1970s and 1994. The amount of information we possess regarding change over time, and the reliability of the conclusions based on this information, will vary between countries. If we have

---

This chapter is a summary of material also used in a subsequent publication (Richard Breen, *Social Mobility in Europe*. Copyright © 2005 by Oxford University Press).

Table 53.1   Sources of Data

Country	# tables	Sources of data	Years for which data are included
Germany	22	Zumabus	1976–77 1979(2) 1980 1982
		Allbus	1980 1982 1984 1986 1988 1990–92 1994 1996 1998
		Politik in der BRD	1978 1980
		Wohlfahrtssurvey	1978
		German socio-economic panel	1986 1999
France	4	Formation-qualification professionnelle Insee surveys	1970 1977 1985 1993
Italy	2	National survey on social mobility	1985
		Italian household longitudinal survey	1997
Ireland	3	Survey of the determinants of occupational status and mobility	1973
		Survey of income distribution and poverty	1987
		Living in Ireland survey	1994
Great Britain	15	General household survey	1973 1975–76 1979–1984 1987–1992
Sweden	24	Annual surveys of living conditions (ULF)	1976–1999
Norway	3	Colbjørnsen et al. 1987	1982
		Moen et al. 1996	1994
		Level of Living Survey	1995
Poland	3	Zagorski 1976	1972
		Slomczynski 1989	1988
		Treiman/ Szelényi	1994
Hungary	4	Social mobility and life history survey	1973 1983 1992
		Way of Life and Time Use Survey (Hungarian Central Statistical Office)	2000
Israel	2	Matras and Weintraub, 1977	1974
		Kraus and Toren 1992	1991
Netherlands	35	Parliamentiary Election Study	1970 1971 1977 1981 1982 1986 1994 1998
		Political Action Survey I	1974 1979
		Justice of Income Survey	1976
		CBS Life Situation Survey	1977 1986
		National Labour Market Survey	1982
		National Prestige and Mobility Survey	1982 1985 1988 1990 1992 1994 1996
		Strategic Labour Market Survey	1998
		Cultural Changes [ISSP]	1987
		Justice of Income Survey	1987
		Primary and Social Relationships	1987
		Social and Cultural Trends	1990
		Justice of Income Survey [ISJP]	1991
		Family Survey I, 1992–93	1992
		Households in the Netherlands pilot	1994
		Households in the Netherlands	1995
		Social Inequality in the Netherlands	1996
		National Crime Study	1996
		Social and Economic Attitudes	1998
		Netherlands Family Survey II	1998
		Use of Information Technology	1999

Table 53.2   The Goldthorpe Class Schema

Goldthorpe Class	Description	Employment relations	CASMIN version
I	Higher-grade professionals, administrators and officials; managers in large industrial establishments; large proprietors	Employer or service relationship	I + II Service class
II	Lower-grade professionals, administrators and officials; higher-grade technicians; managers in small industrial establishments; supervisors of non-manual employees	Service relationship	
IIIa	Routine non-manual employees, higher-grade (administration and commerce)	Intermediate	III Routine non-manual
IIIb	Routine non-manual employees, lower-grade (sales and services)	Labour contract	
IVa	Small proprietors, artisans, etc., with employees	Employer	IVab Non-farm petty-bourgeoisie
IVb	Small proprietors, artisans, etc., without employees	Self-employed	
IVc	Farmers and smallholders; other self-employed workers in primary production	Employer or self-employed	IVc Farmers and other self-employed workers in primary production
V	Lower-grade technicians; supervisors of manual workers	Intermediate	V + VI Technicians, supervisors and skilled manual workers
VI	Skilled manual workers	Labour contract	
VIIa	Semi- and unskilled manual workers (not in agriculture, etc.)	Labour contract	VIIa Semi- and unskilled manual workers (not in agriculture)
VIIb	Semi- and unskilled manual workers in agriculture	Labour contract	VIIb Semi- and unskilled manual workers in agriculture

a small number of observations, any one of them may be very influential in determining whether or not the data display a trend (as we shall see) and this will inevitably lead to uncertainty in the conclusions we draw. All else equal we must, as a consequence, attach more credence to results about temporal trends drawn from countries with a larger number of observations (Sweden, the Netherlands, Great Britain and Germany).

Furthermore, the data that we use are never free of error, and differences in data quality may easily be mistaken for substantive differences. We have used the best quality data available from each of our 11 countries, but we still need to be aware of the potential for differential reliability and validity to induce spurious cross-national variation and temporal change. As far as the differences between countries are concerned, the fieldwork for the surveys we use was in all cases carried out according to internationally accepted procedures and the subsequent coding of the variables—notably class origins and destinations—followed a common, and widely implemented procedure. Nevertheless, while adherence to such norms is some reassurance that the data attain high standards of quality, the surveys in the various countries were carried out independently of each other, and so we should be cautious about what we infer from them concerning cross-national differences. As far as change within countries is concerned, we can have more faith in our findings when the various surveys have been administered in a consistent fashion. In three cases the data always come from the same survey series: these are France (the FQP—Formation-Qualification Professionnelle—surveys), Britain (the General Household Survey) and Sweden (the ULF series). In a further five countries the data sets come from highly comparable sources: these are Ireland (where the three surveys were all carried out by the same fieldwork organization), Hungary (where the four surveys were all fielded by the Hungarian Central Statistical Office), Italy (where a number of the same academics were involved in the design and execution of the two surveys), Germany and Israel. But in the remaining three cases—Norway, Poland and the Netherlands—the data come from various sources within each country and

thus the possibility that variations in data quality might be mistaken for temporal change is greatest here. We believe that more reliance can be placed on estimates of trends *within* countries than measures of differences *between* them: thus our discussion, later in this chapter, of which countries are more or less open in their mobility regime, should be interpreted with some caution. Finally, while the data that we have are probably adequate for presenting a picture of broad trends and differences, we would have less confidence in the extent to which they allow the specifics of the pattern of social fluidity to be compared across either time or countries. This consideration has then dictated our choice of models. Rather than seeking to develop detailed models of the fluidity regime we prefer instead to fit rather general models and to assess their adequacy using several measures (including the conventional chi-squared goodness of fit test and the index of dissimilarity).

Absolute Mobility and Class Structure

In contemporary studies of social mobility a key distinction is drawn between observed patterns of social mobility, sometimes referred to as 'absolute mobility', and social fluidity (or 'relative mobility'). Absolute mobility is concerned with patterns and rates of mobility, where mobility is understood simply as movement between class origins (the social class in which someone was brought up) and class destinations (the class they occupy at the time of the survey). Social fluidity concerns the relationship between class origins and current class position: specifically it is based on the comparison, between people of different

Table 53.3a   Aggregate Class Structures (All Men) in the 11 Countries by Decade

	1970s	1980s	1990s
I + II	23.1	28.6	30.8
III	8.7	9.0	10.1
IVa + b	7.9	8.6	10.4
IVc	8.6	5.7	4.0
V + VI	27.7	27.6	27.1
VIIa	20.6	18.3	15.7
VIIb	3.5	2.3	2.0

Note: Each country is weighted equally in computation of aggregate class structure.

Table 53.3b   Aggregate Class Structures (Women in the Labour Force) in the 10 Countries by Decade

	1970s	1980s	1990s
I + II	22.1	30.5	34.6
III	32.8	32.3	35.1
IVa + b	6.5	6.0	6.1
IVc	8.6	4.4	2.3
V + VI	6.1	6.3	7.1
VIIa	21.1	18.6	13.7
VIIb	2.8	1.7	1.2

Note: Each country is weighted equally in computation of aggregate class structure.

class origins, of their chances of being found in one destination class rather than another. If these chances were the same regardless of origins then the mobility table would display perfect mobility: the class in which a respondent was found would not depend on (would be independent of) the class in which she or he was brought up. Social fluidity is often interpreted as an index of equality in the chances of access to more or less advantageous social positions between people coming from different social origins (in other words, as an index of societal openness),[1] and contemporary research on social mobility accordingly pays much more attention to social fluidity than to absolute mobility. I will follow that precedent here and so will make only a few comments about absolute mobility.

In fact, our results concerning absolute mobility can be summarised quite easily. There has been a marked convergence in the class structures of European countries and in their patterns of absolute mobility, and these things are true for both men and women.

A. Convergence in class structures has been driven by some internationally consistent trends, such as the growth in the service class, I + II, and the decline in manual work, particularly of the unskilled kind. Among women, increased rates of labour force participation have been associated with a reduction in international variation as more and more of them enter occupations in the white collar classes, I + II and III. But the single biggest cause of this convergence has been the declining significance of the farm classes, IVc and VIIb, in those countries (such as Poland, Ireland, and Hungary) where a large farm sector persisted until the last quarter of the 20th century.

B. This trend towards convergence in class structures has occurred together with decreasing variation between countries in their rates of overall mobility, of vertical, of upward and of downward mobility—and, again, this is evident among both sexes, as Tables 53.4 and 53.5 show. But, further, the distribution of people in the mobility tables of the different countries has also grown more similar. If we calculate the index of dissimilarity (Δ) from comparisons, between all pairs of countries, of their entire mobility tables, we find that the average Δ (the average difference between countries) falls from 43 per cent in the 1970s, to 33 in the 1980s and 30 in the 1990s, among women, with the comparable figures for men being 39, 30 and 30 per cent. And the variance around these means has also declined: from 163.2 to 62.6 to 41.6 among women and from 137.5 to 62.9 to 56.1 among men. Although European countries continue to show differences in their absolute mobility flows, these have become smaller.

Absolute mobility concerns the observed rates and patterns of flows between origin and destination classes and, in mobility analysis, is treated as the consequence of social fluidity (the relative chances of people from each origin being found in each destination class) operating within fixed origin and destination distributions. A model in which origins and destinations are independent, given the observed distributions of these two in each country and at each point in time, correctly classifies over 80 per cent of cases, while a model which also assumes a common level and pattern of social fluidity correctly classifies around 95 per cent of cases. It is evident, therefore, that changes over time, and differences between countries, in absolute mobility are driven by variation in the origin and destination distributions rather than in social fluidity.

Can such variation be said to follow a pattern? We believe that the answer, in very broad terms, is yes. We might imagine societies following a developmental path that incorporates two major transitions: from an agricultural to an industrial society, and from an industrial to a post-industrial society. The consequences, for the class structure, of the former transition are a decline in the proportions in classes IVc and VIIb and a growth in the remaining classes, especially (among men) the manual working classes V + VI and VIIa. The transition to a post-industrial society sees the decline of V + VI and VIIa and the growth of I + II and III. Everywhere the decline in agriculture is either more or less complete (Britain, Germany, Sweden, Israel, the Netherlands) or well underway while, in eight of our 11 countries (Ireland, Poland and Hungary being the exceptions), between the 1970s and 1990s, the class structure saw a steady fall in the proportion of men in classes V + VI and VIIa and a consistent increase in the proportion in I + II and III. Among women the pattern was exactly the same. These differences mean that some countries display a post-industrial class structure with a heavy concentration of people in classes I + II and III: this is particularly true of the male class structure in Britain and the Netherlands

Table 53.4 Percentage Mobile by Country in Each Decade (All Men)

Total Mobility

	Germany	France	Italy	Ireland	Great Britain	Sweden	Norway	Poland	Hungary	Israel	N'lands	Mean	Variance
1970s	61.6	66.6	—	56.7	63.0	70.8	—	59.4	77.5	74.4	66.3	66.3	48.0
1980s	62.1	67.5	69.5	61.3	61.8	71.4	71.9	61.0	74.9	—	67.7	66.9	25.8
1990s	60.3	67.0	72.1	66.1	60.8	71.0	68.1	67.4	71.6	74.3	65.7	67.7	19.9

Vertical Mobility

	Germany	France	Italy	Ireland	Great Britain	Sweden	Norway	Poland	Hungary	Israel	N'lands	Mean	Variance
1970s	44.1	43.8	—	39.9	50.7	54.0	—	40.9	53.0	43.7	50.6	46.7	28.5
1980s	45.8	45.9	40.8	42.6	50.8	54.7	55.2	42.9	55.8	—	54.1	48.9	34.6
1990s	46.3	46.3	46.3	45.5	50.7	55.2	52.1	45.9	53.7	50.4	54.0	49.7	13.9

Upward Mobility

	Germany	France	Italy	Ireland	Great Britain	Sweden	Norway	Poland	Hungary	Israel	N'lands	Mean	Variance
1970s	31.7	25.9	—	21.6	32.8	35.1	—	22.1	26.9	20.1	36.1	28.0	37.1
1980s	33.6	29.1	29.0	27.9	33.1	35.3	39.3	24.8	34.7	—	38.9	32.6	22.9
1990s	33.3	29.9	35.9	31.4	31.7	36.6	34.2	26.3	35.9	35.0	37.7	33.4	11.4

Downward Mobility

	Germany	France	Italy	Ireland	Great Britain	Sweden	Norway	Poland	Hungary	Israel	N'lands	Mean	Variance
1970s	12.4	17.9	—	18.4	17.9	19.0	—	18.8	26.2	23.5	14.5	18.7	17.3
1980s	12.2	16.8	11.8	14.7	17.7	19.4	15.9	18.0	21.1	—	15.2	16.3	8.7
1990s	13.0	16.4	10.4	14.1	19.0	18.6	17.9	19.6	17.8	15.4	16.3	16.2	8.0

Table 53.5 Percentage Mobile by Country in Each Decade (Women in the Labour Force)

	Germany	France	Italy	Great Britain	Sweden	Norway	Poland	Hungary	Israel	N'lands	Mean	Variance
Total Mobility												
1970s	74.0	71.4	—	78.8	73.1	—	50.8	81.0	76.5	74.0	72.5	86.4
1980s	75.6	77.6	74.3	76.3	73.6	76.2	66.3	79.5	—	73.9	74.8	13.7
1990s	72.6	77.2	75.0	73.9	73.2	77.4	76.2	76.5	82.2	72.3	75.7	8.8
Vertical Mobility												
1970s	48.6	41.7	—	52.1	55.4	—	34.0	54.1	44.9	51.4	47.8	52.2
1980s	48.8	45.7	51.0	52.6	56.4	54.1	48.5	58.2	—	51.4	51.9	15.7
1990s	47.3	46.0	47.9	53.2	57.9	53.0	50.3	55.7	53.5	53.6	51.8	14.8
Upward Mobility												
1970s	25.8	27.8	—	27.5	23.9	—	19.5	23.3	26.0	30.9	25.6	11.7
1980s	29.6	32.9	38.5	29.0	27.5	34.4	31.7	38.8	—	33.6	32.9	15.7
1990s	32.2	33.2	36.7	30.6	33.5	37.1	34.1	42.0	39.0	34.8	35.3	11.6
Downward Mobility												
1970s	22.8	13.9	—	24.6	31.5	—	14.4	30.8	19.0	20.5	22.2	44.2
1980s	19.2	12.8	12.5	23.7	28.9	19.8	16.8	19.4	—	17.8	19.0	26.0
1990s	15.2	12.8	11.3	22.5	24.4	15.9	16.2	13.7	14.5	18.8	16.5	17.6

and it is true of the female class structure in several countries. But the important thing, from the point of view of the study of absolute mobility, is the recent rapidity of the transition out of agriculture. Similarly, we saw in our comparative analysis that the shift towards a concentration of women in the white-collar classes has been more rapid in countries such as Hungary and Poland where the class distribution in the 1970s differed most from this. The result has been the growing similarity in destination distributions that we have already remarked upon. But because countries embarked on this developmental path long before the first of our surveys was fielded, there is also decreasing variation in class origins. The mean value of the Δ between class origins for each pair of countries fell from 33 per cent in the 1970s to 23 in the 1980s and 24 in the 1990s.[2] Absolute mobility flows converged because their main determinants did.

This convergence chiefly occurred between the 1970s and 1980s and whether the trend will persist, or even strengthen, is, of course, difficult to say. Clearly, if the working classes continue to decline in those countries where the decline has begun, and if this extends from VIIa to V + VI, then further convergence will be inevitable as men, like women, come to be heavily concentrated in classes I + II and III. Recent historical experience of the location of industrial production would suggest that we can expect further convergence; in any event, it seems unlikely that any of these countries will display a growth in classes V + VI and VIIa, while some at least will experience a decline. As for the countries in which these classes have not yet begun to decline (Ireland, Poland and Hungary), the outlook seems less certain. In Ireland the growth of classes I + II and III has out-

stripped that of V + VI and VIIa over this period, but this is not true of the male class structure in Poland and Hungary. On the other hand, among women in Poland and Hungary there has been a steady growth in classes I + II and III and an increase, then a decline, in V + VI and VIIa, suggesting that the second transition may be under way. Much here depends on the nature of economic development. Foreign direct investment in manufacturing, as in the Irish case, is one mechanism by which the size of the working class may be sustained and the rate of convergence consequently slowed.

Social Fluidity

In our comparative analysis we found that trends in social fluidity are very similar among men and women, showing a widespread tendency towards greater fluidity. Britain is the sole clear exception to this: here there has been little or no change. In other cases—notably Germany—there is no statistically significant change, though the trend, at least for men, is towards a weaker association between origins and destinations. Elsewhere—in France, Ireland, Sweden, Poland, Hungary and the Netherlands—there is a statistically significant increase in fluidity, though the small number of observations for Ireland (three), Poland (three), and Hungary (four), and the lack of a consistent pattern of change in these countries, must leave some room for uncertainty. But in contrast to absolute mobility we see no evidence of convergence among countries in their social fluidity. Figures 53.1 (for men) and 53.2 (for women) show these within-country trends in the form of the annual β coefficients from an LmSF model[3] with common local association among all the yearly tables of a given country.

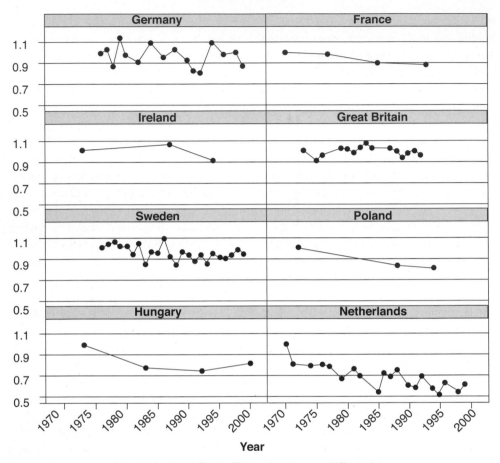

Figure 53.1   Annual LmSF (or Unidiff) Coefficients by Country (All Men)

Figure 53.3 (for men) and Figure 53.4 (for women) show the LmSF β parameters from a model, applied to decade data from each country, which assumes common local association in each table, varying only by β. The value for Britain in the 1980s is set to unity. Among men, Figure 53.3 shows that, in the 1970s, levels of social fluidity were lowest in Germany, France, Italy, Ireland, Hungary and the Netherlands and highest in Britain, Sweden, Norway, Poland and Israel. Fluidity increased in France, Sweden and the Netherlands and possibly in Ireland, Hungary and Poland too. The in-creases in the Netherlands and Hungary were particularly marked. These different trends have left several countries—Sweden, Norway, Poland, Hungary and the Nether-lands—with, as far as we can tell, rather similar rates of fluidity, followed by Britain (where the absence of change has led to a shift in its relative position), Ireland, France, Italy and Germany, which remains the country with the strongest association between class origins and class destinations. At the other extreme, Israel is consistently more open than any other country. Overall, however, we can find no convincing evi-

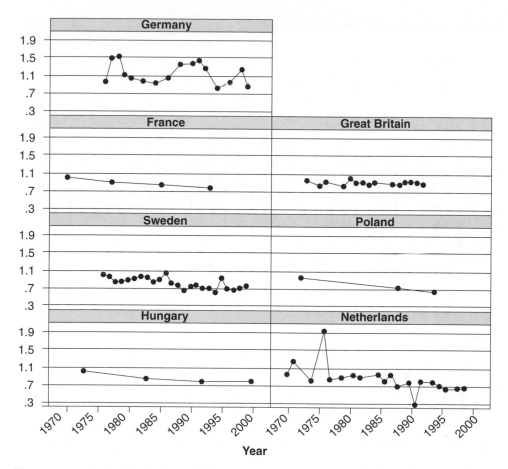

Figure 53.2   Annual LmSF (or Unidiff) Coefficients by Country (Women in the Workforce)

dence of convergence in fluidity regimes: for example, the within decade variance of the βs shown in Figure 53.3 is largest for the 1980s and the Δ for CnSF across countries in each decade is larger for the 1990s than for the 1980s.

The picture among women (Figure 53.4) is very similar. Once again, the points for the 1970s are above those for the 1980s which are above those for the 1990s, indicating a general tendency for fluidity to increase, with Britain being an exception. The average β falls from 1.28 in the 1970s to 1.14 in the 1980s and 1.05 in the 1990s.

France and Germany are the least fluid societies; Britain, Sweden, Poland and, by the 1990s, the Netherlands are the most fluid. Hungary presents a different picture for women than men, the former showing much lower fluidity, compared with other countries, than the latter. In Israel the values are 0.84 in the 1970s and 0.71 in the 1990s. Taken together with the results for men this is evidence of the exceptionally fluid nature of Israeli society.

Overall, the results from our 11 countries point to a clear conclusion: there is a widespread tendency for social fluidity to

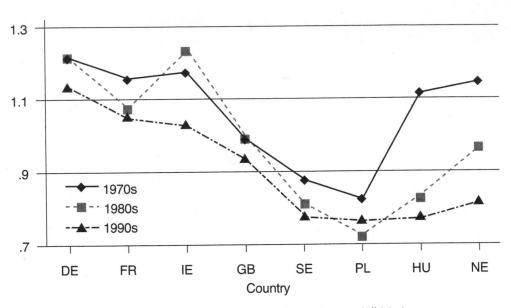

Figure 53.3   LmSF (or Unidiff) Coefficients per Decade, per Country (All Men)

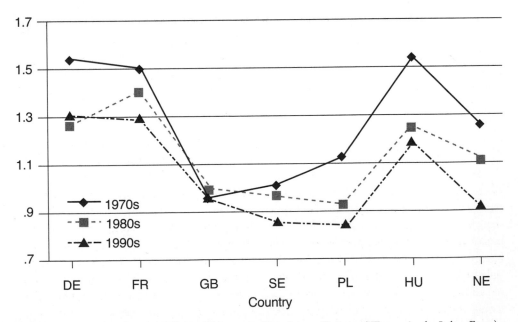

Figure 53.4   LmSF (or Unidiff) Coefficients per Decade, per Country (Women in the Labor Force)

increase, even though this might not be a statistically significant trend in every case. Among men, fluidity is greater at the end of the period than at the start in every country except Britain and Israel (where the values remain the same). Furthermore, of the 20 decade to decade changes in fluidity reported in Breen (2004), we find that in 16 of them fluidity increased and it declined in three—in Ireland and Britain between the 1970s and 1980s and in Norway between the 1980s and 1990s. There is just one further notable case in which fluidity fell (but which is obscured by the use of aggregated decade data) and that is Hungary where fluidity declined significantly between the 1992 and 2000 observations. Although there are some cases (such as Sweden) where we cannot be unequivocal about an increase in fluidity, we can say with confidence that nowhere (with the possible exception of post-Communist Hungary) is there any evidence of a trend in the opposite direction. For women the picture is very similar. Of 18 decade to decade changes, two of them show a decline in fluidity (Germany between the 1980s and 1990s, Britain between the 1970s and 1980s) while 14 show an increase.

Previous Research

These results differ quite substantially from those of the previous major comparative study of social mobility, namely *The Constant Flux,* in which Erikson and Goldthorpe (1993) argue strongly in favour of the so-called FJH hypothesis of a basic similarity in social fluidity in all industrial societies 'with a market economy and a nuclear family system' (Featherman, Jones and Hauser 1975: 340) and they also claim (1992: 367) that 'relative rates possess a high degree of temporal stability'. Indeed, our results are somewhat closer to those of the slightly earlier comparative study by Ganzeboom, Luijkx and Treiman (1989). They used 149 mobility tables for men drawn from 35 countries spanning the period 1947–86. They claim that they show that 'although . . . there is a basic similarity in mobility *patterns . . .* at the same time there are substantial cross-national and cross-temporal differences in the *extent* of mobility.' Furthermore, 'a smaller but significant part of the variance in mobility regimes can be explained by the trend towards increasing openness over time' (Ganzeboom, Luijkx and Treiman 1989: 47). However, although our results and GLT's results are rather similar, it should be noted that the latter have been heavily criticised, notably by Wong (1994: 138), who re-analyses their data and finds that 'the model of temporal invariance cannot be rejected for a majority of countries . . . Hungary and Sweden are the only countries giving irrefutable evidence of temporal variation'.

Why do we find evidence for change and cross-national difference when Erikson and Goldthorpe did not? As far as temporal change is concerned, because Erikson and Goldthorpe have only one mobility table per country, their claim that there is little systematic temporal variation in patterns of social fluidity within countries is based on analyses in which age groups are taken to represent different birth cohorts. But as Breen and Jonsson (2003) have pointed out, this approach confounds lifecycle and cohort effects and makes no allowance for either selective mortality or recall errors. In an assessment of the reliability of measures of class origin and class destination in mobility tables, Breen and Jonsson (1997) found that reliability was lower for origin information from older age groups, implying that the common practice of using age groups to draw conclusions about cohort change over time in mobility regimes may be unsound. More simply, one cannot properly make inferences about change from cross-sectional data.

An important reason why we observe a trend towards increasing social fluidity and Erikson and Goldthorpe do not is that our data, by and large, refer to later-born cohorts. Although our analyses, like those of the overwhelming majority of mobility studies, are based on period data, there is, I believe, good reason to suppose that social fluidity is driven by cohort, rather than period, effects.

Erikson and Goldthorpe's data represents cohorts born between, approximately, 1900 and 1945, whereas our data extends this to cohorts born around 1970. This means that our data contain a larger share of people who benefited from what has been called the Golden Age of Welfare Capitalism—in other words, the long post-war economic boom and the generally more egalitarian educational and social welfare policies that followed in its wake. Work that I have done with Janne Jonsson on Sweden clearly shows that here the major reduction in class inequalities in educational attainment took place among cohorts of people born between 1910 and 1950 and that since then there has been no further equalization. But this means that, as we compare period data for the 1970s, 1980s and 1990s, we gradually lose the older, less fluid cohorts, who are replaced by younger, more fluid cohorts. In the case of Sweden such a process will continue until the second decade of the 21st century, after which we expect to see no further increase in period social fluidity. But it seems likely that the specific cohorts which benefited from the Golden Age will

have differed between countries, so leading to variation between them in the fluidity they display in particular periods.

Whereas we argue that countries display considerable variation in social fluidity, Erikson and Goldthorpe argue the contrary. But in their own analyses (Erikson and Goldthorpe 1992: 381) the logarithm of each odds ratio in their mobility table from Czechoslovakia (which is the country in which they find the greatest fluidity) is two-thirds as strong as in Scotland (the country with the least fluidity). So, for example, given an odds ratio of 3 in Czechoslovakia, the comparable odds ratio would be 5.3 in Scotland. On this basis it is difficult to argue for commonality in the strength of social fluidity, and, indeed, these results are quite similar to ours: in our data the logarithm of the odds ratios in Israel are around half those in Germany. So, an odds ratio of 3 in Israel would be an odds ratio of 7 in Germany. Given this, one might ask why Erikson and Goldthorpe, like many others, conclude that there is little variation in fluidity. The reason is the following. All comparative mobility studies find that the difference in the goodness of fit between a model in which social fluidity is common across all countries (the model of Common Social Fluidity or CnSF) and a model in which fluidity can differ between them is small, relative to the difference between the CnSF model and one in which origins and destinations are independent. It is certainly true that the model of variation in fluidity is a significantly better fit to the data than CnSF, but this incremental improvement to any goodness of fit measure is small. For example, when we analyzed our data according to decade, a very small index of dissimilarity was returned by a model that allowed for no temporal or cross-national variation in social fluidity (3.95 per cent for men and 3.81 for women) and allowing for such variation only improved Δ by, at most, two percentage points. This compares with a Δ of around 15 per cent in models in which origins and destinations are independent. Much the same picture emerged when we used annual data, and arguments like this usually lead to the conclusion that most social fluidity is common and invariant over time. Sometimes the same point is made using the deviance, rather than Δ, as the yardstick, and here the result is even more extreme. For example, 90 per cent of the deviance returned by the model of independence disappears when we add common (among countries and over decades) social fluidity, and a model allowing fluidity to change over time and differ between countries improves it only by a further seven per cent. Taken together, the decompositions of the deviance and of Δ would seem to indicate that more than 85 per cent of social fluidity is common over nations and time.

This then seems to conflict with our finding of large variation between countries in their odds ratios. The problem with using arguments based on Δ or the deviance to support the argument that social fluidity is largely invariant is that variation in fluidity is assessed using measures of the consequences of fluidity for the whole mobility regime (i.e. for absolute mobility), and, as we have seen, these consequences are unanimously agreed to be quite minor. An analogy may help to make the point. In a linear regression, $Y = a + bX$; X (analogous to social fluidity) may display a lot of variation, but it will have little impact on Y (analogous to overall mobility) if the coefficient, b, is close to zero. But simply because b is small we could not then claim that

there was little variation in X. Measures such as the change in Δ or in G^2 might be said to capture the strength of effect of fluidity on overall mobility, but they do not measure the variation in fluidity itself, and it is therefore mistaken to conclude, on this basis, that social fluidity is common and invariant. It is empirically the case that, between countries or over time, large variations in social fluidity can be found which nevertheless have little impact on the overall mobility regime. To illustrate this: if we take the fluidity pattern from the 1997 Italian men's table in our data and insert it into the 1991 Israeli men's table, while preserving the Israeli marginal distributions, the Δ between the real and the constructed Israeli tables is 6 per cent.[4] When we consider that the Israeli and Italian mobility regimes are close to the extremes of the range of fluidity found in our data this suggests that 6 per cent represents the maximum impact of differences in fluidity on the distribution of individuals in the mobility table. The conclusion to be drawn from these apparently contradictory measures of the variation in fluidity is not that it is common or invariant, but, rather, that even quite substantial differences in fluidity have little impact on the distribution of cases over the mobility table—i.e. on observed, absolute mobility flows.

Explanation

Thus far I have said nothing about how we might explain patterns of social mobility or social fluidity, aside from some rather vague remarks about the impact of policies pursued during the Golden Age of Welfare Capitalism. In broad terms, explanations of variations in social fluidity are usually pitched at a macro-sociological level: that is, fluidity is assumed to be related to other, societal level measures. The very influential 'liberal theory of industrialism', for example, argues that fluidity will increase with economic development. In our case, the stage of economic development of our countries varies rather little, but, even so, we could find no evident link between their ranking in fluidity terms and their GDP per capita. Nor did we find any support for Erikson and Goldthorpe's argument that fluidity is related to income inequality: there is no significant association between a country's fluidity and its Gini coefficient. Overall we could discern no tendencies towards either convergence or divergence in fluidity, and thus the hypothesis that, as nations have come to follow different policy trajectories—particularly in economic policy—so we might see growing differences between them in fluidity, receives no support. There is some indication, however, that fluidity is greater in state socialist (Poland and Hungary) and social democratic (Norway and Sweden) countries, and the argument for such a political explanation receives additional support from the finding of declining fluidity in Hungary during the 1990s. But, on the other hand, we observe very high fluidity in Israel and data from the General Social Survey (made available to us by Mike Hout) shows that fluidity is high in the United States. This leads to the conclusion that direct political intervention of the kinds associated with state-socialist and social democratic societies may be one means by which a society can reach relatively high rates of fluidity, but it is not the only one.

One major difficulty in devising theories to explain variation in mobility or fluidity is that mobility tables, especially period-based tables, reflect a large number of underlying processes—artefactual, contingent and substantive. For one thing, this aggregation of processes renders it difficult to explain variations in fluidity; for another, it may also be the case that some of the commonality that has often been observed in comparisons of social fluidity derives from the mixing together in the mobility tables of processes that, when investigated separately, might show greater and more systematic societal and temporal differences.

While it is reasonable to suppose that fluidity in a nation is shaped by government policy, the education system, the workings of the labour market and suchlike, it is also the case that what we observe in a mobility table may also reflect purely artefactual sources of variation arising from differences in the way that the data themselves represent the underlying phenomenon of interest. Furthermore, what we might call contingent factors, which are usually omitted from any theoretical discussion of social fluidity, may play an important role in shaping what we observe. Walter Müller and Reinhard Pollak (see Breen 2004) attribute the high fluidity they find among Germans born in the 1920s to the massive migration from the eastern part of Germany that occurred following the Second World War. The measured class origins of this cohort are thus their pre-migration origins, which had very little relevance in shaping their subsequent mobility patterns: the physical detaching of a large share of the cohort from their true origins led to higher measured social fluidity. The same argument may explain the high level of fluidity in Israel, a country in which a very large share of the population is comprised of immigrants.

Conclusions

The experience of this project should lead us to question the balance that mobility research has struck between social fluidity and absolute mobility. The emphasis has lain heavily on the former but, insofar as we are concerned with the mobility regime, this now seems inappropriate. This is by no means to deny that social fluidity tells us important things about the prevailing degree of inequality in the chances of attaining one class position rather than another, and may be indicative of other characteristics of society. Nevertheless, although one would not want to say that fluidity can never make a difference (since we can easily construct examples in which extreme patterns of fluidity will be highly consequential for the distribution of cases in a mobility table), within the advanced industrial and post-industrial societies, the range of fluidity that we observe is relatively inconsequential in determining variation in mobility flows and in the life chances of individuals and families as these are captured in measures of class position. Many previous authors (such as Grusky and Hauser 1984; Goldthorpe 1985) have called for more attention to be paid to structural change, but, as Erikson and Goldthorpe (1992: 104, 189) suggest, it is not clear how such change should be explained nor, indeed, whether it might not better be approached as a matter of historical description rather than sociological explanation. But while this might be a valid concern if we conceive of class structures as macro-sociological phenomena, it may be less so, and may leave open the possibility of sociological explanation, if we were to turn our attention to the detailed evolution of businesses and firms and of the jobs that constitute classes.

Furthermore, it now seems to me that a period perspective on social mobility may not be the most appropriate if, as I have suggested, social fluidity is driven by factors related to cohorts, rather than periods. The cohort perspective on social mobility has not been entirely neglected, but it has certainly played a very secondary role to the usual period view. Under the cohort approach, change in the association between origins and destinations is believed to occur in specific cohorts, while, from a period point of view, this association is considered to change among all cohorts at similar historical points in time. The importance, for social change, of the replacement of older by younger cohorts has been stressed by several sociologists. In the specific field of mobility research, Erikson and Goldthorpe (1992), for example, argue that equality of condition is essential for equality of opportunity, and that changes in the latter will then predominantly take effect during a person's upbringing and schooling. As a result, the overall level of inequality of opportunity in society will change mainly through cohort replacement, with younger cohorts experiencing a different degree of inequality of educational attainment than older. It has long been education that is the major channel of social mobility: if this is so, then social fluidity should respond to changes in the level of class inequality in educational attainment, which, because educational inequality is itself a characteristic of cohorts, implies a cohort explanation of change in fluidity.

Though rarely spelled out, there is a tension between the cohort interpretation of change in social fluidity and the belief that period effects drive variation in the origin-destination association over the lifecycle through labour market changes that simultaneously affect different birth cohorts. We believe that there are strong arguments for adopting a cohort rather than, or in addition to, a period perspective. It is widely agreed that changes in an individual's social class position are relatively rare after the age of about 35 (Goldthorpe 1980: 51–2, 69–71; Erikson and Goldthorpe 1992: 72). Such stability implies that, except in unusual circumstances in which this stability is disrupted, period effects will be a less important source of change in fluidity when compared with cohort replacement and within-cohort change that occurs during the early years in the labour force.

NOTES

1. The terms association and social fluidity can be used interchangeably: greater social fluidity implies lower origin–destination association. In the log-linear modeling context in which this paper is situated this association is captured by odds ratios.

2. These figures are for men. For women the figures are 36, 24 and 24 per cent. The slight differences arise because our samples of women include only those in the labour force and we have no data for women in Ireland.

3. LmSF means 'log-multiplicative social fluidity' (by analogy with CnSF—'common social fluidity'). We use LmSF to refer to the unidiff (Erikson and Goldthorpe 1992) or log-multiplicative layer effect model (Xie 1992) when the local association is modeled in a completely unspecified way (as it is in CnSF).

4. We use the observed Italian fluidity pattern, and thus the magnitude of the difference that we report does not depend on the adequacy of any particular model of fluidity.

REFERENCES

Breen, Richard (ed.). 2004. *Social Mobility in Europe.* Oxford: Oxford University Press.

Erikson, Robert and John H. Goldthorpe. 1992. *The Constant Flux: A Study of Class Mobility in Industrial Societies.* Oxford: Oxford University Press.

Featherman, David L., F. L. Jones, and Robert M. Hauser. 1975. "Assumptions of Mobility Research in the United States: The Case of Occupational Status." *Social Science Research* 4: 329–60.

Ganzeboom, Harry B. G., Ruud Luijkx, and Donald J. Treiman. 1989. "Intergenerational Class Mobility in Comparative Perspective." *Research in Social Stratification and Mobility* 8: 3–84.

Goldthorpe, John H. 1980. *Social Mobility and Class Structure in Modern Britain.* Oxford: Clarendon Press.

Goldthorpe, John H. 1985. "On Economic Development and Social Mobility." *British Journal of Sociology* 36: 549–573.

Grusky, David B. and Robert M. Hauser. 1984. "Comparative Social Mobility Revisited: Models of Convergence and Divergence in 16 Countries." *American Sociological Review* 49: 19–38.

Wong, Raymond S. 1994. "Postwar Mobility Trends in Advanced Industrial Societies." *Research in Social Stratification and Mobility* 13: 121–44.

54

It's a Decent Bet That Our Children Will Be Professors Too

JAN O. JONSSON,
DAVID B. GRUSKY,
MATTHEW DI CARLO, AND
REINHARD POLLAK

Are children born into privilege very likely to end up privileged themselves? Are children born into less privileged families likewise fated to remain in their social class of origin? We care about such questions for many reasons but perhaps primarily because they speak to whether the competition for money, power, and prestige is fairly run. For many people, the brute facts of extreme poverty or inequality are not in themselves problematic or objectionable, and what really matters is simply whether the competition for riches is a fair one in which everyone, no matter how advantaged or disadvantaged their parents may be, has an equal chance to win. This commitment to a fair competition motivates a quite extensive research literature on how much mobility there is, whether some countries have more of it than others, and whether opportunities for mobility are withering away.

The purpose of this chapter is to ask whether conventional methods of monitoring mobility are adequate for the task. We're concerned that they're not and that, in particular, such methods may overlook some of the most important forms and sources of rigidity. The long-standing convention in the field, and one that we regard as problematic, has been to assume that intergenerational reproduction takes one of two forms, either a categorical form that has parents passing on a big-class position (e.g., manager, professional, craft worker) to their children or a gradational form that has parents passing on their socioeconomic standing to their children. We argue here that these standard approaches ignore the important role that detailed occupations play in reproducing inequality.

The conventional wisdom about how to measure mobility was codified a half century ago. The study of mobility bifurcated

Jan O. Jonsson, David B. Grusky, Matthew Di Carlo, and Reinhard Pollak, "It's a Decent Bet That Our Children Will Be Professors Too." New contribution written for this edition. This chapter is drawn from materials appearing in Jonsson et al. 2009; Grusky et al. 2008; and Jonsson et al. forthcoming.

at that time into one camp that represented social structure in gradational terms (e.g., Svalastoga 1959) and another that represented it in big-class terms (e.g., Carlsson 1958; Glass 1954). These competing representations of social structure were subsequently attached to competing understandings of how inequality is reproduced: The class scholar assumed that parents pass on their social class to children, while the gradational scholar assumed that parents pass on their occupational prestige or socioeconomic standing to their children. Under both approaches, detailed occupations were usually treated as the appropriate starting point in representing the underlying structure of inequality, but they were transformed either by aggregating them into big social classes (i.e., the class approach) or by scaling them in terms of their socioeconomic status or prestige (i.e., the gradational approach). The study of mobility has in this sense been reduced to the study of either class or socioeconomic mobility, yet quite strikingly these simplifying assumptions have come to be adopted with little in the way of evidence that they adequately characterize the structure of opportunity.

Is it possible that both class and gradational representations are incomplete and obscure important rigidities in the mobility regime? We suggest that indeed these simplifying representations provide only partial accounts and that the structure of inequality is best revealed by supplementing them with a third representation that treats detailed occupations as fundamental conduits of reproduction. Because the social, cultural, and economic resources conveyed to children depend so fundamentally on the detailed occupations of their parents, one might expect such occupations to play a featured role in intergenerational reproduction, but in fact this role has gone largely unexplored in most mobility analyses.

It's not just that detailed occupations serve as a main conduit for reproduction. In addition, they index the main communities and identities of workers, and as such they should be understood as a powerful omnibus indicator of the social world within which individuals are located. At a dinner party, we tend to ask a new acquaintance "What do you do?" because the response, almost invariably conveyed in the form of a detailed occupation, provides at once evidence about life chances and capacities (skills and credentials, earnings capacity, networks), honor and esteem (prestige, socioeconomic status), and the social and cultural world within which interactions occur (consumption practices, politics, and attitudes). We care, in other words, about occupations because they are pregnant with information on the life chances, social standing, and social world of their incumbents (see Weeden and Grusky 2005). The (largely untested) bias in this regard is that occupation is far more strongly correlated with these many variables than is income. If we tend to avoid asking acquaintances about their income, it's not just because doing so is viewed as too intrusive and personal but also because we suspect that querying about occupation will yield more in the way of useful information.

Mechanisms of Reproduction

If our main argument, therefore, is that occupations are an important conduit for reproduction, this is obviously not to suggest that inequality is reproduced *exclusively* through occupations. Rather, there's good reason to believe that, while much reproduction occurs through occupations, the more frequently studied big-class and socioeconomic mechanisms are also doing important reproductive work. We suggest below that a comprehensive mobility model should examine at once reproduction at the socioeconomic, big-class, and microclass levels. In most mobility analyses, the three levels are confounded, and conclusions about the structure of mobility may conceal possible differences in how these forms of reproduction play out. We develop this argument below by reviewing each of these three mechanisms of reproduction in turn.[1]

Gradational regime: The gradational (or socioeconomic) approach to studying mobility has inequality taking on a simple unidimensional form in which families are arrayed in terms of either income or occupational status. The life chances of children growing up within such systems are a function, then, of their standing within this unidimensional queue of families. When children are born high in the queue, they tend to secure high-status and highly rewarded occupations by virtue of (1) their privileged access to the economic resources (e.g., wealth, income) needed either to purchase training for the best occupations (e.g., an elite education) or to "purchase" the jobs themselves (e.g., a proprietorship), (2) their privileged access to social networks providing information about and entrée to the best occupations, and (3) their privileged access to cultural resources (e.g., socialization) that motivate them to acquire the best jobs and provide them with the cognitive and interactional skills (e.g., culture of critical discourse) to succeed in them. Under the gradational model, it is the total *amount* of resources that matters, and children born into privileged circum-

stances are privileged because they have access to so many resources (e.g., Hout and Hauser 1992). The imagery here is accordingly that of two unidimensional hierarchies, one for each generation, smoothly joined together through the mediating mechanism of total resources (economic, social, or cultural). In Figure 54.1a, an ideal-typical gradational regime is depicted by projecting a detailed cross-classification of occupational origins and destinations onto a third dimension, one that represents the densities of mobility and immobility. This graph, which orders origin and destination occupations by socioeconomic score, shows the characteristic falloff in mobility chances as the distance between origin and destination scores increases.

Big-class regime: The big-class regime, by contrast, has inequality taking the form of mutually exclusive and exhaustive classes. These classes are often assumed to convey a package of conditions (e.g., employment relations), a resulting social environment that structures behavior and decision making, and a culture that may be understood as an adaptation (or maladaptation) to this environment. For our purposes, the relevant feature of this formulation is that all children born into the same class will have largely the same mobility chances, even though their parents may hold different occupations with different working conditions and socioeconomic standing. The logic of the class situation is assumed, then, to be overriding and to determine the life chances of the children born into it. Obversely, two big classes of similar status will not necessarily convey to their incumbents identical mobility chances, as they may differ on various nonstatus dimensions that have implications for mobility. For example, even though proprietors and routine

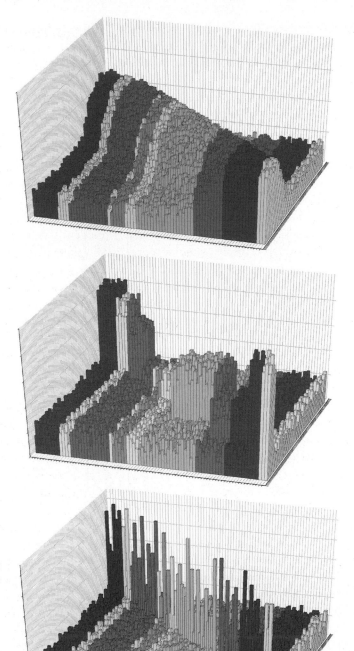

Figure 54.1a
Gradational Regime

Figure 54.1b
Big-Class Regime

Figure 54.1c
Microclass Regime

Note: The base of each figure indexes occupational origin and destination, while the vertical dimension indexes densities of mobility and immobility for each possible combination of origin and destination.

nonmanuals are roughly similar in socioeconomic status, the children of proprietors will tend to become proprietors and the children of routine nonmanuals will tend to become routine nonmanuals. This pattern arises because tastes and aspirations develop in class-specific ways (e.g., the children of proprietors develop tastes for autonomy, and the children of routine nonmanuals develop tastes for stability), because human capital is cultivated and developed in class-specific ways (e.g., the children of proprietors develop entrepreneurial skills, and the children of routine nonmanuals develop bureaucratic skills), because social capital is distributed in class-specific ways (e.g., the children of proprietors are apprised of entrepreneurial opportunities, and the children of routine nonmanuals are apprised of routine nonmanual opportunities), and because the tangible physical capital (e.g., a shop, business) passed on to children of proprietors motivates them to remain proprietors. By virtue of these processes, children do not have generic access to all occupations of comparable standing (as gradationalists would have it), but instead are especially well positioned to assume occupations that align with the culture, training, contacts, and capital that their class origins entail. We represent an ideal-typical class regime of this sort in Figure 54.1b. Because we are focusing on reproduction, we have assumed here (and in Figure 54.1c) that all off-diagonal cells have the same density, save for random noise.

Microclass regime: The occupational, or "microclass," approach shares with the big-class model the presumption that contemporary labor markets are balkanized into discrete categories, but such balkanization is assumed to take principally the form of institutionalized occupations (e.g., doctor, plumber, postal clerk) rather than institutionalized big classes (e.g., routine nonmanuals). By implication, the occupations constituting big classes will have differing propensities for mobility and immobility, a heterogeneity that obtains because the distinctive occupational worlds into which children are born have consequences for the aspirations they develop, the skills they value and to which they have access, and the networks upon which they can draw (see Table 54.1). The children of carpenters, for example, may be especially likely to become carpenters because they are exposed to carpentry skills at home, socialized in ways that render them especially appreciative of carpentry as a vocation, and embedded in social networks that provide them with information about how to become carpenters and how to secure jobs in carpentry. Although a microclass regime again assumes a lumpy class form, the lumpiness is much finer than big-class analysts would allow (see Figure 54.1c). The strong big-class reproduction that we long thought was revealed in mobility tables may instead be artifactual and express little more than the tendency for reproduction at the detailed occupational level.

We have referred above to the occupational skills, culture, and networks that parents transmit to their children. The transmission of skills should, however, be particularly stressed and may well be especially important in understanding why occupations are passed on. The conventional view would have it that the ongoing separation of home and workplace has made it more difficult for parents to transmit such occupational human capital. We agree that its transmission may now be weakened, but this obviously does not mean that it's altogether precluded. The sociologist, for example, may well talk shop with her or his children at the dinner table, litter the home with books and magazines that betray a sociological orientation, and in all other ways inculcate a sociological perspective in the natural course of everyday child rearing. The engineer, by contrast, may bring home toys that involve building things, focus conversation and inquiry on the world of things, and impart a special interest in understanding "how things work." In the aftermath of the World Trade Center collapse, we can imagine the engineer's family talked mainly about why the building failed structurally, whereas the sociologist's family talked mainly about why there is terrorism.

The transmission of occupation-specific human capital is likely to occur outside the professional sector as well. The mechanic is especially likely to spend time at home engaging in repairs, may take her or his children into the repair shop, and may otherwise encourage an interest in taking things apart and fixing them (i.e., a "practical" engineer). Likewise, the seamstress may talk frequently about fashion at home, take her or his children to fashion shows, and train them in sewing and designing clothes. These examples make the simple point that the occupational commitments of parents can affect what they discuss or practice at home, how they spend time with their children, and hence the skills that they impart to their children.

It would be possible to presume that reproduction takes on an exclusively gradational, big-class, or microclass form and build a mobility model that then capitalizes on the imagery underlying that particular form. The field has indeed often proceeded in just that way: That is, big-class analysts

have often insisted on building purist big-class models, while gradationalists have in turn insisted on building purist gradational models. The model that we develop will, by contrast, combine all three forms (big class, microclass, gradational) and thereby make it possible to tease out the net contribution of each. We apply this approach to ask (1) whether the mobility regime contains pockets of extreme microclass rigidity that are concealed when microclasses are aggregated into big classes and (2) whether such microclass reproduction is the main mechanism through which big classes are reproduced. If the answer to these questions is in the affirmative, it will follow that there is more microclass rigidity than is consistent with the practice of ignoring it and less big-class rigidity than is consistent with the practice of building our analyses exclusively around it.

We suspect that a microclass foundation to reproduction is a generic feature of late industrialism rather than something idiosyncratic to the United States. The mechanisms that we've laid out are, after all, in play to a greater or lesser extent in all countries (see Table 54.1). The relative strength of big-class or microclass reproduction in any given society will be affected by the prevailing mix of institutional forms, some supporting big-class structuration (e.g., trade unions) and others supporting microclass structuration (e.g., state-supported occupational closure). We have chosen to analyze four countries (Germany, the United States, Sweden, and Japan) that, by virtue of this different mix of institutional forms, have mobility regimes that support reproduction of different types.

How might mobility vary by country? Whereas Germany and the United States

Table 54.1 Mechanisms of Intergenerational Reproduction

Type of resources	Type of reproduction	
	Big-class	Micro-class
Human capital	General or abstract skills (e.g., cognitive or verbal abilities)	Occupation-specific skills (e.g., acting skills, carpentry skills)
Cultural capital	Abstract culture and tastes (e.g., "culture of critical discourse")	Occupation-specific culture and tastes (e.g., aspirations to become a medical doctor)
Social networks	Classwide networks (typically developed through neighborhood- or job-related interactions)	Occupation-specific networks (typically developed through on-the-job interactions)
Economic resources	Liquid resources (e.g., stocks, bonds, income)	Fixed resources (e.g., business, farm)

are often understood as the home ground of occupationalization, Sweden has a long tradition of big-class organization, and Japan is typically assumed to be stratified more by family and firm than by big class or occupation. We have sought in this fashion to explore the reach of microclass mechanisms into labor markets, like those of Sweden and Japan, that have not historically been regarded as taking a microclass form. If a microclass mechanism nonetheless emerges as fundamental in Sweden or Japan, the case for building that mechanism more systematically into our models is strengthened. This design allows us to assess the strong claim, as recently advanced by Goldthorpe, that "a reliance on occupationally specific factors, which are likely themselves to be quite variable over time and space, would seem especially inadequate" in explaining class reproduction (2007, 144).

In the present analysis, we will not be exploring the structure of cross-national variation in reproduction, and instead we'll be presenting the shared features that hold in approximate form in all countries. We refer the reader elsewhere (Jonsson et al. 2009, forthcoming) for a discussion of cross-national variability in microclass mobility.

The Structure of Contemporary Mobility

The analyses presented here will be carried out with data sets that provide information on the father's occupation, the child's occupation and age, and other variables that aid in occupational and big-class coding (e.g., employment status, branch of industry). Because our analyses are pitched at the occupational level, our father-by-son mobility tables will have many cells, and large data sets for each country are needed. We meet this requirement by drawing on multiple surveys in all countries save Sweden. For Sweden, the occupational data for the children come from the 1990 Census, and the occupational data for the parents are recovered by linking to the 1960 and 1970 Censuses (Erikson and Jonsson 1993). The data from the remaining countries come from the sources listed in Table 54.2. For this chapter, we're forced to focus on the mobility of men, as we've found that women experience more complicated mobility processes that are not as readily summarized in such a short treatment. We have discussed the mobility of women in Jonsson et al. (2009).

We have worked hard to render the data as comparable as possible. Given our need for large data sets, some compromises nonetheless had to be made, most notably pertaining to the period covered and the age of the respondents. The data from the United States, for example, are drawn disproportionately from earlier time periods, although more recent data from the United States are used as well (see Table 54.2 for details). Additionally, the Swedish data set covers only respondents between thirty and forty-seven years old, whereas all other data sets cover respondents between thirty and sixty-four years old. We have elsewhere shown that such differences in coverage don't affect our results much (Jonsson et al. 2009).

The starting point for all of our analyses is the detailed microclass coding scheme represented in Table 54.3. The microclass category may be defined as "a grouping of technically similar jobs that is institutionalized in the labor market through such means as (a) an association or union, (b) licensing or certification requirements, or (c) widely diffused understandings . . . regarding efficient or otherwise preferred ways of organizing production and dividing labor" (Grusky 2005, 66). The scheme used here includes eighty-two microclasses and captures many of the boundaries in the division of labor that are socially recognized and defended. These microclasses were then scaled in terms of the international socioeconomic scale (Ganzeboom, de Graaf, and Treiman 1992). We have applied this scheme to model an 82 × 82 mobility table formed by cross-classifying the father's and offspring's occupation in data pooled from

the United States, Sweden, Germany, and Japan (for details, see Jonsson et al. 2009). The distinctive feature of the resulting analysis is that microclass effects, represented on the main diagonal of Figure 54.2, are layered over more conventional big-class effects.

Given our suspicion that net big-class effects may be weak, it is clearly important to adopt a big-class scheme that fully captures such big-class effects as can be found, as otherwise any possible shortfall in big-class explanatory power might be attributed to poor operationalization. We have accordingly proceeded by fitting a set of nested big-class contrasts that capture the many and varied big-class distinctions that scholars have identified. As shown in Table 54.3, we begin by distinguishing the manual and nonmanual classes, a big-class distinction so important that early class scholars often focused on it alone. We next identify three "macroclasses" in the nonmanual category (i.e., professional-managerial, proprietor, routine nonmanual) and another two macroclasses in the manual category (i.e., manual, primary). Within three of these macroclasses, we then allow further "mesoclass" distinctions to emerge: the professional-managerial class is divided into classical professions, managers and officials, and other professions; the routine nonmanual class is divided into sales workers and clerks; and the manual class is divided into craft, lower manual, and service workers. The resulting scheme, which embodies three layers of big-class distinctions (i.e., manual-nonmanual, macroclass, and mesoclass), may be understood as a nondenominational hybrid of conventional schemes that assembles in one scheme many of the contrasts that have historically been emphasized by big-class scholars.

Table 54.2 Micro-Classes Nested in Manual-Nonmanual Classes, Macro Classes, and Meso Classes

1. NONMANUAL CLASS			2. MANUAL CLASS	
1. Professional-managerial	*2. Proprietors*	*3. Routine nonmanual*	*4. Manual*	*5. Primary*
1. Classical professions	1. Proprietors	**1. Sales**	**1. Craft**	1. Fisherman
1. Jurists		1. Real estate agents	1. Craftsmen, n.e.c	2. Farmers
2. Health professionals		2. Agents, n.e.c.	2. Foremen	3. Farm laborers
3. Professors and instructors		3. Insurance agents	3. Electronics service and repair	
4. Natural scientists		4. Cashiers	4. Printers and related workers	
5. Statistical and social scientists		5. Sales workers	5. Locomotive operators	
6. Architects		**2. Clerical**	6. Electricians	
7. Accountants		1. Telephone operators	7. Tailors and related workers	
8. Authors and journalists		2. Bookkeepers	8. Vehicle mechanics	
9. Engineers		3. Office workers	9. Blacksmiths and machinists	
2. Managers and officials		4. Postal clerks	10. Jewelers	
1. Officials, government and non-profit organizations			11. Other mechanics	
2. Other managers			12. Plumbers and pipe-fitters	
3. Commercial managers			13. Cabinetmakers	
4. Building managers and proprietors			14. Bakers	
3. Other professions			15. Welders	
1. Systems analysts and programmers			16. Painters	
2. Aircraft pilots and navigators			17. Butchers	
3. Personnel and labor relations workers			18. Stationary engine operators	
4. Elementary and secondary teachers			19. Bricklayers and carpenters	
5. Librarians			20. Heavy machine operators	

(continues)

507

508

Table 54.2 *(continued)*

1. NONMANUAL CLASS			2. MANUAL CLASS	
1. Professional-managerial	*2. Proprietors*	*3. Routine nonmanual*	*4. Manual*	*5. Primary*
3. Other professions (continued) 6. Creative artists 7. Ship officers 8. Professional and technical, n.e.c. 9. Social and welfare workers 10. Workers in religion 11. Nonmedical technicians 12. Health semiprofessionals 13. Hospital attendants 14. Nursery school teachers and aides			**2. Lower manual** 1. Truck drivers 2. Chemical processors 3. Miners and related workers 4. Longshoremen 5. Food processing workers 6. Textile workers 7. Sawyers 8. Metal processors 9. Operatives and kindred, n.e.c. 10. Forestry workers **3. Service workers** 1. Protective service workers 2. Transport conductors 3. Guards and watchmen 4. Food service workers 5. Mass transportation operators 6. Service workers, n.e.c. 7. Hairdressers 8. Newsboys and deliverymen 9. Launderers 10. Housekeeping workers 11. Janitors and cleaners 12. Gardeners	

Table 54.3   Surveys for Intergenerational Mobility Analysis

Survey / Sample Size	Period	Ages	Birth Cohorts	Occup.	Scheme[1]
1. Occupational Changes in a Generation I (OCG I)	1962	30–64	1898–1932	1960 SOC	17,544
2. Occupational Changes in a Generation II (OCG II)	1973	30–64	1909–1943	1960–70 SOC	18,856
3. General Social Survey (GSS)	1972–2003	30–64	1908–1970	1970–80 SOC	9,685
4. Survey of Social Stratification & Mobility (SSM)	1955–1995	30–64	1891–1970	Japanese SCO	6,703
5. Japan General Social Survey (JGSS)	2000–2002	30–64	1936–1972	Japanese SCO	1,917
6. German Social Survey[2] (ALLBUS)	1980–2002	30–64	1916–1972	ISCO-68, ISCO-88	5,647
7. German Socioeconomic Panel (GSOEP)	1986, 1999, 2000	30–64	1922–1970	ISCO-68, ISCO-88	2,886
8. German Life History Study LV I-III	1981–1989	30–64	1921–1959	ISCO-68	1,234
9. ZUMA-Standarddemographie Survey	1976–1982	0–64	1912–1952	ISCO-68	2,929
10. 1990 Swedish Census (linked to 1960 and 1970 Censuses)	1990	30–47	1943–1960	NYK80	184,451

[1] SOC = Standard Occupational Classification; SCO = Standard Classification of Occupations; ISCO = International Standard Classification of Occupations; NYK = Nordisk yrkesklassificering.

[2] German data exclude respondents from East Germany (GDR). If a respondent was not gainfully employed at the time of the survey, his last occupation was used.

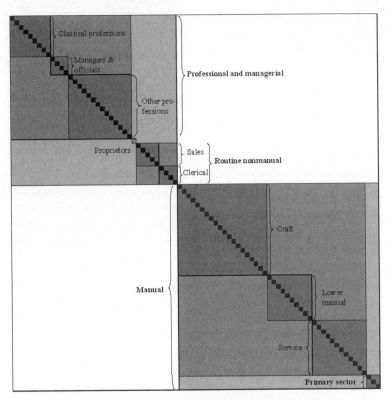

Figure 54.2 Overlapping Inheritance Terms in Mobility Model

Note: The Y axis pertains to occupational origins and the X axis to occupational destinations. The unlabeled microdiagonal squares represent occupational immobility. The size of each big-class category represents the number of microclass categories it encompasses (not the number of workers within the class).

These distinctions are introduced in our mobility models as a nested set of contrasts (see Jonsson et al. 2009). This approach not only allows us to tease out the net residue of reproduction at the mesoclass, macroclass, and manual-nonmanual levels but also allows for patterns of exchange that are more complicated than those conventionally allowed. The stylized parent-to-child mobility table in Figure 54.2 depicts these three sets of overlapping big-class parameters and shows how they capture quite complicated affinities off the microclass diagonal, off the mesoclass diagonal, and even off the macroclass diagonal. If we had

instead proceeded by fitting mesoclass effects alone (as is conventional), we could absorb excess densities in the dark-gray regions of Figure 54.2 but not the surrounding light-gray regions. The cells in the white zones of Figure 54.2 are in fact the only ones that index mobility with respect to *all* class levels. Moreover, even the cells in these zones will be modeled with a gradational term, a parameter that allows us to estimate the extent to which short-distance moves occur more frequently than long-distance ones.

This gradational term captures the tendency of children to assume occupations that are socioeconomically close to their origins. If the apparent clustering at the microclass, mesoclass, macroclass, or manual-nonmanual levels reflects nothing more than this gradational tendency, then the inheritance parameters represented in Figure 54.2 will become insignificant when the gradational parameter is included. The big-class and microclass parameters, taken together, thus speak to the extent to which the mobility regime is lumpy rather than gradational, while the relative size of these parameters speaks to whether conventional big-class analyses have correctly represented the main type of lumpiness. The following model is therefore yielded:

$$m_{ij} = \alpha\beta_i\gamma_j\varphi^{u_iu_j}\delta_{ij}^A\delta_{ij}^B\delta_{ij}^C\delta_{ij}^M$$

where i indexes origins, j indexes destinations, m_{ij} refers to the expected value in the ij^{th} cell, α refers to the main effect, β_i and γ_j refer to row and column marginal effects, φ refers to the socioeconomic effect, μ_i (origin) and μ_j (destination) are socioeconomic scale values assigned to each of the eighty-two microclasses, and δ^A, δ^B, δ^C, and δ^M refer to manual-nonmanual, macroclass, mesoclass, and microclass immobility effects, respectively. The latter parameters are fitted simultaneously and therefore capture net effects. The manual-nonmanual parameter, for example, indexes the average density across those cells pertaining to manual or nonmanual inheritance after purging the additional residue of inheritance that may obtain at the macroclass, mesoclass, and microclass levels.

The Structure of Mobility

When this model is applied to our pooled four-nation sample, the microclass and big-class parameters take on the form represented in Figure 54.3. Although cross-national variations of interest have emerged in our analyses (see Jonsson et al. 2009), Figure 54.3 is based on pooled data that smooth out such variation and thus represent the cross-nationally shared features of mobility.

The most striking feature of this figure is the microdiagonal clustering that appears as a palisade protecting occupational positions from intruders. This palisade bespeaks very substantial departures from equality of opportunity. For example, children born into the classical professions are, on average, 4.2 times more likely to remain in their microclass of origin than to move elsewhere within their mesoclass, while the corresponding coefficients for children born into managerial, craft, and service occupations are 4.6, 7.9, and 5.6, respectively. Although the interior regions of the class structure are typically represented as zones of fluidity (e.g., Featherman and Hauser 1978), we find here substantial microclass reproduction throughout the class structure, even among the "middle classes."

How do the microclass and big-class coefficients compare? Of the fourteen big-class coefficients, the two largest are for proprietors and primary-sector workers, but even these two are smaller than all but the very smallest microclass coefficients. It also bears noting that both of these big classes are big classes in name only. That is, because the proprietor class comprises only shopkeepers, it is not the usual amalgam of many occupations, and there is accordingly good reason to regard proprietors as effectively a microclass. Likewise, the primary sector is not much of an amalgam, dominated as it is by farmers (see Table 54.2). The remaining twelve big-class effects, all of which pertain to true amalgams, are

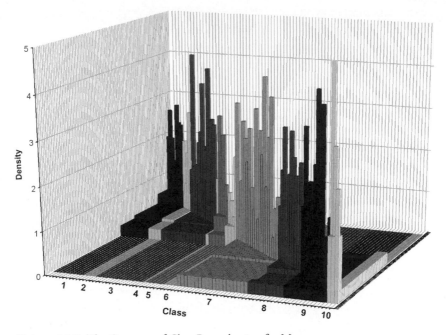

Figure 54.3 The Contours of Class Reproduction for Men

Note: The base indexes occupational origins and destinations, while the vertical dimension indexes densities of mobility and immobility (for each possible combination of origin and destination). 1 = classical professions; 2 = managers and officials; 3 = other professions; 4 = proprietors; 5 = sales; 6 = clerical; 7 = craft; 8 = lower manual; 9 = service; 10 = primary sector.

comparatively weak. The strongest of these effects, those for classical professions, sales work, clerical work, and the manual-non-manual strata, range in size from 1.3 to 1.4 (in multiplicative form).

Is Big-Class Reproduction a Myth?

The foregoing results raise the possibility that the big-class inheritance showing up in generations of mobility studies is largely microclass inheritance in disguise. Have conventional mobility studies indeed created the false impression that big-class reproduction is the dominant form of reproduction? We can address this question by examining whether the big-class effects that appear in conventional mobility analyses are much reduced in size when microclass effects are overlaid on them. It's useful to proceed by reestimating our model after omitting the microclass inheritance terms. The relevant estimates from this trimmed model, which represents a conventional big-class analysis, are shown in Figure 54.4.

We begin by noting that the mesoclass effects under this trimmed model are indeed strong and consistent with the effects secured in conventional mobility analyses. The coefficient for managers, for example, implies that children born into the managerial class are 1.62 times more likely to remain in that class than to exit it (i.e.,

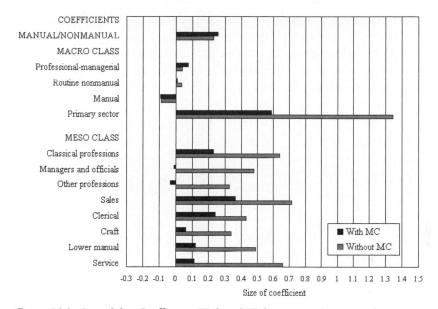

Figure 54.4   Immobility Coefficients With and Without Microclass Controls
Note: For convenience in presentation, the two primary-sector coefficients are each divided by two.

e.$^{48} \cong 1.62$). The corresponding inheritance coefficients for craft workers, lower manual workers, and service workers are 1.40, 1.63, and 1.93, respectively. It is coefficients such as these, all of which are net of gradational effects, that have motivated generations of mobility scholars to regard big-class reproduction as a powerful force.

The results from our full model nonetheless imply that this conclusion is somewhat misleading. When microclass effects are allowed, some of the big-class effects are greatly reduced in strength (i.e., classical professions, sales, clerical), while others disappear altogether or become quite small (i.e., managers and officials, other professionals, craft workers, service workers, lower manual workers). It follows that conventional big-class analyses have generated the appearance of big-class reproduction because it is confounded with microclass reproduction. This is not to suggest that all

big-class reproduction is just microclass reproduction in disguise. Clearly, some big-class reproduction persists even in the presence of microclass controls, a result that was also revealed in Figure 54.3.

We may conclude on the basis of these results that the big-class reproduction appearing in conventional analyses is largely generated by the tendency for children to inherit their microclass. The practical implication of this result is that big-class reproduction may not be easily reduced without interventions that take on inheritance at the occupational level. We return to this issue in the concluding discussion.

Conclusion

The main intellectual backdrop to this analysis is the ongoing sociological debate about the types of social groupings that have taken hold in contemporary industrialism.

Throughout much of the twentieth century, sociologists were fascinated, arguably obsessed, with theorizing about the conditions under which big classes might form, an understandable fascination insofar as individual life chances and even collective outcomes (e.g., revolutions) were believed to depend on class processes. At the same time, class analysts viewed occupations as mere technical positions in the division of labor (rather than meaningful social groups), while scholars in the occupations and professions of literature focused narrowly on individual occupations and how they developed under conditions of professionalization or proletarianization. The occupational form was not understood within either of these traditions as a critical source of inequality and social reproduction (see Grusky 2005). At best, occupations were described as the "backbone" of the inequality system (e.g., Parkin 1971), but such a characterization served principally as an impetus for then reducing occupations to gradational scores (e.g., Hauser and Warren 1997; Ganzeboom, de Graaf, and Treiman 1992) or using them as aggregates in constructing big classes (e.g., Erikson and Goldthorpe 1992).

These characteristic representations of the form of mobility have been treated as assumptions rather than amenable to evidence. The main objective of our research has been to consider whether, when treated as empirical matters, these conventional representations of the structure of mobility are incomplete. We have found that occupations are an important conduit for reproduction and that incorporating this conduit into mobility models can improve our understanding of the mobility process.

There are two main ways in which conventional models misrepresent the structure of opportunity: (1) The most extreme pockets of rigidity are concealed when analysis is carried out exclusively at the big-class level, and (2) the main rigidities in the big-class mobility table have been taken as evidence of big-class reproduction when in fact occupational reproduction is the principal underlying mechanism. These results suggest that the big-class mobility table, long a fixture in the discipline, obscures important mechanisms behind intergenerational reproduction.

Why are occupations such an important conduit for social reproduction? In all countries, parents accumulate much occupation-specific capital, identify with their occupation, and accordingly "bring home" their occupation in ways, both direct and indirect, that then make it salient to their children and lead them to invest in it. It follows that children develop a taste for occupational reproduction, are trained by their parents in occupation-specific skills, have access to occupational networks that facilitate occupational reproduction, and use those skills and networks to acquire more occupation-specific training outside the home. If children are risk averse and oriented principally to avoiding downward mobility, the safest path to realizing this objective may well be to use their occupation-specific resources on behalf of occupational reproduction. Indeed, even in the absence of any intrinsic interest in occupational reproduction, children may still pursue it because it is the best route to big-class reproduction (Erikson and Jonsson 1996). The son of an embalmer, for example, may not have any particular interest in becoming an embalmer but may decide it's foolhardy to fail to exploit the in-house training that is available to him.

It might be tempting to take the position that the extreme microclass inequalities uncovered here are not all that objectionable. Should we really care, for example, that the child of the truck driver has a special propensity to become a truck driver while the child of a gardener has a special propensity to become a gardener? Must we truly commit ourselves to equal access to truck driving and gardening? If pressed, we would argue that all ascriptive constraints on choice, even those pertaining to purely horizontal inequalities, are inconsistent with a commitment to an open society. By this logic, *all* types of origin-by-destination association are problematic because they imply that human choice has been circumscribed, a circumscription that is wholly determined by the accident of birth. We care, in other words, that the truck driver is fated to become a truck driver at birth because that amounts to a stripping away of choice, and most of us would embrace an open society in which choices are expanded, not stripped away. Although our illustrative nonchoice (i.e., being a truck driver versus being a gardener) may not have implications for total rewards (of the sort that are *consensually* valued), it is nonetheless a fateful nonchoice that determines the texture and content of a human life. It is this commitment to an open society, sometimes left quite implicit, that underlies the discipline's long-standing interest in monitoring marital homogamy, occupational sex segregation, and many other forms of ascription that are hybrids of vertical and horizontal processes.

It bears emphasizing, however, that such an argument need not be pursued in the present case, given that the horizontal inequalities uncovered here contribute directly to the perpetuation of vertical ones. That is, we should care about the immobility of truck drivers and gardeners not just because truck driving and gardening imply different styles of life (i.e., "horizontal" inequality), but also because microclass immobility of this sort is the principal mechanism ensuring that the working class reproduces itself. The results from our models make it clear that big-class reproduction arises largely because children frequently remain within their microclass of origin.

We are left with the conclusion that, insofar as microclass reproduction could be eliminated, real declines in big-class reproduction would be observed. It is troubling in this regard that microclass reproduction is deeply rooted in family dynamics and may require unacceptably intrusive policy to root it out. Although our results provide some insight, then, into why contemporary efforts to equalize opportunity have underperformed, they do not necessarily lead us to any wholesale rethinking of those efforts.

NOTE

1. We will often refer to occupations as "microclasses" because they have many of the features and characteristics that are often attributed to big classes.

REFERENCES

Carlsson, G. 1958. *Social Mobility and Class Structure*. Lund: Gleerups.

Erikson, Robert, and John H. Goldthorpe. 1992. *The Constant Flux: A Study of Class Mobility in Industrial Societies*. Oxford: Clarendon Press.

Erikson, Robert, and Jan O. Jonsson. 1993. *Ursprung och utbildning*. SOU 1993:85. Stockholm: Fritzes.

———. 1996. "Explaining Class Inequality in Education: The Swedish Test Case." In *Can Education Be Equalized?* edited by Robert Erikson and Jan O. Jonsson, 1–64. Boulder: Westview.

Featherman, David L., and Robert M. Hauser. 1978. *Opportunity and Change.* New York: Academic Press.

Ganzeboom, Harry B. G., Paul de Graaf, and Donald J. Treiman. 1992. "A Standard International Socio-Economic Index of Occupational Status." *Social Science Research* 21: 1–56.

Glass, D. V. 1954. *Social Mobility in Britain.* London: Routledge and Kegan Paul.

Goldthorpe, John H. 2007. *On Sociology.* Stanford: Stanford University Press.

Grusky, David B. 2005. "Foundations of a Neo-Durkheimian Class Analysis." In *Approaches to Class Analysis,* edited by Erik Olin Wright, 51–81. Cambridge: Cambridge University Press.

Grusky, David B., Yoshimichi Sato, Jan O. Jonsson, Satoshi Miwa, Matthew Di Carlo, Reinhard Pollak, and Mary C. Brinton. 2008. "Social Mobility in Japan: A New Approach to Modeling Trend in Mobility." In *Intergenerational Mobility and Intragenerational Mobility,* edited by Tsutomu Watanabe, 3:1–25. Sendai, Japan: SSM Research Project Series.

Hauser, Robert M., and John R. Warren. 1997. "Socioeconomic Indexes for Occupations: A Review, Update, and Critique." *Sociological Methods* 27: 177–298.

Hout, Michael, and Robert M. Hauser. 1992. "Hierarchy and Symmetry in Occupational Mobility." *European Sociological Review* 8 (December): 239–266.

Jonsson, Jan O., David B. Grusky, Matthew Di Carlo, Reinhard Pollak, and Mary C. Brinton. 2009. "Micro-Class Mobility: Social Reproduction in Four Countries." *American Journal of Sociology* (January).

Jonsson, Jan O., David B. Grusky, Reinhard Pollak, and Matthew Di Carlo. Forthcoming. "Occupations and Social Mobility: Gradational, Big Class, and Micro-Class Reproduction in Comparative Perspective." In *Intergenerational Mobility Within and Across Nations,* edited by Robert Erikson, Markus Jannti, and Timothy Smeeding. New York: Russell Sage Foundation.

Parkin, Frank. 1971. *Class Inequality and Political Order: Social Stratification in Capitalist and Communist Societies.* New York: Praeger.

Svalastoga, Kaare. 1959. *Prestige, Class, and Mobility.* Copenhagen: Gyldendal.

Weeden, Kim A., and David B. Grusky. 2005. "The Case for a New Class Map." *American Journal of Sociology* 111: 141–212.

55

Like Watching Grass Grow?

Assessing Changes in U.S. Intragenerational Economic Mobility over the Past Two Decades

GREGORY ACS AND SETH ZIMMERMAN

Income inequality and economic mobility are two distinct concepts, with *income inequality* denoting the distribution of income at a given point in time and *economic mobility* describing the ability of families to move up and down through the income distribution. Rising mobility can offset the long-term distributional effects of rising income inequality. Indeed, if families are becoming more likely to change their positions in the income distribution, the overall long-term distribution of income may be growing more equal even if income inequality is growing from year to year. Further, the consequences of changes in economic mobility may be offset by economic growth: even if mobility is falling, the standard of living of all individuals, even those in the bottom of the income distribution, may be rising.

This chapter examines changes in economic mobility in the United States over the past two decades and compares mobility today to that of earlier decades. As such, it builds on and extends research that examined economic mobility during the 1970s, 1980s, and early 1990s. Using data from the Panel Study of Income Dynamics (PSID), we find that intragenerational economic mobility between 1994 and 2004 among a cohort of adults ages 25 to 44 in 1994 is quite similar to the mobility experienced by earlier cohorts. In other words, we find very little difference in overall economic mobility over time.

Issues in Measuring Economic Mobility

There are four key components that must be considered when assessing intragenerational economic mobility: (1) the income measure or status metric used; (2) the population assessed; (3) the standard of measurement, whether absolute or relative; and (4) the accounting period considered.

Gregory Acs and Seth Zimmerman, "Like Watching Grass Grow? Assessing Changes in U.S. Intragenerational Economic Mobility over the Past Two Decades," in *U.S. Intragenerational Economic Mobility From 1984 to 2004: Trends and Implications*, pp. 3–23. Washington, D.C.: Economic Mobility Project, an Initiative of the Pew Charitable Trusts, http://economicmobility.org/reports_and_research.

Income Measure

Studies of economic mobility can focus on movements in the distribution of earnings, family incomes, pre- or post-tax and transfer incomes and earnings, and incomes adjusted for family size. Further, the sources of information on incomes and earnings such as self-reported survey data and data from tax records may differ in their ability to accurately measure total income as well as various components of income. As such, assessments of economic mobility and changes in mobility over time may be sensitive to the income concept used.

Population Assessed

Mobility may also differ across populations, and this can influence assessments of mobility in two ways. First, if income is highly volatile for young individuals, studies that include young adults (16- to 24-year-olds) may show more mobility than do studies that focus on adults 25 and up, who are usually more established. Second, studies that try to compare mobility across time periods (e.g., the 1980s and the 1990s) may be influenced by changes in the underlying populations. For example, a large increase in the number of single-parent families could swell the lowest ranks of the income distribution at the start of a time period; if these single parents are less (or more) likely than married parents and childless adults to move up the income distribution, then mobility over the period may appear to be lower (or higher) than in periods marked by smaller shares of single-parent families.

Absolute or Relative Standard

Economic mobility can be measured either relative to one's peer group (relative mobility) or against an absolute standard (ab-solute mobility). Measuring absolute mobility captures the effects of economic growth, but it does not indicate whether one's position in society has changed. Both concepts are useful, but they can produce very different assessments of intragenerational mobility depending on how broadly the population of interest is defined. For example, if the measurement includes younger workers who expect to experience substantial earnings growth, the resulting findings are likely to suggest substantially more absolute mobility than relative mobility.

Accounting Period

Finally, the accounting period used to assess the distribution of income may have significant effects on the assessment of mobility. There are two aspects to this issue: the time span over which mobility is considered and the number of months or years used to measure income at the beginning and end of any particular time span. Most studies of economic mobility assess movements through the income distribution over relatively long time spans, often a decade or longer. Studies that consider mobility over shorter periods, like year to year, are more concerned with volatility—how unstable income or a particular position in the income distribution may be in the short term. Clearly, income volatility and economic mobility are very similar concepts, largely distinguished by the time horizon considered. Much recent research documents a rise over the past two decades in the year-to-year volatility of family income, though not without controversy.

If single-year income is quite volatile, income mobility—as measured over longer time spans, like decades—will appear to be quite high, and if income volatility is increasing over time, mobility will also appear to be increasing. By broadening the accounting period at the start and end of any particular time span to two, three, or even five years, much of the random noise in annual incomes will be averaged away, and the resulting distribution will better reflect "permanent income." Thus, assessments of mobility using longer accounting periods to define starting and end positions will show less mobility than studies that use shorter accounting periods.

Research Review

Given all the factors that can influence assessments of mobility, it is remarkable how consistent the research findings have been over the past three decades. With few exceptions, the research shows that about half of those in the bottom income quintile will rise out of the bottom over a decade, and this is the case in the 1970s, 1980s, and 1990s. For example, Sawhill and Condon (1992) examine relative income mobility of individuals ages 25 to 54, using data from the PSID, and find that 44 percent of those in the bottom income quintile in 1967 moved up and out of the bottom by 1976; between 1977 and 1986, the upward mobility rate rose to 47 percent. Bradbury and Katz (2002) also use PSID data but focus on family heads under age 65 and adjust income for family size. They find that upward mobility rates out of the bottom quintile were 51 percent between 1969 and 1979, 50 percent between 1979 and 1989, and 47 percent between 1988 and 1998. Another PSID-based study, that by Hungerford (2008), reports upward mobility rates of just over 50 percent between both 1980 and 1989 and 1990 and 1999. Finally, Gottschalk and Danziger (1998) also use

PSID data but consider a longer time period, 1968 to 1991, adjust incomes for household size, and focus on 22- to 39-year-olds; they find an upward mobility rate of 53 percent. When they broaden their accounting period, averaging incomes over three years, they find the upward mobility rate falls to 46 percent.

The data in the PSID are self-reported, but even studies using tax records draw similar conclusions about relative income mobility. For example, Carroll, Joulfaian, and Rider (2006) report an upward mobility rate of 54 percent between 1979 and 1995 when using data on taxpayers between the ages of 30 and 50. Focusing on taxpayers aged 25 and over in 1987, Auten and Gee (2007) find that 45 percent of those in the bottom quintile in 1987 moved to higher quintiles between 1987 and 1996. More recent work by the U.S. Department of the Treasury (2008) examines the mobility of taxpayers aged 25 and over between 1996 and 2005 and finds virtually identical upward relative mobility rates: about 45 percent of those in the bottom quintile in 1996 were in a higher quintile in 2005.

Several studies consider absolute mobility and assess the extent to which individuals in the bottom quintile enjoy real income growth and income growth beyond key benchmarks like the threshold for the bottom or top income quintiles. For example, Cox and Alm (1996) use the PSID and find that over 97 percent of those in the bottom income quintile in 1975 had incomes exceeding the 1975 inflation adjusted income threshold for the bottom quintile in 1991. Nearly 40 percent actually crossed the threshold for the top income quintile. The extraordinarily high upward mobility portrayed by Cox and

Alm reflects their use of individual, not family, income and their inclusion of individuals down to the age of 16. Indeed, a 16-year-old with an income of $500 from a summer job who lives with his upper-middle class parents would fall in the bottom quintile in 1975. Sixteen years later, it would not be at all surprising to find his real annual income considerably higher.

Other researchers who assess family income and focus on household heads or restrict their studies to more established individuals find considerably less absolute mobility. For example, Gottschalk and Danziger (1998) find an absolute upward mobility rate from the bottom quintile of 69 percent between 1968–1970 and 1989–1991 when looking at 22- to 39-year-olds and considering family income adjusted for family size. Only 11 percent of those in the bottom quintile saw their incomes cross the threshold for the top quintile. Other studies of absolute income mobility focus on the growth in real income among those in any particular income quintile. For example, Auten and Gee (2007) report that 47 percent of heads of taxpaying units in the bottom income quintile in 1987 saw their real incomes increase at least twofold by 1996 while 23 percent saw no growth or even experienced declines. The trends are quite similar for the 1996 to 2005 period, with half of the heads of taxpaying units (ages 25 and up) in the bottom quintile in 1996 experiencing a doubling of their real income by 2005 while about 18 percent experienced real income declines (U.S. Treasury 2008). Note that even substantial growth in real income may leave individuals below the absolute income threshold for the bottom quintile if their initial incomes are sufficiently low (e.g., experiencing a threefold increase in income from $500 to

$1,500 a year still leaves one well below the 20th percentile in the income distribution). Duncan, Smeeding, and Rodgers (1991) define lower, middle, and upper classes using fixed dollar amounts and assess both upward and downward absolute mobility over two-year periods. They find that about one-third of low-income families climb into the middle class and that about 7 percent of those in the middle class fall into the lower class over any given two-year period. They also note that upward mobility rates were lower in the 1980s than in the 1970s while downward mobility rates rose.

Data and Methods

This paper builds on and extends this prior research by examining mobility trends to 2004, showing how sensitive or robust findings are when different accounting periods and mobility concepts are used, and by assessing the factors associated with upward and downward mobility. Before presenting our results, we first describe our data and analytic approach.

Data

We use data from the PSID. Begun in 1968 with a sample of approximately 5,000 families, the PSID follows individuals and their descendants over time, tracking changes in incomes, behaviors, and living situations. The PSID was administered annually between 1968 and 1997, and biannually thereafter. The most recent wave, administered in 2005, includes weighted data on more than 8,000 families and 16,000 individuals.

The PSID collects data on many types of annual pre-tax income, including earned income, asset income, and cash transfer income. For this paper, we focus on family income—the sum of earned, asset, and transfer income over all family members—on the grounds that an inclusive measure best captures overall economic well-being. For the same reason, we adjust income for family size using the PSID-provided United States Department of Agriculture needs standard.

We limit our sample in five ways. First, we consider only individuals who were either family unit heads or significant others because the PSID only reports comprehensive information for such individuals. Second, we eliminate individuals younger than 25 or older than 45 in the base year to exclude the abrupt income changes that often accompany the shift from school to work and from work to retirement from our analysis. Third, individuals must be observed in both the start and end years of the analysis period. Fourth, we exclude individuals whose family incomes are below $1,200 in 2005 dollars or within the top 1 percent of the adult income distribution in either the base-year or the end-year in order to limit the effect that high- and low-income outliers have on our results. Fifth, and finally, we include only individuals observed as family heads or spouses or partners in both the base and end years. This requirement eliminates about one-quarter of the weighted individuals present in the start year. The attrition rate for individuals in the bottom quintile is somewhat higher than the overall attrition rate, hovering around one-third.

We assess income mobility over two 10-year intervals: 1984 to 1994 and 1994 to 2004. In addition to our primary analysis focusing on annual income, we also consider two-year average income, calculated using data from two PSID waves, to smooth over transitory fluctuations in income. Although we would ideally consider income averaged over consecutive years, the PSID's shift to biannual data collection requires the use of alternate years for a consistent measure. Thus, to compute two-year average income in, say, 1984, we average incomes, adjusted for needs, from 1982 and 1984. When averaging income, we also use income data from 1992 for the 1992–1994 average, and 2002, for the 2002–2004 average. The unweighted samples for our single-year analyses comprise 2,681 individuals in the 1984 to 1994 period and 2,288 in the 1994 to 2004 period. For our two-year average income analyses, our samples comprise 2,441 individuals for the early period and 2,070 for the later period.

The years we use to anchor our analyses are drawn from similar points in the business cycle: 1984, 1994, and 2004 are all early recovery years in which the economy is recovering from a recession but has not yet reached a business cycle peak. Nevertheless, the economy as measured by unemployment rates was a bit stronger in 1994 than in 1984 and a bit stronger in 2004 than in 1994. These differences may influence mobility trends. For either year pair, that unemployment is lower in the end year than the base year may lead us to find higher upward mobility rates: the unemployed are more likely to be in the bottom quintile than in higher quintiles, and when unemployed individuals find work their earnings may move them up and out of the bottom. Thus, when comparing mobility rates across periods, we may find more mobility over periods that start with higher unemployment rates—in other words, there may be more potential mobility in the 1984 to 1994 period than the 1994 to 2004 period because of the overall strengthening of the economy between 1984 and 2004. On net, however, these differences in the strength of the economy are not likely to have large effects on our findings because not all non-workers are in the bottom quintile, starting work does not guarantee moving across quintile lines, and the change in the share of the population that is working is relatively small given the size of the total population.

Methods

We use several straightforward approaches to assess changes in economic mobility over time. First, we follow the work of other researchers and examine transition matrices that show the distribution of individuals across base- and end-year income quintiles. We present transition matrices based on relative mobility as well as absolute mobility (where end-year "quintiles" are not truly quintiles but are based on the real value of the quintile cutoffs from the base year). To assess if mobility is changing over time, specifically, from the early period of 1984–1994 to the later period of 1994–2004, we compare total mobility, that is the share of the population that changed quintiles across the year pairs, as well as upward mobility out of the bottom quintile across the year pairs.

Results

Relative mobility rates for the 1984–1994 and 1994–2004 periods appear in Table 55.1.[1] Computed using single-year income, Table 55.1 demonstrates that overall relative mobility and upward mobility out of the bottom quintile remained nearly static between the 10-year windows beginning in 1984 and 1994. In the earlier period, 60.4 percent of individuals switched quintiles, including 46.5 percent of those who started out in the bottom quintile. The equivalent figures for

the later period were 60.5 percent and 45.4 percent, respectively. Mobility out of the bottom quintile thus accounted for 15.4 percent of total mobility between 1984 and 1994, and 15 percent between 1994 and 2004.

Overall relative mobility trends computed using two-year average income were nearly identical to single-year mobility trends: Table 55.2 shows that approximately 60 percent of individuals moved from one quintile to another over the course of each ten-year period. Income averaging does, however, dampen upward mobility out of the bottom quintile, particularly between 1994 and 2004. Of individuals in the bottom income quintile of average income in 1984, 44.4 percent moved up by 1994, but only 39 percent of the people in the bottom average-income quintile in 1994 had moved up by 2004. However, even this difference is not statistically significant (p = 0.16). Accordingly, mobility out of the bottom quintile made up 14.8 percent of total mobility between 1984 and 1994, and 13.1 percent of total mobility between 1994 and 2004.

Though consistently higher than relative mobility rates, Table 55.3 demonstrates that rates of absolute mobility, when calculated using single-year income, are also fairly stable over time. Between 1984 and 1994, 61.1 percent of individuals saw their positions relative to the initial quintile boundaries change; between 1994 and 2004, that figure was 62.6 percent. In the earlier window, 52.8 percent of individuals in the bottom quintile moved into a higher income group, compared to 54.1 percent in the later window. In each year, mobility out of the bottom quintile accounted for 17.3 percent of total mobility.

Unlike the case for relative mobility, there are a few statistically significant differences

Table 55.1 Quintile Transitions, Single-Year Income (Relative Mobility)

1994 Quintile	2004 Quintile					1984 Quintile	1994 Quintile				
	Lowest	Second	Middle	Fourth	Highest		Lowest	Second	Middle	Fourth	Highest
Lowest	0.546	0.255	0.088	0.076	0.035	Lowest	0.535	0.242	0.106	0.071	0.046
Second	0.215	0.333	0.245	0.144	0.063	Second	0.199	0.370	0.223	0.158	0.050
Middle	0.152	0.204	0.268	0.201	0.176	Middle	0.113	0.209	0.280	0.231	0.166
Fourth	0.067	0.151	0.262	0.312	0.208*	Fourth	0.060	0.119	0.256	0.293	0.271
Highest	0.026	0.056	0.132	0.269	0.517	Highest	0.037	0.045	0.151	0.267	0.501

Overall mobility 0.605   Overall mobility 0.604

Mobility out of bottom quintile 0.454   Mobility out of bottom quintile 0.465

Bottom quintile mobility share 0.150   Bottom quintile mobility share 0.154

Note: *p<.10, **p<.05, ***p<.01

Asterisks indicate significant differences in quintile-to-quintile transition rates between the 1984–94 and 1994–2004 periods.

Note: Tables represent authors' tabulations of PSID data.

Table 55.2 Quintile Transitions, Two-Year Average Income (Relative Mobility)

1994 Quintile	2004 Quintile					1984 Quintile	1994 Quintile				
	Lowest	Second	Middle	Fourth	Highest		Lowest	Second	Middle	Fourth	Highest
Lowest	0.610	0.233	0.090	0.058	0.009**	Lowest	0.556	0.241	0.098	0.072	0.033
Second	0.231	0.335	0.246	0.105	0.083	Second	0.230	0.339	0.235	0.143	0.052
Middle	0.115	0.232	0.255	0.262	0.137	Middle	0.106	0.228	0.285	0.250	0.131
Fourth	0.039	0.129	0.279	0.300	0.252	Fourth	0.034	0.129	0.254	0.292	0.291
Highest	0.013	0.063	0.125	0.277	0.522	Highest	0.016	0.058	0.136	0.265	0.526

Overall mobility 0.596   Overall mobility 0.600

Mobility out of bottom quintile 0.390   Mobility out of bottom quintile 0.444

Bottom quintile mobility share 0.131   Bottom quintile mobility share 0.148

Note: *p<.10, **p<.05, ***p<.01

Asterisks indicate significant differences in quintile-to-quintile transition rates between the 1984–94 and 1994–2004 periods.

in absolute mobility in the middle and top of the income distribution. The probability that an individual in the fourth quintile had income growth that would move him or her across the base-year boundary for the top quintile fell from 49.9 percent in the early period to 41.2 percent in the later period. In addition, an increasing share of individuals in the top quintile saw their real incomes fall below the top income quintile boundary. There is some evidence of increasing upward absolute mobility for individuals in the second and third quintiles as they have become increasingly likely to experience income growth that would lift them above the threshold for the fourth quintile.

Using average incomes rather than single year incomes increases absolute mobility rates for the earlier period but decreases rates for the later period, as reflected in Table 55.4. Overall mobility computed using two-year average incomes was 62.7 percent between 1984 and 1994 (compared with 61.1 percent using single year income), and 59.8 percent between 1994 and 2004 (compared with 62.6 percent using single year income). Over each period, approximately 55 percent of individuals in the bottom quintile moved into a higher income group, with this mobility accounting for 18.5 percent of the total mobility between 1994 and 2004 and 17.5 percent of total mobility between 1984 and 1994.

Again, there are a few specific changes that are statistically significant. Although net movement out of the bottom quintile did not change, those who did move out are far less likely to have crossed the threshold for the top quintile in the later period than in the early period. Indeed those that exceed the bottom quintile threshold are much more likely to only reach the second

quintile during the later period. In addition, as was the case using single year income, we again find that individuals in the fourth quintile are less likely to cross the top quintile income threshold between 1994 and 2004 than they were between 1984 and 1994.

Discussion

Historically, research on relative and absolute economic mobility in the United States focused on whether mobility was different in the 1980s and early 1990s than in the 1960s and 1970s and found that mobility had not changed that much. Since this research, the economy experienced marked growth during the mid- to late-1990s, with particularly strong growth among middle- and lower-income families, and a recession followed by several years of sluggish growth in the early years of the twenty-first century. This paper builds on prior research by assessing absolute and relative income mobility for the 1994–2004 period.

Using data from the PSID, we find that intragenerational economic mobility between 1994 and 2004 among a cohort of adults ages 25 to 44 in 1994 is quite comparable to the mobility experienced by an earlier cohort from 1984 to 1994. In other words, we find very little difference in overall economic mobility over time. Specifically, in both 10-year spans, about 60 percent of individuals changed their income quintiles relative to their peers. Upward mobility rates out of the bottom quintile are quite similar as well, with about 47 percent of those in the bottom rising to higher quintiles. Our findings are quite similar to those reported by other researchers covering various time periods

Table 55.3 Transitions Across Start-Year Quintile Boundaries, Single-Year Income (Absolute Mobility)

1994 Quintile	2004 Quintile					1984 Quintile	1994 Quintile				
	Lowest	Second	Middle	Fourth	Highest		Lowest	Second	Middle	Fourth	Highest
Lowest	0.459	0.228	0.132	0.108	0.073	Lowest	0.472	0.217	0.118	0.094	0.099
Second	0.131	0.214	0.272	0.225**	0.159	Second	0.147	0.249	0.272	0.161	0.171
Middle	0.112	0.115	0.170	0.298***	0.305	Middle	0.076	0.131	0.219	0.226	0.348
Fourth	0.044	0.073	0.136	0.336***	0.412**	Fourth	0.048	0.067	0.123	0.264	0.499
Highest	0.022	0.022	0.056	0.206**	0.693	Highest	0.022	0.036	0.062	0.138	0.741

Overall mobility 0.626

Mobility out of bottom quintile 0.541

Bottom quintile mobility share 0.173

Overall mobility 0.611

Mobility out of bottom quintile 0.528

Bottom quintile mobility share 0.173

Note: *p<.10, **p<.05, ***p<.01
Asterisks indicate significant differences in quintile-to-quintile transition rates between the 1984–94 and 1994–2004 periods.

Table 55.4 Transitions Across Start-Year Quintile Boundaries, Two-Year Average Income (Absolute Mobility)

1994 Quintile	2004 Quintile					1984 Quintile	1994 Quintile				
	Lowest	Second	Middle	Fourth	Highest		Lowest	Second	Middle	Fourth	Highest
Lowest	0.448	0.291**	0.125	0.104	0.033***	Lowest	0.451	0.210	0.156	0.082	0.102
Second	0.111*	0.262	0.259	0.222	0.145	Second	0.156	0.236	0.234	0.199	0.174
Middle	0.059	0.133	0.218	0.281	0.309	Middle	0.064	0.124	0.183	0.266	0.362
Fourth	0.029	0.052	0.128	0.383***	0.408***	Fourth	0.014	0.059	0.132	0.232	0.563
Highest	0.009	0.032	0.053	0.206	0.699*	Highest	0.016	0.023	0.045	0.156	0.761

Overall mobility 0.598

Mobility out of bottom quintile 0.552

Bottom quintile mobility share 0.185

Overall mobility 0.627

Mobility out of bottom quintile 0.549

Bottom quintile mobility share 0.175

Note: *p<.10, **p<.05, ***p<.01
Asterisks indicate significant differences in quintile-to-quintile transition rates between the 1984–94 and 1994–2004 periods.

from 1968 forward. Further, our findings on mobility are rather robust to changes in accounting periods, from single-year to two-year average incomes, as well as to considerations of absolute and relative mobility. For example, total economic mobility rates are slightly over 60 percent regardless of mobility concept, and absolute upward mobility rates hover just above 50 percent while relative upward mobility rates hover just below 50 percent.

It is rather striking that mobility rates have largely remained stable over the past few decades despite notable changes in the economy. Some may point to the levels of mobility in the economy and suggest that the level of mobility should offset concerns about income inequality. Of course, it is hard to know how much economic mobility is enough. Although rising income inequality does not necessarily imply decreasing economic mobility, it is important to note that in the context of rising inequality, stable mobility rates suggest that the distribution of lifetime income must be growing more unequal; that is, lifetime or long-term income inequality is rising.

NOTE

1. The rows in each panel sum to 1 and show where individuals in a given quintile in the base year end up 10 years later, relative to their peers. If there were no mobility at all, then the tables would show "1s" along their diagonals and "0s" on the off-diagonals (i.e., everyone who starts in the bottom quintile stays in the bottom quintile; everyone who starts in the top quintiles stays in the top quintile, and so on). Overall mobility is assessed by examining the share of the population that has changed quintiles (computed by summing the off-diagonal elements and dividing by 5). Upward mobility is assessed by examining the

share of individuals in the first (bottom) quintile who move up to higher quintiles.

REFERENCES

Auten, Gerald E., and Geoffrey Gee. 2007. "Income Mobility in the U.S.: Evidence from Income Tax Returns for 1987 and 1996." Office of Tax Analysis Working Paper 98, U.S. Treasury, May 2007.

Bradbury, Katharine, and Jane Katz. 2002. "Women's Labor Market Involvement and Family Income Mobility When Marriages End." *New England Economic Review* 2002(Q4): 41–74.

Carroll, Robert, David Joulfaian, and Mark Rider. 2006. "Income Mobility: The Recent American Experience." International Studies Program Working Paper 06–20, Andrew Young School of Policy Studies July 2006.

Cox, W. Michael, and Richard Alm. 1996. "By Our Own Bootstraps: Economic Opportunity and the Dynamics of Income Distribution." *Federal Reserve Bank of Dallas Annual Report 1995*.

Duncan, Greg, Timothy Smeeding, and Willard Rodgers. 1991. "W(h)ither the Middle Class? A Dynamic View." The Jerome Levy Economics Institute of Bard College Working Paper 56.

Gottschalk, Peter, and Sheldon Danziger. 1998. "Family Income Mobility: How Much is There and Has It Changed?" In *The Inequality Paradox*, edited by J. Auerbach and R. Belous, 92–111. Washington, DC: National Policy Association.

Hungerford, Thomas. 2008. "Income Inequality, Income Mobility, and Economic Policy: U.S. Trends in the 1980s and 1990s." Congressional Research Service Report RL34434. Washington, DC: Congressional Research Service.

Sawhill, Isabel V., and Mark Condon. 1992. "Is U.S. Income Inequality Really Growing? Sorting Out the Fairness Question." *Policy Bites*. Washington, DC: Urban Institute.

U.S. Department of the Treasury. 2008. *Income Mobility in the U.S. from 1996 to 2005*. http://www.treasury.gov/press/releases/hp673.htm.

56

The Process of Stratification

PETER M. BLAU AND OTIS DUDLEY DUNCAN,
WITH THE COLLABORATION OF ANDREA TYREE

Stratification systems may be characterized in various ways. Surely one of the most important has to do with the processes by which individuals become located, or locate themselves, in positions in the hierarchy comprising the system. At one extreme we can imagine that the circumstances of a person's birth—including the person's sex and the perfectly predictable sequence of age levels through which he is destined to pass—suffice to assign him unequivocally to a ranked status in a hierarchical system. At the opposite extreme his prospective adult status would be wholly problematic and contingent at the time of birth. Such status would become entirely determinate only as adulthood was reached, and solely as a consequence of his own actions taken freely—that is, in the absence of any constraint deriving from the circumstances of his birth or rearing. Such a pure achievement system is, of course, hypothetical, in much the same way that motion without friction is a purely hypothetical possibility in the physical world. Whenever the stratification system of any moderately large and complex society is described, it is seen to involve both ascriptive and achievement principles.

In a liberal democratic society we think of the more basic principle as being that of achievement. Some ascriptive features of the system may be regarded as vestiges of an earlier epoch, to be extirpated as rapidly as possible. Public policy may emphasize measures designed to enhance or to equalize opportunity—hopefully, to overcome ascriptive obstacles to the full exercise of the achievement principle.

The question of how far a society may realistically aspire to go in this direction is hotly debated, not only in the ideological arena but in the academic forum as well. Our contribution, if any, to the debate will consist largely in submitting measurements and estimates of the strength of ascriptive forces and of the scope of opportunities in a large contemporary society. The problem of the relative importance of the two principles in a given system is ultimately a quantitative one. We have pushed our ingenuity to its limit in seeking to contrive relevant quantifications.

The governing conceptual scheme in the analysis is quite a commonplace one. We think of the individual's life cycle as a sequence in time that can be described, however partially and crudely, by a set of classificatory or quantitative measurements taken at successive stages. Ideally we should like to have under observation a cohort of births, following the individuals who make up the cohort as they pass through life. As a practical matter we resorted to retrospective questions put to a representative sample of several adjacent cohorts so as to ascertain those facts about their life histories that we assumed were both relevant to our problem and accessible by this means of observation.

Given this scheme, the questions we are continually raising in one form or another are: how and to what degree do the circumstances of birth condition subsequent status? and, how does status attained (whether by ascription or achievement) at one stage of the life cycle affect the prospects for a subsequent stage? The questions are neither idle nor idiosyncratic ones. Current policy discussion and action come to a focus in a vaguely explicated notion of the "inheritance of poverty." Thus a spokesman for the Social Security Administration writes:

> It would be one thing if poverty hit at random and no one group were singled out. It is another thing to realize that some seem destined to poverty almost from birth—by their color or by the economic status or occupation of their parents.[1]

Another officially sanctioned concept is that of the "dropout," the person who fails to graduate from high school. Here the emphasis is not so much on circumstances operative at birth but on the presumed effect of early achievement on subsequent oppor-

tunities. Thus the "dropout" is seen as facing "a lifetime of uncertain employment,"[2] probable assignment to jobs of inferior status, reduced earning power, and vulnerability to various forms of social pathology.

In this study we do not have measurements on all the factors implicit in a full-blown conception of the "cycle of poverty" nor all those variables conceivably responding unfavorably to the achievement of "dropout" status. . . . This limitation, however, is not merely an analytical convenience. We think of the selected quantitative variables as being sufficient to describe the major outlines of status changes in the life cycle of a cohort. Thus a study of the relationships among these variables leads to a formulation of a basic model of the process of stratification.

A Basic Model

To begin with, we examine only five variables. For expository convenience, when it is necessary to resort to symbols, we shall designate them by arbitrary letters but try to remind the reader from time to time of what the letters stand for. These variables are:

V: Father's educational attainment
X: Father's occupational status
U: Respondent's educational attainment
W: Status of respondent's first job
Y: Status of respondent's occupation in 1962

Each of the three occupational statuses is scaled by the [socioeconomic] index described [elsewhere],[3] ranging from 0 to 96. The two education variables are scored on the following arbitrary scale of values ("rungs" on the "educational ladder") corresponding to specified numbers of years of formal schooling completed:

0: No school
1: Elementary, one to four years
2: Elementary, five to seven years
3: Elementary, eight years
4: High school, one to three years
5: High school, four years
6: College, one to three years
7: College, four years
8: College, five years or more (i.e., one or more years of postgraduate study)

Actually, this scoring system hardly differs from a simple linear transformation, or "coding," of the exact number of years of school completed. In retrospect, for reasons given [elsewhere],[4] we feel that the score implies too great a distance between intervals at the lower end of the scale; but the resultant distortion is minor in view of the very small proportions scored 0 or 1.

A basic assumption in our interpretation of regression statistics—though not in their calculation as such—has to do with the causal or temporal ordering of these variables. In terms of the father's career we should naturally assume precedence of V (education) with respect to X (occupation when his son was 16 years old). We are not concerned with the father's career, however, but only with his statuses that comprised a configuration of background circumstances or origin conditions for the cohorts of sons who were respondents in the Occupational Changes in a Generation (OCG) study. Hence we generally make no assumption as to the priority of V with respect to X; in effect, we assume the measurements on these variables to be contemporaneous from the son's viewpoint. The respondent's education, U, is supposed to follow in time—and

thus to be susceptible to causal influence from—the two measures of father's status. Because we ascertained X as of respondent's age 16, it is true that some respondents may have completed school before the age to which X pertains. Such cases were doubtlessly a small minority and in only a minor proportion of them could the father (or other family head) have changed status radically in the two or three years before the respondent reached 16.

The next step in the sequence is more problematic. We assume that W (first job status) follows U (education). The assumption conforms to the wording of the questionnaire, which stipulated "the first full-time job you had after you left school." In the years since the OCG study was designed we have been made aware of a fact that should have been considered more carefully in the design. Many students leave school more or less definitively, only to return, perhaps to a different school, some years later, whereupon they often finish a degree program.[5] The OCG questionnaire contained information relevant to this problem, namely the item on age at first job. Through an oversight no tabulations of this item were made for the present study. Tables prepared for another study[6] using the OCG data, however, suggest that approximately one-eighth of the respondents report a combination of age at first job and education that would be very improbable unless (a) they violated instructions by reporting a part-time or school-vacation job as the first job, or (b) they did, in fact, interrupt their schooling to enter regular employment. (These "inconsistent" responses include men giving 19 as their age at first job and college graduation or more as their education; 17 or 18 with some college or more; 14, 15, or 16 with high-school graduation or more; and under 14 with some high school or more.) When the two variables are studied in combination with occupation of first job, a very clear effect is evident. Men with a given amount of education beginning their first jobs early held lower occupational statuses than those beginning at a normal or advanced age for the specified amount of education.

Despite the strong probability that the U-W sequence is reversed for an appreciable minority of respondents, we have hardly any alternative to the assumption made here. If the bulk of the men who interrupted schooling to take their first jobs were among those ultimately securing relatively advanced education, then our variable W is downwardly biased, no doubt, as a measure of their occupational status immediately after they finally left school for good. In this sense, the correlations between U and W and between W and Y are probably attenuated. Thus, if we had really measured "job after completing education" instead of "first job," the former would in all likelihood have loomed somewhat larger as a variable intervening between education and 1962 occupational status. We do not wish to argue that our respondents erred in their reports on first job. We are inclined to conclude that their reports were realistic enough, and that it was our assumption about the meaning of the responses that proved to be fallible.

The fundamental difficulty here is conceptual. If we insist on *any* uniform sequence of the events involved in accomplishing the transition to independent adult status, we do violence to reality. Completion of schooling, departure from the parental home, entry into the labor market, and contracting of a first marriage are crucial steps in this transition, which all normally occur within a few short years. Yet they occur at no fixed ages nor in any fixed order. As soon as we aggregate individual data for analytical purposes we are forced into the use of simplifying assumptions. Our assumption here is, in effect, that "first job" has a uniform significance for all men in terms of its temporal relationship to educational preparation and subsequent work experience. If this assumption is not strictly correct, we doubt that it could be improved by substituting any other *single* measure of initial occupational status. (In designing the OCG questionnaire, the alternative of "job at the time of first marriage" was entertained briefly but dropped for the reason, among others, that unmarried men would be excluded thereby.)

One other problem with the U-W transition should be mentioned. Among the younger men in the study, 20 to 24 years old, are many who have yet to finish their schooling or to take up their first jobs or both—not to mention the men in this age group missed by the survey on account of their military service.[7] Unfortunately, an early decision on tabulation plans resulted in the inclusion of the 20 to 24 group with the older men in aggregate tables for men 20 to 64 years old. We have ascertained that this results in only minor distortions by comparing a variety of data for men 20 to 64 and for those 25 to 64 years of age. Once over the U-W hurdle, we see no serious objection to our assumption that both U and W precede Y, except in regard to some fraction of the very young men just mentioned.

In summary, then, we take the somewhat idealized assumption of temporal order to represent an order of priority in a causal or processual sequence, which may be stated diagrammatically as follows:

Table 56.1   Simple Correlations for Five Status Variables

| | Variable | | | | |
Variable	Y	W	U	X	V
Y: 1962 occ. status	—	.541	.596	.406	.322
W: First-job status		—	.538	.417	.332
U: Education			—	.438	.453
X: Father's occ. status				—	.516
V: Father's education					—

$$(V,X) - (U) - (W) - (Y).$$

In proposing this sequence we do not overlook the possibility of what Carlsson calls "delayed effects,"[8] meaning that an early variable may affect a later one not only via intervening variables but also directly (or perhaps through variables not measured in the study).

In translating this conceptual framework into quantitative estimates the first task is to establish the pattern of associations between the variables in the sequence. This is accomplished with the correlation coefficient. Table 56.1 supplies the correlation matrix on which much of the subsequent analysis is based. In discussing causal interpretations of these correlations, we shall have to be clear about the distinction between two points of view. On the one hand, the simple correlation—given our assumption as to direction of causation—measures the gross magnitude of the effect of the antecedent upon the consequent variable. Thus, if $r_{YW} = .541$, we can say that an increment of one standard deviation in first job status produces (whether directly or indirectly) an increment of just over half of one standard deviation in 1962 occupational status. From another point of view we are more concerned with net effects. If both first job and 1962 status have a common antecedent cause—say, father's occupation—we may

want to state what part of the effect of W on Y consists in a transmission of the prior influence of X. Or, thinking of X as the initial cause, we may focus on the extent to which its influence on Y is transmitted by way of its prior influence on W.

We may, then, devote a few remarks to the pattern of gross effects before presenting the apparatus that yields estimates of net direct and indirect effects. Since we do not require a causal ordering of father's education with respect to his occupation, we may be content simply to note that $r_{XV} = .516$ is somewhat lower than the corresponding correlation, $r_{YU} = .596$, observed for the respondents themselves. The difference suggests a heightening of the effect of education on occupational status between the fathers' and the sons' generations. Before stressing this interpretation, however, we must remember that the measurements of V and X do not pertain to some actual cohort of men, here designated "fathers." Each "father" is represented in the data in proportion to the number of his sons who were 20 to 64 years old in March 1962.

The first recorded status of the son himself is education (U). We note that r_{UV} is just slightly greater than r_{UX}. Apparently both measures on the father represent factors that may influence the son's education.

In terms of gross effects there is a clear ordering of influences on first job. Thus

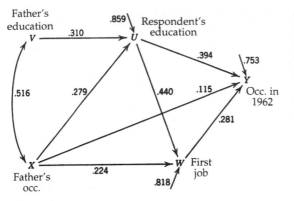

Figure 56.1   Path Coefficients in Basic Model of the Process of Stratification

$r_{WU} > r_{WX} > r_{WV}$. Education is most strongly correlated with first job, followed by father's occupation, and then by father's education.

Occupational status in 1962 (Y) apparently is influenced more strongly by education than by first job; but our earlier discussion of the first-job measure suggests we should not overemphasize the difference between r_{YW} and r_{YU}. Each, however, is substantially greater than r_{YX}, which in turn is rather more impressive than r_{YV}.

Figure 56.1 is a graphic representation of the system of relationships among the five variables that we propose as our basic model. The numbers entered on the diagram, with the exception of r_{XV}, are path coefficients, the estimation of which will be explained shortly. First we must become familiar with the conventions followed in constructing this kind of diagram. The link between V and X is shown as a curved line with an arrowhead at both ends. This is to distinguish it from the other lines, which are taken to be paths of influence. In the case of V and X we may suspect an influence running from the former to the latter. But if the diagram is logical for the respon-

dent's generation, we should have to assume that for the fathers, likewise, education and occupation are correlated not only because one affects the other but also because common causes lie behind both, which we have not measured. The bidirectional arrow merely serves to sum up all sources of correlation between V and X and to indicate that the explanation thereof is not part of the problem at hand.

The straight lines running from one measured variable to another represent *direct* (or net) influences. The symbol for the path coefficient, such as P_{YW}, carries a double subscript. The first subscript is the variable at the head of the path, or the effect; the second is the causal variable. (This resembles the convention for regression coefficients, where the first subscript refers to the "dependent" variable, the second to the "independent" variable.)

Finally, we see lines with no source indicated carrying arrows to each of the effect variables. These represent the residual paths, standing for all other influences on the variable in question, including causes not recognized or measured, errors of measurement, and departures of the true relationship from additivity and linearity, properties that are assumed throughout the analysis.

An important feature of this kind of causal scheme is that variables recognized as effects of certain antecedent factors may, in turn, serve as causes for subsequent variables. For example, U is caused by V and X, but it in turn influences W and Y. The algebraic representation of the scheme is a system of equations, rather than the single equation more often employed in multiple regression analysis. This feature permits a flexible conceptualization of the *modus operandi* of the causal network. Note that Y is shown here as being influenced directly by W, U, and X, but not by V (an assumption that will be justified shortly). But this does not imply that V has no influence on Y. V affects U, which does affect Y both directly and indirectly (via W). Moreover, V is correlated with X, and thus shares in the gross effect of X on Y, which is partly direct and partly indirect. Hence the gross effect of V on Y, previously described in terms of the correlation r_{YV}, is here interpreted as being entirely indirect, in consequence of V's effect on intervening variables and its correlation with another cause of Y.

Path Coefficients

Whether a path diagram, or the causal scheme it represents, is adequate depends on both theoretical and empirical considerations. At a minimum, before constructing the diagram we must know, or be willing to assume, a causal ordering of the observed variables (hence the lengthy discussion of this matter earlier in this chapter). This information is external or *a priori* with respect to the data, which merely describe associations or correlations. Moreover, the causal scheme must be complete, in the sense that all causes are accounted for. Here, as in most problems involving analysis of observational data, we achieve a formal completeness of the scheme by representing unmeasured causes as a residual factor, presumed to be uncorrelated with the remaining factors lying behind the variable in question. If any factor is known or presumed to operate in some other way it must be represented in the diagram in accordance with its causal role, even though it is not measured. Sometimes it is possible to deduce interesting im-

plications from the inclusion of such a variable and to secure useful estimates of certain paths in the absence of measurements on it, but this is not always so. A partial exception to the rule that all causes must be explicitly represented in the diagram is the unmeasured variable that can be assumed to operate strictly as an intervening variable. Its inclusion would enrich our understanding of a causal system without invalidating the causal scheme that omits it. Sociologists have only recently begun to appreciate how stringent are the logical requirements that must be met if discussion of causal processes is to go beyond mere impressionism and vague verbal formulations.[9] We are a long way from being able to make causal inferences with confidence, and schemes of the kind presented here had best be regarded as crude first approximations to adequate causal models.

On the empirical side, a minimum test of the adequacy of a causal diagram is whether it satisfactorily accounts for the observed correlations among the measured variables. In making such a test we employ the fundamental theorem in path analysis, which shows how to obtain the correlation between any two variables in the system, given the path coefficients and correlations entered on the diagram.[10] Without stating this theorem in general form we may illustrate its application here. For example,

$$r_{YX} = p_{YX} + p_{YU}r_{UX} + p_{YW}r_{WX}$$

and

$$r_{WX} = p_{WX} + p_{WU}r_{UX}.$$

We make use of each path leading to a given variable (such as Y in the first example) and the correlations of each of its causes with all other variables in the system. The latter correlations, in turn, may be analyzed; for example, r_{WX}, which appeared as such in the first equation, is broken down into two parts in the second. A complete expansion along these lines is required to trace out all the indirect connections between variables; thus,

$$r_{YX} = p_{YX} + p_{YU}p_{UX} + p_{YU}p_{UV}r_{VX} + p_{YW}p_{WX}$$

$$+ p_{YW}p_{WU}p_{UX} + p_{YW}p_{WU}p_{UV}r_{VX}$$

Now, if the path coefficients are properly estimated, and if there is no inconsistency in the diagram, the correlations calculated by a formula like the foregoing must equal the observed correlations. Let us compare the values computed from such a formula with the corresponding observed correlations:

$$r_{WV} = p_{WX}r_{XV} + p_{WU}r_{UV}$$

$$= (.224)(.516) + (.440)(.453)$$

$$= .116 + .199 = .315$$

which compares with the observed value of .332; and

$$r_{YV} = p_{YU}r_{UV} + p_{YX}r_{XV} + p_{YW}r_{WV}$$

$$= (.394)(.453) + (.115)(.516) + (.281)(.315)$$

$$= .326$$

(using here the calculated rather than the observed value of r_{WV}), which resembles the actual value, .322. Other such comparisons—for r_{YX}, for example—reveal, at most, trivial discrepancies (no larger than .001).

We arrive, by this roundabout journey, at the problem of getting numerical values for the path coefficients in the first place. This involves using equations of the foregoing type inversely. We have illustrated how to obtain correlations if the path coefficients are known, but in the typical empirical problem we know the correlations (or at least some of them) and have to estimate the paths. For a diagram of the type of Figure 56.1 the solution involves equations of the same form as those of linear multiple regression, except that we work with a recursive system of regression equations[11] rather than a single regression equation.

Table 56.2 records the results of the regression calculations. It can be seen that some alternative combinations of independent variables were studied. It turned out that the net regressions of both W and Y on V were so small as to be negligible. Hence V could be disregarded as a direct influence on these variables without loss of information. The net regression of Y on X was likewise small but, as it appears, not entirely negligible. Curiously, this net regression is of the same order of magnitude as the proportion of occupational inheritance in this population—about 10 percent, as discussed [elsewhere].[12] We might speculate that the direct effect of the father's occupation on the occupational status of a mature man consists of this modest amount of strict occupational inheritance. The remainder of the effect of X on Y is indirect, inasmuch as X has previously influenced U and W, the son's education and the occupational level at which he got his start. For reasons noted [elsewhere][13] we do not assume that the full impact of the tendency to take up the father's occupation is registered in the choice of first job.

With the formal properties of the model in mind we may turn to some general problems

Table 56.2 Partial Regression Coefficients in Standard Form (Beta Coefficients) and Coefficients of Determination, for Specified Combinations of Variables

Dependent Variables[a]	Independent Variables[a]				Coefficient of Determination (R2)
	W	U	X	V	
U[b]	—	—	.279	.310	.26
W	—	.433	.214	.026	.33
W[b]	—	.440	.224	—	.33
Y	.282	.397	.120	-.014	.43
Y[b]	.281	.394	.115	—	.43
Y	.311	.428	—	—	.42

[a] V: Father's education
X: Father's occ. status
U: Respondent's education
W: First-job status
Y: 1962 occ. status
[b] Beta coefficients in these sets taken as estimates of path coefficients for Figure 56.1

confronting this kind of interpretation of our results. One of the first impressions gained from Figure 56.1 is that the largest path coefficients in the diagram are those for residual factors, that is, variables not measured. The residual path is merely a convenient representation of the extent to which measured causes in the system fail to account for the variation in the effect variables. (The residual is obtained from the coefficient of determination; if $R^2_{Y(WUX)}$ is the squared multiple correlation of Y on the three independent variables, then the residual for Y is $\sqrt{1 - R^2_{Y(WUX)}}$.) Sociologists are often disappointed in the size of the residual, assuming that this is a measure of their success in "explaining" the phenomenon under study. They seldom reflect on what it would mean to live in a society where nearly perfect explanation of the dependent variable could be secured by studying causal variables like father's occupation or respondent's education. In such a society it would indeed be true that some are "destined to poverty almost from birth . . . by the economic status or occupation of their par-

ents" (in the words of the reference cited in endnote 1). Others, of course, would be "destined" to affluence or to modest circumstances. By no effort of their own could they materially alter the course of destiny, nor could any stroke of fortune, good or ill, lead to an outcome not already in the cards.

Thinking of the residual as an index of the adequacy of an explanation gives rise to a serious misconception. It is thought that a high multiple correlation is presumptive evidence that an explanation is correct or nearly so, whereas a low percentage of determination means that a causal interpretation is almost certainly wrong. The fact is that the size of the residual (or, if one prefers, the proportion of variation "explained") is *no* guide whatever to the validity of a causal interpretation. The best-known cases of "spurious correlation"—a correlation leading to an egregiously wrong interpretation—are those in which the coefficient of determination is quite high.

The relevant question about the residual is not really its size at all, but whether the unobserved factors it stands for are properly represented as being uncorrelated with the measured antecedent variables. We shall entertain [elsewhere][14] some conjectures about unmeasured variables that clearly are not uncorrelated with the causes depicted in Figure 56.1. It turns out that these require us to acknowledge certain possible modifications of the diagram, whereas other features of it remain more or less intact. A delicate question in this regard is that of the burden of proof. It is all too easy to make a formidable list of unmeasured variables that someone has alleged to be crucial to the process under study. But the mere existence of such variables is already acknowledged by the very presence of the residual. It would seem to be part of the task of the critic to *show,* if only hypothetically, but *specifically,* how the modification of the causal scheme to include a new variable would disrupt or alter the relationships in the original diagram. His argument to this effect could then be examined for plausibility and his evidence, if any, studied in terms of the empirical possibilities it suggests.

Our supposition is that the scheme in Figure 56.1 is most easily subject to modification by introducing additional measures of the same kind as those used here. If indexes relating to socioeconomic background other than V and X are inserted we will almost certainly estimate differently the direct effects of these particular variables. If occupational statuses of the respondent intervening between W and Y were known we should have to modify more or less radically the right-hand portion of the diagram. Yet we should argue that such modifications may amount to an enrichment or extension of the basic model rather than an invalidation of it. The same may be said of other variables that function as intervening causes. In theory, it should

be possible to specify these in some detail, and a major part of the research worker's task is properly defined as an attempt at such specification. In the course of such work, to be sure, there is always the possibility of a discovery that would require a fundamental reformulation, making the present model obsolete. Discarding the model would be a cost gladly paid for the prize of such a discovery.

Postponing the confrontation with an altered model, the one at hand is not lacking in interest. An instructive exercise is to compare the magnitudes of gross and net relationships. Here we make use of the fact that the correlation coefficient and the path coefficient have the same dimensionality. The correlation r_{YX} = .405 (Table 56.1) means that a unit change (one standard deviation) in X produces a change of 0.4 unit in Y, in gross terms. The path coefficient, P_{YX} = .115 (Figure 56.1), tells us that about one-fourth of this gross effect is a result of the direct influence of X on Y. (We speculated above on the role of occupational inheritance in this connection.) The remainder (.405 − .115 = .29) is indirect, via U and W. The sum of all indirect effects, therefore, is given by the difference between the simple correlation and the path coefficient connecting two variables. We note that the indirect effects on Y are generally substantial, relative to the direct. Even the variable temporally closest (we assume) to Y has "indirect effects"—actually, common antecedent causes—nearly as large as the direct. Thus r_{YW} = .541 and p_{YW} = .281, so that the aggregate of "indirect effects" is .26, which in this case are common determinants of Y and W that spuriously inflate the correlation between them.

To ascertain the indirect effects along a given chain of causation we must multiply the path coefficients along the chain. The procedure is to locate on the diagram the dependent variable of interest, and then trace back along the paths linking it to its immediate and remote causes. In such a tracing we may reverse direction once but only once, following the rule "first back, then forward." Any bidirectional correlation may be traced in either direction. If the diagram contains more than one such correlation, however, only one may be used in a given compound path. In tracing the indirect connections no variable may be intersected more than once in one compound path. Having traced all such possible compound paths, we obtain the entirety of indirect effects as their sum.

Let us consider the example of effects of education on first job, U on W. The gross or total effect is $r_{WU} = .538$. The direct path is $p_{WU} = .440$. There are two indirect connections or compound paths: from W back to X then forward to U; and from W back to X, then back to V, and then forward to U. Hence we have:

$$r_{WU} = p_{WU} + \underbrace{p_{WX}p_{UX} + p_{WX}r_{XV}p_{UV}}$$

(gross) (direct)   (indirect)

or, numerically,

$$.538 = .440 + (.224)(.279) + (.224)(.516)(.310)$$

$$= .440 + .062 + .036$$

$$= .440 + .098.$$

In this case all the indirect effect of U on W derives from the fact that both U and W have X (plus V) as a common cause. In other instances, when more than one common cause is involved and these causes are them-

selves interrelated, the complexity is too great to permit a succinct verbal summary.

A final stipulation about the scheme had best be stated, though it is implicit in all the previous discussion. The form of the model itself, but most particularly the numerical estimates accompanying it, are submitted as valid only for the population under study. No claim is made that an equally cogent account of the process of stratification in another society could be rendered in terms of this scheme. For other populations, or even for subpopulations within the United States, the magnitudes would almost certainly be different, although we have some basis for supposing them to have been fairly constant over the last few decades in this country. The technique of path analysis is not a method for discovering causal laws but a procedure for giving a quantitative interpretation to the manifestations of a known or assumed causal system as it operates in a particular population. When the same interpretive structure is appropriate for two or more populations there is something to be learned by comparing their respective path coefficients and correlation patterns. We have not yet reached the stage at which such comparative study of stratification systems is feasible. . . .

The Concept of a Vicious Circle

Although the concept of a "cycle of poverty" has a quasi-official sanction in U.S. public policy discussion, it is difficult to locate a systematic explication of the concept. As clear a formulation as any that may be found in academic writing is perhaps the following:[15]

Occupational and social status are to an important extent self-perpetuating. They are associated with many factors which make it difficult for individuals to modify their status. Position in the social structure is usually associated with a certain level of income, education, family structure, community reputation, and so forth. These become part of a vicious circle in which each factor acts on the other in such a way as to preserve the social structure in its present form, as well as the individual family's position in that structure. . . . The cumulation of disadvantages (or of advantages) affects the individual's entry into the labor market as well as his later opportunities for social mobility.

The suspicion arises that the authors in preparing this summary statement were partly captured by their own rhetoric. Only a few pages earlier they had observed that the "widespread variation of educational attainment within classes suggests that one's family background plays an enabling and motivating rather than a determining role."[16] But is an "enabling and motivating role" logically adequate to the function of maintaining a "vicious circle"? In focusing closely on the precise wording of the earlier quotation we are not interested in splitting hairs or in generating a polemic. It merely serves as a convenient point of departure for raising the questions of what is specifically meant by "vicious circle," what are the operational criteria for this concept, and what are the limits of its usefulness.

To begin with, there is the question of fact—or, rather, of how the quantitative facts are to be evaluated. How "difficult" is it, in actuality, "for individuals to modify their status" (presumably reference is to the status of the family of orientation)? We have found that the father-son correlation for occupational status is of the order of .4.

(Assuming attenuation by errors of measurement, this should perhaps be revised slightly upward.) Approaching the measurement problem in an entirely different way, we find that the amount of intergenerational mobility between census major occupation groups is no less than seven-eighths, as much as would occur if there were no statistical association between the two statuses whatsoever, or five-sixths as much as the difference between the "minimum" mobility involved in the intergenerational shift in occupation distributions and the amount required for "perfect" mobility.[17] Evidently a very considerable amount of "status modification" or occupational mobility does occur. (There is nothing in the data exhibited by Lipset and Bendix to indicate the contrary.) If the existing amount of modification of status is insufficient in terms of some functional or normative criterion implicitly employed, the precise criterion should be made explicit: *How much mobility must occur to contradict the diagnosis of a "vicious circle"?*

Next, take the postulate that occupational status (of origin) is "associated with many factors" and that "each factor acts on the other" so as "to preserve . . . the individual family's position." Here the exposition virtually cries out for an explicit *quantitative* causal model; if not one of the type set forth in the first section of this chapter, then some other model that also takes into account the way in which several variables combine their effects. Taking our own earlier model, for want of a better alternative, as representative of the situation, what do we learn about the "associated factors"? Family "position" is, indeed, "associated with . . . education," and education in turn makes a sizable difference in early and subsequent occupational achievement. Yet of the total or gross effect of education (U) on Y, occupational status in 1962 (r_{YU} = .596), only a minor part consists in a transmission of the prior influence of "family position," at least as this is indicated by measured variables V (father's education) and X (father's occupation). . . . A relevant calculation concerns the compound paths through V and X linking Y to U. Using data for men 20 to 64 years old with nonfarm background, we find:

$$p_{YX}p_{UX} = .025$$

$$p_{YX}r_{XV}p_{UV} = .014$$

$$p_{YX}p_{WX}p_{UX} = .014$$

$$p_{YW}p_{WX}r_{XV}p_{UV} = .008$$

$$\overline{}$$

$$Sum = .061$$

This is the *entire* part of the effect of education that has to do with "perpetuating" the "family's position." By contrast, the direct effect is p_{YU} = .407 and the effect via W (exclusive of prior influence of father's education and occupation on respondent's first job) is $p_{YW}p_{WU}$ = .128, for a total of .535. Far from serving in the main as a factor perpetuating initial status, education operates *primarily* to induce variation in occupational status that is independent of initial status. The simple reason is that the large residual factor for U is an indirect cause of Y. But by definition it is quite uncorrelated with X and V. This is not to gainsay the equally cogent point that the degree of "perpetuation" (as measured by r_{YX}) that does occur is mediated in large part by education. . . .

Our model also indicates where the "vicious circle" interpretation is vulnerable. In the passage on the vicious circle quoted there seems to be an assumption that because of the substantial intercorrelations between a number of background factors, each of which has a significant relationship to subsequent achievement, the total effect of origin on achievement is materially enhanced. Here, in other words, the concept of "cumulation" appears to refer to the intercorrelations of a collection of independent variables. But the effect of such intercorrelations is quite opposite to what the writers appear to suppose. They are not alone in arguing from a fallacious assumption that was caustically analyzed by Karl Pearson half a century ago.[18] The crucial point is that if the several determinants are indeed substantially intercorrelated with each other, then their combined effect will consist largely in redundancy, not in "cumulation." This circumstance does not relieve us from the necessity of trying to understand better *how* the effects come about (a point also illustrated in a less fortunate way in Pearson's work). It does imply that a refined estimate of how much effect results from a combination of "associated factors" will not differ greatly from a fairly crude estimate based on the two or three most important ones.

NOTES

1. Mollie Orshansky, "Children of the Poor," *Social Security Bulletin,* 26(July 1963).

2. Forrest A. Bogan, "Employment of High School Graduates and Dropouts in 1964," *Special Labor Force Report,* No. 54 (U.S. Bureau of Labor Statistics, June 1965), p. 643.

3. Peter M. Blau and Otis Dudley Duncan, *The American Occupational Structure,* New York: The Free Press, 1967, ch. 4.

4. *Ibid.*

5. Bruce K. Eckland, "College Dropouts Who Came Back," *Harvard Educational Review,* 34(1964), 402–420.

6. Beverly Duncan, *Family Factors and School Dropout: 1920–1960,* U.S. Office of Education, Cooperative Research Project No. 2258, Ann Arbor: Univ. of Michigan, 1965.

7. Blau and Duncan, *op. cit.,* Appendix C.

8. Gösta Carlsson, *Social Mobility and Class Structure,* Lund: CWK Gleerup, 1958, p. 124.

9. H. M. Blalock, Jr., *Causal Inferences in Non-experimental Research,* Chapel Hill: Univ. of North Carolina Press, 1964.

10. Sewall Wright, "Path Coefficients and Path Regressions," *Biometrics,* 16(1960), 189–202; Otis Dudley Duncan, "Path Analysis," *American Journal of Sociology,* 72(1966), 1–16.

11. Blalock, *op. cit.,* pp. 54 ff.

12. Blau and Duncan, *op. cit.,* ch. 4.

13. *Ibid.,* ch. 3.

14. *Ibid.,* ch. 5.

15. Seymour M. Lipset and Reinhard Bendix, *Social Mobility in Industrial Society,* Berkeley: Univ. of California Press, 1959, pp. 198–199.

16. *Ibid.,* p. 190.

17. U.S. Bureau of the Census, "Lifetime Occupational Mobility of Adult Males: March 1962," *Current Population Reports,* Series P–23, No. 11 (May 12, 1964), Table B.

18. Karl Pearson, "On Certain Errors with Regard to Multiple Correlation Occasionally Made by Those Who Have Not Adequately Studied This Subject," *Biometrika,* 10(1914), 181–187.

57

Family Background and Income in Adulthood, 1961–1999

DAVID J. HARDING, CHRISTOPHER JENCKS, LEONARD M. LOPOO, AND SUSAN E. MAYER

Most Americans endorse the ideal of equal opportunity, and many interpret this ideal as requiring that children from different backgrounds have an equal chance of achieving economic success. Most Americans also recognize that children whose parents have "all the advantages" are more likely to prosper than children whose parents lack these advantages. Understanding this relationship has therefore become a prominent goal of social research, especially since the 1960s. This chapter investigates how the relationship between American family income during adulthood and family background during childhood changed from 1961 to 1999.

Our approach to measuring trends in intergenerational inheritance differs from earlier studies. Almost all earlier studies have focused on the determinants of individuals' occupational rank or earnings. We focus instead on an individual's total family income. This change allows us to assess the impact of family background on the eco-nomic status of individuals who are not working. It also allows us to take account of the fact that individuals' economic status often depends more on how they fare in the "marriage market" than on how they fare in the labor market.

The changing importance of marriage for one's family income is clear when we examine changes in the correlation between a mature adult's own earnings in a given year and his or her total family income in the same year. Among men the correlation[1] between earnings and total family income fell from 0.87 in 1968 to 0.75 in 1996.[2] Among women, the correlation rose from 0.18 in 1968 to 0.39 in 1996. Earnings are still a much better proxy for living standards among men than among women. But since family background influences an individual's chance of having a well-paid spouse, ignoring this fact is likely to bias trend estimates of how background affects economic status among both men and women.

This is a commissioned chapter that draws heavily on material in a previous publication (David J. Harding, Christopher Jencks, Leonard M. Lopoo, and Susan E. Mayer, "The Changing Effect of Family Background on the Incomes of American Adults," in *Unequal Chances: Family Background and Economic Success*, edited by Samuel Bowles, Herbert Gintis, and Melissa Osborne. Copyright © 2005 by the Russell Sage Foundation).

How Family Background Affects Adult Family Income

Figure 57.1 shows some of the pathways by which family background can influence children's eventual income in adulthood.[3] It contains several concepts that require brief discussion.

Genetic Advantages

A growing body of evidence suggests that genetic differences can influence an individual's earnings. Studies based on comparisons of monozygotic (MZ) twins and dizygotic (DZ) twins (Ashenfelter and Rouse 1998; Taubman 1976) suggest that genes are likely to play a significant role in explaining the intergenerational inheritance of economic advantages.[4] However, because estimates based on twin studies require a number of questionable assumptions (Björklund, Jäntti, and Solon 2005; Goldberger 1978), the exact magnitude of the importance of genes is difficult to measure. Björklund and Chadwick's (2002) study of the earnings of fathers and sons in Sweden also suggests that genes play a role.

However, the fact that genetic resemblance helps explain economic resemblance between parents and children does not mean that this source of economic resemblance operates independently of the environment. Suppose, for example, that myopia has a genetic component. Most affluent societies ensure that myopic children get glasses. As a result, myopic children can usually see almost as well as other children. In poor societies where glasses are not available to everyone, the genes that contribute to myopia have a larger impact. People's genes also influence the environments they choose for themselves. Consider two sisters, one of whom finds reading easy and one of whom finds it difficult. The sister who finds reading easier is likely to enjoy reading more and do more of it. As a result, she is likely to score higher on vocabulary and reading tests, get higher grades, stay in school longer, and earn more when she enters the labor force.

Human Capital

Economists use the term "human capital" to describe the skills, knowledge, and character traits that influence a worker's potential earnings. If employers value the same attributes for several generations, parents with above-average human capital are likely to have children with above-average human capital. To begin with, parents with traits that employers value tend to have above-average earnings, so they can invest more in their children's nutrition, health care, and education. Such parents also tend to live in political jurisdictions where the government invests a lot in children.

Although economists use the term "human capital" to describe characteristics that pay off in the labor market, one can easily broaden the concept to include characteristics that pay off in the marriage market. As we shall see, family background explains slightly more of the variation in daughters' family incomes than in sons' family incomes. This difference suggests that family background may exert even more influence on a daughter's success in the marriage market than on a son's success in the labor market.

Taste for Market Goods

Families vary dramatically in the number of hours that their adult members spend doing paid labor. Family members also vary in the extent to which they maximize their hourly wages. Some always take the best-paid

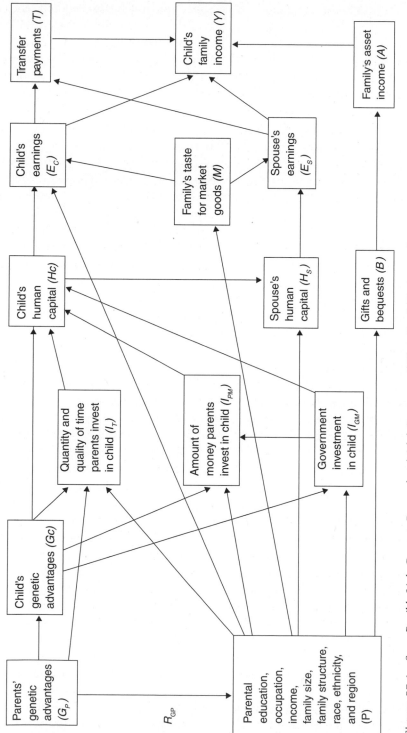

Figure 57.1   Some Possible Links Between Respondents' Adult Incomes and Their Family Background

job they can find, and others settle for less money to get shorter hours, more congenial colleagues, more interesting work, or other nonmonetary advantages. Family background appears to influence how much people work (Altonji and Dunn 2000), and it probably also influences the weight that individuals assign to earnings relative to goals like short hours and interesting work. If these associations change over time, the association between adult income and family background is also likely to change.

Gifts and Bequests

Dividends, interest, and rent accounted for 7 percent of all income received by individuals between the ages of 25 and 64 in 1999.[5] Estimates suggest that income from assets accounts for between 1 and 5 percent of all money income among thirty- to fifty-nine year olds (Gale and Scholz 1994; Wolff 2002). We do not know how this figure has changed over time, but the age at which adults inherit their parents' assets is rising, so the relative importance of inherited assets could be falling for those under the age of sixty.

Two Sources of Change over Time

Figure 57.1 suggests that the effects of family background on incomes can change for two quite different reasons. First, the effects of various family background characteristics on children's characteristics, such as years of schooling, cognitive ability, or taste for market goods, can change. Second, the effects of children's characteristics on their eventual adult income can change. Children's education illustrates both of these possibilities.

The association between parents' socioeconomic advantages and the number of years of school that their children complete declined between World War I and the early 1970s (Hauser and Featherman 1976). As a result, educational disparities among adults from different kinds of families kept shrinking throughout the twentieth century. This trend should have reduced the impact of family background on children's eventual family income. However, the economic value of an extra year of schooling also changed. The effect of an extra year of school on men's annual earnings fell between 1940 and 1975. This change accentuated the declining impact of family background on children's educational attainment, making it doubly difficult for economically advantaged parents to pass along their advantages by keeping their children in school. But after 1975 the labor market returns to schooling rose.

The payoff to schooling also rose in the marriage market. If we compare the most educated third of all mothers to the least educated third, about 93 percent of the most educated and 87 percent of the least educated were living with a husband in both 1940 and 1960. By 1990 the proportions were 84 percent for the most educated and 70 percent for the least educated.[6] The marriage gap between the most and least educated mothers had thus risen from 6 to 14 percentage points. The net result was that although family background had less impact on how much schooling young people got in the last third of the century than earlier in the century, the value of each year of school rose during the last decades of the century.

Mature adults seldom go back to school, so the association between educational attainment and family background when a birth cohort reaches sixty is about the same as when it was thirty. The association does change as more recent birth cohorts replace earlier ones, but this takes a long time. In principle, we can hold changes of this kind constant by tracking the same birth cohort over time. When we do this, almost all the remaining changes in the association between adult family income and family background are attributable to changes in the way employment, marriage, and earnings are distributed among individuals with different background characteristics.

Whereas cohort replacement is slow, the economic value of respondents' characteristics can change relatively rapidly. When job opportunities improved for black workers in the wake of the civil rights movement, for example, young blacks benefited the most, but older blacks also gained. Likewise, when the wage gap between high school and college graduates widened in the 1980s, the change was largest among younger workers but it also affected mature workers. Changes in the marriage market can also change the value of personal characteristics quite rapidly. When divorce rates rise, all women are more likely to experience sudden reductions in family income, but the change is likely to be largest among those with disadvantaged parents, because their divorce rates are likely to rise the most.

Data

We concentrate on trends among men and women between the ages of thirty and fifty-nine, whom we refer to as "mature adults." We use two sources of data, the Occupational Changes in a Generation (OCG) surveys and the General Social Survey (GSS). The OCG surveys were conducted in 1962 and 1973. They both asked men (but not women) about their family background. Our first sample of mature OCG men was born between 1902 and 1932. Our second sample was born between 1913 and 1943. The GSS is a smaller survey that has been conducted either annually or biennially since 1972. The GSS asks both men and women about their family income and family background. We analyze the surveys conducted between 1972 and 2000, so our samples of mature adults were born between 1912 and 1970.

Our primary dependent variable is family income in the year preceding the survey. Although there is some variation across data sources in how our variables are measured, one can think of adult family income as the sum of all sources of income for the respondent and his or her spouse (if married).[7] Variation in income due to survey year, gender, and age has been removed, and we analyze the effect of parental characteristics on the natural logarithm of this adjusted income. We measure family background using seven characteristics of the family in which the respondent grew up, including the family head's occupational ranking (measured by an updated version of Duncan's socioeconomic index, which is based on occupations' educational requirements and economic rewards; see Hauser and Warren 1997), the family head's education in years, the number of siblings, and whether the respondent is black, Hispanic, grew up in the South, and/or grew up in a family with both parents.

Changes in Inequality of Family Background

Suppose that a 10 percent income difference between parents was always associated with a 4 percent income difference between their children. The income gap between children raised by rich and poor parents would then depend on the income gap separating rich and poor parents. If inequality between rich and poor parents falls, as it did during the first two-thirds of the twentieth century, and if all else remains equal, the subsequent income gap between their children will also fall. If inequality between rich and poor parents rises, as it did in the last third of the twentieth century, and if all else remains equal, the income gap between their children will also widen. The same logic holds for other parental advantages, like educational attainment and occupational position.

The degree to which the distribution of background characteristics changed over time varies according to which family background characteristics we examine. Inequality in parental occupation rose by about 15 percent between 1962 and 1999. Inequality in parental years of schooling rose slightly between 1962 and 1973 and declined slightly thereafter, so educational inequality among parents was about the same in 1999 as in 1962. Disparities in the size of children's families declined by about 10 percent between the early 1960s and the 1990s.

Of the four remaining measures of background characteristics—intact family, black, Hispanic, and Southern origins, the only one that changes appreciably is Hispanic. The GSS shows substantial growth in the English-speaking Hispanic population between the 1970s and 1990s. Because Hispanics have relatively low family incomes, the fact that more adults had Hispanic parents implies an increase in the overall level of inequality among parents.

Changes in the Intergenerational Inheritance of Advantage

We turn now to changes in the relationship between mature adults' income and their family background (as measured by the seven background characteristics). We measure this relationship with the multiple correlations between income and family background characteristics, which we denote as R_{pc}.[8] When R_{pc} falls, we can infer that intergenerational changes in rank (what sociologists call "exchange mobility") have become larger or more frequent. When R_{pc} rises, intergenerational changes in rank have become either smaller or less frequent.

Table 57.1 shows multiple correlations between respondents' adult family income and their background characteristics. Among OCG men we see a dramatic decline in R_{pc} between 1961 and 1972. This decline recurs for all age groups. The diagonal arrows track birth cohorts as they age. Here again we see declines between 1961 and 1972. The GSS tells a very different story about changes in R_{pc} after 1972. The multiple correlations for men in different age groups show no consistent trend between the 1970s and the 1990s. When we track the same cohort of men over time, the multiple correlations almost always rise as a cohort ages. This is in sharp contrast to what we saw between 1961 and 1972.

The GSS also provides data on post-1972 trends among women. Table 57.1 shows that although R_{pc} was essentially stable among GSS men, it declined by about one-seventh among GSS women. Whereas R_{pc} was substantially higher among women than men in the 1970s, this gender difference had largely disappeared by the 1990s. This pattern of differences is consistent with the hypothesis that family background influences success in the marriage market somewhat more than it influences success in the labor market, although other explanations are also possible.

Table 57.1   Multiple Correlations of Family Income with Seven Family Background Measures in OCG and GSS, by Age, Sex, and Decade

	OCG Men		GSS Men			GSS Women		
Respondents' Age	1961	1972[a]	1970s	1980s	1990s	1970s	1980s	1990s
30 to 39	.399	.309	.330	.289	.306	.399	.361	.374
40 to 49	.397	.305	.355	.362	.352	.437	.388	.361
50 to 59	.414	.323	.327	.410	.360	.440	.429	.350
Weighted Mean For All 30 to 59 year olds	.403	.312	.337	.342	.335	.423	.385	.364[b]
Approximate Sampling Error of Multiple R[c]	(.008)	(.006)	(.014)	(.017)	(.015)	(.012)	(.015)	(.014)
Sample Size	12,829	23,824	2,382	3,040	3,817	2,761	3,703	4,657

Note: The seven measures of family background are race, ethnicity, Southern origins, living with both parents at age 16, number of siblings, parental education, and parental occupation (see text for details).

[a] The decline between 1961 and 1972 is significant at the .01 level for all age groups.

[b] The average decline between the 1970s and the 1990s is significant at the .01 level.

[c] Approximated using $[(1-R^2)/(N-8)]^{.5}$.

For those who find it hard to decide whether the correlations in Table 57.1 are "large" or "small," Table 57.2 displays the association between family background and income in adulthood in a more intuitively understandable form. Table 57.2 shows the proportion of respondents in the top and bottom quartiles of family background who ended up in each of the four income quartiles as adults. We focus on the probability that those born into the top or bottom quartile were in the top or bottom income quartile as mature adults.

Consistent with the results in Table 48.1, the proportion of men who remained in the bottom or top quartiles declined between 1961 and 1972 and stayed the same afterward.

Among women the story is more complicated. Among GSS women, R_{pc} fell between the 1970s and the 1990s, so we expected a parallel decline in the proportions of GSS women who stayed in both the top and bottom quartiles. Table 57.2 confirms this prediction for women born into the top quartile: their chances of having slipped into a lower quartile were clearly higher in the 1990s than in the 1970s. However, there was little change in the percentage of women born into the bottom quartile who had risen into a higher quartile, although those women who did move up moved further in the 1990s than in the 1970s.

Specific Background Characteristics

Previously we examined the relationship between adult income and family background by combining the seven background measures. Now we separate these characteristics to see which ones became more and less important. Column 1 of Table 57.3 shows the bivariate relationship of logged family income in 1961 to each of the seven family background characteristics. Column 2 shows the change in this coefficient between 1961 and 1972. Almost

Table 57.2   Percent of 30- to 59-Year-Old Sons and Daughters in Each Quartile of Family Income By Quartile of Family Background and Year in OCG and GSS

Parents' Quartile and Survey	Family Income Quartile				Total	Sample Size
	Bottom	Second	Third	Top		
Sons from bottom quartile						
OCG: 1961	46.2	27.7	16.7	9.5	100	2,537
OCG: 1972	40.7	29.8	21.2	8.4	100	6,454
GSS: 1970s	40.3	29.6	19.8	10.2	100	595
GSS: 1980s	39.4	30.0	21.2	9.4	100	840
GSS: 1990s	40.6	25.8	21.1	12.6	100	954
Trend: 1961 to 1990s[a]	−5.3	−1.7	5.7	1.4		
Sons from top quartile						
OCG-I	9.5	20.9	32.1	37.6	100	2,678
OCG-II	11.8	24.0	29.2	35.0	100	4,899
GSS: 1970s	11.6	20.5	30.2	37.8	100	596
GSS: 1980s	12.3	19.7	28.8	39.2	100	728
GSS: 1990s	11.6	21.4	29.0	38.0	100	954
Trend: 1961 to 1990s[a]	2.4	3.9	−4.1	−2.3		
Daughters from bottom quartile						
GSS: 1970s	44.4	26.2	19.6	9.9	100	690
GSS: 1980s	44.5	25.5	18.8	11.2	100	1,070
GSS: 1990s	43.7	25.9	18.8	11.6	100	1,164
Trend: 1970s to 1990s	−0.6	−0.4	−0.8	1.7		
Daughters from top quartile						
GSS: 1970s	10.1	19.1	27.1	42.8	100	691
GSS: 1980s	12.1	19.3	29.7	38.9	100	878
GSS: 1990s	11.7	23.5	27.1	37.7	100	1,164
Trend: 1970s to 1990s	1.5	4.4	0.0	−5.2		

Parents are assigned to quartiles of parental advantages using the same seven measures as in Table 48.1, with each advantage weighted by its coefficient in the equation predicting log family income. Family incomes are assigned to quartiles after eliminating variation due to age, gender, and survey year.

[a] Sum of within-survey changes: (OCG II − OCG I) + (GSS 1990s − GSS 1970s).

all the coefficients decline significantly between 1961 and 1972. However, when we examine each coefficient controlling for the other six, only the changes in the effects of parental occupation, black race, and Southern origins remain statistically significant (results not shown).

The decline in the effect of parental occupation is partly attributable to the steady decline in the proportion of respondents whose fathers were farmers. Among respondents not raised on farms, the main reason for decline was that respondents from the top tenth of the occupational distribution enjoyed less of an economic advantage in 1972 than in 1961 (results not shown). The declining effect of Southern origins probably reflects the narrowing of the income gap between the South and the North. The declining effect of race reflects a decline in the educational gap between blacks and whites, movement of blacks

Table 57.3 Bivariat Regression Coefficients of Seven Family Background Measures When Predicting Log Family Income at Ages 30 to 59 Among OCG Men and GSS Men and Women

Background Measure	OCG Men		GSS Men		GSS Women		GSS Women Minus Men	
	Coefficient for 1961	Change From 1961 to 1972	Coefficient For 1971	Change From 1971 to 1999	Coefficient For 1971	Change From 1971 to 1999	Coefficient For 1971	Change From 1971 to 1999
Father's Occupation								
B	**.257**	**-.089**	**131**	.037	**.207**	-.010	**.076**	-.047
(S.E.)	(.007)	(.009)	(.017)	(.026)	(.017)	(.028)	(.024)	(.038)
Parent's Education								
B	**.053**	**-.012**	**.037**	**.015**	**.057**	-.010	**.020**	**-.025**
(S.E.)	(.002)	(.002)	(.004)	(.006)	(.004)	(.007)	(.006)	(.009)
Number of Siblings								
B	**-.058**	**-.011**	**-.043**	**-.029**	**-.067**	.007	**-.024**	**.036**
(S.E.)	(.002)	(.003)	(.006)	(.010)	(.006)	(.010)	(.008)	(.014)
Intact Family								
B	**.164**	.033	**.090**	**.205**	**.262**	.081	**.172**	-.124
(S.E.)	(.018)	(.024)	(.039)	(.062)	(.039)	(.062)	(.055)	(.088)
Black								
B	**-.824**	**.359**	**-.415**	-.065	**-.770**	**.179**	**-.355**	.244
(S.E.)	(.023)	(.031)	(.051)	(.081)	(.051)	(.079)	(.072)	(.133)
Hispanic								
B	**-.405**	.082	**-.573**	**.443**	**-.482**	.168	.091	-.275
(S.E.)	(.047)	(.055)	(.095)	(.147)	(.095)	(.144)	(.134)	(.206)
Southern Regions								
B	**-.424**	**.191**	**-.260**	.093	**-.367**	**.226**	**-.107**	.133
(S.E.)	(.015)	(.019)	(.035)	(.057)	(.036)	(.060)	(.050)	(.083)
Unweighted Sample	32,242		9,268		11,107			

*Coefficients in boldface are significant at the .05 level

from the South to the North, and some reduction in discrimination.

The remainder of Table 57.3 shows the bivariate results from GSS. Column 3 shows the estimated coefficients of family background measures for men in 1971, and column 4 shows the estimated change in the bivariate coefficients for men between 1971 and 1999. The bivariate relationships of men's family income to their parents' education, number of siblings, and whether they grew up in an intact family become significantly stronger over time. The bivariate effect of parental occupation also grows slightly stronger, but the change is not significant. The bivariate effect of being Hispanic grows weaker over time.

Columns 5 and 7 show that in 1971 almost every family background measure had more impact on women than on men. Columns 6 and 8 show that most of the coefficients for men and women converged between 1971 and 1999. The effects of parental education, race, and Southern origins all weakened significantly for women and were very close to those for men by the late 1990s. The adverse effect of coming from a large family was significantly larger for women than men in 1971, but this difference had also disappeared by the late 1990s. The multivariate GSS results (not shown) are broadly similar to the bivariate results except that the coefficients are smaller.

Summary

Intergenerational Inheritance

The relationship between a mature man's family income in adulthood and his family background fell during the 1960s and then remained stable from the 1970s through the 1990s. But men's incomes began growing more unequal in the 1970s, so the income gap between men raised by advantaged rather than disadvantaged parents widened between the 1970s and the 1990s.

We have no data on trends among women during the 1960s. In the early 1970s intergenerational correlations were higher among daughters than among sons, and daughters' family incomes were also more unequal. The economic cost of having grown up in a disadvantaged family was therefore considerably larger for daughters than for sons. But whereas the association between a mature man's family income and his parents' socioeconomic position was almost constant between the 1970s and the 1990s, this association fell among women. As a result, the economic cost of growing up in a disadvantaged family was roughly constant for women, although it remained larger for women than for men.

Race, Ethnicity, and Region

Disparities in adult family income between blacks and whites, between Hispanics and Anglos, and between those raised in the South and North narrowed between 1961 and 1999.

Parental Education

The effect of parental education on men's family income fell during the 1960s but rose again over the next three decades. Parental education mattered more for mature women's family income than for men's in the 1970s, but this difference had disappeared by the late 1990s.

Parental Occupation

When we rank occupations in terms of their educational requirements and economic rewards, the effect of differences between fathers' occupations on their mature sons' family incomes declined during the

1960s. The effect of a father's occupation shows no clear trend after that for either men or women, but it is consistently larger for women than for men, partly because women's family incomes are more unequal than men's.

Taken together these findings suggest that there were significant changes in equality of opportunity in the United States between 1961 and 1999. For men, equality of opportunity increased during the 1960s but changed little thereafter. Among women there was less equality of opportunity in the early 1970s than among men, but equality of opportunity among women increased during the 1970s. By the late 1990s, the importance of family background for a woman's economic prospects (relative to other women) was similar to its importance for a man's economic prospects (relative to other men). In addition, the importance of race, ethnicity, and region declined between 1961 and 1999. Nevertheless, as we begin the twenty-first century, there are still sizable inequalities of opportunity in the United States. Gender and family background, including race, ethnicity, and region, remain strong predictors of economic well-being in adulthood.

NOTES

1. In this chapter we often measure the relationship between two attributes with a "correlation," which ranges from zero (no relationship) to one (perfect relationship) and which can be thought of as assessing the degree to which two characteristics are associated in the data. A "multiple correlation" can be thought of as a correlation between one attribute and a set of attributes considered together.

2. Men and women without earnings are included and assigned earnings of zero.

3. Figure 57.1 is not a complete causal model. It omits many links that are well established in the research literature, such as the reciprocal ef-

fects of spouses' earnings on one another, to highlight the links that we think are most likely to have changed.

4. Monozygotic (MZ) twins have all their genes in common, and dizygotic (DZ) twins share roughly half their genes.

5. Estimate based on data from U.S. Bureau of the Census (2000, pp. 55 and D–4). Our estimates of family income do not include the implicit return on home equity.

6. These estimates are from tabulations by Andrew Clarkwest using the Integrated Public Use Microsamples from the decennial census.

7. See Harding et al. (2005) for further details on the data and methodology.

8. The square of the multiple correlation is the percentage of the income variance explained by parental characteristics.

REFERENCES

Altonji, Joseph, and Thomas Dunn. 2000. "An Intergenerational Model of Wages, Hours, and Earnings." *Journal of Human Resources* 35(2): 221–258.

Ashenfelter, Orley, and Cecelia Rouse. 1998. "Income, Schooling, and Ability: Evidence from a New Sample of Identical Twins." *Quarterly Journal of Economics* 113: 317–323.

Björklund, Anders, and Laura Chadwick. 2002. "Intergenerational Income Mobility in Permanent and Separated Families." Swedish Institute for Social Research, Stockholm University.

Björklund, Anders, Markus Jäntti, and Gary Solon. 2005. "Influences of Nature and Nurture of Earnings: A Report on a Study of Various Sibling Types in Sweden," in Samuel Bowles, Herbert Gintis, and Melissa Osborne, eds., *Unequal Chances: Family Background and Economic Success.* Princeton, NJ: Princeton University Press and Russell Sage.

Gale, William G., and John Karl Scholz. 1994. "Intergenerational Transfers and the Accumulation of Wealth." *Journal of Economic Perspectives* 8(4): 145–160.

Goldberger, Arthur. 1978. "The Genetic Determination of Income: Comment." *American Economic Review* 68(5): 960–969.

Harding, David J., Christopher Jencks, Leonard M. Lopoo, and Susan E. Mayer. 2005. "The Changing Effect of Family Background on the Incomes of American Adults." In Samuel Bowles, Herbert Gintis, and Melissa Osborne, eds., *Unequal Chances: Family Background and Economic Success*. Princeton, NJ: Princeton University Press and Russell Sage.

Hauser, Robert, and David Featherman. 1976. "Equality of Schooling: Trends and Prospects." *Sociology of Education* 49(2): 99–120.

Hauser, Robert, and John Robert Warren. 1997. "Socioeconomic Indexes for Occupations: A Review, Update, and Critique." *Sociological Methodology* 27: 177–298.

Taubman, Paul. 1976. "The Determinants of Earnings: Genetics, Family, and Other Environments; A Study of Male Twins." *American Economic Review* 66(5): 858–870.

U.S. Bureau of the Census. 2000. "Money Income in the United States, 1999." *Current Population Reports*. Washington, DC: Government Printing Office.

Wolff, Edward. 2002. "Inheritances and Wealth Inequality, 1989–1998." *American Economic Review* 92(2): 260–264.

58

The Educational and
Early Occupational Attainment Process

WILLIAM H. SEWELL, ARCHIBALD O. HALLER,
AND ALEJANDRO PORTES

Blau and Duncan (1967:165–172) have recently presented a path model of the occupational attainment process of the American adult male population. This basic model begins with two variables describing the early stratification position of each person; these are his father's educational and occupational attainment statuses. It then moves to two behavioral variables; these are the educational level the individual has completed and the prestige level of his first job. The dependent variable is the person's occupational prestige position in 1962. That the model is not without power is attested by the fact that it accounts for about 26 percent of the variance in educational attainment, 33 percent of the variance in first job, and 42 percent of the variance in 1962 levels of occupational attainment. Various additions to the basic model are presented in the volume, but none is clearly shown to make much of an improvement in it. These include nativity, migration, farm origin, subgroup position, marriage, and assortative mating. Without detracting from the excellence of the Blau and Duncan analysis, we may make several observations.

1) Because the dependent behaviors are occupational prestige attainments—attainment levels in a stratification system—it is appropriate to single out variables indicating father's stratification position as the most relevant social structural inputs. It is unfortunate that practical considerations prevented the inclusion of psychological inputs in their model, especially considering the repeated references to one such—mental ability—in the literature on differential occupational attainment (Lipset and Bendix, 1959:203–226; Sewell and Armer, 1966). More recently, this gap has been partially filled (Duncan, 1968).

2) Also omitted are social psychological factors which mediate the influence of the input variables on attainment. This, too, is unfortunate in view not only of the speculative theory but also the concrete research in social psychology, which suggests the importance of such intervening variables as reference groups (Merton, 1957:281–386), significant others (Gerth and Mills, 1953: 84–91), self-concept (Super, 1957:80–100), behavior expectations (Gross et al., 1958), levels of educational and occupational

William H. Sewell, Archibald O. Haller, and Alejandro Portes, "The Educational and Early Occupational Attainment Process," *American Sociological Review* 34 (February 1969), pp. 82–92.

aspiration (Haller and Miller, 1963; Ku-vlesky and Ohlendorf, 1967; Ohlendorf et al., 1967), and experiences of success or failure in school (Parsons, 1959; Brookover et al., 1965).

It remains to be seen whether the addition of such psychological and social psychological variables is worthwhile, although there are reasons for believing that at least some of them may be. First, an explanation of a behavior system requires a plausible causal argument, not just a set of path coefficients among temporally ordered variables. As indicated in Duncan's (1969) recent work, the introduction of social psychological mediating variables offers this possibility, but it does not guarantee it. As it stands, the Blau-Duncan model fails to indicate why any connection at all would be expected between the input variables, father's education and occupation, and the three subsequent factors: respondent's education, respondent's first job, and respondent's 1962 occupation. Granting differences among social psychological positions, they all agree that one's cognitions and motivations (including, among others, knowledge, self-concept, and aspirations) are developed in structured situations (including the expectations of others), and that one's actions (attainments in this case) are a result of the cognitive and motivational orientations one brings to the action situation, as well as the factors in the new situation itself. Second, if valid, a social psychological model will suggest new points at which the causal system may be entered in order to change the attainment behaviors of persons, an issue not addressed by the Blau and Duncan volume. Variables such as the expectations of significant others offer other possibilities for manipulating the outcomes, including educational attainments. Third, in addition to the above advantages,

a social psychological model of educational and occupational attainment might add to the explanation of variance in the dependent variables.

The Problem

The present report extends the attempts of the writers (Sewell and Armer, 1966; Sewell and Orenstein, 1965; Sewell and Shah, 1967; Sewell, 1964; Haller and Sewell, 1967; Portes et al., 1968; Haller, 1966; Haller and Miller, 1963; Miller and Haller, 1964; Sewell et al., 1957) to apply social psychological concepts to the explanation of variation in levels of educational and occupational attainment. We assume (1) that certain social structural and psychological factors—initial stratification position and mental ability, specifically—affect both the sets of significant others' influences bearing on the youth, and the youth's own observations of his ability; (2) that the influence of significant others, and possibly his estimates of his ability, affect the youth's levels of educational and occupational aspiration; (3) that the levels of aspiration affect subsequent levels of educational attainment; (4) that education in turn affects levels of occupational attainment. In the present analysis we assume that all effects are linear; also, that the social psychological variables perform only mediating functions.

More specifically, we present theory and data regarding what we believe to be a logically consistent social psychological model. This provides a plausible causal argument to link stratification and mental ability inputs through a set of social psychological and behavioral mechanisms to educational and occupational attainments. One compelling feature of the model is that some of the inputs may be manipulated through

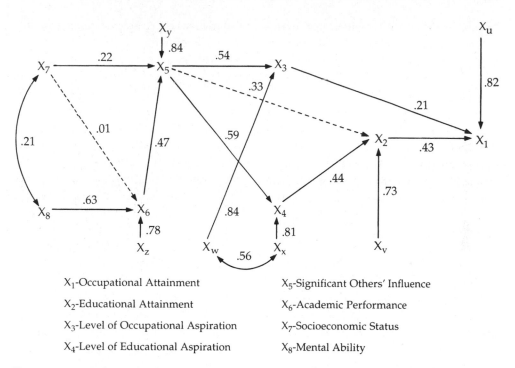

X₁-Occupational Attainment   X₅-Significant Others' Influence

X₂-Educational Attainment   X₆-Academic Performance

X₃-Level of Occupational Aspiration   X₇-Socioeconomic Status

X₄-Level of Educational Aspiration   X₈-Mental Ability

Figure 58.1   Path Coefficients of Antecedents of Educational and Occupational Attainment Levels

experimental or other purposive interventions. This means that parts of it can be experimentally tested in future research and that practical policy agents can reasonably hope to use it in order to change educational and occupational attainments.

A Social Psychological Model

The model treats causal relationships among eight variables. X_1 is the occupational prestige level attained by the adult person, or *occupational attainment* (OccAtt); X_2 is the educational level he had previously attained, or *educational attainment* (EdAtt); X_3 is the occupational prestige level to which he aspired as a youth, or *level of occupational aspiration* (LOA); X_4 is his *level of educational aspiration* as a youth (LEA); X_5 is the influence for educational achievement

exerted upon him by significant others while still in high school, or *significant others' influence* (SOI); X_6 is the quality of his *academic performance* in high school (AP); X_7 is the level of his family in the stratification system, or *socioeconomic status* (SES); and X_8 is his *mental ability* as measured while he was in high school (MA). Path models (Blau and Duncan, 1967:165–172; Wright, 1934; Wright, 1960; Heise, 1969) require a knowledge of the causal order among the variables. Beyond the causal arguments presented below, additional credibility is suggested by the existence of a plausible temporal order among variables. X_7 (SES) and X_8 (MA) precede everything else. X_5 (SOI) and X_6 (AP) precede both aspirations and attainments, and it can be assumed that for the most part X_6 precedes X_5. Youthful aspirations obviously precede later educational and occupational attainments. Pre-adult educational attainments precede adult occupational attainments.

By no means do all of the possible causal linkages seem defensible. The most likely ones are indicated in Figure 58.1. In it straight solid lines stand for causal lines that are to be theoretically expected, dotted lines stand for possible but theoretically debatable causal lines, and curved lines represent unanalyzed correlations among variables which cannot be assigned causal priority in present data.

Commencing from the left of the diagram, we assume, as has often been found before (Sewell and Shah, 1967; Sewell et al., 1957), that a low positive correlation, r_{78}, exists between the youth's measured mental ability (MA) and his parents' socioeconomic status (SES). This is the case: $r_{78} = .21$. We anticipate the existence of substantial effect of MA on academic performance (AP). We theorize that significant others' influence (SOI) is controlled by AP, and by socioeconomic status, as well as by exogenous factors, that they exert profound effects on aspiration, and that the latter in turn influences later attainments. A more detailed examination of the theory follows.

Working with partial conceptions of SOI (and using different terminology), Bordua (1960) and Sewell and Shah (1968) have shown that parents' expectations for the youths' attainments are important influences on later aspirations and attainment. Similarly, Cramer (1967), Alexander and Campbell (1964), Campbell and Alexander (1965), Haller and Butterworth (1960), and Duncan et al. (1968) have investigated peer influences on aspirations and attainments. Each of these sets of actors, plus some others, may be seen as a special case of reference group influence. Building on such

thinking, we have concluded that the key variable here is significant others' influence. Significant others are the specific persons from whom the individual obtains his level of aspiration, either because they serve as models or because they communicate to him their expectations for his behavior (Woelfel, 1967). The term "significant others" is more appropriate than that of "reference group" because it eliminates the implication that collectivities such as one's friends, or work groups, or parents are necessarily the influential agents for all individuals. Experimental research, beginning with Sherif's work (1935), has shown the importance of other persons in defining one's own situation. One obtains his social behavior tendencies largely through the influence of others. Herriott (1963) has carried this line of thinking into the present area of research. He has shown that one's conception of the educational behavior others think appropriate to him is highly correlated with his level of educational aspiration. Thus, significant others' influence is a central variable in a social psychological explanation of educational and occupational attainment. It is obviously important to discover the causal paths determining SOI, as well as those by which it exerts its effects on attainment. We hypothesize a substantial direct path (p_{57}) from socioeconomic status (SES) to SOI. We also hypothesize a substantial effect of mental ability on SOI. This is because we expect that the significant others with whom the youth interacts base their expectations for his educational and occupational attainments in part on his demonstrated abilities. In turn, this implies that the path from mental ability (MA) to SOI is indirect by way of academic performance (AP). Thus, we hypothesize the existence of a pronounced path from MA to

AP (p_{68}) and another from AP to SOI (p_{56}). So far we assume that one's grades in school are based on the quality of his performance. A strong undercurrent in the literature seems to have held, however, that the youth's family's SES has a direct influence on his grades (Havighurst and Neugarten, 1957:236–237). To our knowledge, this has not been adequately demonstrated, and in large high schools, often far removed from the youth's home and neighborhood, this may well be debatable. Nevertheless, since it is at least possible that school grades (the evidences of performance) are partly determined by teachers' desires to please prestigious parents or to reward "middle-class" behavior, we have drawn a dotted path (p_{67}) from SES to AP, allowing for the possibility of such an influence.

We hypothesize that the major effects of significant others' influence (SOI) on attainment are mediated by its effects on levels of aspiration. Thus, we have indicated a path (p_{35}) from SOI to level of occupational aspiration (LOA) and another (p_{45}) from SOI to level of educational aspiration (LEA). It is not inconsistent with this to suspect the possibility that SOI might have a direct influence on later educational attainment (EdAtt); we have thus included a dotted or debatable path (p_{25}) from SOI to EdAtt. Because we are here referring to SOI during late high school, it must necessarily refer largely to college education. There is, therefore, no reason to include such a path from SOI to occupational attainment.

Levels of educational aspiration (LEA) and occupational aspiration (LOA) are known to be highly correlated, since education is widely, and to some extent validly, considered to be a necessary condition for high occupational attainment (Haller and Miller, 1963:30, 39–42, 96). But LOA and LEA are not identical. (In these data, $r_{34.5} = r_{WX} = .56$.) We expect that LEA will have a pronounced effect on EdAtt (p_{24}), and that its entire effect on level of occupational attainment will be expressed through EdAtt. On the other hand, we do not hypothesize any effect of LOA on EdAtt which is not already contained in its correlation with LEA. Hence, there is no hypothetical path for LOA to EdAtt. A direct effect of LOA on OccAtt (p_{13}) is hypothesized, however.

There are 26 possible paths, given the sequence laid out above. As one can see by counting the paths (straight lines) in Figure 58.1, we hypothesize noteworthy effects for only eight of these—ten if the dotted lines are counted. If this were a rigorous theoretical model, path coefficients would be calculated only for these eight (or ten) supposed causal connections. We believe that because of the fact that it is not rigorous, and at this stage of our knowledge probably cannot be, it would be well to calculate all of the possible 26 path coefficients, using the calculated values as rough indicators of the influences operating in the system. If the theoretic reasoning is a fair description of the reality to which it is addressed, the path coefficients for the eight (or ten) predicted causal lines should be considerably greater than those for the remainder where no causal prediction was made. Also, it is entirely possible that some unhypothesized causal lines might turn out to be of importance. This, too, argues for calculating the whole set of 26. These data are presented in tabular form in Table 58.3.

Method

In 1957 all high school seniors in Wisconsin responded to an extensive questionnaire concerning their educational and occupational aspirations and a number of potentially related topics. In 1964 one of the authors (Sewell) directed a follow-up in which data on later educational and occupational attainments were collected from an approximately one-third random sample of the respondents in the original survey.

This study is concerned with those 929 subjects for whom data are available at both times, in 1957 and 1964, and who (a) are males and (b) whose fathers were farmers in 1957. Zero-order correlations are computed on all 929 cases, using a computer program which accepts missing data. All higher order coefficients are based on 739 cases for whom data on each variable were complete. (The matrices of zero-order correlations between all eight variables for those two sets of cases are practically identical.)

Variables

Level of occupational attainment (X_1—OccAtt) was measured by Duncan's (1961) socioeconomic index of occupational status.

Level of educational attainment (X_2—EdAtt) was operationalized with data obtained in 1964 by dividing the sample into those who have had at least some college education and those who have not had any at all.[1]

Level of occupational aspiration (X_3—LOA) was determined by assigning Duncan's (1961) socioeconomic index scores to the occupation indicated by the respondent as the one he desired to fill in the future.

Level of educational aspiration (X_4—LEA) is a dichotomous variable corresponding to the respondent's statement in 1957 of whether or not he planned to attend college after graduating from high school.

Index of significant others' influence (X_5—SOI) is a simple summated score (range: zero to three) of three variables: (a) The

youth's report of his parents' encouragement for college, dichotomized according to whether or not the respondent perceived direct parental encouragement for going to college. (b) The youth's report of his teachers' encouragement for college, dichotomized in a similar manner, according to whether or not direct teacher encouragement for college was perceived by the respondent. (c) Friends' college plans, dichotomized according to the respondent's statement that most of his close friends planned or did not plan to go to college. These variables, all emphasizing education, were combined because they reflect the same conceptual dimension, and that dimension is theoretically more relevant than any of its component parts. That the three components do in fact measure the same dimension is attested by the positive correlations among them and a subsequent factor analysis. These correlations and the correlation of each with the summated variable, significant others' influence, are shown in Table 58.1. It may be relevant to point out the composition of this significant others' index in the light of Kelley's distinction (1952). Clearly, the perceptions of direct parental and teacher pressures toward college conform to the classic case of normative reference groups. The educational plans of close friends, on the other hand, may be thought of as having mixed functions. First, close peer groups may exercise pressure toward conformity, and second, friends' plans also serve for the individual's cognitive comparison of himself with "people like himself." Therefore, though the main character of the dimension indicated by this index is clearly normative, it can be thought of as containing some elements of an evaluative function as well.

Quality of academic performance (X_6—AP) is measured by a reflected arc sine

Table 58.1   Zero-Order Correlations Between Indicators of Significant Others' Influence Regarding College

	Teachers' Influence	Friends' Influence	Index of Significant Others' Influence
Parental Influence	.37	.26	.74
Teachers' Influence	--	.32	.72
Friends' Influence	--	--	.68
Significant Others' Influence	--	--	--

transformation of each student's rank in his high school class.

Socioeconomic status (X_7—SES) is measured by a factor-weighted combination of the education of the respondent's father and mother, his perception of the economic status of the family, his perception of possible parental support should he choose to go to college and the approximate amount of such support, and the occupation of his father.[2]

Measured mental ability (X_8—MA) is indexed by Henmon-Nelson test scores (1942). The data were taken when the youths were in the junior year of high school. The scores, originally recorded as percentile-ranks, were treated with an arc sine transformation to approximate a normal distribution.[3]

Results

The zero-order correlation coefficients among eight variables are presented in Table 58.2. A complete path diagram would involve too many lines to be intelligible, because path coefficients presented in Figure 58.1 were calculated for all 26 possible lines implied in the causal order specified above. With the exception of the theoretically dubious direct path from SES to AP, which turned out to be $p_{67} = .01$, each of the path coefficients for causal lines hypothesized in Figure 58.1 is larger than

those not hypothesized. Both sets of standardized beta (or path) coefficients are presented in Table 58.3.

This table shows that the reasoning presented in the above section, offering a social psychological explanation for educational and occupational attainment, cannot be too far off the mark. We had hypothesized that SOI (significant others' influence) was of central importance. In fact, it has notable direct effects on three subsequent variables, each of which bears ultimately on prestige level of occupational attainment. Both theory and data agree that SOI has direct effects on levels of educational and occupational aspiration, as well as educational (i.e., college) attainment. In turn, each aspiration variable appears to have the predicted substantial effects on its respective attainment variable. Looking at its antecedents, we note theory and data again agree that SOI is affected directly by SES and indirectly by measured mental ability through the latter's effect on the youth's academic performance. The latter variable is crucial because it provides (or is correlated with) palpable evidence that significant others can observe and, thus to a degree, align their expectations for the youth with his demonstrated ability.

None of the unpredicted paths is very strong, but we must recognize that there may be more operating in such a system than we were able to anticipate from previous

Table 58.2 Zero-Order Correlations

	X₁ Occupational Attainment (Prestige Scores: Duncan)	X₂ Educational Attainment (Years College)	X₃ Level of Occupational Aspiration	X₄ Level of Educational Aspiration	X₅ Significant Others' Influence	X₆ Academic Performance (Grade Point)	X₇ Socio-economic Status	X₈ Measured Mental Ability
X₁-Occ. Att.	–	.52	.43	.38	.41	.37	.14	.33
X₂-Ed. Att.	–	–	.53	.61	.57	.48	.23	.40
X₃-LOA	–	–	–	.70	.53	.43	.15	.41
X₄-LEA	–	–	–	–	.59	.46	.26	.40
X₅-SOI	–	–	–	–	–	.49	.29	.41
X₆-AP	–	–	–	–	–	–	.16	.62
X₇-SES	–	–	–	–	–	–	–	.21
X₈-MA	–	–	–	–	–	–	–	–

Table 58.3 Standardized Beta Coefficients for Hypothesized and Non-Hypothesized Causal Paths

Dependent Variables	X_2 EdAtt	X_3 LOA	X_4 LEA	X_5 SOI	X_6 AP	X_7 SES	X_8 MA
				Independent Variables			
X_6 AP	--	--	--	--	--	*(.01)*	.62
X_5 SOI	--	--	--	--	.39	.21	.13
X_4 LEA	--	--	--	.45	.18	.07	.08
X_3 LOA	--	--	--	.42	.12	-.02	.16
X_2 EdAtt	--	.07	.34	(.23)	.17	.05	.03
X_1 OccAtt	.38	.19	-.10	.11	.06	.00	.04

Figures in italics are coefficients for paths hypothesized in Figure 58.1.

Figures in parentheses refer to theoretically debatable causal lines.

thinking. There is a pair of perhaps consequential direct paths from academic performance to educational aspiration (p_{46} = .18) and to educational attainment (p_{26} = .17). There are several possibilities. The data might imply the existence of a mediating factor, such as one's self conception of his ability, a factor which could influence both educational aspirations and attainment. They also suggest that not all of the effect of ability on educational aspiration and attainments is mediated by SOI. Finally, one's ability may exert a continuing effect on his educational attainments quite apart from the mediation of either significant others or aspirations—and therefore apart from one's conception of his ability. Arguments such as these, however, should not be pressed too far because the figures are small. Another unexpected but noteworthy path links mental ability directly to level of occupational aspiration. We offer no speculation regarding it.

So far we have seen that a consistent and plausible social psychological position is at least moderately well borne out by the analysis of lines of apparent influence of its variables when they are arranged in causal order. How well does the total set of independent variables work in accounting for variance in the attainment variables? In brief, $R^2_{1.2345678}$ = .34 and $R^2_{2.345678}$ = .50. Thus, the variables account for 34 percent of the variance in level of occupational attainment and 50 percent of the variance in level of educational attainment. Obviously, variables X_3 through X_8 are much more effective in accounting for educational attainment than in accounting for occupational attainment. Indeed, educational attainment alone accounts for 27 percent of the variance in occupational attainment (from Table 58.3, r^2_{12} = .52² = .27). What we have here, then, is a plausible causal system functioning primarily to explain variation in educational attainment. This, in turn, has considerable effect on occupational attainment. The same set of variables adds a small but useful amount to the explanation of occupational attainment variance beyond that contributed by its explanation of educational attainment.[4]

Discussion and Conclusions

Using father's occupational prestige, the person's educational attainment, and his first job level, Blau and Duncan (1967:165–172) were able to account for 33 percent of the variance in occupational attainment of a nationwide sample of American men. Neither our sample nor our variables are identical with theirs; so it is impossible to assess the total contribution of this study to the state of knowledge as reflected in their work. Educational attainment is strategic in both studies and in this regard the studies are fairly comparable. The present model adds a great deal to the explanation of the social psychological factors affecting that variable. The prospects seem good, too, that if the present model were to be applied to a sample coming from a wider range of the American stratification system with greater age variation, it might prove to be more powerful than it appears with our sample of young farm-reared men. In general, the present take-off on the Blau-Duncan approach to occupational attainment levels seems worthy of further testing and elaboration.

Several comments are appropriate regarding the social psychological position and data presented here. (1) Clearly, the variable we have called significant others' influence is an important factor. The present evidence appears to show that once formed its effects are far-reaching. Also, besides being a powerful explanatory factor, significant others' influence should be amenable to manipulation. It thus suggests itself as a point at which external agents might intervene to change educational and occupational attainment levels. This means that at least part of the system is theoretically amenable to experimental testing. The parts of the present model which are hypothetically dependent upon this variable might be more securely tested if such experiments can be worked out. Also, practical change agents might be able to change levels of attainment, either by inserting themselves or others as new significant others or

by changing the expectations existing significant others have for the individual. There may well be a substantial pay-off from more refined work with this variable.

(2) The results seem to indicate, too, that aspirations (a special class of attitudes) are in fact performing mediational functions in transmitting anterior factors into subsequent behaviors. This has been a subject of recent debate, much of which has in effect held that attitudinal variables are useless epiphenomena. This was recently discussed by Fendrich (1967).

Such encouraging results do not, however, mitigate the need for (a) general experimental determination of the supposed effects of attitudes on behaviors, and (b) specific experimental determination of the effects of aspirations on attainments.

(3) The question may be raised as to the extent to which this system is inherently culture-bound. One might wonder whether attainment behavior within an institutionalized pattern of "sponsored" rather than "contest" achievement (Turner, 1960) would change the path model. Besides this (and perhaps other institutionalized types of achievement patterns), there is also the question of the relevance of the model for ascribed occupational attainment systems. Obviously we do not have data bearing on these questions but we may at least discuss them. Let us suppose that the same eight variables are measured on youth in a "sponsored" achievement context. We speculate that if measured mental ability is the basis of selection of those who are to be advanced, then the direct path from mental ability to significant others' influence would increase because sponsors are significant others. (This would require a more general measure of significant others' influence than was used here.) If a variable other

than mental ability or socioeconomic status is important to the sponsors, then the residual effect of unmeasured variables on significant others' influence would increase. Since one's sponsors presumably influence one's aspirations and aspirations in turn mediate attainment, the rest of the model probably would not change much.

Consider the case of ascribed attainment. Here one's parents' position determines what one's significant others will expect of one; mental ability is either irrelevant or controlled by family position; and one's aspirations are controlled by the family. The importance of higher education may vary among basically ascribed systems: in one it may be unimportant, in another it may merely validate one's status, or in still another it may train ascribed elites to fulfill the key social roles in the society. If educational attainment is important within the social system, aspirations will mediate the influence of significant others upon it, and it in turn will mediate occupational attainment. If not, occupational aspirations will mediate occupational attainment and educational attainment will drop out of the path model. In short, by allowing for variations in the path coefficients, the same basic social psychological model might work well to describe attainment in stratification and mobility systems quite different from that of the present sample.

(4) The linear model used here seems to be an appropriate way to operationalize social psychological positions holding that the function of "intervening" attitudinal variables is to mediate the influence of more fundamental social structural and psychological variables on behavior. By assuming linear relations among variables and applying a path system to the analysis, we have cast the attainment problem in such a framework. It seems to have worked quite well. We are sufficiently encouraged by this attempt to recommend that a parallel tack might be made on problems in which the overt behavior variables are quite different from educational and occupational attainment.

(5) Nonetheless, satisfactory as such a linear model and its accompanying theory seems to be, there is still the possibility that other techniques flowing from somewhat different social psychological assumptions might be better. It is possible that, in the action situation, enduring attitudes (such as educational and occupational aspirations) may function as independent forces which express themselves in relevant overt behaviors to the degree that other personality and situational variables permit. Linear models would thus be effective to the degree that the persons modify their aspirations to bring them in line with potentials for action offered by the latter variables. More importantly, the combined effects of aspirational and facilitational variables would produce nonlinear accelerating curves of influence on behavior variables. For the present types of data, this would imply that parental stratification position, mental ability, and significant others' influence not only produce aspirations, but also, to the extent to which these influences continue more or less unchanged on into early adulthood, they function as differential facilitators for the expression of aspirations in attainments. If this is true, a nonlinear system of statistical analysis handling interaction effects would be even more powerful than the one used in this paper.

(6) It should be remembered that the most highly educated of these young men had just begun their careers when the final data were collected. If the distance between

them and the less educated widens, the occupational attainment variance accounted for by the model may well increase. The direct relations of some of the antecedents to occupational attainment may also change. In particular, mental ability may show a higher path to occupational attainment.

(7) Finally, although the results reported in this paper indicate that the proposed model has considerable promise for explaining educational and early occupational attainment of farm boys, its adequacy should now be tested on populations with a more differentiated socioeconomic background. It is quite possible that in such populations the effects of socioeconomic status on subsequent variables may be significantly increased. The effects of other variables in the system may also be altered when the model is applied to less homogeneous populations.

The present research appears to have extended knowledge of the causal mechanism influencing occupational attainment. Most of this was accomplished by providing a consistent social psychological model which adds to our ability to explain what is surely one of its key proximal antecedents, educational attainment.

NOTES

Revision of paper originally prepared for delivery at the joint sessions of the Rural Sociological Society and the American Sociological Association, San Francisco, August 1967. The research reported here was supported by the University of Wisconsin Graduate School, by the Cooperative State Research Service, and the University's College of Agriculture for North Central Regional Research Committee NC–86, by funds to the Institute for Research on Poverty at the University of Wisconsin provided by the Office of Economic Opportunity pursuant to the provisions of the Economic Opportunity Act of 1964, and by a grant from the National Institute of Health, U. S. Public Health Service (M–6275). The writers wish to thank Otis Dudley Duncan for his careful reading and incisive criticisms and Vimal P. Shah for help in the statistical analysis. The conclusions are the full responsibility of the authors.

1. It is important to note that the timing of the follow-up was such as to allow most individuals to complete their education up to the bachelor's degree and beyond. It is unlikely that the educational attainment of the sample as a whole will change much in the years to come. On the other hand, while the span of seven years allowed those individuals who did not continue their education to find a stable position in the occupational structure and even improve upon it, there was not enough time for those who continued their education to do the same. A few of the latter were still in school; most had just begun their occupational careers. It is therefore possible that a follow-up taken five or ten years from now would show greater differentiation in attainments as the educated group gathers momentum and moves up in the occupational world.

2. Naturally, father's occupation is a constant in this subsample of farm-reared males. It is important to note that the SES mean and standard deviations for this subsample are considerably lower than for the total sample. The low and homogeneous SES levels of this subsample may yield atypical relations among the variables.

3. Our previous research (Sewell and Armer, 1966; Haller and Sewell, 1967) has led us to be skeptical of claims that local ecological and school class compositional factors influence aspirations and attainments. Nevertheless the zero-order intercorrelations of five such variables and their correlations with X_1–X_8 are available (although they are not presented here). Two of these pertain to the county in which the youth attended high school: county level of living and degree of urbanization. Three pertain to his high school senior class: average SES of the class, percentage of the class members whose fathers attended college, and percentage of the class members whose fathers had professional-level

occupations. Though substantially correlated with each other, the variables are uncorrelated with the variables in the above model.

4. Some readers will be interested in the path coefficients as calculated only for the lines hypothesized in the diagram. For this reason and because of the diagram's parsimony, we have calculated the values for each of its eight paths (or ten, including dubious ones). The restricted model explains 47 and 33 percent of the variance in X_2 and X_1, respectively. Data not presented here show that the model reproduces the zero-order correlation matrix quite well. For this reason and because the model is an effective predictor of X_2 and X_1, it may be considered to be fairly valid. Nonetheless, it seems more prudent to rest our case on the less presumptuous data already presented in Table 58.3. This is why the coefficients presented in the diagram are not discussed here.

REFERENCES

Alexander, C. Norman, Jr., and Ernest Q. Campbell. 1964. "Peer influences on adolescent educational aspirations and attainments." American Sociological Review 29 (August):568–575.

Blau, Peter M., and Otis Dudley Duncan. 1967. The American Occupational Structure. New York: Wiley.

Bordua, David J. 1960. "Educational aspirations and parental stress on college." Social Forces 38 (March):262–269.

Brookover, Wilbur B., Jean M. LePere, Don E. Hamachek, Shailer Thomas, and Edsel L. Erickson. 1965. Self-Concept of Ability and School Achievement. East Lansing: Michigan State University, Bureau of Educational Research Services.

Campbell, Ernest Q., and C. Norman Alexander. 1965. "Structural effects and interpersonal relationships." American Journal of Sociology 71 (November):284–289.

Cramer, M. R. 1967. "The relationship between educational and occupational plans of high school students." Paper presented at the meeting of the Southern Sociological Society, Atlanta (unpublished).

Duncan, Otis Dudley. 1961. "A socioeconomic index for all occupations." Pp. 109–138 in Albert J. Reiss, Jr. (ed.), Occupations and Social Status. New York: Free Press.

_____. 1968. "Ability and achievement." Eugenics Quarterly 15 (March):1–11.

_____. 1969. "Contingencies in the construction of causal models." Edgar F. Borgatta, (ed.), Sociological Methodology. San Francisco: Jossey-Bass.

Duncan, Otis Dudley, Archibald O. Haller, and Alejandro Portes. 1968. "Peer influences on aspirations: a reinterpretation." American Journal of Sociology 74 (September):119–137.

Fendrich, James M. 1967. "Perceived reference group support: racial attitudes and overt behavior." American Sociological Review 32 (December):960–970.

Gerth, Hans, and C. Wright Mills. 1953. Character and Social Structure. New York: Harcourt, Brace and World.

Gross, Neal, Ward S. Mason, and Alexander W. McEachern. 1958. Explorations in Role Analysis. New York: Wiley.

Haller, Archibald O. 1966. "Occupational choices of rural youth." Journal of Cooperative Extension 4 (Summer):93–102.

Haller, Archibald O., and Charles E. Butterworth. 1960. "Peer influences on levels of occupational and educational aspiration." Social Forces 38 (May):289–295.

Haller, Archibald O., and Irwin W. Miller. 1963. The Occupational Aspiration Scale: Theory, Structure and Correlates. East Lansing: Michigan Agricultural Experiment Station Bulletin 288.

Haller, Archibald O., and William H. Sewell. 1967. "Occupational choices of Wisconsin farm boys." Rural Sociology 32 (March):37–55.

Havighurst, Robert J., and Bernice L. Neugarten. 1957. Society and Education. Boston: Allyn and Bacon.

Heise, David R. 1969. "Problems in path analysis and causal inference." Edgar F. Borgatta, (ed.), Sociological Methodology. San Francisco: Jossey-Bass.

Henmon, V. A. C., and M. J. Nelson. 1942. The Henmon-Nelson Test of Mental Ability. Boston: Houghton Mifflin Company.

Herriott, Robert E. 1963. "Some social determinants of educational aspiration." Harvard Educational Review 33 (Spring):157–177.

Kelley, Harold H. 1952. "Two functions of reference groups." Pp. 410–414 in Guy E. Swanson et al. (eds.), Readings in Social Psychology. New York: Henry Holt and Company.

Kuvlesky, William P., and George W. Ohlendorf. 1967. A Bibliography of Literature on Status Projections of Youth: I. Occupational Aspirations and Expectations. College Station: Texas A&M University, Department of Agricultural Economics and Sociology.

Lipset, Seymour M., and Reinhard Bendix. 1959. Social Mobility in Industrial Society. Berkeley: University of California Press.

Merton, Robert K. 1957. Social Theory and Social Structure. New York: Free Press.

Miller, I. W., and Archibald O. Haller. 1964. "The measurement of level of occupational aspiration." Personnel and Guidance Journal 42 (January):448–455.

Ohlendorf, George W., Sherry Wages, and William P. Kuvlesky. 1967. A Bibliography of Literature on Status Projections of Youth: II. Educational Aspirations and Expectations. College Station: Texas A & M University, Department of Agricultural Economics and Sociology.

Parsons, Talcott. 1959. "The school class as a social system." Harvard Educational Review 29 (Summer):297–318.

Portes, Alejandro, Archibald O. Haller, and William H. Sewell. 1968. "Professional executive vs. farming as unique occupational choices." Rural Sociology 33 (June):153–159.

Sewell, William H. 1964. "Community of residence and college plans." American Sociological Review 29 (February):24–38.

Sewell, William H., and J. Michael Armer. 1966. "Neighborhood context and college plans." American Sociological Review 31 (April): 159–168.

Sewell, William H., Archibald O. Haller, and Murray A. Straus. 1957. "Social status and educational and occupational aspiration." American Sociological Review 22 (February):67–73.

Sewell, William H., and Alan M. Orenstein. 1965. "Community of residence and occupational choice." American Journal of Sociology 70 (March):551–563.

Sewell, William H., and Vimal P. Shah. 1967. "Socioeconomic status, intelligence, and the attainment of higher education." Sociology of Education 40 (Winter):1–23.

_____. 1968. "Social class, parental encouragement, and educational aspirations." American Journal of Sociology 73 (March):559–572.

Sherif, Muzafer. 1935. "A study of some social factors in perception." Archives of Psychology Number 187.

Super, Donald E. 1957. The Psychology of Careers. New York: Harper.

Turner, Ralph H. 1960. "Sponsored and contest mobility and the school system." American Sociological Review 25 (December):855–867.

Woelfel, Joseph. 1967. "A paradigm for research on significant others." Paper presented at the Joint Session of the Society for the Study of Social Problems and the American Sociological Association, San Francisco (unpublished).

Wright, Sewall. 1934. "The method of path coefficients." Annals of Mathematical Statistics 5 (September):161–215.

_____. 1960. "Path coefficients and regression coefficients: alternative or complementary concept?" Biometrics 16 (June):189–202.

|| 59 ||

Ain't No Makin' It

Leveled Aspirations in a Low-Income Neighborhood

JAY MACLEOD

"Any child can grow up to be president." So maintains the dominant ideology in the United States. This perspective characterizes American society as an open one in which barriers to success are mainly personal rather than social. In this meritocratic view, education ensures equality of opportunity for all individuals, and economic inequalities result from differences in natural qualities and in one's motivation and will to work. Success is based on achievement rather than ascription. Individuals do not inherit their social status—they attain it on their own. Because schooling mitigates gender, class, and racial barriers to success, the ladder of social mobility is there for all to climb. A favorite Hollywood theme, the rags-to-riches story resonates in the psyche of the American people. We never tire of hearing about Andrew Carnegie, for his experience validates much that we hold dear about America, the land of opportunity. Horatio Alger's accounts of the spectacular

mobility achieved by men of humble origins through their own unremitting efforts occupy a treasured place in our national folklore. The American Dream is held out as a genuine prospect for anyone with the drive to achieve it.

"I ain't goin' to college. Who wants to go to college? I'd just end up gettin' a shitty job anyway." So says Freddie Piniella,[1] an intelligent eleven-year-old boy from Clarendon Heights, a low-income housing development in a northeastern city. This statement, pronounced with certitude and feeling, completely contradicts our achievement ideology. Freddie is pessimistic about his prospects for social mobility and disputes schooling's capacity to "deliver the goods." Such a view offends our sensibilities and seems a rationalization. But Freddie has a point. What of Carnegie's grammar school classmates, the great bulk of whom no doubt were left behind to occupy positions in the class structure not much different from those held by their parents? What about the static, nearly permanent element in the working class, whose members consider the chances for mobility remote and thus despair of all hope? These people are shunned, hidden, forgotten—and for good reason—because just as the self-made man is a testament to certain American ideals, so the very existence of an "underclass" in American society is a living contradiction to those ideals.

Utter hopelessness is the most striking aspect of Freddie's outlook. Erik H. Erikson writes that hope is the basic ingredient of all vitality;[2] stripped of hope, there is little left to lose. How is it that in contemporary America a boy of eleven can feel bereft of a future worth embracing? This is not what the United States is supposed to be. The United States is the nation of hopes and dreams and opportunity. As Ronald Reagan remarked in his 1985 State of the Union Address, citing the accomplishments of a young Vietnamese immigrant, "Anything is possible in America if we have the faith, the will, and the heart."[3] But to Freddie Piniella and many other Clarendon Heights young people who grow up in households where their parents and older siblings are unemployed, undereducated, or imprisoned, Reagan's words ring hollow. For them the American Dream, far from being a genuine prospect, is not even a dream. It is a hallucination.

I first met Freddie Piniella in the summer of 1981 when as a student at a nearby university I worked as a counselor in a youth enrichment program in Clarendon Heights. For ten weeks I lived a few blocks from the housing project and worked intensively with nine boys, aged eleven to thirteen. While engaging them in recreational and educational activities, I was surprised by the modesty of their aspirations. The world of middle-class work was entirely alien to them; they spoke about employment in construction, factories, the armed forces, or, predictably, professional athletics. In an ostensibly open society, they were a group of boys whose occupational aspirations did not even cut across class lines. . . .

The male teenage world of Clarendon Heights is populated by two divergent peer groups. The first group, dubbed the Hallway Hangers because of the group's propensity for "hanging" in a particular hallway in the project [i.e., outside doorway #13], consists predominantly of white boys. Their characteristics and attitudes stand in marked contrast to the second group, which is composed almost exclusively of black youths who call themselves the Brothers. Surprisingly, the Brothers speak with relative optimism about their futures, while the Hallway Hangers are despondent about their prospects for social mobility. . . .

Before describing the boys' orientation toward work [in more detail], I would like to make an analytical distinction between aspirations and expectations. Both involve assessments of one's desires, abilities, and the character of the opportunity structure. In articulating one's aspirations, an individual weighs his or her preferences more heavily; expectations are tempered by perceived capabilities and available opportunities. Aspirations are one's preferences relatively unsullied by anticipated constraints; expectations take these constraints squarely into account.[4]

The Hallway Hangers: Keeping a Lid on Hope

Conventional, middle-class orientations toward employment are inadequate to describe the Hallway Hangers' approach to work. The notion of a career, a set of jobs that are connected to one another in a logical progression, has little relevance to these boys. They are hesitant when asked about their aspirations and expectations. This hesitancy is not the result of indecision; rather it stems from the fact that these boys see little choice involved in getting a job. No matter how hard I pressed him, for instance, Jinks refused to articulate his aspirations: "I think you're kiddin' yourself to have any. We're just gonna take whatever we can get." Jinks is a perceptive boy, and his answer seems to be an accurate depiction of the situation. Beggars cannot be choosers, and these boys have nothing other than unskilled labor to offer on a credential-based job market.

It is difficult to gauge the aspirations of most of the Hallway Hangers. Perhaps at a younger age they had dreams for their futures. At ages sixteen, seventeen, and eighteen, however, their own job experiences as well as those of family members have contributed to a deeply entrenched cynicism about their futures. What is perceived as the cold, hard reality of the job market weighs very heavily on the Hallway Hangers; they believe their preferences will have almost no bearing on the work they actually will do. Their expectations are not merely tempered by perceptions of the opportunity structure; even their aspirations are crushed by their estimation of the job market. These generalizations may seem bold and rather extreme, but they do not lack ethnographic support.

The pessimism and uncertainty with which the Hallway Hangers view their futures emerge clearly when the boys are asked to speculate on what their lives will be like in twenty years.

(all in separate interviews)

STONEY: Hard to say. I could be dead tomorrow. Around here, you gotta take life day by day.

BOO-BOO: I dunno. I don't want to think about it. I'll think about it when it comes.

FRANKIE: I don't fucking know. Twenty years. I may be fucking dead. I live a day at a time. I'll probably be in the fucking pen.

SHORTY: Twenty years? I'm gonna be in jail.

These responses are striking not only for the insecurity and despondency they reveal, but also because they do not include any mention of work. It is not that work is unimportant—for people as strapped for money as the Hallway Hangers are, work is crucial. Rather, these boys are indifferent to the issue of future employment. Work is a given; they all hope to hold jobs of one kind or another in order to support themselves and their families. But the Hallway Hangers believe the character of work, at least all work in which they are likely to be involved, is essentially the same: boring, undifferentiated, and unrewarding. Thinking about their future jobs is a useless activity for the Hallway Hangers. What is there to think about?

For Steve and Jinks, although they do see themselves employed in twenty years, work is still of tangential importance.

JM: If you had to guess, what do you think you'll be doing twenty years from now?

(in separate interviews)

STEVE: I don't fucking know. Working probably. Have my own pad, my own

house. Bitches, kids. Fucking fridge full
of brewskies. Fine wife, likes to get laid.

JINKS: Twenty years from now? Probably
kicked back in my own apartment doing
the same shit I'm doing now—getting
high. I'll have a job, if I'm not in the service, if war don't break out, if I'm not
dead. I just take one day at a time.

Although the Hallway Hangers expect to
spend a good portion of their waking hours
on the job, work is important to them not
as an end in itself, but solely as a means to
an end—money.

In probing the occupational aspirations
and expectations of the Hallway Hangers, I
finally was able to elicit from them some
specific hopes. Although Shorty never mentions his expectations, the rest of the Hallway Hangers have responded to my
prodding with some definite answers. The
range of answers as well as how they change
over time are as significant as the particular
hopes each boy expresses.

Boo-Boo's orientation toward work is
typical of the Hallway Hangers. He has
held a number of jobs in the past, most of
them in the summer. During his freshman
year in high school Boo-Boo worked as a
security guard at school for $2.50 an hour
in order to make restitution for a stolen car
he damaged. Boo-Boo also has worked on
small-scale construction projects through a
summer youth employment program called
Just-A-Start, at a pipe manufacturing site,
and as a clerk in a gift shop. Boo-Boo wants
to be an automobile mechanic. Upon graduating from high school, he studied auto
mechanics at a technical school on a scholarship. The only black student in his class,
Boo-Boo was expelled early in his first term
after racial antagonism erupted into a fight.

Boo-Boo was not altogether disappointed,
for he already was unhappy with what he
considered the program's overly theoretical
orientation. (Howard London found this
kind of impatience typical of working-class
students in the community college he studied.[5]) Boo-Boo wanted hands-on training,
but "all's they were doing was telling me
about how it's made, stuff like that." Boo-
Boo currently is unemployed, but he recently had a chance for a job as a cook's
helper. Although he was not hired, the
event is significant nevertheless because
prior to the job interview, Boo-Boo claimed
that his ambition now was to work in a
restaurant. Here we have an example of the
primacy of the opportunity structure in determining the aspirations of the Hallway
Hangers. One job opening in another field
was so significant that the opening
prompted Boo-Boo to redefine totally his
aspirations.

In contrast to the rest of the Hallway
Hangers who are already on the job market,
Steve wants to stay in school for the two
years required to get his diploma. Yet he has
a similar attitude toward his future work as
do the other youths. He quit his summer
job with the Just-A-Start program and has
no concrete occupational aspirations. As for
expectations, he believes he might enlist in
the Air Force after graduation but adds, "I
dunno. I might just go up and see my
uncle, do some fuckin' construction or
something."

Many of these boys expect to enter military service. Jinks and Frankie mention it as
an option; Stoney has tried to enlist, but
without success. Although Jinks refuses to
think in terms of aspirations, he will say
what he expects to do after he finishes
school.

JM: What are you gonna do when you get out?

JINKS: Go into the service, like everybody else. The navy.

JM: What about after that?

JINKS: After that, just get a job, live around here.

JM: Do you have any idea what job you wanna get?

JINKS: No. No particular job. Whatever I can get.

Jinks subsequently quit school. He had been working twenty hours a week making clothes-racks in a factory with his brother. He left school with the understanding that he would be employed full-time, and he was mildly content with his situation: "I got a job. It ain't a good job, but other things will come along." Two weeks later, he was laid off. For the past three months he has been unemployed, hanging full-time in doorway #13.

Shorty has worked construction in the past and has held odd jobs such as shoveling snow. Shorty, an alcoholic, has trouble holding down a steady job, as he freely admits. He was enrolled in school until recently. Ordered by the court to a detoxification center, Shorty apparently managed to convince the judge that he had attended enough Alcoholics Anonymous meetings in the meantime to satisfy the court. He has not returned to school since, nor has he landed a job. Given that Shorty is often on the run from the police, he is too preoccupied with pressing everyday problems to give serious thought to his long-term future. It is not surprising that my ill-timed query about his occupational aspirations met with only an impatient glare. . . .

The definitions of aspirations and expectations given [earlier] suggest that an assessment of the opportunity structure and of one's capabilities impinge on one's preferences for the future. However, the portrait of the Hallway Hangers painted in these pages makes clear that "impinge" is not a strong enough word. But are the leveled aspirations and pessimistic expectations of the Hallway Hangers a result of strong negative assessments of their capabilities or of the opportunity structure?

This is not an easy question to answer. Doubtless, both factors come into play, but in the case of the Hallway Hangers, evaluation of the opportunity structure has the dominant role. Although in a discussion of why they do not succeed in school, the Hallway Hangers point to personal inadequacy ("We're all just fucking burnouts"; "We never did good anyways"), they look to outside forces as well. In general, they are confident of their own abilities.

(In a group interview)

JM: If you've got five kids up the high school with all A's, now are you gonna be able to say that any of them are smarter than any of you?

SLICK: *(immediately)* No.

JM: So how'd that happen?

SLICK: Because they're smarter in some areas just like we're smarter in some areas. You put them out here, right? And you put us up where they're living—they won't be able to survive out here.

SHORTY: But we'd be able to survive up there.

FRANKIE: See, what it is—they're smarter more academically because they're taught by teachers that teach academics.

JM: Not even streetwise, just academically, do you think you could be up where they are?

FRANKIE: Yeah.

CHRIS: Yeah.

SHORTY: Yeah.

JM: When it comes down to it, you're just as smart?

FRANKIE: Yeah.

SLICK: (*matter-of-factly*) We could be smarter.

FRANKIE: Definitely.

CHRIS: On the street, like.

FRANKIE: We're smart, we're smart, but we're just smart [inaudible]. It's fucking, y'know, we're just out to make money, man. I know if I ever went to fucking high school and college in a business course. . . .

SLICK: And concentrated on studying. . . .

FRANKIE: I know I could make it. I am a businessman.

JM: So all of you are sure that if you put out in school. . . .

FRANKIE: Yeah! If I went into business, I would, yeah. If I had the fucking money to start out with like some of these fucking rich kids, I'd be a millionaire. Fucking right I would be.

Although these comments were influenced by the dynamics of the group interview, they jibe with the general sense of self-confidence the Hallway Hangers radiate and indicate that they do not have low perceptions of their own abilities.

If their assessments of their own abilities do not account for the low aspirations of the Hallway Hangers, we are left, by way of explanation, with their perceptions of the job opportunity structure. The dominant view in the United States is that American society is an open one that values and differentially rewards individuals on the basis of their merits. The Hallway Hangers question this view, for it runs against the grain of their neighbors' experiences, their families' experiences, and their own encounters with the labor market.

The Clarendon Heights community, as a public housing development, is by definition made up of individuals who do not hold even modestly remunerative jobs. A large majority are on additional forms of public assistance; many are unemployed. Like most old housing projects, Clarendon Heights tends to be a cloistered, insular neighborhood, isolated from the surrounding community. Although younger residents certainly have external points of reference, their horizons are nevertheless very narrow. Their immediate world is composed almost entirely of people who have not "made it." To look around at a great variety of people—some lazy, some alcoholics, some energetic, some dedicated, some clever, some resourceful—and to realize all of them have been unsuccessful on the job market is powerful testimony against what is billed as an open society.

The second and much more intimate contact these boys have with the job market is through their families, whose occupational histories only can be viewed as sad and disillusioning by the Hallway Hangers. These are not people who are slothful or slow-witted; rather, they are generally industrious, intelligent, and very willing to work. With members of their families holding low-paying, unstable jobs or unable to find work at all, the Hallway Hangers are unlikely to view the job opportunity structure as an open one.

The third level of experience on which the Hallway Hangers draw is their own. These boys are not newcomers to the job market. As we have seen, all have held a variety of jobs. All except Steve are now on the job market year round, but only Stoney has a steady job. With the exceptions of Chris, who presently is satisfied with his success peddling drugs, and Steve, who is still in school, the Hallway Hangers are actively in search of decent work. Although they always seem to be following up on some promising lead, they are all unemployed. Furthermore, some who were counting on prospective employment have had their hopes dashed when it fell through. The work they have been able to secure typically has been in menial, dead-end jobs paying minimum wage.

Thus, their personal experience on the job market and the experiences of their family members and their neighbors have taught the Hallway Hangers that the job market does not necessarily reward talent or effort. Neither they nor their parents, older siblings, and friends have shared in the "spoils" of economic success. In short, the Hallway Hangers are under no illusions about the openness of the job opportunity structure. They are conscious, albeit vaguely, of a number of class-based obstacles to economic and social advancement. Slick, the most perceptive and articulate of the Hallway Hangers, points out particular barriers they must face.

SLICK: Out here, there's not the opportunity to make money. That's how you get into stealin' and all that shit.

(*in a separate interview*)
SLICK: That's why I went into the army—cuz there's no jobs out here right now

for people that, y'know, live out here. You have to know somebody, right?

In discussing the problems of getting a job, both Slick and Shorty are vocal.

SLICK: All right, to get a job, first of all, this is a handicap, out here. If you say you're from the projects or anywhere in this area, that can hurt you. Right off the bat: reputation.
SHORTY: Is this dude gonna rip me off, is he. . . .
SLICK: Is he gonna stab me?
SHORTY: Will he rip me off? Is he gonna set up the place to do a score or somethin'? I tried to get a couple of my buddies jobs at a place where I was working construction, but the guy says, "I don't want 'em if they're from there. I know you; you ain't a thief or nothing."

Frankie also points out the reservations prospective employers have about hiring people who live in Clarendon Heights. "A rich kid would have a better chance of getting a job than me, yeah. Me, from where I live, y'know, a high crime area, I was prob'ly crime-breaking myself, which they think your nice honest rich kid from a very respected family would never do."

Frankie also feels that he is discriminated against because of the reputation that attaches to him because of his brothers' illegal exploits. "Especially me, like I've had a few opportunities for a job, y'know. I didn't get it cuz of my name, because of my brothers, y'know. So I was deprived right there, bang. Y'know they said, 'No, no, no, we ain't havin' no Dougherty work for us.'" In a separate discussion, Frankie again makes this point. Arguing that he would have almost no chance to be hired as a fireman, despite ostensibly meritocratic hiring procedures, even if he scored very highly on the test, Frankie concludes, "Just cuz fuckin' where I'm from and what my name is."

The Hallway Hangers' belief that the opportunity structure is not open also emerges when we consider their responses to the question of whether they have the same chance as a middle- or upper-class boy to get a good job. The Hallway Hangers generally respond in the negative. When pushed to explain why, Jinks and Steve made these responses, which are typical.

(*in separate interviews*)
JINKS: Their parents got pull and shit.
STEVE: Their fucking parents know people.

Considering the boys' employment experiences and those of their families, it is not surprising that the Hallway Hangers' view of the job market does not conform to the dominant belief in the openness of the opportunity structure. They see a job market where rewards are based not on meritocratic criteria, but on "who you know." If "connections" are the keys to success, the Hallway Hangers know that they are in trouble.

Aside from their assessment of the job opportunity structure, the Hallway Hangers are aware of other forces weighing on their futures. A general feeling of despondency pervades the group. As Slick puts it, "The younger kids have nothing to hope for." The Hallway Hangers often draw attention to specific incidents that support their general and vague feelings of hopelessness and of the futility of nurturing aspirations or high expectations. Tales of police

brutality, of uncaring probation officers and callous judges, and of the "pull and hookups of the rich kids" all have a common theme, which Chris summarizes, "We don't get a fair shake and shit." Although they sometimes internalize the blame for their plight (Boo-Boo: "I just screwed up"; Chris: "I guess I just don't have what it takes"; Frankie: "We've just fucked up"), the Hallway Hangers also see, albeit in a vague and imprecise manner, a number of hurdles in their path to success with which others from higher social strata do not have to contend.

Insofar as contemporary conditions under capitalism can be conceptualized as a race by the many for relatively few positions of wealth and prestige, the low aspirations of the Hallway Hangers, more than anything else, seem to be a decision, conscious or unconscious, to withdraw from the running. The competition, they reason, is not a fair one when some people have an unobstructed lane. As Frankie maintains, the Hallway Hangers face numerous barriers: "It's a steeplechase, man. It's a motherfucking steeplechase." The Hallway Hangers respond in a way that suggests only a "sucker" would compete seriously under such conditions.

Chris's perspective seems a poignant, accurate description of the situation in which the Hallway Hangers find themselves.

CHRIS: I gotta get a job, any fucking job. Just a job. Make some decent money. If I could make a hundred bucks a week, I'd work. I just wanna get my mother out of the projects, that's all. But I'm fucking up in school. It ain't easy, Jay. I hang out there [in doorway #13] 'til about one o'clock every night. I never want to go to school. I'd much rather hang out and get high again. It's not that I'm dumb. You gimme thirty bucks today, and I'll give you one hundred tomorrow. I dunno. It's like I'm in a hole I can't get out of. I guess I could get out, but it's hard as hell. It's fucked up.

The Brothers: Ready at the Starting Line

Just as the pessimism and uncertainty with which the Hallway Hangers view their futures emerges when we consider what they perceive their lives will be like in twenty years, so do the Brothers' long-term visions serve as a valuable backdrop to our discussion of their aspirations. The ethos of the Brothers' peer group is a positive one; they are not resigned to a bleak future but are hoping for a bright one. Nowhere does this optimism surface more clearly than in the Brothers' responses to the question of what they will be doing in twenty years. Note the centrality of work in their views of the future.

(all in separate interviews)
SUPER: I'll have a house, a nice car, no one bothering me. Won't have to take no hard time from no one. Yeah, I'll have a good job, too.
JUAN: I'll have a regular house, y'know, with a yard and everything. I'll have a steady job, a good job. I'll be living the good life, the easy life.
MIKE: I might have a wife, some kids. I might be holding down a regular business job like an old guy. I hope I'll be able to do a lot of skiing and stuff like that when I'm old.

CRAIG: I'll probably be having a good job on my hands, I think. Working in an office as an architect, y'know, with my own drawing board, doing my own stuff, or at least close to there.

James takes a comic look into his future without being prompted to do so. "The ones who work hard in school, eventually it's gonna pay off for them and everything, and they're gonna have a good job and a family and all that. Not me though! I'm gonna have *myself*. I'm gonna have some money. And a different girl every day. And a different car. And be like this (*poses with one arm around an imaginary girl and the other on a steering wheel*)."

The Brothers do not hesitate to name their occupational goals. Although some of the Brothers are unsure of their occupational aspirations, none seems to feel that nurturing an aspiration is a futile exercise. The Brothers have not resigned themselves to taking whatever they can get. Rather, they articulate specific occupational aspirations (although these often are subject to change and revision).

Like all the Brothers, Super has not had extensive experience on the job market; he only has worked at summer jobs. For the past three summers, he has worked for the city doing maintenance work in parks and school buildings through a CETA-sponsored summer youth employment program. During the last year, Super's occupational aspirations have fluctuated widely. His initial desire to become a doctor was met with laughter from his friends. Deterred by their mocking and by a realization of the schooling required to be a doctor, Super immediately decided that he would rather go into business:

"Maybe I can own my own shop and shit." This aspiration, however, also was ridiculed. "Yeah, right," commented Mokey, "Super'll be pimping the girls, that kinda business." In private, however, Super still clings to the hope of becoming a doctor, although he cites work in the computer field as a more realistic hope. "Really, I don't know what I should do now. I'm kinda confused. First I said I wanna go into computers, right? Take up that or a doctor." The vagueness of Super's aspirations is important; once again, we get a glimpse of how little is known about the world of middle-class work, even for somebody who clearly aspires to it. Of one thing Super is certain: "I just know I wanna get a good job."

Although Super does not distinguish between what constitutes a good job and what does not, he does allude to criteria by which the quality of a job can be judged. First, a good job must not demand that one "work on your feet," a distinction, apparently, between white and blue-collar work. Second, a good job implies at least some authority in one's workplace, a point Super makes clearly, if in a disjointed manner. "Bosses—if you don't come on time, they yell at you and stuff like that. They want you to do work and not sit down and relax and stuff like that, y'know. I want to try and be a boss, y'know, tell people what to do. See, I don't always want people telling me what to do, y'know—the low rank. I wanna try to be with people in the high rank." Although Super does not know what occupation he would like to enter, he is certain that he wants a job that is relatively high up in a vaguely defined occupational hierarchy. . . .

The Brothers display none of the cockiness about their own capabilities that the Hallway Hangers exhibit. Instead, they attribute lack of success on the job market exclusively to personal inadequacy. This is particularly true when the Brothers speculate about the future jobs the Hallway Hangers and their own friends will have. According to the Brothers, the Hallway Hangers (in Super's words) "ain't gonna get nowhere," not because of the harshness of the job market but because they are personally lacking. The rest of the Brothers share this view.

JM: Some of those guys who hang with Frankie, they're actually pretty smart. They just don't channel that intelligence into school, it seems to me.

CRAIG: I call that stupid, man. That's what they are.

JM: I dunno.

CRAIG: Lazy.

(in a separate interview)

SUPER: They think they're so tough they don't have to do work. That don't make sense, really. You ain't gonna get nowhere; all's you gonna do is be back in the projects like your mother. Depend on your mother to give you money every week. You ain't gonna get a good job. As you get older, you'll think about that, y'know. It'll come to your mind. "Wow, I can't believe, I should've just went to school and got my education."

(in a separate interview)

MOKEY: They all got attitude problems. They just don't got their shit together. Like Steve. They have to improve themselves.

In the eyes of the Brothers, the Hallway Hangers have attitude problems, are incapable of considering their long-term future, and are lazy or stupid.

Because this evidence is tainted (no love is lost between the two peer groups), it is significant that the Brothers apply the same criteria in judging each other's chances to gain meaningful employment. James thinks Mokey is headed for a dead-end job because he is immature and undisciplined. He also blames Juan for currently being out of work. "Juan's outta school, and Juan does *not* have a job (*said with contempt*). Now that's some kind of a senior. When I'm a senior, I'm gonna have a job already. I can see if you're gonna go to college right when you get out of school; but Juan's not doin' nothin'. He's just stayin' home." Juan, in turn, thinks that Mokey and Super will have difficulty finding valuable work because of their attitudes. He predicts that Derek and Craig will be successful for the same reason.

These viewpoints are consistent with the dominant ideology in America; barriers to success are seen as personal rather than social. By attributing failure to personal inadequacy, the Brothers exonerate the opportunity structure. Indeed, it is amazing how often they affirm the openness of American society.

(*all in separate interviews*)
DEREK: If you put your mind to it, if you want to make a future for yourself, there's no reason why you can't. It's a question of attitude.
SUPER: It's easy to do anything, as long as you set your mind to it, if you wanna do it. If you really want to do it, if you really want to be something. If you don't want to do it . . . you ain't gonna make it. I gotta get that through my mind: I

wanna do it. I wanna be somethin'. I don't wanna be livin' in the projects the rest of my life.
MOKEY: It's not like if they're rich they get picked [for a job]; it's just mattered by the knowledge of their mind.
CRAIG: If you work hard, it'll pay off in the end.
MIKE: If you work hard, really put your mind to it, you can do it. You can make it.

This view of the opportunity structure as an essentially open one that rewards intelligence, effort, and ingenuity is shared by all the Brothers. Asked whether their chances of securing a remunerative job are as good as those of an upper-class boy from a wealthy district of the city, they all responded affirmatively. Not a single member of the Hallway Hangers, in contrast, affirms the openness of American society. . . .

Reproduction Theory Reconsidered

This basic finding—that two substantially different paths are followed within the general framework of social reproduction—is a major challenge to economically determinist theories. Two groups of boys from the same social stratum who live in the same housing project and attend the same school nevertheless experience the process of social reproduction in fundamentally different ways. This simple fact alone calls into question many of the theoretical formulations of Bowles and Gintis.[6] If, as they argue, social class is the overriding determinant in social reproduction, what accounts for the variance in the process between the Brothers and Hallway Hangers?

Bowles and Gintis, in considering a single school, maintain that social reproduction takes place primarily through educational tracking. Differential socialization through educational tracking prepares working-class students for working-class jobs and middle-class students for middle-class jobs. But the Hallway Hangers and the Brothers, who are from the same social class background and exposed to the curricular structure of the school in the same manner, undergo the process of social reproduction in substantially different manners. The theory of Bowles and Gintis cannot explain this difference.

Bourdieu's notion of habitus, however, can be used to differentiate the Hallway Hangers and the Brothers.[7] The habitus, as defined by Giroux, is "the subjective dispositions which reflect a class-based social grammar of taste, knowledge, and behavior inscribed in . . . each developing person."[8] According to Bourdieu, the habitus is primarily a function of social class. Bourdieu does not give an adequate sense of the internal structure of the habitus, but there is some precedent in his work for incorporating other factors into constructions of the habitus; for example, he differentiates people not only by gender and class, but also by whether they come from Paris or not. Although Bourdieu sometimes gives the impression of a homogeneity of habitus within the boundaries of social class, I understand habitus to be constituted at the level of the family and thus can include, as constitutive of the habitus, factors such as ethnicity, educational histories, peer associations, and demographic characteristics (e.g., geographical mobility, duration of tenancy in public housing, sibling order, and family size) as these shape individual

action. Although Bourdieu never really develops the notion along these lines, he does allude to the complexity and interplay of mediations within the habitus. "The habitus acquired in the family underlies the structuring of school experiences, and the habitus transformed by schooling, itself diversified, in turn underlies the structuring of all subsequent experiences (e.g. the reception and assimilation of the messages of the culture industry or work experiences), and so on, from restructuring to restructuring."[9] When understood along the lines I have indicated, the concept of habitus becomes flexible enough to accommodate the interactions among ethnicity, family, schooling, work experiences, and peer associations that have been documented [here].

Although we may accept the notion of habitus as a useful explanatory tool, we must reject the inevitability of its *function* in Bourdieu's theoretical scheme. According to Bourdieu, the habitus functions discreetly to integrate individuals into a social world geared to the interests of the ruling classes; habitus engenders attitudes and conduct that are compatible with the reproduction of class inequality. The outstanding example of this process is the development by working-class individuals of depressed aspirations that mirror their actual chances for social advancement.

The circular relationship Bourdieu posits between objective opportunities and subjective hopes is incompatible with the findings [presented here]. The Brothers, whose objective life chances probably were lower originally than those available to the Hallway Hangers because of racial barriers to success, nevertheless nurture higher aspirations than do the Hallway Hangers. By emphasizing structural determinants at the expense of mediating factors that influence subjective renderings of objective probabilities, Bourdieu presumes too mechanistic and simplistic a relationship between aspiration and opportunity. This component of his theory fails to fathom how a number of factors lie between and mediate the influence of social class on individuals; Bourdieu cannot explain, for instance, how ethnicity intervenes in the process of aspiration formation and social reproduction.

Thus, the theoretical formulations of Bowles and Gintis and the deterministic elements of Bourdieu's theory, although elegant and intuitively plausible, are incapable of accounting for the processes of social reproduction as they have been observed and documented in Clarendon Heights. These theories give an excellent account of the hidden structural and ideological determinants that constrain members of the working class and limit the options of Clarendon Heights teenagers. What the Hallway Hangers and the Brothers demonstrate quite clearly, however, is that the way in which individuals and groups respond to structures of domination is open-ended. Although there is no way to avoid class-based constraints, the outcomes are not predefined. Bowles and Gintis and Bourdieu pay too little attention to the active, creative role of individual and group praxis. As Giroux maintains, what is missing from such theories "is not only the issue of resistance, but also any attempt to delineate the complex ways in which working-class subjectivities are constituted."[10]

From Ethnography to Theory

Once we descend into the world of actual human lives, we must take our theoretical bearings to make some sense of the social landscape, but in doing so we invariably find that the theories are incapable of accounting for much of what we see. The lives of the Hallway Hangers and the Brothers cannot be reduced to structural influences or causes; although structural forces weigh upon the individuals involved, it is necessary, in the words of Willis, "to give the social agents involved some meaningful scope for viewing, inhabiting, and constructing their own world in a way which is recognizably human and not theoretically reductive."[11] We must appreciate both the importance and the relative autonomy of the cultural level at which individuals, alone or in concert with others, wrest meaning out of the flux of their lives.

The possibilities open to these boys as lower-class teenagers are limited structurally from the outset. That they internalize the objective probabilities for social advancement to some degree is beyond question. The process by which this takes place, however, is influenced by a whole series of intermediate factors. Because gender is constant in the study discussed in these pages, race is the principal variable affecting the way in which these youths view their situation. Ethnicity introduces new structurally determined constraints on social mobility, but it also serves as a mediation through which the limitations of class are refracted and thus apprehended and understood differently by different racial groups. The Brothers comprehend and react to their situation in a manner entirely different from the response the Hallway Hangers make to a similar situation; ethnicity introduces a new dynamic that makes the Brothers more receptive to the achievement ideology. Their acceptance of this ideology affects their aspirations but also influences, in tandem with parental encouragement, their approach to school and the character of their peer group, factors that in turn bear upon their aspirations.

If we modify the habitus by changing the ethnicity variable and altering a few details of family occupational and educational histories and duration of tenancy in public housing, we would have the Hallway Hangers. As white lower-class youths, the Hallway Hangers view and interpret their situation in a different light, one that induces them to reject the achievement ideology and to develop aspirations and expectations quite apart from those the ideology attempts to generate. The resultant perspective, which is eventually reinforced by the Hallway Hangers' contact with the job market, informs the boys' approach to school and helps us understand the distinctive attributes of this peer group. Thus, although social class is of primary importance, there are intermediate factors at work that, as constitutive of the habitus, shape the subjective responses of the two groups of boys and produce quite different expectations and actions.

Having grown up in an environment where success is not common, the Hallway Hangers see that the connection between effort and reward is not as clearcut as the achievement ideology would have them believe. Because it runs counter to the evidence in their lives and because it represents a forceful assault on their self-esteem, the Hallway Hangers repudiate the achievement ideology. Given that their parents are inclined to see the ideology in the same light, they do not counter their sons' rejection of the American Dream.

A number of important ramifications follow from the Hallway Hangers' denial of the dominant ideology: the establishment of a peer group that provides alternative means of generating self-esteem, the rejection of school and antagonism toward teachers, and, of course, the leveling of aspirations. In schematizing the role of the peer group, it is difficult not to appear tautological, for the group does wield a reciprocal influence on the boys: It attracts those who are apt to reject school and the achievement ideology and those with low aspirations and then deepens these individuals' initial proclivities and further shapes them to fit the group. But at the same time, the peer subculture itself, handed down from older to younger boys, is the product of the particular factors that structure the lives of white teenagers in Clarendon Heights.

In addition to the peer group, the curricular structure of the school solidifies the low aspirations of the Hallway Hangers by channeling them into programs that prepare students for manual labor jobs. Low aspirations, in turn, make the Hallway Hangers more likely to dismiss school as irrelevant. Once on the job market, the Hallway Hangers' inability to secure even mediocre jobs further dampens their occupational hopes. Thus although each individual ultimately retains autonomy in the subjective interpretation of his situation, the leveled aspirations of the Hallway Hangers are to a large degree a response to the limitations of social class as they are manifest in the Hallway Hangers' social world.

The Brothers' social class origins are only marginally different from those of the Hallway Hangers. Being black, the Brothers also must cope with racially rooted barriers to success that, affirmative action measures notwithstanding, structurally inhibit the probabilities for social advancement, although to a lesser degree than do shared class limitations. What appears to be a comparable objective situation to that of the Hallway Hangers, however, is apprehended in a very different manner by the Brothers.

As black teenagers, the Brothers interpret their families' occupational and educational records in a much different light than do the Hallway Hangers. Judging by the Brothers' constant affirmation of equality of opportunity, the boys believe that racial injustice has been curbed in the United States in the last twenty years. Whereas in their parents' time the link between effort and reward was very tenuous for blacks, the Brothers, in keeping with the achievement ideology, see the connection today as very strong: "If you work hard, it'll pay off in the end" (Craig). Hence, the achievement ideology is more compatible with the Brothers' attitudes than with those of the Hallway Hangers, for whom it cannot succeed against overwhelming contrary evidence. The ideology is not as emotionally painful for the Brothers to accept because past racial discrimination can help account for their families' poverty, whereas the Hallway Hangers, if the ideology stands, are afforded no explanation outside of laziness and stupidity for their parents' failures. The optimism that acceptance of the achievement ideology brings for the Brothers is encouraged and reinforced by their parents. Thus, we see how in the modified habitus ethnicity affects the Brothers' interpretation of their social circumstances and leads to acceptance of the achievement ideology, with all the concomitant results.

Postscript: The Hallway Hangers and Brothers Eight Years Later

"Hey, Jay, what the fuck brings you back to the Ponderosa?" Greeted by Steve in July 1991, I surveyed a Clarendon Heights that had changed considerably since 1983. Steve jerked his thumb over his shoulder at a group of African American teenagers lounging in the area outside doorway #13, previously the preserve of the Hallway Hangers. "How do you like all the new niggers we got here? Motherfuckers've taken over, man." I asked Steve about Frankie, Slick, and the other Hallway Hangers. "I'm the only one holding down the fort," he answered. "Me and Jinks—he lives in the back. The rest of 'em pretty much cut loose, man."

In their mid-twenties, the seven Hallway Hangers should be in the labor force full time. Most of them aren't: They are unemployed or imprisoned, or are working sporadically either for firms "under the table" or for themselves in the drug economy. . . . The Hallway Hangers have been trapped in what economists call the secondary labor market—the subordinate segment of the job structure where the market is severely skewed against workers. Jobs in the primary labor markets provide wages that can support families and an internal career structure, but the rules of the game are different in the secondary labor market. Wages are lower, raises are infrequent, training is minimal, advancement is rare, and turnover is high.

When the legitimate job market fails them, the Hallway Hangers can turn to the underground economy. Since 1984 almost all of the Hallway Hangers have at least supplemented their income from earnings in the burgeoning, multibillion-dollar drug market. The street economy promises better money than does conventional employment. It also provides a work site that does not demean the Hallway Hangers or drain their dignity. As workers in the underground economy, they won't have to take orders from a boss's arrogant son, nor will they have to gossip with office colleagues and strain to camouflage their street identities. . . .

Although they have certainly fared better than the Hallway Hangers, the Brothers have themselves stumbled economically in the transition to adulthood. Even more so than the Hallway Hangers, the Brothers have been employed in the service sector of the economy. They have bagged groceries, stocked shelves, flipped hamburgers, delivered pizzas, repaired cars, serviced airplanes, cleaned buildings, moved furniture, driven tow trucks, pumped gas, delivered auto parts, and washed dishes. They have also worked as mail carriers, cooks, clerks, computer operators, bank tellers, busboys, models, office photocopiers, laborers, soldiers, baggage handlers, security guards, and customer service agents. Only Mike, as a postal service employee, holds a unionized position. Although their experiences on the labor market have been varied, many of the Brothers have failed to move out of the secondary labor market. Instead, like the Hallway Hangers, they have been stuck in low-wage, high-turnover jobs. . . .

These results are depressing. The experiences of the Hallway Hangers since 1984 show that opting out of the contest—neither playing the game nor accepting its rules—is not a viable option. Incarceration and other less explicit social penalties are applied by society when the contest is taken on one's own terms. There is no escape: The Hallway Hangers must still generate income, build relationships, and establish households. Trapped inside the game, the Hallway Hangers now question their youthful resistance to schooling and social norms. Granted the opportunity to do it over again, the Hallway Hangers say they would have tried harder to succeed.

But the Brothers *have* always tried, which is why their experiences between 1984 and 1991 are as disheartening as the Hallway Hangers'. If the Hangers show that opting out of the contest is not a viable option, the Brothers show that dutifully playing by the rules hardly guarantees success either. Conservative and liberal commentators alike often contend that if the poor would only apply themselves, behave responsibly, and adopt bourgeois values, then they will propel themselves into the middle class. The Brothers followed the recipe quite closely, but the outcomes are disappointing. They illustrate how rigid and durable the class structure is. Aspiration, application, and intelligence often fail to cut through the firm figurations of structural inequality. Though not impenetrable, structural constraints on opportunity, embedded in both schools and job markets, turn out to be much more debilitating than the Brothers anticipated. Their dreams of comfortable suburban bliss currently are dreams deferred, and are likely to end up as dreams denied.

NOTES

1. All names of neighborhoods and individuals have been changed to protect the anonymity of the study's subjects.

2. Erik H. Erikson, *Gandhi's Truth* (New York: Norton, 1969), p. 154.

3. Ronald Reagan, "State of the Union Address to Congress," *New York Times,* 6 February 1985, p. 17.

4. Kenneth I. Spenner and David L. Featherman, "Achievement Ambitions," *Annual Review of Sociology* 4 (1978):376–378.

5. Howard B. London, *The Culture of a Community College* (New York: Praeger, 1978).

6. Samuel Bowles and Herbert Gintis, *Schooling in Capitalist America* (New York: Basic Books, 1976).

7. See Pierre Bourdieu, *Outline of a Theory of Practice* (Cambridge: Cambridge University Press, 1977).

8. Henry A. Giroux, *Theory & Resistance in Education* (London: Heinemann Educational Books, 1983), p. 89.

9. Bourdieu, *Outline of a Theory of Practice,* p. 87.

10. Giroux, *Theory & Resistance,* p. 85.

11. Paul E. Willis, *Learning to Labor* (Aldershot: Gower, 1977), p. 172.

60

The Pecking Order

Which Siblings Succeed and Why

DALTON CONLEY

Once upon a time a future president was born. William Jefferson Blythe IV entered the world one month premature but at a healthy six pounds and eight ounces. At twenty-three, his mother, Virginia, was young by today's standards, but perhaps a touch old for Arkansas in the 1940s. She was a widow, so times were tight during Bill's early years. In fact, times would be tough during all of Bill's childhood. Nonetheless, he seemed destined for great things. According to family lore, in second grade Bill's teacher "predicted that he would be President someday."

His mother eventually married Roger Clinton, but that didn't make life any easier for Bill. Roger was a bitterly jealous alcoholic who often became physically abusive to his wife. Bill cites the day that he stood up to his stepfather as the most important marker in his transition to adulthood and perhaps in his entire life. In 1962, when Bill was sixteen, Virginia finally divorced Roger, but by then there was another Roger Clinton in the family, Bill's younger half brother.

Though Bill despised his stepfather, he still went to the Garland County courthouse and changed his last name to Clinton after his mother's divorce from the man— not for the old man's sake, but so that he would have the same last name as the younger brother he cherished. Though they were separated by ten years, were only half siblings, and ran in very different circles, the brothers were close. The younger Roger probably hated his father more than Bill did, but he nonetheless started to manifest many of the same traits as he came of age. He was a fabulous salesman: at age thirteen, he sold twice as many magazines as any of his classmates for a school project, winning a Polaroid camera and a turkey for his superior effort. He also had an affinity for substance abuse: by eighteen, he was heavily into marijuana. During Bill's first (unsuccessful) congressional campaign in 1974, Roger spent much of his time stenciling signs while smoking joints in the basement of campaign headquarters.

As Bill's political fortunes rose, Roger's prospects first stagnated and then sank. He tried his hand at a musical career, worked odd jobs, and eventually got into dealing drugs. And it was not just pot; in 1984, then-governor Bill Clinton was informed that his brother was a cocaine dealer under investigation by the Arkansas state police. The governor did not stand in the way of a sting operation, and Roger was caught on tape boasting how untouchable he was as the brother of the state's chief executive. Then the axe fell. After his arrest, Roger was beside himself in tears, threatening suicide for the shame he had brought upon his family—in particular, his famous brother. Upon hearing this threat Bill shook Roger violently. (He, in truth, felt responsible for his brother's slide.)

The next January, Roger was sentenced to a two-year prison term in a federal corrections facility in Fort Worth, Texas. Bill describes the whole ordeal as the most difficult episode of his life. David Maraniss—the author of *First in His Class,* the most comprehensive biography of Clinton to date—summarizes the family situation as follows:

> How could two brothers be so different: the governor and the coke dealer, the Rhodes scholar and the college dropout, one who tried to read three hundred books in three months and another who at his most addicted snorted cocaine sixteen times a day, one who could spend hours explaining economic theories and another whose economic interests centered on getting a new Porsche? In the case of the Clinton brothers, the contrasts become more understandable when considered within the context of their family history and environment. They grew up in a town of contrast and hypocrisy, in a family of duality and conflict. Bill and Roger were not so much opposites as two sides of the same coin.

If asked to explain why Bill succeeded where Roger failed, most people will immediately point to genetic differences. After all, they were only half siblings to begin with. Others will pin it on birth order, claiming that firstborns are more driven and successful. But both of these accounts rely on individual explanations—ones particular to the unique biology or psychology of Bill and Roger—and both are incomplete. Was Bill more favored and more driven because he was a firstborn? My research shows that in families with two kids, birth order does not really matter that much. In fact, just under one-fourth of U.S. presidents were firstborns—about what we would expect from chance. The fact is that birth position only comes into play in larger families. But what about genes: was Bill simply luckier in the family gene pool? That may be so, but it still does not explain why sibling disparities are much more common in poor families and broken homes than they are in rich, intact families. In fact, when families have limited resources, the success of one sibling often generates a negative backlash among the others.

Sure, if one kid is born a mathematical genius and the other with no talents whatsoever, their respective dice may be cast at birth. But for most of us, how genes matter depends on the social circumstances around us. A child in one family may be born with innate athletic talent that is never nurtured because the parents in that family value reading ability over all else. Yet in another family, the fit between the individual talents of a particular child—say spatial reasoning—and the values of the parents may be perfect, and those abilities are realized. Finally, what kind of rewards talent brings depends entirely on the socioeconomic structure of the time. Fifty years ago, musical talent might have led to a decent living. Today—in an economy that rewards the most popular musicians handsomely at the expense of everyone else—innate musical ability is more often a route to financial struggle.

In Bill Clinton's case, he obviously had good genes—which contributed to his sharp mind, quick wit, tall stature, and verbal charisma—but there was not much advantage to being the firstborn. What really made a difference in his life was the good fit between his particular talents, the aspirations of those around him, and the political opportunities in a small state like Arkansas. This good fit combined with his family's lack of economic resources to generate an enormous sibling difference in success. However, had Virginia had money, she might not have had to put all her eggs—all her hopes and dreams—in Bill's basket. She might have been able to actively compensate for Bill's success by giving Roger extra financial and nonfinancial support—sending him, for example, to an elite private school when he started to veer off track. Instead, Bill's success seemed to come at the expense of Roger's—particularly when it led Roger to a false sense of invincibility.

On the surface, it may seem that the case of the Clintons is atypical. And, of course, a pair of brothers who are, respectively, the president and an ex-con is a bit extreme. But the basic phenomenon of sibling differences in success that the Clintons represent is not all that unusual. In fact, in explaining economic inequality in America, sibling differences represent about three-quarters of all the differences between individuals. Put another way, only one-quarter of all income inequality is between families. The remaining 75 percent is within families. Sibling differences in accumulated wealth (i.e., net worth) are even greater, reaching 90-plus percent. What this means is that if

we lined everyone in America up in rank order of how much money they have—from the poorest homeless person to Bill Gates himself—and tried to predict where any particular individual might fall on that long line, then knowing about what family they came from would narrow down our uncertainty by about 25 percent (in the case of income). In other words, the dice are weighted by which family you come from, but you and your siblings still have to roll them. For example, if you come from a family that ranks in the bottom 5 percent of the income hierarchy, then you have a 40 percent chance of finding yourself in the lowest 10 percent, a 21 percent chance of making it to somewhere between the 30th and 70th percentile, and only a one in a thousand chance of making it to the top 10 percent. If you come from the richest 5 percent of families in America, then your odds are flipped. And if you start at the dead middle of the American income ladder, then you are about 63 percent likely to end up somewhere in that 30th- to 70th-percentile range, with a 4 percent chance of ending up either in the top or the bottom 10 percent. A similar pattern holds for educational differences. For example, if you attended college there is almost a 50 percent chance that one of your siblings did not (and vice versa).

What do sibling disparities as large as these indicate? They imply an American landscape where class identity is ever changing and not necessarily shared between brothers and sisters. Taken as a whole, the above statistics present a starkly darker portrait of American family life than we are used to. We want to think that the home is a haven in a heartless world. The truth is that inequality starts at home. These statistics also pose problems for those concerned with what seems to be a marked erosion of the idealized nuclear family. In fact, they hint at a trade-off between economic opportunity and stable, cohesive families.

While it may be surprising to realize how common sibling inequality is on the whole, my analysis of national data shows that Americans are quite aware of sibling disparities within their own families. For instance, when given a choice of fourteen categories of kin ranging from parents to grandparents to spouses to uncles, a whopping 34 percent of respondents claimed that a sibling was their most economically successful relative. When the question is flipped, 46 percent of respondents report a sibling being their least successful relative. Both these figures dwarf those for any other category. When respondents were asked to elaborate about why their most successful relative got that way, their most common answer was a good work ethic (24.5 percent); when we add in other, related categories like "responsible, disciplined," "perseverance, motivation," or "set goals, had a plan," the total is well over half of all responses. Contrast that with the 22.6 percent that covers all categories of what might be called socioeconomic influences, such as "inheritance," "coming from a family with money," "marrying money," and so on. When accounting for the success of our kin, individual characterological explanations win out.

The pattern becomes even more striking when we flip the question to ask about the misfortune of the least successful relative. Only 9.6 percent of respondents cite social forces like poverty, lack of opportunity, or the pitfalls of a particular field as an explanation. Meanwhile, a whopping 82.4 percent cite individualistic reasons—having a "bad attitude" or "poor emotional or men-

tal health." The single largest category was "lack of determination."

That shows us how harsh we are on our brothers and sisters. Are we fair when we pass this kind of judgment, or terribly biased? I think the latter. In my book *The Pecking Order*, I challenge the perceived split between individual personality-based explanations for success and failure, and sociological ones. I argue that in each American family there exists a pecking order between siblings—a status hierarchy, if you will. This hierarchy emerges over the course of childhood and both reflects and determines the siblings' positions in the overall status ordering in society. It is not just the will of the parents or the "natural" abilities of the children themselves that determines who is on top in the family pecking order; the pecking order is conditioned by the swirling winds of society, which envelop the family. Gender expectations, the economic cost of schooling in America, a rising divorce rate, geographic mobility, religious and sexual orientations— all of these societal issues weigh in heavily on the pecking order between siblings. In other words, in order to truly understand the pecking orders within American families, you cannot view them in isolation from the larger economy and social structures in which we live. The family is, in short, no shelter from the cold winds of capitalism; rather it is part and parcel of that system. What I hope you end up with is a nuanced understanding of how social sorting works—in America writ large, and in your family writ small. And just maybe— along the way—we will all have a little more sympathy for our less fortunate brothers and sisters.

Books about siblings debate why children raised by the same parents in the same house under the same circumstances turn out differently—sometimes very differently. They offer genetic explanations, or focus on birth order or the quality of parenting. The *Pecking Order* takes all these issues into account, but, based on years of research with three separate studies, it now moves us beyond those factors. Why is there a pecking order in American families, and how does it work? The reasons go way beyond relationships between family members. Americans like to think that their behavior and their destiny are solely in their own hands. But the pecking order, like other aspects of the social fabric, ends up being shaped by how society works.

In fact, siblings serve merely as a tool by which I hope to shed light on why some of us are rich and others poor; on why some are famous and others in America are anonymous. However, in figuring this all out, we do not gain much traction by comparing Bill Clinton with Joe Q. Public, Bill Gates with the average reader of this book, or any pair of randomly associated people. Some books tell you that the best way to understand why one person succeeds and another does not is to examine big amorphous categories like class or economics or race. I say the best way to do it is to examine differences within families, specifically to compare siblings with one another. Only by focusing in on the variety of outcomes that arise within a given family can we gain a real understanding of the underlying forces, of the invisible hands of the marketplace, that push each of us onto our chosen (or assigned) path in life. Siblings provide a natural experiment of sorts. They share much of their genetic endowment. They also share much of the same environment. So it's logical to ask: how and why is it that some siblings end up in radically different positions in life? If we find an answer to that question, I think we will understand something very fundamental to American life.

61

The Strength of Weak Ties

MARK S. GRANOVETTER

Most intuitive notions of the "strength" of an interpersonal tie should be satisfied by the following definition: the strength of a tie is a (probably linear) combination of the amount of time, the emotional intensity, the intimacy (mutual confiding), and the reciprocal services which characterize the tie. Each of these is somewhat independent of the other, though the set is obviously highly intracorrelated. Discussion of operational measures of and weights attaching to each of the four elements is postponed to future empirical studies. It is sufficient for the present purpose if most of us can agree, on a rough intuitive basis, whether a given tie is strong, weak, or absent.

Consider, now, any two arbitrarily selected individuals—call them A and B—and the set, $S = C, D, E, \ldots$, of all persons with ties to either or both of them. The hypothesis which enables us to relate dyadic ties to larger structures is: the stronger the tie between A and B, the larger the proportion of individuals in S to whom they will both be tied, that is, connected by a weak or strong tie. This overlap in their friendship circles is predicted to be least when their tie is absent, most when it is strong, and intermediate when it is weak.

The proposed relationship results, first, from the tendency (by definition) of stronger ties to involve larger time commitments. If A-B and A-C ties exist, then the amount of time C spends with B depends (in part) on the amount A spends with B and C, respectively. (If the events "A is with B" and "A is with C" were independent, then the event "C is with A and B" would have probability equal to the product of their probabilities. For example, if A and B are together 60% of the time, and A and C 40%, then C, A, and B would be together 24% of the time. Such independence would be less likely after than before B and C became acquainted.) If C and B have no relationship, common strong ties to A will probably bring them into interaction and generate one. Implicit here is Homans's idea that "the more frequently persons interact with one another, the stronger their sentiments of friendship for one another are apt to be" (1950, p. 133).

Mark S. Granovetter, "The Strength of Weak Ties," *American Journal of Sociology* 78 (May 1973), pp. 1361–1366, 1371–1373, 1378–1380. Copyright © 1973 by The University of Chicago Press. Used by permission of The University of Chicago Press and the author.

The hypothesis is made plausible also by empirical evidence that the stronger the tie connecting two individuals, the more similar they are, in various ways (Berscheid and Walster 1969, pp. 69–91; Bramel 1969, pp. 9–16; Brown 1965, pp. 71–90; Laumann 1968; Newcomb 1961, chap. 5; Precker 1952). Thus, if strong ties connect A to B and A to C, both C and B, being similar to A, are probably similar to one another, increasing the likelihood of a friendship once they have met. Applied in reverse, these two factors—time and similarity—indicate why weaker A-B and A-C ties make a C-B tie less likely than strong ones: C and B are less likely to interact and less likely to be compatible if they do. . . .

To derive implications for large networks of relations, it is necessary to frame the basic hypothesis more precisely. This can be done by investigating the possible triads consisting of strong, weak, or absent ties among A, B, and any arbitrarily chosen friend of either or both (i.e., some member of the set S, described above). A thorough mathematical model would do this in some detail, suggesting probabilities for various types. This analysis becomes rather involved, however, and it is sufficient for my purpose in this paper to say that the triad which is most unlikely to occur, under the hypothesis stated above, is that in which A and B are strongly linked, A has a strong tie to some friend C, but the tie between C and B is absent. This triad is shown in Figure 61.1. To see the consequences of this assertion, I will exaggerate it in what follows by supposing that the triad shown never occurs—that is, that the B-C tie is always present (whether weak or strong), given the other two strong ties. Whatever results are inferred from this supposition should tend to

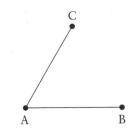

Figure 61.1   Forbidden Triad

occur in the degree that the triad in question tends to be absent.

Some evidence exists for this absence. Analyzing 651 sociograms, Davis (1970, p. 845) found that in 90% of them triads consisting of two mutual choices and one nonchoice occurred less than the expected random number of times. If we assume that mutual choice indicates a strong tie, this is strong evidence in the direction of my argument. Newcomb (1961, pp. 160–65) reports that in triads consisting of dyads expressing mutual "high attraction," the configuration of three strong ties became increasingly frequent as people knew one another longer and better; the frequency of the triad pictured in Figure 61.1 is not analyzed, but it is implied that processes of cognitive balance tended to eliminate it.

The significance of this triad's absence can be shown by using the concept of a "bridge"; this is a line in a network which provides the *only* path between two points (Harary, Norman, and Cartwright 1965, p. 198). Since, in general, each person has a great many contacts, a bridge between A and B provides the only route along which information or influence can flow from any contact of A to any contact of B, and, consequently, from anyone connected *indirectly* to A to anyone connected indirectly to B. Thus, in the study of diffusion, we can expect bridges to assume an important role.

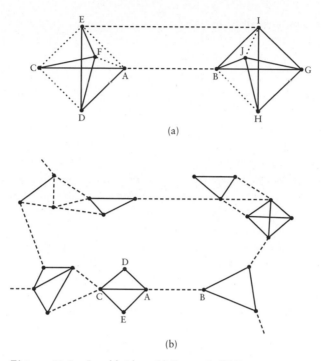

Figure 61.2   Local bridges. (a) Degree 3; (b) Degree 13.
Straight line = strong tie; dotted line = weak tie.

Now, if the stipulated triad is absent, it follows that, except under unlikely conditions, *no strong tie is a bridge.* Consider the strong tie *A-B:* if *A* has another strong tie to *C,* then forbidding the triad of Figure 61.1 implies that a tie exists between *C* and *B,* so that the path *A-C-B* exists between *A* and *B;* hence, *A-B* is not a bridge. A strong tie can be a bridge, therefore, *only if* neither party to it has any *other* strong ties, unlikely in a social network of any size (though possible in a small group). Weak ties suffer no such restriction, though they are certainly not automatically bridges. What is important, rather, is that all bridges are weak ties.

In large networks it probably happens only rarely, in practice, that a specific tie provides the *only* path between two points. The bridging function may nevertheless be served *locally.* In Figure 61.2a, for example, the tie *A-B* is not strictly a bridge, since one can construct the path *A-E-I-B* (and others). Yet, *A-B is* the shortest route to *B* for *F, D,* and *C.* This function is clearer in Figure 61.2b. Here, *A-B* is, for *C, D,* and others, not only a local bridge to *B,* but, in most real instances of diffusion, a much more likely and efficient path. Harary et al. point out that "there may be a distance [length of path] beyond which it is not feasible for *u* to communicate with *v* because of costs or distortions entailed in each act of transmission. If *v* does not lie within this critical distance, then he will not receive messages originating with *u*" (1965, p. 159). I will refer to a tie as a "local bridge of degree *n*" if *n* represents the shortest path between its two points (other than itself), and *n* > 2. In Figure 61.2a, *A-B* is a local bridge of degree 3, in 2b, of degree 13. As with bridges in a highway system, a local bridge in a social network will be more significant as a connection between two sectors to the extent that it is the only alternative for many people—that is, as its degree increases. A bridge in the absolute sense is a local one of infinite degree. By the same logic used above, only weak ties may be local bridges.

Suppose, now, that we adopt Davis's suggestion that "in interpersonal flows of most any sort the probability that 'whatever it is' will flow from person i to person j is (a) directly proportional to the number of all-positive (friendship) paths connecting i and j; and (b) inversely proportional to the length of such paths" (1969, p. 549). The significance of weak ties, then, would be that those which are local bridges create more, and shorter, paths. Any given tie may, hypothetically, be removed from a network; the number of paths broken and the changes in average path length resulting between arbitrary pairs of points (with some limitation on length of path considered) can then be computed. The contention here is that removal of the average weak tie would do more "damage" to transmission probabilities than would that of the average strong one.

Intuitively speaking, this means that whatever is to be diffused can reach a larger number of people, and traverse greater social distance (i.e., path length), when passed through weak ties rather than strong. If one tells a rumor to all his close friends, and they do likewise, many will hear the rumor a second and third time, since those linked by strong ties tend to share friends. If the motivation to spread the rumor is dampened a bit on each wave of retelling, then the rumor moving through strong ties is much more likely to be limited to a few cliques than that going via weak ones; bridges will not be crossed. . . .

I will develop this point empirically by citing some results from a labor-market study I have recently completed. Labor economists have long been aware that American blue-collar workers find out about new jobs more through personal contacts than by any other method. (Many studies are reviewed by Parnes 1954, chap. 5.) Recent studies suggest that this is also true for those in professional, technical, and managerial positions (Shapero, Howell, and Tombaugh 1965; Brown 1967; Granovetter 1970). My study of this question laid special emphasis on the nature of the *tie* between the job changer and the contact person who provided the necessary information.

In a random sample of recent professional, technical, and managerial job changers living in a Boston suburb, I asked those who found a new job through contacts how often they *saw* the contact around the time that he passed on job information to them. I will use this as a measure of tie strength. A natural a priori idea is that those with whom one has strong ties are more motivated to help with job information. Opposed to this greater motivation are the structural arguments I have been making: those to whom we are weakly tied are more likely to move in circles different from our own and will thus have access to information different from that which we receive.

I have used the following categories for frequency of contact: often = at least twice a week; occasionally = more than once a year but less than twice a week; rarely = once a year or less. Of those finding a job through contacts, 16.7% reported that they saw their contact often at the time, 55.6% said occasionally, and 27.8% rarely ($N = 54$). The skew is clearly to the weak end of the continuum, suggesting the primacy of structure over motivation.

In many cases, the contact was someone only marginally included in the current network of contacts, such as an old college friend or a former workmate or employer, with whom sporadic contact had been maintained (Granovetter 1970, pp. 76–80). Usually such ties had not even been very strong when first forged. For work-related ties, respondents almost invariably said that they never saw the person in a nonwork context. Chance meetings or mutual friends operated to reactivate such ties. It is remarkable that people receive crucial information from individuals whose very existence they have forgotten. . . .

From the individual's point of view, then, weak ties are an important resource in making possible mobility opportunity. Seen from a more macroscopic vantage, weak ties play a role in effecting social cohesion. When a man changes jobs, he is not only moving from one network of ties to another, but also establishing a link between these. Such a link is often of the same kind which facilitated his own movement. Especially within professional and technical specialties which are well defined and limited in size, this mobility sets up elaborate structures of bridging weak ties between the more coherent clusters that constitute operative networks in particular locations.

REFERENCES

Berscheid, E., and E. Walster. 1969. *Interpersonal Attraction*. Reading, Mass.: Addison-Wesley.

Bramel, D. 1969. "Interpersonal Attraction, Hostility and Perception." In *Experimental Social Psychology*, edited by Judson Mills. New York: Macmillan.

Brown, David. 1967. *The Mobile Professors*. Washington, D.C.: American Council on Education.

Brown, Roger. 1965. *Social Psychology*. New York: Free Press.

Davis, James A. 1969. "Social Structures and Cognitive Structures." In R. P. Abelson et al., *Theories of Cognitive Consistency*. Chicago: Rand McNally.

———. 1970. "Clustering and Hierarchy in Interpersonal Relations." *American Sociological Review* 35 (October): 843–52.

Granovetter, M. S. 1970. "Changing Jobs: Channels of Mobility Information in a Suburban Community." Doctoral dissertation, Harvard University.

Harary, F., R. Norman, and D. Cartwright. 1965. *Structural Models*. New York: Wiley.

Homans, George. 1950. *The Human Group*. New York: Harcourt, Brace & World.

Laumann, Edward. 1968. "Interlocking and Radial Friendship Networks: A Cross-sectional Analysis." Mimeographed. Ann Arbor: University of Michigan.

Newcomb, T. M. 1961. *The Acquaintance Process*. New York: Holt, Rinehart & Winston.

Parnes, Herbert. 1954. *Research on Labor Mobility*. New York: Social Science Research Council.

Precker, Joseph. 1952. "Similarity of Valuings as a Factor in Selection of Peers and Near-Authority Figures." *Journal of Abnormal and Social Psychology* 47, suppl. (April): 406–14.

Shapero, Albert, Richard Howell, and James Tombaugh. 1965. *The Structure and Dynamics of the Defense R & D Industry*. Menlo Park, Calif.: Stanford Research Institute.

62

Social Networks and Status Attainment

NAN LIN

Status attainment can be understood as a process by which individuals mobilize and invest resources for returns in socioeconomic standings. These resources can be classified into two types: personal resources and social resources. *Personal resources* are possessed by the individual who can use and dispose of them with freedom and without much concern for compensation. *Social resources* are resources accessible through one's direct and indirect ties. The access to and use of these resources are temporary and borrowed. For example, a friend's occupational or authority position, or such positions of this friend's friends, may be ego's social resource. The friend may use his or her position or network to help ego to find a job. These resources are "borrowed" and useful to achieve ego's certain goal, but they remain the property of the friend or his or her friends.

The theoretical and empirical work for understanding and assessing the status attainment process can be traced to the seminal study reported by Blau and Duncan (1967). Their major conclusion was that, even accounting for both the direct and in-direct effects of ascribed status (parental status), achieved status (education and prior occupational status) remained the most important factor accounting for the ultimate attained status. The study thus set the theoretical baseline for further modifications and expansions. All subsequent theoretical revisions and expansions must be evaluated for their contribution to the explanation of status attainment beyond those accounted for by the Blau-Duncan paradigm (Kelley 1990; Smith 1990). Several lines of contributions since then, including the addition of sociopsychological variables (Sewell and Hauser 1975), the recasting of statuses into classes (Wright 1979; Goldthorpe 1980), the incorporation of "structural" entities and positions as both contributing and attained statuses (Baron and Bielby 1980; Kalleberg 1988), and the casting of comparative development or institutions as contingent conditions (Treiman 1970), have significantly amplified rather than altered the original Blau-Duncan conclusion concerning the relative merits of achieved versus ascribed personal resources in status attainment.

Nan Lin, "Social Networks and Status Attainment," *Annual Review of Sociology* 25 (1999), pp. 467–470, 485–487. Copyright © 1999 by *Annual Review of Sociology*. Used by permission.

In the last three decades, a research tradition has focused on the effects on attained statuses of social resources. The principal proposition is that social resources exert an important and significant effect on attained statuses, beyond that accounted for by personal resources. Systematic investigations of this proposition have included efforts in (1) developing theoretical explanations and hypotheses, (2) developing measurements for social resources, (3) conducting empirical studies verifying the hypotheses, and (4) assessing the relative importance of social resources as compared to personal resources in the process of status attainment. . . .

Contributions of social network analysis to status attainment can be traced to the seminal study conducted by Mark Granovetter (1974), who interviewed 282 professional and managerial men in Newton, Massachusetts. The data suggested that those who used interpersonal channels seemed to land more satisfactory and better (e.g., higher income) jobs. Inferring from this empirical research, substantiated with a review of job search studies, Granovetter proposed (1973) a network theory for information flow. The hypothesis of "the strength of weak ties" was that weaker ties tend to form bridges that link individuals to other social circles for information not likely to be available in their own circles, and such information should be useful to the individuals.

However, Granovetter never suggested that access to or help from weaker rather than stronger ties would result in better statuses of jobs thus obtained (1995:148). Clues about the linkage between strength of ties and attained statuses came indirectly from a small world study conducted in a tri-city metropolitan area in upstate New York (Lin, Dayton, and Greenwald 1978).

The task of the participants in the study was to forward packets containing information about certain target persons to others they knew on a first-name basis so that the packets might eventually reach the target persons. The study found that successful chains (those packets successfully forwarded to the targets) involved higher-status intermediaries until the last nodes (dipping down in the hierarchy toward the locations of the targets). Successful chains also implicated nodes that had more extensive social contacts (who claimed more social ties), and yet these tended to forward the packets to someone they had not seen recently (weaker ties). The small world study thus made two contributions. First, it suggested that access to hierarchical positions might be the critical factor in the process of status attainment. Thus, the possible linkage between strength of ties and status attainment might be indirect: The strength of weak ties might lie in their accessing social positions vertically higher in the social hierarchy, which had the advantage in facilitating the instrumental action. Second, the study implicated behavior rather than a paper-and-pencil exercise, as each step in the packet-forwarding process required actual actions from each participant. Thus, the study results lend behavioral validity to those found in previous status attainment paper-pencil studies.

Based on these studies, a theory of social resources has emerged (Lin 1982, 1990). The theory begins with an image of the macro-social structure consisting of positions ranked according to certain normatively valued resources such as wealth, status, and power. This structure has a pyramidal shape in terms of accessibility and control of such resources: The higher the position, the fewer the occupants; and the higher the position, the better the view it has of the structure (especially down below). The pyramidal structure suggests advantages for positions nearer to the top, both in terms of number of occupants (fewer) and accessibility to positions (more). Individuals within these structural constraints and opportunities take actions for expressive and instrumental purposes. For instrumental actions (attaining status in the social structure being one prime example), the better strategy would be for ego to reach toward contacts higher up in the hierarchy. These contacts would be better able to exert influence on positions (e.g., recruiter for a firm) whose actions may benefit ego's interest. This reaching-up process may be facilitated if ego uses weaker ties, because weaker ties are more likely to reach out vertically (presumably upward) rather than horizontally relative to ego's position in the hierarchy.

REFERENCES

Baron, J. N., and W. T. Bielby. 1980. "Bringing the Firm Back in: Stratification, Segmentation, and the Organization of Work." *American Sociological Review* 45:737–65.

Blau, P. M., and O. D. Duncan. 1967. *The American Occupational Structure.* New York: Wiley.

Goldthorpe, J. H. 1980. *Social Mobility and Class Structure in Modern Britain.* New York: Oxford University Press.

Granovetter, M. 1973. "The Strength of Weak Ties." *American Journal of Sociology* 78: 1360–80.

Granovetter, M. 1974. *Getting a Job.* Cambridge, MA: Harvard University Press.

Granovetter, M. 1995. *Getting a Job.* Rev. ed. Chicago: University of Chicago Press.

Kalleberg, A. 1988. "Comparative Perspectives on Work Structures and Inequality." *Annual Review of Sociology* 14:203–25.

Kelley, J. 1990. "The Failure of a Paradigm: Log-Linear Models of Social Mobility." Pages 319–46, 349–57 in *John H. Goldthorpe: Consensus and Controversy,* edited by J. Clark, C. Modgil, and S. Modgil. London: Falmer.

Lin, N. 1982. "Social Resources and Instrumental Action." Pages 131–45 in *Social Structure and Network Analysis,* edited by P. V. Marsden and N. Lin. Beverly Hills, CA: Sage Publications.

Lin, N. 1990. "Social Resources and Social Mobility: A Structural Theory of Status Attainment." Pages 247–71 in *Social Mobility and Social Structure,* edited by R. L. Breiger. New York: Cambridge University Press.

Lin, N., P. Dayton, and P. Greenwald. 1978. "Analyzing the Instrumental Use of Relations in the Context of Social Structure." *Sociological Methods and Research* 7:149–66.

Sewell, W. H., and R. M. Hauser. 1975. *Education, Occupation & Earnings: Achievement in the Early Career.* New York: Academic Press.

Smith, M. R. 1990. "What Is New in New Structuralist Analyses of Earnings?" *American Sociological Review* 55:827–41.

Treiman, D. J. 1970. "Industrialization and Social Stratification." Pages 207–34 in *Social Stratification: Research and Theory for the 1970s,* edited by E. O. Laumann. Indianapolis: Bobbs-Merrill.

Wright, E. O. 1979. *Class Structure and Income Determination.* New York: Academic Press.

63

Structural Holes

RONALD S. BURT

Some people enjoy higher incomes than others. Some are promoted faster. Some are leaders on more important projects. The human capital explanation is that inequality results from differences in individual ability. The usual evidence is on general populations, as is Becker's (1975) pioneering analysis of income returns to education, but the argument is widely applied by senior managers to explain who gets to the top of corporate America—managers who make it to the top are smarter or better educated or more experienced. But, while human capital is surely necessary to success, it is useless without the social capital of opportunities in which to apply it.

Social capital can be distinguished in its etiology and consequences from human capital (e.g., Coleman, 1990; Bourdieu and Wacquant, 1992; Burt, 1992; Putnam, 1993; Lin, 1998). With respect to etiology, social capital is a quality created between people, whereas human capital is a quality of individuals. Investments that create social capital are therefore different in fundamental ways from the investments that create human capital (Coleman, 1988, 1990). I focus in this paper on consequences, a focus in network analysis for many years (Breiger, 1995). With respect to consequences, social capital is the contextual complement to human capital. Social capital predicts that returns to intelligence, education, and seniority depend in some part on a person's location in the social structure of a market or hierarchy. While human capital refers to individual ability, social capital refers to opportunity. Some portion of the value a manager adds to a firm is his or her ability to coordinate other people: identifying opportunities to add value within an organization and getting the right people together to develop the opportunities. Knowing who, when, and how to coordinate is a function of the manager's network of contacts within and beyond the firm. Certain network forms deemed social capital can enhance the manager's ability to identify and develop opportunities. Managers with more social capital get higher returns to their human capital because they are positioned to identify and develop more rewarding opportunities.

Ronald S. Burt, "The Contingent Value of Social Capital," *Administrative Science Quarterly* 42 (June 1997), pp. 339–343, 363–365. Copyright © 1997 by *Administrative Science Quarterly*. Used by permission.

The Network Structure of Social Capital

Structural hole theory gives concrete meaning to the concept of social capital. The theory describes how social capital is a function of brokerage opportunities in a network (see Burt, 1992, for detailed discussion). The structural hole argument draws on several lines of network theorizing that emerged in sociology during the 1970s, most notably, Granovetter (1973) on the strength of weak ties, Freeman (1977) on betweenness centrality, Cook and Emerson (1978) on the power of having exclusive exchange partners, and Burt (1980) on the structural autonomy created by network complexity. More generally, sociological ideas elaborated by Simmel (1955) and Merton (1968), on the autonomy generated by conflicting affiliations, are mixed in the structural hole argument with traditional economic ideas of monopoly power and oligopoly to produce network models of competitive advantage. In a perfect market, one price clears the market. In an imperfect market, there can be multiple prices because disconnections between individuals, holes in the structure of the market, leave some people unaware of the benefits they could offer one another. Certain people are connected to certain others, trusting certain others, obligated to support certain others, dependent on exchange with certain others. Assets get locked into suboptimal exchanges. An individual's position in the structure of these exchanges can be an asset in its own right. That asset is social capital, in essence, a story about location effects in differentiated markets. The structural hole argument defines social capital in terms of the information and control advantages of being the broker in relations between people otherwise disconnected in social structure. The disconnected people stand on opposite sides of a hole in social structure. The structural hole is an opportunity to broker the flow of information between people and control the form of projects that bring together people from opposite sides of the hole.

Information Benefits

The information benefits are access, timing, and referrals. A manager's network provides access to information well beyond what he or she could process alone. It provides that information early, which is an advantage to the manager acting on the information. The network that filters information coming to a manager also directs, concentrates, and legitimates information received by others about the manager. Through referrals, the manager's interests are represented in a positive light, at the right time, and in the right places.

The structure of a network indicates the redundancy of its information benefits. There are two network indicators of redundancy. The first is cohesion. Cohesive contacts—contacts strongly connected to each other—are likely to have similar information and therefore provide redundant information benefits. Structural equivalence is the second indicator. Equivalent contacts—contacts who link a manager to the same third parties—have the same sources of information and therefore provide redundant information benefits.

Nonredundant contacts offer information benefits that are additive rather than redundant. Structural holes are the gaps between nonredundant contacts (see Burt, 1992: 25–30, on how Granovetter's weak ties generalize to structural holes). The hole

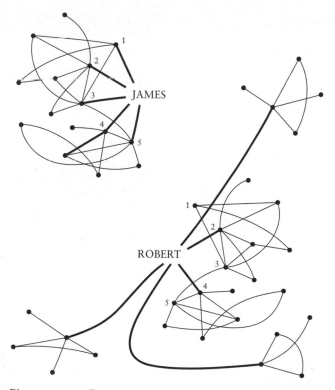

Figure 63.1 Illustrative Manager's Networks. Thick lines represent a manager's direct contacts.

is a buffer, like an insulator in an electric circuit. A structural hole between two clusters in a network need not mean that people in the two clusters are unaware of one another. It simply means that they are so focused on their own activities that they have little time to attend to the activities of people in the other cluster. A structural hole indicates that the people on either side of the hole circulate in different flows of information. A manager who spans the structural hole, by having strong relations with contacts on both sides of the hole, has access to both information flows. The more holes spanned, the richer the information benefits of the network.

Figure 63.1 provides an example. James had a network that spanned one structural hole. The hole is the relatively weak connection between the cluster reached through contacts 1, 2, and 3 and the cluster reached through contacts 4 and 5. Robert took over James's job and expanded the social capital associated with the job. He preserved connection with both clusters in James's network but expanded the network to a more diverse set of contacts. Robert's network, with the addition of three new clusters of people, spans ten structural holes.

Information benefits in this example are enhanced in several ways. The volume is higher in Robert's network simply because he reaches more people indirectly. Also, the diversity of his contacts means that the quality of his information benefits is higher. Each cluster of contacts is a single source of information because people connected to one another tend to know the same things at about the same time. Nonredundant clusters provide Robert with a broader information screen and, therefore, greater assurance that he will be informed of opportunities and impending disasters (access benefits). Further, since Robert's contacts are only linked through him at the center of the network, he is the first to see new opportunities created by needs in one group that could be served by skills in other groups (timing benefits). He stands at the crossroads of social organization. He has the option of bringing together otherwise disconnected individuals in the network when it would be rewarding. And because Robert's contacts are more diverse, he is more likely to be a candidate for inclusion in new opportunities (referral benefits). These benefits are compounded by the fact that having a network that yields such benefits makes Robert more attractive to other people as a contact in their own networks.

Control Benefits

The manager who creates a bridge between otherwise disconnected contacts has a say in whose interests are served by the bridge. The disconnected contacts communicate through the manager, giving the manager an opportunity to adjust his or her image with each contact, which is the structural foundation for managerial robust action (Padgett and Ansell, 1993). Simmel and Merton introduced the sociology of people who derive control benefits from structural holes: The ideal type is the *tertius gaudens*

(literally, "the third who benefits"), a person who benefits from brokering the connection between others (see Burt, 1992: 30–32, for review). As the broker between otherwise disconnected contacts, a manager is an entrepreneur in the literal sense of the word—a person who adds value by brokering the connection between others (Burt, 1992: 34–36; see also Martinelli, 1994). There is a tension here, but not the hostility of combatants. It is merely uncertainty. In the swirling mix of preferences characteristic of social networks, where no demands have absolute authority, the *tertius* negotiates for favorable terms. Structural holes are the setting for *tertius strategies,* and information is the substance. Accurate, ambiguous, or distorted information is strategically moved between contacts by the *tertius.* The information and control benefits reinforce one another at any moment in time and cumulate together over time.

Networks rich in structural holes present opportunities for entrepreneurial behavior. The behaviors by which managers develop these opportunities are many and varied, but the opportunity itself is at all times defined by a hole in the social structure around the manager. In terms of the structural hole argument, networks rich in the entrepreneurial opportunities of structural holes are entrepreneurial networks, and entrepreneurs are people skilled in building the interpersonal bridges that span structural holes.

Predicted Social Capital Effect

Managers with contact networks rich in structural holes know about, have a hand in, and exercise control over the more rewarding opportunities. They monitor information more effectively than it can be monitored bureaucratically. They move information faster, and to more people, than memos. These entrepreneurial managers know the parameters of organization problems early. They are highly mobile relative to people working through a bureaucracy, easily shifting network time and energy from one solution to another. More in control of their immediate surroundings, entrepreneurial managers tailor solutions to the specific individuals being coordinated, replacing the boiler-plate solutions of formal bureaucracy. There is also the issue of costs: entrepreneurial managers offer inexpensive coordination relative to the bureaucratic alternative. Managers with networks rich in structural holes operate somewhere between the force of corporate authority and the dexterity of markets, building bridges between disconnected parts of the firm where it is valuable to do so. They have more opportunity to add value, are expected to do so, and are accordingly expected to enjoy higher returns to their human capital. The prediction is that in comparisons between otherwise similar people like James and Robert in Figure 63.1, it is people like Robert who should be more successful.

REFERENCES

Becker, Gary. 1975 Human Capital, 2d ed. Chicago: University of Chicago Press.

Bourdieu, Pierre, and Loïc J. D. Wacquant. 1992 An Invitation to Reflexive Sociology. Chicago: University of Chicago Press.

Breiger, Ronald L. 1995 "Socioeconomic achievement and social structure." In Annual Review of Sociology, 21: 115–136. Palo Alto, CA: Annual Reviews.

Burt, Ronald S. 1980 "Autonomy in a social topology." American Journal of Sociology, 85: 892–925.

_____. 1992 Structural Holes. Cambridge, MA: Harvard University Press.

Coleman, James S. 1988 "Social capital in the creation of human capital." American Journal of Sociology, 94: S95–S120.

_____. 1990 Foundations of Social Theory. Cambridge, MA: Harvard University Press.

Cook, Karen S., and Richard M. Emerson. 1978 "Power, equity and commitment in exchange networks." American Sociological Review, 43: 712–739.

Freeman, Linton C. 1977 "A set of measures of centrality based on betweenness." Sociometry, 40: 35–40.

Granovetter, Mark S. 1973 "The strength of weak ties." American Journal of Sociology, 78: 1360–1380.

Lin, Nan. 1998 Social Resources and Social Action. New York: Cambridge University Press (forthcoming).

Martinelli, Alberto. 1994 "Entrepreneurship and management." In Neil J. Smelser and Richard Swedberg (eds.), The Handbook of Economic Sociology: 476–503. Princeton, NJ: Princeton University Press.

Merton, Robert K. 1968 "Continuities in the theory of reference group behavior." In Robert K. Merton, Social Theory and Social Structure: 335–440. New York: Free Press.

Padgett, John F., and Christopher K. Ansell. 1993 "Robust action and the rise of the Medici, 1400–1434." American Journal of Sociology, 98: 1259–1319.

Putnam, Robert D. 1993 Making Democracy Work: Civic Traditions in Modern Italy. Princeton, NJ: Princeton University Press.

Simmel, Georg. 1955 Conflict and the Web of Group Affiliations. Trans. by Kurt H. Wolff and Reinhard Bendix. New York: Free Press.

64

Networks, Race, and Hiring

ROBERTO M. FERNANDEZ AND
ISABEL FERNANDEZ-MATEO

It is common for scholars interested in race and poverty to invoke a lack of access to job networks as a reason why minorities face difficulties in the labor market (e.g., Royster 2003; Wilson 1996). Previous studies on this issue, however, have produced mixed results. Minorities have been found to be *more* likely to have obtained their job through networks than nonminorities (e.g., Elliott 1999). Yet, these jobs pay *less* than jobs obtained by other means (e.g., Falcon 1995). Rather than exclusion from white networks (e.g., Royster 2003), the emphasis in the literature has shifted to minorities' over-reliance on ethnic networks. Thus, the imagery that emerges from these studies is that minorities are stuck in the "wrong networks," that is, those that lead to low-wage jobs.

There is something slippery about the way these network arguments are currently being used, however. Because "wrong network" is defined in terms of the eventual outcome (a network is "good" if it leads to a good outcome, otherwise, it is a "wrong network"), such explanations run the danger of circular reasoning. To give network accounts

of minority underperformance analytical bite, we need to specify the mechanisms by which minorities are "excluded" from productive networks or "stuck" in unproductive ethnic networks.

We argue that being "stuck" in the "wrong network" can be produced by minority underrepresentation in *any* of a number of steps in the recruitment and hiring process. Using unique data from one employer, we illustrate the mechanisms by which minorities can be isolated from good job opportunities. To avoid circular reasoning, we form proper baselines of comparison using data on both networked and nonnetworked minorities and nonminorities at each stage of the hiring pipeline and identify the specific points in the process where network factors could lead minorities to have less access to these desirable jobs than nonminorities.

Race and Networks in the Labor Market

A common argument in sociology is that jobs found through networks pay better and

This is a commissioned chapter that draws heavily on material in a previous publication (Roberto M. Fernandez and Isabel Fernandez-Mateo, "Networks, Race, and Hiring," *American Sociological Review* 71 [2006], pp. 42–71).

are of higher status than those found through formal channels (Lin 2002). Evidence on this issue, however, is mixed, especially for minority groups. Reingold (1999) suggests that social networks lead to racial insularity and contribute to the economic marginalization of minorities. However, since many of these studies analyze samples of job incumbents, they often suffer from causal ambiguity (do ties to higher status people cause superior labor market outcomes, or is it that people with superior labor market outcomes gain access to high-status people?). In order to avoid the causal ambiguity problem, a number of studies use samples of job seekers and examine the chances of obtaining employment for various search methods (e.g., Elliott 1999). Employer surveys (e.g., Holzer 1996) are an alternative way of studying this issue, by fleshing out the employer side of the hiring process.

Neither of these approaches, however, examines actual hiring processes and their role in social isolation from good jobs. Without baseline information on the presence or absence of social ties for the pool of competing applicants, some of whom are hired and others are not, it is impossible to identify the effect of social contacts on hiring per se. In order to address this issue, some authors have used single-firm screening studies (e.g., Fernandez, Castilla, and Moore 2000; Fernandez and Sosa 2005), but most of this research has not analyzed the role of race in hiring due to lack of appropriate data (a prominent exception is Petersen, Saporta, and Seidel 2000).

"Wrong Networks"

A key component of understanding whether minorities are cut off from em-ployment opportunities is to understand why they may be underrepresented in networks that lead to *good* jobs. That is, in order to attribute logically the exclusion of minorities to the absence of network ties to good jobs, we would need to feel confident that minorities might plausibly have been hired except for the lack of the contact. It is critical to define the various processes whereby network factors could limit minorities' access to desirable jobs. In our conceptualization, the "wrong network" account is consistent with underrepresentation of minorities in any of a number of stages in the recruitment and hiring process. Figure 64.1 represents a conceptual map of the ways in which networks might affect the various stages. These are separated into two sets of processes, referring and screening.

The referral process may contribute to minorities' isolation either if there are no minority employees available to refer in the pool of workers (as in Kasinitz and Rosenberg's [1996] account), or if these employees are reluctant to pass on information about good jobs (see Smith 2005). Even if there are potential referrers who are willing to refer someone, minorities could still be cut off if these referrers were not to refer minority applicants (step 1c.). This could happen if job referral networks are less than perfectly homophilous by race (see Rubineau and Fernandez 2005). If all these conditions are met (steps 1a.–1c.), there will be a set of networked minority candidates in the applicant pool. At this point the screening stage on the demand side of the hiring interface begins.

The effect of screening processes on minorities' access to desirable jobs depends on the employer's attitude towards referrals. If

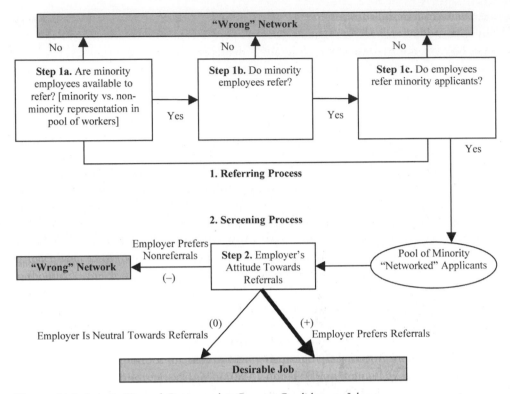

Figure 64.1 Steps in Network Processes that Connect Candidates to Jobs

firms prefer to recruit employee referrals (Fernandez, Castilla, and Moore 2000), they will tend to hire minority workers in proportion to their representation in the *networked* pool of applicants. In this case, minorities would thus be cut off from good jobs only if they are underrepresented in the networked applicant pool. However, if employers avoid hiring through networks (see Ullman 1966), being well represented in the pool of referred applicants is bad news for minorities. Finally, if the employer is neutral toward hiring referrals, access to desirable jobs for minorities will be provided in step 2 (screening) in proportion to the *overall applicant pool,* as opposed to the networked applicant pool. In such case the employers' preferences would have no effect in cutting off minorities from desirable jobs.

Analyses

We illustrate these processes using unique data on employees working at one company site and trace their networks of job contacts to applicants for desirable entry-level jobs. Minorities account for 50 percent of employees at this site, with Asian Americans and Hispanics being the largest groups. We collected all 2,065 paper applications to the plant's entry-level production jobs from September 1997 to November 30, 2000. We coded data on applicants' education, work history, and other human capital characteristics and geocoded candidates to the addresses they listed on the application form. Most importantly, and unusually, we have data on the applicants' race. All applicants must turn in their form in person, and when they do so the receptionist at the company (who is the same one for the whole period) records the applicant's apparent race and gender. Race is thus not self-identified as in most surveys and is well suited to our purposes of understanding the role of race in the screening process.

As mentioned above, in order to ensure that we are not misattributing the effect of networks to the effect of human capital factors, we must show that the candidates for these jobs might plausibly have been hired even without network ties. In this setting, it is clear that these entry-level jobs are within reach for people with modest education and labor force experience. The median years of education and experience for the people hired into these jobs are 12 and 7.9, respectively. Moreover, the local labor market was experiencing high rates of unemployment during the period (between 6.76 and 14.1 percent). Data from the local labor market (see Table 64.1) shows that the wages offered by the firm were attractive—particularly for females and minorities. Starting wages were $7.75/hr for the first eight months of the study, and $8.05 afterwards. These wages fell in the 25th and 27th percentiles of the overall wage distribution for males in the area (35th and 36th percentiles for females). For whites, these starting wages fell in the 18th and 19th percentiles of the male wage distribution, while they were more attractive for minority males (27th and 28th percentiles for African Americans; 35th and 36th for His-

panics; 32nd and 35th for Asian Americans). The pattern is similar for females, although for them the wages are even more attractive than for males in every case. Furthermore, most hires receive pay raises after a 90-day probation period (to $8.50, $10.05, or $10.35), which makes wages even more attractive. In fact, the top wage approaches the median of the wage distribution for white and African American women in the area and well exceeds the median for Hispanic and Asian American females.

Are Minority Employees Available to Refer?

In order to study the role of job-referral networks in the application process, we distinguish networked candidates using data from the original application forms. Employee referrals made up 30.2 percent of the applications for which we could identify recruitment source (2,556 out of 2,605). Using the company's employee database, we have been able to link referrers with their referral for 83.7 percent of the "employee referral" applications. For studying who among company employees produces referrals, we use the firm's personnel records. Five hundred fifty-seven workers were employed at the focal plant at any point over the study period, and for these we coded their self-identified race and gender.

We address step 1a in Figure 64.1 by studying the race and gender distribution of employees who could have produced referral applications during the period. For both genders, over half the workers are minorities (this percentage increases to over 60 percent for entry-level employees). Relatively large percentages of Asian Americans and Hispanics, but more modest percentages of

Table 64.1   Percentile Ranks of Company Offered Wages in Wage Distribution of All Non-College Population in Local Metro Area by Racial Group

	All Racial Groups		Non-Hispanic White		African American	
	Male	Female	Male	Female	Male	Female
Starting Wages (N = 192)						
Hired 9/97–4/98						
8.3% ($7.75)	25	35	18	30	27	37
Hired 5/98–11/00						
91.7% ($8.05)	27	36	19	31	28	38
Wages after 90-Day						
Probation (N = 109)						
15.6% ($8.05)	27	36	19	31	28	38
62.4% ($8.50)	29	40	21	34	32	41
21.1% ($10.05)	37	51	27	45	40	48
0.1% ($10.35)	38	52	28	46	41	48

	Hispanic		Asian American		All Minorities	
	Male	Female	Male	Female	Male	Female
Starting Wages (N = 192)						
Hired 9/97–4/98						
8.3% ($7.75)	35	43	32	39	33	41
Hired 5/98–11/00						
91.7% ($8.05)	36	44	35	41	35	42
Wages after 90-Day						
Probation (N = 109)						
15.6% ($8.05)	36	44	35	41	35	42
62.4% ($8.50)	39	49	37	45	37	46
21.1% ($10.05)	49	61	43	55	46	58
0.1% ($10.35)	50	62	45	57	48	59

Source: Persons in the U.S. Census Bureau's 5 percent 2000 Public Use Micro Sample for the local metro area who are at least 15 years of age and have fewer than 16 years of education with positive wage and salary income in 1999. Data are weighted to reflect the population.

African Americans, are represented. Women make up 69.4 percent of entry-level workers, and they are overrepresented irrespective of race.

We also compare these race and gender distributions of workers with the composition of persons employed in the local area (Table 64.2). We find that white workers are underrepresented in this factory compared to their proportion in the area. Asian Americans, however, are extremely overrepresented. While they make up 6.1 percent of employed males in the local labor market, they account for 26.8 percent of male employees. Hispanics are slightly underrepresented (24.9 percent of employees, 35.3 percent in the area), while the percentages of African Americans employed at the factory are quite similar to their proportion in the area (5.9 versus 4.0 percent for males). In sum, minorities are definitely available to refer in this setting.

Table 64.2 Racial and Gender Distributions of Workers Employed During Hiring Window (September 1997–November 2000), and Persons Employed in Metropolitan Area

| | All Plant Employees[a] | | Entry Level Employees Only | | 2000 PUMS[b] | |
	Female	Male	Female	Male	Female	Male
Non-Hispanic White	44.0	41.5	38.5	28.6	54.3	50.4
African American	3.1	5.9	3.1	5.6	5.0	4.0
Hispanic	28.7	24.9	30.1	28.6	29.8	35.3
Asian American	23.3	26.8	27.6	35.7	6.5	6.1
Native American	0.9	1.0	0.7	1.6	0.9	0.7
Other, Multirace	—	—	—	—	—	—
Total	100.0	100.0	100.0	100.0	100.0	100.0
Total N	352	205	286	126	174838	208174

[a]Each person is counted equally if they were employed at any time during hiring window (September 1, 1997–November 30, 2000).

[b]Persons in the 5 percent 2000 PUMS who are at least 15 years of age and less than 16 years of education with positive wage and salary income in 1999. Data are weighted to reflect the population.

Do Minority Employees Refer?

Of the 557 employees, 200 of them originated a total of 580 applications. Asian Americans refer the most (50.9 percent of male Asian Americans originated at least one referral applicant). Interestingly, whites show the lowest rates of producing referrals (27.7 percent for females and 18.8 percent for males). To determine whether background factors might account for the observed race differences in referral behavior, we estimate a set of negative binomial regressions (see Fernandez and Fernandez-Mateo 2006, Table 5). These models show that there are no significant gender differences in the counts of referrals originated by employees at the company. There are race differences, however, as minorities generate more referrals than whites (with Asian Americans producing the most). These effects remain even when adding the extensive controls for individual background mentioned above. Thus, at step 1b in Figure 64.1, we have no evidence that minorities are less likely than whites to produce referral applicants.

Do Minority Employees Refer Minority Applicants?

The simplest criterion to assess if this is a point of disconnection for minorities is whether there are any minorities at all produced by the referral process, irrespective of the race of the referrer. We analyze the race distribution of applicants produced by referrers of different racial backgrounds. We find that there is a strong relationship between the race of the referrer and the race of the referral applicant (for both genders). Most important, 61.8 percent of male and 57.2 percent of female referred applicants are minorities. Clearly, by this first criterion, minorities are not cut off at step 1c.

A more stringent criterion would be to assess whether the referral process is reproducing the racial distribution of the referring population (the 200 employees identified above). We find that whites are the most insular of the groups in referring (76.9 percent of the referrals produced by white employees are white). The percentage of African Americans and Asian Americans in the referral pool matches the percentage of the referring population quite closely (5.6 vs. 4.0 percent for African Americans; 34.6 vs. 32.5 percent for Asian Americans). Hispanics, however, constitute a third of referrers, but only 19 percent of referrals. Hispanics, therefore, seem to be somehow cut off, in relative terms, from the networks leading to these jobs.

A final criterion depends on whether minorities refer minority applicants less than they refer white applicants. We find, however, that irrespective of which minority group one considers, the percentage referring whites is lower than the percentage referring minorities. By this final criterion, we find no evidence that a lack of racial homophily in minorities' referring patterns is weakening their access to this company. In sum, there is little evidence that minorities in this setting are cut off from the job networks that lead to employment at this company due to the behavior of the originators of referral networks (the "referring" process).

Hiring Interface

Even if networked minorities are well represented in the application pool, this does not necessarily mean that they will be similarly represented at subsequent stages of the screening process. This step depends on the employer's racial biases and attitudes towards referrals ("screening process" in Figure 64.1). Our fieldwork and interviews with HR managers at this site suggest that the employer has neither a strong preference nor distaste for referred applicants. We assembled data on all applicants for entry-level jobs and tracked their progress through the hiring pipeline (from application, to interview, to offer, to hire).

For females (see Figure 64.2a), there is little evidence of a preference for networked candidates (33.9 percent of female applicants and 35.3 percent of female hires were referrals). Also, the race distribution did not change much across stages. Similarly for males (Figure 64.2b), the percentage of networked applicants does not increase across the various stages of the screening process. If anything, it decreases (networked candidates constitute 35.3 percent of the overall male applicant pool and 28.6 percent of hires).

We also performed multivariate (probit) analyses of who is hired versus not hired, in order to introduce controls into the analysis. For female applicants, both recruitment source and race do not significantly influence the probability of hire. This does not change when human capital and controls are added to the model (although some of these controls such as "years of experience" are significant). There is thus no evidence of a preference for networked candidates among females, and the race distribution of hires is not different from the distribution of applicants. For males, the results show that all minority racial groups are more likely to be hired than whites—irrespective of whether the person was a referral or not. The only significant pattern is that Asian American nonnetworked males are 8.5 percent more prevalent among hires than among applicants, even after everything else is controlled for.

In sum, the regression results show that there is little evidence of an employer's preference either for, or against, candidates who were referred to the company at the hiring interface. The one exception is the case of Asian American males, where nonnetworked candidates are more likely to be hired compared with networked applicants. We can only speculate whether this reflects a conscious effort to limit the num-

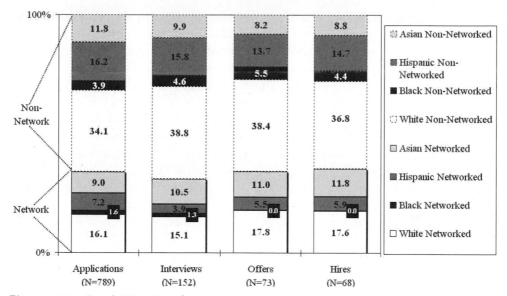

Figure 64.2a Female Hiring Interface

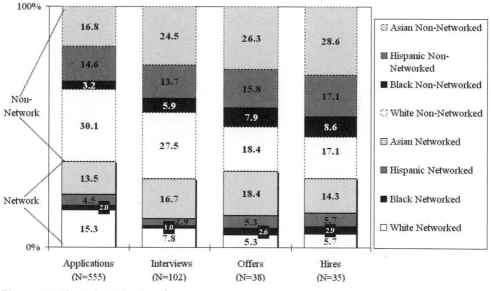

Figure 64.2b Male Hiring Interface

ber of Asian Americans—who are overrepresented in the application pool relative to the population in the local labor market. The hiring interface is thus a point of disconnection for Asian American males (i.e.,

the arrow labeled "(-)" in step 2 of Figure 64.1), but this employer is otherwise neutral with respect to networked candidates (i.e., the arrow labeled "0" in step 2 of Figure 64.1).

Summary and Conclusion

This paper makes a number of theoretical contributions to the study of racial inequality and networks. First, it contributes to specifying the mechanisms operating in network accounts of racial inequality in the labor market. Past accounts in this area often run the danger of circular reasoning because "wrong network" is defined in terms of the eventual outcome. We argue that much more analytical precision is needed to specify what it means to be "stuck" in the "wrong network," as these stories are consistent with minority underrepresentation in *any* of a number of steps in the recruitment and hiring process. Indeed, this study is the first to analyze comprehensively the racial implications of *both* the referring process and the screening mechanisms at the point of hire. We found that network factors operate at several stages of the recruitment process, but we found scant evidence that these factors serve to cut off minorities from employment at this company.

This study also has significant implications for policy. Since policies are often designed to target distinct steps in the recruitment process (National Research Council 2004), understanding each of these steps is crucial for crafting effective policy interventions. Affirmative action, for example, is focused on affecting the behavior of labor market screeners (Reskin 1998). Assessing the effect of these policies will be very difficult without data on both hires and nonhires. Other policy prescriptions recommend that companies open up their recruitment practices by broad advertising and use of formal recruitment systems, on the theory that informal, referral-based recruitment is inherently exclu-sionary (LoPresto 1986). The results presented here, however, suggest that this heuristic is too simple. Relying on referrals can help reproduce the distribution of the referring population. Therefore, in settings where the current workforce is racially diverse—as is the case in this setting—the referral processes can actually help *perpetuate* diversity (see Rubineau and Fernandez 2005).

Although the "wrong network" account does not fit the facts in this setting, this is not to say that in another, less diverse setting, where referrals may be preferred by screeners, the empirical results would not be markedly different. While we can make no claims of empirical generalizability, however, this study has important methodological implications. Its value is apparent in the light it sheds on mechanisms that are normally hidden from view. We suggest that the fine-grained processes that we have uncovered here need to be addressed to render the "wrong network" hypothesis testable in other settings. Moreover, it is important to realize that the race and network effects that are often reported in analyses of highly aggregated survey data are likely conflating the effects of the multiple mechanisms that we have delineated. Distinguishing among these steps should be a high priority in future research at the intersection of networks and race in the labor market.

REFERENCES

Elliott, James R. 1999. "Social Isolation and Labor Market Insulation: Network and Neighborhood Effects on Less-Educated Urban Workers." *Sociological Quarterly* 40: 199–216.

Falcon, Luis M. 1995. "Social Networks and Employment for Latinos, Blacks, and Whites." *New England Journal of Public Policy* 11: 17–28.

Fernandez, Roberto M., Emilio J. Castilla, and Paul Moore. 2000. "Social Capital at Work: Networks and Employment at a Phone Center." *American Journal of Sociology* 105: 1288–1356.

Fernandez, Roberto M., and Isabel Fernandez-Mateo. 2006. "Networks, Race and Hiring." *American Sociological Review* 71: 42–71.

Fernandez, Roberto M., and M. Lourdes Sosa. 2005. "Gendering the Job: Networks and Recruitment at a Call Center." *American Journal of Sociology* 111: 859–904.

Holzer, Harry J. 1996. *What Employers Want: Job Prospects for Less-Educated Workers.* New York: Russell Sage Foundation.

Kasinitz, Philip, and Jan Rosenberg. 1996. "Missing the Connection: Social Isolation and Employment on the Brooklyn Waterfront." *Social Problems* 43: 180–93.

Lin, Nan. 2002. *Social Capital: A Theory of Social Structure and Action.* New York: Cambridge University Press.

LoPresto, Robert. 1986. "Recruitment Sources and Techniques." Pp. 13–1 to 13–26 in *Handbook of Human Resource Administration*, 2nd ed., edited by J. J. Famularo. New York: McGraw-Hill.

National Research Council. 2004. *Measuring Racial Discrimination.* Panel on Methods for Assessing Discrimination, edited by Rebecca M. Blank, Marilyn Dabady, and Constance F. Citro. Committee on National Statistics, Division of Behavioral and Social Sciences and Education. Washington, DC: National Academies Press.

Petersen, Trond, Ishak Saporta, and Marc-David Seidel. 2000. "Offering a Job: Meritocracy and Social Networks." *American Journal of Sociology* 106: 763–816.

Reingold, David A. 1999. "Social Networks and the Employment Problem of the Urban Poor." *Urban Studies* 36: 1907–32.

Reskin, Barbara F. 1998. *The Realities of Affirmative Action.* Washington, DC: American Sociological Association.

Royster, Deirdre A. 2003. *Race and the Invisible Hand: How White Networks Exclude Black Men from Blue-Collar Jobs.* Berkeley: University of California Press.

Rubineau, Brian, and Roberto M. Fernandez. 2005. "Missing Links: Referral Processes and Job Segregation." MIT Sloan School of Management, Massachusetts Institute of Technology, Cambridge, MA. Unpublished manuscript.

Smith, Sandra. 2005. "'Don't Put My Name on It': Social Capital Activation and Job-Finding Assistance Among the Black Urban Poor." *American Journal of Sociology* 111: 1–57.

Ullman, Joseph C. 1966. "Employee Referrals: A Prime Tool for Recruiting Workers." *Personnel* 43: 30–35.

Wilson, William Julius. 1996. *When Work Disappears: The World of the New Urban Poor.* New York: Alfred A. Knopf.

PART VIII

The Consequences
of Inequality

65

Life at the Top in America
Isn't Just Better, It's Longer

JANNY SCOTT

Jean G. Miele's heart attack happened on a sidewalk in Midtown Manhattan in May 2004. He was walking back to work along Third Avenue with two colleagues after a several-hundred-dollar sushi lunch. There was the distant rumble of heartburn, the ominous tingle of perspiration. Then Miele, an architect, collapsed onto a concrete planter in a cold sweat.

Will L. Wilson's heart attack came four days earlier in the bedroom of his brownstone in Bedford-Stuyvesant in Brooklyn. He had been regaling his fiancée with the details of an all-you-can-eat dinner he was beginning to regret. Wilson, a Consolidated Edison office worker, was feeling a little bloated. He flopped onto the bed. Then came a searing sensation, like a hot iron deep inside his chest.

Ewa Rynczak Gora's first signs of trouble came in her rented room in the noisy shadow of the Brooklyn-Queens Expressway. It was the Fourth of July. Gora, a Polish-born housekeeper, was playing bridge. Suddenly she was sweating, stifling an urge to vomit. She told her husband not to call an ambulance; it would cost too much. In-

stead, she tried a home remedy: salt water, a double dose of hypertension pills, and a glass of vodka.

Architect, utility worker, maid: heart attack is the great leveler, and in those first fearful moments, three New Yorkers with little in common faced a single common threat. But in the months that followed, their experiences diverged. Social class—that elusive combination of income, education, occupation, and wealth—played a powerful role in Miele's, Wilson's, and Gora's struggles to recover.

Class informed everything from the circumstances of their heart attacks to the emergency care each received, the households they returned to, and the jobs they hoped to resume. It shaped their understanding of their illness, the support they got from their families, their relationships with their doctors. It helped define their ability to change their lives and shaped their odds of getting better.

Class is a potent force in health and longevity in the United States. The more education and income people have, the less likely they are to have and die of heart

---

disease, strokes, diabetes, and many types of cancer. Upper-middle-class Americans live longer and in better health than middle-class Americans, who live longer and better than those at the bottom. And the gaps are widening, say people who have researched social factors in health.

As advances in medicine and disease prevention have increased life expectancy in the United States, the benefits have disproportionately gone to people with education, money, good jobs, and connections. They are almost invariably in the best position to learn new information early, modify their behavior, take advantage of the latest treatments, and have the cost covered by insurance.

Many risk factors for chronic diseases are now more common among the less educated than the better educated. Smoking has dropped sharply among the better educated, but not among the less. Physical inactivity is more than twice as common among high school dropouts as among college graduates. Lower-income women are more likely than other women to be overweight, though the pattern among men may be the opposite.

There may also be subtler differences. Some researchers now believe that the stress involved in so-called high-demand, low-control jobs further down the occupational scale is more harmful than the stress of professional jobs that come with greater autonomy and control. Others are studying the health impact of job insecurity, lack of support on the job, and employment that makes it difficult to balance work and family obligations.

Then there is the issue of social networks and support, the differences in the knowledge, time, and attention that a person's family and friends are in a position to offer. What is the effect of social isolation? Neighborhood differences have also been studied: How stressful is a neighborhood? Are there safe places to exercise? What are the health effects of discrimination?

Heart attack is a window on the effects of class on health. The risk factors—smoking, poor diet, inactivity, obesity, hypertension, high cholesterol, and stress—are all more common among the less educated and less affluent, the same group that research has shown is less likely to receive cardiopulmonary resuscitation, to get emergency room care, or to adhere to lifestyle changes after heart attacks.

"In the last twenty years, there have been enormous advances in rescuing patients with heart attack and in knowledge about how to prevent heart attack," said Ichiro Kawachi, a professor of social epidemiology at the Harvard School of Public Health. "It's like diffusion of innovation: whenever innovation comes along, the well-to-do are much quicker at adopting it. On the lower end, various disadvantages have piled onto the poor. Diet has gotten worse. There's a lot more work stress. People have less time, if they're poor, to devote to health maintenance behaviors when they are juggling two jobs. Mortality rates even among the poor are coming down, but the rate is not anywhere near as fast as for the well-to-do. So the gap has increased."

Bruce G. Link, a professor of epidemiology and sociomedical sciences at Columbia University, said of the double-edged consequences of progress: "We're creating disparities. It's almost as if it's transforming health, which used to be like fate, into a commodity. Like the distribution of BMWs or goat cheese."

The Best of Care

Jean Miele's advantage began with the people he was with on May 6, when the lining of his right coronary artery ruptured, cutting off the flow of blood to his sixty-six-year-old heart. His two colleagues were knowledgeable enough to dismiss his request for a taxi and call an ambulance instead.

And because he was in Midtown Manhattan, there were major medical centers nearby, all licensed to do the latest in emergency cardiac care. The emergency medical technician in the ambulance offered Miele a choice. He picked Tisch Hospital, part of New York University Medical Center, an academic center with relatively affluent patients, and passed up Bellevue, a city-run hospital with one of the busiest emergency rooms in New York.

Within minutes, Miele was on a table in the cardiac catheterization laboratory, awaiting angioplasty to unclog his artery—a procedure that many cardiologists say has become the gold standard in heart attack treatment. When he developed ventricular fibrillation, a heart rhythm abnormality that can be fatal within minutes, the problem was quickly fixed.

Then Dr. James N. Slater, a fifty-four-year-old cardiologist with some twenty-five thousand cardiac catheterizations under his belt, threaded a catheter through a small incision in the top of Miele's right thigh and steered it toward his heart. Miele lay on the table, thinking about dying. By 3:52 P.M., less than two hours after Miele's first symptoms, his artery was reopened and Slater implanted a stent to keep it that way.

Time is muscle, as cardiologists say. The damage to Miele's heart was minimal.

Miele spent just two days in the hospital. His brother-in-law, a surgeon, suggested a few specialists. His brother, Joel, chairman of the board of another hospital, asked his hospital's president to call New York University. "Professional courtesy," Joel Miele explained later. "The bottom line is that someone from management would have called patient care and said, 'Look, would you make sure everything's okay?'"

Things went less flawlessly for Will Wilson, a fifty-three-year-old transportation coordinator for Con Ed. He imagined fleetingly that he was having a bad case of indigestion, though he had had a heart attack before. His fiancée insisted on calling an ambulance. Again, the emergency medical technician offered a choice of two nearby hospitals—neither of which had state permission to do angioplasty, the procedure Jean Miele received.

Wilson chose the Brooklyn Hospital Center over Woodhull Medical and Mental Health Center, the city-run hospital that serves three of Brooklyn's poorest neighborhoods. At Brooklyn Hospital, he was given a drug to break up the clot blocking an artery to his heart. It worked at first, said Narinder P. Bhalla, the hospital's chief of cardiology, but the clot re-formed.

So Bhalla had Wilson taken to the Weill Cornell Center of New York–Presbyterian Hospital in Manhattan the next morning. There, Bhalla performed angioplasty and implanted a stent. Asked later whether Wilson would have been better off if he had had his heart attack elsewhere, Bhalla said the most important issue in heart attack treatment was getting the patient to a hospital quickly.

But he added, "In his case, yes, he would have been better off had he been to a hospital that was doing angioplasty."

Wilson spent five days in the hospital before heading home on many of the same high-priced drugs that Miele would be taking and under similar instructions to change his diet and exercise regularly. After his first heart attack, in 2000, he quit smoking; but once he was feeling better, he stopped taking several medications, drifted back to red meat and fried foods, and let his exercise program slip.

This time would be different, he vowed: "I don't think I'll survive another one."

Ewa Gora's experience was the rockiest. First, she hesitated before allowing her husband to call an ambulance; she hoped her symptoms would go away. He finally insisted; but when the ambulance arrived, she resisted leaving. The emergency medical technician had to talk her into going. She was given no choice of hospitals; she was simply taken to Woodhull, the city hospital Will Wilson had rejected.

Woodhull was busy when Gora arrived around 10:30 p.m. A triage nurse found her condition stable and classified her as "high priority." Two hours later, a physician assistant and an attending doctor examined her again and found her complaining of chest pain, shortness of breath, and heart palpitations. Over the next few hours, tests confirmed she was having a heart attack.

She was given drugs to stop her blood from clotting and to control her blood pressure, treatment that Woodhull officials say is standard for the type of heart attack she was having. The heart attack passed. The next day, Gora was transferred to Bellevue, the hospital Jean Miele had turned down, for an angiogram to assess her risk of a second heart attack.

But Gora, who was fifty-nine at the time, came down with a fever at Bellevue, so the angiogram had to be canceled. She remained at Bellevue for two weeks, being treated for an infection. Finally, she was sent home. No angiogram was ever done.

Comforts and Risks

Jean Miele is a member of New York City's upper middle class. The son of an architect and an artist, he worked his way through college, driving an ice-cream truck and upholstering theater seats. He spent two years in the military and then joined his father's firm, where he built a practice as not only an architect but also an arbitrator and an expert witness, developing real estate on the side.

Miele is the kind of person who makes things happen. He bought a $21,000 house in the Park Slope section of Brooklyn, sold it about fifteen years later for $285,000, and used the money to build his current house next door, worth over $2 million. In Brookhaven, on Long Island, he took a derelict house on a single acre, annexed several adjoining lots, and created what is now a four-acre, three-house compound with an undulating lawn and a fifteen-thousand-square-foot greenhouse he uses as a workshop for his collection of vintage Jaguars. . . .

His approach to his health was utilitarian. When body parts broke, he got them fixed so he could keep doing what he liked to do. So he had had disk surgery, rotator cuff surgery, surgery for a carpal tunnel problem. But he was also not above an occasional bit of neglect. In March 2004, his doctor suggested a stress test after Miele complained of shortness of breath. On May 6, the prescription was still hanging on the kitchen cabinet door.

An important link in the safety net that caught Miele was his wife, a former executive at a sweater manufacturing company who had stopped work to raise Emma but managed the Mieles' real estate as well. While Miele was still in the hospital, she was on the Internet, Googling stents.

She scheduled his medical appointments. She got his prescriptions filled. Leaving him at home one afternoon, she taped his cardiologist's business card to the couch where he was sitting. "Call Dr. Hayes and let him know you're coughing," she said, her fingertips on his shoulder. Thirty minutes later, she called home to check.

She prodded Miele, gently, to cut his weekly egg consumption to two, from seven. She found fresh whole wheat pasta and cooked it with turkey sausage and broccoli rabe. She knew her way around nutrition labels.

Lori Miele took on the burden of dealing with the hospital and insurance companies. She accompanied her husband to his doctor's appointments and retained pharmaceutical dosages in her head.

"I can just leave and she can give you all the answers to all the questions," Miele said to his cardiologist, Dr. Richard M. Hayes, one day.

"Okay, why don't you just leave?" Hayes said back. "Can she also examine you?"

With his wife's support, Miele set out to lose thirty pounds. His pasta consumption plunged to a plate a week from two a day. It was not hard to eat healthfully from the Mieles' kitchens. Even the "junk drawer" in Park Slope was stocked with things like banana chips and sugared almonds. Lunches in Brookhaven went straight from garden to table: tomatoes with basil, eggplant, corn, zucchini flower tempura.

At his doctor's suggestion, Miele enrolled in a three-month monitored exercise program for heart disease patients, called cardiac rehab, which has been shown to reduce the mortality rate among heart patients by 20 percent. Miele's insurance covered the cost. He even managed to minimize the inconvenience, finding a class ten minutes from his country house.

He had the luxury of not having to rush back to work. By early June, he had decided he would take the summer off, and maybe cut back his workweek when he returned to the firm.

"You know, the more I think about it, the less I like the idea of going back to work," he said. "I don't see any real advantage. I mean, there's money. But you've got to take the money out of the equation."

So he put a new top on his 1964 Corvair. He played host to a large family reunion, replaced the heat exchanger in his boat, and transformed the ramshackle greenhouse into an elaborate workshop. His weight dropped to 189 pounds, from 211. He had doubled the intensity of his workouts. His blood pressure was lower than ever. . . .

Lukewarm Efforts to Reform

Will Wilson fits squarely in the city's middle class. His parents had been sharecroppers who moved north and became a machinist and a nurse. He grew up in Bedford-Stuyvesant and had spent thirty-four years at Con Ed. He had an income of $73,000, five weeks' vacation, health benefits, a house worth $450,000, and plans to retire to North Carolina when he is fifty-five.

Wilson, too, had imagined becoming an architect. But there had been no money for college, so he found a job as a utility worker. By age twenty-two, he had two children. He considered going back to school, with the company's support, to study engineering. But doing shift work, and with small children, he never found the time.

For years he was a high-voltage cable splicer, a job he loved because it meant working outdoors with plenty of freedom and overtime pay. But on a snowy night in the early 1980s, a car skidded into a stanchion, which hit him in the back. A doctor suggested that Wilson learn to live with the pain instead of having disk surgery, as Jean Miele had done.

So Wilson became a laboratory technician, then a transportation coordinator, working in a cubicle in a low-slung building in Astoria, Queens, overseeing fuel deliveries for the company's fleet. Some people might think of the work as tedious, Wilson said, "but it keeps you busy."

"Sometimes you look back over your past life experiences and you realize that if you would have done something different, you would have been someplace else," he said. "I don't dwell on it too much because I'm not in a negative position. But you do say, 'Well, dag, man, I should have done this or that.'"

Wilson's health was not bad, but far from perfect. He had quit drinking and smoking, but had high cholesterol, hypertension, and diabetes. He was slim, five foot nine, and just under 170 pounds. He traced his first heart attack to his smoking, his diet, and the stress from a grueling divorce.

His earlier efforts to reform his eating habits were half-hearted. Once he felt better, he stopped taking his cholesterol and hypertension drugs. When his cardiologist moved and referred Wilson to another doctor, he was annoyed by what he considered the rudeness of the office staff. Instead of demanding courtesy or finding another specialist, Wilson stopped going.

By the time Dr. Bhalla encountered Wilson at Brooklyn Hospital, there was damage to all three main areas of his heart. Bhalla prescribed a half-dozen drugs to lower Wilson's cholesterol, prevent clotting, and control his blood pressure.

"He has to behave himself," Bhalla said. "He needs to be more compliant with his medications. He has to really go on a diet, which is grains, no red meat, no fat. No fat at all."

Wilson had grown up eating his mother's fried chicken, pork chops, and macaroni and cheese. He confronted those same foods at holiday parties and big events. There were doughnut shops and fried chicken places in his neighborhood; but Wilson's fiancée, Melvina Murrell Green, found it hard to find fresh produce and good fish.

"People in my circle, they don't look at food as, you know, too much fat in it," Wilson said. "I don't think it's going to change. It's custom."

At Red Lobster after his second heart attack, Green would order chicken and Wilson would have salmon—plus a side order of fried shrimp. "He's still having a problem with the fried seafood," Green reported sympathetically. . . .

Ignoring the Risks

Ewa Gora is a member of the working class. A bus driver's daughter, she arrived in New York City from Kraków in the early 1990s, leaving behind a grown son. She worked as a housekeeper in a residence for the elderly in Manhattan, making beds and cleaning toilets. She said her income was $21,000 to $23,000 a year, with health insurance through her union.

For $365 a month, she rented a room in a friend's Brooklyn apartment on a street lined with aluminum-sided row houses and American flags. She used the friend's bathroom and kitchen. She was in her seventh year on a waiting list for a subsidized one-bedroom apartment in the adjacent Williamsburg neighborhood. In the meantime, she had acquired a room-mate: Edward Gora, an asbestos-removal worker newly arrived from Poland and ten years her junior, whom she met and married in 2003.

Like Jean Miele, Ewa Gora had never imagined she was at risk of a heart attack, though she was overweight, hypertensive, and a thirty-year smoker, and heart attacks had killed her father and sister. She had numerous health problems, which she addressed selectively, getting treated for back pain, ulcers, and so on, until the treatment became too expensive or inconvenient, or her insurance declined to pay.

"My doctor said, 'Ewa, be careful with cholesterol,'" recalled Gora, whose vestigial Old World sense of propriety had her dressed in heels and makeup for every visit to Bellevue. "When she said that, I think nothing; I don't care. Because I don't believe this touch me. Or I think she have to say like that because she doctor. Like cigarettes: she doctor, she always told me to stop. And when I got out of the office, lights up."

Gora had a weakness for the peak of the food pyramid. She grew up on her mother's fried pork chops, spare ribs, and meatballs—all cooked with lard—and had become a pizza, hamburger, and french fry enthusiast in the United States. Fast food was not only tasty but also affordable. "I eat terrible," she reported cheerily from her bed at Bellevue. "I like grease food and fast food. And cigarettes." . . .

If Jean Miele's encounters with the health care profession in the first months after his heart attack were occasional and efficient, Ewa Gora's were the opposite. Whereas he saw his cardiologist just twice, Gora, burdened by complications, saw hers a half-dozen times. Meanwhile, her heart attack seemed to have shaken loose a host of other problems.

A growth on her adrenal gland had turned up on a Bellevue CAT scan, prompting a visit to an endocrinologist. An old knee problem flared up; an orthopedist recommended surgery. An alarming purple rash on her leg led to a trip to a dermatologist. Because of the heart attack, she had been taken off hormone replacement therapy and was constantly sweating. She tore open a toe stepping into a pothole and needed stitches. . . .

And Gora was gaining weight. To avoid smoking, she was eating. Her work had been her exercise and now she could not work. Jad Swingle, her doctor, suggested cardiac rehab, leaving it up to Gora to find a program and arrange it. Gora let it slide. As for her diet, she had vowed to stick to chicken, turkey, lettuce, tomatoes, and low-fat cottage cheese. But she got tired of that. She began sneaking cookies when no one was looking—and no one was.

She cooked separate meals for her husband, who was not inclined to change his eating habits. She made him meatballs with sauce, liver, soup from spare ribs. Then one day she helped herself to one of his fried pork chops, and was soon eating the same meals he was. As an alternative to eating cake while watching television, she turned to pistachios, and then ate a pound in a single sitting.

When the stress test was finally done, Dr. Swingle said the results showed she was not well enough to return to full-time work. He gave her permission for part-time work, but her boss said it was out of the question. By November, four months after her heart attack, her weight had climbed to 197 pounds from 185 in July. Her cholesterol levels were stubbornly high and her blood pressure was up, despite drugs for both.

In desperation, Gora embarked upon a curious, heart-unhealthy diet clipped from a Polish-language newspaper. Day 1: two hardboiled eggs, one steak, one tomato, spinach, lettuce with lemon and olive oil. Another day: coffee, grated carrots, cottage cheese, and three containers of yogurt. Yet another: just steak. She decided not to tell her doctor. "I worry if he don't let me, I not lose the weight," she said.

Uneven Recoveries

Nearly a year after his heart attack, Jean Miele was, remarkably, better off. He had lost thirty-four pounds and was exercising five times a week and taking subway stairs two at a time. He had retired from his firm on the terms he wanted. He was working from home, billing $225 an hour. More money in less time, he said. His blood pressure and cholesterol were low. "You're doing great," Dr. Hayes had said. "You're doing better than ninety-nine percent of my patients."

Will Wilson's heart attack had been a setback. His heart function remained impaired, though improved somewhat. At one checkup in the spring of 2005, his blood pressure and his weight had been a little high. He still enjoyed fried shrimp on occasion, but he took his medications diligently. He graduated from cardiac rehab with plans to join a health club with a pool. And he was looking forward to retirement.

Ewa Gora's life and health were increasingly complex. With Dr. Swingle's reluctant approval, she returned to work in November 2004. She had moved into the subsidized apartment in Williamsburg, which gave her her own kitchen and bathroom for the first time in seven years. But she began receiving menacing phone calls from a collection agency about an old bill her health insurance had not covered. Her husband, with double pneumonia, was out of work for weeks.

She had her long-awaited knee surgery in January 2005. But it left her temporarily unable to walk. Her weight hit two hundred pounds. When the diet failed, she considered another consisting largely of fruit and vegetables sprinkled with an herbal powder. Her blood pressure and cholesterol remained ominously high. She had been warned that she was now a borderline diabetic.

"You're becoming a full-time patient, aren't you?" Swingle remarked.

66

Health, Income, and Inequality

JOHN MULLAHY, STEPHANIE ROBERT, AND BARBARA WOLFE

The idea that income is associated with health goes back a long way in the literature. Perhaps the most influential work affecting contemporary work in this area was by Samuel Preston (1975), who observed, in comparing mortality rates across countries, that the impact of additional income on health (as measured by mortality) is greater on those with low income than on those with higher income. This effect is illustrated in Figure 66.1, which shows the health of individuals on the vertical axis, plotted against the income of the individual's family group on the horizontal axis. The concave shape of the curve conveys the idea that because a dollar transferred from the rich to the poor improves the health of the poor person more than it decreases the health of the rich person, this transfer increases the average level of health of the members of a community.

This is called the *absolute income hypothesis,* and in its simplest form it argues that if all that matters to health at the level of an individual is income, a community with more equal income will tend to have better average health than a community with more

inequality when comparing two communities with equal average income. In an international context, Angus Deaton (2001) points out that, according to the absolute income hypothesis, redistribution could improve health even if average income was not increased, and that redistribution from rich to poor countries would in principle improve worldwide average health.

A related concept is the *absolute deprivation* or *poverty hypothesis.* According to this hypothesis, those with the lowest incomes face poorer health and a greater risk of mortality owing to a variety of factors associated with extreme poverty, such as inadequate nutrition, lack of quality health care, exposure to a variety of physical hazards, and heightened stress. In this hypothesis, a dollar redistributed from rich to poor would improve the health of the poor and improve the average health of the entire population. The difference between the absolute income hypothesis and the absolute deprivation or poverty hypothesis is that in the former greater income improves the health of all persons, although in a nonlinear way, while

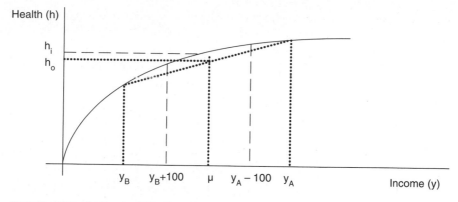

Source: Wagstaff and Van Doorslaer (2000, 546, fig. 2).

Figure 66.1   Implications of the Concavity of the Health-Income Relationship

in the latter only those who have low incomes are expected to see health improvements as a result of an increase in income.

The *relative income hypothesis* focuses on an individual's income relative to that of others in that individual's "group" rather than on his or her absolute income. According to this hypothesis, if the income of everyone but one in a group increases, that one person's health is expected to deteriorate. A related hypothesis is the *relative position* or *relative deprivation hypothesis*. According to this hypothesis, it is an individual's relative rank in society that is tied to health outcomes. This hypothesis encompasses the relative income hypothesis, but it extends the concept of relative position to measures of rank other than income, such as occupational rank or educational rank. These hypotheses are consistent with some research in the United States and the United Kingdom that demonstrates that the association between socioeconomic position and health occurs at all levels of the socioeconomic hierarchy, with even those in the highest socioeconomic groups having better health than those just below them in the socioeconomic

hierarchy, which is referred to as a "gradient effect" of socioeconomic position on health (Adler et al. 1994; Marmot et al. 1991).

The relative income and relative position hypotheses imply that it is not just the conditions experienced by those in absolute poverty that lead to poor health. Rather, there are psychosocial and other factors that remain unevenly distributed all the way up the income scale that perpetuate income inequalities in health. Perceptions of being relatively deprived ("keeping up with the Joneses"), stress, and other more psychosocial and behavioral than material factors may play a role in perpetuating income inequalities in health at the upper income levels. Health effects at the upper end of the income distribution may reflect relative position, whereas health effects at the lower end may reflect absolute deprivation (Adler and Newman 2002).

The hypothesis that focuses most directly on the tie between health inequality and income inequality is the *income inequality hypothesis*. According to the strong version of this hypothesis, societies with greater inequality produce worse health among their citizens, holding constant the average income of societies. Although these arguments were first made in comparisons of income inequality between countries, research has more recently examined whether regions, states, counties, and cities with greater income inequality have worse health than their more equal counterparts.

A Brief Review of the Evidence

Although all of these hypotheses initially seem testable, controversy arises because they are not always mutually exclusive. For example, tests of the income inequality hypothesis at the aggregate level may be empirically consistent with tests of the absolute poverty or relative income hypotheses at the individual level. Such overlap continues to obscure our understanding of the relationship between income, income inequality, and health. Without a clearer conceptual and empirical understanding of these relationships, program and policy recommendations about how to reduce income-related inequalities in health remain elusive and hotly debated.

In general, two empirical approaches have been taken to examine these hypotheses. Research examining the absolute deprivation, relative income, and relative position hypotheses has usually examined individual-level data on income and health or mortality to examine the existence and shape of the income-health relationship among individuals. Recent research has extended examination of these hypotheses by including aggregate measures of *community* socioeconomic level, such as the percentage of persons in poverty or community median family income, along with individual-level income data. In contrast, research examining the income inequality hypothesis has employed aggregate data either exclusively or at least at the level of measuring income inequality. We divide our brief review of the literature into these two general types of studies, focusing particularly on the recent research testing the income inequality hypothesis.

Income and Health

Voluminous empirical studies and reviews demonstrate a robust association between income and morbidity and mortality, using various measures of both income and health across samples and at various time points (Adler et al. 1993, 1994; Antonovsky 1967; Feinstein 1993; Williams and Collins 1995; Robert and House 2000a). To date, most of the evidence demonstrates a nonlinear rather than linear gradient relationship between income and mortality (Backlund, Sorlie, and Johnson 1996; McDonough et al. 1997; Ettner 1996) and between income and morbidity (House et al. 1990, 1994; Mirowsky and Hu 1996).

Although most research on income and health is cross-sectional, there is some evidence that there may be widening socioeconomic inequalities in health in the United Kingdom (Black et al. 1982), the United States (Pappas et al. 1993), and other developed countries (Evans, Barer, and Marmor 1994; Marmot, Kogevinas, and Elston 1987). However, Deaton (2001, 60) suggests that the rapid increases in income inequality in the 1970s and 1980s in Britain and the United States "have not been associated with any slowdown in the rate of mortality decline." To date, datasets have been of insufficiently long duration or too incomplete in terms of longitudinal information on both income and health to explore the relationship between income, income inequality, and health over time.

Figure 66.2 reports on trends in family income from 1974 to 1996. It illustrates the

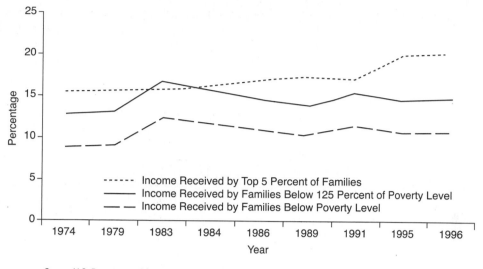

Source: U.S. Department of Commerce (2000, tables 745, 760).

Figure 66.2   Trends in Income of U.S. Families, 1974 to 1996

growing share of income received by the top 5 percent of families and shows the proportion of U.S. families below the official poverty line and the proportion who are near-poor (those below 125 percent of the poverty line). The growing share of the top 5 percent is indicative of growing inequality; the proportion poor and near-poor shows a more complicated picture—an increase from 1974 to 1983, a decline through 1989, followed by a smaller increase to 1991, with little change in the next few years.

Figure 66.3 reports the proportion of the population who reported poor or fair health by income group over these same years. Consistent with both the absolute income and deprivation hypotheses and the relative income and deprivation hypotheses, the health of the poor is always worse than that of the nonpoor, and the health of the near-poor is between the two. The trends over time show a continual improvement in the health of the non-poor, but not among the poor and near-poor: in both cases, after some improvement over the period 1974 to 1989, there was some deterioration in health from 1991 to 1996. Caution should be used in viewing these trends, however, since the way in which these health statistics are reported changed over this time period; hence the "jump" may be due to the reporting change. The increase after 1991, however, cannot be explained by the change in reporting, since there were no further changes.

Health status also differs systematically by race, and increasing attention is being paid to racial inequalities in health in the United States. There is a strong but far from complete overlap between racial and income inequalities in health (Williams 2002; Hayward et al. 2000; Williams and Collins 1995; Sorlie, Backlund, and Keller 1995; Ren and Amick 1996). Although this overlap is often acknowledged, it is not explicitly examined in much research on income and health.

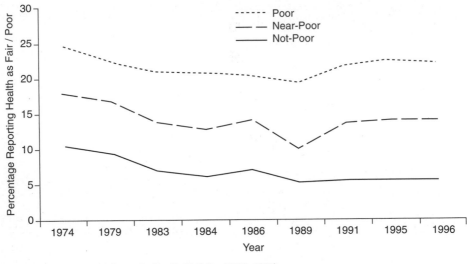

Source: National Center for Health Statistics (1998–1999).

Figure 66.3   Trends in Self-Reported Health of U.S. Families by Family Income, 1974 to 1996

Figures 66.4 and 66.5 present the trend in poverty and in poor and fair health for white and African American respondents. Figure 66.5 highlights the well-known higher poverty rates among African Americans and the higher proportion of African Americans with poor or fair health relative to the white population. The trends in health are of interest, for they are consistent with a tie between poverty and overall health for whites but not for African Americans. After 1983, the two lines track closely for whites. For African Americans, Figure 66.5 shows generally improving health, while the poverty rate fluctuates more. In this case, the figure does not illustrate or suggest a link between the two, although if the trend lines began in 1983, both would show some steady decline and hence improvement in health and reduction of poverty. Clearly, more attention should be paid to measuring trends in the relationship between income, race, and health and mortality over time in the United States.

Some recent research examines not only the relationship between individual or family income and health but also the impact of the neighborhood or community income level on individual health (see reviews in Robert 1999; Bond Huie 2001; Pickett and Pearl 2001; Robert and House 2000b; Diez-Roux 2000, 2001). This research finds evidence that living in communities with a higher proportion of poverty households, or with overall lower income (for example, low median family income), is associated with poor health and mortality over and above the effects of individual or family income in the United States (Haan, Kaplan, and Camacho 1987; Waitzman and Smith 1998a; Robert 1998; Diez-Roux et al. 1997; Anderson et al. 1997; Blakely, Lochner, and Kawachi 2002). Living in poorer communities may be detrimental to the health of all residents, regardless of their own income.

Most of this multilevel research, however, finds that individual- or family-level

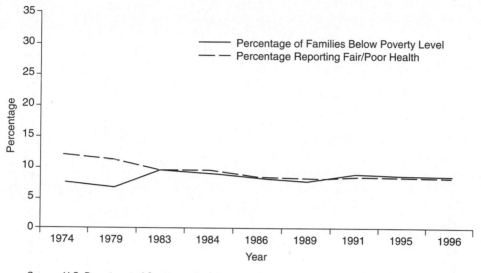

Source: U.S. Department of Commerce (2000) National Center for Health Statistics (1981 to 1999).

Figure 66.4   Comparing Self-Reported Health and Poverty Status of U.S. Families: White Families, 1974 to 1996

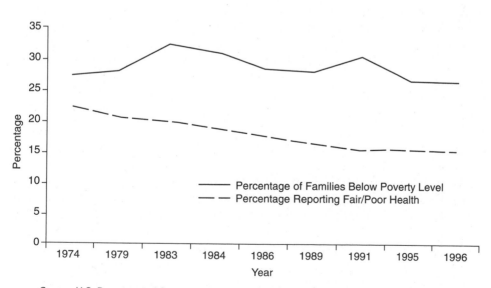

Source: U.S. Department of Commerce (2000) National Center for Health Statistics (1981 to 1999).

Figure 66.5   Comparing Self-Reported Health and Poverty Status of U.S. Families: African American Families, 1974 to 1996

socioeconomic characteristics are more significant correlates of health than are community variables (Robert 1998; Brooks-Gunn,
Duncan, and Aber 1997; Elliott et al. 1996).

Combining multilevel research on the individual and community socioeconomic
context and health with research on race, income, and health may be particularly important. For example, because the United States
is residentially segregated by race (Jargowsky
1997; Massey and Denton 1993; Wilson
1987), African American and non-Hispanic
white people of the same family income level
live in very different neighborhoods. In a
study by Stephanie Robert and Kum Yi Lee
(2002), the disadvantaged health status of
African American older adults that remains
after controlling for individual SES is further
explained after considering community socioeconomic characteristics. The higher
number of chronic conditions experienced
by African American older adults is explained
only after considering both individual-level
and community-level socioeconomic characteristics. Moreover, Robert and Lee demonstrate that African American older adults may
even have slightly better self-rated health
than non-African American older adults once
the individual SES and the community socioeconomic context are controlled.

A number of researchers have also
demonstrated the necessity of exploring
more explicitly how the community racial
context and individual race and ethnicity
are related to community and individual
income and health (Deaton and Lubotsky
2003; Collins and Williams 1999; Robert
and House 2000b; Haan, Kaplan, and Camacho 1987; LeClere, Rogers, and Peters
1997, 1998; Robert 2002; Nazroo 2003;
Krieger 2003; Acevedo-Garcia et al. 2003;
Miller and Paxson 2001). What role do
racial distribution, concentration, and seg-

regation play in determining or explaining
community-, family-, and individual-level
income inequalities in health? We turn to
these questions.

Income Inequality and Health

Whereas the evidence for a relationship between individual income and health is
strong and relatively consistent, the evidence for a relationship between aggregate
measures of income inequality and health is
weak and controversial. There has been
much focus in recent years on the latter research, with heated and excited debate
about the importance to health and well-
being of living in more or less unequal
places. Ironically, the focus on this latter,
more speculative, research may have unwittingly diverted attention from the former,
more consistent, research.

The literature regarding the income inequality hypothesis must refer to Richard
Wilkinson, given the influence of his writings on the field. In various writings over
the last decade (see, for example, Wilkinson 1992, 1994, 1996), he has provided
evidence of a relationship between income
inequality in a country and life expectancy,
both at a point in time and over time.
However, other researchers have raised
questions about this evidence, calling into
doubt the reliability of the data Wilkinson
uses to measure income inequality (Gravelle, Wildman, and Sutton 2002; Mellor
and Milyo 2001). Using two more recent
datasets considered to be of superior quality, two teams of researchers, Ken Judge,
Jo-Ann Mulligan, and Michaela Benzeval
(1998) and Hugh Gravelle, John Wildman, and Matthew Sutton (2002), find no
significant relationship between income inequality and life expectancy across developed countries.

The idea that income inequality per se may influence health has caught the attention of many researchers, and a growing body of literature tests this hypothesis not only at the level of countries but across regions, states, counties, and cities within nations. For example, using states as the unit of comparison, George Kaplan and his colleagues (1996) and Bruce Kennedy, Ichiro Kawachi, and Deborah Prothrow-Stith (1996) find a significant relationship between several mortality rates and income inequality. Kennedy and his colleagues (1998) also find similar associations between self-rated health and income inequality. Kaplan and his colleagues find a tie between mortality rates and inequality in household income at the state level in the United States, even when median incomes are included. Kennedy and his colleagues (1996) use an alternative index of inequality, the "Robin Hood Index," also using state data for the United States. In their analysis of a variety of mortality rates, inequality is a statistically significant predictor. A follow-up study by Kawachi and Kennedy (1997) explores additional measures of inequality and mortality with similar results: a statistically significant link between measures of income inequality at the state level and health as measured by mortality rates. Examining 283 metropolitan areas as units of analysis rather than states, John Lynch, George Kaplan, and Elsie Pamuk (1998) similarly look at the relationships between multiple measures of inequality and mortality. The inequality measures predict mortality over and above other community-level factors, such as per capita income and the proportion of the population with incomes under 200 percent of the poverty level. Using county and tract-level data, Felicia LeClere and Mah-

Jabeen Soobader (2000) find independent income inequality effects primarily at the county level, but only for some specific subgroups by age, race, and gender. In these studies, various controls were added for median income, for proportion below the poverty line or near poverty, per capita income, and average household size.

Although most researchers accept this raw association between income inequality and health, even after controlling for median income levels or poverty, debate arises primarily over potential *explanations* for this relationship. Lynch and his colleagues (2000) describe three types of explanations for the association between income inequality and health: the individual income interpretation, the psychosocial environment interpretation, and the neomaterial interpretation. According to the *individual income interpretation,* aggregate associations between income inequality and health simply reflect the nonlinear (concave) relation between income and health at the individual level. According to the *psychosocial environment interpretation,* perceptions of inequality produce instabilities in social capital—perceived mistrust, lack of social cohesion, and so on—that work through behaviors and psychosocial responses that affect an individual's biological responses and ultimate health. The *neomaterial interpretation* suggests that places with the greatest income inequality are places that also have inequalities in human, physical, health, and social infrastructure that ultimately affect health.

The individual income interpretation suggests that, theoretically, if the relationship between individual income and health is nonlinear, then there should be an aggregate-level association between income inequality and health (Ecob and

Davey Smith 1999; Gravelle 1998; Preston 1975; Rodgers 1979). Empirically, this has been tested in several studies that control for individual income while examining the association between income inequality and health. The association between income inequality and health or mortality sometimes remains after controlling for individual SES (Waitzman and Smith 1998b; Soobader and LeClere 1999; Fiscella and Franks 2000; Kennedy et al. 1998; LeClere and Soobader 2000; Lochner et al. 2001), and sometimes it does not (Fiscella and Franks 1997, 2000; Mellor and Milyo 1999; LeClere and Soobader 2000; Blakely, Lochner, and Kawachi 2002; Daly et al. 1998). For example, Tony Blakely, Kimberly Lochner, and Ichiro Kawachi (2002) use individual-level data from the 1996 and 1998 Current Population Survey in conjunction with 1990 Gini coefficient measures at the metropolitan area (MA) levels to look at self-rated health. They find no significant association between MA-level income inequality and health self-rated as poor or fair after controlling for sex, age, race, individual-level household income, and MA-level household income. In a recent review, Subramanian, Blakely, and Kawachi (2003) suggest that the only consistent associations between income inequality and health in multilevel studies may be seen at the state level in the United States, rather than at either smaller levels of aggregation within the United States or between or within other countries.

It seems crucial to explore further the extent to which the relationship between measures of inequality at the aggregate level and health reflects the nonlinear association between individual income and health. However, even if the aggregate relationship were fully explained by the individual-level

relationship, the interpretation of this finding would still be open for debate. Should the aggregate relationship then be seen as an artifact of the individual-level data, and therefore not meaningful, or does income inequality at more macro levels play a more causal role in producing or reproducing income inequalities in health?

Much of the heated debate in the literature on income inequality and health seems to stem from reactions to the so-called psychosocial environment interpretation. A number of researchers have explored the possibility that inequality per se produces a social environment that ultimately affects an individual's health (see, for example, Wilkinson 1996). For example, Kawachi and his colleagues (1997) suggest that high income inequality within states is associated with low social cohesion and disinvestment in social capital, which then affect mortality. Examples of this would be the relative income and deprivation hypotheses, which suggest that an individual's perceived relative income or position may affect health through psychosocial pathways (Adler et al. 1994).

Proponents of the neomaterial interpretation believe that more consideration should be given to factors that exist outside of, or as precursors to, psychosocial pathways. For example, Lynch and his colleagues (2000) point out that there are structural, political, and economic processes that generate inequality, and that these processes exist before individuals experience or perceive their effects. Therefore, focusing on the structural, political, and economic processes that both produce and result from inequality may be more appropriate than attending primarily to individual perceptions or experiences that occur downstream from these processes.

Examples of research exploring neomaterial interpretations of the link between income inequality and health include research that explores the potential intermediating role of public investment in, for instance, health care, public safety, education, and environmental quality. To the extent that such investments are concentrated in higher-income areas, or in less unequal areas, then an individual living in such areas gains more access to such goods and services (Kaplan et al. 1996; Lynch, Kaplan, and Pamuk 1998; Davey Smith 1996). The neomaterial interpretation implies that greater income inequality in society leads to greater differences in resources across communities that are associated with greater differences in health across communities. This finding highlights deprivation, but in this view deprivation at the individual level is compounded by deprivation at the community level as socioeconomic segregation and greater income inequality make the indirect costs of acquisition of health care and a healthy lifestyle more expensive to those with the lowest incomes. This suggests interaction effects between income inequality and individual income level. A number of studies suggest that income inequality may be a significant determinant of health, but only for those with the lowest incomes (Mellor and Milyo 1999; Soobader and LeClere 1999).

Critiquing the Literature on Income Inequality and Health

To summarize our primary understanding of the literature on income, income inequality, and health: there is a strong relationship between individual income and health that persists, and perhaps strengthens, over time. The shape of the relationship between income and health appears to be nonlinear, such that increases in income among those at the low end of the distribution should have greater positive consequences for their health than similar increases in income would have for the health of those at the top end of the income distribution. Much attention has been paid recently to the possibility that income inequality per se is related to health. The results of this research are still tenuous, though deserving of further study. However, it appears that the focus on this more tenuous research has unwittingly diverted attention from the former research on individual income and health. We conclude that (1) more research is needed to examine the relationship between income inequality and health, although (2) the greater advances in our understanding of the relationship between income and health will come from research that refocuses attention on the relationship between individual income level and health. Nevertheless, even if the primary relationship between income and health should be examined at the individual level, mediators of this relationship may very well operate at more aggregate levels such as households or neighborhoods.

REFERENCES

Acevedo-Garcia, Dolores, Kimberly A. Lochner, Theresa L. Osypuk, and Sukanya V. Subramanian. 2003. "Future Directions in Residential Segregation and Health Research: A Multilevel Approach." *American Journal of Public Health* 93(2): 215–21.

Adler, Nancy E., Thomas Boyce, Margaret A. Chesney, Sheldon Cohen, Susan Folkman, Robert L. Kahn, and S. Leonard Syme. 1994. "Socioeconomic Status and Health: The Challenge of the Gradient." *American Psychologist* 49(1): 15–24.

Adler, Nancy E., W. Thomas Boyce, Margaret A. Chesney, Susan Folkman, and S. Leonard

Syme. 1993. "Socioeconomic Inequalities in Health: No Easy Solution." *Journal of the American Medical Association* 269: 3140–45.

Adler, Nancy E., and Katherine Newman. 2002. "Socioeconomic Disparities in Health: Pathways and Policies." *Health Affairs* 21(2): 60–76.

Anderson, Roger T., Paul Sorlie, Eric Backlund, Norman Johnson, and George A. Kaplan. 1997. "Mortality Effects of Community Socioeconomic Status." *Epidemiology* 8: 42–47.

Antonovsky, Aaron. 1967. "Social Class, Life Expectancy, and Overall Mortality." *Milbank Memorial Fund Quarterly* 45: 31–73.

Backlund, Eric, Paul D. Sorlie, and Norman J. Johnson. 1996. "The Shape of the Relationship Between Income and Mortality in the United States: Evidence from the National Longitudinal Mortality Study." *Annals of Epidemiology* 6(1): 12–20.

Black, Douglas, J. N. Morris, Cyril Smith, and Peter Townsend. 1982. *Inequalities in Health: The Black Report.* New York: Penguin.

Blakely, Tony A., Kimberly Lochner, and Ichiro Kawachi. 2002. "Metropolitan-Area Income Inequality and Self-Rated Health: A Multilevel Study." *Social Science and Medicine* 54(1): 65–77.

Bond Huie, Stephanie A. 2001. "The Concept of Neighborhood in Health and Mortality Research." *Sociological Spectrum* 21: 341–58.

Brooks-Gunn, Jeanne, Greg J. Duncan, and J. Lawrence Aber, eds. 1997. *Neighborhood Poverty: Context and Consequences for Children,* vol. 1. New York: Russell Sage Foundation.

Collins, Chiquita A., and David R. Williams. 1999. "Segregation and Mortality: The Deadly Effects of Racism?" *Sociological Forum* 14(3): 495–523.

Daly, Mary C., Greg J. Duncan, George A. Kaplan, and John W. Lynch. 1998. "Macro-to-Micro Links in the Relation Between Income Inequality and Mortality." *Milbank Memorial Fund Quarterly* 76(3): 303–4, 315–39.

Davey Smith, George. 1996. "Income Inequality and Mortality: Why Are They Related?" *British Medical Journal* 313: 987–88.

Deaton, Angus. 2001. "Health, Inequality, and Economic Development." Working paper

8318. Cambridge, Mass.: National Bureau of Economic Research (June).

Deaton, Angus, and Darren Lubotsky. 2003. "Mortality, Inequality, and Race in American Cities and States." *Social Science and Medicine* 56(6): 1139–53.

Diez-Roux, Ana V. 2000. "Multilevel Analysis in Public Health Research." *Annual Review of Public Health* 21: 171–92.

_____. 2001. "Investigating Neighborhood and Area Effects on Health." *American Journal of Public Health* 91: 1783–89.

Diez-Roux, Ana V., F. Javier Nieto, Carles Muntaner, Herman A. Tyroler, George W. Comstock, Elad Shahar, Leslie S. Cooper, Robert L. Watson, and Moyses Szklo. 1997. "Neighborhood Environments and Coronary Heart Disease: A Multilevel Analysis." *American Journal of Epidemiology* 146(1): 48–63.

Ecob, Russell, and George Davey Smith. 1999. "Income and Health: What Is the Nature of the Relationship?" *Social Science and Medicine* 48(5): 693–705.

Elliott, Delbert S., William J. Wilson, David Huizinga, Robert J. Sampson, Amanda Elliott, and Bruce Rankin. 1996. "The Effects of Neighborhood Disadvantage on Adolescent Development." *Journal of Research in Crime and Delinquency* 33: 389–426.

Ettner, Susan L. 1996. "New Evidence on the Relationship Between Income and Health." *Journal of Health Economics* 15(1): 67–86.

Evans, Robert G., Morris L. Barer, and Theodore R. Marmor, eds. 1994. *Why Are Some People Healthy and Others Not? The Determinants of Health of Populations.* New York: Aldine de Gruyter.

Feinstein, Jonathan S. 1993. "The Relationship Between Socioeconomic Status and Health: A Review of the Literature." *Milbank Memorial Fund Quarterly* 71: 279–322.

Fiscella, Kevin, and Peter Franks. 2000. "Individual Income, Income Inequality, Health, and Mortality: What Are the Relationships?" *Health Services Research* 35(1): 307–18.

Gravelle, Hugh. 1998. "How Much of the Relationship Between Population Mortality and Unequal Distribution of Income Is a Statistical

Artifact?" *British Medical Journal* 316: 382–85.

Gravelle, Hugh, John Wildman, and Matthew Sutton. 2002. "Income, Income Inequality, and Health: What Can We Learn from the Aggregate Data?" *Social Science and Medicine* 54: 577–89.

Haan, Mary, George A. Kaplan, and Terry Camacho. 1987. "Poverty and Health: Prospective Evidence from the Alameda County Study." *American Journal of Epidemiology* 125(6): 989–98.

Hayward, Mark D., Toni P. Miles, Eileen M. Crimmins, and Yu Yang. 2000. "The Significance of Socioeconomic Status in Explaining the Racial Gap in Chronic Health Conditions." *American Sociological Review* 65: 910–30.

House, James S., Ronald C. Kessler, A. Regula Herzog, Richard P. Mero, Ann M. Kinney, and Martha J. Breslow. 1990. "Age, Socioeconomic Status, and Health." *Milbank Memorial Fund Quarterly* 68(3): 383–411.

House, James S., James M. Lepkowski, Ann M. Kinney, Richard P. Mero, Ronald C. Kessler, and A. Regula Herzog. 1994. "The Social Stratification of Aging and Health." *Journal of Health and Social Behavior* 35: 213–34.

Jargowsky, Paul A. 1997. *Poverty and Place: Ghettos, Barrios, and the American City.* New York: Russell Sage Foundation.

Judge, Ken, Jo-Ann Mulligan, and Michaela Benzeval. 1998. "Income Inequality and Population Health." *Social Science and Medicine* 46(4–5): 567–79.

Kaplan, George A., Elsie R. Pamuk, John W. Lynch, Richard D. Cohen, and Jennifer L. Balfour. 1996. "Inequality in Income and Mortality in the United States: Analysis of Mortality and Potential Pathways." *British Medical Journal* 312: 999–1003.

Kawachi, Ichiro, and Bruce P. Kennedy. 1997. "The Relationship of Income Inequality to Mortality: Does the Choice of Indicator Matter?" *Social Science and Medicine* 45: 1121–27.

Kawachi, Ichiro, Bruce P. Kennedy, Kimberly Lochner, and Deborah Prothrow-Stith. 1997. "Social Capital, Income Inequality, and Mortality." *American Journal of Public Health* 87(9): 1491–98.

Kennedy, Bruce P., Ichiro Kawachi, Roberta Glass, and Deborah Prothrow-Stith. 1998. "Income Distribution, Socioeconomic Status, and Self-rated Health in the United States: Multilevel Analysis." *British Medical Journal* 317: 917–21.

Kennedy, Bruce P., Ichiro Kawachi, and Deborah Prothrow-Stith. 1996. "Income Distribution and Mortality: Cross-sectional Ecological Study of the Robin Hood Index in the United States." *British Medical Journal* 312: 1004–7.

Krieger, Nancy. 2003. "Does Racism Harm Health? Did Child Abuse Exist Before 1962? On Explicit Questions, Critical Science, and Current Controversies: An Ecosocial Perspective." *American Journal of Public Health* 93(2): 194–99.

LeClere, Felicia B., and Mah-Jabeen Soobader. 2000. "The Effect of Income Inequality on the Health of Selected U.S. Demographic Groups." *American Journal of Public Health* 90(12): 1892–97.

Lynch, John W., George A. Kaplan, and Elsie R. Pamuk. 1998. "Income Inequality and Mortality in Metropolitan Areas of the United States." *American Journal of Public Health* 88: 1074–80.

Lynch, John W., George Davey Smith, George A. Kaplan, and James S. House. 2000. "Income Inequality and Mortality: Importance to Health of Individual Income, Psychosocial Environment, or Material Conditions." *British Medical Journal* 320(7243): 1200–4.

Marmot, Michael G., Manolis Kogevinas, and Mary Ann Elston. 1987. "Social/Economic Status and Disease." *Annual Review of Public Health* 8: 111–35.

Marmot, Michael G., G. Davey Smith, Stephen A. Stansfeld, C. Patel, F. North, J. Head, I. White, E. J. Brunner, and A. Feeney. 1991. "Health Inequalities Among British Civil Servants: The Whitehall II Study." *Lancet* 337(8754):1387–93.

Massey, Douglas S. 1990. "American Apartheid: Segregation and the Making of the Underclass." *American Journal of Sociology* 96: 329–58.

Massey, Douglas S., and Nancy A. Denton. 1993. *American Apartheid: Segregation and the Making of the Underclass.* Cambridge, Mass.: Harvard University Press.

McDonough, Peggy, Greg J. Duncan, David Williams, and James House. 1997. "Income Dynamics and Adult Mortality in the United States, 1972 Through 1989." *American Journal of Public Health* 87(9): 1476–83.

Mellor, Jennifer M., and Jeffrey D. Milyo. 1999. "Income Inequality and Individual Health: Evidence from the Current Population Survey." Working paper 8. Boston: Robert Wood Johnson Foundation Scholars in Health Policy Research Program.

_____. 2001. "Reexamining the Evidence of an Ecological Association Between Income Inequality and Health." *Journal of Health Politics, Policy, and Law* 26(3): 487–522.

Miller, Douglas, and Christina Paxson. 2001. "Relative Income, Race, and Mortality." Working paper. Princeton, N.J.: Princeton University, Center for Health and Wellbeing.

Mirowsky, John, and Paul Nongzhuang Hu. 1996. "Physical Impairment and the Diminishing Effects of Income." *Social Forces* 74: 1073–96.

National Center for Health Statistics. Various years. *Health, United States.* Washington: U.S. Government Printing Office.

Nazroo, James Y. 2003. "The Structuring of Ethnic Inequalities in Health: Economic Position, Racial Discrimination, and Racism." *American Journal of Public Health* 93(2): 277–84.

Pappas, Gregory, Susan Queen, Wilbur Hadden, and Gail Fisher. 1993. "The Increasing Disparity in Mortality Between Socioeconomic Groups in the United States, 1960 and 1986." *New England Journal of Medicine* 329: 103–9.

Pickett, Kate E., and Michelle Pearl. 2001. "Multilevel Analyses of Neighborhood Socioeconomic Context and Health Outcomes: A Critical Review." *Journal of Epidemiology and Community Health* 55: 111–22.

Preston, Samuel. 1975. "The Changing Relation Between Mortality and Level of Development." *Population Studies* 29: 231–48.

Ren, Xinhua S., and Benjamin Amick. 1996. "Race and Self-assessed Health Status: The Role of Socioeconomic Factors in the United States." *Journal of Epidemiology and Community Health* 50: 269–73.

Robert, Stephanie A. 1998. "Community-Level Socioeconomic Status Effects on Adult Health." *Journal of Health and Social Behavior* 39: 18–37.

_____. 1999. "Socioeconomic Position and Health: The Independent Contribution of Community Context." *Annual Review of Sociology* 25: 489–516.

Robert, Stephanie A., and James S. House. 2000a. "Socioeconomic Inequalities in Health: An Enduring Sociological Problem." In *Handbook of Medical Sociology,* edited by Chloe E. Bird, Peter Conrad, and Allen M. Fremont. New York: Prentice-Hall.

_____. 2000b. "Socioeconomic Inequalities in Health: Integrating Individual-, Community-, and Societal-Level Theory and Research." In *Handbook of Social Studies in Health and Medicine,* edited by Gary L. Albrecht, Ray Fitzpatrick, and Susan C. Scrimshaw. London: Sage Publications.

Robert, Stephanie A., and Kum Yi Lee. 2002. "Explaining Race Differences in Health Among Older Adults: The Contribution of Community Socioeconomic Context." *Research on Aging* 24(6): 654–83.

Rodgers, Gerry B. 1979. "Income and Inequality as Determinants of Mortality: An International Cross-section Analysis." *Population Studies* 33: 343–51.

Soobader, Mah-Jabeen, and Felicia B. LeClere. 1999. "Aggregation and the Measurement of Income Inequality: Effects on Morbidity." *Social Science and Medicine* 48: 733–44.

Sorlie, Paul D., Eric Backlund, and Jacob B. Keller. 1995. "U.S. Mortality by Economic, Demographic, and Social Characteristics: The National Longitudinal Mortality Study." *American Journal of Public Health* 85: 949–56.

Subramanian, Sukanya V., Tony Blakely, and Ichiro Kawachi. 2003. "Income Inequality as a Public Health Concern: Where Do We Stand?" *Health Services Research* 38: 153–67.

U.S. Department of Commerce. U.S. Census Bureau. 2000. *Statistical Abstract of the United*

States: 2000. Washington: U.S. Government Printing Office.

Wagstaff, Adam, and Eddy van Doorslaer. 2000. "Income Inequality and Health: What Does the Literature Tell Us?" *Annual Review of Public Health* 21: 543–67.

Waitzman, Norman J., and Ken R. Smith. 1998a. "Phantom of the Area: Poverty-Area Residence and Mortality in the United States." *American Journal of Public Health* 88(6): 973–76.

———. 1998b. "Separate but Lethal: The Effects of Economic Segregation on Mortality in Metropolitan America." *Milbank Memorial Fund Quarterly* 76(3): 341–73.

Wilkinson, Richard G. 1992. "Income Distribution and Life Expectancy." *British Medical Journal* 304: 165–68.

———. 1994. "The Epidemiological Transition: From Material Scarcity to Social Disadvantage?" *Daedalus* 123: 61–77.

———. 1996. *Unhealthy Societies: The Affliction of Inequality.* London: Routledge.

Williams, David R. 2002. "Racial/Ethnic Variations in Women's Health: The Social Embeddedness of Health." *American Journal of Public Health* 92(4): 588–97.

Williams, David R., and Chiquita Collins. 1995. "U.S. Socioeconomic and Racial Differences in Health: Patterns and Explanations." *Annual Review of Sociology* 21: 349–86.

Wilson, William Julius. 1987. *The Truly Disadvantaged: The Inner City, the Underclass, and Public Policy.* Chicago: University of Chicago Press.

67

The Social Stratification of Theatre, Dance, and Cinema Attendance

TAK WING CHAN AND
JOHN H. GOLDTHORPE

In current sociological literature the relationship between social inequality and patterns of cultural taste and consumption is the subject of a large and complex debate. This paper starts by outlining the leading positions that have been taken up in this debate, and then presents some illustrative findings from a research programme in which the authors are currently engaged. These findings are used chiefly as the basis for a critical evaluation of the rival positions that have been set out, although they may also be of interest in their own right. In addition, attention is drawn to the methodology on which the paper rests. Although this may appear somewhat daunting, at least to readers who lack a statistical background, it is, we would argue, only by following such an approach that the issues with which we are concerned can be adequately addressed.

In the sociological literature referred to, it is possible to identify three main lines of argument. In their essentials, these arguments can be stated as follows, although each has variant forms.

1. *The homology argument:* this claims that social stratification—that is, the prevailing structure of inequality within a society—and cultural stratification map onto each other very closely. Individuals in higher social strata are those who prefer and predominantly consume 'high' or 'elite' culture, and individuals in lower social strata are those who prefer and predominantly consume 'popular' or 'mass' culture—with, usually, various intermediate situations being also recognized. In some versions of the argument (e.g. Bourdieu, 1984) it is further claimed that the arrogation of 'distinction' in cultural taste and, conversely, processes of 'aesthetic distancing' are actively used by members of dominant social classes as means of symbolically demonstrating and confirming their superiority.

2. *The individualization argument:* this seeks in effect to relegate the homology argument to the past. In modern, relatively affluent and highly commercialized societies, it is held that differences

Tak Wing Chan and John H. Goldthorpe, "The Social Stratification of Theatre, Dance, and Cinema Attendance," *Cultural Trends* 14 (September 2005), pp. 194–201, 203–205, 207–208, 211–212.

in cultural taste and consumption are rapidly losing any clear grounding in social stratification: age, gender, ethnicity or sexuality, for example, all can, and do, serve as alternative social bases of cultural differentiation. And in more radical forms of the argument (e.g. Bauman, 1988; Featherstone, 1987), emphasis is placed on the growing ability of individuals to free themselves from social conditioning and influence of any kind and to choose and form their own distinctive identities and lifestyles—patterns of cultural consumption included.

3. *The omnivore–univore argument:* this in effect challenges both the homology and individualization arguments (see especially Peterson & Kern, 1996; Peterson & Simkus, 1992). As against the latter, it sees cultural differentiation as still mapping closely onto social stratification; but, as against the former, it does not see this mapping as being on 'elite-to-mass' lines. Rather, it claims that the cultural consumption of individuals in higher social strata differs from that of individuals in lower social strata in that it is *greater and much wider in its range.* It comprises not only more 'high-brow' culture, but also more 'middle-brow' and more 'low-brow' culture as well, while the consumption of individuals in lower social strata tends to be largely restricted to more popular cultural forms. Thus, the crucial distinction is not between elite and mass but rather between cultural omnivores and cultural univores.

In other work (Chan & Goldthorpe, 2005), we seek to evaluate these three argu-

ments by analysing data on musical consumption. Far stronger, even if still somewhat qualified, support is found for the omnivore–univore argument than for either the homology or individualization argument, as explained further below. However, it has to be noted that the omnivore–univore argument was initially developed with specific reference to musical consumption (Peterson & Simkus, 1992); and while, in this context, it has in fact received support additional to that of the present authors (see e.g. Coulangeon, 2003; Van Eijck, 2001), its wider application has been rather little studied. The present paper, therefore, aims to examine how well it fares in another domain of cultural consumption, that of theatre, dance and cinema. This differs from music in several ways, but perhaps most obviously for present purposes in that consumption generally requires attendance at some venue and, with the main exception of video film (which is discounted in what follows), there is no equivalent to the home consumption via various media that is of major importance in the domain of music.

Data and Concepts

As in the authors' work on musical consumption, data is used from the Arts in England survey which was carried out by the Office for National Statistics on behalf of Arts Council England. The survey was based on a stratified probability sample of individuals aged over 16 and living in private households in England in 2001. In all, 6,042 interviews were completed, representing a response rate of 64 per cent (for further details, see Skelton *et al.,* 2002). However, here attention is restricted to respondents aged 20 to 64. With this limitation, and after deleting all cases with missing values on variables of interest here, there is an effective sample of $N = 3,819$.

As regards theatre and cinema attendance, attention is concentrated on the results obtained in the survey from six questions. Respondents were asked whether or not, in the last 12 months, they had attended a performance of a play/drama, a musical, a pantomime, a ballet, some other form of dance (including contemporary dance, African People's dance and South Asian dance), or had seen a film at a cinema (or other venue rather than at home). It should be stressed that interest in these results lies not primarily in the answers given to each question taken separately, but rather in the possibility that the answers to the six questions *taken together* can reveal *patterns* of theatre and cinema consumption and in turn serve to identify *types of consumer* in this domain. As will be seen, this interest is reflected in the way in which the data are analysed.

As regards social stratification, we believe it important to do more than treat this through some single classification or scale of an essentially *ad hoc* kind—such as, say, the Market Research Society categories (AB, C1, C2, D) or the old Registrar General's Social Classes. Therefore information collected in the Arts in England survey on respondents' employment and occupation is drawn on in order to allocate them by both *social class* and *social status,* which are viewed, following a long-established tradition in sociology, as *conceptually separate forms of stratification.*

The class structure overall, and likewise individuals' positions within it, are seen as being defined in a quite objective way by economic relations or, more precisely, by relations in labour markets and production units. To allocate individuals by class, the new National Statistics Socio-Economic Classification (NS-SEC) is used—in its seven-category version—which is specifically designed to capture differences in employment relations (Rose & Pevalin, 2003). The categories of the classification are shown in Table 67.4. In contrast, the status order is seen as reflecting inter-subjective assessments of individuals' social superiority, equality and inferiority as expressed most directly in relations of social intimacy. Such relations, where present among members of different social groupings, imply a basic equality of status and, where absent, a recognition of inequality. To allocate individuals by status, a 31-category occupationally based scale developed by the authors from analyses of patterns of close friendship in contemporary British society is used (Chan & Goldthorpe, 2004). The categories of this scale are shown in rank order, from high to low status, in Table 67.5. The closer together any two categories in the scale are, the more similar, occupationally, are their members' friends; the further apart they are, the less similar are their members' friends.

In any society, the positions of individuals within the class structure and the status order will tend to be correlated—but not perfectly so. Instances of discrepancy between class and status position are always likely to occur. For example, the authors' own results indicate that in present-day Britain salaried professionals and associate professionals tend to have higher status than do salaried managers, and especially managers in manufacturing, construction or transport, despite holding similar class positions as defined in terms of employment relations; or again that routine wage workers in services, especially personal services, tend to have higher status than even skilled manual workers. Since class and status are only imperfectly correlated, it is possible to ask whether it is the one or the other that exerts the greater influence on individuals' experience and action across different areas of social life. There is, for example, evidence that class is the dominant influence so far as individuals' economic life-chances are concerned—i.e. in determining their degree of economic security and their prospects—and also in shaping their political orientations and affiliations. But, in contrast, the expectation would be that in regard to cultural consumption it is status that will carry the greater weight. This is because differences in status are typically expressed in lifestyles, and cultural consumption is one important aspect of lifestyle through which status 'markers' can be readily laid down. In order to test whether this expectation holds good, it is of course essential that one should be able to distinguish class and status, conceptually and operationally.

In addition to treating class and status separately, we also draw on information available from the Arts in England Survey on respondents' incomes and on their educational qualifications. The latter are coded to the six National Vocational Qualification levels that range from 'no qualifications' to 'degree-level qualification or higher'. In sociological analyses of cultural consumption, income and education are often taken as substitutes or proxies for more direct measures of class or status of the kind to be used in the present study. However, income and education are here considered *along with* such measures of class and status, so that their independent effects, if any, can be established.

Finally, also included in the present analyses is socio-demographic information

Table 67.1   Percentage of Respondents Who Have Visited a Cinema or a Theatre for Various Kinds of Performance in the Past Twelve Months

Ballet	1.9
Other dance	12.7
Pantomime	14.6
Musical	25.4
Play/drama	29.0
Cinema	62.7

collected in the Arts in England survey, in particular regarding respondents' sex, age, marital status, family composition and region of residence. Given that the primary concern is with the social stratification of theatre, dance and cinema attendance, these socio-demographic variables are intended to serve primarily as 'controls': that is to say, they are brought into analyses chiefly in order to remove the possibility of any hidden confounding of their effects with those of class, status, income and education on which present interest centres.

Analytical Strategy

In Table 67.1 we show the percentage of respondents who in the last year had attended a theatre, for performances of the kinds previously indicated, or a cinema. As can be seen, there is some wide variation in the probabilities of attendance, although much on lines that might be expected. Cinema attendance is by far the most frequently reported, while, at the other extreme, going to the theatre for a ballet performance is at a very low level.

As earlier remarked, we wish to treat the data in question primarily as basis for obtaining an understanding of individuals' patterns of theatre and cinema attendance and of the different types of consumer in this cultural domain. To this end, a statistical

Table 67.2 · Latent Class Models Fitted to Data on Cultural Participation in the Domain of Theatre, Dance and Cinema

Model	Number of classes	G^2	df	p
1	1	1583.64	57	0.00
2	2	268.16	50	0.00
3	2[a]	53.22	49	0.31

[a]A local dependence term is included in this model to allow for an association between attendance at ballet and other dance events.

technique known as latent class analysis is employed, which can be intuitively understood as follows.

There are six questions that serve as indicators of theatre or cinema attendance. Since each question has a two-option (yes/no) answer, there are in fact 2^6 or 64 different possible response sets. The overall pattern of individuals' responses will therefore be complex. But the answers given by respondents to the six questions can be expected to show some degree of association. Thus, for example, those who say that they have been to a play are also likely to report having been to a cinema. Conversely, those who say that they have not been to a ballet are also likely to report that they have not been to other dance events, and so on. What the technique of latent class analysis aims to do is to simplify matters by exploiting this association among the six indicators. It seeks to identify a limited number of discrete classes, or categories, of respondents such that, *conditional on their belonging to one or other of these classes,* individuals' responses on the indicator items become independent of each other—i.e. there is no longer any association between them. Insofar as this can be done, it can be said that it is individuals' membership of the latent classes that is the *source* of the association initially found among their responses, and each latent class can be taken as representing a quite distinctive pattern of response.

Results

Latent Class Analysis of Theatre and Cinema Attendance

It turns out in fact that, as is shown in Table 67.2, a very simple latent class solution can be obtained for our data on theatre and cinema attendance. With the minor technical modification that is noted in Table 67.2, a model proposing just two latent classes fits the data satisfactorily: that is, just two latent classes prove sufficient to capture virtually all of the association that exists among responses on the six indicator items. Or, one could say, it emerges that underlying the results previously reported in Table 67.1 on these six different kinds of attendance, a clear, essentially dichotomous, patterning prevails.

On the basis of this solution we can then go on to assign each individual in the sample to one or other of the two latent classes that are identified—that is, to whichever he or she has the highest probability of belonging to, given his or her own set of responses on the six indicator items; in this way the respondents are divided into two types of consumer of theatre, dance and cinema. In Table 67.3 it is shown, first of all, that this process of assignment does not result in any major change in the relative size of the latent classes from that initially estimated under the model; or, in other words, no great degree of uncertainty appears to arise about the latent

Table 67.3   Estimated Size of the Latent Classes and Conditional Probabilities (Percent) of Attendance Under Our Preferred Model

	Latent class	
	1	2
Relative size (%), initial	62.5	37.5
Relative size (%), post-assignment	64.2	35.8
Probabilities of attendance (%)		
Ballet	0.1	5.0
Other dance	5.6	24.6
Pantomime	6.7	27.9
Musical	6.9	56.2
Play/drama	6.1	67.1
Cinema	48.0	87.1

class with which particular respondents should be affiliated. Second, the probabilities of individuals reporting each of the six different kinds of attendance considered are shown, given their latent class membership.

What, then, can be discovered about the two types of consumer that are derived from the latent class analysis? Our findings are in fact rather clear cut. As can be seen, latent class 1, which accounts for almost two-thirds of the sample, comprises individuals who have a very low probability—less than 10 per cent—of having attended a theatre in the year before the interview for any of the kinds of performance distinguished, and whose consumption is effectively limited to a fairly modest—48 per cent—probability of having visited a cinema. Latent class 2, in contrast, which accounts for somewhat over one-third of the sample, comprises individuals who have a relatively high probability (i.e. as compared to the overall rates shown in Table 67.1) of having attended a theatre for each of the kinds of performance covered and of having been to the cinema as well.

These findings would then, so far as they go, appear highly consistent with the omnivore–univore argument initially referred to. The latent Class 2 represents the theatre and cinema omnivores, and latent Class 1 the univores, whose consumption is in fact more or less restricted to the cinema. Certainly, we find no evidence of the kind that might be expected from the homology argument of a cultural elite who, in pursuit of 'distinction', attend the theatre for, say, drama and ballet performances but who at the same time display 'aesthetic distancing' in shunning musicals and pantomime. Members of latent Class 2 have the highest probability of attendance at not only drama and ballet but also all other kinds of theatre performance covered and the cinema. Furthermore, the very fact that the sample divides so readily into just two types of consumer is in itself sufficient to throw serious doubt on the individualization argument. There is no evidence here of the kind of individual diversity in cultural consumption that would, were it present, effectively defy latent class analysis or at all events require that an unmanageably large number of latent classes be distinguished, and ones to which individuals could be assigned only with great uncertainty.

Table 67.4   Distribution of Univores (U) and Omivores (O) Within NS Social Classes

NS social class	U (%)	O (%)	N
1 Higher managerial and professional occupations	43.9	56.2	488
2 Lower managerial and professional occupations	49.4	50.6	1023
3 Intermediate occupations	63.2	36.8	574
4 Small employers and own-account workers	72.7	27.3	275
5 Lower supervisory and technical occupations	77.7	22.3	359
6 Semi-routine occupations	77.1	22.9	620
7 Routine occupations	85.8	14.2	480
	64.2	35.8	3819

Theatre, Dance and Cinema Attendance and Social Stratification

As already noted, in our work on musical consumption (Chan & Goldthorpe, 2005), we also find, with some qualification, support for the omnivore–univore argument. Our latent class analyses in this case point in fact to three types of musical consumer: univores, whose consumption is largely restricted to pop and rock, and then two kinds of omnivore—'true' omnivores and omnivore listeners. The former have a high probability both of attending musical events and of listening to music across all the genres distinguished, while the latter are omnivorous only in their listening to broadcast or recorded music. Further analysis then reveals that the chances of being an omnivore, and especially a true omnivore, rather than a univore, increase with status, although—following the expectations earlier mentioned—the effects of class are negligible once status is included in the analysis. In addition, it is shown that even when the effects of status (and class) are controlled, the chances of being a musical omnivore rather than a univore still increase fairly steadily with level of educational qualifications, but that, in contrast,

these chances do not appear to be affected by income when other stratification variables are controlled. How far, then, are similar results obtained in regard to cultural consumption in the form of theatre and cinema attendance?

To begin with, we may examine the simple two-way relationships that exist between the chances of being in this regard an omnivore or a cinema-only univore (according to the previous analyses) and class and status respectively. In Table 67.4 we show the distribution of univores (latent Class 1) and omnivores (latent Class 2) within the seven classes of NS-SEC. It is evident that omnivores are most common in the professional and managerial classes, 1 and 2, where they are in fact in a slight majority, while univores dominate in Classes 5, 6 and 7, those of lower supervisory and technical, semi-routine and routine workers.

Figure 67.1 is then analogous to Table 67.4, but with the 31 categories of our status scale replacing the seven NS-SEC classes. An obvious 'status gradient' exists in the chances of being an omnivore rather than a univore.

These results are then consistent with the general idea that it is members of higher social strata who are more likely to be culturally omnivorous, and members of lower strata who are more likely to be univorous.

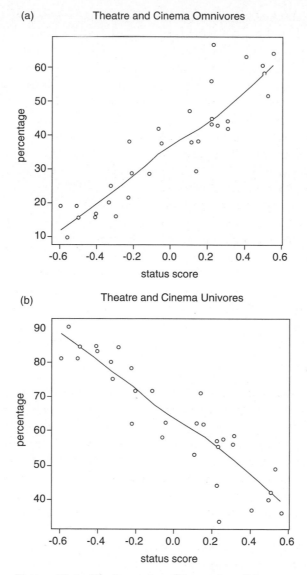

Figure 67.1   The Proportion of Respondents Being Univores and Omnivores Within Status Categories by Status Score

But to test this idea more rigorously against the data on theatre and cinema attendance, it is necessary to move on from merely two-way, or bivariate, analysis to analysis of a multivariate kind. That is to say, it is necessary to relate the chances of an individual being an omnivore rather than a univore to the full range of stratification variables referred to earlier and also to the socio-demographic variables of sex, age, marital status, family composition and region of residence that are introduced as controls. Only if the effects of all these variables are considered simultaneously can we hope to gain some reliable idea of their relative importance.

In Table 67.5 we report results from a binary logistic regression analysis. Such an analysis is appropriate where the 'dependent' variable—that on which our explanatory interest centres—has just two possible values, 'x' or 'not x': or, in our case, being an omnivore or not being an omnivore, and thus a univore. The β coefficients shown in the second column of the table represent the estimated effects of the variables listed in the first column. A positive coefficient implies that the higher the value of the explanatory variable, the higher the probability of being an omnivore rather than a univore, and a negative coefficient implies the opposite. Coefficients that are starred are statistically significant.

In assessing the results obtained from our regression analysis, we may begin with those relating to the socio-demographic control variables at the top of the table, since these turn out to be methodologically instructive. First, we may note a result that serves to confirm what several other investigators (e.g. O'Hagan, 1999; Quine, 1999) have previously reported: namely, that a highly significant gender effect exists in that women are more likely to be theatre goers than men; or, in our terms, women are more likely than men to be theatre and cinema omnivores rather than simply cinema-only univores. Second, though, the further finding of other investigators that the probability of theatre attendance increases with age cannot be confirmed. What we do find is that having a family that includes children below age 5, as compared with having no children, has a significant negative effect on the chances of being an omnivore. This would then suggest that where positive age

effects on theatre attendance do show up in two-way analyses, or indeed in multivariate analyses in which family composition variables are not included, they should be very cautiously interpreted, and with the possibility being kept in mind that they may well reflect life-cycle stage rather than generation.

A third result likewise brings out the advantage of multivariate analysis. It can be seen that the coefficients for living in regions outside London, although often negative in sign, in no case achieve significance (though that for the North comes close). Again, then, the implication is that where in two-way analyses living outside London (or the South East) appears to have a negative effect on theatre attendance, this finding could easily mislead. If stratification variables are not simultaneously considered, it could be that what region variables largely pick up is not any specifically geographical effects, such as the location of venues, travelling times, etc., but rather the (concealed) effects of stratification variables, on account of the populations of regions differing in their class and status composition and in their average levels of income and educational attainment.

Now turning to the effects of stratification variables in our own analysis, which is our main focus of interest, the following points stand out. First, it can be seen that when class and status are included in the analysis together, the effect of status is highly significant and positive—i.e. the chances of being an omnivore rather than a univore increase with status—while class effects are for the most part insignificant. Only membership of Class 7, that of routine, largely manual wage workers, has a significant—negative—effect on the chances of being an omnivore. In other words, our

Table 67.5   Coefficients from Binary Logistic
Regression Analysis for Effects of Covariates on the
Probability of Being an Omnivore Rather than a Univore

	$\hat{\beta}$	SE
Female[a]	0.615**	0.092
Married[b]	0.148	0.112
Separated	0.188	0.139
Age[c]	0.005	0.004
Child (0–4)[d]	−0.562**	0.113
Child (5–10)	0.070	0.100
Child (11–15)	0.088	0.105
The North[e]	−0.231	0.124
Midlands	−0.207	0.123
South East	0.083	0.135
South West	−0.189	0.153
Income	0.026**	0.005
CSE/others[f]	0.169	0.152
O levels	0.668**	0.128
A levels	1.130**	0.145
Sub-degree	1.027**	0.160
Degree	1.223**	0.151
Class 2[g]	0.078	0.126
Class 3	−0.161	0.160
Class 4	−0.205	0.203
Class 5	−0.134	0.218
Class 6	−0.199	0.195
Class 7	−0.507*	0.230
Status	0.631**	0.179
Constant	−2.118**	0.292

Notes: [a] Male is reference category. [b] Single is the reference
category. [c] Centred at age 20. [d] Not having children is the
reference category. [e] London is the reference category. [f] No
qualifications is the reference category. [g] Class 1 is the reference
category. * $p < 0.05$, ** $p < 0.01$.

results in the domain of theatre, dance and cinema do in this regard largely replicate those obtained in the domain of music, even if in the present case the preponderance of status over class effects is somewhat less marked, and thus our general theoretical expectation that status will be more closely associated with cultural consumption than will class, because such consumption represents an aspect of lifestyle through which status is readily expressed and displayed, is further borne out.

Second, Table 67.5 reveals that level of educational qualification tends also to have a significant and positive effect, over and above that of status (and class), on the chances of being an omnivore rather than a univore. Thus, in this regard, too, our findings in the case of music are broadly confirmed, although it should be noted that with theatre and cinema attendance, in contrast with musical consumption, the effects of education are not entirely 'monotonic'. That is to say, the effects of having some educational qualifications rather than none on the chance of being an omnivore do not consistently increase with level of qualification. As can be seen, having CSE-level qualifications rather than none has no significant effect, and having tertiary but sub-degree qualifications has a weaker effect than having only A levels.

Third, our regression analysis also shows that even when all other stratification variables are taken into account, a highly significant and positive effect of income on theatre and cinema attendance still remains: the higher an individual's income the more likely he or she is to be an omnivore rather than a univore. This result is then that which is most at variance with what we find in the analysis of musical consumption in which, as earlier noted, income proved to have no significant effect on the probability of being an omnivore rather than a univore, or in fact on the probability of being a true omnivore rather than an omnivore listener.

Conclusions

Three rival arguments concerning the relationship between social stratification and cultural consumption have been advanced and widely discussed in the sociological literature: what we have labelled as the homology, individualization and omnivore–univore arguments. In previous work on musical consumption in England, we have presented findings that broadly favour the omnivore–univore argument, while lending little support to its competitors. In the present paper, we turn to the domain of theatre, dance and cinema, and ask how far the results of the analyses of musical consumption can be replicated.

In one respect, it could be said that the case of theatre, dance and cinema provides a yet more straightforward confirmation of the omnivore–univore argument than that of music. Our latent class analyses indicate just two main patterns of attendance, and, in turn, two main types of consumer: those, around one-third of the sample, who do appear omnivorous in having a relatively high probability of attending theatre performances of *all* the kinds considered *and* of going to the cinema; and those, around two-thirds of the sample, who are univorous in being cinema-goers only, if indeed they are consumers in the domain of theatre and cinema at all. That it is these two types of consumer that are empirically identifiable, and only these types, does then in itself serve to call both the homology and the individualization arguments into question. Our latent class analyses fail to reveal a cultural elite who systematically discriminate among different kinds of theatre performance; but at the same time, theatre and cinema attendance clearly cannot be regarded as simply forms of individual expression, devoid of all social patterning. Moreover, when stratification variables are introduced into the analyses the results obtained are generally those that would be expected under the omnivore–univore argument. Higher status, higher educational qualifications and a higher income all increase individuals' chances of being an omnivore rather than a univore. In sum, theatre and cinema attendance, like musical consumption, is quite evidently socially stratified, but on omnivore–univore rather than elite–mass lines.

At the same time, though, some differences from our findings in the domain of music have also to be recognized. To begin with, while status effects do generally dominate class effects on theatre and cinema attendance, as would be expected to be the case, class is not so completely overshadowed as it is in relation to musical consumption. The chances of being a theatre and cinema omnivore significantly decrease for those holding the least advantaged class positions (Class 7), even when status is controlled for. Further, while education is clearly an important influence on theatre and cinema attendance, its effects would appear to be somewhat less consistent and also relatively less strong than they are on musical consumption. And finally, and most notably, income, which appears statistically non-significant in regard to musical omnivorousness, exerts a highly significant and fairly substantial effect on the probability of being a theatre and cinema omnivore, even when other stratification variables are included in the analysis.

REFERENCES

Bauman, Z. (1988). *Freedom.* Milton Keynes: Open University Press.

Bourdieu, P. (1984). *Distinction: A social critique of the judgement of taste.* London: Routledge & Kegan Paul.

Chan, T. W., & Goldthorpe, J. H. (2004). Is there a status order in contemporary British society? Evidence from the occupational structure of friendship. *European Sociological Review, 20*(5), 383–401.

Chan, T. W., & Goldthorpe, J. H. (2005). *Social stratification and cultural consumption: music in England.* Paper presented at a one-day workshop on 'The social bases of cultural consumption', Oxford, March 18.

Coulangeon, P. (2003). La stratification sociale des gôuts musicaux. *Revue francaise de sociologie, 44,* 3–33.

Featherstone, M. (1987). Lifestyle and consumer culture. *Theory, Culture and Society, 4*(1), 55–70.

McCutcheon, A. L. (1987). *Latent class analysis.* Newbury Park, CA: Sage.

O'Hagan, J. (1999). Policy analysis of theatre in the UK. *Cultural Trends, 9*(34), 25–29.

Peterson, R. A., & Kern, R. M. (1996). Changing highbrow taste: from snob to omnivore. *American Sociological Review, 61*(5), 900–907.

Peterson, R. A., & Simkus, A. (1992). How musical tastes mark occupational status groups. In M. Lamont & M. Fournier (Eds.), *Cultivating differences: Symbolic boundaries and the making of inequality* (pp. 152–186). Chicago, IL: University of Chicago Press.

Quine, M. (1999). Audiences for live theatre in Britain: the present situation and some implication. *Cultural Trends, 9*(34), 1–24.

Rose, D., & Pevalin, D. J. (Eds.). (2003). *A researcher's guide to the National Statistics Socio-economic Classification.* London: Sage.

Skelton, A., Bridgwood, A., Duckworth, K., Hutton, L., Fenn, C., Creaser, C., & Babbidge, A. (2002). *Arts in England: Attendance, participation and attitudes in 2001* (Res. report 27). London: Arts Council England.

Van Eijck, K. (2001). Social differentiation in musical taste patterns. *Social Forces, 79*(3), 1163–1184.

Weber, M. (1922/1968). *Economy and society.* Berkeley, CA: University of California Press.

68

Unequal Childhoods

Class, Race, and Family Life

ANNETTE LAREAU

There are many studies that tell us of the detrimental effects of poverty on children's lives, but it is less clear what the mechanisms are for the transmission of class advantage across generations.

I suggest that social class has an important impact on the cultural logic of childrearing (see Lareau 2003 for details). Middle-class parents, both white *and* black, appear to follow a cultural logic of childrearing that I call "concerted cultivation." They enroll their children in numerous age-specific organized activities that come to dominate family life and create enormous labor, particularly for mothers. Parents see these activities as transmitting important life skills to children. Middle-class parents also stress language use and the development of reasoning. Talking plays a crucial role in the disciplinary strategies of middle-class parents. This "cultivation" approach results in a frenetic pace for parents, creates a cult of individualism within the family, and emphasizes children's performance.

Among white and black working-class and poor families, childrearing strategies emphasize the "accomplishment of natural growth." These parents believe that as long as they provide love, food, and safety, their children will grow and thrive. They do not focus on developing the special talents of their individual children. Working-class and poor children have more free time and deeper and richer ties within their extended families than the middle-class children. Some participate in organized activities, but they do so for different reasons than their middle-class counterparts. Working-class and poor parents issue many more directives to their children and, in some households, place more emphasis on physical discipline than do middle-class parents.

The pattern of concerted cultivation, with its stress on individual repertoires of activities, reasoning, and questioning, encourages an *emerging sense of entitlement* in children. Of course, not all parents and children are equally assertive, but the pattern of questioning and intervening among the white and black middle-class parents in the study contrasts sharply with the definitions of how to be helpful and effective observed among the white and black working-class and poor families. The pattern of the ac-

---

Table 68.1   Argument of Unequal Childhoods: Class Differences in Childrearing

	Childrearing Approach	
	Concerted Cultivation	*Accomplishment of Natural Growth*
Key Elements	Parent actively fosters and assesses child's talents, opinions, and skills	Parent cares for child and allows child to grow
Organization of Daily Life	*multiple child leisure activities orchestrated by adults	*child "hangs out" particularly with kin
Language Use	*reasoning/directives *child contestation of adult statements *extended negotiations between parents and child	*directives *rare for child to question or challenge adults *general acceptance by child of directives
Interventions in Institutions	*criticisms and interventions on behalf of child *training of child to take on this role	*dependence on institutions *sense of powerlessness and frustrations *conflict between childrearing practices at home and at school
Consequences	Emerging sense of entitlement on the part of the child	Emerging sense of constraint on the part of the child

complishment of natural growth, with its emphasis on child-initiated play, autonomy from adults, and directives, encourages an *emerging sense of constraint.* Members of these families, adults as well as children, tend to be deferential and outwardly accepting (with sporadic moments of resistance) in their interactions with professionals such as doctors and educators. At the same time, however, compared to their middle-class counterparts, the white and black working-class and poor families are more distrustful of professionals in institutions. These are differences with long-term consequences. In a historical moment where the dominant society privileges active, informed, assertive clients of health and educational services, the various strategies employed by children and parents are not equally valuable. In sum, differences in family life lie not only in the advantages parents are able to obtain for their children, but also in the skills being transmitted to children for negotiating their own life paths.

Methodology

Study Participants

The study is based on interviews and observations of children eight to ten years of age and their families. A team of graduate research assistants and I collected the data. The first phase involved observations in third-grade public school classrooms, mainly in a metropolitan area in the Northeast. The schools serve neighborhoods in a white suburban area and two urban locales—one a white working-class neighborhood and the other a nearby poor black neighborhood. About one-half of the children are white and about one-half are black. One child is interracial. The research assistants and I carried out individual interviews (averaging two hours each) with all of the mothers and most of the fathers (or guardians) of 88 children, for a total of 137 interviews. We also observed children as they took part in organized activities in the communities surrounding the schools. The most intensive part of the research, however, involved home observations of 12 children and their families. Nine of the 12 families came from the classrooms I observed, but the boy and girl from the two black middle-class families and the boy from the poor white family came from other sites. Most observations and interviews took place between 1993 and 1995, but interviews were done as early as 1990 and as late as 1997. This chapter focuses primarily on the findings from the observations of these 12 families since the key themes discussed here surfaced during this part of the fieldwork. I do include some information from the larger study to provide a context for understanding the family observations. All names are pseudonyms.

Intensive Family Observations

The research assistants and I took turns visiting the participating families daily, for a total of about 20 visits in each home, often in the space of one month. The observations were not limited to the home. Fieldworkers followed children and parents as they took part in school activities, church services and events, organized play, kin visits, and medical appointments. Most field observations lasted about three hours; sometimes, depending on the event (e.g., an out-of-town funeral, a special extended family event, or a long shopping trip), they lasted much longer. In most cases, there was one overnight visit. We often carried tape recorders with us and used the audiotapes for reference in writing up field notes. Families were paid $350, usually at the end of the visits, for their participation.

A Note on Class

My purpose in undertaking the field observations was to develop an *intensive,* realistic portrait of family life. Although I deliberately focused on only 12 families, I wanted to compare children across gender and race lines. Adopting the fine-grained differentiation of categories characteristic of current neo-Marxist and neo-Weberian empirical studies was not tenable. My choice of class categories was further limited by the school populations at the sites I had selected. Very few of the students were children of employers or of self-employed workers. I decided to concentrate exclusively on those whose parents were employees. Various criteria have been proposed to differentiate within this heterogeneous group, but authority in the workplace and "credential barriers" are the two most commonly used. I assigned the families in the study to a working-class or middle-class category based on discussions with each of the employed adults. They provided extensive information about the work they did, the nature of the organization that employed them, and their educational credentials. I added a third category: families not involved in the labor market (a population traditionally excluded from social class groupings) because in the first school I studied, a substantial number of children were from households supported by public assistance. To ignore them would have restricted the scope of the study arbitrarily. The final subsample contained 4 middle-class, 4 working-class, and 4 poor families.

Children's Time Use

In our interviews and observations of white and black middle-class children, it was striking how busy they were with organized activities. Indeed, one of the hallmarks of middle-class children's daily lives is a set of adult-run organized activities. Many children have three and four activities per week. In some families, every few days activities conflict, particularly when one season is ending and one is beginning. For example in the white middle-class family of the Tallingers, Garrett is on multiple soccer teams—the "A" traveling team of the private Forest soccer club and the Intercounty soccer team—he also has swim lessons, saxophone lessons at school, private piano lessons at home, and baseball and basketball. These organized activities provided a framework for children's lives; other activities were sandwiched between them.

These activities create labor for parents. Indeed, the impact of children's activities takes its toll on parents' patience as well as their time. For example, on a June afternoon at the beginning of summer vacation, in a white-middle-class family, Mr. Tallinger comes home from work to take Garrett to his soccer game. Garrett is not ready to go, and his lackadaisical approach to getting ready irks his father:

Don says, "Get your soccer stuff—you're going to a soccer game!" Garrett comes into the den with white short leggings on underneath a long green soccer shirt; he's number 16. He sits on an armchair catty-corner from the television and languidly watches the World Cup game. He slowly, abstractedly, pulls on shin guards, then long socks. His eyes are riveted to the TV screen. Don comes in: "Go get your other stuff." Garrett says he can't find his shorts. Don: "Did you look in your drawer?" Garrett nods. . . . He gets up to look for his shorts, comes back into the den a few min-

utes later. I ask, "Any luck yet?" Garrett shakes his head. Don is rustling around elsewhere in the house. Don comes in, says to Garrett, "Well, Garrett, aren't you wearing shoes?" (Don leaves and returns a short time later): "Garrett, we HAVE to go! Move! We're late!" He says this shortly, abruptly. He comes back in a minute and drops Garrett's shiny green shorts on his lap without a word.

This pressured search for a pair of shiny green soccer shorts is a typical event in the Tallinger household. Also typical is the solution—a parent ultimately finds the missing object, while continuing to prod the child to hurry. The fact that today's frenzied schedule will be matched or exceeded by the next day's is also par:

Don: (describing their day on Saturday) Tomorrow is really nuts. We have a soccer game, then a baseball game, then another soccer game.

This steady schedule of activity—that none of the middle-class parents reported having when they were a similar age—was not universal. Indeed, while we searched for a middle-class child who did not have a single organized activity we could not find one, but in working-class and poor homes, organized activities were much less common and there were many children who did not have any. Many children "hung out." Television and video games are a major source of entertainment but outdoor play can trump either of these. No advanced planning, no telephone calls, no consultations between mothers, no drop-offs or pickups—no particular effort at all—is required to launch an activity. For instance, one afternoon, in a black working-class family, Shannon (in

7th grade) and Tyrec (in 4th grade) walk out their front door to the curb of the small, narrow street their house faces. Shannon begins playing a game with a ball; she soon has company:

> (Two boys from the neighborhood walk up.) Shannon is throwing the small ball against the side of the row house. Tyrec joins in the game with her. As they throw the ball against the wall, they say things they must do with the ball. It went something like this: Johnny Crow wanted to know. . . . (bounces ball against the wall), touch your knee (bounce), touch your toe (bounce), touch the ground (bounce), under the knee (bounce), turn around (bounce). Shannon and Tyrec played about four rounds.

Unexpected events produce hilarity:

> At one point Shannon accidentally threw the ball and it bounced off of Tyrec's head. All the kids laughed; then Tyrec, who had the ball, went chasing after Shannon. It was a close, fun moment—lots of laughter, eye contact, giggling, chasing.

Soon a different game evolves. Tyrec is on restriction. He is supposed to remain inside the house all day. So, when he thinks he has caught a glimpse of his mom returning home from work, he dashes inside. He reappears as soon as he realizes that it was a false alarm. The neighborhood children begin an informal game of baiting him:

> The kids keep teasing Tyrec that his mom's coming—which sends him scurrying just inside the door, peering out of the screen door. This game is enacted about six times. Tyrec also chases Shannon around the street,

trying to get the ball from her. A few times Shannon tells Tyrec that he'd better "get inside"; he ignores her. Then, at 6:50 [P.M.] Ken (a friend of Tyrec's) says, "There's your mom!" Tyrec scoots inside, then, says, "Oh, man. You were serious this time."

Informal, impromptu outdoor play is common in Tyrec's neighborhood. A group of boys approximately his age, regularly numbering four or five but sometimes reaching as many as ten, play ball games together on the street, walk to the store to get treats, watch television at each other's homes, and generally hang out together.

Language Use

In addition to differences by social class in time use, we also observed differences in language use in the home. As others have noted (Bernstein, 1971; Heath, 1983) middle-class parents used more reasoning in their speech with children while working-class and poor parents used more directives. For example, in observations of the African American home of Alex Williams, whose father was a trial lawyer and mother was a high level corporate executive, we found that the Williamses and other middle-class parents use language frequently, pleasurably, and instrumentally. Their children do likewise. For example, one January evening, Alexander is stumped by a homework assignment to write five riddles. He sits at the dinner table in the kitchen with his mother and a fieldworker. Mr. Williams is at the sink, washing the dinner dishes. He has his back to the group at the dinner table. Without turning around, he says to Alex, "Why don't you go upstairs to the third floor and get one those books and see if there is a riddle in there?"

Alex [says] smiling, "Yeah. That's a good idea! I'll go upstairs and copy one from out of the book." Terry turns around with a dish in hand, "That was a joke—not a valid suggestion. That is not an option." He smiled as he turned back around to the sink. Christina says, looking at Alex: "There is a word for that you know, plagiarism." Terry says (not turning around), "Someone can sue you for plagiarizing. Did you know that?" Alex: "That's only if it is copyrighted." They all begin talking at once.

Here we see Alex cheerfully (though gently) goading his father by pretending to misunderstand the verbal instruction to consult a book for help. Mr. Williams dutifully rises to the bait. Ms. Williams reshapes this moment of lightheartedness by introducing a new word into Alexander's vocabulary. Mr. Williams goes one step further by connecting the new word to a legal consequence. Alex upstages them both. He demonstrates that he is already familiar with the general idea of plagiarism and that he understands the concept of copyright, as well.

In marked contrast to working-class and poor parents, however, even when the Williamses issue directives, they often include explanations for their orders. Here, Ms. Williams is reminding her son to pay attention to his teacher:

I want you to play close attention to Mrs. Scott when you are developing your film. Those chemicals are very dangerous. Don't play around in the classroom. You could get that stuff in someone's eye. And if you swallow it, you could die.

Alex chooses to ignore the directive in favor of instructing his misinformed mother:

Alex corrects her, "Mrs. Scott told us that we wouldn't die if we swallowed it. But we would get very sick and would have to get our stomach pumped." Christina does not follow the argument any further. She simply reiterates that he should be careful.

Possibly because the issue is safety, Ms. Williams does not encourage Alex to elaborate here, as she would be likely to do if the topic were less charged. Instead, she restates her directive and thus underscores her expectation that Alex will do as she asks.

Although Mr. and Ms. Williams disagreed on elements of how training in race relations should be implemented, they both recognized that their racial and ethnic identity profoundly shaped their and their son's everyday experiences. They were well aware of the potential for Alexander to be exposed to racial injustice, and they went to great lengths to try to protect their son from racial insults and other forms of discrimination. Nevertheless, race did not appear to shape the dominant cultural logic of child-rearing in Alexander's family or in other families in the study. All of the middle-class families engaged in extensive reasoning with their children, asking questions, probing assertions, and listening to answers. Similar patterns appeared in interviews and observations with other African American middle-class families.

A different pattern appeared in working-class and poor homes where there was simply less verbal speech than we observed in middle-class homes. There was also less speech between parents and children, a finding noted by other observational studies (Hart and Risley, 1995). Moreover, interspersed with intermittent talk are adult-issued directives. Children are told to do certain things (e.g., shower, take out the garbage) and not to do others (e.g., curse, talk back). In an African American home of a family living on public assistance in public housing, Ms. McAllister uses one-word directives to coordinate the use of the single bathroom. There are almost always at least four children in the apartment and often seven, plus Ms. McAllister and other adults. Ms. McAllister sends the children to wash up by pointing to a child, saying, "Bathroom," and handing him or her a washcloth. Wordlessly, the designated child gets up and goes to the bathroom to take a shower.

Children usually do what adults ask of them. We did not observe whining or protests, even when adults assign time-consuming tasks, such as the hour-long process of hair-braiding Lori McAllister is told to do for the four-year-old daughter of Aunt Dara's friend Charmaine:

> Someone tells Lori, "Go do [Tyneshia's] hair for camp." Without saying anything, Lori gets up and goes inside and takes the little girl with her. They head for the couch near the television; Lori sits on the couch and the girl sits on the floor. [Tyneshia] sits quietly for about an hour, with her head tilted, while Lori carefully does a multitude of braids.

Lori's silent obedience is typical. Generally, children perform requests without comment. For example, at dinner one night, after Harold McAllister complains he doesn't like spinach, his mother directs him to finish it anyway:

> Mom yells (loudly) at him to eat: "EAT! FINISH THE SPINACH!" (No response. Harold is at the table, dawdling.) Guion and Runako and Alexis finish eating and

leave. I finish with Harold; he eats his spinach. He leaves all his yams.

The verbal world of Harold McAllister and other poor and working-class children offers some important advantages as well as costs. Compared to middle-class children we observed, Harold is more respectful towards adults in his family. In this setting, there are clear boundaries between adults and children. Adults feel comfortable issuing directives to children, which children comply with immediately. Some of the directives that adults issue center on obligations of children to others in the family ("don't beat on Guion" or "go do [her] hair for camp"). One consequence of this is that Harold, despite occasional tiffs, is much nicer to his sister (and his cousins) than the siblings we observed in middle-class homes. The use of directives and the pattern of silent compliance are not universal in Harold's life. In his interactions with peers, for example on the basketball "court," Harold's verbal displays are distinctively different than inside the household, with elaborated and embellished discourse. Nevertheless, there is a striking difference in linguistic interaction between adults and children in poor and working-class families when compared to that observed in the home of Alexander Williams. Ms. McAllister has the benefit of being able to issue directives without having to justify their decisions at every moment. This can make childrearing somewhat less tiring.

Another advantage is that Harold has more autonomy than middle-class children in making important decisions in daily life. As a child, he controls his leisure schedule. His basketball games are impromptu and allow him to develop important skills and talents. He is resourceful. He appears less exhausted than ten-year old Alexander. In addition, he has important social competencies, including his deftness in negotiating the "code of the street."[1] His mother has stressed these skills in her upbringing, as she impresses upon her children the importance of "not paying no mind" to others, including drunks and drug dealers who hang out in the neighborhoods which Harold and Alexis negotiate.

Still, in the world of schools, health care facilities, and other institutional settings, these valuable skills do not translate into the same advantages as the reasoning skills emphasized in the home of Alexander Williams and other middle-class children. Compared to Alexander Williams, Harold does not gain the development of a large vocabulary, an increase of his knowledge of science and politics, a set of tools to customize situations outside the home to maximize his advantage, and instruction in how to defend his argument with evidence. His knowledge of words, which might appear, for example, on future SAT tests, is not continually stressed at home.

In these areas, the lack of advantage is *not* connected to the intrinsic value of the McAllister family life or the use of directives at home. Indeed, one can argue raising children who are polite and respectful children and do not whine, needle, or badger their parents is a highly laudable childrearing goal. Deep and abiding ties with kinship groups are also, one might further argue, important. Rather, it is the specific ways that institutions function that ends up conveying advantages to middle-class children. In their standards, these institutions also permit, and even demand, active parent involvement. In this way as well, middle-class children often gain an advantage.

Intervention in Institutions

Children do not live their lives inside of the home. Instead, they are legally required to go to school, they go to the doctor, and many are involved in church and other adult-organized activities. In children's institutional lives, we found differences by social class in how mothers monitored children's institutional experiences. While in working-class and poor families children are granted autonomy to make their own way in organizations, in the middle-class homes, most aspects of the children's lives are subject to their mother's *ongoing* scrutiny.

For example in an African American middle-class home, where both parents are college graduates and Ms. Marshall is a computer worker and her husband a civil servant, their two daughters have a hectic schedule of organized activities including gymnastics for Stacey and basketball for Fern. When Ms. Marshall becomes aware of a problem, she moves quickly, drawing on her work and professional skills and experiences. She displays tremendous assertiveness, doggedness, and, in some cases, effectiveness in pressing institutions to recognize her daughters' individualized needs. Stacey's mother's proactive stance reflects her belief that she has a duty to intervene in situations where she perceives that her daughter's needs are not being met. This perceived responsibility applies across all areas of her children's lives. She is no more (or less) diligent with regard to Stacey and Fern's leisure activities than she is with regard to their experiences in school or church or the doctor's office. This is clear in the way she handles Stacey's transition from her township gymnastics classes to the private classes at an elite private gymnastic program at Wright's.

Ms. Marshall describes Stacey's first session at the club as rocky:

> The girls were not warm. And these were little . . . eight and nine year old kids. You know, they weren't welcoming her the first night. It was kinda like eyeing each other, to see, you know, "Can you do this? Can you do that?"

More importantly, Ms. Marshall reported that the instructor is brusque, critical and not friendly toward Stacey. Ms. Marshall cannot hear what was being said, but she could see the interactions through a window. A key problem is that because her previous instructor had not used the professional jargon for gymnastic moves, Stacey does not know these terms. When the class ends and she walks out, she is visibly upset. Her mother's reaction is a common one among middle-class parents: She does not remind her daughter that in life one has to adjust, that she will need to work even harder, or that there is nothing to be done. Instead, Ms. Marshall focuses on Tina, the instructor, as the source of the problem:

> We sat in the car for a minute and I said, "Look, Stac," I said. She said, "I-I," and she started crying. I said, "You wait here." The instructor had come to the door, Tina. So I went to her and I said, "Look." I said, "Is there a problem?" She said, "Aww . . . she'll be fine. She just needs to work on certain things." Blah-blah-blah. And I said, "She's really upset. She said you-you-you [were] pretty much correcting just about everything." And [Tina] said, "Well, she's got—she's gotta learn the terminology."

Ms. Marshall acknowledges that Stacey isn't familiar with specialized and technical gymnastics terms. Nonetheless, she continues to defend her daughter:

> I do remember, I said to her, I said, "Look, maybe it's not all the student." You know, I just left it like that. That, you know, sometimes teaching, learning and teaching, is a two-way proposition as far as I'm concerned. And sometimes teachers have to learn how to, you know, meet the needs of the kid. Her style, her immediate style was not accommodating to—to Stacey.

Here Ms. Marshall is asserting the legitimacy of an individualized approach to instruction. She frames her opening remark as a question ("Is there a problem?"). Her purpose, however, is to alert the instructor to the negative impact she has had on Stacey ("She's really upset."). Although her criticism is indirect ("Maybe it's not all the student . . . "), Ms. Marshall makes it clear that she expects her daughter to be treated differently in the future. In this case, Stacey does not hear what her mother says, but she knows that her wishes and feelings are being transmitted to the instructor in a way that she could not do herself.

Although parents were equally concerned about their children's happiness, in working-class and poor homes we observed different patterns of oversight for children's institutional activities. For example in the white working-class home of Wendy Driver, Wendy's mother does not nurture her daughter's language development like Alexander Williams' mother does her son's. She does not attempt to draw Wendy out or follow up on new information when Wendy introduces the term mortal sin while the family is sitting around watching television. But, just like Ms. Williams, Ms. Driver cares very much about her child and just like middle-class parents she wants to help her daughter succeed. Ms. Driver keeps a close and careful eye on Wendy's schooling. She knows that Wendy is having problems in school. Ms. Driver immediately signs and returns each form Wendy brings home from school and reminds her to turn the papers in to her teacher.

Wendy is "being tested" as part of an ongoing effort to determine why she has difficulties with spelling, reading, and related language-based activities. Her mother welcomes these official efforts but she did not request them. Unlike the middle-class mothers we observed, who asked teachers for detailed information about every aspect of their children's classroom performance and relentlessly pursued information and assessments outside of school as well, Ms. Driver seems content with only a vague notion of her daughter's learning disabilities. This attitude contrasts starkly with that of Stacey Marshall's mother, for example. In discussing Stacey's classroom experiences with fieldworkers, Ms. Marshall routinely described her daughter's academic strengths and weaknesses in detail. Ms. Driver never mentions that Wendy is doing grade-level work in math but is reading at a level a full three years below her grade. Her description is vague:

> She's having problems. . . . They had a special teacher come in and see if they could find out what the problem is. She has a reading problem, but they haven't put their finger on it yet, so she's been through all kinds of special teachers and testing and everything. She goes to Special Ed, I think it's two

classes a day . . . I'm not one hundred percent sure—for her reading. It's very difficult for her to read what's on paper. But then— she can remember things. But not everything. It's like she has a puzzle up there. And we've tried, well, they've tried a lot of things. They just haven't put their finger on it yet.

Wendy's teachers uniformly praise her mother as "supportive" and describe her as "very loving," but they are disappointed in Ms. Driver's failure to take a more active, interventionist role in Wendy's education, especially given the formidable nature of her daughter's learning problems. From Ms. Driver's perspective, however, being actively supportive means doing whatever the teachers tell her to do.

> Whatever they would suggest, I would do. They suggested she go to the eye doctor, so I did that. And they checked her and said there was nothing wrong there.

Similarly, she monitors Wendy's homework and supports her efforts to read:

> We listen to her read. We help her with her homework. So she has more attention here in a smaller household than it was when I lived with my parents. So, we're trying to help her out more, which I think is helping. And with the two [special education] classes a day at the school, instead of one like last year, she's learning a lot from that. So, we're just hoping it takes time and that she'll just snap out of it.

But Ms. Driver clearly does not have an *independent* understanding of the nature or degree of Wendy's limitations, perhaps because she is unfamiliar with the kind of terms the educators use to describe her daughter's needs (e.g., a limited "sight vocabulary," underdeveloped "language arts skills"). Perhaps, too, her confidence in the school staff makes it easier for her to leave "the details" to them: "Ms. Morton, she's great. She's worked with us for different testing and stuff." Ms. Driver depends on the school staff's expertise to assess the situation and then share the information with her:

> I think they just want to keep it in the school till now. And when they get to a point where they can't figure out what it is, and then I guess they'll send me somewhere else. . . .

Her mother is not alarmed, because "the school" has told her not to worry about Wendy's grades:

> Her report card—as long as it's not spelling and reading—spelling and reading are like F's. And they keep telling me not to worry, because she's in the Special Ed class. But besides that, she does good. I have no behavior problems with her at all.

Ms. Driver wants the best possible outcome for her daughter and she does not know how to achieve that goal without relying heavily on Wendy's teachers:

> I wouldn't even know where to start going. On the radio there was something for children having problems reading and this and that, call. And I suggested it to a couple different people, and they were like, wait a second, it's only to get you there and you'll end up paying an arm and a leg. So I said to my mom, "No, I'm going to wait until

the first report card and go up and talk to them up there."

Thus, in looking for the source of Ms. Driver's deference toward educators, the answers don't seem to lie in her having either a shy personality or underdeveloped mothering skills. To understand why Wendy's mother is accepting where Stacey Marshall's mother would be aggressive, it is more useful to focus on social class position, both in terms of how class shapes worldviews and how class affects economic and educational resources. Ms. Driver understands her role in her daughter's education as involving a different set of responsibilities from those perceived by middle-class mothers. She responds to contacts from the school—such as invitations to the two annual parent-teacher conferences—but she does not initiate them. She views Wendy's school life as a separate realm, and one in which she, as a parent, is only an infrequent visitor. Ms. Driver expects that the teachers will teach and her daughter will learn and that, under normal circumstances, neither requires any additional help from her as a parent. If problems arise, she presumes that Wendy will tell her; or, if the issue is serious, the school will contact her. But what Ms. Driver fails to understand, is that the educators expect her to take on a pattern of "concerted cultivation" where she actively monitors and intervenes in her child's schooling. The teachers asked for a complicated mixture of deference and engagement from parents; they were disappointed when they did not get it.

Conclusions

I have stressed how social class dynamics are woven into the texture and rhythm of children and parents' daily lives. Class position influences critical aspects of family life: time use, language use, and kin ties. Working-class and middle-class mothers may express beliefs that reflect a similar notion of "intensive mothering," but their behavior is quite different. For that reason, I have described sets of paired beliefs and actions as a "cultural logic" of childrearing. When children and parents move outside the home into the world of social institutions, they find that these cultural practices are not given equal value. There are signs that middle-class children benefit, in ways that are invisible to them and to their parents, from the degree of similarity between the cultural repertoires in the home and those standards adopted by institutions.

NOTE

1. Elijah Anderson, *Code of the Street*, New York: W. W. Norton (1999).

BIBLIOGRAPHY

Anderson, Elijah. 1999. *Code of the Street*. New York, NY: W. W. Norton.

Bernstein, Basil. 1971. *Class, Codes, and Control: Theoretical Studies Towards a Sociology of Language*. New York, NY: Schocken.

Hart, Betty and Todd R. Risley. 1995. *Meaningful Differences in the Everyday Experiences of Young American Children*. New Haven: Yale University Press.

Heath, Shirley Brice. 1983. *Ways with Words: Language, Life, and Work in Communities and Classrooms*. Cambridge: Cambridge University Press.

Lareau, Annette. 2003. *Unequal Childhoods: Class, Race, and Family Life*. Berkeley, CA: University of California Press.

69

The Digital Reproduction of Inequality

ESZTER HARGITTAI

By the beginning of the twenty-first century, information and communication technologies (ICT) had become a staple of many people's everyday lives. The level of instantaneous connectivity—to others and to an abundance of information—afforded by advances in ICT is unprecedented. With economies increasingly dependent on knowledge-intensive activities, the unequal distribution of knowledge and information access across the population may be linked increasingly to stratification. No sooner did the Internet start diffusing to the general population in the mid-1990s than did debates spring up about its implications for social inequality. From the perspective of social mobility, digital media could offer people, organizations, and societies the opportunity to improve their positions regardless of existing constraints. From the point of view of social reproduction, however, ICT could exacerbate existing inequalities by increasing the opportunities available to the already privileged while leading to the growing marginalization of the disadvantaged.

Most initial attention concerning ICT's implications for social stratification focused on what segments of the population have access to the Internet or are Internet users (e.g., Bimber 2000; Hoffman and Novak 1998). Access is usually defined as having a network-connected machine in one's home or workplace. Use more specifically refers to people's actual use of the medium beyond merely having access to it. The term "digital divide" became a popular expression to sum up concerns about the unequal diffusion of the medium. The concept is most often understood in binary terms: someone either has access to the medium or does not, someone either uses the Internet or does not.

However, as an increasing portion of the population has gone online, a dichotomous approach is no longer sufficient to address the different dimensions of inequality associated with digital media uses. The term *digital inequality* better captures the spectrum of differences associated with ICT uses (DiMaggio et al. 2004). A more re-

Original chapter commissioned for this book. The author is grateful for valuable comments from David Grusky and for helpful discussions with Paul DiMaggio and Russ Neuman (who also deserves credit for the title). She thanks the Center for Advanced Study in the Behavioral Sciences and the John D. and Catherine T. MacArthur Foundation for their support.

fined approach considers different aspects of the divide, focusing on such details as quality of equipment, autonomy of use, the presence of social support networks, experience and user skills, in addition to differences in types of uses (Barzilai-Nahon 2006; Dewan and Riggins 2006; DiMaggio et al. 2004; Mossberger, Tolbert, and Stansbury 2003; Norris 2001; van Dijk 2005; Warschauer 2003).

Variation in basic usage rates continues to exist, so considering the core digital divide of access versus no access remains an important undertaking. However, to understand in a nuanced manner the implications of ICT for social inequality, it is important to analyze differences among users as well. This chapter will do both, starting with a historical look at connectivity patterns by population segments. This discussion is then followed by an explanation of why it is important to distinguish among users of digital media. A conceptual framework lays out the processes through which users' social position influences their ICT uses and how this in turn may contribute to social inequality even among the connected. Although the primary focus here is on Internet use in the United States, the main arguments made can be extended to the use of other digital devices in other national contexts as well.

The Haves and Have Nots

In 1995, the National Telecommunications Information Administration of the U.S. Department of Commerce published a report entitled "Falling Through the Net: A Survey of the 'Have Nots' in Rural and Urban America" in which policy makers analyzed data from the Current Population Survey about computer and modem use among Americans. Findings suggested that different segments of the population were using digital technologies at varying rates. In subsequent years, these reports began to focus increasingly on Internet access as opposed to computer use only, documenting continued differences among various population groups (NTIA 1998, 1999, 2000). The reports' titles highlighted concerns about inequality as they all began with the phrase "Falling Through the Net."

Breaking with tradition, the fifth report of the NTIA published in 2002, based on data collected in 2001, was called "A Nation Online: How Americans Are Expanding Their Use of the Internet" (NTIA 2002). The title of this last report no longer focused on differences. Rather, it highlighted the fact that more and more Americans were going online. While significant differences remained among various population segments regarding their rates of connectivity, the report focused on the growing number of people accessing the Internet through high-speed connections. This change in focus may imply that Internet use had reached universal levels, but that was not the case.

Overall findings from the reports suggested that while the Internet may have been spreading to an increasing portion of the American population, certain segments were much more likely to be online than others. In particular, men, younger people, whites, non-Hispanics, urban residents, the more highly educated, and those with higher income were more connected than their counterparts. Gender differences leveled off after a few years with respect to basic access (Ono and Zavodny 2003) although not regarding amount of use and skill (Hargittai and Shafer 2006). In contrast, all other differences in access among different population segments remained throughout the years.

Looking at adoption figures over time, we find that while all segments increased their participation significantly, disparities continued to persist. Figures 69.1 and 69.2 illustrate this point for income and education, respectively. As Figure 69.1 shows, people in all income brackets increased their participation over time, but the slopes in the higher income brackets are somewhat steeper, leading to an increased gap among groups over time. The data points in Figure 69.2 tell a similar story. Although the gap between those who have a college degree and graduate education narrowed over the years, all other gaps widened over time. In particular, the least educated—those with less than a high school degree—increased their connectivity minimally over the eight-year period. Overall, these trend data suggest that while all population segments may have become increasingly connected, serious divides persist with the most disadvantaged trailing behind the more privileged in significant ways.

We have less data on the diffusion of cell phones, but the little evidence that has surfaced suggests similar patterns of unequal distribution among the population. Looking at the earlier years of diffusion using data from 1994–1998, researchers found that mobile technology adoption was positively related to both income and education (Wareham, Levy, and Shi 2004). Based on data from 2006, Horrigan showed that people with lower levels of income were less likely to be users (Horrigan 2006). Analyses (by Hargittai for this chapter) of these same data collected by the Pew Internet and American Life Project also found that those

with higher levels of education were more likely to own cell phones, and these findings are robust (also for income) when controlling for other factors. Moreover, those with higher income tend to own cell phones with more functionality (e.g., the ability to send and receive text messages, take photos, and go online). While this literature is not as elaborate as the one on different rates of Internet connectivity, these findings clearly suggest that the digital divide expands beyond Internet use into the domain of mobile technology adoption as well.

Differences Among the Connected

The uses of ICT can differ considerably with divergent outcomes for one's life chances. Therefore, it is imperative to examine variations in use among those who have crossed the digital divide fault line to the land of the connected. Baseline Internet use statistics do not distinguish among those who go online for no more than checking sports scores or TV schedules and those who use the medium for learning new skills, finding deals and job opportunities, participating in political discussions, interacting with government institutions, and informing themselves about health matters. Yet such differentiated uses can have significant implications for how ICT uses may relate to life outcomes. This section describes how various user characteristics and one's social surroundings influence digital media uses.

People's Internet uses do not happen in isolation of their societal position and the social institutions they inhabit. A refined approach to digital inequality recognizes that people's socioeconomic status influences the ways in which they have access to and use ICT. In addition to factors such as

(Age>=18)

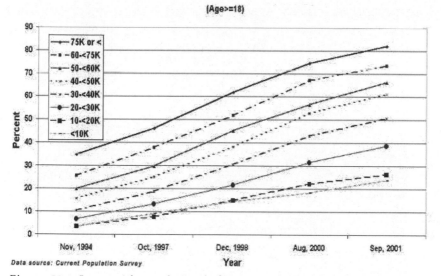

Figure 69.1 Internet Adoption by Level of Income in the United States, 1994–2001

(Age >=18)

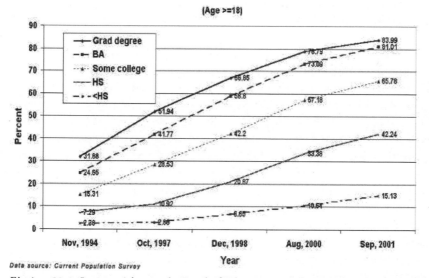

Figure 69.2 Internet Adoption by Level of Education in the United States, 1994–2001

age, gender, race, ethnicity, disability status, education, and wealth, one's social surroundings are also relevant to one's ICT experiences. Figure 69.3 presents a graphical representation of this framework.

The basic premise is that the societal position that users inhabit influences aspects of their digital media uses, such as the technical equipment to which they have access and the level of autonomy they posses when using the medium. Autonomy of use is understood as the freedom to use digital media when and where one wants to. Twenty-four-hour access at home can yield

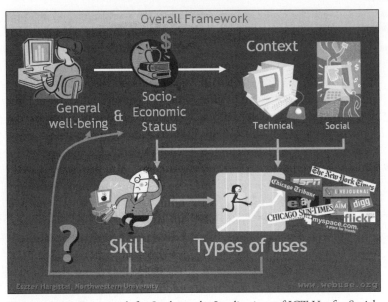

Figure 69.3 Framework for Studying the Implications of ICT Use for Social Inequality

a much more autonomous user experience than having to drive half an hour to a public library where one competes with others for usage time and where filtering software limits the types of materials within reach. Similarly, a workplace that allows Web use without constraints results in a very different experience from a job environment where one's online actions are constantly monitored. Quality of equipment (available hardware, software, and connection speed) and autonomy of use can both be a function of one's socioeconomic status.

The use of and learning about digital media both happen in social contexts. In addition to autonomy of use, which itself is a certain social context, the availability of other users in one's social circles can have important implications for one's online experiences. The relevant mechanisms through which social networks matter can be grouped into two main categories: informal and more directed information exchange. The former refers to knowledge one amasses through everyday discussions with peers about digital media uses and includes suggestions passed along by others through email or at the water cooler. The latter highlights the importance of support networks when users encounter a specific problem during their experiences with ICT. When faced with a difficulty, it makes a difference to have access to knowledgeable networks that help in finding a solution.

All of these factors then influence users' online abilities and what they are able to accomplish using digital media. While many online actions may seem trivial to the experienced user, most activities require some level of know-how. From recognizing what material is available online to being able to find it efficiently, from knowing how to contribute to online content production to knowing where to find relevant networks, from having the ability to evaluate content credibility to being vigilant about privacy and security concerns, informed uses of digital media rely on many important skills (Hargittai 2007b).

One's social position, the context of one's use, and one's online abilities then all have the potential to influence the types of uses to which one puts the medium. Some uses are more likely to yield beneficial outcomes than others. The next section will enumerate the ways in which ICT uses may improve, or in some cases impede, one's life chances.

How ICT Use Matters

The most pressing question for students of social inequality is whether the usage dimensions described above then loop back and translate into differences in users' socioeconomic position. What are the processes through which more informed and frequent uses of ICT may privilege some users over others? There are several ways in which differential ICT uses may influence access to the types of assets, resources, and valued goods that underlie stratification systems (Grusky 2008). The overarching idea is that certain types of ICT uses can result in increased human capital, financial capital, social capital, and cultural capital while other types of uses may outright disadvantage the uninformed.

With more and more jobs requiring the synthesis and analysis of varying types of information, employees with advanced Internet user skills can perform their jobs more effectively and efficiently. The Internet makes vast amounts of information available *so long as* one knows how to locate desired material. While theoretically all public Web pages are equally available to all users, not everybody possesses the necessary skills to (1) recognize in all situations the types of content relevant to a task that can be found online; (2) find the information; (3) do so efficiently; and (4) carefully evaluate the results to avoid misinformation or, worse, fraudulent outcomes.

Even if people do not know how to perform certain tasks, advanced skills will allow them to find assistance online. Since skill encompasses the ability to find others who may have the desired information and efficiently contact them for guidance, even when lacking know-how most relevant to the task at hand, the skilled user can benefit through informed use of the medium. This all leads to more tasks getting done quicker and more efficiently with possibly higher-quality results than would be possible if relying on fewer resources. In addition to helping with the performance of on-the-job tasks, ICT also allow people to develop additional skills that may advantage them in the labor market. Free tutorials exist online for training in a myriad of domains from foreign languages to software applications, from design skills to networking to productivity enhancement tips.

Enterprising ways of using the Internet can save a person significant amounts of money. Several services exist that make comparison shopping very easy, allowing the user to find the best deals on an item without spending money on gas and time on driving from one store to the next. The use of auction sites expands options even further. Moreover, the especially knowledgeable can take advantage of other people's mistakes by searching for items with spelling mistakes thereby avoiding bidding wars given that misspelled items are seen by few (Hargittai 2006). In addition to savings through informed purchasing, people can also make money by selling products on the Web. While putting one's items on the market used to require significant up-front investment, ICT have lowered the barriers to entry for putting things up for sale accessible to a large buyer base, assuming one knows what services help with reaching the largest or most relevant purchasers.

The potential of ICT for expanding one's social networks is enormous, although efficient and relevant ways of doing so are not trivial and require some amount of know-how. In some cases the Internet simply complements more traditional methods of networking while in others the medium is the main facilitator of a new relationship. The former refers to use of the tool to contact people who are already in one's extended network. The latter occurs thanks to various online interactions that can range from the exchange of information on a mailing list to the exchange of goods and services extending well beyond the Web. People find rides, coordinate meetings, and get emotional support from others online. But as with all other aspects of Internet use, skill matters. Finding the relevant communities and being sufficiently vigilant not to place oneself in harm's way are all important aspects of building social capital on the Web.

Familiarity with the latest trends can serve as status markers. Being able to discuss special topics in depth can help create bonds between people. Thanks to the Internet, certain subjects formerly much less accessible to the general public are more widely available. It is no longer necessary to go see a museum's special exhibition to have the facility to discuss what is on display since many galleries now put their pieces online. It is possible to develop a reasonably informed opinion about a restaurant halfway across the world simply by reading the many reviews available and constantly updated online. Knowing how to locate information about travel destinations—from driving directions to entertainment options—can yield more influence to the informed. Being able to draw on a myriad of topics while conversing with higher-ups can leave a good impression. While resources about diverse topics have long been available to the public, the ease and speed with which the Internet delivers information is unprecedented.

Informed users can be more engaged in the political process than those who rely exclusively on broadcast media for their political information seeking. Whether finding like-minded people or informing oneself in depth about the other side's perspective, the Internet allows for the exchange of political opinions much more than any other medium. Creating petitions and mobilizing others around a cause can be facilitated significantly with various online tools. Again, however, knowledge of what is available in this domain and how one can implement the services to benefit one's specific needs and interests is an essential part of any such undertaking.

The above are examples of how informed uses can have beneficial outcomes. There is another side to online actions, however. Uninformed uses may have outright problematic if not detrimental consequences. Do users stop to think about the context of, for example, an email message that requests confidential information from them? If everyone was aware of these issues, then phishing emails—messages that pretend to be from a reputable source to extract confidential information from users—would not lead to people giving up their passwords to Web sites that contain private information such as their bank accounts. Yet, we know that even among young adults—the generation that is growing up with these media—many lack the necessary knowledge to approach possibly malicious email with care (Hargittai In press). While fraud has always existed, the scope of malicious activities and their consequences have skyrocketed.

Related to online social interactions discussed above, but sufficiently distinct to merit its own discussion, is one's reputation developed from one's online pursuits. Sending emails from the privacy of one's home or office leads many to behave less carefully than they would in a public social setting. Few interactions on the Web are truly anonymous yet many people do not realize this when sending critical messages or posting comments on Web sites. An unwelcome remark can have negative consequences if targeting the wrong person. Alternatively, critical comments by others can tarnish the reputation of the person under attack. In contrast, a well-thought-out online presence can result in significant benefits. Those who participate regularly in online discussions and maintain Web sites frequented by many can amass fame that can later translate into fortune as well.

Generally speaking, many of the skills needed to reap the benefits listed here—or sidestep negative implications—can be learned from one's immediate networks. Growing up in a household that has the latest gadgets and digital media resources will make a difference when a student then encounters these tools in the classroom. Having siblings who can navigate the technologies will help in the transfer of relevant know-how. Living in neighborhoods where many in one's proximity are also discovering the latest ICT options will allow for more opportunities to develop savvy in the domain of digital media than a situation in which one is isolated without access to rele-vant technologies and knowledgeable networks. Bourdieu's cultural capital (1973) applied to the twenty-first century must incorporate the differential exposure to, understanding, and use of ICT. Work looking at young adults' digital literacy has found a statistically significant positive relationship between Internet savvy and the parental education of respondents (Hargittai 2007b).

Overall, it is important to recognize that ICT do not nullify the effects of other variables on one's life chances. People's ICT uses happen in the context of their lives, influenced by their socioeconomic status and social surroundings. The question is whether ICT uses have an independent effect on life outcomes. Given the relative newness of the Internet and other digital media uses at a mass societal level, this field is in its infancy and lacks the longitudinal data necessary to answer many of the questions raised here. Nonetheless, preliminary findings seem to suggest that ICT reinforce inequalities more than alleviating differences. Although not without its critics (DiNardo and Pischke 1997), the general consensus seems to be that skill-biased technological change, and especially computerization, is an important source of the rise in earnings inequality in recent years (Krueger 1993). A more recent study found Internet use to have an independent effect on wage differences, suggesting tangible outcomes of being among the connected (DiMaggio and Bonikowski 2006).

Luxury Good or Essential Tool?

In 2001, then chair of the Federal Communication Commission Michael Powell likened the digital divide to a luxury car divide, stating : "I think there is a Mercedes divide, I would like to have one, but I can't afford one" (quoted in Clewley 2001).

Is Internet use simply a luxury item with people's connectivity—or lack thereof—merely a reflection of their preferences for the medium? As ICT become ever more central to our social infrastructure one can no longer participate meaningfully in our society without deep and ongoing usage of digital media. Once an entire society is built around these tools, they can no longer be considered simply as luxury goods. While the car and the telephone may have, at one time, been regarded as extravagant expenditures of the wealthy, once contemporary society was thoroughly built around these innovations they became necessities for operating in society and those who lacked them were socially excluded.

While it may be that some people opt out of ICT use based on an informed understanding of all that the Internet has to offer, much more likely is that people do not realize the many necessities and benefits of digital media. As an increasing number of activities between institutions and individuals move online—concerning both the public and the private sector—being a nonuser will have growing implications for people's access to various services. If government institutions assume a familiarity with and access to the medium, then lacking access to and understanding of such resources some will be unable to interact with and navigate the system optimally.

Take, for example, the case of Medicare Part D in 2006. The government introduced a new system and required the elderly to make important choices about their health insurance. In response to concerns about the difficulty of navigating the system, the administration created a Web site and directed people to it for assistance with the program (Freese, Rivas, and Hargittai 2006). However, the resource was very complicated to navigate for many and the assumption that the elderly could access and understand the site was unfounded, as many were uninformed about or confused by the system. Similarly, more and more commercial services make material available on the Web and charge extra fees to those who interact with the company offline. When important government services are primarily accessible online and when there is an extra financial cost to handling matters with businesses offline, then having access to the Internet and knowing how to use it can no longer be considered an optional luxury item.

Conclusion

Disparities in people's Web-use abilities and uses have the potential to contribute to social inequalities rather than alleviate them. Those who know how to navigate the Web's vast landscape and how to use digital media to address their needs can reap significant benefits from it. In contrast, those who lack abilities in these domains may have a harder time dealing with certain logistics of everyday life, may miss out on opportunities, and may also obtain incorrect information from unreliable sources or come to rely on unsubstantiated rumors. Differentiated uses of digital media have the potential to lead to increasing inequalities benefiting those who are already in advantageous positions and denying access to better resources to the underprivileged. Merton's (1973) observation "Unto every one who hath shall be given" applies to this domain. Preliminary findings from this emerging field suggest that initial advantages translate into increasing returns over time for the digitally connected and digitally skilled.

REFERENCES

Barzilai-Nahon, Karine. 2006. "Gaps and Bits: Conceptualizing Measurements for Digital Divide/s." *Information Society* 22: 269–278.

Bimber, B. 2000. "The Gender Gap on the Internet." *Social Science Quarterly* 81: 868–876.

Bourdieu, Pierre. 1973. "Cultural Reproduction and Social Reproduction." Pp. 71–112 in *Knowledge, Education, and Cultural Change*, edited by Richard Brown. London: Tavistock.

Clewley, Robin. 2001. "I Have a (Digital) Dream." In *Wired*. http://www.wired.com/politics/law/news/2001/04/43349.

Dewan, S., and F. Riggins. 2006. "The Digital Divide: Current and Future Research Directions." *Journal of the Association of Information Systems* 6: 298–337.

DiMaggio, Paul, and Bart Bonkowski. Forthcoming. "Make Money Surfing the Web? The Impact of Internet Use on the Earnings of U.S. Workers." *American Sociological Review.*

DiMaggio, Paul, Eszter Hargittai, Coral Celeste, and Steven Shafer. 2004. "Digital Inequality: From Unequal Access to Differentiated Use." Pp. 355–400 in *Social Inequality*, edited by Kathryn Neckerman. New York: Russell Sage Foundation.

DiNardo, John E., and Jorn-Steffen Pischke. 1997. "The Returns to Computer Use Revisited: Have Pencils Changed the Wage Structure Too?" *Quarterly Journal of Economics* 112: 291–303.

Freese, Jeremy, Salvador Rivas, and Eszter Hargittai. 2006. "Cognitive Ability and Internet Use Among Older Adults." *Poetics* 34: 236–249.

Grusky, David B. 2008. *Social Stratification: Class, Race, and Gender in Sociological Perspective.* Boulder, CO: Westview Press.

Hargittai, Eszter. 2006. "Hurdles to Information Seeking: Explaining Spelling and Typographical Mistakes in Users' Online Search Behavior." *Journal of the Association of Information Systems* 7. http://jais.aisnet.org/articles/default.asp?vol=7&art=1.

———. 2007a. "Beyond Gigs of Log Data: The Social Aspects of Internet Use." In *Tech Talks*. Mountain View, CA: Google, Inc. January 30.

http://video.google.com/videoplay?docid=6884513936578531954.

———. 2007b. "A Framework for Studying Differences in People's Digital Media Uses." In *Cyberworld Unlimited?*, edited by Nadia Kutscher and Hans-Uwe Otto. Wiesbaden: VS Verlag für Sozialwissenschaften/GWV Fachverlage GmbH. Pp. 121-137.

———. In press. "The Role of Expertise in Navigating Links of Influence." In *The Hyperlinked Society*, edited by Joseph Turow and Lokman Tsui. Ann Arbor: University of Michigan Press.

Hargittai, Eszter, and Steven Shafer. 2006. "Differences in Actual and Perceived Online Skills: The Role of Gender." *Social Science Quarterly* 87(2):432-448. June.

Hoffman, D. L., and T. P. Novak. 1998. "Bridging the Racial Divide on the Internet." Pp. 390–391 in *Science* 280(5362).

Horrigan, John. 2006. "Tech Users: What They Have, How It Matters." In KMB Video Journal Conference. St. Petersburg Beach, Florida.

Krueger, Alan. 1993. "How Computers Have Changed the Wage Structure: Evidence from Microdata, 1984–1989." *Quarterly Journal of Economics* 108: 33–60.

Merton, R. K. 1973. *The Sociology of Science: Theoretical and Empirical Investigations.* Chicago: University of Chicago Press.

Mossberger, Karen, Caroline J. Tolbert, and Mary Stansbury. 2003. *Virtual Inequality: Beyond the Digital Divide.* Washington, DC: Georgetown University Press.

National Telecommunications and Information Administration. 1998. "Falling Through the Net II: New Data on the Digital Divide." Washington, DC: NTIA.

———. 1999. "Falling Through the Net: Defining the Digital Divide." Washington, DC: NTIA.

———. 2000. "Falling Through the Net: Toward Digital Inclusion." Washington, DC: NTIA.

———. 2002. "A Nation Online: How Americans Are Expanding Their Use of the Internet." Washington, DC: NTIA.

Norris, P. 2001. *Digital Divide: Civic Engagement, Information Poverty and the Internet in Democratic Societies.* New York: Cambridge University Press.

Ono, Hiroshi, and Madeline Zavodny. 2003. "Gender and the Internet." *Social Science Quarterly* 84: 111–121.

van Dijk, Jan A. G. M. 2005. *The Deepening Divide.* London: Sage Publications.

Wareham, Jonathan, Armando Levy, and Wei Shi. 2004. "Wireless Diffusion and Mobile Computing: Implications for the Digital Divide." *Telecommunications Policy* 28: 439–457.

Warschauer, M. 2003. *Technology and Social Inclusion.* Cambridge, MA: MIT Press.

PART IX

Globalization and Inequality

70

Globalism's Discontents

JOSEPH E. STIGLITZ

Few subjects have polarized people throughout the world as much as globalization. Some see it as the way of the future, bringing unprecedented prosperity to everyone, everywhere. Others, symbolized by the Seattle protestors of December 1999, fault globalization as the source of untold problems, from the destruction of native cultures to increasing poverty and immiseration. In this article, I want to sort out the different meanings of globalization. In many countries, globalization has brought huge benefits to a few with few benefits to the many. But in the case of a few countries, it has brought enormous benefit to the many. Why have there been these huge differences in experiences? The answer is that globalization has meant different things in different places.

The countries that have managed globalization on their own, such as those in East Asia, have, by and large, ensured that they reaped huge benefits and that those benefits were equitably shared; they were able substantially to control the terms on which they engaged with the global economy. By contrast, the countries that have, by and large, had globalization managed for them by the International Monetary Fund (IMF) and other international economic institutions have not done so well. The problem is thus not with globalization but with how it has been managed.

The international financial institutions have pushed a particular ideology—market fundamentalism—that is both bad economics and bad politics; it is based on premises concerning how markets work that do not hold even for developed countries, much less for developing countries. The IMF has pushed these economics policies without a broader vision of society or the role of economics within society. And it has pushed these policies in ways that have undermined emerging democracies.

More generally, globalization itself has been governed in ways that are undemocratic and have been disadvantageous to developing countries, especially the poor within those countries. The Seattle protestors pointed to the absence of democracy and of transparency, the governance of the international economic institutions by and for special corporate and financial interests, and the absence of countervailing democratic checks to ensure that these informal and *public* institutions serve a general interest. In these complaints, there is more than a grain of truth.

Beneficial Globalization

Of the countries of the world, those in East Asia have grown the fastest and done most to reduce poverty. And they have done so, emphatically, via "globalization." Their growth has been based on exports—by taking advantage of the global market for exports and by closing the technology gap. It was not just gaps in capital and other resources that separated the developed from the less-developed countries, but differences in knowledge. East Asian countries took advantage of the "globalization of knowledge" to reduce these disparities. But while some of the countries in the region grew by opening themselves up to multinational companies, others, such as Korea and Taiwan, grew by creating their own enterprises. Here is the key distinction: Each of the most successful globalizing countries determined its own pace of change; each made sure as it grew that the benefits were shared equitably; each rejected the basic tenets of the "Washington Consensus," which argued for a minimalist role for government and rapid privatization and liberalization.

In East Asia, government took an active role in managing the economy. The steel industry that the Korean government created was among the most efficient in the world—performing far better than its private-sector rivals in the United States (which, though private, are constantly turning to the government for protection and for subsidies). Financial markets were highly regulated. My research shows that those regulations promoted growth. It was only when these countries stripped away the regulations, under pressure from the U.S. Treasury and the IMF, that they encountered problems.

During the 1960s, 1970s, and 1980s, the East Asian economies not only grew rapidly but were remarkably stable. Two of the countries most touched by the 1997–1998 economic crisis had had in the preceding three decades not a single year of negative growth; two had only one year—a better performance than the United States or the other wealthy nations that make up the Organization for Economic Cooperation and Development (OECD). The single most important factor leading to the troubles that several of the East Asian countries encountered in the late 1990s—the East Asian crisis—was the rapid liberalization of financial and capital markets. In short, the countries of East Asia benefited from globalization because they made globalization work for them; it was when they succumbed to the pressures from the outside that they ran into problems that were beyond their own capacity to manage well.

Globalization can yield immense benefits. Elsewhere in the developing world, globalization of knowledge has brought improved health, with life spans increasing at a rapid pace. How can one put a price on these benefits of globalization? Globalization has brought still other benefits: Today there is the beginning of a globalized civil society that has begun to succeed with such reforms as the Mine Ban Treaty and debt forgiveness for the poorest highly indebted countries (the Jubilee movement). The globalization protest movement itself would not have been possible without globalization.

The Darker Side of Globalization

How then could a trend with the power to have so many benefits have produced such opposition? Simply because it has not only failed to live up to its potential but frequently has had very adverse effects. But this forces us to ask, why has it had such adverse effects? The answer can be seen by looking at each of the economic elements of globalization as pursued by the international financial institutions and especially by the IMF.

The most adverse effects have arisen from the liberalization of financial and capital markets—which has posed risks to developing countries without commensurate rewards. The liberalization has left them prey to hot money pouring into the country, an influx that has fueled speculative real-estate booms; just as suddenly, as investor sentiment changes, the money is pulled out, leaving in its wake economic devastation. Early on, the IMF said that these countries were being rightly punished for pursuing bad economic policies. But as the crisis spread from country to country, even those that the IMF had given high marks found themselves ravaged.

The IMF often speaks about the importance of the discipline provided by capital markets. In doing so, it exhibits a certain paternalism, a new form of the old colonial mentality: "We in the establishment, we in the North who run our capital markets, know best. Do what we tell you to do, and you will prosper." The arrogance is offensive, but the objection is more than just to style. The position is highly undemocratic: There is an implied assumption that democracy by itself does not provide sufficient discipline. But if one is to have an external disciplinarian, one should choose a good disciplinarian who knows what is good for growth, who shares one's values. One doesn't want an arbitrary and capricious taskmaster who one moment praises you for your virtues and the next screams at you for being rotten to the core. But capital markets are just such a fickle taskmaster; even ardent advocates talk about their bouts of irrational exuberance followed by equally irrational pessimism.

Lessons of Crisis

Nowhere was the fickleness more evident than in the last global financial crisis. Historically, most of the disturbances in capital flows into and out of a country are not the result of factors inside the country. Major disturbances arise, rather, from influences outside the country. When Argentina suddenly faced high interest rates in 1998, it wasn't because of what Argentina did but because of what happened in Russia. Argentina cannot be blamed for Russia's crisis.

Small developing countries find it virtually impossible to withstand this volatility. I have described capital-market liberalization with a simple metaphor: Small countries are like small boats. Liberalizing capital markets is like setting them loose on a rough sea. Even if the boats are well captained, even if the boats are sound, they are likely to be hit broadside by a big wave and capsize. But the IMF pushed for the boats to set forth into the roughest parts of the sea before they were seaworthy, with untrained captains and crews, and without life vests. No wonder matters turned out so badly!

To see why it is important to choose a disciplinarian who shares one's values, consider a world in which there were free mobility of skilled labor. Skilled labor would then provide discipline. Today, a country that does not treat capital well will find capital quickly withdrawing; in a world of free labor mobility, if a country did not treat skilled labor well, it too would withdraw. Workers would worry about the quality of their children's education and their family's health care, the quality of their environment and of their own wages and working conditions. They would say to the government: If you fail to provide these essentials, we will move elsewhere. That is a far cry from the kind of discipline that free-flowing capital provides.

The liberalization of capital markets has not brought growth: How can one build factories or create jobs with money that can come in and out of a country overnight? And it gets worse: Prudential behavior requires countries to set aside reserves equal to the amount of short-term lending; so if a firm in a poor country borrows $100 million at, say, 20 percent interest rates short-term from a bank in the United States, the government must set aside a corresponding amount. The reserves are typically held in U.S. Treasury bills—a safe, liquid asset. In effect, the country is borrowing $100 million from the United States and lending $100 million to the United States. But when it borrows, it pays a high interest rate, 20 percent; when it lends, it receives a low interest rate, around 4 percent. This may be great for the United States, but it can hardly help the growth of the poor country. There is also a high *opportunity* cost of the reserves; the money could have been much better spent on building rural roads or constructing schools or health clinics. But instead, the country is, in effect, forced to lend money to the United States.

Thailand illustrates the true ironies of such policies: There, the free market led to investments in empty office buildings, starving other sectors—such as education and transportation—of badly needed resources. Until the IMF and the U.S. Treasury came along, Thailand had restricted bank lending for speculative real estate. The Thais had seen the record: Such lending is an essential part of the boom-bust cycle that has characterized capitalism for 200 years. It wanted to be sure that the scarce capital went to create jobs. But the IMF nixed this intervention in the free market. If the free market said, "Build empty office buildings," so be it! The market knew better than any government bureaucrat who mistakenly might have thought it wiser to build schools or factories.

The Costs of Volatility

Capital-market liberalization is inevitably accompanied by huge volatility, and this volatility impedes growth and increases poverty. It increases the risks of investing in the country, and thus investors demand a risk premium in the form of higher-than-normal profits. Not only is growth not enhanced but poverty is increased through several channels. The high volatility increases the likelihood of recessions—and the poor always bear the brunt of such downturns. Even in developed countries, safety nets are weak or nonexistent among the self-employed and in the rural sector. But these are the dominant sectors in developing countries. Without adequate safety nets, the recessions that follow from capital-market liberalization lead to impoverishment. In the name of imposing budget discipline and reassuring investors, the IMF invariably demands expenditure reductions, which almost inevitably result in cuts in outlays for safety nets that are already threadbare.

But matters are even worse—for under the doctrines of the "discipline of the capital markets," if countries try to tax capital, capital flees. Thus, the IMF doctrines inevitably lead to an increase in tax burdens on the poor and the middle classes. Thus, while IMF bailouts enable the rich to take their money out of the country at more favorable terms (at the overvalued exchange rates), the burden of repaying the loans lies with the workers who remain behind.

The reason that I emphasize capital-market liberalization is that the case against it—and against the IMF's stance in pushing it—is so compelling. It illustrates what can go wrong with globalization. Even economists like Jagdish Bhagwati, strong advocates of free trade, see the folly in liberalizing capital markets. Belatedly, so too has the IMF—at least in its official rhetoric, though less so in its policy stances—but too late for all those countries that have suffered so much from following the IMF's prescriptions.

But while the case for trade liberalization—when properly done—is quite compelling, the way it has been pushed by the IMF has been far more problematic. The basic logic is simple: Trade liberalization is supposed to result in resources moving from inefficient protected sectors to more efficient export sectors. The problem is not only that job destruction comes before the job creation—so that unemployment and poverty result—but that the IMF's "structural adjustment programs" (designed in ways that allegedly would reassure global investors) make job creation almost impossible. For these programs are often accompanied by high interest rates that are often justified by a single-minded focus on inflation. Sometimes that concern is deserved; often, though, it is carried to an extreme. In the United States, we worry that small increases in the interest rate will discourage investment. The IMF has pushed for far higher interest rates in countries with a far less hospitable investment environment. The high interest rates mean that new jobs and enterprises are not created. What happens is that trade liberalization, rather than moving workers from low-productivity jobs to high-

productivity ones, moves them from low-productivity jobs to unemployment. Rather than enhanced growth, the effect is increased poverty. To make matters even worse, the unfair trade-liberalization agenda forces poor countries to compete with highly subsidized American and European agriculture. . . .

An Unfair Trade Agenda

The trade-liberalization agenda has been set by the North, or more accurately, by special interests in the North. Consequently, a disproportionate part of the gains has accrued to the advanced industrial countries, and in some cases the less-developed countries have actually been worse off. After the last round of trade negotiations, the Uruguay Round that ended in 1994, the World Bank calculated the gains and losses to each of the regions of the world. The United States and Europe gained enormously. But sub-Saharan Africa, the poorest region of the world, lost by about 2 percent because of terms-of-trade effects: The trade negotiations opened their markets to manufactured goods produced by the industrialized countries but did not open up the markets of Europe and the United States to the agricultural goods in which poor countries often have a comparative advantage. Nor did the trade agreements eliminate the subsidies to agriculture that make it so hard for the developing countries to compete.

The U.S. negotiations with China over its membership in the WTO displayed a double standard bordering on the surreal. The U.S. trade representative, the chief negotiator for the United States, began by insisting that China was a developed country. Under WTO rules, developing countries are allowed longer transition periods in which state subsidies and other departures from the WTO strictures are permitted. China certainly wishes it were a developed country, with Western-style per capita incomes. And since China has a lot of "capitas," it's possible to multiply a huge number of people by very small average incomes and conclude that the People's Republic is a big economy. But China is not only a developing economy; it is a low-income developing country. Yet the United States insisted that China be treated like a developed country! China went along with the fiction; the negotiations dragged on so long that China got some extra time to adjust. But the true hypocrisy was shown when U.S. negotiators asked, in effect, for developing-country status for the United States to get extra time to shelter the American textile industry.

Trade negotiations in the service industries also illustrate the unlevel nature of the playing field. Which service industries did the United States say were *very* important? Financial services—industries in which Wall Street has a comparative advantage. Construction industries and maritime services were not on the agenda, because the developing countries would have a comparative advantage in these sectors.

Consider also intellectual-property rights, which are important if innovators are to have incentives to innovate (though many of the corporate advocates of intellectual property exaggerate its importance and fail to note that much of the most important research, as in basic science and mathematics, is not patentable). Intellectual-property rights, such as patents and trademarks, need to balance the interests of producers with those of users—not only users in developing countries, but researchers in developed countries. If we underprice the profitability of innovation to the inventor, we deter invention. If we overprice its cost to the research community and the end user, we retard its diffusion and beneficial effects on living standards.

In the final stages of the Uruguay negotiations, both the White House Office of Science and Technology Policy and the Council of Economic Advisers worried that we had not got the balance right—that the agreement put producers' interests over users'. We worried that, with this imbalance, the rate of progress and innovation might actually be impeded. After all, knowledge is the most important input into research, and overly strong intellectual-property rights can, in effect, increase the price of this input. We were also concerned about the consequences of denying lifesaving medicines to the poor. This issue subsequently gained international attention in the context of the provision of AIDS medicines in South Africa [see "Medicine as a Luxury" by Merrill Goozner, on page A7]. The international outrage forced the drug companies to back down—and it appears that, going forward, the most adverse consequences will be circumscribed. But it is worth noting that initially, even the Democratic U.S. administration supported the pharmaceutical companies.

What we were not fully aware of was another danger—what has come to be called "biopiracy," which involves international drug companies patenting traditional medicines. Not only do they seek to make money from "resources" and knowledge that rightfully belong to the developing countries, but in doing so they squelch domestic firms who long provided these traditional medicines. While it is not clear whether these patents would hold up in court if they were effectively challenged, it is clear that the less-developed countries may not have the legal and financial resources required to mount such a challenge. The issue has become the source of enormous emotional, and potentially economic, concern throughout the developing world. This fall, while I was in Ecuador visiting a village in the high Andes, the Indian mayor railed against how globalization had led to biopiracy. . . .

Trickle-Down Economics

We recognize today that there is a "social contract" that binds citizens together, and with their government. When government policies abrogate that social contract, citizens may not honor their "contracts" with each other, or with the government. Maintaining that social contract is particularly important, and difficult, in the midst of the social upheavals that so frequently accompany the development transformation. In the green eye-shaded calculations of the IMF macroeconomics there is, too often, no room for these concerns.

Part of the social contract entails "fairness," that the poor share in the gains of society as it grows, and that the rich share in the pains of society in times of crisis. The Washington Consensus policies paid little attention to issues of distribution or "fairness." If pressed, many of its proponents would argue that the best way to help the poor is to make the economy grow. They believe in trickle-down economics. *Eventually*, it is asserted, the benefits of that growth *trickle down* even to the poor. Trickle-down economics was never much more than just a belief, an article of faith. Pauperism seemed to grow in nineteenth-century England even though the country as a whole prospered. Growth in America in the 1980s provided the most recent dramatic example: while the economy grew,

those at the bottom saw their real incomes decline. The Clinton administration had argued strongly against trickle-down economics; it believed that there had to be active programs to help the poor. And when I left the White House to go to the World Bank, I brought with me the same skepticism of trickle-down economics; if this had not worked in the United States, why would it work in developing countries? While it is true that sustained reductions in poverty cannot be attained without robust economic growth, the converse is not true: growth need not benefit all. It is not true that "a rising tide lifts all boats." Sometimes, a quickly rising tide, especially when accompanied by a storm, dashes weaker boats against the shore, smashing them to smithereens.

In spite of the obvious problems confronting trickle-down economics, it has a good intellectual pedigree. One Nobel Prize winner, Arthur Lewis, argued that inequality was good for development and economic growth, since the rich save more than the poor, and the key to growth was capital accumulation. Another Nobel Prize winner, Simon Kuznets, argued that while in the initial stages of development inequality increased, later on the trend was reversed.[1]

The history of the past fifty years has, however, not supported these theories and hypotheses. East Asian countries—South Korea, China, Taiwan, Japan—showed that high savings did not require high inequality, that one could achieve rapid growth without a substantial increase in inequality. Because the governments did not believe that growth would automatically benefit the poor, and because they believed that greater *equality* would actually enhance growth, governments in the region took active steps to ensure that the rising tide of growth did lift most boats, that wage inequalities were kept in bounds, that some educational opportunity was extended to all. Their policies led to social and political stability, which in turn contributed to an economic environment in which businesses flourished. Tapping new reservoirs of talent provided the energy and human skills that contributed to the dynamism of the region.

Elsewhere, where governments adopted the Washington Consensus policies, the poor have benefited less from growth. In Latin America, growth has not been accompanied by a reduction in inequality, or even a reduction in poverty. In some cases poverty has actually increased, as evidenced by the urban slums that dot the landscape. The IMF talks with pride about the progress Latin America has made in market reforms over the past decade (though somewhat more quietly after the collapse of the star student Argentina in 2001, and the recession and stagnation that have afflicted many of the "reform" countries during the past five years), but has said less about the numbers in poverty.

Clearly, growth alone does not always improve the lives of all a country's people. Not surprisingly, the phrase "trickle-down" has disappeared from the policy debate. But, in a slightly mutated form, the idea is still alive. I call the new variant *trickle-down-plus.* It holds that growth is necessary and *almost* sufficient for reducing poverty—implying that the best strategy is simply to focus on growth, while mentioning issues like female education and health. But proponents of trickle-down-plus failed to implement policies that would effectively address either broader concerns of poverty or even specific issues such as the education of women. In practice, the advocates of trickle-down-plus continued with much

the same policies as before, with much the same adverse effects. The overly stringent "adjustment policies" in country after country forced cutbacks in education and health: in Thailand, as a result, not only did female prostitution increase but expenditures on AIDS were cut way back; and what had been one of the world's most successful programs in fighting AIDS had a major setback.

The irony was that one of the major proponents of trickle-down-plus was the U.S. Treasury under the Clinton administration. Within the administration, in domestic politics, there was a wide spectrum of views, from New Democrats, who wanted to see a more limited role for government, to Old Democrats, who looked for more government intervention. But the central view, reflected in the annual Economic Report of the President (prepared by the Council of Economic Advisers), argued strongly against trickle-down economics—or even trickle-down-plus. Here was the U.S. Treasury pushing policies on other countries that, had they been advocated for the United States, would have been strongly contested *within the administration,* and almost surely defeated. The reason for this seeming inconsistency was simple: The IMF and the World Bank were part of Treasury's turf, an arena in which, with few exceptions, they were allowed to push their perspectives, just as other departments, within their domains, could push theirs. . . .

Global Social Justice

Today, in much of the developing world, globalization is being questioned. For instance, in Latin America, after a short burst of growth in the early 1990s, stagnation and recession have set in. The growth was not sustained—some might say, was not sustainable. Indeed, at this juncture, the growth record of the so-called post-reform era looks no better, and in some countries much worse, than in the widely criticized import-substitution period of the 1950s and 1960s when Latin countries tried to industrialize by discouraging imports. Indeed, reform critics point out that the burst of growth in the early 1990s was little more than a "catch-up" that did not even make up for the lost decade of the 1980s.

Throughout the region, people are asking: "Has reform failed or has globalization failed?" The distinction is perhaps artificial, for globalization was at the center of the reforms. Even in those countries that have managed to grow, such as Mexico, the benefits have accrued largely to the upper 30 percent and have been even more concentrated in the top 10 percent. Those at the bottom have gained little; many are even worse off. The reforms have exposed countries to greater risk, and the risks have been borne disproportionately by those least able to cope with them. Just as in many countries where the pacing and sequencing of reforms has resulted in job destruction outmatching job creation, so too has the exposure to risk outmatched the ability to create institutions for coping with risk, including effective safety nets.

In this bleak landscape, there are some positive signs. Those in the North have become more aware of the inequities of the global economic architecture. The agreement at Doha to hold a new round of trade negotiations—the "Development Round"—promises to rectify some of the imbalances of the past. There has been a marked change in the rhetoric of the international economic institutions—at least they talk about poverty. At the World Bank, there have been some real reforms; there has been some progress in translating the rhetoric into reality—in ensuring that the voices of the poor are heard and the concerns of the developing countries are listened to. But elsewhere, there is often a gap between the rhetoric and the reality. Serious reforms in governance, in who makes decisions and how they are made, are not on the table. If one of the problems at the IMF has been that the ideology, interests, and perspectives of the financial community in the advanced industrialized countries have been given disproportionate weight (in matters whose effects go well beyond finance), then the prospects for success in the current discussions of reform, in which the same parties continue to predominate, are bleak. They are more likely to result in slight changes in the shape of the table, not changes in who is *at* the table or what is on the agenda.

September 11 has resulted in a global alliance against terrorism. What we now need is not just an alliance *against* evil, but an alliance *for* something positive—a global alliance for reducing poverty and for creating a better environment, an alliance for creating a global society with more social justice.

NOTE

1. See W. A. Lewis, "Economic Development with Unlimited Supplies of Labor," *Manchester School* 22 (1954), pp. 139–91, and S. Kuznets, "Economic Growth and Income Inequality," *American Economic Review* 45(1) (1955), pp. 1–28.

71

The New Geography of Global Income Inequality

GLENN FIREBAUGH

The new geography of inequality—not to be confused with the "new economic geography" that arose in economics in the 1990s (Fujita, Krugman, and Venables 1999)—refers to the new pattern of global income inequality caused by the recent phenomenon of declining inequality across nations accompanied by (in many places) rising inequality within nations. This phenomenon, which began in the last third of the twentieth century and continues today, results in a "new geography" because it represents the reversal of trends that trace back to the early stages of Western industrialization. Put in the perspective of an individual, the new geography of global income inequality means that national location—while still paramount—is declining in significance in the determination of one's income.

Despite a recent surge of interest in global inequality, researchers have largely overlooked its changing contour. Studies of global income inequality over the last decades of the twentieth century have been preoccupied with the problem of global divergence, that is, the presumed problem of worsening income inequality for the world as a whole (for example, Wade 2001; Milanovic 2002). This preoccupation with global divergence is misguided, first, because global income inequality almost certainly declined over this period and, second, because the focus on the level of global income inequality has diverted attention from the changing nature of global income inequality in recent decades. Global income inequality is no worse today than it was in the 1960s and 1970s, but global income inequality is nevertheless changing—it is gradually shifting from inequality across nations to inequality within nations. The rising importance of within-nation inequality and declining importance of between-nation inequality represents a historic change, since it involves the reversal of a trend that began with the uneven industrialization of the world that started more than two centuries ago.

This chapter contrasts the New Geography Hypothesis with the popular view that globalization—by which I mean the increased interconnectedness of localities, particularly the deepening of economic links between countries—has led to growing global income inequality:

Globalization $\longrightarrow$ global inequality.

For short, I call this popular view the Trade Protest Model, because the protests against the World Trade Organization in Seattle and elsewhere were driven at least in part by the assumption that global trade is exacerbating global inequality. To place the New Geography Hypothesis in context, it is useful first to examine five myths that underlie the globalization $\longrightarrow$ global inequality model.

Myths of the Trade Protest Model

Under the heading "Siege in Seattle," the December 13, 1999, issue of the U.S. magazine *Newsweek* gave this account of the protests surrounding the meeting of the World Trade Organization in Seattle, Washington:

> Until last week, not so many Americans had even heard of the WTO. Fewer still could have identified it as the small, Geneva-based bureaucracy that the United States and 134 other nations set up five years ago to referee global commerce. To Bill Clinton, it is a mechanism that can allow America to do well and good at the same time. But to many of the 40,000 activists and union members who streamed into Seattle—a clean, scenic city that has grown rich on foreign trade—the WTO is something else again: a secretive tool of ruthless multinational corporations. They charge it with helping sneaker companies to exploit Asian workers, timber companies to clear-cut rain forests, shrimpers to kill sea turtles and a world of other offenses.

Media accounts grappled with the sheer diversity of the protesters, from leaders of U.S. labor to members of environmental groups to a leading Chinese dissident. The common thread seemed to be, as the *New York Times* (1999) put it, the view that the WTO is a "handmaiden of corporate interests whose rulings undermine health, labor and environmental protections around the world." According to *The Economist* (1999), "The WTO has become a magnet for resistance to globalisation by both old-fashioned protectionists and newer critics of free trade."

Some of the protest groups emphasized rising inequality as among the most noxious consequences of increasing trade globalization. For example, Ralph Nader's Public Citizen group portrays the WTO as a tool of big business "which is harming the environment and increasing inequality" (*The Economist* 1999), and representatives of 1,448 nongovernmental organizations protesting the WTO signed a statement claiming that "globalisation has three serious consequences: the concentration of wealth in the hands of the multinationals and the rich; poverty for the majority of the world's population; and unsustainable patterns of production and consumption that destroy the environment" (*New Scientist* 1999). Note that two of the three consequences— concentration of wealth and impoverishment of the majority—tie globalization directly to growth in inequality.

Global income inequality is the result of the interplay of multiple causes, of course, so serious analyses are unlikely to give an unqualified endorsement to the notion that globalization has automatically resulted in an explosion in global income inequality. Global inequality existed before the recent growth in world trade, and it would persist if nations suddenly stopped trading. Nonetheless, popular literature on globalization has tended to fuel the belief in a globalization-led explosion in global income inequality by making claims that purport to be grounded in the findings of serious scholarly analyses. Upon closer inspection, however, many of the claims fly in the face of available empirical evidence. This section examines the key myths that underlie the globalization → global inequality model.

Myth 1. The Myth of Exploding Global Income Inequality. A steady drumbeat of reports and articles claims that the world's income is becoming more and more unequally distributed. Here is a sample:

- "Globalization has dramatically increased inequality between and within nations" (Jay Mazur, 2000, in *Foreign Affairs*).
- "The very nature of globalization has an inherent bias toward inequality. . . . One would have to be blind not to see that globalization also exacerbates the disparity between a small class of winners and the rest of us" (Paul Martin, Canada's prime minister, June 1998, quoted in Eggertson 1998).
- "Along with ecological risk, to which it is related, expanding inequality is the most serious problem facing world society" (Anthony Giddens, 1999).
- "Thus, overall, the ascent of informational, global capitalism is indeed characterized by simultaneous economic development and underdevelopment, social inclusion and social exclusion. . . . There is polarization in the distribution of wealth at the global level, differential evolution of intra-country income inequality, and substantial growth of poverty and misery

in the world at large" (Manuel Castells, 1998, p. 82, emphasis omitted).

What I have found (Firebaugh 2003) is that global income inequality has not exploded but in fact leveled off and then declined in the last part of the twentieth century. Although income inequality rose somewhat in the average nation, income inequality declined across nations. Since between-nation inequality is the larger component of global income inequality, the decline in between-nation income inequality more than offset the rise in within-nation income inequality. As a result, global income inequality declined in the last years of the twentieth century. Sherlock Holmes was right: it *is* a capital mistake to theorize in advance of the facts (Doyle 1955, p. 507). With respect to global income inequality, much mischief has been done by theorizing about global income inequality on the basis of the views expressed above. Theorizing based on the widespread view of exploding global income inequality is theorizing based on facts that aren't.

Myth 2. The Myth of Growing Income Inequality Across Nations, as Rich Nations Surge Ahead and Poor Nations Fall Further Behind. The first myth—exploding global inequality—is based on a second myth, the myth that inequality is growing across nations. The second myth is as widespread as the first, and it has been fueled by widely circulated reports of international agencies:

- "Figures indicate that income inequality between countries has increased sharply over the past 40 years" (World Bank 2000b, *World Development Report 2000/2001*, p. 51).

- "The average income in the richest 20 countries is 37 times the average in the poorest 20—a gap that has doubled in the past 40 years" (International Monetary Fund 2000, p. 50).
- "Gaps in income between the poorest and richest people and countries have continued to widen. In 1960 the 20% of the world's people in the richest countries had 30 times the income of the poorest 20%—in 1997, 74 times as much. . . . Gaps are widening both between and within countries" (United Nations Development Program 1999, *Human Development Report 1999,* p. 36).
- "It is an empirical fact that the income gap between poor and rich countries has increased in recent decades" (Ben-David, Nordström, and Winters 1999, World Trade Organization special study, p. 3).
- "In 1960, the Northern countries were 20 times richer than the Southern, in 1980 46 times. . . . [I]n this kind of race, the rich countries will always move faster than the rest" (Sachs 1992, *The Development Dictionary,* p. 3).

The myth of growing income inequality across nations is based in large part on a misinterpretation of the widely cited finding (for example, World Bank 2000b, p. 50) that income growth has tended to be slower in poor nations than in rich nations. As we shall see, this positive cross-country association between income level and income growth rate conceals the critical fact that the poor nations that are falling badly behind contain no more than 10 percent of the world's population, whereas the poor nations that are catching up (largely in Asia)

contain over 40 percent of the world's population. When nations are weighted by population size—as they must be if we want to use between-nation inequality to draw conclusions about global income inequality— we find that income inequality across nations peaked sometime around 1970 and has been declining since. This peaking of between-nation income inequality circa 1970 is particularly interesting in light of Manuel Castells's (1998, p. 336) well-known claim that a "new world" originated in the late 1960s to mid-1970s. Ironically, though, Castells characterizes the world born in this period as a world of sharply increasing global inequality, and many other globalization writers make the same error.

I have debunked myth number 2 first by replicating the United Nations/World Bank results and then by demonstrating how they have been misinterpreted (Firebaugh 2003). In addition to the weighting problem just mentioned, the claims of growing inequality often ignore nations in the middle of the income distribution, focusing instead on selected nations at the tails. When the entire income distribution is used, and when individuals are given equal weight, we find that—far from growing—income inequality across nations declined in the late twentieth century.

Myth 3. The Myth That Globalization Historically Has Caused Rising Inequality Across Nations.   Contrary to this myth, the trend in between-nation inequality historically has not followed changes in the trend in world economic integration. First, although it is true that between-nation income inequality increased dramatically over the nineteenth and early twentieth centuries, Peter Lindert and Jeffrey Williamson (2000) argue that the period of rising inequality across nations began *before* the period of true globalization started, so globalization apparently did not cause the upturn. Second, the sharp decline in globalization between World War I and World War II did not result in declining inequality across nations (to the contrary, between-nation income inequality shot up rapidly over the period). Finally, income inequality across nations has declined in recent decades, during a period when globalization has presumably reached new heights. (I say "presumably" because globalization is itself a contentious issue: see Guillén 2001. Nonetheless virtually all agree that the world has become more economically integrated over recent decades, even if the degree of globalization is often overstated, as Chase-Dunn, Kawano, and Brewer 2000, among others, have noted.) In short, the rise in global inequality predates the rise in globalization, global inequality has risen while globalization was declining, and currently global inequality is declining while globalization is rising. It is hard then to make the case historically that globalization is the cause of rising income inequality across nations (O'Rourke 2001).

Myth 4. The Myth of a Postindustrial World Economy. In reading the globalization literature it is easy to lose sight of the fact that, until recently, most of the world's people were engaged in agriculture. So the world's workforce is barely postagricultural, much less postindustrial. This book makes the point that the primary engine still driving the growth in world production is more manufacturing. A new information age might be on the way, but it is not here yet—at least it is not here for most of the world's people. It is important to look ahead, of course, and

it is hard to argue against the view that the world will eventually be postindustrial. The death of industrialization is nonetheless much exaggerated, as is the view that we are rapidly approaching an information-based global economy (Quah 1997). Estimates of the composition of global output, albeit rough approximations, rule out the claims of some globalization writers that we live in a new economic era quite unlike the era of the last generation. Industrialization was important in the nineteenth century, it was important in the twentieth century, and it remains important in most regions of the world in the twenty-first century. A preoccupation with postindustrialization in the face of the continuing diffusion of industrialization results in an incomplete and distorted story of global income inequality that deemphasizes the critical role of the continuing spread of industrialization to all regions of the world. Computers are important, but they are not all-important. In accounting for recent trends in global income inequality, the bigger story is industrial growth in Asia, not technological growth in the West.

Myth 5. The Myth of International Exchange as Inherently Exploitative. Globalization involves increased exchange over national boundaries. One might posit that increased exchange worsens global inequality under some historical conditions and reduces it under other conditions. Until those historical conditions are identified and understood, the effect of globalization on global income inequality at any point in time is an open question to be settled empirically.

But if international exchange is inherently exploitative, as some theories of world stratification insist, then rising exchange implies rising exploitation, and the Trade

Protest Model is true virtually by definition. The Trade Protest Model then becomes:

> Globalization $\longrightarrow$ more exploitation of poor nations by rich nations $\longrightarrow$ greater global inequality

Note that this elaboration of the Trade Protest Model reveals how high the theoretical stakes are with regard to empirical tests of the globalization $\longrightarrow$ global income inequality model, since the failure of globalization to lead to rising global income inequality would undermine exploitation theories (for example, dependency theories) as well as undermining the Trade Protest Model.

I have presented evidence that increasing international exchange over recent decades has been accompanied by declining—not rising—income inequality across nations (Firebaugh 2003). Other studies also document declining between-nation income inequality over recent decades. The decline in between-nation inequality has significant theoretical implications. The assumption of inherent exploitation favoring rich nations in international exchange is the linchpin of some theoretical schools. But if international exchange were inherently exploitative, we would not expect to observe declining inequality across nations during a period of rising international trade. Yet the assumption persists, suggesting that in some theories the notion of inherent exploitation is so essential that it enjoys creedal status as a doctrine to be believed rather than as a hypothesis to be tested.

Causes of the Reversal: An Overview

I argue that the world's spreading industrialization and growing economic integration in the late twentieth century and the early twenty-first have reversed the historical pattern of uneven economic growth favoring richer nations. The conventional view, just elaborated, is that globalization has exacerbated global income inequality. The evidence challenges that view. In reality globalization has offsetting effects—by spurring industrialization in poor nations, globalization raises inequality within many nations and compresses inequality across nations. The net effect has been a reduction in global income inequality in recent decades, since the reduction in between-nation income inequality has more than offset the growth in within-nation income inequality.

The new pattern of rising within-nation and falling between-nation income inequality has multiple causes. The most important cause is spreading industrialization—the diffusion of industrialization to the world's large poor nations. The diffusion of industrialization to poor regions compresses inequality across nations and boosts inequality within them. The effect of spreading industrialization on between-nation inequality is reinforced by the effect of the growing integration of national economies. Growing economic integration tends to dissolve institutional differences between nations. The convergence of institutional economic goals and policies compresses inequality across nations by (in some instances at least) removing impediments to growth in poor nations.

There are at least four other significant causes of the new geography of global inequality. The first is technological change that reduces the tyranny of space in general and more particularly reduces the effect of labor immobility across national boundaries. This technological change works to reduce inequality across nations. The second is a demographic windfall that has benefited some poor Asian nations in recent decades and promises to benefit other poor nations in the near future. This effect also operates to compress global income inequality, by reducing between-nation inequality. The third is the rise of the service sector, especially in richer nations. Growth in this sector has boosted income inequality within nations, and it is likely to do so in the future as well. The fourth is the collapse of communism, which also boosted within-nation inequality. This is a nonrecurring event, however, so its effect on within-nation inequality is limited to a specific point in history, the 1990s.

In short, the decline in between-nation income inequality that began in the late twentieth century was caused by deepening industrialization of poor nations, by growing economic integration that dissolves institutional differences between nations, by technological change that reduces the effects of labor immobility across national boundaries, and by a demographic windfall that has benefited some poor nations and promises to benefit others in the future. The growth in within-nation income inequality was caused by the deepening industrialization of poor nations, by the growth of the service sector, and by the collapse of communism.

The Inequality Transition

The industrialization of richer nations in the nineteenth century and first half of the twentieth caused income inequality across nations to explode. As a result, global income inequality shifted from inequality within nations to inequality across nations. Now, however, poorer nations are industrializing faster than richer ones are, and between-nation inequality is declining while within-nation inequality appears to be rising. If this turnaround continues, future historians will refer to an inequality transition that accompanied world industrialization. That transition is from within-nation inequality to between-nation inequality back to within-nation inequality, with the late twentieth century as the period when the shift back to within-nation income inequality began.

Phase 1 of the Transition: From Within- to Between-Nation Inequality

Phase 1 of the inequality transition coincides with the period of Western industrialization that began in the late eighteenth century and ended in the second half of the twentieth century. The first phase of the inequality transition was characterized by unprecedented growth in income inequality across nations. As Lant Pritchett (1996, p. 40) puts it, "the overwhelming feature of modern economic history is a massive divergence in per capita incomes between rich and poor countries." The evidence is incontrovertible. First, it is clear that current levels of between-nation income inequality would not have been possible earlier in human history. Again quoting Pritchett (1997, pp. 9–10): "If there had been no divergence, then we could extrapolate backward from present income of the poorer countries to past income assuming they grew at least as fast as the United States. However, this would imply that many poor countries must have had incomes below $100 in 1870 [in 1985 U.S. dollars]. Since this cannot be true, there must have been divergence."

Second, Pritchett's conclusion that "there must have been divergence" is supported by estimates of between-nation income inequality in the nineteenth century. Consider the recent estimates of Bourguignon and Morrisson (1999). Bourguignon and Morrisson use the Maddison (1995) data to estimate changes in the level of between-nation income inequality from 1820 to 1992. Because their objective is to estimate total world income inequality—not just between-nation income inequality—Bourguignon and Morrisson begin by disaggregating national income data into vintiles (5 percent groups, that is, twenty income groups per nation). National boundaries have changed over the past two centuries, of course, and nations have come and gone over the past two centuries. Even in nations where boundaries remained constant, we do not always have income data for the entire period. To overcome these problems, Bourguignon and Morrisson grouped the 199 nations with income data in 1992 into 33 homogeneous groups, each of which represented at least 1 percent of the world population or world GDP in 1950. The 33 groups include single nations (such as China and the United States) as well as large groups of small nations and small groups of medium-sized nations. From these 660 data points (33 nation groups x 20) it is a straightforward matter to apply the population-weighted formulas for the Theil index and the mean logarithmic deviation (MLD)—two measures of inequality—to calculate summary measures of the world's total inequality for different years. By collapsing the 199 nations into 33 groups, Bourguignon and Morrisson are able to extend their inequality series back to 1820. Note that, to the extent that their grouping strategy introduces bias, the bias is in the direction of underestimating between-nation inequality and inflating within-nation inequality, since some of the inequality within the nation groups is actually between-nation inequality. But that bias should not affect our basic conclusions about the relative growth in between-nation and within-nation income inequality over the past two centuries.

The results are striking (Figure 71.1). Two facts stand out. First, the B/W ratio— the ratio of between-nation to within-nation income inequality—is much higher now than it was in the early stages of Western industrialization. The increase in the B/W ratio reflects both a rise in between-nation income inequality and a decline in within-nation income inequality since 1820 (Table 71.1). By far the greater change is in between-nation income inequality, however. The Theil index for between-nation income inequality (actually, inequality between nation *groups*) shot up from 0.061 in 1820 to 0.513 in 1992, and the MLD shot up from 0.053 in 1820 to 0.495 in 1992. As anticipated, then, the Industrial Revolution of the past two centuries has increased income inequality across nations, but the magnitude of the increase is stunning. There has been a metamorphosis from a world where poverty was the norm in all nations to a richer world with much lower poverty rates (Bourguignon and Morrisson 1999, table 1) but also with much greater income inequality across nations. Because the steep rise in between-nation income inequality was not accompanied by an increase in inequality within nations, where you live—your nation—is much more important in determining your income in today's world than it was in the preindustrial world.

The second fact that stands out is that the growth in the B/W ratio stalled in the second half of the twentieth century. The B/W ratio stopped growing in the second half of the twentieth century because

The Reversal of Historical Inequality Trends

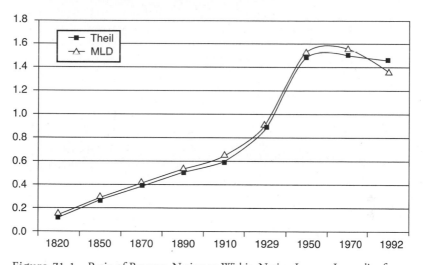

Figure 71.1   Ratio of Between-Nation to Within-Nation Income Inequality for
Thirty-three Nation Groups, 1820–1992.
Based on Table 71.1. Theil and MLD are measures of inequality

growth in inequality across the nation groups has slowed dramatically since 1950. In the four decades after 1950, income inequality across the nation groups increased by 6 percent using the Theil index and by 5 percent using the MLD. Over the four decades prior to 1950, the Theil had grown about 60 percent and the MLD had grown about 75 percent. Apparently the most dramatic effects of Western industrialization on between-nation inequality are over. After more than a century of sharp divergence in national incomes, the trend has been much more stable in recent years. This finding is in line with the findings of others (for example, Schultz 1998; Firebaugh 1999; Melchior, Telle, and Wiig 2000; Goesling 2001) who, drawing on data for individual nations instead of nation groups, find that between-nation income inequality is no longer rising. As we shall see later, between-nation income inequality declined

in the late twentieth century when income data for the 1990s are added to data for the 1970s and 1980s.

Finally, it should be emphasized that the results here are so strong that the historical story they tell of increasing inequality across nations and of a rising *B/W* ratio cannot be dismissed as due to error in the data. To be sure, income estimates for the nineteenth century are gross approximations for many nations. But even if we make the extreme assumption that incomes are so drastically overstated for poorer nations in 1820 (or so drastically understated for richer nations in 1820) that the Theil and the MLD estimates understate between-nation income inequality in 1820 by a factor of three, that would still mean that between-nation income inequality tripled from 1820 to 1992 (from 0.18 to 0.51 based on the Theil index and from 0.16 to 0.50 for the MLD), and the *B/W* ratio still

Table 71.1   Trends in Income Inequality Between and Within Thirty-three Homogeneous Nation Groups, 1920–1992

Year	Between nation groups		Within nation groups	
	Theil	MLD	Theil	MLD
1820	.061	.053	.472	.388
1850	.128	.111	.477	.393
1870	.188	.162	.485	.399
1890	.251	.217	.498	.408
1910	.299	.269	.500	.413
1929	.365	.335	.413	.372
1950	.482	.472	.323	.309
1970	.490	.515	.324	.330
1992	.513	.495	.351	.362

Source: Bourguignon and Morrison (1999), table 3.

Estimates: Between nation groups: From Bourguignon and Morrison (1999), based on Maddison (1995) data set. *Within nation groups:* From Bourguignon and Morrison (1999), based on updating of Berry, Bourguignon, and Morrison (1983a,b) for the post–World War II period and on various sources (for example, Lindert 1999; Morrison 1999) for the pre–World War II period. Bourguignon and Morrison (2002) published modestly revised estimates for inequality. By collapsing vintiles to deciles, they report slightly lower estimates of inequality within the nation groups, but the fundamental conclusions are the same.

Note: Income measures are adjusted for purchasing power parity, and inequality measures are based on income vintiles (see Bourguignon and Morrison 1999 for elaboration).

would have more than tripled for both inequality measures.

Phase 2 of the Transition: From Between-Nation Back to Within-Nation Inequality

The second phase of the inequality transition began in the second half of the twentieth century, with the stabilization of between-nation income inequality in the 1960–1990 period and the decline in between-nation inequality beginning in earnest in the 1990s. Social scientists hardly have a stellar track record for predictions, especially with regard to sweeping predictions such as the one made here. Nonetheless there is sufficient theory and evidence that we can plausibly forecast that the *B/W* ratio will continue to decline in the twenty-first century.

The prediction of a declining *B/W* ratio is based on two separate conjectures. The first conjecture is that between-nation income inequality will decline, and the second conjecture is that within-nation income inequality will rise, or at least will not decline. These conjectures are based on the causes of the current trends, which I expect to continue and in some cases to intensify. (I am assuming that there will be no cataclysmic upheaval in the twenty-first century, such as a global war or a worldwide plague.) Recall the causes listed earlier for the inequality turnaround in the late twentieth century. I expect the major causes to continue, so between-nation income inequality will decline because of the continued industrialization of poor nations, because of the continued convergence of national economic policies and institutions arising from growing economic integration of national economies, because of the declining significance of labor immobility across national borders, and because of a demographic windfall for many poor nations. Within-nation income inequality will rise—or at least not decline—because of the continued industrialization of poor nations and because of continued growth in the service sector. Because between-nation inequality is the larger component, global income inequality will decline.

The conjecture of declining global income inequality is out of step with much of the globalization literature. A recurring theme in that literature is that we have entered a new information-based economic era where productive activity is becoming less dependent on physical space, as a rising share of the world's economic output is produced in electronic space that knows no national borders (Sassen 2000). This phenomenon is possible because of the emergence of a global economy where income—and hence income inequality—is becoming increasingly rooted in knowledge rather than in capital goods (Reich 1991). What do these developments imply for global income inequality? For many globalization writers, the answer is clear: global inequality is bound to worsen because of the growing "global digital divide" that enlarges the gap between the "haves" and the "have-nots" (Campbell 2001; Ishaq 2001; Norris 2001).

The theoretical argument that a shift to a knowledge-based global economy would worsen global income inequality is shaky. It is not hard to think of reasons why the shift from an industrial-based to a knowledge-based global economy would reduce, not increase, inequality across nations. Knowledge is mobile, especially with today's telecommunication technologies that permit virtually instant worldwide codification and distribution of knowledge. In addition, because knowledge can be given away without

being lost, the notion of property rights is more problematic in the case of knowledge, so it is harder to concentrate and monopolize knowledge across nations than it is to concentrate and monopolize capital goods across nations. Hence the switch to a knowledge-based global economy should mean that one's income is increasingly determined by how much knowledge one obtains and uses as opposed to where one lives. The tighter link between knowledge and income in turn implies declining income inequality across nations and rising inequality within nations since—absent institutional barriers—the variance in individuals' ability to obtain and benefit from knowledge is greater within nations than between them.

The issue of how the new information age will affect global inequality in the near term is not as decisive as often imagined, since as already noted, the coming of the information age is often much exaggerated. What is still most important in today's world is industrialization for the many, not digitization for the few. Historically the spread of industrialization has been the primary force driving the growth in between-nation income inequality. The initially richer nations of the West were the first to industrialize, and the poorer nations of Asia and Africa lagged behind. The new geography of inequality is also driven by the spread of industrialization, but the effects are different today: now the spread of industrialization means the diffusion of manufacturing technology to the world's largest poor regions. In recent decades inequality has declined across nations as industrialization has been an engine of growth in the most populous poor regions of the world, especially East Asia. That growth has worked both to compress inequality across

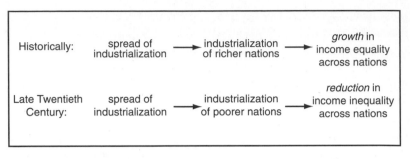

Figure 71.2   Industrialization and Between-Nation Income Inequality:
Historically and in the Late Twentieth Century

nations (Figure 71.2) and to boost inequality within the industrializing nations.

The significance of this continuation of world industrialization has been lost in much of the literature on globalization, because of preoccupation with the idea that we are witnessing the emergence of a new knowledge-based technology regime. To be sure, in the categories used to classify world production, the output of the so-called service sector is estimated to exceed the output of the industrial sector for the world as a whole (World Bank 1997, table 12). Yet much of the service sector—an amorphous sector that includes wholesale and retail trade, the banking industry, government, the transportation industry, the commercial real estate industry, and personal services (including health care and education)—has arisen to grease the wheels of industry. Aside from the growth in personal services and government, much of the growth in the service sector has been for services for producers, not consumers—for example, the rise of an engineering industry to design better machines, and the growth of a banking industry and a commercial real estate industry for commercial transactions. In addition, many of the other so-called service industries—the transportation industry that distributes manufactured goods, for example,

and the specialized retailing industry that sells the goods—benefit producers as well as consumers. In short, a significant portion of the growth in service industries over the past century can be seen as ancillary to the industrialization process.

With regard to income inequality within nations, we expect the continuing spread of world industrialization to boost inequality along the lines of the classic argument, from Simon Kuznets (1955), that industrialization boosts inequality (at least initially) as workers move from the lower-wage but larger agricultural sector to the higher-wage industrial sector. Importantly, this argument suggests that income inequality increases in poor nations as they industrialize because of income gains, not income losses. In other words, inequality grows not because some people are becoming poorer but because some people are becoming richer, so the growth in income inequality in poor nations as they industrialize reflects rising rather than declining fortunes. If the industrialization of large poor nations does boost income inequality in those nations, at this juncture in history the continued spread of industrialization implies growth in income inequality in the average nation, because those nations are home to such a large fraction of the world's population. And there are no obvious counterforces on the horizon. Although the jump in income inequality following the collapse of communism in Eastern Europe and the former USSR is not likely to be repeated, there is no good reason to expect income inequality in those nations to fall in the near future. Nor is there any good reason to expect income inequality to decline notably in the West in the near future, either. We lack reliable inequality data for many African nations, but even if inequality were falling rapidly (which is unlikely), the effect of falling within-nation inequality in Africa would not offset the effect of rising within-nation inequality in Asia, given the relative sizes of the two regions. Few expect within-nation income inequality to decline sharply in Latin America in the near future, even though Latin America currently exhibits the highest level of within-nation income inequality of the world's major regions. Indeed, because of the advantage enjoyed by North American farmers with respect to some types of produce, economic integration in the Americas could exacerbate inequality by removing protections for farmers in Latin America. If that reasoning is correct, there is merit in the concern of WTO protesters that globalization may exacerbate income inequality within some poor nations by driving down incomes in the lower-income agricultural sector. But the bigger story is that industrialization (not the collapse of farm prices) will tend to drive up inequality within nations, at least initially. Because many nations are still on the part of the Kuznets (1955) curve where migration from farm to factory boosts inequality, we can anticipate further growth in within-nation income inequality in the early decades of the twenty-first century.

REFERENCES

Ben-David, Dan, Håkan Nordström, and L. Alan Winters. 1999. *Trade, Income Inequality, and Poverty.* WTO Special Study no. 5. Geneva: World Trade Organization.

Berry, Albert, François Bourguignon, and Christian Morrisson. 1983a. "Changes in the world distribution of income between 1950 and 1977." *Economic Journal* 93:331–350.

———. 1983b. "The level of world inequality: How much can one say?" *Review of Income and Wealth* 29:217–241.

Bourguignon, François, and Christian Morrisson. 1998. "Inequality and development: The role of dualism." *Journal of Development Economics* 57:233–257.

———. 1999. "The size distribution of income among world citizens: 1820–1990." Draft. June.

———. 2002. "Inequality among world citizens: 1820–1992." *American Economic Review* 92:727–744.

Campbell, Duncan. 2001. "Can the digital divide be contained?" *International Labour Review* 140:119–141.

Castells, Manuel. 1998. *End of Millennium.* Malden, Mass.: Blackwell.

Chase-Dunn, Christopher, Yukio Kawano, and Benjamin D. Brewer. 2000. "Trade globalization since 1795: Waves of integration in the world-system." Special millennium issue, edited by Glenn Firebaugh, of the *American Sociological Review* 65:77–95.

Doyle, Arthur Conan. 1955. *A Treasury of Sherlock Holmes.* Selected and with an introduction by Adrian Conan Doyle. Garden City, N.Y.: Hanover House.

The Economist. 1999. "The battle in Seattle." U.S. edition. November 27.

Eggertson, Laura. 1998. "Rich-poor gap next issue for Martin." *Toronto Star.* June 3, p. A6.

Firebaugh, Glenn. 1999. "Empirics of world income inequality." *American Journal of Sociology* 104:1597–1630.

———. 2003. *The New Geography of Global Income Inequality.* Cambridge: Harvard University Press.

Fujita, Masahisa, Paul Krugman, and Anthony J. Venables. 1999. *The Spatial Economy: Cities, Regions, and International Trade.* Cambridge: MIT Press.

Giddens, Anthony. 1999. "Globalization: An irresistible force." *The Daily Yomiuri,* June 7, p. 8.

Goesling, Brian. 2001. "Changing income inequalities within and between nations: New evidence." *American Sociological Review* 66:745–761.

Guillén, Mauro F. 2001. "Is globalization civilizing, destructive, or feeble? A critique of five key debates in the social science literature." *Annual Review of Sociology* 27:235–260.

International Monetary Fund (IMF). 2000. "How we can help the poor." *Finance and Development* (December). (http://www.imf.org/external/pubs.)

Ishaq, Ashfaq. 2001. "On the global digital divide." *Finance and Development* 38:44–47.

Kuznets, Simon. 1955. "Economic growth and income inequality." *American Economic Review* 45:1–28.

Lindert, Peter, and Jeffrey G. Williamson. 2000. "Does globalization make the world more unequal?" Paper presented at the "Globalization in Historical Perspective" preconference, National Bureau of Economic Research, Cambridge, Mass. November.

Maddison, Angus. 1995. *Monitoring the World Economy, 1820–1992.* Paris: OECD.

Mazur, Jay. 2000. "Labor's new internationalism." *Foreign Affairs* 79:79–93.

Melchior, Arne, Kjetil Telle, and Henrik Wiig. 2000. *Globalization and Inequality: World Income Distribution and Living Standards, 1960–1998.* Studies on Foreign Policy Issues. Oslo: Royal Norwegian Ministry of Foreign Affairs.

Milanovic, Branko. 2002. "True world income distribution, 1988 and 1993: First calculation based on household surveys alone." *Economic Journal* 112:51–92.

Morrisson, Christian. 1999. "Historical perspectives on income distribution: The case of Europe." In *Handbook of Income Distribution,* ed. A. B. Atkinson and F. Bourguignon. Amsterdam: Elsevier.

New Scientist. 1999. Editorial. December 4.

New York Times. 1999. "National guard is called to quell trade talk protests." December 1.

Norris, Pippa. 2001. *Digital Divide: Civic Engagement, Information Poverty, and the Internet Worldwide.* Cambridge and New York: Cambridge University Press.

O'Rourke, Kevin H. 2001. "Globalization and inequality: Historical trends." National Bureau of Economic Research. Draft. April.

Pritchett, Lant. 1996. "Forget convergence: Divergence past, present, and future." *Finance and Development* (June):40–43.

———. 1997. "Divergence, big time." *Journal of Economic Perspectives* 11:3–17.

Quah, Danny T. 1997. "Increasingly weightless economies." *Bank of England Quarterly Bulletin* (February):49–55.

Reich, Robert B. 1991. *The Work of Nations: Preparing Ourselves for Twenty-first-Century Capitalism.* New York: Knopf.

Sachs, Wolfgang, ed. 1992. *The Development Dictionary: A Guide to Knowledge as Power.* London: Zed Books.

Sassen, Saskia. 2000. "Territory and territoriality in the global economy." *International Sociology* 15:372–393.

Schultz, T. Paul. 1998. "Inequality in the distribution of personal income in the world: How it is changing and why." *Journal of Population Economics* 11:307–344.

United Nations Development Program. 1999. *Human Development Report 1999.* New York: Oxford University Press.

PART X

What Is To Be Done?

72

Little Labor

How Union Decline Is Changing the American Landscape

JAKE ROSENFELD

A recent *Wall Street Journal* editorial decrying the role of Big Labor in shaping the Obama administration's domestic policy expressed worry that unions' outsize clout would force higher taxes on investment income. Such articles are typical fare for a newspaper long critical of the labor movement's role in American life. But what's strange is the continued use of "Big Labor" as a shorthand moniker for trade unions in the contemporary United States. If organized labor remains big today, then back in its post–World War II peak, it was positively enormous. Fully one-third of the private sector workforce belonged to a labor union during the 1950s, and millions more resided in households reliant on a union wage. During the heyday of collective bargaining in this country, unions helped pattern pay and benefit packages among nonunion workers, as employers matched union contracts to forestall organizing drives and maintain a competitive workforce. Politicians, Democrats especially, depended on organized labor's support during elections and consulted closely with labor leaders when devising policy in office. Big Labor, then, was once quite big indeed.

The only thing that remains big about labor unions today is their problems. Figure 72.1 tracks unionization rates for private and public sector workers between 1973 and 2009. By the early 1970s, organized labor had already begun its decades-long decline, but still nearly a quarter of all private-sector employees belonged to a labor union at this time. The late 1970s and 1980s proved especially brutal for organized labor, with unionization rates halving during the period. The nation's intellectuals and journalists covered this phenomenon extensively, linking union decline to a new post-industrial economy increasingly open to global trade. Recent trends have garnered less attention, yet private-sector unionization rates *nearly halved again* between 1990 and 2009. The story for public sector unions has been a bit brighter. Rates of organization among government workers increased steadily during the 1970s, settling

Jake Rosenfeld, "Little Labor: How Union Decline is Changing the American Landscape," *Pathways* (Summer 2010), pp. 3–6.

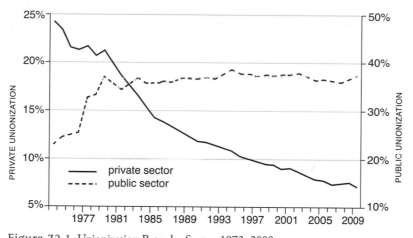

Figure 72.1 Unionization Rates by Sector, 1973–2009

Data are provided by Barry T. Hirsch and David A. McPherson's www.unionstats.com database (2010), and are based on Current Population Survey (CPS) data. Unionization data for 1982 are unavailable; I generate 1982 estimates by averaging 1981 and 1983 rates.

at slightly over one-third of all public sector workers, where they have remained relatively consistently up to the present. Three decades of stasis in public-sector organization rates suggests that the earlier expansion may have reached its limit. And over four-fifths of the U.S. workforce is employed in the private sector. Moreover, recent research has demonstrated that the benefits of union membership are much smaller in the public sector, due to the relative transparency and standardization that govern many public-sector contracts. Organized labor, then, is disappearing in the sector where historically it has had the greatest impact on people's livelihoods.

But even less understood than the overall decline in unions' *prevalence* is the concomitant decline in unions' *activity*. Academics have long debated whether high levels of unionization are a net good when it comes to global competitiveness or overall economic performance. But fewer dispute

that unions have been a historically positive force in bolstering the economic prospects of union members themselves. Unions bolster workers' clout in confrontations with employers, historically winning them higher wages, better benefits, and greater workplace protections than might be offered otherwise. Strikes represent unions' most potent weapon in confrontations with employers, and this weapon used to be a regular feature of America's industrial landscape, affecting millions of workers each year. But this has changed. Figure 72.2 below presents two series: the first shows the number of large strikes (involving 1,000 or more workers) over the last 45 years. The number of strikes involving 1,000 or more workers peaked at over 400 in 1974. In 2009, there were five. While the sheer precipitousness of this decline is staggering, we know that strikes of such magnitude are often unrepresentative of more typical work stoppages. But to date,

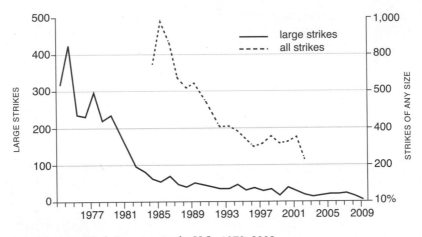

Figure 72.2 Work Stoppages in the U.S., 1973–2009

Data for large strikes provided by the Bureau of Labor Statistics (BLS) Historical Work
Stoppage Database (http://www.bls.gov/wsp/data.htm). The BLS defines large strikes as those
including 1,000 or more workers. Data for strikes of any size provided to the author by the
Federal Mediation and Conciliation Service (FMCS).

no public data has been available to document strikes of all sizes in recent decades.
Because of this, I filed a Freedom of Information Act (FOIA) request to obtain information on all strikes for the years in which
data were collected. Figure 72.2 presents
this data, and the trend mirrors what's been
happening with large strikes. As late as the
mid-1980s, nearly 1,000 walkouts occurred
in a single year. By the dawn of the 21st
century, that number had fallen to just over
200, a decline of nearly 80 percent in less
than 20 years. What we've seen, then, is a rise
in what might be called "union dormancy,"
whereby unions are no longer routinely
agitating on behalf of their membership,
at least not in the traditional form of the
labor strike.

So what happened to Big Labor? Organized labor's penetration was especially
deep in core manufacturing industries. The
transformation to a post-industrial economy hit union workers in these industries
hard, as jobs become increasingly vulnera-

ble to outsourcing, deskilling, and technological innovations rendering many positions redundant. The process accelerated
throughout the 1970s and 1980s, as traditionally protected industries like auto manufacturing opened up to competition from
abroad, pushing domestic manufacturers to
search for less labor-friendly jurisdictions.
Yet private sector deunionization was not
limited to the manufacturing sector; across
all major industries with some union presence, membership rates remain lower today
than in the past. This is true even in those
industries not threatened by cheaper labor
overseas, such as transportation and retail.
The wave of deregulation that began in the
Carter administration opened up some of
these sectors to cutthroat competition,
pressuring employers to shed expensive
contracts and the unions that bargained for
them. Partly as a response to deindustrialization and deregulation, there arose a concerted, broad-based effort by employers to
shift bargaining power away from labor

unions. By the early 1980s, innovative tactics adopted by management and used against organizing drives and existing unions shattered the relative détente between business and labor that had predominated for decades. These sophisticated strategies took full advantage of existing policies governing labor-management relations and proved incredibly effective at pushing back at what employers felt was overreach by unions.

A New Landscape

While the causes of organized labor's decades-long decline in the private sector are well known, the broad consequences are not. Existing research tends to focus on deunionization's consequences for the earnings of male, blue-collar workers. But the removal of organized labor from much of the private sector also affects the economic assimilation of recent immigrants and their offspring, widens black-white wage inequality among female workers, redistributes political power, and redefines the nature of strikes in modern America. I touch on each of these consequences below.

The Disappearing Economic Ladder for Hispanic Immigrants

Unionization has always been unevenly spread across demographic groups. The labor movement's great upsurge between the Great Depression and World War II relied heavily on European immigrants and their children, with many arrivals assuming top leadership posts in the nation's fastest growing unions. During the labor movement's peak, unions helped provide a firm economic foundation for these otherwise disadvantaged populations, propelling millions into the middle class. Some have argued that labor's future is brightening once again, given the influx of Hispanic immigration since the 1960s. That is, if labor can organize recent immigrants, unions might once again reclaim a powerful position in the economic landscape. This optimism is driven by events like the labor movement's success in organizing largely Hispanic janitors in Southern California, many of them recent immigrants.

But how is organized labor actually interacting with this new wave of immigration? Despite the historical role immigrants played in building the U.S. labor movement, in more recent decades top unions have eyed immigrant workers warily. Many assumed immigrants were largely unorganizable, due to the precarious legal status of some recent arrivals, the lower labor standards immigrants were accustomed to in their home countries, and the resulting worry that employers would use immigrant labor to undercut existing wages and benefits of native-born workers. The "Justice for Janitors" campaign in Southern California helped counter such claims and helped galvanize organizers across the nation, who sought to capitalize on the class-based solidarity exhibited by many Hispanic immigrants. And indeed, certain Hispanic subgroups, including immigrants who have lived in the United States for a number of years and immigrants who are citizens, are joining unions at higher rates than native-born Whites. Figure 72.3 displays the odds of joining a union over a one-year period for various Hispanic subgroups compared to U.S.-born Whites. Odds ratios above one indicate that the Hispanic subgroup is more likely to join a union than a White nonimmigrant. U.S.-born Hispanics have over 40 percent higher odds of joining a

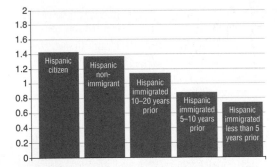

Figure 72.3 Odds of Joining a Union, 1973–2009
Odds ratios refer to the relative odds of joining a union over a one-year period where the reference category is non-immigrant whites. Data come from matched files of the Current Population Survey (CPS), and estimates adjust for a range of factors influencing unionization. For more on the estimation procedure, see Rosenfeld, Jake, and Meredith Kleykamp. 2009. "Hispanics and Organized Labor in the United States, 1973 to 2007." *American Sociological Review* 74:916–37.

union compared to U.S.-born whites, echoing the historical pattern of immigrant groups and their children seeking unionized employment to assimilate upward into the middle class. Hispanic immigrant citizens and Hispanic immigrants who have lived in the United States for many years are also joining unions at higher rates than native-born Whites.

But there are limits to such trends. Despite the highly publicized organizing drives of the "Justice for Janitors" campaign, the percentage of Hispanic janitors in labor unions has actually declined since 1990, as has the fraction of all janitors who claim union membership. Unlike the Southern and Eastern European migrants who once swelled the ranks of the union workforce, recent arrivals face an economic context largely hostile to trade unions. In those remaining parts of the private sector where unions remain active, Hispanics' and Hispanic subgroups' *relative* unionization rates are high, but their *overall* unionization rates

are low—along with nearly everyone else's. Thus, contemporary immigrants and their offspring enter labor markets that increasingly lack an established unionized pathway to the middle class, a pathway that past immigrant populations relied upon extensively.

The Declining Significance of Unions for Black Females

Aside from limiting mobility for low-skilled immigrant populations, the decline of organized labor exacerbates economic inequality between African Americans and Whites. Unionization rates for African Americans have exceeded those of Hispanics and Whites for decades now. As the labor movement began integrating its ranks, African-American workers, eager to escape discriminatory treatment institutionalized in U.S. labor markets, sought out organized labor as a partial refuge against economic inequity. This is especially true for females. Despite the stereotypical image of the blue-collar male union worker, unionization rates for African-American females rose drastically during the 1960s and 1970s, with nearly one in four Black women in the private sector belonging to a union by the end of the 1970s. In the heavily industrialized Midwest, rates of unionization for African-American females working in the private sector peaked at 40 percent. Past work by economists John Bound and Richard Freeman has found that union decline widened wage gaps between young Black and White males, especially in the Midwest. But the ramifications of deunionization for racial wage inequality are actually larger for *females*, given that differences in private sector unionization rates between Black and White females far exceed differences between Black and White males. Indeed, had unionization rates remained at their peak levels, Black–White wage differences among private sector females would be nearly 30 percent smaller than where they stand today.

A Political Force Diminished

As unions vanish from the economic landscape, their presence in the political realm is reduced as well. Historically, the labor movement has channeled and organized the political energies of the working class, helping to counter the robust, positive connection between civic participation and socioeconomic status. Indeed, trade unions have historically stood as one of the few institutions equalizing political participation across income and educational divides. Nowhere was this role more pronounced than in the private sector, where voting rates run comparatively low, especially among those lacking a college education. This is not true in the public sector. The combined effects of unionization and public-sector employment are not simply additive; public-sector employment bolsters political participation, but being in a public-sector union results in only a slight increase in the propensity to vote. Figure 72.4 presents predicted probabilities of voting for public- and private-sector union members and nonmembers. The difference in voting turnout among public sector members and nonmembers is only 2.5 percentage points. The effect of union membership on voting in the private sector is nearly three times as large.

Today, the number of public sector union members equals the number of private sector union members, marking a dramatic break from when private sector union rolls dwarfed those of government employees. This shift has important politi

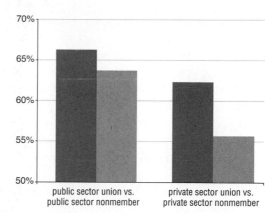

Figure 72.4 Predicted Probabilities of Voting for Union Members and Nonmembers, 1984–2006
Probabilities generated from voter turnout models that adjust for a range of demographic, economic, and geographic factors found to influence voting. Sample is restricted to employed citizens only, age 18 and over. Data come from the November series of the Current Population Survey (CPS). For more on the estimation procedure, see Rosenfeld, Jake, 2010. "Economic Determinants of Voting in an Era of Union Decline." *Social Science Quarterly* 91:379–96.

cal consequences. The already high voter turnout rates—and educational levels—among government workers, union and nonunion alike, leave little room for unions to raise turnout in the public sector. Meanwhile, in the private sector, union status remains a significant indicator of whether an *individual* will vote or not. However, given the reduced fraction of private-sector workers in labor unions, the *aggregate* effect of unionization on voting turnout is now quite small, and shrinking union rolls reduce the ability of unions to drive up turnout among nonunion citizens.

The consequences of union decline described above largely focus on nonunion workers—those who in the past would have benefited from union membership but who no longer will, whether they be an immigrant employee who once would have been organized, a female African-American worker no longer able to rely on a union wage to reduce pay gaps with her white counterpart, or a less-educated worker lacking the training, resources, and knowledge to participate in politics. But union decline affects remaining union workers as well. Research by economists John DiNardo and David S. Lee suggests that the union wage benefits for newly organized manufacturing firms are negligible. This may be due, in part, to the dramatic decline in strikes described earlier. In decades past, unions often authorized a walkout during contract negotiations, pressuring employers to raise wages and benefits. These pressure tactics worked; union members who had participated in a strike had higher wages, on average, than non-striking members. This no longer seems true today. While we lack direct measures of strikes' impacts on an individual striker's pay, the Federal Mediation and Conciliation Service data presented in Figure 72.2 allow for comparisons between pay scales in industries and regions in which strike activity remains relatively high and those in which strikes have disappeared. I find that the positive wage–strike relationship has been severed; workers in high-strike locales see no wage gains compared to workers in relatively quiescent sectors. Strikes now are often last-ditch attempts to hold the line on wages and benefits, as union leaders simply refrain from striking except in the most desperate situations. Thus, unions are not only failing to bolster the fortunes of those who once would have been organized, they are also struggling to protect the fortunes of those still in their ranks.

Where from Here?

It is difficult indeed to counter the self-perpetuating dynamic behind the foregoing trends. As union ranks shrink, so too does the constituency directly mobilized to press for change, and with it, labor's leverage in convincing lawmakers to risk the political consequences of business opposition. The present economic climate further dampens enthusiasm for worker activism, as employees cling to their positions, while millions of others less fortunate scramble to find work.

Organized labor's signature legislative effort is the Employee Free Choice Act (EFCA). In its most robust form, the proposed legislation would radically recast how union elections are held in the United States, bypassing the traditional election campaign in favor of a "card check" policy whereby a union is recognized after over half of workers sign up in support of collective bargaining. A compromise version of the bill would retain the "secret ballot" election procedure but would reduce election times, grant organizers greater access to employees on the worksite, and institute binding arbitration if a contract has not been agreed upon after a specified period of time. Passage of either version would shift some of the power in organizing drives to labor, although it would not address the broader economic challenges labor faces, such as the continuing decline of manufacturing employment, the pressures of international competition among remaining manufacturing firms, and aggressive competition in many deregulated domestic industries.

There are other institutional changes that, if implemented, might alter the balance of power somewhat. The Obama administration has, for example, floated a proposal to revamp the way the government allocates federal contracts to companies. The proposal would prioritize firms that offer high wages while penalizing those that had committed labor violations, thereby giving an edge to unionized companies and benefiting millions of non-union workers by providing an incentive to nonunion firms to raise wages and improve treatment of workers. An estimated one in four workers is employed by a company that contracts with the government, so the scale of the regulatory change could be enormous. Importantly, the administration is exploring ways to change regulations through executive order, thus avoiding difficulties in generating a filibuster-proof majority in the Senate.

Any policy effort to help organized labor faces formidable political opposition, although we can't rule out the possibility that the administration will creatively short-circuit the full legislative process. For many employers, the costs of unionization are substantial, and thus the benefits of continuing inaction are clear. Unions often reduce flexibility in hiring and firing decisions, may slow managers' abilities to shift resources and capital as soon as opportunities arise, and substantially reduce managerial discretion in setting pay, all the while increasing wage and benefit bills. Strong employer opposition has helped push unionization down to levels unseen since before the Great Depression. Because such declines are self-perpetuating, at this point, it will take decisive legal and institutional action to reverse or even halt the trend—action that, if not taken soon, won't have much of a constituency behind it any longer. The simple fact: Big Labor cannot get much smaller.

73

Crisis No More

The Success of Obama's Stimulus Program

GARY BURTLESS

The recession that began in December 2007 ranks as the worst since World War II. It carved a huge slice out of Americans' financial wealth and caused the biggest percentage decline in employment of the post-war era. Even though the stock market rebounded in 2009 and U.S. output began to grow in the second half of that year, the recession continues to take a terrible toll on the incomes and psychological health of many families.

No one should confuse the recent recession with the Great Depression, however. Two key features of that depression made it "Great"—its severity and its duration. Between 1929 and 1933, real GDP in the United States fell almost 27 percent. U.S. GDP did not return to its 1929 level until 1936. Real personal consumption declined more than 18 percent. In 1933, about one out of every four Americans in the labor force was jobless. The National Bureau of Economic Research (NBER), which is in the business of dating recessions, estimates that after reaching a cyclical peak in August 1929, the U.S. economy shrank for the next 43 months, by far the longest period of uninterrupted economic decline in the twentieth century. In the 10 downturns since World War II, excluding the most recent one, the average recession lasted just 10 months. Even the longest post-war recessions, in 1973–1975 and 1981–1982, lasted only 16 months.

As of this writing, NBER has dated the onset of the recession (December 2007) but has not yet determined its end date. The recession will not last 43 months, however. The economy began to grow again in the summer of 2009, and the unemployment rate started to decline late in the same year, less than 24 months after the recession began. Real GDP probably fell less than 5 percent from its previous peak. The number of private payroll jobs began to increase in the first quarter of 2010. The peak unemployment rate will almost certainly be less than 10.5 percent, far below the peak unemployment rate attained in the 1930s and somewhat below the peak unemployment rate hit during the 1981–1982 recession.

Gary Burtless, "Crisis No More: The Success of Obama's Stimulus Program," *Pathways* (Summer 2010), pp. 24–28.

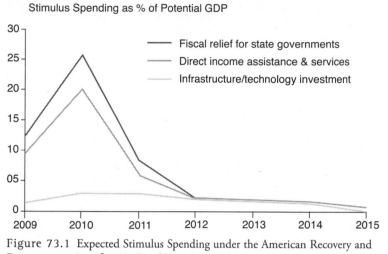

Figure 73.1 Expected Stimulus Spending under the American Recovery and Reinvestment Act of 2009, Fiscal Years 2009–2015

Source: Congressional Budget Office and Joint Committee on Taxation

The Scope of the Response

In fiscal year 2009, the federal government pumped stimulus amounting to about 1.25 percent of national income into the economy. In 2010, the stimulus package will inject about twice that amount (see Figure 73.1). The stimulus dollars are targeted toward four main objectives: (1) protecting the incomes and health insurance of newly laid-off workers and other economically vulnerable populations; (2) providing immediate stimulus to consumer spending by raising after-tax household income through temporary tax reductions and increases in some transfers; (3) offering temporary fiscal relief to state and local governments in order to reduce their need to boost taxes or reduce spending in the recession; and (4) providing direct federal support for infrastructure investments and research and development projects in health, science, and efficient energy production. Figure 73.1 combines spending on the first two items into a single category, direct income assistance and services. In the first two years of the stimulus program, spending on this category represents by far the largest component of the federal response. Understanding the composition of the response is key to understanding how the stimulus succeeded in pushing the economy toward recovery. As I argue below, the stimulus packages enacted in 2008 and 2009 contained both standard and nonstandard responses as compared to prior recessions. Understanding the scope and mix of the packages points us to a broader understanding of how and why the government response was crucial for heading off a much deeper crisis.

Standard Responses

It is not unusual for the government to accelerate spending on public infrastructure projects during a recession. Congress also often provides temporary tax cuts to stimulate consumption and business investment when the economy is weak. It did so again in this recession. In fact, the tax cuts in the American Recovery and Reinvestment Act (ARRA), mostly for households, account for about 45 percent of total stimulus spending in 2009 and 2010. In addition, Congress nearly always offers extensions of unemployment benefits when joblessness is high. It did so in this recession too.

The most important protection American workers receive when they are laid off is unemployment insurance (UI). Newly laid-off workers are typically eligible for up to six months of UI benefits after they lose their jobs. By the standards of other industrial countries, the six-month limit on benefits is rather short. Of the 21 richest industrial countries, 15 provide jobless benefits that last a year or more. Unemployed workers in these countries receive much better social protection if their unemployment lasts a long time. Unemployment protection lasts longer in the United States when the jobless rate soars. When a state's unemployment rate rises above a certain threshold, workers in that state are supposed to receive additional weeks of benefits, with the number of extra weeks linked to the increase in the state's unemployment rate.

In every recession since the late 1950s, Congress has enacted a federally funded extension of UI benefits. The extension in 1975–1977 was particularly generous, providing the unemployed with benefits that could last up to 65 weeks. Congress provided somewhat less generous special benefit extensions in more recent recessions. The benefit extension provided in the 2009 ARRA was far more generous than that offered in any previous U.S. recession. By the fall of 2009, laid-off workers in high-unemployment states were eligible for federally funded benefit extensions that could last up to 73 weeks, providing them with a total of up to 99 weeks of benefits after a layoff. In 2009, Congress also funded an increase in unemployment benefits equal to $25 per week, or about 8 percent of the previous average benefit amount. In sum, the 2008 and 2009 stimulus packages greatly expanded the income protection available to the unemployed, both in comparison to the protection ordinarily available in a recession and in relation to the protection offered in other industrial countries. The generosity of U.S. benefits is still far less than it is in some other rich countries, but at least in this recession we are closer to the Organisation for Economic Co-operation and Development's (OECD) average.

Nonstandard Responses

In addition to these traditional actions, the Obama administration and Congress also took a number of more unusual steps to lessen the adverse effects of the recession. One of the most surprising was the provision of generous federal subsidies to help unemployed workers pay for health insurance. This subsidy, which was originally limited to nine months per worker, covers 65 percent of the cost to laid-off workers of continuing their coverage under their former employer's health insurance plan.

Most working Americans who are not poor receive health insurance through an employer or the employer of another wage earner in the family. Employers typically pay for most of the premium cost of the insurance. When workers are laid off they ordinarily lose the employer subsidy. The total, unsubsidized cost of health insurance is notoriously high, around $5,000 a year for single workers and $13,000 for workers with a spouse and one or more child dependents. These premiums are 10 percent and 32 percent, respectively, of the average year-round wage of American workers. Not surprisingly, comparatively few workers can afford to pay the full cost of these premiums after they are laid off. The result is that many laid-off workers lose their health insurance when they lose their jobs. In no previous recession were laid-off workers offered a generous public subsidy to pay for an extension of their private health coverage.

Two other aspects of the 2009 stimulus package were exceptional. First the ARRA provided unusually generous fiscal relief to state governments. Second, it offered large, though temporary, incentives for states and young adults to invest in education and training.

By my estimate a little more than one-fifth of the 2009 stimulus package, or a total of $175 billion, will be devoted to providing fiscal relief to state governments. This relief is provided in a variety of forms. Some federal grants were authorized to help pay for local law enforcement, for example. Nearly $30 billion was authorized to fund aid for particular aspects of state and local education. Most of this was targeted at education for the economically disadvantaged and for children who have learning or other disabilities. Since state educational spending is fungible, however, it is likely that the extra federal funds earmarked for one educational purpose can be reallocated to other educational functions at the discretion of state and local policymakers.

Congress created two temporary programs to provide general fiscal relief to the states. One gives almost $50 billion to be divided among the states "in order to minimize and avoid reductions in education and other essential services." In exchange for the grants, state governments must show they are making unspecified progress in a number of broad areas. All 50 states have submitted applications for these funds, and the applications will receive nearly automatic approval from federal officials.

A second form of fiscal relief was provided through a temporary change in the funding formula for Medicaid, the federal–state public health insurance program for low-income Americans. Medicaid is administered by state governments, but most of its costs are financed with large federal grants. The fraction of costs paid by the federal government is determined by a formula that links a state's federal reimbursement rate to the state's per capita income. States with high average incomes ordinarily get 50 percent of their Medicaid program costs reimbursed, while states with low average incomes receive a higher federal subsidy rate. Medicaid is one of the most costly government programs. In 2007, benefit payments under the program represented 2.8 percent of GDP. This means the federal government's Medicaid grants to state governments are a major source of state revenues. By changing the funding formula, the federal government can dramatically raise or lower total state revenues. The 2009 stimulus package temporarily changed the matching formula to make it much more favorable to states. The CBO estimates that the cost of the temporary formula change to the U.S. Treasury will be $90 billion spread over three years.

All of the temporary measures just described provide immediate relief to state governments. Unlike the federal government, which can borrow unlimited funds to pay for its operations, state governments must generally cover the cost of their operations with current tax revenues, fees, or grants from the federal government. Because states were given generous fiscal relief, state legislatures did not have to cut spending or increase taxes as much as would have been necessary in the absence of federal aid.

Federal fiscal relief to the states is particularly important for education and for maintaining social protection to the poor. In the United States, education is primarily the responsibility of state and local governments. The federal government typically pays for only about 10 percent to 12 percent of the total cost of public primary and secondary schools. State and local governments pay for the rest. Since balanced budget rules make state and local budgets pro-cyclical, state legislatures face pressure to reduce school budgets during recessions. The federal government pays for most of the cost of social safety net programs for the poor, but state governments still pay for a substantial share of these costs. Equally important, state governments are responsible for administering some of the biggest programs targeted toward the poor, including Medicaid and Temporary Assistance for Needy Families (TANF). State governments make the rules that help determine who is eligible for benefits, and they set the level of many benefits. Even though they do not pay for the full cost of the programs, when a recession occurs, many states are tempted to curtail eligibility or cut benefits. This is the opposite policy from the one urged by most economists, who think it is important for benefits to be maintained or even improved in a recession. Thus, the federal government's unconventional policy of temporarily easing states' strained budgets almost certainly prevented a weakening of the state and local social safety net.

A Success or a Failure?

Before 2009, state fiscal relief and temporary incentives for human capital investment rarely, if ever, played a big role in federal stimulus programs. As a result, we have little evidence to predict the short-term impact of these measures on government and household consumption. Based on evidence of state spending patterns and post-secondary educational investments in the current recession, we will learn more about the counter-cyclical effectiveness of these two kinds of policies. One encouraging sign is that payroll employment in state and local government and in education has not been badly hurt by the recessions. In spite of the sharp decline in state and local tax revenues, governments have been able to maintain their pre-recession employment levels. It may be that state and local employees' annual wages and benefit costs have been trimmed, because many governments have forced their workers to accept unpaid furloughs. However, the payroll employment statistics provide little evidence of a massive cutback in the number of state and local employees.

Anecdotal evidence suggests the federal government's efforts to support education and human capital investment have probably succeeded. Many public and private post-secondary institutions report strong demand for places in their entering classes. Profit-making training institutions also report surging demand. If the recession has made post-secondary education and training unaffordable to more students, the application data provide little evidence for it. Some hard data on college enrollment also

December 2007=100

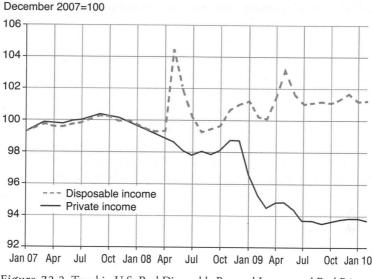

Figure 73.2 Trend in U.S. Real Disposable Personal Income and Real Private Income, January 2007–February 2010

Source: Bureau of Economic Analysis, U.S. Department of Commerce

suggest college attendance remains high. The Bureau of Labor Statistics reports that 70.1 percent of 2009 high school graduates were enrolled in college last October. This is an all-time high in the percentage of graduates going on to college. The enrollment rate should have plummeted if students couldn't afford to attend college or if post-secondary institutions had been forced by budget cuts to slash their staffs.

Another tangible sign of a payoff from the ARRA stimulus is the continued strength in consumer spending. The severity of the recession caused private incomes to plunge. The solid dark line in Figure 73.2 shows the trend in real private income— labor compensation, self-employment income, interest, dividends, and other capital income—between 2007 and February 2010. Private income began to fall in the fourth quarter of 2007, fell sharply immediately after the worst of the financial crisis in late 2008, and did not stabilize until the

summer of 2009. After June 2009, Americans' private incomes were more than 6 percent below their pre-recession level.

The broken line in Figure 73.2 shows the trend in real personal disposable income— that is, private income plus government transfers minus personal tax payments. Federal government programs and stimulus dollars cushioned the massive blow to private family incomes. Disposable income fell less than 1 percent after the start of the recession, a stunning fact too often ignored given the severity and length of the current downturn. Reduced federal taxes and increased government benefit payments, partly funded out of the stimulus package, have kept Americans' spendable incomes from falling as fast as their private incomes. Household consumption fell in the recession, in spite of the massive swing in taxes and public transfers, but it only fell modestly. Americans were made cautious in their spending because of the drop in their personal wealth and fear of losing their jobs. But government benefits helped boost the spending of the unemployed, and lower taxes helped insulate middle class families from some of the effect of the drop in wealth. By the beginning of 2010, personal consumption spending was close to its pre-recession level.

Could the administration and Congress have done better? The 2009 stimulus package should almost certainly have been larger. The administration's own forecast implied that the gap between actual and potential national output was big enough to justify a bigger package than the one Congress adopted. The political reality, however, is that opposition to stimulus spending by conservatives in the Senate precluded a larger package. In fact, Congress passed a smaller stimulus than the one the president asked for. In retrospect the package should also have included a much bigger allocation for new government capital spending—on roads, mass transit, public buildings, and environmental capital projects. This investment would directly provide jobs to workers in construction and capital goods manufacturing, industries hard hit by the recession. The objection to this kind of spending is that the money often funds questionable projects and is spent with too great a lag to do much good. These objections carry more weight when a recession is short and when petty political considerations play a big role in deciding which projects deserve funding. In this recession, the job market downturn is likely to last a long time, so even delayed capital spending is likely to do some good.

74

Skill Formation and the Economics of Investing in Disadvantaged Children

JAMES J. HECKMAN

Four core concepts important to devising sound social policy toward early childhood have emerged from decades of independent research in economics, neuroscience, and developmental psychology (*1*). First, the architecture of the brain and the process of skill formation are influenced by an interaction between genetics and individual experience. Second, the mastery of skills that are essential for economic success and the development of their underlying neural pathways follow hierarchical rules. Later attainments build on foundations that are laid down earlier. Third, cognitive, linguistic, social, and emotional competencies are interdependent; all are shaped powerfully by the experiences of the developing child; and all contribute to success in the society at large. Fourth, although adaptation continues throughout life, human abilities are formed in a predictable sequence of sensitive periods, during which the development of specific neural circuits and the behaviors they mediate are most plastic and therefore optimally receptive to environmental influences.

A landmark study concluded that "virtually every aspect of early human development, from the brain's evolving circuitry to the child's capacity for empathy, is affected by the environments and experiences that are encountered in a cumulative fashion, beginning in the prenatal period and extending throughout the early childhood years" (*2*). This principle stems from two characteristics that are intrinsic to the nature of learning: (i) early learning confers value on acquired skills, which leads to self-reinforcing motivation to learn more, and (ii) early mastery of a range of cognitive, social, and emotional competencies makes learning at later ages more efficient and therefore easier and more likely to continue.

Early family environments are major predictors of cognitive and noncognitive abilities. Research has documented the early (by ages 4 to 6) emergence and persistence of gaps in cognitive and noncognitive skills (*3*, *4*). Environments that do not stimulate the young and fail to cultivate these skills at early ages place children at an

James J. Heckman, "Skill Formation and the Economics of Investing in Disadvantaged Children," *Science* 312 (June 2006), pp. 1900–1902.

early disadvantage. Disadvantage arises more from lack of cognitive and noncognitive stimulation given to young children than simply from the lack of financial resources.

This is a source of concern because family environments have deteriorated. More U.S. children are born to teenage mothers or are living in single parent homes compared with 40 years ago (5). Disadvantage is associated with poor parenting practices and lack of positive cognitive and noncognitive stimulation. A child who falls behind may never catch up. The track records for criminal rehabilitation, adult literacy, and public job training programs for disadvantaged young adults are remarkably poor (3). Disadvantaged early environments are powerful predictors of adult failure on a number of social and economic measures.

Many major economic and social problems can be traced to low levels of skill and ability in the population. The U.S. will add many fewer college graduates to its workforce in the next 20 years than it did in the past 20 years (6, 7). The high school dropout rate, properly measured with inclusion of individuals who have received general educational development (GED) degrees, is increasing at a time when the economic return of schooling has increased (8). It is not solely a phenomenon of unskilled immigrants. Over 20% of the U.S. workforce is functionally illiterate, compared with about 10% in Germany and Sweden (9). Violent crime and property crime levels remain high, despite large declines in recent years. It is estimated that the net cost of crime in American society is $1.3 trillion per year, with a per capita cost of $4,818 per year (10). Recent research documents the importance of deficits in cognitive and noncognitive skills in explaining these and other social pathologies (11).

Noncognitive Skills and Examples of Successful Early Interventions

Cognitive skills are important, but noncognitive skills such as motivation, perseverance, and tenacity are also important for success in life. Much public policy, such as the No Child Left Behind Act, focuses on cognitive test score outcomes to measure the success of interventions in spite of the evidence on the importance of noncognitive skills in social success. Head Start was deemed a failure in the 1960s because it did not raise the intelligence quotients (IQs) of its participants (12). Such judgments are common but miss the larger picture. Consider the Perry Preschool Program (13), a 2-year experimental intervention for disadvantaged African-American children initially ages 3 to 4 that involved morning programs at school and afternoon visits by the teacher to the child's home. The Perry intervention group had IQ scores no higher than the control group by age 10. Yet, the Perry treatment children had higher achievement test scores than the control children because they were more motivated to learn. In followups to age 40, the treated group had higher rates of high school graduation, higher salaries, higher percentages of home ownership, lower rates of receipt of welfare assistance as adults, fewer out-of-wedlock births, and fewer arrests than the controls (13). The economic benefits of the Perry Program are substantial (Table 74.1). Rates of return are 15 to 17% (14). (The rate of return is the increment in earnings and other outcomes, suitably valued, per year for each dollar invested in the child.) The benefit-cost ratio (the ratio of the aggregate program benefits over the life of the child to the input costs) is over eight to one.

Table 74.1 Economic benefits and costs of the Perry Preschool Program (*27*). All values are discounted at 3% and are in 2004 dollars. Earnings, Welfare, and Crime refer to monetized value of adult outcomes (higher earnings, savings in welfare, and reduced costs of crime). K–12 refers to the savings in remedial schooling. College/adult refers to tuition costs.

	Perry Preschool
Child care	$986
Earnings	$40,537
K–12	$9184
College/adult	$–782
Crime	$94,065
Welfare	$355
Abuse/neglect	$0
Total benefits	$144,345
Total costs	$16,514
Net present value	$127,831
Benefits-to-costs ratio	8.74

Perry intervened relatively late. The Abecedarian program, also targeted toward disadvantaged children, started when participants were 4 months of age. Children in the treatment group received child care for 6 to 8 hours per day, 5 days per week, through kindergarten entry; nutritional supplements, social work services, and medical care were provided to control group families. The program was found to permanently raise the IQ and the noncognitive skills of the treatment group over the control group. However, the Abecedarian program was intensive, and it is not known whether it is the age of intervention or its intensity that contributed to its success in raising IQ (*15–17*).

Reynolds *et al.* present a comprehensive review of early childhood programs directed toward disadvantaged children and their impact (*18*). Similar returns are obtained for other early intervention programs (*19, 20*), although more speculation is involved in these calculations because the program participants are in the early stages of their life cycles and do not have long earnings histories.

Schools and Skill Gaps

Many societies look to the schools to reduce skills gaps across socioeconomic groups. Because of the dynamics of human skill formation, the abilities and motivations that children bring to school play a far greater role in promoting their performance in school than do the traditional inputs that receive so much attention in public policy debates. The Coleman Report (*21*) as well as recent work (*22, 23*) show that families and not schools are the major sources of inequality in student performance. By the third grade, gaps in test scores across socioeconomic groups are stable by age, suggesting that later schooling and variations in schooling quality have little effect in reducing or widening the gaps that appear before students enter school (*4, 24*). Figure 74.1 plots gaps in math test scores by age across family income levels. The majority of the gap at age 12 appears at the age of school enrollment. Carneiro and Heckman performed a cost-benefit analysis of classroom size reduction on adult earnings (*3*).

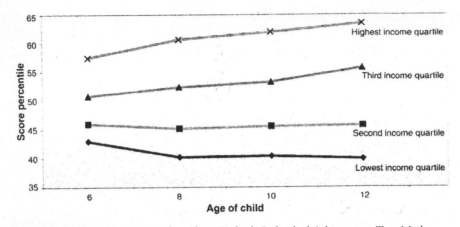

Figure 74.1 Average percentile rank on Peabody Individual Achievement Test–Math score by age and income quartile. Income quartiles are computed from average family income between the ages of 6 and 10. Adapted from (3) with permission from MIT Press.

Although smaller classes raise the adult earnings of students, the earnings gains received by students do not offset the costs of hiring additional teachers. The student-teacher achievement ratio (STAR) randomized trial of classroom size in Tennessee shows some effect of reduced classroom size on test scores and adult performance, but most of the effect occurs in the earliest grades (25, 26). Schools and school quality at current levels of funding contribute little to the emergence of test score gaps among children or to the development of the gaps.

Second Chance Programs

America is a second chance society. Our educational policy is based on a fundamental optimism about the possibility of human change. The dynamics of human skill formation reveal that later compensation for deficient early family environments is very costly (4). If society waits too long to compensate, it is economically inefficient to invest in the skills of the disadvantaged. A serious trade-off exists between equity and efficiency for ado-lescent and young adult skill policies. There is no such trade-off for policies targeted toward disadvantaged young children (28).

The findings of a large literature are captured in Fig. 74.2. This figure plots the rate of return, which is the dollar flow from a unit of investment at each age for a marginal investment in a disadvantaged young child at current levels of expenditure. The economic return from early interventions is high, and the return from later interventions is lower. Remedial programs in the adolescent and young adult years are much more costly in producing the same level of skill attainment in adulthood. Most are economically inefficient. This is reflected in Fig. 74.2 by the fact that a segment of the curve lies below the opportunity cost of funds (the horizontal line fixed at r). The opportunity cost is the return from funds if they were invested for purposes unrelated to disadvantaged children.

Conclusions

Investing in disadvantaged young children is a rare public policy initiative that pro-

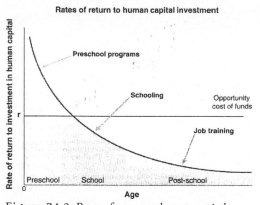

Figure 74.2 Rates of return to human capital investment in disadvantaged children. The declining figure plots the payout per year per dollar invested in human capital programs at different stages of the life cycle for the marginal participant at current levels of spending. The opportunity cost of funds (r) is the payout per year if the dollar is invested in financial assets (e.g., passbook savings) instead. An optimal investment program from the point of view of economic efficiency equates returns across all stages of the life cycle to the opportunity cost. The figure shows that, at current levels of funding, we overinvest in most schooling and post-schooling programs and underinvest in preschool programs for disadvantaged persons. Adapted from (3) with permission from MIT Press.

motes fairness and social justice and at the same time promotes productivity in the economy and in society at large. Early interventions targeted toward disadvantaged children have much higher returns than later interventions such as reduced pupil-teacher ratios, public job training, convict rehabilitation programs, tuition subsidies, or expenditure on police. At current levels of resources, society overinvests in remedial skill investments at later ages and underinvests in the early years.

Although investments in older disadvantaged individuals realize relatively less return overall, such investments are still clearly beneficial. Indeed, the advantages

gained from effective early interventions are sustained best when they are followed by continued high-quality learning experiences. The technology of skill formation shows that the returns on school investment and postschool investment are higher for persons with higher ability, where ability is formed in the early years. Stated simply, early investments must be followed by later investments if maximum value is to be realized.

REFERENCES AND NOTES

1. E. I. Knudsen, J. J. Heckman, J. Cameron, J. P. Shonkoff, *Proc. Natl. Acad. Sci. U.S.A.*, in press.

2. J. P. Shonkoff, D. Phillips, *From Neurons to Neighborhoods: The Science of Early Child Development* (National Academies Press, Washington, DC, 2000).

3. P. Carneiro, J. J. Heckman, in *Inequality in America: What Role for Human Capitol Policies?* J. J. Heckman, A. B. Krueger, B. Friedman, Eds. (MIT Press, Cambridge, MA, 2003), ch. 2, pp. 77–237.

4. F. Cunha, J. J. Heckman, L. J. Lochner, D. V. Masterov, in *Handbook of the Economics of Education*, E. A. Hanushek, F. Welch, Eds. (North Holland, Amsterdam, in press).

5. J. J. Heckman, D. V. Masterov, "The productivity argument for investing in young children," (Working Paper No. 5, Committee on Economic Development, Washington, DC, 2004).

6. J. B. DeLong, L. Katz, C. Goldin, in *Agenda for the Nation*, H. Aaron, J. Lindsay, P. Nivola, Eds. (Brookings Institution Press, Washington, DC, 2003), pp. 17–60.

7. D. T. Ellwood, in *The Roaring Nineties: Can Full Employment Be Sustained?* A. Krueger, R. Solow, Eds. (Russell Sage Foundation, New York, 2001), pp. 421–489.

8. J. J. Heckman, P. LaFontaine, *J. Lab. Econ.*, in press.

9. *International Adult Literacy Survey, 2002: User's Guide*, Statistics Canada, Special Surveys Division, National Literacy Secretariat, and

Human Resources Development Canada (Statistics Canada, Ottawa, Ontario, 2002).

10. D. A. Anderson, *J. Law Econ.* **42**, 611 (1999).

11. J. J. Heckman, J. Stixrud, S. Urzua, *J. Lab. Econ.*, in press.

12. Westinghouse Learning Corporation and Ohio University, *The Impact of Head Start: An Evaluation of the Effects of Head Start on Children's Cognitive and Affective Development*, vols. 1 and 2 (Report to the Office of Economic Opportunity, Athens, OH, 1969).

13. L. J. Schweinhart *et al.*, *Lifetime Effects: The High/Scope Perry Preschool Study Through Age 40* (High/Scope, Ypsilanti, MI, 2005).

14. A. Rolnick, R. Grunewald, "Early childhood development: Economic development with a high public return" (Tech. rep., Federal Reserve Bank of Minneapolis, Minneapolis, MN, 2003).

15. C. T. Ramey, S. L. Ramey, *Am. Psychol.* **53**, 109 (1998).

16. C. T. Ramey, S. L. Ramey, *Prev. Med.* **27**, 224 (1998).

17. C. T. Ramey *et al.*, *Appl. Dev. Sci.* **4**, 2 (2000).

18. A. J. Reynolds, M. C. Wang, H. J. Walberg, *Early Childhood Programs for a New Century* (Child Welfare League of America Press, Washington, DC, 2003).

19. L. A. Karoly *et al.*, *Investing in Our Children: What We Know and Don't Know About the Costs and Benefits of Early Childhood Interventions* (RAND, Santa Monica, CA, 1998).

20. L. N. Masse, W. S. Barnett, *A Benefit Cost Analysis of the Abecedarian Early Childhood Intervention* (Rutgers University, National Institute for Early Education Research, New Brunswick, NJ, 2002).

21. J. S. Coleman, *Equality of Educational Opportunity* (U.S. Department of Health, Education, and Welfare, Office of Education, Washington, DC, 1966).

22. S. W. Raudenbush, "Schooling, statistics and poverty: Measuring school improvement and improving schools" Inaugural Lecture, Division of Social Sciences, University of Chicago, Chicago, IL, 22 February 2006.

23. J. J. Heckman, M. I. Larenas, S. Urzua, unpublished data.

24. D. A. Neal, in *Handbook of Economics of Education*, E. Hanushek, F. Welch, Eds. (Elsevier, Amsterdam, in press).

25. B. Krueger, D. M. Whitmore, *Econ. J.*, **111**, 1 (2001).

26. B. Krueger, D. M. Whitmore, in *Bridging the Achievement Gap*, J. E. Chubb, T. Loveless, Eds. (Brookings Institution Press, Washington, DC, 2002).

27. W. S. Barnett, Benefit-Cost Analysis of Preschool Education, 2004, (http://nieer.org/resources/files/BarnettBenefits.ppt).

28. F. Cunha, J. J. Heckman, *J. Hum. Resour.*, in press.

29. This paper was generously supported by NSF (grant nos. SES-0241858 and SES-0099195), National Institute of Child Health and Human Development (NIH grant no. R01HD043411), funding from the Committee for Economic Development, with a grant from the Pew Charitable Trusts and from the Partnership for America's Economic Success. This research was also supported by the Children's Initiative project at the Pritzker Family Foundation and a grant from the Report to the Nation of America's Promise. The views expressed in this paper are those of the author and not necessarily those of the sponsoring organizations. See our Web site (http://jenni.uchicago.edu/econ_neurosci) for more information.

75

The Harlem Miracle

DAVID BROOKS

The fight against poverty produces great programs but disappointing results. You go visit an inner-city school, job-training program or community youth center and you meet incredible people doing wonderful things. Then you look at the results from the serious evaluations and you find that these inspiring places are only producing incremental gains.

That's why I was startled when I received an e-mail message from Roland Fryer, a meticulous Harvard economist. It included this sentence: "The attached study has changed my life as a scientist."

Fryer and his colleague Will Dobbie have just finished a rigorous assessment of the charter schools operated by the Harlem Children's Zone. They compared students in these schools to students in New York City as a whole and to comparable students who entered the lottery to get into Harlem Children's Zone schools, but weren't selected.

They found that the Harlem Children's Zone schools produced "enormous" gains. The typical student entered the charter middle school, Promise Academy, in sixth grade and scored in the 39th percentile among New York City students in math.

By the eighth grade, the typical student in the school was in the 74th percentile. The typical student entered the school scoring in the 39th percentile in English Language Arts (verbal ability). By eighth grade, the typical student was in the 53rd percentile.

Forgive some academic jargon, but the most common education reform ideas—reducing class size, raising teacher pay, enrolling kids in Head Start—produce gains of about 0.1 or 0.2 or 0.3 standard deviations. If you study policy, those are the sorts of improvements you live with every day. Promise Academy produced gains of 1.3 and 1.4 standard deviations. That's off the charts. In math, Promise Academy eliminated the achievement gap between its black students and the city average for white students.

Let me repeat that. It eliminated the black-white achievement gap. "The results changed my life as a researcher because I am no longer interested in marginal changes," Fryer wrote in a subsequent e-mail. What Geoffrey Canada, Harlem Children's Zone's founder and president, has done is "the equivalent of curing cancer for these kids. It's amazing. It should be celebrated. But it almost doesn't matter if we stop there. We

---

David Brooks, "The Harlem Miracle," *New York Times*, May 8, 2009, p. 31.

don't have a way to replicate his cure, and we need one since so many of our kids are dying—literally and figuratively."

These results are powerful evidence in a long-running debate. Some experts, mostly surrounding the education establishment, argue that schools alone can't produce big changes. The problems are in society, and you have to work on broader issues like economic inequality. Reformers, on the other hand, have argued that school-based approaches can produce big results. The Harlem Children's Zone results suggest the reformers are right. The Promise Academy does provide health and psychological services, but it helps kids who aren't even involved in the other programs the organization offers.

To my mind, the results also vindicate an emerging model for low-income students. Over the past decade, dozens of charter and independent schools, like Promise Academy, have become no excuses schools. The basic theory is that middle-class kids enter adolescence with certain working models in their heads: what I can achieve; how to control impulses; how to work hard. Many kids from poorer, disorganized homes don't have these internalized models. The schools create a disciplined, orderly and demanding counterculture to inculcate middle-class values.

Basically, the no excuses schools pay meticulous attention to behavior and attitudes. They teach students how to look at the person who is talking, how to shake hands. These schools are academically rigorous and college-focused. Promise Academy students who are performing below grade level spent twice as much time in school as other students in New York City. Students who are performing at grade level spend 50 percent more time in school.

They also smash the normal bureaucratic strictures that bind leaders in regular schools. Promise Academy went through a tumultuous period as Canada searched for the right teachers. Nearly half of the teachers did not return for the 2005–2006 school year. A third didn't return for the 2006–2007 year. Assessments are rigorous. Standardized tests are woven into the fabric of school life.

The approach works. Ever since welfare reform, we have had success with intrusive government programs that combine paternalistic leadership, sufficient funding and a ferocious commitment to traditional, middle-class values. We may have found a remedy for the achievement gap. Which city is going to take up the challenge? Omaha? Chicago? Yours?

76

Flexicurity

JOSHUA COHEN AND
CHARLES SABEL

Ten years ago, the stylized story about poverty and inequality went something like this: "You can be the United States, with lots of income inequality, very flexible labor markets, and very high levels of employment; or you can be Germany, with not so much inequality, rigid labor markets, and lots of unemployment; or you can be Sweden, with pretty low levels of inequality and unemployment. But you can be Sweden only if you employ lots of workers (especially women) in an expanded public sector providing services to families, as inflexible labor market rules keep private sector firms from expanding employment."

Given these options, our system did not seem so bad. Sober analysts acknowledged the costs of American inequality and poverty, especially for African-Americans. But sobriety also compelled recognition of the benefits of the great American jobs machine: creating lots of low-wage work was a large compensation, not least to middle-class families who could afford to hire domestic workers to provide some of the services provided publicly in Sweden. It was hard to see an alternative, as we lacked Sweden's cultural homogeneity, its solidaristic political culture,

and the associated willingness to maintain outsized public employment.

And really: How could there have been an alternative with better results for low-wage workers, given our deeply rooted concern that the protections provided by rigid labor markets or substantial public employment ultimately limit the life chances of the vulnerable by undermining their sense of personal responsibility? Short-term gains in security sound good, but aren't they overwhelmed by the long-term risks of dependency? Low unemployment with high levels of labor force participation and high growth rates; greater income equality and reduced poverty; and a sense of personal responsibility resistant to the moral hazards of solidaristic subsidies: That mix is nice work if you can get it, and good for the utopian fantasies that some call "political philosophy." But such a package is simply unrealistic here, and probably impossible (except in a Sweden) given the hard trade-offs that life imposes and that grown-ups understand.

That was then, this is now. The grown-ups who managed the miracle of global finance have been sent to their (generously

Joshua Cohen and Charles Sabel, "Flexicurity," *Pathways* (Spring 2009), pp. 9, 10–14.

appointed) rooms. Leading policymakers look openly to Japan for lessons about anti-deflationary policy when interest rates hover just above the "zero bound" and to Sweden for lessons about how to nationalize, revitalize, and reprivatize a financial system after a bad-mortgage binge. Fears are great, but hopes are also high. And the idea that the United States might have something to learn about public policy from the rest of the world seems a little less like the carping of academics constitutionally incapable of appreciating what awed the rest of the world about this country, and a little more like the thing that sensible adults do when they are having "issues."

As it happens, when it comes to addressing inequality and poverty, there is something to learn from the far reaches of Old Europe.

Consider the case of Denmark. In the early 1990s, facing high unemployment, low growth, a public sector nearly immobilized in the face of economic decline, and a long-smoldering revolt against an apparently incapacitated state, Denmark reconfigured its welfare state to create a system called *flexicurity*. The essential idea of flexicurity—conveyed by the name—is to combine high *flexibility* in labor markets with high levels of *security* for workers. The flexibility includes both wage flexibility and relative ease for firms in laying off workers, with much lower levels of job protection than other OECD countries. The security comes from a mix of high levels of unemployment insurance—a considerably higher "replacement rate," or ratio of average weekly benefits to average weekly earnings, than any other OECD country—and an active labor market policy providing education and training. This training ensures successful integration into the labor market

for younger and older workers, and it offers life-long learning. The idea, in a slogan, is: *Employment security, not job security.* It means a career at varied, increasingly skilled work, not a lifetime climbing the job ladder in a single firm.

The cumulative effect of flexicurity for individuals, moreover, is to encourage an economy-wide shift in favor of more skilled jobs, as well as innovative firms that can make use of them. Low unemployment rates and rising skill levels give the most skilled, desirable workers (who are, of course, likely to be the ones most attentive to skill acquisition) their pick of jobs. Employers have to attract them with work that is not only interesting, but offers the prospect of further learning. Firms can afford to offer such jobs only if they undertake projects that make productive and well-remunerated use of these workers—and such projects, being the opposite of routine, will naturally require innovative exploration of new possibilities. The robust, adaptable security of individuals fosters the adaptive robustness of the whole economy.

Two other features of flexicurity, not built into the name, are essential to its success. In contrast with our conventional picture of public goods as (by their nature) standardized for broad categories of recipients (e.g., primary education for children ages, say, 5 to 10), flexicurity is individualized. The guiding assumption—based on many recent studies of life on Earth—is that individuals have distinct lives, and that (especially when people are experiencing troubles) those lives cannot easily or constructively be compartmentalized into discrete pieces—work, family, education, training, income, health, transportation, housing—addressed by distinct policies.

On the contrary, family problems are likely to aggravate, or be aggravated by, problems in school or work; addressing any one of these effectively requires attention to at least some of the others. So, support for younger and older adult jobseekers requires not just *customized* services, but *bundles* of customized services adjusted to the needs of individuals and meshing with one another.

Moreover, because education and training require the engagement of workers in ways that simple income support (or in-kind assistance) does not, there is also an important role for *personal responsibility*. Customized services are effective only if those to whom the services are directed participate actively in their production—indeed, that participation is required for the services to be customized to particular needs in the first place. Flexicurity is not what a "nanny state" does when it is taking charge of its responsibility-challenged, incapacitated wards; it is not what a sadder-but-wiser, post-nanny welfare state does when it compensates citizens for some hard luck in youth before sending them out to face the tough, cold world. It is what a democracy does to ensure the continuing inclusion of all its equal members, in a world where we face, individually and collectively, the continuing risks of economic, social, and political exclusion thrown up by rapidly changing labor markets in largely open economies.

This low-resolution description of flexicurity focuses on design principles rather than specific policies and corresponding institutions. But this level of description is entirely faithful to the self-understandings of actors in the system (especially to some of the leading social democrats, such as Mogens Lykketoft, who helped create Danish flexicurity in the 1990s, and the many local and regional actors who customize services today) and of the many outsiders who have tried to learn from the Danish experience. As the appeal of flexicurity has spread from Denmark to Ireland, Finland, and the Netherlands, and become a focus of EU debate over labor market policy, participants in that debate have come to understand that flexicurity takes different forms in different settings. Jeremy Bentham once wrote a constitutional code with a blank space left for the name of the country. The participants in the debate about flexicurity are less abstractly universal in their thinking. As they understand it, the right way to think about flexicurity's broader dispersion is not to simply take a Danish operating manual, translate, enter another country's name, and apply. Instead, the point is to adapt the five design principles just described—flexibility in employment and compensation, robust security for workers, lifelong learning, customization, and personal responsibility to make use of changing opportunities—then pursue mutual comparisons across different versions of flexicurity (first internationally, then domestically) for improvement. Thus, a sixth principle of flexicurity is its adaptability—to changes in Denmark, and, at least potentially, to settings in other countries.

Transforming flexibility and security from competing goods to mutually supportive complements is immensely appealing in an age of deep uncertainty. This appeal has made flexicurity the active subject of EU discussion in recent years, as the European Commission has urged other countries to adopt their own versions of the Danish system. The main European debate acknowledges the merits of the scheme as applied in Denmark, which has experienced persistently low unemployment, high labor force participation, and low inequality. (Some critics have argued that Denmark's strong economic performance is not a result of flexicurity. They point to very slight reductions in labor supply resulting from high replacement rates and the detailed rules covering short-term unemployment. But they ignore what appear to be the significant structural benefits of increased mobility and skill acquisition to the economy.) The concern has been whether the essentials of the system, including its adaptability to changing domestic conditions, can translate across national boundaries, especially because of different regulatory institutions (and associated capacities to sustain active labor market policy), varying levels of trust and solidarity (e.g., how much can people be trusted not to game the unemployment insurance system), and different traditions of labor market flexibility and volatility.

Some of the concerns that have been raised in the European portability debate arguably carry over to the United States, with even greater force:

- The Danes have trust and solidarity; the United States, in contrast, is a famously fractious place, with an abstractly constitutional patriotism, not the deeper ethno-national solidarities needed to provide the assurances against cheating on which flexicurity depends.
- Americans have an exceptionally passionate attachment to individual responsibility. Yes, we like our equality of opportunity, too: Indeed, that value lies at the heart of our shared civic convictions. But the conventional idea of mixing equal opportunity and responsibility is to ensure equality at

life's starting gate, whether through initial education and training, or—as in the post-nanny welfare state Bruce Ackerman and Anne Alstott proposed—a wealth gift for each citizen at age 21 that he or she can use to fund a career, or through some other form of early equalization, after which responsibility kicks in and (but for occasions of personal disaster) individuals are the agents of their own failure and success.

- The Danes like to pay taxes: They have 50 percent tax rates. We don't like taxes. But you have to like them some to support the customized system of lifelong learning.
- The Danes have unions; the United States' unionization rate is about one-tenth Denmark's. How can a country run an active labor market policy with high levels of security and flexibility if it lacks unions with the local knowledge to help ensure the flexibility, or the national power to help guard the state's commitment to security?

These concerns are all forceful, but we are living through unusual times, and we wonder whether we should let ourselves be guided by a knee-jerk invocation of American exceptionalism. All four criticisms remind us that a move to flexicurity would require a sharp departure from past practice, freeing ourselves from the tight grip of the past's famously cold, dead hand. But just a few quick reminders: In November 2008, the country elected a black president, defying conventional expectations. And we are now passing through the largest economic crisis in 75 years, a crisis that looks like it will issue in some entirely unanticipated shifts in national policy. We have already thrown caution to the winds. It would be a tragic mistake to think we could do that, yet remain otherwise as constrained as we often take ourselves to be.

These general observations about unusual circumstances and possibilities apply with particular force to the first concern—the sufficiency of national trust and solidarity. Who knows how much trust and solidarity are really essential to make flexicurity work, or how much we can muster?

As for the second, personal responsibility plays, as we have said, a large and essential role in flexicurity. While it is not about finger-wagging, it does accept that a person's success and failure in life depend importantly on her aspirations and efforts. Flexicurity is about lifelong learning in a public policy system that does not deny personal responsibility (you cannot learn without playing an active role), but rather reconceptualizes the conventional notion that we are victims of (a slightly corrigible) fate until 18 or 21, and nearly self-sufficient thereafter.

What about taxes? One pertinent observation is that no one loves taxes, not even the Danes. In fact, flexicurity was, in part, a reaction to a Danish tax revolt dating to the 1970s. That revolt was animated by a simple idea: Taxes are fine if they are used for good purposes (Danes, like the rest of us, are allergic to throwing money away). But aren't things different in the United States? Doesn't the American allergy extend even to taxes that are used efficiently for public purposes? Isn't the point here to keep "our own money"?

Maybe. But maybe not. In his interesting book *Why Trust Matters*, Mark Hetherington argues that variations in willingness to spend on social welfare in the United States since the 1960s are explained not by shifts to an ideological conservativism, but by shifts in trust, particularly in the government's capacity to make good use of tax resources: "When government programs require people to make sacrifices, they need to trust that the result will be a better future for everyone. Absent that trust, people will deem such sacrifices as unfair, even punitive, and, thus, will not support the programs that require them" (p. 4). Hetherington's argument is that the relevant kinds of trust declined after the mid-1960s. His case is hardly conclusive, but his point has considerable force, at least against the knee-jerk idea that intense tax allergies here make an otherwise attractive labor market policy—good for growth and for distribution—ineligible.

As for unions, we are not expecting a large expansion in American unionization rates. But we need to be careful about the role of unions in the flexicurity system. Danish unions helped push for innovations in the system of lifelong learning, and they play an important part in managing regional services (especially at the plant level). But the national unions are not, at the moment, active in extending or further adapting the system at the national level, and they have been reluctant to encourage too much local initiative for fear of authorizing a decentralization that they would be unable to control. That said, the power of unions to protect workers from employer offensives helps create a political environment in which employers and government are more inclined to look for a reasonable social bargain that does not impose large burdens on workers. A balance of power helps public reason work its magic.

But even here, the lessons for the United States may not be as dim as the point suggests. The last election and the current crisis are creating possibilities that do not exist in more normal times, and there is broad agreement that larger investments in worker training are important. With some foresight and a great deal of good fortune, it might be possible to improve the balance of power here, too, in a way that gives a reinvigorated labor movement a role in constructing a national framework for life-long learning and contributing to that framework's local adaptability.

The Republicans are accusing President Obama of wanting to turn the United States into a northern European "welfare state." When it comes to flexicurity—with its embrace of equality, dynamic efficiency, and a sensible understanding of responsibility—we hope they are right.

77

A Golden Parachute for Everyone?

DALTON CONLEY

In the standard, industrial society model of Keynesian economics, job growth drives the economy, and consumption, in turn, is what drives job growth. As a result, most politicians are obsessed with jobs as the main avenue to economic security—they push the idea that we need to create more and more jobs, and find people to fill those jobs. This obsession leads to a tilting at windmills on the part of political leaders, particularly during election years—and doubly so during recessionary years.

Mainstream Democratic politicians are right about the fact that productivity gains are not equally distributed among workers. But they are mendacious in promising that they can fix the problem by scuttling trade deals or cutting tax rebate checks. In a globalized economy where wages are always lower somewhere else, keeping manufacturing jobs here is a losing battle. Instead we should focus on de-linking—to the maximum extent possible—economic security from the vagaries of the labor market by helping average Americans become part of an investor class. We Americans should be thinking about ourselves as an investor society, as global capital managers. Yes, this may take a feat of imagination to envision

during a period of recession, but if we don't take stock of our fundamental policy strategies during a downturn, when will we?

With the current consumption-based approach to social and economic policy, there will always be a disconnect between the macroeconomic health of the U.S. economy and the fortunes of the typical American family. Productivity growth results in the shedding of jobs and a windfall for the few—the executives and major shareholders—instead of the many. By contrast, if everyone were an investor, productivity gains could instead be distributed in the form of dividends. When productivity increases, we could actually work less, taking more time off when our kids were born or our parents were ailing, for instance. Such a work-deemphasizing approach would represent nothing short of a whole new economic policy, one more appropriate for a post-industrial knowledge economy than the New Deal's vestigial, social insurance model.

This need for a national family investment policy is made all the more pressing by recent trends in private savings rates nationwide. In 1984, the rate stood at 10.4 percent of national income. By 2006 it had slid into the red (-1 percent). We have the

Dalton Conley, "A Golden Parachute for Everyone?" *Pathways* (Summer 2008), pp. 13–15.

lowest savings rate among the world's largest economies, and the lowest domestic savings rate since the Great Depression. How is it possible that we had negative savings even in the early 2000s, a time of economic growth? Answering this question is key to understanding the recent disconnect between the macroeconomic health of the economy (as traditionally measured) and poll numbers showing an American public anxious about their economic prospects.

We need to do something drastic to raise our savings rates in this country—across the socioeconomic spectrum—or face a future in which we do not control our own financial destiny.

Obstacles to Savings

Today's relentless consumption and depressed savings is a relatively new development, not a long-standing feature of American culture. These outcomes may be understood as the result of outmoded social arrangements that depress savings in general and retirement savings in particular. The following four factors are especially problematic.

Over-reliance on employer-based plans: Like our health care system, our savings system is broken partially due to its historic link to employers. But today, in an era of flex time and frequent job change, only about half of all workers are covered by an employer retirement plan. And less than 30 percent of low-income workers (the bottom fifth of the income distribution) have the opportunity to take advantage of such plans. Just as it does not make sense from a competitiveness or efficiency standpoint for the United States to lean on employers to provide health care, the same can be said for savings policy. It is time

to recognize that a system created in a previous labor market does not work in today's climate. Individuals should be able to enjoy all the tax and match benefits of savings regardless of who their employer may be or whether they are employed at all.

Overly complicated tapestry of plans: The number of savings plan types is truly dizzying: traditional IRAs, Roth IRAs, 401(k) plans, simple 401(k), 403(b) plans, 457 plans, thrift savings plans, simple IRAs. The list goes on and on. Worse yet, given the nature of politics and the policy-making process, legislators often just add to the existing smorgasbord of programs. As with tax reform, it comes time every so often to overhaul the system and simplify. That time has come. Why is less more? With a smaller number of clearly delineated plans, it becomes easier to explain which plans should be used for which purposes, and the public is accordingly less likely to abandon all hope of understanding.

Silo-ed savings plans: In addition to the various retirement savings options listed above, we also have savings plans for health and education (health savings accounts, Coverdell IRAs, 529 plans). However, an integrated, lifetime savings policy would create a single mechanism to incentivize savings for a variety of productive purposes. Of course, we would need to rethink bankruptcy and other laws to protect essential savings from creditors in much the same way that retirement savings currently enjoy a privileged position. In other words, if we were to link all tax-privileged savings plans into a single account, we would need new rules to protect some portion of those savings for retirement—in case, for instance, a family were devastated by medical bills.

Lack of commitment mechanisms: We know from behavioral economics that future commitments to save are easier to make than current commitments, since people tend to discount the future more than they "should." Yet we continue to have a policy that does not take into consideration this fundamental aspect of human nature. We need a policy that allows individuals to commit to future withholdings, even if they do not feel ready to contribute at a particular point in time. We also need to offer individuals the option of electing "covenant" savings plans. Borrowing from the covenant marriage movement, this election would stiffen rules for withdrawal and strengthen future contribution commitments.

If we were to achieve a consensus that traditional social insurance is simply not enough in a post-industrial economy, what would an investor society policy environment look like? An attractive approach is outlined below.

Toward an Investor Society Policy

The hard part of saving, everyone knows, is being able to forget about all the other seemingly endless needs and wants that arise each pay cycle and instead squirrel away part of our check. Those in the middle and working classes have it particularly rough in this regard. They have more financial pressures, and they frequently do not have an employer who is willing to match savings with company funds.

In fact, H&R Block recently conducted an experiment in which one group of income-tax filers was offered a 50 percent match to divert some of their tax refund to an individual retirement account. Only 14 percent took the company up on its offer (though this figure was lower for those who were offered no match or a smaller one). This relatively low figure may dumbfound some economists as irrational. But it makes complete sense to sociologists. Many of Block's clientele are folks who can barely make ends meet on a day-to-day basis. Plus, they are uncertain about the future, and rightly so. Will they hold onto their present jobs in an age of employment instability? Will they even live long enough to enjoy the fruits of their IRA? They may be figuring that $500 in hand now is a lot more valuable than $750, plus compounded interest, 20 or 30 years in the future.

But if it is true that future uncertainties combine with the financial stresses of today to put the squeeze on lower-income families' savings, then there is a silver lining, a way to provide these families an easy savings mechanism over the long haul: no-money-down, long-term matches (thereby using the logic of the balloon mortgage payment and other tricks of the sub-prime lending market toward better ends).

This is how it would work: Instead of having to make repeated "savings decisions" to fork over my tax refund year after year in order to qualify for a saver's credit (under the current IRS policy) or an IRA match (under the Block experiment or a similar policy), the individual would agree to set aside future wages—say 4 percent annually for 15 years. In return, the individual gets a $1,000 initial deposit into a savings account, and a 50 percent government match for that 4 percent over the course of the next decade and a half. The key is that the government would be asking low-income savers to commit to squirreling away future earnings, not current tax refunds (as compared with the H&R Block experiment or the current U.S. saver's credit). This commitment structure gives savers something now while paying later—thus promoting savings by taking full advantage of what we know about human behavior.

Building on this idea, such a plan could borrow inspiration from the covenant marriage movement to strengthen the savings commitment even further. Here, penalties for non-qualified withdrawals would be more severe. We could use the future match rate as an incentive for individuals to commit to greater savings by offering, for example, a 50 percent match for the first 3 percent of earnings committed to savings; 55 percent for the next 1 percent; and 60 percent for the following 1 percent. This creates the maximum incentive for everyone to put away 5 percent annually. Individuals could save more of their pretax income (up to, say, 10 percent) on this tax-preferred basis; however, the match would end at 5 percent. The entire system would be limited in the same way FICA is currently limited to the first $102,000 of compensation in order to ensure some progressivity.

Lest more stringent withdrawal penalties seem draconian, universal savings plans could be designed for lifetime use. In other words, we could have one tax-preferred asset account that would work as a 529 college savings plan, a health spending account, and a universal IRA. Thus, withdrawals (up to certain percentage limits for each category) could be made for a wide range of qualifying reasons at any point. Such a plan would be intended to replace all retirement savings plans—employer- or individual-based—as well as savings policies not intended for retirement (such as tax credits on savings).

Evidence from savings experiments also suggests that once the initial barriers to saving have been surmounted, individuals tend to save more. In other words, savings is ad-

dictive. I therefore propose that we create a series of universal "family savings accounts," seeded with $1,000 at birth, mimicking Tony Blair's "baby bonds" policy that has been successfully implemented in the United Kingdom. Parents could then direct a proportion of their matched savings to their children's accounts with no tax penalty. This will make every child grow up with an asset and savings orientation. A successful retirement security orientation must begin with the right policies from the cradle.

While I have focused on improving savings opportunities for low-income Americans here, such policies could (and should) be made universal. This ensures both fairness and political support. But it should be noted that, in general, it is lower-income Americans (and minorities in particular) who face a savings/assets crisis. This is most true in today's recessionary economic climate, making action all the more urgent and necessary. Key to righting American savings rates as a whole is fixing the system for the poorest among us.

The Covenant Savings Plan

The Pension Protection Act takes a step in the right direction by encouraging (though not requiring) companies to make 401(k) deductions the default upon employment unless a participant does the paperwork to withdraw. But for the increasing numbers of Americans who are self-employed, temporarily employed, or who work for a company that does not offer a 401(k), we need to create the same structure of savings.

A "covenant savings plan" along the lines of what I've outlined here would do exactly that—provide a mechanism by which those who don't have the option of a 401(k) at work can check a box once and save for years. This family savings plan should garner appeal on both sides of the aisle. Republicans have long desired private savings accounts for all Americans. Democrats, meanwhile, want to protect Social Security and augment it for those at the bottom of the income distribution. This proposal accomplishes both goals.

Is now the right time to recast ourselves as an investor society? It might well be argued that, however attractive such a recasting might be, we haven't the luxury of undertaking major reform in the context of dire economic circumstances. But economic history suggests otherwise: It was, after all, precisely the dire circumstances of the Depression that ushered in major institutional reform (in the form of Keynesian economics), reform that served us well for the bulk of the 20th century. Some 70 years later, difficult economic circumstances again cast in sharp relief the deficiencies of consumption-based approaches, shortcomings that can no longer be ignored. These circumstances, for all the short-term pain they cause, will be a long-term blessing insofar as they force us to chart a new and more productive course for the 21st century.

78

The Pragmatic Case for Reducing Income Inequality

ROBERT H. FRANK

Moral arguments alone are often insufficient to persuade affluent voters to accept higher taxes. Here I will argue for an expanded social safety net on purely pragmatic grounds. As I will explain, a more effective safety net would benefit not only the low-income citizens who receive services from it directly, but also the more affluent citizens whose higher tax payments would be necessary to support it. The reason is that income inequality has prevented us from adopting efficient solutions to many problems that affect rich and poor alike.

A case in point is the regulations on auto emissions we adopt to promote cleaner air. Because these regulations increase car prices, legislators in most jurisdictions exempt older vehicles to avoid imposing unacceptable costs on the mostly low-income motorists who drive them. Yet the cost to society of this exemption far outweighs its benefit for the poor.

For example, although fewer than 10 percent of the vehicles in Los Angeles are more than 15 years old, these cars account for more than half the smog. Exempting old cars thus necessitates much stricter reg-

ulations for new ones. But the cheapest ways of reducing emissions from new cars have long since been adopted. Meeting air quality targets by further tightening new-car standards is several times as costly as meeting those targets by eliminating the exemption for older vehicles.

By raising taxes on high-income motorists, the government could pay for vouchers that would enable low-income motorists to scrap their older vehicles in favor of cleaner used cars of more recent vintage. The required taxes would be much smaller than the resulting savings from not having to adopt such costly standards for new vehicles. Both rich and poor motorists would win.

If everyone could be made better off by the policy change just described, why hasn't it been implemented? In recent decades, potent anti-government rhetoric has made it difficult even to discuss such proposals, let alone adopt them. This rhetoric rests on two claims that anti-government conservatives hold to be self-evident. One is that government spending is always and everywhere wasteful, the other that it is morally

Robert H. Frank, "The Pragmatic Case for Reducing Income Inequality," *Pathways* (Winter 2008), pp. 25–27.

illegitimate for the state to transfer resources from rich to poor.

A proposal to levy higher taxes on the affluent to pay for a vehicle buyout program for the poor runs up against both claims. If I were running for office and made such a proposal, conservatives would pounce. They might say, "Frank thinks the bureaucrats in Washington know how to spend your money more wisely than you do!" Or, "You worked hard for your money. You can make charitable contributions if you want to, but the government has no right to take your money by force and give it to the poor!" With voter opinion increasingly shaped largely by 15-second sound bites, these have proved extremely difficult slogans to run against.

Yet the claims on which these slogans rest are shaky at best. Government is often wasteful, yes, but so are actors in other sectors. For example, the privately organized health insurance system in the United States delivers worse outcomes at substantially higher cost than the government-managed single-payer systems in virtually every other industrial country. But proposals to adopt a single-payer system would require higher taxes and increased benefits for low-income citizens, steps that reliably unleash the full power of anti-government rhetoric. ("Socialized medicine!!") So for now, we remain saddled with a system that everyone agrees is dysfunctional.

The claim that taxpayers have a moral right to spend their pre-tax income as they see fit also has considerable rhetorical force. But it, too, collapses under scrutiny. If government couldn't compel tax payments under penalty of law, there could be no government. With no government, we would have no army. In short order, we would be invaded by some other government's army and then be compelled to pay taxes to that government.

All countries have governments with the power to compel tax payments. Under our constitution, citizens have the right to spend their *post-tax* incomes as they see fit, provided they do not violate the law. But our elected representatives are empowered to vote on what services the government should provide and how taxes should be collected to pay for them. It is ridiculous to insist that the government has no right to tax and transfer.

The real question isn't whether the government knows how to spend our money more wisely than we do. Rather, it's how we as a society want to apportion our scarce resources between public and private spending. As our current practices in the health care and emissions regulation domains demonstrate clearly, the insistence that government cannot tax and transfer often prevents us from achieving outcomes that would be better for every citizen.

Similar examples abound in other domains. In the realm of antipoverty policy, for instance, most economists agree that raising the earned-income tax credit would be the most efficient way of increasing the living standard of the working poor. The program employs general tax revenues to support income subsidies to those whose earnings fall below a given threshold. Its compelling advantage is that, unlike a higher minimum wage, it does not discourage hiring. But proposals to increase the earned-income tax credit would require higher taxes on the affluent.

Because the most efficient antipoverty policy is deemed politically unfeasible, many economists supported the 2007 legislation that raised the minimum wage for the first time in a decade. But this was less than a complete victory for the working poor. For unlike an increase in the earned-income tax credit, an increase in the minimum wage not only limits job creation for the least-skilled workers, it also raises the prices of goods they produce. Overall, it would have been cheaper to raise the earned-income tax credit.

Anti-government rhetoric has also prevented the adoption of energy policies that would produce better outcomes for all. For example, economists of all political stripes have argued that a stiff tax on gasoline would relieve traffic congestion, reduce greenhouse gases, accelerate the development of energy-saving technologies, and reduce dependence on foreign oil. But it would also impose significant economic hardship on low-income families, making it necessary to increase transfer payments to those families. Both the tax on gasoline and the transfer to low-income families, however, are prime targets for anti-government rhetoric. ("Social engineering!!") So gasoline taxes continue to be far lower in the United States than in other industrial countries.

Whatever else it may have accomplished, potent anti-government rhetoric of recent decades has sharply lowered the income tax rates on the nation's wealthiest families. It is an iron law of politics that when an interest group wins favorable treatment from the government, it will fight bitterly to protect its gains. Accordingly, the prospect of making the tax system more progressive to pay for an expanded social safety net may seem naïve.

Yet a careful reading of the evidence suggests that even the wealthy have been made worse off, on balance, by recent tax cuts. The private benefits of these cuts have been much smaller, and their indirect costs much larger, than many recipients appear to have anticipated.

On the benefit side, tax cuts have led the wealthy to spend more money, in the seemingly plausible expectation that doing so would make them happier. As social scientists increasingly recognize, however, well-being depends less on how much people consume in absolute terms than on the social context in which consumption occurs. As the economist Richard Layard has written, "In a poor country, a man proves to his wife that he loves her by giving her a rose, but in a rich country, he must give a dozen roses." The rich are spending more, but the effect has often been just to raise the bar that defines adequate.

On the cost side of the ledger, the federal budget deficits created by the recent tax cuts have had serious consequences, even for the wealthy. For example, they have led to cuts in federal financing for basic scientific research that threaten the very basis of our long-term economic prosperity.

Large deficits also threaten our public health. Thus, despite the increasing threat from micro-organisms like E. coli 0157, the government inspects beef processing plants at only a quarter the rate it did in the early 1980s. Poor people have died from eating contaminated beef, but so have rich people.

Citing revenue shortfalls, the nation postpones maintenance of its highways and bridges, even though doing so means having to spend two to five times as much on repairs in the long run. Poor people died when the I-35 bridge over the Mississippi collapsed in Minneapolis, but so did rich people.

Deficits have also compromised the nation's security. In 2004, for example, the

Bush administration reduced financing for the Energy Department's program to secure loosely guarded nuclear stockpiles in the former Soviet Union by 8 percent. And despite the rational fear that terrorists may try to detonate a nuclear bomb in an American city, most cargo containers are not inspected before they enter our nation's ports.

A surprisingly simple remedy is at hand. By replacing federal income taxes with a steeply progressive consumption tax, we could erase the federal deficit, stimulate additional savings, pay for valuable public services, and reduce overseas borrowing—all without requiring difficult sacrifices from taxpayers.

Under such a tax, people would report not only their income but also their annual savings, as many already do under 401(k) plans and other retirement accounts. A family's annual consumption is simply the difference between its income and its annual savings. That amount, minus a standard deduction—say, $30,000 for a family of four—would be the family's taxable consumption. Rates would start low—say, 10 percent. A family that earned $50,000 and saved $5,000 would thus have taxable consumption of $15,000. It would pay only $1,500 in tax, about half what it pays under the current tax system.

As taxable consumption rises, the tax rate on additional consumption would also rise. With a progressive income tax, marginal tax rates cannot rise beyond a certain threshold without threatening incentives to save and invest. Under a progressive consumption tax, however, higher marginal tax rates actually strengthen those incentives.

Consider a family that spends $10 million a year and is deciding whether to throw a $2 million coming-of-age party for its daughter. If the top marginal tax rate on

consumption were 100 percent, the party would cost $4 million. The additional tax payment would reduce the federal deficit by $2 million. Alternatively, the family could scale back, throwing only a $1 million party. Then it would pay $1 million in additional tax and could deposit $2 million in savings. The federal deficit would fall by $1 million, and the additional savings would stimulate investment, promoting growth. Either way, the nation would come out ahead with no real sacrifice required of wealthy families, because when all spend less on parties, the result is merely to redefine what must be spent to mark a special occasion.

Without displacing any urgent private purchases, a progressive consumption tax would generate sufficient new revenue to fund the very best antipoverty programs. A progressive consumption tax would also reduce the growing financial pressures confronting most families. Top earners, having received not only the greatest income gains over the last three decades but also substantial tax cuts, have been building larger houses simply because they have more money. Those houses have shifted the frame of reference for people with slightly lower incomes, leading them to build larger as well. The resulting expenditure cascade has affected families at all income levels.

The median new house in the United States, for example, now has over 2,300 square feet, over 40 percent more than in 1979, even though real median family earnings have risen little since then. The problem is not that middle-income families are trying to "keep up with the Gateses." Rather, these families feel pressure to spend beyond what they can comfortably afford because more expensive neighborhoods tend to have better schools. A family that spends less than its peers on housing must thus send its children to lower-quality schools.

Some people worry that tax incentives for reduced consumption might throw the economy into recession. But total spending, not just consumption, determines output and employment. If a progressive consumption tax were phased in gradually, its main effect would be to shift spending from consumption to investment, causing productivity and incomes to rise faster.

Should a recession occur, a temporary cut in consumption taxes would provide a much more powerful stimulus than the traditional temporary cut in income taxes. People would benefit from a temporary consumption tax cut only if they spent more right away. In contrast, consumers who fear that they might lose their jobs in a recession are often reluctant to spend temporary income-tax rebates.

Failure to address the current fiscal crisis is not an attractive option. With baby boomers retiring and most voters now favoring universal health coverage, budget shortfalls will grow sharply. Annual borrowing from abroad, now more than $800 billion, will also increase, causing further declines in the slumping dollar. And the personal savings rate, which has been negative for the last two years, will fall still farther, causing future reductions in economic growth.

The progressive consumption tax is perhaps the only instrument that can reverse these trends at acceptable political cost. It has been endorsed by a long list of distinguished economists of varying political orientations. It was proposed in the Senate in 1995 by Sam Nunn, the Georgia Democrat then serving his final term, and Pete Domenici, Republican of New Mexico, who called it the Unlimited Savings Allowance tax. In short, this tax is not a radical idea.

Although the Bush tax cuts for the nation's wealthiest families threaten American economic prosperity, they have done little for their ostensible beneficiaries. Even purely in terms of self-interest, they would have fared much better if the same money had been spent to repair our aging bridges. And they would fare better still if we replaced the federal income tax with a progressive consumption tax and used some of the resulting revenue to fund safety net programs.

79

Tackling the Managerial Power Problem

The Key to Improving Executive Compensation

LUCIAN A. BEBCHUK AND JESSE M. FRIED

Executive pay continues to attract much attention from investors, financial economists, regulators, the media, and the public at large. The dominant paradigm for economists' study of executive compensation has long been that pay arrangements are the product of arm's-length bargaining—bargaining between executives attempting to get the best possible deal for themselves and boards seeking only to serve shareholder interests. According to this "official story," directors can be counted on to act as guardians of shareholders' interests. This assumption has also been the basis for corporate rules governing compensation in publicly traded firms.

But the actual pay-setting process has deviated far from this arm's-length model. Managerial power and influence have played a key role in shaping the amount and structure of executive compensation. Directors have had various economic incentives to support, or at least go along with, arrangements favorable to the company's top executives. Collegiality, team spirit, a natural desire to avoid conflict within the board, and sometimes friendship and loyalty have also pulled board members in that direction. Although many directors own shares in their firms, their financial incentives to avoid arrangements favorable to executives have been too weak to induce them to take the personally costly, or at the very least unpleasant, route of haggling with their CEOs.

The inability or unwillingness of directors to bargain at arm's length has enabled executives to obtain pay that is higher and more decoupled from performance than would be expected under arm's-length bargaining. Indeed, there is a substantial body of evidence indicating that pay has been higher, or less sensitive to performance, when executives have more power over directors. Executives have less power over directors when shareholders are larger or more sophisticated and thus can more easily exert influence over the board. Not surprisingly,

Lucian A. Bebchuk and Jesse M. Fried, "Tackling the Managerial Power Problem: The Key to Improving Executive Compensation," *Pathways* (Summer 2010), pp. 10–12.

executive pay is lower and better tied to performance when there is a large outside shareholder or a greater concentration of institutional owners. Conversely, executive pay increases significantly after the adoption of anti-takeover provisions that give managers more power. Executive pay is also higher when the compensation committee chair has been appointed under the current CEO and may feel some obligation or gratitude toward that CEO.

One of the main constraints on executives' ability to extract even more value from boards is fear of shareholder outrage. Boards thus aggressively "camouflage" the amount and performance-insensitivity of executive pay in an attempt to reduce such outrage. Before 1992, for example, firms were required to disclose executive pay but were not told how they had to disclose it. Many firms thus chose to provide shareholders with long, dense narratives in which any dollar amounts were spelled out rather than expressed in numbers. A shareholder would need to spend a considerable amount of time just to find the dollar amounts, and there was generally not enough information provided to accurately add up the executive's total compensation. In 1992, the SEC required firms to disclose most compensation elements in a standardized, easy-to-read "Summary Compensation Table." Firms responded to the new disclosure requirements by coming up with pay arrangements, such as Supplemental Executive Retirement Plans (SERPs), that did not have to be reported in the table. In 2006, the SEC revised disclosure requirements to better capture the value of such "stealth compensation." But history has shown that compensation designers will try to develop other schemes to deliver pay to executives under shareholders' radar screens.

The desire to camouflage executive pay can explain the widespread practice of backdating executives' option grants, which came to light a few years ago. Most firms grant options to executives that are at-the-money: the exercise price is set to the grant-date stock price. The executive profits to the extent that the sale-date stock price exceeds the exercise price. It turns out that thousands of firms covertly backdated option grants to dates when the stock price was lower. This backdating secretly lowered the exercise price on executives' stock options and boosted the value of their option grants. Backdating also enabled firms to report lower compensation for executives than they actually received.

The existing flaws in compensation arrangements impose substantial costs on shareholders. First, there is the excess pay that managers receive as a result of their power—that is, the difference between what managers' influence enables them to obtain and what they would get under arm's-length contracting. The excess amounts paid to executives come directly at shareholders' expense, and these amounts are not mere pocket change. Second, and perhaps more important, executives' influence leads to compensation arrangements that dilute and distort executives' incentives. In particular, the decoupling of pay from performance reduces executives' incentives to make value-creating decisions and may even lead them to take steps that generate short-term gains at the expense of long-term shareholder value. In our view, the reduction in shareholder value caused by these inefficiencies—rather than that caused by excessive managerial pay—could well be the biggest cost arising from managerial influence over compensation.

The Need for Shareholder-Serving Directors

The problems of executive compensation arrangements are rooted in boards' failure to bargain at arm's length with executives. Greater transparency, improved board procedures, additional shareholder approval requirements, and a better understanding by shareholders of the desirability of various compensation arrangements can all help improve the situation. But these remedies cannot substitute completely for effective decision making by directors striving to serve shareholder interests.

The problems of executive compensation would be best addressed by improving directors' incentives. We need to turn the "official story" of executive compensation and board governance—which portrays directors as faithfully serving shareholders' interests—from fiction into reality.

Directors who safeguard shareholder interests are needed not only to address executive compensation problems but also to tackle the myriad corporate governance problems that would continue to arise even if compensation arrangements were optimized. For example, having such directors is essential for our ability to rely on boards to prevent managers from engaging in empire building or from impeding acquisition offers that would benefit shareholders. The foundation of our board-monitoring system of corporate governance is the existence of directors who select, supervise, and compensate executives with shareholders' interests in mind. Shareholders' ability to rely on such directors is, so to speak, the Archimedean point on which this system stands. The critical question, then, is how to make directors more focused on shareholder interests.

The Limits of Director Independence

The main way that the corporate governance system has responded to perceived governance problems over the years is by trying to bolster board independence. Reforms have sought to make nominally independent directors more independent and expand the presence and role of such independent directors on the board. Strengthened director independence is now widely believed to be key to the effectiveness of the board-monitoring model. Attributing past governance problems to insufficient director independence, many believe that strengthened independence will prevent such governance problems in the future.

We agree that director independence is likely to be beneficial. But director independence cannot by itself ensure that boards properly carry out their critical role. Rules governing director independence cannot deliver nearly as much as their enthusiastic supporters claim.

A fundamental limitation of independence requirements is that they fail to provide affirmative incentives for directors to enhance shareholder value. These requirements merely reduce, and do not fully eliminate, directors' incentives and inclinations to favor executives. Thus, any residual tendency among directors to favor executives may still have a substantial impact in the absence of any countervailing incentives to enhance shareholder value. What we need, then, is to provide directors with *affirmative* incentives to focus on shareholder interests.

Invigorating Corporate Elections

In our view, the most effective way to improve board performance is to increase the power of shareholders vis-à-vis directors. We should make directors not only more independent from executives but also less independent from shareholders. The appointment of directors should substantially depend on shareholders, not only in theory but in practice. Such dependence would give directors better incentives to serve shareholder interests.

Making directors dependent on shareholders could counter some of the factors that incline directors to pursue their own interests or those of executives rather than those of shareholders. Such dependence could make the desire for re-election a positive force rather than a negative one. It could also provide directors with an incentive to develop reputations for serving shareholders. And lastly, it could help instill in directors a sense of loyalty toward shareholders, especially if institutional investors take an active role in putting directors on boards.

For all of these reasons, we support the removal of barriers that have historically insulated directors from shareholders. Because of shareholders' collective action problems, increasing shareholder power vis-à-vis directors would hardly be a perfect solution. But movement in this direction has substantial potential for improving the incentives and performance of boards.

Shareholders' power to replace directors plays a critical role in the corporation. Although this power is not supposed to be used routinely, it should provide a critical fail-safe. "If the shareholders are displeased with the action of their elected representatives," emphasized the Delaware Supreme Court in its well-known opinion in the case of *Unocal Corp. v. Mesa Petroleum Co.*, "the powers of corporate democracy are at their disposal to turn the board out."

In reality, however, this safety valve is weak. Attempts by shareholders to replace incumbents with a team that would do a better job—the kind of action referred to in the *Unocal* opinion above—face considerable impediments. To make directors more focused on shareholder interests, it would be desirable to reduce these impediments.

To begin, shareholders should get access to the corporate ballot. Under existing rules, only incumbents' nominees are placed on the corporate ballot, and outside challengers have to bear the costs of distributing and collecting proxies supporting challengers' nominees. When a significant group of shareholders wishes to run a candidate, this candidate should simply be placed on the corporate ballot.

Beyond providing shareholders with easier access to the corporate ballot, additional measures to strengthen electoral threats should be adopted. Under existing rules of corporate law, incumbents' "campaign" costs are fully covered by the company—providing them with a great advantage over outside candidates, who must pay their own way. To lower the financial barrier for challengers, companies should be required to reimburse reasonable costs incurred by such nominees when they garner sufficient support in the ultimate vote.

Such reimbursement arrangements could be opposed, of course, on grounds that they would be costly to shareholders. But an improved corporate elections process would be in the interests of both companies and shareholders. The proposed measures would not expend corporate resources on nominees whose initial support and chances of winning are negligible; the limited amounts expended on serious challenges would be a small and worthwhile price to pay for an improved system of corporate governance.

Incumbent directors are currently protected from removal not only by the substantial cost to challengers of putting forward a competing slate, but also by staggered boards. In a staggered board, only one-third of the members come up for election each year. As a result, no matter how dissatisfied shareholders are, they must prevail in two annual elections in order to replace a majority of the incumbents and take control away from current management. A substantial fraction of public companies have such an arrangement.

The entrenching effect of staggered boards is costly to shareholders. Companies with a charter-based staggered board have a significantly lower value than other companies, controlling for relevant differences. Legal reforms that would require or encourage firms to have all directors stand for election together could thus contribute significantly to shareholder wealth.

Another way to reduce directors' ability to ignore shareholder interests is to remove the board's veto power over changes to the company's basic governance arrangements. These arrangements are set forth either in the rules of the state in which the company is incorporated or in the company's charter. Under longstanding corporate law, only the board—not a group of shareholders, however large—can initiate and bring to a shareholder vote a proposal to change the state of incorporation or to amend the corporate charter.

Federal securities laws give shareholders the power to express their sentiments in precatory shareholder resolutions, but these resolutions are nonbinding. In recent years, shareholders of companies with staggered boards have increasingly initiated proposals recommending annual election of all directors. However, boards often choose to ignore these proposals, even when they attract a majority of the shareholder vote.

Directors' control over the corporate agenda is often justified on grounds that the U.S. corporation is a completely "representative democracy," in which shareholders can act only through their representatives, the directors. In theory, if shareholders could easily replace directors, that power would be sufficient to induce directors not to stray from shareholders' wishes on major corporate issues.

As we have seen, however, the removal of directors is rather difficult under existing arrangements. It would be far from easy even under a reformed system of corporate elections. Furthermore, shareholders may be pleased with management's general performance but still wish to put in place governance arrangements that restrict management's power or discretion in certain ways. Shareholders should be able to make a change in governance arrangements without concurrently having to replace the board.

The absence of shareholder power to initiate and approve changes in firms' basic corporate governance arrangements has, over time, tilted these arrangements excessively in management's favor. As new issues and circumstances have arisen, firms have tended to adopt charter amendments that address these changes efficiently only when the amendments were favored by management. Additionally, states seeking to attract incorporating and reincorporating firms have had incentives to give substantial weight to management preferences, even at the expense of shareholder interests.

Giving shareholders the power to initiate and approve by vote a proposal to reincorporate or to adopt a charter amendment could produce, in one bold stroke, a substantial improvement in the quality of corporate governance. Shareholder power to change governance arrangements would reduce the need for intervention from outside the firm by regulators, exchanges, or legislators.

Indeed, if shareholders had the power to set the ground rules of corporate governance, they could use it to address some of the problems we have discussed above. Shareholders could establish rules that dismantle staggered boards or invigorate director elections. Shareholders could also adopt charter amendments that improve the process by which executive pay is set or place whatever limits they deem desirable on pay arrangements.

Executive pay problems reflect underlying flaws in corporate governance. To fix these problems, the structure of corporate governance arrangements must be reformed. The power of the board and the weakness of shareholders are often viewed as an inevitable corollary of the modern corporation's widely dispersed ownership. But this weakness is partly due to the legal rules that insulate management from shareholder intervention. Changing these rules would reduce the extent to which boards can stray from shareholder interests and would much improve corporate governance—including flawed executive pay arrangements.

80

Poverty and Marriage, Income Inequality and Brains

CHARLES MURRAY

All manner of remedies for poverty and inequality have been tried repeatedly since 1964. They typically were greeted with early and well-publicized claims of success. When the technical evaluations were published (and seldom publicized), it turned out that the early successes were temporary or that they never really existed. It was this monotonous pattern that led Peter Rossi, the nation's leading scholar in the evaluation of social programs, to formulate Rossi's Iron Law of Program Evaluation: "The expected value of any net impact assessment of any large scale social program is zero."

The cycle of optimistic promises and zero results will repeat itself, because once again the politicians are ignoring causes that don't fit the way they want the world to be. In the case of poverty, they ignore the causal role of the failure to marry. In the case of increasing income inequality, they ignore the causal role of the rising market value of brains.

Poverty and Marriage

The first-order effect of the failure to marry is to create poverty among lone women with children. In 2005, 91 percent of married couples with children under the age of 18 had enough family income to put them above the poverty line even without counting government transfers, compared to only 56 percent of single mothers. A young woman with children and no husband is an inherently vulnerable economic unit.

The second-order effects arise from the consequences to the next generation when large numbers of children within a neighborhood are raised without fathers. I focus the discussion on African Americans because historically they quit marrying first and have been the subject of the most research.

As black nonmarital births rose from 22 percent of live births in 1960 to 55 percent in 1980, most policy scholars still held that the black extended family compensated for the lack of fathers and that single mothers can raise children just as well as the old-fashioned two-parent family if they are given a decent level of economic support. By the end of the 1980s, when black nonmarital births had reached 67 percent of live births, both positions had become empirically untenable. The extended-family argument had overlooked a brutal reality: If

---

Charles Murray, "Poverty and Marriage, Income Equality and Brains," *Pathways* (Winter 2008), pp. 21–24.

there is no marriage in generation I, grand-fathers and uncles become scarce in generation II and are gone by generation III. The fathers-aren't-that-important argument ran up against the results of the research that was supposed to confirm it. Study after study found that children raised by unmarried women did worse than children raised by the biological father and mother, even after controlling for income, education, and other socioeconomic background variables. They did not do worse on a few selected outcomes, but on everything from educational achievement and emotional development in childhood to employment and criminal activity in adulthood. The accumulated technical literature was so large and one-sided that by the mid-1990s the consensus among scholars that the failure to marry was damaging to children had crossed ideological boundaries.

Exactly why the damage is so great is not as settled as the fact that damage occurs. I will offer some explanations that are consistent with the literature but that still have speculative elements.

One explanation is painful to state publicly: In the aggregate, unmarried women tend to make bad mothers. It sounds harsh, but the evidence, derived from systematic data collection on parenting behaviors for large, nationally representative samples, needs to be faced: The chances that a child born to an unmarried woman will grow up severely deprived of stimulation, warmth, consistent discipline, and an organized environment are multiples of the chances facing a child born to a married couple, even after controlling for income. Why? The empirical realities that unmarried women are disproportionately immature, ignorant, and with low cognitive ability probably play roles.

A second explanation involves the functions that fathers serve for daughters who are coping with sexual maturation. Daughters of never-married women are more likely to have sex in early adolescence, with all its negative consequences, than girls who have grown up with the biological father in the home. Fathers can delay sex through two routes. One is a father's authority—it may be hard to restrain adolescent sexual momentum in the heat of the moment, but "My daddy would kill me" has been known to do the job. The other route may be the father's role as first boyfriend. In early adolescence, girls without fathers have a hole in their emotional lives that they tend to fill with the males who are available—i.e., boyfriends who demand sex.

A third explanation involves the functions that fathers serve for sons. Little boys instinctively pick an older male to idolize, and, given a chance, the person he will choose first is his father. A father who behaves responsibly toward the mother and gets up and goes to work every day is teaching his son about how a grown-up male is supposed to behave, even if he never says a word about what he is doing. Boys who do not have fathers tend not to learn those lessons. Boys who live in neighborhoods where they do not even have friends with fathers have an even stronger tendency not to learn those lessons.

Lacking fathers, boys will find role models somewhere. For African-American boys in inner-cities, there is a ready substitute in the form of adolescent males who have the most money, the most bling, the most women, and the most attitude—the role models who tell little boys that drugs are cool, crime is cool, living off women is cool, low-paying jobs are demeaning, and that a man is supposed to retaliate immedi-

ately and violently whenever he is disre-
spected. They are not lessons that make for
good employees.

Ignore the figures on unemployment and
imprisonment among young black males,
bad as they are, and consider just this:
About a quarter of young black males who
are not in prison and not in school are also
not in the labor force. Lest it be thought
that this number reflects discouraged workers who have given up, the percentage of
black males ages 16–24 who are not in
school but not in the labor force has risen
during the hottest economies. It stood at 21
percent as of 1992, when the national unemployment rate was a high 7.5 percent. In
2000, the year that had the lowest national
unemployment rate in three decades, after
seven consecutive years of plentiful jobs for
low-skill workers, it had risen to 26 percent. Young black male dropout from the
labor force is not a jobs problem. It is a socialization problem.

The aggregate effects of the inherent financial vulnerability of the single-mother
household, bad parenting by unmarried
mothers, and the lack of fathers mean that
the failure to marry plays an important role
in producing each year's black poverty statistics. Just how large a role is a matter of
debate, but a few basics are undeniable. As
long as half of black families with children
under 18 are headed by a lone female, and
as long as a quarter of young black males
who are out of prison and out of school are
not even looking for work, the poverty
numbers for blacks are not going to come
down much no matter how good the economy is and no matter what new social programs the politicians try.

Meanwhile, the poverty-inducing effects
of nonmarital births are growing for Latino
and Anglo populations. Nonmarital births

now account for half of all Latino births
and a quarter of all Anglo births. Both figures have risen steadily and show no signs
of slowing down.

Income Inequality and Brains

Consider the classic geek. He is 22 years old
with a new bachelor's degree *summa cum
laude* in mathematics, his fingers dance
across a computer keyboard like Vladimir
Horowitz's danced across a piano keyboard,
but socially he is a klutz. He will never be a
success at any career that requires people
skills. How is he going to make a living? If
the year is 1908, he can become a teacher
of mathematics or an accountant who will
never rise to management. He will make a
modest income all his life. If the year is
2008, employers from microchip companies
to quant funds are aggressively recruiting
him with offers of big starting salaries, signing bonuses, and stock options. He is likely
to be a millionaire before he reaches thirty.
Or as Bill Gates once said to a reporter, Microsoft's real competitor is not Apple or
IBM, but Goldman Sachs. "I mean the
competition for talent," he continued. "It's
all about IQ. Our only competition for IQ
is the top investment banks."

The story of the mathematics geek is em-
blematic of much of the story behind increasing income inequality. Over the course
of the 20th century, the job market
changed in three respects, all of which lead
to higher incomes for people lucky enough
to be born with high cognitive ability.

First, the proportion of jobs that are
screened for high cognitive ability doubled
from 1900 to 1950, and then doubled
again from 1950 to 2000. By "screened for
high cognitive ability," I mean occupations
such as engineer, physician, or attorney

with advanced educational requirements that can be met only by people with high cognitive ability. For many of these occupations, the proportion of jobs they represented far more than quadrupled over the century. Engineering jobs in 2000 accounted for 12 times the proportion they had in 1900. College and university teaching jobs accounted for 30 times the 1900 proportion. In computer science, the two million jobs that existed in 2000 had no counterpart at all in 1900.

Second, the link between cognitive ability and managerial jobs not formally screened for cognitive ability also increased. In part, this reflected credentialing—many entry-level managerial jobs that were routinely filled by people with high school educations in 1900 were restricted to people with college degrees by 2000. But the cognitive demands of managerial jobs also increased over the course of the century, as the size of organizations and the complexity of managing their operation increased in tandem.

Third, the dollar value of these jobs in the marketplace, already higher than the value of skilled and unskilled labor, increased disproportionately. For the first half of the century, for example, the average engineer made a little more than twice the income of the average manufacturing employee, and the ratio remained roughly constant. Then, beginning in the 1950s, their incomes began to diverge sharply. By the 1960s, the average engineer made three times the income of the average manufacturing employee. The same thing happened throughout the economy.

The most obvious factor leading to this situation is technology. If a robot can replace a worker with a strong back, pay for strong backs must stay below the break-even point for buying robots instead. Meanwhile, the economic incentives to invent better and cheaper robots generates high-paying jobs for people with the cognitive ability to design robots.

The scale of modern enterprises also makes cognitive ability more valuable. The average revenue of a *Fortune* 500 company increased by 5.5 times from 1960 to 2000 in constant dollars. This increase in scale changes the value of the marginal contribution that a talented employee can make. How much money will a company pay someone who can create an advertising campaign that increases its annual revenue by half a percentage point? If a half a percentage point represents $63 million (the average for the *Fortune* 500 in 2000), that person is worth a lot more money than he was in 1960, when it represented $11 million in comparable dollars. Similarly, the scale of the stakes in lawsuits, corporate mergers, and favorable rulings from regulatory agencies have multiplied, and so has the value of people who can increase the odds of getting the right outcome.

Other dynamics are at work too, but they are variations on a common theme: American society is increasingly complex and has ever more money in play. Wealth will gravitate toward those who are best at dealing with complexity. Dealing with complexity is what high cognitive ability is good for.

Controlling rising income inequality in the face of these dynamics is impossible with anything short of 90 percent marginal tax rates, and perhaps not even then. Consider the excoriated CEOs with compensation packages worth tens of millions of dollars even though their companies are losing money. Such CEOs exist, and better rules for corporate governance could probably reduce their incidence. But the trend that underlies these notorious cases, the rapidly increasing ratio of the pay of the senior executive to the pay of the average worker, is not irrational. Exceptionally able managers are correlated with exceptional corporate performance—that's an empirical relationship that Warren Buffet has relied upon to choose stocks and thereby make his own fortune, and it is the reason that Microsoft's most important competitor is Goldman Sachs. As long as that underlying relationship exists—and there is no way to get rid of it—corporations are going to bid up the price of the most able executives. The richer corporations become, the higher the bidding will go.

Don't look to more and better education as a way of damping rising income inequality. More education of the right kind is useful for almost everyone as a way of raising personal earning potential. But raising skills is not the same thing as reducing income inequality. Another aspect of today's economy is what Robert Frank and Philip Cook have called the "winner take all" phenomenon. To illustrate, suppose the problem were unequal income for cellists, and we were to borrow from John Edwards's "College for Everyone" idea proposed in the 2008 (election season) and undertake a "Cellos for Everyone" initiative. It would surely increase the number of proficient cellists. But as long as we can go to iTunes and download any recording of Beethoven's cello sonatas we prefer, we will still download the ones played by Yo Yo Ma and a handful of others at the top of the cellist hierarchy. A Cellos for Everyone initiative may affect who is at the very top, but it will not reduce income inequality among cellists. Similarly, a College for Everyone initiative will not reduce income inequality in

the labor force as a whole. There are many reasons it won't, but the relevant one here is that the most radical increases in income inequality are not driven by differences in education among people at the center of the cognitive bell curve. They are driven by the rising economic value of people at the far right-hand tail.

I should not pick on John Edwards. College for Everyone would be no more ineffectual than the solutions for poverty and rising income inequality that others have proposed. They all depend on assumptions about the nature of the problems that ignore reality. Perhaps the public understands that, which would help explain why those problems barely register on the list of political issues that will decide their votes. An old joke from the Soviet Union had as its punch line, "We pretend to work and they pretend to pay us." We in the United States appear to have reached a similar modus Vivendi when it comes to poverty and income inequality. The politicians pretend to have answers and we pretend to listen to them.

REFERENCES

For the evidence regarding the evaluations of the social programs of the 1960s and 1970s, see C. Murray (1984), *Losing Ground: American Social Policy 1950–1980* (New York: Basic Books). Rossi's laws are found in P. Rossi (1987), "The iron law of evaluation and other metallic rules," in J. Miller & M. Lewis (Eds.), *Research in Social Problems and Public Policy* (Vol. 4, pp. 3–20), Greenwich, Conn.: JAI Press.

Data on single-female households and poverty come from the Bureau of the Census, http://pubdb3.census.gov/macro/032006/rdcall/2_001.htm. Figures regarding percentages of nonmarital births come from the National Center for Health Statistics *Vital Statistics* series, available online at http://www.cdc.gov/nchs/about/major/

dvs/Vitalstatsonline.htm. For evidence regarding unmarried mothers, some basic compendia are S. McLanahan, & G. Sandefur (1994), *Growing Up with a Single Parent*, Cambridge: Harvard Univ. Press; M. Lamb (Ed.), (1998), *Parenting and Child Development in Nontraditional Families*, Mahwah, NJ: Lawrence Erlbaum Associates Inc.; and K.S. Hymowitz (2006), *Marriage and Caste in America: Separate and Unequal Families in a Post-Marital Age*, Chicago: Ivan R. Dee. For perspectives on young black males, parenting, and work, see the above plus M.L. Sullivan (1989), *"Getting Paid": Youth Crime and Work in the Inner City*, Ithaca, N.Y.: Cornell University Press; R.I. Lerman & T.J. Ooms, (Eds.), (1993) and *Young Unwed Fathers: Changing Roles and Emerging Policies*, Philadelphia: Temple Univ. Press. Evidence for the relationship between IQ and nonmarital births and between IQ and parenting are given in R.J. Herrnstein & C. Murray (1994), *The Bell Curve: Intelligence and Class Structure in American Life*, New York: Free Press, chapter 8.

Data on labor force participation of young black males come from the Bureau of Labor Statistics, available online at http://www.bls.gov/data/home .htm#calc.

The discussion of inequality and cognitive ability is also drawn from *The Bell Curve*, chapters 2, 3, and 4, with updated figures using 2000 data from the Bureau of Labor Statistics, http://www.bls.gov/oes/home.htm. The Bill Gates' quote comes from R. Kaarlgaard (2004, 28 July), "Microsoft's IQ dividend," *Wall Street Journal*. For evidence about why Cellos for Everyone would not narrow income inequality among cellists, see R.H. Frank & P.J. Cook (1995), *The Winner-Take-All Society: Why the Few at the Top Get So Much More Than the Rest of Us*, New York: The Free Press. Historical data on the *Fortune* 500 are available online at http://www.aggdata.com/business/fortune_500. For polling data showing the low priority of poverty and income inequality as a political issue, see http://www.pollingreport .com/priority.htm.

About the Editors

David B. Grusky is Professor of Sociology at Stanford University, Director of the Center for the Study of Poverty and Inequality at Stanford University, and coeditor (with Paula England) of the Studies in Social Inequality Series. He received his B.A. at Reed College, his M.S. and Ph.D. at the University of Wisconsin–Madison, and has held positions at the University of Chicago, Cornell University, and Stanford University. He is a Fellow of the American Association for the Advancement of Science, recipient of the 2004 Max Weber Award (with Maria Charles), founder of the Cornell University Center for the Study of Inequality, and a former Presidential Young Investigator. Although his research ranges widely, much of it examines whether and why gender, racial, and class-based inequalities are growing stronger or weaker, whether and why they differ in strength across countries, and how such changes and differences are best measured. His recent books are *The Inequality Puzzle* (coauthored with Roland Berger, Tobias Raffel, Geoffrey Samuels, and Chris Wimer, Springer Press, 2010), *Social Stratification* (coedited with Szonja Szelényi and Manwai C. Ku, Westview Press, 3rd edition, 2008), *Poverty and Inequality* (coedited with Ravi Kanbur, Stanford University Press, 2006), *Mobility and Inequality* (coedited with Stephen Morgan and Gary Fields, Stanford University Press, 2006), *Occupational Ghettos* (coauthored with Maria Charles, Stanford University Press, 2004), *The Declining Significance of Gender?* (coedited with Francine Blau and Mary Brinton, Russell Sage, 2006), and *Inequality: Classic Readings in Race, Class, and Gender* (coedited with Szonja Szelényi, Westview Press, 2006).

Szonja Szelényi has taught courses in poverty, inequality, and gender at the University of Wisconsin, Stanford University, and Cornell University. Her books are *Equality by Design* (Stanford University Press, 1998) and *Inequality: Classic Readings in Race, Class, and Gender* (coedited with David Grusky, Westview Press, 2006).

About the Book

THE INEQUALITY READER AND OUR NEW SERIES
OF INEQUALITY ANTHOLOGIES

The publication of the *Inequality Reader* completes the recently undertaken expansion of our series of inequality anthologies into a full three-volume set. This expansion is a response to the burgeoning interest in poverty and inequality, the increasingly diverse research literature within the poverty and inequality field, and the increasingly diverse needs of consumers of this literature. The three books making up our series fill the following niches:

> *A comprehensive introduction.* The *Inequality Reader* is intended for undergraduate and graduate readers requiring an introduction to the field as well as for scholars and general readers who would profit from a compilation of the most influential scholarship on poverty and inequality. This volume draws broadly from classic theoretical and conceptual pieces, qualitative and ethnographic studies, quantitative analyses of the sources of poverty and inequality, and "experiential pieces" that convey the lived experience of poverty and inequality. In assembling this volume, a special effort was made to include articles that cast light on recent changes in the structure of poverty and inequality, not only the spectacular takeoff in income inequality but also equally dramatic developments in contemporary race, class, and gender inequalities.
>
> *A compilation of the classics.* Published in 2006, *Classic Readings in Race, Class, and Gender* is a slimmer volume of essential readings in poverty and inequality, readings that define the conceptual and empirical foundations of the field. This book, which represents the classical core alone, may be supplemented with contemporary articles that are tailored to the particular interests of the reader.
>
> *An advanced reader.* The final book in our three-part series, the venerable *Social Stratification* (3rd edition), combines a full roster of classic readings with the most advanced, cutting-edge scholarship on poverty and inequality. Not for the faint of heart, *Social Stratification* is appropriate for anyone requiring full exposure to advanced scholarship in the field, including the most influential quantitative and technical pieces. The introductory graduate student should consider coupling this book with the new *Inequality Reader.*

Index

Aaronson, Daniel, 188
Absolute deprivation hypothesis, 622
Absolute income hypothesis, 622
Absolute mobility, 484–489
Academic achievement, 217; stereotype threat and, 276–281
Academic performance, 555–557, 558–561
Acculturation, 240
Achievement: academic, 217, 276–281; "contest," 562; gap, 717–718; sponsored, 562
Adaptation, 238, 240, 243, 246, 247
Affirmative action, 276
African American(s): college and, 276–277; dropout rates for, 276; health of, 626, 628; incarceration of, 208, 209–210; neighborhoods of, 185, 628; police and, 315. *See also* Blacks
Afrocentrism, 226
Alexander, C., 556
Allocative discrimination, 412, 421–422
Alm, Richard, 519–520
Altman, Drew, 28
Ambient hazards, 188
An American Dilemma (Myrdal), 171–172
American Dream, 567, 568
American Recovery and Reinvestment Act (ARRA), 706–710
Amsbary, Sarah McArthur, 335–336
Anders, Björklund, 542
Anderson, Deborah J., 366
Aneshensel, Carol S., 188
Animus theory of discrimination, 379
Antipathy-based theory of discrimination, 378
Antipoverty program, 90–91
Apartheid, 9, 176–180
Aronson, Joshua, 276, 277
ARRA. *See* American Recovery and Reinvestment Act
Arrow, Kenneth, 351

Arrow impossibility theorem, 26
Ascription, 392, 567
Aspirations: of Brothers, 575–577; expectations versus, 568; of Hallway Hangers, 568–575; in low-income neighborhoods, 567–582; occupational, 568
Assessment: of teachers, 718
Asset(s): of groups, 8; human, 4; opportunity, 302
Assimilation: as problem, 239–240; segmented, 237–248
Atkinson, Anthony, 26
Attribution error, 382–383, 385–386
Auditions: blind, 351–363; democratization of, 351, 356; orchestral, 351–352, 356–358
Auten, Gerald E., 519, 520
Authority, 53

Babbidge, A., 637
Bakunin, M., 121
Bakunin's doctrine, 120
Balance, 25, 30
Balfour, Jennifer L., 629
Baltzell, Digby, 130–131
Banfield, Edward, 173
Barnes, Brenda C., 334
Baron, James N., 472
Baumer, Eric, 188
Becker, Gary, 351, 429, 432–433, 597
Begue, Brian, 222
Behrman, Jere, 31
Belcher, Richard, 335
Bell, Daniel, 121
The Bell Curve (Herrnstein/Murray), 22, 276
Benabou, Roland, 29
Bendix, Reinhard, 538
Benson, John, 28
Bentham, Jeremy, 721
Benzeval, Michaela, 628